2016

the best ca[r

in France

over 1100 independent reviews

Compiled by: Alan Rogers Travel Ltd

Designed by: Vine Design Ltd

Additional photography: T Lambelin, www.lambelin.com
Maps created by Customised Mapping (01769 540044)
contain background data provided by GisDATA Ltd

Published by: Alan Rogers Travel Ltd,
Spelmonden Old Oast, Goudhurst, Kent TN17 1HE
www.alanrogers.com Tel: 01580 214000

British Library Cataloguing-in-Publication Data:
A catalogue record for this book is available
from the British Library.

ISBN 978-1-909057-79-1

Printed in Great Britain by Stephens & George Print Group

Contents

Alan Rogers - in search of 'the best'

Alan Rogers Guides were first published almost 50 years ago. Since Alan Rogers published the first campsite guide that bore his name, the range has expanded and now covers 27 countries in five separate guides. No fewer than 20 of the campsites selected by Alan for the first guide are still featured in our 2016 editions.

There are over 11,000 campsites in France of varying quality: this guide contains impartially written reports on 1,118, including many of the very finest, each being individually inspected and selected. We aim to provide you with a selection of the best, rather than information on all – in short, a more selective, qualitative approach. New, improved maps and indexes are also included, designed to help you find the choice of campsite that's right for you.

We hope you enjoy some happy and safe travels – and some pleasurable 'armchair touring' in the meantime!

" ...the campsites included in this book have been chosen entirely on merit, and no payment of any sort is made by them for their inclusion."

Alan Rogers, 1968

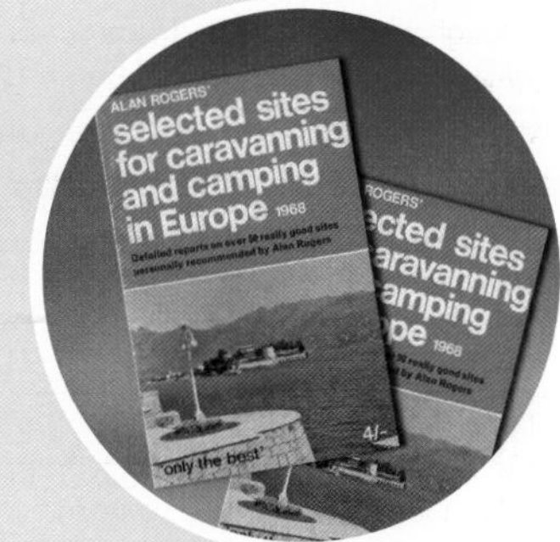

How do we find the best?

The criteria we use when inspecting and selecting campsites are numerous, but the most important by far is the question of good quality. People want different things from their choice of site so we try to include a range of campsite 'styles' to cater for a wide variety of preferences: from those seeking a small peaceful campsite in the heart of the countryside, to visitors looking for an 'all singing, all dancing' site in a popular seaside resort. Those with more specific interests, such as sporting facilities, cultural events or historical attractions, are also catered for.

The size of the site, whether it's part of a chain or privately owned, makes no difference in terms of it being required to meet our exacting standards in respect of its quality and it being 'fit for purpose'. In other words, irrespective of the size of the site, or the number of facilities it offers, we consider and evaluate the welcome, the pitches, the sanitary facilities, the cleanliness, the general maintenance and even the location.

Expert opinions

We rely on our dedicated team of Site Assessors, all of whom are experienced campers, caravanners or motorcaravanners, to visit and recommend campsites. Each year they travel some 100,000 miles around Europe inspecting new campsites for the guide and re-inspecting the existing ones. Our thanks are due to them for their enthusiastic efforts, their diligence and integrity.

We also appreciate the feedback we receive from many of our readers and we always make a point of following up complaints, suggestions or recommendations for possible new campsites. Of course we get a few grumbles too – but it really is a few, and those we do receive usually relate to overcrowding or to poor maintenance during the peak school holiday period. Please bear in mind that, although we are interested to hear about any complaints, we have no contractual relationship with the campsites featured in our guides and are therefore not in a position to intervene in any dispute between a reader and a campsite.

Independent and honest

Whilst the content and scope of the Alan Rogers guides have expanded considerably since the early editions, our selection of campsites still employs exactly the same philosophy and criteria as defined by Alan Rogers in 1968.

'telling it how it is'

Firstly, and most importantly, our selection is based entirely on our own rigorous and independent inspection and selection process. Campsites cannot buy their way into our guides – indeed the extensive Site Report which is written by us, not by the site owner, is provided free of charge so we are free to say what we think and to provide an honest, 'warts and all' description. This is written in plain English and without the use of confusing icons or symbols.

Looking for the best

Highly respected by site owners and readers alike, there is no better guide when it comes to forming an independent view of a campsite's quality. When you need to be confident in your choice of campsite, you need the Alan Rogers Guide.

- Sites only included on merit
- Sites cannot pay to be included
- Independently inspected, rigorously assessed
- Impartial reviews
- Almost 50 years of expertise

Written in plain English, our guides are exceptionally easy to use, but a few words of explanation regarding the layout and content may be helpful. Regular readers will see that our site reports are grouped into 22 official regions (including the Vendée) and then listed alphabetically by town within each region.

Region

Index town

Site name

Postal address (including département) T: telephone number. E: email address

alanrogers.com web address (including Alan Rogers reference number)

A description of the site in which we try to give an idea of its general features – its size, its situation, its strengths and its weaknesses. This section should provide a picture of the site itself with reference to the facilities that are provided and if they impact on its appearance or character. We include details on pitch numbers, electricity (with amperage), hardstandings etc. in this section as pitch design, planning and terracing affects the site's overall appearance. Similarly we include reference to pitches used for caravan holiday homes, chalets, and the like. Importantly at the end of this column we indicate if there are any restrictions, e.g. no tents, no children, naturist sites.

Facilities

Lists more specific information on the site's facilities and amenities and, where available, the dates when these facilities are open (if not for the whole season). Off site: here we give distances to various local amenities, for example, local shops, the nearest beach, plus our featured activities (bicycle hire, fishing, horse riding, boat launching). Where we have space we list suggestions for activities and local tourist attractions.

Open: Site opening dates.

Directions

Separated from the main text in order that they may be read and assimilated more easily by a navigator en-route. Bear in mind that road improvement schemes can result in road numbers being altered.

GPS: references are provided in decimal format. All latitudes are North. Longitudes are East unless preceeded by a minus sign e.g. 48.71695 is North, 0.31254 is East and -0.31254 is West.

Charges guide

Maps, campsite listings and indexes

For this 2016 guide we include a map immediately after our Introduction to each region. These maps show the towns near which one or more of our featured campsites are located.

Within each regional section of the guide, we list these towns and the site(s) in that vicinity in alphabetical order.

You will certainly need more detailed maps for navigation, for example the Michelin atlas. We provide GPS coordinates for each site to assist you. Our indexes will also help you to find a site by its region and site name, or by the town where the site is situated.

Understanding the entries

Regions and départements

For administrative purposes, France is divided into 22 official regions covering the 95 départements (similar to our counties). The départements included in each region are stated in our introductions, together with their official number (eg. the département of Manche is number 50). We use these département numbers as the first two digits of our campsite reference numbers, so any campsite in the Manche département will start with the number 50, prefixed with FR.

Facilities

Toilet blocks

Unless we comment otherwise, toilet blocks will be equipped with WCs, washbasins with hot and cold water and hot showers with dividers or curtains, and will have all necessary shelves, hooks, plugs and mirrors. We also assume that there will be an identified chemical toilet disposal point, and that the campsite will provide water and waste water drainage points and bin areas. If not the case, we comment. We do mention certain features that some readers find important: washbasins in cubicles, facilities for babies, facilities for those with disabilities and motorcaravan service points. Readers with disabilities are advised to contact the site of their choice to ensure that facilities are appropriate to their needs.

Shop

Basic or fully supplied, and opening dates.

Bars, restaurants, takeaway facilities and entertainment

We try hard to supply opening and closing dates (if other than the campsite opening dates) and to identify whether there are discos or other entertainment.

Children's play areas

Fenced and with safety surface (e.g. sand, bark or pea-gravel).

Swimming pools

If particularly special, we cover in detail in our main campsite description but reference is always included under our Facilities listings. We will also indicate the existence of water slides, sunbathing areas and other features. Opening dates, charges and levels of supervision are provided where we have been notified. There is a regulation whereby Bermuda shorts may not be worn in swimming pools (for health and hygiene reasons). It is worth ensuring that you do take 'proper' swimming trunks with you.

Leisure facilities

For example, playing fields, bicycle hire, organised activities and entertainment.

Dogs

If dogs are not accepted or restrictions apply, we state it here. Check the quick reference list at the back of the guide.

Off site

This briefly covers leisure facilities, tourist attractions, restaurants etc. nearby.

Charges

These are the latest provided to us by the sites. In those cases where 2016 prices have not been provided to us by the sites, we try to give a general guide.

Reservations

Necessary for high season (July/August) in popular holiday areas. You can reserve many sites via The Caravan Club Travel Service or through other tour operators. Or be wholly independent and contact the campsite(s) of your choice direct. However, do bear in mind that many sites are closed all winter.

Telephone numbers

All numbers assume that you are phoning from within France. To phone France from outside that country, prefix the number shown with the relevant International Code (00 33) and drop the first 0, shown as (0) in the numbers indicated.

Non-geographic telephone numbers

In this guide we do not include any numbers that impose an extra charge on callers to that number (e.g. 084x or 03xx). Where Freephone numbers appear (0800 or 0808), calls to these numbers are free of charge.

Opening dates

These are advised to us during the early autumn of the previous year – sites can, and sometimes do, alter these dates before the start of the following season, often for good reasons. If you intend to visit shortly after a published opening date, or shortly before the closing date, it is wise to check that it will actually be open at the time required. Similarly some sites operate a restricted service during the low season, only opening some of their facilities (e.g. swimming pools) during the main season; where we know about this, and have the relevant dates, we indicate it – again if you are at all doubtful it is wise to check.

Sometimes, campsite amenities may be dependent on there being enough customers on site to justify their opening and, for this reason, actual opening dates may vary from those indicated.

Some French site owners are very relaxed when it comes to opening and closing dates. They may not be fully ready by their stated opening dates – grass and hedges may not all be cut or perhaps only limited sanitary facilities open. At the end of the season they also tend to close down some facilities and generally wind down prior to the closing date. Bear this in mind if you are travelling early or late in the season – it is worth phoning ahead.

The Camping Cheque low season touring system goes some way to addressing this in that many participating campsites will have all key facilities open and running by the opening date and these will remain fully operational until the closing date.

Taking a tent?

In recent years, sales of tents have increased dramatically. With very few exceptions, the campsites listed in this guide have pitches suitable for tents, caravans and motorcaravans. Tents, of course, come in a dazzling range of shapes and sizes. Modern family tents with separate sleeping pods are increasingly popular and these invariably require large pitches with electrical connections. Smaller lightweight tents, ideal for cyclists and hikers, are also visible on many sites and naturally require correspondingly smaller pitches. Many (but not all) sites have special tent areas with prices adjusted accordingly. If in any doubt, we recommend contacting the site of your choice beforehand.

Our Accommodation section

512

Over recent years, more and more campsites have added high quality mobile home and chalet accommodation. In response to feedback from many of our readers, and to reflect this evolution in campsites, we have now decided to include a separate section on mobile homes and chalets. If a site offers this accommodation, it is indicated above the site report with a page reference where full details are given. We have chosen a number of sites offering some of the best accommodation available and have included full details of one or two accommodation types at these sites.

Please note however that many other campsites listed in this guide may also have a selection of accommodation for rent.

You're on your way!

Whether you're an 'old hand' in terms of camping and caravanning or are contemplating your first trip, a regular reader of our Guides or a new 'convert', we wish you well in your travels and hope we have been able to help in some way.

We are, of course, also out and about ourselves, visiting sites, talking to owners and readers, and generally checking on standards and new developments.

We wish all our readers thoroughly enjoyable Camping and Caravanning in 2016 – favoured by good weather of course! **The Alan Rogers Team**

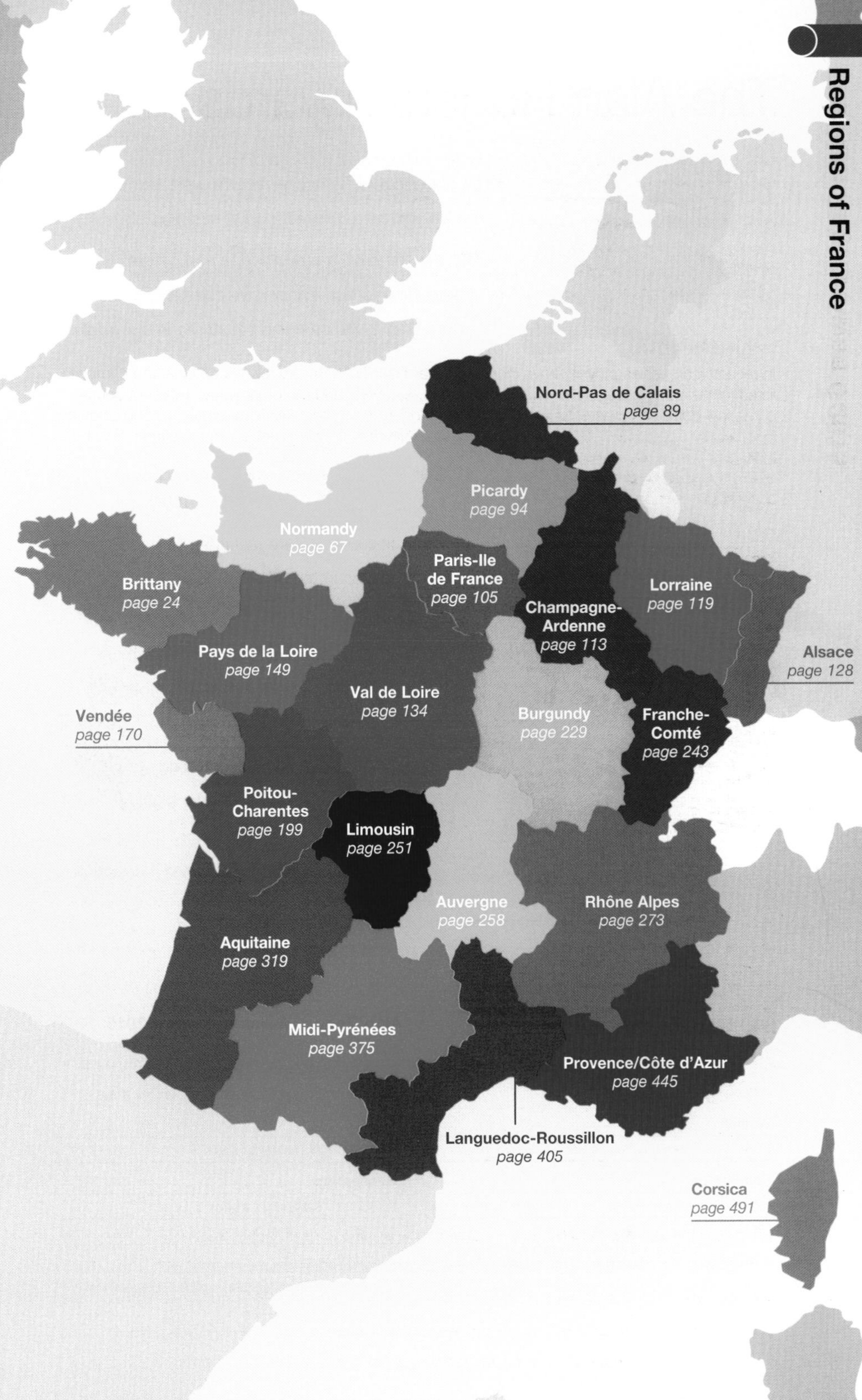
Nord-Pas de Calais
page 89
Picardy
page 94
Normandy
page 67
Paris-Ile de France
page 105
Brittany
page 24
Champagne-Ardenne
page 113
Lorraine
page 119
Alsace
page 128
Pays de la Loire
page 149
Val de Loire
page 134
Vendée
page 170
Burgundy
page 229
Franche-Comté
page 243
Poitou-Charentes
page 199
Limousin
page 251
Auvergne
page 258
Rhône Alpes
page 273
Aquitaine
page 319
Midi-Pyrénées
page 375
Provence/Côte d'Azur
page 445
Languedoc-Roussillon
page 405
Corsica
page 491

The Alan Rogers Awards

The Alan Rogers Campsite Awards were launched in 2004 and have proved a great success.

Our awards have a broad scope and before committing to our winners, we carefully consider more than 2,000 campsites featured in our guides, taking into account comments from our site assessors, our head office team and, of course, our readers.

Our award winners come from the four corners of Europe, from Spain to Croatia, and this year we are making awards to campsites in ten different countries.

Needless to say, it's an extremely difficult task to choose our eventual winners, but we believe that we have identified a number of campsites with truly outstanding characteristics.

In each case, we have selected an outright winner, along with two highly commended runners-up. Listed below are full details of each of our award categories and our winners for 2015.

Alan Rogers Progress Award 2015

This award reflects the hard work and commitment undertaken by particular site owners to improve and upgrade their site.

Winner	
ES84800	Camping Resort Sanguli Salou *Spain*
Runners-up	
FR31000	Sites et Paysages Le Moulin *France*
UK2450	The Orchards Holiday Caravan and Camping Park *England*

Alan Rogers Welcome Award 2015

This award takes account of sites offering a particularly friendly welcome and maintaining a friendly ambience throughout readers' holidays.

Winner	
FR35080	Domaine du Logis *France*
Runners-up	
ES88020	Camping Cabopino *Spain*
NL5840	Veluwecamping de Pampel *Netherlands*

Alan Rogers Active Holiday Award 2015

This award reflects sites in outstanding locations which are ideally suited for active holidays, notably walking or cycling, but which could extend to include such activities as winter sports or watersports.

Winner	
AU0180	Sportcamp Woferlgut *Austria*
Runners-up	
DE30030	Camping Wulfener Hals *Germany*
IT62040	Camping Seiser Alm *Italy*

Alan Rogers Innovation Award 2015

Our Innovation Award acknowledges campsites with creative and original concepts, possibly with features which are unique, and cannot therefore be found elsewhere. We have identified innovation both in campsite amenities and also in rentable accommodation.

Winner	
IT60200	Camping Union Lido Vacanze *Italy*
Runners-up	
FR29010	Castel Camping Ty Nadan *France*
FR24350	RCN Le Moulin de la Pique *France*

Alan Rogers Small Campsite Award 2015

This award acknowledges excellent small campsites (less than 75 pitches) which offer a friendly welcome and top quality amenities throughout the season to their guests.

Winner	
IT64045	Camping Tenuta Squaneto *Italy*
Runners-up	
FR02020	Camping Les Etangs du Moulin *France*
DE34380	Camping Am Möslepark *Germany*

Alan Rogers Seaside Award 2015

This award is made for sites which we feel are outstandingly suitable for a really excellent seaside holiday.

Winner	
FR17010	Camping Bois Soleil *France*
Runners-up	
NL6870	Kennemer Duincamping de Lakens *Netherlands*
CR6782	Zaton Holiday Resort *Croatia*

Alan Rogers Country Award 2015

This award contrasts with our former award and acknowledges sites which are attractively located in delightful, rural locations.

Winner	
AU0265	Park Grubhof *Austria*
Runners-up	
FR12160	Camping Les Peupliers *France*
SW2630	Röstånga Camping & Bad *Sweden*

Alan Rogers Family Site Award 2015

Many sites claim to be child friendly but this award acknowledges the sites we feel to be the very best in this respect.

Winner	
ES80400	Camping Las Dunas *Spain*
Runners-up	
UK0845	Hillhead Caravan Club Site *England*
LU7620	Europacamping Nommerlayen *Luxembourg*

Alan Rogers Readers' Award 2015

We believe our Readers' Award to be the most important. We simply invite our readers (by means of an on-line poll at www.alanrogers.com) to nominate the site they enjoyed most.

The outright winner for 2015 is:

Winner	
FR38010	Camping Le Coin Tranquille *France*

Our warmest congratulations to all our award winners and our commiserations to all those not having won an award on this occasion.

The Alan Rogers Team

Getting the most from off peak touring

£14.95 night outfit+ 2people

There are many reasons to avoid high season, if you can. Queues are shorter, there's less traffic, a calmer atmosphere and prices are cheaper. And it's usually still nice and sunny!

And when you use Camping Cheques you'll find great quality facilities that are actually open and a welcoming conviviality.

Did you know?

Camping Cheques can be used right into mid-July and from late August on many sites. Over 90 campsites in France alone accept Camping Cheques from 20th August.

Save up to 60% with Camping Cheques

Camping Cheque is a fixed price scheme allowing you to go as you please, staying on over 600 campsites across Europe, always paying the same rate and saving you up to 60% on regular pitch fees. One Cheque gives you one night for 2 people + unit on a standard pitch, with electricity. It's as simple as that.

Special offers mean you can stay extra nights free (eg 7 nights for 6 Cheques) or even a month free for a month paid! Especially popular in Spain during the winter, these longer-term offers can effectively halve the nightly rate. See Site Directory for details.

Check out our amazing Ferry Deals!

Why should I use Camping Cheques?

- It's a proven system, recognised by all 600+ participating campsites - so no nasty surprises.
- It's flexible, allowing you to travel between campsites, and also countries, on a whim - so no need to pre-book. (It's low season, so campsites are rarely full, though advance bookings can be made).
- Stay as long as you like, where you like - so you travel in complete freedom.
- Camping Cheques are valid at least 2 years - so no pressure to use them up. (If you have a couple left over after your trip, simply keep them for the following year, or use them up in the UK).

Tell me more... (but keep it brief!)

Camping Cheques was started in 1999 and has since grown in popularity each year (nearly 2 million were used last year). That should speak for itself. There are 'copycat' schemes, but none has the same range of quality campsites that save you up to 60%.

Ask for your **FREE** continental road map, which explains how Camping Cheque works

01342 336621

Order your 2016 Directory

campingcheque.co.uk

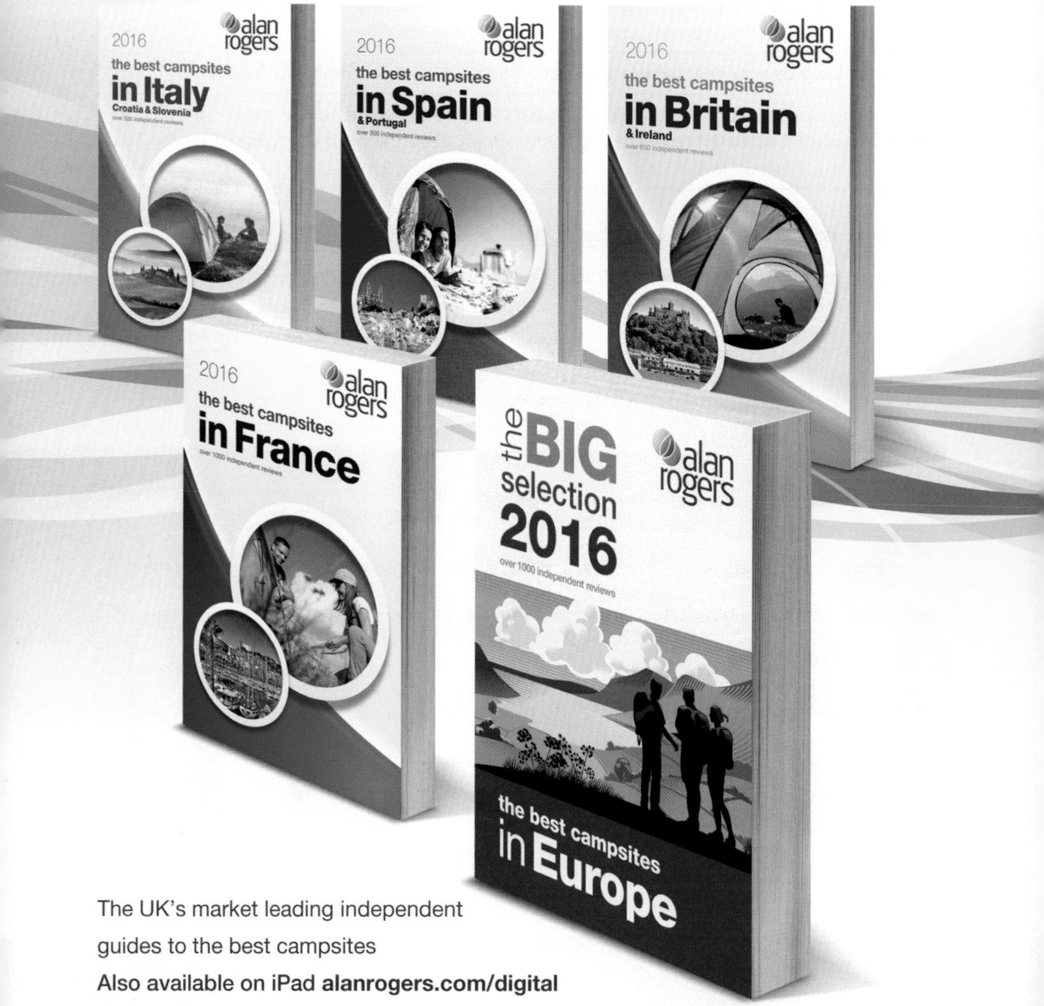

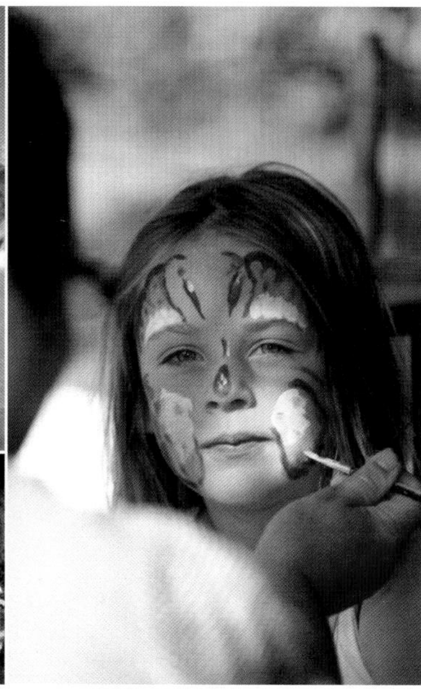

What's In A Name?

Differentiating between the groups

At Alan Rogers we have been inspecting and reviewing campsites since 1968. There's no question things are very different today: facilities, standards, professionalism, technology have all evolved beyond all recognition. But we find there is still room for individuality, style and personality.

Campsites may still be small and uncommercial with modest facilities and the charm of a family-run establishment. Others may be larger and offer the impressive amenities of a modern resort. Some may favour highlighting their historic pedigree and ambience, others prefer to stress their rural location.

To achieve these various aims, many have joined forces with other like-minded campsites to raise their profile via glossy brochures and the like. Of course it's not black and white but over the following pages we try to clarify the distinctions between some of these groups of campsites, each of which claim to be unique in their own way.

Les Castels is a well-established and highly regarded group of 4&5 star campsites set in the grounds of stunning châteaux, beautiful manors and charming country houses. This ensures unique natural settings for some of France's finest touring sites. You will be assured of a warm and courteous welcome, tranquil surroundings, great service and a taste of authentic French 'art de vivre'.

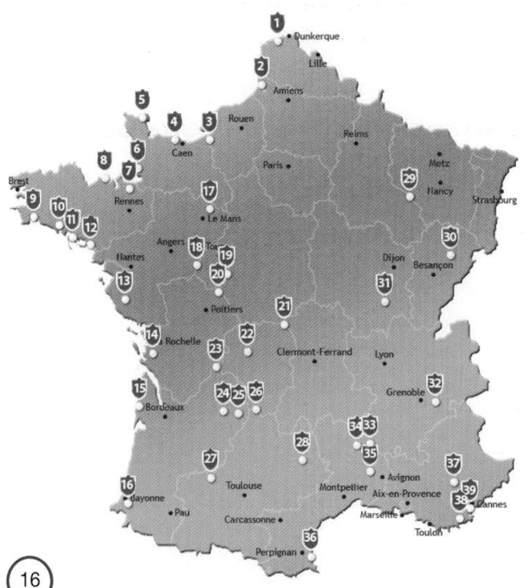

Campsites

1. Castel La Bien Assise
2. Castel Domaine de Drancourt
3. Castel Le Brévedent
4. Castel Le Château de Martragny
5. Castel L'Anse du Brick
6. Castel Château de Lez Eaux
7. Castel Domaine des Ormes
8. Castel Château de Galinée
9. Castel Domaine de L'Orangerie de Lanniron
10. Castel Le Ty Nadan
11. Castel La Grande Métairie
12. Castel Manoir De Ker an Poul
13. Castel La Garangeoire
14. Castel Séquoia Parc
15. Castel Le Village Western
16. Castel Le Ruisseau des Pyrénées
17. Castel Le Château de Chanteloup
18. Castel Domaine de la Brèche
19. Castel Parc de Fierbois
20. Castel Le Petit Trianon de Saint Ustre
21. Castel Château de Poinsouze
22. Castel Château de Leychoisier
23. Castel Les Gorges du Chambon
24. Castel Saint Avit Loisirs
25. Castel Le Moulin du Roch
26. Castel Domaine de La Paille Basse
27. Castel Le Camp de Florence
28. Castel Le Caussanel
29. Castel La Forge de Sainte Marie
30. Castel Val de Bonnal
31. Castel Château de L'Epervière
32. Castel Le Château de Rochetaillée
33. Castel Domaine de Sévenier
34. Castel L'Ardéchois
35. Castel Château de Boisson
36. Castel Les Criques de Porteils
37. Castel Domaine du Verdon
38. Castel Douce Quiétude
39. Castel Domaine de la Bergerie

Les Castels

In Their Own Words...

Dreaming of a holiday in exceptional surroundings? Do you want to combine relaxation with activities for the whole family? If so then choose one of the 39 Les Castels campsites in France - all are either 4 or 5 star rated.

Quality Assured

Very large pitches, exceptionally comfortable top-of-the-range accommodation and flawless service await you on Les Castels campsites. All campsites subscribe to the Les Castels Quality Charter - a guarantee of excellence in facilities and services.

4 and 5 star services

Let Les Castels wait on you hand and foot, with the full 5 star services such as wellness spa, restaurant with enticing menus, from breakfast to half board or a la carte options.

Whether you're on the move or just lazing

Many Les Castels campsites offer supervised activities for children: organised games, fun workshops, outings and picnics, singing, dancing and real shows. There is a wide range of activities for the whole family: football, tennis, mountain biking, aqua aerobics, tree climbing, pedal boats, canoeing, archery and more.

Fancy glamping

For authentic and original holidays that blend nature and comfort, stay in a safari tent, gipsy caravan, tree house, or a raft-house! You won't forget this unique and discovery-filled experience.

Preserving our environmental heritage

With sites that are all located in areas of outstanding natural beauty, Les Castels have always been respectful of the environment, ensuring that your holiday brings you as close as possible to unspoilt nature. Each property contributes largely to the historical, environmental and architectural heritage of its region.

Premium offer: the freedom of the outdoor life plus the very best in contemporary comfort

Try the premium offer and enjoy the Les Castels 'art of living' package: a spacious pitch or accommodation plus all you need to enjoy a fabulous holiday with VIP services: bed linen and towels included, cleaning supply kit, television or hi-fi sound system, free internet access, etc.

www.camping-castels.co.uk

•Rennes
Paris•
•Nantes
Le Petit Rocher
Bel Air
Les Peupliers
Signol
•Bordeaux
Le Boudigau
•Toulouse
La Pergola
Perpignan•

Camp'Atlantique

In Their Own Words...

Wonderful holidays on 3 and 4 star campsites

Stay at one of Camp'Atlantique's campsites and discover the friendly, family atmosphere at each one of them. Whether travelling as a couple, a family or with friends, you will find everything you need to get the most from your holiday! From the moment you book until the end of your stay, our professional and dynamic team will help with everything you can imagine. We do everything we can to guarantee the very best comfort and quality, always supported by free entertainment and by being just two steps from the beach.

Services and facilities beyond your expectations

At 4 of our campsites you will find spacious pitches for tents, caravans and motorhomes and at all of them accommodation such as mobile homes (from 3 to 12 people), chalets (up to 8 people) or Ecolodges. Enjoy a range of facilities during your stay: heated swimming pools with waterslides and super paddling pools with water games for children, bars, restaurants, snacks/take aways, groceries, sports grounds*, free entertainment, free kids clubs,... You can also benefit from numerous optional services (bed linen, equipment for babies, barbecues...) in fact, all the comforts of home!

*depending on campsite

Exceptional destinations

Wherever you choose to stay, in the Vendée, Charente-Maritime, Aquitaine or on the Western Mediterranean coast, every Camp'Atlantique campsite is situated in an exceptional environment. Get close to nature within a short walk of the beach and stay near to well-known seaside resorts and typical French villages. Come and visit our fascinating regions and discover cultures, rich in history and tradition.

www.camp-atlantique.co.uk

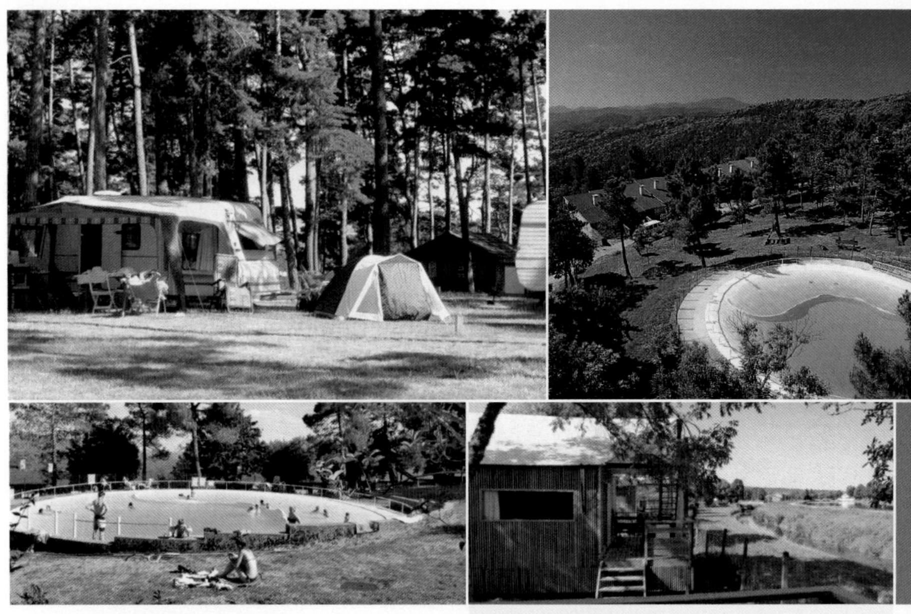

The Revea Camping offer 6 destinations throughout many of France's most alluring regions. Holiday options include chalets, mobile homes and other types of high quality accommodation.

Revea campsites operate on a human scale and invariably offer great service and a friendly, convivial environment for holidays, whether 'en famille' or between friends.

Campsites

1. Tonnerre, La Cascade
2. Ruynes en Margeride, Le Petit Bois
3. Montpezat de Quercy Le Faillal
4. Bagnols les Bains, Le Tivoli
5. St Rémy sur Durolle, Les Demeures du Lac
6. St Germain de Calberte, Lou Serre de la Can

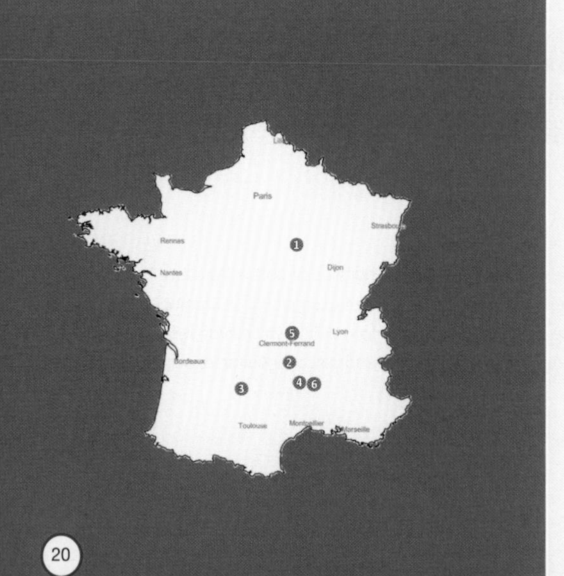

Revea

In Their Own Words...

Revea Camping offers various accomodation options throughout France, in the countryside or in the mountains. A wide range of destinations for every kind of holiday : hiking in Auvergne, relaxing in Lozère, culture and gastronomy in Burgundy.

Holidays for everyone

Our aim is to offer great value, nature holidays for everyone. We have special offers throughout the year : week-end breaks, one week or two weeks holidays, and always attractive prices whether you holiday with your partner, your family or your friends.

Revea – environment and heritage

Revea welcome you to a natural and authentic holiday environment. A great way to discover wonderful places, amazing landscapes and unspoiled villages.

www.revea-camping.fr/en

alan rogers

Want independent campsite reviews at your fingertips?

You'll find them here...

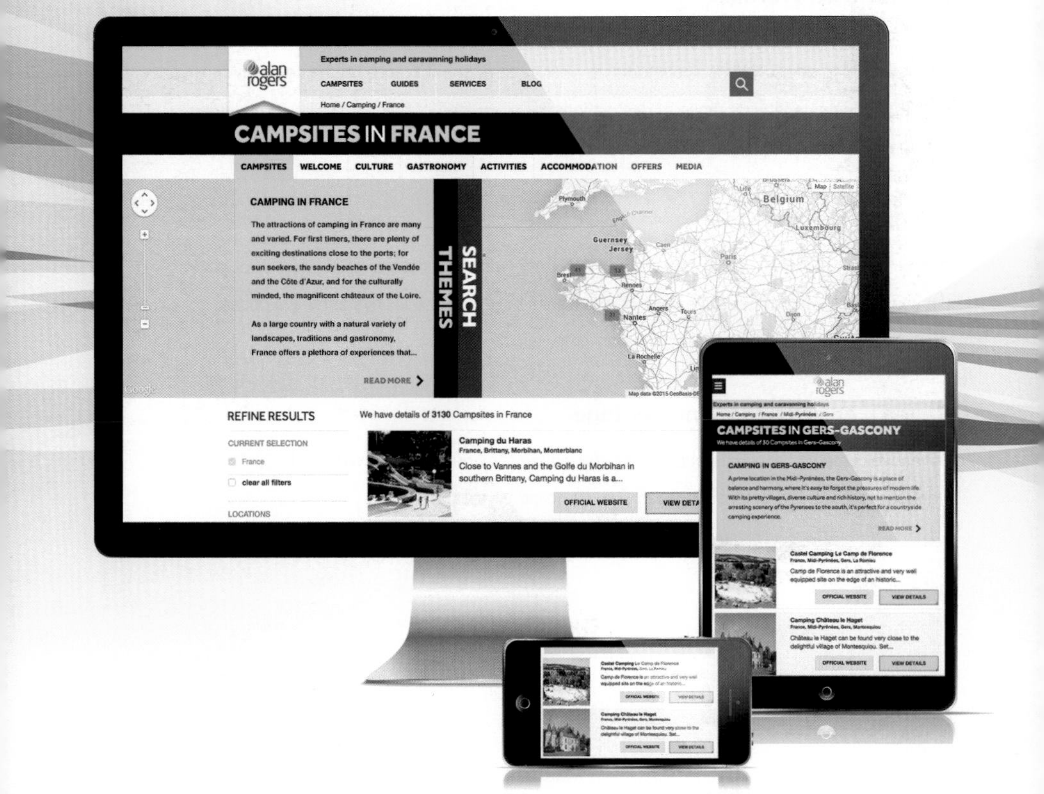

With over 8,000 campsites listed and 4,000 in-depth reviews at **alanrogers.com**

DÉPARTEMENTS: 22 CÔTES D'ARMOR, 29 FINISTÈRE, 35 ILLE-ET-VILAINE, 56 MORBIHAN

MAJOR CITIES: RENNES AND BREST

Rolling sandy beaches, hidden coves, pretty villages and a picturesque coastline all combine to make Brittany a very popular holiday destination. Full of Celtic culture steeped in myths and legends, Brittany is one of the most distinctive regions of France.

Secluded bays, busy little fishing villages and broad sandy beaches dotted with charming seaside resorts are all to be found along the 2,700 km. of Brittany's coastline. The rugged north shore is a maze of rocky coves, while to the south, there are miles of golden sandy beaches. Inland, tiny country roads weave their way through farmland dotted with stone cottages, alternating with the mysterious forests of Arthurian legend.

Brittany's rich Celtic heritage is evident today in its festivals, folklore and customs, and the area is famous for its standing stones, notably the granite megaliths at Carnac. Castles and manor houses, ornate churches and cathedrals are waiting to be explored, as are the bustling weekly markets displaying the freshest regional produce.

The abbey fortress of Mont Saint-Michel on the north coast (in Normandy) should not be missed and Concarneau in the south is a lovely walled town enclosed by granite rocks.

Places of interest

Cancale: small fishing port and the 'oyster capital' of Brittany.

Carnac: 3,000 standing stones (menhirs).

Concarneau: fishing port, old walled town.

Dinan: historic walled town.

Perros-Guirec: leading resort of the Pink Granite Coast.

Quiberon: boat service to three islands: Belle Ile (largest of the Breton islands), Houat, Hoëdic.

Rennes: capital of Brittany, medieval streets, half-timbered houses; Brittany Museum.

St Malo: historic walled city, fishing port.

Cuisine of the region

Fish and shellfish are commonplace; traditional *crêperies* abound and welcome visitors with a cup of local cider.

Agneau de pré-salé: leg of lamb from animals pastured in the salt marshes and meadows.

Beurre blanc: sauce for fish dishes made with shallots, wine vinegar and butter.

Cotriade: fish soup with potatoes, onions, garlic and butter.

Crêpes Bretonnes: the thinnest of pancakes with a variety of sweet fillings.

Galette: can be a biscuit, cake or pancake; with sweet or savoury fillings.

Gâteau Breton: rich cake.

Poulet blanc Breton: free-range, quality, white Breton chicken.

www.brittanytourism.com
tourism-crtb@tourismebretagne.com
(0)2 99 28 44 30

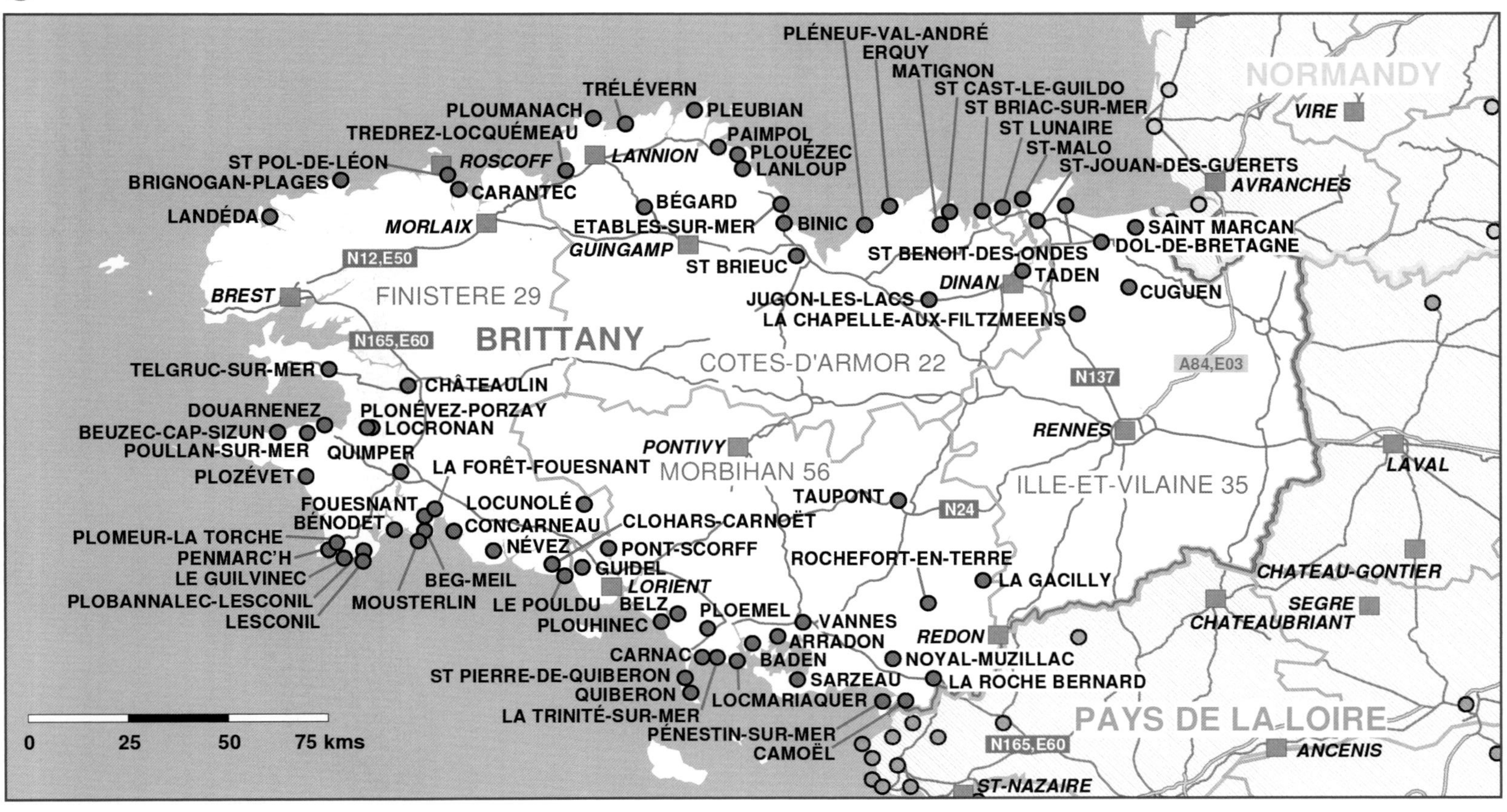
PLÉNEUF-VAL-ANDRÉ
ERQUY
MATIGNON
ST CAST-LE-GUILDO
ST BRIAC-SUR-MER
ST LUNAIRE
ST-MALO
ST-JOUAN-DES-GUERETS
NORMANDY
VIRE
AVRANCHES
TRÉLÉVERN
PLOUMANACH
PLEUBIAN
TREDREZ-LOCQUÉMEAU
PAIMPOL
PLOUËZEC
LANLOUP
ST POL-DE-LÉON
ROSCOFF
LANNION
BRIGNOGAN-PLAGES
CARANTEC
BÉGARD
LANDÉDA
MORLAIX
ETABLES-SUR-MER
BINIC
SAINT MARCAN
DOL-DE-BRETAGNE
GUINGAMP
ST BENOIT-DES-ONDES
N12,E50
ST BRIEUC
DINAN
TADEN
CUGUEN
BREST
FINISTERE 29
JUGON-LES-LACS
LA CHAPELLE-AUX-FILTZMEENS
N165,E60
BRITTANY
COTES-D'ARMOR 22
TELGRUC-SUR-MER
CHÂTEAULIN
N137
A84,E03
DOUARNENEZ
PLONÉVEZ-PORZAY
BEUZEC-CAP-SIZUN
LOCRONAN
RENNES
POULLAN-SUR-MER
QUIMPER
PONTIVY
LAVAL
PLOZÉVET
LA FORÊT-FOUESNANT
MORBIHAN 56
ILLE-ET-VILAINE 35
FOUESNANT
LOCUNOLÉ
TAUPONT
N24
BÉNODET
CONCARNEAU
CLOHARS-CARNOËT
PLOMEUR-LA TORCHE
NÉVEZ
PONT-SCORFF
PENMARC'H
ROCHEFORT-EN-TERRE
GUIDEL
LE GUILVINEC
BEG-MEIL
LA GACILLY
CHATEAU-GONTIER
LORIENT
PLOBANNALEC-LESCONIL
MOUSTERLIN
LE POULDU
BELZ
SEGRE
PLOEMEL
LESCONIL
VANNES
CHATEAUBRIANT
PLOUHINEC
REDON
ARRADON
CARNAC
BADEN
NOYAL-MUZILLAC
ST PIERRE-DE-QUIBERON
SARZEAU
LA ROCHE BERNARD
QUIBERON
LOCMARIAQUER
LA TRINITÉ-SUR-MER
PAYS DE LA LOIRE
0 25 50 75 kms
PÉNESTIN-SUR-MER
CAMOËL
N165,E60
ANCENIS
ST-NAZAIRE

Arradon

Sites et Paysages de Penboch

9 chemin de Penboch, F-56610 Arradon (Morbihan) T: 02 97 44 71 29. E: camping.penboch@wanadoo.fr

alanrogers.com/FR56040

Penboch is 200 metres by footpath from the shores of the Golfe du Morbihan with its many islands, with plenty to do, including watersports, fishing and boat trips. The site, in a peaceful, rural area, is divided into two – the main part, on open ground with hedges and young trees, the other across a minor road in woodland with lots of shade. Penboch has 192 pitches on flat grass, 112 are for touring and they are mostly divided into groups. There is electricity (10A) on all pitches and most have water and drainage.

Facilities

Three sanitary blocks, two on the main part (one heated) and one in the annex, include washbasins in cabins. New washing facilities include private family cabins (extra charge). Laundry. Motorcaravan services. Shop, bar and takeaway (all 15/5-10/9). Heated outdoor pool with slide and paddling pool (15/5-15/9). Indoor pool (all season) with jacuzzi and massage tables. Good playground. Games room. Bicycle hire arranged. American-style motorhomes accepted in low season. WiFi (charged).

Open: 2 April - 25 September.

Directions

From N165 at Auray or Vannes, take D101 along northern shores of Golfe du Morbihan; or leave N165 at D127 signed Ploeren and Arradon. Take turn to Arradon and site is signed. GPS: 47.62206, -2.8007

Charges guide

Per unit incl. 2 persons and electricity	€ 21.40 - € 41.30
extra person	€ 4.50 - € 6.80
child (2-6 yrs)	€ 3.50 - € 5.00
dog	€ 1.50 - € 3.50

Baden

Camping Mané Guernehué

52 rue Mané er Groez, F-56870 Baden (Morbihan) T: 02 97 57 02 06. E: info@camping-baden.com

alanrogers.com/FR56130

Located close to the Morbihan gulf, Mané Guernehué is a smart, modern site with excellent amenities, including an equestrian centre, and a variety of pitches. Some are terraced beneath pine trees, others in a former orchard with delightful views of the surrounding countryside. The 377 pitches are generally large, 210 being occupied by mobile homes and chalets. Most pitches have 10A electricity and a few also have water and drainage. Many are level but a few, particularly in the centre of the site, slope to varying degrees. An impressive indoor pool complex has been added to the existing complex of outdoor pools and there is an equally impressive new spa and wellness facility.

Facilities

Three modern toilet blocks include washbasins in cabins. Facilities for disabled visitors. Washing machines and dryers. Small shop, bar and takeaway (3/4-30/9). Heated outdoor pool with slides (1/5-30/9). Heated indoor pool (all season), water slide. Spa complex. Fishing. Minigolf. Equestrian centre and pony trekking. Fitness room. Teenagers' room with games and TV. Play area. Tree top adventure area. Varied entertainment programme in high season. Mobile homes for rent. WiFi (charged).

Open: 3 April - 1 November.

Directions

From Auray or Vannes use the D101 to Baden and watch for signs to site. GPS: 47.61419, -2.92596

Charges guide

Per unit incl. 2 persons and electricity	€ 21.80 - € 47.50
extra person	€ 6.20 - € 8.40
child (under 7 yrs)	€ 3.60 - € 3.80
dog	€ 3.10 - € 4.20

Camping Cheques accepted.

Bégard

Camping du Donant

Guénézan, F-22140 Bégard (Côtes d'Armor) T: 04 73 93 60 00. E: camping.begard@wanadoo.fr

alanrogers.com/FR22220

Camping du Donant is a purpose-built municipal site conveniently situated for visiting the Trégor countryside, the pink granite coast, the beaches at Trégastel and the sculptured rocks of Ploumanach. The well maintained site has 91 pitches of which 71 are for touring units; 41 have 10A electricity with the remainder being more suitable for tents. The pitches are separated by young trees and bushes providing shade in some places. This is a very pleasant, spacious and reasonably priced campsite. Although there is no shop, bar, restaurant or takeaway, these are available in the town, a short walk away.

Facilities

Toilet facilities are modern and clean. The main block has controllable showers and some washbasins in cubicles, facilities for disabled visitors and laundry with washing machine and dryer. A small block near the more distant pitches has two wet rooms and WCs. TV room. Play area. Boules. Entertainment programme (July/Aug). Bicycle hire. WiFi over site (charged). Chalets and tents for rent.

Open: 1 April - 30 September.

Directions

Site is on southern edge of Bégard between Guingamp and Lannion, just off the D767. Leave at St Laurent exit onto D32 and site is across the Amoripark roundabout. GPS: 48.617477, -3.28311

Charges guide

Per unit incl. 2 persons and electricity	€ 13.40 - € 17.00
extra person	€ 3.30 - € 4.00
child	€ 1.40 - € 5.50

Beg-Meil

Camping de la Piscine

B.P. 12 Kerleya, Beg-Meil, F-29170 Fouesnant (Finistère) T: 02 98 56 56 06.
E: contact@campingdelapiscine.com **alanrogers.com/FR29170**

There are many campsites in this area but la Piscine is notable for the care and attention to detail that contribute to the wellbeing of its visitors. Created by the Caradec family from an apple orchard, the 199 level, grass pitches are of a generous size and are separated by an interesting variety of hedges and trees. Water, drainage and 10A electricity points are provided, normally one stand between two pitches. Several mobile homes are also available to hire. The small bar and takeaway with terrace overlooking the pool complex provides a relaxing focal point. A quiet site set back from the sea, la Piscine will appeal to families looking for good quality without too many on-site activities.

Facilities

Two refurbished toilet units include washbasins in cabins and showers. Facilities for disabled visitors. Laundry facilities. Motorcaravan services. Shop (15/6-11/9). Bar and takeaway (4/7-30/8). Pool complex with three slides, waterfall and jacuzzi. Covered, heated pool (all season). Wellness centre with jacuzzi, massage, sauna and Turkish bath. Play area. BMX track. Bicycle hire. Half-court tennis. Multisports pitch. TV room. Entertainment organised in high season. Free WiFi. Off site: Beach 1 km.

Open: 10 May - 11 September.

Directions

Site is 5 km. south of Fouesnant. Turn off N165 expressway at Coat Conq signed Concarneau and Fouesnant. At Fouesnant join D45 signed Beg-Meil and shortly turn right on D145 signed Mousterlin. In 1 km. turn left and follow signs to site.
GPS: 47.86667, -4.01556

Charges guide

Per unit incl. 2 persons
and electricity € 23.80 - € 37.40
extra person € 4.70 - € 7.60

Belz

Camping le Moulin des Oies

21 rue de la Côte, F-56550 Belz (Morbihan) T: 02 97 55 53 26. E: lemoulindesoies@orange.fr
alanrogers.com/FR56500

This delightful rural site is lovingly cared for by the owners, M. and Mme. Guillois. The 68 generously sized pitches, all with 6A electricity, four also with water and drainage, are grassy, level and marked by trees and shrubs. Separated from the sea by the width of a small road, the campsite has its own salt water inlet, controlled by a sluice; not being affected by the tide and with a small sandy beach, there is safe bathing at all times. To the side of this, there is a shaded, grassy picnic area. The site is ideal for small tents, cycle and motorcycle camping, as there is a kitchen with cooking facilities and a covered picnic area for dining. The nearby town of Belz is within walking distance.

Facilities

Sanitary block with showers. Facilities for disabled visitors. Washing machine, games room, TV. Multisports court. Bar, restaurant and takeaway (Apr-Sept). Saltwater swimming pool with beach. Kitchen with dining area for campers. Bicycle hire. Fishing. Only certain breeds of dog accepted. WiFi (charged). Off site: Bicycle hire 500 m. Belz town 1 km. Beach 3.5 km. Golf and riding 6 km.

Open: 2 April - 1 October.

Directions

Leave the N165 at Auray and take the D22 signed Lorient. At Belz the site is signed on the right after entering the town and the site is 1 km. further.
GPS: 47.680403, -3.175821

Charges guide

Per unit incl. 2 persons
and electricity € 18.80 - € 20.80
extra person € 5.00
No credit cards.

Belz

Camping de Saint Cado

3 rue Pen Perleieu, Saint Cado, F-56550 Belz (Morbihan) T: 02 97 55 31 98. E: info@camping-saintcado.com
alanrogers.com/FR56700

The Ria d'Etel is a small gulf, which although much smaller than the nearby Golfe du Morbihan, has a similar appeal, thanks to its mild climate and attractive scenery. Saint Cado is a delightful spot, famed for its artists' community. This campsite overlooks the little harbour and the Ria d'Etel. There are 109 pitches, 86 for touring units with electricity (3/6/10A), and a degree of shade, some with excellent river views. Ten mobile homes are available for rent. If you are seeking a small, peaceful site in idyllic surroundings, then look no further.

Facilities

Bread delivery van (July/Aug). Bar and takeaway (July/Aug). TV room. Play area. Tennis. Volleyball. Mobile homes for rent. WiFi over site (charged). Off site: Shops, cafés and restaurants 300 m. Fishing and beach 1 km. Golf and riding 5 km. Canoe and boat hire. Coastal footpaths. Sailing.

Open: 1 April - 30 September.

Directions

From the north (N165) take the exit to Etel and Belz. In Belz, follow signs to St Cado and then follow signs to the site. GPS: 47.682996, -3.18869

Charges guide

Per unit incl. 2 persons
and electricity € 13.00 - € 20.00
extra person € 3.80

Bénodet

Camping du Letty

Chemin de Creisanguer, F-29950 Bénodet (Finistère) T: 02 98 57 04 69. E: reception@campingduletty.com

alanrogers.com/FR29030

The Guyader family have ensured that this excellent and attractive site has plenty to offer for all the family. With a charming ambience, it is on the outskirts of the popular resort of Bénodet and spreads over 22 acres with 542 pitches, all for touring units. Groups of four to eight pitches are set in cul-de-sacs with mature hedging and trees to divide each group. All pitches have 10A electricity, water and drainage. As well as direct access to a small sandy beach with a floating pontoon (safe bathing depends on the tides), the site has a grand aquatic parc with heated open-air and indoor pools including pools for children, jacuzzi, and slides. At the attractive floral entrance, former farm buildings provide a host of facilities including a well equipped fitness room and new wellness rooms for massages and jacuzzis. There is also a modern nightclub and bar providing quality live entertainment most evenings.

Facilities

Six well placed toilet blocks are of good quality and include washbasins in large cabins and controllable hot showers. One block includes a separate laundry and dog washing areas. Baby rooms. Provision for disabled visitors. Launderette. Hairdressing room. Motorcaravan services. Well stocked shop. Extensive snack bar and takeaway. Bar with games room and night club. Library/reading room with four computer stations. Entertainment room with satellite TV. Pool complex with indoor and outdoor pools, children's pool, jacuzzi and slide. Fitness centre (no charge). Sauna (charged). Tennis and squash (charged). Boules. Archery. Play area. Entertainment (July/Aug). WiFi (charged).

Open: 20 June - 4 September.

Directions

From N165 take D70 Concarneau exit. At first roundabout take D44 to Fouesnant. Turn right at T-junction. After 2 km. turn left to Fouesnant (still D44). Continue through La Forêt Fouesnant and Fouesnant, picking up signs for Bénodet. Shortly before Bénodet at roundabout turn left (Le Letty). Turn right at next mini-roundabout and site is 500 m. on left. GPS: 47.86700, -4.08783

Charges guide

Per unit incl. 2 persons and electricity	€ 24.00 - € 43.00
extra person	€ 5.00 - € 10.00
child (2-6 yrs)	€ 4.00 - € 7.00

Bénodet

Sunêlia l'Escale Saint-Gilles

Corniche de la Mer, F-29950 Bénodet (Finistère) T: 02 98 57 05 37. E: sunelia@stgilles.fr

alanrogers.com/FR29430

This is a large and busy holiday-style campsite with 467 pitches but only around 90 for tourers. It is facing the Glénan Islands, 50 m. from the beach and close to the River Odet, and offers various types of accommodation. Families with young children rather than teenagers could find that the wide range of activities and entertainment offered, as well as a large sports and fitness complex (100 m. away) make l'Escale St-Gilles a good choice. The touring pitches are small to medium in size and nicely hedged. The whole family will enjoy the indoor and outdoor pools with flumes, slides and moving river.

Facilities

Two toilet blocks with showers and washing facilities in cubicles. Baby room. Facilities for disabled visitors. Laundry facilities. Large shop. Restaurant (28/5-3/9). Bar (Apr-Sept). Takeaway. Indoor heated swimming pool complex and fun pool. Spa and massage (Apr-Sept). Fitness room. Games room. Entertainment. Multisports court. Bicycle hire. WiFi (charged). No dogs in July/Aug.

Open: 2 May - 18 September.

Directions

From Quimper take D34 south to Bénodet. Before entering town take D44 east, signed Fouesnant. Site is signed on right as you leave Bénodet. GPS: 47.862888, -4.095776

Charges guide

Per unit incl. 2 persons and electricity	€ 21.00 - € 44.00
extra person	€ 5.00 - € 10.00

Bénodet

Camping de la Plage

20 rue du Poulquer, F-29950 Bénodet (Finistère) T: 02 98 57 00 55. E: laplagebenodet@orange.fr

alanrogers.com/FR29500

This is a large, well organised site that has a rural feel, although it is only 300 m. from the beach and 800 m. from the popular seaside town of Bénodet. There is a great variety of shrubs and trees offering ample shade and privacy for the 270 grassy pitches. There are 160 for touring (electricity 6/10A), attractively and informally laid out on one side of the site, with some hardstandings for motorcaravans. Access for large units may be difficult. A further 100 pitches are used for mobile homes to rent. A splendid pool complex has an indoor swimming pool, two water chutes, toddlers' pool and a jacuzzi.

Facilities

Four large adequate toilet blocks with facilities for children, families and campers with disabilities although access is not easy. Motorcaravan services. Shop, bar with TV and takeaway (all July/Aug). Heated swimming and paddling pools (one can be covered), flumes, toboggan, jacuzzi (all season). Multisports court. Boules. Exercise bikes. Play areas. Games room. Miniclub and entertainment (July/Aug). Bicycle hire. Mobile homes and chalets for rent (18/4 to 13/9). WiFi (charged). Off site: Beach 300 m.

Open: 13 June - 13 September.

Directions

From Fouesnant take D44 west towards Bénodet. After 10 km. take Le Letty road south. Site is well signed. GPS: 47.86768, -4.09626

Charges guide

Per unit incl. 2 persons and electricity	€ 25.70 - € 26.70
extra person	€ 7.00
child (2-12 yrs)	€ 4.00
dog	€ 3.60

Bénodet

Camping du Poulquer

Rue du Poulquer, F-29950 Bénodet (Finistère) T: 02 98 57 04 19. E: campingdupoulquer@wanadoo.fr

alanrogers.com/FR29760

Camping du Poulquer is well located within 200 metres of Bénodet's large sandy beach and just 800 metres from the town centre with its promenades, restaurants and shops. Family run with a friendly ambience, and very popular with a high level of returning campers, this is a pretty site with many trees and attractive floral displays. The 148 touring pitches are set away from the entertainment areas in a tranquil environment. They are on grass and are a mixture of flat and slightly sloping. Electricity (10A) is provided. The nearby Iles Glénan are ideal for a summer daytrip and offer a small nature reserve and idyllic sandy beaches.

Facilities

Sanitary facilities include some private cabins and provision for visitors with disabilities. Washing machine. Shop. Bar with snacks and takeaway (July/Aug). Indoor pool (15/5-15/9) with sauna, steam room and jacuzzi. Outdoor pool with flumes (1/6-5/9). Entertainment room. Games and play areas for children. Boules. Free WiFi in bar area. Off site: Beach 200 m. Golf, bicycle hire, tennis and watersports nearby.

Open: 15 May - 30 September.

Directions

Travel east from Lorient on N165, take exit 51 on to D70 then D44 signed Fouesnant, and follow road to outskirts of Bénodet. After Bénodet sign, follow signs left for Letty, then turn right and follow signs to site on left. GPS: 47.86779, -4.09848

Charges guide

Per unit incl. 2 persons and electricity	€ 21.10 - € 26.40
extra person	€ 5.70 - € 7.20

Beuzec-Cap-Sizun

Camping Pors Peron

F-29790 Beuzec-Cap-Sizun (Finistère) T: 02 98 70 40 24. E: info@campingporsperon.com

alanrogers.com/FR29540

This small site situated on the Cap Sizun peninsula is lovingly cared for by English owners, Graham and Nikki Hatch. The site is hilly but the terrain has been terraced to provide 98 fairly level pitches. Many mature trees and shrubs provide some shade and areas of privacy. Long leads are required for the 60 electricity hook-ups (10A). The owners have recently purchased new wooden mobile homes to blend in with the rural ambiance of their site. These are all equipped with televisions receiving English and French channels. A 200 m. walk takes you to a delightful sandy bay and you can access a coastal path.

Facilities

One central toilet block has open style washbasins and preset showers. Facilities for disabled visitors and babies (kept locked). Laundry facilities. Small shop in reception, bread delivered daily. Small, unfenced but safe play area with trampoline. Bicycle hire. Boules. Library and board games. WiFi. Off site: Medieval town of Pont Croix 5 km. Douarnenez for shops, market and restaurants 12 km.

Open: 1 April - 31 October.

Directions

West from Douarnenez on D7 for 12 km. Site signed on right towards Pors Peron. GPS: 48.08435, -4.48191

Charges guide

Per unit incl. 2 persons and electricity	€ 16.00 - € 19.00
extra person	€ 4.00 - € 5.00
child (2-7 yrs)	€ 3.00 - € 4.00

Binic

Camping le Panoramic

Rue Gasselin, F-22520 Binic (Côtes d'Armor) T: 02 96 73 60 43. E: camping.le.panoramic@wanadoo.fr

alanrogers.com/FR22310

You will receive a warm welcome from the owners of this site on the Goëlo coast. It is in a woodland setting, yet only 800 m. from the beaches and the popular resort of Binic. It is ideally situated for visiting the many charming little resorts along this coast. There are 176 pitches in total, 69 are available for touring of which 50 have 10A electricity. All are divided by neat hedging and are easily accessible. A feature of this campsite is the vast range of activities for all ages. These are arranged during July and August and include themed soirées, night markets and Breton games.

Facilities

Two well appointed toilet blocks with all necessary facilities, including those for disabled visitors. Bar with basic shop (all season). Restaurant (Tues/Thurs. in low season, daily in high season). Bread to order. Covered and heated pool (all season). Fenced play area. Boules. Games/TV room. Good range of entertainment (July/Aug). WiFi throughout. Off site: Casino. Zoo. Fishing and sailing 800 m. Riding 4 km. Golf 7 km.

Open: 29 March - 28 September.

Directions

From N12 St Brieuc bypass head north on D786 towards Paimpol. On approaching Binic look for campsite sign to right. GPS: 48.591895, -2.824237

Charges guide

Per unit incl. 2 persons and electricity	€ 16.00 - € 27.00
extra person	€ 4.00 - € 6.30
child (under 7 yrs)	€ 2.75 - € 4.00

Brignogan-Plages

Camping de la Côte des Légendes

Rue Douar ar Pont, F-29890 Brignogan-Plages (Finistère) T: 02 98 83 41 65.

E: camping-cote-des-legendes@orange.fr alanrogers.com/FR29340

With direct access to a safe, sandy beach on the Baie de Brignogan and adjacent to a Centre Nautique (sailing, windsurfing, kayaking), this site could be ideal for a family seaside holiday in high season. It is very quiet in low season. There are 102 level touring pitches arranged in rows and protected by hedges, together with 31 privately owned mobile homes and 14 for rent. A small shop and bar are open all season. Activities are arranged for adults and children by the helpful owner, Manuelle; she and her husband, Pierre, both speak good English.

Facilities

Main toilet facilities (open only in July/Aug) are at the rear of the site in a large block that provides washbasins in cubicles, laundry room, baby baths and facilities for disabled visitors. A second small block near the beach is open all season. Motorcaravan services. Bar and small shop (July/Aug). Playground and playing field. WiFi (charged). Off site: Watersports centre adjacent. Village services 700 m. Bicycle hire 1 km. Riding 6 km.

Open: 29 March - 12 November.

Directions

From Roscoff ferry terminal take D58 towards Morlaix. After 6 km. turn right on D10 towards Plouescat and then Plouguerneau. Turn right on D770 to Brignogan-Plages. At top of main street bear left following signs (NOT sat nav!) for site and Club Nautique. GPS: 48.67278, -4.32929

Charges guide

Per unit incl. 2 persons and electricity	€ 15.85 - € 19.85
extra person	€ 3.85 - € 4.80

Camoël

Camping les Embruns

Camoëlin, F-56130 Camoël (Morbihan) T: 02 99 90 07 65. E: contact@camping-lesembruns.com

alanrogers.com/FR56480

This small site is situated midway between the busy town of La Roche Bernard and some of Brittany's finest beaches. The young owners, Anita and Nicholas Thaunoux, keep the site immaculate and have made it attractive with well tended flowers and shrubs. The 20 touring pitches are modest in size and some offer shade. All have 10A electricity. On-site activities are rather limited, but its location is good for walking and cycling. Families with young children would find the site and the area ideal.

Facilities

One old toilet block. Washing machine. Reception sells a limited range of food. Small play area. Bicycle hire. Boules. Volleyball. Off site: Shops and restaurants 3 km. in Camoël. Large town of Roche Bernard 15 km. with beaches, boat launching, fishing and riding.

Open: 30 March - 11 November.

Directions

Leave N165 at Arzal exit and head south on D139 to Camoël. Exit Camoël on D34 west. In 500 m. turn right. Site well signed. GPS: 47.48758, -2.42098

Charges guide

Per unit incl. 2 persons and electricity	€ 16.50 - € 25.00
extra person	€ 3.00 - € 5.50
child (under 10 yrs)	€ 2.50 - € 4.00
dog	€ 3.00

Carantec

Yelloh! Village les Mouettes

50 route de la Grande Grève, F-29660 Carantec (Finistère) T: 02 98 67 02 46. E: contact@les-mouettes.com
alanrogers.com/FR29000

Les Mouettes is a sheltered site on the edge of an attractive bay, with access to the sea at the front of the site. In a wooded setting with many attractive trees and shrubs, the 474 pitches include 125 for touring units, all with electricity, water and drainage. The remainder are taken by tour operators and by 348 mobile homes and chalets for rent. At the centre of the 'village' are shops, a bar, a restaurant, an entertainment stage, sports facilities and an impressive heated pool complex with swimming, paddling and water slide pools, plus a 'tropical river', jacuzzi and sauna.

Facilities

Two clean sanitary blocks include controllable showers and washbasins in cabins. Facilities for children, babies and disabled visitors. Laundry. Shop (limited hours outside the main season). Takeaway. Bar with TV. Restaurant/pizzeria/grill. Heated pool complex indoor (all season) and outdoor (from 12/5). Beauty salon. Games rooms. Play area. Half-court tennis. Minigolf. Bicycle hire. Entertainment. Large units should phone first. WiFi over site (charged). Off site: Beach 2 km.

Open: 17 April - 6 September.

Directions

Carantec is 15 km. northwest of Morlaix and 15 km. by road from Roscoff. From D58 Roscoff-Morlaix road, turn east to Carantec on D173. In 4 km. site is signed to the left at roundabout immediately after supermarket on right. GPS: 48.65807, -3.92833

Charges guide

Per unit incl. 2 persons, electricity and water	€ 18.00 - € 50.00
extra person	€ 6.00 - € 9.00

Carnac

Castel Camping la Grande Métairie

Route des Alignements de Kermario-Kerlescan, B.P. 85, F-56342 Carnac (Morbihan) T: 02 97 52 24 01.
E: info@lagrandemetairie.com **alanrogers.com/FR56010**

La Grande Métairie is a good quality site situated back from the sea, close to the impressive rows of the famous Carnac menhirs (giant prehistoric standing stones). The site has 581 individual pitches (112 for touring units), surrounded by hedges and trees. All have 10A electricity (some need long leads). The site is well known and popular and has many British visitors, with 314 pitches taken by tour operators. It is ideal for families with children of all ages. It is lively and busy over a long season with new activities added each year. Musical evenings, barbecues and other organised events including occasional dances are held in an outdoor amphitheatre (pitches near these facilities may be noisy late at night – the bar closes at midnight). Paddocks with ponds are home for ducks, goats and ponies to watch and feed. There are also pony rides around the site. A super pool complex comprises heated indoor and outdoor pools, water slides and toboggans and a jacuzzi. A local market takes place at Carnac.

Facilities

Three large, well maintained toilet blocks with washbasins in cabins. Facilities for babies and disabled visitors. Laundry facilities. Motorcaravan services. Shops (from 17/5). Bar lounge and terrace, takeaway (from 21/5) and restaurant. TV and games rooms. Swimming pool complex with bar. Playgrounds and playing field. Tennis. Minigolf. BMX track. Bicycle hire. Fishing. Zip-wire. Paintball. Helicopter rides (July/Aug). Amphitheatre. Events and entertainment. American-style motorhomes accepted up to 27 ft. WiFi throughout (charged).

Open: 5 April - 14 September.

Directions

From N165 take Quiberon/Carnac exit onto the D768. After 5 km. turn south onto D119 (Carnac). At roundabout and after 4 km. turn left (northeast) onto D196 to the site. GPS: 47.5973, -3.0607

Charges guide

Per unit incl. 2 persons and electricity	€ 18.00 - € 51.00
extra person	€ 4.00 - € 8.00
child (4-7 yrs)	free - € 5.40
dog	€ 5.00

Carnac

Camping Moulin de Kermaux

Route de Kerlescan, F-56340 Carnac (Morbihan) T: 02 97 52 15 90. E: moulin-de-kermaux@wanadoo.fr

alanrogers.com/FR56090

Only 100 m. from the famous Carnac megaliths, Moulin de Kermaux is an excellent base from which to see these ancient stones as they portray their ever changing mood, colour and profile. Family run, the site has 156 pitches, 45 for tourers; all have 10/15A electricity and 35 have water and drainage. They are mostly separated by hedges and have many mature trees offering welcome shade. The compact nature of the site offers a safe environment for parents and children of all ages. There is an aquatic complex with heated indoor and outdoor pools and a separate toboggan pool. This is a well run, quiet and immaculately kept site.

Facilities

The modern, fully equipped, heated sanitary block has washbasins in cabins. Facilities for disabled visitors. Baby room. Laundry facilities. Motorcaravan services. Shop (July/Aug). Bar with satellite TV. Takeaway (26/6-31/8). Swimming and paddling pools. Sauna and jacuzzi. Adventure playground. Minigolf. Organised activities (July/Aug). Bicycle hire. WiFi over part of site (charged).

Open: 2 April - 17 September.

Directions

From N165 take Quiberon/Carnac exit onto D768. After 5 km. turn south on D119 towards Carnac. After 4 km. at roundabout turn left (northeast) on D196 to site. GPS: 47.59675, -3.06162

Charges guide

Per unit incl. 2 persons and electricity	€ 24.00 - € 38.00
extra person	€ 6.50

Carnac

Camping le Moustoir

Route du Moustoir, F-56340 Carnac (Morbihan) T: 02 97 52 16 18. E: info@lemoustoir.com

alanrogers.com/FR56110

Camping le Moustoir is a friendly, family run site situated about three kilometres inland from the many beaches of the area and close to the famous alignments of standing stones. The 65 touring pitches (of 165) are grassy and separated by shrubs and hedges, with several shaded by tall pine trees. All have 10A electricity. There is a popular pool area with slides, swimming pool and a paddling pool with mushroom fountain and a second covered pool complex. The bar and terrace become the social centre of the site in the evenings. A high season entertainment programme includes a daily miniclub attracting children of several nationalities.

Facilities

Toilet block is in traditional style and is well maintained. Facilities for disabled visitors and babies. Motorcaravan services. Shop, bar, restaurant and takeaway. Heated swimming pool (21x8 m), water slides, and paddling pool (10/5-30/9). Heated indoor swimming pool (all season). Wellness area. Adventure playground. Tennis. Boules. Volleyball. Football. Basketball. Table tennis. Pool. Miniclub. WiFi near bar (free).

Open: 11 April - 19 September.

Directions

From N165, take exit to D768 (Carnac, Quiberon). After 5 km. at second crossroads turn left (D119) towards Carnac. After 3 km. turn left (oblique turning) after a hotel. Site is 500 m. on left. GPS: 47.60825, -3.06587

Charges guide

Per unit incl. 2 persons and electricity	€ 24.00 - € 41.00

Camping Cheques accepted.

Carnac

Camping les Druides

55 chemin de Beaumer, F-56340 Carnac (Morbihan) T: 02 97 52 08 18. E: contact@camping-les-druides.com

alanrogers.com/FR56370

Situated in a small village just two kilometres from the town of Carnac, this very pleasant site has 110 pitches on level grass, most having high mature hedges that give a good feel of privacy. Of these, 81 have good access to 6/10A electricity while 30 also have water and waste water. You will receive a very warm welcome from Mme. Geneviève and her daughter, who have built this site up over many years. This is a lovely base from which to explore the region; the famous megaliths are close by and the beaches are only 500 metres away. Nearby Carnac offers a good choice of restaurants, bars and shops.

Facilities

Two modern sanitary blocks, some washbasins in cubicles, preset showers and British style WCs. Baby room. Laundry room with washer/dryer and sinks (all kept very clean). Excellent facilities for disabled visitors. Bread and snacks from reception. Superb fenced swimming pool open from 5/5 (heated 1/6-10/9) with jacuzzi and tropical plants. Games room with TV. Play areas. Multisports court. Pétanque. WiFi (charged).

Open: 23 April - 10 September.

Directions

From N165 Vannes-Lorient dual carriageway south of Auray, take exit for Carnac. Head southwest on D768 for 7 km. Turn south on D119 (Carnac). In Carnac centre, east on D781 towards St Philibert. Turn right and follow signs to site on right before Carnac-Plage area. GPS: 47.58033, -3.05685

Charges guide

Per unit incl. 2 persons and electricity	€ 24.30 - € 38.80

Carnac

Flower Camping du Lac

F-56340 Carnac (Morbihan) T: 02 97 55 78 78. E: info@lelac-carnac.com

alanrogers.com/FR56390

Overlooking the lake and situated between the Morbihan Gulf and the Quiberon peninsula, this site is only 3 km. from the port of La Trinité-sur-Mer while the famous megaliths are even closer. The site is well maintained, with flowering landscaped gardens and mature trees and shrubs giving plenty of shade and some privacy. The 120 pitches are of various sizes, many giving superb views of the lake; there is good access for larger units. The owner is aiming to appeal to young families and couples looking for a quiet holiday in an idyllic setting.

Facilities

Two sanitary blocks, kept clean and well maintained. Baby bath. Laundry units. Facilities for disabled visitors. Small shop (all season) with limited takeaway (1/7-30/8). Heated swimming pool (15/5-30/9). Play area with trampolines. Games room with electronic games and table football. TV room. Fishing. Bicycle hire. Cycling and canoe activities arranged regularly. Kayaks, surfboards and cars for hire. WiFi (free).

Open: 1 April - 30 October.

Directions

From N165 Vannes-Lorient dual carriageway, take exit for Carnac. Head southwest on D768 for 4 km, turn south on D186 La Trinité-sur-Mer road. Site is well signed from here and at end of a long access road (1.5 km). GPS: 47.61135, -3.0288

Charges guide

Per unit incl. 2 persons and electricity	€ 21.10 - € 34.10
extra person	€ 5.00

Carnac

Camping le Rosnual

2 chemin de Rosnual, F-56340 Carnac (Morbihan) T: 02 52 20 01 26. E: info@vagues-oceanes.com

alanrogers.com/FR56420

Situated just 3 km. from Carnac, this is a well maintained and well organised, large village-style site with 316 mobile homes and chalets for hire and eight pitches available for touring. The pitches are well set out in small separate areas with plenty of established trees and shrubs, but this is essentially a mobile home park. With the all-singing, all-dancing facilities, you usually find this type of site is a good choice for families who are looking for an action packed holiday. The modern reception has information about this beautiful part of Brittany, the staff are very helpful and English is spoken. A free bus and the tourist mini-train both stop at the gate to take you into town.

Facilities

One large modern and well maintained sanitary block. Large laundry room. Supermarket. Snack bar with takeaway and bar with TV. Restaurant. Heated indoor pool (all season), outdoor (May-Sept). Entertainment and activities (July/Aug) include two children's clubs (4-8 yrs, 8-12 yrs), aerobics and discos. Games room. Multisports court. Bicycle hire. WiFi throughout.

Open: 2 April - 25 September.

Directions

From N165 Vannes-Lorient dual carriageway south of Auray, head southwest on D768 towards Carnac and follow signs for Carnac. Camping Rosnual is well signed from here and is to east of D119, 2 km. before Carnac town. GPS: 47.602228, -3.069391

Charges guide

Per unit incl. 2 persons and electricity	€ 39.00
extra person	€ 9.00

Châteaulin

Camping la Pointe

La Pointe, Saint Coulitz, F-29150 Châteaulin (Finistère) T: 02 98 86 51 53. E: lapointecamping@aol.com

alanrogers.com/FR29280

This small rural campsite is situated by the River Aulne on the outskirts of Châteaulin. The English owners, Julie and Marcus Gregory, have developed the site to provide a friendly and relaxed atmosphere. The 60 pitches vary in size and quality, 50 have 10A electricity and a few provide hardstanding for heavier units. There is a small kitchen garden complete with chickens, where campers can purchase free range eggs and other produce and are also welcome to just sit and relax. A family/games room can be found above the well maintained toilet block. Weekly crêpe evenings are organised in July and August.

Facilities

The toilet and shower block also provides facilities for disabled visitors. Baby changing area. Laundry facilities. Motorcaravan services. Family/games room. Small shop for basics and bread. Fresh eggs and produce available from the kitchen garden. Free WiFi over site. Bicycle and kayak hire. Off site: Fishing in the Aulne 200 m. (permit needed). Châteaulin 1.5 km. with shops, bars and restaurants. Beach 20 km.

Open: 15 March - 15 October.

Directions

From Quimper or Brest on N165, exit at 'Châteaulin Centre'. From Châteaulin follow signs to St Coulitz. After 1.5 km. turn left and continue 100 m. GPS: 48.18746, -4.0848

Charges guide

Per unit incl. 2 persons and electricity	€ 19.50 - € 22.00

Camping Cheques accepted.

Châteaulin

Camping de Rodaven

Rocade de Prat Bihan, F-29150 Châteaulin (Finistère) T: 02 98 86 32 93. E: contact@campingderodaven.fr

alanrogers.com/FR29640

This riverside campsite is located within a short walk of Châteaulin and has been transformed by its enthusiastic owner, M. Gerente, into a most delightful place to stay. There are 94 reasonably sized, level, grassy pitches (40 with 10A electricity). They are divided by various flowering shrubs, small trees and, in the more open area of the site, by white lines on the grass. A pleasant focal point is a small bar with a covered terrace. The site is alongside the Nantes Brest canal, which offers good fishing (permit required). The nearest sandy beach is at Pentrez (15 km).

Facilities

Toilet and shower block with facilities for disabled campers. Washing machine and dryer. Bar, snack bar with takeaway (from 1/5). Play area. Bicycle hire. Pedalo and canoe hire. Archery. Boules. Fishing on canal (permit required). Free WiFi over part of site. Off site: Swimming pool and tennis courts 200 m. Town centre 350 m. Beach 15 km. Locronan and Quimper.

Open: 1 April - 30 September.

Directions

From the direction of Brest on N165 leave at first sign for Châteaulin and follow D770 to the town. Within the town follow signs for Piscine. Opposite Piscine you will see sign for the campsite. GPS: 48.18985, -4.09012

Charges guide

Per unit incl. 2 persons and electricity	€ 15.50 - € 16.50

Camping Cheques accepted.

Châteaulin

Camping Ty Provost

Dinéault, F-29150 Châteaulin (Finistère) T: 02 98 86 29 23. E: contact@typrovost.com

alanrogers.com/FR29645

Ty Provost is a small, simple campsite in a village outside the historic riverside town of Châteaulin in Finistère, near the western tip of Brittany. There are 40 large pitches on level ground, some occupied by modern wooden chalets. Many are separated by hedges and 6/10A electricity connections are provided on 20 pitches. Reception provides tourist information and a few basic food supplies. Châteaulin has shops, bars and restaurants while the ancient town of Quimper offers a wider choice by day and by night. M. Nicolas is a keen walker and is able to supply notes on detailed walking and cycling routes in the area. He will also lead walks himself.

Facilities

Central toilet block and separate baby room. Facilities for disabled visitors. Laundry room. Reception with bar, small shop for basic food supplies and adjacent picnic room. Games room. Free WiFi. Off site: Fishing and bicycle hire 3 km. Châteaulin 3.5 km. Douarnenez 26 km. Quimper 35 km. Audierne with boat trips to Ile de Sein 46 km.

Open: 1 June - 14 September.

Directions

Châteaulin is 35 km. north of Quimper off the N165 Brest-Quimper expressway. From the town take D887 west signed Crozon, turn north on Route de Toul Ar C'hoat then fork left towards Dinéault. Site is signed to right. GPS: 48.207095, -4.124004

Charges guide

Per unit incl. 2 persons and electricity	€ 21.70
extra person	€ 3.90

Clohars-Carnoët

Flower Camping le Kergariou

Kervec, F-29360 Clohars-Carnoët (Finistère) T: 02 98 71 54 65. E: camping.lekergariou@wanadoo.fr

alanrogers.com/FR29950

Le Kergariou is a pleasant family site close to the pretty village of Clohars-Carnoët, and is located around a mile from the beach. There are 100 grassy pitches here and most have electrical connections. The site boasts an attractive swimming pool with an adjoining paddling pool, and also has a football pitch and well equipped play area. A number of mobile homes and chalets are available for rent. The pretty, and typically Breton, port of Doëlan is around 1.5 km. away and has proved a popular film location. The larger resort of Le Pouldu is also close at hand.

Facilities

One modern toilet block has a baby room and facilities for disabled campers. Family shower room. Washing machines and dryers. No shop, but bread can be ordered. Swimming pool (15/6-30/8). Paddling pool. Games room. Play area. Sports field. Mobile homes and caravans for rent. Bicycle hire. Off site: Shops and restaurants in Doëlan and Clohars-Carnoët. Cycling and coastal walking trails. Sailing. Fishing 1.5 km. Riding 3 km.

Open: 1 April - 7 September.

Directions

From north (N165) leave at Quimperlé exit (D28) and head south on D16 to Clohars-Carnoët. Continue on D16 towards Doëlan and you will see the site before reaching Doëlan. GPS: 47.782737, -3.588833

Charges guide

Per unit incl. 2 persons and electricity	€ 8.00 - € 19.00
extra person	€ 3.00 - € 4.00
child (under 7 yrs)	€ 2.00 - € 2.50

Concarneau

Flower Camping le Cabellou Plage

Avenue du Cabellou, F-29185 Concarneau (Finistère) T: 02 98 97 37 41. E: info@le-cabellou-plage.com

alanrogers.com/FR29520

Le Cabellou Plage is a very pleasant, well maintained site located close to Concarneau. The large, grassy pitches are divided by young hedges, all have 10A electricity and some also have water and drainage. Many have fine views to the nearby beach and the old walled town beyond. The enthusiastic owner has tastefully landscaped many areas of the site with a profusion of shrubs and flowers. A large swimming pool on site is overlooked by a terrace and bar, and the beach is just 25 m. away. The wide and attractive bay is ideal for canoeing and canoes are available for hire from the site. The area for mobile homes is most attractive and cars are parked in an adjacent parking area. A number of safari tents are also available to hire. La Cabellou is ideally situated for those wishing to visit Concarneau with shops, restaurants and bars and its twice weekly market. A regular bus service is available from outside the campsite. There are plenty of walking and cycling opportunities direct from the site. Pont Aven and the cathedral city of Quimper are also within easy reach.

Facilities

One modern toilet block is bright and cheerful and provides mainly open style washbasins and preset showers. Baby room. Facilities for disabled visitors. Laundry room. Motorcaravan Services. Shop (July/Aug). Bar with TV and Internet access (July-Aug). Outdoor heated swimming pool (all season). Play area. Sea fishing. Scuba lessons and water gymnastics. Bicycle hire. Free WiFi over part of site. Off site: Supermarkets, shops and restaurants in Concarneau 4 km. Tennis 3 km.

Open: 25 April - 12 September.

Directions

Site is just south of Concarneau. Take the D783 towards Tregunc. Turn right onto Avenue Cabellou. Site is well signed from here.
GPS: 47.85616, -3.90005

Charges guide

Per unit incl. 2 persons and electricity	€ 19.50 - € 34.50
extra person	€ 3.00 - € 6.00
child (3-6 yrs)	€ 2.50 - € 4.50
dog	€ 2.00 - € 4.00

Concarneau

Camping les Sables Blancs

Avenue Le Dorlett, F-29900 Concarneau (Finistère) T: 02 98 97 16 44.
E: contact@camping-lessablesblancs.com **alanrogers.com/FR29150**

This is an attractive terraced site overlooking the sea on the outskirts of Concarneau. Most of the 105 touring pitches are shaded by mature trees and shrubs. All with 10A electricity (long leads may be required), they are level and well shaded though access to some could prove a little difficult for large units. A traditionally styled bar, restaurant and conservatory opens out onto a terrace with a swimming pool overlooking the Baie de la Forêt. Although the site is terraced with steep steps in places, the main touring pitches are on the top part of the site close to the main facilities.

Facilities

One new modern toilet block provides very good facilities including washbasins (some in cubicles) and showers. Facilities for babies and disabled visitors. New laundry facilities. Bar and restaurant (3/4-30/9). Heated outdoor swimming pool (12/4-14/9). Play area. Evening entertainment (July/Aug). Billiards room. Free WiFi in bar. Off site: Concarneau with shops, bars and restaurants. Beach 150 m. Riding 1 km. Bicycle hire 1.5 km.

Open: 1 April - 31 October.

Directions

Leave the N165 for Concarneau on D70. Site is situated on the northern edge of town on the coast road. Well signed. GPS: 47.88195, -3.92195

Charges guide

Per unit incl. 2 persons and electricity (10A)	€ 18.00 - € 30.00
extra person	€ 4.00 - € 7.00
child (2-16 yrs)	€ 2.00 - € 4.00
dog	€ 2.00

Concarneau

Camping les Prés Verts

B.P. 612, Kernous-Plage, F-29186 Concarneau (Finistère) T: 02 98 97 09 74. E: info@presverts.com

alanrogers.com/FR29190

This quiet, rural family run site has all the basic features expected of a campsite but its stylish pool complex with Romanesque style columns and statue, plants and flower tubs is a more unusual feature. The 142 pitches are mostly arranged on long, open, grassy areas either side of main access roads. Specimen trees, shrubs and hedges divide the site into smaller areas. There is an area towards the rear of the site where the pitches have sea views. There is direct access to the sandy beach with no roads to cross (300 m). Concarneau is just 2.5 km.

Facilities

Two toilet blocks provide unisex WCs, but separate washing facilities for ladies and men. Preset hot showers and washbasins in cabins, both closed 21.00-08.00. Some child size toilets. Facilities for disabled visitors. Laundry facilities. Shop (1/7-25/8). Pizza service twice weekly. Heated swimming pool (1/6-31/8) and paddling pool. Playground (0-5 yrs). Minigolf (charged). Off site: Path to sandy/rocky beach 300 m. Coastal path. Riding 1 km. Bicycle hire 1.5 km. Supermarket 2 km.

Open: 1 May - 30 September.

Directions

Turn off C7 road, 2.5 km. north of Concarneau, where site is signed. Take third left after Hotel de l'Océan. GPS: 47.8907, -3.9383

Charges guide

Per unit incl. 2 persons and electricity (6A)	€ 22.00 - € 28.90
extra person	€ 5.20 - € 6.20
child (2-9 yrs)	€ 3.20 - € 4.20
dog	€ 2.00 - € 2.50

Cuguen

Camping le Bois Coudrais

F-35270 Cuguen (Ille-et-Vilaine) T: 02 99 73 27 45. E: info@vacancebretagne.com

alanrogers.com/FR35010

This gem of a campsite, owned and run by Claire and Philippe Ybert, a delightful couple from Jersey, is the kind of small, rural site that is becoming a rarity in France. It has 25 well kept, grassy pitches (19 with electrical connections nearby), some separated by young shrubs, others with mature trees. They are spread over three small fields, one for tents with an area set aside for ball games. The owners are intent on keeping their site a peaceful and natural retreat. An enclosure, home to a group of friendly goats and some chickens, is a magnet for children. Four attractive gîtes and a tent are available to rent but there are no mobile homes, organised games or music.

Facilities

The toilet block beside the house provides washbasins in cubicles, showers, plus facilities for disabled visitors. Bar (all season) with takeaway (June-Sept). Fresh bread can be ordered night before. Small heated swimming pool (15/5-15/9). Animal enclosure. Games field. Free WiFi over site. Gîtes for hire. Off site: Shops and restaurants in Combourg 10 km. Fishing 13 km. Golf, riding, lake with beach, sailing and boat launching 15 km. Dinan, Dinard, St Malo and Rennes all within 50 km.

Open: 28 April - 30 September.

Directions

Cuguen is 40 km. south east of St Malo. From N137 St Malo-Rennes road turn east on D794 to Combourg and on towards Fougères. Turn north on D83 for Mont St-Michel. Site is 1 km. past Cuguen on the left, well signed. GPS: 48.45395, -1.651333

Charges guide

Per unit incl. 2 persons and electricity	€ 23.40
extra person	€ 4.00
child (0-14 yrs)	€ 3.00

No credit cards.
20% off in May, June and September when booked in advance.

Dol-de-Bretagne

Castel Camping Domaine des Ormes

Epiniac, F-35120 Dol-de-Bretagne (Ille-et-Vilaine) T: 02 99 73 53 00. E: info@lesormes.com

alanrogers.com/FR35020

This impressive site in the grounds of the Château des Ormes is in the north east part of Brittany, in an estate of wooded parkland and lakes. It is busy in high season but peaceful at other times, with an impressive range of facilities and a wide range of accommodation. Of the 700 pitches, 140 are for tourers (most with 6A electricity, some with 16A and their own water and waste water). They are of varying sizes (80-150 sq.m) and there is a choice of terrain – flat or gently sloping, wooded, walled or open. The rest are occupied by tour operators (550) and by mobile homes (120 to rent).

Facilities

The heated sanitary blocks are of a good standard, with family cubicles and facilities for babies, children and disabled visitors. Motorcaravan services. Supermarket, bar, restaurant, pizzeria and takeaway. Games room, bar and disco. Indoor and outdoor pools, an impressive aqua park and wave pool. Adventure play area. Golf (charged). Bicycle hire. Fishing. Equestrian centre (charged). Minigolf. Tennis. Sports ground. Paintball. Archery. Zip wire. Climbing wall. Cricket club. WiFi over site (charged).

Open: 1 April - 24 September.

Directions

Site is off D795 8 km. south of Dol-de-Bretagne, 11 km. north of Combourg. GPS: 48.4903, -1.7278

Charges guide

Per unit incl. 2 persons and electricity	€ 30.40 - € 54.10
extra person	€ 4.70 - € 8.30
child (3-13 yrs)	€ 3.10 - € 5.20
dog	€ 2.10

Douarnenez

Camping Indigo Douarnenez

69 avenue du Bois d'Isis, F-29100 Douarnenez (Finistère) T: 02 98 74 05 67.

E: douarnenez@camping-indigo.com **alanrogers.com/FR29940**

The Indigo group is renowned for its 'natural' campsites. Indigo Douarnenez has an attractive forest setting just 400 m. from the superb Plage des Sables Blancs. There are 124 pitches here, of which 86 are reserved for touring, some with excellent views across the vast sweep of the Bay of Douarnenez. They are well shaded and grassy, and all have 13A electricity. There are also a number of fully equipped safari-style tents (some with wood burning stoves) for hire as well as a handful of Romany-style caravans. An impressive range of amenities includes a swimming pool and bar/restaurant, and a large safari tent with a wood fire for communal entertainment.

Facilities

Two modern toilet blocks have hot showers and washbasins in cubicles. Facilities for disabled visitors. Washing machines and dryers. Bar, snack bar, takeaway (July/Aug). Outdoor heated swimming pool (all season). Play area. Multisports court. Boules. Activity programme. Fully equipped safari-style tents and Romany-style caravans for rent. WiFi (free). Off site: Beach and fishing 400 m. Riding 2.5 km. Bicycle hire 4 km.

Open: 29 April - 30 September.

Directions

The site is located west of the centre of Douarnenez. From Quimper head north on D765 to Douarnenez and then follow D207 passing to the western side of the Pouldavid. The site is on Avenue du Bois d'Isis and is well signed. GPS: 48.103056, -4.358889

Charges guide

Per unit incl. 2 persons and electricity	€ 13.20 - € 23.10
extra person	€ 3.90 - € 5.80

Erquy

Camping le Vieux Moulin

14 rue des Moulins, F-22430 Erquy (Côtes d'Armor) T: 02 96 72 34 23. E: camp.vieux.moulin@wanadoo.fr

alanrogers.com/FR22050

Le Vieux Moulin is a family run site, just 2 km. from the little fishing port of Erquy on Brittany's Emerald Coast, on the edge of a pine forest and nature reserve. It is about 900 m. from a beach of sand and shingle. Taking its name from the old mill opposite, the site has 199 pitches all with 10A electricity and some with electricity, water and drainage. One section of 39 pitches is arranged around a pond. Most pitches are of a fair size, arranged in square boxes, with trees giving shade. Evening entertainment is organised and there is a friendly pizzeria. The excellent pool complex includes a paddling pool, water slides and an indoor pool with jacuzzi. The site becomes quite lively in high season.

Facilities

Two good quality toilet blocks with facilities for disabled visitors and babies. A further small block provides toilets and dishwashing only. Washing machines and dryer. Motorcaravan services. Shop (1/7-5/9). Pizzeria and takeaway (1/5-1/9). Bar and terrace. Heated, covered pool complex. Play areas. Tennis. Gym. TV/games room. Bicycle hire. No electric barbecues. WiFi throughout (free).

Open: 18 April - 12 September.

Directions

Site is 2 km. east of Erquy. Take minor road towards Les Hôpitaux and site is signed from junction of D786 and D34 roads. GPS: 48.63858, -2.44189

Charges guide

Per unit incl. 2 persons and electricity	€ 23.00 - € 39.00

Camping Cheques accepted.

Erquy

Sites et Paysages Bellevue

Route de la libération, F-22430 Erquy (Côtes d'Armor) T: 02 96 72 33 04. E: info@campingbellevue.fr

alanrogers.com/FR22210

Situated a mile from the beaches between Erquy and Pléneuf Val-André, Camping Bellevue offers a quiet country retreat with easy access to the cliffs of Cap Fréhel, Sables d'Or and Saint Cast. There are 160 pitches of which 120 are available for touring units, all with electricity (10A) and 50 extra large ones with water and drainage. The site also has 20 mobile homes and tents to rent. Children are well catered for at this campsite – there are heated swimming and paddling pools, three play areas with minigolf, pétanque and volleyball.

Facilities

Two modern, unisex toilet blocks are of a high standard. Some washbasins in cubicles. Facilities for disabled visitors. Laundry facilities. Shop and bar (15/6-10/9). Crêperie and takeaway (12/4-31/8). Swimming and paddling pools. Play areas. Games room and library. Minigolf. Pétanque. Entertainment and organised activities in high season. There is also a multisports area with basketball, football etc. Max. 2 dogs. WiFi (free).

Open: 12 April - 15 September.

Directions

From St Brieuc road take D786 towards Erquy. Site is adjacent to the D786 at St Pabu and is well signed. GPS: 48.59426, -2.48475

Charges guide

Per unit incl. 2 persons and electricity	€ 22.50 - € 29.00
child (0-12 yrs)	free - € 4.70
extra person	€ 4.60 - € 5.70

Erquy

Camping la Plage de Saint Pabu

Saint Pabu, F-22430 Erquy (Côtes d'Armor) T: 02 96 72 24 65. E: camping@saintpabu.com

alanrogers.com/FR22500

Saint Pabu is a pretty site beside a broad, sandy beach close to Erquy. There is a fine panoramic view of the sea from the site. Pitches here are mostly divided by mature hedges and are of a good size. All 333 touring pitches have 10A electrical connections. A number of large, family pitches (130 sq.m) and 'grand confort' pitches are available (with electricity, water and drainage). It is also possible to rent mobile homes (one, two or three-bedroom models). On-site amenities include a bar and well stocked shop. Takeaway meals are available in high season.

Facilities

Four toilet blocks (one large and three smaller) provide hot showers and washbasins in cubicles. Facilities for babies and disabled visitors. Laundry facilities. Motorcaravan services. Dog shower. Shop (1/5-30/9). Bar/snack bar (1/5-30/9). Restaurant. Takeaway (high season). Play area. Games room. Mobile homes for rent. Direct beach access. WiFi (free). Off site: Watersports. Fishing. Boat trips. Shops and restaurants in Erquy 4 km.

Open: 27 March - 9 October.

Directions

St Pabu can be found just south of Erquy. Approaching from Erquy, head south on D34 and follow signs to St Pabu and then to site. GPS: 48.6067, -2.49674

Charges guide

Per unit incl. 2 persons and electricity	€ 21.80 - € 30.30
extra person	€ 4.40 - € 5.60
child (under 7 yrs)	€ 2.40 - € 3.00

Etables-sur-Mer

Camping l'Abri Côtier

Ville Es Rouxel, F-22680 Etables-sur-Mer (Côtes d'Armor) T: 02 96 70 61 57.

E: camping.abricotier@wanadoo.fr **alanrogers.com/FR22100**

L'Abri Côtier is a family run site 500 m. from a sandy beach. It is arranged in two sections which are separated by a lane. The first is in an orchard setting and mainly occupied by privately owned mobile homes. The second section has 125 touring pitches, all with 6-10A electricity (long leads may be required) and most also have water and drainage. Pitches are set out on level or part sloping grass and the whole site is divided up by mature trees and shrubs. Some pitches are within a pleasant walled area. The beach is within walking distance and there are restaurants in the village.

Facilities

Clean sanitary facilities include some washbasins in cabins and pushbutton showers. Facilities for disabled visitors. Baby bath/shower. Laundry room. Well stocked shop. Bar providing a simple takeaway service (plus set menu in high season). Covered terrace and games area. Sheltered outdoor, heated swimming pool with paddling pool and jacuzzi. Small play area. Some entertainment in peak season. WiFi (charged). Off site: Beach and sailing 500 m. Restaurants and indoor pool in the village. Riding 1 km.

Open: 1 May - 16 September.

Directions

Etables-sur-Mer is 20 km. north of St Brieuc. From N12 (St Brieuc bypass) take D786 towards St Quay Portrieux. After 12 km. ignore signs to Etables centre, at a roundabout, turn left and immediately right (site signed). GPS: 48.63559, -2.83546

Charges guide

Per unit incl. 2 persons and electricity (10A)	€ 20.40 - € 23.60
extra person	€ 4.70 - € 5.80
child (under 7 yrs)	€ 3.30 - € 4.10

Fouesnant

Camping de PenHoat

Pointe de Mousterlin, 15 route du Grand Parge, F-29170 Fouesnant (Finistère) T: 02 98 56 51 89.
E: info@camping-penhoat.com **alanrogers.com/FR29630**

This small rural campsite is set in two acres of trees, shrubs and well tended flowerbeds. The 87 touring pitches are level, grassy, generous in size and separated by hedges and/or small trees. The 58 pitches with electricity (5/10A) may need long leads. The 40 mobile homes are mostly separated from the touring pitches. There are also six traditional gîtes for hire. The pleasant wooden chalet-style bar and takeaway has a covered terrace. Kayaks can be hired at the campsite. The long sandy beach is 300 m. away. And for lovers of wildlife, the protected Mousterlin nature reserve is next to the campsite.

Facilities

Two toilet and shower blocks with facilities for campers with disabilities. Laundry. Baby room. Bar, takeaway and restaurant. Games room. Playground. Trampoline. Bicycle and kayak hire. Gîtes for hire. WiFi (charged).
Off site: Beach 300 m. Riding 1 km. Shops in Fouesnant 6 km. Golf 6 km.

Open: 3 April - 15 September.

Directions

Site is 5 km. south of Fouesnant. Turn off N165 at Coat Cong signed Concarneau and Fouesnant. Join D45 signed Beg-Meil and shortly turn right on D145 signed Mousterlin. Site signed in 5 km.
GPS: 47.851024, -4.035341

Charges guide

Per unit incl. 2 persons and electricity	€ 16.00 - € 18.40
extra person	€ 4.10 - € 4.80

Fouesnant

Camping le Kervastard

56 chemin Kervastard, Beg-Meil, F-29170 Fouesnant (Finistère) T: 02 98 94 91 52.
E: camping.le.kervastard@wanadoo.fr **alanrogers.com/FR29690**

Camping le Kervastard has a pleasant situation at the heart of the pretty Breton resort of Beg-Meil. The owner, M. Rupp, is always keen to practise his English. It is 300 m. from the pleasure port and 600 m. from a magnificent sandy beach (other good beaches are nearby). The 122 pitches (55 for touring) are of a good size and grassy. Most have electrical connections (6-10A). On-site amenities include a swimming pool (and separate paddling pool). The centre of Beg-Meil can easily be reached on foot and there are plenty of shops, cafés, restaurants and crêperies there. The atmosphere on site is relaxed, particularly in low season.

Facilities

Two modern toilet blocks with facilities for babies and disabled visitors. Washing machines and dryers. Swimming pool (15/6-15/9). Paddling pool. Play area. TV/Games room. Occasional activities (high season). Accommodation to rent. WiFi over site (charged).
Off site: Fishing and beach 300 m. Beg-Meil centre (shops and restaurants). Golf and riding 5 km. Bicycle hire 1 km.

Open: 15 April - 15 October.

Directions

Approachng from N165 (Vannes-Quimper), leave at the Concarneau exit and follow D44 to Fouesnant (passing through La Forêt-Fouesnant). Follow signs to Beg-Meil and continue to the village, where the site is well signed. GPS: 47.86652, -4.01481

Charges guide

Per unit incl. 2 persons and electricity	€ 16.00 - € 32.50

Camping Cheques accepted.

Guidel

Camping les Jardins de Kergal

Route de Guidel Plages, F-56520 Guidel (Morbihan) T: 02 97 05 98 18. E: jardins.kergal@wanadoo.fr
alanrogers.com/FR56220

This is a long established campsite that offers a variety of well cared for pitches (106 for tourers, all with 16A electricity). Most are shaded by mature trees and, unusually, some are triangular in shape. Access could be tricky for larger units. The toilet facilities have been refurbished to a very high standard, complete with soft music and potted plants. A comfortable lounge contains a small library, board games and a television. The site's pool complex is impressive with a heated, covered pool, an open pool with slides and a paddling pool. Many sporting facilities are provided, and in high season there is entertainment and activities for children.

Facilities

The good toilet block includes facilities for disabled visitors and babies. Washing machine and dryer. Shop (all season). Bar (July/Aug). Pizza and rôtisserie vans visit (high season). Covered swimming pool (all season). Outdoor pool and slides (1/6-15/9). Multisports court. Bicycle hire. Minigolf. WiFi in bar (first 30 mins. free).
Off site: Beaches 1.5 km. Fishing 3 km. Riding 6 km.

Open: 1 April - 11 November.

Directions

From the RN165 west of Lorient take exit for Guidel, then the D306 from Guidel towards the beach (plage). Site is well signed on the left.
GPS: 47.77466, -3.50616

Charges guide

Per unit incl. 2 persons and electricity	€ 19.00 - € 31.00
extra person	€ 5.00 - € 7.00

Jugon-les-Lacs

Camping Au Bocage du Lac

Rue du Bocage, F-22270 Jugon-les-Lacs (Côtes d'Armor) T: 02 96 31 60 16.

E: contact@campinglacbretagne.com **alanrogers.com/FR22200**

This well kept former municipal site has been updated over the past few years by the current owners, M. and Mme. Rivière. It is on the edge of a small village beside a lake, a short drive from the sea. It offers 138 large touring pitches, all with electrical connections, set on gently sloping grass and divided by shrubs and bushes, with mature trees providing shade. Some 45 wooden chalets and mobile homes are interspersed with the touring pitches. On-site facilities include an excellent swimming pool complex with both heated outdoor and covered pools with children's sections and sunbathing patio. There is also an extensive play area and a small animal park.

Facilities

Two sanitary blocks, one updated with controllable showers, the other (open in high season) is more traditional. British and Turkish style WCs and some washbasins in cabins. Facilities for disabled visitors. Washing machines and dryers. Small shop sells basics. Bar with restaurant. Outdoor swimming pools (1/5-15/9), covered pool (all season). Tennis. Boules. Play area. Small animal park. Activity programmes July/Aug. Fishing. WiFi in bar area (charged).

Open: 12 April - 5 October.

Directions

Jugon is 40 km. southeast of St Brieuc. From N12 (St Brieuc/Rennes) turn east after Lamballe on N176 towards Dinan. In 7 km. take exit for Jugon-les-Lacs. In village turn south and follow signs to lake and site. GPS: 48.40120, -2.31736

Charges guide

Per unit incl. 2 persons and electricity (10A) € 17.35 - € 28.05

Camping Cheques accepted.

La Chapelle-aux-Filtzméens

Camping le Domaine du Logis

Le Logis, F-35190 La Chapelle-aux-Filtzméens (Ille-et-Vilaine) T: 02 99 45 25 45.

E: domainedulogis@wanadoo.fr **alanrogers.com/FR35080**

This is an attractive rural site with enthusiastic owners, set in the grounds of an old château. The site's upgraded modern facilities are housed in traditional converted barns and farm buildings, which are well maintained and equipped. There is a total of 203 pitches, 85 of which are for touring units. The grass pitches are level, of a generous size and divided by mature hedges and trees. All have 10A electricity connections, water and drainage. This site would appeal to most age groups, with plenty to offer the active, including a fitness room with a good range of modern equipment and a sauna for those who prefer to relax, or perhaps enjoy a quiet day's fishing by the lake. For the evenings, there is a pleasant bar and an excellent restaurant. Although set in a quiet, rural part of the Brittany countryside, the nearby village of La Chapelle-aux-Filtzmeens has a bar, restaurant and shops. A 20-minute car ride will bring you into the large town of Rennes, or perhaps travel north for 30 minutes to Mont Saint-Michel, Dinan, Dinard and the old fishing port of Saint Malo to sample the famous Brittany seafood.

Facilities

One comfortable toilet block with washbasins and showers. Toilet and shower for disabled visitors. Laundry facilities. Bar with Sky TV. Restaurant and takeaway (1/7-29/8). Outdoor swimming pool and whirlpool (1/5-30/9). Fitness and games rooms. Sauna. BMX circuit. Bicycle hire. Lake fishing. Unfenced play areas. Club for children (high season). WiFi throughout (free). Off site: Boating on the canal. Riding 10 km.

Open: 1 April - 2 November.

Directions

Turn south off N176 onto D795 (Dol-de-Bretagne). Continue to Combourg and then take D13 to La Chapelle-aux-Filtzméens. Continue for 2 km. to site on right. GPS: 48.3275, -1.83481

Charges guide

Per unit incl. 2 persons and electricity € 24.00 - € 35.00

Camping Cheques accepted.

La Forêt-Fouesnant

Camping du Manoir de Penn Ar Ster

2 chemin de Penn Ar Ster, F-29940 La Forêt-Fouesnant (Finistère) T: 02 98 56 97 75.

E: info@camping-pennarster.com **alanrogers.com/FR29100**

This site will appeal to those who prefer a quiet place to stay away from the noise and bustle of busier sites. In the grounds of an old Breton house and arranged on terraces up the steep sides of a valley, the site has a picturesque, garden-like quality. There are 105 pitches, of which about half are for touring units (the remainder are used for mobile homes). Pitches vary in size (80-100 sq.m) and some are accessed by steep slopes, but all are on flat, grassy terraces, with low hedging and all have electricity (6/10A), water and drainage. The campsite is open for a long season and its location in the village of La Forêt-Fouesnant makes it popular with those camping by bicycle, motorbike or in a motorcaravan.

Facilities

Two sanitary blocks include mixed British and Turkish style toilets, cabins with washbasins and showers, baby areas and children's toilets. One block is heated in low season and contains facilities for disabled campers. At the rear of the old house is a laundry room with washing machines and dryers. Play area. Tennis. Bicycle hire. Barrier with card. Off site: Baker 50 m. Village with all amenities 150 m. Golf 800 m. Riding 2 km.

Open: 1 March - 14 November.

Directions

From N165 take D70 Concarneau exit. At first roundabout take D44 (Forêt-Fouesnant). Follow to T-junction and turn right on D783. After 2 km. turn left back onto D44 to Forêt-Fouesnant. In village take first exit right at roundabout to site 150 m. on left. GPS: 47.911316, -3.979679

Charges guide

Per unit incl. 2 persons and electricity (6A) € 20.80 - € 27.80

No credit cards. Less 20% outside 1/7-26/8.

La Forêt-Fouesnant

Camping de Kéranterec

Route de Port la Forêt, F-29940 La Forêt-Fouesnant (Finistère) T: 02 98 56 98 11.

E: info@camping-keranterec.com **alanrogers.com/FR29240**

A well established family run site with a very French ambience, Kéranterec has 265 grassy pitches in two distinct areas. The upper part of the site is more open and has little shade, and is also largely taken up by private mobile homes. The lower and more mature area is predominantly for tourers, with terraced pitches set in a former orchard. Spacious and divided by mature hedging, all pitches have electrical connections (25 m. cable advised) and most also offer water and drainage. Some pitches have shade from the many trees on the lower part of the site, and some also overlook the little cove at the rear.

Facilities

Two modern, fully equipped toilet blocks kept very clean include washbasins in cubicles, baby baths and facilities for disabled visitors. Laundry facilities. Small shop and bar (24/5-6/9) and takeaway (July/Aug). TV room. Heated outdoor swimming pool (1/5-10/9) with paddling pool, jacuzzi and slides. Covered, heated pool (19/4-10/9). Tennis. Boules. Play area. Children's club and family activities (July/Aug). Free WiFi. Off site: Beach 10 mins.

Open: 12 April - 20 September.

Directions

From N165 take D70 Concarneau exit. At first roundabout take D44 (Fouesnant). After 2.5 km. turn right at T-junction, and follow for 2.5 km. and turn left (Port La Forêt). Go over roundabout, (Port La Forêt). After 1 km. turn left (site signed), then in 400 m. turn left to site. GPS: 47.89923, -3.95505

Charges guide

Per unit incl. 2 persons and electricity € 16.00 - € 34.00

La Gacilly

Camping Art Nature Village

Le Bout du Pont, Sixt-sur-Aff, F-35550 La Gacilly (Ille-et-Vilaine) T: 02 99 08 10 59.

E: contact@art-nature-village.com **alanrogers.com/FR35220**

In peaceful, rural Southern Brittany on the edge of the town of La Gacilly and next to the River Aff, the small campsite of Art Nature Village offers a variety of pitches and accommodation. The 25 touring pitches are spacious (all 120 sq.m) and divided by hedges and there are also luxury tents, trailer caravans and cottages to rent. Vehicles are restricted to certain zones. The nature pitches are green and private, next to the river and near sanitary facilities. Larger comfort pitches have 6A electricity. There is provision for cyclists and ramblers. Designated motorcaravan stopover pitches (16.00-10.00) have hardstanding and are near sanitary and service facilities, but have no electricity.

Facilities

Sanitary blocks with washbasins in individual cabins, family bathroom, baby bathroom and facilities for disabled visitors. Breakfast room. Bar (July/Aug). Washing machine and dryer. Beauty salon. Secure shed for cyclists' and ramblers' equipment. Motorcaravan services. Play area. Entertainment (July/Aug). Fishing in river. WiFi area (free).

Open: 3 April - 1 November.

Directions

From Redon take the D164 south and then D873 and D773 to La Gacilly. Follow signs for the site. GPS: 47.76362, -2.125518

Charges guide

Per unit incl. 2 persons and electricity € 18.00 - € 23.50

extra person € 4.00 - € 5.00

La Roche Bernard

Camping Municipal le Pâtis

3 chemin du Pâtis, F-56130 La Roche-Bernard (Morbihan) T: 02 99 90 60 13. E: camping.lrb56@gmail.com
alanrogers.com/FR56080

This is another of those excellent municipal sites one comes across in France. Situated beside the River Vilaine, five minutes' walk from the centre of the very attractive old town of La Roche-Bernard and beside the port and marina, it provides 61 level grass, part-hedged pitches in bays of four, with 6A electricity and water. Eighteen special pitches for motorcaravans have been created at the entrance, along with two wooden chalets to hire. Next door is a sailing school, boats to hire, fishing, tennis, archery, etc. A restaurant and bar are on the quayside, with others uphill in the town.

Facilities

Two fully equipped sanitary blocks, one new and very modern, the other fully refurbished. Facilities for disabled visitors. Motorcaravan services. Laundry room behind reception with washing machine and dryer. Bicycle hire. WiFi (free). Off site: Fishing 500 m. Riding 5 km. Golf 15 km.

Open: April - mid October.

Directions

From Vannes on D165, exit at J17 for La Roche-Bernard D765. Once across bridge, follow signs for Le Port Neuf and site. GPS: 47.51817, -2.30317

Charges guide

Per unit incl. 2 persons and electricity	€ 15.10 - € 21.10
extra person	€ 3.10 - € 3.80

La Trinité-sur-Mer

Camping de la Plage

Plage de Kervillen, F-56470 La Trinité-sur-Mer (Morbihan) T: 02 97 55 73 28.
E: camping@camping-plage.com **alanrogers.com/FR56020**

The Carnac and La Trinité area of Brittany is popular with British holidaymakers. Camping de la Plage is a well established site with direct access to the safe, sandy beach of Kervillen Plage. There are 195 grass pitches, some of which are used by tour operators and others occupied by mobile homes (available to rent), but many are available for touring. Pitches are all hedged and of a good size (100 sq.m) and have 6/10A electricity, water and drainage. The site has a slight slope and a few pitches reflect this. With narrow roads and sharp bends, La Plage may not be suitable for larger units.

Facilities

Two sanitary blocks (one heated) have free hot water, washbasins in cubicles, baby baths and facilities for children and disabled visitors. Laundry facilities. Swimming pool with water slides. Play areas including ball pool. Tennis. TV. Entertainment programme in high season for all ages. Bicycle hire. Canoe hire. Beach. Guided tours. WiFi throughout (charged). Communal barbecue areas (no charcoal on pitches). Off site: Fishing 50 m. Shop with bakery. Bar, restaurant, crêperie and takeaway all 200 m. Sailing 1.5 km. Riding 3.5 km.

Open: 30 April - 19 September.

Directions

From N165 at Auray take D28 (La Trinité-sur-Mer). On through town following signs to Carnac-Plage on D186. Site signed off this road to the south. Take care to take road signed to Kervillen Plage where it forks. At seafront turn right. Site is 300 m. on right and is well signed. GPS: 47.57563, -3.02890

Charges guide

Per unit incl. 2 persons and electricity (10A)	€ 23.90 - € 47.00
extra person	€ 6.20
child (2-17 yrs)	€ 3.00 - € 4.65

La Trinité-sur-Mer

Camping de la Baie

Plage de Kervillen, F-56470 La Trinité-sur-Mer (Morbihan) T: 02 97 55 73 42.
E: contact@campingdelabaie.com **alanrogers.com/FR56030**

This site is one of two owned by members of the same family. It is situated on the coast overlooking the safe, sandy beach of Kervillen Plage, with its little rocky outcrops providing a naturally enclosed swimming area. This is a very friendly site, which is ideal for quiet or family holidays in an area with lots of local interest. There are 168 pitches, of which around 50 are used by tour operators. The 92 touring pitches are all of good size, hedged and all have electricity (6/10A) water and drainage. Some shade is provided by mature and maturing trees. American style motorhomes should book ahead.

Facilities

Two very clean toilet blocks include well equipped baby rooms and full en-suite facilities for disabled visitors. Laundry facilities. Bar, restaurant and takeaway (open to the public, all season). Well stocked shop. Small (12 m) swimming pool with slide. Play areas. Multisports pitches. TV room. Games room. Bicycle hire. WiFi over site (charged). Off site: Beach, fishing and boat ramp 50 m. Tennis and minigolf 200 m. (shared with Camping de la Plage). Sailing school 1.5 km. Golf 5 km.

Open: 25 April - 20 September.

Directions

From N165 at Auray take D28 (La Trinité-sur-Mer). Go through town following signs to Carnac Plage on D186. Site is well signed off this road to the south. Be careful to take the road signed to Kervillen Plage where it forks. GPS: 47.57364, -3.02758

Charges guide

Per unit incl. 2 persons and electricity (10A)	€ 22.10 - € 52.05
extra person	€ 2.65 - € 3.70
child (under 2 yrs)	free

La Trinité-sur-Mer

Camping de Kervilor

Kervilor, F-56470 La Trinité-sur-Mer (Morbihan) T: 02 97 55 76 75. E: camping.kervilor@wanadoo.fr
alanrogers.com/FR56050

Kervilor may be a good alternative for those who find the beachside sites in La Trinité too busy and lively. In a village on the outskirts of the town, it has 250 pitches on flat grass and is attractively landscaped with trees (silver birch) and flowers giving a sense of spaciousness. The pitches are in groups divided by hedges, separated by shrubs and trees and all have 6/10A electricity. Around 167 are used for touring units. The site has a central pool complex with outdoor and covered swimming and paddling pools, slides and fountains. Activities and entertainment are organised in high season. The pleasant port of La Trinité is only 1.5 km. away, with sandy beaches within 2 km.

Facilities

Two modern toilet blocks of a good standard with further facilities in an older block. They include many washbasins in cabins, facilities for babies and disabled visitors. Fridge hire. Small laundry. Small shop. Bar with terrace and takeaway (both from 8/5). Pool complex with covered pool. Play area. Minigolf. Pétanque. Tennis. Volleyball. Bicycle hire. Electric barbecues not permitted. WiFi in bar area (free). Off site: Town facilities 1.5 km. Sandy beach, fishing and riding 2 km. Golf 12 km.

Open: 12 April - 21 September.

Directions

Site is north of La Trinité-sur-Mer and is signed in the town centre. From Auray take D186 Quiberon road; turn left at site sign at Kergroix on D186 to La Trinité-sur-Mer, and left again at outskirts of town. GPS: 47.60213, -3.03672

Charges guide

Per unit incl. 2 persons and electricity (10A)	€ 20.60 - € 35.65
extra person	€ 3.95 - € 5.80
child (under 7 yrs)	€ 2.55 - € 3.85

Landéda

Camping des Abers

Dunes de Sainte Marguerite, F-29870 Landéda (Finistère) T: 02 98 04 93 35.
E: camping-des-abers@wanadoo.fr **alanrogers.com/FR29130**

This delightful 12-acre site is in a beautiful location almost at the tip of the Presqu'île Sainte Marguerite on the northwestern shores of Brittany. The peninsula lies between the mouths (abers) of two rivers, Aber Wrac'h and Aber Benoît. Camping des Abers is set just back from a wonderful sandy beach with rocky outcrops and islands you can walk to at low tide. There are 180 pitches (158 for touring), landscaped and terraced, some with amazing views, others sheltered by mature hedges, trees and flowering shrubs. Hubert le Cuff and his team make you very welcome and speak excellent English. With its soft, white sand beach the setting is ideal for those with younger children and this quiet, rural area provides a wonderful, tranquil escape from the hustle and bustle of life, even in high season.

Facilities

Three toilet blocks provide washbasins in cubicles and showers (token from reception € 0.65-0.85). Facilities for disabled visitors and babies. Fully equipped laundry. Motorcaravan services. Shop stocks basics (14/5-22/9). Takeaway (July/Aug). Play area. Games room. Hairdresser. The site is famous for its Breton music; dancing, cooking classes and guided walks arranged. Splendid beach with good bathing, fishing, windsurfing and other watersports. WiFi throughout. Off site: Bus service just outside site. Pizzeria next door. Tennis. Sailing club 3 km. Riding 7 km. Golf 30 km. Miles of superb coastal walks. The nearby town of L'Aber Wrac'h, a well known yachting centre, has many memorable restaurants.

Open: 1 May - 30 September.

Directions

Landéda is 55 km. west of Roscoff via D10 to Plougerneau then D13 crossing river bridge (Aber Wrac'h) and turning west to Lannilis. From N12 Morlaix-Brest road turn north on D59 to Lannilis. Continue through town taking road to Landéda and from there follow signs for Dunes de Ste Marguerite, Camping and des Abers. GPS: 48.59344, -4.60281

Charges guide

Per unit incl. 2 persons and electricity	€ 16.30 - € 19.00
extra person	€ 3.70 - € 4.30
child (under 7 yrs)	€ 2.30 - € 2.70
dog	€ 2.13 - € 2.50

Lanloup

Camping le Neptune

Ker Guistin, F-22580 Lanloup (Côtes d'Armor) T: 02 96 22 33 35. E: contact@leneptune.com

alanrogers.com/FR22160

Situated on the Côte de Goëlo at Lanloup, le Neptune offers a peaceful, rural retreat for families. The friendly owners, François and Marie Jo Camard, keep the site neat and tidy and there is a regular programme of renovation. There are 84 level, grass pitches (65 for touring units) separated by trimmed hedges providing privacy and all with electricity (10A). There are also 22 mobile homes to rent. Within walking distance is the local village, with a restaurant and a shop, and sandy beaches are only a short drive away. The area is good for cycling and walking.

Facilities

The modern, heated, toilet block is of a good standard, clean and well maintained and provides washbasins in cubicles and pushbutton showers. Facilities for disabled visitors. Laundry. Motorcaravan services. No restaurant but good takeaway (all season). Small well stocked shop for basic needs. Bar with indoor and outdoor seating. Heated swimming pool with retractable roof. Pétanque. Play area. Entertainment and children's activities in high season. WiFi over site (charged).

Open: 1 April - 17 October.

Directions

Lanloup is 30 km. north west of St Brieuc and 100 km. from both Roscoff and St Malo. From N12 St Brieuc bypass take D786 Paimpol (par la côte). After 28 km. on approaching Lanloup, site is well signed, turning right at crossroads by café. GPS: 48.71372, -2.96704

Charges guide

Per unit incl. 2 persons and electricity	€ 19.00 - € 29.00

Camping Cheques accepted.

Le Guilvinec

Yelloh! Village la Plage

Hent Maner ar Ster, F-29730 Le Guilvinec (Finistère) T: 02 98 58 61 90. E: info@yellohvillage-la-plage.com

alanrogers.com/FR29110

La Plage is a spacious site with direct access to a long sandy beach between the fishing town of Le Guilvinec and the watersports beaches of Penmarc'h on the southwest tip of Brittany. It is surrounded by tall trees (tree houses for rent) which provide shelter and is made up of several flat, sandy meadows. The 410 pitches (200 for touring units) are arranged on either side of sandy access roads, mostly not separated but all numbered. There is less shade in the newer areas. Electricity is available on most pitches. Like all beach-side sites, the facilities receive heavy use.

Facilities

Four sanitary blocks are of differing designs but all provide modern, bright facilities including washbasins in cabins, good facilities for children and disabled visitors. Laundry facilities. Motorcaravan services. Shop with gas supplies. Bright, airy, well furnished bar, restaurant and takeaway (all open all season). Covered heated swimming pool with paddling pool and slide. Sauna and fitness complex. Play area. TV room. Tennis. Minigolf. Pétanque. Giant chess. Bicycle hire. Beach. Multisports and football fields. Entertainment all season. WiFi over part of site (free).

Open: 11 April - 13 September.

Directions

Site is west of Le Guilvinec. From Pont l'Abbé, take the D785 road towards Penmarc'h. In Plomeur, turn left on D57 (Le Guilvinec). On entering Le Guilvinec fork right signed port and camping. Follow road along coast to site on left. GPS: 47.80427, -4.31241

Charges guide

Per unit incl. 2 persons and electricity	€ 18.00 - € 47.00
extra person	€ 6.00 - € 8.00
child (3-7 yrs)	free - € 6.00

Lesconil

Camping des Dunes

67 rue Paul Langevin, F-29740 Lesconil (Finistère) T: 02 98 87 81 78. E: campingdesdunes@gmail.com

alanrogers.com/FR29270

On the edge of the sand dunes near the village of Lesconil, this campsite has the great advantage of providing direct access to an excellent sandy beach. The 160 sandy and grassy pitches have little shade, but are quite spacious and all have electricity (10A). The site is only 800 m. from the village of Lesconil, a delightfully unspoilt fishing port where you can still see the small fishing fleet return each day. There is a good choice of restaurants and cafés, and a Centre Nautique offering a range of watersports.

Facilities

Two central, unisex toilet blocks have some washbasins in cubicles. Baby area. Two toilet/shower rooms for disabled visitors. Washing machine and dryer. Baker's van visits every morning in high season. Play area for younger children. Sauna and jacuzzi. Trampolines. Bowling alley game. Free WiFi in bar area. Off site: Tennis nearby. Beach 100 m. Bicycle hire and sailing 800 m.

Open: 5 April - 30 September.

Directions

From Pont l'Abbé follow D102 to Lesconil. Just before village (sports stadium on right) the site is signed just past stadium. Site is 1.5 km. on right, just past Camping de la Grande Plage. GPS: 47.79715, -4.22868

Charges guide

Per unit incl. 2 persons and electricity	€ 24.50
extra person	€ 4.90

No credit cards.

Le Pouldu

Camping les Embruns

2 rue du Philosophe Alain, le Pouldu Plages, F-29360 Clohars-Carnoët (Finistère) T: 02 98 39 91 07.
E: contact@camping-les-embruns.com**alanrogers.com/FR29180**

This site is unusual in that it is located in the heart of a village, yet is only 250 metres from a sandy cove. The entrance with its code operated barrier and wonderful floral displays, is the first indication that this is a well tended and well organised site, and the owners have won numerous regional and national awards for its superb presentation. The 176 pitches (100 occupied by mobile homes) are separated by trees, shrubs and bushes, and most have electricity (16A, Europlug), water and drainage. A dedicated area has been created for motorcaravans at a special rate. On-site facilities include a heated swimming pool, a circular paddling pool, a water play pool and a wellness centre with sauna and massage facilities. It is only a short walk to the village centre with all its attractions and services. It is also close to beautiful countryside and the Carnoët Forest which are good for walking and cycling.

Facilities

Two modern sanitary blocks, recently renovated and heated in winter, include mainly British style toilets, some washbasins in cubicles, baby baths and good facilities for disabled visitors. Family bathrooms. Laundry facilities. Motorcaravan services (€ 4). Shop. Restaurant, bar and terrace, takeaway (26/3-19/9). Covered, heated swimming and paddling pools (2/7-26/8). Wellness centre with fitness equipment. Large games hall. Play area. Football field. Minigolf. Communal barbecue area. Daily activities for children and adults organised in July/Aug. Bicycle and car hire. Internet access and WiFi in reception area (charged). Off site: Nearby sea and river fishing and watersports. Beach 250 m. Riding 2 km. Golf 20 km.

Open: 26 March - 1 October.

Directions

From N165 take either exit for Kervidanou, Quimperlé Ouest or Kergostiou, Quimperlé Centre, Clohars-Carnoët exit and follow D16 to Clohars-Carnoët. Then take D24 for Le Pouldu and follow site signs in village. GPS: 47.76867, -3.54508

Charges guide

Per unit incl. 2 persons and electricity	€ 17.50 - € 37.50
extra person	€ 4.50 - € 7.50
child (under 7 yrs)	€ 3.10 - € 5.00
dog	€ 3.50

Less in low seasons.

Lesconil

Flower Camping de la Grande Plage

71 rue Paul Langevin, F-29740 Lesconil (Finistère) T: 02 98 87 88 27. E: contact@campinggrandeplage.com
alanrogers.com/FR29710

Lesconil is a pleasant, traditional seaside resort, south west of Quimper. La Grande Plage has direct access to an excellent sandy beach and is close to the village centre. There are 120 pitches here, most with electrical connections, as well as a number of mobile homes and bungalow-style tents available for rent. Most pitches are well shaded. Leisure facilities include a recently constructed swimming pool with water slides and a separate paddling pool. A welcome drink is organised every week and other activities are on offer in high season, including themed meals and sports contests.

Facilities

Sanitary facilities include hot showers and provision for children and disabled visitors. Washing machine. Motorcaravan services. Bar and snack bar (15/6-15/9). Heated, outdoor swimming pool complex with water slides and paddling pool (1/5-30/9). Play area. Accommodation for rent. Entertainment and activity programme. Bicycle hire. WiFi (charged). Max. 2 dogs.

Open: 12 April - 30 September.

Directions

From Pont l'Abbé, head south on D2 and D102, passing through Plobannalec-Lesconil. Continue to Lesconil and follow signs to the site on rue Paul Langevin. GPS: 47.7979, -4.22895

Charges guide

Per unit incl. 2 persons and electricity (6A)	€ 20.40 - € 25.55
extra person	€ 4.20 - € 5.50

Locmariaquer

Camping Lann Brick

Lann Brick, F-56740 Locmariaquer (Morbihan) T: 02 97 57 32 79. E: camping.lannbrick@wanadoo.fr
alanrogers.com/FR56690

Lann Brick can be found close to Carnac and La Trinité-sur-Mer, on the western side of the Morbihan gulf. The site is just 200 m. from the sea. Pitches here are generally sized between 70 and 90 sq.m, and are grassy with reasonable shade and high hedges. Most have electricity (6/10A). This small family site is lovingly cared for with manicured trees, shrubs and flowers. It has a very small, convivial bar with an outdoor terrace alongside a modest pool complex, and these are the focal point of the site. Various activities are organised in peak season, including themed evenings and dances.

Facilities

One traditional, clean toilet block has preset showers and washbasins in cabins. Facilities for babies and disabled visitors, although gravel paths could challenge wheelchair users. Washing machines and dryers. Small shop for essentials. Takeaway food. Swimming pool. Paddling pool. Bicycle hire. Small play area. Entertainment programme. Mobile homes and caravans for rent.
Off site: Shops and restaurants in Locmariaquer. Cycling and walking trails around the gulf. Sailing and watersports.

Open: 1 April - 14 October.

Directions

Approaching from north (N165) leave at second Auray exit (D28) and head south on D28 to Le Chat Noir. Here, join the southbound D781 and at Kercadoret follow local signs to site on right. GPS: 47.578567, -2.97443

Charges guide

Per unit incl. 2 persons and electricity	€ 20.60 - € 26.60
extra person	€ 4.10 - € 5.10

Locronan

Camping Locronan

Rue de la Troménie, F-29180 Locronan (Finistère) T: 02 98 91 87 76. E: contact@camping-locronan.fr
alanrogers.com/FR29650

Camping Locronan is a well cared for, friendly site on the edge of the village of Locronan (400 m). The site has a heated covered pool and a children's play area. The 100 pitches (76 for touring) are level, grassy and divided by low hedges. These are arranged on four different levels as the site is on the side of a steep hill. Vehicle access between the levels is steep and pedestrian access is by wooden steps which may be unsuitable for children and disabled visitors. Many of the pitches offer panoramic views across the countryside to the distant bay of Douarnenez.

Facilities

Two modern toilet blocks have facilities for disabled campers. Laundry facilities. Shop. Covered swimming pool. Small bar area (all season). Play area. WiFi over part of site (free). Mobile homes and equipped tents for rent. Off site: Shops and restaurants in Locronan 300 m. Tennis 300 m. Beach 5 km. Riding 8 km. Walking and cycling tracks. Quimper 13 km.

Open: April - September.

Directions

Locronan is northwest of Quimper. From there, head north on D39 and D63 (towards Douarnenez) until you reach the village. The site is clearly signed in the village. GPS: 48.095824, -4.199181

Charges guide

Per unit incl. 2 persons and electricity (10A)	€ 19.22 - € 23.92
extra person	€ 4.20 - € 5.50

Camping Cheques accepted.

Matignon

Camping Vert le Vallon aux Merlettes

43 rue du Docteur Jobert, F-22550 Matignon (Côtes d'Armor) T: 02 96 80 37 99.
E: contact@campingdematignon.com **alanrogers.com/FR22260**

Le Vallon aux Merlettes is situated on the edge of the town and has a quiet, simple and rural ambience. The friendly owners are very welcoming and take care to maintain the site well. There are some 100 grass touring pitches which are level and numbered and all have electricity (10A). Many shrubs and trees provide shade to some areas. Although there are limited leisure facilities on site, there are several sporting opportunities adjacent. The magnificent beaches of Saint Cast and a swimming pool with sea water are within 5 km. This site is ideally situated for excursions to Cap Fréhel, Erquy, Dinard, Saint Malo and Mont Saint-Michel.

Facilities

One modern and centrally located toilet block includes washbasins, both open style and in cabins, and preset showers. Facilities for disabled visitors. Laundry facilities. Motorcaravan services. Small shop in reception for basics. Bar and basic snack bar. TV. Small unfenced play area. Internet access. WiFi (charged). Off site: Leisure facilities adjacent. Beach and swimming pool 5 km.

Open: 1 May - 30 September.

Directions

From N12 take D786 northeast to Erquy. Matignon is 16 km. east of Erquy still on the D786. Site is well signed in the town. GPS: 48.59111, -2.29578

Charges guide

Per unit incl. 2 persons and electricity	€ 14.60 - € 19.50
child (2-13 yrs)	free - € 2.40
extra person	€ 3.00 - € 4.20

Locunolé

Castel Camping le Ty-Nadan

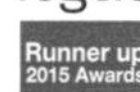

Route d'Arzano, F-29310 Locunolé (Finistère) T: 02 98 71 75 47. E: info@tynadan-vacances.fr

alanrogers.com/FR29010

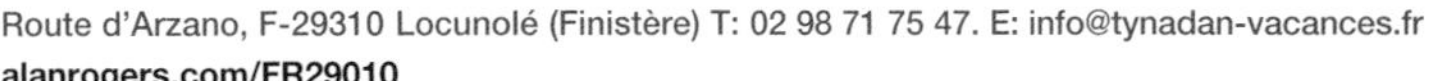

Castel Camping le Ty-Nadan is a well organised site set in wooded countryside in southern Brittany, along the bank of the River Elle (renowned for fishing). There are 200 grassy pitches for touring units, many with shade, and 67 fully serviced, some with private sanitary facilities. A variety of outdoor family pursuits is on offer, including canoeing, horse riding, walking, mountain biking, rock climbing. An interesting option is excursions on Segway electric vehicles. All activities are supervised by qualified staff. The pool complex with slides and paddling pool is very popular as are the large indoor pool complex and indoor games area. There is an adventure play park and another play park for 5-8 year olds. There are tennis courts, table tennis, pool tables and archery. A varied programme of entertainment for all ages is provided all season, including clubs and activities for younger children, teenagers and adults. There are concerts, Breton evenings with hog roasts, dancing, etc. (be ready to be actively encouraged to join in!). This is a wonderful site for families with children.

Facilities

Three sanitary blocks are equipped with showers, private washing cubicles and facilities for babies. Washing machines and dryers. Well stocked shop. Bar. Restaurant and takeaway. Heated outdoor pools. Indoor pool with changing rooms. Small river beach (unfenced). Indoor badminton. Activity and entertainment programmes (during school holidays). Riding centre. Bicycle hire. Canoe trips. Fishing. Segways. Zip wire. Internet access and WiFi (charged). Shuttle service to the beaches. Booking service for island trips. Off site: Beaches 20 minutes by car (or shuttle service). Golf 20 km.

Open: 4 May - 5 September.

Directions

Make for Arzano which is northeast of Quimperlé on the Pontivy road and turn off D22 after 8 km, just west of village site sign. Site is 3 km. further. GPS: 47.90468, -3.47477

Charges guide

Per unit incl. 2 persons and electricity	€ 20.80 - € 49.00
extra person	€ 4.45 - € 9.10
child (2-6 yrs)	€ 2.10 - € 5.60
dog	€ 2.20 - € 6.10

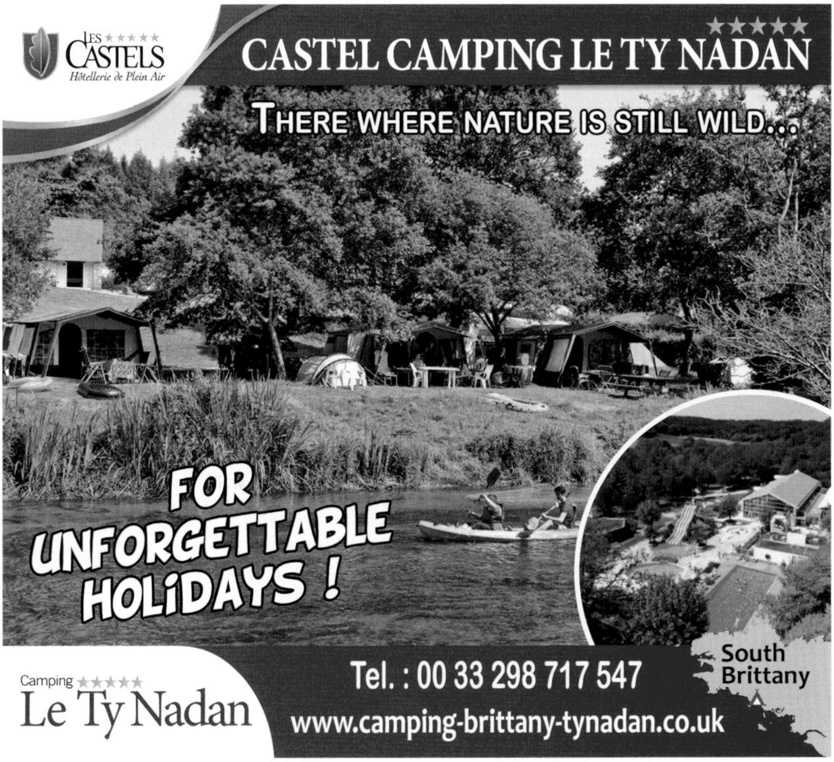

Mousterlin

Camping le Grand Large

48 route du Grand Large, Mousterlin, F-29170 Fouesnant (Finistère) T: 02 98 56 04 06.
E: grandlarge@franceloc.fr **alanrogers.com/FR29290**

Le Grand Large is a beach-side site situated on the Pointe de Mousterlin in natural surroundings. The site is separated from the beach by the road that follows the coast around the point. It is also protected from the wind by an earth bank with trees and a fence. There are 300 pitches with 89 on grass for tourers. Electricity (10A) is available throughout (long leads useful). The focal point of the site is an imaginative pool complex with slides, flumes and water features. A small river runs through the site but it is fenced. The ground is rather sandy in places with some shrubs and mature trees.

Facilities

Two neat toilet blocks (one only open in high season, with facilities for children and disabled visitors), have washbasins in cabins. Laundry facilities. Shop. Bar overlooking the sea with attractive terrace. Grill restaurant. Takeaway (July/Aug). New covered pool complex and outdoor, heated swimming pool with paddling pool and water slides in a separate pool. Tennis. Multisports court. Small play area. Games rooms. Bicycle hire. WiFi (free).

Open: 17 April - 6 September.

Directions

Site is 7 km. south of Fouesnant. Turn off N165 expressway at Coat Conq, signed Concarneau and Fouesnant. At Fouesnant take A45 signed Beg-Meil, then follow signs to Mousterlin. In Mousterlin turn left and follow camping signs. GPS: 47.84826, -4.03702

Charges guide

Per unit incl. 2 persons and electricity	€ 19.00 - € 35.00
extra person	€ 4.70 - € 7.00

Mousterlin

Sunêlia l'Atlantique

Kerbader, B.P 11, F-29170 Fouesnant (Finistère) T: 02 98 56 14 44. E: sunelia@latlantique.fr
alanrogers.com/FR29350

L'Atlantique is quietly situated just outside Beg-Meil. The 432 pitches are predominantly used by tour operators with about 130 for touring visitors. Pitches are level and grassy, all with electricity, separated by low shrubs. Apple orchards used for cider production are also on the site. All the facilities are grouped together in the centre including an innovative play area and pool complex with both indoor and outdoor pools, water slides and a paddling pool. The sandy beach faces the Glénan Islands and is a pleasant 400 m. walk away through a nature reserve. Coastal paths await exploration and Concarneau, Pont-Aven and La Pointe du Raz are all nearby. Eight pitches with their own sanitary facilities have been added and some with hardstandings.

Facilities

Fully equipped toilet blocks (cleaned three times a day) have facilities for disabled visitors. Restaurant (July/Aug). Shop, bar, snack bar with takeaway meals and pizza. Heated outdoor and indoor pools, water complex with slides (all season). Tennis. TV room. Billiards. Minigolf. Sports ground. Play area. Children's club (4-12 yrs) and evening entertainment in July/Aug. Play room (0-4 yrs). Bicycle hire. WiFi (charged). Dogs are not accepted.

Open: 20 April - 8 September.

Directions

From Fouesnant follow directions for Mousterlin for 2 km, then follow Chapelle de Kerbader. Site is signed. GPS: 47.856564, -4.020658

Charges guide

Per unit incl. 2 persons and electricity (6A)	€ 22.00 - € 41.00
with own sanitary facility	€ 33.00 - € 62.00

Camping Cheques accepted.

Névez

Camping les 2 Fontaines

Feunteun Vihan, Raguénes, F-29920 Névez (Finistère) T: 02 98 06 81 91. E: info@les2fontaines.fr
alanrogers.com/FR29470

Les 2 Fontaines is a large site with 288 pitches;105 are for touring, 118 are used by tour operators, and the remainder for mobile homes. The well cared for pitches are on grass, level and attractively laid out amongst mature trees and shrubs. All have 10A electricity connections. Trees have been carefully planted creating one area with silver birch, one with apple trees and another with palms and tropical plants. The pool complex is an excellent feature complete with chutes, flumes and waterfalls, and a covered pool with adjacent gym and massage room. There are numerous daytime activities for all the family to enjoy and a variety of entertainment in the evening.

Facilities

Two toilet blocks are of good quality with washbasins in cabins and preset showers. Separate facilities for disabled visitors. Laundry facilities. Basic motorcaravan services. Well stocked shop. Bar and takeaway. Large indoor and outdoor swimming pool complex. Fitness. Play area. 6-hole golf course. Driving range. Rollerblade hire. Archery. Scuba diving. WiFi in bar (free). Bicycle hire.

Open: 30 April - 4 September.

Directions

Travel south from Névez towards Raguénes. The site is on the left after 3 km. and is well signed. GPS: 47.79879, -3.79166

Charges guide

Per unit incl. 2 persons and electricity	€ 20.90 - € 40.80

Camping Cheques accepted.

Névez

Camping le Raguénès-Plage

19 rue des Iles, F-29920 Névez (Finistère) T: 02 98 06 80 69.
E: info@camping-le-raguenes-plage.com **alanrogers.com/FR29090**

Mme. Guyader and her family will ensure you receive a warm welcome on arrival at this well kept and pleasant site. Le Raguénès-Plage is an attractive and well laid out campsite with many shrubs and trees. The 287 pitches are a good size, flat and grassy, separated by trees and hedges. All have electricity (6/10/15A), water and drainage. The site is used by tour operators (51 pitches), and has 60 mobile homes of its own. A pool complex complete with heated indoor pool and water toboggan is a key feature and is close to the friendly bar, restaurant, shop and takeaway. From the far end of the campsite, a delightful five-minute walk along a path and through a cornfield takes you down to a pleasant, sandy beach looking out towards the Ile Verte and the Presqu'île de Raguénès.

Facilities

Two clean, well maintained sanitary blocks include a mixture of British and Turkish style toilets, washbasins in cabins, baby baths and facilities for disabled visitors. Laundry room. Motorcaravan services. Small shop, restaurant, bar and takeaway (all 1/5-14/9). Reading and TV room. Heated indoor and outdoor pools with sun terrace and paddling pool. Sauna (charged). Play areas. Games room. Large variety of activities organised in July/Aug. Bicycle hire. WiFi over site (charged).
Off site: Bus service to nearby towns. Beach, fishing and watersports 300 m. Supermarket 3 km. Riding 10 km.

Open: 9 April - 30 September.

Directions

From N165 take D24 Kerampaou exit. After 3 km. turn right towards Nizon and bear right at church in village following signs to Névez (D77). Continue through Névez, following signs to Raguénès. Continue for 3 km. to site on left (entrance is quite small and easy to miss). GPS: 47.79337, -3.80049

Charges guide

Per unit incl. 2 persons and electricity	€ 21.90 - € 39.10
extra person	€ 4.60 - € 6.20
child (under 7 yrs)	€ 2.00 - € 3.90
dog	€ 1.50 - € 3.20

Noyal-Muzillac

Camping Moulin de Cadillac

Route de Berric, F-56190 Noyal-Muzillac (Morbihan) T: 02 97 67 03 47. E: infos@moulin-cadillac.com
alanrogers.com/FR56430

Le Moulin de Cadillac is a riverside site located 15 minutes by car from the beaches of the Morbihan. Set in the heart of rural Brittany, this attractive site has 192 pitches, 123 of which are for touring (10A electricity). Pitches are generous (100-150 sq.m) although access to some is tight and may not be suitable for larger units. They are well laid out on grass and a profusion of trees and shrubs provide both shade and privacy. There is a great indoor pool complex and the fishing lake ensures that there is plenty to keep the family entertained. Boat trips to local islands and around the Gulf of Morbihan are popular.

Facilities

Three well appointed toilet blocks include facilities for children and disabled visitors. Covered laundry area. Shop. Bar (July/Aug). Large, indoor aquatic park with slides flumes and fountains. Outdoor pool with slides (1/6-2/9; heated July/Aug) and paddling pool. Games room. TV room. All-weather sports pitch. Tennis. Minigolf. Three play areas. Two fishing lakes. Children's zoo. Some entertainment in high season. No electric barbecues. Mobile homes, chalets and tents for rent. Off site: Muzillac for shopping, restaurants etc. 8 km. Beaches 10 km.

Open: 13 April - 15 September.

Directions

From Vannes travel southeast on the N165. Exit on D140 towards Berric. After 3 km. at Lauzach, site is well signed on the right. Continue for a further 4 km. GPS: 47.61310, -2.50140

Charges guide

Per unit incl. 2 persons and electricity	€ 19.40 - € 31.80
extra person	€ 4.50 - € 6.20
child (under 7 yrs)	€ 2.00 - € 3.00
dog	€ 1.00 - € 2.20

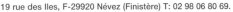

Paimpol

Camping Municipal de Cruckin

Rue de Cruckin, Kérity, F-22500 Paimpol (Côtes d'Armor) T: 02 96 20 78 47.
E: contact@camping-paimpol.com **alanrogers.com/FR22250**

A neat and well managed municipal site situated close to the historic fishing port of Cité des Islandais and within easy reach of the Ile de Bréhat. This is an ideal location for many interesting walks. The site has 130 well maintained, mostly level pitches set in both wooded and open areas and all have electricity connections (5-12A). A very large area has been provided for sports, a play area and picnic tables. Although the site does not have its own swimming pool, the beach is just a short walk away.

Facilities

One modern and heated toilet block. Washbasins in cabins and showers. Facilities for babies and disabled visitors. Laundry facilities. Bread and milk (high season). Snack bar/takeaway (July/Aug). Motorcaravan services. Large field for football. Pétanque. Fenced play area. Internet access on request. Bicycle hire. Fishing.
Off site: Beach. Kérity village with shops, restaurants and cafés. Riding 2 km. Golf 10 km.

Open: 1 April - 10 October.

Directions

From N12 St Brieuc bypass, take D786 north towards Paimpol. Village of Kérity is 3 km. south of Paimpol. Site is signed. GPS: 48.76966, -3.02209

Charges guide

Per unit incl. 2 persons and electricity	€ 17.80 - € 20.60
extra person	€ 3.50 - € 4.00
child (under 10 yrs)	€ 2.00 - € 2.50

Pénestin-sur-Mer

Camping les Iles Pénestin

La Pointe du Bile, B.P. 4, F-56760 Pénestin-sur-Mer (Morbihan) T: 02 99 90 30 24.
E: contact@camping-des-iles.fr **alanrogers.com/FR56120**

You will receive a warm, friendly welcome at this family run campsite. The owner, Madame Communal, encourages everyone to make the most of this beautiful region. Of the 184 pitches, 109 are for touring. Most are flat, hedged and of a reasonable size (larger caravans and American-style motorhomes are advised to book) and all have electricity (10A, Europlug). Some pitches have sea views and overlook the beach. There is direct access to cliff-top walks and local beaches (you can even walk to small off-shore islands at low tide). The heated swimming pool complex provides a focal point for all ages.

Facilities

The new large central toilet block is spotlessly clean with washbasins in cabins and showers. Laundry facilities. Facilities for disabled visitors and baby room. Shop, bar and restaurant, takeaway, heated outdoor pool complex (all open all season). Bicycle hire. Riding. Activities and entertainment in July/Aug. Across the road in Parc des Iles (mobile home section of site): Motorcaravan services. TV room. Multisports pitch. Tennis court. No electric barbecues. WiFi over site (charged).

Open: 10 April - 30 September.

Directions

From D34 (La Roche-Bernard), at roundabout just after entering Pénestin take D201 south (Assérac). Take right fork to Pointe-du-Bile after 2 km. Turn right at crossroads just before beach. Site is on left. GPS: 47.44543, -2.48396

Charges guide

Per unit incl. 2 persons and electricity	€ 21.00 - € 43.00
extra person (over 7 yrs)	€ 4.00 - € 6.00

Camping Cheques accepted.

Pénestin-sur-Mer

Domaine d'Inly

514

Route de Couarne, F-56760 Pénestin-sur-Mer (Morbihan) T: 02 99 90 35 09. E: inly-info@wanadoo.fr
alanrogers.com/FR56240

This very large site is mainly taken up with mobile homes and cottages, some belonging to the site owner, some private and some belonging to tour operators. Most of these pitches are arranged in groups of 10 to 14 around a central stone circle with a water point in the centre. The many large trees have been sensibly pruned to provide an acceptable level of shade. Of the 500 pitches, 80 are for touring units and all are large (100 sq.m) with 10A electrical connections (Europlug). Most are level and are situated by the attractive lake at the bottom of the site where one can fish or canoe. Pony rides are possible around the lake. There is a variety of sporting and leisure activities on offer.

Facilities

Two toilet blocks include facilities for disabled visitors, and a baby room. Laundry. Shop. Small, comfortable bar with large screen satellite TV, attractive restaurant and takeaway (all season). Heated indoor and outdoor pool complex with slide (outdoor 15/5-20/9, indoor all season). Games room. Play areas. Football pitch (weekly games organised in July/Aug). Lake for fishing/canoeing. Pony rides. Bicycle hire. Sports and activities. WiFi (free).

Open: 2 April - 30 September.

Directions

On D34 from La Roche-Bernard, at roundabout just after entering Pénestin, take D201 south signed Assérac. After 100 m. turn left (site signed) opposite Carrefour supermarket. After 650 m. turn right, again signed, and campsite is 400 m. on left.
GPS: 47.471483, -2.467267

Charges guide

Per unit incl. 2 persons and electricity	€ 18.00 - € 42.00
extra person	€ 6.00 - € 7.00

Pénestin-sur-Mer

Camping le Cénic

F-56760 Pénestin-sur-Mer (Morbihan) T: 02 99 90 45 65. E: info@lecenic.com

alanrogers.com/FR56180

Le Cénic has a rural setting amidst trees and shrubs and provides activities for all tastes. An attractive covered aquatic complex has water slides, bridges, rivers and a jacuzzi, whilst the outdoor pool comes complete with water slide, mushroom fountain and sunbathing areas. You may fish in the lake or use inflatables, watched by the peacock, the geese and turkeys. There is a hall for table tennis and a range of indoor games. There are 310 pitches, 160 of which are for touring. Of these, 90 have 6A electricity, but long leads will be required. The area has much to offer from the beaches of La Mine d'Or, the harbour at Trébiguier-Pénestin, the Golfe du Morbihan with its numerous islands, La Baule with its magnificent beach and the medieval city of Guérande to the unique Brière nature reserve.

Facilities

Good new toilet block includes washbasins in cabins. Facilities for disabled visitors. Baby room. Separate laundry. Bar and shop (July/Aug). TV and games rooms (July/Aug). Indoor swimming pool (15/4-15/9) and outdoor pool (July/Aug). Play area. Fishing. WiFi in part of site. Off site: Bicycle hire 1 km. Sailing 2 km. Riding 3 km. Pénestin town 2 km. Sandy beaches 2.5 km.

Open: 11 April - 13 September.

Directions

From D34 (La Roche-Bernard), at roundabout just after entering Pénestin take D201 south (Assérac). After 100 m. take first turning on left. After 800 m. turn left and campsite is 300 m. on right down a narrow winding lane. GPS: 47.47910, -2.45643

Charges guide

Per unit incl. 2 persons and electricity	€ 19.60 - € 33.00
extra person	€ 4.80 - € 6.50
child (under 7 yrs)	€ 2.00 - € 3.00
dog	€ 2.00 - € 2.50

Pénestin-sur-Mer

Camping les Pins

Route du val, F-56760 Pénestin-sur-Mer (Morbihan) T: 02 99 90 33 13. E: camping.lespins@wanadoo.fr

alanrogers.com/FR56630

Located in the South Morbihan region, 2 km. from the beach and 1 km. from Pénestin, les Pins is spread over 4.5 hectares, with 197 marked pitches in either shaded or sunny spots, in a calm environment. There are mobile homes and chalets for rent accommodating between three and six people. 69 touring pitches from 80 to 140 sq.m. are available with 6A electricity. Amenities include an outdoor heated swimming pool with water slides and play pool and an indoor pool with jacuzzi. Entertainment and activities for young and old are organised in high season. Surrounded by ocean, Pénestin offers 25 km. of coastline to lovers of the sea and hiking.

Facilities

Two sanitary blocks, one heated and with facilities for babies and disabled campers. Washing machines and dryer. Bar and takeaway (15/4-15/9). Heated outdoor swimming pool with slides and paddling pool (1/7-31/8). Heated indoor pool with whirlpool and jacuzzi (15/4-15/9). Games room. Playground. Organised events and activities. Charcoal barbecues not permitted. WiFi in some areas (free). Off site: Fishing, bicycle hire and sailing 2 km. Beach 2 km. Riding 15 km. Golf 20 km.

Open: 1 April - 18 October.

Directions

From the D34 towards Pénestin turn south at the first roundabout after crossing the D192 (Tréhiguier-Assérac) and site is shortly on right. GPS: 47.47653, -2.4521

Charges guide

Per unit incl. 2 persons and electricity	€ 13.80 - € 31.20
extra person	€ 3.20 - € 5.90
child (0-7 yrs)	€ 1.70 - € 3.60
dog	€ 0.80 - € 1.50

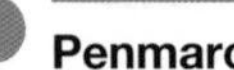

Penmarc'h

Flower Camping les Genêts

20 rue de Gouesnac'h Nevez, F-29760 Penmarc'h (Finistère) T: 02 98 58 66 93.

E: campinglesgenets29@orange.fr **alanrogers.com/FR29260**

Les Genêts' owners, Bridgette and Pascal Rohart, bought this rural campsite a few years ago and have enthusiastically transformed it beyond recognition. The modern reception is in front of a modestly sized swimming pool complex with flumes, a slide and a section for small children. A covered pool has been added. The 176 pitches are divided by trees and hedges and vary in both size and quality. The clever design of the flower beds and shrubs around the site is particularly attractive. There are 45 pitches for mobile homes which are placed to one side of the campsite.

Facilities

Two heated toilet blocks with showers and wash cubicles. Laundry room. Motorcaravan services. Bar and snack bar (all season). Bread available (July/Aug). Covered swimming pool (1/5-30/9). Play area and trampoline. Bicycle hire. Free WiFi by pool and office. Off site: Shops and restaurants 1.5 km. Riding, beach, fishing and boat launching 1.5 km. Golf 3 km.

Open: 2 April - 30 September.

Directions

From Pont l'Abbé, take the D785 southwest towards Penmarc'h. Before the town turn left eastwards on the D53 (Loctudy) and site is on left in 2 km. GPS: 47.81838, -4.309452

Charges guide

Per unit incl. 2 persons and electricity	€ 16.50 - € 27.00
extra person	€ 3.50 - € 5.50

Camping Cheques accepted.

Pléneuf-Val-André

Campéole les Monts Colleux

26 rue Jean Lebrun, F-22370 Pléneuf-Val-André (Côtes d'Armor) T: 02 96 72 95 10.

E: monts-colleux@campeole.com **alanrogers.com/FR22380**

Les Monts Colleux has a hilltop setting in Le Val André yet is within easy reach of the town. Some pitches have fine views of the sea. This was formerly a municipal site and is well managed with well kept hedges and pitches. The reception area and shop are modern, although the sanitary blocks are older. The 114 pitches (all with 6A electricity) are generally flat, although, given its hillside location, some are sloping. Although there is no swimming pool on site, there is a large covered municipal pool adjacent, with limited free access for campers. A member of the Campéole group.

Facilities

Two toilet blocks, one with special facilities for children, the other also includes facilities for disabled visitors. Motorcaravan services. Shop, snack bar and takeaway meals (all high season). Games/TV room. Play area. Bouncy castle. Bicycle hire. Activity and entertainment programme. Communal barbecue. Mobile homes and chalets for rent. Off site: Municipal covered swimming pool. Val-André centre, fishing and beach 300 m.

Open: 3 April - 27 September.

Directions

Approaching from the east (St Malo and Dinard) on the D786, bypass Erquy and continue to Pléneuf-Val-André and then to Le Val-André. Follow signs to Piscine Municipale – the site is adjacent. GPS: 48.5894, -2.5508

Charges guide

Per unit incl. 2 persons and electricity	€ 15.70 - € 23.60

Camping Cheques accepted.

Pleubian

Camping de Port la Chaine

F-22610 Pleubian (Côtes d'Armor) T: 02 96 22 92 38. E: info@portlachaine.com

alanrogers.com/FR22140

Michelle and Thierry Suquet offer a warm welcome to this comfortable, quiet, family site with stunning views. In a beautiful location on the Presqu'île Sauvage between Paimpol and Perros-Guirec, attractive trees and shrubs provide a balance of sun and shade for the 200 pitches. Of these, 140 are for touring, all with electricity (long leads may be needed in places) and some also have water and drainage. Pitches are on grassy terraces on the gradual descent towards the bay and the sea (a sandy bay with rocks). Most terraces have a slight slope, so those with motorcaravans will need to choose their pitch carefully.

Facilities

Two traditional style toilet blocks are comfortable and fully equipped. Washbasins in cabins, British and Turkish style toilets. Cabins for families or disabled visitors. Washing machines and dryer. Bar/snacks with terrace and takeaway (30/6-24/8). Bread and croissants (all season). New covered and heated swimming pool (all season) and outdoor heated pool (1/7-3/9). Play area. Games room. Pétanque. Children's entertainer in July/Aug. Beach, fishing and sailing. WiFi in reception area.

Open: 7 April - 22 September.

Directions

Pleubian is 37 km. north of Guingamp and 87 km. by road east of Roscoff. From D786 Lannion-Paimpol road, east of Tréguier turn north on D20 to Pleubian and on for 2 km. towards l'Armor Pleubian. Site signed to left. GPS: 48.8555, -3.1327

Charges guide

Per unit incl. 2 persons and electricity	€ 18.90 - € 27.90
extra person	€ 4.40 - € 6.90
child (2-7 yrs)	€ 3.80 - € 4.50

Plobannalec-Lesconil

Yelloh! Village l'Océan Breton

Lieu-dit le Manoir de Kerlut, F-29740 Plobannalec-Lesconil (Finistère) T: 02 98 82 23 89.
E: info@yellohvillage-loceanbreton.com **alanrogers.com/FR29120**

L'Océan Breton is a comfortable site in the grounds of a manor house on a river estuary near Pont l'Abbé. The campsite itself has neat, modern buildings and is laid out on flat grass providing 220 pitches (60 for touring units). All have electricity connections (6/10A), some also have water and drainage and around ten pitches have hardstanding. One area is rather open with separating hedges planted, the other part being amongst more mature bushes and some trees which provide shade. Site amenities are of excellent quality.

Facilities

New sanitary facilities including washbasins all in cabins, and facilities for babies and disabled visitors. Laundry. Small shop. Restaurant. Takeaway. Large modern bar with TV (satellite) and entertainment all season. Large aquapark with slides and children's pool. Covered, heated swimming pool. Sauna, solarium and small gym. Fitness centre. Play area. Tennis. Pétanque. Games room. Bicycle hire. Off site: Riding 1 km. Beach and fishing 2 km.

Open: 2 May - 4 September.

Directions

From Pont l'Abbé, on D785, take D102 road towards Lesconil. Site is signed on the left, shortly after the village of Plobannalec.
GPS: 47.81234, -4.22105

Charges guide

Per unit incl. 2 persons and electricity	€ 19.00 - € 45.00
extra person	€ 6.00 - € 8.00
child (3-7 yrs)	free - € 6.00

Ploemel

Camping Saint Laurent

Kergonvo, F-56400 Ploemel (Morbihan) T: 02 97 56 85 90. E: contact@camping-saint-laurent.fr
alanrogers.com/FR56330

This is an attractive, peaceful and rural site ten minutes from the beaches and 10 km. from Carnac. There are 60 touring pitches out of a total of 90 which are set among pine trees and wiry hedges giving some shade. Long leads are required for the 10A electricity. There is a more casual camping area being developed further away amongst some trees. A new covered, heated swimming and paddling pool has sun loungers. The welcoming bar and patio area also has a communal barbecue. Basic provisions are available from reception where good English is spoken. This pleasant, wooded site is now part of a group of seven sites called Camp'in Ouest.

Facilities

One bright modern heated sanitary block provides adequate facilities with excellent en suite facilities for disabled visitors and is centrally located. Shop (1/6-30/9). Small bar (1/5-25/10). Restaurant (1/6-30/9). Takeaway (1/6-25/10). Covered, heated swimming pool and paddling pool (1/5-30/9). Volleyball. Basketball. Small play area. Bicycle hire. WiFi (free). Off site: Golf 1 km. Riding 5 km. Fishing and beaches 10 km.

Open: April - October.

Directions

From the N165 Vannes-Lorient dual carriageway, take the exit signed D768 Ploemel/Carnac. After 4 km. turn right heading northwest towards Ploemel. Once in the village centre follow signs to St Laurent Camping. GPS: 47.66406, -3.09985

Charges guide

Per unit incl. 2 persons and electricity	€ 16.70 - € 21.60
extra person	€ 3.90 - € 5.00

Plomeur-la Torche

Sites et Paysages la Torche

Pointe de la Roche, F-29120 Plomeur-la Torche (Finistère) T: 02 98 58 62 82. E: info@campingdelatorche.fr
alanrogers.com/FR29370

Probably a 'must stay' site for surfers, this rural, family owned, wooded campsite, like so many in this part of Brittany, comes to life in July and August. The natural beauty of the wide sandy beaches of la Torche can be accessed directly from the site via a footpath (1.5 km). La Torche is internationally renowned as a paradise for all boardsports, particularly windsurfing. The site has 155 pitches (99 for tourers), divided by trees and hedges and tending to the generous in size. Most have 6A electricity connections and 50 have water and drainage also. Around 56 chalets and mobile homes are discreetly positioned amongst the trees.

Facilities

The main toilet block provides hot showers, washing cubicles and good facilities for disabled visitors. A second block opens in high season. Laundry facilities. Shop, bar and terrace, with snacks (all July/Aug). Covered swimming pool (15/6-15/9). Play area. Games/TV room. Entertainment in July/Aug. Free WiFi in bar.
Off site: Riding 500 m. Beach 1.5 km.

Open: 1 April - 30 September.

Directions

From Pont l'Abbé the D785 south to Plomeur, then follow signs for Pointe de La Torche. After 3 km. site is signed to left. GPS: 47.832859, -4.326355

Charges guide

Per unit incl. 2 persons and electricity	€ 16.00 - € 22.00
extra person	€ 3.50 - € 5.50
child (0-7 yrs)	€ 2.50 - € 3.50

Plonévez-Porzay

Camping La Plage de Tréguer

Plage de Sainte Anne-la-Palud, F-29550 Plonévez-Porzay (Finistère) T: 02 98 92 53 52.
E: camping-treguer-plage@wanadoo.fr **alanrogers.com/FR29590**

Set right on the dunes adjacent to a large, sandy beach on the huge sweep of Douarnenez Bay, this is apparently one of only seven campsites in Brittany with direct access to a beach, with no paths or roads to cross. It certainly is an impressive location, not manicured but on the 'wild' side, being a protected area. Tall hedges provide wind shelter, tamarisk grows in profusion and there are uninterrupted views out to sea. Some pitches nestle in the shelter of the dunes (sandier ground), others are in groups of four or eight, bordered by hedging. There are mobiles homes available for rent.

Facilities

One central toilet block has showers, washbasins in cabins, and facilities for babies and disabled visitors. Bar, takeaway and shop (July/Aug). Heated outdoor swimming pool with jacuzzi, waterfall for children and paddling pool (1/6-30/9). Play area. Bouncy castle. Multisports court. Games room/TV. Organised entertainment (July/Aug). Direct access to beach. Off site: Restaurant 2 km. Shops 3 km. Boat launching 3 km. Sailing 5 km. Bicycle hire 10 km. Riding 15 km. Golf 18 km. Fishing.

Open: 6 April - 29 September.

Directions

Situated on the north side of the village, it is well signed from Plonévez-Porzay.
GPS: 48.14485, -4.26882

Charges guide

Per unit incl. 2 persons and electricity	€ 17.40 - € 25.50
extra person	€ 3.60 - € 5.50
child (2-7 yrs)	€ 2.60 - € 3.60

Camping Cheques accepted.

Plouézec

Camping le Cap de Bréhat

Route de Port Lazo, F-22470 Plouézec (Côtes d'Armor) T: 02 96 20 64 28. E: info@cap-de-brehat.fr
alanrogers.com/FR22320

Camping Cap de Bréhat is in a magnificent setting with exceptional views of the Bay of Paimpol and the Ile de Bréhat. The enthusiastic owners are keen to make visitors welcome at their site which is well positioned for exploring the Goëlo Coast, Paimpol and the Pink Granite Coast. The campsite is in two sections and slopes down to the beach. The upper section is mostly devoted to mobile homes and is reached by a road or a series of steep steps, the lower section is for tourers. There are 141 pitches with 120 good sized grass pitches for touring (90 with 6A electricity).

Facilities

Two toilet blocks include facilities for disabled visitors but the site is not ideal for those with walking difficulties. Bar and restaurant with terrace and views over the bay. Takeaway. New covered swimming pool and paddling pool. Play area. Boules. Fishing. Sports area. Bicycle hire. Organised activities (July/Aug). Internet access. WiFi throughout (free in bar area). Off site: Beach 200 m. Boat ramp 300 m. Riding 6 km. Golf 12 km. Amenities in Plouézec and Paimpol.

Open: 1 March - 25 September.

Directions

From St Brieuc take D786 north towards Paimpol. Site is at Plouézec, south of Paimpol, well signed from D786. GPS: 48.759792, -2.962795

Charges guide

Per unit incl. 2 persons and electricity	€ 20.00 - € 30.00
extra person	€ 3.60 - € 6.20
child (2-11 yrs acc. to age)	€ 2.00 - € 4.70
dog (max. 1)	€ 4.50

Plouhinec

Camping Moténo

Route du Magouër, F-56680 Plouhinec (Morbihan) T: 02 97 36 76 63. E: camping-moteno@wanadoo.fr
alanrogers.com/FR56440

This site is situated on the east side of the River d'Etel, just before it enters the sea. The grass pitches are of average size, hedged and shaded by large trees. Of the 256 pitches, 140 are occupied by mobile homes, mostly for rent. The remaining 75 pitches for touring units all have 10A electricity. The site's new aquapark complex with covered and open areas is superb and includes slides, flumes and various pools. The beach is easily accessible, just 800 m. away, as is the little port facing Etel which can be reached by a regular ferry service. Plouhinec, the nearest town, is 5 km. by road where you will find shops and restaurants. A little further is the large town of Lorient.

Facilities

New modern, heated toilet block. Facilities for disabled visitors. Washing machines and dryer. Shop, bar and takeaway (July/Aug). New pool complex including spa pool. Multisports court. Gym. Bicycle hire. Play area. Entertainment (July/Aug). Charcoal barbecues are not permitted (communal available). WiFi throughout (charged). Off site: Fishing 100 m. Beach 800 m.

Open: 4 April - 27 September.

Directions

From Plouhinec, southeast of Lorient, take the D781 towards Carnac. Site is signed on right in 4 km. Follow signs for Plage. GPS: 47.66457, -3.22098

Charges guide

Per unit incl. 2 persons and electricity	€ 18.70 - € 35.50
extra person	€ 3.70 - € 7.00
child (0-7 yrs)	€ 2.60 - € 4.95

Ploumanach

Yelloh! Village le Ranolien

Ploumanach, F-22700 Perros-Guirec (Côtes d'Armor) T: 02 96 91 65 65. E: info@yellohvillage-ranolien.com
alanrogers.com/FR22080

Le Ranolien has been attractively developed around a former Breton farm – everything here is either made from, or placed on or around, the pink rocks, some of them massive. Of the 520 pitches 110 are for touring, mostly large and flat, but some quite small, all with electricity (10A) and some with water and drainage. The rest of the site is taken up with mobile homes and chalets for hire and pitches used by two tour operators. The site is on the coast, with beaches and coves within walking distance and there are spectacular views from some pitches.

Facilities

The main toilet block is heated in cool weather and has washbasins in cabins, mostly British style WCs and good showers, some spacious and with washbasins. Facilities for disabled visitors. Laundry. Motorcaravan services. Supermarket and gift shop. Restaurant, crêperie and bar. Indoor (all season) and outdoor (from end May) swimming pool complex. Wellness centre. Disco (July/Aug). Minigolf. Games room. Play area. Cinema. Gym. New Romany-style caravans and luxury chalets for rent. WiFi (charged). Off site: Beach 1.5 km. Riding 3 km.

Open: 11 April - 21 September.

Directions

Perros-Guirec is 12 km. north of Lannion. From Lannion take D788 to Perros-Guirec. Follow signs to Centre Ville past harbour area, then turn right along coast road (Centre Ville par la Corniche and Trégastel). Continue through north of town and on to La Clarté. After a sharp left hand bend site is immediately on the right. GPS: 48.82798, -3.476233

Charges guide

Per unit incl. 2 persons and electricity	€ 18.00 - € 45.00
extra person	€ 6.00 - € 9.00

Plozévet

Camping la Corniche

Chemin de la Corniche, F-29710 Plozévet (Finistère) T: 02 98 91 33 94. E: infos@campinglacorniche.com
alanrogers.com/FR29330

A well presented site, La Corniche is conveniently placed for both coast (1.5 km), with large sandy beaches, and the delights of inland Brittany. Large level fields are divided into smaller areas by mature hedging and there is some shade from trees. There are 120 generously sized grass pitches with 10A electricity available to the 88 touring units. There are some mobile homes and safari tents to rent. Many visitors return to la Corniche each year. The town of Plozévet is a ten-minute stroll away. There are several restaurants, most specialising in typically Breton food, bars and a small supermarket.

Facilities

Toilet facilities are excellent, one block having being completely rebuilt. Comprehensively equipped, they include individual wash cubicles. Provision for disabled visitors. Small shop and bar (from 1/4), takeaway (July/Aug). Swimming pool and paddling pool (heated, 15/5-15/9). Play area. Games/TV room. Bicycle hire. Entertainment (July/Aug). WiFi over site (charged). Off site: Beach and fishing 2 km. Riding 6 km.

Open: 28 March - 30 September.

Directions

Head west from Quimper and pick up the D784 towards Landudec and Plozévet. After 26 km, where the road makes a sharp right in the centre of Plozévet, take a left towards the coast (Plage). Site is on right after 1 km. GPS: 47.98039, -4.43051

Charges guide

Per unit incl. 2 persons and electricity	€ 19.30 - € 23.90

Camping Cheques accepted.

Pont-Scorff

Camping Entre Terre et Mer

Route d'Arzano, lieu-dit Sapin en Gam, F-56620 Pont-Scorff (Morbihan) T: 02 97 32 56 56.
E: camping.etem@wanadoo.fr **alanrogers.com/FR56750**

This small rural site is only 1 km. from the small bustling Breton town of Pont-Scorff (perhaps best known for its large zoo). The immaculate site has been recently acquired by M. and Mme. Didier. It has 17 very large touring pitches, all with 16A electricity (three also have water and drainage). They are level, grassy and many have some shade. The small swimming and paddling pool is overlooked by a pleasant terrace. For families and couples looking for a peaceful holiday, this would be a real find. Cars must be parked away from pitches.

Facilities

One small heated toilet block with some private cabins and facilities for disabled visitors. Washing machine and dryer. Motorcaravan services. Takeaway food (July/Aug). Covered heated swimming pool (1/4-15/10; no Bermuda shorts). Meeting room with TV, library and board games. Play area. Sports field. Limited entertainment in high season. WiFi (charged). Off site: Bicycle hire 200 m.

Open: 15 February - 15 December.

Directions

From Vannes west on N165 take exit 42 onto D769 north signed Morlaix. After 6 km exit onto D26 to Pont-Scorff. Follow signs for the high town and the campsite on D6. GPS: 47.84947, -3.41214

Charges guide

Per unit incl. 2 persons and electricity	€ 13.50 - € 24.50
extra person	€ 3.10 - € 6.00

Poullan-sur-Mer

Camping de la Baie de Douarnenez

30 rue Luc Robet, F-29100 Poullan-sur-Mer (Finistère) T: 02 98 74 26 39. E: info@camping-douarnenez.com
alanrogers.com/FR29060

This is an attractive, family run site just back from the sea near Douarnenez in Finistère. It has 190 pitches on fairly flat ground, marked out by separating hedges, though varying in size, shape and quality. With 77 pitches used for touring units, the site also has a number of mobile homes and chalets. These are sympathetically positioned amongst the trees and shrubs, away from the touring pitches. All pitches have electrical connections and the original trees provide shade in some areas. A large room, the Woodpecker Bar, is used for entertainment with discos and cabaret in July and August. Weekly outings and clubs for children are organised in high season.

Facilities

Two modern toilet blocks include washbasins, mostly in cabins, and facilities for disabled visitors. Laundry facilities. Motorcaravan services. Gas. Small shop for basics. Bar (July/Aug). Restaurant and takeaway (6/7-30/8). Heated, indoor and outdoor swimming and paddling pools (no Bermuda-style shorts). Tennis. Minigolf. Fishing. Bicycle hire. Playground. WiFi throughout (charged).

Open: 7 April - 16 September.

Directions

Site is 500 m. east of centre of Poullan on D7 road towards Douarnenez. From Douarnenez take circular bypass route towards Audierne. Turn onto D7, (Poullan). Site is signed. GPS: 48.0824, -4.40805

Charges guide

Per unit incl. 2 persons and electricity	€ 17.00 - € 34.00
extra person	€ 3.60 - € 5.90

Quiberon

Camping le Conguel

Boulevard de la Teignouse, B.P. 20599, F-56175 Quiberon (Morbihan) T: 02 97 50 19 11.
E: info@campingduconguel.com **alanrogers.com/FR56260**

Camping Le Conguel is situated on the coast near the southern tip of the Quiberon peninsula, about 2 km. from the town centre. The beach is just across the road (not busy except at weekends) and a national sailing school is 500 m. along the coast. The 75 touring pitches are in two groups along the seaward side of the site. They are flat, hedged and rather worn, and all have electricity (10A), water and drainage. The remaining 175 pitches are taken up by mobile homes, some for tour operators. The focus of the campsite is a superb complex comprising the swimming pool, restaurants, a bar and shop, all enclosed by terraces with seating areas.

Facilities

Two modern, well designed toilet blocks with baby rooms and facilities for disabled visitors. Laundry with washing machines and dryers. Heated swimming pool complex with slides (4/4-13/9). Bar (with TV). Restaurant, takeaway and shop (all 4/4-13/9). Tennis. Multi-gym. Sauna. Jacuzzis. Bicycle hire. Internet access. Off site: Beach and fishing 50 m. Boat ramp 200 m. Golf 500 m.

Open: 4 April - 30 September.

Directions

From N165 take Quiberon/Carnac exit onto D768. Follow road south towards Quiberon town centre. Turn left (east) signed Port Haliguen. At port follow road round to right towards aerodrome. Site is on right 1.5 km. along coast. GPS: 47.47450, -3.09310

Charges guide

Per unit incl. 2 persons and electricity	€ 21.95 - € 52.95

Quiberon

Camping Do Mi Si La Mi

31 rue de la Vierge, Saint Julien-Plage, F-56170 Quiberon (Morbihan) T: 02 97 50 22 52.
E: camping@domisilami.com **alanrogers.com/FR56360**

Occupying a five-hectare site on the Quiberon Peninsula, just 100 metres from the sandy beaches, this campsite has plenty to offer and is particularly quiet and laid back in low season. Of the 350 pitches, 189 are for touring and are set amongst high mature hedges and colourful shrubs giving plenty of shade and privacy; some have sea views. Long leads are required on a few pitches as the 10A electricty points can be shared between three or four pitches. The excellent amenities for children are in a well fenced area and include climbing frames, bouncy castles and multisports courts.

Facilities

New, high quality sanitary block with hot showers. Facilities for disabled campers and young children. Separate laundry. Shop. Bar, restaurant and takeaway (1/4-15/9). TV room. Bouncy castles. Multisports courts. Bicycle hire. Children's club. WiFi throughout (charged). Off site: Restaurant and supermarket 50 m. Beaches 100 m. Town centre 2 km. Golf and riding 3 km.

Open: 1 April - 1 November.

Directions

From N165 Vannes-Lorient dual carriageway south of Auray, take Carnac exit. Continue southwest on D768 via Plouharmel following signs for Quiberon. 25 km. from N165, before Quiberon, site is signed to left at St Julien-Plage. GPS: 47.49974, -3.12026

Charges guide

Per unit incl. 2 persons and electricity	€ 17.80 - € 27.80
extra person	€ 2.90 - € 5.00

Quiberon

Flower Camping Bois d'Amour

87 rue de Saint-Clément, F-56170 Quiberon (Morbihan) T: 02 97 50 13 52.
E: camping.boisdamour@flowercampings.com **alanrogers.com/FR56520**

Le Bois d'Amour faces toward Belle Ile and lies just 150 m. from the attractive, sandy Goviro beach at the southern end of the Quiberon peninsula. There are 259 pitches here, of which around 120 are for touring units, most with electricity. Other pitches are occupied by mobile homes and chalets (for rent). On-site amenities include a large indoor pool and a separate children's pool. There is also a safari tent village. Quiberon is explored by bicycle and these are available to rent on site. In high season, a regular programme of activities and entertainment is organised including activities for children.

Facilities

Three good toilet blocks include facilities for children and disabled visitors. Laundry facilities. Shop. Bar/snack bar. Takeaway. Heated indoor swimming and paddling pools. Games room. Playground. Activity and entertainment programme. Mobile homes and chalets for rent. Bicycle hire. Free WiFi throughout. Off site: Nearest beach 150 m. Fishing. Riding 200 m. Golf 500 m. Tennis. Quiberon. Carnac. Excursions to Belle Ile.

Open: 4 April - 27 September.

Directions

From Auray (RN 165) take the southbound D768 to Plouharnel and on to Quiberon. Upon arrival in Quiberon, follow signs to Thalassotherapie and then the site GPS: 47.47634, -3.110364

Charges guide

Per unit incl. 2 persons and electricity	€ 19.00 - € 41.00
extra person	€ 4.20 - € 6.50

Quimper

Castel Camping l'Orangerie de Lanniron

Château de Lanniron, F-29000 Quimper (Finistère) T: 02 98 90 62 02. E: camping@lanniron.com
alanrogers.com/FR29050

L'Orangerie is a beautiful and peaceful family site set in ten acres of a 17th-century, 38-hectare country estate on the banks of the Odet river, formerly the home of the Bishops of Quimper. The site has 199 grassy pitches (156 for touring units) of three types varying in size, services and price. They are on flat ground, laid out in rows alongside access roads with shrubs and bushes providing separation. All have electricity and 88 have three services. The original outbuildings have been attractively converted around a walled courtyard. Used by tour operators (30 pitches).

Facilities

Excellent heated block in the courtyard and second modern block serving the top areas of the site. Facilities for disabled visitors and babies. Washing machines and dryers. Motorcaravan services. Shop (15/5-10/9). Bar (23/5-7/9). Restaurant and takeaway. Swimming and paddling pool. Aquapark with slides. Small play area. Tennis. Minigolf. Golf course (9 holes). Fishing. Archery. Bicycle hire. TV/video and games rooms. Karaoke. Pony rides and tree climbing (July/Aug). WiFi over site (charged).

Open: 28 March - 15 November.

Directions

From Quimper follow Quimper Sud signs, then Toutes Directions and general camping signs, finally signs for Lanniron. GPS: 47.97685, -4.11102

Charges guide

Per unit incl. 2 persons and electricity	€ 23.50 - € 46.30
extra person	€ 4.20 - € 8.80
child (2-9 yrs)	€ 3.30 - € 5.80
dog	€ 3.60 - € 5.40

Rochefort-en-Terre

Sites et Paysages Au Gré des Vents

2 chemin de Bogeais, F-56220 Rochefort-en-Terre (Morbihan) T: 02 97 43 37 52. E: gredesvents@orange.fr
alanrogers.com/FR56100

This quiet family site is in wooded countryside, 600 m. from the town. Philippe and Benedicte Lambert have recently purchased this neat, tidy and organised site. There are 85 pitches (66 for tourers, 43 with 6/10A electricity) of good size (80-150 sq.m) on neat grass, with two levels. The upper level, with a limited number of electrical hook-ups, is flat and pitches are divided by young shrubs. The entrance, reception and bar are located here, just beyond the security gate. The lower level is partly sloping with mature trees, shade and electricity on all pitches.

Facilities

The modern heated sanitary block is kept very clean and includes large, comfortable showers and cabins with washbasins. Provision for disabled visitors. Baby room. Laundry facilities. Motorcaravan services. Bread delivered each morning. Bar. Takeaway. Indoor heated swimming pool (12/4-21/9). Tennis. Football area. Two play areas. WiFi (charged). Off site: Lake 500 m. with fishing and watersports.

Open: 29 March - 28 September.

Directions

From Redon take D775 Vannes road west for 25 km. Branch north on D774 (Rochefort-en-Terre). Follow road past the lake on left, in 800 m. pass car park, then turn at next sharp left, follow sign to site up a narrow lane. GPS: 47.69515, -2.34913

Charges guide

Per unit incl. 2 persons and electricity	€ 20.20 - € 26.40
extra person	€ 4.00 - € 5.65

Saint Benôit-des-Ondes

Camping de l'Ile Verte

42 rue de l'Ile Verte, F-35114 Saint Benôit-des-Ondes (Ille-et-Vilaine) T: 02 99 58 62 55.

E: bienvenue@campingdelileverte.com **alanrogers.com/FR35180**

L'Ile Verte is located at the heart of the bay of Le Mont Saint-Michel, close to Cancale and Saint Malo, and is a good base for discovering the culture, gastronomy and coast of this beautiful area. The campsite is just 400 m. from the sea and has 21 mobile homes for rent, as well as 39 generously sized touring pitches, all with 6A electricity. On-site amenities include a covered, heated swimming pool and a good children's play area. Special kitchen facilities have been provided for visitors with tents. In peak season, activities and events are organised including evening swimming and local folk groups.

Facilities

One older style toilet block (renovated in 2013) has new shower fittings and provides washbasins in cubicles. Facilities for disabled visitors (key access). Laundry area. Motorcaravan services. Bar/takeaway in high season. Pizza van once a week and seafood platters delivered in July/Aug. Covered and heated swimming pool. Play area. Boules. Activity and entertainment. Mobile homes for rent. Bicycle hire. WiFi (charged). Off site: Restaurants and shops in the village and Cancale. Golf 15 km.

Open: 1 April - 1 November.

Directions

The site can be found on the edge of the village of St Benôit-des-Ondes. Approaching from St Malo, follow D155 and D6, via St Meloir-des-Ondes until St Benôit-des-Ondes. Follow signs to the site. GPS: 48.615779, -1.851835

Charges guide

Per unit incl. 2 persons and electricity	€ 19.70 - € 24.00
extra person	€ 3.10 - € 4.20
child (3-12 yrs)	€ 2.20 - € 3.10

Saint Briac-sur-Mer

Camping Emeraude

7 chemin de la Souris, F-35800 Saint Briac-sur-Mer (Ille-et-Vilaine) T: 02 99 88 34 55.

E: info@seagreen-campingemeraude.com **alanrogers.com/FR35100**

M. Senghor has created a pleasant site with a French feel and some surprising features for such a compact site. Notably these include an attractive heated leisure pool with water slides, whirlpool and a paddling pool, safely separated from the main pool and with its own little slide. There are 77 level pitches for touring, separated by hedges or shrubs and all with electricity connection adjacent (6A). Beyond these are 121 mobile homes and chalets (80 for rent). Although in an urban setting, the sandy beaches of the attractive Côte Eméraude are only a short drive away.

Facilities

Large heated toilet block with washbasins in cubicles and controllable showers. Facilities for disabled visitors. Baby room. Washing machine and dryer. Motorcaravan services. Swimming pool (15/5-15/9). Shop and takeaway. Bar (July/Aug). Games room. Excellent play area. Minigolf. Bicycle hire. Children's activities and evening entertainment for families (July/Aug). Gas barbecues for hire. No twin-axle caravans or large motorcaravans. Only dogs under 15 kg. accepted in rental accommodation. WiFi throughout (charged).

Open: 4 April - 21 September.

Directions

St Briac is 7 km. west of Dinard. From ferry terminal follow signs for Dinard. Turn west onto D168. Keep west onto D603 and follow signs for 'Camping Eméraude par la côte' (avoids town centre); site is well signed from there. From other directions take D976/N176 following signs for Dinard. GPS: 48.62776, -2.130865

Charges guide

Per unit incl. 2 persons and electricity	€ 23.00 - € 32.55
extra person	€ 5.50 - € 6.60

Saint Brieuc

Flower Camping des Vallées

Boulevard Paul Doumer, Parc de Brézillet, F-22000 Saint Brieuc (Côtes d'Armor) T: 02 96 94 05 05.

E: campingdesvallees@wanadoo.fr **alanrogers.com/FR22000**

A well managed town centre campsite, just one kilometre from the TGV rail station. Neat and tidy, it has 85 good sized pitches, 35 with electricity (10A), water and drainage, set mainly on flat terraced grass and separated by shrubs and bushes, with 12 hardstandings for large motorcaravans. Mature trees are plentiful, providing shade if required, and a small stream winds through the middle of the site creating a quiet, peaceful atmosphere. Saint Brieuc's pedestrianised centre is filled with small shops and boutiques and several speciality food emporia, all within a short walk.

Facilities

The two main toilet blocks include some washbasins in cabins, facilities for disabled visitors and baby room. Laundry facilities. Motorcaravan services. Two further smaller blocks are at the bottom of the site. Shop with basic, compact bar with snacks and takeaway (July/Aug). Play area. Arcade games. Bicycle hire. Entertainment and weekly pony days for children (July/Aug). WiFi (charged).

Open: 15 March - 20 December.

Directions

From the east, on entering St Brieuc, look for the sign to the railway station and from there, signs for Brézillet or site. GPS: 48.50042, -2.75921

Charges guide

Per unit incl. 2 persons and electricity	€ 16.50 - € 24.90
extra person	€ 4.00 - € 5.20

No credit cards.

Saint Cast-le-Guildo

Camping le Châtelet

Rue des Nouettes, F-22380 Saint Cast-le-Guildo (Côtes d'Armor) T: 02 96 41 96 33. E: chateletcp@aol.com

alanrogers.com/FR22040

Carefully developed over the years from a former quarry, le Châtelet is pleasantly and quietly situated with lovely views over the estuary from many pitches. It is well laid out, mainly in terraces with fairly narrow access roads. There are 216 good sized pitches separated by hedges, all with electricity (8A). A safari, cocoon and teepee tent village is positioned around a little lake (unfenced) which can be used for fishing. Used by one tour operator (23 pitches). A green walking area is a nice feature around the lower edge of the site and a path leads directly down to a beach (about 200 m. but with steps).

Facilities

Four toilet blocks with access at different levels include washbasins in cabins and facilities for children. Three small toilet blocks on the lower terraces. Some facilities are closed outside July/Aug. Motorcaravan services. Heated swimming and paddling pools (all season). Shop for basics and bar (8/5-4/9), takeaway (19/6-4/9), lounge and general room with satellite TV and pool table. Zen room for rest, meditation and massage (high season). Games room. Play area. Organised games and activities in season. Dancing (June-Aug). WiFi throughout (charged).

Open: 13 April - 11 September.

Directions

Best approach is to turn off D786 road at Matignon towards St Cast (ignore sat nav); just inside St Cast limits turn left at sign for Campings and follow site signs on C90. GPS: 48.63723, -2.26934

Charges guide

Per unit incl. 2 persons and electricity	€ 25.10 - € 41.10
extra person	€ 4.20 - € 7.20
child (0-14 yrs acc. to age)	free - € 5.10
dog	€ 4.20

Saint Cast-le-Guildo

Castel Camping le Château de Galinée

La Galinée, F-22380 Saint Cast-le-Guildo (Côtes d'Armor) T: 02 96 41 10 56. E: chateaugalinee@wanadoo.fr

alanrogers.com/FR22090

Situated a few kilometres back from Saint Cast and owned and managed by the Vervel family, Galinée is in a parkland setting on level grass with numerous and varied mature trees. It has 273 pitches, all with electricity, water and drainage and separated by many mature shrubs and bushes. The top section is mostly for mobile homes. An attractive outdoor pool complex has swimming and paddling pools and two pools with a water slide and a stream. A new indoor complex has now also been added and includes a swimming pool, bar, restaurant and large entertainment hall.

Facilities

The large modern sanitary block includes washbasins in private cabins, facilities for babies and a good unit for disabled visitors. Laundry room. Shop for basics, bar and excellent takeaway menu (all 25/5-4/9). Attractive outdoor heated pool complex with swimming and paddling pools. Covered complex with heated swimming pool, bar, restaurant, entertainment hall and outside terrace with large play area. Tennis. Fishing. WiFi over site (charged).

Open: 11 May - 5 September.

Directions

From D168 Ploubalay-Plancoet road turn onto D786 towards Matignon and St Cast. Site is very well signed 1 km. after leaving Notre Dame de Guildo. GPS: 48.58475, -2.25656

Charges guide

Per unit incl. 2 persons and electricity	€ 23.60 - € 35.60
extra person	€ 4.20 - € 7.30

Camping Cheques accepted.

Saint Jouan-des-Guerets

Yelloh! Village le P'tit Bois

La Lande Chaladouze, F-35430 Saint Jouan-des-Guerets (Ille-et-Vilaine) T: 02 99 21 14 30.
E: contact@ptitbois.com **alanrogers.com/FR35040**

On the outskirts of Saint Malo, this neat, family oriented site, which is ideal for both younger and older children, is very popular with visitors of all nationalities. It is good for stopovers or for longer stays. Le P'tit Bois provides 275 level pitches with 95 for touring units, which are divided into groups by mature hedges and trees, separated by shrubs and flowers and have access from tarmac roads. Half of them have electrical hook-ups and over half have water taps. There are site-owned mobile homes and chalets so facilities are open throughout the season.

Facilities

One fully equipped, heated toilet block with washbasins in cabins, baby baths and sanitary facilities specially for children. Laundry. Simple facilities for disabled visitors. Motorcaravan services. Shop. Bar (entertainment in July/Aug), snack bar with takeaway. TV room. Games rooms. Heated swimming pool, paddling pool and two water slides (from 15/5). Heated indoor pool. Playground. Multisports court. Tennis. Minigolf. WiFi (free).

Open: 1 April - 18 September.

Directions

St Jouan is west of St Malo-Rennes road (N137) just outside St Malo. Site is signed from N137 (take 2nd exit for St Jouan on D4). GPS: 48.60993, -1.98665

Charges guide

Per unit incl. 2 persons and electricity	€ 19.00 - € 47.00
extra person	€ 6.00 - € 9.00
child (3-7 yrs)	free - € 7.00

Saint Lunaire

Camping la Touesse

171 rue de la Ville Gehan, F-35800 Saint Lunaire (Ille-et-Vilaine) T: 02 99 46 61 13.
E: camping.la.touesse@wanadoo.fr **alanrogers.com/FR35060**

This family campsite was purpose built and has been developed since 1987 by Alain Clément, who is keen to welcome more British visitors. Set just back from the coast road, 300 metres from a sandy beach, it is in a semi-residential area. It is, nevertheless, a pleasant, sheltered site with a range of trees and shrubs. Of the 141 level, grass pitches in bays, 90 are for touring units, all with electricity (5/10A). A plus factor of this site, besides its proximity to Dinard, is the fine sandy beach which is sheltered – so useful in early season – and safe for children. An Aqua Park, featuring both covered and outdoor heated swimming pools, a water slide and whirlpool opened in 2015. The owners speak English.

Facilities

The central toilet block is well maintained, heated in low season with all modern facilities. Part of it may not be open outside July/Aug. Baby bath. Toilet for disabled campers. Laundry facilities. Motorcaravan services. Shop for basics, pleasant bar/restaurant with TV and takeaway (1/4-20/9). Video games for children. Heated indoor (all season) and outdoor (1/5-15/9) swimming pools, waterslide and whirlpool. Sauna. Bouncy castle. Bicycle hire. Internet access in reception. WiFi over site (charged).

Open: 1 April - 30 September.

Directions

From ferry terminal follow signs for Dinard on D168 across the dam until 1st roundabout where north onto D266 (Dinard) for 1.1 km. Left onto D786 for 1.3 km. Take 3rd exit from roundabout (rue de la Ville Es Lemetz), after 700 m. right onto rue de la Ville Géhan for 700 m. to site on right.
GPS: 48.63084, -2.08418

Charges guide

Per unit incl. 2 persons and electricity (10A)	€ 19.70 - € 26.00

Saint Lunaire

Flower Camping Longchamp

Boulevard de Saint-Cast, F-35800 Saint Lunaire (Ille-et-Vilaine) T: 02 99 46 33 98.
E: contact@camping-longchamp.com **alanrogers.com/FR35070**

Flower Camping Longchamp lies on the Emerald Coast just 100 m. from a magnificent sandy beach. Set in a wooded area this site gives the impression of being a large landscaped garden. Of the 270 pitches, 170 are for touring and 140 have 10A electricity. They are large and well kept, some level and others on a slope. Hedges divide off certain areas and some shade is provided by Cypress trees. There are 39 privately owned mobile homes. The addition of an indoor pool and an outdoor aqua park make this a very good holiday destination. The restaurant on site has a cosy atmosphere and an extensive menu.

Facilities

Two very clean toilet blocks with some washbasins in cabins and large showers. Facilities for disabled visitors. Laundry. Small shop, restaurant, bar and takeaway (June-Sept). Indoor swimming pool (all season) and outdoor pool complex with slides (15/6-10/9). TV/games room. Play area. Bouncy castle (July/Aug). Minigolf. Tennis. Boules. Some entertainment in high season. Torches useful. WiFi in some areas (charged).

Open: 1 April - 30 September.

Directions

From ferry terminal follow signs for Dinard. From other directions take D976/N176 and follow signs for Dinard. Turn west onto D168. Keep west onto D603 and in 3 km. turn north on D503 (St Lunaire). Site signed from village. GPS: 48.63384, -2.12052

Charges guide

Per unit incl. 2 persons and electricity	€ 18.80 - € 32.70
extra person	€ 4.00 - € 6.70

Saint Marcan

Camping le Balcon de la Baie

Le Verger, F-35120 Saint Marcan (Ille-et-Vilaine) T: 02 99 80 22 95. E: contact@lebalcondelabaie.com
alanrogers.com/FR35210

Camping le Balcon de la Baie is owned by an enthusiastic young couple. It is close to Mont Saint-Michel, Saint Malo, Dinard and Dinan, and only a two-hour drive from Cherbourg. This quiet little site has just 39 touring pitches set amongst mature trees and well tended shrubs and plants. Some have sea views and many have 6A electricity. There are also mobile homes for rent. An attractive small pool complex offers a main pool (20 m) merging into a paddling pool and a whirlpool. A bistro/crêperie is a short walk from the campsite and there are shops and a restaurant in the nearby village of Saint Broladre.

Facilities

Sanitary block includes hot showers and facilities for babies and disabled visitors. Washing machine, dryer and ironing board. Baker calls daily. Basic supplies at reception. Heated swimming pool with paddling area and jacuzzi (15/5-15/9). Playground. Pétanque. Volleyball. In high season: playroom with TV; sale of local produce, pizzas, moules-frites evenings. WiFi in some areas (charged). Off site: Crêperie 550 m. Fishing 5 km.

Open: 1 April - 31 October.

Directions

From A84/N175 exit 34 south of Avranches, take N175 then N176 (St Malo/St Brieuc). In 23 km. take D89 for St Marcan. Site is signed to right in 2.5 km. GPS: 48.589432, -1.629404

Charges guide

Per unit incl. 2 persons and electricity	€ 18.00 - € 21.40

Camping Cheques accepted.

Saint Malo

Domaine de la Ville Huchet

Route de la Passagère, Quelmer, F-35400 Saint Malo (Ille-et-Vilaine) T: 02 99 81 11 83.
E: info@villehuchet.com **alanrogers.com/FR35050**

Domaine de la Ville Huchet has been transformed in recent years into a site with modern facilities and lots of character. The 107 touring pitches are well laid out and mainly of generous size, most with 6A electricity and some with shade. There are six 'grand comfort' pitches and four with 16A hook-ups. An older manor house, undergoing renovation, is at the centre of the site. A splendid pool complex with slides and toboggans has been created alongside a large, covered pool. Entertainment for young and old takes place in the spacious bar during high season, while a crêperie provides a range of food. This is a useful site positioned on the edge of Saint Malo with easy access to the ferry terminal, old town and beaches. A bus service to take you into the town is 400 m. away. The site is in the process of gradual renovation. In addition to works on the manor house, which now has a new roof and front door, a new sanitary block with living walls is being built. A small third block is open in high season only. At one end of the site, an area without electricity is reserved for tents.

Facilities

One main sanitary block, a small additional block opens in high season. A new block opened in 2015. Facilities for children and disabled visitors. Motorcaravan services. Shop. Bar. Crêperie (July/Aug). Snack bar. Aqua park with water slides (June-Aug). Covered pool. Bicycle hire. Play area. Entertainment programme in peak season (including live bands). Communal barbecue. WiFi over site (charged). Off site: Aquarium 700 m. Fishing 2 km. St Malo 3.5 km.

Open: 1 April - 18 September.

Directions

From St Malo take D137 towards Rennes. Take exit for St Jouan (D4) heading south. The site is well signed (2 km). GPS: 48.61507, -1.98782

Charges guide

Per unit incl. 2 persons and electricity	€ 19.90 - € 37.90
extra person	€ 3.80 - € 7.30
child (2-12 yrs)	€ 2.80 - € 4.70
dog	€ 4.00

Saint Pierre-de-Quiberon

Flower Camping l'Océan

16 avenue de Groix, B.P. 18 Kerhostin, F-56510 Saint Pierre-de-Quiberon (Morbihan) T: 02 97 30 91 29.
E: info@relaisdelocean.com **alanrogers.com/FR56470**

L'Océan is a member of the Flower group and can be found just 100 m. from the nearest beach, halfway down the Quiberon peninsula. There are 267 sandy pitches which are generally level and well shaded, although some sunnier pitches are also available. A selection of mobile homes and fully equipped tents are for rent. In peak season, a varied entertainment programme is on offer, including traditional Celtic folk evenings and magic shows, as well as discos and concerts. The site's bar/restaurant,'Ty Mouss', is the focal point and specialises in pizzas and crêpes as well as other light meals. In low season, these facilities are unavailable.

Facilities

Sanitary facilities provide hot showers, but are a little dated. Facilities for disabled visitors. Laundry facilities. Motorcaravan services. Shop, bar/restaurant and takeaway (July/Aug). Heated outdoor swimming pool (May-Sept). Multisports terrain. Tennis. Bicycle hire. Canoe hire. Play area. TV/games room. Activity and entertainment programme. Mobile homes and equipped tents for rent. WiFi (charged). Charcoal barbecues are not allowed (communal available). Off site: Beach 100 m.

Open: 1 April - 4 October.

Directions

Leave the N165 at the Quiberon exit and head south on the D768. Continue towards St Pierre-de-Quiberon, passing through Plouharnel. Site is located at Kerhostin and is signed to the right, before St Pierre. GPS: 47.534327, -3.139558

Charges guide

Per unit incl. 2 persons and electricity	€ 16.40 - € 26.80
extra person	€ 3.60 - € 5.20
child (3-6 yrs)	€ 2.30 - € 4.00

Saint Pol-de-Léon

Camping Ar Kleguer

Avenue de la Mer, F-29250 Saint Pol-de-Léon (Finistère) T: 02 98 69 18 81. E: info@camping-ar-kleguer.com

alanrogers.com/FR29040

Ar Kleguer is less than 20 minutes from the Roscoff ferry terminal in the heart of the Pays du Léon in north Finistère. One section of the site (used in high season) has a country feel and incorporates a small domestic animal park. The main section is divided into several areas, some on terraces at the edge of the sea with spectacular views overlooking the Bay of Morlaix. There are 182 large and well kept pitches, 122 for touring units, all with 10A electricity connections. This neat site is decorated with attractive flowers, shrubs and trees.

Facilities

Three modern, tiled toilet blocks are well maintained and kept clean. One new block includes a kitchen area for walkers and cyclists. Facilities for babies, children and disabled visitors. Family room. Laundry room. Shop, bar and takeaway (July/Aug). New indoor (all season) and outdoor (30/6-30/8) heated pool complex with paddling pools and slide. Pool table. Tennis. Bicycle hire. Animal park. Play area. Entertainment and activities for children (July/Aug). Free WiFi over part of site. Off site: Restaurant at site entrance. Beach adjacent with fishing and sailing. Riding 4 km. Golf 7 km.

Open: 2 April - 25 September.

Directions

St Pol is 18 km. northwest of Morlaix just off the D58 Morlaix-Roscoff road. Site is best approached from south, leaving D58 on the D769 signed St Pol Littoral. Turn right at cemetery following signs for Plages et Port and campsites. Turn left along seafront to site at end. GPS: 48.69075, -3.96734

Charges guide

Per unit incl. 2 persons and electricity	€ 22.55 - € 29.90
extra person	€ 4.70 - € 6.50
child (2-7 yrs)	€ 2.80 - € 4.35

Saint Pol-de-Léon

Camping de Trologot

Grève du Man, F-29250 Saint Pol-de-Léon (Finistère) T: 02 98 69 06 26. E: camping-trologot@wanadoo.fr

alanrogers.com/FR29490

This small and attractive riverside site has a comfortable ambience and is only a short drive from the port of Roscoff. There are 100 pitches, 85 for touring, all level, grassy and hedged and with electricity (10A). Many small trees give a little shade. A comfortable bar opens onto a large terrace that surrounds the swimming and paddling pools. There is little in the way of sports provision other than table tennis and boules. Young children are catered for with an excellent play area and, for the not so young, there is entertainment in the bar during high season.

Facilities

One central toilet block includes facilities for campers with disabilities. Washing machine and dryer. Heated swimming and paddling pools (15/6-10/9). Small shop and bar (July/Aug). Play area. Boules. Billiards. Visiting food vans (July/Aug). Organised activities (July/Aug). Fishing. WiFi (free). Off site: St Pol-de-Léon 2 km.

Open: 1 May - 30 September.

Directions

From Morlaix go north on D58 to St Pol-de-Léon. Follow signs for Plage/Port. Site is well signed. GPS: 48.69347, -3.96944

Charges guide

Per unit incl. 2 persons and electricity	€ 18.20 - € 23.30

Camping Cheques accepted.

Sarzeau

Lodge Club Presqu'île de Rhuys

Route d'Arzon, F-56370 Sarzeau (Morbihan) T: 02 97 41 29 93. E: info@lodgeclub.fr

alanrogers.com/FR56250

Lodge Club Presqu'île de Rhuys is a 13-hectare site close to the Gulf of Morbihan and the medieval towns of Vannes and Auray. It is divided into three main areas by trees. The larger area by the entrance was an orchard and some mature apple trees have been left to mark the touring pitches and provide some shade. The second area has a mixture of mobile homes and touring pitches divided into small groups by hedges. All the pitches are flat and of a good size, and have electricity (10A). The third area is being developed for privately owned mobile homes. The converted farm building houses reception and a pleasant bar overlooking the swimming pool.

Facilities

Three toilet blocks, one fairly new, with some washbasins in cabins. Baby rooms and facilities for disabled visitors. Laundry facilities. Basic motorcaravan services. Shop (28/4-13/9). Bar and takeaway (23/5-31/8). Heated swimming and paddling pools (28/4-13/9). Games tent. TV room. Three graded play areas. Kids' club (July/Aug). BMX track. Bicycle hire. WiFi (charged).

Open: 28 March - 30 September.

Directions

East of Vannes on N165, join D780 towards Sarzeau. Bypass Sarzeau, keeping on D780, following signs to Arzon. Take 4th exit at roundabout (Le Bohat) after 2 km. and site is 300 m. on right. GPS: 47.5225, -2.797067

Charges guide

Per unit incl. 2 persons and electricity	€ 21.50 - € 34.30

Sarzeau

Camping la Ferme de Lann-Hoëdic

Rue Jean de la Fontaine, Lann-Hoëdic, F-56370 Sarzeau (Morbihan) T: 02 97 48 01 73.
E: contact@camping-lannhoedic.fr **alanrogers.com/FR56200**

Camping la Ferme de Lann-Hoëdic is an attractively landscaped site with many flowering shrubs and trees. The 108 touring pitches, all with 10A electricity, are large and mostly level with maturing trees which offer some shade. The 20 pitches with mobile homes are in a separate area. The working farm produces cereal crops and the summer months are an interesting time for children to see the harvest in progress. Mireille and Tim, the owners, go out of their way to make this a welcoming and happy place to stay. Located in the countryside on the Rhuys Peninsula, Golfe du Morbihan, it is an ideal base for cycling, walking and water-based activities. Since the site opened in 2002, it has developed into one of the prettiest campsites in the Morbihan region. A visitor remarked that it is like "camping in a garden". Ecology is taken very seriously with solar panels for water heating and a composting system that you are encouraged to use for any waste food.

Facilities

Two high quality toilet blocks with facilities for disabled visitors and babies. Washing machines and dryers. Bar. Bread delivery. Ice creams and soft drinks from reception. Takeaway and traditional Breton 'soirées' (high season). Meeting room with TV and library. Sauna and massage. Bicycle hire. Playground with modern, well designed equipment. Pétanque. Internet access. WiFi in some areas (charged). Off site: Beach 800 m. Sarzeau 2 km. Riding 4 km. Golf 6 km.

Open: 1 April - 31 October.

Directions

East of Vannes on the N165, join the D780 towards Sarzeau. Exit D780 at the Super U roundabout south of Sarzeau, following signs for Le Roaliguen. Campsite is signed. GPS: 47.50745, -2.76092

Charges guide

Per unit incl. 2 persons and electricity	€ 17.00 - € 22.60
extra person	€ 3.80 - € 5.00
child (under 7 yrs)	€ 1.80 - € 2.50
dog	€ 2.50

Camping Cheques accepted.

LA FERME DE LANN HOËDIC
Sarzeau
Camping ★★★
★★★
The comfort of a 3-star campsite, the charm of a country setting.
Rue Jean de la Fontaine - 56370 Sarzeau Tél : +33 297 48 01 73
www.camping-lannhoedic.fr

Sarzeau

Castel Camping Manoir de Ker An Poul

Lieu-dit Penvins, F-56370 Sarzeau (Morbihan) T: 02 97 67 33 30. E: info@manoirdekeranpoul.com
alanrogers.com/FR56450

Le Manoir de Ker An Poul has an attractive location, close to the sea (700 m) in the southern Morbihan region. The old manor house is charming and the site has been developed in the grounds. This is quite a large site with around 299 pitches, around half of which are occupied by mobile homes and chalets. There is a large indoor and outdoor pool complex. Many activities are on offer in high season, including evening entertainment and a club for children.

Facilities

Sanitary facilities include hot showers, washbasins in cabins and facilities for disabled visitors. Laundry facilities. Shop. Bar, restaurant and snack bar. Indoor pool. Outdoor swimming pool and paddling pools. Games room. Multisports pitch. Play area. Bicycle hire. Activity and entertainment programme. Mobile homes and chalets for rent. WiFi in some areas (charged). Off site: Beach and fishing 800 m. Golf 4 km. Sarzeau 7 km. Cycle and walking tracks. Morbihan gulf.

Open: 25 March - 25 September.

Directions

From Vannes, head south on D780 towards Sarzeau. At St Armel join the D199 (Route de Menez) to Penvins and site is clearly signed. GPS: 47.50542, -2.68325

Charges guide

Per unit incl. 2 persons and electricity	€ 19.00 - € 35.00
extra person	€ 6.00 - € 7.00
child (under 7 yrs)	€ 3.00 - € 4.00

Taden

Camping International la Hallerais

4 rue de la Robardais, F-22100 Taden (Côtes d'Armor) T: 02 96 39 15 93.
E: camping.la.hallerais@wanadoo.fr **alanrogers.com/FR22060**

La Hallerais has a lot more to offer than most municipal sites. It is ideally located for exploring this fascinating area and is a short run from Saint Malo and from the resorts of the Côte d'Armor. It is just outside the attractive old medieval town of Dinan, beyond and above the little harbour on the River Rance. There is a pleasant riverside walk to the port and up into the town. Of the 226 pitches, 107 are for touring, all with electricity (6A), water and drainage, and are mainly on level, shallow terraces, with trees and hedges giving a park-like atmosphere. The staff are very friendly and speak excellent English.

Facilities

Two toilet blocks, one refurbished to a high standard, are of good quality and heated in cool weather. They include pushbutton showers and washbasins in cubicles and also some spacious cabins with shower and washbasin. Unit for disabled visitors. Launderette. Shop. Attractive bar/restaurant with outside terrace and good-value takeaway. Swimming and paddling pools (1/6-30/9). Tennis. Minigolf. Games room with TV room above. Play area. Fishing. Mobile homes for rent. Free WiFi.

Open: 10 March - 11 November.

Directions

Dinan is due south of St Malo (32 km. by road). From N176 (Avranches/St Brieuc) take Taden exit north of Dinan, turn towards Taden and follow blue signs to site. Do not attempt Dinan centre.
GPS: 48.47148, -2.02284

Charges guide

Per unit incl. 2 persons and electricity	€ 16.58 - € 20.90
extra person	€ 3.44 - € 4.07

Taupont

Camping la Vallée du Ninian

Le Rocher, Le Ville Bonne, F-56800 Taupont (Morbihan) T: 02 97 93 53 01. E: infos@camping-ninian.fr
alanrogers.com/FR56160

Murielle and Stéphane Veaux have recently acquired this peaceful family run site in central Brittany, formerly a farm. They continue to make improvements to ensure that their visitors have an enjoyable holiday. The level site falls into three areas – the orchard with 83 large, hedged touring pitches with electricity (3-10A), the wood with about 13 pitches more suited to tents, and the meadow by the river providing a further 35 pitches delineated by small trees and shrubs, with electricity. The bar has, as its centrepiece, a working cider press with which Stéphane makes his own cider.

Facilities

Central building houses unisex toilet facilities including washbasins in cubicles, large cubicle with facilities for families and disabled visitors. Laundry area with washing machines, dryer and ironing board. Shop (26/3-30/9) selling bread. Bar, restaurant and takeaway (9/7-27/8). Indoor heated swimming pool and children's pool with slide and fountain. Swings, slides and large trampoline. Boules. Trout fishing (permits from office). Bicycle hire. Free WiFi over site.

Open: 26 March - 30 September.

Directions

From Ploërmel follow signs to Taupont north on N8. Continue through Taupont and turn left (east) signed Vallée du Ninian. Follow road for 3 km. to site on left. From Josselin follow signs for Hellean. Through village, sharp right after River Ninian bridge. Site is 400 m. on right. GPS: 47.96931, -2.47014

Charges guide

Per unit incl. 2 persons and electricity	€ 15.80 - € 19.70
extra person	€ 3.70 - € 4.90

Telgruc-sur-Mer

Sites et Paysages le Panoramic

Route de la Plage-Penker, F-29560 Telgruc-sur-Mer (Finistère) T: 02 98 27 78 41.
E: info@camping-panoramic.com **alanrogers.com/FR29080**

This medium sized, traditional site is situated on quite a steep, ten-acre hillside with fine views. It is personally run by M. Jacq and his family who all speak good English. The 200 pitches are arranged on flat, shady terraces, in small groups with hedges and flowering shrubs, and 23 pitches have services for motorcaravans. Divided into two parts, the main upper site is where most of the facilities are located, with the swimming pool, its terrace and a playground located with the lower pitches across the road.

Facilities

The main site has two well kept toilet blocks with another very good block opened for main season across the road. All three include showers, washbasins in cubicles, facilities for disabled visitors, baby baths, plus laundry facilities. Motorcaravan services. Small shop (July/Aug). Refurbished bar/restaurant with takeaway (1/5-31/8). Barbecue area. Heated pool, paddling pool and jacuzzi (15/5-15/9). Playground. Games and TV rooms. Tennis. Bicycle hire. Free WiFi. Off site: Beach and fishing 700 m.

Open: 1 May - 15 September.

Directions

Site is just south of Telgruc-sur-Mer. On D887 pass through Ste Marie du Ménez Horn. Turn left on D208 signed Telgruc-sur-Mer. Continue straight on through town and site is on right within 1 km. GPS: 48.22409, -4.37186

Charges guide

Per unit incl. 2 persons and electricity (10A)	€ 26.50
extra person	€ 5.00

Tredrez-Locquémeau

Flower Camping les Capucines

Ancienne Voie Romaine, F-22300 Tredrez-Locquémeau (Côtes d'Armor) T: 02 96 35 72 28.
E: les.capucines@wanadoo.fr **alanrogers.com/FR22010**

A warm welcome awaits at this beautifully kept, family run site, quietly situated about a kilometre from the village of Saint-Michel-en-Grève with its good, sandy beach and close to Locquémeau, a pretty fishing village. There are 106 pitches on terraces or on slightly sloping ground, separated by hedges, with mature trees providing shade in places; 69 have electricity (10A), water and drainage, 20 are more suitable for tents and there are chalets and mobile homes for hire including a luxury model with its own hot tub. A pleasant bar overlooks the modern swimming pool. A mini-farm and skate park have been added. A good value restaurant/crêperie can be found at Trédrez and other bars and restaurants at Saint-Michel, while Locquémeau has a delightful Café du Port and an up-market restaurant. There are numerous towns and villages along this stretch of coastline, so there is a good choice of markets, shops and supermarkets. The nearest big towns are Lannion, 10 km. northeast, and Morlaix, 28 km. southwest. It is, however, the rugged coastline with its pretty bays that is the real attraction of this part of Brittany.

Facilities

Two traditional toilet blocks, clean and very well kept, include controllable showers, washbasins in cabins and facilities for babies and disabled campers. Laundry with washing machines and dryer. Small shop for essentials (bread to order). Takeaway, bar with TV and games room. New covered and heated swimming pool. Paddling pool. Playground. Bouncy giraffe. Minigolf. Multisports court. Aviaries. No electric barbecues. Chalets and mobile homes to rent. WiFi (charged). Off site: Bars, restaurants, beach, riding and fishing within 2 km. Golf 15 km.

Open: 25 March - 30 September.

Directions

Site is just off D786 Lannion/Morlaix road. From Lannion turn right in about 8 km. onto D88 to Trédrez and Locquémau, then first left three times following signs to site (last left turn is sharp and blind). GPS: 48.69274, -3.55663

Charges guide

Per unit incl. 2 persons and electricity	€ 19.00 - € 28.20
extra person	€ 4.20 - € 5.80
child (3-6 yrs)	€ 3.00 - € 4.00

Trélévern

RCN Port l'Epine

Venelle de Pors Garo, F-22660 Trélévern (Côtes d'Armor) T: 02 96 23 71 94. E: portlepine@rcn.fr
alanrogers.com/FR22130

Port l'Epine is a very pretty site in a unique situation on a promontory with direct access to the sea, and with superb views across the bay to Perros Guirec. The site is now part of the Dutch RCN group and is managed by a very enthusiastic young couple who are keen to ensure that all visitors enjoy their stay. There are 101 pitches for touring units, all on closely mown, level grass with electricity (16A). They are well defined and separated by attractive hedging and trees. There are 47 mobile homes for rent. This site is ideal for families with young children, though not necessarily for teenagers looking for lots to do!

Facilities

The original toilet block is well equipped; a second block has been refurbished in modern style with thermostatically controllable showers and washbasins in cubicles. Baby room. Facilities for disabled visitors. Modern launderette. Shop, bar, restaurant with takeaway, small heated swimming pool and paddling pool (all season). Fenced play area near the bar/restaurant. Activity programme. Fishing and boat launching. WiFi (free in bar).

Open: 19 April - 20 September.

Directions

Trélévern is 14 km. northeast of Lannion. From D778 turn east at roundabout south of Perros-Guirec, take D6 towards Tréguier. After Louannec, turn left on D38 for Trélévern. Go through village following camping signs. Port l'Epine is clearly marked and opposite municipal site. GPS: 48.81311, -3.38598

Charges guide

Per unit incl. 2 persons and electricity	€ 17.00 - € 45.00

Vannes
Camping du Haras

5 rue de Kersimon, Vannes-Meucon, F-56250 Monterblanc (Morbihan) T: 02 97 44 66 06.
E: contact@campingvannes.com **alanrogers.com/FR56150**

Close to Vannes and the Golfe du Morbihan in southern Brittany, Camping du Haras is a small, family run site in a rural location. There are 140 pitches, in a variety of settings, both open and wooded, the pitches are well kept and of a good size, all with electricity (4-16A) and most with water and drainage. Whilst M. Danard intends keeping the site quiet and in keeping with its rural setting, he provides plenty of activities for lively youngsters, including some organised games and evening parties. Adults will enjoy the new wellness area with indoor pool, spa, sauna and massage facilities. There is a good pool with waves, three slides, fountains and plenty of sunbathing space. Small animals are kept at the animal park on site and there is a riding school nearby. An artificial beach has been created to provide facilities for beach volleyball and other beach games. The beaches are 15 km. away.

Facilities

The two modern toilet blocks (heated in winter) provide a few washbasins in cabins and controllable showers. Facilities for babies and disabled visitors. Laundry facilities. No shop but basics are kept in the bar. Bar with snacks (May-Oct). Restaurant and takeaway (July/Aug). Outdoor pool with waves and slide (1/5-31/10). Indoor pool complex and spa (1/4-31/10). Play area. Animal park. Trampoline. Minigolf. Organised activities (high season). Bicycle hire. WiFi (free in reception and bar). Off site: Riding 400 m. Fishing 3 km. Beach 15 km.

Open: 15 March - 12 November.

Directions

From Vannes on N165 take exit signed Pontivy and airport on the D767. Follow signs for airport and Meucon. Turn right on the D778, follow airport and yellow campsite signs. GPS: 47.730477, -2.72801

Charges guide

Per unit incl. 2 persons and electricity (10A)	€ 24.00 - € 34.00
extra person	€ 5.00
child (0-7 yrs)	€ 3.00
dog	€ 4.00

Vannes
Flower Camping de Conleau

188 avenue Maréchal Juin, F-56000 Vannes (Morbihan) T: 02 97 63 13 88.
E: camping.conleau@flowercampings.com **alanrogers.com/FR56410**

This well maintained site on the edge of the Gulf of Morbihan in southern Brittany, has been recently acquired by the Flower group and is being upgraded to a high standard. It is divided into three areas: one for new mobile homes, one for ready erected tents, and the third for tourers. Some hardstandings are available for larger motorcaravans. The 216 pitches are grassy, some slightly sloping, and many have views over the Morbihan. The new bar and restaurant has a patio that overlooks the covered swimming pool. A bus stop outside the site entrance will take you to Vannes town centre.

Facilities

Three well positioned sanitary blocks provide very good modern facilities and are kept very clean. Separate laundry room. Bar/restaurant (July/Aug). New heated, covered swimming pool. TV/games room with pool tables and electronic games. Bicycle hire. Bouncy castle. Children's club and evening entertainment. Free WiFi throughout. Off site: Bus stop nearby. Small seawater swimming pool and beach 500 m. Boat trips 500 m. Town centre 3 km. Cinema 4 km. Beach 15 km.

Open: 4 April - 27 September.

Directions

From N165 Vannes-Lorient dual carriageway, take any of the four exits south towards Vannes town centre. Site is well signed from any of these points, as is the Port of Conleau, where site is located. GPS: 47.63365, -2.78008

Charges guide

Per unit incl. 2 persons and electricity	€ 18.00 - € 29.00
extra person	€ 3.50 - € 6.00
child (3-6 yrs)	€ 2.50 - € 4.00
dog	€ 2.00 - € 3.00

DÉPARTEMENTS: 14 CALVADOS, 27 EURE, 50 MANCHE, 61 ORNE, 76 SEINE MARITIME

MAJOR CITIES: CAEN AND ROUEN

A striking area whose beauty lies not only in the landscape. Famed for its seafood and Celtic tradition, certain areas of Normandy remain untouched and wonderfully old fashioned.

Normandy has a rich landscape full of variety. From the wild, craggy granite coastline of the northern Cotentin to the long sandy beaches and chalk cliffs of the south. It also boasts a superb coastline including the Cotentin Peninsula, cliffs of the Côte d'Albâtre and the fine beaches and fashionable resorts of the Côte Fleurie. Plus a wealth of quiet villages and unspoilt countryside for leisurely exploration.

The history of Normandy is closely linked with our own. The famous Bayeux Tapestry chronicles the exploits of the Battle of Hastings and there are many museums, exhibitions, sites and monuments, including the Caen Memorial Museum, which commemorate operations that took place during the D-Day Landings of 1944.

Normandy is known as the dairy of France and its dishes often feature cream, butter, and fine cheeses such as Camembert and Pont l'Evêque. The cider route takes in the countryside and pretty villages of the Pays d'Auge, where Calvados, the distinctive apple brandy, and cider are produced.

Places of interest

Bayeux: home to the famous tapestry; 15th-18th-century houses; cathedral; museums.

Cherbourg: La Cité de la Mer; Château des Ravalet; Thomas Henry Museum.

Omaha Beach: D-Day beaches; landing site monuments; American cemetery.

Deauville: seaside resort; horse racing centre.

Giverny: home of impressionist painter Claude Monet; Monet Museum.

Honfleur: picturesque port city with old town.

Lisieux: pilgrimage site, shrine of Ste Thérèse.

Mont St-Michel: world famous abbey on an island.

Rouen: Joan of Arc Museum; Gothic churches, cathedrals, abbey, clock tower.

Cuisine of the region

Andouillette de Vire: small chitterling (tripe) sausage.

Barbue au cidre: brill cooked in cider and Calvados.

Douillon aux pommes à la Normande: baked apples in pastry.

Escalope (Vallée d'Auge): veal sautéed and flamed in Calvados with cream and apples.

Teurgoule: rice pudding with cinnamon.

Tripes à la mode de Caen: stewed beef tripe with onions, carrots, leeks, garlic, cider and Calvados.

www.normandy-tourism.co.uk
info@normandie-tourisme.org
(0)2 32 33 79 00

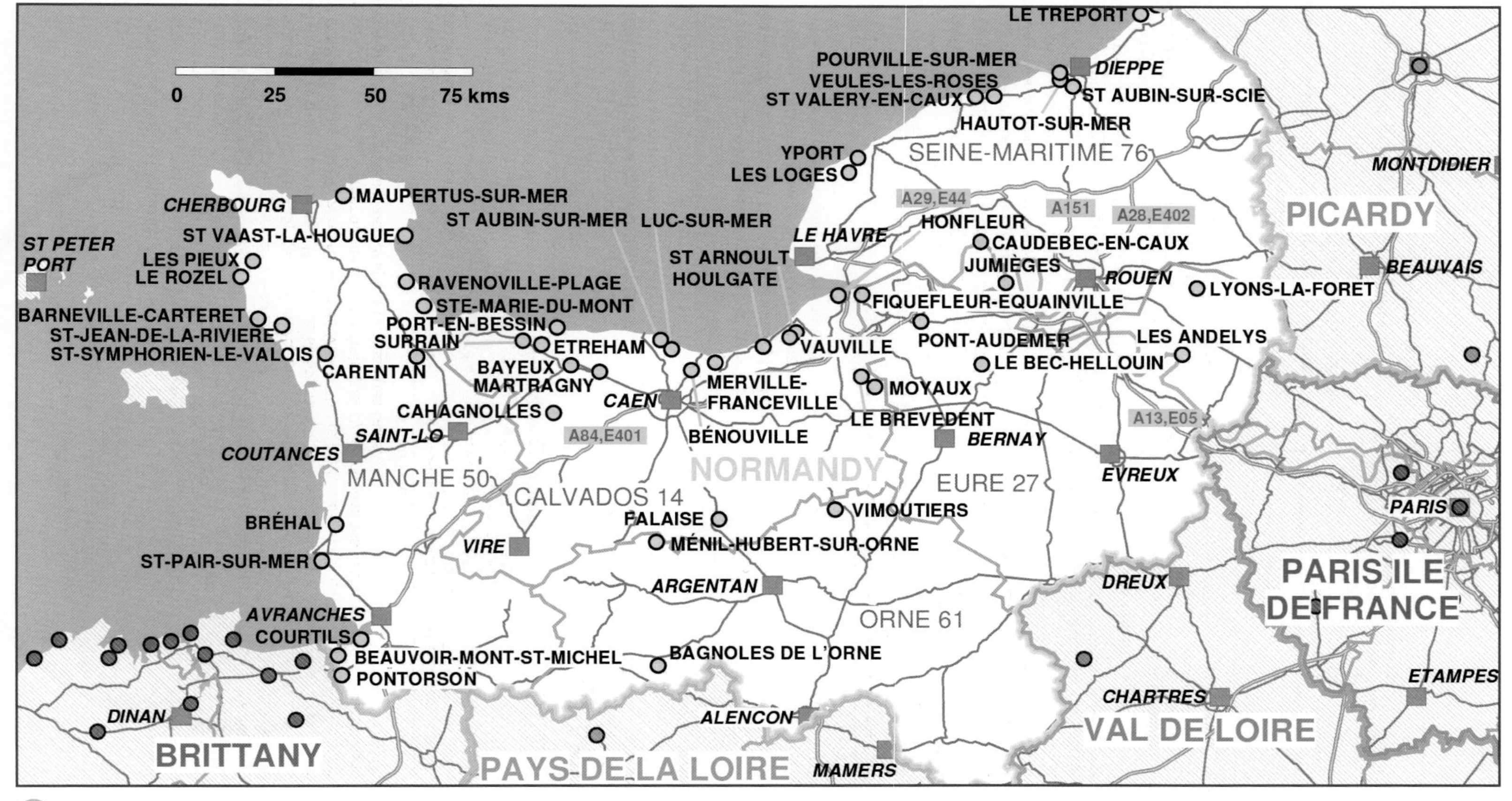

0
25
50
75 kms
LE TREPORT
POURVILLE-SUR-MER
DIEPPE
VEULES-LES-ROSES
ST VALERY-EN-CAUX
ST AUBIN-SUR-SCIE
HAUTOT-SUR-MER
YPORT
LES LOGES
SEINE-MARITIME 76
MONTDIDIER
CHERBOURG
MAUPERTUS-SUR-MER
ST AUBIN-SUR-MER
LUC-SUR-MER
A29,E44
A151
A28,E402
HONFLEUR
PICARDY
LE HAVRE
CAUDEBEC-EN-CAUX
ST VAAST-LA-HOUGUE
ST PETER PORT
LES PIEUX
LE ROZEL
ST ARNOULT
HOULGATE
JUMIÈGES
ROUEN
BEAUVAIS
RAVENOVILLE-PLAGE
LYONS-LA-FORET
STE-MARIE-DU-MONT
FIQUEFLEUR-EQUAINVILLE
BARNEVILLE-CARTERET
PORT-EN-BESSIN
ST-JEAN-DE-LA-RIVIERE
SURRAIN
ETREHAM
VAUVILLE
PONT-AUDEMER
LES ANDELYS
ST-SYMPHORIEN-LE-VALOIS
CARENTAN
BAYEUX
MARTRAGNY
LE BEC-HELLOUIN
MERVILLE-FRANCEVILLE
MOYAUX
CAEN
CAHAGNOLLES
LE BREVEDENT
A13,E05
SAINT-LO
A84,E401
BÉNOUVILLE
BERNAY
COUTANCES
NORMANDY
EVREUX
MANCHE 50
EURE 27
CALVADOS 14
VIMOUTIERS
FALAISE
BRÉHAL
PARIS
VIRE
MÉNIL-HUBERT-SUR-ORNE
ST-PAIR-SUR-MER
PARIS ILE DE FRANCE
ARGENTAN
DREUX
AVRANCHES
ORNE 61
COURTILS
BAGNOLES DE L'ORNE
BEAUVOIR-MONT-ST-MICHEL
PONTORSON
ETAMPES
CHARTRES
DINAN
ALENCON
VAL DE LOIRE
BRITTANY
PAYS-DE-LA LOIRE
MAMERS

Bagnoles de l'Orne

Camping de la Vée

5 avenue du Président Coty, F-61140 Bagnoles-de-l'Orne (Orne) T: 02 33 37 87 45.
E: info@campingbagnolesdelorne.com **alanrogers.com/FR61030**

Camping de la Vée is a pleasant municipal site in the town of Bagnoles de l'Orne, and is open for a long season (March to November). The 246 pitches (228 for touring) are large and grassy and are grouped around the two well maintained toilet blocks. All have 10A electricity. Some 51 hardstandings are available for motorcaravan users. On-site amenities include a snack bar with special meal offers in peak season, a play area and free WiFi. A number of fully equipped mobile homes are available for rent. Bagnoles is an important thermal spa centre and can be reached on the shuttle bus. The town's Belle Epoque quarter is deservedly famous, lined with fine villas with extravagant polychrome façades, influenced by the Art Deco style. Bagnoles is surrounded by the vast Andaines forest, which forms a part of the Parc Naturel Régional de Normandie Maine. This is great walking country and the site managers will be pleased to recommend routes. A little further away, Alençon to the east is the region's capital and has a great deal of interest including the Château des Ducs.

Facilities

Sanitary facilities specially for children. Snack bar. Play area. Mobile homes for rent. Shuttle bus to spa. Bar. WiFi throughout (free). Only electric barbecues permitted. Off site: Shops, restaurants and spa in Bagnoles de l'Orne. Bicycle hire 1 km. Golf 2 km. Riding 3 km. Alençon. Walking and cycling tracks.

Open: 5 March - 13 November.

Directions

Approaching from the north (La Ferté Macé), head south on D916 to Bagnoles de l'Orne. The site is on the Avenue du Président René Coty, to the south of the town centre and is well signed.
GPS: 48.54778, -0.41983

Charges guide

Per unit incl. 2 persons and electricity	€ 16.70 - € 18.10
extra person	€ 3.85 - € 4.35
child (under 13 yrs)	€ 2.30 - € 2.40
dog	€ 1.70

Barneville-Carteret

Camping du Golf

43 chemin des Mielles, Saint Jean-de-la-Rivière, F-50270 Barneville-Carteret (Manche) T: 02 33 04 78 90.
E: contact@camping-du-golf.fr **alanrogers.com/FR50250**

Camping du Golf is a friendly, family campsite on the western side of the Cotentin peninsula on the Côte des Isles (the Channel Islands). Day excursions are possible to Jersey. The site is only ten minutes from the nearest sandy beach, and an hour and forty-five minutes north of Mont Saint-Michel. On-site amenities include a covered, heated swimming pool, a bar and a shop, and in high season a programme of activities and entertainment is organised. There are 106 pitches for touring units, all with 6A electricity, water and drainage and 110-180 sq.m. in size. There are plenty of holiday activities available at Camping du Golf for all the family. Children are provided with open grass and sandy areas for play and an indoor games area with table tennis tables and electronic games. A new covered and heated swimming pool is open all season. There are facilities for pétanque and golfers will enjoy practising their sport right on the doorstep. It is just a five-minute walk to a riding centre. Barneville Carteret to the north is a popular resort with good opportunities for watersports and there are museums and the Landing Beaches for excursion opportunities.

Facilities

New toilet block and further small block by pool. Family shower rooms. Facilities for disabled visitors. Laundry facilities. Shop. Bar. Snack bar/takeaway. Swimming pool (from 1/4). Play area. Basketball, football and volleyball pitch. TV room. Entertainment and activities in July/Aug. Bicycle hire. Bouncy castle. WiFi over site (charged). Mobile homes for hire. Off site: Shops, cafés and restaurants in Barneville Carteret. Golf 50 m. (accessed via gate at rear of site). Riding 400 m. Cycling and walking trails. Sailing and other watersports. Fishing 1 km. Ferry crossings to the Channel Islands. Museums and D-day Landing sites.

Open: 1 April - 1 November.

Directions

The site is 40 km. south of Cherbourg. Take the southbound D650 to Barneville-Carteret and from the centre take the beach road towards St Jean-des-Rivières, from where the site is clearly signed.
GPS: 49.36224, -1.74649

Charges guide

Per unit incl. 2 persons and electricity	€ 22.00 - € 33.00
extra person	€ 5.00 - € 7.00
child (2-6 yrs)	€ 4.00 - € 5.00
dog	€ 4.00

Camping Cheques accepted.

Bayeux

Camping des Bords de l'Aure

Boulevard Eindhoven, F-14400 Bayeux (Calvados) T: 02 31 92 08 43. E: campingmunicipal@mairie-bayeux.fr

alanrogers.com/FR14020

This is an excellent municipal site, only a few kilometres from the coast and D-Day landing beaches. Pleasantly laid out with grassy lawns and bushes, its neat, cared for appearance makes a good impression. It is very useful for a stopover or for a longer stay, and ideal if you wish to visit Bayeux, the cathedral and the tapestry. The 140 pitches (many hardstanding) are in two areas, well marked and generally of good size with 6A electricity. The site is busy over a long season and reception is open 08.00-12.30 and 14.00-19.00 (all day in July and August). There is a queueing area outside the entrance.

Facilities

The two good quality toilet blocks have washbasins in cabins in main block and units for disabled visitors. Baby changing. Covered laundry area. Motorcaravan services. Takeaway food van (Mon-Fri. pm). Bread delivered. Two playgrounds. Reading room with TV. Games room. Bicycle hire. 10 mobile homes to rent. WiFi (free). Off site: Free admission to large public indoor swimming pool with children's pool and jacuzzi adjacent to site. Supermarket nearby (closes 8 pm). Bayeux centre 1 km.

Open: 3 April - 1 November.

Directions

On the northernmost point of the inner ring road (D613), just west of the junction to Arromanches (D516), the site is well signed in this area. GPS: 49.2839, -0.6976

Charges guide

Per unit incl. 2 persons and electricity	€ 18.13
extra person	€ 4.57
child (under 7 yrs)	€ 2.67

Less 10% for stay over 5 days.

Beauvoir-Mont Saint-Michel

Camping Caravaning Aux Pommiers

28 route du Mont Saint-Michel, F-50170 Beauvoir-Mont Saint-Michel (Manche) T: 02 33 60 11 36.

E: campingauxpommiers@gmail.com **alanrogers.com/FR50120**

This site changed hands in 2011 and the resident owners offer a warm, friendly welcome at their quiet site in the small village of Beauvoir, just 4 km. from Le Mont Saint-Michel. The 68 well defined grass touring pitches, 50 with 10A electricity, are of a reasonable size, well maintained and level. Some are separated by hedges and there are trees providing some shade. The large fenced, heated swimming pool has a paved terrace with ample sun loungers, and next to the reception is a bar serving takeaway food during July and August.

Facilities

Two clean, well equipped toilet blocks with free showers. Facilities for disabled visitors. Laundry facilities. Motorcaravan services. Shop, bar with TV and pool table (all season). Takeaway food (July/Aug). Heated, indoor pool (all season). Bicycle hire. Small play area. WiFi over site (charged). Chalet and mobile homes for hire. Off site: Riding 1 km. Beach 5 km.

Open: 28 March - 13 November.

Directions

Beauvoir is 50 km. east of St Malo and 5 km. north of Pontorson. From N175/N176 (E401), follow signs for Le Mont St-Michel on D976. Site is on right in the village of Beauvoir. GPS: 48.596344, -1.511725

Charges guide

Per unit incl. 2 persons and electricity	€ 20.20 - € 26.30
extra person	€ 4.70 - € 6.90

Bénouville

Camping les Hautes Coutures

Avenue de la Côte de Nacre, F-14970 Bénouville (Calvados) T: 02 31 44 73 08.

E: info@campinghautescoutures.com **alanrogers.com/FR14060**

Les Hautes Coutures is a pleasant site beside the Caen ship canal and a short walk from Pegasus Bridge. Being ten minutes from the ferry, it is very good for overnight stops although there is a minimum stay of two nights in the peak season. However, with the D-Day Beaches on your doorstep, one day is not enough. This well laid out site has 277 pitches, many occupied by mobile homes, both private and rental. There are 99 grassy touring pitches, all with 10A electricity; some are among the mobiles and are of variable sizes and separated by mature hedging, while those by the canal are larger and more open.

Facilities

Two main sanitary blocks have showers and washbasins in cabins (warm water), but facilities can be under pressure at peak times. A third small block of WCs serves canalside pitches. Facilities for disabled visitors. Laundry. Motorcaravan services. Small shop and bar. Restaurant and takeaway (July/Aug and Sat. pm). Outdoor heated pool complex. Small lounge/TV area and games room. Play area. Outdoor fitness equipment. Multisports court. Children's club (July/Aug). Boules. WiFi (charged).

Open: 1 April - 30 October.

Directions

From Ouistreham ferry, follow D84 towards Caen for 4.5 km. Take first exit (Z.A. Bénouville). At T-junction turn right and after 400 m. turn left and site is on right in 300 m, just before re-joining dual carriageway. GPS: 49.24948, -0.27217

Charges guide

Per unit incl. 2 persons and electricity	€ 24.00 - € 35.10
extra person	€ 9.80

Camping Cheques accepted.

Bréhal

Camping la Vanlée

Rue des Gabions, F-50290 Bréhal (Manche) T: 02 33 61 63 80. E: camping.valee@wanadoo.fr
alanrogers.com/FR50220

La Vanlée is a large, traditional municipal site with direct access to a huge sandy beach and dunes. Recently taken over by a new resident manager, the site is undergoing modernisation (new 10A electricity supply on a third of the site and a new reception). All of the 466 marked pitches are on open, sandy grass, some on uneven but firm ground. The roads are tarmac, but driving for some distance over grass is required to reach most pitches, giving a feeling of wild camping. Some 25 per cent of the site is occupied by semi-residential caravans, but there is usually plenty of free space away from them.

Facilities

Five toilet blocks (only two were open at the time of our visit), two with upgraded heating systems. Washbasins in cabins (no doors) with hot water. Pushbutton showers. Hairdryer points. Good facilities for disabled campers. Washing and drying facilities. Shop, bar, brasserie and takeaway (July/Aug). TV room. Games room. Multisports pitch. Boules. (July/Aug). Activity programme including live concerts and theatre. WiFi (charged). Torches useful.

Open: 1 May - 30 September.

Directions

From north or south on D971 enter Bréhal. Leave on D592, signed Camping la Vanlée. Entering St Martin-de-Bréhal follow signs for 'camping-golf'. Continue alongside golf course directly to site. GPS: 48.908405, -1.564897

Charges guide

Per unit incl. 2 persons and electricity (6A)	€ 18.00 - € 25.90
extra person	€ 4.30 - € 5.80

Cahagnolles

Camping l'Escapade

Rue de l'Eglise, F-14490 Cahagnolles (Calvados) T: 02 31 21 63 59. E: escapadecamping@orange.fr
alanrogers.com/FR14390

L'Escapade is in an attractive countryside location in the heart of Normandy, west of Caen and within easy reach of both Ouistreham (Caen) and Cherbourg ferry terminals. The spacious entrance is flanked by an attractive fishing lake and by the smart reception and bar linked by decking and a terrace, with the pool complex beyond. The camping area is at the top of a hill on gently sloping ground. Of the 92 grassy pitches, 31 are for tourers, all with electricity connections (10A) and water taps to hand. The remainder are occupied by well kept mobile homes, including 28 for rent.

Facilities

The central sanitary block includes five hot pushbutton showers (8 mins/day free), vanity-style open washbasins plus some in cabins. Baby room. Second block with facilities for disabled visitors. Washing machine and dryer. Shop. Bar/snack bar with TV. Covered, heated pool with water slides and paddling pool (4/4-30/9). Evening entertainment. Activities for children. Multisports court. Tennis. Boules. Play area. Bouncy castles. Fishing lakes. Pond with ducks. Mini farm and aviary. Free WiFi in bar.

Open: 1 April - 1 October.

Directions

Cahagnolles is 30 km. west of Caen. From N13 Bayeux bypass, leave at exit 37 (Balleroy/St Lô) on D572. In 2.6 km. take exit, cross over main road and head south on D99 for 10 km. through St Paul-du-Vernay, then turn east to Cahagnolles. Site on right in 550 m. GPS: 49.155496, -0.762461

Charges guide

Per unit incl. 2 persons and electricity	€ 19.50 - € 26.00
extra person	€ 5.50 - € 6.50

Carentan

Flower Camping le Haut Dick

30 chemin du Grand Bas Pays, F-50500 Carentan (Manche) T: 02 33 42 16 89.
E: contact@camping-lehautdick.com **alanrogers.com/FR50240**

Le Haut Dick is located at the heart of the south Cotentin peninsula. On the banks of the Haut Dick canal, this is a simple campsite but has a pleasant bar/snack bar and a well maintained sanitary block. It comprises 100 good sized pitches which are flat, grassy and well divided by hedges, 71 for touring, with 10A electricity. The town of Carentan is a ten-minute walk away and features a brand new pool complex. This site is an ideal departure point for visiting the World War Two Landing Beaches and the Marais of the Cotentin Peninsula.

Facilities

The main sanitary block has showers, baby rooms and facilities for disabled visitors. A second basic block serves the upper pitches in high season. Washing machine. Shop with fresh bread. Bar, snack bar and takeaway (all season). Outdoor swimming pool (15/6-15/9). Minigolf. Play area. Bicycle and go-kart hire. Boules. Accommodation to rent. WiFi (free in bar). Off site: Fishing 200 m. Riding 4 km. Beach 12 km.

Open: 1 April - 27 September.

Directions

From north on N13 leave at exit for Carentan and head east on D971, then south on D913 to town centre. Bear left onto rue Seblin, left at square and right at green. Pass the port and turn right to site in 500 m. GPS: 49.309859, -1.238869

Charges guide

Per unit incl. 2 persons and electricity	€ 19.00 - € 27.50
extra person	€ 3.50 - € 5.50

Caudebec-en-Caux

Camping Barre Y Va

Route de Villequier (RD 81), F-76490 Villequier (Seine-Maritime) T: 02 35 96 26 38.
E: campingbarreyva@orange.fr **alanrogers.com/FR76280**

Camping Barre Y Va is a gem of a site, close to the riverside town of Caudebec-en-Caux with its attractive promenade and landing stage for the passing cruise ships. Across the road, the River Seine is full of interest with all manner of shipping. Of the 70 pitches, there are 48 for touring spread along the length of the site, divided by small trees and bushes, and with 10A electricity. There is a special gravel area for motorcaravans. The owners take great care of their customers and have recently installed a very well designed covered pool complex with slides and jacuzzi chair. The road alongside the site does get busy on weekdays during the early morning and evening rush hours.

Facilities

Two unheated unisex toilet blocks with washbasins in cabins, preset showers and British style toilets (no seats). Basic facilities for disabled visitors. Laundry facilities. Motorcaravan services. Fresh bread available (4/4-22/10). Bar and snack bar with small shop. Covered and heated swimming and paddling pools, slides and jacuzzi chair. Bicycle hire. Play area. Trampoline. Pétanque. Minigolf. Mobile homes for rent. WiFi throughout (charged).

Open: 26 March - 22 October.

Directions

Villequier is 50 km. east of Le Havre via A131/D982. At Lillebonne head southeast on D81. Site is east of village before Caudebec-en-Caux. The entrance is narrow, larger units may struggle. Late arrivals area 50 m. west of entrance. GPS: 49.521761, 0.702153

Charges guide

Per unit incl. 2 persons and electricity	€ 21.15 - € 27.25
extra person	€ 4.40 - € 5.25

Courtils

Camping Saint-Michel

35 route du Mont Saint-Michel, F-50220 Courtils (Manche) T: 02 33 70 96 90.
E: infos@campingsaintmichel.com **alanrogers.com/FR50110**

This delightful, quiet site is located in a peaceful, rural setting, yet is only 8 km. from the busy tourist attraction of Mont Saint-Michel. The site has 100 pitches which include 45 for touring units and 42 for mobile homes to rent. Electricity connections (6/10A) are available to all pitches and many trees and shrubs provide a good amount of shade. A welcoming reception has a terrace overlooking the pool. The owners intend to maintain a quiet and peaceful site, hence there are no discos or organised clubs.

Facilities

Two small, well maintained toilet blocks have washbasins in cubicles and pushbutton showers. Baby room. Laundry. En-suite facilities for disabled visitors. Motorcaravan services. Shop (all season). Bar (15/3-15/10). Heated swimming pool (1/5-20/9). Mini farm. Play area. Games room. Bicycle hire. WiFi (free in reception area). Off site: Fishing (sea) 2 km, (river) 6 km. Beaches 2 km. and (for swimming) 30 km. Riding 9 km. Sailing 25 km.

Open: 15 March - 11 November.

Directions

Courtils is 8 km. east of Mont St-Michel. From St Malo take D137 south and join N176 east to Pontorson where it becomes N175. In 12 km. turn northwest on D43 signed Courtils. Site is through village on the left. GPS: 48.627616, -1.416

Charges guide

Per unit incl. 2 persons and electricity	€ 19.00 - € 25.00

Camping Cheques accepted.

Etreham/Bayeux

Camping la Reine Mathilde

Route de Sainte Honorine, F-14400 Etreham/Bayeux (Calvados) T: 02 31 21 76 55.
E: campingreinemathilde@gmail.com **alanrogers.com/FR14300**

In the countryside, close to a pleasant little village, Camping la Reine Mathilde is within easy reach of the historic town of Bayeux, the D-Day beaches and the interesting fishing port of Port-en-Bessin. The site is in the grounds of a large stone farmhouse. The 76 grassy touring pitches are mainly of a good size and equipped with electrical connections (6A). There are some 49 chalets and mobile homes, with 14 available for rent. Walkers and cyclists are well provided for in the area, with cycle routes into and around Bayeux. Port-en-Bessin has shops, bars and restaurants and the Omaha Beach Golf Course.

Facilities

The sanitary facilities are housed in a beautifully converted stone outbuilding and include separate male and female toilets, preset showers, washbasins in cabins, baby changing and facilities for disabled visitors. Laundry room. Motorcaravan services. Reception in farmhouse with small shop (bread and pastries to order). New bar and snack bar serving simple meals. Heated swimming and paddling pool (20/6-15/9). Play area. Entertainment and activities (high season). Accommodation to rent. WiFi (free by bar).

Open: 1 April - 30 September.

Directions

Etreham is northwest of Bayeux. From there take westbound N13 and leave after Tour-en-Bessin, following signs to Etreham (D206). The site is well signed in the village. Continue through village to boundary sign, take first right and follow signs to campsite. GPS: 49.331316, -0.802447

Charges guide

Per unit incl. 2 persons and electricity	€ 16.00

Camping Cheques accepted.

Falaise

Camping Municipal du Château

1 rue du Val d'Ante, F-14700 Falaise (Calvados) T: 02 31 90 16 55. E: camping@falaise.fr
alanrogers.com/FR14100

The location of this site is really quite spectacular, lying in the shadow of the Château of William the Conqueror, within walking distance of the historic town of Falaise in the heart of Normandy. The site itself is small, with only 60 pitches (most with 10A electricity) either beside the little river, on a terrace above or on gently sloping ground. There are plans for some new terracing which will provide more level pitches. With trees and hedges providing some shade as well as open grassed areas, this site has a pleasant, rather intimate feel about it. Charges are reasonable and the reception friendly.

Facilities

Although the sanitary facilities are dated, they are of good quality and kept clean. Some Turkish-style WCs. Free hot water to preset showers, washbasins (some in cubicles), laundry and dishwashing sinks (all closed overnight).
No provision for disabled visitors. Motorcaravan services. Excellent play area. Tennis courts and boules pitch.
TV room with free WiFi. Off site: Bicycle hire 300 m. Town with château, museums, shops, and restaurants 400 m.

Open: 1 May - 30 September.

Directions

Approach from north is strongly advised to avoid town. From north on N158 or south on A88 leave at exit 10 for Falaise and head south on D658. Cross roundabout and in 600 m. at 2nd mini-roundabout bear right onto Voie Panoramique (D243B) signed to château and site. GPS: 48.89556, -0.20468

Charges guide

Per unit incl. 2 persons and electricity € 17.10 - € 18.50

Fiquefleur-Equainville

Sites et Paysages Domaine de la Catinière

Route de Honfleur, F-27210 Fiquefleur-Equainville (Eure) T: 02 32 57 63 51.
E: info@camping-catiniere.com **alanrogers.com/FR27020**

This is a peaceful, rural site close to the Normandy coast and the pretty harbour town of Honfleur, where you are assured of a friendly welcome from the new resident owners. There are 130 pitches, 90 for tourers, all with 4/8/13A electricity. Some have shade, while others are more open. There are 20 mobile homes and a thatched cottage for rent. An open field houses tents and other units not requiring electricity. Well fenced streams, popular with young anglers, run through the site. Improvements have not compromised the French atmosphere, and this is an ideal base for exploring this part of Normandy.

Facilities

A single heated toilet block contains mostly British style WCs, hot showers, some washbasins in cubicles, and basic facilities for babies and disabled visitors.
One section is enclosed and heated when required.
Washing machine and dryer. Reception with small shop.
Bar/restaurant with simple regional dishes and snacks.
Heated swimming pool with slides and flume (1/6-15/9).
Two playgrounds. Trampoline. Children's farm. Boules.
WiFi throughout (charged). Off site: Supermarket nearby.

Open: 1 April - 16 October.

Directions

From Pont de Normandie (toll bridge) take first exit on leaving bridge (exit 3, A29) signed Honfleur. At roundabout turn left under motorway towards Le Mans on D580/D180. Take 2nd exit on right after 2.5 km, onto D22 (Beuzeville). Site is on right after 1 km. GPS: 49.40090, 0.30608

Charges guide

Per unit incl. 2 persons and electricity € 21.00 - € 34.50

Hautot-sur-Mer

Camping la Source

Petit Appeville, F-76550 Hautot-sur-Mer (Seine-Maritime) T: 02 35 84 27 04. E: info@camping-la-source.fr
alanrogers.com/FR76040

This friendly, attractive site with a heated outdoor pool is just four kilometres from Dieppe and is useful for those using the Newhaven-Dieppe ferry crossing, either as a one night stopover or for a few days break before heading on. The 120 pitches (70 for touring) are flat and there is some shade. Electricity (10A) is available to all. There are good hardstandings for motorcaravans but other pitches may suffer after heavy rain. The site is quietly located in a valley with the only disturbance from the occasional passing train. A fast flowing small river runs along one border (not protected for young children).

Facilities

One large, heated toilet block is clean and includes washbasins in cubicles, good sized showers. Baby room. Unit for disabled visitors, but the unmade gravel roads may cause problems, especially for wheelchair users. Laundry facilities. Motorcaravan services. Small bar and terrace. Heated swimming pool (15/5-15/9). Playing field. TV and games rooms. Fishing. Bicycle hire. Six mobile homes for rent. WiFi throughout (charged).

Open: 15 March - 15 October.

Directions

From Dieppe follow D925 west (Fécamp). At foot of descent at traffic lights in Petit Appeville turn left. Just after railway, turn left under bridge (3.5 m) then ahead on narrow unmade road (limited passing places). Site is on left. GPS: 49.89846, 1.05694

Charges guide

Per unit incl. 2 persons and electricity € 26.20 - € 28.40
Camping Cheques accepted.

Honfleur

Camping la Briquerie

Equemauville, F-14600 Honfleur (Calvados) T: 02 31 89 28 32. E: info@campinglabriquerie.com

alanrogers.com/FR14180

La Briquerie is a large, busy site on the outskirts of the attractive and popular harbour town of Honfleur. Very well cared for and efficiently run by a family team, the site has 420 pitches, many of which are let on a seasonal basis. There are also 130 medium to large, hedged touring pitches. All have electricity (5/10A), water and drainage. Among the main attractions here are the splendid swimming complex with indoor and outdoor pools, and its close proximity to Honfleur. The site is just half an hour from the ferry terminal at Le Havre.

Facilities

Modern, clean sanitary blocks with good facilities for children and disabled visitors. Laundry room with washing machines and dryers. Grocery and crêperie (July/Aug). Large restaurant, bar and takeaway. Large pool complex with two flumes. Covered pool (April-Sept). Outdoor pool and slides (July/Aug). Sauna. Jacuzzi. Well equipped fitness room. Boules. Minigolf. Multisports court. TV. WiFi over site (free). Off site: Bus stop 200 m.

Open: 1 April - 30 September.

Directions

Site is well signed from Honfleur on D579, beside the Intermarché on D62. GPS: 49.39735, 0.20849

Charges guide

Per unit incl. 2 persons, electricity, water and drainage	€ 22.60 - € 34.90
extra person	€ 5.20 - € 9.30
child (3-7 yrs)	€ 3.20 - € 4.20

No credit/debit cards.

Houlgate

Yelloh! Village la Vallée

88 route de la Vallée, F-14510 Houlgate (Calvados) T: 02 31 24 40 69. E: camping.lavallee@wanadoo.fr

alanrogers.com/FR14070

Camping de la Vallée is an attractive site with good, well maintained facilities, situated on the rolling hillside above Houlgate. The original farmhouse building has been converted to house a bar/brasserie and a comfortable TV lounge and billiards room overlooking the aqua park. The site has 365 pitches with 170 for touring units (including 12 hardstandings). Open and separated by hedges, all the average sized pitches have 6/10A electricity and some also have water and drainage. Most of the site is sloping, some level, with gravel or tarmac roads. Shade is provided by a variety of well kept trees and shrubs.

Facilities

Three good toilet blocks include washbasins in cabins, facilities for disabled visitors, and baby rooms. Laundry facilities. Motorcaravan services. Shop. Bar. Restaurant and takeaway. Aqua park with covered pool and heated outdoor pool (May-Sept). Games room. Playground. Bicycle hire. Volleyball. Football. Tennis. Pétanque. Entertainment (July/Aug). WiFi (charged). Off site: Riding 500 m. Town, golf, beach and fishing, all 1 km. Watersports.

Open: 1 April - 1 November.

Directions

From A13 take Cabourg exit, follow D400 to Dives-sur-Mer, then D513 (Houlgate) as far as seafront. After 1 km. at lights, straight on for Centre Ville, then just before main centre turn right, folllow site sign to the town hall roundabout, straight on past tourist office on left, turn first right and follow signs to site in 1 km. GPS: 49.2940, -0.0683

Charges guide

Per unit incl. 2 persons and electricity	€ 21.00 - € 49.00

Jumièges

Camping de la Forêt

Rue Mainberthe, F-76480 Jumièges (Seine-Maritime) T: 02 35 37 93 43. E: info@campinglaforet.com

alanrogers.com/FR76130

This is a pleasant family site with a friendly, relaxed atmosphere. It has recently been taken over by the Commare family who have started a programme of improvements by adding a cover to the pool and rebuilding the main toilet block. The 110 grassy pitches (80 for tourers, all with 10A electricity) are attractively located in woodland. Most pitches have some shade at different times of the day. The nearby village of Jumièges, a short walk away, is surrounded on three sides by one of the huge bends of the River Seine – it is located in the Parc Naturel Régional des Boucles de la Seine.

Facilities

The central toilet block has been rebuilt and fitted out to a high standard with washbasins in cubicles and preset showers. A second, smaller block (refurbishment is planned) has toilets and open-style washbasins, baby room, facilities for disabled visitors and laundry facilities. Motorcaravan services. Shop (bread to order). Small swimming pool with retractable roof and paddling pool (both heated 1/6-15/9). Playground. Boules. TV/games room. Outdoor fitness equipment. Bicycle hire. WiFi.

Open: 1 April - 31 October.

Directions

From A29 exit 8 follow Yvetot-Pont de Brotonne. Before bridge, turn left and follow Le Trait and Jumièges. Site clearly signed to left on entering village. GPS: 49.43487, 0.82897

Charges guide

Per unit incl. 2 persons and electricity	€ 24.00 - € 28.00
extra person	€ 5.00 - € 5.50

Le Bec-Hellouin

Camping Saint Nicolas

15 rue Saint Nicolas, F-27800 Le Bec-Hellouin (Eure) T: 02 32 44 83 55. E: campingstnicolas@orange.fr

alanrogers.com/FR27030

This lovely site, operated by the municipal authority and still run by the same resident wardens, is located on a forested hillside above the interesting and attractive small town of Le Bec-Hellouin. The town is quite photogenic, has the usual tourist shops, several bars and restaurants and horse-drawn carriage rides. There are 126 marked grassy pitches, 30 used for seasonal units, leaving about 82 for touring units, all with 10A hook-ups and some with water taps. There is limited shade from a few mature trees. A rather steep footpath leads down to the town and the imposing Abbey of Bec.

Facilities

A modern heated unit has good showers and some washbasins in cubicles. Extra facilities in the old unit by reception, where you will find the laundry. Reception stocks snacks, soft drinks and ices. Baker calls each morning. Covered outdoor swimming pool. Playground. Playing field and tennis courts. Free WiFi over site. Off site: Le Bec-Hellouin and its abbey 1.5 km.

Open: 15 March - 15 October.

Directions

From A28 take exit 13 onto the D438 southbound. Turn right on D581 to Malleville-sur-le-Bec. The site is on the right 1 km. after Malleville and is well signed. GPS: 49.23477, 0.72532

Charges guide

Per unit incl. 2 persons and electricity	€ 15.50 - € 17.60

Camping Cheques accepted.

Le Brévedent

Castel Camping du Brévedent

Route du Pin, F-14130 Le Brévedent (Calvados) T: 02 31 64 72 88. E: contact@campinglebrevedent.com

alanrogers.com/FR14090

Le Brévedent is a well established, traditional site with 132 pitches (105 for touring units, 31 used by tour operators) set in the grounds of an elegant, 18th-century hunting pavilion. Pitches are either around the fishing lake in the lower gardens (level), or in the old orchard (gently sloping). All have 10A electricity. It is an excellent holiday destination within easy reach of the Channel ports and its peaceful, friendly environment makes it ideal for mature campers or families with younger children (note: the lake is unfenced). Reception provides a good selection of tourist information and English is spoken.

Facilities

Three toilet blocks include washbasins in cubicles and facilities for disabled visitors. One has been refurbished with spacious en-suite cubicles; a second is due to be replaced for 2016. Laundry facilities. Kitchen for mothers with babies. Motorcaravan services. Shop (baker delivers each morning). Bar in château (evenings). Restaurant (15/5-15/9). Takeaway (1/5-15/9). Café (July/Aug). Heated swimming and paddling pools (1/5-15/9, unsupervised). Playgrounds. Minigolf. Boules. Games room. Fishing. Children's club (July/Aug). WiFi (free in café). No dogs.

Open: 30 April - 17 September.

Directions

Le Brévedent is 13 km. southeast of Pont-l'Evêque: take D579 toward Lisieux for 4 km. then south on D51 towards Moyaux. At Blangy-le-Château stay on D51 to Le Brévedent. Site is on left just after village. GPS: 49.22525, 0.30438

Charges guide

Per unit incl. 2 persons and electricity	€ 22.20 - € 34.00
extra person	€ 5.10 - € 8.20
child (0-12 yrs)	€ 3.40 - € 6.10

Le Rozel

Camping le Ranch

La Mielle, F-50340 Le Rozel (Manche) T: 02 33 10 07 10. E: contact@camping-leranch.com

alanrogers.com/FR50230

Le Ranch is a pleasantly situated, family run site with direct access to a long and wide sandy beach that extends to some 3 km. The reception area is well presented and has a small shop that stocks all the basic provisions. An excellent outdoor pool complex is enclosed by clear glass screening and has ample space with sun loungers. Access to site is controlled by a magnetic key, which is also used to activate the showers in the splendid sanitary block. The 35 touring pitches are large and well defined by small hedges; some are on raised terraces but are easily accessed. All have 10A electricity, water and waste water. Booking is essential in high season.

Facilities

One modern heated toilet block is kept spotlessly clean and has washbasins in cabins. Showers operated by barrier entry key. Baby area. Facilities for disabled visitors. Laundry and dishwashing area. Shop for basics and beach toys. Bar with TV, pizzeria (eat in or take away). Outdoor pool complex (1/5-30/9). Indoor pool (all season). Play area. Boules. Barbecue areas. WiFi (first hour free).

Open: 1 April - 30 September.

Directions

To or from Cherbourg on D650, 3 km. south of Les Pieux take D62 (Le Rozel). D62 leads directly to site which is well signed. GPS: 49.480199, -1.842055

Charges guide

Per unit incl. 2 persons and electricity	€ 24.20 - € 40.20
extra person	€ 4.90 - € 8.40
child (3-11 yrs)	€ 3.70 - € 6.30

Les Andelys

Camping l'Ile des Trois Rois

1 rue Gilles Nicolle, F-27700 Les Andelys (Eure) T: 02 32 54 23 79. E: campingtroisrois@aol.com
alanrogers.com/FR27070

One hour from Paris, on the banks of the Seine and overlooked by the impressive remains of Château Gaillard (Richard Coeur de Lion), this attractive and very spacious ten-hectare site will appeal to couples and young families. There is easy access to the 115 level, grassy touring pitches in a well landscaped setting, all with electricity (6A), although some long leads may be required. Many pitches back onto the River Seine where you can watch the barges, and most have views of the château. Of the 80 mobile homes, there are seven for rent, leaving lots of space to enjoy the surroundings, including the large lake full of perch and bream for those eager fishermen. Others can try their luck in the Seine. A nearby station will whisk you to Paris for the day, while a short drive will bring the delights of Monet's house and garden. A Medieval Festival is held in Les Andelys in the last weekend of June. Walk along the banks of the Seine and watch the huge passenger boats cruising there, or stroll into the main town for shopping and restaurants.

Facilities

Four small, heated toilet blocks have showers and washbasins in cubicles. One has facilities for disabled visitors, another has a laundry facility. Motorcaravan services. Heated swimming and paddling pools (15/5-15/9). Bar, restaurant and takeaway (1/6-30/8). Fenced play area. Adult open-air exercise area. Evening entertainment (4/7-30/8). Bicycles and barbecues for hire. Satellite TV. Internet access. WiFi throughout (charged). Off site: Cycling and walking trails. Riding and golf 5 km. Giverny 20 km. Rouen 40 km.

Open: 15 March - 15 November.

Directions

Les Andelys is 40 km. southeast of Rouen. From the town centre, continue on D125 and follow signs until roundabout by bridge where second exit leads directly into site. GPS: 49.23564, 1.40005

Charges guide

Per unit incl. 2 persons and electricity	€ 23.00 - € 27.00
extra person	€ 7.00
child (under 3 yrs)	free
dog	€ 3.00

Camping Cheques accepted.

Le Tréport

Camping Municipal les Boucaniers

Rue Pierre Mendès France, F-76470 Le Tréport (Seine-Maritime) T: 02 35 86 35 47.
E: camping@ville-le-treport.fr **alanrogers.com/FR76110**

This is a large, good quality, modern municipal site. It has an attractive floral entrance, tarmac roads and easy access to pitches. The 193 touring pitches (176 with 6A electricity: some long leads necessary) are on level grass, some with dividing hedges, and trees to provide a little shade. There are 50 good quality wooden chalets for rent, and some privately owned mobile homes. A small unit acts as shop, bar and takeaway all season. The baker calls daily in high season, and every day except Wednesday in low season. The town centre is within walking distance with a choice of many good seafood restaurants. The resort is popular with the French, and has been so for more than a century.

Facilities

Three well equipped sanitary blocks (the larger one can be heated) provide mainly British style WCs, washbasins in cubicles, preset hot showers, with facilities for small children and disabled visitors in one block. Multisports court. Minigolf. Boules. Max. 2 dogs. Motorcaravan parking and services adjacent (€ 5.00) Off site: Tennis, football and gymnasium nearby. Fishing, golf and beach 2 km. Riding 3 km. Markets at Le Tréport (Mon. and Sat) and at Eu (Fri).

Open: 1 April - 30 September.

Directions

From D925 Abbeville-Dieppe road take D1915 towards Le Tréport centre. At new roundabout take first exit to right and site entrance is 150 m. on the right in rue Pierre Mendès-France.
GPS: 50.05772, 1.38870

Charges guide

Per unit incl. 2 persons and electricity	€ 20.90 - € 22.90
extra person	€ 4.30 - € 4.90
child (3-12 yrs)	€ 2.85 - € 3.15
dog	€ 1.30 - € 1.60

L'Ile des Trois Rois

The park Ile des Trois Rois is situated in the most beautiful bend of the Seine nearby Castle Gaillard in Normandy and is a haven of peace. Paris is situated of less than an hour and Rouen is half an hour driving from the campsite.

Facilities:

- Two heated swimming pools
- Ping pong
- Camper service
- Bar and restaurant (high season)
- Play Area

1, Rue Gilles Nicole - F-27700 Les Andelys - France
Tel. 0033 (0) 2 32 54 23 79 - Fax 0033 (0) 2 32 51 14 54
Email campingtroisrois@aol.com - www.camping-troisrois.com

Les Loges

Camping Airotel l'Aiguille Creuse

F-76790 Les Loges (Seine-Maritime) T: 02 35 29 52 10. E: camping@aiguillecreuse.com

alanrogers.com/FR76160

L'Aiguille Creuse, conveniently close to Le Havre, is named after a rock, alleged to be hollow, near Etretat. The site is set back from the Côte d'Albâtre in the village of Les Loges, between Etretat and the fishing port of Fécamp. There are 135 good sized grassy pitches, slightly sloping in parts and divided by neat hedges. Of these, 78 are for touring, all with 10A electricity and 14 also with water and drainage. The remainder are occupied by mobile homes for rent. The village is within easy walking distance and buses run from here to Fécamp and to Etretat and Le Havre. An alternative and more adventurous way of getting to Etretat is by booking a rail buggy and pedaling yourselves down the hill – you are then brought back up to the village by road in a 'petit train'. The picturesque villages of Etretat and Yport were an attraction for the Impressionist painters and have largely remained unspoiled. The cliffs at Etretat continue to attract artists and photographers and one way to enjoy them is from a boat – there are trips from Fécamp passing beneath the famous arches; or become a 'crew member' on a traditional sailing boat. Fécamp has many festivities connected with the sea and offers various conducted tours including one of WW2 bunkers and the military hospital buried in the cliffs. Many will enjoy a visit to the distillery and cellars of the Palais Bénédictine. There is also plenty to appeal to younger visitors in the area.

Facilities

Two modern toilet blocks (one heated, the other open in July/Aug) with unisex toilets (no seats), controllable showers, washbasins in cubicles, baby changing and facilities for children and disabled visitors. Laundry. Motorcaravan services. Smart new bar (with 30 mins. free WiFi daily). Takeaway (9/7-22/8). Heated pool with retractable roof. New playground. WiFi (charged). Card-operated barrier. Off site: Shops and bars within 1 km.

Open: 2 April - 17 September.

Directions

From Fécamp, take D940 towards Etretat. Passing through Les Loges site is well signed to the left. GPS: 49.698782, 0.275602

Charges guide

Per unit incl. 2 persons and electricity	€ 22.00 - € 28.50
extra person	€ 4.50 - € 6.00
child (2-6 yrs)	€ 3.00 - € 4.50

Camping Cheques accepted.

Luc-sur-Mer

Camping la Capricieuse

2 rue Brummel, F-14530 Luc-sur-Mer (Calvados) T: 02 31 97 34 43. E: info@campinglacapricieuse.com

alanrogers.com/FR14170

La Capricieuse is an excellent municipal site situated an the edge of the delightful small seaside town of Luc-sur-Mer. It is an ideal location for visiting the D-Day landing beaches and Le Mémorial (Peace Museum) at Caen. This immaculate site has 192 touring pitches of varying sizes, most are on level grass with hedges and a variety of trees giving some shade. One hundred and fifty have electricity (6/10A) and 52 also have water and drainage. Although the site does not have its own shop, bar or restaurant, these can be found within walking distance in Luc-sur-Mer.

Facilities

Three modern, heated toilet blocks with washbasins in cubicles and showers are kept very clean. Fully equipped facilities for disabled visitors. Laundry facilities. Motorcaravan services. Large TV room. Games room. Adventure playground (unfenced). Tennis. Boules. Multisports court. Free WiFi in TV room.

Open: 1 April - 30 September.

Directions

Take the D514 from Ouistreham car ferry and head west to Luc-sur-Mer. Campsite is well signed from western end of St Luc. GPS: 49.31797, -0.35780

Charges guide

Per unit incl. 2 persons and electricity (10A)	€ 24.50
extra person	€ 5.80

Les Pieux

Camping le Grand Large

F-50340 Les Pieux (Manche) T: 02 33 52 40 75. E: info@legrandlarge.com

alanrogers.com/FR50060

Le Grand Large is a well established, quality family site with direct access to a long sandy beach and within a 20 km. drive of Cherbourg. It is a neat and tidy site with 119 touring pitches divided and separated by hedging giving an orderly, well laid out and attractive appearance. Almost all have electricity (10A, Europlug), water and drainage. There are 49 mobile homes for rent in three separate areas. The reception area is at the entrance (with a security barrier) and the forecourt is decorated with flower beds. To the rear of the site and laid out in the sandhills is an excellent play area. Not surprisingly, the sandy beach is the big attraction. The length of units is restricted to eight metres to prevent any problems accessing pitches. Roads around the site are tarmac and many of the delightful plants and shrubs that you see bordering these carry name tags in four languages. The pleasant views from the site stretch across the bay to the tip of the Cherbourg peninsula. Every effort is made at le Grand Large to attract and cater for families with young children, so noisy entertainment is not an option.

Facilities

Two well maintained toilet blocks. The main one is modern and includes washbasins in cubicles and some family rooms. Some showers and WCs have access to the outside of the building. Provision for disabled visitors. Baby bathroom. Laundry area. Motorcaravan services. Shop for basics, bar (all season). Snacks (July/Aug). Heated swimming and paddling pools (indoor all season, outdoor 13/6-6/9). Play area. Tennis. Boules. Fishing. TV room. Some entertainment (July/Aug). WiFi over site (charged). Off site: Two supermarkets in Les Pieux.

Open: 11 April - 20 September.

Directions

From Cherbourg port take N13 south for 2 km. Branch right on D650 (Carteret). Continue for 18 km. to Les Pieux. Take D4 in town and turn left just after 'Super U' supermarket. Follow site signs via D117/517. GPS: 49.49452, -1.84246

Charges guide

Per unit incl. 2 persons and electricity	€ 23.00 - € 40.00
extra person	€ 5.00 - € 8.70

Camping Cheques accepted.

Lyons-la-Forêt

Camping Municipal Saint Paul

2 route de Saint Paul, F-27480 Lyons-la-Forêt (Eure) T: 02 32 49 42 02. E: camping-saint-paul@orange.fr

alanrogers.com/FR27050

The village of Lyons-la-Forêt, with its medieval covered market and wonderfully preserved, half-timbered buildings is classified as one of 'Les Plus Beaux Villages de France'. Within walking distance of the village, next to the playing field and public pool, this quiet municipal campsite is a delightful and peaceful spot. The site has 100 level grass, numbered pitches, separated by hedges with a variety of mature trees providing shade. There are 53 for touring units, each with 6A electricity, water and drainage; hardstandings are available. Seven chalets for rent occupy some of the pitches overlooking the clear shallow stream which runs the length of the site.

Facilities

Central toilet block with controllable showers and washbasins in cubicles; facilities for disabled visitors are on ladies' side (basic shower room, washbasin and WC). Washing machine and dryer. Motorcaravan services. Reception sells some basics. TV/games room. Small play areas. Pétanque. Bicycle hire. WiFi throughout (charged). Off site: Tennis courts 100 m (book at reception).

Open: 1 April - 31 October.

Directions

Lyons-la-Forêt is 35 km. east of Rouen via N31 Beauvais road. Turn south at La Feuillie on D921/D321 to Lyons-la-Forêt. Site is on left on bend at foot of hill. GPS: 49.40308, 1.47822

Charges guide

Per unit incl. 2 persons and electricity	€ 16.50 - € 20.50

No credit cards.

Martragny

Castel Camping le Château de Martragny

52 Hameau Saint Leger, F-14740 Martragny (Calvados) T: 02 31 80 21 40. E: chateau.martragny@wanadoo.fr
alanrogers.com/FR14030

Martragny is an attractive site in the parkland of a château. Close to D-Day beaches and Bayeux, it is also convenient for the ports of Caen and Cherbourg, and has the facilities and charm to encourage both long stays and stopovers. The pleasant lawns surrounding and approaching the château take 160 touring units, with electricity connections (10A, some longer leads required). Most pitches are divided by either a small hedge or a few trees. In contrast to the busyness of Bayeux, the de Chassey family ensure you can enjoy the peace and calm of their home when you enjoy a glass of wine in the lovely courtyard, surrounded by the warm ancient stonework.

Facilities

Three sanitary blocks (one new) include washbasins in cabins, showers, sinks for dishwashing and laundry, and a baby room. Disabled visitors are well catered for. Good laundry. Shop. Bar, brasserie and takeaway (all season). Heated outdoor swimming pool (20x6 m) and paddling pool. Play areas. Tennis. Minigolf. Games and TV room. Fishing pond. Family entertainment (July/Aug). WiFi over site (free). Off site: Riding 1 km. Bayeux Tapestry 8 km.

Open: 23 May - 26 August.

Directions

From Caen on N13 take exit for Martragny, ignore turning to village, continue for 100 m, site signed on right. GPS: 49.24299, -0.60588

Charges guide

Per unit incl. 2 persons and electricity	€ 31.40 - € 40.50
extra person	€ 7.00 - € 9.50

Camping Cheques accepted.

Maupertus-sur-Mer

Castel Camping Caravaning l'Anse du Brick

Route du Val de Saire, 18 Anse du Brick, F-50330 Maupertus-sur-Mer (Manche) T: 02 33 54 33 57.
E: welcome@anse-du-brick.com **alanrogers.com/FR50070**

A friendly, family site, l'Anse du Brick overlooks a picturesque bay on the northern tip of the Cotentin Peninsula, eight kilometres east of Cherbourg port. This quality site makes a pleasant night halt or an ideal longer stay destination for those not wishing to travel too far. Its pleasing location offers direct access to a small sandy beach and a woodland walk. This is a mature, terraced site with magnificent views from certain pitches. Tarmac roads lead to the 117 touring pitches (all with 10A electricity) which are level, separated and mostly well shaded by many trees, bushes and shrubs.

Facilities

New sanitary facilities with washbasins, mainly in cubicles, and pushbutton showers. All kept spotlessly clean and well maintained. Provision for children, families and disabled visitors. Laundry area. Motorcaravan services. Shop. Restaurant and bar/pizzeria. Heated swimming pools (indoor all season, outdoor from 1/5). Tennis. Play area. Organised entertainment (July/Aug). Miniclub (6-12 yrs). Bicycle and kayak hire. WiFi over site (charged). Off site: Fishing 200 m. Riding 4 km.

Open: 9 April - 18 September.

Directions

From Cherbourg port follow signs for Caen and Rennes. After third roundabout, take slip road to right towards Bretteville-en-Saire (D116). Continue for 7 km. Site signed to right.
GPS: 49.66715, -1.48704

Charges guide

Per unit incl. 2 persons and electricity	€ 23.50 - € 44.00
extra person	€ 4.80 - € 8.70

Ménil-Hubert-sur-Orne

Camping de la Rouvre

Lieu-dit le bas Rouvrou, F-61430 Ménil-Hubert-sur-Orne (Orne) T: 02 33 64 82 40. E: larouvre@gmail.com
alanrogers.com/FR61090

Camping de la Rouvre is set on the banks of the River Rouvre, 2 km. from its confluence with the River Orne. There are 17 grassy touring pitches (ten adjacent to the river), almost all with 16A electricity (long leads required) and separated by hedges. An open field accommodates a further 30 units. There are two tents and a wooden chalet for hire. The site is convenient for several ferry ports, with the famous tourist sites of Mont Saint-Michel, Bayeux, and the Normandy landing beaches on the doorstep.

Facilities

One clean sanitary block has adequate provision with hot showers, one private cabin and facilities for disabled visitors (gravel path). Washing machine. Boules. Communal barbecue. Fishing. Bouncy castle. Bicycle hire. WiFi throughout (charged). Off site: Mountain biking, climbing, kayaking, hiking and fishing. Riding 2 km. Golf 8 km.

Open: 1 April - 15 October.

Directions

From Caen take N158 south towards Falaise then exit D511 towards Pont d'Ouilly. Turn left onto D25 until Ménil-Hubert-sur-Orne.
GPS: 48.84327, -0.39821

Charges guide

Per unit incl. 2 persons and electricity	€ 20.40
extra person	€ 4.65
child (under 13 yrs acc. to age)	€ 3.55 - € 4.65

No credit cards.

Merville-Franceville

Camping les Peupliers

F-14810 Merville-Franceville (Calvados) T: 02 31 24 05 07. E: contact@camping-peupliers.com

alanrogers.com/FR14190

Les Peupliers is run by friendly, family managers who keep it attractive and tidy. It is just 300 metres from a long, wide, sandy beach. The touring pitches, of which there are 109, are on level open ground, all with 10/16A electricity. Those in the newest part are hedged but, with just a few trees on the edge of the site, there is little shade. The campsite amenities are near the entrance, housed in neat modern buildings. An animation programme for children and various activities are organised in high season. This site is ideally located for visiting Caen, Bayeux and the traditional seaside towns of Deauville and Trouville. The site is ideal for couples and families who are looking for a variety of activities.

Facilities

Two excellent heated toilet blocks with washbasins in cabins and showers. Good facilities for disabled visitors and for babies. Laundry room. Small shop, bar with terrace and takeaway (all July/Aug). Heated outdoor swimming pool and paddling pool (June-Sept). Indoor heated pool (Apr-Oct). Play area. Games room. Entertainment in high season. WiFi over part of site (free).

Open: 1 April - 31 October.

Directions

From Ouistreham take D514 to Merville-Franceville. Site is well signed off Allée des Pins. From Rouen on A13 (exit 29B), take D400 to Cabourg then D514 to Merville-Franceville. GPS: 49.28326, -0.17053

Charges guide

Per unit incl. 2 persons and electricity	€ 23.00 - € 31.20
extra person	€ 4.80 - € 8.10

Merville-Franceville

Camping le Point du Jour

Route de Cabourg, F-14810 Merville-Franceville-Plage (Calvados) T: 02 31 24 23 34.
E: camp.lepointdujour@wanadoo.fr **alanrogers.com/FR14210**

Camping le Point du Jour has a very French flavour and is an ideal location for family holidays as it has direct access to a fine sandy beach. It is becoming popular with British visitors who will receive a warm welcome from the owner and staff. There are 142 pitches bordered by shrubs and hedging, including 30 occupied by mobile homes and chalets (ten for hire). There are some seasonal units but most have to be removed for high season. All touring pitches have 10A electricity, including those on the sea-dyke, and 12 also have water and drainage. Fishing is possible from the beach and small boats may be launched. Kite surfing is popular and sailing and other watersports are possible further along the beach.

Facilities

Two toilet blocks (one heated, the other unisex in low season) provide washbasins in cubicles, pushbutton showers, and facilities for babies and disabled visitors. Laundry. Motorcaravan services. Small bar (serving basic drinks and snacks except in very low season; bread delivery). Pool table. Exercise machines. Indoor swimming pool with section for children. Wellness cabin for hire with sauna, jacuzzi and body care sessions. Play area. Bicycle hire. Children's club. Entertainment and activities (high season). WiFi over site (charged).

Open: 1 April - 7 November.

Directions

Merville-Franceville is 17 km. northeast of Caen. From Ouistreham car ferry port (16 km) follow signs for Caen and turn east on D514 over Pegasus Bridge and through Merville to site on left. GPS: 49.28319, -0.19098

Charges guide

Per unit incl. 2 persons and electricity	€ 23.00 - € 39.00
extra person	€ 4.80 - € 8.60
child (4-10 yrs)	€ 2.30 - € 4.90

Moyaux

Château Camping le Colombier

Le Val Sery, F-14590 Moyaux (Calvados) T: 02 31 63 63 08. E: chateau@camping-lecolombier.com

alanrogers.com/FR14050

Le Colombier is a real gem of a campsite, situated in the grounds of a Normandy château, which is home to the owner. Within the attractive, landscaped gardens there is a large, rectangular swimming pool and an impressive former dovecote now houses a cosy bar and library. There are no mobile homes or chalets here; all 178 pitches are dedicated to touring, most with electricity connections. They are large and marked out by trees at the corners, but with no dividing hedges. Reception is in a restored building and the staff are efficient and friendly. The site's main amenities are open all season.

Facilities

Two toilet blocks include private cabins and a unit for disabled visitors. Motorcaravan services. Laundry facilities. Bar. Shop. Crêperie. Takeaway. Occasional dinners (limited numbers) served in the château. Heated swimming pool (25x12 m). Tennis. Minigolf. Indoor and outdoor play areas. Organised events all season. Free WiFi on part of site. Off site: Free fishing on nearby lake.

Open: 1 May - 15 September.

Directions

Site is 3 km. northeast of Moyaux on the D143, well signed from the Cormeilles-Lisieux road. GPS: 49.20974, 0.389792

Charges guide

Per unit incl. 2 persons and electricity	€ 28.00 - € 38.00
extra person	€ 6.00 - € 8.00

Pont-Audemer

Flower Camping Caravaning des Etangs Risle-Seine

19 route des Etangs, F-27500 Toutainville (Eure) T: 02 32 42 46 65. E: infos@camping-risle-seine.com

alanrogers.com/FR27010

This attractive and well maintained quiet, rural site is well laid out with 51 hedged touring pitches on level grass, 38 with 10A electricity, and 20 with water and waste water connections also. There is a separate tent field for groups or 'free' camping. Fishing and watersports are possible as the site is positioned next to some large lakes. The River Risle runs close to the site too. In Pont-Audemer you will find shops, restaurants and a good swimming complex.

Facilities

Two basic toilet blocks include washbasins in cabins and preset showers. Facilities for disabled visitors. Laundry. Bar area with terrace (soft drinks only as there is no alcohol licence). Bread delivery. Takeaway food. New heated outdoor swimming pool (1/5-30/9). Playing field. TV. Fishing. Some family entertainment (July/Aug). WiFi throughout (free). Off site: Golf adjacent. Base Nautique 500 m. Bicycle hire 5 km. Supermarkets within 2.5 km.

Open: 1 April - 30 October.

Directions

Leave Toutanville centre on D675 (Avenue des Peupliers). After 300 m, just before motorway bridge, turn left and then immediately right (between motorway bridge pillars!) and travel 1.5 km. on rue des Etangs (small country lane between motorway and fields). Site is signed. GPS: 49.3666, 0.48739

Charges guide

Per unit incl. 2 persons and electricity	€ 16.90 - € 21.00

Pontorson

Camping Haliotis

Chemin des Soupirs, F-50170 Pontorson (Manche) T: 02 33 68 11 59. E: camping.haliotis@wanadoo.fr

alanrogers.com/FR50080

The staff at this beautiful campsite offer a warm welcome to visitors. Situated on the edge of the little town of Pontorson, 9 km. from Mont Saint-Michel, the site has 152 pitches, including 118 for touring units. Most have 16A electricity and 24 really large ones also have water and drainage. Excellent private sanitary facilities are also available on 12 luxury pitches. The comfortable reception area incorporates a pleasant bar where breakfast is served. This opens onto the swimming pool terrace. The site is attractively laid out and includes a Japanese garden. Haliotis (which takes its name from a large shell) is by the River Couesnon and it is possible to walk, cycle and canoe along the river to Mont Saint-Michel.

Facilities

Well equipped, heated toilet block with controllable showers and washbasins in cubicles. Good facilities for disabled visitors. Baby room. Laundry facilities. Bar serving breakfast. Bread to order. Shop. Outdoor heated swimming pool (1/5-30/9) with jacuzzi and separate paddling pool. Sauna and solarium. Fenced play areas. Pétanque. Archery. Games room. Tennis. Golf practice range. Multisports court. Bicycle hire. Japanese garden and animal park. Miniclub. Free WiFi over site.

Open: 15 March - 11 November.

Directions

Pontorson is 22 km. southwest of Avranches and bypassed by the N176 which links with D137 from St Malo to the west and (via N175) with A84 (Caen-Rennes) to the east. Site is 300 m. north of town centre. Note: Entrance is on rue du Général Patton. Follow signs, not sat nav! GPS: 48.55836, -1.51429

Charges guide

Per unit incl. 2 persons and electricity	€ 19.50 - € 25.50

Camping Cheques accepted.

Port-en-Bessin

Camping Port'land

Chemin du Castel, F-14520 Port-en-Bessin (Calvados) T: 02 31 51 07 06. E: campingportland@wanadoo.fr

alanrogers.com/FR14150

Port'land, now a mature site, lies on the western edge of the delightful little resort of Port-en-Bessin, one of Normandy's busiest fishing ports. The 279 pitches are large and grassy with 156 for touring units, all with electricity (mainly 16A), water and waste water, and 35 with hardstandings. There are 98 mobile homes for rent. The camping area has been imaginatively landscaped, many pitches overlooking small fishing ponds. A modern building houses the refurbished reception and a smart bar/restaurant with an interesting menu. A coastal path leads to the little town, which has shops and waterfront restaurants.

Facilities

Main sanitary block is well maintain with controllable showers, washbasins in cubicles and an attractive baby room. En-suite unit for disabled visitors. Covered, heated swimming pool with paddling pool. Open-air pool with slides (July/Aug). Shop. Bar. Restaurant with takeaway. Wood-fired pizza oven (July/Aug). Large TV and games room (1st floor with lift). Multisports pitch. Fishing. Play area. Free WiFi in main building.

Open: 1 April - 1 November.

Directions

Port-en-Bessin is 43 km. northwest of Caen. Site is clearly signed off D514, 4 km. west of Port-en-Bessin. GPS: 49.3463, -0.7732

Charges guide

Per unit incl. 2 persons and electricity	€ 22.00 - € 47.00
extra person	€ 6.00 - € 10.00
child (2-10 yrs)	€ 3.00 - € 6.00

Pourville-sur-Mer

Camping le Marqueval

1210 rue de la Mer, F-76550 Pourville-sur-Mer (Seine-Maritime) T: 02 35 82 66 46.
E: contact@campinglemarqueval.com **alanrogers.com/FR76010**

Le Marqueval is a well established, family site of 290 pitches, located close to the seaside town of Hautot-sur-Mer, just west of Dieppe. The site has been developed around three small lakes (one unfenced, suitable for fishing). There are 60 grass pitches for touring units, all of a good size, separated by hedges and 40 with electrical connections (6A). The majority of the pitches here are used for privately owned mobile homes. Leisure amenities include a swimming pool and smaller children's pools. The site's bar also functions as a snack bar and in high season hosts occasional evening entertainment.

Facilities

The single toilet block is at the entrance to the site. Motorcaravan services (charged). Shop. Bar, snack bar, takeaway (July/Aug and w/ends). Outdoor, heated swimming pool (15/6-15/9), hot tub and spa. Fishing (charged). Playground. Basketball court. Entertainment and activity programme. Mobile homes for rent. WiFi throughout (charged). Off site: Beach 1.3 km. Riding, bicycle hire, golf and boat launching 3 km. Tennis. Cycle and walking tracks. Supermarket in Dieppe 5 km.

Open: 17 March - 15 October.

Directions

Head west from Dieppe on the D925 as far as Hautot-sur-Mer. Then turn right onto the D153 towards Pourville. Site is well signed from here. GPS: 49.9088, 1.0406

Charges guide

Per unit incl. 2 persons and electricity	€ 19.00 - € 25.00
extra person	€ 4.00 - € 7.50
child (2-6 yrs)	€ 3.00 - € 4.00

Ravenoville-Plage

Camping le Cormoran

2 le Cormoran, F-50480 Ravenoville Plage (Manche) T: 02 33 41 33 94. E: lecormoran@wanadoo.fr
alanrogers.com/FR50050

This welcoming, environmentally friendly, family run site close to Cherbourg and Caen is just across the road from a long sandy beach. It is also close to Utah beach and is ideally located for those wishing to visit the many museums, landing beaches and remembrance gardens of WW2. On flat, quite open ground, the site has 110 good sized pitches on level grass, all with 6/10A electricity (Europlug). Some extra large pitches are available. The well kept pitches are separated by mature hedges and the site is decorated with flowering shrubs. A covered pool, a sauna and a gym are among recent improvements. These facilities, plus a shop, comfortable bar and takeaway, are open all season.

Facilities

Four toilet blocks, three heated, are of varying styles and ages but all are maintained to a good standard. Laundry facilities. Shop. Bar and terrace. Snacks and takeaway. Outdoor pool (30/6-1/9, unsupervised). New covered pool, sauna and gym (all season). Play areas. Tennis. Boules. Entertainment, TV and games room. Billiard golf (one of only three in Europe). Playing field with archery (July/Aug). Hairdresser and masseuse. Bicycle and shrimp net hire. Riding (July/Aug). Communal barbecues. BMX park for children. WiFi (charged). Off site: Beach 20 m.

Open: 5 April - 30 September.

Directions

From N13 take Ste Mère-Eglise exit and in centre of town take road to Ravenoville (6 km), then Ravenoville-Plage (3 km). Just before beach turn right and site is 500 m. GPS: 49.46643, -1.23533

Charges guide

Per unit incl. 2 persons and electricity	€ 23.00 - € 35.00
extra person	€ 4.70 - € 8.20
child (5-10 yrs)	€ 2.30 - € 3.30

Camping Cheques accepted.

Saint Arnoult

Camping la Vallée de Deauville

Avenue de la Vallée, F-14800 Saint Arnoult (Calvados) T: 02 31 88 58 17. E: contact@camping-deauville.com
alanrogers.com/FR14200

This large, modern site is close to the traditional seaside resorts of Deauville and Trouville. With a total of 450 pitches, there are many mobile homes, both for rent and privately owned, and 150 for touring units (including a 70-pitch tent field). The main pitches are level, of a reasonable size and mostly hedged, 80 have 10A electricity. A new swimming pool complex with flumes, lazy river, jacuzzi and fun pool makes an attractive focal point near the entrance, and there is a large fishing lake.

Facilities

Two heated toilet blocks with showers and washbasins in cubicles. Good facilities for babies and disabled visitors. Laundry facilities. Small shop. Bar and restaurant. Takeaway. Outdoor heated swimming pool (1/6-15/9). Spa. Good play area and games room. New multisports court. Bicycle hire. Entertainment in high season. WiFi (charged). Off site: Golf and riding 2 km. Beach 3 km.

Open: 1 April - 31 October.

Directions

From A13 at Pont l'Eveque join N177 (Deauville) and after 9 km. take D27 signed St Arnoult. Site is well signed on edge of village. GPS: 49.32864, 0.08634

Charges guide

Per unit incl. 2 persons and electricity	€ 21.80 - € 35.70
extra person	€ 5.70 - € 9.50

Saint Aubin-sur-Mer

Yelloh! Village la Côte de Nacre

17 rue du Général Moulton, F-14750 Saint Aubin-sur-Mer (Calvados) T: 02 31 97 14 45.

E: info@yellohvillage-cote-de-nacre.com **alanrogers.com/FR14010**

La Côte de Nacre is a large, popular, commercial site with many facilities, all of a high standard. It is an ideal holiday location for families. Two thirds are given over to mobile homes and there are four tour operators on the site. The 150 touring pitches are reasonable, both in size and condition, all having 10A electricity. There is some hedging and a few trees, and pleasant, well cared for flowerbeds. A state-of-the-art, heated pool complex includes both open and covered (sliding roof) areas, slides, whirlpools and water jets, and on a hot day becomes the focal point of the campsite.

Facilities

The sanitary block provides hot showers, washbasins in cubicles and a large room for toddlers and babies. Facilities for disabled visitors. Dishwashing and laundry room. Motorcaravan services. Grocery with fresh bread baked on site. Bar, restaurant and takeaway. Swimming pool complex. Hammam, sauna and body treatments (charged). Play area with bouncy castle and climbing frames. Multisports court. Synthetic skating rink. Library. Games room. Bicycle hire. Kids' clubs and mini-discos. Entertainment. WiFi. Mobile homes for rent.

Open: 4 April - 14 September.

Directions

Travel west from Ouistreham on D514 to St Aubin-sur-Mer. Site is well signed, to the left, just off the main road in a residential area. Take care as signage is small and you are in an urban area with no turning back. GPS: 49.32600, -0.39052

Charges guide

Per unit incl. 2 persons and electricity	€ 18.00 - € 47.00
extra person	€ 6.00 - € 9.00
child (3-6 yrs)	free - € 6.00

Saint Aubin-sur-Scie

Camping Vitamin

865 rue des Vertus, F-76550 Saint Aubin-sur-Scie (Seine-Maritime) T: 02 35 82 11 11.

E: camping.vitamin@wanadoo.fr **alanrogers.com/FR76030**

Although the address is Saint Aubin, this compact site is actually on the outskirts of Dieppe and is only a couple of kilometres from the seafront and the shops. Those arriving or leaving by ferry could find it useful for a stopover as it is just off the main N27 to Rouen. It has a very French atmosphere, with 106 privately owned mobile homes and 39 for hire. The 44 touring pitches (all with 10A electricity) are attractively laid out on level grass, and some are positioned between the mobile homes. The Morelle family work hard to ensure that everything is as it should be, but they speak very little English, so be prepared to practise your French.

Facilities

Two excellent and well maintained unisex toilet blocks provide free showers and washbasins in cubicles. Facilities for disabled visitors. Baby bath. Washing machines and dryers. Motorcaravan services. Bar serving snacks (1/6-30/9) and entertainment (July/Aug). Heated swimming pools, outdoor (1/7-31/8), indoor (1/4-15/10). Adventure playground and field for games. Multisports court. Games barn. Large pétanque pitch. Sports tournaments in high season. WiFi over site (charged).

Open: 1 April - 15 October.

Directions

From Dieppe ferry terminal head southeast to turn west onto ring road and follow this, keeping right at large roundabout (Leclerc), left at next (Intermarché) onto N27 (Rouen). At roundabout (Auchan), turn south on N27. Take sliproad and turn right to site. GPS: 49.90063, 1.0747

Charges guide

Per unit incl. 2 persons and electricity	€ 19.90 - € 25.90
extra person	€ 5.10 - € 5.90

Saint Jean-de-la-Rivière

Yelloh! Village les Vikings

4 rue des Vikings, Saint Jean-de-la-Rivière, F-50270 Barneville-Carteret (Manche) T: 04 66 73 97 39.

E: info@yellohvillage-lesvikings.com **alanrogers.com/FR50200**

Les Vikings is located close to the attractive resort of Barneville-Carteret on the western side of the Cherbourg Peninsula. The site is just 400 m. from a sandy beach. There are 250 pitches of which around 70 are reserved for touring, the rest being occupied by mobile homes and chalets, some of which are for rent. Pitches are grassy and of a reasonable size, with 6A electricity, but long leads may be required. Most of the site's amenities are grouped around the entrance and these include a swimming pool (covered and heated), a restaurant/pizzeria and bar as well as a grocery shop.

Facilities

The main toilet block is outstanding, the second block is due for refurbishment. Well stocked shop. Bar. Restaurant, snack bar and takeaway. Swimming pool complex with flume. Games room. Play area. Small farm with chickens, goats, a pony and a llama. Activity and entertainment programme (high season).

Open: 4 April - 28 September.

Directions

From Cherbourg, head southwest on D650 to Barneville-Carteret. Site is at St Jean-de-la-Rivière, just to south of town. GPS: 49.3641, -1.75347

Charges guide

Per unit incl. 2 persons and electricity	€ 18.00 - € 40.00
extra person	€ 7.00 - € 8.00

Saint Pair-sur-Mer

Castel Camping le Château de Lez Eaux

240 avenue de Lez Eaux, F-50380 Saint Pair-sur-Mer (Manche) T: 02 33 51 66 09. E: bonjour@lez-eaux.com
alanrogers.com/FR50030

Set in the grounds of a château, Lez Eaux lies in a rural situation just off the main route south, under two hours from Cherbourg. Of the 229 pitches, 124 are for touring units, all with electricity (10A, Europlug) and 84 with water and drainage. Most of the pitches are of a very good size, partly separated by trees and shrubs on flat or slightly sloping, grassy ground overlooking Normandy farmland and a small fishing lake. The indoor pool complex has a fun pool for very small children and there is a heated outdoor pool.

Facilities

Three modern clean toilet blocks (one heated in low season) include hot showers and washbasins in cabins, facilities for disabled visitors and children. Shop. Bar. snacks and takeaway. Small heated swimming pool and indoor tropical-style fun pool with paddling pool and slide (all season, no T-shirts or Bermuda-style shorts). Play area. Tennis. Games and TV rooms. Bouncy castle. Children's club and music evenings (July/Aug). Bicycle hire. Lake fishing. Torches useful. WiFi in bar area (charged). Max. 1 dog per pitch.

Open: 1 April - 11 September.

Directions

Lez Eaux is just to the west of the D973 17 km. northwest of Avranches and 7 km. southeast of Granville. Site is between the two turnings east to St Aubin-des-Préaux and is well signed.
GPS: 48.79778, -1.52498

Charges guide

Per unit incl. 2 persons and electricity	€ 21.00 - € 55.00
extra person	€ 8.00

No credit cards.

Saint Symphorien-le-Valois

Camping l'Etang des Haizes

43 rue Cauticotte, F-50250 Saint Symphorien-le-Valois (Manche) T: 02 33 46 01 16.
E: info@campingetangdeshaizes.com **alanrogers.com/FR50000**

This is an attractive and very friendly site with a swimming pool complex that has a four-lane slide, a jacuzzi and a paddling pool. L'Etang des Haizes has 160 good sized pitches, of which 100 are for touring units, on fairly level ground and all with electricity (10A, Europlug). They are set in a mixture of conifers, orchard and shrubbery, with some very attractive, slightly smaller pitches overlooking the lake and 60 mobile homes inconspicuously sited. The fenced lake has a small beach (swimming is permitted), with ducks and pedaloes, and offers good coarse fishing for huge carp (we are told!).

Facilities

Two well kept and modern unisex toilet blocks with washbasins in cabins, units for disabled visitors, and two family cabins. Small laundry. Motorcaravan services. Milk, bread and takeaway snacks (no gas). Snack bar/bar with TV and terrace (28/6-29/8). Swimming pool complex (28/5-4/9). Play areas. Bicycle hire. Pétanque. Organised activities (6/7-22/8). Well stocked tourist information cabin. WiFi (charged).

Open: 4 April - 30 September.

Directions

Site is 24 km. south of N13 at Valognes and 29 km. north of Coutances: leave D900 at roundabout at northern end of bypass (towards town). Site signed on right. GPS: 49.300413, -1.544775

Charges guide

Per unit incl. 2 persons and electricity	€ 18.00 - € 38.00
extra person	€ 4.00 - € 8.50
child (2-10 yrs)	€ 4.00 - € 6.00

Saint Valery-en-Caux

Camping Etennemare

Hameau d'Etennemare, F-76460 Saint Valery-en-Caux (Seine-Maritime) T: 02 35 97 15 79.
E: contact@camping-etennemare.com **alanrogers.com/FR76090**

This comfortable, neat site is two kilometres from the picturesque harbour and town, 30 km. west of Dieppe. Quietly located, it has 116 pitches of which 49 are available for touring units. The grassy pitches are all on a slight slope, with electricity (6/10A), but very little shade. Reception is open all day in July and August, but in low season is closed 12.00-15.00 daily and all day Wednesday: a card-operated security barrier is in use. The site is close to the municipal sports complex and there are shops and restaurants in the bustling town and a Casino, pools and plenty of entertainment along the seafront.

Facilities

Two modern, clean and well maintained sanitary buildings are side by side, one containing showers and the other toilets, some washbasins in cubicles and facilities for disabled visitors. Both blocks are heated in winter. Washing machines. Small shop (July/Aug). Playground. Off site: Hypermarket 1.5 km. Pebble beach 2 km.

Open: 4 April - 5 November.

Directions

From Dieppe keep to D925 Fécamp road (not through town). At third roundabout turn right on D925E towards hypermarket. From Fécamp turn left on D925E as before. Take first right (site signed) to site on left in 1 km. GPS: 49.8585, 0.7046

Charges guide

Per unit incl. 2 persons and electricity	€ 18.50 - € 26.00

Camping Cheques accepted.

Saint Vaast-la-Hougue

Camping la Gallouette

10 bis rue de la Gallouette, F-50550 Saint Vaast-la-Hougue (Manche) T: 02 33 54 20 57.
E: contact@camping-lagallouette.fr **alanrogers.com/FR50010**

Claudine and Jean Luc Boblin will give you a warm welcome at their seaside campsite, which is ideally placed for visiting Barfleur, Ste-Mère-Eglise and the Normandy landing beaches. There are 183 level pitches in total, 123 for touring and all with 10A electricity. Some are separated by hedges and there are many colourful flower beds, shrubs and trees, but little shade. A light and airy bar faces onto a terrace and swimming pool and there is also a state-of-the-art multisports court. The site is close to the Channel ferry terminal at Cherbourg. Saint Vaast-la-Hougue is a busy fishing port with freshly caught fish on sale and a good choice of fish restaurants. Just a couple of hundred yards from the site, on a Saturday morning, you will find a bustling, traditional French market. A regular bus service from near the site entrance will take you to most of the surrounding areas including Barfleur and Cherbourg. For those wanting to take a leisurely stroll there is a pleasant walk along the raised sea wall to Fort de la Hougue which can be seen from the site. There is a dedicated area within the site for some 16 motorcaravans to overnight on hardstandings, with access to all facilities at a reduced rate.

Facilities

Three sanitary blocks, one open (and rather tired) and two enclosed, have British style toilets, showers and washbasins (some in cabins). Area for disabled visitors and for babies. Laundry facilities. Small shop. Snack bar. Bar with terrace. Swimming pool (15/5-15/9). Multisports court. Play area. Pétanque. WiFi over site (charged). Entertainment in high season. Off site: Beach 300 m. Shops and restaurant in St Vaast 300 m. Riding 5 km. Golf 11 km. Fishing. Sailing. Boat trips to Ile de Tatihou.

Open: 1 April - 30 September.

Directions

The D902 runs between Barfleur and Valognes on eastern side of Cherbourg peninsula. About halfway, at Quettehou, take D1 to St Vaast. Site signed on right on entering town. GPS: 49.58494, -1.26858

Charges guide

Per unit incl. 2 persons and electricity	€ 21.30 - € 30.05
extra person	€ 4.80 - € 6.80
child (2-10 yrs)	€ 3.00 - € 3.85

Sainte Marie-du-Mont

Flower Camping Utah Beach

F-50480 Sainte Marie-du-Mont (Manche) T: 02 33 71 53 69. E: utah.beach@wanadoo.fr
alanrogers.com/FR50140

Situated in an area rich in modern history, this family run campsite has a very French atmosphere. It is very well cared for, with landscaped areas, flower beds and shrubs. The 32 spacious pitches reserved for touring units are on level grass, separated by hedges and all have 6A electricity. A feature of the site is the heated swimming pool with adjacent sauna and jaccuzzi, and there is a well stocked aviary and a BMX facility. The site is only 50 m. from Utah Beach, one of the D-Day landing beaches.

Facilities

One well equipped and clean sanitary block provides British style toilets, washbasins in cabins and showers. Baby bath. Facilities for disabled visitors. Laundry facilities. Motorcaravan services. Shop. Bar, restaurant and takeaway. Swimming pool (15/5-30/9). Multisports court. BMX area. Play area (unfenced). Volleyball. Tennis. Games room. Aviary. Free WiFi over site. Entertainment in high season. Mobiles homes for rent. Off site: Riding 10 km. Bicycle hire and golf 15 km.

Open: 1 April - 17 September.

Directions

From the N13 south of Ste Mère-Église take D70 west to Ste Marie du-Mont, then D913 to the coast. Turn left on D421 coast road and site is 500 m. on left. GPS: 49.41931, -1.18058

Charges guide

Per unit incl. 2 persons and electricity	€ 20.50 - € 29.50
extra person	€ 4.00 - € 6.00
child (3-7 yrs)	€ 3.00 - € 4.50

Surrain

Camping la Roseraie d'Omaha

Rue de l'Eglise, F-14710 Surrain (Calvados) T: 02 31 21 17 71. E: camping-laroseraie@orange.fr

alanrogers.com/FR14340

Near a quiet little village in the Calvados region of Normandy, Camping La Roseraie d'Omaha is a rural family site just 4 km. from the sea and close to the D-Day landing beaches. The 51 touring pitches all have electricity (10A, Europlug) and 30 also have a water tap and drain; there is some shade in places. There are also 37 mobile homes and bungalows, most available to rent. The site is close to the N13 Cherbourg-Caen dual carriageway, so is convenient for an overnight stop as well as being a good base from which to explore the Normandy countryside and coastline. Some noise should be expected from the nearby dual carriageway.

Facilities

Brightly-decorated sanitary facilities with preset showers and most washbasins in cubicles. Unit for disabled visitors. Baby room. Laundry. Bar, snack bar with TV (1/5-15/09). Takeaway. Grocery. Fresh bread. Heated indoor swimming pool with slides and paddling pool (1/4-30/9). Playground. Volleyball. Minigolf (charged). Boules pitch. Tennis court (charged). Children's and family entertainment (July/Aug). Bicycle and mountain bike hire. WiFi over site (charged).

Open: 1 April - 30 September.

Directions

Surrain is 44 km northwest of Caen. From N13 take exit 38 (Mosles) and continue northeast on N2013/D613 for 9 km. towards Surrain; site is on left before village. GPS: 49.32571, -0.86448

Charges guide

Per unit incl. 2 persons and electricity	€ 19.10 - € 23.50
extra person	€ 5.00 - € 6.20
child (under 7 yrs)	€ 2.80 - € 3.50

Vauville

Camping l'Orée de Deauville

Lieu dit 'Le Lieu Roti', D27, F-14800 Vauville (Calvados) T: 02 31 87 96 22.

E: contact@camping-normandie-loreededeauville.com **alanrogers.com/FR14410**

Camping l'Orée de Deauville is situated close to the village of Vauville in the heart of the Calvados stud farms, near the famous resort of Deauville. There are 150 large, level, grass pitches. The 100 for touring (10A electricity) are separated by neat hedging and a variety of mature trees give good shade in places. The enthusiastic new owners have brought order to an over-run site; grass and hedges are well maintained and there is an on-going programme of improvements. The aim is to continue to provide a relaxed, family friendly environment from which to explore the many attractions of this interesting area.

Facilities

The sanitary block has pushbutton showers and some washbasins in cubicles. Basic provision for disabled visitors (shower/washbasin and separate WC). Washing machines and dryer. Bread to order. Bar, snack bar and takeaway (1/7-1/9). Small heated pool, children's pool and sunbathing area (20/6-1/9; no Bermuda shorts). Play areas. Table tennis. Boules. WiFi by reception (free). Bicycle, go-kart and barbecue hire. Off site: Beach 3 km.

Open: 28 March - 1 November.

Directions

Leave Le Havre on A131 east, turn south on A29 to cross Normandy Bridge. Take exit 2, D579, towards Deauville. After 6 km. turn right on D228 then in 8 km. turn left to roundabout and cross onto D27. Site is on left in 6 km. GPS: 49.32194, 0.06078

Charges guide

Per unit incl. 2 persons and electricity	€ 20.00 - € 26.00
extra person	€ 5.00 - € 7.00

Veules-les-Roses

Camping les Mouettes

Avenue Jean Moulin, F-76980 Veules-les-Roses (Seine-Maritime) T: 02 35 97 61 98.

E: contact@camping-lesmouettes-normandie.com **alanrogers.com/FR76060**

Les Mouettes is set back from the cliffs, with the pretty seaside resort of Veules-les-Roses below. It is a busy site, attracting many visitors en route from Dieppe. There are 152 pitches in total but many are occupied by mobile homes and seasonal caravans, leaving only 82 for touring, all with 6A electricity, and 21 for tents without electricity. They are level, grassy and divided by hedges, but have no shade. The narrow roads may cause difficulty for larger units. A special area for 16 motorcaravans is by the entrance. The site is open for a longer season and may be useful for those travelling south for winter.

Facilities

Toilet facilities are in a central group of buildings and provide separate male and female facilities, and those for disabled visitors. Washbasins in cubicles, showers, toilets (no seats) and baby changing. Motorcaravan services. Covered heated swimming pool (15/4-15/10). Play area. WiFi throughout (charged). Off site: Village centre and beach 300 m. Tennis. Walking and cycle trails. Cinema, shops and restaurants.

Open: 4 April - 2 November.

Directions

Veules-les-Roses is west of Dieppe. From there, head west on the D925 towards St Valéry-en-Caux. On arrival at town sign for Veules-les-Roses, site is immediately on left. GPS: 49.876239, 0.802935

Charges guide

Per unit incl. 2 persons and electricity	€ 18.90 - € 27.00
extra person	€ 3.70 - € 5.40
child (5-10 yrs)	€ 2.60 - € 3.60

Vimoutiers

Camping Municipal la Campière

Boulevard du Docteur Dentu, F-61120 Vimoutiers (Orne) T: 02 33 39 18 86. E: mairie.vimoutiers@wanadoo.fr
alanrogers.com/FR61010

In a valley on the northern side of the pleasant little town of Vimoutiers, which is on both the Normandy cheese and cider routes, this is a delightful municipal site. The 36 pitches are flat and grassy, separated by laurel hedging and laid out amongst attractive and well maintained flower and shrub beds. There is some shade around the perimeter and all pitches have electricity (8A). Also, there are four mobile homes to rent. The town is famous for its cheese and has a Camembert museum. Nearby, at Mont-Ormel, the events of the Falaise Gap are brought vividly to life. La Campière enjoys a great sense of spaciousness, overlooking the town's sports fields and tennis courts and with a pleasant park on the other side of the road. The shops, bars and restaurants of Vimoutiers are just five minutes' walk away and there is a supermarket even closer.

Facilities

The central sanitary block, although rather dated, is clean and heated. It provides open washbasins, good sized, well designed showers, children's toilets and provision for disabled visitors. Play area. Off site: Tennis courts and a park adjacent. Large supermarket 300 m. Restaurant and shops in town 400 m. Outdoor fitness course 1.5 km. Watersports facilities and riding 2 km. Camembert 5 km. Livarot 8 km. Lisieux 28 km.

Open: 1 April - 31 October.

Directions

Vimoutiers is 50 km. east of Caen. Site is on northern edge of town, on the main Lisieux-Argentan road (D517/D916), next to large sports complex. GPS: 48.93245, 0.19609

Charges guide

Per unit incl. 2 persons and electricity	€ 12.45 - € 15.05
extra person	€ 3.55
child (0-10 yrs)	€ 2.20

Reductions for 7th and subsequent days.

Yport

Flower Camping la Chênaie

Rue Henry Simon, F-76111 Yport (Seine-Maritime) T: 02 35 27 33 56.
E: camping.yport@flowercampings.com **alanrogers.com/FR76170**

La Chênaie, part of the Flower Camping group, is set in a wooded valley, just 1 km. from the traditional fishing village of Yport, renowned for its fishermen's houses and beautiful 19th-century villas. Of the 101 pitches, 39 are for touring and the rest are wooden chalets, mobile homes and FreeFlower tents, all for rent. The touring pitches are on open level grass with no shade, so may not offer the privacy some may require. All have 6A electricity. The nearby village of Etretat, with its famous chalk cliffs, inspired the paintings of Claude Monet and Gustave Courbet. This whole coastline is littered with small inlets and pretty villages while, inland, there is the rest of Normandy to explore, including farms producing cheese and Calvados.

Facilities

Modern toilet block with toilets, washbasins in cubicles and showers. Facilities for babies and disabled visitors. Laundry. Shop. Snack bar. Takeaway. Heated covered pool. Games room and play area. WiFi throughout (free). Off site: Local shops, bars, restaurants in village. Fishing 800 m. Riding 4 km. Bicycle hire, sailing and boat launching 6 km. Golf 12 km.

Open: 4 April - 27 September.

Directions

Yport is between Etretat and Fécamp. From Fécamp (42 km. northeast of Le Havre), take D940 southwest for 5 km, turn right on D104 towards Yport and site is on the left in 1 km. GPS: 49.732805, 0.320682

Charges guide

Per unit incl. 2 persons and electricity	€ 19.00 - € 30.00
extra person	€ 3.00 - € 5.50
child (2-7 yrs)	€ 2.00 - € 4.00
dog	€ 2.00 - € 3.00

DÉPARTEMENTS: 59 NORD, 62 PAS DE CALAIS

MAJOR CITY: LILLE

Nord-Pas de Calais, with its lush countryside and market towns, is much more than just a stopover en-route to or from the ports. The peaceful rural unspoilt charms of the region provide a real breath of fresh air.

Whether travelling by ferry or through the tunnel, this is one of the most accessible regions of France and has much to offer – the elegant resorts and sandy beaches of the opal coast, beautiful Flemish architecture in Arras, and all the attractions of the region's bustling capital, Lille. The landscape around Flanders is most closely associated with the battles of the First World War, and is the site of numerous military cemeteries and monuments to those who fell.

The area however is predominately rural. Inland and south are long vistas of rolling farmland broken by little rivers and well scattered with pockets of forest woodland. The coastline is characterised by sandy beaches, shifting dunes and ports. It is a quiet and sparsely populated area with peaceful villages and churches that provide evidence of the glorious achievements of French Gothic architecture. Boulogne is home to Nausicaa, the world's largest sea-life centre and from Cap Griz-Nez you may be able to see the White Cliffs of Dover. There are also many huge hypermarkets where you may stock up on wine, beer and cheese.

Places of interest

Arras: on the River Scarpe, has beautiful 13th- and 14th-century houses and the lovely Abbey of Saint Waast.

Boulogne: best entered by way of the lower town with the 13th-century ramparts of the upper town in the background. The castle next to the Basilica of Notre Dame is impressive.

Lille: Palais des Beaux-Arts; Cathedral; Sunday market; Euralille shopping complex.

Le Touquet: pleasant, all-year-round, coastal resort town with six miles of sandy beaches.

Cuisine of the region

Hearty stews and game from the forests of the Ardennes feature strongly, and in the north beer is commonly used in dishes such as carbonnade flamande.

Caudière (Chaudière, Caudrée): versions of fish and potato soup.

Croquelots or Bouffis: lightly salted and smoked herring.

Gris de Lille: a really salty square of cheese with a strong smell.

Hochepot: a thick Flemish soup with virtually everything in it but the kitchen sink.

Waterzooï: a cross between soup and stew, usually of fish or chicken.

www.northernfrance-tourism.com
contact@crt-nordpasdecalais.fr
(0)3 20 14 57 57

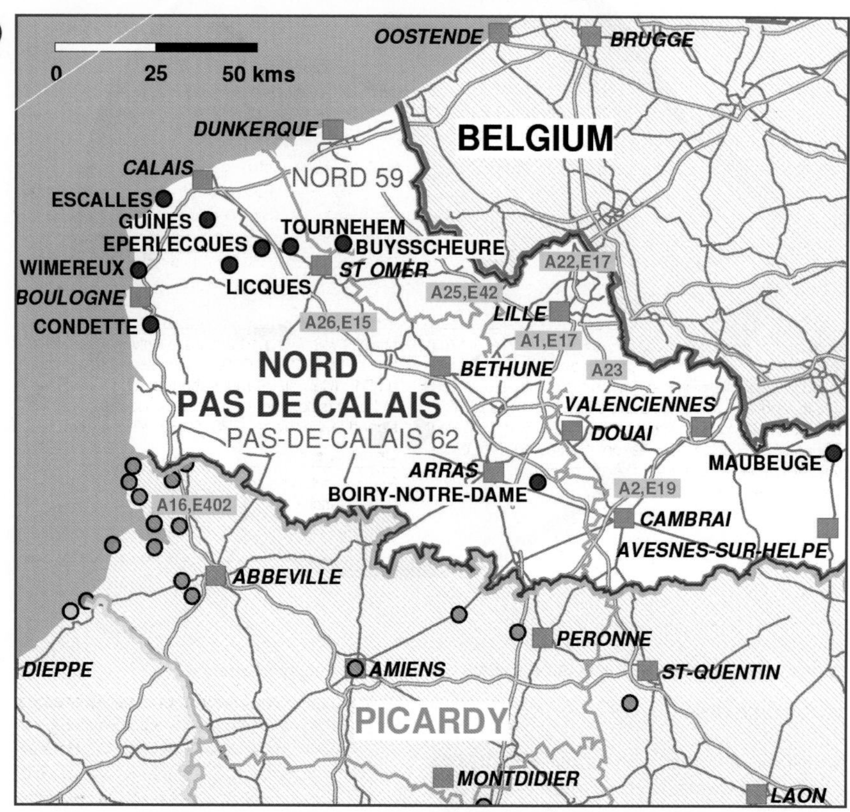

Boiry-Notre-Dame

Camping la Paille Haute

145 rue de Sailly, F-62156 Boiry-Notre-Dame (Pas-de-Calais) T: 03 21 48 15 40. E: lapaillehaute@wanadoo.fr

alanrogers.com/FR62080

La Paille Haute is quietly situated in a small village overlooking beautiful countryside, yet easily accessed from the A1, A2 and A26 autoroutes. It is an ideal overnight stop on your holiday route as well as a great base for exploring the Flemish city of Arras with its underground tunnels (begun in the tenth century and used in both World Wars), the battlefields of the Somme and the Thiépval Memorial. Of the 149 pitches, 65 are for touring on level grass and all with 6/10A electricity. Three places for late night arrivals (with electricity) are outside the barrier. The friendly owner has worked hard over the years expanding and developing this site to what it is today. Northern France is often overlooked by holidaymakers but is full of folklore and traditions. Many carnivals are centred around giant figures based on historical people and events; there are belfries with chimes played from ancient keyboards, unique in this region, and the unusual vertical archery begun in the Middle Ages and still practised today. The nearby town of Cambrai is famous for its cambric linen and chitterling sausages and, once war-torn, is now more at peace with its architecture and history.

Facilities

One modern, basic unisex toilet block. Extra toilet block by pool. One toilet/shower room for disabled visitors. Washing machine and dryer under canopy. Motorcaravan services. Baker calls twice daily (except Sun). Swimming pool (15/5-8/9). Poolside bar, snacks and pizza oven and restaurant (15/6-8/9). TV in bar. Fishing pond (securely fenced). Large playground. Boules. Entertainment (in season). WiFi over part of site (free). Off site: Supermarket in Vis-en-Artois 3 km. Riding 10 km. WW1 Canadian memorial at Vimy Ridge, 15 km. Golf 15 km.

Open: 1 April - 31 October.

Directions

From A1 exit 15 take D939 southeast. After 3 km. turn left for Boiry-Notre-Dame and follow camping signs to site. GPS: 50.273533, 2.948667

Charges guide

Per unit incl. 2 persons and electricity (6A)	€ 23.00 - € 26.50
extra person	€ 4.50 - € 5.00
child (under 7 yrs)	€ 3.50 - € 3.00

Buysscheure

Camping Caravaning la Chaumière

529 Langhemast straete, F-59285 Buysscheure (Nord) T: 03 28 43 03 57.
E: camping.LaChaumiere@wanadoo.fr **alanrogers.com/FR59010**

This is a very friendly, pleasant site, in the départment du Nord with a strong Flanders influence. … is a really warm welcome here. Set just behind the village of Buysscheure, the site has just 29 pitche… separated by trees and bushes. All are for touring units and each pair shares a light, 6A electricity connections, water point and rubbish container. Access from narrow approach roads can be difficult, although once on site there are several pitches available for extra large units. A small, fenced fishing lake contains some large carp. Bernadette can arrange all the documentation for British visitors' pets.

Facilities

Modern unisex toilet facilities are simple and small in number, with two WCs, one shower and one washbasin cabin. Facilities for disabled visitors may also be used (a toilet and separate washbasin/shower room). Laundry facilities. Motorcaravan services. Bar (daily) and restaurant (weekends only, all day in season). Heated outdoor pools (July/Aug). Play area. Minigolf. Archery. Fishing. Dog exercise area. WiFi in the bar (free).

Open: 1 April - 31 October.

Directions

From Calais take A16 towards Dunkirk. Take exit 53 on the D600 (St Omer). At crossroads turn left on D11 (Cassel). At roundabout turn right on D928 to Lederzeele. Turn left signed Buysscheure. Site is signed in the village. GPS: 50.80152, 2.33924

Charges guide

Per unit incl. 2 persons and electricity	€ 20.00 - € 23.00

No credit cards.

Condette

Caravaning du Château d'Hardelot

21 rue Nouvelle, F-62360 Condette (Pas-de-Calais) T: 03 21 87 59 59.
E: contact@camping-caravaning-du-chateau.com **alanrogers.com/FR62040**

Within about 15 minutes' drive of Boulogne and only five minutes by car from the long sandy beach at Hardelot, this modern site has 70 pitches with around 35 for touring units, the rest occupied by long stay or units to rent. Pitches are of varying size on level grass, all with access to electricity (10A). Hedging plants between the pitches are maturing well and there is shade from mature trees around the site. With friendly and accommodating owners, this site provides a useful overnight stop, but is also an excellent base for longer stays. British visitors enjoy the welcome they receive here and return year after year.

Facilities

Modern sanitary facilities in two small units (one heated) include large hot showers and baby bath. Laundry. Motorcaravan services. Excellent playground and entertainment for children (in season). Small fitness room. WiFi (charged). Off site: English-run pub/restaurant within walking distance. Château d'Hardelot (800 m) offers a variety of shows (April-Sept). Fishing 800 m. Riding 1 km. Golf 2 km. Bicycle hire and boat launching 3 km.

Open: 1 April - 31 October.

Directions

South of Boulogne, take N1 Amiens (Paris) road, then on outskirts take right fork for Le Touquet-Paris Plage (D940). Continue for 5 km. passing garage and signs for Condette, turn right at roundabout. Turn right again at next roundabout. Site entrance (narrow) is ahead on right. GPS: 50.6466, 1.6256

Charges guide

Per unit incl. 2 persons and electricity	€ 22.20 - € 27.90

No credit cards.

Eperlecques

Camping Château du Gandspette

133 rue de Gandspette, F-62910 Eperlecques (Pas-de-Calais) T: 03 21 93 43 93.
E: contact@chateau-gandspette.com **alanrogers.com/FR62030**

This spacious, family run site is set in the grounds of a 19th-century château. It is conveniently situated for the Channel ports and tunnel, providing overnight accommodation together with a range of facilities for longer stays. There are 110 touring pitches, all with 6A electricity hook-ups and 21 with hardstanding. These are interspersed with 20 privately owned mobile homes and caravans with a further 18 for hire. Most pitches are delineated by trees and hedging. Mature trees form the perimeter of the site, through which there is access to woodland walks. Even when the site is busy, there is still a sense of space with large green areas kept free of caravans and tents.

Facilities

Two sanitary blocks with some washbasins in cubicles. Good facilities for babies and disabled visitors. Laundry facilities. Motorcaravan services. Bar, grill restaurant and takeaway (all 1/5-15/9). Swimming pools (15/5-15/9). Playground. Multisports court. Tennis. Pétanque. Children's room. Entertainment in season. No electric barbecues. WiFi over site (charged).

Open: 1 April - 30 September.

Directions

From Dunkirk ferry follow signs for St Omer D300. At Watten roundabout exit right (Gandspette) following site signs. GPS: 50.81924, 2.17753

Charges guide

Per unit incl. 2 persons and electricity	€ 22.50 - € 33.00
extra person	€ 6.20 - € 7.20

Camping Cheques accepted.

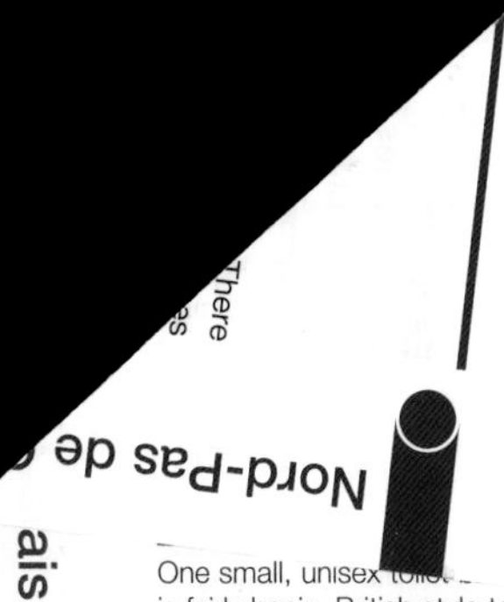

9 Escalles (Pas-de-Calais) T: 03 21 85 25 36.

fr **alanrogers.com/FR62200**

)pale is very convenient for the Calais ferries and Eurotunnel as well as the A16. The 41 pitches are terraced and set on open ground separated , some shade around the perimeter and all pitches have electricity (6/10A, es from the beach, the pitches have spectacular views over the coast lanc-Nez and the English coastline. Most pitches have hardcore wheel ctivities for children, this site is ideal for those who enjoy peace and quiet.

One small, unisex ... eated in low season, is fairly basic. British style toilets, washbasins (some in cubicles) and pushbutton showers (charged). Facilities for disabled visitors. Washing machine and dryer. Motorcaravan services (charged). Bread to order. Ice packs frozen. Caravan storage. WiFi to some areas (free). Off site: Hotel and restaurants in village 1 km. Beach 2 km. Coastal walks. Cap Blanc-Nez 2 km. Riding 3 km. Golf 4 km. Fishing and bicycle hire 5 km.

Open: 1 April - 11 November.

Directions

Escalles is 14 km southwest of Calais. Leave A16/E402 (Dunkerque, Calais, Boulogne) at exit 40. Join D243 westbound, pass through Peuplingues. After Escalles village sign, take second turning on left (watch for small site sign at road junction). The site entrance is 300 m. on left. GPS: 50.91229, 1.72047

Charges guide

Per unit incl. 2 persons and electricity	€ 16.00

No credit cards.

Guînes

Castel Camping Caravaning la Bien-Assise

D231, F-62340 Guînes (Pas-de-Calais) T: 03 21 35 20 77. E: castels@bien-assise.com

alanrogers.com/FR62010

Now a mature and well developed campsite, the history of la Bien-Assise goes back to the 1500s. There are 198 pitches here, including four with hardstanding, mainly set among mature trees with others on a newer field. Connected by surfaced and gravel roads and of a good size (up to 300 sq.m), shrubs and bushes divide most of the pitches. Being close to Calais, the Channel Tunnel exit and Boulogne, makes this a good stopping point en-route, but la Bien-Assise is well worth a longer stay. It is a very popular site which is also used by tour operators, but is well managed and there are no adverse effects.

Facilities

Three well equipped toilet blocks provide many washbasins in cubicles, showers and baby rooms. Laundry facilities. The main block is in four sections, two unisex. Two motorcaravan service points. Shop. Restaurant. Bar/grill and takeaway (all from mid April). TV room. Pool complex (mid April-mid Sept) with toboggan, covered paddling pool and outdoor pool. Play areas. Minigolf. Tennis. Bicycle hire. WiFi (charged, but free with a drink in the bar). Off site: Riding 3 km.

Open: 20 April - 15 September.

Directions

From ferry or tunnel follow signs for A16 Boulogne. Leave A16 at exit40 and take D215 towards Fréthun and Guines. At first roundabout take third exit (Fréthun, Guines). Follow signs for Guines at next five roundabouts. Site is at next roundabout, well signed. GPS: 50.86632, 1.85698

Charges guide

Per unit incl. 2 persons and electricity	€ 25.60 - € 34.40
extra person	€ 4.70 - € 6.70

Licques

Camping les Pommiers des 3 Pays

273 rue du Breuil, F-62850 Licques (Pas-de-Calais) T: 03 21 35 02 02. E: contact@pommiers-3pays.com

alanrogers.com/FR62190

This delightful site, close to the Channel ports and the A26 and A16 autoroutes, is on the outskirts of Licques in the beautiful Boulonnais countryside. Of the 58 level, grassy pitches, 27 are for touring. All have 16A electricity, water tap and drain, some have rubberised hardstanding. Motorcaravans are especially welcome. The pretty brasserie caters for dining and takeaway in pleasant surroundings near the brand new, heated pool. There is a small, fenced play area for children. A longer stay enables visits to the beaches of the Opal Coast, and many sites of both World Wars, including Dunkirk and Ypres.

Facilities

One heated toilet block with hot showers, washbasins, baby changing and a separate facility for disabled visitors. A small second block has WCs only. Laundry. Bar and restaurant with snacks (1/4-15/10). Heated swimming and paddling pools with retractable roof (25/4-15/9). Small play area. Children's activities (July/Aug). Bicycle hire. TV/games room. Field for groups/rallies. WiFi (free).

Open: 15 March - 15 November.

Directions

Licques is 27 km. south of Calais. From A26 leave at exit 2 (Licques) head southwest on D217 to Licques. Turn south on D215/D191 and site is on left in 1 km. GPS: 50.779825, 1.947707

Charges guide

Per unit incl. 2 persons and electricity	€ 22.90 - € 27.10
extra person	€ 5.10 - € 6.50

Maubeuge

Camping Municipal du Clair de Lune

212 route de Mons, F-59600 Maubeuge (Nord) T: 03 27 62 25 48. E: camping@ville-maubeuge.fr
alanrogers.com/FR59050

This is an attractive site convenient for a night stop close to the RN2 road or for longer stays if touring in the area. It is a neat and tidy municipal site with 91 marked pitches of fair size. Mainly on slightly sloping ground and separated by trim hedges, most have 6/10A electrical connections and some have hardstanding. A variety of broad-leaved trees provide shade. Reception staff are friendly and helpful and live on the site. Although there are few amenities on the site, the interesting town centre of Maubeuge itself is only about 1 km. away.

Facilities

Two circular sanitary blocks (one for men, the other for women) provide good modern facilities. Adventure-style playground. Boules. WiFi in some areas (free).
Off site: Supermarket 1.5 km. Riding and bicycle hire 2 km. Golf 2.5 km.

Open: 1 April - 30 September.

Directions

Site is on the RN2 road (the N6 in Belgium) north of the town, on the right going towards Mons.
GPS: 50.29572, 3.97645

Charges guide

Per unit incl. 2 persons and electricity	€ 14.25 - € 14.40
extra person	€ 3.61

Tournehem

Camping Caravaning Bal

500 rue du Vieux Chateau, F-62890 Tournehem sur le Hem (Pas-de-Calais) T: 03 21 35 65 90.
E: contact@hotel-bal.com **alanrogers.com/FR62170**

Camping Bal is a natural site laid out in 4.5-hectare grounds and adjacent to Hotel Bal. The site is within easy reach of the A26 (7 km). This is an excellent overnight stop and very convenient for Calais. There are 15 pitches with hardstanding for touring units, 12 in one area separated by grass. A few additional grass pitches are scattered around the site. Electricity is available. Visitors may dine in the attractive restaurant and bar at the adjacent hotel where free WiFi is provided. The local village is within walking distance and offers a bakery, pharmacy and further amenities.

Facilities

In low season there are very limited facilities for the touring pitches (a single toilet, shower and washbasin). The main sanitary block is opened for July/Aug. Small play area. Tennis court. Boules. Games room (July/Aug). Hotel bar and restaurant (from 18.00 all year). WiFi in the hotel (free). Off site: Site is five minutes' walk from the village. Fishing 5 km. Riding and bicycle hire 10 km. Golf 15 km.

Open: 1 April - 31 October.

Directions

Site and hotel well signed in Tournehem. N.B. watch out for bridge (3.1 m. high, 2.4 m. wide). Alternative route is available. GPS: 50.80852, 2.05553

Charges guide

Per unit incl. 2 persons and electricity	€ 18.00

Wimereux

Camping l'Eté Indien

Hameau Honvault, F-62930 Wimereux (Pas-de-Calais) T: 03 21 30 23 50. E: ete.indien@wanadoo.fr
alanrogers.com/FR62120

L'Eté Indien is located near the resort of Wimereux, a little to the north of Boulogne. It offers a quiet and tranquil environment in which to enjoy your holiday – despite some occasional (every 30 mins) train noise during the day. Of the 170 pitches, 44 for tourers vary in size, are well marked and are on a terraced incline furthest from the site entrance and pool complex and 41 have electrical connections (10/16A). In keeping with its Wild West theme, there is a small village of eight Indian teepees for rent, as well as 36 conventional mobile homes and chalets. Other amenities include a fishing pond and a snack bar.

Facilities

Two toilet blocks include facilities for babies and disabled visitors. Laundry. Motorcaravan services. Small shop. Bar, snack bar and takeaway, swimming pool, paddling pool (all 1/5-30/9). Play area with trampoline. Boules. Games room. Internet access and WiFi. Fishing pond. Off site: Riding adjacent. Beach 1 km. Golf 1.5 km. Wimereux, Le Touquet, Boulogne and the Nausicaa museum. Cité de l'Europe shopping complex at Calais.

Open: All year.

Directions

From the A16 take exit 32 (Wimereux) and follow signs to Wimereux (D96 and D940). After 1.5 km. turn right. Site is well signed from here and is on the left, close to a riding centre. Approach is rather narrow, with speed ramps and is poorly surfaced.
GPS: 50.75142, 1.60728

Charges guide

Per unit incl. 2 persons and electricity	€ 19.00 - € 26.00
extra person	€ 5.00 - € 7.00
child (2-7 yrs)	€ 4.00 - € 6.00
dog	€ 2.00 - € 3.00

DÉPARTEMENTS: 02 AISNE, 60 OISE, 80 SOMME

MAJOR CITY: AMIENS

The birthplace of Gothic architecture in France with no less than six cathedrals, the region is still predominately rural with deep river valleys, forests of mature beech and oak, peaceful lakes and sandy beaches, providing plenty of contrast.

Picardy lies between the Marne and Somme rivers. It has a rich history, being the settlement site of the Franks around 600 AD, undergoing periods of rule by the English and the Spanish, and as the site of some of Europe's most famous battles, notably Crécy and the Somme. More recently, two world wars have left their indelible marks on the area, with preserved World War One trenches, pristine military cemeteries and poignant memorials, from small village crosses to the towering edifices of Thiepval and Vimy.

Picardy's unspoilt coastline with its wild beauty and changing light has inspired generations of artists, Degas and Seurat among them. Today's visitors can enjoy a wide range of activities – cycling, windsurfing, kayaking, sand-yachting, horse riding and hot-air ballooning. The region also has some of the best golf courses in France. Do not miss the spectacular 'Baie de Somme' with its dunes and saltwater meadows, and the magnificent Gothic cathedral at Amiens.

Places of interest

Abbeville: church of St Vulfran; Bagatelle Château; Baie de Somme nature reserve.

Amiens: Notre Dame cathedral, impressive for its size and richly sculpted façade and the stone carvings of the choir; monument to the 1918 Battle of the Somme; remarkable 'hortillonnages' (water gardens) and interlocking canals.

Chantilly: Château of Chantilly with a 17th-century stable with a 'live' Horse Museum.

Compiègne: Seven miles east of the town is Clairière de l'Armistice. The railway coach here is a replica of the one in which the 1918 Armistice was signed and in which Hitler received the French surrender in 1942.

Laon: 12th-century cathedral; WW1 trenches; Vauclair Abbey.

Marquenterre: one of Europe's most important bird sanctuaries.

Vervins: surrounded by 60 fortified churches.

Cuisine of the region

Fresh fish and seafood are popular, as is chicory-flavoured coffee.

Carbonnade de Boeuf à la Flamande: braised beef with beer, onions and bacon.

Caudière (Chaudière, Caudrée): versions of fish and potato soup.

Ficelles Picardes: ham pancakes with mushroom sauce.

Flamiche aux poireaux: puff pastry tart with cream and leeks.

Soupe courquignoise: soup with white wine, fish, moules, leeks and Gruyère cheese.

www.picardietourisme.com/en
documentation@picardietourisme.com
(0)3 22 22 33 63

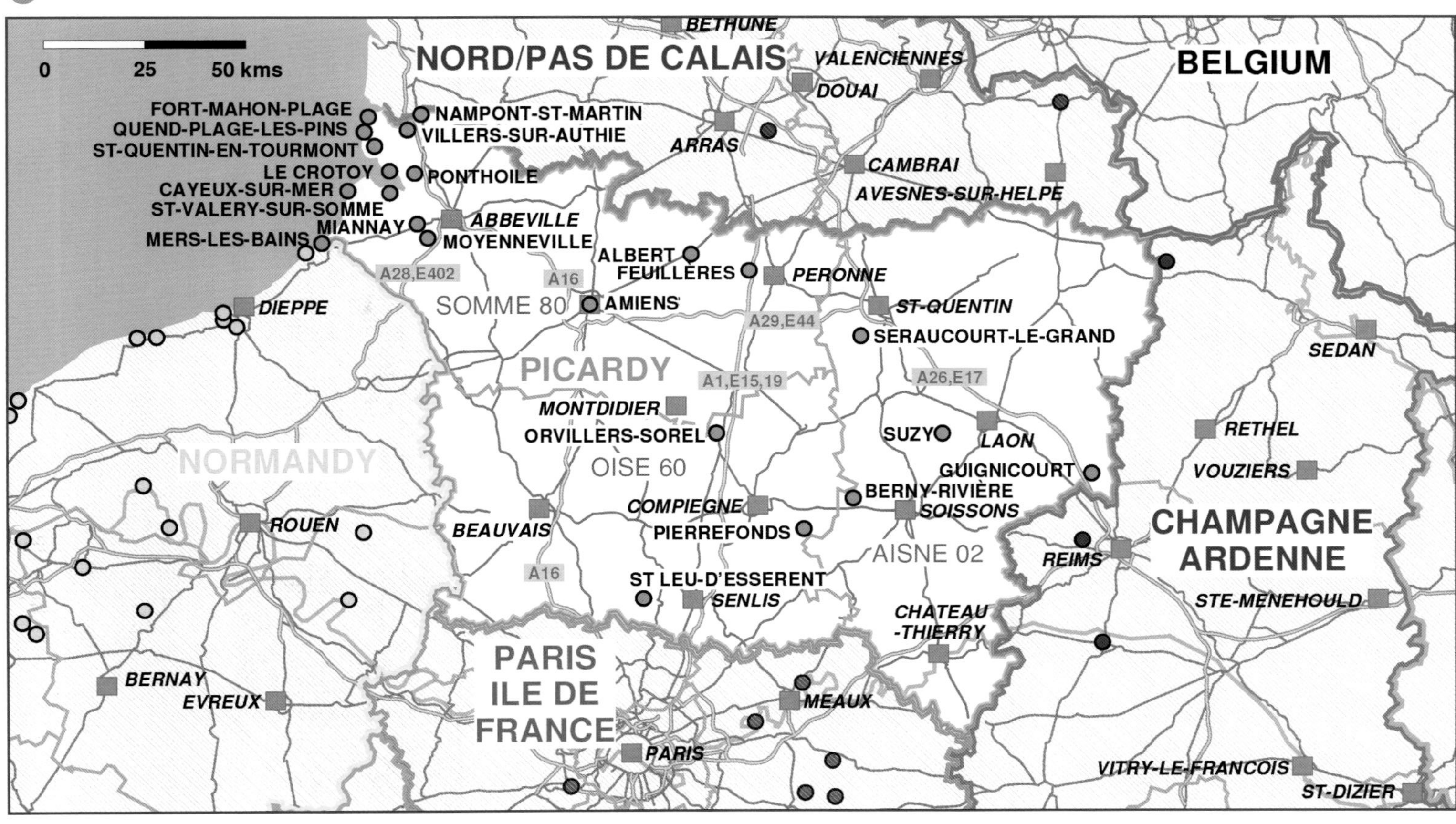

0 25 50 kms
NORD/PAS DE CALAIS
BETHUNE
VALENCIENNES
DOUAI
BELGIUM
FORT-MAHON-PLAGE
QUEND-PLAGE-LES-PINS
ST-QUENTIN-EN-TOURMONT
LE CROTOY
CAYEUX-SUR-MER
ST-VALERY-SUR-SOMME
MIANNAY
MERS-LES-BAINS
NAMPONT-ST-MARTIN
VILLERS-SUR-AUTHIE
PONTHOILE
ABBEVILLE
MOYENNEVILLE
ARRAS
CAMBRAI
AVESNES-SUR-HELPE
ALBERT
FEUILLERES
PERONNE
A28,E402
A16
SOMME 80
AMIENS
A29,E44
ST-QUENTIN
SERAUCOURT-LE-GRAND
DIEPPE
SEDAN
PICARDY
A1,E15,19
A26,E17
MONTDIDIER
ORVILLERS-SOREL
SUZY
LAON
RETHEL
NORMANDY
OISE 60
GUIGNICOURT
VOUZIERS
BERNY-RIVIÈRE
SOISSONS
COMPIEGNE
ROUEN
BEAUVAIS
PIERREFONDS
CHAMPAGNE
ARDENNE
AISNE 02
REIMS
A16
ST LEU-D'ESSERENT
SENLIS
STE-MENEHOULD
CHATEAU
-THIERRY
PARIS
ILE DE
FRANCE
BERNAY
EVREUX
MEAUX
PARIS
VITRY-LE-FRANCOIS
ST-DIZIER

Albert

Camping le Vélodrome

Rue Henry Dunant, F-80300 Albert (Somme) T: 03 64 62 22 53. E: campingalbert@laposte.net

alanrogers.com/FR80310

Camping le Vélodrome is a former municipal site that is now managed by M. Francis Lebon, who is enthusiastically developing it. The area is well laid out with mature trees. There are 82 touring pitches (seven with hardstandings for motorcaravans) on two levels with electricity hook ups (6/10A) and almost half have water and waste water disposal. The pitches are separated by young shrubs. The village of Albert is a five-minute walk away and has several places of interest, including the Somme Museum.

Facilities

The central unisex toilet block is clean and well maintained and provides free preset showers, vanity style washbasins and washing up facilities. Suite for disabled visitors with easy access. Laundry facilities. Boules. Free WiFi over part of site. Off site: Lake fishing and golf driving range within 50 m. Bicycle hire 500 m.

Open: 1 April - 15 October.

Directions

Leave N25 at exit 37 (northeast of Amiens) and take D929 to Albert. The site is signed to the east of the town. GPS: 50.01171, 2.65517

Charges guide

Per unit incl. 2 persons and electricity	€ 18.20
extra person	€ 4.00
child (under 12 yrs)	€ 3.00

Amiens

Sites et Paysages Parc des Cygnes

111 avenue des Cygnes, F-80080 Amiens (Somme) T: 03 22 43 29 28. E: alban@parcdescygnes.com

alanrogers.com/FR80100

Parc des Cygnes is just a few minutes from the N1, the A16 Paris-Calais motorway and the A29/A26 route to Rouen and the south, so it is useful as a stopover, being about 50 km. from the ports. It enjoys a riverside position with good access to Amiens. The 3.2 hectares have been completely levelled and attractively landscaped. Bushes and shrubs divide the site into areas, and trees around the perimeter provide some shade. Of the 145 pitches, 136 are for touring, with nine mobile homes for rent. All pitches are grassed with plenty of space on the tarmac roads in front of them for motorcaravans to park in wet conditions. There are 81 pitches with electricity (10A), of which 37 also have water and drainage, further water points can be accessed throughout the rest of the site.

Facilities

Two toilet blocks (both open when site is busy) with separate toilet facilities but unisex shower and washbasin area. Baby bath. Facilities for disabled visitors. Reception building also has toilets, showers and washbasins (heated as required). Laundry facilities. Shop (open on request all season), bar and takeaway (4/5-8/9; weekends only in low season). TV/games room. Bicycle hire. Fishing. WiFi over part of site (charged).

Open: 1 April - 14 October.

Directions

From A16, leave at exit 20. Take Rocade Nord (northern bypass) to exit 40, follow signs for Amiens Longpré. At roundabout take 2nd exit to Parc de Loisirs, then right to site. For satnav use rue du Grand Marais. GPS: 49.92077, 2.25962

Charges guide

Per unit incl. 2 persons and electricity	€ 21.30 - € 27.70
extra person	€ 6.70

Berny-Rivière

Caravaning la Croix du Vieux Pont

F-02290 Berny-Rivière (Aisne) T: 03 23 55 50 02. E: info@la-croix-du-vieux-pont.com

alanrogers.com/FR02030

In an idyllic setting on a bank of the River Aisne, la Croix du Vieux Pont is a smart, modern, 34-hectare site offering a wide range of high quality facilities. Many pitches are occupied by chalets and mobile homes and there is a large tour operator presence, but there are 100 pleasant touring pitches, all with 6A electrical connection and water tap. They are mostly in the older part of the site; some have concrete bases, a grass verge and a quaint stone-built barbecue with covered patio. It is easy to escape the noise and find peace around the lakes.

Facilities

The 10 toilet blocks vary in style but are all modern and kept very clean, with washbasins in cabins, some with en-suite WC or shower and washbasin. Facilities for babies and disabled visitors. Laundry. Motorcaravan services. Large supermarket and bakery. Bar, pizza and burger bars and takeaway. Poolside restaurant and lakeside bar, café and restaurant (1/4-30/9). Evening entertainment (high season). Swimming pool complex. Games rooms. Multisports area. Play areas. Fishing. Bicycle hire. Minigolf. Archery. WiFi in bar area (charged).

Open: Two weeks before Easter - 31 October.

Directions

From Compiègne take N31 towards Soissons. At site sign, turn left onto D2 to Vic-sur-Aisne then right on D91 towards Berny-Riviere and follow signs to site on right at La Fabrique. Entrance is clearly signed. GPS: 49.40487, 3.12840

Charges guide

Per unit incl. 2 persons and electricity	€ 15.00 - € 15.50
extra person	€ 9.00 - € 12.50
dog	€ 2.00

Cayeux-sur-Mer

Camping les Galets de la Mollière

Rue Faidherbe, La Mollière, F-80410 Cayeux-sur-Mer (Somme) T: 03 22 26 61 85.
E: info@campinglesgaletsdelamolliere.com **alanrogers.com/FR80190**

Cayeux-sur-Mer is a traditional seaside resort close to the Somme estuary, and les Galets de la Mollière is located just to the north of the town. Formerly a municipal site, it has undergone a recent renovation programme and now provides the opportunity to experience a typical French family holiday. The site extends over six hectares and has 195 pitches on level grass, of which 125 are reserved for touring units. All have 10A electrical connections (most French-style two-pin). The amenities include an attractive swimming pool complex, bar, shop and a games room. A fine sandy beach is adjacent to the site, a short walk across the sand dunes. Cayeux is just 3 km. away and has a good range of shops and restaurants.

Facilities

Toilet blocks include hot showers, washbasins in cabins and facilities for babies and disabled visitors. Washing machines and dryers. Small shop. Bar, snack bar and takeaway (all July/Aug). Games room. Play area. Heated outdoor swimming pool (1/5-16/9). Boules. WiFi (charged). Mobile homes for rent. Off site: Motorcaravan services (across the road from the site entrance). Beach 300 m. Riding and fishing 1 km. Bicycle hire 2 km.

Open: 1 April - 1 November.

Directions

From A16 take exit 24 (Le Crotoy) and join D32 to Rue, then D940 to St Valéry. Bypass St Valéry on D940 then join D3 (Cayeux-sur-Mer). After 4 km. you will arrive at La Mollière. Site is well signed from here. GPS: 50.2026, 1.5251

Charges guide

Per unit incl. 3 persons and electricity	€ 19.00 - € 33.00
extra person (over 1 yr)	€ 7.00

Feuillères

Camping du Château et de l'Oseraie

10 rue du Château, F-80200 Feuillères (Somme) T: 03 22 83 17 59. E: jsg-bred@wanadoo.fr
alanrogers.com/FR80180

Being very close to the A1 autoroute and in the heart of the Somme region, this site is ideally placed for either a stopover or a longer stay to investigate the many sites associated with World War I. Despite the closeness to the autoroute and the railway, the site is very quiet and peaceful and immaculately kept. There are just 30 good-sized grass pitches available for touring, each with 6/10A electricity. The rest of the site is occupied by ten modern chalets for hire and 80 privately owned mobile homes. It is an easy stroll into the pleasant village of Feuillères.

Facilities

Excellent toilet facilities, modern and spotlessly clean, include free, controllable showers. Separate en-suite room for disabled visitors. Laundry facilities. Motorcaravan services. Small shop in reception sells basics; baker calls daily in low season, bread to order in high season. Bar with TV. Simple snacks (from frozen). Heated swimming pool with linked paddling section (27/4-1/10). Games for children in high season. Multisports court. Playground for younger children. Torches useful. WiFi over site (free). Off site: Restaurant 500 m. Bicycle hire 10 km.

Open: 1 April - 31 October.

Directions

Feuillères is just off the A1 (Lille/Paris) motorway, 89 km. south of Lille. Leave at exit 13.1 and take D938 westwards towards Albert. After crossing the autoroute take D146 south to Feuillères (site well signed); in village turn right at small church to site in 200 m. GPS: 49.94813, 2.84364

Charges guide

Per unit incl. 2 persons and electricity	€ 21.40 - € 22.40
extra person	€ 5.50 - € 5.70

Fort-Mahon-Plage

Camping le Royon

1271 route de Quend, F-80120 Fort-Mahon-Plage (Somme) T: 03 22 23 40 30. E: info@campingleroyon.com
alanrogers.com/FR80040

This busy site, some two kilometres from the sea, has 376 pitches of which just 30 are used for touring units. Fourteen are near the entrance, the remainder are set amongst the mobile homes. They are of either 95 or 120 sq.m, level, marked, numbered and divided by hedges. There is also an additional space for 50 tents. Electricity (6A) and water points are available to all. The remaining 296 pitches are used for mobile homes. The site is well lit, fenced and guarded at night (€ 30 deposit for barrier card). Entertainment is organised for adults and children in July and August when it will be very full.

Facilities

Four toilet blocks provide unisex facilities with British and Turkish style WCs and washbasins in cubicles. Units for disabled visitors. Baby baths. Laundry facilities. Shop. Gas supplies. Mobile takeaway calls evenings in July/Aug. Clubroom and bar. Heated, open-air and covered pools, children's pool (15/6-15/9). Play area. TV/games room. Multisports court. Tennis. Boules. Bicycle hire. WiFi.

Open: 18 March - 1 November.

Directions

From A16 exit 24, take D32 around Rue (becomes D940 then continues as D32 Fort-Mahon-Plage). Site is on right after 19 km. GPS: 50.33229, 1.5796

Charges guide

Per unit incl. up to 3 persons and electricity	€ 19.00 - € 34.00
extra person (over 1 yr)	€ 7.00

Fort-Mahon-Plage

Camping le Vert Gazon

741 route de Quend, F-80120 Fort-Mahon-Plage (Somme) T: 03 22 23 37 69.
E: camping@camping-levertgazon.com **alanrogers.com/FR80140**

Discover the French seaside resort of Fort-Mahon-Plage by staying at this small, family run site with its 123 pitches on level grass. There are 40 places for touring units and two dedicated sections for tents. The enthusiastic owner organises entertainment in high season which will be very French in style. The whole area gets very busy in high season with all the aquatic activities you could wish for; the local council even provides free hand-drawn tri-cars to enable disabled visitors to be taken across the wide sandy beaches. There are flat cycle routes through the pine forest and down to the coast.

Facilities

The large, heated toilet block is old but renovated, giving a clean, bright feel, with unisex showers, washbasins in cubicles and British style WCs. Ramped facilities for disabled visitors. Snack bar and disco (July/Aug). Small heated swimming pool and children's pool (June-Sept). Pétanque. Play area. Entertainment (July/Aug). Bicycle hire. Free WiFi over part of site. Off site: Supermarket 1 km. Golf and beach 2 km.

Open: 1 April - 7 October.

Directions

From A16 exit 24, take D32 around Rue, when road becomes the D940 for a while, then continues again as D32 towards Fort-Mahon-Plage. Site is on right 18 km. from the A16. GPS: 50.334395, 1.57403

Charges guide

Per unit incl. 2 persons and electricity	€ 23.50 - € 26.50
extra person	€ 5.00 - € 7.00
dog	€ 2.00

Guignicourt

Camping Au bord de l'Aisne

14 rue des Godins, F-02190 Guignicourt (Aisne) T: 03 23 79 74 58. E: campingguignicourt@orange.fr
alanrogers.com/FR02060

Its enthusiastic young owners took over this former municipal site in 2011 and have transformed it into a delightful location for an overnight stop or for a longer stay. It has 100 pitches of which 80 are available for touring units with ten occupied by chalets for rent and eight by seasonal units. Pitches are generally large and level, separated by young bushes and all with 10A electrical connections available. Those along the river bank have delightful views along the tree-lined Aisne, though access is via a coded gate in the secure fence. The town is quite attractive and is worthy of an evening stroll. All amenities, including reception, pool and sanitary blocks are accessed by steps or a ramp from the pitches on the lower level.

Facilities

The new sanitary block is fully equipped, with sensor-controlled showers (one on each 'side' with en-suite washbasin), washbasins in cubicles and hairdryers. En-suite units for disabled visitors. Baby bath on ladies' side. Laundry room. Bar serving snacks and takeaways. Covered heated swimming and paddling pools with disabled access. Play area (2-4 yrs). Swings. Trampoline. Boules. Fishing. Bicycle and Segway hire. Chalets for rent.

Open: 1 April - 31 October.

Directions

From A26 exit 14, head east on D925 3.5 km. to the village and continue for a short distance. Site is signed to the right (ignore sat nav if it tries to take you down a very narrow street on left). Site is to right and immediately left at the end of the (fairly narrow) street GPS: 49.4320, 3.9704

Charges guide

Per unit incl. 2 persons and electricity	€ 28.00 - € 29.60
extra person	€ 8.80

Le Crotoy

Camping le Ridin

Lieu-dit Mayocq, F-80550 Le Crotoy (Somme) T: 03 22 27 03 22. E: leridin@baiedesommepleinair.com
alanrogers.com/FR80110

Le Ridin is a popular family site set in the countryside just 2 km. from Le Crotoy with its beaches and marina, and 6 km. from the famous bird reserve of Le Marquenterre. The site has 161 pitches, including 41 for touring; the remainder are occupied by mobile homes (for rent). There is some shade and all pitches have 4/6/10A electricity. The pitches and roads are unsuitable for large units. The site amenities are housed in beautifully converted barns across the road and these include a heated pool, fitness centre, bar/restaurant and bicycles for hire.

Facilities

Toilet blocks are heated in cool weather and provide good showers and facilities for children. Laundry facilities. Motorcaravan services. Restaurant/bar. Small shop. Swimming and paddling pools (15/5-15/9). Fitness centre. Games room. Play area. TV room. Entertainment and activity programme in high season. Bicycle hire. WiFi over site (charged). Off site: Golf 2 km. Fishing and riding 3 km.

Open: 1 April - 30 September.

Directions

From A16 (Calais-Abbéville) take exit 24 and follow signs to Le Crotoy. At roundabout at Le Crotoy turn towards St Férmin, then second road on right. GPS: 50.23905, 1.63182

Charges guide

Per unit incl. 2 persons and electricity	€ 19.00 - € 31.00
extra person	€ 5.30 - € 5.50

Le Crotoy

Flower Camping les Aubépines

800 rue de la Maye, Saint Firmin, F-80550 Le Crotoy (Somme) T: 03 22 27 01 34.

E: lesaubepines@baiedesommepleinair.com **alanrogers.com/FR80120**

This peaceful, family run site is on the edge of the Parc Ornithologique du Marquenterre and is just 1 km. from a beach on the Baie de Somme, a river estuary famous for its resident population of seals. There are 194 pitches, although 128 are occupied by privately owned mobile homes with a few available for rent. Consequently there are just 66 touring pitches scattered throughout the site. All on level ground, they are of a reasonable to good size, separated by hedges and trees and with water taps and electricity (3-10A) close by.

Facilities

Two unisex toilet blocks, fairly basic but clean and in good order. Washbasins in cubicles, pushbutton showers and some larger cubicles with shower and basin. Baby bath and toilet. Facilities for disabled visitors are minimal (no grab rails). Laundry room. Small well stocked shop. Heated outdoor pool (1/5-15/9). Indoor games. Small play area. Bicycle hire. Outdoor fitness machines. WiFi over site (charged). Off site: Beaches 1 km. and 10 km. Fishing 2 km. Riding, bird sanctuary, tennis 3 km. Golf 10 km.

Open: 1 April - 1 November.

Directions

Le Crotoy is on the D940 Berck-Le Tréport road. At roundabout for town, take D4 to St Firmin, turn right at next roundabout. After village sign, turn left to site (signed) on right in 500 m. GPS: 50.24976, 1.61196

Charges guide

Per unit incl. 2 persons and electricity	€ 19.00 - € 31.00
extra person	€ 5.00 - € 6.00
child (3-7 yrs)	€ 4.00 - € 5.00

Mers-les-Bains

Flower Camping le Rompval

Lieu-dit Blengues, F-80350 Mers-les-Bains (Somme) T: 02 35 84 43 21.

E: lerompval@baiedesommepleinair.com **alanrogers.com/FR80220**

Le Rompval is a former municipal site located in the pleasant seaside resort of Mers-les-Bain, around 25 km. west of Abbéville, at the mouth of the Bresle river. There are 132 pitches (77 for touring) and these are grassy and of a good size. All are equipped with 8A electricity, and 30 also have water and waste water connections. Around 46 pitches are occupied by chalets (21 available for rent). The site boasts some interesting architecture and a number of amenities including a small shop and takeaway food service and a heated, covered pool and paddling pool. The nearest beach is 2.5 km. distant. This is a great sweep of sand, ideal for sand yachting and windsurfing.

Facilities

Facilities for disabled visitors. Motorcaravan services. Bar and takeaway (10/7-25/8). Shop. Play area. Activity programme (high season). Heated, indoor pool. Chalets for rent. WiFi over part of site (free). Off site: Beach 2.5 km. Windsurfing and sand yachting. Mers-les-Bains (attractive seaside resort with Belle Epoque villas). Cliff top walks. Supermarket.

Open: 1 April - 6 November.

Directions

From north, leave A16 at exit 23 (Abbeville Nord). Briefly join southbound A28 then take D925 to Eu. Here, head west on D1015 to Mers-les-Bains and follow signs to the site. GPS: 50.077262, 1.414474

Charges guide

Per unit incl. 2 persons and electricity	€ 18.00 - € 25.50

Camping Cheques accepted.

Miannay

Sites et Paysages le Clos Cacheleux

12 route de Bouillancourt, F-80132 Miannay (Somme) T: 03 22 19 17 47.

E: raphael@camping-lecloscacheleux.fr **alanrogers.com/FR80210**

Le Clos Cacheleux is a well situated campsite of eight hectares bordering woodland in the park of the Château Bouillancourt, which dates from the 18th century. The site was first opened in July 2008. It is 11 km. from the Bay of the Somme, regarded as being amongst the most beautiful bays in France. There are 90 very large, grassy pitches (230-250 sq.m) and all have electricity (10A, Europlug), five also have water and waste water. The aim of the owners is to make your stay as enjoyable as possible by providing a high quality site, and improvements are being made each year. All visitors have access to the swimming pool, shop, bar and miniclub of the sister site, le Val de Trie, 500 m. away along a steep road.

Facilities

Two modern sanitary blocks are well maintained and clean, with a baby room and facilities for disabled visitors. Washing machine and dryer. Fridge hire. Adult fitness area. Fishing pond. Free WiFi. Torch essential. At the sister site: shop, bar with terrace. Restaurant and takeaway (27/4-1/9). Covered pool (13/4-30/9). Library and TV room. Play area. Boules. Picnic tables. Freezer for ice packs. Four tree houses to rent.

Open: 1 April - 15 October.

Directions

From A28 at Abbeville take D925 towards Eu and Le Tréport; not towards Moyenville. Turn left in Miannay onto D86 towards Toeufles. After 2 km. site is on right. GPS: 50.08676, 1.71515

Charges guide

Per unit incl. 2 persons and electricity	€ 19.50 - € 27.90
extra person	€ 3.40 - € 5.80

Moyenneville

Camping le Val de Trie

Rue des Sources, Bouillancourt-sous-Miannay, F-80870 Moyenneville (Somme) T: 03 22 31 48 88.
E: raphael@camping-levaldetrie.fr **alanrogers.com/FR80060**

Le Val de Trie is a natural countryside site in woodland, near a small village. The 80 numbered, grassy touring pitches are of a good size, divided by hedges and shrubs with mature trees providing good shade in most areas, and all have electricity (10A). Eleven also have water and waste water. It can be very quiet in April, June, September and October. If there is no-one on site, just choose a pitch or call at the farm to book in. This is maturing into a well managed site with modern facilities and a friendly, relaxed atmosphere. It is well situated for the coast and also the cities of Amiens and Abbeville.

Facilities

Two clean, recently renovated sanitary blocks include washbasins in cubicles, units for babies and disabled visitors. Laundry facilities. Microwave. Shop. Bar with TV. Bread to order and butcher visits in season. Snack bar with takeaway (27/4-30/8). Room above bar for children. Covered heated swimming pool with jacuzzi (13/4-29/9). Outdoor pool for children (27/4-8/9). WiFi (free).

Open: 1 April - 4 October.

Directions

From A28 take exit 2 near Abbeville and D925 to Miannay. Turn left on D86 to Bouillancourt-sous-Miannay: site signed in village.
GPS: 50.0855, 1.71492

Charges guide

Per unit incl. 2 persons and electricity	€ 18.90 - € 27.10
extra person	€ 3.30 - € 5.60

Camping Cheques accepted.

Nampont-Saint Martin

Camping la Ferme des Aulnes

Fresne, F-80120 Nampont-Saint Martin (Somme) T: 03 22 29 22 69. E: contact@fermedesaulnes.com
alanrogers.com/FR80070

This peaceful site with 144 pitches has been developed on the meadows of a small, 17th-century farm on the edge of Fresne and is lovingly cared for by its new enthusiastic owners, Marie and Denis Lefort, and their hard working team. Restored outbuildings house reception and the facilities, around a central courtyard that boasts a fine heated swimming pool. A new development includes a bar and entertainment room. Outside, facing the main gate, are 20 large, level grass pitches for touring. There is also an area for tents. The remaining 22 touring pitches are in the main complex, hedged and fairly level.

Facilities

Both sanitary blocks are heated and include washbasins in cubicles, with a large cubicle for disabled visitors. Motorcaravan services. Shop, piano bar and restaurant. TV room. Swimming pool (16x9 m; heated and with cover for cooler weather). Jacuzzi and sauna. Fitness room. Aquagym. Balnéotherapy. Playground. Boules. Archery. Fishing. WiFi throughout (free). Shuttle service to stations and airports. Off site: Private lake fishing (free) 2 mins. away. River fishing 100 m.

Open: 25 March - 1 November.

Directions

From Calais, take A16 to exit 25 and turn for Arras for 2 km. and then towards Abbeville on N1. At Nampont-St Martin turn west on D485 and site will be found in 2 km. GPS: 50.33645, 1.71285

Charges guide

Per unit incl. 2 persons and electricity	€ 27.00 - € 37.00
extra person	€ 7.00
child (under 7 yrs)	€ 4.00

Camping Cheques accepted.

Orvillers-Sorel

Aestiva Camping de Sorel

Rue Saint-Claude, F-60490 Orvillers-Sorel (Oise) T: 03 44 85 02 74. E: contact@aestiva.fr
alanrogers.com/FR60020

Aestiva Camping de Sorel is north of Compiègne, close to the A1 motorway and is ideal as an overnight stop. There are 120 large grassy pitches, of which 70 are available for touring, all with electricity connections (three with water and drainage). The original farm buildings have been carefully converted to house the site's main amenities including a bar, restaurant and the toilet facilities. The site is open for a long season but most amenities are only open from April to September. The site is, however, close to the village of Sorel with its shops and restaurants. There are five mobile homes for rent.

Facilities

Toilet block with facilities for children and disabled visitors. Laundry facilities. Motorcaravan services. Shop (15/5-30/10). Bar, restaurant, snack bar (all season) and takeaway 15/5-15/10). Play area. Boules. Hairdressing service. Multigym and sauna. WiFi throughout (charged). Off site: Tennis. Fishing 5 km. Riding and golf 8 km. Compiègne 15 km. Parc Astérix 57 km. Paris 95 km.

Open: 1 February - 15 December.

Directions

Take exit 11 from the A1 motorway (Lille-Paris) and join the northbound N17. Site is signed to the right on reaching village of Sorel after 8 km.
GPS: 49.56688, 2.70841

Charges guide

Per unit incl. 2 persons and electricity	€ 21.00
extra person	€ 6.00

Camping Cheques accepted.

Pierrefonds

Camping le Coeur de la Forêt

34 rue de l'Armistice, F-60350 Pierrefonds (Oise) T: 03 44 42 80 83. E: camping-de-pierrefonds@orange.fr

alanrogers.com/FR60070

The town of Pierrefonds is dominated by an impressive château that will be instantly recognised by followers of the TV series Merlin. The campsite is on the edge of the town and aims to attract traditional campers as well as holiday-makers looking for something different in the way of accommodation. You are sure of a warm welcome from the very friendly manager. There are currently 59 pitches, including five occupied by seasonal or rental units. All have 10A electrical connections, water and drain. They are separated by well trimmed hedges and are mainly level and of a good size, though a few are sloping.

Facilities

Traditional building at entrance houses all facilities: separate toilet provision for men and ladies (well maintained and kept very clean) with controllable showers and some washbasins in cubicles. Washing machine. Reception from which drinks and ices are served on the little terrace and where bread and meal baskets can be ordered. Small play unit (3-8 yrs). Bicycle hire. WiFi around reception (free) Two small vintage caravans, a wooden cabin and a 'Hobbit's House' for hire.

Open: 12 April - 2 October.

Directions

From A1 exit 9 (from south) or 10 (from north) follow signs for Compiègne (D200 or N31) and follow ring road (Rocade Sud) east; this becomes D973. Continue southeast on D973 (Pierrefonds) when ring road turns north. Site is on left just before village. GPS: 49.35437, 2.97574

Charges guide

Per unit incl. 2 persons and electricity	€ 16.00 - € 18.00

No credit cards.

Ponthoile

Camping la Safrière

82 RD 140, Morlay, F-80860 Ponthoile (Somme) T: 03 22 27 07 09. E: camping-la-safriere@wanadoo.fr

alanrogers.com/FR80320

A beautifully laid out and well maintained, family run site, la Safrière is a 500 m. walk from the coast and its cycle paths and walks around the Baie de Somme. The site has 125 pitches including 30 touring pitches in various parts of the site. Most with 6/10A electricity, the pitches are large, flat and very well cared for. Almost all are separated by neatly trimmed hedges giving good privacy. This is a quiet, peaceful site but still provides a range of facilities for children. Six gravel pitches for motorcaravans (up to 10 m) are in a dedicated part of the site beside fields, a stream and a fishing pool. Four have electricity connections. Many customers return to this site again and again.

Facilities

Main sanitary block in centre of site. Part unisex plus separate showers and toilets for ladies. Baby room. Toilet and separate shower room for disabled visitors. Two smaller blocks with WCs and washbasins. Boules. Minigolf. Fishing. Bicycle hire. Bouncy castle, trampolines, climbing frame on sand. Games room. WiFi by reception and games room (free). Off site: Riding 1 km. Beach and boat launching 4 km. Golf and sailing 15 km.

Open: 1 April - 31 October.

Directions

Leave A16 at exit 24 and take D32. At second roundabout take D235 (Route de Ponthoile). In Ponthoile keep on D235 (route de Morlay). In Morlay turn left on D140 and site is on the left after 300 m. GPS: 50.20928, 1.69149

Charges guide

Per unit incl. 2 persons and electricity	€ 23.00 - € 23.50
extra person	€ 5.00

Quend-Plage-les-Pins

Flower Camping les Vertes Feuilles

25 route de la Plage Monchaux, F-80120 Quend-Plage-les-Pins (Somme) T: 03 22 23 55 12.
E: contact@lesvertesfeuilles.com **alanrogers.com/FR80130**

Situated on the Picardy coast, four kilometres from the beach, this three-hectare site provides 60 touring pitches out of a total of 150, all with electricity hook-ups (6/10A). The remainder contain a mix of mobile homes and semi-residential caravans. The site roads are slightly narrow, but one or two larger units can be accommodated with care. Some of the very reasonably sized pitches are a little uneven with patchy grass. This whole area is bustling in high season with many campsites and holiday villages but this makes for a wonderful French-style seaside holiday. Some entertainment is provided in high season.

Facilities

One large toilet block, dated but clean, has unisex showers, washbasins in cubicles and three family rooms. Ramped facilities for disabled visitors. Small shop, brasserie and snack bar. Bread delivery. Covered heated swimming pool. Play area and indoor games room. Bicycle hire. WiFi over site (charged). Off site: Golf 2 km. Fishing 3 km. Beach 4 km. Riding 5 km. Local markets. Free access to tennis courts in Rue and Le Crotoy.

Open: 26 March - 2 November.

Directions

From A16 exit 24 (Rue), take D32 around Rue, when road becomes D940, then continues again as D32 towards Fort-Mahon-Plage. After left turn for Quend-Plage, site on left. GPS: 50.31950, 1.60583

Charges guide

Per unit incl. 2 persons and electricity	€ 19.50 - € 33.00
extra person	€ 4.50 - € 6.00

Saint Leu-d'Esserent

Camping Campix

B.P. 37, F-60340 Saint Leu-d'Esserent (Oise) T: 03 44 56 08 48. E: campix@orange.fr

alanrogers.com/FR60010

This informal site has been unusually developed in a former sandstone quarry on the outskirts of the small town. The quarry walls provide a sheltered, peaceful environment and trees soften the slopes. Not a neat, manicured site, the 160 pitches are in small groups on different levels with stone and gravel access roads (some fairly steep). Electricity (6A) is available to all the pitches. There are many secluded corners, mostly for smaller units and tents, and space for children to explore (parents must supervise – some areas, although fenced, could be dangerous). There are roulottes and wooden chalets for rent.

Facilities

A large building houses reception and two clean, heated sanitary units – one for touring units, the other (open July/Aug) usually reserved for groups. Two suites for disabled campers double as baby rooms. Laundry area. Facilities may be congested at peak times. Motorcaravan services. Shop (July/Aug). Bread and milk daily. Pizza and other Italian food delivered in the evenings (July/Aug). Outdoor swimming pool (10/5-10/9). Play area. Volleyball. Basketball. Bicycle hire. Torches are advised.
Off site: Fishing 1 km. Riding and golf 5 km.

Open: 7 March - 30 November.

Directions

St Leu-d'Esserent is 11 km. west of Senlis, 5 km. northwest of Chantilly. From north on A1 autoroute take Senlis exit, from Paris the Chantilly exit. Site north of town off D12 towards Cramoisy, and signed in village. Do not use sat nav for final approach.
GPS: 49.22487, 2.42709

Charges guide

Per unit incl. 2 persons and electricity	€ 17.00 - € 25.00
extra person	€ 4.50 - € 7.00

Camping Cheques accepted.

Saint Quentin-en-Tourmont

Camping Le Champ Neuf

8 rue du Champ Neuf, F-80120 Saint Quentin-en-Tourmont (Somme) T: 03 22 25 07 94.
E: contact@camping-lechampneuf.com **alanrogers.com/FR80020**

Le Champ Neuf is located in Saint Quentin-en-Tourmont on the Bay of the Somme. It is a quiet site, 900 m. from the ornithological reserve of Marquenterre, the favourite stop for thousands of migratory birds; birdwatchers will appreciate the dawn chorus and varied species. This eight-hectare site has 161 pitches with 34 for touring, on level grass with 6/10A electricity. The site is only 75 minutes from Calais and 18 km. from the motorway. An excellent covered pool complex has been added, including a flume, jacuzzi and pool for toddlers, and a fitness room and sauna. This area is particularly good for cycling with several level, traffic-free routes nearby. The Bay of the Somme, Saint Valéry, watersports and the cathedral city of Amiens are all close.

Facilities

Four unisex toilet blocks have showers, washbasins in cubicles, family cubicles and facilities for disabled visitors. Laundry facilities. Motorcaravan services. Bar, snack bar and entertainment area. Play area. TV. Games room. Covered, heated pool complex including slides (from 5/4), jacuzzi and children's pool. Fitness room. Sauna. Multisports court. WiFi over site (free). Gas barbecues not accepted. Off site: Shops, restaurants and bars in Rue 7 km.

Open: 1 April - 31 October.

Directions

From A16 exit 24, take D32 towards and around Rue. At second roundabout take second exit on D940, then left on D4 for 1.5 km. before turning right on D204 to Le Bout des Crocs. Site is signed to the left. GPS: 50.26895, 1.60263

Charges guide

Per unit incl. 2 persons and electricity	€ 20.00 - € 31.00
extra person	€ 5.50 - € 6.50
child (2-7 yrs)	€ 4.00 - € 5.00
dog	€ 2.00

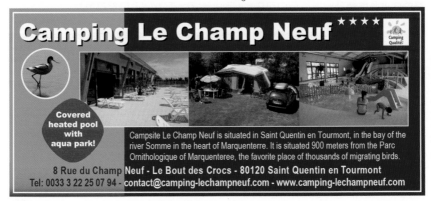

Saint Valery-sur-Somme

Camping Airotel Le Walric

345 route d'Eu, F-80230 Saint Valery-sur-Somme (Somme) T: 03 22 26 81 97.

E: info@campinglewalric.com **alanrogers.com/FR80150**

A clean, well kept and well managed site, Le Walric is about 75 minutes from Calais. It has completely updated with a bar and snack bar, a pool complex (now with a cover), two play areas entertainment in high season. There are 263 well laid out, large and level grass pitches. Of these, 47 with 6A electricity connections are for touring, with the remainder used for a mix of mobile homes and semi-residential caravans. The site's situation on the outskirts of the town make it an ideal holiday location. Medieval Saint Valéry is renowned for its association with William the Conqueror. The cathedral cities of Amiens and Abbeville are nearby.

Facilities

Two heated toilet blocks include British style toilets, washbasins in cubicles and hot showers. Facilities for disabled visitors. Laundry room with baby changing. Motorcaravan services. Shop. Bar with snacks and TV. Heated outdoor pool with retractable roof. Play areas. Tennis. Volleyball. Boules. Outdoor fitness equipment for adults. Bicycle hire can be arranged. Children's club and entertainment (July/Aug). WiFi throughout (charged).

Open: 1 April - 1 November.

Directions

From A16 exit 24, follow D32 across N1. At roundabout take D235 to Morlay; turn left on D940 and continue around St Valery until fourth roundabout where take first exit on D3 to site on right. GPS: 50.1838, 1.61791

Charges guide

Per unit incl. 3 persons and electricity	€ 19.00 - € 35.00
extra person	€ 7.00

Saint Valéry-sur-Somme

Castel Camping le Château de Drancourt

B.P. 80022, F-80230 Saint Valery-sur-Somme (Somme) T: 03 22 26 93 45. E: chateau.drancourt@wanadoo.fr **alanrogers.com/FR80010**

This is a popular, busy and lively site within easy distance of the Channel ports. There are 340 pitches in total, of which 167 are for touring units. These are mainly on level grass, of good size, some in shade and others in the open, all with electricity (10A). The remaining pitches are divided between mobile homes/chalets for rent, privately owned accommodation and several tour operators. The site is well landscaped and, in spite of the numbers in high season, does not feel overcrowded. Two of the pools have been renovated and the wide range of activities on offer will keep children occupied. A full programme of events for all ages take place on a daily basis throughout most of the season.

Facilities

Three toilet blocks include washbasins in cubicles, family bathrooms and facilities for disabled visitors. Laundry facilities. Shop. Two bars. Restaurant and takeaway. TV rooms, one for children. Games room. Three pools (two covered, all heated 15/5-31/8). Tennis. Golf practice range. Minigolf. Bicycle hire. Fishing. Large field for ball games. Pony riding in season. WiFi in bar area (charged).

Open: 12 April - 14 September.

Directions

Site is 2.5 km. south of St Valery and signed from the D940 Berck-Le Tréport road. Turn south on D48 Estréboeuf road. Turn immediately left to Drancourt and site. GPS: 50.15281, 1.63614

Charges guide

Per unit incl. 2 persons and electricity	€ 21.00 - € 37.00
extra person	€ 4.00 - € 8.00

Seraucourt-le-Grand

Camping du Vivier aux Carpes

10 rue Charles Voyeux, F-02790 Seraucourt-le-Grand (Aisne) T: 03 23 60 50 10.

E: contact@camping-picardie.com **alanrogers.com/FR02000**

Vivier aux Carpes is a small quiet site close to the A26, two hours from Calais, so is an ideal overnight stop but is also worthy of a longer stay. The 65 well spaced pitches are at least 100 sq.m, mainly on flat grass with dividing hedges. The 40 for touring units all have 10A electricity and there are special pitches on gravel for motorcaravans. This is a neat, purpose designed site imaginatively set out around attractive fishing ponds, which are naturally unfenced, and has a comfortable feel. The enthusiastic owners speak excellent English and are keen to welcome British visitors.

Facilities

The clean, modern toilet block has spacious cubicles with pushbutton showers and a couple of washbasins in cabins. Toilet facilities may be under a little pressure at busy times. Separate, heated suite for disabled visitors. Laundry facilities. Basic motorcaravan services. Open-air snack bar and takeaway (July/Aug). Large games room. Small play area. Bicycle hire. Pétanque. Fishing (€ 6/day, € 35/week). Rallies welcome. WiFi over site (charged).

Open: 1 March - 31 October.

Directions

Leave A26 (Calais-Reims) at exit 11. Take D1 left (Soissons) for 4 km, then take Seraucourt-le-Grand exit onto D8; at Essigny-le-Grand (4 km) turn sharp right on D72 to Seraucourt (5 km). Site entrance is on right between houses. GPS: 49.78217, 3.21403

Charges guide

Per unit incl. 2 persons and electricity	€ 21.00
extra person	€ 4.50
child (under 10 yrs)	€ 3.50

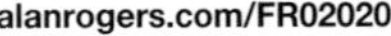

Suzy

Camping les Etangs du Moulin

F-02320 Suzy (Aisne) T: 03 23 80 92 86. E: contact@etangsdumoulin.fr
alanrogers.com/FR02020

515

alan rogers Runner up 2015 Awards

Camping les Etangs du Moulin is a unique, small and friendly site to the south of Saint Quentin, which over the last few years has been transformed into a Wild West-themed holiday village. As well as the 61 touring pitches (with 6A electricity), an assortment of teepees, wagons and cabins are available to rent. There are no fewer than eight lakes here, two stocked with trout and two with carp, making this site a good choice for anglers (fishing materials available for hire). The reception, restaurant and bar also follow the Wild West theme. Mountain bikes can be hired and the site's owners can recommend a number of routes.

Facilities

Two well maintained and modern unisex toilet blocks include hot showers and washbasins in cubicles. Family shower room with baby bath. Laundry facilities. Restaurant, bar/snack bar. Heated outdoor swimming pool. Play area. Trampolines. Volleyball. Fishing. Mountain bike and go-kart hire. Teepees, wagons and cabins for rent. WiFi throughout (charged).

Open: 1 April - 30 September.

Directions

The site is close to the village of Suzy, to the west of Laon. From Laon, head west on D7 to Cessieres and then follow signs to Suzy and the site. GPS: 49.548957, 3.470092

Charges guide

Per unit incl. 2 persons and electricity	€ 23.10 - € 25.60

Villers-sur-Authie

Sites et Paysages le Val d'Authie

20 route de Vercourt, F-80120 Villers-sur-Authie (Somme) T: 03 22 29 92 47.
E: camping@valdauthie.fr **alanrogers.com/FR80090**

In a village location, this well organised site is within 12 km. of several beaches, but also has its own excellent pool complex, small restaurant and bar. The owner has carefully controlled the size of the site, leaving space for a leisure area with an indoor pool complex. There are 164 pitches in total, but with many holiday homes and chalets (some for hire), there are only 50 for touring units. These are on grass, some are divided by small hedges, with 6/10A electric hook-ups, and ten have full services. Amenities on the site include a fitness trail and running track, a mountain bike circuit and plenty of good paths for evening strolls. Excellent meals can be taken in the site's own lovely restaurant which has a superb upstairs room overlooking the pool and gardens (book at busy times). Ideas for excursions include the 15/16th-century chapel and hospice and the Aviation Museum at Rue, Valloire Abbey and gardens, and the steam railway which runs from Le Crotoy to Cayeux-sur-Mer around the Baie de Somme. Another enjoyable family day out would be to cycle the traffic-free route around the bay.

Facilities

Good toilet facilities, some unisex, include shower and washbasin units, washbasins in cubicles. Limited facilities for babies and disabled visitors. Shop. Bar/restaurant (2/4-25/9; hours vary). Swimming and paddling pools (lifeguards in July/Aug). Playground, club room with TV. Weekend entertainment in season. Multisports court, beach volleyball, football, boules and tennis court. Trampoline. Fitness room including sauna (charged). Bicycle hire. Internet access (free). WiFi (charged).

Open: 1 April - 3 October.

Directions

Villers-sur-Authie is 25 km. northwest of Abbeville. From A16 exit 24 take N1 to Vron, then left on D175 to Villers-sur-Authie. Or use D85 from Rue, or D485 from Nampont-St Martin. Site is at southern end of village at road junction. GPS: 50.31357, 1.69488

Charges guide

Per unit incl. 2 persons and electricity	€ 25.50 - € 31.00
extra person	€ 6.50

Camping Cheques accepted.

DÉPARTEMENTS: 75 PARIS, 77 SEINE-ET-MARNE, 78 YVELINES, 91 ESSONE, 92 HAUTS-DE-SEINE, 93 SEINE-ST-DENIS, 94 VAL DE MARNE, 95 VAL D'OISE

MAJOR CITIES: PARIS, VERSAILLES, IVRY, MELUN, NANTERRE, BOBIGNY, CRETEIL AND PONTOISE

With its tree-lined boulevards, museums, art galleries, the Arc de Triomphe and, of course, the famous Eiffel Tower, this cosmopolitan city has plenty to offer. Less than 30 miles from the heart of the capital, a fun-packed trip to Disneyland Paris is also within reach.

It is almost impossible to capture the magic and sophistication of Paris, an elegant city that enchants every visitor, whether they are scaling the heights of the Eiffel Tower, gliding along the Seine on a 'bateau mouche', or just watching the world go by from a romantic pavement café.

Away from the famous sights and luxurious shops, a verdant oasis awaits in the hills and secret woodlands of the Ile de France. Square bell towers in gentle valleys, white silos on endless plains of wheat; soft and harmonious landscapes painted and praised by La Fontaine, Corot and all the landscape painters. Paris is surrounded by forests, Fontainebleau, Compiègne, Saint-Germain-en-Laye and majestic châteaux such as Fontainbleau and Vaux-le-Vicomte.

Disneyland Resort Paris provides a great day out for all the family with two fantastic theme parks with over 70 attractions and shows to choose from. On the outskirts of Paris is Parc Astérix, with one of Europe's most impressive roller-coasters.

Places of interest

Fontainebleau: château and national museum, history of Napoléon from 1804-1815.

Malmaison: château and national museum.

Meaux: agricultural centre; Gothic cathedral, chapter house and palace.

Paris: obviously! The list of places is too extensive to include here.

St Germain-en-Laye: château; Gallo-roman and Merovingian archaeological museum.

Sèvres: ceramics museum.

Thoiry: château and Parc Zoologique, 450-hectare park with gardens and African reserve containing 800 animals.

Versailles: Royal Castle, Royal Apartments, Hall of Mirrors, Royal Opera and French History Museum.

Cuisine of the region

Although it has no specific regional cuisine, Paris and the Ile de France offer a wide selection of dishes from all the regions of France. Paris also has a wide choice of restaurants serving dishes from around the world.

www.new-paris-idf.com
info@nouveau-paris-idf.com
(0)1 44 50 19 98

Boulancourt

Camping Ile de Boulancourt

6 allée des Marronniers, F-77760 Boulancourt (Seine-et-Marne) T: 01 64 24 13 38.

E: campingiledeboulancourt@orange.fr **alanrogers.com/FR77180**

In pleasant countryside south of Paris and within easy reach of the Palais de Fontainebleau, this is a traditional, no-frills campsite occupying an attractive location on the bank of the River Essonne. There are 110 pitches on level grassland with groups of trees providing some shade; electricity connections (6A) are available. Nature lovers will be in their element, with woodland paths and waterways surrounding the site, and the forest of Fontainebleau with its major climbing sites and the Parc Naturel Régional du Gatinais Français both a short drive (or an energetic ride) away. A few mobile homes and chalets can be hired, and two new ones are planned for 2016. The village of Boulancourt is just round the corner and has a small shop and a bar/restaurant where fresh bread is delivered. Nearby Malesherbes offers a wider choice of shops and restaurants. If you would like a day out in Paris but don't fancy driving, it is possible to take a train from Malesherbes.

Facilities

Heated sanitary block with facilities for babies and disabled visitors. Motorcaravan services. Pétanque. Playground. Trampoline. New hospitality room (library, games, kitchen and space for campers). Fishing. Botanical walks. Bicycle hire. WiFi throughout (charged). Picnic evenings and floral workshops in high season. Off site: Village (shop and bar/restaurant) 250 m. Tennis, football field and golf course 800 m. Spa 800 m. Swimming pool and archery 3 km. River swimming, sailing, canoeing, kayaking, climbing wall and acrobranches 5 km. Malesherbes 7 km. Milly-la-Forêt 20 km. Nemours 25 km. Fontainebleau 30 km.

Open: All year excl. Christmas week.

Directions

Boulancourt is 75 km. due south of Paris (88 km. by road). From A6 Paris/Lyon motorway, leave at exit 14 (Malesherbes) and head southwest on D152 to Malesherbes. In 15 km. turn south on D948 (Orléans), bear left on D948/D410 (site signed) and continue south on D410 (Puiseaux). Turn right then left on D103A2 to Boulancourt and to site on right after village. GPS: 48.25657, 2.43575

Charges guide

Per unit incl. 2 persons and electricity	€ 18.50
extra person	€ 4.90
child (2-12 yrs)	€ 3.60
dog	€ 1.50

Crèvecoeur-en-Brie

Caravaning des 4 Vents

22 rue de Beauregard, F-77610 Crèvecoeur-en-Brie (Seine-et-Marne) T: 01 64 07 41 11. E: f.george@free.fr

alanrogers.com/FR77040

This peaceful, pleasant site has been owned and run by the same family for over 50 years. There are around 200 pitches, with a few permanent and seasonal units, however, there are 140 spacious grassy pitches for touring units, well separated by good hedges, all with 6A electricity and a water tap shared between two pitches. The whole site is very well cared for and landscaped with flowers and trees everywhere. This is a great family site with the swimming pool and games facilities located at the top end of the site so that campers are not disturbed. Some aircraft noise can be expected.

Facilities

Three sanitary blocks (two heated in cooler weather) provide washbasins (mainly in cubicles) and pushbutton showers. Facilities for disabled visitors. Laundry facilities. Motorcaravan services. Mobile snack bar and pizzeria (July/Aug, 16.00-23.00) and a baker (07.30-11.00). Well fenced but unsupervised, circular swimming pool (16 m. diam; June-Sept). Playground. Games room. Volleyball. Boules pitch. WiFi (free).

Open: 20 March - 1 November.

Directions

Crèvecoeur is just off the D231 between A4 exit 13 and Provins. From north, pass obelisk and turn right onto the C3 in 3 km. From south 19 km. after junction with N4, turn left at signs to village. Follow site signs. GPS: 48.75060, 2.89714

Charges guide

Per unit incl. 2 persons and electricity	€ 30.00
extra person (over 5 yrs)	€ 6.00
dog	€ 4.00

Jablines

International de Jablines

Base de Loisirs, F-77450 Jablines (Seine-et-Marne) T: 01 60 26 09 37. E: welcome@camping-jablines.com

alanrogers.com/FR77030

Jablines is a modern site which, with the leisure facilities of the adjacent Espace Loisirs, offers an interesting alternative to other sites in the region. Man-made lakes provide opportunities for many water-based activities. The Grand Lac is said to have the largest beach on the Ile-de-France. The site itself has 154 pitches, of which 143 are for touring units. Most are of a good size (100-120 sq.m), often slightly sloping, with gravel hardstanding and grass, accessed by tarmac roads and marked by young trees. All have 10A electrical connections; 60 are fully serviced. There are 11 wooden chalets for rent. The whole complex close to the Marne has been developed around old gravel workings. Whilst staying on the campsite admission to the Base de Loisirs is free. Water activities include catamaran sailing, windsurfing, water boarding, canoeing, fishing and supervised bathing, plus a large equestrian centre, an orienteering course, a multisports court and mountain bike trails. In high season, the activities at the leisure complex are supplemented by a bar/restaurant and a range of very French-style group activities.

Facilities

Two toilet blocks, heated in cool weather, include pushbutton showers, some washbasins in cubicles. Facilities for disabled visitors. Laundry facilities. Motorcaravan services (charged). Shop. Play area. Boules. Public telephone. WiFi throughout (free). Ticket sales for Disneyland and Parc Astérix. Mobile homes for rent. Off site: Bar/restaurant adjacent (500 m) at Base de Loisirs with watersports, riding, tennis and minigolf.

Open: 26 March - 29 October.

Directions

From A1 south, follow signs for Marne-la-Vallée using A104. Take exit 6A Clay-Souilly on N3 (Meaux). After 6 km. turn south on D404 and follow signs. At park entry keep left for campsite. GPS: 48.91378, 2.73451

Charges guide

Per unit incl. 2 persons and electricity	€ 26.00 - € 33.00
extra person	€ 7.00 - € 8.00
child (3-11 yrs)	€ 5.00 - € 6.00

Maisons-Laffitte

Camping Caravaning International

1 rue Johnson, F-78600 Maisons-Laffitte (Yvelines) T: 01 39 12 21 91. E: maisonslaffitte@sandaya.fr
alanrogers.com/FR78010

This site on the banks of the Seine is consistently busy, has multilingual, friendly reception staff and occupies a grassy, tree covered area bordering the river. There are 336 pitches, 111 occupied by mobile homes and tour operators, plus two areas dedicated to tents. Most pitches are separated by hedges, are of a good size with some overlooking the Seine (unfenced access), and all 225 touring pitches have electricity hook-ups (10A). The roads leading to the site are a little narrow so large vehicles need to take care. There is a frequent train service and occasional noise from aircraft.

Facilities

Three sanitary blocks, two insulated for winter use and one more open (only used in July/Aug). Facilities are clean with constant supervision necessary due to volume of visitors. Provision for disabled visitors. Motorcaravan services. Self-service shop. Restaurant/bar. Takeaway food and pizzeria (all open all season). TV in restaurant. Badminton. Football area. Fishing possible with licence. Internet point and WiFi throughout (charged).

Open: Week before Easter - 3 November.

Directions

From A13 take exit 7 (Poissy) and follow D153, D308 (Maisons-Laffitte), then site signs before town centre. From A15 exit 7 take D184 (St Germain), after 11 km. turn left on D308 (Maisons-Laffitte). Follow signs. GPS: 48.9399, 2.14589

Charges guide

Per unit incl. 2 persons and electricity	€ 32.50 - € 37.50
extra person	€ 6.90 - € 7.50

Melun

Camping la Belle Etoile

Quai Joffre, La Rochette, F-77000 Melun (Seine-et-Marne) T: 01 64 39 48 12.
E: info@campinglabelleetoile.com **alanrogers.com/FR77070**

Alongside the River Seine, this site has an overall mature and neat appearance. Although the approach road passes through an industrial area, you will discover that la Belle Etoile enjoys a pleasant position with pitches to the fore of the site within view of the barges passing back and forth. The 162 touring pitches, 130 with 6A electricity connections, are on grass and laid out between the many shrubs and trees. There are 18 chalets for hire. A friendly, family run site with pleasant and helpful English-speaking owners, it is ideally situated for visiting Fontainebleau and Paris.

Facilities

The three sanitary blocks are not new but they are kept very clean and the water is very hot. Laundry room. Baby bath. A small block for disabled visitors (shower, washbasin and WC). Motorcaravan services. Shop, small bar, snacks and takeaway (July/Aug, w/ends in low season). Bread to order. Heated outdoor swimming pool (1/5-1/9). Play area. Bouncy castle. Trampoline. Bicycle hire. WiFi over site (charged). Tickets for Disney and Vaux le Vicomte.

Open: 4 April - 27 September.

Directions

Travelling north on RD606 Fontainebleau-Melun road, on entering La Rochette, pass petrol station on left. Turn immediately right into Ave de la Seine. Pass under single-lane bridge. At end of road turn left at river, site on left in 500 m. GPS: 48.52502, 2.66940

Charges guide

Per unit incl. 2 persons and electricity	€ 22.00 - € 26.00

Camping Cheques accepted.

Paris

Camping Indigo Paris - Bois de Boulogne

2 allée du Bord de l'Eau, F-75016 Paris (Paris) T: 01 45 24 30 00. E: paris@camping-indigo.com
alanrogers.com/FR75020

A busy site and the only one within Paris, set in a wooded area between the Seine and the Bois de Boulogne. The site is quite extensive but nevertheless becomes very full with many international visitors, with noise well into the night, despite the rules. There are 459 pitches of varying sizes (including mobile homes) of which 280 are marked, with electricity (10A), water, drainage and TV aerial connections. An improvement and development programme including a new toilet block and restaurant was recently carried out. Reservations are made for pitches – if not booked, arrive early in season (mornings).

Facilities

Four toilet blocks, two of which are showing signs of age. Newest block has facilities for disabled visitors but there is no ramped access. All these facilities have heavy use in season. Laundry room. Two motorcaravan service points. Shop, bar, restaurant and takeaway all year. Bar open 07.00-24.00 most times and until 02.00 in peak season. New central lodge for relaxation. New playground. Bicycle hire. Shuttle bus to Paris. WiFi.

Open: All year.

Directions

Site is between River Seine and Bois de Boulogne, just north of the Pont de Suresnes. Approach from Port Maillot. Site is on one-way street with no left turn from Bvd. Richard Wallace into allé du Bord de l'Eau. Traffic lights at site entrance. Follow signs and use a good map. GPS: 48.86885, 2.234734

Charges guide

Per unit incl. 2 persons and electricity	€ 30.90 - € 41.80
extra person	€ 5.60 - € 8.00

Pommeuse

Camping le Chêne Gris

24 place de la Gare de Faremoutiers, F-77515 Pommeuse (Seine-et-Marne) T: 01 64 04 21 80.
E: info@lechenegris.com **alanrogers.com/FR77020**

This attractive and well managed site is owned and run by a Dutch holiday company. A principal building houses reception on the ground floor and also an airy restaurant/bar plus a takeaway. Of the 340 pitches, 45 are for touring, all with electricity and the majority with water. The remainder (higher up the hill on which the site is built) are occupied by over 220 mobile homes and some 70 tents belonging to a Dutch tour operator. The pitches will easily accommodate units up to seven metres. Terraces look out onto the heated leisure pool complex and an outdoor adventure-style play area for over-fives, whilst the indoor soft play area is in a large tent at the side of the bar. The site is next to a railway station with trains direct to Paris. Disneyland is only 20 km. Reservation is recommended.

Facilities

The sanitary facilities have been refurbished. Facilities for disabled visitors. Family rooms. Laundry area. Bar, restaurant, takeaway and swimming pool complex (all from Easter weekend). Motorcaravan services. Indoor and outdoor play areas. Chalets and tents for rent. WiFi (charged). Off site: Shops, bars and restaurants within walking distance. Fishing and riding 2 km.

Open: 27 March - 1 November.

Directions

Pommeuse is 55 km. east of Paris. From A4 at exit 16 take D934 towards Coulommiers. In 10 km. turn south for 2 km. on D25 to Pommeuse; site on right after level-crossing. Also signed from south on D402 Guignes-Coulommiers road, taking D25 to Faremoutiers. Site is well signed from D25.
GPS: 48.808213, 2.993935

Charges guide

Per unit incl. 2 persons and electricity	€ 25.00 - € 44.00
extra person	€ 3.50 - € 6.00
child (3-11 yrs)	€ 3.00 - € 4.50
dog	€ 5.00 - € 5.50

Rambouillet

Huttopia Rambouillet

Route du Château d'Eau, F-78120 Rambouillet (Yvelines) T: 01 30 41 07 34. E: rambouillet@huttopia.com
alanrogers.com/FR78040

This pleasant site is part of the Huttopia group, whose philosophy is to rediscover the camping spirit. It is in a peaceful forest location beside a lake, with good tarmac access roads and site lighting. The 116 touring pitches, 100 with electricity connections (10A), are set among the trees and in clearings. As a result, shade is plentiful and grass sparse. The main area is kept traffic-free but there is a section for motorcaravans and those who need or prefer to have their car with them. There is an Espace Nature with 40 large pitches for camping. As part of their efforts to be environmentally friendly, Huttopia have built a natural swimming pool. The water is filtered by reeds and it was used for the first time in 2008 and passed the stringent tests of France's Ministry of Health. The opening date each year depends on how quickly the reeds do their work, but it will certainly be open from June to September.

Facilities

The heated sanitary block has controllable showers, some washbasins in cubicles and a number of more spacious family cubicles. Facilities for disabled visitors. Laundry facilities. Three outlying 'rondavels' each with two family rooms. Motorcaravan services. Small shop selling basics. Bar/restaurant/takeaway with terrace (daily in July/Aug, weekends in low season). Only electric barbecues allowed. Communal barbecue area. Games room with TV. Play area. Natural swimming pool (June-Sept, earlier if possible). Boules. Volleyball. Picnic area. Bicycle hire. Fishing. Children's and family activities with a nature theme (July/Aug). Off site: Golf 2 km. Riding 3 km. Lake with beach 15 km. Sailing 20 km.

Open: 4 March - 4 November.

Directions

Rambouillet is 52 km. southwest of Paris. Site is southeast of town: from N10 southbound take Rambouillet/Les Eveuses exit, northbound take Rambouillet centre exit, loop round (site signed) and rejoin N10 southbound, taking next exit. Pass under N10, following signs to site in 1.7 km.
GPS: 48.62638, 1.84375

Charges guide

Per unit incl. 2 persons and electricity	€ 24.20 - € 41.00
extra person	€ 5.90 - € 8.30
child (2-7 yrs)	free - € 5.30
dog	€ 2.60 - € 4.20

Touquin

Camping les Etangs Fleuris

Route Couture, F-77131 Touquin (Seine-et-Marne) T: 01 64 04 16 36. E: contact@etangs-fleuris.com
alanrogers.com/FR77090

This is a pleasant, peaceful site which has a very French feel. Of the 225 pitches, the 90 for touring are grouped in two separate areas. Fifty are on level ground around the three attractive lakes, separated by hedges and with shade from mature trees. Another 50 are on a newly constructed part of the site, mostly on level grass bordered by young trees. All touring pitches have water and electricity (10A). Also in this area is a new sanitary block with facilities for disabled visitors. The life of the site centres round a smart bar/function room which doubles as reception and a shop, as well as the lakes and an attractive, irregularly shaped pool with waterslide. The lakes are home to some sizeable carp as well as being restocked daily with trout (fishing € 5 for half a day). Surrounded by forests and crops, this is a good area for hiking and mountain biking. It is also an ideal base to go to Paris (50 km) and Disneyland (23 km) and to provide a practical alternative to the busier sites nearer the centre.

Facilities

Three heated toilet blocks (one new, one closed in low season) offer pushbutton showers and open washbasins (with dividers and hooks) for men but mainly in cubicles for ladies. Laundry facilities. Heated pool with paddling section (15/5-17/9). Takeaway and snacks (every night high season, weekends and B.Hs in low season). WiFi on part of site (charged). Multisports pitch. Minigolf. Trampoline. Off site: Zoo 7 km. Golf 20 km.

Open: 4 April - 17 September.

Directions

Touquin is off the D231, 21 km. from exit 13 of A4 motorway and 30 km. northeast of Provins. From D231 follow signs for Touquin, then Etangs Fleuris. Site is 2.5 km. west of village. Well signed from D231. GPS: 48.733054, 3.046978

Charges guide

Per unit incl. 2 persons and electricity	€ 22.00
extra person	€ 11.00
child (3-11 yrs)	€ 4.50
dog	€ 1.50

Varreddes

Le Village Parisien

Route de Congis (D121), F-77910 Varreddes (Seine-et-Marne) T: 01 64 34 80 80.
E: contact@villageparisien.com **alanrogers.com/FR77050**

If you are intending to visit Disneyland, this site is ideally situated, just 12 km. away. Tickets can be purchased at the site and taxi travel can be arranged. However, the site has more to offer than its proximity to the theme park. There are 260 pitches in total with 100 for touring units. They are reasonably well cared for with mature hedges dividing them (access to some could be difficult for larger units). They include 50 smaller touring pitches, more suitable for tents and motorcaravans, with electricity on a flat, grassy area with young trees. The site is close to Charles de Gaulle airport and beneath the flight path.

Facilities

Three toilet blocks are old, but adequate (one closed in low season). Facilities for disabled visitors. Laundry facilities. Motorcaravan services. Small shop and takeaway. Bar with entertainment and TV (1/5-15/9). Swimming and paddling pools (1/5-15/9, unheated). Tennis. Play area. Minigolf. Bicycle and kayak hire. Pétanque. Football, volleyball and basketball. Tickets and taxis for Disneyland. WiFi on part of site (charged). Off site: Fishing and kayaking 50 m. Golf 10 km.

Open: 1 April - 1 November.

Directions

Heading south on the A1 towards Paris, turn southeast on N330 at Senlis. Head towards Meaux, then turn left on D405 for Varreddes. Site is well signed from here (about 2 km). GPS: 49.002938, 2.941412

Charges guide

Per unit incl. 2 persons and electricity	€ 20.00 - € 36.00
extra person (over 4 yrs)	€ 4.00
dog	€ 2.00

Veneux-les-Sablons

Camping les Courtilles du Lido

Chemin du Passeur, F-77250 Veneux-les-Sablons (Seine-et-Marne) T: 01 60 70 46 05.
E: lescourtilles-dulido@wanadoo.fr **alanrogers.com/FR77130**

Les Courtilles du Lido is an attractive, family run site located just outside the 14th-century village of Moret-sur-Loing on the edge of the Forêt de Fontainebleau. There are 180 well shaded grassy pitches with 10A electricity dispersed throughout the five-hectare terrain, although access to some may be difficult due to overhanging branches. A good range of amenities includes a heated outdoor pool and minigolf, as well as a pizzeria and bar with a lovely terrace around a central fountain. There are 19 mobile homes for rent. Paris lies 55 km. to the north and can be accessed by either the A5 or A6 motorways or by rail from the local station (within walking distance). Some train noise is audible.

Facilities

A single toilet block provides adequate facilities including those for children. Motorcaravan services (€ 4). Shop, pizzeria, bar and takeaway (all season). Outdoor heated swimming pool (15/5-22/9). Play area. Games room. Minigolf (€ 2). Short tennis. Boules. Free WiFi. Off site: Fishing 500 m. Canoeing. Moret-sur-Loing (Gallo-Roman village) 2 km. Fontainebleau 5 km.

Open: 21 March - 27 September.

Directions

From Fontainebleau take the southbound D606 (towards Sens). At Veneux-les-Sablons follow signs for Moret-sur-Loing and then St Mammès. Final approach is through a short, single-lane tunnel (unsuitable for large RVs). Site is well signed. GPS: 48.38321, 2.80303

Charges guide

Per unit incl. 2 persons and electricity	€ 19.50
extra person	€ 4.00

Versailles

Huttopia Versailles

31 rue Berthelot, F-78000 Versailles (Yvelines) T: 01 39 51 23 61. E: versailles@huttopia.com
alanrogers.com/FR78060

This Huttopia site is rather different. When the French owners visited Canada and experienced 'back to nature' camping, they were so impressed that they decided to introduce the idea to France. This is probably a little like camping as it used to be, but with some big differences. Gone are the formal pitches with neatly trimmed hedges, and instead there are 125 of varying sizes arranged informally amongst the trees, 93 with electricity (10A). The terrain is as nature intended with very little grass and much of it steep and rugged. Long electricity leads are required and be prepared to use blocks and corner steadies on many pitches. Most pitches have good shade.

Facilities

Three well designed toilet blocks (one closed in low season) provide basic facilities, including those for children and disabled visitors. Laundry. Motorcaravan services. Special bivouacs for cooking and washing up. No shop but supermarket nearby. Restaurant with takeaway (July/Aug and w/ends). Bar. Heated outdoor swimming and paddling pools (30/4-18/9). Playground. Games room. Boules. Bicycle hire. No charcoal barbecues.

Open: 24 March - 2 November.

Directions

From the front of the Château de Versailles take the Avenue de Paris and follow signs rather than using sat nav. Narrow roads leading to site so care needed with larger outfits. GPS: 48.79396, 2.16075

Charges guide

Per unit incl. 2 persons and electricity	€ 34.80 - € 50.30
extra person	€ 7.20 - € 10.20
child (2-7 yrs)	€ 3.60 - € 5.70

Villiers-sur-Orge

Camping le Beau Village de Paris

1 voie des Prés, F-91700 Villiers-sur-Orge (Essonne) T: 01 60 16 17 86. E: contact@campingaparis.com
alanrogers.com/FR91010

This is a pleasant, typically French campsite just 25 km. south of Paris and conveniently located at the centre of a triangle formed by the A6 motorway, the N20/A10 to Orleans and the N104 east/west link road, La Francilienne. Half of its 124 pitches are occupied on a seasonal basis by Parisians and 20 mobile homes to rent; the remainder are touring pitches, all hedged and with 10A electricity. Trees provide some shade. Reception, in a traditionally-styled building, also has a pleasant little bar, a games room and an attractive terrace with wooden tables, benches, thatched canopies and a barbecue.

Facilities

Three toilet blocks, heated as required, have controllable showers and some washbasins in cabins. The main block has baby changing and laundry facilities. A second (older) block has adequate facilities for disabled visitors, the third is in a prefabricated unit. Small bar (July/Aug and on demand). Games room. Pool table. Adventure play area. Free loan of canoes. Boules. Free WiFi on part of site.

Open: All year.

Directions

From N104 join N20 north, exit at La Ville-du-Bois and Carrefore on D35 towards Villiers-sur-Orge. In village, turn right at lights immediately before river on Voie des Prés along riverbank to site on left. Tight turn into entrance. GPS: 48.65527, 2.30409

Charges guide

Per unit incl. 2 persons and electricity	€ 20.60 - € 22.50
extra person	€ 5.15 - € 6.00

DÉPARTEMENTS: 08 ARDENNES, 51 MARNE, 10 AUBE, 52 HAUTE-MARNE

MAJOR CITY: REIMS

The varied landscapes of Champagne-Ardenne include dense forests, vineyards and winding rivers. The whole area is dotted with ancient churches and castles, towns and villages.

Situated on the flatlands of Champagne are the most northerly vineyards in France where special processing turns the light, dry wine into 'le Champagne'. Nowhere else in the world are you allowed to make sparkling wine and call it Champagne. Reims and Epernay are the centres for the wine trade. It is not the names of the vineyards that have become famous but those of the shippers, such as Veuve Clicquot and Moët & Chandon.

This is essentially a place of rural peace, with chalky rolling fields, although there is some heavy industry in the north. This north-eastern slice of France has seen many European battles and the hilly terrain and deep forests of the Ardennes gave some advantage to the Resistance fighters of the last war when Ardennes was annexed to Germany. Its main city of Charleville-Mezieres was two distinct towns lying on either side of the Meuse river until their amalgamation in 1966 and each retains its individuality.

Places of interest

Charleville-Mezieres: arcaded Palace Ducale, similar in style to the Place des Vosges in Paris; birthplace of the poet Arthur Rimbaud.

Chalons-sur-Marne: perfect Gothic-style cathedral with 12th-century tower.

Épernay: home of Champagne production. Guided tours and tastings are available at some of the larger Champagne houses.

Reims: 13th-century Gothic cathedral. In 406, Clovis, the first king of France, was baptised here and the kings of France from Louis V11 to Charles X were crowned here.

Troyes: ancient capital of the Champagne region with a beautifully preserved city centre with a Gothic cathedral, dozens of churches and 15th-century houses; a system of boulevards shaped like a Champagne cork; Musée d'Art Moderne including works by Dégas and Gaugin.

Cuisine of the region

Andouillettes de Troyes: chitterlings sausage made from pork and onions and seasoned with herbs.

Madeleine de Commercy: small, shell-shaped, buttery pastries with orange flavouring.

Flamiche aux Maroilles/Goyere: a hot creamy tart based on local cheese.

Biscuits roses: traditional pink biscuits made with eggs, flour and sugar, originally baked to accompany Champagne.

www.tourisme-champagne-ardenne.com
contact@tourisme-champagne-ardenne.com
(0)3 26 21 85 80

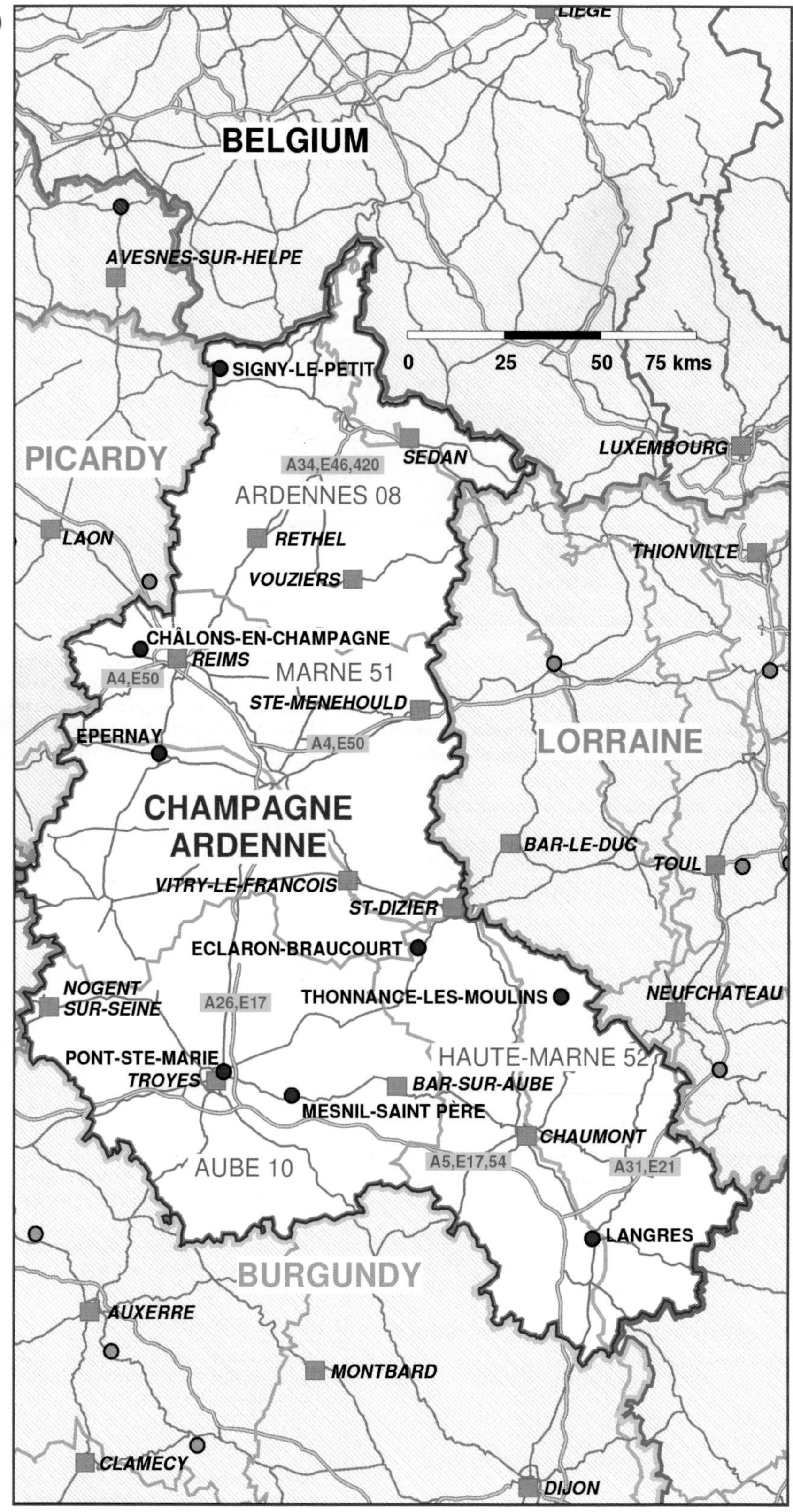
LIEGE
BELGIUM
AVESNES-SUR-HELPE
SIGNY-LE-PETIT
0 25 50 75 kms
SEDAN
LUXEMBOURG
PICARDY
A34,E46,420
ARDENNES 08
LAON
RETHEL
THIONVILLE
VOUZIERS
CHÂLONS-EN-CHAMPAGNE
REIMS
MARNE 51
A4,E50
STE-MENEHOULD
EPERNAY
A4,E50
LORRAINE
CHAMPAGNE
ARDENNE
BAR-LE-DUC
TOUL
VITRY-LE-FRANCOIS
ST-DIZIER
ECLARON-BRAUCOURT
NOGENT
SUR-SEINE
A26,E17
THONNANCE-LES-MOULINS
NEUFCHATEAU
HAUTE-MARNE 52
PONT-STE-MARIE
TROYES
BAR-SUR-AUBE
MESNIL-SAINT PÈRE
CHAUMONT
A5,E17,54
A31,E21
AUBE 10
LANGRES
BURGUNDY
AUXERRE
MONTBARD
CLAMECY
DIJON

Châlons-en-Champagne

Camping de Châlons-en-Champagne

Rue de Plaisance, F-51000 Châlons-en-Champagne (Marne) T: 03 26 68 38 00.
E: camping.chalons@orange.fr **alanrogers.com/FR51020**

The location of Châlons, south of Reims and near the A4 and A26 autoroutes, about 30 and Boulogne, makes this an ideal stopover. This site on the southern edge of town nov Aquadis-Loisirs group. The wide entrance with its neatly mown grass and flowerbeds lea of large pitches separated by hedges, many with taps and drains adjacent. Of the 140 p ... 69 are on gravel, the rest on grass; 96 have electricity (10A). Some overlook a small lake.

Facilities

Two fairly basic toilet blocks (one open only in high season, the other can be heated) include washbasins in cabins, baby room and hairdressing station. Unit for disabled visitors. Laundry facilities. Shop. Bread to order. Open-air bar, snack bar and takeaway (1/5-30/9). Games (pool and babyfoot) and TV rooms. Fishing lake. Playground. Minigolf. Tennis. Volleyball. Boules. Mini-football. Motorcaravan services. Bicycle hire. WiFi throughout (charged). Four mobile homes to rent. Off site: Bus stop 800 m. Fishing. Riding 1 km.

Open: 7 March - 6 November.

Directions

Châlons-en-Champagne is 50 km. southeast of Reims. From north on A4, take La Veuve exit (27) onto N44 Reims-Vitry road which bypasses town. Leave at St Memmie exit and follow camping signs. From south on A26, take exit 18 and take D5/D977 into town. Turn right at roundabout on to D1, signed 'Camping'. GPS: 48.9359, 4.3832

Charges guide

Per unit incl. 2 persons and electricity	€ 22.90
extra person	€ 5.50

Camping Cheques accepted.

Eclaron-Braucourt

Yelloh! Village en Champagne

F-52290 Eclaron-Braucourt (Haute-Marne) T: 03 25 06 34 24. E: info@yellohvillage-en-champagne.com
alanrogers.com/FR52050

Also known as Les Sources du Lac, this Yelloh! Village site is located close to the village of Eclaron and has direct access to the Lac du Der. This is a very large lake with 77 km. of shoreline and is home to over 270 species of birds. Part of the lake is an ornithological reserve but a wide range of water-based activities are on offer in other areas. These include fishing, windsurfing and sailing, and a separate area is reserved for motorboats. There are just 30 touring pitches here and around 120 mobile homes and chalets for rent.

Facilities

Two toilet blocks include facilities for babies. The facilities may be under pressure at busy times. Shop for basics. Bar. Restaurant. Takeaway. Swimming pool. Paddling pool. Direct access to the lake and beach. Play area. Bicycle hire. Fishing. Ornithological activities. Activity and entertainment programme. Off site: Sailing 6 km. Riding 10 km. Golf 30 km. Walking and cycle trails. Fishing. The Champagne route.

Open: 1 May - 30 November.

Directions

Eclaron is 7 km. southwest of St Dizier. From the N4 (Paris-Nancy) on the St Dizier southern bypass take the D384 towards Montier-en-Der and after passing Eclaron look for signs to the site on right. GPS: 48.57213, 4.84891

Charges guide

Per unit incl. 2 persons and electricity	€ 18.00 - € 36.00
extra person (over 7 yrs)	€ 5.00 - € 7.00

Epernay

Camping d'Epernay

Allées de Cumières, F-51200 Epernay (Marne) T: 03 26 55 32 14. E: camping.epernay@free.fr
alanrogers.com/FR51040

This very well maintained municipal site in the heart of the Champagne region is well worth a visit. Although situated between two sports stadia the site is a peaceful oasis on the banks of the River Marne. There are 109 level, grass pitches of which 80 have electricity (5/10A). These are bordered by well trimmed hedges of varying heights and numerous mature trees offering some shade. The whole site is arranged neatly and uniformly in rows. The tarmac roads around the site are in first class condition with no speed humps. The traditional sanitary block may struggle to cope with demand in high season. Caravans over six metres and twin axles are not permitted.

Facilities

One traditional toilet block contains washbasins, pushbutton controllable showers. Facilities for disabled visitors. Motorcaravan services. Laundry facilities. Open-air restaurant, snack bar and takeaway (1/5-30/9). Play area. Multisports pitch. Fishing. Bicycle hire. Sailing. Boat launching. WiFi throughout (free). Off site: Epernay centre with shops and restaurants 2 km.

Open: 1 May - 30 September.

Directions

The site is on the north side of Epernay on D301 and is clearly signed throughout the city. Travelling south on N51/D951 from Reims, after crossing the river turn right at the roundabout. Site is on the right. GPS: 49.05769, 3.95028

Charges guide

Per unit incl. 2 persons and electricity	€ 20.00 - € 21.50

...s

...nping Lac de la Liez

Rue des Voiliers, F-52200 Peigney (Haute-Marne) T: 03 25 90 27 79. E: contact@camping-liez.fr
alanrogers.com/FR52030

Managed by the charming Baude family, this excellent lakeside site is near the city of Langres. Only twenty minutes from the A5/A31 junction, Camping Lac de la Liez provides an ideal spot for an overnight stop en route to the south of France. However, there is also a lot on offer for a longer stay. The site provides 157 fully serviced pitches, 16 with private sanitary units. Attractive terracing on the lower part of the site means that some have views of the 250-hectare lake with its sandy beach and small harbour where boats and pedaloes may be hired. Perfect for watersports, access to the lake is down steps and across quite a fast road. It is possible to cycle or even walk the 18 km. circuit around the lake. As well as all the activities on the lake, sporting provision on site includes tennis, volleyball, boules, archery and bicycle hire. There are pony rides in high season. Langres with its old ramparts and ancient city centre is within easy reach – it was elected one of the 50 most beautiful towns in France and it is well worth a visit. There are markets in Langres and many of the nearby towns and villages. The surrounding countryside has much to offer walkers and cyclists and motorists will find plenty of scenic drives.

Facilities

Two older heated toilet blocks (one closed in low season) have all facilities including controllable showers and washbasins in cabins. Facilities for babies and disabled campers. A more recent block has eight en-suite units along with 16 pitches with private sanitary facilities. Laundry facilities. Motorcaravan services. Shop (from 15/4). Bar and restaurant with takeaway (from 15/4). Indoor pool with spa and sauna. Heated outdoor pool with slide. Games room. Playground. Tennis (free in low season). Bicycle hire. WiFi over site (charged).

Open: 29 March - 25 September.

Directions

From A5/A31 motorways follow signs for Langres. From Langres via N19 towards Vesoul. After 3 km. turn right, straight after the large river bridge, then follow site signs. Also signed from D74 (Neufchâteau). GPS: 47.87317, 5.38069

Charges guide

Per unit incl. 2 persons and electricity	€ 25.00 - € 36.00
extra person	€ 6.00 - € 8.50
child (2-12 yrs)	€ 3.50 - € 5.00

Camping Cheques accepted.

Langres

Camping de la Croix d'Arles

Route de Dijon, Saint Geosmes, F-52200 Bourg Langres (Haute-Marne) T: 03 25 88 24 02.
E: croix.arles@yahoo.fr **alanrogers.com/FR52040**

Only 10 km. from autoroute A31 (exit Langres Sud), this site is ideally located for an overnight stop on your holiday journey, but also has the basics for a longer stay. There are 180 pitches, of which 150 are for touring units with 10A electricity. Most facilities are near the entrance, as is a flat grassy area mostly used by caravans and motorcaravans for overnight stops. A wooded area, where nature has been worked with rather than controlled, provides groups of numbered pitches with lots of shade (leads for electricity of up to 40 m. could be needed). Further on is an area for tents with no electricity supply.

Facilities

Two modern toilet blocks with some washbasins in cabins and controllable showers. Facilities for disabled visitors. Baby room. Laundry facilities. Small shop for basics. Bar. Restaurant and takeaway (1/4-31/10). Swimming and paddling pools (15/5-15/9). Playground. Minigolf. Games rooms. Boules. WiFi on part of site.

Open: 15 March - 31 October.

Directions

From north on A31 exit 6 (Langres) then D974 (towards Dijon). After 5 km. site is on right and is well signed. GPS: 47.8128, 5.32056

Charges guide

Per unit incl. 2 persons and electricity	€ 18.00 - € 21.00
extra person	€ 3.00 - € 4.00

Mesnil-Saint Père

Camping Lac d'Orient

17 rue du Lac, F-10140 Mesnil-Saint Père (Aube) T: 03 25 40 61 85. E: info@camping-lacdorient.com

alanrogers.com/FR10020

Le Lac d'Orient opened in 2009 equipped with a good range of leisure amenities and with an attractive rural location. The site can be found at the centre of the large Forêt d'Orient natural park and is just 100 m. from the Lac d'Orient which is ideal for all manner of watersports. Previously a small municipal site, it has been rebuilt and offers a modern restaurant, bar and takeaway as well as a heated indoor pool and outdoor swimming pools with slides, all in one complex with the reception and the shop. The pitches here are large and are semi-shaded with mature trees. There are 206 pitches, 180 for touring units and a few occupied by mobile homes and chalets. All have 10A electrical connections and some also offer water and drainage.

Facilities

One purpose built toilet block and one totally refurbished, both of a high standard. Facilities for children and disabled visitors. Laundry facilities. Restaurant, bar and takeaway (9/4-18/9). Shop. Heated indoor pool (all season) and outdoor swimming pools with slides (14/5-11/9). Paddling pool. Spa bath. TV room. Play area. Multisports court. Max. 1 dog per pitch accepted. WiFi (free). Off site: Motorcaravan services outside site. Lac d'Orient 100 m. Windsurfing and sailing. Canoe and pedalo hire. Fishing. Cycling and walking tracks. Troyes centre 20 km.

Open: 9 April - 24 September.

Directions

Mesnil-St Père is 20 km. east of Troyes. From the north, leave A26 at exit 23 and join eastbound D619 (Lac d'Orient). Turn left on D43 following signs to Mesnil-St Père and then site. GPS: 48.26331, 4.34666

Charges guide

Per unit incl. 2 persons and electricity	€ 24.40 - € 34.40
extra person	€ 6.50 - € 8.50
child (under 7 yrs)	€ 3.50 - € 4.50
dog	€ 3.00

Camping Cheques accepted.

Pont-Sainte-Marie

Camping Municipal de Troyes

7 rue Roger Salengro, F-10150 Pont-Sainte-Marie (Aube) T: 03 25 81 02 64. E: info@troyescamping.net

alanrogers.com/FR10010

This municipal campsite, within the Troyes city boundary and about 2 km. from the centre, is on one of the main routes from Luxembourg to the southwest of France, and on the main route from Calais to the Mediterranean. There are 150 level, grassy pitches (20 with hardstanding) for touring units, evenly divided between shaded and open, with electricity (10A, Europlug). Troyes makes a good night stop or a base for discovering the lively city. As the old capital of the Champagne region, it has a marvellous Mediaeval centre and interesting museums, and is well worth a longer stay. The cathedral is renowned for its stained glass windows. In addition, not far from the site is the biggest centre in Europe for factory shops and designer outlets, run by the same company that has six such centres in Great Britain.

Facilities

Two toilet blocks contain washbasins and preset showers. Facilities for children and disabled visitors. Motorcaravan services. Washing machines and dryer. Shop for basics. Gas supplies. Bar, restaurant, snack bar and takeaway (1/6-10/9). Heated outdoor swimming pool (1/6-15/9). WiFi on part of site (free). TV room. Games room. Play area (for under 5s). Minigolf. Boules. Bicycle hire. Off site: Bus to Troyes centre 100 m. Supermarket 400 m. Other shops, restaurants, bars and ATM 300 m. Riding 8 km.

Open: 1 April - 15 October.

Directions

From all routes follow signs for Troyes and Pont-Ste Marie (just north of the old city centre), then signs for Camping Municipal. GPS: 48.31124, 4.09683

Charges guide

Per unit incl. 2 persons and electricity	€ 20.50 - € 24.80
extra person	€ 5.20 - € 6.20
child (2-12 yrs)	€ 3.40 - € 4.40
dog	€ 1.15

…-Petit

…ine de la Motte

…680 Signy-le-Petit (Ardennes) T: 03 24 53 54 73. E: contact@domainedelamotte.eu

…nrogers.com/FR08170

Domaine de la Motte is located between fields and forest, and is ideally situated for visiting Belgium and Luxembourg. The Ardennes region will charm you with its beautiful shady forests, lakes and rivers, and lovers of architecture can see many fine examples of fortified churches and public buildings. This ten-hectare family-oriented site has 87 level grassy touring pitches enclosed by hedges; all have 10A electricity and water, but only a few have shade. There are gîtes, chalets and mobile homes for hire. Just a few hundred metres from the site, there is a lake with a beach, and a separate fishing lake. Walks around the campsite will lead you to 'the Stone Virgin' or the old laundry. Nearby, you can visit a Forestry Museum where many of the forest crafts of days gone by are still practised. Some of the most beautiful views of the Ardennes can be seen in Monthermé, including the famous Loop of the Meuse.

Facilities

Two toilet blocks (one traditional and unheated) have showers, washbasins and toilets in cubicles. Dishwashing and laundry facilities. Facilities for children and disabled visitors. Basic motorcaravan services. Bar, restaurant and takeaway (all year). Heated swimming pool. Gym. Sauna. Solarium, Spa treatments. Small play area. Bouncy castle and trampoline. Multisports pitch. Minigolf (charged). Entertainment for adults and children (July/Aug). Bicycle and go-kart hire. Free WiFi over site. Off site: Bathing area at Lake Motte 500 m. Shops in Signy-le-Petit 1.5 km. Riding 2 km.

Open: All year.

Directions

From A26/E17 take exit 13 and join N2 towards Vervins. At roundabout north of Vervins take D963 towards Hirson. At roundabout on approach to Hirson turn right onto D1043/E44, at next roundabout turn right (southeast) then D10 north to Signy-le-Petit. Continue straight on through the village onto rue Dugard and continue for 1.5 km, site is on left. GPS: 49.91279, 4.28705

Charges guide

Per unit incl. 2 persons and electricity	€ 20.00
extra person	€ 4.00
child (under 12 yrs)	€ 2.00
dog	€ 2.00

Thonnance-les-Moulins

Castel Camping la Forge de Sainte Marie

R.D. 427, F-52230 Thonnance-les-Moulins (Haute-Marne) T: 03 25 94 42 00.

E: info@laforgedesaintemarie.com **alanrogers.com/FR52020**

This attractive campsite in a secluded valley is entered through a narrow arched gateway. It was created in 1995 by careful conservation of original forge buildings and the surrounding land. The River Rongeant meanders through the site widening into a small fishing lake. A picturesque bridge links the upper part of the site to the reception area. Grass pitches, 147 for touring units, are of varying sizes on terraces, amongst trees or in more open areas. Electricity (6A, Europlug) and water are available and 120 pitches are fully serviced. Ten premium pitches have garden furniture, fridge and barbecue. There are also 39 mobile homes and chalets. Larger units should take care with manoeuvring. The department of Haute-Marne is situated between the better known areas of Champagne and the Vosges. It is a sleepy land of rolling hills, forests and farmland. In the heart of this lies Thonnance-les-Moulins, a small village 12 km. east of Joinville and the north-south N67 main road between Saint Dizier and Chaumont.

Facilities

Two sanitary blocks provide all facilities including those for children and disabled visitors. Family shower room. Additional facilities at reception and pool complex. Laundry facilities. Shop, restaurant and bar with terrace. Pizzeria in high season. Heated indoor pool and paddling pool. Play areas. Bicycle hire. Fishing (charged). Games room. Archery. Organised games for children (July/Aug). Programme for adults including wine and cheese tasting and guided walks. WiFi (charged). Off site: Joinville with shops, restaurants and ATM 12 km. Golf 45 km. Birthplaces of Joan of Arc 30 km. and General de Gaulle 53 km.

Open: 18 April - 4 September.

Directions

Site is 12 km. southeast of Joinville between Poissons and Germay on road D427. The site entrance and access roads may be a little tight for large units. GPS: 48.40644, 5.27109

Charges guide

Per unit incl. 2 persons and electricity	€ 22.50 - € 39.50
extra person	€ 4.50 - € 10.00
child (2-9 yrs)	€ 2.50 - € 5.00
dog	€ 2.00

Camping Cheques accepted.

DÉPARTEMENTS: 54 MEURTHE-ET-MOSELLE, 55 MEUSE, 57 MOSELLE, 88 VOSGES

MAJOR CITIES: NANCY, METZ

For centuries, Lorraine has been a major European crossroads, resulting in a rich mixture of cultural influences. Today it is an idyllic setting for holidays, with a diverse historical and cultural heritage, plus endless forests, lakes, rivers and mountains to explore.

Lorraine's position on the French border has made it vulnerable to war, and the history of those conflicts can be seen in many of the region's museums. It underwent periods of German rule, most recently from 1872-1918, and this is evident in its architecture, cuisine and language.

With a strong industrial tradition, Lorraine is a treasure trove of arts and crafts, in particular crystalware, earthenware and enamelwork, with many historical examples on display in specialist museums.

There are no less than three outstanding country parks, home to deer and wild boar, while mountain goats scale the high pastures of the Vosges mountains. The Vosges crests formed part of the battle front in World War One and military requirements led to the building of the road now known as the Route des Cretes which runs near to the highest peaks. It goes past more WWI sites than vineyards, and more 'ballons' (the highest peaks are so-called because they are round and bald) than villages but the view from the top is utterly breathtaking.

Places of interest

Epinal: picturesque town and capital of the Vosges.

Fermont: underground fort at Longuyon, 50 km. north of Verdun.

Metz: 13th-century cathedral of St Etienne; Centre Pompidou Metz museum of modern art; Place St. Louis; Old City with Renaissance and medieval architecture.

Nancy: Place Stanislas, a UNESCO World Heritage Site; 14th-century Porte de la Craffe; Arc de Triomphe.

Verdun: hill forts such as Fort de Vaux and Fort de Douaumont; large military cemetery at Douaumont.

Amnéville: 40-acre zoological park, one of the three largest in France, has 2,000 animals and a primate facility.

Cuisine of the region

The cooking is peppery and hearty and quite unlike any other region.

Bar-le-Duc ('Lorraine caviar'): redcurrant jam de-seeded with a goose quill.

Quiche Lorraine: made only in the classical manner with cream, eggs and bacon.

Potée Lorraine: smoked meats combined with carrots, leeks and sometimes beans.

Eau-de-vie: a strong, white alcohol liqueur distilled from fermented fruit juices, including mirabelles (small yellow plums), cherries and pears.

www.tourism-lorraine.com
contact@tourisme-lorraine.fr
(0)3 83 80 01 80

Anould

Camping les Acacias

191 rue Léonard de Vinci, F-88650 Anould (Vosges) T: 03 29 57 11 06. E: contact@acaciascamp.com
alanrogers.com/FR88270

Les Acacias is a small, comfortable site in an area surrounded by stunning lakes, waterfalls and rivers, and is a haven for walkers, mountain bikers and nature enthusiasts. The 75 pitches, 55 for touring units and tents, are mainly level and most have shade. All have 6A electricity. There is a heated pool for the whole family and all the amenities of the town are close by. There is a choice of accommodation to rent, including chalets, roulottes and bungalows. In summer, forest camping is available with access to all site facilities and to the 'Parcours de Santé' trim trail.

Facilities

The heated sanitary block has showers, washbasins and toilets in cubicles. Family wash room. Children's facilities. Laundry. Clothes drying room. Small shop (baker calls). Gas sales. Snack bar and takeaway. Covered bar/terrace. Heated, open-air pool (10/6-10/9). Games room. Games field and play area. Volleyball. Basketball. Trampoline. Table football. Barbecues allowed (communal area). WiFi on part of site. Off site: Supermarket 1 km. Bicycle hire and riding 3 km. Tennis 12 km. Hohneck 17 km.

Open: 1 January - 25 September.

Directions

From N59 at St Dié-des-Vosges/Ste Marguerite, take D415 south. In Anould continue on D415 eastwards and in a short distance turn right into rue Léonard de Vinci. Site is on your left. GPS: 48.18359, 6.95791

Charges guide

Per unit incl. 2 persons and electricity	€ 15.50
extra person	€ 3.90
child (under 7 yrs)	€ 2.00 - € 3.90
dog	€ 1.00

Bulgnéville

Camping Porte des Vosges

ZA la Grande Tranchée, F-88140 Bulgnéville (Vosges) T: 03 29 09 12 00.
E: contact@camping-portedesvosges.com **alanrogers.com/FR88290**

At Camping Porte des Vosges you are assured of a very warm welcome from the new owners, Sylvie Drode and her husband. This spacious, clean and very well cared for site is situated in Lorraine, on the outskirts of the historic town of Bulgnéville and is just off the E21/A31 making it an ideal stopover as well as for longer holidays. The sloping site has trees and bushes which shade the 97 spacious touring pitches (70-150 sq.m) that are on gravel or grass and there are two equipped tents and a vintage caravan to rent. All the pitches have access to electricity (6A, Europlug) and water points are distributed throughout the site.

Facilities

One sanitary block with showers, toilets and basins all in cubicles. Facilities for disabled visitors. Snack bar with TV. Takeaway (all season). Fresh bread and pastries can be ordered (1/4-10/10). Small playground. Communal barbecue. Free WiFi (in snack bar). Off site: Fishing, tennis, multisports pitch and adventure playground 500 m. Riding 3 km. Sailing 4 km. Bicycle hire and golf 6 km.

Open: 1 April - 31 October.

Directions

Camping Porte des Vosges is south of Nancy. From Nancy take E21/A31 south to exit 9 towards Vittel/Contrexéville/Bulgnéville. At roundabout take third exit onto D164. Turn right to D14 then left. Site is on left. GPS: 48.1990, 5.84481

Charges guide

Per unit incl. 2 persons and electricity	€ 16.00 - € 18.00
extra person	€ 4.60

Burtoncourt

Camping la Croix du Bois Sacker

F-57220 Burtoncourt (Moselle) T: 03 87 35 74 08. E: camping.croixsacker@wanadoo.fr
alanrogers.com/FR57080

This very attractive site is quiet and child friendly and has been run for the last few years by a young and enthusiastic couple who have made many improvements to this former municipal site. For example, the terrace has been enlarged, a small shop added and the facilities for disabled visitors improved. There are 60 small to medium, uneven and open pitches, some with shade and all with electricity and water taps. The site is not far from Metz and is well suited for travellers going south to Germany, Switzerland or Italy. Forming part of the site, a lake is good for fishing (carp).

Facilities

The seasonal and touring parts of the site have separate facilities. Showers are on payment (token). Turkish style toilets outnumber British style. Washbasins, some in cabins. Facilities for disabled visitors. Facilities may become stretched at peak times. Washing machine. Shop. Bar. Sports field and tennis court. Play area. Lake swimming (July/Aug). Fishing. WiFi.

Open: 1 April - 20 October.

Directions

From the A4 take exit 37 (Argancy) and follow signs for Malroy, Chieulles and Vany on RD3 towards Bouzonville. Then take D53 to Burtoncourt and site. GPS: 49.22499, 6.39943

Charges guide

Per unit incl. 2 persons and electricity	€ 19.50
extra person	€ 5.00
child (2-12 yrs)	€ 3.00

No credit cards.

Bussang

Domaine de Champé

14 rue des Champs-Navés, F-88540 Bussang (Vosges) T: 03 29 61 61 51. E: info@domaine-de-champe.com
alanrogers.com/FR88050

Bordered by the Moselle river, surrounded by the mountains of the Vosges and located just off the town square, this site is open all year making it a good base from which to explore in summer, and ideal for skiing in winter, when you might be tempted to rent one of the 40 chalets. Domaine de Champé is a level site with 80 touring pitches, all with 4/12A electricity, spread over a fairly large area on both sides of a tributary stream, so some are quite a distance from the facilities. There are two heated pools, one large outside and a smaller one inside. The village boasts a Theatre of the People, founded in 1895, giving shows in July and August. The Casino is open all year and is very popular.

Facilities

One new, large sanitary building has all necessary facilities including for babies and disabled campers. Motorcaravan services. Bar and restaurant (all year), takeaway (July/Aug). Swimming pools (outdoor 1/5-30/9). Wellness centre (charged) including sauna, Hammam and relaxation room. Tennis. Two large play areas. Electric bike hire. Internet access. WiFi in parts (charged). Off site: Skiing 3 km.

Open: All year.

Directions

Bussang is between Remiremont and Mulhouse on N66, almost due north of Belfort. Site is signed from the town centre. GPS: 47.888617, 6.85715

Charges guide

Per unit incl. 2 persons and electricity	€ 19.00 - € 34.00
extra person	€ 4.00 - € 6.50

Camping Cheques accepted.

Celles-sur-Plaine

Camping des Lacs

F-88110 Celles-sur-Plaine (Vosges) T: 03 29 41 28 00. E: camping@paysdeslacs.com

alanrogers.com/FR88140

This is a well organised site with its own pool, close to the village centre, with many water-based and sporting activities available at the nearby lakes. There are 123 level touring pitches, 109 with electricity (16A) and 20 chalets and tents for rent. Some shaded pitches border the tiny Plaine river, 35 pitches have gravel hardstanding, others are on grass, but all are surrounded by well trimmed mature hedges. The site is owned by a collaboration of regional and local organisations, with a very active and enthusiastic resident manager.

Facilities

Three good sanitary units equally spaced along the site have been completely refurbished to a very high standard. Each has controllable showers and washbasins in cabins, baby room with bath, children's unit, en-suite units for disabled visitors. Laundry facilities. Small shop for basics (1/6-27/9). Bar (1/5-27/9). Takeaway. Heated outdoor swimming and paddling pools (1/6-15/9). Play area. Fishing. Entertainment in high season. Eco-friendly chalets for hire. WiFi in bar area (free). Off site: Beach with supervised lake swimming (July/Aug).

Open: 11 April - 27 September.

Directions

Celles is 80 km. southeast of Nancy. From N59 Nancy/St Dié, take exit for Raon l'Etape, from north turn right at T-junction in town, then take D392a northeast for 10 km. to Celles-sur-Plaine, and follow camping signs. GPS: 48.454933, 6.94725

Charges guide

Per unit incl. 2 persons and electricity	€ 18.00 - € 24.00
extra person	€ 6.00 - € 7.00
child (4-7 yrs)	€ 4.50 - € 5.50

Corcieux

Yelloh! en Vosges Domaine des Bans

Rue James Wiese, F-88430 Corcieux (Vosges) T: 03 29 51 64 67.

E: info@yellohvillage-domaine-des-bans.com **alanrogers.com/FR88080**

Domaine des Bans is a large holiday village with plenty of activities to keep you occupied. Open all year, this family oriented site has a total of 630 pitches, mainly taken by static and tour operator units, leaving just 80 available for touring. These pitches are numbered, vary in size and are scattered around the campsite with some on low terraces. Most have good shade and all have electricity, water and a drain. Some are tucked away in quiet areas with others nearer to where activities take place. This site is more suited for longer stays or as a base for exploring the varied and interesting countryside.

Facilities

Three toilet blocks provide all necessary facilities including for disabled visitors and babies. Shop and bar (30/5-6/9). Restaurant (1/5-6/9). Takeaway (30/4-6/9). Large swimming pool complex (outdoor 1/6-6/9, indoor 1/5-6/9). Playground and area for ball games. Tennis. Minigolf. Archery. Bicycle hire. Riding. Three lakes for fishing and boating. Entertainment including discos, theatre performances and live music (high season). Goat Castle. Internet. WiFi. Max. weight 3.5 tons.

Open: 26 April - 6 September.

Directions

Corcieux is 25 km. south of St Dié. From St Dié-Gérardmer road (N415, then D8), turn west on D60 just north of Gerbépal to Corcieux. Site is signed and is just south of the town. GPS: 48.16903, 6.88028

Charges guide

Per unit incl. 2 persons and electricity	€ 18.00 - € 44.00
extra person	€ 6.00 - € 8.00
child (3-6 yrs)	free - € 7.00

Corcieux

Sites et Paysages Au Clos de la Chaume

21 rue d'Alsace, route de Gerardmer, F-88430 Corcieux (Vosges) T: 03 29 50 76 76.

E: info@camping-closdelachaume.com **alanrogers.com/FR88120**

This pleasant site is within walking distance of the town, on level ground with a small stream. The friendly family owners, who are British and French, live on site and do their best to ensure campers have an enjoyable relaxing stay. There are 94 level grassy pitches of varying sizes and with varying amounts of sun and shade. All 64 touring pitches have electricity hook-ups (6/10A) and some are divided by shrubs and trees. The site carries the LPO (League for Bird Protection) label with over 30 species present. There is an attractive, well fenced, new swimming pool and an excellent small adventure-style playground.

Facilities

Two modern sanitary blocks provide all the necessary facilities for families and disabled visitors. Children's sanitary facilities. Laundry with washing machines and dryers. Motorcaravan services. Reception keeps basics (June/Aug). New covered swimming pool (1/5-20/9). Play area. Games room with pool table and library. Boules. Volleyball. WiFi throughout (charged). Off site: Bicycle hire 800 m. Riding 2 km. Fishing 3 and 10 km. Golf 30 km.

Open: 27 April - 20 September.

Directions

Corcieux is 17 km. southwest of St Dié-des-Vosges. Site is on the D60, east of town centre, by the town boundary sign. GPS: 48.16826, 6.89025

Charges guide

Per unit incl. 2 persons and electricity	€ 16.00 - € 26.10
extra person	€ 6.50
child (2-6 yrs)	€ 3.60

Granges-sur-Vologne

Flower Camping la Sténiole

1 le Haut Rain, F-88640 Granges-sur-Vologne (Vosges) T: 03 29 51 43 75. E: steniole@wanadoo.fr

alanrogers.com/FR88110

Set in a lovely rural area in the heart of the Vosges Massif, this attractive site is run by a dedicated young couple who are constantly improving the site and its facilities. A new indoor pool opened in 2015. The 125 pitches (4/10A electricity), either separated by hedges or beside the water, offer little shade. A small river has been used to form a small lake for fishing and swimming and a series of separate ponds (water quality is checked regularly). An atmosphere of relaxation is encouraged and the whole family can have a good time here. The final approach is on a steep, single-track road, a 250-metre climb in 2 kilometres.

Facilities

Two new toilet blocks and further facilities in the main building include amenities for children and disabled visitors. Washing machines and dryers. Bar. Restaurant (July/Aug). Pizza takeaway (June-Aug). WiFi over site (charged). Lake swimming. Fishing. Games room with TV and library. Play area. Football. Volleyball. Trampoline. Tennis. WiFi throughout (free). Accommodation to rent.

Open: 1 May - 30 September.

Directions

Take D420 from Epinal towards St-Dié-des-Vosges, at Bruyères turn southeast on D423 to Granges-sur-Vologne. Go through town towards Gérardmer, the site is signed right. GPS: 48.12045, 6.83084

Charges guide

Per unit incl. 2 persons and electricity	€ 17.00 - € 21.00
extra person	€ 3.50 - € 4.00

Granges-sur-Vologne

Camping Gadémont Plage

2 Gadémont, F-88640 Granges-sur-Vologne (Vosges) T: 03 29 51 44 60. E: deleeuw697@aol.com

alanrogers.com/FR88400

Camping Gadémont Plage is open all year and can be found within the Parc Naturel Régional des Ballons des Vosges, close to the town of Granges-sur-Vologne. Pitches here are terraced and are generally well shaded. A number of pitches can be found on the banks of the little river which runs through the site. There is also direct access to a small lake (canoeing is possible – courses available) with fishing (free to campers). This is a good base for exploring the Vosges, which is, of course, a very popular region for adventure sports. Various activities are organised on site in peak season including occasional discos and sports competitions.

Facilities

Two modern, clean toilet blocks, one by reception is heated. Showers by token in July/Aug. Facilities for disabled visitors in one block. Restaurant/snack bar. Takeaway. Activity and entertainment programme. Canoeing. Fishing. Play area. Fully equipped chalets and mobile homes for rent. WiFi. English and Dutch spoken. Off site: Shops and restaurants in Granges-sur-Vologne 2 km. Bicycle hire 3 km. Gérardmer 10 km.

Open: All year.

Directions

Approaching from Gérardmer, head north on D423 to Granges-sur-Vologne. You will see the site signed to the left 100 m. before reaching the village. GPS: 48.123783, 6.818449

Charges guide

Per unit incl. 2 persons and electricity	€ 15.40 - € 20.50
extra person	€ 4.75

Herpelmont

Camping Caravaning Domaine des Messires

1ac rue des Messires, F-88600 Herpelmont (Vosges) T: 03 29 58 56 29. E: mail@domainedesmessires.com

alanrogers.com/FR88070

Nestling in woods beside a lake, des Messires is a haven of peace and tranquillity and is perfect for nature lovers – not only are there birds and flowers but beavers, too. The Vosges is famous for its mountains and you can easily explore the Moselle vineyards and the medieval villages with their old walls and storks on chimneys. The 114 good sized and serviced pitches are on grass over stone, with some directly by the lakeside, excellent for fishing. When the day is over, enjoy a leisurely meal at the welcoming restaurant overlooking the lake or relax in the bar. There are 22 mobile homes for rent.

Facilities

The fully equipped, airy toilet block includes all washbasins in cabins, provision for disabled visitors (key from reception), baby room and laundry. Bar (20/4-27/9) and restaurant (15/5-10/9) with terrace overlooking the lake. Takeaway (15/5-10/9). Two small play areas. Games and TV room. Canoeing and lake swimming. Programme of activities for children and adults in high season. Torches handy. WiFi (charged).

Open: 17 April - 27 September.

Directions

From Épinal, exit N57 on N420 for St Dié and follow signs until you pick up signs for Bruyères. Lac du Messires is signed as you leave Bruyères on D423, at Laveline go south to Herpelmont and site. GPS: 48.1787, 6.74309

Charges guide

Per unit incl. 2 persons and electricity	€ 18.00 - € 26.00
extra person	€ 4.00 - € 6.50

La Bresse

Camping de Belle Hutte

1bis Vouille de Belle-Hutte, F-88250 La Bresse (Vosges) T: 03 29 25 49 75.

E: camping-belle-hutte@wanadoo.fr **alanrogers.com/FR88020**

Belle Hutte is a pleasant family run site in the heart of the Vosges mountains on one of the southern routes to the Col de la Schlucht. Surrounded by mountains and trees, it occupies an open hill slope with 130 numbered grass pitches (110 for touring) on six terraces. Pitches of 80-150 sq.m. are divided by hedges and all have electrical connections (2-10A, Europlug). This site is well worth the detour from the usual main through routes and access is easy via good roads. Situated adjacent to a ski resort, this site makes a perfect base for winter skiing and summer walking. Chalets are also available to rent.

Facilities

The well built, central sanitary block is of excellent quality. Heated in cool weather, it also has facilities for disabled visitors and babies. Laundry facilities. Motorcaravan services. Shop for gifts and basic food supplies. Takeaway and bar (Dec-Mar, July/Aug). TV room. Swimming pool complex (June-Sept; no Bermuda shorts). Playground. Play room. Ski storage room. Picnic area. Pétanque. Badminton. WiFi throughout (charged).

Open: 16 December - 15 November.

Directions

Site is 9 km. from La Bresse on D34 road towards the Col de la Schlucht. GPS: 48.035, 6.96268

Charges guide

Per unit incl. 2 persons and electricity	€ 13.90 - € 29.80
extra person	€ 3.90 - € 8.30
child (0-13 yrs acc. to age)	€ 3.20 - € 6.20
dog	€ 1.95

Higher prices are for winter.

La Bresse

Domaine du Haut des Bluches

5 route des Planches, F-88250 La Bresse (Vosges) T: 03 29 25 64 80. E: hautdesbluches@labresse.fr

alanrogers.com/FR88210

Le Domaine du Haut des Bluches is attractively located in the rolling hills of the Vosges and is close to the ski resorts of Gérardmer and La Bresse. The site is open most of the year with skiing possible in winter and it is a good base for nature lovers in summer. There are 128 slightly uneven and sloping grass/gravel pitches informally laid out in groups on terraces. These include 100 for touring, all with electricity (4/8/13A, Europlug), long leads and rock pegs advised. Across the road there are special areas of hardstanding for motorcaravans, including some electricity hook-ups, all at a special rate. Although there is little organised on the site, La Bresse (4 km) has a wide range of activities on offer.

Facilities

Two well appointed, modern, heated toilet blocks include cabins with WC, basin and shower. Facilities for babies and disabled visitors. Motorcaravan services. Small shop (bread to order) and bar (all year). Restaurant and takeaway (high season, weekends only in low season). Fishing. Games/TV room. Play area. Multisports court. Boules. Internet. Luge and skating rink. WiFi (free).
Off site: Zip wire 1 km. Ski resorts, 5-8 km. Luge and skating rink 5 km. Riding 15 km.

Open: All year excl. mid November to early December.

Directions

La Bresse is 25 km. south of Gérardmer on the D486. At the eastern end of the town turn south on Route des Planches. Site is signed, entrance in 350 m. GPS: 47.998986, 6.918324

Charges guide

Per unit incl. 2 persons and electricity	€ 15.10 - € 25.10
extra person	€ 3.40
child (4-12 yrs)	€ 2.20

Le Tholy

JP Vacances - Camping de Noirrupt

15 chemin de l'Etang, F-88530 Le Tholy (Vosges) T: 03 29 61 81 27. E: info@jpvacances.com

alanrogers.com/FR88030

An attractive, modern, family run site, Camping de Noirrupt has a commanding mountainside position with some magnificent views, especially from the upper terraces. This is a comfortable, high quality site that is sure to please. The tarmac road winds up through the site with pitches (all with access to electricity and water) being terraced and provided with tarmac car parking spaces. The 77 lawn-like touring pitches are generally spacious, and the whole site is beautifully landscaped with many attractive shrubs, flower beds, decking and trees. There are also 12 cottage-style chalets available to rent.

Facilities

Two modern, clean buildings at different levels, plus a small unit behind reception. Washbasins in cubicles, facilities for babies and disabled campers. Washing machines and dryer. Shop. Bar, snack bar and takeaway (6/7-22/8). Swimming pool (15x10 m. 1/6-15/9). TV room (1/6-15/9). Tennis. Organised activities in high season. WiFi (charged). Chalets for rent. No electric barbecues

Open: 1 May - 31 September.

Directions

From Gérardmer take D417 west (Remiremont). In Le Tholy turn right on D11, continue up hill for 2 km, and site is signed to left. GPS: 48.0889, 6.728483

Charges guide

Per unit incl. 2 persons and electricity	€ 20.47 - € 27.10
extra person	€ 4.27 - € 6.10

No credit cards.

Metz

Camping Municipal de Metz-Plage

Allée de Metz-Plage, F-57000 Metz (Moselle) T: 03 87 68 26 48. E: campingmetz@mairie-metz.fr

alanrogers.com/FR57050

As this site is just a short way from the autoroute exit and within easy walking distance for the city centre, it could make a useful night stop if travelling from Luxembourg to Nancy or for a longer stay if exploring the area. By the Moselle river, the 151 pitches are on fairly level grass and most are under shade from tall trees. Sixty-five pitches are fully serviced and 84 have electricity (10A). Tent pitches have a separate place beside the river.

Facilities

The two sanitary blocks, one newer than the other, are acceptable if not luxurious. Facilities for disabled visitors. Baby room. Laundry facilities. Motorcaravan services. Shop. Bar, restaurant and takeaway. Hardstanding pitches for overnight stops for motorcaravans without electricity. WiFi (free). Bicycle hire. Fishing (permits for sale). Off site: Indoor pool adjacent (free entry). Riding 5 km. Golf 8 km.

Open: 24 April - 5 October.

Directions

From autoroute take Metz-Nord-Pontiffray exit (no. 33) and follow site signs. GPS: 49.12402, 6.16917

Charges guide

Per unit incl. 2 persons and electricity	€ 16.00 - € 29.50
extra person	€ 3.10
child (4-10 yrs)	€ 2.10
dog	€ 0.50

Saint Maurice-sur-Moselle

Camping les Deux Ballons

17 rue du Stade, F-88560 Saint Maurice-sur-Moselle (Vosges) T: 03 29 25 17 14. E: stan0268@orange.fr

alanrogers.com/FR88010

Run by the same family for over 50 years, les Deux Ballons is set in a narrow valley near the source of the River Moselle in the Vosges. The 150 pitches (all fully serviced, 4/10A electricity) are on level grass, some under trees and others in the open by a stream that runs through the site. Wild birds are abundant, including kingfishers. This is the perfect location from which to commence the climb of the Ballon d'Alsace, which is hugely popular with cyclists. Theatre lovers should visit Bussang (6 km) and see the large wooden People's Theatre, built in 1895 and still performing in July and August every year; you will marvel at the raked stage and the enormous backstage areas which may be visited at any time.

Facilities

Two stylish and modern toilet blocks (all season) and two older ones (high season only). Facilities for babies and disabled visitors. Laundry. Motorcaravan services. Gas supplies. Bar and takeaway (July/Aug). Large heated swimming pool with slide and paddling pool (June-Aug). Fishing. Tennis. Bicycle hire. Boules. TV. Internet point. WiFi in parts (charged). Off site: Shops and restaurant nearby. Riding 3 km. Paragliding 6 km. Mulhouse and car museum 30 minutes.

Open: 10 April - 15 September.

Directions

Site is on main N66 Le Thillot-Bussang road on western edge of St Maurice behind Avia filling station (entrance partly obscured so keep a look out). GPS: 47.85517, 6.81108

Charges guide

Per unit incl. 2 persons and electricity	€ 23.70 - € 36.50
extra person	€ 6.20 - € 7.20
child (2-7 yrs)	€ 4.50 - € 5.20

No credit cards.

Sanchey

Camping Club Lac de Bouzey

19 rue du Lac, F-88390 Sanchey (Vosges) T: 03 29 82 49 41. E: lacdebouzey@orange.fr

alanrogers.com/FR88040

Open all year, Camping Lac de Bouzey is 8 km. west of Épinal, at the start of the Vosges Massif. The 134 reasonably level grass pitches are separated by tall trees and neat hedging giving varying amounts of shade. There are 100 for touring, all with access to 6/10A electricity and water. They are on a gently sloping hillside above the lake with its sandy beaches. In high season, an extensive timetable of activities is arranged for all ages, especially teenagers, and the site will be very lively. Golf can be arranged at a local course with discounted rates. English is spoken.

Facilities

The toilet block includes a baby room and one for disabled visitors (there are some gradients). Small, heated section in the main building with toilet, washbasin and shower is used in winter. Family shower room. Facilities for children. Laundry facilities. Motorcaravan services. Shop. Bar (1/5-1/11). Restaurant and takeaway (1/3-1/11). Heated pool (1/5-30/9). Games room. Archery. Fishing. Riding. Bicycle hire. Soundproofed room for cinema shows and discos (high season). WiFi throughout.

Open: All year.

Directions

Site is 8 km. west of Épinal on the D460. From Épinal follow signs for Lac de Bouzey and Sanchey. At western end of Sanchey turn south, site signed. GPS: 48.16692, 6.35990

Charges guide

Per unit incl. 2 persons and electricity	€ 27.00 - € 32.00
extra person	€ 7.00 - € 11.00

Camping Cheques accepted.

Saulxures-sur-Moselotte

Base de Loisirs du Lac de la Moselotte

336 route des Amias, F-88290 Saulxures-sur-Moselotte (Vosges) T: 03 29 24 56 56.

E: contact@lac-moselotte.fr **alanrogers.com/FR88090**

This neat, well run, spacious lakeside site, part of a leisure village complex, has 105 grassy pitches with 63 for touring units. All of these have 10A electricity and 30 also have water and a drain. They are individually hedged and a variety of young trees give only a little shade. The site is fully fenced and a security barrier with a key used for the gates to the lakeside. The adjacent Base de Loisirs offers a wide variety of activities and the area is very good for walking and cycling. This is a good base for both summer and winter. Due to its location, expect some traffic noise.

Facilities

The heated toilet block has key entry, controllable hot showers, some washbasins in cubicles and good facilities for babies and disabled campers. Laundry facilities. Shop (July/Aug). Bread to order. Bar/snack bar and terrace. Bicycle hire. Play area. Outdoor skittle alley. Entertainment programme (July/Aug). WiFi in parts (free). Base de Loisirs adjacent with lake (swimming supervised July/Aug), sandy beach, play area, climbing wall, fishing, archery and hire of pedaloes, canoes and kayaks.

Open: All year.

Directions

Saulxures-sur-Moselotte is 20 km. east of Remiremont. From Remiremont take D417 east (St Amé), then right (southeast) on D43 towards La Bresse for 10.5 km. Turn left into Saulxures (site signed), entrance on right by lake after 700 m. GPS: 47.95273, 6.75212

Charges guide

Per unit incl. 2 persons and electricity	€ 18.80 - € 21.80
extra person	€ 4.00 - € 5.00

Verdun

Camping les Breuils

Allée des Breuils, F-55100 Verdun (Meuse) T: 03 29 86 15 31. E: contact@camping-lesbreuils.com

alanrogers.com/FR55010

Thousands of soldiers of many nations are buried in the cemeteries around this famous town and the city is justly proud of its determined First World War resistance. Les Breuils is a neat, attractive site beside a small fishing lake and close to the town and citadel. It provides 162 flat pitches of varying sizes on two levels (144 for touring units), many with shade. Separated by trees or hedges, they are beside the lake and 120 offer 6A electricity connections (long leads will be necessary for some). The Citadelle Souterraine is well worth a visit and is within walking distance of the site.

Facilities

Two sanitary blocks are a mixture of old and new, including washbasins in cabins for ladies. Facilities for babies and disabled visitors. Cleaning variable. Laundry. Motorcaravan services. Shop. Bar. Restaurant (1/5-15/9). Swimming pool (200 sq.m) and children's pool (1/5-15/9). Fenced gravel play area. Multisports complex. Bicycle hire. WiFi. Off site: Town and boat launching 1 km. Riding 5 km.

Open: 15 March - 15 October.

Directions

The RN3 forms a sort of ring road round the north of the town. Site is signed from this on the west side of the town (500 m. to site). GPS: 49.15404, 5.36573

Charges guide

Per unit incl. 2 persons and electricity	€ 17.70 - € 21.40
extra person	€ 4.30 - € 5.90
child (2-10 yrs)	€ 3.10 - € 3.80

Villers-les-Nancy

Campéole le Brabois

Avenue Paul Muller, F-54600 Villers-les-Nancy (Meurthe-et-Moselle) T: 03 83 27 18 28.

E: brabois@campeole.com **alanrogers.com/FR54000**

This site is within the Nancy city boundary and just 5 km. from the centre. Situated within a forest area, there is shade in most parts and, although the site is on a slight slope, the 174 good sized, numbered and separated pitches are level. Of these, 140 pitches have electricity connections (5A) and ten also have 15A electricity, water and drainage. There are many plans for this site, including refurbishment of the playground for 2016. Being on one of the main routes from Luxembourg to the south of France, le Brabois makes a good night stop. However, Nancy is a delightful city in the heart of Lorraine and well worth a longer stay.

Facilities

Four sanitary blocks have been completely updated. Facilities for babies and disabled visitors. Laundry. Motorcaravan services. Shop (incl. eggs and other produce grown on site). Bread to order. Restaurant with bar and takeaway (15/4-15/9). Library. Two playgrounds. WiFi (free from 2nd night). Off site: Shops and restaurants 1 km. Riding 1 km. Bicycle hire 2 km. Walking and cycling. Regular buses to Nancy.

Open: 1 April - 15 October.

Directions

From A33, exit 2b for Brabois. Continue for 500 m. to 'Quick' restaurant on left. Turn left, pass racetrack to T-junction, turn right and after 400 m. turn right on to site entrance road. GPS: 48.66440, 6.14330

Charges guide

Per unit incl. 2 persons and electricity	€ 17.00 - € 21.00

Credit cards minimum € 15.

Camping Cheques accepted.

Villey-le-Sec

Camping de Villey-le-Sec

34 rue de la Gare, F-54840 Villey-le-Sec (Meurthe-et-Moselle) T: 03 83 63 64 28.

E: info@campingvilleylesec.com **alanrogers.com/FR54010**

This neat campsite is a popular overnight stop, but the area is worth a longer stay. Villey-le-Sec has its own fortifications, part of the defensive system built along France's frontiers after the 1870 war, and a long cycle track passes near the site. On a bank of the Moselle river, there are 86 level, grassy, marked touring pitches with electricity (6/10A) and plenty of water taps. There are also individual water taps and waste water drainage for eight of these pitches. Another area without electricity accommodates 11 tents. Just outside the site is an overnight stopping place for motorcaravans. This site is conveniently near the motorway from Luxembourg to the Mediterranean. Toul, with its 2000 years of history and Vauban fortifications, is well worth a visit.

Facilities

Two modern toilet blocks (one heated) with controllable hot showers and washbasins in cabins. Facilities for babies and disabled visitors. Motorcaravan services. Washing machine and dryer. Shop. Bar/restaurant. Snack bar and takeaway (all 15/4-20/9). Playground. Playing field. Boules. Fishing (permit required). Charcoal barbecues are not permitted. WiFi on part of site (charged). Off site: Rock climbing 4 km. Golf 15 km.

Open: 1 April - 30 September.

Directions

Villey-le-Sec is 7 km. east of Toul. Leave A31 west of Nancy at exit 15 and after 1 km. at roundabout (Leclerc supermarket) take D909 to Villey-le-Sec. In village follow signs 'Camping' to the right, proceed down a steep hill for 600 m. then at bottom of hill turn left into site. GPS: 48.65281, 5.99151

Charges guide

Per unit incl. 2 persons and electricity (6A)	€ 18.80 - € 21.50
extra person	€ 3.80
child (0-7 yrs)	€ 2.70
dog	€ 1.80

Xonrupt Longemer

Flower Camping Verte Vallée

4092 route du Lac, F-88400 Xonrupt Longemer (Vosges) T: 03 29 63 21 77.

E: contact@campingvertevallee.com **alanrogers.com/FR88410**

In one of France's most picturesque regions, amongst the Vosges mountains and the vineyards of Alsace, Verte Vallée enjoys an enviable location just 300 m. from the shore of the Lac de Longemer, and within easy reach of the popular towns of Kaysersburg and Colmar. Of the 147 pitches, 132 are for touring with 4-10A electricity (long leads advisable). The site is open much of the year and winter sports enthusiasts can leave their vehicles on site and use the shuttle bus to their destinations. There are chalets and tent lodges to rent and a large cottage for parties of up to 22. Sitting some 610 m. above sea level and surrounded by wooded hills and mountains, Verte Vallée offers a myriad of hiking and cycling opportunities throughout the year. This campsite is a most attractive and scenic base for a truly rural holiday.

Facilities

Shower blocks (one heated with drying room). Washing machines and dryer. Baby room. Shop (fresh bread daily) and takeaway (July/Aug). Motorcaravan services. Cooked meat vendor and a pizza van call twice weekly. Bar (1/6-30/9). Heated indoor and outdoor pools (1/5-30/9). Tennis. Trampoline. Playground. Indoor games room and TV room. WiFi on part of site. Off site: Sailing, fishing, lakeside beach and bar and pedalo hire within 500 m. Skiing 4 km. Bicycle hire 5 km. Riding 8 km. National Park. Kaysersburg. Colmar. German and Swiss borders.

Open: All year excl. 2 November - 14 December.

Directions

From Metz/Nancy take E23 to Epinal. Then D11 and D417 to Gerardmer. Continue on 417 and D67A. Site will be found on the left, shortly after passing the Lac de Longemer. GPS: 48.062418, 6.964747

Charges guide

Per unit incl. 2 persons and electricity	€ 19.00 - € 27.00
extra person	€ 5.50 - € 6.00
child (3-6 yrs)	€ 3.20 - € 3.50
dog	€ 2.00 - € 3.00

DÉPARTEMENTS: 67 BAS-RHIN, 68 HAUT-RHIN

MAJOR CITY: STRASBOURG

Lying between the Rhine and the Vosges mountains, to the north and east, Alsace shares a border with Germany, to the south with German-speaking Switzerland and to the west with Lorraine and Franche Comté.

Alsace lies between the River Rhine and the Vosges mountains. It is largely regarded as the Germanic region of France, bordering Germany in the north and east, and German-speaking Switzerland in the south. Indeed, a significant number of its inhabitants speak the Alsacian dialect, a form of German similar to that spoken in Switzerland. Having been under both German and French rule during the development of modern day Europe, it shows the influence of both countries.

Alsace has two départements, both geographically similar, with the Vosges mountains in the west sweeping down to the Rhine Valley and the fertile plains of the east. The capital of the Lower Rhine is Strasbourg, home of the European Parliament, and a vibrant city with an attractive medieval centre and an outlying industrial belt. The capital of the Upper Rhine is Colmar, with its beautifully preserved medieval houses; however, the largest city is Mulhouse, a major manufacturing centre with a wealth of museums and attractions.

Places of interest

Colmar: interesting for its 16th-century timber houses; Musée d'Unterlinden.

Kayserberg: small town, birthplace of Albert Schweitzer; special Christmas market.

Haut-Koenigsberg: legendary hilltop castle in the Vosges mountains, close to Strasbourg.

Mulhouse: famous for the Musée National de l'Automobile and the Musée Français de Chemin de Fer.

Riquewihr: almost untouched since the 18th century (whilst almost every other village was decimated by war) with 13/14th-century fortifications and medieval houses.

Cuisine of the region

Beckenoffe (Baeckeoffe): a hotpot of potatoes, lamb, beef, pork and onions, cooked in local wine.

Choucroute: sauerkraut with peppercorns, boiled ham, pork, Strasbourg sausages and boiled potatoes.

Flammekuche: bread dough topped with cream, onions and bacon.

Munster: a soft, strong tasting cheese with orange rind, believed to have been invented by the monks of the Benedictine Abbey.

Tarte à l'oignon Alsacienne: onion and cream tart.

www.tourisme-alsace.com
crt@tourisme-alsace.com
(0)3 89 24 73 50

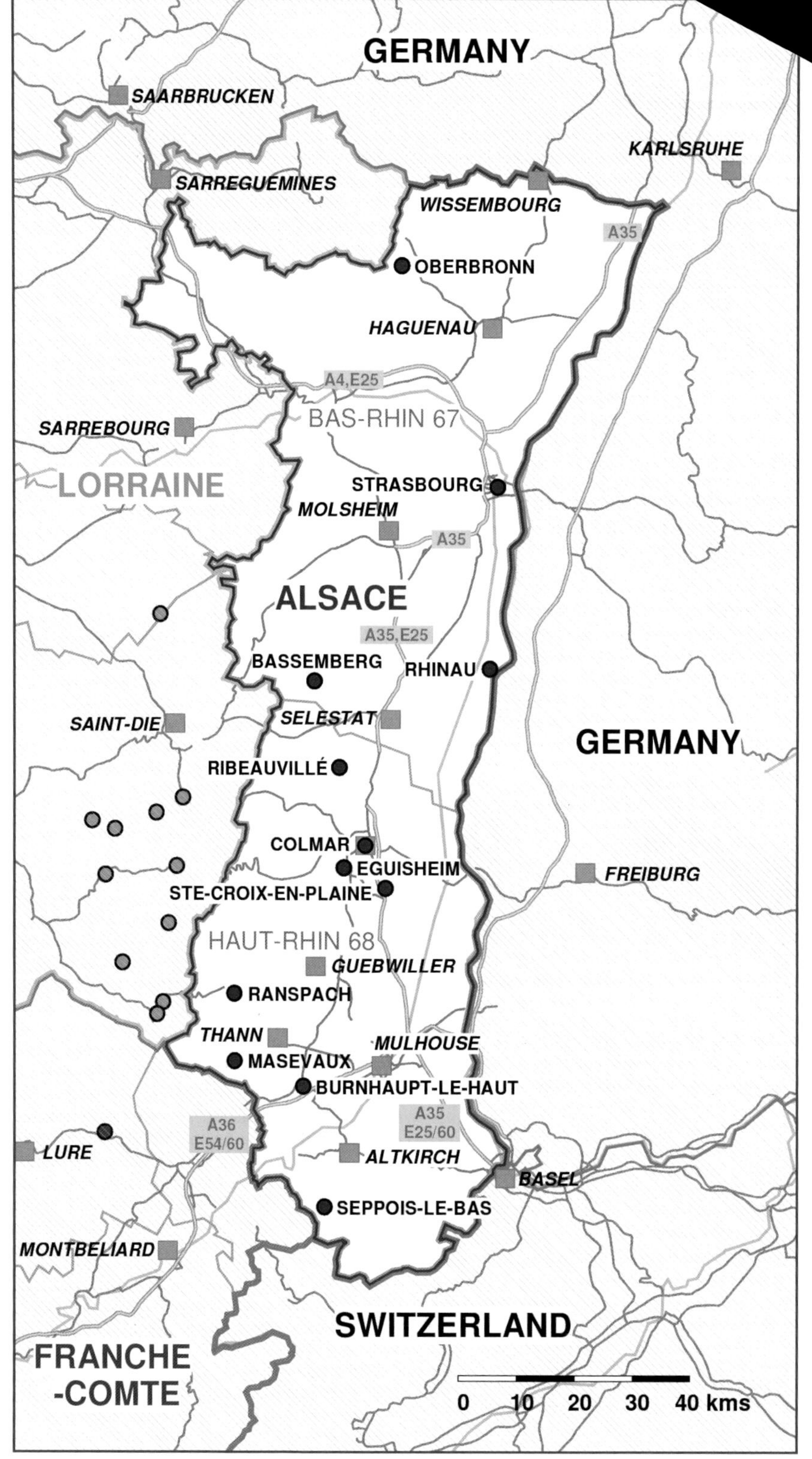
GERMANY
SAARBRUCKEN
KARLSRUHE
SARREGUEMINES
WISSEMBOURG
A35
OBERBRONN
HAGUENAU
A4,E25
BAS-RHIN 67
SARREBOURG
LORRAINE
STRASBOURG
MOLSHEIM
A35
ALSACE
A35,E25
BASSEMBERG
RHINAU
SAINT-DIE
SELESTAT
GERMANY
RIBEAUVILLÉ
COLMAR
EGUISHEIM
FREIBURG
STE-CROIX-EN-PLAINE
HAUT-RHIN 68
GUEBWILLER
RANSPACH
THANN
MULHOUSE
MASEVAUX
BURNHAUPT-LE-HAUT
A36
E54/60
A35
E25/60
LURE
ALTKIRCH
BASEL
SEPPOIS-LE-BAS
MONTBELIARD
SWITZERLAND
FRANCHE
-COMTE
0 10 20 30 40 kms
ace

…iessen

…-67220 Bassemberg (Bas-Rhin) T: 03 88 58 98 14. E: giessen@campeole.com
…m/FR67070

… is a member of the Campéole group and can be found at the foot of the Vosges mountains … access to many of the best loved sights in Alsace. Although there is no pool on site, a large …x comprising indoor and outdoor pools with a water slide can be found adjacent to the site, with … admission for all campers. The 69 touring pitches here are grassy and of a good size, mostly with 6A electrical connections and some shaded by mature trees. A number of mobile homes and fully equipped tents are available for rent. A supplement is payable for twin-axle caravans.

Facilities

Two toilet blocks with all facilities including controllable hot showers and facilities for disabled visitors. Laundry. Bar. Snack bar/takeaway (July/Aug). Play area. Multisports court. Activities and entertainment. Bicycle hire. Mobile homes and equipped tents for rent. WiFi (charged).
Off site: Swimming pool complex adjacent. Tennis. Roller-blading rink. Hiking and mountain biking. Fishing 1.5 km. Riding 5 km. Strasbourg 50 km.

Open: 4 April - 15 September.

Directions

Leave the A35 autoroute at exit 17 (Villé) and follow the N59 then D424 to Villé from where site is signed. Turn south onto D39 to Bassemberg and follow signs. GPS: 48.33722, 7.28862

Charges guide

Per unit incl. 2 persons and electricity	€ 15.70 - € 27.50
extra person	€ 4.20 - € 6.90

Camping Cheques accepted.

Burnhaupt-le-Haut

Camping les Castors

4 route de Guewenheim, F-68520 Burnhaupt-le-Haut (Haut-Rhin) T: 03 89 48 78 58.
E: camping.les.castors@wanadoo.fr **alanrogers.com/FR68300**

Camping les Castors provides a convenient starting point from which to explore Alsace. It is close to the Vosges mountains which are dominated by the Ballon d'Alsace (1,427 m). This well cared for site with its stream and small lake offers 135 pitches with electricity (10A). Most are of a reasonable size and some have some shade. Fishing is possible in the lake and the site is on the banks of the river. Bicycles can be hired and there are walks in the adjacent forest and the surrounding countryside. The small village of Burnhaupt-le-Haut is within 1.5 km. and has a supermarket, ATM and pharmacy.

Facilities

A new sanitary block offers modern facilities with hot showers and washbasins in cubicles. Facilities for babies and disabled visitors. Laundry facilities. Attractive bar and restaurant with terrace, serving traditional local food. Takeaway. Bread can be ordered from reception. Small play area. Fishing. Bicycle hire. WiFi on terrace (charged).
Off site: Excursions. Supermarket 1.5 km.

Open: 1 April - 31 October.

Directions

Exit D38 (Masevaux and Burnhaupt-le-Haut). Take the D466 towards Masevaux. The site is signed to the right after 1 km. GPS: 47.746877, 7.124494

Charges guide

Per unit incl. 2 persons and electricity	€ 18.30
extra person	€ 3.50
child (under 10 yrs)	€ 2.30

Camping Cheques accepted.

Colmar

Camping Indigo Colmar

1 allée du Camping, Horbourg-Wihr, F-68180 Colmar (Haut-Rhin) T: 03 89 41 15 94.
E: colmar@camping-indigo.com **alanrogers.com/FR68110**

Stretching alongside the Ill river in urban Colmar, this site has 150 unseparated pitches, 120 for touring, arranged on terraces. Due to the danger of flooding on the lowest terrace during the winter months, this part of the site is closed during that period. Despite noise from the A35 motorway, this is a pleasant, well maintained setting with some shade from mature trees. All pitches have 10A electricity connections (Europlug, some pitches require long leads). The reception is comfortable and welcoming with English spoken. Rental accommodation includes wood and canvas tents and wooden lodges. A supplement is payable for twin-axle caravans.

Facilities

One modern heated sanitary block next to the main building and two older blocks (one closed in low season). Washbasins in cubicles, hot showers and facilities for disabled visitors. Washing machine and dryer. Motorcaravan services. Bar (April-Dec). Restaurant and takeaway (May-Sept). Bread to order at reception. New heated pool and paddling pool. Play area. Outdoor chess. TV room. Boules pitch. Table football. Fishing. Bicycle hire. Barbecue hire. WiFi (free in TV lounge).

Open: 27 March - 4 January.

Directions

Using the RN83 or D415 roads into Colmar, follow signs for Horbourg-Wihr and site is well signed from here. GPS: 48.07962, 7.38652

Charges guide

Per unit incl. 2 persons and electricity	€ 19.30 - € 22.60
extra person	€ 3.90 - € 4.80
child (2-7 yrs)	free - € 3.00
dog	€ 2.20 - € 4.40

Eguisheim

Camping des Trois Châteaux

10 rue du Bassin, F-68420 Eguisheim (Haut-Rhin) T: 03 89 23 19 39. E: camping.eguisheim@orange.fr

alanrogers.com/FR68040

The village of Eguisheim, 'cradle of the Alsace vineyards', lies on the Alsace Route des Vins to the west of Colmar. The three châteaux from which the site gets its name are clearly visible on the hill behind the site. Being close to the village, Les Trois Châteaux is always busy. Flowers, shrubs and trees, and well tended grass areas make this a very pleasant place. The 121 pitches, 115 with electricity (6/10A), are either on a slight slope or a terrace, and are marked and numbered, most with good shade. Around 80% of pitches have some gravel hardstandings, most of irregular shape and size. We see this site as being suitable primarily for adults rather than families.

Facilities

The single heated sanitary block in the centre of the site has hot showers and warm water only to washbasins. Some washbasins in cubicles and facilities for disabled visitors. Men's showers to be reconstructed for 2016. Motorcaravan services. Playground. WiFi (free). Chalets to rent. Off site: Bicycle hire in town. Fishing 3 km. Golf and riding 10 km.

Open: 23 March - 23 December, excl. 2-24 November.

Directions

Eguisheim is just off the D83 and the site is well signed in the village. GPS: 48.04255, 7.29989

Charges guide

Per unit incl. 2 persons and electricity	€ 16.30 - € 19.80
extra person	€ 3.90 - € 4.40
child (3-13 yrs)	€ 1.00 - € 2.50

Masevaux

Camping de Masevaux

3 rue du Stade, F-68290 Masevaux (Haut-Rhin) T: 03 89 82 42 29. E: camping-masevaux@tv-com.net

alanrogers.com/FR68030

Masevaux is a pleasant little town in the Haut-Rhin department of Alsace, just north of the A36 Belfort-Mulhouse motorway. The neatly mown 110 pitches for tourers are on level grass, of reasonable size, marked by trees and hedges, and all have electricity (3/6A). Most are well shaded with good views of the surrounding hills. The new French manager would like to welcome more British visitors. A good choice for stopover or a longer stay to explore this interesting region; an ideal site for serious walkers.

Facilities

A modern, well designed and well equipped sanitary block has most washbasins in private cabins. Baby room. Laundry. Café/bar serving snacks. Baker calls in high season. Ice creams and soft drinks from reception. TV room, small library. Boules. Play area. Tennis (extra charge). Fishing. WiFi. Off site: Supermarket, restaurants and indoor pool. Wednesday market in Masevaux. Bicycle hire 300 m. Golf 7 km. Riding 10 km. Beach 15 km.

Open: 10 January - 10 December.

Directions

From D466 in Masevaux follow signs for Belfort and then Camping Complexe Sportif. GPS: 47.7782, 6.9909

Charges guide

Per unit incl. 2 persons and electricity	€ 15.00 - € 17.00
extra person	€ 3.00 - € 4.00
child (3-16 yrs)	€ 1.50 - € 2.50

Oberbronn

Flower Camping l'Oasis

3 rue du Frohret, F-67110 Oberbronn (Bas-Rhin) T: 03 88 09 71 96. E: oasis.oberbronn@laregie.fr

alanrogers.com/FR67010

This is an attractively situated, inexpensive site, amidst the mountains and forests of northern Alsace, not far from the German border. There are good views over the valley to one side and the pretty village with trees sheltering the other. The circular internal road has pitches around the outside (139 for touring units, 15 for seasonal units, 39 accommodation units for rent), and space in the centre where there is a playground. The solar-heated swimming pool and children's pool are of excellent quality. A Centre de Vacances provides a covered swimming pool, sauna and fitness room.

Facilities

Sanitary facilities can be heated in cool weather and include hot showers and washbasins, a baby room and facilities for disabled visitors. Laundry facilities. Small shop. Fresh bread (1/4-30/9). Bar. Restaurant, snack bar and takeaway (all 1/4-30/9). Outdoor swimming pool and children's pool (July/Aug). Heated indoor swimming pool (1/5-30/9). Sauna and Jacuzzi. Playground. Games room. Tennis. Excursions (July/Aug). WiFi on most of site (charged). Off site: Walking and cycle routes. Supermarket 1 km. Bicycle hire 8 km. Fishing 12 km. Riding 19 km.

Open: 15 March - 15 November.

Directions

Travel northwest from Haguenau on N62 for 20 km. South of Niederbronn turn left on D28 for Oberbronn-Zinswiller. Site is signed from here. From A4 take exit 42 to Sarreguemines, then N62 and D620 towards Haguenau and as above. GPS: 48.9291, 7.6041

Charges guide

Per unit incl. 2 persons and electricity	€ 13.70
extra person	€ 3.70
child (under 7 yrs)	€ 2.20

No credit cards.

Ranspach

Flower Camping les Bouleaux

8 rue des Bouleaux, F-68470 Ranspach (Haut-Rhin) T: 03 89 82 64 70. E: contact@alsace-camping.com

alanrogers.com/FR68140

Les Bouleaux is a well maintained site with 100 touring pitches of a rather small size (80 sq.m), although they are flat and grassy. The site is open all year round, but the shop is only opened during the high season. The site is ideally situated if you are coming by motorbike or are planning to go paragliding or skiing. Les Bouleaux is set in the heart of the Thur valley, at the foot of the Vosges mountains. It offers many possibilities for outdoor activities such as climbing, playing golf, hiking and fishing, to name just a few. Also recommended is a visit to the Wesserling park and its beautiful gardens, which were established in 1699!

Facilities

Two traditional, clean sanitary blocks with showers. Good baby room. Facilities for disabled visitors. Shop (July/Aug). Bar, excellent restaurant, snack bar/takeaway (all year except Nov). New indoor swimming and paddling pools (caps compulsory, no Bermudas). Boules. Volleyball. Minigolf. Play area. WiFi (charged). Accommodation to rent. Off site: Fishing 1 km. Bicycle hire and beach 3 km.

Open: All year.

Directions

Leave the A31 and follow signs for Epinal on E23. Approaching Epinal follow E512 towards Mulhouse. Continue on the E512 until Ranspach. Drive 700 m. on N66, then turn right on rue des Bouleaux to site. GPS: 47.880743, 7.010334

Charges guide

Per unit incl. 2 persons and electricity	€ 19.50 - € 27.00
extra person	€ 4.50 - € 6.00

Rhinau

Camping la Ferme des Tuileries

1 rue des Tuileries, F-67860 Rhinau (Bas-Rhin) T: 03 88 74 60 45. E: camping.fermetuileries@neuf.fr

alanrogers.com/FR67040

Close to the German border, this ten-hectare, family run site has 150 large open pitches, hardstanding for 15 motorcaravans and room for 50 seasonal caravans. The site buildings have a traditional external appearance but all have modern interiors. Welcoming reception staff will provide information about the site and the local area. A small lake with two water slides is used for swimming and boating (separate areas) and there is also a small unsupervised and unheated swimming pool. A newly built restaurant and bar are at the lakeside. A ferry crosses the Rhine river into Germany.

Facilities

Three modern, bright and cheerful blocks with the usual facilities. Two washing machines and two dryers. Controllable showers. Family bathroom at no extra charge. Fully equipped facilities for disabled visitors (key access). Motorcaravan services. Bar, restaurant and takeaway (1/7-15/8). Small lake for swimming, fishing, boating, two water slides. Unsupervised swimming pool (July/Aug, caps compulsory). Tennis. Pétanque. Minigolf. Bicycle hire. Dogs are not accepted. Off site: Supermarket 500 m. Ferry across the Rhine 1 km.

Open: 1 April - 30 September.

Directions

Coming from Colmar (A35) take exit 14 (Kogenheim-Benfeld-Erstein) then the N83 to exit for Benfeld-Rhinau, following site signs. From Strasbourg on A35 take exit 7 (Erstein-Fegersheim) then the N83. GPS: 48.321, 7.698

Charges guide

Per unit incl. 2 persons and electricity	€ 15.60
extra person	€ 4.00
child (under 7 yrs)	€ 2.00

No credit cards or cheques.

Ribeauvillé

Camping Municipal Pierre de Coubertin

23 rue de Landau, F-68150 Ribeauvillé (Haut-Rhin) T: 03 89 73 66 71. E: camping.ribeauville@wanadoo.fr

alanrogers.com/FR68050

The fascinating medieval town of Ribeauvillé on the Alsace Route des Vins is within walking distance of this attractive, quietly located site. Popular and well run, it has 208 touring pitches, all with 16A electricity and some separated by shrubs or railings. There are tarmac and gravel access roads. This is a site solely for touring units – there are no mobile homes or seasonal units here. The small shop is open daily for most of the season (hours vary) providing bread, basic supplies and some wines.

Facilities

Large, heated block provides modern facilities with washbasins in cubicles. Baby facilities. Large laundry room. A smaller unit at the far end of the site is opened for July/Aug. Very good facilities for disabled campers at both units. Shop (Easter-Oct). Excellent adventure-style play area with rubber base. Tennis. Boules. TV room. Free WiFi over site. Off site: Outdoor pool (June-Aug). Bicycle hire 200 m. Fishing and riding 500 m. Golf 12 km.

Open: 15 March - 15 November.

Directions

Ribeauvillé is 13 km. southwest of Sélestat. Turn north off the D106 at traffic lights by large car park, east of the town centre. GPS: 48.19482, 7.33654

Charges guide

Per unit incl. 2 persons and electricity	€ 16.30 - € 17.30
extra person	€ 4.20
child (0-7 yrs)	€ 2.00

Saint Croix-en-Plaine

Camping ClairVacances

D1 route de Herrlisheim, F-68127 Saint Croix-en-Plaine (Haut-Rhin) T: 03 89 49 27 28.
E: reception@clairvacances.com **alanrogers.com/FR68080**

ClairVacances is a very neat, tidy and pretty garden site with 135 level pitches (120 for touring) of generous size, numbered and mostly separated by trees and shrubs. All have 16A electricity connections and 12 are fully serviced with water and drainage. The site has been imaginatively laid out with the pitches reached from hard access roads. This is a quiet family site. The friendly couple who own and run it will be pleased to advise on the attractions of the area. The site is 1 km. from the A35 exit, not far from Colmar in the region of Alsace, a popular and picturesque area.

Facilities

Two excellent, modern toilet blocks include washbasins in cabins, well equipped baby rooms and good facilities for disabled visitors. Laundry facilities. Motorcaravan services. Takeaway (July/Aug). Swimming and paddling pools (heated) with large sunbathing area (1/5-30/9). Playground. Community room. Camping Gaz. Dogs are not accepted. No football. Gas and electric barbecues only. American-style motorhomes and twin-axle caravans are not accepted. Free WiFi throughout.

Open: 23 April - 10 October.

Directions

Site is signed from exit 27 of the A35 on D1, halfway between St Croix-en-Plaine and Herrlisheim.
GPS: 48.01606, 7.35016

Charges guide

Per unit incl. 2 persons and electricity	€ 17.00 - € 32.00
extra person	€ 4.50 - € 7.50
child (2-12 yrs acc. to age)	€ 1.50 - € 5.50

Seppois-le-Bas

Village Center les Lupins

1 rue de la Gare, F-68580 Seppois-le-Bas (Haut-Rhin) T: 04 99 57 21 21. E: contact@village-center.fr
alanrogers.com/FR68120

Only ten kilometres from the Swiss border and within walking distance of a small village, this is a pleasant, traditional site. It has 138 level, grass touring pitches, all with electrical connections (6A), a few seasonal units and 13 chalets (ten available to rent). Shade is provided in places by mature trees. The main site building (formerly a railway station) houses reception which has a few basic supplies, tourist information, a pool table and electronic games. Snacks and drinks are served on the terrace overlooking the small, fenced swimming pool. The site is a member of the Village Center group.

Facilities

The central toilet block provides plenty of facilities in a traditional style. A second block (open in high season) is older but with similar facilities. En-suite units for disabled visitors. Laundry facilities. Bread to order and basic supplies from reception. Drinks and simple snacks served on the terrace. Swimming pool (15/5-15/9). Play area. Bicycle hire. Internet access and WiFi (charged). Gas barbecues only. Off site: Restaurant across the road. Village 400 m. Fishing 2 km. Golf 4 km. Riding 8 km.

Open: 4 April -17 September.

Directions

Seppois is 30 km. southwest of Mulhouse. On A36 from Besançon at exit 11, take N1019 to Grandvillars, then D463 east to Seppois. From Mulhouse on A36 at exit 15, take D466 to Altkirch, D432 towards Ferrette, then D17 to Seppois. Site is signed in village. GPS: 47.53913, 7.17998

Charges guide

Per unit incl. 2 persons and electricity	€ 14.00 - € 15.00

Camping Cheques accepted.

Strasbourg

Camping Indigo Strasbourg

9 rue de l'Auberge de Jeunesse, F-67200 Strasbourg (Bas-Rhin) T: 03 88 30 19 96.
E: strasbourg@camping-indigo.com **alanrogers.com/FR67060**

Reopened in July 2015 after a lengthy refurbishment, Camping Indigo Strasbourg is a beautifully designed and built, brand new city site in south west Strasbourg. During the low season you pick your pitch but in high season and during the time of the Christmas market (when there may be snow!), reservations are advised as the site becomes full. There are currently 90 pitches with electricity hook-ups (6-9A, Europlug). A new central lodge has been added, the sanitary facilities completely rebuilt and a modern café/restaurant opened on site. There is a bus stop 200 m. from the site and the city tram runs into town. The city centre is only 30 minutes' walk so this site is an ideal base from which to explore it.

Facilities

Two brand new, heated sanitary blocks with facilities for families and disabled visitors. Washing machines and dryer. Motorcaravan services. Bar, restaurant and takeaway (all 6/7-31/8). Outdoor heated swimming pool (30/4-18/9). Bicycle hire. Free WiFi on part of site. Wood and canvas tents and Romany-style caravans for rent. Off site: The city of Strasbourg is a 30-minute walk.

Open: All year.

Directions

From the D35 take exit 4 (Montagne Verte) follow site signs. From the city centre follow directions for Oswald and Illskirch to Montagne Verte.
GPS: 48.575507, 7.71506

Charges guide

Per unit incl. 2 persons and electricity	€ 21.80 - € 31.80
extra person	€ 4.20 - € 5.30

DÉPARTEMENTS: 18 CHER, 28 EURE-ET-LOIR, 36 INDRE, 37 INDRE-ET-LOIRE, 41 LOIR-ET-CHER, 45 LOIRET

MAJOR CITIES: ORLÉANS, TOURS

With over one hundred of France's finest châteaux, this is a region to inspire the imagination. The Loire valley is a charming region of lush countryside, rolling vineyards, fields of sunflowers and of course the great river itself.

For centuries the Loire valley was frequented by French royalty, and the great river winds its way past some of France's most magnificent châteaux: Amboise, Azay-le-Rideau, Chenonceau with its famous arches that span the river and appear to 'float' on the water, and the fairytale Ussé with myriad magical turrets, are just some of the highlights.

Known as the Garden of France, the Loire Valley is a patchwork of lush fields, cool forests and meandering rivers. Following the course of the Loire are the vineyards that produce some of France's most renowned wines, notably Sancerre and the sparking Vouvray. Its stunning architecture, troglodyte caves, tiny Romanesque churches and magical son-et-lumière productions are just an hour from Paris by TGV. The Loire à Vélo long-distance cycle path offers visitors the chance to discover the region's charming villages and historic cities while enjoying all that nature has to offer.

Places of interest

Amboise: château; Leonardo da Vinci museum.

Beauregard: château with Delft tiled floors.

Blois: château with architecture from Middle Ages to Neo-Classical periods.

Chambord: Renaissance château.

Chartres: cathedral with stained glass windows.

Chinon: old town; Joan of Arc museum

Loches: old town; château and its fortifications.

Orléans: Holy Cross cathedral; house of Joan of Arc.

Tours: Renaissance and Neo-Classical mansions; cathedral of St Gatien.

Vendôme: Tour St Martin; La Trinité.

Villandry: famous Renaissance gardens.

Cuisine of the region

Wild duck, pheasant, hare, deer, and quail are classics, and freshwater fish such as salmon, perch and trout are favourites. Specialities include rillettes, andouillettes, tripe, mushrooms, and regional cheeses such as Pouligny St. Pierre and Ste. Maure de Touraine, and Petit Sable and Ardoises d'Angers cookies.

Bourdaines: baked apples stuffed with jam.

Tarte à la citrouille: pumpkin tart.

Tarte Tatin: upside-down tart of caramelised apples and pastry.

www.visaloire.com
crtcentre@visaloire.com
(0)2 38 79 95 28

EVREUX MEAUX
0 25 50 75 kms
PARIS
NORMANDY
DREUX
PARIS
ILE DE FRANCE
SENONCHES
CHARTRES
ETAMPES
EURE-ET-LOIR 28
MAMERS
A11,E50
LOIRET 45
PAYS DE LA LOIRE
CHATEAUDUN
PITHIVIERS
MONTARGIS
BURGUNDY
VAL DE LOIRE
LE MANS
LOIR-ET-CHER 41
ORLEANS
CHECY
A77
A10,E05,60
VENDOME
GIEN
POILLY-LEZ-GIEN
BRIARE-LE-CANAL
SUÈVRES
MUIDES-SUR-LOIRE
BLOIS
NOUAN-LE-FUZELIER
BRACIEUX
CANDÉ-SUR-BEUVRON
PIERREFITTE-SUR-SAULDRE
SONZAY
MESLAND
AUBIGNY-SUR-NÈRE
CHEVERNY
NEUNG-SUR-BEUVRON
RILLÉ
LA VILLE-AUX-DAMES
LUYNES
FAVEROLLES-SUR-CHER
BALLAN-MIRÉ
TOURS
FRANCUEIL-CHENONCEAU
INDRE-ET-LOIRE 37
VIERZON
A71,E11
CHINON
CHEMILLÉ-SUR-INDROIS
BOURGES
TROGUES
LOCHES-EN-TOURAINE
STE CATHERINE-DE-FIERBOIS
CHER 18
INDRE 36
CHATEAUROUX
CHATELLERAULT
VELLES
AUVERGNE
A20,E09
POITIERS
POITOU CHARENTES
LIMOUSIN
MONTLUCON

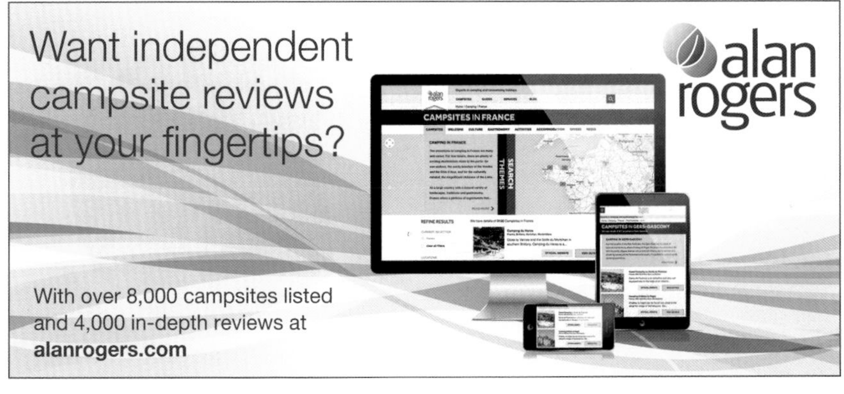

Aubigny-sur-Nère

Camping les Etangs

Route de Sancerre, F-18700 Aubigny-sur-Nère (Cher) T: 02 48 58 02 37. E: camping.aubigny@orange.fr

alanrogers.com/FR18010

Les Etangs is a site of 100 pitches, close to the Sancerre vineyards and the lakes of the Sologne. A member of the Flower group, this site extends over two hectares and borders a small lake (suitable for fishing). Pitches are large and grassy (most have electrical connections). There are chalets available for rent. The town of Aubigny-sur-Nère is very close (1 km) and has a close attachment with Scotland, thanks to the 'Auld Alliance'. The town is the only one in France to celebrate French-Scottish friendship on Bastille Day. Bring your bicycle as there are many tracks running through the surrounding forests.

Facilities

Two heated toilet blocks are a good provision and are well located. Bar (high season). New swimming pool complex should be completed. Play area. Fishing (permit required). Activity and entertainment programme. WiFi over site (free). Communal barbecue areas. Chalets and tents to rent. Off site: Swimming pool with aqua-gym 50 m. Aubigny-sur-Nère 1 km. Golf 20 km. Riding 25 km. Sancerre vineyards. Walking and cycle tracks.

Open: 1 April - 30 September.

Directions

Aubigny is southeast of Orléans. Approaching from the north (Orléans) on the A71 autoroute take exit 4 for Salbris and head east on D724 and D924 until Aubigny. Take the D923 towards Sancerre and site is 1 km. GPS: 47.48435, 2.45703

Charges guide

Per unit incl. 2 persons and electricity	€ 16.50 - € 21.00
extra person	€ 3.00 - € 4.50
child (3-7 yrs)	€ 2.00 - € 3.00
dog	€ 2.00 - € 3.00

Ballan-Miré

Camping de la Mignardière

22 avenue des Aubépines, F-37510 Ballan-Miré (Indre-et-Loire) T: 02 47 73 31 00. E: info@mignardiere.com

alanrogers.com/FR37010

Southwest of the city of Tours, this site is within easy reach of several of the Loire châteaux, notably Azay-le-Rideau. There are also many varied sports amenities on the site or very close by. The site has 168 numbered pitches of which 130 are for touring units, all with electricity (10A) and 37 with drainage and water. Pitches are of a good size (60-130 sq.m) on rather uneven grass, accessed by tarmac roads. The barrier gates (coded access) are closed 22.30-07.30. Reservation is essential for most of July and August. There is also a watersports complex within 300 m. of the site.

Facilities

Three very clean toilet blocks (one recently upgraded) include washbasins in private cabins, good facilities for disabled campers, baby room and laundry facilities. Motorcaravan services. Well stocked shop sells snacks (all season). Takeaway. Indoor heated swimming pools and outdoor heated pool (all season). Paddling pool. Tennis. Bicycle hire. WiFi over site (charged). Torch useful. Off site: Attractive lake 300 m. Family fitness run. Fishing and sailing 500 m. Boat launching 1.5 km. Golf and riding 4 km. Tours centre 8 km.

Open: 4 April - 17 September.

Directions

From A10 autoroute take exit 24 and D751 towards Chinon. Turn right after 5 km. at Campanile Hotel following signs to site. From Tours take D751 towards Chinon. GPS: 47.35509, 0.63408

Charges guide

Per unit incl. 2 persons and electricity	€ 21.60 - € 26.00
incl. water and drainage	€ 23.00 - € 37.00
extra person	€ 4.40 - € 6.00
child (2-12 yrs)	€ 3.00 - € 4.00

Bracieux

Camping Indigo les Châteaux

11 rue Roger Brun, F-41250 Bracieux (Loir-et-Cher) T: 02 54 46 41 84. E: chateaux@camping-indigo.com

alanrogers.com/FR41120

Indigo les Châteaux is a well situated, wooded site on the outskirts of the small town of Bracieux, and convenient for many of the best known châteaux of the Loire valley. There are 350 pitches, 282 of which are reserved for touring. Some are grouped in blocks of four between hedges, and all have access to 6/10A electricity and water. Mature trees provide shade throughout most of the site. Accommodation to rent includes mobile homes, chalets, Romany-style caravans and wood and canvas tents. Camping Indigo have a policy of continually updating their sites, and there is a new heated swimming pool. In addition, there is a good municipal outdoor swimming pool next door. Of the many châteaux close at hand, Chambord and Cheverny are amongst the most celebrated.

Facilities

The four toilet blocks are well spaced among the pitches, with modern, clean facilities, including those for families and disabled visitors. Motorcaravan services. Small shop. Bar. Snack bar/pizzeria (July/Aug). Heated indoor swimming pool. Fishing. Play area. Games/TV room and small library. Activity and entertainment programme (July/Aug). Mobile homes and tents for rent. Bicycle hire. Barbecue hire. Internet access. WiFi at café (free). Off site: Municipal outdoor swimming pool adjacent (15/6-31/8). Bicycle hire 300 m. Shops and restaurants 300 m. Château de Chambord 8 km. Cheverny 9 km. Golf and riding 10 km.

Open: 24 March - 2 November.

Directions

From Blois take D765 south towards Cheverny. At roundabout (junction with D956) turn east on D923, signed Bracieux. Turn south on D112 at roundabout and the site is 300 m. on right, just over the river. GPS: 47.550883, 1.537867

Charges guide

Per unit incl. 2 persons and electricity	€ 21.20 - € 34.50
extra person	€ 5.30 - € 6.35
child (2-13 yrs)	free - € 4.10
dog	€ 2.20 - € 4.40

Briare-le-Canal

Camping le Martinet

Val du Martinet, F-45250 Briare-le-Canal (Loiret) T: 02 38 31 24 50. E: contact@campinglemartinet.fr

alanrogers.com/FR45100

Only Camp le Martinet is located between the Loire river and the Briare canal, just ten minutes from the picturesque town of Briare with its famous bridge. The site is well laid out with hardcore roads and 160 grass touring pitches. These are surrounded by low hedging and trees provide some shade. Electricity and water points are easily accessible. A little English is spoken and what the site lacks in the way of facilities, it makes up for in its tranquillity, views and walking opportunities. You will find a full range of shops and restaurants in the town.

Facilities

One central toilet block is well appointed and modern and includes free showers. Facilities for children. Laundry facilities. Motorcaravan services. Visiting snack van. Small play area. Free WiFi around reception area. Off site: Town with shops and restaurants 10 mins. walk. Walking and cycle tracks.

Open: 1 April - 30 September.

Directions

Leave the A77 south of Gien at exit 20 for Briare. Site is 2 km. to the northwest of Briare and is well signed from the D952. GPS: 47.641628, 2.72567

Charges guide

Per unit incl. 2 persons and electricity	€ 17.80
extra person	€ 3.80
child (2-13 yrs)	€ 2.00
dog	€ 1.20

No credit cards.

Candé-sur-Beuvron

Camping la Grande Tortue

3 route de Pontlevoy, F-41120 Candé-sur-Beuvron (Loir-et-Cher) T: 02 54 44 15 20.
E: camping@grandetortue.com **alanrogers.com/FR41070**

In the region that the Kings of France chose to build their most beautiful residences, this pleasant, shady site has been developed in the surroundings of an old 800-hectare forest, just 1 km. from the banks of the Loire river. For those seeking a relaxing holiday, it provides 169 pitches, including 111 for touring units, all with 10A electricity (119 Europlugs) and 58 with full services. The friendly family owners continue to develop the site with a multisports court and an attractive swimming pool complex. During July and August, they organise a programme of trips including canoeing and riding excursions, as well as twice weekly concerts and shows. La Grande Tortue is very well placed for visiting the châteaux of the Loire and the cities of Orléans and Tours. There are several good restaurants close at hand, although the site restaurant is also recommended with a range of good value meals in a pleasant environment.

Facilities

Three sanitary blocks offer washbasins in cabins and pushbutton showers. Facilities for disabled visitors in one block. Laundry facilities. Motorcaravan services. Shop, terraced bar and restaurant with takeaway. Heated swimming pool covered in poor weather, shallow outdoor pools for children (1/5-17/9). Trampolines, ball crawl with slide and climbing wall, two bouncy inflatables. Club for children (July/Aug). Multisports court. Bicycle hire (13/4-17/9). WiFi over site (charged). No electric barbecues. Off site: Walking and cycling. Fishing 1 km. Riding 3 km. Golf 10 km. Châteaux at Blois 10 km. Chambord 20 km. Chenonceau 20 km.

Open: 9 April - 17 September.

Directions

Site is just outside Candé-sur-Beuvron on D751, between Amboise and Blois. From Amboise, turn right just before Candé, then left into site.
GPS: 47.4900069, 1.2583208

Charges guide

Per unit incl. 2 persons and electricity	€ 23.00 - € 35.00
extra person	€ 7.00 - € 10.00
child (5-11 yrs)	€ 4.25 - € 6.75
dog	€ 4.00

Camping Cheques accepted.

Chécy

Camping Municipal les Pâtures

55 chemin du Port, F-45430 Chécy (Loiret) T: 02 38 91 13 27. E: camping@checy.fr
alanrogers.com/FR45180

Once upon a time, all small French towns had a municipal campsite; Chécy still has. If you want a campsite with all services and facilities, then this is not for you. However, it is personal, pretty, perfectly clean and outside the gate you have the wide reaches of the Loire all to yourself. There is no restaurant, bar, shop or swimming pool, but these are all provided by the town, which is a ten-minute walk away. With 34 neat, shaded pitches (6A electricity and water) and a social marquee, this could be the authentic Loire-side experience you have been waiting for. Franck and Valérie direct this site on behalf of the Mairie. It is very basic but organised, tidy and well cared for. Bicycle and kayak hire can be arranged by the site, which is right next to the Loire and the Orléans - Chécy canal, so there are many opportunities for canoeing, walking and cycling, or just enjoying the flora and fauna of the riverbank. Swimming is dangerous at this point of the river, but there is a public pool in town with concessions for campers.

Facilities

One sanitary block with hot showers, washbasins in cubicles and facilities for disabled visitors. Motorcaravan services. Social area marquee. Small playground. Bread (July/Aug). WiFi throughout (free). Off site: Shops, bars and restaurants and swimming pool in Chécy 10 mins. on foot. Buses/trams to Orléans every 15 mins. (high season). Birdwatching area. Kayak and bicycle hire. Boat trips 3 km. Supermarket 3 km.

Open: 1 May - 28 September.

Directions

From A10 take exit 14 and follow signs to Chécy. Camping is signed from the edge of town and is next to the river. GPS: 47.88577, 2.02802

Charges guide

Per unit incl. 2 persons and electricity	€ 17.00
extra person	€ 3.70
child (3-10 yrs)	€ 2.00
dog	€ 1.00

Chemillé-sur-Indrois

Camping les Coteaux du Lac

Base de Loisirs, F-37460 Chemillé-sur-Indrois (Indre-et-Loire) T: 02 47 92 77 83.
E: lescoteauxdulac@wanadoo.fr **alanrogers.com/FR37150**

This former municipal site has been completely refurbished to a high standard and is being operated by a private company owned by the present manager, Emmanuel Dugas. There are 47 touring pitches, all with 10A electricity and individual water tap; four have hardstanding for motorcaravans. At present there is little shade apart from that offered by a few mature trees, but new trees and bushes have been planted and flower beds are to be added. In a few years this promises to be a delightful site; meanwhile it is smart and very well tended. The site is in pleasant countryside above a lake and next to a rapidly developing Base de Loisirs with watersports provision and a bar/restaurant. There is a good, well equipped little swimming pool with paddling area securely separated from the main pool (open and heated 1/6-30/9). The site is near the town of Loches which has an attractive château, and is an easy drive from Tours and from the many châteaux along the Loire and the Indre, including Chenonceau.

Facilities

Excellent sanitary block with controllable showers, some washbasins in cabins and en-suite facilities for disabled visitors. Special facilities for children. Laundry facilities. Reception sells a few basic supplies and bread can be ordered. Swimming and paddling pools (14/4-15/9). Playing field. Play equipment for different ages. Fishing. Bicycle hire. WiFi over site (charged). Chalets to rent (15) are grouped at far end of site. Off site: Fishing 100 m. Lakeside beach, sailing and other watersports 200 m. Riding 4 km. Golf 15 km.

Open: 1 April - 4 October.

Directions

Chemillé-sur-Indrois is 55 km. southeast of Tours and 14 km. east of Loches, just off the D760 from Loches to Montrésor. Site is to the north of this road and is signed just west of Montrésor.
GPS: 47.15786, 1.15986

Charges guide

Per unit incl. 2 persons and electricity	€ 18.00 - € 26.90
extra person	€ 3.90 - € 5.90
child (3-6 yrs)	€ 2.50 - € 3.90
dog	€ 2.00

Chinon

Camping de l'Ile Auger

Quai Danton, F-37500 Chinon (Indre-et-Loire) T: 02 47 93 08 35. E: camping-chinon@cc-cyl.fr
alanrogers.com/FR37070

This traditional, good value site is well placed for exploring the old medieval town of Chinon. It lies alongside the River Vienne with views of the impressive château, which has a museum to Joan of Arc and was once the home of England's Henry II. A five-minute walk over the bridge takes you to the château and town centre. The 277 level pitches are numbered but not separated and trees provide some shade. All have 8/12A electricity (long leads may be needed). Four tents are now available to rent. Nearby are châteaux at Ussé, Azay-le-Rideau and Villandry and the abbey at Fontevraud.

Facilities

The main toilet block by the entrance is in need of refurbishment but is clean and sound with all the usual facilities. Three small blocks around the rest of the site have WCs and washbasins with cold water. Laundry facilities. Motorcaravan services. Playground. Boules court. Fishing. Canoes. Barrier locked 22.00-07.00. A warden lives on site. WiFi (charged). Off site: Indoor and outdoor swimming pools nearby. Bicycle hire 100 m. Town with shops and restaurants 400 m.

Open: 1 April - 31 October.

Directions

Chinon is 45 km. southwest of Tours. West of Chinon, at roundabout, leave Chinon bypass (D751) and take D8 east to town centre (3 km). Turn south, cross river and immediately turn west to site in 300 m. GPS: 47.163776, 0.235208

Charges guide

Per unit incl. 2 persons and electricity (12A)	€ 13.55 - € 15.90
extra person	€ 2.45 - € 3.10

Cheverny

Sites et Paysages les Saules

Les Saules, F-41700 Cheverny (Loir-et-Cher) T: 02 54 79 90 01. E: contact@camping-cheverny.com

alanrogers.com/FR41100

Set in the heart of the château region, les Saules has developed into a popular, friendly campsite run by a local family. The well renovated, traditional reception buildings in their lakeside setting give a very pleasant welcome. There are 164 good size, level pitches with 148 for touring units. All have shade from the many trees on the site, and 10A electricity connections (a few will require leads longer than 25 m), and there are ample water taps. A large, grassy field provides room for youngsters to play safely. There are many designated cycle paths and walking circuits in the area, often linking châteaux through attractive, sleepy countryside. Cheverny, just a five-minute cycle ride away, is considered to have the best interior and furnishings of all the châteaux in the Loire region, and many others are within easy reach (Chambord, Chenonceau, Chaumont and more).

Facilities

Two sanitary blocks with toilets, showers, washbasins in cubicles and facilities for disabled visitors. Laundry. Motorcaravan services. Gas supplies. Shop, snack bar and takeaway (14/5-12/9). Restaurant (July/Aug). Bar. Heated swimming and paddling pools (1/4-17/9). TV/social room with toys, board games, books. Two play areas. Large grass area for ball games. Minigolf (free). Fishing. Bicycle hire. Internet and WiFi. Off site: Golf and riding 3 km.

Open: 1 April - 20 September.

Directions

From Cheverny take D102 south towards Contres. Site is on right after 2 km. GPS: 47.4811, 1.450106

Charges guide

Per unit incl. 2 persons and electricity	€ 22.50 - € 36.00
extra person	€ 4.50
child (4-10 yrs)	€ 2.00
dog	€ 2.00

Faverolles-sur-Cher

Camping Couleurs du Monde

1 rondpoint de Montparnasse, F-41400 Faverolles-sur-Cher (Loir-et-Cher) T: 02 54 32 06 08.
E: contact@camping-couleurs-du-monde.com **alanrogers.com/FR41150**

Les Couleurs du Monde is a welcoming site in the heart of the Loire Valley. It is close to the River Cher and the small, medieval town of Montrichard, and well placed for exploring some of the region's best known sights. The 96 touring pitches are of a very good size, grassy and well shaded, most with electrical connections. On-site amenities include a swimming pool, paddling pool and a snack bar/takeaway. A supermarket with ATM is nearby (50 m). The barrier is closed 22.00-07.00. Reservation is essential for July and August.

Facilities

One very clean, newly refurbished toilet block has vanity style washbasins and hot water. Baby room. Facilities for disabled visitors (key access). Washing machine and dryer. Shop for basics. Snack bar and takeaway (all season). Swimming pool (no Bermuda shorts). Paddling pool. Games room. Play areas. Minigolf. Boules pitch. Volleyball. Go-carts. Canoe trips. Entertainment (July/Aug). Mobile homes and chalets to rent. Bicycle hire. WiFi over site (charged). Off site: Supermarket with ATM 50 m. Shops, cafés and restaurants in Montrichard. Walking and cycling trails. Chenonceau. Chaumont.

Open: 21 March - 24 October.

Directions

The site is situated on south side of River Cher. From A85/E604 leave at exit 11. Follow signs for Montrichard on D976. Site is next to Carrefour market on the Montrichard roundabout.
GPS: 47.33399, 1.18768

Charges guide

Per unit incl. 2 persons and electricity	€ 15.94 - € 24.94
extra person	€ 3.50 - € 6.00
child (0-7 yrs)	€ 2.50 - € 4.50
dog	€ 2.00

Francueil-Chenonceau

Camping le Moulin Fort

F-37150 Francueil-Chenonceau (Indre-et-Loire) T: 02 47 23 86 22. E: lemoulinfort@wanadoo.fr

alanrogers.com/FR37030

Camping le Moulin Fort is a tranquil, riverside site with British owners, John and Sarah Scarratt. The 130 pitches are enhanced by trees and shrubs offering plenty of shade and 110 pitches have electricity (6A). From the snack bar terrace adjacent to the restored mill building, a timber walkway over the mill race leads to the unheated swimming pool and paddling pools. The site is ideal for couples and families with young children, although the river is unfenced. There is occasional noise from trains passing on the opposite bank of the river.

Facilities

Two toilet blocks with all the usual amenities of a good standard, include washbasins in cubicles, baby baths and facilities for disabled visitors. Washing machines and dryer. Motorcaravan services. Shop (1/5-30/9). Bar, restaurant and takeaway (all 21/5-20/9). Swimming pool (21/5-25/9). Excellent play area. Minigolf. Pétanque. Games room and TV. Library. Fishing. Bicycle hire. Family entertainment (July/Aug). WiFi in bar area (charged).

Open: 7 May - 27 September.

Directions

Site is 35 km. east of Tours off D976 Vierzon road. From A85 at exit 11 take D31 towards Bléré and turn east on D976 (Vierzon) for 7 km. then north on D80 (Chenonceau) to site. GPS: 47.32735, 1.08936

Charges guide

Per unit incl. 2 persons and electricity	€ 19.50 - € 28.00
extra person	€ 3.00 - € 5.00
child (4-12 yrs)	€ 3.00 - € 4.00

Gien

Camping les Bois du Bardelet

Le Petit Bardelet, Poilly-lez-Gien, F-45500 Gien (Loiret) T: 02 38 67 47 39. E: contact@bardelet.com

alanrogers.com/FR45010

This attractive, high quality site, ideal for families with young children, is in a rural setting and well situated for exploring the less well known eastern part of the Loire Valley. Two lakes (one for boating, one for fishing) and a pool complex have been attractively landscaped in 18 hectares of former farmland, blending old and new with natural wooded areas and more open grassland with rural views. There are 245 large, level grass pitches with 120 for touring units. All have at least 10A electricity, 15 have water, waste water and 16A electricity, and some 30 have hardstanding. Eight have an individual en-suite sanitary unit beside the pitch.

Facilities

Two heated toilet blocks (effectively unisex) have some washbasins in cubicles, controllable showers, an en-suite unit for disabled visitors and a baby room. Laundry facilities. Shop, bar, takeaway and restaurant. Heated outdoor pool (4/5-4/9). Heated indoor pool and children's pool (all season). Wellness centre. Fitness and jacuzzi rooms. Beach on lake. Games area. Canoeing and fishing. Tennis. Minigolf. Volleyball. Pétanque. Play area. Kids' club, sports tournaments, excursions and activities (July/Aug). Bicycle hire. WiFi.

Open: 9 April - 25 September.

Directions

Leave A77 autoroute at exit 19 and take D940 (Bourges) to bypass Gien. Continue on D940 for 5 km. At junction with D53 (no left turn) turn right and right again to cross D940 (site signed). Follow signs for 1.5 km. to site. GPS: 47.64152, 2.61528

Charges guide

Per unit incl. 2 persons and electricity	€ 21.70 - € 36.20
extra person (over 2 yrs)	€ 5.60 - € 7.40

Camping Cheques accepted.

La Ville-aux-Dames

Camping les Acacias

Rue Berthe Morisot, F-37700 La Ville-aux-Dames (Indre-et-Loire) T: 02 47 44 08 16.
E: contact@camplvad.com **alanrogers.com/FR37210**

Les Acacias is a pretty, family run site, named after the surrounding acacia trees. In a rural location, the site is within easy reach of the A10 (5.5 km). Many gardens, museums and chateaux are nearby to visit and the picturesque site is set just a short distance from the Loire river. Probably the main reason one would stay here is that there is direct access along the river bank to Tours city centre. Separated by trees and shrubs, the 88 touring pitches are 100 sq.m. in size and have grass and gravel surfaces; 10A electricity is provided to 66 pitches. Mobile homes are available to rent.

Facilities

Sanitary facilities in a single, central block are heated in winter and include washbasins in cubicles. Laundry facilities. Fridge hire. Motorcaravan services. Small shop in reception. Bar with TV (15/6-15/9). Restaurant and takeaway (15/6-15/9). Boules. Bicycle hire. Play area (new in 2015). Open areas for ball games. Twin-axle caravans are not accepted. WiFi throughout (free).

Open: All year.

Directions

From the A10 take exit 21 (Tours-centre). Follow signs for Autres Directions/Ambroise. At roundabout take first exit (Ambroise) on D751. In 5.5 km. turn right (site signed), take first turning left and entrance is on the left. GPS: 47.40209, 0.77846

Charges guide

Per unit incl. 2 persons and electricity	€ 20.00
extra person	€ 3.50

Loches-en-Touraine

Camping la Citadelle

Avenue Aristide Briand, F-37600 Loches-en-Touraine (Indre-et-Loire) T: 02 47 59 05 91.
E: camping@lacitadelle.com **alanrogers.com/FR37050**

A pleasant, well maintained site, la Citadelle's best feature is probably that it is within walking distance of Loches, noted for its perfect architecture and its glorious history, yet at the same time the site has a rural atmosphere. The 102 standard touring pitches are all level, of a good size and have 10A electricity. Numerous trees offer varying degrees of shade. The 27 larger serviced pitches have 16A electricity but little shade, a further six luxury pitches have all facilities including furniture, fridge and barbecue. Mobile homes (28 for hire) occupy the other 48 pitches. Loches with its château and dungeons is a gentle 500 m. walk along the river.

Facilities

Three sanitary blocks provide mainly British style WCs, washbasins (mostly in cabins) and controllable showers. Laundry facilities. Motorcaravan services. Two baby units and provision for disabled visitors. Heated swimming pool (May-Sept). Paddling pool and play area (adult supervision strongly recommended). Small bar. Snack bar (July/Aug; bread to order at reception). Boules. Volleyball. Games room. Miniclub (July/Aug). WiFi (charged).

Open: 19 March - 30 September.

Directions

Loches is 45 km. southeast of Tours. Site is well signed from most directions. Do not enter town centre. Approach from roundabout by supermarket at southern end of bypass (D943). Site signed towards town centre and is on right in 800 m.
GPS: 47.12303, 1.00223

Charges guide

Per unit incl. 2 persons and electricity	€ 16.50 - € 49.50

Luynes

Flower Camping les Granges

Avenue de l'Europe, F-37230 Luynes (Indre-et-Loire) T: 02 47 55 79 05. E: reception@campinglesgranges.fr
alanrogers.com/FR37250

Camping les Granges is located on the edge of Luynes, a pretty town with a choice of bars, restaurants and shops. Its small château can be seen from the entrance to this modest site with its 26 touring pitches and a wide choice of rental accommodation on the remaining 37. Pitches have 10A electricity and access to water. There is a heated swimming pool and a snack bar which is open all season. In the centre of the site is a green space for games, and a children's club is held every morning in high season. English is spoken at reception in high season.

Facilities

Sanitary facilities with preset showers, open washbasins and provision for disabled visitors. Washing machines and dryer. Motorcaravan services. Shop and fresh bread in reception. Bar and takeaway. Heated outdoor swimming pool. Play area. Grassed area for outdoor games. Games room with TV, billiards, table football and darts. Kids' club (4-8 yrs, July/Aug). Musical evenings weekly (July/Aug). No electric barbecues. WiFi throughout (free).

Open: 30 March - 30 September.

Directions

Luynes is west of Tours. Take exit 7 from A85 and the D952 to Luynes. Campsite is signed in town.
GPS: 47.38111, 0.55881

Charges guide

Per unit incl. 2 persons and electricity	€ 18.50 - € 26.00
extra person	€ 3.00 - € 4.00
child (2-13 yrs)	€ 2.00 - € 2.50

Mesland

Yelloh! Village Parc du Val de Loire

155 route de Fleuray, F-41150 Mesland (Loir-et-Cher) T: 02 54 70 27 18. E: parcduvaldeloire@wanadoo.fr
alanrogers.com/FR41010

Between Blois and Amboise, quietly situated among vineyards away from the main roads and towns, this site is nevertheless centrally placed for visits to the châteaux; Chaumont, Amboise and Blois (21 km) are the nearest in that order. There are 130 touring pitches (80-120 sq.m) with four different levels of provision including six premium pitches. All the pitches have electricity (10A). Activities and events are organised in July and August and at weekends in low season, and there is likewise a range of family evening entertainment. Careful attention is paid to the needs of different age groups, ranging from a baby playroom to organised events for teenagers and adults.

Facilities

A state-of-the-art sanitary block in the touring area, plus an additional older unit only open in July/Aug. Good provision for children, babies and disabled visitors. Laundry. Motorcaravan services. Shop with bakery. Bar, restaurant, snacks, pizzeria and takeaway. TV rooms. Three swimming pools, one heated and covered (outdoor 25/4-11/9), one larger one with slide and flume. Balnéo. Tennis. Three playgrounds. Bicycle hire. Minigolf. WiFi.

Open: 10 April - 13 September.

Directions

From A10 exit 18 (Château-Renault, Amboise) take D31 south to Autrèche (2 km). Turn left on D55 for 3.5 km. In Dame-Marie Les Bois turn left, then right onto D43 to Mesland. Follow site signs.
GPS: 47.51002, 1.10481

Charges guide

Per unit incl. 2 persons and electricity	€ 18.00 - € 36.00
extra person	€ 6.00 - € 8.00

Muides-sur-Loire

Camping Château des Marais

27 rue de Chambord, F-41500 Muides-sur-Loire (Loir-et-Cher) T: 02 54 87 05 42.

E: info@camping-marais.com **alanrogers.com/FR41040**

The Château des Marais campsite is a good base for visiting the château at Chambord and the other châteaux in the Vallée des Rois. The site, providing 115 large touring pitches in avenues, all with electricity (10A), access to water and drainage and ample shade, is situated in the oak and hornbeam woods of its own attractive, small château. Twenty-five designated motorcaravan pitches are on hardstanding and grass. An excellent swimming complex offers pools with two slides, two flumes and a lazy river. There is an on-site tourism office where bookings can be made. Used by a UK tour operator.

Facilities

Four sanitary blocks have good facilities including some large showers and washbasins en-suite, suitable for visitors with disabilities. Washing machines and dryers. Motorcaravan services. Shop. Bar/restaurant with large terrace. Takeaway (7/5-11/9). Breakfast service. Swimming complex with heated and unheated pools, slide and cover for cooler weather. Wellness spa centre with massage. New minigolf course. Bicycle and go-kart hire. Games room. Children's club (high season). Fishing pond. Excursions to Paris in high season. Free WiFi in bar area.

Open: 2 May - 11 September.

Directions

From A10 autoroute take exit 16 to Mer-Chambord. Follow signs for Chambord, cross the River Loire, then go straight on for 1 km. before turning right and following signs to site. GPS: 47.66580, 1.52877

Charges guide

Per unit incl. 2 persons and electricity	€ 21.00 - € 40.00
extra person	€ 13.80 - € 19.20
child (1-17 yrs)	free - € 8.00

Credit cards accepted for amounts over € 80.

Neung-sur-Beuvron

Camping Municipal de la Varenne

34 rue de Veillas, F-41210 Neung-sur-Beuvron (Loir-et-Cher) T: 02 54 83 68 52.

E: camping.lavarenne@wanadoo.fr **alanrogers.com/FR41090**

This is a particularly well organised site in a peaceful location, just 16 km. from the A71 autoroute. The site has a slight slope but most of the 69 grass touring pitches are fairly level, all with electricity hook-ups (10A). Some pitches are individual, others in bays of four, and some for tents amongst trees. There is good shade in most areas. To the rear is a large open field which slopes down to the small river. Each evening the manager visits every pitch to take bread orders; these are available from reception at 08.00 the following morning. Four mobile homes are for rent.

Facilities

Excellent, clean and well equipped modern building includes spacious showers, baby changing facilities and a suite for disabled visitors. A second unit at the rear of the reception building has additional older facilities. Washing machine and dryer. Freezer for ice blocks. Another building houses a leisure room, microwave and fridges. Motorcaravan services. Playground. Two tennis courts. Bicycle hire. Communal barbecue. WiFi.

Open: Easter - 30 September.

Directions

Neung-sur-Beuvron is 40 km. east of Blois, and 2 km. west of the D922, 22 km. north of Romarantin-Lanthenay. From the east, in the town centre, turn right at church and follow signs for camping. GPS: 47.53822, 1.81508

Charges guide

Per unit incl. 2 persons and electricity	€ 12.20
extra person	€ 2.80

Nouan-le-Fuzelier

Camping la Grande Sologne

Rue des Peupliers, F-41600 Nouan-le-Fuzelier (Loir-et-Cher) T: 02 54 88 70 22.

E: info@campingrandesologne.com **alanrogers.com/FR41180**

The experienced owners here, who speak many languages, are working hard to raise this site to a high standard. It is in a parkland setting on the southern edge of Nouan-le-Fuzelier close to the A71, making this an ideal spot to spend some time relaxing whilst en route north or south. It has 165 spacious, level, grass pitches with a variety of mature trees giving some shade, with 150 for touring. All have 10A electricity, but long leads may be necessary. They are marked but not delineated and access is easy for large outfits. The site is entered through a very attractive park which has some interesting sculptures and houses the excellent municipal swimming pool (free for campers) and tennis courts (reduced price).

Facilities

Three modern toilet blocks with all necessary facilities including those for campers with disabilities. Washing machine, dryer. Snack bar (July/Aug). Small shop (all season). Games/TV room. Motorcaravan services. Fishing. Bicycle hire. Play area. WiFi. Mobile homes and tents for hire. Off site: Adjacent municipal swimming pool (free), tennis courts (reduced price). Equestrian centre 7 km.

Open: 1 April - 15 October.

Directions

Nouan-le-Fuzelier is between exits 3 and 4 on A71 autoroute, south of Orléans. Take D2020 to site at southern edge of Nouan-le-Fuzelier, opposite railway station. Well signed. GPS: 47.533863, 2.037674

Charges guide

Per unit incl. 2 persons and electricity	€ 18.70 - € 23.60

Camping Cheques accepted.

Pierrefitte-sur-Sauldre

Leading Camping les Alicourts Resort

Domaine des Alicourts, F-41300 Pierrefitte-sur-Sauldre (Loir-et-Cher) T: 02 54 88 63 34.

E: info@lesalicourts.com **alanrogers.com/FR41030**

A secluded holiday village set in the heart of the forest, with many sporting facilities and a super spa centre, Camping les Alicourts is midway between Orléans and Bourges, to the east of the A71. There are 490 pitches, 153 for touring and the remainder occupied by mobile homes and chalets. All pitches have 6A electricity connections and good provision for water, and most are 150 sq.m. (min. 100 sq.m). Locations vary from wooded to more open areas, thus giving a choice of amount of shade. All facilities are open all season and the leisure amenities are exceptional. The Senseo Balnéo centre offers indoor pools, hydrotherapy, massage and spa treatments for over 18s only (some special family sessions are provided). An inviting, part-covered outdoor water complex includes two swimming pools, a pool with wave machine and a beach area, not forgetting three water slides. Competitions and activities are organised for all ages and in high season there is a miniclub with an entertainer twice a day, a disco once a week and a dance for adults. A member of Leading Campings group.

Facilities

Three modern sanitary blocks include some washbasins in cabins and baby bathrooms. Laundry facilities. Facilities for families and disabled visitors. Motorcaravan services. Shop. Boutique. Restaurant. Takeaway in bar with terrace. Pool complex. Spa centre. Library. 7-hectare lake (fishing, bathing, canoes, pedaloes, cable-ski). 9-hole golf course. Adventure play area. Tennis. Minigolf. Boules. Roller skating/skateboarding (bring own equipment). Bicycle hire. Internet access and WiFi (charged). Off site: Riding 6 km.

Open: 29 April - 4 September.

Directions

From A71, take Lamotte-Beuvron exit (no 3) or from N20 Orléans to Vierzon turn left on to D923 towards Aubigny. After 14 km. turn right at camping sign on to D24E. Site signed in 2 km.
GPS: 47.54398, 2.19193

Charges guide

Per unit incl. 2 persons and electricity	€ 20.00 - € 52.00
extra person	€ 7.00 - € 12.00
child (1-17 yrs. acc. to age)	free - € 10.00
dog	€ 5.00 - € 7.00

Reductions for low season longer stays.

Poilly-lez-Gien

Sites et Paysages Camping Touristique de Gien

Rue des Iris, F-45500 Poilly-lez-Gien (Loiret) T: 02 38 67 12 50. E: camping-gien@wanadoo.fr

alanrogers.com/FR45030

This open, attractive, well cared for site lies on a bank of the Loire with views of the town of Gien and its château. It has a long river frontage, which includes a good expanse of sandy beach. There are 200 good sized, level, grassy pitches with 150 for touring. All have 10A electricity. Some are shaded by mature trees and many have good views over the river. The bar and restaurant, with a pleasant outdoor area, are open to the public and meals are reasonably priced. Soirées with different themes are held weekly in July and August. A long distance cycle path passes the entrance. This is an excellent base for exploring the eastern end of the Loire valley, and Gien has a festival celebrating the heritage of this part of the Loire at Ascensiontide. The tourist office organises a range of activities, both sporting and cultural. There is a regular bus service to Orléans, an ancient city well known for its association with Joan of Arc.

Facilities

Two unisex toilet blocks, one heated, are fairly basic but clean and have washbasins in cabins, controllable showers and facilities for disabled visitors. Laundry. Bar and restaurant (15/5-15/9), both open to the public. Inflatable swimming pool (with removable roof) and paddling pools (15/6-15/9). Play area and grassed games area. Outdoor exercise equipment. Minigolf. Bicycle and pedal cart hire. Canoe hire. Fishing. Large sandy beach. Some organised activities (July/Aug). WiFi over site (charged). Off site: Shop 50 m. outside gates (all year; closed Sun. outside July/Aug). Children's club on beach.

Open: 12 March - 31 October.

Directions

Gien is 70 km. southeast of Orléans. Leave A77 autoroute at exit 19 and take D940 (Bourges) to bypass Gien to east; cross Loire and turn north at roundabout towards town centre. At traffic lights before bridge, turn west to Poilly-lez-Gien and site is on right in 800 m. GPS: 47.68229, 2.62315

Charges guide

Per unit incl. 2 persons and electricity	€ 20.00 - € 24.00
extra person	€ 6.00
child (under 12 yrs)	€ 4.00

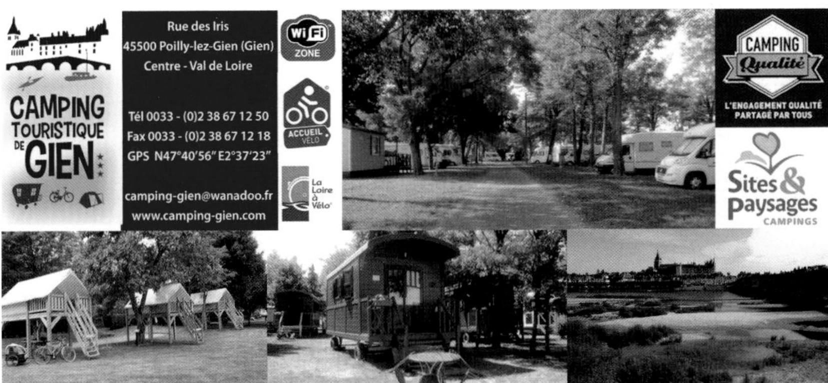

Rillé

Huttopia Rillé

Lac de Rillé, F-37340 Rillé (Indre-et-Loire) T: 02 47 24 62 97. E: rille@huttopia.com

alanrogers.com/FR37140

Huttopia Rillé is a rural site ideal for tent campers seeking a more natural, environmentally friendly, peaceful campsite close to a lake. Cars are parked outside the barrier but allowed on site to unload and load. The 133 slightly uneven and sloping pitches, 72 for touring, all have 10A electricity (very long leads needed). They vary in size and are numbered but not marked. This site is designed for those with tents, though small caravans and motorcaravans (special area) are accepted. Several types of accommodation for hire (cabin, hut, trailer or wood and canvas tents). It is not ideal for those with walking difficulties.

Facilities

Modern central toilet block with family rooms and facilities for disabled visitors (no ramps and difficult access for wheelchairs). A smaller block has separate showers, washbasins and facilities for disabled visitors. Motorcaravan services. Shop. Bar, restaurant and takeaway (July/Aug and weekends). Bicycle hire. Small heated swimming pool with paddling area (4/5-18/9). Play area. Fishing. Canoes on lake. Communal barbecue areas (no charcoal barbecues). Max. 1 dog.

Open: 4 May - 17 October.

Directions

Rillé is 40 km. west of Tours. Leave D766 Angers-Blois road at Château la Vallière take D749 southwest. In Rillé turn west on D49. Site is on right in 2 km. GPS: 47.44600, 0.33291

Charges guide

Per unit incl. 2 persons and electricity	€ 21.90 - € 35.50
extra person	€ 5.50 - € 8.40
child (2-7 yrs)	free - € 5.50

Sainte Catherine-de-Fierbois

Castel Camping Parc de Fierbois

F-37800 Sainte Catherine-de-Fierbois (Indre-et-Loire) T: 02 47 65 43 35. E: contact@fierbois.com

alanrogers.com/FR37120

Parc de Fierbois is set among 250 acres of lakes and forest in the heart of the Loire Valley. In all, there are 320 pitches including 185 for touring units. These include 24 high quality, premium pitches which have fridges, barbecues, sun loungers and free WiFi. A small part of the site is used by tour operators whilst there is a range of accommodation to rent, including chalets, mobile homes and even some tree houses. This is a lively family holiday site which can accommodate up to 1,500 people in the summer, with a very wide range of activities and facilities on offer for all ages. There is a super pool complex with toboggans and a sandy beach on the shores of the lake. There is plenty here to occupy and entertain children of all ages. Activities range from pony rides to electric cars and from zip wires over the lake to a skateboard park for teenagers. Bikes are useful to get around. A token system operates for payment.

Facilities

Two toilet blocks provide preset hot showers and washbasins in cubicles. Baby room. Good facilities for disabled visitors. Laundry facilities. Motorcaravan services. Well stocked supermarket. Restaurant, pizzas and takeaway (June-Aug). Bar. Indoor heated pool. Water park complex (pools, slides, paddling pool, sunbathing areas). Wellness. Gym. Multisports area. Riding. Tennis. Pétanque. Minigolf. Skateboard park. Go-karts and electric cars. Fishing. TV/video room. Indoor entertainment and games bar. Club for children. Entertainment programme (July/Aug). Bicycle hire. WiFi throughout (charged). Off site: Sainte Catherine-de-Fierbois 1.5 km. Golf 30 km.

Open: 2 May - 4 September.

Directions

Travelling south on N10 from Tours, go through Montbazon and on towards St Maure and Chatellerault. Site signed 16 km. outside Montbazon near Ste Catherine. Turn off main road. Follow site signs. From A10 autoroute use St Maure exit and turn north up N10. GPS: 47.1487, 0.6548

Charges guide

Per unit incl. 2 persons and electricity	€ 25.00 - € 52.00
extra person (from 4 yrs)	€ 7.00 - € 9.00

Senonches

Huttopia Senonches

Etang de Badouleau, avenue de Badouleau, F-28250 Senonches (Eure-et-Loir) T: 02 37 37 81 40.
E: senonches@huttopia.com **alanrogers.com/FR28140**

Huttopia Senonches is a ten-hectare site hidden away in the huge Forêt Dominiale de Senonches, and, in keeping with other Huttopia sites, combines a high standard of comfort with a real sense of backwoods camping. There are 84 touring pitches here, some with 10A electricity. The pitches are very large, ranging from 100 sq.m. to no less than 300 sq.m. There are also 36 Canadian-style log cabins and tents available for rent. A good range of on-site amenities includes a shop and a bar/restaurant. The chlorine-free natural pool, with terrace, overlooks an unfenced lake and is open from early July until September. The forest can be explored on foot or by bicycle (hire available on site), and beyond the forest the great city of Chartres is easily visited; with its stunning Gothic cathedral it is widely considered to be the finest in France. Senonches town is just one kilometre away.

Facilities

The modern sanitary blocks are heated in low season, and have special facilities for disabled visitors. Shop (all season). Bread to order. Breakfast service. Bar, snack bar and takeaway (w/ends in low season). Swimming pool (June-Sept). Living area with library, TV, games and coffee machine. Fishing. Play area. Bicycle hire. Entertainment and activity programme. Kids' club (July/Aug, 5-12 yrs). Wood and canvas tents, Cahuttes and chalets for rent. Gas barbecues only. Max. 1 dog. Off site: Tennis and riding 200 m. Shops, bars and restaurants in Senonches 1 km. Cycle and walking tracks. Chartres 40 km.

Open: 4 May - 3 October.

Directions

Approaching from Chartres, use the ring road (N154) and then take the D24 in a northwesterly direction. Drive through Digny and continue to Senonches, from where the site is well signed.
GPS: 48.5533, 1.04146

Charges guide

Per unit incl. 2 persons and electricity	€ 21.80 - € 39.30
extra person	€ 4.50 - € 7.00
child (2-7 yrs)	free - € 4.80
dog	€ 2.60 - € 4.20

Sonzay

Camping l'Arada Parc

Rue de la Baratière, F-37360 Sonzay (Indre-et-Loire) T: 02 47 24 72 69. E: info@laradaparc.com

alanrogers.com/FR37060

A good, well maintained site in a quiet location, easy to find from the motorway and popular as an overnight stop, Camping l'Arada Parc is an attractive family site nestling in the heart of the Tourangelle countryside between the Loire and Loir valleys. The 62 grass touring pitches all have 10A electricity (Europlug) and 18 have water and drainage. The clearly marked pitches, some slightly sloping, are separated by trees and shrubs, some of which are hardstanding and now provide a degree of shade. An attractive, heated pool is on a pleasant terrace beside the restaurant. Entertainment, themed evenings and activities for children are organised in July and August. This is a new site with modern facilities which include a superb covered pool and fitness room.

Facilities

Two modern toilet blocks provide unisex toilets, showers and washbasins in cubicles. Baby room. Facilities for disabled visitors recently improved. Laundry facilities. Motorcaravan services. Shop, bar, restaurant and takeaway. Outdoor swimming pool with slide and new terrace surround (no Bermuda-style shorts; 1/5-15/9). Heated, covered pool (all season). Fitness room. Small play area. Games area. Boules. TV room. Bicycle hire. Internet access. WiFi throughout (charged). Footpath to village. Off site: Tennis 200 m. Riding 5 km. Fishing 9 km. Golf 12 km.

Open: 3 April - 11 October.

Directions

Sonzay is northwest of Tours. From the new A28 north of Tours take exit 27 to Neuillé-Pont-Pierre which is on the D938 Le Mans-Tours road. Then take D766 towards Château la Vallière and turn southwest to Sonzay. Follow campsite signs. GPS: 47.526228, 0.450865

Charges guide

Per unit incl. 2 persons and electricity	€ 22.50 - € 32.00
extra person	€ 4.20 - € 5.80
child (3-12 yrs. acc. to age)	free - € 4.00
dog	€ 2.50

Suèvres

Camping Parc de la Grenouillère

RN 152, F-41500 Suèvres (Loir-et-Cher) T: 02 54 87 80 37. E: la.grenouillere@wanadoo.fr

alanrogers.com/FR41020

La Grenouillère is an attractive site set in a 28-acre park midway between Orléans and Tours, well situated for visiting many of the Loire châteaux. The 280 pitches, with 130 for touring, are in three distinct areas. The majority are in a wooded area, with about 60 in the old orchard and the remainder in open meadows. There are varying amounts of shade from the trees. There is one water point for every four pitches and all have electric hook-up (10A). Additionally, there are 14 fully serviced pitches with a separate sanitary block in the outbuildings of the château. There are some overnight places outside the barrier. Though an ideal site for touring in the region, there are enough attractions on site and locally to make it suitable for a longer holiday. A canoe/kayak trip, wine cellar and cheese tasting visits, musical evenings and children's entertainment are organised in high season.

Facilities

Three excellent sanitary blocks are well appointed and include facilities for disabled visitors. Laundry facilities. Shop. Bar. Pizzeria with takeaway. Restaurant and grill takeaway (20/5-31/8). Swimming complex of four pools (one covered) and slide. Spa with whirlpool, jacuzzi, sauna, massage. Tennis. Games room. Bicycle and canoe hire (July/Aug). Fishing. WiFi (charged). Pets are not accepted. Off site: Suèvres 3 km. Riding and watersports 5 km. Golf 10 km.

Open: 18 April - 12 September.

Directions

Site is on the D2152 between Suèvres and Mer (3 km) and is well signed. GPS: 47.68557, 1.48686

Charges guide

Per unit incl. 2 persons and electricity	€ 22.00 - € 33.00
incl. full services	€ 33.00 - € 58.00
extra person	€ 6.00 - € 8.00
child (3-6 yrs)	€ 4.00 - € 6.00

Trogues

Château de La Rolandière

Château de La Rolandière, F-37220 Trogues (Indre-et-Loire) T: 02 47 58 53 71. E: contact@larolandiere.com
alanrogers.com/FR37090

This is a charming site set in the grounds of a château and you are assured of a very warm welcome here. There are 50 medium sized, level or gently sloping pitches, separated by hedges with a variety of trees giving some shade. Most have 6A electricity (long leads advised) with water taps nearby. There is a large chalet and mobile homes for hire, and bed and breakfast is also available. The site has a pleasant swimming pool, paddling pool, fitness room and games/TV room. The bar and restaurant have a sunny terrace overlooking the château. Minigolf, swings, slides and an area for ball games are adjacent. The site is a delightfully peaceful spot from which to visit the châteaux at Chinon, Loches, Villandry or Azay-le-Rideau, and the villages of Richelieu and Crissay-sur-Manse. There are many interesting excursions to beautiful gardens and grottos and you should find time to enjoy the local gastronomy and wines. In July and August, there is a good programme of activities for families with younger children.

Facilities

The older style toilet block has been refurbished to provide good facilities with modern showers, washbasin and laundry areas. Provision for disabled visitors and children. Small shop for basics. Bar with terrace. Snacks and takeaway (July/Aug). Swimming pool (15/5-24/9). Minigolf. Play area. Fitness room. TV lounge. WiFi.
Off site: Fishing 1 km. on River Vienne. River beach and boat launching 4 km. Restaurant 4 km. Bicycle hire and shops 6 km. St Maure 7 km. Golf 15 km.

Open: 23 April - 24 September.

Directions

Trogues is 40 km. southwest of Tours on the D760 Loches-Chinon road. Site is on D760, midway between Trogues and A10 (exit 25). Entrance is signed and marked by a model of the château. GPS: 47.10767, 0.51052

Charges guide

Per unit incl. 2 persons and electricity	€ 22.90 - € 31.40
extra person	€ 4.70 - € 6.70
child (under 13 yrs)	€ 3.00 - € 4.00
dog	€ 2.50 - € 3.50

No credit cards.

Velles

Camping les Grands Pins

Les Maisons-Neuves (D920), F-36330 Velles (Indre) T: 02 54 36 61 93. E: contact@les-grands-pins.fr
alanrogers.com/FR36100

Les Grands Pins is an attractive, spacious site situated twelve kilometres from the lively town of Châteauroux. It is probably more of a transit site, with most visitors stopping only one or two nights whilst travelling north or south on the A20. There are 49 pitches for touring, half of which are on open grassland, the rest are set amongst pine trees which offer plenty of shade. There is no hedging so pitches are open to each other. Electricity (10A) and water are available to all. At the site entrance there is a very pleasant, recently renovated restaurant with bar and a takeaway service. There are no mobile homes for rent or seasonal units. All the facilities of Châteauroux are within a ten-minute drive.

Facilities

Two small sanitary blocks with washbasins and showers in cubicles. Facilities for disabled visitors. Restaurant, bar and takeaway at site entrance. Bread to order. Small outdoor swimming pool (July/Aug; unheated). Minigolf. Football. Tennis. Play area. TV room. Free WiFi over part of site. Off site: Shops, bars and restaurants in Châteauroux (10 mins. drive). Riding 3 km. Fishing 5 km. Riding 6 km. Golf 15 km.

Open: 19 March - 19 October.

Directions

From north, leave A20 at exit 14 and in 500 m. turn right onto D920. Continue south parallel with motorway. Follow signs to Les Maisons Neuves and campsite signs. GPS: 46.74214, 1.61983

Charges guide

Per unit incl. 2 persons and electricity	€ 21.00
extra person	€ 5.40
child (under 7 yrs)	€ 3.50

No credit cards.

DÉPARTEMENTS: 44 LOIRE-ATLANTIQUE, 49 MAINE-ET-LOIRE, 53 MAYENNE, 72 SARTHE

Strictly speaking, the département of 85 Vendée is also part of this region. Because of its importance as a holiday destination for British people, we have featured it separately in this guide.

MAJOR CITIES: ANGERS, NANTES

The Pays de la Loire covers the area of Western France to the south of Brittany and Normandy. It lies along the lower stretches of the River Loire, the longest river in France, downstream from the châteaux of the Val de Loire region.

Created in the late 20th century, the Pays de la Loire is a relatively new region embracing parts of the old provinces of Anjou, Brittany, Maine and Poitou. Two of its five departments are coastal, with over 450 km. of Atlantic shoreline and some of France's most popular seaside resorts – La Baule, Le Croisic, Saint Jean-de-Monts – and includes the islands of Yeu and Noirmoutier.

Further inland, Anjou is dominated by the historic city of Angers with its medieval castle, once home to the Plantagenet kings of England. Much of this area is rural, with a strong agricultural heritage, but every year visitors flock to Le Mans, capital of Sarthe, for its 24-hour motor race.

Other attractions include the small town of La Flèche on the River Loir, home to France's oldest zoo, while Laval has some fine 16th- and 18th-century houses and two châteaux. It lies on the River Mayenne, a navigable waterway with 85 km. of towpaths, ideal for walkers and cyclists.

Places of interest

Angers: art town; medieval castle and tapestries; cathedral.

Brissac: 15th-century castle.

Le Croisic: small fishing port; Naval Museum.

Fontevraud: 11th-century Royal abbey.

Guérande: walled city with historic centre.

La Baule: holiday resort with lovely sandy bay.

Le Mans: the annual 24-hour car race attracting visitors from all over the world; car museum, old town, cathedral.

Le Puy de Fou: 15-16th-century castle, son-et-lumière production; popular theme park.

Les Sables d'Olonne: fishing port and seaside resort.

Nantes: major city with sightseeing and shopping opportunities; boat trips along the River Erdre.

Saumer: 13th-century castle; Cadre Noir National School of Horse Riding; wine cellars and Mushroom Museum.

Cuisine of the region

Beurre blanc: a buttery sauce that goes well with fish.

Rillauds d'Anjou: muscadet sausages.

Curé Nantais and Port-Salut: local cheeses.

Pâté aux prunes: A speciality of the Angers region and found in all good local bakers in July and August, this sugary pastry is filled with plums.

www.paysdelaloire.co.uk
infotourisme@sem-paysdelaloire.fr
(0)2 40 48 24 20

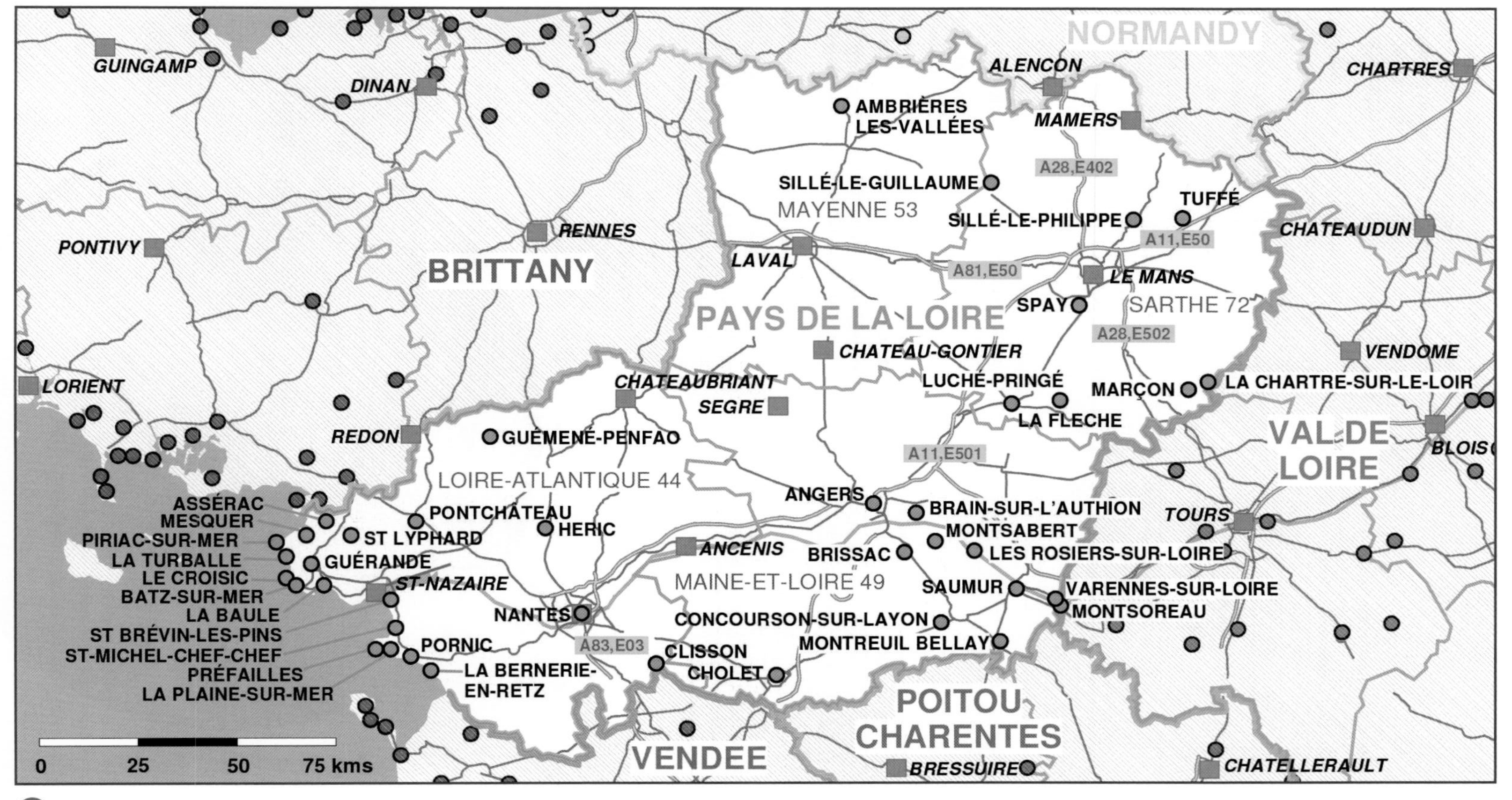

NORMANDY
BRITTANY
PAYS DE LA LOIRE
VAL DE LOIRE
POITOU CHARENTES
VENDEE
MAYENNE 53
SARTHE 72
LOIRE-ATLANTIQUE 44
MAINE-ET-LOIRE 49
GUINGAMP
DINAN
ALENCON
CHARTRES
AMBRIÈRES LES-VALLÉES
MAMERS
A28,E402
SILLÉ-LE-GUILLAUME
TUFFÉ
SILLÉ-LE-PHILIPPE
A11,E50
CHATEAUDUN
RENNES
PONTIVY
LAVAL
A81,E50
LE MANS
SPAY
A28,E502
CHATEAU-GONTIER
VENDOME
LORIENT
CHATEAUBRIANT
LUCHÉ-PRINGÉ
MARÇON
LA CHARTRE-SUR-LE-LOIR
SEGRE
LA FLECHE
REDON
GUÉMENÉ-PENFAO
BLOIS
A11,E501
ANGERS
BRAIN-SUR-L'AUTHION
TOURS
ASSÉRAC
MESQUER
PONTCHÂTEAU
PIRIAC-SUR-MER
ST LYPHARD
HERIC
MONTSABERT
LA TURBALLE
GUÉRANDE
ANCENIS
BRISSAC
LES ROSIERS-SUR-LOIRE
LE CROISIC
BATZ-SUR-MER
ST-NAZAIRE
SAUMUR
VARENNES-SUR-LOIRE
LA BAULE
NANTES
MONTSOREAU
CONCOURSON-SUR-LAYON
ST BRÉVIN-LES-PINS
PORNIC
A83,E03
MONTREUIL BELLAY
ST-MICHEL-CHEF-CHEF
CLISSON
PRÉFAILLES
LA BERNERIE-EN-RETZ
CHOLET
LA PLAINE-SUR-MER
BRESSUIRE
CHATELLERAULT
0
25
50
75 kms

Ambrières-les-Vallées

Flower Camping Parc de Vaux

35 rue des Colverts, F-53300 Ambrières-les-Vallées (Mayenne) T: 02 43 04 90 25.
E: parcdevaux@camp-in-ouest.com **alanrogers.com/FR53010**

Parc de Vaux is an ex-municipal site which was acquired in 2010 by the owners of FR72080. This 3.5-hectare site has 90 pitches, 18 occupied by mobile homes, chalets and bungalow tents available to rent. The 59 touring pitches are generally grassy and well sized (mostly with 10A electricity and water). The site is located close to the pretty village of Ambrières-les-Vallées and there is direct access to the village from the site by a footbridge over the river. The village is around 12 km. north of Mayenne, and may prove a convenient en-route stop. There is a swimming pool adjacent (with water slide) and the site also has access to a lake and a good range of amenities.

Facilities

Three small toilet blocks, one with facilities for disabled visitors. No facilities for children. Laundry. Motorcaravan services. Bar and snack bar/takeaway in high season. Heated outdoor swimming pool (5/6-12/9). Sports field. Fishing. Football. Basketball. Minigolf. Boules. Canoes. Pedalos. Bicycle hire. Archery and tennis adjacent. Games room with TV and library. Play area. Mobile homes/chalets/bungalow tents for rent. Free WiFi on part of site. Off site: Amenities in Ambrières-les-Vallées.

Open: 12 April - 27 October.

Directions

From Mayenne head north on D23 to Ambrières-les-Vallées. The site is clearly signed on your right-hand side from here. GPS: 48.391908, -0.61709

Charges guide

Per unit incl. 2 persons and electricity	€ 14.80 - € 17.80
extra person	€ 3.50 - € 4.60
child (under 13 yrs)	€ 1.90 - € 2.60

Camping Cheques accepted.

Angers

Camping du Lac de Maine

Avenue du Lac de Maine, F-49000 Angers (Maine-et-Loire) T: 02 41 73 05 03. E: camping@lacdemaine.fr
alanrogers.com/FR49000

The Lac de Maine campsite is situated in the heart of the Anjou region. Most of the 143 level touring pitches are part grass and part gravel hardstanding, with the remainder all gravel. All have water, a drain and 10A electricity. Some pitches are not suitable for awnings. The main entrance has a height restriction of 3.2 m, although there is an alternative gate for higher vehicles. This is a useful site, open for a long season and only five minutes from the centre of Angers. With wide access roads, it is also suitable for American RVs. This site has the advantage of being at the southern end of the Parc de Loisirs du Lac de Maine. The adjacent 220 acre lake has a sandy beach for swimmers, windsurfing, sailing and pedaloes, while the parkland provides tennis courts and a nature reserve.

Facilities

Two sanitary blocks, one which can be heated and includes some washbasins in cubicles. British style WCs. Facilities for babies and disabled visitors. Laundry facilities. Motorcaravan services. Restaurant and takeaway (July/Aug). Bar (20/6-10/9). Heated L-shaped swimming pool (1/5-30/9). Spa. Pétanque. Bicycle hire. Play area. Internet point and WiFi (free). Barrier card deposit (€ 20). Off site: Supermarket within walking distance. Lake beach 500 m. Fishing 1 km. Riding 3 km. Golf 5 km.

Open: 25 March - 10 October.

Directions

Site is just west of Angers near the N23 (Angers-Nantes road). Turn south at signs for Quartier de Maine and Lac de Maine. Follow signs for Pruniers and Bouchemaine. Site on D111 and signed. GPS: 47.45434, -0.59619

Charges guide

Per unit incl. 2 persons and electricity	€ 19.30 - € 27.00
extra person	€ 3.40
child (under 13 yrs)	€ 2.30

Camping Cheques accepted.

Assérac

Camping le Moulin de l'Eclis

Pont Mahé, 5 bis rue de la Plage, F-44410 Assérac (Loire-Atlantique) T: 02 40 01 76 69.
E: info@camping-leclis.com **alanrogers.com/FR44330**

Le Moulin de l'Eclis is an attractive, rural site with direct access to a safe sandy beach. There are 180 pitches of which around half are available for tourers, most with 10A electricity. Most pitches are of a generous size on grass and are divided by small trees and shrubs. There are many tall pine trees which provide good shade. A newer area has somewhat sloping pitches and here there is no shade. A solar heated, covered pool is ideal for when the tide goes out from the wide shallow bay, and there is direct access to the beach. Watersports are popular and some are organised. This site appeals to windsurfers.

Facilities

Three bright, modern, heated toilet blocks include some washbasins in cabins and large preset showers with dividers. A new block has family cabins and facilities for children. Good facilities provided for disabled visitors. Laundry facilities. Small shop sells fresh bread (1/5-30/9). Butcher's van calls (July/Aug). Bar with snacks and takeaway (July/Aug). Covered, solar heated pool and paddling pool. Play area. Watersports. WiFi (free).

Open: 1 April - 11 November.

Directions

Take the D82 from Asserac in a northwest direction for 5 km. Site is on left and well signed.
GPS: 47.44548, -2.45161

Charges guide

Per unit incl. 2 persons and electricity	€ 20.06 - € 41.50
extra person	€ 3.80 - € 6.20
child	€ 2.60 - € 4.10

Assérac

Flower Camping Domaine du Pont Mahé

Pont Mahé, F-44410 Assérac (Loire-Atlantique) T: 02 40 01 74 98. E: contact@pont-mahe.com
alanrogers.com/FR44400

La Grande Brière is a vast area of marshland to the north of the Loire estuary. This is an area rich in flora and fauna, arguably best explored using the traditional punts (chalands). Domaine du Pont Mahé is a seaside site to the north of the Brière. The new owners are working to improve the site and its amenities. Of the 81 pitches, 36 are for touring and the remainder are occupied by mobile homes (27 for rent). The pitches are generally well shaded and of a good size. The site's covered swimming pool is a focal point and is attractively surrounded by a terrace with straw parasols. Bicycle hire is on offer and a number of cycle tracks run close to the site.

Facilities

Sanitary facilities include hot showers and washbasins in cabins. Facilities for disabled visitors. Laundry. Shop (July/Aug). Bar, restaurant and takeaway (21/5-31/8). Covered swimming pool (11/4-30/9). Children's pool. Play area. Games room. Bicycle and canoe hire. Activity and entertainment programme. Mobile homes and equipped tents for rent. WiFi throughout (charged). Off site: Nearest beach 250 m. Fishing. Cycle tracks.

Open: 1 April - 31 October.

Directions

Leave the N165 at Arzal exit and head south on the D139 (which becomes the D83) as far as Assérac. Head west here on D82 to Pont Mahé and site is well signed. GPS: 47.44737, -2.45043

Charges guide

Per unit incl. 2 persons and electricity	€ 14.90 - € 28.50
extra person	€ 3.00 - € 4.50

Batz-sur-Mer

Flower Camping les Paludiers

Rue Appert, F-44740 Batz-sur-Mer (Loire-Atlantique) T: 02 40 60 17 28. E: paludiers@flowercampings.com
alanrogers.com/FR44360

Les Paludiers is pleasantly situated at Batz-sur-Mer, a typical Breton town between La Baule and the fortified town of Guérande. The site has 260 pitches with 157 used for touring units on grass and sandy ground, marked and divided by shrubs. There are 70 comfort pitches with 10A electricity. The remainder of the pitches are occupied by mobile homes, chalets and six tented lodges on stilts. At the rear of the modern reception building there is a bar and games room. Outside, a patio area overlooks a small heated swimming and paddling pool and a large play area.

Facilities

Three modern sanitary blocks, each with good facilities for disabled visitors and a baby room. Laundry facilities. Motorcaravan services. Shop with essentials. Bar and snacks. Heated swimming and paddling pools. Play area. Games room with stage. Activities and entertainment. Communal barbecue. Bicycle hire. WiFi throughout (free). Off site: Beach 100 m. Town centre 800 m. Golf 1 km.

Open: 26 March - 2 October.

Directions

From Nantes take N171 to St Nazaire then D213 towards Guérande. At D774 follow signs to Batz-sur-Mer, go through village and take 3rd exit from roundabout into rue Appert. Site entrance is on left.
GPS: 47.2788, -2.4913

Charges guide

Per unit incl. 2 persons and electricity	€ 15.00 - € 30.00
extra person	€ 4.00 - € 7.00

Brain-sur-l'Authion

Camping du Port Caroline

Route de la Bohalle, F-49800 Brain-sur-l'Authion (Maine-et-Loire) T: 02 41 80 42 18.
E: info@campingduportcaroline.fr **alanrogers.com/FR49030**

Camping du Port Caroline is an attractive site lying alongside a small river and close to the little village of Brain-sur-l'Authion, which is at the heart of the Anjou region. This is a quiet, relaxing site with little in the way of organised activities. There are 121 large, level, grassy pitches, 100 for touring, all with 10A electricity. They are separated by a variety of hedging and tall grees give most pitches ample shade. On site are a new small swimming and paddling pool with a jacuzzi, plus a bar/takeaway, games room and two small play areas. This is a useful base for visiting the vineyards of the Anjou which are all around.

Facilities

The two sanitary blocks of very different designs are clean and well maintained. Facilities for disabled visitors. Outdoor heated swimming and paddling pools (15/5-8/9). Shop. Snack bar. Takeaway (Tues. and Thurs). Play area. Bicycle hire. Mobile homes and chalets (one for disabled visitors) for hire. WiFi. Off site: Tennis. Fishing (charge applies). Boating. Multisports pitch. Walking and cycle trails. Boat trips on the Loire.

Open: 1 April - 31 October.

Directions

From Angers take D347 east towards Saumur for 7 km. At roundabout turn south onto D113 for 2 km. to Brain-sur-l'Authion. Site is signed just south of village. GPS: 47.44278, -0.40832

Charges guide

Per unit incl. 2 persons and electricity	€ 17.00 - € 21.00
extra person	€ 4.00 - € 4.50

Camping Cheques accepted.

Brissac

Sites et Paysages de l'Etang

Route de Saint Mathurin, F-49320 Brissac-Quincé (Maine-et-Loire) T: 02 41 91 70 61.
E: info@campingetang.com **alanrogers.com/FR49040**

At Camping de l'Etang many of the 125 very large, level touring pitches have pleasant views across the countryside. Separated and numbered, some have a little shade and all have electricity (16A) with water and drainage nearby; 24 are fully serviced. A small bridge crosses the River Aubance which runs through the site (well fenced) and there are two lakes where free fishing can be enjoyed. The site has its own vineyard and the wine produced can be purchased on the campsite. The adjacent Parc de Loisirs is a paradise for young children with many activities (discounts for campers).

Facilities

Three well maintained toilet blocks provide all the usual facilities. Laundry facilities. Baby room. Disabled visitors are well catered for. Motorcaravan services. The farmhouse houses reception, a shop (all season) and takeaway snacks (July/Aug) when bar is closed. A bar/restaurant serves crêpes, salads, etc. (evenings July/Aug). Swimming pool (heated and covered) and paddling pool. Fishing. Play area. Bicycle hire. Family entertainment in high season. WiFi throughout (charged).

Open: 23 April - 11 September.

Directions

Brissac-Quincé is 17 km. southeast of Angers on D748 towards Poitiers. Do not enter the town but turn north on D55 (site signed) towards St Mathurin. GPS: 47.3611, -0.4353

Charges guide

Per unit incl. 2 persons and electricity	€ 20.00 - € 35.00
extra person	€ 4.40 - € 6.60
child (0-10 yrs)	€ 1.00 - € 3.85

Cholet

Centre Touristique Lac de Ribou

Allée Léon Mandin, F-49300 Cholet (Maine-et-Loire) T: 02 41 49 74 30. E: lacderibou@franceloc.fr
alanrogers.com/FR49120

Situated just 58 km. southeast of Nantes and a similar distance from the River Loire at Angers and Saumur, this could be a useful place to break a journey or to spend a few days relaxing. Camping Lac de Ribou is a holiday complex in pleasant parkland next to an extensive lake on the outskirts of the busy market town of Cholet. One hundred touring pitches are on undulating land, divided by hedges and with mature trees providing shade. Most have electricity (10A, long leads required on some) and water.

Facilities

One sanitary block provides preset showers and washbasins in cabins. Facilities for children and disabled visitors. Laundry. Motorcaravan services. Small shop (July/Aug). Bar and snack bar with takeaway (July/Aug). Swimming pool complex with slides, flumes, toboggan and paddling pool. Upgraded indoor pool (from 11/4). Play area. Multisports pitch. Boules. Activities for all ages (July/Aug). Cabaret evenings. Communal barbecue. WiFi in snack bar and reception (free).

Open: 28 March - 4 October.

Directions

From N249 take exit 10 onto D160 into Cholet. Follow signs in town to Parc de Loisirs de Ribou. The site is well signposted in town. GPS: 47.036367, -0.843733

Charges guide

Per unit incl. 2 persons and electricity	€ 17.00 - € 27.00
extra person	€ 4.00 - € 6.00
dog	free - € 3.50

Clisson

Camping du Moulin

Route de Nantes, ZA de Câlin, F-44190 Clisson (Loire-Atlantique) T: 02 40 54 44 48.
E: camping@valleedeclisson.fr **alanrogers.com/FR44020**

This good value, small site, conveniently situated on one of the main north-south routes on the edge of the interesting old town of Clisson, in the middle of the wine growing region, was completely renovated in 2013. There are 50 good sized, marked and level pitches with electricity, divided by floral hedges and trees, plus six individual motorcaravan pitches and five chalets to rent. There is also an unmarked, wooded area for small tents. A barbecue and campfire area is to the rear of the site above the river where one can fish or canoe (via a steep path).

Facilities

The fully equipped and newly renovated sanitary facilities, cleaned each afternoon, include some washbasins in cabins and others in a separate large room, with hot and cold water. Unit for disabled visitors. Laundry facilities. Motorcaravan services. Small playground. Fishing. Five mobile homes for hire. Play area. Electric barbecues for hire. Club room with TV and table-football. Excursions and entertainment (July/Aug). WiFi over site (free). Off site: Supermarket with fuel just across the road.

Open: 1 April - 18 October.

Directions

From N249 Nantes-Cholet road, take exit for Vallet/Clisson and D763 south for 7 km. then fork right towards Clisson town centre. At roundabout after passing Leclerc supermarket on your right take second exit (into site). GPS: 47.09594, -1.28271

Charges guide

Per unit incl. 2 persons and electricity	€ 17.00 - € 19.00
extra person	€ 4.40

No credit cards.

Concourson-sur-Layon

Camping Caravaning la Vallée des Vignes

La Croix Patron, F-49700 Concourson-sur-Layon (Maine-et-Loire) T: 02 41 59 86 35.
E: info@campingvdv.com **alanrogers.com/FR49070**

The enthusiasm of the English owners here comes across instantly in the warm welcome received by their guests. Bordering the Layon river, the 79 good sized grass pitches (50 for tourers) are reasonably level and fully serviced (10A electricity, water tap and drain) but have little shade. Five pitches have a hardstanding for cars. Attractions include an enclosed bar and restaurant overlooking a generously sized sun terrace surrounding the pool. In high season there are activities for children and adults. This is an ideal base for visiting the châteaux of the Loire and the many local caves and vineyards.

Facilities

The toilet block includes washbasins in cabins and dishwashing facilities. Baby room. Facilities for disabled visitors. Washing machine. Bar meals and takeaway (15/5-15/9). Swimming and paddling pools (15/5-15/9). Playground, games area and football pitch. Minigolf. Volleyball. Basketball. Internet access and WiFi over part of site (free). Fishing. Caravan storage. Off site: Bicycle hire 4 km. Golf 20 km. Grand Parc Puy du Fou.

Open: 15 April - 30 September.

Directions

Site is 20 km. southwest of Saumur. Take D347 then D960, bypass Doué-la-Fontaine. Site entrance is on right 500 m. beyond Concourson-sur-Layon. GPS: 47.17431, -0.34730

Charges guide

Per unit incl. 2 persons and electricity	€ 23.50 - € 43.00
extra person	€ 4.00 - € 6.00
child (2-12 yrs)	€ 2.00 - € 4.00

Guémené-Penfao

Flower Camping l'Hermitage

36 avenue du Paradis, F-44290 Guémené-Penfao (Loire-Atlantique) T: 02 40 79 23 48.
E: camping.hermitage@wanadoo.fr **alanrogers.com/FR44130**

L'Hermitage is a pretty, wooded site set in the Vallée du Don and would be useful for en-route stops or for longer stays. The enthusiastic staff, even though their English is a little limited, provide a warm welcome and maintain this reasonably priced site to a good standard. There are 110 pitches of which 80 are a good size for touring and camping. Some are formally arranged on open, level grass pitches, whereas others are informal amongst light woodland. Electricity (6A) is available to all (a long lead may be useful). A further 18 pitches are taken by mobile homes, most of which are for rent.

Facilities

Clean and well serviced toilet block includes some washbasins in cabins with warm water. Laundry and dishwashing sinks under cover (cold water but a hot tap is provided). Smallish pool, paddling pool and slide (renovation in progress May 2015). Small play area. Pétanque. Bicycle hire. Games room with video games. WiFi (free). Off site: Leisure complex with indoor pool opposite. Fishing 500 m. Village 1 km. for all facilities.

Open: 4 April - 1 November.

Directions

Exit N137 at Derval (Châteaubriant) but take D775 for Redon. Guémené-Penfao is 13 km. Watch for site signs before centre. Site is on outskirts in a semi-residential area. GPS: 47.62595, -1.8181

Charges guide

Per unit incl. 2 persons and electricity	€ 17.00 - € 22.50
extra person	€ 3.50 - € 5.00

Guérande

516

Le Domaine de Léveno

Lieu-dit Léveno, F-44350 Guérande (Loire-Atlantique) T: 02 40 24 79 30.
E: domaine.leveno@wanadoo.fr **alanrogers.com/FR44220**

There have been many changes to this extensive site over the years and considerable investment has been made to provide a range of excellent new facilities. The number of mobile homes and chalets has increased considerably, leaving only around 76 of the 600 pitches for touring. These are in small groups or scattered among the mobiles, on pitches divided by hedges and with mature trees which offer good shade. All have electricity (6A). When we visited in mid May they were rather overgrown. Access to some is challenging and the site is not recommended for larger units.

Facilities

Main toilet block offers preset showers, washbasins in cubicles and facilities for disabled visitors. A second, smaller block has been refurbished to a high standard. Laundry facilities. Motorcaravan services. Small shop selling basics and takeaway snacks. Restaurant. Bar with TV and games (all April-Sept). Indoor pool. Heated outdoor pool complex with paddling pool (15/5-15/9). Fitness room. Excellent, safe play areas. Multisports court, tennis and crazy golf. Activities and events (high season). No electric barbecues. WiFi in bar (free).

Open: 12 April - 28 September.

Directions

Guérande is 80 km. west of Nantes. From Nantes via N165/N171/D213 and from Vannes on D774 take D99E Guérande bypass. Turn east following signs for Villejames and Leclerc hypermarket and continue on D247 to site on right.
GPS: 47.33352, -2.3906

Charges guide

Per unit incl. 2 persons, electricity and water	€ 22.00 - € 40.00
extra person	€ 3.00 - € 7.00

Guérande

Camping la Fontaine

Route de Saint Molf, Kersavary, F-44350 Guérande (Loire-Atlantique) T: 02 40 24 96 19.
E: contact@camping-lafontaine.com **alanrogers.com/FR44530**

Visitors to this pleasant little site, close to the historic walled town of Guérande, will find a relaxed ambiance and receive a warm welcome from owners Marc and Joëlle. There are just 110 level, grassy pitches (77 for tourers), most divided by hedges and with electrical connections (6A) and water points nearby. The remainder are occupied by mobile homes, 12 of which are available for rent. The salt marshes that produce the famous Sel de Guérande, the fishing port of La Turballe and a wide variety of sandy beaches and little coves are all within easy reach.

Facilities

Central modern toilet block with controllable showers and some washbasins in cubicles, one cubicle with shower and washbasin. Baby room. En-suite unit for disabled visitors. Washing machine and dryer. Hairdryer, iron and board available from reception. Bread can be ordered and a small snack bar/takeaway has occasional themed evenings (both July/Aug). Playground. Boules. Electric barbecues are not permitted. Free WiFi over site.

Open: 30 March - 27 October.

Directions

Guérande is 80 km. west of Nantes. From Nantes via N165/N171/D213 take D99E Guérande bypass and head north on D233 (St Molf). From Vannes on D774 at junction with D99E take first exit (D233). Site is on left in 1 km. GPS: 47.349167, -2.434167

Charges guide

Per unit incl. 2 persons and electricity	€ 16.70 - € 23.90
extra person	€ 4.00 - € 5.50

Heric

Camping la Pindière

La Denais, F-44810 Heric (Loire-Atlantique) T: 02 40 57 65 41. E: contact@camping-la-pindiere.com
alanrogers.com/FR44430

Camping la Pindière can be found between Nantes and Rennes, close to the Nantes-Brest canal. The site is open all year and may appeal as an en-route stop, although there is much to see in the area. Pitches here are of a good size and generally well shaded (48 for touring). Most have electrical connections. Mobile homes and roulottes are available for rent. The adjacent Auberge des Pyrénées is a pleasant restaurant, open throughout the year. Cycling is popular in the area, with a number of excellent cycle tracks, including routes alongside the canal. The great city of Nantes, the largest in Brittany, is within easy reach.

Facilities

New, heated toilet block. Facilities for disabled visitors. Laundry facilities. Motorcaravan services. Bar, restaurant and takeaway. Heated, covered swimming pool and paddling pool (July/Aug). Play area. Volleyball. Mobile homes for rent. WiFi (free). Off site: Shops, bars and restaurants in Heric. Riding 1 km. Fishing 5 km.

Open: All year.

Directions

Heric is north of Nantes. From the north, use N137 Rennes-Nantes road and leave at Fay-de-Bretagne exit. Follow signs from here. GPS: 47.41329, -1.6705

Charges guide

Per unit incl. 2 persons and electricity	€ 18.40 - € 21.20

No credit cards.

La Baule

Camping les Ajoncs d'Or

Chemin du Rocher, F-44500 La Baule (Loire-Atlantique) T: 02 40 60 33 29. E: contact@ajoncs.com

alanrogers.com/FR44170

This site is situated in pine woods, 1.5 km. inland of La Baule and its beautiful bay. A well maintained, natural woodland setting provides a wide variety of pitch types (just over 200), some level and bordered with hedges and tall trees to provide shade and many others that maintain the natural characteristics of the woodland. Most pitches have 6A electricity and water nearby and are usually of a larger size. There is a wooded area that young campers are encouraged to pitch. A central building provides a shop and an open friendly bar that serves snacks and takeaways. The owner, M. Garnier, is continually looking for ways to improve his site.

Facilities

The single sanitary block is clean and well maintained providing plenty of facilities including a baby room and facilities for disabled campers. Washing machines and dryers. Shop, bar and snack bar (July/Aug and w/ends). Good size swimming pool and paddling pool (1/6-15/9). Sports and playground areas. Bicycle hire. Entertainment and aquagym classes (July/Aug). WiFi in some areas.

Open: 1 March - 30 November.

Directions

From N171 take exit for La Baule-les Pins. Follow signs for La Baule Centre, then left at roundabout in front of Carrefour supermarket and follow site signs. GPS: 47.29361, -2.37833

Charges guide

Per unit incl. 2 persons and electricity	€ 15.00 - € 24.00
extra person	€ 8.00

La Baule

Airotel la Roseraie

20 avenue Jean Sohier, F-44500 La Baule (Loire-Atlantique) T: 02 40 60 46 66. E: camping@laroseraie.com

alanrogers.com/FR44280

This is a lively site with plenty of potential and some good features. There is a warm welcome from the Burban family and their reception staff in very pleasant and smart surroundings. An excellent pool complex by the entrance is open all season and includes a heated pool with a roof that is opened when the sun shines, a separate flume and a paddling pool. There are 223 level pitches of which 55 are for touring units, all with 6/10A electricity and 18 with water and drainage. There is a lively programme of activities for children and families in high season. A comfortable sitting room with a TV is handy for poor weather. The site is just 2 km. from the sophisticated seaside resort of La Baule.

Facilities

One traditional sanitary block has controllable showers, washbasins in cubicles, facilities for disabled visitors, washing machines and dryers. A modern extension to another block has en-suite showers and washbasins and an attractively decorated children's section. Small shop. Bar with snacks and restaurant facility and separate takeaway. Play area. Games/TV and fitness rooms. Multisports court. Tennis. Bicycle hire. Boules. WiFi (free).

Open: 4 April - 29 September.

Directions

Site is beside N171/D99 Nantes and St Nazaire-Guérande road (Route Bleue). Leave at exit for La Baule-les Pins and Escoublac and go towards La Baule. At church in Escoublac turn right and site is 500 m. on right. GPS: 47.29884, -2.3566

Charges guide

Per unit incl. 2 persons and electricity	€ 23.00 - € 41.20
extra person	€ 5.00 - € 8.30

La Bernerie-en-Retz

Camping les Ecureuils

24 avenue Gilbert Burlot, F-44760 La Bernerie-en-Retz (Loire-Atlantique) T: 02 40 82 76 95.
E: camping.les-ecureuils@wanadoo.fr **alanrogers.com/FR44050**

Close to both the sea and the centre of the little village of La Bernerie, les Ecureuils is a pleasant and spacious family run site. The sandy beach here is great for children; swimming is restricted to high tide, since the sea goes out a long way, although at low tide a shallow lagoon remains which is perfect for young children. The site has 170 touring pitches, all with 10A electricity close by and 19 with their own water tap and drain. There are also 89 mobile homes and chalets for rent and a further 50 privately owned. The village has several shops, bars and restaurants, and a sailing school.

Facilities

Two toilet blocks have been renovated to an excellent standard with controllable showers and washbasins in cubicles. En-suite units for disabled visitors. Baby rooms. Motorcaravan services. Bar with terrace, also selling bread, plus snack bar and takeaway (July/Aug). Pool complex with water slides and flume (15/5-15/9). Renovated playground with trampolines. New multisports court. Communal barbecue area. WiFi (free in bar).

Open: 1 May - 16 September.

Directions

La Bernerie-en-Retz is 26 km. south of St Nazaire bridge via D213. From the D213/D13 some 6 km. from junction east of Pornic, turn west on D66 to La Bernerie. Site is signed to right by railway station before reaching town. GPS: 47.0845, -2.036667

Charges guide

Per unit incl. 2 persons and electricity	€ 22.00 - € 44.00
extra person	€ 4.00 - € 8.00

La Chartre-sur-le-Loir

Camping du Vieux Moulin

Chemin des Bergivaux, avenue des Déportés, F-72340 La Chartre-sur-le-Loir (Sarthe) T: 02 43 44 41 18.
E: campingduvieuxmoulin72@gmail.com **alanrogers.com/FR72070**

Le Vieux Moulin is a pleasant family site, located on the banks of the Loir, close to the pretty town of La Chartre-sur-le-Loir, to the south east of Le Mans. The 67 touring pitches here are grassy and of a good size. There are also a number of mobile homes and fully equipped tents available for rent. On-site amenities include a heated swimming pool, a paddling pool and a sports field. Canoeing is popular here and canoes can be rented on site. The site becomes livelier in peak season with a limited entertainment and activity programme, including a children's club and occasional karaoke evenings.

Facilities

A modern sanitary block provides pushbutton showers and washbasins in cubicles. Facilities for disabled visitors and babies. Washing machine and dryer. Motorcaravan services. Small shop selling basics, restaurant and takeaway with licence (weekends and July/Aug). Swimming and paddling pools (1/5-30/9). Fishing. Canoeing. Bicycle hire. Large sports field. Play area. Mobile homes and equipped tents for rent. WiFi.
Off site: Village with shops, bars and restaurants 1 km.

Open: 28 March - 30 November.

Directions

La Chartre-sur-le-Loir is 47 km. SE of Le Mans. From A28 exit 26, head east to Château du Loir, turn south on D938/D338 (Caen-Tours road) and cross the Loir. Then northeast on D305 to La Chartre-sur-le-Loir. After one-way system follow signs to the site, turning left immediately after crossing river. GPS: 47.7324, 0.57095

Charges guide

Per unit incl. 2 persons and electricity	€ 19.50
extra person	€ 4.00

La Flèche

Camping la Route d'Or

Allée du camping, F-72200 La Flèche (Sarthe) T: 02 43 94 55 90. E: info@camping-laroutedor.com
alanrogers.com/FR72010

This is a very busy site as La Flèche lies at the junction of the Le Mans-Angers and Laval-Saumur roads. Set in quiet, park-like surroundings on the south bank of the River Loir (not to be confused with the River Loire, a few miles to the south), the site is a pleasant stroll from the town centre where there are plenty of shops and restaurants. There are 190 touring pitches marked out on flat grass, many in excess of 100 sq.m. and some with dividing hedges. A further ten pitches offer mobile homes for rent. Some are in the open park, others are shaded by tall trees. Electricity (10A) is available in all areas (long leads are frequently needed). There are 35 shady pitches with water and drainage and one overnight hardstanding suitable for larger units or American RVs – phone in advance.

Facilities

Two original sanitary blocks are of the older style with rather cramped showers, and British and Turkish style WCs. The central block is more modern and includes a second unit for disabled visitors. A separate block with laundry can be heated in cool weather (used by other campers in winter). Motorcaravan services. Bakery service each morning. Swimming pool and paddling pool. Tennis. Boules. Play area. Pedalos and canoes for hire on the river. Bicycle hire (routes in English from reception). WiFi area. Twin-axle caravans are not accepted.
Off site: Indoor pool in La Flèche. Shops 300 m.

Open: 1 March - 31 October.

Directions

Exit the A11 Angers-Le Mans motorway at exit 10. Take the D306 southeast. Avoid signs for La Flèche town centre, but continue on the D306 towards Bouge. The municipal campsite is well signed off this road. GPS: 47.69514, -0.07927

Charges guide

Per unit incl. 1 person	€ 6.50 - € 7.30
extra person	€ 2.25 - € 2.70
child (under 10 yrs)	€ 1.70 - € 2.00
electricity (10A)	€ 3.60

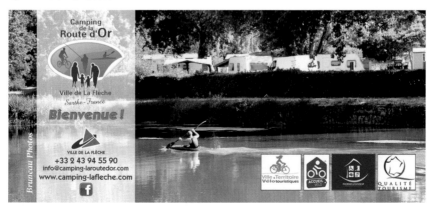

La Plaine-sur-Mer

Camping le Ranch

Les Hautes Raillères, F-44770 La Plaine-sur-Mer (Loire-Atlantique) T: 02 40 21 52 62.
E: info@camping-le-ranch.com **alanrogers.com/FR44240**

This is a pleasant, family run campsite with a very friendly, French ambience. It is close to the beaches of the Jade Coast between Pornic and Saint Brévin-les-Pins, yet not right on the seashore. The 88 touring pitches all have access to 10A electricity, although on some a long cable may be required. These occupy the central part of the site with the fringe areas taken up by mobile homes and chalets, 28 for rent and 74 privately owned (although 30 of these are also available for rent in high season). The rows of pitches are separated by well kept hedges and small trees mark the corners of most plots.

Facilities

The central sanitary block has preset showers and washbasins in cubicles. Facilities for disabled visitors. Baby room. Further small toilet block. Motorcaravan services. Bar has small shop selling bread, basics and camping gas. Good takeaway (6/7-31/8). Heated swimming pool complex with slides and flume (1/5-30/9). Activities for children and entertainment and sports events for families in high season. Electric barbecues are not permitted. WiFi (charged). Off site: Beach and fishing 800 m. Bicycle hire 1.5 km. Boat launching 3 km.

Open: 1 April - 30 September.

Directions

La Plaine-sur-Mer is 16 km. south of the St Nazaire bridge. Site is on D96 5 km. northeast of the town. From D213 (Route Bleue) just south of St Michel-Chef-Chef turn southwest on D96 towards La Plaine. Site on left in 2 km. GPS: 47.155216, -2.1649

Charges guide

Per unit incl. 2 persons and electricity	€ 19.20 - € 33.70
extra person	€ 3.50 - € 6.50
child (under 8 yrs)	€ 2.00 - € 4.50
dog	€ 3.00 - € 3.20

La Plaine-sur-Mer

Camping la Tabardière

2 route de la Tabardière, F-44770 La Plaine-sur-Mer (Loire-Atlantique) T: 02 40 21 58 83.
E: info@camping-la-tabardiere.com **alanrogers.com/FR44150**

Owned and managed by the Barré family, this campsite is pleasant, peaceful and immaculate. It will suit those who want to enjoy the local coast and towns but return to an oasis of relaxation. However, it still provides activities and fun for those with energy remaining. The 150 pitches for touring are mostly terraced and care needs to be taken in manoeuvring caravans into position – although the effort is well worth it. The pitches have access to electricity (4-10A) and water taps are conveniently situated nearby. The site is probably not suitable for people using wheelchairs. Whilst this is a rural site, its amenities are excellent with a covered swimming pool, paddling pool and water slides, volleyball, tennis, boules and a very challenging 18-hole minigolf course to keep you occupied, plus a friendly bar. The beautiful beaches are 3 km. away, with the fishing harbour town, Pornic, some 5 km, ideal for cafés, restaurants and evening strolls.

Facilities

Two good, clean toilet blocks are well equipped and include laundry facilities. Motorcaravan services. Shop (1/6-31/8). Takeaway (July/Aug). Bar (1/6-5/9). Good sized covered swimming pool, paddling pool and slides (from 15/4). Playground. Minigolf. Volleyball. Basketball. Half-size tennis courts. Boules. Fitness programme. Bicycle hire (July/Aug). WiFi throughout (free). Off site: Beach and sea fishing 3 km. Golf 4 km.

Open: 2 April - 24 September.

Directions

Site is well signed, inland off the D13 Pornic-La Plaine-sur-Mer road. GPS: 47.14111, -2.152285

Charges guide

Per unit incl. 2 persons and electricity	€ 20.00 - € 36.00
extra person	€ 4.30 - € 7.90
child (2-9 yrs)	€ 3.30 - € 5.20

Camping Cheques accepted.

La Plaine-sur-Mer

Flower Camping la Guichardière

2 rue de Mouton, F-44770 La Plaine-sur-Mer (Loire-Atlantique) T: 02 40 21 55 09.
E: contact@camping-laguichardiere.net **alanrogers.com/FR44500**

An easy stroll from the sea and the fishing and yachting port of la Gravette, Camping la Guichardière is situated in the Loire-Atlantique between La Baule and Noirmoutier. In a green and flowery setting, there are 210 pitches, of which 63 are for tourers. They are mainly in an area close to the facilities and are separated by hedges. Fifty-five have electricity connections (6A). There are 25 mobile homes and chalets for hire. The welcome from the Oursel family and their English-speaking staff is warm. The amenities of La Plaine-sur-Mer and Préfailles are within easy reach.

Facilities

Traditional, well maintained sanitary block with hot showers and some washbasins in cubicles. Baby bath. Facilities for disabled visitors. Laundry facilities. Motorcaravan services. Bar with small shop, snack bar and takeaway (July/Aug, busy w/ends). Heated pool and paddling pools (1/5-15/9). Entertainment for children and families (July/Aug weekdays). Tennis. Pétanque. Playground. Games area. Bicycle hire. Free WiFi in bar.

Open: 6 April - 30 September.

Directions

From N844 Nantes Périphérique at exit 52, follow Noirmoutier/Pornic D723 then D751 to Pornic. Head northwest on D213 St Nazaire, then turn west on D286 to La Plaine-sur-Mer from where site is signed. GPS: 47.152626, -2.208196

Charges guide

Per unit incl. 2 persons and electricity	€ 21.44 - € 33.44

La Turballe

Camping le Parc Sainte Brigitte

Domaine de Bréhet, chemin des Routes, F-44420 La Turballe (Loire-Atlantique) T: 02 40 24 88 91.
E: saintebrigitte@wanadoo.fr **alanrogers.com/FR44040**

Le Parc Sainte Brigitte is a well established site in the attractive grounds of a manor house, under three kilometres from the beaches. It is a spacious site with 158 good pitches, 74 with electricity, water and drainage. Some are arranged in a circular, park-like setting near the entrance, others are in wooded areas under tall trees and the remainder are on more open grass in an unmarked area near the pool. This is a quiet place to stay outside the main season, whilst in high season, it can become very busy yet it still retains its family atmosphere. One can walk around many of the areas of the estate that are not used for camping; there are farm animals to see and a carp fishing lake will be popular with anglers.

Facilities

The main toilet block, supplemented by a second block, is of good quality. They include washbasins in cabins and two bathrooms. Laundry facilities and lines provided. Motorcaravan services. Small shop. Pleasant restaurant/bar with takeaway (both 1/4-30/9). Heated swimming pool with sliding roof and paddling pool. Playground. Bicycle hire. Boules. TV room and traditional 'salle de réunion'. Fishing. Charcoal barbecues are tolerated. WiFi throughout (free). Off site: Riding 2 km.

Open: 1 April - 1 October.

Directions

Entrance is off the busy La Turballe-Guérande D99 road, 3 km. east of La Turballe. A one-way system operates. GPS: 47.34253, -2.47168

Charges guide

Per unit incl. 2 persons, water, waste water and electricity	€ 31.50
extra person	€ 6.70
child (under 7 yrs)	€ 5.30
dog	€ 1.60

La Turballe

Camping la Falaise

1 boulevard de Belmont, F-44420 La Turballe (Loire-Atlantique) T: 02 40 23 32 53.
E: info@camping-de-la-falaise.com **alanrogers.com/FR44340**

La Falaise is a simple site enjoying direct access to a wide sandy beach. There are 150 pitches of which 63 are available to touring units with water and electricity (Europlugs). Other pitches are occupied by mobile homes and chalets (some to rent). The pitches are of a reasonable size and marked by low hedges, but are not shaded. This is a quiet site in low season becoming much livelier in July and August. A small bar and takeaway on the site are open all season and nearby La Turballe has a good selection of shops and restaurants. A heated covered pool, new sanitary facilities and a play area are all of a very high standard. This site suits those with motorcaravans as a rental service for small cars is available.

Facilities

New heated sanitary block. Bar, snack bar and takeaway (1/4-30/10). Heated covered pool (all season). Play area (unfenced). Bicycle hire. Car rental. Mobile homes and chalets for rent. Direct access to the beach. WiFi throughout (free). Off site: Shops 300 m. Fishing. Boat launching 500 m. Shops in La Turballe 2 km.

Open: 1 April - 1 November.

Directions

Take the D99 from Guérande to La Turballe and then continue towards Piriac-sur-Mer. Bypass La Turballe and the site is on this road after a further kilometre. GPS: 47.353833, -2.517333

Charges guide

Per unit incl. 2 persons and electricity	€ 19.40 - € 30.00

Le Croisic

Camping de l'Océan

15 route de la Maison Rouge, F-44490 Le Croisic (Loire-Atlantique) T: 02 40 23 07 69.
E: camping-ocean@wanadoo.fr **alanrogers.com/FR44210**

Camping de l'Océan is situated on the Le Croisic peninsula, an attractive part of the Brittany coastline. Out of a total of 400 pitches, some 50 are available for touring units with the remainder being taken by mobile homes either privately owned or for rent. The pitches are level and 80-100 sq.m. in size (they were rather worn when we visited). The leisure facilities, which include a restaurant, bar and pool complex, are of an excellent standard. This site, probably more suitable for families with young teenagers, can be very lively in high season with a wealth of activities and entertainment for all ages. Sports are well catered for and there are tournaments in high season. After an excellent meal in the restaurant you can enjoy a range of entertainment on most evenings in July and August. The site is within walking distance of the Atlantic Ocean and white sandy beaches, just 150 m. away.

Facilities

Three adequate toilet blocks with facilities for disabled visitors. Washing machines and dryers. Restaurant, bar, takeaway and shop (all season). Motorcaravan services. Swimming pool complex comprising an indoor pool, outdoor pool and paddling pool (15/5-27/9). Spa and wellness facility. Volleyball. Football. Basketball. Tennis. Bicycle hire. Charcoal barbecues are permitted. WiFi over site (charged; free in bar area). Mobile homes and maisonettes for rent. Off site: Riding, fishing and beach 150 m. Golf 400 m. Sailing 2 km. Market (most days). Shops, bars and restaurants in Le Croisic.

Open: 10 April - 27 September.

Directions

From Le Pouliguen, travel west on N171 to Le Croisic. Site is well signed from here and found in 1.5 km. GPS: 47.29752, -2.53593

Charges guide

Per unit incl. 2 persons and electricity	€ 26.00 - € 54.00
extra person	€ 6.00 - € 9.00
child (2-7 yrs)	€ 4.00 - € 7.00
dog	€ 5.00 - € 7.00

Le Croisic

Camping la Pierre Longue

B.P. 13 rue Henri Dunant, F-44490 Le Croisic (Loire-Atlantique) T: 02 40 23 13 44.
E: lapierrelongue@orange.fr **alanrogers.com/FR44320**

La Pierre Longue is on a peninsula which stretches over 5 km. into the ocean. The friendly owners have a great sense of humour at this delightful site. There are a total of 55 grass touring pitches of ample size which are well tended and divided by small trees and young shrubs. There is some shade but not a great deal. A comfortable bar and a restaurant with a comprehensive menu serving speciality seafood dishes open out onto a terrace and small swimming pool. This site is open for a long season and has a very pleasant ambience.

Facilities

The main modern toilet block is heated with washbasins both open and in cubicles. Large shower area. Facilities for disabled visitors. Laundry facilities. Small shop, bar, restaurant and takeaway (22/6-5/9). Outdoor heated swimming and paddling pools (May-Sept). Bicycle hire. WiFi (free). Off site: Riding 300 m. Golf 400 m. Fishing 500 m. Medieval town of Guérande. Beaches of La Baule.

Open: 15 March - 30 November.

Directions

Take D774 from Guérande south to Pouliguen. Follow northwest to Le Croisic. Site is well signed and on left after 1.5 km. GPS: 47.29244, -2.52923

Charges guide

Per unit incl. 2 persons and electricity	€ 16.90 - € 26.80
extra person	€ 4.00 - € 7.10

Les Rosiers-sur-Loire

Camping Val de Loire

6 rue Sainte-Baudruehe, F-49350 Les Rosiers-sur-Loire (Maine-et-Loire) T: 02 41 51 94 33.
E: contact@camping-valdeloire.com **alanrogers.com/FR49180**

This small, attractive site is on the outskirts of the village close to the River Loire between Saumur and Angers. There are 84 touring pitches, all with 10A electricity, individual water taps and waste water drainage. A further 28 pitches are used for mobile homes, mostly for hire. Beech hedging provides good privacy. Recent additions include a pleasant little bar with a terrace and an adjacent marquee used for games and entertainment. There are two new heated swimming pools, one covered, the other surrounded by sunbathing terraces and with a large (linked) paddling pool. When we visited in late June, everything was very quiet, but in July/August there is a busy programme of activities.

Facilities

The main toilet block is modern and offers all the necessary facilities, including those for babies and campers with disabilities. Two older blocks and a new prefabricated unit provide additional facilities. Bar with TV serves snacks (fresh bread to order; June-Aug). Covered pool (1/4-30/9). Outdoor pool (1/6-15/9). Children's activities. Evening entertainment in high season. Play area. Minigolf. Tennis. Bicycle hire. WiFi over site.

Open: 1 April - 30 September.

Directions

From A85 motorway at exit 1 take D144 south to Beaufort-en-Vallée. Continue south on D59. Site is signed to right on approach to village.
GPS: 47.35877, -0.22604

Charges guide

Per unit incl. 2 persons and electricity	€ 21.00 - € 60.90
extra person	€ 4.00 - € 5.50

Luché-Pringé

Camping la Chabotière

Place des Tilleuils, rue de La Plage, F-72800 Luché-Pringé (Sarthe) T: 02 43 45 10 00.
E: contact@lachabotiere.com **alanrogers.com/FR72100**

This is a delightful little municipal site on the River Loir, just a few steps from the main square of an interesting village classed as a Petite Cité de Caractère. There are 85 pitches, 65 for touring and all with access to electricity and the remainder used for wooden chalets and canvas bungalows for rent. The main part of the site down by the river is kept vehicle free in July and August, ensuring a safer and quieter environment. A child-proof gate leads out onto the river bank and footpath. There are many opportunities for walking, cycling and sightseeing in the area.

Facilities

The traditional toilet block is well maintained and kept clean; it has pushbutton showers and some washbasins in cubicles. Baby room and washbasins for children. Facilities for disabled visitors. Washing machines and dryer. Motorcaravan services. Quiet room with tables for playing cards and games plus free Internet access (adults only). Adventure play area. Large sports field. Bicycle hire. Fishing. Activities for children and in the evening. Free WiFi over site. Chalets for rent. No electric barbecues.

Open: 1 April - 15 October.

Directions

From A11 between Le Mans and Angers, leave at exit 10 or 11 and head eastwards to La Flèche, then north on D323 (Le Mans). At Clermont-Créans turn east on D13 to Luché-Pringé. In main square (ignore earlier campsite sign) turn sharp right then left, signed 'Minigolf' then site. GPS: 47.70253, 0.07365

Charges guide

Per unit incl. 2 persons and electricity	€ 12.10 - € 14.70

No credit cards.

Marçon

Flower Camping Lac des Varennes

Saint Lezin, route de Port-Gauthier, F-72340 Marçon (Sarthe) T: 02 43 44 13 72.

E: lacdesvarennes@camp-in-ouest.com **alanrogers.com/FR72080**

This extensive site is located near the massive forest of Bercé in the Vallée du Loir and is on the shore of the lake from which it takes its name. There are 250 pitches here, with 175 for tourers, all grassy and with electrical connections (10A). Many also have lake views. The site has its own sandy beach (with a beach volleyball court) and canoes are available for rent. In high season, various activities are organised including a club for children and riding. Mobile homes are available for rent. A gate gives free access to the Base de Loisirs which offers a variety of water- and land-based activities.

Facilities

Three traditional sanitary blocks are kept clean and provide pushbutton showers, some washbasins in cubicles and a mix of British and Turkish style toilets. Washing machines and dryer. Basic facilities for disabled visitors. Motorcaravan services. Shop, snack bar and takeaway (July/Aug). Simple bar with games and TV. Play area. Organised entertainment (July/Aug). Direct access to lake with fishing and swimming. WiFi on part of site. Off site: Base de Loisirs with sailing and sports. Riding 5 km. Walking and cycling in the forest 8 km.

Open: 12 April - 27 October.

Directions

Marçon is 50 km. southeast of Le Mans. From A28 exit 26, head east to Château du Loir, turn south on D938/D338 (Caen-Tours) and cross the Loir. Then head northeast on D305 to Marçon, and turn west in village centre to Base de Loisirs and site on right in 1 km. GPS: 47.7125, 0.4993

Charges guide

Per unit incl. 2 persons and electricity	€ 15.50 - € 20.00
extra person	€ 4.00 - € 5.50

Mesquer

Camping le Château du Petit Bois

1820 route de Kerlagadec, F-44420 Mesquer (Loire-Atlantique) T: 02 40 42 68 77.

E: info@campingdupetitbois.com **alanrogers.com/FR44270**

This pleasant campsite is located in the wooded grounds of a small château. The 125 good sized touring pitches, all with electricity (10A) have varying degrees of shade and a few are in the open for those who like a sunny plot. Reception is housed in a wooden chalet and is welcoming and informative. The Marin family and their staff are friendly and helpful and the site is very well run. The village of Mesquer is just over a kilometre away and there is a good choice of beaches and little coves nearby.

Facilities

The central sanitary block has preset showers and open style washbasins together with some cubicles with controllable shower and a washbasin. Washing machine and dryer. Facilities for babies and disabled visitors. Bar/snack bar/takeaway. Bread can be ordered (July/Aug and holiday weekends). Shop. Attractive pool complex (15/5-15/9) with heated main pool, paddling pool and a pool with water slides (July/Aug only, supervised). Programme of activities (all July/Aug). WiFi (free).

Open: 1 April - 15 October.

Directions

Mesquer is 90 km. west of Nantes. From Nantes Périphérique take N165 (Vannes) and at exit 8 (Saveney) turn west on N171/D213 to Guérande bypass, then north to St Molt and turn west on D52 to Mesquer. GPS: 47.39902, -2.47132

Charges guide

Per unit incl. 2 persons and electricity	€ 13.20 - € 28.00
extra person	€ 5.00 - € 6.50

Montreuil-Bellay

Flower Camping les Nobis d'Anjou

Rue Georges Girouy, F-49260 Montreuil-Bellay (Maine-et-Loire) T: 02 41 52 33 66.

E: contact@campinglesnobis.com **alanrogers.com/FR49250**

Close to the impressive Château de Montreuil-Bellay, les Nobis is part of the Flower group of campsites and occupies a quiet location on the bank of the River Thouet, yet is conveniently located for visits to Saumur and the many other châteaux of the western Loire Valley. There are 120 pitches, 33 occupied by mobile homes and 'Kiwi' tents; the 87 touring pitches have electrical connections (10A). A short walk takes you to the château built in the 15th century but whose history goes back to the Plantagenet Kings and from there you can stroll through the narrow streets of the historic town.

Facilities

Two sanitary blocks (one up a flight of steps) with facilities for children and disabled visitors. Baby area. Launderette. Motorcaravan service point. Restaurant and snack bar with takeaway. Bar. Small shop in reception. Bakery. Heated outdoor pool (from 1/5). Games room. TV room. Playground. Trampoline. Table tennis. Boules court. Fishing. Aquagym classes. Organised entertainment and activities in high season. Barbecue rental. WiFi (free).

Open: 2 April - 2 October.

Directions

Montreuil-Bellay is 16 km. south of Saumur via D347. At roundabout north of town turn south to cross river and follow signs to site by château. NB: do not go down very narrow road on right just after bridge. GPS: 47.13196, -0.15913

Charges guide

Per unit incl. 2 persons and electricity	€ 17.50 - € 28.00
extra person	€ 4.00

Montsabert

Yelloh! Village Parc de Montsabert

150 route de Montsabert, F-49320 Coutures (Maine-et-Loire) T: 02 41 57 91 63.
E: info@yellohvillage-parcdemontsabert.com **alanrogers.com/FR49060**

This extensive site has recently been taken over by a friendly French couple who already have plans for improvements. It has a rural atmosphere in the shadow of Montsabert château, from where visiting peacocks happily roam in the spacious surroundings. The main features are the heated swimming pool (with cover) and the adjoining refurbished, rustic-style restaurant. There are 157 pitches with 93 large, well marked touring pitches, divided by hedges and all with water tap, drain and electricity (10A). Picnic tables are provided. This partially wooded site offers the peace of the countryside and a wealth of activities in high season.

Facilities

The main toilet block can be heated and has all necessary facilities including a baby room and facilities for disabled visitors. Laundry facilities. A second block serves the pool and another provides more WCs. Shop, bar and takeaway. Restaurant. Heated pool (can be covered) and paddling pool. Sports hall. Minigolf. Tennis. Play area. Archery. Riding. Bicycle hire. Entertainment (high season). Max. 2 dogs. WiFi throughout (charged).

Open: 1 April - 4 September.

Directions

Coutures lies on D751, 25 km. southeast of Angers. In village, turn north to site (well signed).
GPS: 47.3744, -0.3469

Charges guide

Per unit incl. 2 persons and electricity	€ 18.00 - € 31.00
extra person	€ 5.00 - € 7.00
child (3-7 yrs)	free - € 6.00

Montsoreau

Camping l'Isle Verte

Avenue de la Loire, F-49730 Montsoreau (Maine-et-Loire) T: 02 41 51 76 60. E: isleverte49@orange.fr
alanrogers.com/FR49090

This friendly, natural site, with pitches overlooking the Loire, is just 200 m. from the nearest shop, bar and restaurant in Montsoreau and is an ideal base from which to explore the western Loire area. Most of the 90 shaded, level and good sized touring pitches are separated by low hedges but grass tends to be rather sparse during dry spells. All have 16A electricity. Excellent English is spoken in the reception and bar/restaurant. Attractions within walking distance include the château, troglodyte caves (used for traditional mushroom production) and restaurant, wine tasting in the cellars nearby and a Sunday market in the village.

Facilities

A modern, well maintained building provides all necessary facilities, including those for disabled campers. Baby room. Laundry facilities. Motorcaravan services. Bar and restaurant (15/5-30/9). Heated swimming and paddling pools (15/4-30/9). Small play area. Bouncy castle. Trampoline. Tennis. Boules. Fishing. Organised family activities. Boat launching. WiFi (charged). Off site: Boat launching and river beach 300 m. Bicycle hire 1 km.

Open: 1 April - 12 October.

Directions

Montsoreau lies on the south bank of the River Loire, on D947 Saumur-Chinon road, 12 km. from Saumur. Site is clearly signed on western side of village.
GPS: 47.21820, 0.05265

Charges guide

Per unit incl. 2 persons and electricity	€ 19.50 - € 27.50

Camping Cheques accepted.

Nantes

Nantes Camping

21 boulevard du Petit Port, F-44300 Nantes (Loire-Atlantique) T: 02 40 74 47 94.
E: nantes-camping@nge-nantes.fr **alanrogers.com/FR44010**

Those readers who visited this site when it was Camping du Petit Port would be amazed at the recent transformation; it is now a modern, well equipped site with several types of pitch and different types of accommodation for rent. It lies within the city limits in a peaceful, park-like setting with mature trees. It has 57 flat, good sized pitches for tourers. Some are on grass, some on hardstanding, some are both. All have electricity (16A), water connections and drainage with taps nearby. There are 36 tent pitches on separate grass areas, all with electricity and water to hand.

Facilities

Two excellent heated sanitary blocks include large shower cubicles with washbasins and good facilities for disabled visitors. Hairdryers. Baby rooms. Washing machines and dryers. Motorcaravan services. Bar/restaurant serving regional dishes prepared on the premises (July/Aug daily; Sept-June midday excl. Sat. plus w/end evenings). Bread to order. Breakfasts. Shop for basics (July/Aug). Play area. Boules. Minigolf. Bicycle hire. WiFi over site (€1 fee).

Open: All year.

Directions

Site is on northern edge of city near the university. From Périphérique Est leave at exit 29 (Porte de la Chapelle) and follow signs for Nantes Centre. Site entrance is on right on fifth roundabout.
GPS: 47.2433, -1.55679

Charges guide

Per unit incl. 2 persons and electricity	€ 25.60 - € 35.60
extra person	€ 4.00 - € 6.00

Piriac-sur-Mer

Camping Parc du Guibel

Route de Kerdrien, F-44420 Piriac-sur-Mer (Loire-Atlantique) T: 02 40 23 52 67.
E: camping@parcduguibel.com **alanrogers.com/FR44070**

This is a very large site situated in extensive woodland and just back from the coast. A keen birdwatcher once told the owner that he had seen 50 different species of birds. There are 450 pitches of which 300 are for touring, mainly shaded but some in small clearings. One section at the top of the site, across a minor road, is always quiet and peaceful. Half of the pitches have electricity (10A), some also have a water tap. A number of mobile homes and chalets are for rent.

Facilities

Five sanitary blocks of varying ages, the newer ones with controllable showers. Facilities for disabled visitors. Baby room. Laundry facilities. Motorcaravan services. Bar, snack bar, takeaway and restaurant (July/Aug only). Swimming pool complex with slide, flume and paddling pool (1/4-30/9). Play area. Electronic games (July/Aug). Multisports pitch. Minigolf. WiFi (charged). Off site: Riding 400 m. Fishing 1 km. Beach 1.2 km. Sailing 3.5 km. Golf 18 km.

Open: 1 April - 30 September.

Directions

On N165 from Vannes, leave at exit 15 towards La Roche Bernard, turn left to join D774 towards La Baule. 8 km. after Herbignac, turn right on D48 to St Molt and Mesquer towards Piriac. Do not take coast road but turn left on D52. Site signed on right in 3 km. GPS: 47.38616, -2.51029

Charges guide

Per unit incl. 2 persons and electricity	€ 15.10 - € 18.60
extra person	€ 3.60 - € 6.50

Pontchâteau

Camping Le Deffay

B.P. 18 Le Deffay, Sainte Reine-de-Bretagne, F-44160 Pontchâteau (Loire-Atlantique) T: 02 40 88 00 57.
E: info@camping-le-deffay.com **alanrogers.com/FR44090**

A family managed site, Camping Le Deffay is a refreshing departure from the usual formula in that it is not over organised or supervised and has no tour operator units. The 170 good sized, fairly level pitches (103 for touring) have pleasant views and are either on open grass, on shallow terraces divided by hedges or informally arranged in a central, slightly sloping wooded area. All have 10A electricity. The bar, restaurant and covered pool are located within the old courtyard area of the smaller château that dates from before 1400. A significant attraction of the site is the large, unfenced lake which is well stocked for fishermen and even has free pedaloes for children. The landscape is wonderfully natural and the site blends well with the rural environment of the estate, lake and farmland which surround it. Alpine-style chalets overlook the lake and fit in well with the environment and the larger château (built in 1880 and now offering B&B) stands slightly away from the camping area but provides a wonderful backdrop for an evening stroll. The site is close to the Brière Regional Park, the Guérande Peninsula and La Baule and is just 20 minutes' drive from the nearest beach.

Facilities

The main toilet block is well maintained, if a little dated, and is well equipped including washbasins in cabins, provision for disabled visitors and a baby bathroom. Laundry facilities. Shop. Bar and small restaurant with takeaway. Heated swimming pool with sliding cover and paddling pool (all season). Play area. TV. Entertainment in season including miniclub. Fishing and pedaloes on the lake. Torches useful. WiFi throughout (charged).

Open: 1 May - 30 September.

Directions

Site is signed from D33 Pontchâteau-Herbignac road near Ste Reine. Also signed from the D773 and N165-E60 (exit 13). GPS: 47.44106, -2.15981

Charges guide

Per unit incl. 2 persons and electricity	€ 17.80 - € 29.80
extra person	€ 3.00 - € 5.90
child (2-12 yrs)	€ 2.00 - € 4.30

Camping Cheques accepted.

Pornic

Yelloh! Village La Chênaie

36 rue du Patisseau, F-44210 Pornic (Loire-Atlantique) T: 02 40 82 07 31. E: accueil@campinglachenaie.com

alanrogers.com/FR44080

La Chênaie is a pleasant, family run campsite in countryside close to the fishing port of Pornic and less than three kilometres from the nearest beach. There are 114 touring pitches in three areas on gently sloping ground with the pool and other leisure facilities in the dip between. All the pitches are well tended with 10A electricity available (long leads may be needed in places) and there is some shade in places from maturing trees and bushes. There are mobile homes scattered among the touring pitches and others at the top of the site with some for rent. A new wellness centre was opened in 2014. This joins amenities that also include outdoor pools and a covered, heated pool.

Facilities

Three good sanitary blocks, one central to each area. Some washbasins in cubicles. Baby room. Facilities for disabled visitors. Large washing machines and dryer. Motorcaravan services. Shop selling bread and basics. Bar, restaurant and snack bar with takeaway. Two heated indoor swimming pool and paddling pools. Outdoor pools (30/5-31/8). Wellness centre. Bicycle hire. Play area. Some activities for children and adults. WiFi (charged).

Open: 29 April - 4 September.

Directions

Pornic is 19 km. south of the St Nazaire bridge. From north take exit for D751 Nantes. At roundabout on D751 north of D213 take exit for la Chênaie and follow signs to site. GPS: 47.118483, -2.070817

Charges guide

Per unit incl. 2 persons and electricity	€ 19.00 - € 43.00
extra person	€ 6.00 - € 8.00

Pornic

Camping le Patisseau

29 rue du Patisseau, F-44210 Pornic (Loire-Atlantique) T: 02 40 82 10 39. E: contact@lepatisseau.com

alanrogers.com/FR44100

Just a short drive from the fishing village of Pornic, le Patisseau is a relaxed site with a large number of mobile homes and chalets, and is popular with young families and teenagers. The 67 touring pitches, all with electrical connections (10A), are in the forest with plenty of shade from mature trees. Some are on a slight slope and access to others might be tricky for larger units. A railway runs along the bottom half of the site with trains several times a day, but none overnight, and the noise is minimal.

Facilities

Modern heated toilet block is very spacious and well fitted; most washbasins are open style, but the controllable showers are all in large cubicles with washbasins. Also good facilities for disabled visitors and babies. Laundry rooms. Shop (25/6-27/8). Restaurant, bar and takeaway. Indoor heated pool with sauna, jacuzzi and spa (all season). Small heated outdoor pools and water slides (30/5-24/9). Play areas. Bouncy castle. Multisports court. Bicycle hire. WiFi in bar area (charged).

Open: 2 April - 24 September.

Directions

Pornic is 48 km. west of Nantes via D273/D751 and 19 km. south of the St Nazaire bridge via D213. From north take exit for D751 Nantes. At roundabout take exit for le Patisseau and follow signs to site. Avoid town centre. GPS: 47.118833, -2.072833

Charges guide

Per unit incl. 2 persons and electricity	€ 22.00 - € 39.00
extra person	€ 5.00 - € 8.00

Pornic

Camping de la Boutinardière

Rue de la Plage de la Boutinardière 23, F-44210 Pornic (Loire-Atlantique) T: 02 40 82 05 68.
E: info@laboutinardiere.com **alanrogers.com/FR44180**

This is truly a holiday site to suit all the family, whatever their ages, just 200 m. from the beach. It has 103 individual, good sized pitches, 90-120 sq.m. in size, many bordered by three metre high, well maintained hedges for shade and privacy. All pitches have electricity available (6/10A). It is a family owned site and part of the Airotel group. English is spoken by the helpful, obliging reception staff. There is an excellent site shop and, across the road, a water complex comprising indoor and outdoor pools, a paddling pool and a twin toboggan water slide in addition to sports and entertainment areas.

Facilities

Toilet facilities are in three good blocks, one large and centrally situated and two supporting blocks. Washbasins are in cabins. Laundry facilities. Shop. New complex of bar, restaurant, terraces. Three heated swimming pools, one indoor (April-Sept), a paddling pool and water slides (15/5-15/9). Games room. Sports and activity area. Playground. Minigolf. Fitness equipment and wellness. Maisonette accommodation for rent. WiFi throughout.

Open: 2 April - 25 September.

Directions

From north or south on D213, take Nantes D751 exit. At roundabout (with McDonalds) take D13 signed La Bernarie-en-Retz. After 4 km. site is signed to right. Note: do NOT exit from D213 at Pornic Ouest or Centre. GPS: 47.09805, -2.05176

Charges guide

Per unit incl. 2 persons and electricity	€ 36.60 - € 67.90
extra person	€ 5.50 - € 8.50
child (under 8 yrs)	€ 4.50 - € 6.50

Préfailles

Camping EléoVic

Route de la Pointe Saint Gildas, F-44770 Préfailles (Loire-Atlantique) T: 02 40 21 61 60.

E: contact@camping-eleovic.com **alanrogers.com/FR44230**

This is a well situated site overlooking the sea on the attractive Jade Coast, west of Pornic. There are 70 touring pitches which are rather worn, some with wonderful views of the sea, and a similar number of mobile homes, many of which are for rent. All pitches have access to 10A electricity, although on some you may need a long cable. Much of the ground is sloping so a really level pitch may not be available and access for larger units to some pitches may be tricky. The site has so much to offer, however, that any extra effort that may be needed to get installed is likely soon to be forgotten.

Facilities

Central sanitary block has spacious preset showers and washbasins in cabins. Facilities for disabled visitors and children. Family room. Room for dishwashing and laundry. Further facilities are in the pool building and another smaller block. Motorcaravan services. Good restaurant (July/Aug; not Wednesdays) with small bar and terrace. Heated swimming pool with sliding cover and paddling pool (4/4-27/9). Fitness room. Playground. Boules. Activities for families (high season). Bicycle hire. Direct access to small rocky cove. WiFi throughout (charged).

Open: 5 April - 28 September.

Directions

From north on D213 turn southwest just south of St Michel-Chef-Chef on D96 to La Plaine-sur-Mer and follow signs for Préfailles. Continue on D313 towards La Pointe St Gildas and at 50 km. sign turn left, then left again to site. GPS: 47.132616, -2.2315

Charges guide

Per unit incl. 2 persons and electricity	€ 19.00 - € 36.00
extra person	€ 3.80 - € 7.00

Saint Brévin-les-Pins

Camping le Fief

57 chemin du Fief, F-44250 Saint Brévin-les-Pins (Loire-Atlantique) T: 02 40 27 23 86.

E: camping@lefief.com **alanrogers.com/FR44190**

If you are a family with young children or lively teenagers, this could be the campsite for you. Le Fief is a well established site 800 m. from sandy beaches on the southern Brittany coast. It has a magnificent aquapark with outdoor and covered swimming pools, paddling pools, slides, river rapids, fountains, jets and more. The site has 125 pitches for touring units, all with 8A electricity and varying slightly in size and accessibility. There are also 205 mobile homes and chalets to rent and 40 privately owned units. An impressive Taos mobile home village includes a new Sunny Club for children.

Facilities

One excellent new toilet block and three others of a lower standard. Laundry. Shop (1/6-31/8). Bar, restaurant and takeaway with terrace. Heated outdoor pools (1/5-15/9). Covered pool (all season). Wellness centre. Play area. Tennis. Pétanque. Archery. Games room. Organised entertainment and activities (weekends April/June, daily July/Aug). Bicycle hire. WiFi over site (charged). Off site: Shops, bars and restaurants nearby. Beach 800 m. Bus stop 1 km.

Open: 4 April - 27 September.

Directions

From the St Nazaire bridge take the fourth exit from the D213 signed St Brévin-l'Océan. Continue over first roundabout and bear right at the second to join Chemin du Fief. The site is on the right, well signed. GPS: 47.23486, -2.16757

Charges guide

Per unit incl. 2 persons and electricity	€ 25.00 - € 47.00

No credit cards.

Saint Lyphard

Camping Fleur de Brière

Route d'Herbignac, F-44410 Saint Lyphard (Loire-Atlantique) T: 09 53 63 11 88.

E: contact@campingfleurdebriere.com **alanrogers.com/FR44480**

This former municipal campsite, on the edge of the charming village of Saint Lyphard, stood empty for two years before it was taken into private ownership by Carl Pelleteur in 2011. He has already worked wonders. The pitches are large, level and most have some shade provided by well kept, mature shrubs and trees. Amenities are few and simple, but satisfactory. A yurt village is on one side of the site. The village of Saint Lyphard is only 500 m. away where you will find a small supermarket and shops. The intention of the owner is to maintain this eco-friendly, natural site.

Facilities

One sanitary block with showers and washbasins in cubicles. Washing machine. Bar/restaurant and takeaway (15/6-15/9). Communal barbecues only. Off site: Shops, bar and restaurant, lake for swimming all within 1 km. Riding 5 km. Golf 10 km.

Open: 15 March - 14 November.

Directions

Leave the N165 (Nantes-Vannes) at exit 15 and follow D774 south to Herbignac. Then take the D47 to St Lyphard. The site is on the left at entry to the village. GPS: 47.396761, -2.301636

Charges guide

Per unit incl. 2 persons and electricity	€ 16.00 - € 24.00
extra person	€ 5.00 - € 7.00

Saint-Michel-Chef-Chef

Camping du Bord de Mer

1 bis, boulevard de l'Océan, F-44730 Saint-Michel-Chef-Chef (Loire-Atlantique) T: 02 40 27 93 16.
E: contact@borddemer-camping.com **alanrogers.com/FR44520**

This small campsite is delightful, although the pitches are on the small side and the grass is rather sparse. All have 10A electricity. Mature trees provide some shade. A small bar with takeaway food opens on one side on to a terrace and the covered pool. On the other side it is open with seating that looks out over the sea and some of the iconic fishing towers and their nets suspended over the water. In high season there is a good programme of entertainment for young and old. This site is ideally suited to young families looking to spend a lot of their holiday on the magnificent sandy beach which is only 20 metres from the campsite. For restaurants, bars and shops a visit to nearby Pornic is a must.

Facilities

One central sanitary block includes washbasins in cabins. Facilities for disabled visitors (although access poor for wheelchairs). Multi-purpose bar and games room with TV and Internet access (July/Aug). Snack bar and takeaway (all season). Covered pool (April-Nov). Solarium. Boules. WiFi (charged). Off site: Beach 20 m. Sailing and minigolf 500 m. Supermarket and shops nearby.

Open: 1 March - 12 November.

Directions

South of St Nazaire bridge on D213, take exit for D77 (St Michel-Chef-Chef). Follow signs for La Plage and site is on seafront. GPS: 47.18195, -2.16156

Charges guide

Per unit incl. 2 persons and electricity	€ 17.50 - € 37.50
extra person	€ 6.00 - € 9.50

Saumur

Camping Chantepie

La Croix, Saint Hilaire-Saint Florent, F-49400 Saumur (Maine-et-Loire) T: 02 41 67 95 34.
E: info@campingchantepie.com **alanrogers.com/FR49020**

On arriving at Camping Chantepie with its colourful, floral entrance, a friendly greeting awaits you. The site is set beside a restored farmhouse with beautiful views from one end over the Loire Valley. It is owned by a charitable organisation that provides employment for local people with disabilities. The 120 grass touring pitches are level and spacious, with some new larger ones (200 sq.m. at extra cost – state preference when booking). All pitches have electricity (16A, ten also with water and waste water) and are separated by low hedges of flowers and trees which offer some shade. Water points are easily accessible around the site. This is a good site for families. A member of Sites et Paysages.

Facilities

The sanitary block is clean and equipped with washbasins in cubicles, hot showers (men and women separately) and good facilities for disabled visitors. Baby room. Laundry. Motorcaravan services. Small shop in reception. Bar, terraced café, restaurant and takeaway (all 21/6-31/8). Covered, heated pool, outdoor pool and paddling pool. Fitness centre. Play area. Minigolf, TV. Miniclub (July/Aug). Pony rides (July/Aug). Bicycle hire. WiFi over site (free).

Open: 25 April - 12 September.

Directions

St Hilaire-St Florent is 2 km. west of Saumur. Take D751 (Gennes). Right at roundabout in St Hilaire-St Florent and on until Le Poitrineau and campsite sign, then turn left. Continue for 3 km. then turn right into site road. GPS: 47.29382, -0.14285

Charges guide

Per unit incl. 2 persons and electricity	€ 22.60 - € 40.00
extra person	€ 4.40 - € 6.60

Saumur

Flower Camping de l'Ile d'Offard

Boulevard de Verden, Ile d'Offard, F-49400 Saumur (Maine-et-Loire) T: 02 41 40 30 00.
E: iledoffard@flowercampings.com **alanrogers.com/FR49080**

This site occupies a prime position on an island in the River Loire, within walking distance of the centre of the historic town of Saumur. The 207 touring pitches are mainly on grass with plenty of shade provided by mature trees. Twelve hardstandings nearer the entrance can be rather dusty in dry weather. There are 150 pitches with access to 10A electricity and some also have water and drainage. Ile d'Offard is useful as an overnight stop on the journey south (or north) but it is also an excellent base from which to visit the numerous châteaux in the region.

Facilities

Three unisex sanitary blocks, one heated in winter, include provision for disabled visitors. Block one has a well equipped laundry. The other blocks are only open in high season. These facilities are generally kept reasonably clean but are fairly basic. Motorcaravan services. Restaurant and bar (1/5-30/9) with takeaway. Heated swimming, paddling and spa pools (15/4-30/9). Play area. Activities, children's club, wine tastings etc. in high season. Internet access and WiFi (charged).

Open: 1 March - 15 November.

Directions

From north and A85 exit 3, take D347 (Saumur). After 2.5 km, left at roundabout (Saumur touristique). Follow old road towards river and town. Cross bridge onto island, immediately left at roundabout. Site is ahead in 1 km. GPS: 47.25762, -0.06100

Charges guide

Per unit incl. 2 persons and electricity	€ 17.50 - € 31.90
extra person	€ 3.00 - € 6.50

Sillé-le-Guillaume

Camping Indigo les Molières

Sillé Plage, F-72140 Sillé-le-Guillaume (Sarthe) T: 02 43 20 16 12. E: molieres@camping-indigo.com

alanrogers.com/FR72040

Les Molières is an attractive recent addition to the Indigo group and is a good choice for families looking for an active holiday in a verdant setting. It can be found close to Sillé-le-Guillaume, around 30 km. north of Le Mans. There are 166 large shady pitches here; 129 for tourers. Most are equipped with electricity connections (10A). A large lake of 32 hectares is ideal for sailing and windsurfing and the forested surrounds of the Parc Naturel Régional provide an excellent environment for cycling or walking. Swimming is also popular from the large sandy beach. The Maison du Lac et de la Forêt is an interesting centre with a wealth of information about the area. In high season, a little tourist train circles the lake.

Facilities

Sanitary facilities include those for disabled visitors. Washing machine and dryer (token). Motorcaravan services. Small shop for essentials and regional produce. Bread and pastries to order. Weekly market. Snack bar and takeaway (July/Aug). Heated outdoor pool. Direct access to lake. Sailing. Fishing. Bicycle hire. Play area. Children's entertainment (5-11 yrs, 9/7-26/8). Max. 1 dog. Electric barbecues only. WiFi by snack bar (free).

Open: 4 May - 26 September.

Directions

From Le Mans head north on D338 and then D304 to Sillé-le-Guillaume. Then follow signs to the Parc Naturel Régional and the site.
GPS: 48.20422, -0.12858

Charges guide

Per unit incl. 2 persons and electricity	€ 19.80 - € 30.10
extra person	€ 3.60 - € 5.50

Sillé-le-Philippe

Castel Camping le Château de Chanteloup

Chanteloup, F-72460 Sillé-le-Philippe (Sarthe) T: 02 43 27 51 07. E: chanteloup.souffront@wanadoo.fr

alanrogers.com/FR72030

This attractive and peaceful site, close to Le Mans, is situated in the park of a 19th-century château in the heart of the Sarthe countryside. There are 90 very large pitches, all with 8A electricity, although long leads may be required in some places. Some pitches adjoin woodland, many are around the edges of the lawns and completely open, and a few overlook a small fishing lake. New premium pitches are also equipped with unlimited WiFi, furniture and parasol, barbecue and fridge. The pitches are unobtrusively marked out and this enhances the feeling of spaciousness around the old château.

Facilities

All sanitary facilities are in the château outbuildings and are clean and well maintained. Washbasins in cabins. Baby facilities and good en-suite unit for disabled visitors. Laundry. Small shop (10/7-30/8). Fresh bread daily. Takeaway and restaurant with covered outdoor seating (10/6-30/8). Bar and TV room. Outdoor swimming pool (heated July/Aug). Play area (supervision essential). Games room. Volleyball. Organised activities (July/Aug). Bicycle hire. WiFi over site (charged).

Open: 1 June - 31 August.

Directions

From autoroute take exit 23, follow signs for Le Mans and Tours, then Le Mans and Savigné l'Evèque. Site is to east, just off main road and signed on edge of Sillé. GPS: 48.10586, 0.34108

Charges guide

Per unit incl. 2 persons and electricity	€ 31.60 - € 39.00
extra person	€ 7.50 - € 9.50

Charges higher during Le Mans race week.

Spay

Domaine du Houssay

Route d'Arnage, F-72700 Spay (Sarthe) T: 02 43 21 16 58. E: camping-spay@wanadoo.fr

alanrogers.com/FR72250

This campsite is located within the leisure centre of Houssay, close to the River Sarthe. Set in forty hectares, it is also the closest campsite to the 24-hour race circuit at Le Mans, some 6 km. away. There are 86 pitches arranged in a horseshoe shape around a lake. Pitches are of a good size and all have electricity (10A). This is a green and open site with varying degrees of shade. The leisure centre offers a range of activities and it is a short walk into the local village of Spay for any daily needs.

Facilities

The centrally located toilet block provides toilets, showers and dishwashing and laundry sinks. Facilities for children, babies and disabled visitors. Washing machine and dryer. Motorcaravan services. Communal room with TV area. Bicycle, canoe and pedalo hire. Caravans and chalets for rent. Lake swimming (beach showers). Free WiFi over part of site. Waymarked trails from campsite. Off site: Leisure centre adjacent. Water park with lifeguard (July/Aug). Bakery, butchers, pharmacy and small supermarket 1 km.

Open: 15 April - 30 September.

Directions

From Le Mans, southwest on D323 then left on D147S towards Arnage. Turn right on D212 at big crossroads towards Spay, under motorway bridge then sharp right turn to narrow single lane bridge over Sarthe. After bridge is sports centre on right, then site on right. GPS: 47.92117, 0.15677

Charges guide

Per unit incl. 2 persons and electricity	€ 12.50
extra person	€ 2.50
child (under 8 yrs)	€ 1.30

Tuffé

Camping du Lac

Impasse du Plan d'Eau, F-72160 Tuffé (Sarthe) T: 02 43 93 88 34. E: campingdulac.tuffe@wanadoo.fr
alanrogers.com/FR72260

A few miles to the east of Le Mans, this attractive and peaceful site, as the name would suggest, is situated on the banks of a lake. There are 130 grass pitches with a variety of settings, shade and size. All the pitches have 16A electricity and a water point nearby, and many have attractive lake views. A group of 15 pitches designed for motorcaravans have hardstanding strips. This is a neat and well maintained campsite. There is direct access to the lake where there is a beach and a watersports centre. A vintage railway line runs alongside the site in high season. The annual 24-hour car race attracts visitors from all over the world and takes place just a 20 minute drive away. The site also offers mobile homes and chalets to rent.

Facilities

Three toilet blocks (one heated in low season) are well maintained and kept very clean. Washbasins and preset showers in cubicles. Baby bathroom. Facilities for disabled campers. Laundry. Motorcaravan services. Small shop. Restaurant/snack bar adjacent. Swimming pool with sliding cover and children's area (April-Sept; shorts forbidden). Games/TV room. Volleyball. Play area. Boules. Bicycle hire. WiFi in parts (charged). Off site: Tennis. Minigolf. Pedalos. Tuffé and its Abbey 3 km. Supermarket 6.5 km.

Open: 12 April - 4 October.

Directions

From A11 exit 6 travel south on A28. At next junction turn east on D323. In Connerré turn north on D33 and continue on this road to Tuffé (take care on narrow roads in Connerré and Beillé). Site is then easy to find – follow signs for Base de Loisirs.
GPS: 48.11866, 0.51148

Charges guide

Per unit incl. 2 persons and electricity	€ 14.80 - € 20.65
extra person	€ 3.70 - € 5.20
child (2-9 yrs)	€ 1.95 - € 3.20
dog	€ 2.10 - € 2.75

Varennes-sur-Loire

Castel Camping Domaine de la Brèche

L'Etang de la Brèche, 5 impasse de la Brèche (RN152), F-49730 Varennes-sur-Loire (Maine-et-Loire)
T: 02 41 51 22 92. E: contact@domainedelabreche.com **alanrogers.com/FR49010**

The Saint Cast family have developed Domaine de la Brèche with care and attention. The attractive site occupies a 24-hectare estate, 4 km. northeast of Saumur on the edge of the Loire, behind the levees. There are 235 spacious, level, grass pitches, with 135 for touring, including ten premium pitches. Trees and bushes give some shade. All have electricity (some require long cables). Eighty have a water supply and drainage. The restaurant (open to the public), bar and terrace provide an attractive social base and are popular with British visitors. The pool complex includes a heated indoor pool, flumes and toboggans and a paddling pool. Domaine de la Brèche is a good base from which to explore the famous châteaux, abbeys, wine cellars, mushroom caves and troglodyte villages in this region. With numerous cycle routes, a bicycle is a useful asset. A British tour operator uses a small area of the site.

Facilities

Three modern toilet blocks with all necessary facilities including those for babies and disabled campers. Washing up sinks and laundry. Good shop and épicerie. Bar. Restaurant (open to public), pizzeria and takeaway. Outdoor swimming pool (from 18/5) and heated indoor swimming pool (from 25/4). Tennis. Multisports pitch. Go-karts. Minigolf. Bicycle hire. Games and TV rooms. Sporting and entertainment programme (10/7-25/8). Pony riding. Torch useful. WiFi over site (charged; free in reception area). Off site: Saumur 3 km. Boat launching 5 km. Golf 7 km.

Open: 14 April - 13 September.

Directions

Site is well signed on the north bank of the River Loire, 100 m. north of the main D952, Saumur-Tours road, 5 km. northeast of Saumur.
GPS: 47.24731, -0.00048

Charges guide

Per unit incl. 2 persons and electricity	€ 16.00 - € 42.00
with water and drainage	€ 18.50 - € 56.00
extra person	€ 4.00 - € 9.00
child (4-12 yrs)	€ 2.50 - € 5.00

7th night free in low season.

DÉPARTEMENT: VENDÉE

Because of its importance as a holiday destination for British visitors to France, we have decided in this guide to list the Vendée département as a region in its own right. Administratively the département lies in the region of Pays de la Loire.

MAJOR CITY: LA ROCHE-SUR-YON

It's not only the fine beaches that make this holiday region so appealing – sleepy fishing harbours, historic ports and charming towns all create a great holiday atmosphere.

With a sunshine record to rival the south of France, the Vendée is among the most popular areas in France. Visitors flock to the region to enjoy the exceptionally mild climate and 160 km. stretch of gently shelving, mostly sandy beaches. Popular resorts include Les Sables-d'Olonne, La Tranche-sur-Mer, and St Jean-de-Monts. Explore the coasts for traditional fishing villages or head inland for fields of sunflowers and unspoilt rural villages.

The Vendée was the centre of the counter-revolutionary movement between 1793 and 1799 and a 'son et lumière' held at Le Puy-du-Fou tells the whole story. Les Sables-d'Olonne is its main resort renowned for its excellent sandy beach. The area between the Vendée and Charente, the Marais Poitevin, is one of the most unusual in France – a vast tract of marshland with a thousand or more tree-lined canals and slow moving streams.

Places of interest

L'Aiguillon-sur-Mer: famous for its mussels and other shellfish; site of migrating birds between August and November.

Apremont: pretty village with a Renaissance castle; Vendée's largest lake with a sandy beach, watersports and boat hire.

Île-d'Yeu: one hour by boat from the coast, a major tourist destination with colourful shops, cafés and restaurants; art galleries and exhibitions; bicycles and cars for hire.

Jard-sur-Mer: Abbey of Lieu-Dieu (financed by Richard the Lionheart); seaside with attractive, colourful houses.

Le Puy-du-Fou: 15/16th-century castle; son-et-lumière production and historical theme park.

Les Sables-d'Olonne: the start and finish line of the grand Vendée Globe yacht race; arts and crafts shops.

Cuisine of the region

Locally produced meat and poultry include Charolais beef, salt-marsh lamb, duck from Challans and foie gras. Seafood includes sole sablaise, cooked with lemon, barbecued sardines from Saint Gilles-Croix-de-Vie, baked white tuna and mussels from the Baie de l'Aiguillon cooked in white wine.

Samphire: a herb that grows on the edges of the salt marshes.

Mogette: slow-cooked baby haricot beans, traditionally served with gammon.

Jambon de Vendee: local raw-cured ham.

www.vendee-tourisme.com/en
info@vendee-tourisme.com
(0)2 51 47 88 20

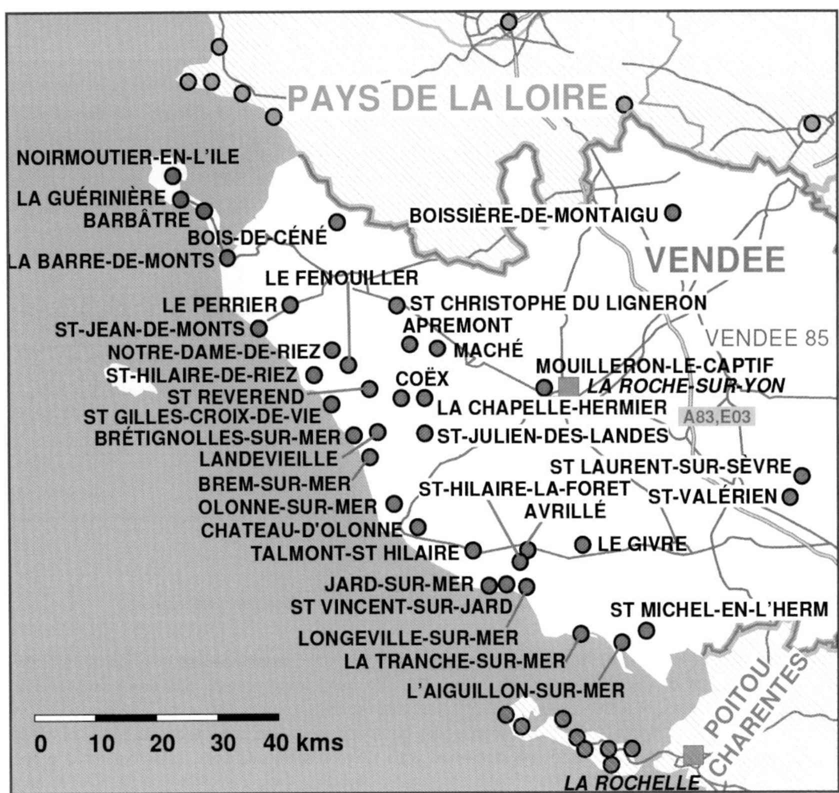

Apremont

Camping les Charmes

Route de la Roussière, F-85220 Apremont (Vendée) T: 02 51 54 48 08. E: campinglescharmes@wanadoo.fr

alanrogers.com/FR85380

Les Charmes is a peaceful, well laid out campsite, 3 km. from Apremont and 20 minutes from the Vendée's sandy beaches. It is suitable for families with young children and for those seeking a quiet, peaceful holiday. There are 55 pitches, including 35 spacious and grassy, level touring pitches with dividing hedges, some under shade from the mature trees around the perimeter. Electrical connections are available for most (6/10A, long cables required for some pitches), plus communal water points nearby. There is also mobile home and chalet accommodation for rent all year. The campsite has an indoor swimming pool with a smaller area for children within the main pool and a new jacuzzi and sauna. Access may not be suitable for large vehicles.

Facilities

Two sanitary blocks have washbasins and showers in cubicles and facilities for children and disabled visitors. Washing machine and dryer. Small shop. Bread to order (July/Aug). Swimming pool with paddling pool (15/5-30/9). Sauna and jacuzzi. Small play area. Pétanque. Barbecue area with picnic tables. TV room. Football pitch. WiFi over site (charged). Torches useful. Off site: Lake for swimming. Shop, bar and restaurant within 1.5 km. Fishing and sailing 1.5 km. Golf 8 km. Bicycle hire 12 km. Beach 20 km. Château in Apremont open July/Aug.

Open: 14 April - 15 September.

Directions

At Aizenay, take D948 to Noirmoutier Challans. Ignore right turn to Maché/Apremont, go under bridge and after 4 km. turn left after wind turbines. Continue on D94 to Commequiers, after 3 km. turn left after sign for 'Le Potager du ventre à choux'. Follow site signs for 500 m to site on right.
GPS: 46.77858, -1.733952

Charges guide

Per unit incl. 2 persons and electricity	€ 16.50 - € 22.60
extra person	€ 3.60 - € 4.90
child (under 10 yrs)	€ 2.10 - € 4.00
dog	€ 1.10 - € 2.80

Avrillé

Camping Domaine des Forges

Rue des Forges, F-85440 Avrillé (Vendée) T: 02 51 22 38 85. E: forges@franceloc.fr
alanrogers.com/FR85930

Arranged in the beautiful grounds of a 16th-century manor house, the 20 touring pitches here are very generous in size (100-200 sq.m) with 16A electricity, water and drainage. Some of the premium pitches with additional services such as Internet access and cable TV carry an extra charge. The owners' aim is to develop a prestige campsite with the highest quality of services and they have made a very good start. A further 150 pitches are occupied by mobile homes, chalets, roulottes and tents available for hire. A large lake is available for fishing.

Facilities

Four heated sanitary blocks include facilities for babies and disabled visitors. Laundry facilities. Motorcaravan services. Shop (Apr-Sept). Bar and takeaway. Heated indoor pool with whirlpool. Two heated outdoor pools with flumes, slides, wading and fun pools for children. Play area. Minigolf. Fishing lake. Multisports area. Boules. Fitness room. Bicycle hire. WiFi (charged). Max. 1 dog.

Open: 11 April - 27 September.

Directions

Travel south from La Roche-sur-Yon on the D747 for 21 km. At the D19, turn right for Avrillé (about 6 km). At junction with the D949 turn right and first right again into rue des Forges. Site at the end of the road. GPS: 46.47609, -1.49454

Charges guide

Per unit incl. 2 persons, electricity, water and drainage € 19.00 - € 33.00

Barbâtre

Domaine le Midi

Rue du camping, F-85630 Barbâtre (Vendée) T: 02 51 39 63 74. E: midi@originalcamping.com
alanrogers.com/FR85014

This family site is a member of the Original Camping group and is located close to the village of Barbâtre, on the west coast of the island of Noirmoutier. The site has direct access to a fine sandy beach. There are 412 pitches, of which around 208 are available for touring units (the rest are occupied by an imaginative range of chalets, mobile homes and fully equipped tents, including teepees, many of which are for rent). Touring pitches are mostly equipped with 16A electricity. On-site amenities include two swimming pools and a paddling pool. These are surrounded by a wide sunbathing area. A children's beach club is organised in peak season and evening entertainment is also on offer.

Facilities

Heated sanitary facilities include provisions for children and disabled visitors. Laundry facilities. Motorcaravan service point. Shop (July/Aug). Two heated swimming pools, one covered (all season), one open (15/5-28/9). Games room. Play area. Tennis. Sailing school. Activity and entertainment programme. No charcoal barbecues. WiFi throughout (charged). Off site: Shops and restaurants in Barbâtre 5 minutes' walk. Riding. Watersports. Fishing.

Open: April - September.

Directions

Noirmoutier can be accessed either by the Gois causeway (at low tide only) or by the bridge from Fromentine, to the south of the island. From the bridge head north to Barbâtre on D944 and the site is well signed. GPS: 46.94508, -2.1853

Charges guide

Per unit incl. 2 persons and electricity € 18.00 - € 34.90
extra person € 4.90 - € 7.90

Bois-de-Céné

Camping le Bois Joli

2 rue de Châteauneuf, F-85710 Bois-de-Céné (Vendée) T: 02 51 68 20 05.
E: contact@camping-leboisjoli.com **alanrogers.com/FR85510**

A warm welcome is given by the English-speaking owners, Martine and Eric Malard, who make every effort to ensure that your stay is enjoyable. On site is a small, attractive lake with fishing and a large sports field. There are 178 pitches of which 94 are for touring units, all with 6A electricity (Europlug). The site has 24 mobile homes for rent, including one equipped for disabled visitors, and there are 60 which are privately owned. Indoor and outdoor swimming pools. This is a hidden gem in a small village away from the hustle and bustle of the seaside resorts. Ideal for those looking for a quiet holiday, it is still within a short drive of the Vendée coast and the Ile de Noirmoutier.

Facilities

Three toilet blocks have washbasins in cubicles, some controllable showers, family shower cubicles with baby bath and child's toilet. Facilities for disabled visitors. Laundry. Motorcaravan services. Shop (bread to order), bar serving simple meals (all season) with takeaway service (July/Aug and busy w/ends). Heated swimming pools, (outdoor 1/6-15/9). WiFi (charged). Activities and entertainment (July/Aug). Communal barbecue.

Open: 1 April - 15 October.

Directions

Bois-de-Céné is 47 km. southwest of Nantes and 10 km. north of Challans, at junction of D21 Bouin-La Garnache and D28 Châteauneuf-Machecoul. Site is south of the village where the D58 from Challans meets the D21 and D28. GPS: 46.93382, -1.88791

Charges guide

Per unit incl. 2 persons and electricity € 18.00 - € 24.00

Camping Cheques accepted.

Boissière-de-Montaigu

Domaine de l'Eden

Bois de la Raillère, F-85600 Boissière-de-Montaigu (Vendée) T: 02 51 41 62 32.
E: contact@camping-domaine-eden.fr **alanrogers.com/FR85540**

Hidden in the Haut Bocage hinterland of the Vendée, le Domaine de l'Eden is a haven of tranquillity. Open all year and just 10 km. from the A83, it is ideal for a stopover. This 15 hectare site has 56 spacious, level touring pitches made up of grass and sand with mature trees providing varying amounts of shade. Four hardstanding pitches are suitable for motorcaravans. There are also mobile homes/chalets scattered throughout the site, many available for rent. Amenities include outdoor heated swimming pools for adults and children and some evening entertainment in high season. Le Domaine de l'Eden offers the chance to taste the real France for oneself and a good network of well marked footpaths and cycle ways is easily accessible.

Facilities

Two sanitary blocks with hot showers and some washbasins in cubicles, facilities for children and disabled visitors. Laundry. Motorcaravan services. Small shop, bar with TV, and snack bar (all July/Aug). Heated outdoor swimming pool with paddling area (15/6-15/9). Play area. Tennis courts. Multisports court. Football. Minigolf. Volleyball. Fitness course. Lake fishing. Entertainment marquee. WiFi over site (charged). Bicycle hire.

Open: All year.

Directions

Site is signed from N137 Nantes-La Rochelle road, 7 km. south of Montaigu and 30 km. north of Chantonnay. At tourist office, take D62 northeast for 5 km, through Le Pont Lege and follow signs. GPS: 46.937774, -1.219826

Charges guide

Per unit incl. 2 persons and electricity € 18.00 - € 23.00

Brem-sur-Mer

Camping l'Océan

17 rue du Brandais, F-85470 Brem-sur-Mer (Vendée) T: 02 51 90 59 16. E: locean@cybelevacances.com
alanrogers.com/FR85110

Set amongst grapevines and fir trees, Camping l'Océan is only 600 metres from a beautiful sandy beach, while the village centre is also within walking distance. A warm welcome awaits you at the modern reception area which is well stocked with local information. The 168 touring pitches, all with 10A electric connections (Europlug) reasonably close, are of a good size, separated by bushes (and in some cases vines) and with some mature trees providing shade. They are located in two main sections and you are largely unaware of the 364 mobile homes (175 available to rent) on either side.

Facilities

Two bright, modern toilet blocks serve the touring areas. Free preset showers and washbasins in cubicles. Separate toilet and shower for disabled visitors. Facilities for children. Washing machines and dryers. Shop, bar, snack bar and takeaway. Heated outdoor swimming pool (15/6-15/9) with slide. Heated indoor pool with slide, flume and lazy river. Fitness room. Playgrounds (2-6 yrs and 6-12 yrs). Bicycle hire. WiFi over site (charged).

Open: 4 April - 1 November.

Directions

From A87 at La Roche-sur-Yon continue on D160 towards Les Sables-d'Olonne. Take exit for La Mothe-Achard and Bretignolles-sur-Mer. Follow D54 to Brem-sur-Mer. Site is to north of village on D38 to Bretignolles. GPS: 46.60411, -1.84060

Charges guide

Per unit incl. 2 persons and electricity € 18.00 - € 28.00

Brem-sur-Mer

Camping le Chaponnet

16 rue du Chaponnet, F-85470 Brem-sur-Mer (Vendée) T: 02 51 90 55 56. E: contact@le-chaponnet.com
alanrogers.com/FR85480

This well established, family run site is within five minutes' walk of Brem village and 1.5 km. from a sandy beach. The 85 touring pitches are level with varying amounts of grass, some with shade from mature trees. Pitches are separated by tall hedges and serviced by tarmac or gravel roads and have frequent water and 10A electricity points (long leads may be required). Premium pitches are available for an additional charge. Tour operators have mobile homes and tents on 85 pitches and there are 165 other mobile homes and chalets, over half available for rent.

Facilities

Five sanitary blocks (two open in low season) are well maintained and have showers and washbasins in cubicles. Facilities for babies and disabled visitors. Laundry. Motorcaravan services. Bar (June-Sept). Restaurant, snack bar and pizzeria (1/6-28/8). Indoor and outdoor (1/5-29/9) heated pools. Play area. Multisports area. Tennis. Miniclub (July/Aug). WiFi (charged).

Open: 2 April - 30 September.

Directions

From A87 at La Roche-sur-Yon continue on D160 towards Les Sables-d'Olonne. Take exit for La Mothe-Achard and Bretignolles-sur-Mer. Follow D54 to Brem-sur-Mer. Site is clearly signed, just off one-way system in village. GPS: 46.60433, -1.83244

Charges guide

Per unit incl. 2 persons and electricity € 26.40 - € 39.50

Bretignolles-sur-Mer

Camping les Dunes

50 avenue des Dunes, F-85470 Bretignolles-sur-Mer (Vendée) T: 02 51 90 55 32.
E: infos@campinglesdunes.fr **alanrogers.com/FR85002**

If you want a site close to a fantastic beach with great surfing, this is the place for you. Camping les Dunes has a fine location between the fishing port of Saint Gilles-Croix-de-Vie and the larger resort of Les Sables-d'Olonne. It enjoys direct access to one of the Vendée's finest beaches. The site has 30 sandy pitches of around 90 sq.m, all surrounded by one metre high hedges and fully serviced (10A electricity). There are also mobile homes to rent. A water park has two outdoor pools and a heated indoor pool with jacuzzi, lazy river and water slide. Evening entertainment is organised every night except Saturday during high season, including discos, bingo, karaoke, folk dancing and live music. There is a choice of watersports at the Dunes beach opposite.

Facilities

Nine sanitary blocks are clean and adequately equipped with preset showers in cubicles. Facilities for disabled visitors. Washing machines and dryer. Well stocked shop (15/4-5/9). Bar. Small restaurant and snack bar/crêperie. Outdoor and indoor swimming pools with paddling pool and jacuzzi. Play area. Library. Minigolf. Tennis. TV room. Children's club. Evening entertainment. Beach volleyball. Multisports pitch. Boules. Bicycle hire. WiFi throughout (charged). Off site: Shops and restaurants in St Gilles-Croix-de-Vie. Zoo at Les Sables-d'Olonne. Surf school. Bowling. Amusement park.

Open: 1 April - 11 November.

Directions

Take A83 south from Nantes and exit 4 towards La Roche-sur-Yon. Take D763 continuing along D937 and then along D160 towards Les Sables-d'Olonne. Continue on D38 north through Ile d'Olonne and Brem-sur-Mer. At end of village, follow signs to site. GPS: 46.607591, -1.850955

Charges guide

Per unit incl. 2 persons and electricity	€ 21.00 - € 37.80
extra person	€ 4.90 - € 8.40
child (0-13 yrs)	€ 2.40 - € 5.20
dog	€ 2.35 - € 5.10

Bretignolles-sur-Mer

Chadotel Camping la Trévillière

1 rue de Bellevue, F-85470 Bretignolles-sur-Mer (Vendée) T: 02 51 90 09 65. E: info@chadotel.com
alanrogers.com/FR85310

In a pleasant rural setting, la Trévillière is on the edge of the little resort town of Brétignolles. There are 200 pitches, 105 for touring, all with 10A electricity (Europlug, long leads required on some). Some are level, some sloping; all are separated by hedges or low bushes either with shade or more open. Although just 2 km. from the nearest beach and less than 5 km. from the Plage des Dunes (one of southern Vendée's best beaches), la Trévillière has a more laid back feel than many other sites in the area, particularly in low season. The site has 70 mobile homes and chalets, half available for rent, but it remains very much a camping and caravanning site. There is a wide choice of activities and tourist attractions in the area if you want to get away from the beach. Les Sables d'Olonne has fashionable shops, bars and restaurants as well as discos and night clubs.

Facilities

Three traditional unheated sanitary blocks, a little tired in parts, include showers and washbasins in cubicles, a unit for disabled visitors and a baby room with bath, shower and toilet. Laundry facilities. Bar, small shop and snack bar with takeaway (10/6-15/9). Heated indoor and outdoor pools, slide and paddling pool. Play area. Games room. Multisports court. Basketball. Minigolf. Max. 1 dog. No charcoal barbecues. Bicycle hire. WiFi throughout (charged). Off site: Shops, restaurants and bars 1 km. Beach 2 km. Fishing, sailing and riding all 3 km. Golf 10 km. In Bretignolles-sur-Mer there are buses to Les Sables-d'Olonne (20 km) to the south and St Gilles-Croix-de-Vie (8 km) and St Jean-de-Monts (25 km) to the north.

Open: 5 April - 19 September.

Directions

Brétignolles is 40 km. west of La Roche-sur-Yon on D38 coast road. From north, after St Gilles go through Bretignolles-La Sauzaie (left fork) and before Bretignolles turn left on sharp right hand bend, heading for stade municipal. Site on right in 800 m. GPS: 46.63632, -1.85844

Charges guide

Per unit incl. 2 persons and electricity	€ 15.50 - € 32.00
extra person	€ 6.00
child (2-13 yrs)	€ 4.00
dog	€ 3.50

Coëx

RCN Camping la Ferme du Latois

Le Latoi, F-85220 Coëx (Vendée) T: 02 51 54 67 30. E: ferme@rcn.fr

alanrogers.com/FR85770

Originally a simple 'camping à la ferme', this site has been developed by a Dutch organisation into an extensive, very well equipped and well maintained campsite. Located around two attractive fishing lakes, the 215 pitches, most available for touring, are spacious and attractively laid out with plenty of grass, hedges and trees, some young, some mature. All have electricity (6/10A) and a few are very large. There are 30 mobile homes for rent. An old barn has been converted into a large restaurant offering an extensive French menu, including a 'menu du jour'. Also here are a small bar, a shop selling basic provisions and the reception area. The busy fishing port of Saint Gilles-Croix-de-Vie with its quayside bars and restaurants, its attractive pedestrianised streets, its extensive marina and its 'Grande Plage' is just a short drive away. This stretch of coast offers a good choice of other sandy beaches and there are plenty of well documented places to go and things to do in the area.

Facilities

Two large, modern sanitary blocks built in traditional style have excellent toilets, showers and washbasins in cubicles. Good facilities for disabled visitors. Attractively tiled areas for babies and children, with special toilets, washbasins and showers. Two smaller blocks provide additional facilities. Laundry room with washing machines and dryers. Motorcaravan services. Small shop. Bar counter with terrace. Restaurant. All facilities available all season. Heated outdoor swimming pool with slides. Play area. Bicycle hire. Fishing lakes. Archery (July/Aug). WiFi over site (charged). Internet point. Max. 1 dog. Mobile homes for rent. Off site: Shops and restaurants in Coëx 2 km. Golf and riding 3 km. Beach, sea fishing and boat launching 12 km. St Gilles-Croix-de-Vie 12 km.

Open: 25 April - 19 September.

Directions

Coëx is 29 km. west of La Roche-sur-Yon via the D948 to Aizenay, then the D6 Coëx south ring road. Site is south of Coëx. Take first left off D40 to La Chaize-Giraud and site is clearly signed.
GPS: 46.677033, -1.76885

Charges guide

Per unit incl. 2 persons and electricity	€ 14.00 - € 35.50
extra person	€ 2.50 - € 4.95
dog	€ 7.00

Jard-sur-Mer

Chadotel Camping l'Océano d'Or

84 rue Georges Clémenceau, F-85520 Jard-sur-Mer (Vendée) T: 02 51 33 05 05. E: info@chadotel.com

alanrogers.com/FR85270

This eight-hectare site should appeal to families with children of all ages. It is very lively in high season but appears to be well managed with a full programme of activities (it can therefore be noisy, sometimes late at night). The site is only 1 km. from the excellent beach. There are 450 flat, grass and sand pitches, 121 are for touring units with the remainder occupied by tour operators and mobile homes for rent. All touring pitches have 10A electricity (French sockets, long leads may be required) and are quite large (about 100 sq.m). Some are separated by high hedges, others are more open with low bushes between them. There is a good aquatic area – the flume takes you past rocks before plunging into the pool. There are shops, bars and restaurants, and a weekly market in the pleasant little town of Jard-sur-Mer.

Facilities

Four recently refurbished unisex toilet blocks include washbasins in cubicles and hot showers. Facilities for disabled visitors and children. Laundry facilities. Shop (1/6-10/9). Bar with large screen TV, snack bar and takeaway (1/6-10/9, limited hours outside high season). Swimming pool (heated 15/5-10/9) with slides, waterfalls and children's pool. Fitness suite. Walled (three sides) boat-themed play area. Games room. Tennis. Bicycle hire. Pétanque. Multisports pitch. Electric barbecues are not allowed. Max. 1 dog. Internet and WiFi throughout (charged). Off site: Cycle paths adjacent. Excellent beach within walking distance. Shops and restaurant 400 m. Château de Talmont 6 km. Riding 1 km. Golf 10 km. Karting and other activities within 15 km.

Open: 5 April - 20 September.

Directions

Site is on the D21 Talmont-St Hilaire-Longeville-sur-Mer, just east of the turning to the town centre.
GPS: 46.42075, -1.5694

Charges guide

Per unit incl. 2 persons and electricity	€ 18.50 - € 34.50
extra person	€ 6.00
child (2-13 yrs)	€ 4.00
dog	€ 3.50

L'Aiguillon-sur-Mer

Camping Bel Air

2 route de Bel Air, F-85460 L'Aiguillon-sur-Mer (Vendée) T: 02 51 20 41 94. E: contact@camp-atlantique.com
alanrogers.com/FR85004

Camping Bel Air is close to the Atlantic coast and about 60 km. north of La Rochelle. This large and lively site has entertainment for all ages ranging from painting classes for the young through to evening soirées and water aerobics for the older children and adults. Of the 362 pitches, 63 are for touring units, on grass with small hedges for separation. Mature trees provide shade and 10A electricity hook-ups are available. A variety of chalets and mobile homes are available for rent. A good restaurant and bar provides locally sourced meals during the day. There is a well equipped gym and a good shop.

Facilities

Two, unisex toilet blocks provide showers, washbasins in cubicles and facilities for children and disabled visitors. Motorcaravan service point. Large shop. Bar. Restaurant. Indoor and outdoor swimming pools with water slide and water garden for toddlers. Wellness centre. Play area. Multisports court. Minigolf. Badminton and volleyball. Bicycle hire. Max. 1 dog. Only gas barbecues permitted. WiFi throughout (charged).

Open: 2 April - 25 September.

Directions

Camping Bel Air can be found 60 km. north of La Rochelle. From the A83 motorway take exit 7 for Luçon. From Luçon take the D746 to L'Agillion-sur-Mer. Site is well signed on entering the town. GPS: 46.34343, -1.31988

Charges guide

Per unit incl. 2 persons and electricity € 18.00 - € 29.00

Camping Cheques accepted.

La Barre-de-Monts

Campéole la Grande Côte

Route de la Grande Côte, F-85550 La Barre-de-Monts (Vendée) T: 02 51 68 51 89.
E: grande-cote@campeole.com **alanrogers.com/FR85840**

A site that lives up to its name, this one is very large, with 810 pitches. However, 265 are occupied by Bengali tents to rent, 80 by private caravans and 29 by tour operators. There are still 396 numbered touring pitches in rows, all with 10A electricity and spread over undulating sand dunes with sparse grass under pine trees. The site is served by eight fairly modern and fairly well maintained toilet blocks around the site. Some of the terraced pitches at the rear of the site have views of the impressive bridge onto the Ile de Noirmoutier and there is direct access to a sandy beach via a gate. Some road noise is to be expected from the nearby bridge.

Facilities

Eight toilet blocks (two renovated) include some washbasins in cubicles, seatless toilets, baby bath, and a good unit for disabled campers. Laundry room. Outdoor heated swimming pools (15/5-20/9). Shop for bread and basics, bar and takeaway (1/7- 31/8). Playgrounds and bouncy castle. Games room. TV room. Entertainment and clubs for children (July/Aug). Multisports court. Boules. Minigolf. Bicycle hire. WiFi (charged). Off site: Fishing 50 m.

Open: 3 April - 20 September.

Directions

From north take D758 to Beauvoir-sur-Mer, then D22 to La Barre-de-Monts. Continue through town ignoring road to Fromentine. At town boundary turn right on D38b. In 500 m, straight on at roundabout for 1 km. then right (Grand Côte). Next left for 1 km. to site. GPS: 46.8858, -2.1477

Charges guide

Per unit incl. 2 persons and electricity € 18.20 - € 30.70

La Chapelle-Hermier

Camping le Pin Parasol

Lac du Jaunay, Châteaulong, F-85220 La Chapelle-Hermier (Vendée) T: 02 51 34 64 72.
E: contact@campingpinparasol.fr **alanrogers.com/FR85680**

Tucked away in the Vendée countryside, yet just 15 minutes' drive from the beach, this attractive friendly campsite enjoys a pleasant rural setting above the Lac du Jaunay, well away from the bustle of the coast. There are 184 good sized touring pitches, all with 10A electricity (Europlug) and 33 with water tap and drainage. Some have shade, others are in the open with maturing hedges and trees. The keen family owners are very hands-on and the facilities are of a high standard, most notably the elegant entrance and reception building and the very well equipped pool area.

Facilities

Four excellent toilet blocks (one heated) with hot showers, washbasins in cabins and facilities for babies and disabled visitors. Washing machines and dryers. Shop (15/5-15/9). Bar with terrace (24/4-25/9). Takeaway (15/6-30/8). Heated outdoor pool with paddling pool, slides and flumes (1/6-15/9). Indoor pool. Wellness centre. Fitness equipment. Play areas. Games room. Multisports pitch. Boules. Children's club. Fishing. Bicycle hire. WiFi.

Open: 24 April - 25 September.

Directions

La Chapelle-Hermier is 26 km. west of La Roche-sur-Yon. Site is to the south of the D42 La Chapelle-Hermier-l'Aiguillon-sur-Vie road, 2 km. east of the junction with the D40 Coëx-La Chaize-Giraud road and is well signed. GPS: 46.66622, -1.75528

Charges guide

Per unit incl. 2 persons and electricity € 18.00 - € 40.25

La Guérinière

Camping le Caravan'île

1 rue de la Tresson B.P. 4, la Guérinière, F-85680 Ile de Noirmoutier (Vendée) T: 02 51 39 50 29.

E: contact@caravanile.com **alanrogers.com/FR85620**

This well appointed, family run site, on the island of Noirmoutier, has direct access across a dune to an extensive sandy beach, although swimming is only possible at high tide. It has good, heated pools and a variety of entertainment is arranged in high season. Most of the 103 reasonably level touring pitches are on sand behind the dunes. All have electricity (8A, Europlug) and are separated by bushes and the occasional maturing tree; there is little shade. The site has a very French ambience with 192 privately owned mobile homes, plus 90 for rent.

Facilities

Three very clean sanitary blocks with preset showers and washbasins in cabins. Facilities for babies and disabled visitors. Washing machines and dryers. Motorcaravan services. Small supermarket, snack bar and takeaway (all 15/4-15/9). Heated indoor pool and paddling pool with sauna, jacuzzi, steam room and solarium. Outdoor pool with waterslides and paddling pool (15/5-15/9; heated July/Aug). Fitness room. Small play area. Multisports court. Tennis. Minigolf. TV/games room. WiFi (charged).

Open: 15 March - 15 November.

Directions

The Ile de Noirmoutier is 70 km. southwest of Nantes. At La Barre-de-Monts, take D38 across bridge to island and continue to fifth roundabout. Take exit for La Guérinière and immediately turn left to site. GPS: 46.96631, -2.216073

Charges guide

Per unit incl. 2 persons and electricity	€ 20.50 - € 33.00
extra person	€ 4.00 - € 7.50

La Tranche-sur-Mer

Camping Baie d'Aunis

10 rue du Pertuis Breton, F-85360 La Tranche-sur-Mer (Vendée) T: 02 51 27 47 36.

E: info@camping-baiedaunis.com **alanrogers.com/FR85870**

This very popular 2.5-hectare site has direct access to a sandy beach through a pedestrian gate (with key code) and across a car park. The town centre is also only 500 m. away. Shady and level, there are 130 touring pitches, all with 10A electricity. A good number of pitches are on a gravel base and a few are suitable only for smaller units. There are chalets and mobile homes (23) to rent. On-site amenities include a heated swimming pool and a good restaurant and bar. This is a popular seaside resort with 13 km. of good quality sandy beaches. All have first aid posts, lifeguards in season and dogs are forbidden on the sands. From the pier by the Centre Nautique, just 50 m. from the site's rear pedestrian gate, you can catch ferries to the islands of Aix and Ré and to the larger resort of La Rochelle across the bay. You can also learn to fly or take pleasure flights from the aerodrome behind the town.

Facilities

The main, centrally located sanitary unit is large, good quality and very well appointed. A smaller unit at the far end of the site has been renovated to a high standard. Washbasins in cubicles, provision for children and disabled visitors. Laundry rooms. Motorcaravan services. Bar/restaurant and takeaway (24/5-13/9, Thurs. and Sun. only in low season). Outdoor heated swimming pool. Playground. Games room. TV room. Library. Multisports area. Dogs not accepted July/Aug. WiFi over site (free). Off site: Bicycle hire adjacent. Sea fishing within 50 m. Boat launching 100 m. Town centre 500 m. Riding 12 km.

Open: 24 April - 13 September.

Directions

From La Roche-sur-Yon take D747 to La Tranche. At roundabout (D747 and D1046) carry straight on to next roundabout and turn right towards town centre. At next roundabout continue straight on to site on left (well signed). GPS: 46.34638, -1.43184

Charges guide

Per unit incl. 2 persons and electricity	€ 26.60 - € 36.00
extra person	€ 6.30 - € 8.00
child (under 5 yrs)	€ 4.10 - € 5.00
dog	€ 2.30

La Tranche-sur-Mer

Camping du Jard

123 boulevard Maréchal de Lattre de Tassigny, F-85360 La Tranche-sur-Mer (Vendée) T: 02 51 27 43 79.
E: info@campingdujard.fr **alanrogers.com/FR85020**

Camping du Jard is a well maintained site situated between La Rochelle and Les Sables-d'Olonne. First impressions are good with a friendly welcome from M. Marton and his staff. The 150 touring pitches, all with 10A electricity (Europlug) and 60 also with water and drainage, are level and grassy; many are hedged by bushes and a large variety of trees provide shade in places. A small number of pitches are used by tour operators and 50 accommodation units are available to rent. An impressive pool complex has a heated outdoor pool with toboggan and paddling pool, plus an indoor pool with jacuzzi. The site is 700 m. from a sandy beach with many shops and restaurants nearby.

Facilities

Three toilet blocks (unheated, only one open in low season) provide washbasins and showers in cubicles. Facilities for babies and disabled visitors. Washing machines and dryers. Shop, restaurant and bar (all July/Aug). Heated outdoor pool (from 18/5); heated indoor pool. Sauna, solarium and fitness room. Tennis. Minigolf. Bicycle hire. Play area, games and TV rooms. Internet point; free WiFi around bar. No American-style motorcaravans. No pets. Off site: Beach 700 m.

Open: 16 May - 12 September.

Directions

From A87 Cholet/La Roche-sur-Yon leave at exit 32 for La Tranche-sur-Mer and take D747 to La Tranche. Turn east following signs for La Faute-sur-Mer along bypass. Take exit for La Grière and then turn east to site. GPS: 46.34836, -1.38738

Charges guide

Per unit incl. 2 persons and electricity	€ 24.50 - € 33.00
extra person	€ 6.00 - € 7.00

La Tranche-sur-Mer

Camping les Blancs Chênes

Route de la Roche-sur-Yon, F-85360 La Tranche-sur-Mer (Vendée) T: 02 52 20 01 26.
E: info@vagues-oceanes.com **alanrogers.com/FR85580**

Part of the Vagues Océanes group, this is a very well managed site with good facilities, excellent children's activities and a programme of high season entertainment for all. The manager and his staff take real pride in their work. The 25 level touring pitches are on sandy grass, are separated by hedges and have access to electricity (5A). They are close to the entrance and some have shade. The site is 1.8 km. from the town of La Tranche with its many shops, restaurants and sandy beach. In high season a free bus service to the beach is provided.

Facilities

Three modern toilet blocks have showers and washbasins in cabins, baby units and facilities for disabled visitors. Shop (July/Aug). Bar with TV. Restaurant and takeaway. Large pool complex with terrace, indoor pool (15/4-10/9) with spa beds, outdoor pool (15/6-10/9) with jacuzzi, paddling pool, flume and slides. Good sports facilities include minigolf (charged), table tennis and 2 multisports areas. Bicycle hire. Spa pool and sauna. Entertainment centre with bar. Fitness centre. WiFi (free in bar).

Open: 9 April - 10 September.

Directions

Site is well signed on the western side of the D747 (La Tranche-La Roche) road, 2 km. north of La Tranche. Units must turn right on leaving site. GPS: 46.3631, -1.4205

Charges guide

Per unit incl. 2 persons and electricity	€ 18.00 - € 44.00
extra person	€ 5.00 - € 9.00
child (under 5 yrs)	free - € 7.00

Landevieille

Camping l'Evasion

Route des Sables, F-85220 Landevieille (Vendée) T: 02 51 22 90 14. E: contact@camping-levasion.fr
alanrogers.com/FR85885

Camping l'Evasion is located close to the Lac de Jaunay, well known for its water-based activities. This is a modern, well equipped site and boasts a natural swimming pool bordered by white sand. There is also a traditional outdoor swimming pool with slides, plus a large, covered pool with jacuzzi. There are just 12 good sized touring pitches here, all equipped with electrical connections. There are also numerous mobile homes available for rent. Other amenities at l'Evasion include a bar/restaurant (with takeaway food service). The nearest beach is 5 km. away (at Bretignolles-sur-Mer).

Facilities

Shop. Bar/restaurant. Takeaway. Outdoor swimming pool and paddling pool with jacuzzi and water slides. Covered heated pool, paddling pool and jacuzzi. Paddling pool (15/5-14/9). Aqua gym. Multisports pitch. Bicycle hire. Play area. Activity and entertainment programme. Mobile homes for rent. WiFi throughout (charged). Off site: Shops and restaurants at Bretignolles-sur-Mer.

Open: 12 April - 14 September.

Directions

Approaching from the north (Challans), head south on D32 towards Les Sables-d'Olonne. Pass through Landevieille and continue on D32 (rue des Sables). The site is well signed. GPS: 46.635, -1.79747

Charges guide

Per unit incl. 2 persons and electricity	€ 34.00 - € 50.00

No credit cards.

Le Château-d'Olonne

Camping le Bel Air

6 chemin de Bel Air, F-85180 Le Château-d'Olonne (Vendée) T: 02 51 22 09 67.
E: lebelair@cybelevacances.com **alanrogers.com/FR85710**

Le Bel Air is a well established site close to the Vendée's largest resort, Les Sables-d'Olonne. It is now very much dedicated to mobile homes and chalets. Of its 286 pitches, just 46 are for touring – 40 on grass mostly with electricity (9-16A), water and drainage plus six on concrete for motorcaravans. This is a very well equipped site with the focal point being a new and impressive pool complex including a large covered pool and separate outdoor pool.

Facilities

Five well equipped small sanitary blocks with facilities for babies and disabled visitors. Laundry with washing machines and dryers. Motorcaravan services. Bar, snack bar, takeaway and shop. Heated outdoor pool with children's pool and waterslides (April-Sept). Heated indoor pool with sauna, spa and gym (all season). TV room. Games room. Multisports court. Playground. Bicycle hire. Activities in high season. Mobile homes and chalets for rent. Charcoal barbecues not permitted. WiFi over site (charged). Off site: Beach, fishing and sailing 3 km.

Open: 4 April - 1 November.

Directions

Château d'Olonne is 40 km. southwest of La Roche-sur-Yon. From end of A87 Cholet/La Roche-sur-Yon at exit 33, continue on D160 to Les Sables ring road, then follow signs to Château d'Olonne. Site is off the Sables-Talmont road 2 km. east of the Géant Casino supermarket roundabout and is well signed to the south. GPS: 46.47207, -1.72646

Charges guide

Per unit incl. 2 persons and electricity	€ 22.00 - € 36.00
extra person	€ 4.00 - € 6.00

Le Fenouiller

Camping SHH le Pas Opton

Route de Nantes, F-85800 Le Fenouiller (Vendée) T: 02 51 55 11 98. E: enquiries@springharvestholidays.com
alanrogers.com/FR85060

A quiet, well established site, le Pas Opton is managed by Spring Harvest Holidays which has developed the site and its facilities. The site is now operated as a Christian holiday centre. Touring visitors on daily rates are only accepted outside July and August. It is 6 km. inland from Saint Gilles-Croix-de-Vie. With a well ordered atmosphere, it offers a range of on-site amenities including a heated swimming pool and water slide. There are 67 standard or premium touring pitches, all with electricity (6A Europlug) and some with hardstanding, water and drainage. There are also 190 mobile homes and fixed tents.

Facilities

Two unheated sanitary blocks include washbasins mainly in cabins for women, partly for men, and units for babies and disabled visitors. Laundry facilities. Shop (30/6-1/9). Bar with fresh bread, café and takeaway (all July/Aug). Heated swimming pool (20/5-10/9) with water slide and children's pools. Playground. Pool table. Multisports area. Volleyball court. Boules pitch. 5-a-side football pitch. Entertainment and some dancing organised in season. Shuttle bus to beach and village (May-Sept). WiFi in bar area (charged). Off site: Sailing and windsurfing 2 km.

Open: 11 May - 21 September.

Directions

Site is northeast of St Gilles, on the D754 past Le Fenouiller towards the junction with D32. GPS: 46.73043, -1.8776

Charges guide

Contact site for details.

Le Givre

Camping la Grisse

F-85540 Le Givre (Vendée) T: 02 51 30 83 03. E: lagrisse@wanadoo.fr
alanrogers.com/FR85345

Camping la Grisse is one of a very few sites in this area which is open all year. Located just ten minutes from the beaches, the site is run by Didier Martineau, who will be delighted to welcome you and speaks very good English. He is keen to retain the relaxed ambiance of the site. It is centred on the family farm and was first opened in 1995. The family have been improving it ever since. The 2.5-hectare site has a total of 79 pitches with just 36 huge, grassy, level touring pitches, all with 16A electricity (Europlug). There is also easy access to water. There is no shop, bar, restaurant or swimming pool on site. Family barbecues are organised at weekends in high season. There are mobile homes and chalets for hire.

Facilities

Small toilet block provides washbasins and showers in cubicles. Laundry. Facilities for children and visitors with disabilities. Motorcaravan service point. Bread delivered in high season. Play area. Volleyball. Boules. Bouncy castle. WiFi throughout (free). Off site: Supermarket 5 km. Riding 5 km. Beach 7 km. Golf 20 km.

Open: All year.

Directions

From Lucon take D949 and turn left at junction with D747 (La Tranche road). Turn left in 3 km. and follow site signs. GPS: 46.444821, -1.398171

Charges guide

Per unit incl. 2 persons and electricity	€ 8.00 - € 13.10
extra person	€ 4.10 - € 7.70

Le Perrier

Domaine le Jardin du Marais

208 route de Saint-Gilles, F-85300 Le Perrier (Vendée) T: 02 51 68 09 17. E: info@lejardindumarais.eu
alanrogers.com/FR85635

Le Perrier is a small village in the heart of the marshes, characterised by the flat land and vast prairies surrounding it. Le Jardin du Marais is a delightful, family site in a country setting on the edge of the marshes. It is beautifully kept and has excellent facilities including a well stocked shop, a pleasant bar/restaurant and a good pool complex. The enthusiastic and hardworking owners are keen to welcome more British visitors who will be sure of a warm reception. Of the 120 pitches, 50 are available for touring – the established pitches offer some shade and have electricity and water nearby, a new area offers large pitches with electricity, water and drainage. The beaches are just seven kilometres away.

Facilities

Two bright, modern sanitary blocks provide showers and washbasins in cubicles. Baby bath. En-suite facility for disabled visitors. Laundry. Motorcaravan services arranged. Shop (fresh food in high season), bar/restaurant and takeaway. Outdoor pool with paddling pool and flume (15/6-15/9), terrace and loungers. Indoor heated pool (15/4-15/9). Solarium. Fitness room. Play area. Fishing in small lake (fenced and gated). Children's club (July/Aug). Games area. Volleyball. Go-karts. Children's cycle circuit. Bicycle hire. Internet. WiFi over site (charged).

Open: 3 April - 2 October.

Directions

Le Perrier is 51 km. northwest of La Roche-sur-Yon and 11 km. southwest of Challans. Site is 2 km. to south on D59 to Le Pissot and St Gilles; from the new route of the D205 Challans-St Jean-de-Monts road turn south on D59 and site is on right in 300 m. GPS: 46.80133, -1.980656

Charges guide

Per unit incl. 2 persons and electricity	€ 18.00 - € 33.00
extra person	€ 5.00 - € 7.50

Longeville-sur-Mer

Camping le Petit Rocher

1250 avenue du Docteur Mathevet, F-85560 Longeville-sur-Mer (Vendée) T: 02 51 20 41 94.
E: contact@camp-atlantique.com **alanrogers.com/FR85000**

Le Petit Rocher has a seaside location (150 m. from the beach) set in a pine forest, with an air of peace and tranquillity. Although the area is undulating, the 132 good sized touring pitches are flat and arranged in terraces throughout the wooded area. Electricity hook-ups are available (10A Euro plugs) and there are adequate water points. A grassy play area for children is thoughtfully situated in a hollow, but has limited equipment. Various accommodation types are available to rent.

Facilities

Three spacious sanitary blocks are clean and well maintained. Heated indoor pool, snacks and takeaway (all open all season). Multisports area. Bicycle hire. WiFi throughout (charged). Max. 1 dog. Only gas barbecues permitted. Communal barbecue. Off site: Bars, restaurant, and small shops nearby. Beach 150 m. Riding 2 km. Boat launching 11 km. Fishing 15 km. Golf 20 km.

Open: 2 April - 25 September.

Directions

From Longeville-sur-Mer follow signs for Le Rocher towards La Tranche-sur-Mer. Turn right at first roundabout, following camping signs to site on right. GPS: 46.403767, -1.507183

Charges guide

Per unit incl. 2 persons and electricity	€ 18.00 - € 32.00
extra person	€ 5.00 - € 9.00

Longeville-sur-Mer

Camping les Dunes

Les Conches, F-85560 Longeville-sur-Mer (Vendée) T: 02 51 33 32 93. E: contact@camping-lesdunes.com
alanrogers.com/FR85015

The name gives a clue to its location! This well run site is on the edge of a pine forest and just a 600 m. walk to the sea. The 255 pitches are mainly occupied by mobile homes, with 90 for rent and 50 owned by a small British tour operator, but there are 52 mainly level touring pitches in groups and divided by hedges. Forty have 10A electricity, water and drainage whilst a few are tucked away among the trees and are ideal for smaller tents. Quiet in low season, the site comes to life in July and August with activities arranged for all the family. There is a children's club daily except Saturdays.

Facilities

Two unheated sanitary blocks are bright, clean and well maintained. Hot water to dishwashing and laundry sinks. Washing machines and dryers. Facilities for children and disabled visitors. Shop, bar with restaurant, games and TV. Snack bar with takeaway (limited opening in low season). Heated outdoor pool with paddling pool and slides (supervised July/Aug). Indoor pool (all season). Adventure play area on sand. Bouncy castle. Activities and entertainment (July/Aug). Bicycle hire. WiFi (charged).

Open: 11 April - 13 September.

Directions

Site is 6 km. south of Longeville-sur-Mer on D105 From A87 Cholet/La Roche leave at exit 32 for La Tranche and follow D747 to town. Turn northwest on D105 for 6 km. to Les Conches where site is signed to left. GPS: 46.388027, -1.478181

Charges guide

Per unit incl. 2 persons and electricity	€ 21.90 - € 35.40
extra person	€ 6.40 - € 7.00
child (under 5 yrs	€ 4.10 - € 4.80

Longeville-sur-Mer

MS Vacances Camping Club Les Brunelles

Le Bouil, F-85560 Longeville-sur-Mer (Vendée) T: 02 53 81 70 00. E: reservation@ms-vacances.com

alanrogers.com/FR85440

This is a well managed site with a wide range of facilities and a varied programme of high season entertainment for all the family. A busy site in high season, there are plenty of activities to keep younger children and teenagers happy and occupied. Les Brunelles has 612 pitches of which 113 are for touring units; all have electricity (10A) and 40 also have water and drainage. Most are 90 sq.m. to allow easier access for larger units. The touring pitches are mainly level on sandy grass and separated by hedges, away from most of the mobile homes. A good sandy beach is 800 m. away.

Facilities

Six well maintained and modernised sanitary blocks have British style toilets and washbasins/showers in cubicles. Facilities for children and disabled visitors. Laundry. Motorcaravan services. Shop, restaurant, takeaway and large modern, airy bar. Covered pool with jacuzzi. Outdoor heated pool with slides and paddling pools. Solarium. Tennis. Play area. Entertainment for all ages. Bicycle hire. Max. 1 dog. WiFi over site (charged). Gas barbecues only. Off site: Beach 800 m.

Open: 11 April - 20 September.

Directions

Longeville-sur-Mer is 28 km. south of A87 exit 32 at La Roche-sur-Yon via D747 (La Tranche), D949 (Les Sables) and in 3 km, D91. Site is 3.5 km. southwest of village and signed from D21 (Jard-sur-Mer).
GPS: 46.41330, -1.52313

Charges guide

Per unit incl. 2 persons and electricity	€ 25.00 - € 47.00
extra person	€ 6.20 - € 12.40

Camping Cheques accepted.

Maché

Camping Caravaning Val de Vie

Rue du Stade, F-85190 Maché (Vendée) T: 02 51 60 21 02. E: campingvaldevie@orange.fr

alanrogers.com/FR85320

Opened in 1999, Val de Vie is a good quality, three-hectare site run with enthusiasm and dedication by its new owners, Florence and Pascal Faudrit, on the outskirts of a rural village set back from the coast. There are 92 pitches in total, 71 for touring units, with electricity (6/10A), that vary in size from 70-130 sq.m. on mostly level grass with hedging. There are nine extra large super pitches (booking essential for high season). The ground can become very hard so steel pegs are advised. The pitches are arranged in a circular fashion around the toilet block which, with reception, is built in the local style with attractive, red tiled roofs. If you are looking for a beach, the Vendée coast is 20 km. away. There are no tour operators at this peaceful site.

Facilities

The two toilet blocks have excellent, modern facilities with some washbasins and showers in cubicles. Baby bath. Facilities for disabled campers. Laundry facilities. Basic motorcaravan service point. Reception also stocks wine, beer, soft drinks and ice-cream. Bread to order (high season). Small play area. Bouncy castle and trampoline. Heated swimming pool (from mid May). Bicycle hire. Off site: Shops, bar and tabac within walking distance.

Open: 1 April - 30 September.

Directions

From La Roche-sur-Yon take D948 northwest. At end of Aizenay bypass continue for 2 km; cross River Vie and take next right, following the signs for Maché into the village centre.
GPS: 46.75268, -1.68633

Charges guide

Per unit incl. 2 persons and electricity	€ 17.30 - € 31.10
extra person	€ 3.00 - € 4.40

Mouilleron-le-Captif

Camping Ambois

13 lieu-dit l'Ambois, F-85000 Mouilleron-le-Captif (Vendée) T: 02 51 37 29 15. E: camping-ambois@voila.fr

alanrogers.com/FR85045

La Roche-sur-Yon is an interesting Napoleonic town and capital of the Vendée. The town has easy access to fine sandy beaches. L'Ambois is an attractive three-hectare site, located just 2 km. from La Roche, and open all year. There are just ten 120 sq.m. grassy pitches for touring, with 6/10A electrical connections (Europlug), water and waste water. Fifty-eight mobile homes and chalets are available for rent. Leisure facilities include a covered swimming pool, a children's farm, and during the peak season, occasional evening entertainment is organised.

Facilities

Two heated sanitary blocks include provision for babies and disabled visitors. Laundry. Bar (all year). Snack bar and takeaway food (1/4-30/9). Heated, covered swimming pool (15/4-30/9). Entertainment and activity programme. Playground. Trampoline. Bouncy castle. Boules. Minigolf. Children's farm. Bicycle hire. Mobile homes and chalets to rent. WiFi over site (charged). Off site: Supermarket 2 km.

Open: All year.

Directions

Head north from La Roche-sur-Yon following signs to Aizenay, Noirmoutier and Challans. Join D948 and take the exit to Le Vigneau. The site is well signed from here. GPS: 46.69638, -1.46116

Charges guide

Per unit incl. 2 persons and electricity	€ 17.90 - € 19.20

Noirmoutier-en-l'Ile

Camping Indigo Noirmoutier

Rue des Sableaux, Bois de la Chaize, F-85330 Noirmoutier-en-l'Ile (Vendée) T: 02 51 39 06 24.

E: noirmoutier@camping-indigo.com **alanrogers.com/FR85720**

Located in woodland and on dunes along a two kilometre stretch of sandy beach, just east of the attractive little town of Noirmoutier on the island of the same name, this could be paradise for those who enjoy a simple campsite in a natural setting. On land belonging to France's forestry commission, this site is operated by Huttopia whose aim is to adapt to the environment rather than take it over. The 386 touring pitches, all with electricity (10A), are situated among the pine trees and accessed along tracks. Those on the sand dunes have fantastic views across the Baie de Bourgneuf. They cost a few euros extra – if you are lucky enough to get one. Some pitches may experience noise from a nearby bar.

Facilities

Five unheated sanitary blocks provide preset showers and washbasins in cubicles. The central one is larger and more modern. Facilities for children and disabled visitors. Laundry. Motorcaravan services. Freezer service. Bread to order. Snack bar and takeaway (July/Aug). Picnic tables. New play area. Boules. Volleyball. Bicycle and canoe hire. Only electric barbecues allowed. Free WiFi over part of site. Off site: Beach 100 m. Shops, bars and restaurants in Noirmoutier-en-l'Ile 2 km. Riding 4 km. Sailing 5 km. Golf 25 km.

Open: 15 April - 3 October.

Directions

The Ile de Noirmoutier is 70 km. southwest of Nantes. At La Barre-de-Monts, take D38 across bridge to island and continue 20 km. to Noirmoutier-en-l'Ile. Go through town (narrow streets!) past three sets of traffic lights and at roundabout turn right following blue signs to Campings. Site is ahead at roundabout in 2 km. Do not use sat nav.
GPS: 46.9969, -2.2201

Charges guide

Per unit incl. 2 persons and electricity	€ 20.80 - € 36.30
extra person	€ 3.90 - € 5.80
child (2-7 yrs)	free - € 3.40
dog	€ 2.20 - € 4.40

Notre-Dame-de-Riez

Camping Domaine des Renardières

13 chemin du Chêne Vert, F-85270 Notre-Dame-de-Riez (Vendée) T: 02 51 55 14 17.

E: caroline.raffin@free.fr **alanrogers.com/FR85520**

Just 7 km. from the busy coastal strip, Domaine des Renardières is an oasis of calm in the traditional French manner. Converted from the family farm in 1970, the site comprises five fields with varying amounts of shade. Two have touring pitches, all with electricity (10A), are well grassed and level. Solar lighting. Torches and long cables are advisable. Mme. Raffin's benevolent authority is to be seen everywhere and the welfare of her clients is of paramount importance to her. Recycling of waste is encouraged – there are collection points for batteries and green waste. There is an entertainment programme in high season. Large units are accepted.

Facilities

The unisex toilet block has private cubicles, baby changing room and a bathroom for disabled visitors. Showers are closed at night except for one cold shower. Laundry. Motorcaravan services. Shop. Air-conditioned bar with TV and takeaway (1/7-27/8). Pizza van calls. Solar-heated pool (covered for 2016). Play area. Boules. Gas and electric barbecues only. Bicycle hire. WiFi throughout (charged). Off site: Fishing 1 km. Vélorail 5 km. Bicycle hire and Atlantic Toboggan 7 km. St Hilaire-de-Riez 7 km. with good sandy beach. Sailing 10 km. Riding and golf 11 km. Puy du Fou 80 km.

Open: 1 April - 30 October.

Directions

Site is northeast of the village of Notre-Dame-de-Riez. Turn in centre of village and cross railway. Fork right and site is on left. Well signed.
GPS: 46.75523, -1.89814

Charges guide

Per unit incl. 2 persons and electricity	€ 18.00 - € 24.00
extra person	€ 3.60 - € 4.70
child (under 5 yrs)	€ 1.80 - € 2.60
dog	€ 1.60

Reductions out of high season.
No credit cards.

Olonne-sur-Mer

MS Vacances Camping Club Le Trianon

95 rue du Maréchal Joffre, F-85340 Olonne-sur-Mer (Vendée) T: 02 53 81 70 00.
E: reservation@ms-vacances.com **alanrogers.com/FR85005**

On the edge of the bustling village of Olonne-sur-Mer and close to the popular resort of Les Sables-d'Olonne, Le Trianon is a large site very much geared to mobile homes and chalets, of which 374 are available for rent. There are 68 touring pitches scattered amongst the statics. They vary in size and shape but all have water taps and drainage with electricity (10A) nearby, and there is plenty of shade. The site is under new ownership and there are ambitious development plans. Nearby Olonne-sur-Mer has shops, bars, restaurants and a large supermarket. Free transport to the beach in July and August.

Facilities

Three toilet blocks with controllable showers and washbasins in cubicles, facilities for babies and disabled visitors. Washing machines and dryers. Well stocked shop, bar and restaurant, snack bars and takeaway. New water park with indoor and outdoor heated pools. Fitness room. Massage and hairdressing. Adventure playground. Bouncy castle. Tennis. Basketball. Beach volleyball. Minigolf. Small fenced fishing lake. Bicycle hire. Activity programme. Children's clubs and entertainment at busy times. WiFi over site (charged). Gas barbecues only.

Open: 11 April - 20 September.

Directions

From A87 at La Roche-sur-Yon, head southwest on D160 towards Les Sables-d'Olonne and leave at exit for Olonne-sur-Mer (D80). Continue on this road, crossing D760 and you will see the site (well signed) on right. Use loop in car park opposite while booking in. GPS: 46.53172, -1.758279

Charges guide

Per unit incl. 2 persons
and electricity € 25.00 - € 47.00
extra person € 6.20 - € 12.40

Camping Cheques accepted.

Olonne-sur-Mer

Camping Sunêlia la Loubine

1 route de la Mer, F-85340 Olonne-sur-Mer (Vendée) T: 02 51 33 12 92. E: info@la-loubine.fr
alanrogers.com/FR85030

On the edge of a forest and just 1.8 kilometres from a sandy beach, la Loubine is a busy campsite close to Les Sables-d'Olonne. Under new ownership from 2011, the site has 80 grass touring pitches which are mostly shaded, all with electricity and with water points nearby. Mobile homes and chalets, many for rent, and tour operator tents occupy the remaining 300 pitches. The camping areas have many mature trees and hedges, some quite high, providing plenty of shade. A shuttle bus to the beach (2 km) operates in high season. Olonne-sur-Mer has shops, bars, restaurants and a hypermarket.

Facilities

Four toilet blocks have washbasins in cubicles and controllable showers. Facilities for disabled visitors. Washing machines and dryers. Shop (July/Aug). Bar (9/4-27/8), restaurant and takeaway. Complex of outdoor and heated indoor pools. Activity programme (July/Aug). Tennis. Fitness room. Minigolf. New play area. Bicycle hire. WiFi over site (charged). Internet (charged). Gas barbecues only. Dogs are not allowed in high season.

Open: 9 April - 11 September.

Directions

Site is off D80 coast road between Olonne-sur-Mer and Brem-sur-Mer, signed at small roundabout. From La Roche-sur-Yon via A87/D160, turn west on D80 to Olonne-sur-Mer, then on to site, signed to left in 4 km. GPS: 46.54626, -1.80556

Charges guide

Per unit incl. 2 persons
and electricity € 21.50 - € 41.90
extra person € 3.50 - € 7.50

Olonne-sur-Mer

Camping Domaine de l'Orée

13 route des Amis de la Nature, F-85340 Olonne-sur-Mer (Vendée) T: 02 51 33 10 59. E: loree@free.fr
alanrogers.com/FR85180

On the edge of a national forest, close to marshes and a bird sanctuary, and just 1,500 m. from a fine sandy beach, Domaine de l'Orée will provide ample opportunities for an active holiday whether in the impressive pool complex, using the many sports facilities, venturing out onto the network of footpaths and cycle tracks or just going to the beach. The 53 touring pitches are level and separated by bushes; all have electricity (10A, Europlug), 40 also have a water tap and drainage and ten have their own private toilet and fridge. The remaining 243 pitches are occupied by chalets and mobile homes, many for rent.

Facilities

Two blocks providing adequate sanitary facilities have good, hot showers (preset) and washbasins in cabins. Baby bath. Basic facilities for disabled visitors. Washing machines and dryers. Well stocked shop (July/Aug). Bar, snack bar and takeaway (from 1/5). Heated outdoor pool and fun pool with slides (from 1/5). Heated indoor pool. Fitness equipment. Play areas. Trampolines. Tennis (free). Bicycle hire. WiFi over site (charged). Gas barbecues only.

Open: 25 April - 17 September.

Directions

From La Roche-sur-Yon via A87/D160, turn west on D949 Les Sables ring road then north on D32 to Olonne-sur-Mer. Site is signed to left in town centre. GPS: 46.54951, -1.80664

Charges guide

Per unit incl. 2 persons
and electricity € 20.50 - € 39.00
extra person € 4.00 - € 6.50

Olonne-sur-Mer

Camping le Nid d'Eté

2 rue de la Vigne Verte, F-85340 Olonne-sur-Mer (Vendée) T: 02 51 95 34 38. E: info@leniddete.com

alanrogers.com/FR85290

This campsite of 1.5 hectares has a mixture of rental chalets (36) and touring pitches (90). One chalet has been fully equipped to cater for disabled guests. Some larger touring pitches (130 sq.m) are available in a new section but they have no shade. Set on the edge of Olonne-sur-Mer, the site is arranged on both sides of a narrow approach road and is therefore probably unsuitable for large units. The level, grass pitches are well maintained with some small hedges inbetween. All have electricity hook-ups (10A) with Europlugs and ample water points.

Facilities

One sanitary block for each area with showers and washbasins in cubicles. Facilities for children and disabled visitors. Laundry facilities. Heated outdoor pool (1/5-30/9). Heated indoor pool. Shop, bar with TV and takeaway (all 15/4-30/9). Play area. Bicycle hire. WiFi throughout (charged). Off site: Shop and bar within 1.5 km. Supermarket 2 km. Fishing and riding 2 km. Beach 4 km.

Open: 1 April - 30 September.

Directions

Follow blue and white camping signs from Olonne-sur-Mer. GPS: 46.53315, -1.79365

Charges guide

Per unit incl. 2 persons and electricity	€ 19.40 - € 33.00
extra person	€ 3.70 - € 5.20
child (2-7 yrs)	€ 3.00 - € 3.80
dog	€ 1.00 - € 3.10

Olonne-sur-Mer

Flower Camping Bois Soleil

94 chemin des Barres, F-85340 Olonne-sur-Mer (Vendée) T: 02 51 33 11 97.

E: camping.boissoleil@wanadoo.fr **alanrogers.com/FR85400**

A pleasant, traditionally laid out site with just 199 pitches, separated by hedges, on flat or gently sloping ground, Bois Soleil has a large number of mobile homes and chalets, leaving just 32 pitches for tourers and tents. All have electricity (6A) and water points and most are grouped in a pleasant corner with views out over the marshes and bird reserve to distant villages. There is an excellent swimming pool complex with water slides plus an attractive indoor pool with hammam, while the nearby forest and marais provide fine opportunities for walkers and nature lovers.

Facilities

The two toilet blocks (one heated, the other open in high season) have mainly British style toilets, pushbutton showers and washbasins in cubicles (in newer block). Baby bath. En-suite unit for disabled visitors. Blocks are locked overnight but basic facilities provided. Laundry facilities. Shop (July/Aug). Bar, snack bar and takeaway (July/Aug and busy w/ends). Outdoor pool with waterslides and flume (heated July/Aug). Heated indoor pool with slide, paddling pool and hammam. Fitness room with sauna. Activities (July/Aug). Play areas. Trampoline. Minigolf. Bicycle hire. WiFi (charged). Gas barbecues only.

Open: 12 April - 13 September.

Directions

From La Roche-sur-Yon via A87/D160, turn west on D80 to Olonne-sur-Mer and continue to site (signed on right in 4 km). GPS: 46.55446, -1.80601

Charges guide

Per unit incl. 2 persons and electricity	€ 19.10 - € 31.15
extra person	€ 3.50 - € 5.00
child (under 7 yrs)	€ 2.60 - € 3.50
dog	€ 3.00

Saint Christophe-du-Ligneron

Camping du Domaine de Bellevue

Bellevue de Ligneron, F-85670 Saint Christophe-du-Ligneron (Vendée) T: 02 51 93 30 66.

E: campingdebellevue85@orange.fr **alanrogers.com/FR85385**

Domaine de Bellevue is a family site in the northern Vendée, close to the town of Challans (famous for its market), and around 20 minutes from the broad, sandy beaches at Saint Gilles-Croix-de-Vie. There are 126 large (minimum 110 sq.m) pitches; 30 for tourers, ten fully serviced with 16A electricity, dispersed around a large park which has two generous fishing ponds stocked with carp and other species. An entertainment programme runs during July and August and includes special activities for children. There is a range of mobile homes, chalets and bungalow-style tents for rent.

Facilities

Two sanitary blocks with washbasins and showers in cubicles and facilities for children and disabled visitors. Laundry. Bar, snack bar (July/Aug and w/ends). Covered, heated swimming pool and children's pool. Play area. Games room. Trampoline. Volleyball. Pétanque pitch. Activity and entertainment programme (July/Aug). Mobile homes and chalets for rent. Fishing. Small animal farm. WiFi throughout (charged). Off site: Restaurant 500 m.

Open: 1 March - 31 October.

Directions

From Challans, head south on D2948 towards Aizenay. On reaching St Christophe du Ligneron, follow signs to site. GPS: 46.81511, -1.77472

Charges guide

Per unit incl. 2 persons and electricity	€ 14.00 - € 23.00
extra person	€ 3.50 - € 5.00
child (under 7 yrs)	€ 3.00 - € 4.00
dog	€ 3.00

Saint Gilles-Croix-de-Vie

Camping les Cyprès

41 rue du Pont Jaunay, F-85806 Saint Gilles-Croix-de-Vie (Vendée) T: 02 51 55 38 98.
E: contact@camping-lescypres85.com **alanrogers.com/FR85495**

On the edge of a pine forest and just a short walk across the dunes from a fine sandy beach, this could be an ideal spot for a seaside holiday. Les Cyprès is a very French campsite with good basic facilities and a pleasant modern pool complex. The 300 pitches are in an arc curving out towards the sea in both directions from reception; the 141 touring pitches of varying shapes and sizes occupy the southern end of the arc. All have access to electricity (10A) and water, though long leads are required in places and some are more suitable for tents because of the trees. Seasonal units occupy a number of these pitches except in high season. Other sections are for mobile homes and chalets for rent or privately owned. A walking and cycle route passes the site linking to an extensive network of tracks. The site is a short drive from the busy fishing port and resort of Saint Gilles-Croix-de-Vie with a good range of shops, bars and restaurants along its pedestrianised streets and on the quayside. An impressive new hypermarket has been built on the edge of town and there are lively weekly markets here and in neighbouring towns and villages. The resort of Les Sables-d'Olonne is 28 km. to the south and busy Saint Jean-de-Monts is closer still to the northwest; buses run between the two and pass along the nearby main road.

Facilities

Two traditional toilet blocks serving the touring areas. Baby bath in ladies' section of main block. Unit for disabled visitors opposite reception plus laundry facilities. Motorcaravan services. Shop (April-Aug). Bar (July/Aug). Snack bar and takeaway with shared terrace (July/Aug and weekends). Outdoor pool (from 1/5). Heated indoor pool with jacuzzi. Paddling pools. Games room. Play area. Multisports court. Bicycle hire and children's go-karts. Free WiFi in bar area. Off site: Beach 500 m. Fishing 1 km.

Open: 4 April - 20 September.

Directions

St Gilles-Croix-de-Vie is 45 km. west of La Roche-sur-Yon on the D38 coast road. From roundabout at southern end of St Gilles bypass, head towards town and take first left in 400 m. Site is signed and is in 1 km. GPS: 46.67089, -1.909132

Charges guide

Per unit incl. 2 persons and electricity	€ 21.50 - € 30.50
extra person	€ 6.10 - € 6.70
child (2-5 yrs)	€ 4.30 - € 4.70

CAMPING les Cyprès ***
• Access to the beach at 400 m
• Cycling routes directly from the site
• Open air and covered swimming pools
• Touring pitches and mobile homes from April to September
Vendée - 41 rue du Pont Jaunay - 85800 ST GILLES CROIX DE VIE
Tel: 00 33 2 51 55 38 98 • Email: contact@camping-lescypres85.com

Saint Gilles-Croix-de-Vie

Chadotel Camping le Bahamas Beach

168 route des Sables, F-85800 Saint Gilles-Croix-de-Vie (Vendée) T: 02 51 54 69 16. E: info@chadotel.com
alanrogers.com/FR85500

A member of the Chadotel group, le Bahamas Beach is separated from the sandy beach by 600 m. of sand dunes and the River Jaunay. It is a modern, well equipped site, very well placed on one of the most popular stretches of the Vendée coast. The 81 touring pitches are scattered amongst the total of 235, of which 154 are mobile homes. The pitches are grassy and level on sandy soil, separated by hedges or low bushes and all have easy access to electricity and water. There are few trees and little shelter from the wind off the sea. Maximum unit length permitted is 8.5 m.

Facilities

Two well maintained toilet blocks include washbasins in cubicles, a unit for disabled visitors and baby rooms. Laundry facilities. Bar, snacks and takeaway (25/5-15/9, limited hours in low season). Shop (25/5-15/9). Heated outdoor pool with cover. Children's pool. Play area. Minigolf. Football, basketball and volleyball. Bicycle hire. WiFi over site (charged). Off site: Beach 15 mins. on foot.

Open: 5 April - 20 September.

Directions

From roundabout at southern end of D38 St Gilles bypass, take exit signed St Gilles-Grande-Plage. Site is 500 m. on left. GPS: 46.67833, -1.91571

Charges guide

Per unit incl. 2 persons and electricity	€ 18.50 - € 34.50
extra person	€ 6.00

Saint Gilles-Croix-de-Vie

Camping le Petit Pavillon

181 route des Sables, F-85800 Saint Gilles-Croix-de-Vie (Vendée) T: 02 51 55 14 63.
E: contact@lepetitpavillon.fr **alanrogers.com/FR85880**

A delightful and surprising site, there is a warm welcome from the resident owners. With 171 pitches, including 75 lovingly tended, privately owned chalets, and 11 units for rent, there are 85 touring pitches on grass, all with electricity (4/10A, some Europlug). The site roads are a little narrow and some pitches are rather shallow and therefore more suitable for tents, trailer tents and small motorcaravans. Some pitches are marked by low hedges, others are more open. Background traffic noise can affect some pitches closest to the adjacent bypass at busy times, but it quietens at night. This is a pure traditional camping site with no frills, only a takeaway two days a week in July and August.

Facilities

Two of the three sanitary blocks are of excellent quality with modern fittings. Facilities for disabled visitors. Motorcaravan services. Takeaway twice weekly (July/Aug). Games room. Minigolf. Playground and animation. Site is unsuitable for American RVs and large motorcaravans over 8 m. Gas barbecues only. Internet access. WiFi over part of site (free). Off site: Fishing 200 m. (with a permit). Bicycle hire and boat launching 3 km. Riding 4 km.

Open: 1 April - 30 September.

Directions

St Gilles-Croix-de-Vie is 30 km. north of Les Sables-d'Olonne. Site is south of town by roundabout at start of by-pass (D38B). At roundabout turn towards town (D38) and site is a short distance on right. GPS: 46.67623, -1.9121

Charges guide

Per unit incl. 2 persons and electricity	€ 14.90 - € 18.50
extra person	€ 3.60 - € 4.60

Saint Hilaire-de-Riez

Camping le Château

Rue du Château Vieux, F-85270 Saint Hilaire-de-Riez (Vendée) T: 02 28 11 63 18. E: loisirs85@free.fr
alanrogers.com/FR85008

An excellent choice for families, this site is situated in a green park, 2.5 km from the beaches, between marshes and forest. It is one of three sites owned by the Sun Marina group. The four-hectare site is split into two areas either side of the road. It offers 30 level, separated touring pitches on grass with some shade. They are of a good size and most have 10A electricity (Europlug) and water. A large proportion of the site (316 pitches) is occupied by privately owned mobile homes. A bar and restaurant opens during July and August and a swimming pool complex with both indoor and outdoor pools is open all season. A good choice of activities are available for all ages.

Facilities

Two, unheated toilet blocks provide hot showers, washbasins in cubicles and facilities for children and disabled visitors. Laundry facilities. Small shop, bar, restaurant and takeaway (July/Aug). Large pool complex with heated indoor pool and jacuzzi and an outdoor pool with water slide and flume. Sun terrace. Play area. Tennis. Football and volleyball. Boules. Kids' club. Entertainment in high season. WiFi throughout (charged).

Open: 10 May - 15 September.

Directions

Follow the coastal road of St Jean-de-Monts south towards St Hilaire-de-Riez. After having passed the village sign continue on the D38 for 0.7 km, turning right at the roundabout. Site is just off roundabout on a one-way road. GPS: 46.7267, -1.9559

Charges guide

Per unit incl. 2 persons and electricity	€ 14.00 - € 34.00
extra person	€ 5.00

Saint Hilaire-de-Riez

Camping les Ecureuils

100 avenue de la Pège, F-85270 Saint Hilaire-de-Riez (Vendée) T: 02 51 54 33 71.
E: info@camping-aux-ecureuils.com **alanrogers.com/FR85230**

Of the seaside sites on the Vendée, les Ecureuils has to be one of the best, run by a friendly and most helpful family. Just 300 m. from a superb beach, the site is ideally situated for exploring from Les Sables-d'Olonne to Noirmoutier. Developed on what was originally a farm, there are 215 pitches (39 for touring units). On sandy grass, all have electricity (6A, Europlug adaptors available free of charge), water and drainage. Well kept hedges and mature trees give shade and privacy, although some more open pitches are also available for sun lovers. The site is popular with British tour operators (60%).

Facilities

The two main sanitary blocks are spacious and include some washbasins in cubicles and facilities for babies and disabled visitors. Laundry facilities. Motorcaravan services. Dog shower. Small shop. Restaurant. Large, airy bar with screened terrace. Swimming pool complex including fun pool for small children and water slide with splash pool. Indoor pool. Wellness. Gym. Tennis court. Games room. New play area. Children's club. Facilities open all season.

Open: 25 April - 6 September.

Directions

Driving south D38 (St Jean-de-Monts-St Gilles), turn right at L'Oasis hotel/restaurant in Orouet (6 km. outside St Jean), signed Les Mouettes. After 1.5 km. at roundabout turn left (St Hilaire-de-Riez). Site is 500 m. on left. GPS: 46.74473, -2.00869

Charges guide

Per unit incl. 2 persons and electricity	€ 25.00 - € 42.00

Saint Hilaire-de-Riez

Camping la Ningle

Chemin des Roselières 66, F-85270 Saint Hilaire-de-Riez (Vendée) T: 02 51 54 07 11.

E: campingdelaningle@wanadoo.fr **alanrogers.com/FR85350**

At Camping la Ningle you are guaranteed to receive a warm welcome from M. et Mme. Guibert-Guilbald, who have created a very pleasant campsite with a friendly, family atmosphere. There are 148 pitches; 45 available for touring units. All are fully serviced (electricity 6/10A, water and drainage). Pitches are spacious with dividing hedges and all have some shade. The nearest beach is a 500 m. walk through a pine forest. There is also a heated aquatic park on site with one covered swimming pool and one outdoor swimming pool with its slide and a paddling pool for children.

Facilities

Two very clean toilet blocks include washbasins and showers in cubicles. Toilet/shower room for disabled visitors and a large family shower room. Laundry facilities. Bread available and takeaway three evenings per week (July/Aug). Bar (July/Aug). Main swimming pool, larger children's pool, paddling pool and slide (all season). Fitness suite. Tennis court. Games field. Games room. Fishing lake. Children's activities (July/Aug) and regular pétanque competitions. Free WiFi in bar area.

Open: 1 May - 15 September.

Directions

Driving south on D38 (St Jean-de-Monts-St Gilles), turn right at L'Oasis hotel/restaurant in Orouet, signed Les Mouettes. After 1.5 km. at roundabout, turn left (St Hilaire-de-Riez). Pass two campsites, then next left, (la Ningle). GPS: 46.74476, -2.0044

Charges guide

Per unit incl. 2 persons and electricity	€ 20.50 - € 34.20
extra person	€ 3.80 - € 5.50

Saint Hilaire-de-Riez

Camping les Chouans

108 avenue de la Faye, F-85270 Saint Hilaire-de-Riez (Vendée) T: 02 51 54 34 90.

E: info@camping-leschouans.com **alanrogers.com/FR85640**

This family run campsite is within a short drive of some wonderful beaches. In high season it is bustling and lively with a children's club and a full programme of activities for youngsters and the whole family. A smart bar, refreshment and entertainment area is next to the imaginative open-air pool complex. There are 105 privately owned mobile homes, 98 for hire and 49 touring pitches scattered round the site (80-100 sq.m) with 10A electricity and water reasonably close by, some shaded. Late night discos may be noisy in July and August.

Facilities

Two basic sanitary blocks (with unisex toilets). Shower room and separate toilet for disabled campers. Baby room. Laundry. Fridge hire. Well stocked shop, large modern bar with food to eat in or take away. Heated swimming pool with lazy river, water slides and jacuzzi (all season). Bicycle hire. Tennis. Multisports courts. Boules. Table tennis. Small fitness gym (charged). Play area. Games room. Children's club. Archery (July/Aug). Good entertainment programme for all ages (July/Aug). WiFi throughout (free in bar). Off site: Beach 1.8 km.

Open: 10 April - 13 September.

Directions

St Hilaire-de-Riez is 45 km. west of La Roche-sur-Yon just off the D38 St Jean-de-Monts-St Gilles road. From D38/D38bis at roundabout northwest of town, turn southeast towards St Hilaire (D38), take first right and at T-junction turn right to site on right in 650 m. GPS: 46.73415, -1.973591

Charges guide

Per unit incl. 2 persons and electricity	€ 20.00 - € 38.00
extra person	€ 7.00 - € 11.00
child (4-13 yrs)	free - € 7.00

Saint Hilaire-la-Forêt

Camping la Grand Métairie

8 rue de la Vineuse en Plaine, F-85440 Saint Hilaire-la-Forêt (Vendée) T: 02 51 33 32 38.

E: info@camping-grandmetairie.com **alanrogers.com/FR85300**

Just five kilometres from the super sandy beach at Jard-sur-Mer, la Grand Métairie offers many of the amenities of its seaside counterparts, but with the important advantage of being on the edge of a delightful, sleepy village otherwise untouched by tourism. It is a busy, well run site with a programme of lively entertainment in high season. The site has 172 pitches (39 touring pitches), all with electricity (10A). The pitches have good shade, are all separated by mature trees and hedges and are reasonable in size, although access to some may prove difficult for larger units. Minimum stay in high season.

Facilities

Two modern toilet blocks are very clean and include some washbasins in cabins. Units for babies and disabled visitors. Washing machines and dryers. Fridge hire. Smart bar/restaurant and takeaway (from 2/7). Attractive, heated outdoor pool and paddling pool (20/5-10/9). Indoor pool. Gym. Minigolf. Games room. Play area. Multisports area. Mini farm. Miniclub. Bicycle hire. WiFi (charged).

Open: 3 April - 26 September.

Directions

From Les Sables take D949 (La Rochelle) towards Talmont-St Hilaire and Luçon; 7 km. after Talmont turn right on D70 to St Hilaire-la-Forêt. Site is on left before village centre. GPS: 46.44862, -1.52626

Charges guide

Per unit incl. 2 persons and electricity	€ 16.00 - € 28.00
extra person	€ 4.00 - € 7.00

Saint Hilaire-la-Forêt

Camping des Batardières

2, rue des Batardières, F-85440 Saint Hilaire-la-Forêt (Vendée) T: 02 51 33 33 85.

alanrogers.com/FR85390

Camping des Batardières is a haven of tranquillity on the edge of an unspoilt village, yet just 5 km. from the sea. It is an attractive, unsophisticated little site, lovingly maintained by its owners for more than 25 years. Many visitors return year after year. There are 75 good sized, manicured, grassy pitches (a few up to 130 sq.m) and all are available for touring units (there are no mobile homes and no tour operators!). All have easy access to water and electricity (6A). Otherwise there are few facilities on site.

Facilities

The sanitary block is kept very clean and visitors are encouraged to keep it that way (no shoes in the shower cubicles, for instance). Some washbasin and shower combination cubicles. Laundry facilities. Tennis court. Play area and field for games, kite-flying etc. Not suitable for American motorhomes or twin-axle caravans.
Off site: Village shop and bar 200 m. Jard-sur-Mer 5 km. Bicycle hire 3 km. Fishing 5 km. Golf 16 km.

Open: 1 July - 1 September.

Directions

From Les Sables-d'Olonne take D949 (La Rochelle) towards Talmont-St Hilaire and Luçon. 7 km. after Talmont turn right on D70 to St Hilaire-la-Forêt. Site signed to the right approaching village.
GPS: 46.4486, -1.5286

Charges guide

Per unit incl. 2 persons and electricity	€ 21.00 - € 25.00
extra person	€ 4.00

No credit cards.

Saint Jean-de-Monts

Camping l'Abri des Pins

Route de Notre-Dame-de-Monts, F-85160 Saint Jean-de-Monts (Vendée) T: 02 51 58 83 86.

E: contact@abridespins.com **alanrogers.com/FR85090**

L'Abri des Pins is situated on the outskirts of Saint Jean-de-Monts and is separated from the sea and a long sandy beach by a strip of pine forest. The site has 218 pitches, 30 of which are for touring units, most with electricity and water; they are separated by hedges and most have shade. Seventy pitches have mobile homes and chalets for rent, the rest being occupied by privately owned mobiles. It has an impressive entrance and good leisure facilities which include a recently added indoor pool and unusual children's pool. The sanitary blocks are modern and clean. From the site, it is a pleasant 15-minute walk to the beach.

Facilities

The two traditional sanitary blocks are modern and clean. Washbasins in cabins, preset showers, basic facilities for babies and disabled visitors. Laundry. Snack bar with takeaway (July/Aug). Heated indoor and outdoor pools, water slide, new pool for children and decked sunbathing area. Sauna and steam room. Gym equipment. Miniclub daily. Activities and entertainment (July/Aug). Play area. Games rooms. Tennis. Pétanque. Bicycle hire arranged. WiFi over site (charged). Off site: Supermarket 500 m.

Open: 15 June - 16 September.

Directions

St Jean-de-Monts is 55 km. northwest of La Roche-sur-Yon. Site is 4 km. north of town centre on western side of D38 Notre Dame-de-Monts road, almost opposite Les Places Dorées.
GPS: 46.8093, -2.109

Charges guide

Per unit incl. 3 persons and electricity	€ 25.00 - € 39.00
extra person	€ 4.10 - € 7.25

Saint Jean-de-Monts

Camping le Tropicana

Chemin des Bosses, F-85160 Saint Jean-de-Monts (Vendée) T: 02 51 58 62 98. E: contact@le-tropicana.com

alanrogers.com/FR85145

Le Tropicana is in the heart of a vast pine forest, a few kilometres south of Saint Jean-de-Monts. It is only minutes away from a fine sandy beach (gate from site) and all the amenities in Saint Hilaire-de-Riez. This seven-hectare site has a total of 332 pitches with 59 for tourers. They are generous (100-130 sq.m), on sandy grass, and all have 10A electricity (long leads may be required). The whole family will enjoy the water park with its three heated swimming pools with water slides and a toddlers' pool. The extensive high season entertainment and leisure programme caters for all ages.

Facilities

Three toilet blocks with showers and washbasins in cubicles and facilities for disabled visitors. Baby room. Laundry. Shop (bread to order), bar/restaurant/takeaway (29/6-1/9). Heated indoor swimming pool and paddling pool. Heated outdoor pool with slide, flume and jacuzzi. Wellness. Play area. Beach volleyball. Games room. Entertainment (July/Aug). TV room. WiFi (charged).

Open: 14 May - 18 September.

Directions

Site is signed off D38 6 km. south of St Jean-de-Monts in village of Orouet. From St Jean-de-Monts turn right at L'Oasis restaurant towards Mouette and follow signs to site. GPS: 46.75563, -2.00781

Charges guide

Per unit incl. 3 persons, electricity and water	€ 24.70 - € 37.40
extra person	€ 4.00 - € 7.00

Saint Jean-de-Monts

Camping la Yole

13 chemin des Bosses, Orouet, F-85160 Saint Jean-de-Monts (Vendée) T: 02 51 58 67 17.
E: contact@la-yole.com **alanrogers.com/FR85150**

La Yole is an attractive and well run site, two kilometres from a sandy beach. It offers 369 pitches, of which 76 are occupied by tour operators and 133 mobile homes are either privately owned or available to rent. There are 170 touring pitches, most with shade and separated by bushes and trees. An area at the rear of the site is a little more open. All the pitches are of at least 100 sq.m. and have electricity (10A), water and drainage. The pool complex includes an attractive outdoor pool, a paddling pool, slide and an indoor heated pool with jacuzzi. An extension to the pool area is planned for 2016. There are also gym facilities and entertainment is organised in high season. This is a clean and tidy site, ideal for families with children and you will receive a helpful and friendly welcome. It is well placed for visiting many of the attractions the Vendée has to offer. Lively Saint Jean-de-Mont has a good choice of shops, bars and restaurants plus a daily market. The busy fishing port of Saint Gilles-Croix-de-Vie with its extensive marina also offer quayside bars and restaurants. If you get the chance, take an unforgettable trip to the historical, world class theme park and evening spectacular, le Puy du Fou.

Facilities

Four toilet blocks (one heated in low season) include washbasins in cabins, hot showers and facilities for disabled visitors and babies. Laundry. Shop (20/5-5/9). Bar with TV, restaurant and takeaway (2/4-7/9). Outdoor pool and paddling pool. Indoor heated pool with jacuzzi (all season). Gym centre. Play area (4-10 yrs). Tennis. Games room. Children's club. Bicycle hire. Entertainment in high season. WiFi on part of site (charged). Gas barbecues only. Communal barbecue area provided. Max. 1 dog. Off site: Bus service. Riding 1 km. Beach 2 km. Fishing, golf and watersports 6 km.

Open: 2 April - 25 September.

Directions

Site is signed off the D38, 6 km. south of St Jean-de-Monts in the village of Orouet. Coming from St Jean-de-Monts turn right at l'Oasis restaurant towards Mouette and follow signs to site.
GPS: 46.75659, -2.00792

Charges guide

Per unit incl. 2 persons, electricity, water and drainage	€ 22.00 - € 38.50
extra person	€ 4.00 - € 7.20
child (0-9 yrs)	free - € 6.70
dog	€ 5.00 - € 7.00

Camping Cheques accepted.

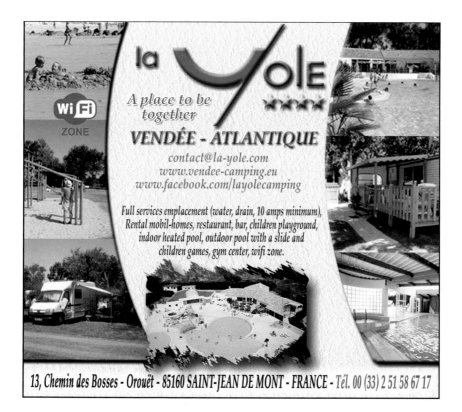

Saint Jean-de-Monts

Camping Acapulco

63 avenue des Epines, F-85160 Saint Jean-de-Monts (Vendée) T: 02 28 11 63 18. E: loisirs85@free.fr

alanrogers.com/FR85220

Ideal for family beach holidays, this large, friendly site is just 700 m. from the beach. The majority of the 450 pitches here are taken by mobile homes; at present there are 40 available for touring, although some of these are destined for more mobiles. The few existing touring pitches, which have electricity and water nearby, are of average size on grass and divided by hedges. There is an excellent pool complex with water slides, a children's pool, an imaginative new balnéo area and a sunbathing terrace. Adjacent to this is a spacious bar/snack bar. Acapulco is between the popular resort of Saint Jean-de-Monts and the more laid back Saint Hilaire-de-Riez, so the opportunities for shopping and eating out are numerous.

Facilities

Three unheated sanitary blocks are clean and include washbasins in cabins and preset showers. Facilities for babies and disabled visitors. Laundry. Shop, takeaway and bar/snack bar. Heated, open-air pool complex. Play area. Tennis. Boules. Multisports area. Games room. Bicycle hire. Children's club (4-11 yrs) and full programme of activities and entertainment plus excursions (July/Aug). WiFi over site (charged). Off site: Sandy beach 600 m.

Open: 26 April - 12 September.

Directions

The site is off D38 St Jean-de-Monts-St Gilles road at Orouët. At mini roundabout by l'Oasis hotel turn southwest (Les Mouettes) and campsite. Site is on left in 2 km. GPS: 46.7637, -2.009

Charges guide

Per unit incl. 2 persons and electricity	€ 22.00 - € 46.00
extra person	€ 5.00 - € 6.00

Saint Jean-de-Monts

Camping les Places Dorées

Route de Notre-Dame-de-Monts, F-85160 Saint Jean-de-Monts (Vendée) T: 02 51 59 02 93.

E: contact@placesdorees.com **alanrogers.com/FR85280**

Les Places Dorées is, in high season, a busy, popular site with a lively programme of activities and entertainment. At other times it is quieter, but still has plenty to offer. There are 288 grassy pitches, of which just 60 are available for touring units, the quietest being towards the back of the site. Those nearer the leisure complex can be noisy in high season with the bar and disco closing late. Pitches are separated by hedges and there is some shade from maturing trees. A 20-minute walk will take you to a long sandy beach. Nearby Saint Jean is a busy resort with plenty of shops, bars and restaurants.

Facilities

Three traditional toilet blocks are beginning to show their age but seem to be kept clean. Preset showers and washbasins in cubicles. Facilities for babies and disabled visitors. Laundry facilities. Bread to order. Bar, snack bar and takeaway (July/Aug). Outdoor pool complex with slides, jacuzzi and waterfall. Covered, heated pool, spa facilities and gym. Multisports pitch. Miniclub (July/Aug). Games room. Trampoline. Bicycle hire arranged. WiFi over site (charged). Facilities at L'Abri des Pins (opposite).

Open: 11 June - 11 September.

Directions

St Jean-de-Monts is 55 km. northwest of La Roche-sur-Yon. Site is 4 km. north of St Jean-de-Monts on the D38 St Jean-de-Monts-Notre Dames-de-Monts road on the eastern side, almost opposite L'Abri des Pins. GPS: 46.80993, -2.10992

Charges guide

Per unit incl. 3 persons and electricity	€ 25.00 - € 39.00

No credit cards.

Saint Jean-de-Monts

Camping la Forêt

190 chemin de la Rive, F-85160 Saint Jean-de-Monts (Vendée) T: 02 51 58 84 63.

E: camping-la-foret@wanadoo.fr **alanrogers.com/FR85360**

Camping la Forêt is an attractive, well run site with a friendly family atmosphere, thanks to the hard working owners, M. and Mme. Jolivet. Many visitors return year after year. It provides just 61 pitches with 46 for touring units. They are of a reasonable size and surrounded by mature hedges; all have water and electricity (10A), and some also have drainage. A variety of trees provide shade to every pitch. There are 16 mobile homes for rent (from 5 April) and one tour operator on site (11 pitches), but their presence is not intrusive and the site has a quiet and relaxed atmosphere. You are advised not to enter the site without checking pitch availability. Staff offer assistance with pitching your caravan.

Facilities

The central toilet block has hot showers and washbasins in cubicles and a family room. Laundry facilities. Baby bath. Facilities for disabled visitors. Motorcaravan tanks emptied on request. Basics sold in reception, including fresh bread (June-Aug). Takeaway (15/5-15/9). Small heated outdoor swimming pool (1/5-15/9). TV/games room. Play area. Bicycle hire. Fishing. WiFi (charged).

Open: 1 May - 28 September.

Directions

The site is 6 km. north of St Jean just off D38 towards Notre Dame-de-Monts. At southern end of Notre Dame, turn west at sign for site and Plage de Pont d'Yeu. Bear left and site is on left in 200 m. GPS: 46.81828, -2.13004

Charges guide

Per unit incl. 2 persons and electricity	€ 19.00 - € 35.90

Saint Jean-de-Monts

Flower Camping Plein Sud

246 route de Notre-Dame-de-Monts, F-85160 Saint Jean-de-Monts (Vendée) T: 02 51 59 10 40.

E: info@campingpleinsud.com **alanrogers.com/FR85590**

Plein Sud is a small, friendly site, immaculately kept and with a very French ambience. Of the 110 grassy pitches separated by hedges, 40 are available for touring. They are of a reasonable size and all have electricity and water; most also have drainage. Twenty pitches have site owned mobile homes, cabins or tents for rent, the rest have privately owned mobiles. The touring pitches at the far end of this long, narrow site are particularly peaceful. Only 800 m. away, via another campsite across the road and through a strip of forest, is a long stretch of safe, sandy beach.

Facilities

Two well maintained and immaculate sanitary blocks provide pushbutton showers and washbasins in cabins. Good facilities for disabled visitors. Baby room. Laundry facilities. Small bar with TV and terrace (July/Aug). Attractive heated pool with paddling pool (15/5-13/9). Waterpark. Play areas. Multisports court. Bread and milk to order (high season). Outside caterers provide takeaways (Tues-Sun). Bicycle hire. New stocked fridge. Pony and trap rides for young children. Children's club and family entertainment (July/Aug). WiFi (charged).

Open: 11 April - 13 September.

Directions

Site is 4 km. north of St Jean-de-Monts on D38 towards Notre Dame-de-Monts. Site is on right after passing a number of restaurants.
GPS: 46.809805, -2.109557

Charges guide

Per unit incl. 2 persons and electricity	€ 18.50 - € 31.50
extra person	€ 2.00 - € 5.00
child (0-7 yrs)	free

Saint Jean-de-Monts

Camping Aux Coeurs Vendéens

251 route de Notre-Dame-de-Monts, F-85160 Saint Jean-de-Monts (Vendée) T: 02 51 58 84 91.

E: info@coeursvendeens.com **alanrogers.com/FR85740**

This is a delightful little site, a real find for those wishing to enjoy the beaches and lifestyle of this stretch of coastline without the razzmatazz of some of the neighbouring sites. It is family run and everywhere there is attention to detail: flower tubs beside the road as you drive in, whitewashed stones for the pitch numbers, engraved designs on the washbasin mirrors, even plugs for the dishwashing sinks! There are 46 touring pitches, all with electricity available (10A), and a further 69 with mobile homes and chalets, all but five available for rent.

Facilities

Two rather dated sanitary blocks are bright, cheerful and kept very clean. Controllable showers, washbasins in cubicles, two pleasant baby rooms. En-suite facilities for disabled visitors (wheelchair users might have minor difficulties accessing this). Laundry. Small shop with takeaway. Bar. Swimming pools (outdoor 1/6-7/9). Fitness equipment. TV/games room. Playgrounds. Trampoline and bouncy castle. Miniclub (5-12 yrs, July/Aug). Bicycle hire. WiFi throughout (free).

Open: 23 April - 23 September.

Directions

Site is on the D38 just over 3 km. north of St Jean-de-Monts, roughly halfway between St Jean-de-Monts and Notre Dame-de-Monts, on the western side of the road. GPS: 46.809133, -2.110167

Charges guide

Per unit incl. 2 persons and electricity	€ 19.00 - € 33.50
extra person	€ 3.00 - € 5.20
child (under 5 yrs)	free - € 3.50

Saint Jean-de-Monts

Camping les Amiaux

223 rue de Notre-Dame-de-Monts, F-85160 Saint Jean-de-Monts (Vendée) T: 02 51 58 22 22.

E: accueil@amiaux.fr **alanrogers.com/FR85760**

This is a busy, family run campsite that is very popular with British holidaymakers and is used by a number of tour operators who occupy 150 of the 544 pitches. However, there are still 300 touring pitches, all with electricity (10A), water tap and drain; there are also 32 mobile homes for hire. The site is on both sides of the main road, linked by a tunnel. Most of the larger pitches are on the far side, so owners of high units would need to ask for a pitch on the main part of the site. There are outstanding leisure facilities. From the back gate there is a coastal cycle track and a forest path to the beach.

Facilities

Seven sanitary blocks provide washbasins in cubicles, controllable showers and facilities for children and disabled visitors. Washing machines and dryers. No motorcaravan services. Indoor (all season) and outdoor pools (July/Aug). Shop, bar, restaurant and takeaway (8/5-30/8). Play areas. Multisports court. Volleyball. Tennis. Minigolf. Miniclub. Bicycle hire. WiFi (charged).

Open: 8 May - 13 September.

Directions

Site is on D38 3 km. north of St Jean-de-Monts, halfway between St Jean-de-Monts and Notre-Dame-de-Monts, with the entrance on the western side of the road. GPS: 46.808533, -2.104467

Charges guide

Per unit incl. 2 persons and full services	€ 20.00 - € 35.70
extra person	€ 5.00

Saint Jean-de-Monts

Camping Caravaning le Bois Joly

46 route de Notre-Dame-de-Monts, B.P. 507, F-85165 Saint Jean-de-Monts (Vendée) T: 02 51 59 11 63.
E: info@camping-leboisjoly.com **alanrogers.com/FR85780**

This is an attractive, family run holiday site with indoor and outdoor pool complexes and 382 pitches, most of which are fully serviced. Over half are taken by mobile homes and chalets leaving 183 good sized, hedged pitches with 10A electricity hook-ups (2 pins) for touring units. Grassy and level, these are served by tarmac roads. A good family holiday location, there are lots of activities and entertainment in July and August. The indoor pool is open all season, the L-shaped outdoor pool complex has a menhirs theme and attractive flower beds. On site there are several small playgrounds for younger children, plus a very large and comprehensive adventure playground. The river behind the site offers opportunities for fishing and canoeing.

Facilities

Four clean modern sanitary blocks with controllable showers, washbasins in cubicles. Facilities for babies and disabled visitors. Laundry facilities. One block is heated for low season. Drive-over motorcaravan services. Bar, snack bar and takeaway (2/4-25/9). Indoor pool (all season). Outdoor pools (15/6-15/9). Playgrounds. Multisports court. Pétanque. TV room. Games room. Events, entertainment and canoeing on site (July/Aug). Children's clubs. River fishing. Safety deposit boxes. No charcoal barbecues allowed. No twin-axle caravans accepted. Bicycle hire. WiFi throughout (charged).
Off site: Riding and tennis 500 m. Beach 1.5 km. Shops, restaurants and other services all within 2 km. Golf 2 km.

Open: 2 April - 25 September.

Directions

Site is at the northern end of St Jean-de-Monts, on the eastern side of the D38, 300 m. north of junction (roundabout) with D51. GPS: 46.79963, -2.07442

Charges guide

Per unit incl. 2 persons and electricity	€ 20.00 - € 34.00
extra person	€ 7.00 - € 9.00
child (5-12 yrs)	€ 1.00 - € 3.00
dog	€ 1.50 - € 3.00

Saint Jean-de-Monts

Camping Zagarella

Route des Sables, F-85160 Saint Jean-de-Monts (Vendée) T: 02 51 58 19 82. E: zagarella@zagarella.fr
alanrogers.com/FR85940

Camping Zagarella is an ideal site for happy family holidays, with many facilities for children of all ages. A family run site, the management and staff are very friendly and do all they can to ensure everyone has a good time. There are 301 pitches with just 25 used for touring units, all with electricity (10A), water and waste water. These vary in size and shape but are mainly level and grassy and divided by shrubs. Some areas of the site are heavily wooded but there are more open parts for sun lovers. There are three tour operators here which leads to a nice mix of nationalities. The site has both indoor and outdoor heated swimming pools with a water chute and slides and the play areas provided for younger children are very well equipped. Children's clubs and family entertainment are organised in high season.

Facilities

Two modern, unheated toilet blocks are clean and well maintained. Both contain good facilities for disabled visitors and baby baths. An additional block is rather dated. Laundry. Bar, snack bar and takeaway (12/4-13/9). Small shop. Heated indoor pool (all season). Heated outdoor pool (15/5-13/9). Play area. Bouncy castle. Games room. Club for children (high season). Tennis. Multisports court. Bicycle hire. Only gas barbecues are permitted. Free WiFi in bar. Off site: Supermarket 1 km. Riding 1.5 km. Fishing and beach 3 km. Golf 3.5 km.

Open: 11 April - 13 September.

Directions

Travelling south on the D38 St Jean-de-Monts-St Gilles road. 4 km. south of St Jean keep a sharp look out for a blue site sign on the right. Turn right and site is on the right. GPS: 46.781389, -2.018056

Charges guide

Per unit incl. 2 persons and electricity	€ 21.50 - € 33.40
extra person	€ 6.40 - € 7.00
child (under 5 yrs)	€ 4.10 - € 4.80
dog	€ 3.60 - € 5.00

Saint Jean-de-Monts

Campéole Plage des Tonnelles

18 route de la Tonnelle, B.P. 10115, F-85161 Saint Jean-de-Monts (Vendée) T: 02 51 58 81 16.

E: plage-tonnelles@campeole.com **alanrogers.com/FR85960**

Le Campéole Plage des Tonnelles is an extensive site (25 hectares) located on land belonging to the French forestry commission and close to the popular resort of Saint Jean-de-Monts. The site has direct access to a superb sandy beach and is divided by a road. It also has a good sized heated swimming pool. The 229 touring pitches, all with electricity (6A), are mostly sandy and of a reasonable size. A few are on uneven ground. A range of chalets, fully equipped bungalow tents and mobile homes are available for rent. The site has a small bar and snack bar (open in July and August) just along the road.

Facilities

Four sanitary blocks, two recently refurbished to a very high standard with modern preset showers, washbasins in cubicles and excellent facilities for children and disabled visitors. Laundry. Motorcaravan services. Bar, snack bar and takeaway (July/Aug). Heated swimming and paddling pools (1/6-13/9, supervised July/Aug). Archery (July/Aug). Multisports court. Minigolf. Trampoline. Bouncy castle. Play area. Bicycle hire. WiFi (charged) in reception.

Open: 3 April - 13 September.

Directions

The site is 6 km. north of St Jean-de-Monts on D38 towards Notre Dame-de-Monts. Turn west at roundabout at Les Tonnelles where site is signed and on right in 300 m. GPS: 46.8094, -2.1208

Charges guide

Per unit incl. 2 persons and electricity	€ 18.20 - € 30.70
extra person	€ 4.70 - € 7.80

Saint Jean-de-Monts

Campéole les Sirènes

71 avenue des Demoiselles, B.P. 427, F-85164 Saint Jean-de-Monts (Vendée) T: 02 51 58 01 31.

E: sirenes@campeole.com **alanrogers.com/FR85970**

Les Sirènes is a large campsite located in the forest behind the popular resort of Saint Jean-de-Monts. The nearest beach, just 700 m. away, is long and sandy, shelving very gradually into the sea. The 338 touring pitches vary considerably in size and level; some, ideal for tents, are among the tall pine trees, whilst others are on flat ground but still have shade provided by a variety of younger trees (190 have 6-10A electrical connections – long leads required on some – and water taps nearby). Fully equipped tents and mobile homes (with specially adapted models for disabled visitors) are for rent.

Facilities

Several small sanitary blocks serve the different parts of the site (only main block open in low season). They are fairly basic but a programme of refurbishment has begun. Some modern preset showers and mainly open style washbasins (a few in cabins) with only cold water. Washing machines and dryers. Shop, bar and takeaway (July/Aug). Heated outdoor swimming pools with paddling pool (1/6-11/9, supervised July/Aug). Multisports pitch. Bicycle hire. Bouncy castle. Archery. Play area. Children's and teens' clubs (July/Aug). WiFi by reception (charged).

Open: 1 April - 30 September.

Directions

From southern end of D38/D38bis St Jean bypass turn north on D38 Route des Sables towards town. At next roundabout go left on D123 Avenue Valentin, (La Plage). Right at 2nd roundabout, after 1.2 km. right at roundabout along Ave des Mimosas into Ave des Demoiselles. Site on right in 400 m. GPS: 46.780083, -2.055881

Charges guide

Per unit incl. 2 persons and electricity	€ 18.20 - € 30.70
extra person	€ 4.10 - € 8.20

Saint Julien-des-Landes

Castel Camping la Garangeoire

Route de la Chapelle-Hermier, F-85150 Saint Julien-des-Landes (Vendée) T: 02 51 46 65 39.

E: info@garangeoire.com **alanrogers.com/FR85040**

La Garangeoire is a stunning campsite that celebrated its 50th anniversary in 2014 and is situated some 15 km. inland, near the village of Saint Julien-des-Landes. Set in 200 hectares of parkland surrounding the small château of la Garangeoire, of which there is an outstanding view as you approach through the gates. With a spacious, relaxed atmosphere, the main camping areas are on either side of the old road which is edged with mature trees. The 356 pitches (153 for touring), all named rather than numbered, are individually hedged, some with shade. They are well spaced and large (150-200 sq.m), 100 have electricity (16A, Europlug), 45 have water and drainage also, and four have a private WC facility.

Facilities

Ample, first class sanitary facilities. All have washbasins in cabins and showers. Facilities for babies and disabled visitors. Laundry facilities. Motorcaravan services. Shop, restaurant and takeaway (8/5-18/9). Pool complex and children's pool. Multisports court. Bicycle hire. Minigolf. Archery (July/Aug). Riding (July/Aug). Fishing and boating. Bouncy castle. Trampolines. Children's clubs (4-12 yrs).

Open: 18 April - 20 September.

Directions

Site is signed from St Julien; entrance is to the east off the D21 road, 2.5 km. north of St Julien-des-Landes. GPS: 46.663648, -1.713395

Charges guide

Per unit incl. 2 persons and electricity	€ 19.75 - € 41.50
extra person	€ 5.05 - € 8.70

Saint Julien-des-Landes

Village de la Guyonnière

La Guyonnière, F-85150 Saint Julien-des-Landes (Vendée) T: 02 51 46 62 59. E: info@laguyonniere.com
alanrogers.com/FR85260

La Guyonnière is a spacious (30 hectare) rural site. It is Dutch owned but English is spoken and all visitors are made very welcome. The pitches are arranged on eight different fields, each one reasonably level. There are 298 mostly large pitches (225 sq.m) with a mix of sun and shade and large units are welcome. Some are open, others are separated by a tree and a few bushes. All have access to electricity connections (10A, Europlug) and 117 are occupied by mobile homes and chalets. The pool complex includes an outdoor pool with a wild water river and a heated indoor pool with a waterfall. Bar and restaurant facilities are housed in original farm buildings, attractively converted. Evening entertainment is provided in high season. This is a perfect place for families, with large play areas on sand and grass, and a paddling pond with shower. There are no tour operators and, needless to say, no road noise. This site is popular for many reasons, the main one being the relaxed atmosphere.

Facilities

Five toilet blocks (two open in low season and recently upgraded) provide washbasins in cubicles and hot showers. Provision for children and disabled visitors. Laundry facilities. Motorcaravan service point. Shop, bar with TV and pool table, pizzeria with takeaway (all season). Restaurant (15/6-13/9). Pool complex with outdoor pool (all season) and wild water river and covered pool (all season) with waterfall and disability lift. Paddling pool. Wellness facility. Play areas. Sand pit. Tennis. Multisports pitch. Bicycle hire. WiFi throughout (charged). Off site: Riding 3 km. Golf 8 km. Beaches 10 km.

Open: 25 April - 13 September.

Directions

Site is signed off the D12 road (La Mothe Achard-St Gilles-Croix-de-Vie), 4 km. west of St Julien-des-Landes. The site is 1 km. from the main road. GPS: 46.65273, -1.74987

Charges guide

Per unit incl. 2 persons and electricity	€ 21.00 - € 39.00
extra person	€ 10.00
child (3-12 yrs)	€ 8.00
dog	€ 4.00

Camping Cheques accepted.

Saint Julien-des-Landes

Yelloh! Village Château La Forêt

3 Rue de La Forêt, Route de Martinet, F-85150 Saint Julien-des-Landes (Vendée) T: 02 51 46 62 11.
E: camping@chateaulaforet.com **alanrogers.com/FR85820**

Set in the tranquil and beautiful natural parkland surrounding a 19th-century château, this lovely site has 266 large pitches, of which 161 are for touring units. There are also 30 units for rent and 60 pitches are occupied by tour operators. All are on grass and fully serviced including 10A electricity; some are in shady woodland and others, for sun worshippers, are more open. The camping area is only a small part of the 50-hectare estate with a mix of woodland, open meadows and fishing lakes, all accessible to campers. The many outbuildings around the courtyard have been tastefully converted and include a bar and restaurant in the old stables. Children will have a great time here exploring the vast, unrestricted area and sometimes hidden corners of this site in Swallows and Amazons style. However, parents should note there are open, unfenced fishing lakes and barns with tractors and machinery. The attractive small village with shops and services is within walking distance.

Facilities

Three sanitary blocks are newly refurbished and include washbasins in cubicles, with good provision for babies and disabled campers. No motorcaravan service point. Laundry facilities with washing machines and dryers. Shop, bar, small restaurant and takeaway (all season). Two swimming pools, one outdoor (1/6-31/8), one heated and covered with children's pool and slide (all season). Play area. Regular evening entertainment, children's clubs and disco (July/Aug). Large adventure playground (charged). Trampoline. Games room. Tennis. Boules. Fishing lakes. 6-hole swing golf course (pitch and putt with soft balls) and minigolf. Canoeing trips. Bicycle hire. Free WiFi. Bubble room for hire (includes breakfast). Only gas barbecues permitted. No twin-axle caravans. Off site: Equestrian centre. Surf school. Puy du Fou.

Open: 28 April - 3 September.

Directions

St Julien-des-Landes is 25 km. west of La Roche-sur-Yon, northwest of La Mothe-Achard. From La Mothe-Achard take D12 to St Julien, turn northeast on D55 at crossroads towards Martinet. Site is on left almost immediately (signed). GPS: 46.6432, -1.71198

Charges guide

Per unit incl. 2 persons and electricity	€ 15.00 - € 41.00
extra person	€ 5.00 - € 7.00
child (3-6 yrs)	free - € 6.00
dog	€ 5.00

Saint Julien-des-Landes

Flower Camping la Bretonnière

La Bretonnière, F-85150 Saint Julien-des-Landes (Vendée) T: 02 51 46 62 44.
E: info@la-bretonniere.com **alanrogers.com/FR85850**

An attractive, modern site on a family farm surrounded by beautiful, peaceful countryside, this site is sure to please. With 165 pitches in an area of six hectares, there is plenty of space for everyone. There are 101 touring pitches, eight tents, eighteen mobile homes and 20 alpine-style chalets, spread around several fields, some quite open, others with some shade from perimeter hedges. The grassy pitches are all of a really generous size with 12/16A electricity (Europlug, long leads may be required). Two swimming pools, both covered, are surrounded by a pleasant terrace, with the bar and reception nearby.

Facilities

Four modern, clean and well appointed toilet blocks with baby rooms and facilities for disabled visitors at 2 blocks (may not be open April/May). Motorcaravan services. Small shop, bar, snack bar and takeaway (July/Aug). Two covered swimming pools and play pool for children. Wellness. Playgrounds. Games/TV room. Tennis. Boules. Basketball. Volleyball. Indoor and outdoor football pitches. Fishing lake. Bicycle hire. WiFi (free by bar and reception).

Open: 9 April - 30 September.

Directions

From La Mothe-Achard take D12 west towards Bretignolles-sur-Mer, pass through St Julien and after 2 km. take first turn right (site signed). Site is 500 m. GPS: 46.64463, -1.73328

Charges guide

Per unit incl. 2 persons and electricity	€ 17.00 - € 32.00
extra person	€ 3.50 - € 6.00
child (3-7 yrs)	€ 2.50 - € 5.00

Saint Laurent-sur-Sèvre

Camping le Rouge Gorge

Route de la Verrie, F-85290 Saint Laurent-sur-Sèvre (Vendée) T: 02 51 67 86 39.
E: campinglerougegorge@wanadoo.fr **alanrogers.com/FR85890**

A family run site, le Rouge Gorge has 72 touring pitches, plus some units for rent and privately owned caravans and chalets. The site does accept a small number of workers' units. Slightly sloping and undulating pitches are on grass in a garden-like setting and a small wildlife pond (fenced) is in the centre of the site. It would make a suitable base from which to visit the spectacles of Puy de Fou and the steam railway which runs from Mortagne-sur-Sèvre to Les Herbiers. This is also an excellent stopover for those heading to and from southern France and Spain, or the ski-resorts.

Facilities

Two toilet blocks (one heated and open in low season), with washbasins in cubicles and facilities for disabled visitors and babies. Laundry facilities. No motorcaravan services or chemical disposal. Bar and shop (bread and basics, July/Aug). Snack bar and takeaway (15/6-15/9). Breakfast service (order day before). Heated swimming pool (8/5-23/9). Miniclub and some evening entertainment (July/Aug). Boules. Playground. TV room. Free WiFi on part of site. Twin-axle caravans should book in advance.

Open: 1 March - 25 October.

Directions

St Laurent-sur-Sèvre is 10 km. due south of Cholet, just south of the N149. Site is on D111 west of town towards la Verrie, entrance at top of hill on right. GPS: 46.95781, -0.90309

Charges guide

Per unit incl. 2 persons and electricity	€ 18.00 - € 23.10
extra person	€ 3.90 - € 4.50
child (2-9 yrs)	€ 2.50 - € 3.10

Saint Michel-en-l'Herm

Camping la Dive

12 route de la Mer, F-85580 Saint Michel-en-l'Herm (Vendée) T: 02 51 30 26 94.
E: contact@camping-la-dive.com **alanrogers.com/FR85013**

Camping la Dive can be found south of the popular resort of La Tranche-sur-Mer, close to the broad, sweeping bay of l'Aiguillon-sur-Mer. The nine-hectare site is located on the edge of the pleasant village of Saint Michel-en-l'Herm. The beach can be accessed in around five minutes by car. The 125 touring pitches here are of average to large in size, grassy, part shaded and have 6A electricity. A wide range of mobile homes, chalets, roulottes and tents are available for rent in a new area of the site. On-site amenities include an outdoor swimming pool complex with slides, flume, sauna and jacuzzi, minigolf and pony rides. There is a good range of shops in the village (500 m).

Facilities

Three toilet blocks have facilities for children and disabled visitors. Laundry. Bar, restaurant and takeaway (1/5-30/8). Outdoor swimming and paddling pools. Jacuzzi. Sauna. Gym. Small games room. Bouncy castles. Multisports pitch. Boules. Bicycle hire. Pony rides. Minigolf. Children's farm. Play area. Entertainment and activity programme (July/Aug). No electric barbecues. WiFi over site (charged). Off site: Weekly market (Thu). Beach five minutes' drive.

Open: 1 April - 30 September.

Directions

St Michel-en-l'Herm is 8 km. east of l'Aiguillon-sur-Mer. From there, head east on D746. Site is 500 m. from village centre and well signed. Beware of tight right hand turn into site. GPS: 46.34912, -1.24786

Charges guide

Per unit incl. 2 persons and electricity	€ 19.50 - € 30.00
extra person	€ 4.90 - € 6.00

Saint Révérend

Camping le Pont Rouge

Rue Clémenceau, F-85220 Saint Révérend (Vendée) T: 02 51 54 68 50. E: camping.pontrouge@wanadoo.fr
alanrogers.com/FR85660

This small, tranquil site is situated down a short tree-lined lane just 600 metres from a small village. It is suitable for people who prefer to be away from the nearby coastal resorts. The pitches are on grass and vary in shape and size (80-100 sq.m). Most are near mature trees giving ample shade and are separated by tall hedges, some flowering, ensuring peace and privacy. The 42 mobile homes are away from the 31 touring pitches, in an open sunny aspect. All pitches have electricity (6A) but long leads may be required on some. Ample water points are situated close to all pitches. The site is not suitable for American motorhomes or twin-axle caravans.

Facilities

Two unheated toilet blocks, one by reception building with separate facilities for ladies and gents. The second block has separate showers and washbasins in cubicles with unisex WCs and facilities for babies and disabled visitors. Laundry room. Very small shop and small bar with TV (July/Aug). Snack bar and takeaway (15/6-15/9). Small, fenced pool complex with separate children's pool and slide. Play area. Badminton. Boules. Games room. No charcoal barbecues. WiFi on part of site (charged).

Open: 4 April - 26 September.

Directions

From D6 Aizenay to St Gilles-Croix-de-Vie turn north onto D94 St Révérend 4 km. west of Coëx. Site on left in 400 m. GPS: 46.69651, -1.83345

Charges guide

Per unit incl. 2 persons and electricity	€ 15.00 - € 24.00
extra person	€ 4.00 - € 5.00
child (1-13 yrs)	€ 3.00 - € 4.00

Saint Valérien

Village des Rulières

185 route de Ligne, le Pré des Rulières, F-85570 Saint Valérien (Vendée) T: 02 51 28 00 28.
E: f.lesrulieres@club-internet.fr **alanrogers.com/FR85135**

Developed adjacent to two large fishing lakes, les Rulières is a compact and peaceful site at the heart of the Vendée region, close to the Marais Poitevin. There are 25 modern chalets to rent and just seven very large, grassy pitches for tourers, all with water and electricity (10A) nearby, though a long lead may be needed on some. It is a great retreat for anglers, and for those who enjoy walking and cycling as there is an extensive and expanding network of waymarked paths in the area. The coast is around 30 km. away, while La Rochelle and the Ile de Ré are also an easy drive.

Facilities

Small basic toilet block with pushbutton showers and washbasins in cubicles. Washing machine. Heated swimming pool with retractable roof. Bread van calls. Private fishing lake (€ 5/day, € 15/week). In high season: activities organised for children on demand; welcome drink Saturdays; weekly themed family meal with music and entertainment and carriage rides for children pulled by Coquette, one of the site's donkeys (charged). Small playground (2-5 yrs). WiFi throughout (charged).

Open: 1 May - 30 September.

Directions

St Valérien is 50 km. northwest of Niort. From A83 leave at exit 8 (Fontenay-le-Comte), go north on D206 then west on D148 (Ste Hermine). In Pouill turn north on D104/D99 to St Valérien. Site is off D52, 1.5 km. north of village. GPS: 46.54199, -0.95953

Charges guide

Per unit incl. 2 persons and electricity	€ 16.00 - € 23.00
extra person	€ 6.00
child (under 4 yrs)	€ 4.00

Saint Vincent-sur-Jard

Chadotel Camping la Bolée d'Air

Route de Bouil, F-85520 Saint Vincent-sur-Jard (Vendée) T: 02 51 90 36 05. E: info@chadotel.com
alanrogers.com/FR85430

This is a well managed site with good facilities and a varied programme of high season entertainment, just 900 m. away from a sandy beach. The 120 touring pitches are all level and well grassed on sandy soil. Many are situated around the perimeter and separated by hedges giving good privacy but little shade. Long electricity cables may be required on some. The main road runs along one side of the site, which may result in traffic noise at busy times. The site is used by two small tour operators.

Facilities

Two modernised, unisex toilet blocks provide washbasins in cabins and facilities for children and disabled visitors. Washing machine and dryer. Shop with takeaway (1/6-31/8). Bar (1/6-19/9). Heated indoor and outdoor (1/6-19/9) pools with slide, jacuzzi and paddling pool. Tennis. Minigolf. Bicycle hire. Boules. Good all-weather, multisports terrain. WiFi (charged). Off site: Beach 900 m.

Open: 3 April - 19 September.

Directions

Site is just off the D21 Les Sables-La Tranche road, just east of St Vincent-sur-Jard and is well signed from the main road. GPS: 46.41839, -1.52791

Charges guide

Per unit incl. 2 persons and electricity	€ 15.50 - € 32.00
extra person	€ 6.00
child (2-13 yrs)	€ 4.00

Saint-Vincent-sur-Jard

Camping la Mouette Cendrée

Les Malécots, F-85520 Saint-Vincent-sur-Jard (Vendée) T: 02 51 33 59 04. E: camping.mc@orange.fr

alanrogers.com/FR85275

La Mouette Cendrée is a green site surrounded by mature trees and farmland but conveniently close to a main road. It is ideally situated on the Atlantic Coast for the beach and close to pretty seaside villages. The owners aim to create a peaceful and friendly atmosphere at this small and simple site. The 101 grassy, flat pitches are of 70/110 sq.m. and are separated by a mixture of tall and low hedges with 10A electricity available throughout. A special entertainment area is where paella, moules-frites and disco nights are held in high season. There is a pleasant pool area with a heated outdoor pool, a paddling pool and a fun water slide. It is an attractive, small family-run site with a convivial vibe.

Facilities

The unheated toilet block is well equipped and includes washbasins and showers in cubicles. Facilities for disabled visitors. Washing machines. Bread to order. Swimming pool, paddling pool and slide. Entertainment evenings (July/Aug)). Multisports pitch. Boules. Bicycle hire (July/Aug). No charcoal barbecues. WiFi by reception (free). Off site: Supermarket 800 m. Beach 1.5 km.

Open: 1 April - 31 October.

Directions

Site is signed from D21 between Talmont-St-Hilaire and La Tranche-sur-Mer, 1 km. from St Vincent-sur-Jard town centre. GPS: 46.425412, -1.565718

Charges guide

Per unit incl. 2 persons and electricity	€ 21.50 - € 29.50
extra person	€ 5.00

Talmont-Saint-Hilaire

Yelloh! Village le Littoral

Le Porteau, F-85440 Talmont-Saint-Hilaire (Vendée) T: 02 51 22 04 64. E: info@campinglelittoral.com

alanrogers.com/FR85250

One hundred metres from the sea, five minutes from Les Sables-d'Olonne, le Littoral is situated on the south Vendée coast. It has been fully modernised over recent years by the Boursin family. The site's 460 pitches are mainly used for mobile homes and chalets, but there are 90 touring pitches, hedged, of a good size and all with water, electricity (10A) and drainage. The site has a heated pool complex with outdoor and indoor pools. The mini-market, bar and restaurant are open all season with frequent themed evenings and lots of entertainment and activities in high season.

Facilities

Two sanitary blocks have both British and Turkish style WCs, showers and washbasins in cubicles. Baby rooms. Facilities for disabled visitors. Laundry facilities. Fridge hire. Shop, bar, restaurant and takeaway, pizzeria and crêperie, outdoor pool complex with slides, indoor pool (all open all season). Bicycle hire. Multisports court. Good play areas. TV/games room. Miniclub (all season), teens club (July/Aug). Bicycle hire. WiFi (free at bar). Free shuttle to beach and town (July/Aug). Accommodation to rent.

Open: 15 April - 11 September.

Directions

From Les Sables or Talmont, follow signs for 'Aquarium 7ème continent'. The site is beside the next roundabout after the aquarium. GPS: 46.451633, -1.702017

Charges guide

Per unit incl. 2 persons and electricity	€ 18.00 - € 49.00
extra person	€ 6.00 - € 7.00
child (3-6 yrs)	free - € 6.00

Talmont-Saint-Hilaire

Camping Loyada

Avenue de l'Atlantique, F-85440 Talmont-Saint-Hilaire (Vendée) T: 02 51 21 28 10.
E: contact@camping-loyada.fr **alanrogers.com/FR85920**

Camping Loyada is a spacious family campsite covering five hectares with 226 grassy pitches, most of which are used for accommodation to rent. The 35 touring pitches are scattered among the mobiles and separated by hedges; all have electricity (10A) and drainage, with water taps nearby. The enthusiastic and friendly owners are working hard to maintain the excellent standards and to create a family holiday atmosphere. There are beaches within four to five kilometres, including the very pleasant beach of Le Veillon, which is situated between dunes and forest. The nearby village of Talmont-Saint-Hilaire has a castle and a few shops, bars and restaurants.

Facilities

Two modern toilet blocks with all the necessary facilities, including those for disabled visitors, a baby room and a WC and shower for children. Washing machines. Shop (April-Sept). Bar, snack bar and takeaway (July/Aug). Indoor heated swimming pool. Outdoor pool (heated 15/6-15/9). TV room. Playground. Miniclub (July/Aug). Bicycle hire. WiFi over site (charged).

Open: 1 April - 15 October.

Directions

Talmont-St Hilaire is 100 km. west of Niort. From A10 at Niort take A83 (Nantes), then exit 7 (Ste Hermine) towards Luçon and Talmont-St Hilaire. Bypass village, then turn back and follow signs for Port Bourgenay. GPS: 46.465838, -1.652852

Charges guide

Per unit incl. 2 persons and electricity	€ 15.00 - € 29.50

alan rogers

On the move? Take your guides

You'll find them here...

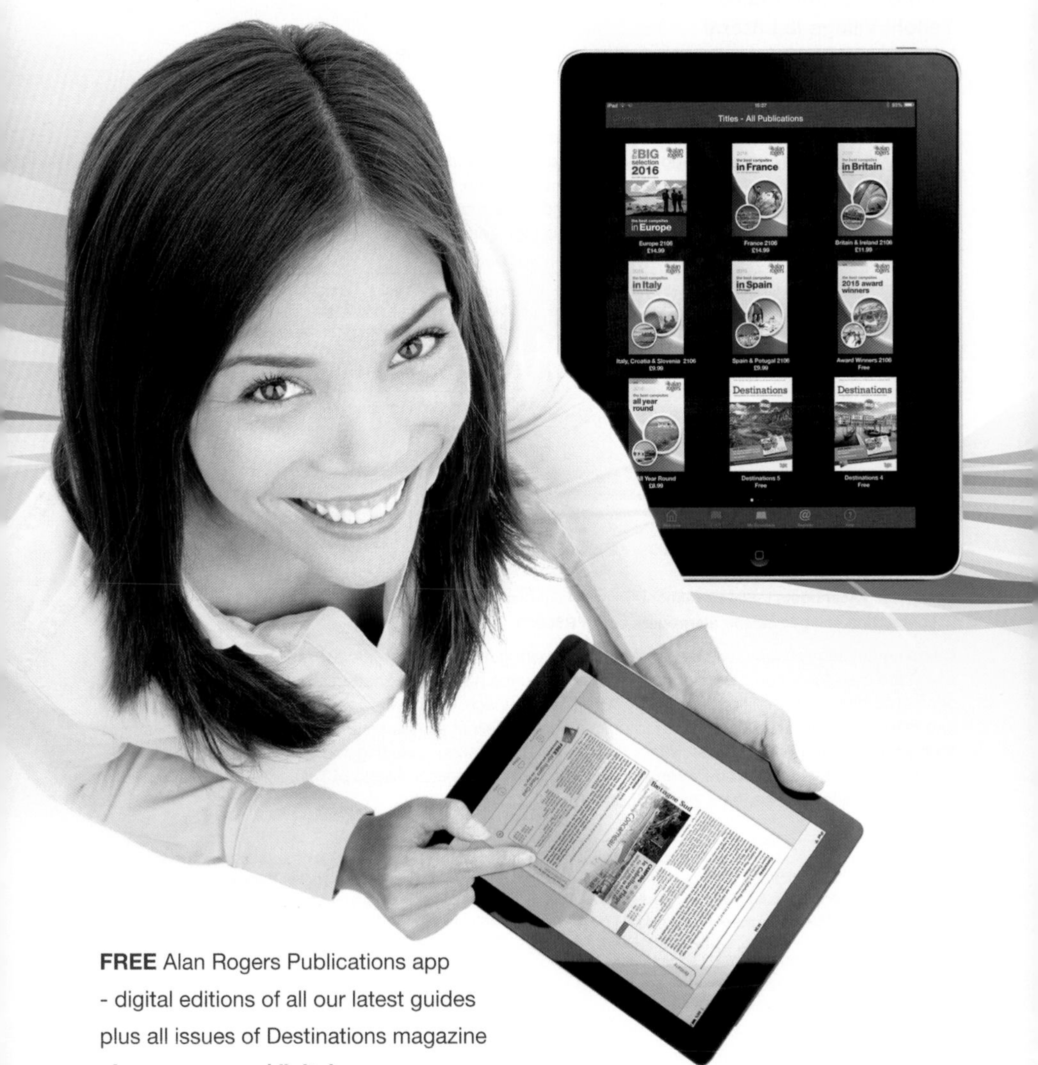

FREE Alan Rogers Publications app
- digital editions of all our latest guides
plus all issues of Destinations magazine
alanrogers.com/digital

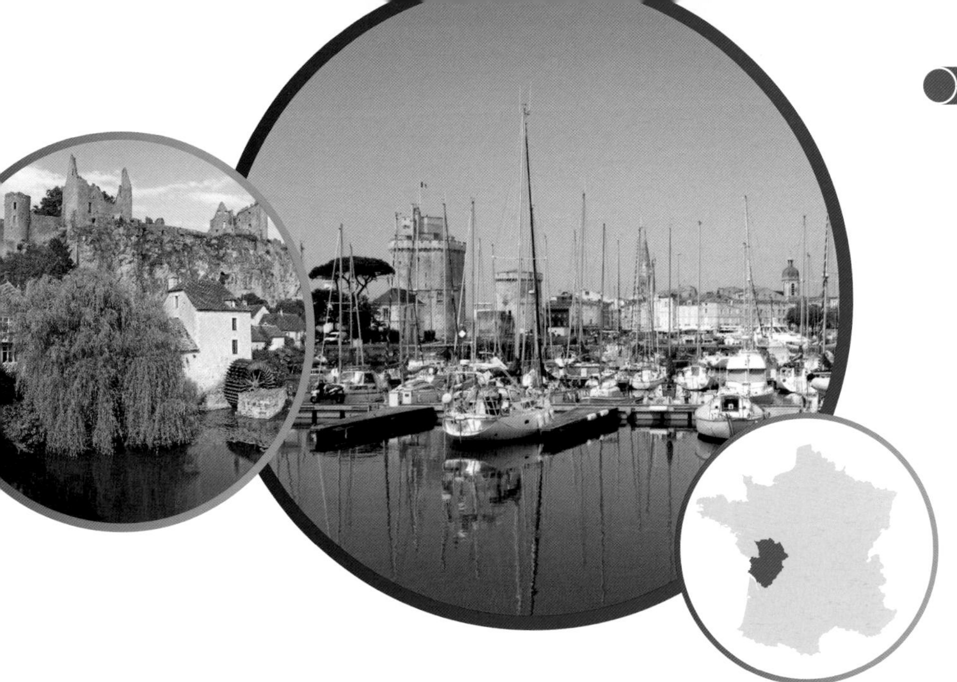

DÉPARTEMENTS: 16 CHARENTE, 17 CHARENTE-MARITIME, 79 DEUX SÈVRES, 86 VIENNE

MAJOR CITIES: POITIERS, LA ROCHELLE, COGNAC

On the Atlantic coast, between the châteaux of the Loire Valley and the Bordeaux vineyards, lies Poitou-Charentes, one of the sunniest parts of the French western coast. Its mild climate, with 2,250 hours of sunshine per year, makes it popular with visitors from early spring to late autumn.

The Poitou-Charentes region was formed as recently as 1956 and comprises the central section of the Atlantic coast, with undulating inland regions extending to the foothills of the Massif Central. It is the sunniest area of France outside the Mediterranean, and with miles of beautiful, sandy beaches and bustling resorts such as Royan and La Rochelle, it is a magnet for holidaymakers and sailing enthusiasts.

In the south, the area around Cognac is home to extensive vineyards that produce the grapes for the famous brandy and for the local apéritif, Pineau des Charentes. The familiar names of Rémy Martin, Hennessy and Martell can be seen above the distilleries that line the River Charente.

The region's capital, Poitiers, is one of France's oldest cities and sits on a hilltop overlooking the River Clain. Its historic centre has a wealth of Romanesque art and ancient buildings. In complete contrast, the technological theme park, Futuroscope, is just 8 km. away and with some 3 million visitors annually is among the top 20 visitor attractions in France.

Places of interest

Angoulême: hilltop town surrounded by ramparts, cathedral, Renaissance château.

Cognac: the most celebrated 'eau de vie' in the world; cellars; Valois castle.

Marais Poitevin: marshes also known as the 'Green Venice'.

Poitiers: Palais de Justice; Notre Dame la Grande Romanesque church; old city.

La Rochelle: port; Porte de la Grosse Horloge (clock gate); Museum of the New World.

Saint Savin: 17th-century abbey; mural painting.

Cuisine of the region

Fish predominates, both fresh water (eel, trout, pike) and sea water (shrimps, mussels, oysters).

Bouilliture (bouilleture): eel stew with shallots and prunes in Sauvignon white wine.

Boulaigou: thick sweet or savoury pancake.

Bréjaude: cabbage, leek and bacon soup.

Cagouilles: snails from Charente.

Casserons en matelote: squid in red wine sauce with garlic and shallots.

Farcidure: a dumpling (poached or sautéed).

Farci Poitevin: paté of cabbage, spinach and sorrel, encased in cabbage leaves.

Tourteau Fromage: cake baked with sugar, eggs, flour and goat's cheese and having a unique caramelised top.

www.visit-poitou-charentes.com
crt@poitou-charentes-vacances.com
(0)5 49 50 10 50

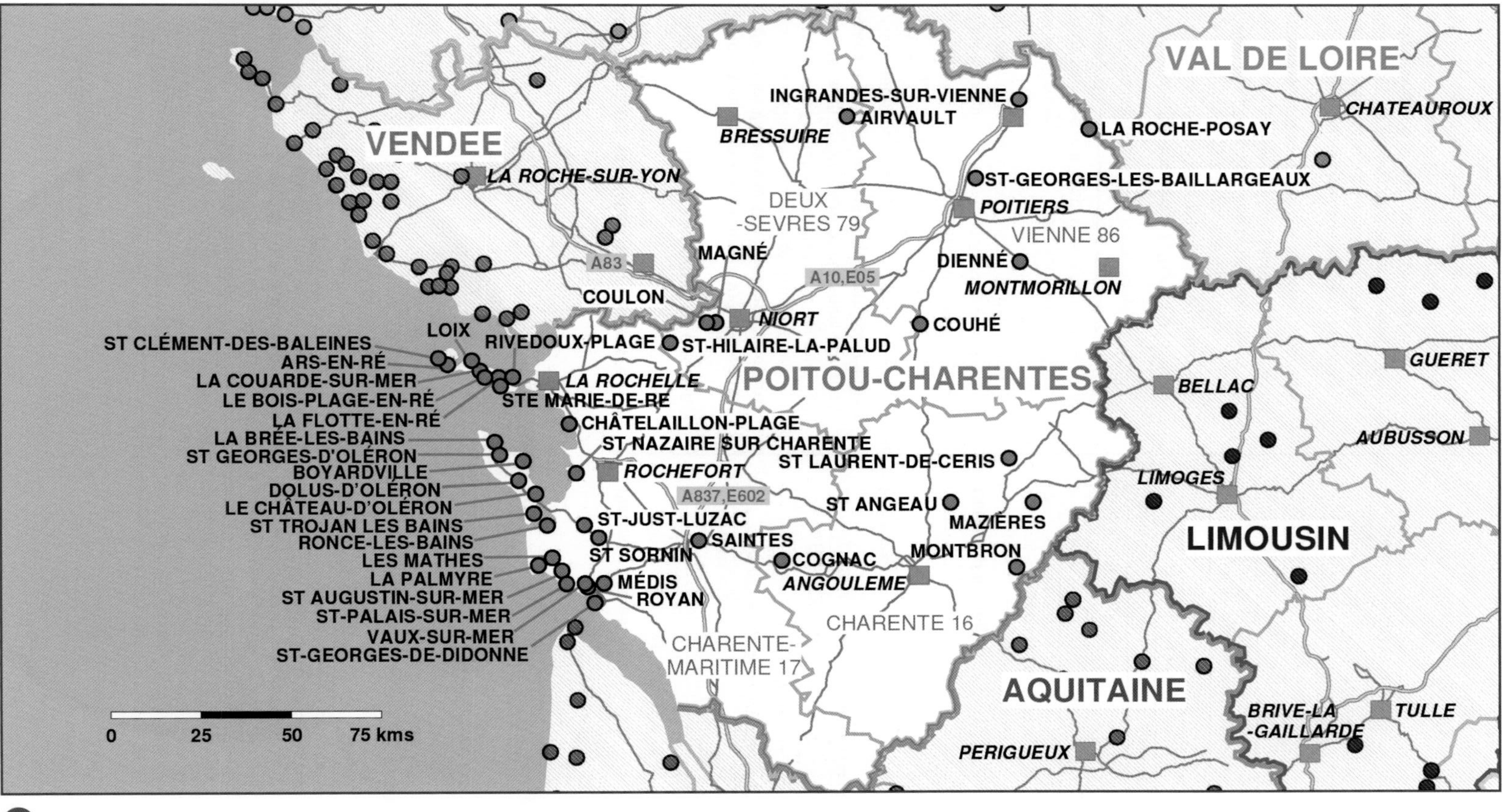

For latest campsite news, availability and prices visit
alanrogers.com

Ars-en-Ré

Camping le Cormoran

Route de Radia, F-17590 Ars-en-Ré (Charente-Maritime) T: 05 46 29 46 04. E: info@cormoran.com

alanrogers.com/FR17260

On the outskirts of Ars-en-Ré, le Cormoran offers a quiet rural holiday. There are 91 mobile homes, many for hire, and 27 pitches of varying sizes for touring units (all with 10A electricity). A lovely new bar/restaurant serves imaginative meals and takeaway dishes all season. Being just 500 m. from a sandy beach, close to the local oyster beds and with numerous cycle paths that include routes through a nature reserve, this campsite is popular with families of all ages. The village church can be seen from miles around, so much so that the spire is painted white with a black apex as an aid to navigation for shipping. This western end of the island is generally quiet and unspoilt, with some excellent sandy beaches, vineyards and salt marshes. At the furthest point is the Phare des Baleines, an historic monument dating back to 1854, surrounded by pleasant gardens with a museum and an older tower from 1682; the lighthouse is still fully operational and the views from the top can be well worth the climb.

Facilities

The two toilet blocks provide excellent facilities for babies, young children and disabled visitors. Laundry. Motorcaravan services. Bar, restaurant and takeaway meals (all season). Heated swimming pool and terrace with paddling pools, spa pools and jacuzzi. Sauna and Hammam. Fitness centre. Tennis. Games room. Play areas and bouncy castle. Multisports court. Boules. Children's entertainment and family activities (July/Aug). Bicycle hire. No charcoal barbecues. WiFi throughout (free). Off site: Nearest beach and fishing 500 m. Ars-en-Ré 800 m. Boat launching, sailing and riding 1 km. Golf 9 km.

Open: 3 April - 27 September.

Directions

Cross the toll bridge from La Rochelle onto the Ile de Ré and follow signs for Phare des Baleines via D201/D735 to Ars-en-Ré. Site is to west of village and is well signed from main road.
GPS: 46.21121, -1.5298

Charges guide

Per unit incl. 2 persons (3 in high season) and electricity	€ 24.65 - € 50.50
extra person	€ 5.90 - € 11.80
child (1-9 yrs)	€ 3.80 - € 11.80
dog	€ 2.95 - € 4.85

Airvault

Camping de Courte Vallée

8 rue de Courte Vallée, F-79600 Airvault (Deux-Sèvres) T: 05 49 64 70 65.
E: camping@caravanningfrance.com **alanrogers.com/FR79020**

Jane and James have recently taken ownership of this small, landscaped site set in ten acres of parkland, close to the small River Thouet. In the heart of rural France and off the main tourist tracks, the site offers tranquillity in surroundings maintained to the highest standards. It is only 15 minutes' walking distance from the small, medieval market town of Airvault (the birthplace of Voltaire). There are 65 level or slightly sloping grass pitches, all with electricity (13A), and five have water and drainage. They are separated by a variety of shrubs and tall trees offering some shade.

Facilities

A clean, modern and well maintained unisex block has spacious cubicles for showers and washbasins, and shower and WC cubicles for disabled visitors. A new block is planned for the 2016 season. Laundry facilities. Bar/coffee shop selling snacks and ice-cream (bread to order). Heated swimming pool (20/5-30/9). Boules. Play area. Free WiFi over site. Wine tasting and barbecues. Off site: Airvault (Sat. market) is a 10-15 minute walk.

Open: 1 March - 1 November.

Directions

From south on D938 (Parthenay-Thouars) take the D725 Airvault. Site is well signed, follow blue and white signs. Note: caravans are not allowed in village. From north on D938 use only D725 to Airvault. Ignore sat nav. GPS: 46.833056, -0.148333

Charges guide

Per unit incl. 2 persons
and electricity € 29.00 - € 33.00
extra person € 7.00 - € 8.00

Boyardville

Camping Signol

121 avenue des Albatros, F-17190 Boyardville (Charente-Maritime) T: 02 51 20 41 94.
E: contact@camp-atlantique.com **alanrogers.com/FR17600**

Occupying an eight-hectare site just 800 metres from the sandy beaches, and a short walk from the little port of Boyardville, this campsite has plenty to offer. Of the 340 pitches, just 52 are for touring, set amongst high pine trees, some occupying hillocks, others tucked away among mobile homes. The pitches vary in size and access to some is tight making them unsuitable for larger units. Levelling blocks may be required. Electricity (6A) is available to all, although long leads are sometimes required. There may be a short walk to the water supply.

Facilities

Three traditional, fully equipped toilet blocks provide washbasins in cubicles and preset showers. Basic facilities for disabled campers and for children. Laundry. Motorcaravan services. Shop, bar/snack bar, takeaway. Two heated swimming pools. Sauna, steam room and fitness room. Massage and beauty parlour. Play area. Children's club (July/Aug). Boules. Evening entertainment. WiFi over site (charged). Gas barbecues only on pitches. Mobile homes and chalets available to rent. Max. 1 dog. Off site: Fishing 500 m. Beach, sailing and windsurfing 800 m. Golf 2 km.

Open: 2 April - 25 September.

Directions

Cross the bridge to the Ile d'Oléron, continue on D26/D734 to Dolus and turn right on D126 signed Boyardville. Continue on this road for 7 km. until the canal bridge at the edge of the town. Cross bridge and turn immediately sharp right along the quayside. Site signed from here. GPS: 45.96807, -1.24456

Charges guide

Per unit incl. 2 persons
and electricity € 22.00 - € 39.00
extra person € 5.00 - € 9.00

Camping Cheques accepted.

Cognac

Camping de Cognac

Boulevard de Châtenay, route de Sainte Sévère, F-16100 Cognac (Charente) T: 05 45 32 13 32.
E: info@campingdecognac.com **alanrogers.com/FR16050**

Situated close to the historic town of Cognac, this municipal site is set in parkland beside the River Charente. It has 168 pitches, 160 for touring, all have 6A electricity (long leads required), ten have hardstanding and a water tap but no drainage. The pitches are separated by shrubs and some hedging, with a variety of trees giving varying amounts of shade. Access for large units is good, though twin-axle caravans are not accepted. There is some noise from the adjacent road. Public transport is available to the town centre (daily July/Aug; Saturdays at other times).

Facilities

Two well equipped, fairly modern toilet blocks (access by steps) include toilets for children, baby bath and washing machines. Ground level facilities for disabled visitors (key). Motorcaravan services. Small swimming pool (July/Aug). Small shop. Snack bar (July/Aug). Fishing. Play area on grass. Minigolf. WiFi throughout. Off site: Bicycle hire 1 km. Restaurants, bars and shops in the town (2.3 km).

Open: 4 May - 22 September.

Directions

Site is 2.4 km. northwest of the town on the D24 to Ste Sévère just after crossing the river. GPS: 45.70916, -0.31289

Charges guide

Per unit incl. 2 persons
and electricity € 18.40 - € 21.40
extra person € 5.00 - € 6.00

Châtelaillon-Plage

Camping Au Port-Punay

Allée Bernard Moreau, Les Boucholeurs, F-17340 Châtelaillon-Plage (Charente-Maritime) T: 05 17 81 00 00.
E: contact@camping-port-punay.com **alanrogers.com/FR17340**

Au Port-Punay is a friendly, well run site that celebrated its 50th anniversary in 2014. It is just 200 metres from the beach and 3 km. from the centre of the resort of Châtelaillon-Plage. There are 115 touring pitches laid out on well trimmed grass, with many mature poplars and low shrubs. The site has a well stocked shop, open all season, and a small bar and restaurant open mid June-mid September. A heated swimming pool has a separate gated area for paddling. A good range of activities is available and in high season some entertainment is arranged. This is a family run site (Famille Moreau) and the son of the family speaks excellent English, as does his wife, Angelique. Rochefort to the south and La Rochelle to the north are well worth a visit (buses from outside the site), as is the nearby town of Châtelaillon-Plage, which has an all-year covered market and, in summer, a street market every day. Au Port-Punay has just one large toilet block, centrally positioned on the site, with very good facilities.

Facilities

One large toilet block with good facilities including washbasins in cubicles and large shower cubicles. Facilities for babies and disabled visitors. Washing machines and dryers. Motorcaravan services. Shop. Bar, restaurant and takeaway (18/6-11/9). Swimming pool (heated May-Sept). Fitness equipment. Games area. Play area. Bicycle hire. WiFi over site (charged). Off site: Buses to Rochefort and La Rochelle from outside site. Beach 200 m. Food market in village. Châtelaillon-Plage 1.5 km. along the seafront on foot or bike, 3 km. by road. Riding 2 km. Golf 10 km.

Open: 2 May - 25 September.

Directions

From N137 (La Rochelle-Rochefort) take the exit for Châtelaillon-Plage. At first roundabout follow sign for town centre. At second roundabout turn left. Follow signs to site at seaside hamlet of Les Boucholeurs. Drive to the sea wall then turn left through village to site. GPS: 46.05480, -1.08340

Charges guide

Per unit incl. 2 persons and electricity	€ 23.50 - € 33.50
extra person	€ 5.50 - € 6.50
child (2-7 yrs)	€ 4.00 - € 5.00
dog	€ 2.50 - € 3.00

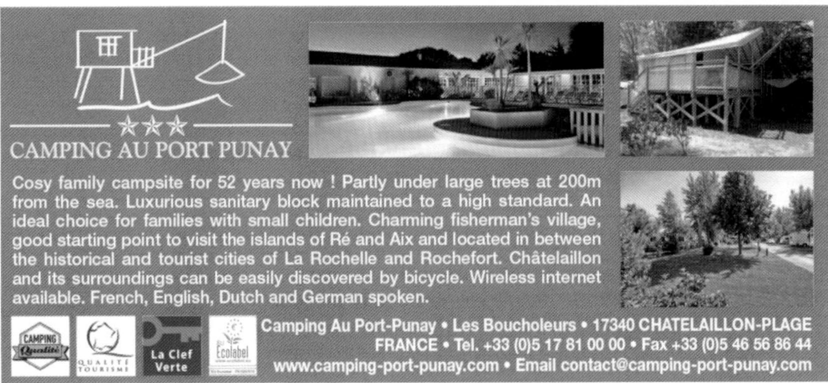

★★★
CAMPING AU PORT PUNAY
Cosy family campsite for 52 years now ! Partly under large trees at 200m from the sea. Luxurious sanitary block maintained to a high standard. An ideal choice for families with small children. Charming fisherman's village, good starting point to visit the islands of Ré and Aix and located in between the historical and tourist cities of La Rochelle and Rochefort. Châtelaillon and its surroundings can be easily discovered by bicycle. Wireless internet available. French, English, Dutch and German spoken.
Camping Qualité
Qualité Tourisme
La Clef Verte
Ecolabel
Camping Au Port-Punay • Les Boucholeurs • 17340 CHATELAILLON-PLAGE
FRANCE • Tel. +33 (0)5 17 81 00 00 • Fax +33 (0)5 46 56 86 44
www.camping-port-punay.com • Email contact@camping-port-punay.com

Couhé

Sites et Paysages Caravaning les Peupliers

Avenue de Paris, F-86700 Couhé (Vienne) T: 05 49 59 21 16. E: info@lespeupliers.fr
alanrogers.com/FR86080

Les Peupliers is situated in a valley just 25 km. south of Poitiers and close to the N10 motorway. The site has been family owned and run since 1968 and continually updated to provide good facilities. The camping area is divided in the middle by a small river (unfenced) with crossing points at various intervals. There are 187 pitches, 43 of which are for mobile homes available to rent. The 144 level touring pitches are on grass and separated by trees and shrubs; 101 have 16A electricity and 86 are fully serviced. The site enjoys a rural position within this region and tends to benefit from long hours of sunshine.

Facilities

Three sanitary blocks also provide facilities for babies and disabled visitors. Laundry facilities. Motorcaravan services. TV and fridge rental. Shop. Restaurant, bar and snack bar (July/Aug). Pool complex. Playgrounds. Fishing lake. Minigolf. Multisport court. Entertainment in high season. WiFi throughout (charged). Off site: Tennis 800 m. Bicycle hire 1 km. Riding 5 km. Golf 40 km.

Open: 2 May - 30 September.

Directions

Couhé is 30 km. south of Poitiers on N10. From north, follow signs to Couhé town centre and campsite (a short distance from slip road on right). From south, take second Couhé exit from N10. Site entrance is opposite end of slip road. GPS: 46.31263, 0.18216

Charges guide

Per unit incl. 2 persons and electricity	€ 35.60
extra person	€ 8.30

Coulon

Camping de la Venise Verte

178 route des Bords de Sèvre, F-79510 Coulon (Deux-Sèvres) T: 05 49 35 90 36.
E: accueil@camping-laveniseverte.fr **alanrogers.com/FR79040**

The new owners, Marie and Bruno, will be pleased to welcome you to their site on the edge of the Sèvre Nortaise and the Marais Poitevin, which is ideal for short or long stays. With canoe and bicycle hire on site you have no excuse for not exploring the local area. In the Deux-Sèvres, the department of discovery, so named because it has two rivers named Sèvre, the Noirtaise and Nantaise, the Venise Verte provides an excellent site. There are 120 flat pitches here with 94 used for touring units, the remainder occupied by 26 mobile homes. The pitches are of a good size, most with 10A electricity, water and drainage, and with some shade.

Facilities

Modern toilet facilities are of a high standard with free showers. Facilities for disabled visitors. Washing machine and dryer. Motorcaravan services. Heated swimming pool (15/6-15/9). Play area. Bicycle hire. Boules area. Fishing. WiFi on part of site (free). Off site: Fishing 200 m. Coulon 1 km. Boat trips in the Marais. Ideal for walking, fishing, cycling or canoeing. Golf and riding 15 km.

Open: 1 April - 31 October.

Directions

From Niort take N11 (La Rochelle). Turn on the D3 (Sansais) and then north on D1 (Coulon). At traffic lights head towards Centre Ville (Coulon) at mini-roundabout turn slightly right. Follow Sèvre Noirtaise for 1.5 km. to site on the right. Beware of tight turn after site barrier. GPS: 46.31492, -0.60835

Charges guide

Per unit incl. 2 persons and electricity	€ 20.00 - € 29.00
extra person	€ 5.00 - € 7.00

Dienné

Camping Domaine de Dienné

F-86410 Dienné (Vienne) T: 05 49 45 87 63. E: info@domaine-de-dienne.fr
alanrogers.com/FR86120

This is without doubt a wonderful site and unique in what it offers. It concentrates on your well being and provides all the facilities you could wish for in achieving that aim. The whole site extends over 47 hectares but there are just 14 pitches for touring units and these are on generous plots of 250 sq.m. All have their own water supply, drainage and 16A electricity (Europlug) and access for even the largest of units will not cause a problem. The accommodation to rent includes Romany-style caravans, tree houses, yurts, a gîte and cottages, which are all of superb quality and again on large plots. Domaine de Dienné cannot fail to impress from the moment you arrive.

Facilities

Toilet block with washbasins and showers. Facilities for disabled visitors. Shop, bar, restaurant and takeaway. Heated indoor swimming pool (all season). Outdoor pool (July/Aug). Health and fitness centre. Riding centre. Mountain biking. Bicycle hire. Adventure park. Climbing tower. Children's games. Walking trails. Fishing. Cooking lessons. Free WiFi over site. Communal barbecue area. Off site: Poitiers airport 25 km. Futuroscope.

Open: 12 February - 31 December.

Directions

From Poitiers take N147 towards Limoges. After the village of Fleure the site is well signed. GPS: 46.445028, 0.559294

Charges guide

Per unit incl. 2 persons and electricity	€ 21.00 - € 39.00
extra person	€ 4.00 - € 7.50

Dolus-d'Oléron

Camping Indigo Oléron les Chênes Verts

9 passe de l'Ecuissiere, F-17550 Dolus-d'Oléron (Charente-Maritime) T: 05 46 75 32 88.
E: chenes-verts@camping-indigo.com **alanrogers.com/FR17985**

Les Chênes Verts, peacefully situated on the eastern side of the Ile d'Oléron, was completely renovated in 2012 and has direct access to the Passe de l'Ecuissière beach. The 105 touring pitches are of a good size and 80 have electricity connections. Several are occupied by fully equipped safari-style tents. Recent improvements include a small shop (with bread and croissants) and snack bar. Various activities are organised, including workshops for children and opportunities to discover more about the island and its inhabitants. Cycling is popular across the island, with miles of dedicated cycle tracks.

Facilities

Two comfortable shower blocks. Family cubicle. Facilities for disabled visitors. Washing machine and dryer. Bar, snack bar/takeaway (July/Aug). Play area. Fully equipped tents for hire. WiFi at bar terrace (free). Electric barbecues only. Bicycle hire. Off site: Nearest beach and fishing 50 m. Shops and restaurants in Dolus-d'Oléron. Boat trips. Cycle tracks across the island. Riding 3.5 km.

Open: 4 May - 26 September.

Directions

Dolus-d'Oléron is north of Le Château d'Oléron. Approaching from the mainland, cross the (toll-free) bridge at Marennes and head north on D26 to Dolus-d'Oléron. GPS: 45.886995, -1.275433

Charges guide

Per unit incl. 2 persons and electricity	€ 20.30 - € 32.30
extra person	€ 4.00 - € 6.20

Ingrandes-sur-Vienne

Castel Camping le Petit Trianon

Saint Ustre, 1 rue du Moulin de Saint-Ustre, F-86220 Ingrandes-sur-Vienne (Vienne) T: 05 49 02 61 47.

E: chateau@petit-trianon.fr **alanrogers.com/FR86010**

A family owned site, le Petit Trianon is situated halfway between Tours and Poitiers. It enjoys a countryside position within the lovely grounds of a small 18th-century château. Visitors to the site often return several times after their first visit for the calm and tranquil atmosphere here. There are 116 fairly open pitches, all with electricity (10A), set in seven hectares, which gives a real sense of spaciousness. Plants are well tended and shade is provided in parts by the many attractive trees. Access around the site is good and large units are accepted by prior arrangement. There is an English owned bar and restaurant (with a French chef) within 50 m. offering a good menu.

Facilities

The sanitary facilities include washbasins in cabins, some washbasin and shower units, baby baths, washing machines and dryer. Facilities for disabled visitors. Motorcaravan services. Shop. Snack bar. Takeaway. Heated swimming pool and paddling pool. Playground. Minigolf. Badminton, croquet, volleyball and boules. Satellite TV. Reading room. Children's club and entertainment (July/Aug). Bicycle hire. Bread making (July/Aug). Internet access. WiFi (charged). Caravan storage. Off site: Restaurant 50 m. Tennis 2 km. Fishing 3 km. Riding 6 km. Local markets. Châtellerault 9 km. Poitiers with Futuroscope.

Open: 18 April - 11 September.

Directions

Take the N10 to Ingrandes-sur-Vienne and take the D75 towards Oyre. Follow D161 to St Ustre (1.5 km) and site is then well signed.
GPS: 46.885533, 0.586133

Charges guide

Per unit incl. 2 persons and electricity	€ 24.40 - € 33.80
extra person	€ 7.00 - € 8.60
child (4-13 yrs)	€ 2.90 - € 4.60
dog	€ 2.00

La Brée-les-Bains

Antioche d'Oléron

16 route de Proires, F-17840 La Brée-les-Bains (Charente-Maritime) T: 05 46 47 92 00.

E: info@camping-antiochedoleron.com **alanrogers.com/FR17570**

Close to the northern point of the Ile d'Oléron, Antioche is quietly located within a five minute walk of the beach. There are 130 pitches, of which 87 are occupied by mobile homes, half available for rent, and 43 are for touring units. The pitches are set amongst attractive shrubs and palm trees and all have electricity (16A), water and a drain. The site becomes livelier in season with regular evening entertainment and activities for all the family. A thriving market selling local produce and products is within easy reach on foot and is held daily in high season. Along the road at Saint Denis-d'Oléron is a busy port and marina with a choice of bars and restaurants, many specialising in seafood.

Facilities

The modern sanitary block is of a good standard and is kept clean and fresh. Cubicle with controllable shower and washbasin. Facilities for babies and disabled visitors. No chemical disposal point (drains on pitches used). Laundry. Bar and snack bar with takeaway. Two heated swimming pools (one covered). Paddling pool. Jacuzzi. Play area. Children's club, evening entertainment and activities for all the family (July/Aug). WiFi over site (charged July/Aug). Bicycle hire. Off site: Beach and fishing 150 m. Village with market (daily 15/6-15/9) 1 km. Riding 1.5 km. Sailing and boat launching 2.5 km. Golf 7 km.

Open: 6 April - 28 September.

Directions

Cross the bridge to the Ile d'Oléron and continue on the D26/D734 through St Pierre and St Georges, then turn right onto the D273E1 towards La Brée-les-Baines. Bear left at roundabout, then at T-junction turn left from where the campsite is signed. GPS: 46.02007, -1.35764

Charges guide

Per unit incl. 2 persons and electricity	€ 23.10 - € 40.95
extra person	€ 7.80 - € 9.40
child (1-14 yrs)	€ 4.40 - € 5.60
dog	€ 4.30

La Couarde-sur-Mer

Camping l'Océan

50 route d'Ars, F-17670 La Couarde-sur-Mer (Charente-Maritime) T: 05 46 29 87 70.
E: info@campingocean.com **alanrogers.com/FR17230**

L'Océan lies close to the centre of the Ile de Ré, just 50 m. from a sandy beach. There are 339 pitches here with 153 for touring units, the remainder occupied by mobile homes and chalets. The camping area is well shaded and pitches are of a reasonable size, all with electricity (10A). A pleasant bar/restaurant overlooks the large heated swimming pool which is surrounded by an attractive sunbathing terrace. Bicycle hire is popular here as the island offers over 100 km. of interesting cycle routes.

Facilities

The two toilet blocks are modern and well maintained with facilities for children and disabled visitors. Laundry. Dog shower. Motorcaravan services. Shop, bar, restaurant and takeaway, swimming pool. Spa with sauna, Turkish bath, jacuzzi etc. Play area. Games room. Riding. Tennis. Minigolf. Trampolines. Boules. Multisports area. Bicycle hire. Entertainment in high season. Fishing pond adjacent. No charcoal barbecues. WiFi (free). Mobile homes for rent. Off site: Beach 50 m. La Couarde 2.5 km. Riding 3 km.

Open: 8 April - 25 September.

Directions

After toll bridge, join D735 which runs along the north side of island until you pass La Couarde. The site is 2.5 km. beyond village (towards Ars-en-Ré). GPS: 46.20433, -1.46767

Charges guide

Per unit incl. 1 or 2 persons and electricity	€ 26.00 - € 49.00
extra person	€ 5.00 - € 13.00

Camping Cheques accepted.

La Couarde-sur-Mer

Camping la Tour des Prises

Route d'Ars, F-17670 La Couarde-sur-Mer (Charente-Maritime) T: 05 46 29 84 82.
E: camping@lesprises.com **alanrogers.com/FR17630**

La Tour des Prises is a friendly, family site surrounded by vineyards, close to the village of La Couarde-sur-Mer on the southern side of the Ile de Ré. There are 140 pitches here (80-110 sq.m), 55 of which are occupied by fully equipped mobile homes and chalets (for rent). The 85 touring pitches are of a good size with electricity (16A) nearby. The site is just 500 m. from a fine sandy beach, the Plage des Prises. Cycling is particularly popular on the island thanks to the quality and extent of its cycle tracks, one of which passes the site. La Couarde is a pleasant resort with 5 km. of beaches.

Facilities

Two unisex toilet blocks provide good facilities and are kept clean. The second block has been extended and refurbished to a high standard and includes excellent facilities for babies, children and disabled visitors. Laundry. Basic motorcaravan services. Small shop (1/6-15/9). Takeaway (2/6-20/9). Heated, covered swimming pool. Children's pool. Entertainment for adults, and a children's club in high season. Free WiFi over site. Games room. Play area. Bicycle hire. Mobile homes and chalets to rent. Off site: Nearest beach 500 m.

Open: 1 April - 30 September.

Directions

From La Rochelle, cross the toll bridge to the Ile de Ré and follow signs for La Phare des Baleines, St Martin and then La Couarde-sur-Mer (D201/D735). Avoid village. Stay on D735 towards Ars-en-Ré. Site is signed to right in 1.5 km. GPS: 46.20447, -1.44641

Charges guide

Per unit incl. 2 persons and electricity	€ 25.60 - € 42.60
extra person	€ 4.00 - € 8.50

La Flotte-en-Ré

Flower Camping le Bel Air

5 route de la Noue, F-17630 La Flotte-en-Ré (Charente-Maritime) T: 05 46 09 63 10.
E: camping.bel-air@flowercampings.com **alanrogers.com/FR17285**

La Flotte is a typical Atlantic fishing village on the Ile de Ré, with narrow, wallflower-lined streets, brightly painted shutters and a port filled with sailing boats. Close to the star-shaped citadel at Saint Martin-de-Ré and just 900 m. from the long, sandy Plage de l'Arnérault, le Bel Air makes an ideal base for exploring the island on foot, by bicycle or by boat. There are over 220 pitches, with 6A electricity, separated by hedges or low fences and with plenty of mature trees providing shade. There are tents and modern canvas homes for hire. The site surrounds a rugby club on three sides.

Facilities

Four unheated sanitary blocks provide washbasins and hot showers in cubicles. Facilities for families, children and disabled visitors. Motorcaravan services (€ 4). Laundry. Snack bar with fresh bread daily (July/Aug). Outdoor heated pool (May-September). Play area. Boules court. Tennis. Activities room. Occasional children's activities (July/Aug). Bicycle hire. WiFi on part of site (free). No charcoal barbecues. Off site: Shops 500 m.

Open: 4 April - 27 September.

Directions

La Flotte is on the north coast of the Ile de Ré. From La Rochelle take N237 to Ile de Ré, crossing toll bridge. Follow D735 for 11 km, then turn north at roundabout to La Flotte. Site is on right in 300 m. GPS: 46.18202, -1.33137

Charges guide

Per unit incl. 2 persons and electricity	€ 16.00 - € 34.00
extra person	€ 4.00 - € 6.50

La Flotte-en-Ré

Camping la Grainetière

Route de Saint Martin, Chemin des Essarts, F-17630 La Flotte-en-Ré (Charente-Maritime)

T: 05 46 09 68 86. E: la-grainetiere@orange.fr **alanrogers.com/FR17280**

A truly friendly welcome awaits you from Isabelle, Eric and Fanny at la Grainetière. It is a peaceful campsite set in almost three hectares of pine trees which provide some shade for the 51 touring pitches of various shapes and sizes. There are also 80 well spaced chalets, mobile homes and roulottes for rent. Some pitches are suitable for units up to seven metres (these should be booked in advance). There are no hedges for privacy and the pitches are sandy with some grass. Most pitches have a water point, electricity (10A) and waste water drainage. The site is well lit. The site is situated just 1.5 kilometres from the beach and La Flotte-en-Ré with its harbour-side restaurants is even closer.

Facilities

The unisex, heated sanitary block is first class, with washbasins in cubicles, showers, British style WCs, facilities for children and disabled visitors. Laundry facilities. Shop. Takeaway. Covered swimming pool (heated all season) and jacuzzi. Bicycle hire. Fridge hire. Play area. Games room. Library. TV room. Charcoal barbecues are not permitted. Free WiFi over site. Off site: Beach, fishing, boat launching and sailing 2 km. Bar and restaurant 2 km. Riding 3 km. Golf 10 km.

Open: 1 April - 2 October.

Directions

Follow the signs for St Martin. The site is on the main road between La Flotte and St Martin. GPS: 46.18755, -1.344933

Charges guide

Per unit incl. 2 persons and electricity	€ 23.00 - € 45.00
extra person	€ 5.50 - € 9.00
child (0-7 yrs)	€ 3.50 - € 5.00
dog	€ 3.00 - € 4.50

La Flotte-en-Ré

Camping les Peupliers

Route de Rivedoux, F-17630 La Flotte-en-Ré (Charente-Maritime) T: 02 51 20 41 94.

E: contact@camp-atlantique.com **alanrogers.com/FR17290**

On the Ile de Ré, les Peupliers is just 800 metres from the sea with sea views from some of the pitches. There are just 20 touring pitches here, and 144 chalets for rent, set within a five hectare area of light woodland with the trees providing some shade. English is spoken at reception and the staff go out of their way to make your stay enjoyable. The site is close to the shops and restaurants of the pretty fishing port of Flotte-en-Ré. With 100 km. of cycle tracks, sandy beaches, local markets and a uniquely sunny micro-climate, this is a great place to sample island life. Historic La Rochelle on the mainland is one of France's most captivating ports. Subject to demand, a daily programme of entertainment for adults and children is possible throughout the season.

Facilities

The toilet block includes washbasins and showers in cubicles. Good disabled facilities. Laundry facilities. Shop, restaurant, takeaway and bar with TV. Heated outdoor swimming pools with flume. Play area. Trampoline. Multisports pitch. Fitness suite. Sauna. Hammam. Children's club and entertainment. Bicycle hire. Max. 1 dog. WiFi throughout. Only gas barbecues allowed. Communal barbecue provided. Off site: Riding 500 m. Beach, fishing, boat launching and sailing 800 m.

Open: 2 April - 2 November.

Directions

Over the toll bridge and turn left at second roundabout. Site is well signed. GPS: 46.18461, -1.3080

Charges guide

Per unit incl. 2 persons and electricity	€ 24.00 - € 42.00
extra person	€ 5.00 - € 9.00
child (under 5 yrs)	free - € 6.00

La Flotte-en-Ré

Camping l'Ile Blanche

Chemin des Bardonnieres, F-17630 La Flotte-en-Ré (Charente-Maritime) T: 05 46 09 52 43.
E: ileblanche@wanadoo.fr **alanrogers.com/FR17520**

Pitches at this four-hectare site are exclusively for mobile homes and chalets. The Ile de Ré is known as l'Ile Blanche because of its dazzling white beaches and this park lies between the villages of La Flotte, St Martin and Le Bois-Plage. Camping l'Ile Blanche has a range of mobile homes and chalets available for rent, attractively dispersed throughout the wooded terrain. There are no touring pitches here. The site provides a peaceful family atmosphere in a quiet location, 1 km. from the nearest beach and from the village centre. Leisure facilities include a covered swimming pool and a popular restaurant. Between June and September electric shuttle buses serve the entire island.

Facilities

Laundry facilities. Covered, heated swimming pool (12/4-30/9) and children's pool (June-Sept). Tennis. Volleyball. Bar, restaurant and takeaway. Unfenced play area. Electric barbecues only. Bicycle hire. WiFi on part of site (free). Off site: Riding 500 m. Fishing 1 km. Beach 2 km. Golf 10 km. Bicycle trails.

Open: 12 April - 30 September.

Directions

After the toll bridge (from La Rochelle), take the D735 signed La Flotte and St Martin. Upon reaching La Flotte, take the ring road, avoiding the village centre. Site is well signed from here and is on the left. GPS: 46.18982, -1.34796

Charges guide

Contact site for details.

La Palmyre

Yelloh! Village Parc de la Côte Sauvage

La Coubre, F-17570 La Palmyre (Charente-Maritime) T: 05 46 22 40 18.
E: campingparccotesauvage@gmail.com **alanrogers.com/FR17750**

Set amongst terraced woodlands and with direct access to sandy beaches on both the open sea and the more protected Bonne Anse, this large family run campsite has 200 touring pitches of varying sizes. Some are randomly set amongst the trees and bushes on sandy grass, others, larger and well defined, offer more open aspects and are interspersed with chalets and mobile homes, many available for rent. Côte Sauvage has access to the many country cycle and walking trails in the area and is next to the lighthouse of Pointe de la Coubre. The charming town of La Palmyre has many restaurants, bars and shops and its zoo, the second largest in France, is very popular.

Facilities

Four traditional heated sanitary blocks with usual facilities and of varying ages are being gradually upgraded; one modern block has bright cubicles for showers and washbasins. Facilities for disabled visitors. Laundry. Motorcaravan services. Shop. Bar and restaurant with takeaway. Heated outdoor and indoor swimming pools with water slides and attractive terraces. Fitness room. Multisports court. Boules. Games/TV rooms. Children's club and organised activities and entertainment for all the family. Bicycle hire. Only gas or electric barbecues on pitches. WiFi over part of site (charged). Dogs are not accepted. Off site: Beach 300 m. Town 3 km. Riding 4 km. Golf 4 km.

Open: 9 April - 15 September.

Directions

La Palmyre is 57 km. west of Saintes. From A10 at Saintes, take N150 to Royan and turn north on D25 to La Palmyre. Continue ahead on D25 (campsite signed). After 3 km. turn left at sign for site. GPS: 45.697098, -1.229396

Charges guide

Per unit incl. 2 persons and electricity	€ 18.00 - € 49.00
extra person	€ 7.00 - € 9.00
child (3-6 yrs)	free - € 7.00

La Roche-Posay

Airotel la Roche Posay Vacances

Route de Lesigny, F-86270 La Roche-Posay (Vienne) T: 05 49 86 21 23.

E: info@larocheposay-vacances.com **alanrogers.com/FR86050**

Camping la Roche Posay is set in eight hectares and has direct access to the Creuse river on which fishing and canoes are popular. There are 200 pitches, of which 78 are used for mobile homes to rent. Access around the site is good for larger units. The pitches are all large and 10A electricity is available. This is a good, well run site in very natural surroundings. There is a sense of spaciousness where you can relax in a convivial atmosphere. Many different types of trees offer a mix of shade and the site is pleasantly landscaped. A free shuttle bus runs from the site to town.

Facilities

Two fully equipped, heated toilet blocks, one in each section. Excellent facilities for disabled visitors and children. Bar and takeaway. Snack bar (July/Aug). Outdoor swimming pool with toboggan (May-Sept). Heated, covered swimming and paddling pools. Play area. Games room. Fishing. Canoes. Boules. Riding. Bicycle hire. Entertainment in high season. WiFi (free in bar). Off site: Spa (20% discount) shops and restaurants in La Roche Posay 2 km. Golf 2 km.

Open: 11 April - 26 September.

Directions

Site is signed from the D725 town bypass, turning north at roundabout onto D5 towards Lesigny. Site is 50 m. on right. GPS: 46.799646, 0.80945

Charges guide

Per unit incl. 2 persons and electricity	€ 18.00 - € 34.00
extra person	€ 6.00 - € 8.00
child (1-17 yrs acc. to age)	free - € 6.00
dog	€ 3.00

Le Bois-Plage-en-Ré

Camping les Varennes

Raise Maritaise, BP 20026, F-17580 Le Bois-Plage-en-Ré (Charente-Maritime) T: 05 46 09 15 43.

E: info@les-varennes.com **alanrogers.com/FR17390**

Situated in the middle of the Ile de Ré, les Varennes is a good quality, well maintained site, 500 m. from a long, sandy golden beach. There are 142 pitches, 57 for touring units with 10A electricity and 85 for chalets which are all available for rent. The pitches are level and half of them are shaded by tall pine trees. They are easily accessible but it is recommended to telephone in advance for availability of pitches for larger outfits. There is a pleasant heated swimming pool which has a retractable cover so that users can enjoy the facility from early in the year.

Facilities

Two sanitary blocks (one heated) with facilities for children, babies and disabled visitors. Laundry facilities. Basic motorcaravan services. Small bar with TV and shop (1/5-1/9). Bread to order. Heated swimming pool, covered in bad weather. Children's club in July/Aug. Playground. Bicycle hire. Boules. WiFi throughout (free). Communal barbecue area. Max. one dog per unit. Off site: Fishing, sailing and beach 500 m. Riding 2 km. Golf 20 km.

Open: 11 April - 27 September.

Directions

After crossing onto the island, take the D201 to Le Bois-Plage. Turn left at roundabout to beach along Avenue de Gros Joncs. After 200 m, turn right and site is on right. If coming from Nantes, avoid Marans in high season. GPS: 46.17873, -1.38307

Charges guide

Per unit incl. 2 persons and electricity	€ 23.70 - € 38.70
extra person (over 2 yrs)	€ 4.00 - € 8.00

Le Bois-Plage-en-Ré

Campéole les Amis de la Plage

68 avenue du Pas des Boeufs, F-17580 Le Bois-Plage-en-Ré (Charente-Maritime) T: 05 46 09 24 01.

E: les-amis-de-la-plage@campeole.com **alanrogers.com/FR17610**

Les Amis de la Plage, a former municipal site, and now a member of the Campéole group, is located on the southern side of the Ile de Ré, at Le Bois-Plage-en-Ré. The site has direct gated access across the sand dunes to a superb sandy beach. There are 219 pitches, some of which are occupied by mobile homes, chalets and fully equipped tents. The 136 touring pitches are sandy with varying degrees of shade, some are rather small and others are on undulating land. Most have electrical connections (10A). The island's largest market is held daily, just 500 m. from the site.

Facilities

Four toilet blocks (two closed low season) provide some washbasins in cubicles and facilities for disabled visitors and children. Laundry. Motorcaravan services. No shop, but bread to order daily. Play area. Boules. Activities and entertainment (high season). Direct access to beach. Communal barbecue area. Mobile homes, chalets and tents for rent. WiFi (charged in high season). Bicycle hire. Off site: Swimming pool (charged) and bar/pizzeria opposite site entrance. Fishing and market 500 m.

Open: 3 April - 27 September.

Directions

From La Rochelle, cross the toll bridge and take D201 along the southern coast of the island until you reach Le Bois-Plage-en-Ré, and then turn south following signs to site. GPS: 46.177401, -1.386514

Charges guide

Per unit incl. 2 persons and electricity	€ 20.90 - € 26.90
extra person	€ 4.30 - € 7.20
child (2-5 yrs)	free - € 4.30

Le Château-d'Oléron

Camping la Brande

Route des Huitres, F-17480 Le Château-d'Oléron (Charente-Maritime) T: 05 46 47 62 37.
E: info@camping-labrande.com **alanrogers.com/FR17220**

An environmentally friendly site, run and maintained to a high standard, la Brande offers an ideal holiday environment on the delightful Ile d'Oléron. It is situated on the oyster route and close to a sandy beach. Pitches here are generous and mostly separated by hedges and trees, the greater number for touring outfits. All are on level grassy terrain and have electricity hook-ups, some are fully serviced. Some of the most attractive pitches are in a newer section towards the back of the site. Activities during the high season, plus the natural surroundings, make this an ideal choice for families. A feature of this site is the heated indoor pool (29°C) which is open all season. The Barcat family ensures that their visitors not only enjoy quality facilities, but Gerard Barcat offers guided bicycle tours and canoe trips. This way you discover the oyster farming, vineyards and history of Oléron (joined to the mainland by a 3 km. bridge).

Facilities

Three clean, unheated sanitary blocks have spacious, well equipped showers and washbasins (mainly in cabins). Baby facilities. Excellent facilities for disabled visitors. Private facilities to rent. Laundry rooms. Motorcaravan services. Superb restaurant/takeaway and bar (July/Aug). Shop (July/Aug). Heated indoor swimming pool. Jacuzzi. Sauna. Playground. Games room. Football field. Tennis. Minigolf. Fishing. Archery (high season). Bicycle hire. Canoe hire. Free WiFi on part of site. Kids' club. Lending library. Off site: Beach 300 m. Supermarket 2 km. Sailing 2 km. Riding 6 km. Golf 7 km.

Open: 28 March - 8 November.

Directions

After crossing bridge to l'Ile d'Oléron turn right towards Château d'Oléron. Continue through village and follow sign for Route des Huitres. Site is on left after 2.5 km. GPS: 45.90415, -1.21525

Charges guide

Per unit incl. 2 persons and electricity	€ 21.90 - € 44.00
extra person	€ 5.50 - € 8.50
dog	€ 3.50

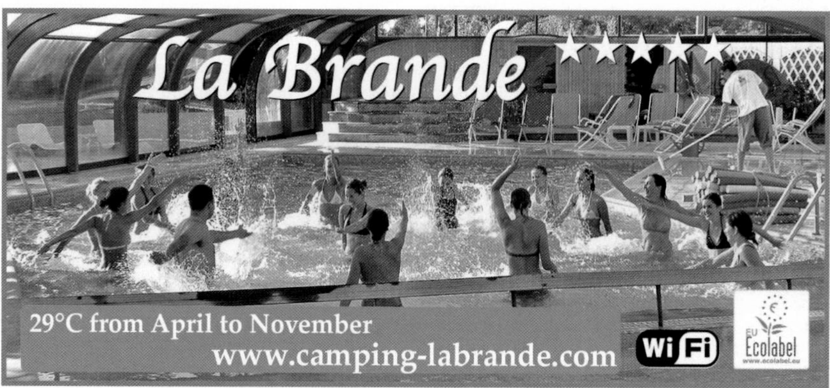

Le Château-d'Oléron

Airotel Oléron

Domaine de Montravail, 19 rue de la Libération B.P. 31, F-17480 Le Château-d'Oléron (Charente-Maritime)
T: 05 46 47 61 82. E: info@camping-airotel-oleron.com **alanrogers.com/FR17060**

This family run site on the outskirts of Le Château-d'Oléron has very good facilities, including a superb equestrian centre, a full range of sporting activities and an attractive heated pool complex. This is a mature site with 265 pitches of a good size, with varying degrees of shade provided by trees and attractive shrubs. It is well laid out and most of the 110 touring pitches have electricity (10A), four with individual water and drainage. The remaining pitches are used for mobile homes, chalets and bungalows of which 72 are for rent. A full entertainment programme is provided in high season. Visitors can enjoy exploring the island with its fine sandy beaches on the Atlantic coast.

Facilities

Two modern toilet blocks with facilities for disabled visitors and babies. Washing machine and dryer. Motorcaravan services. Shop. Bar, restaurant and takeaway (15/6-15/9). Heated swimming and paddling pools. Equestrian centre. Playground. Multisports court. Tennis. Minigolf. Fishing. Bicycle hire. TV and games room. WiFi throughout (charged). Lending library. Off site: Supermarket 500 m. Local markets. Zoo. Aquarium.

Open: Easter - 15 October.

Directions

Cross bridge onto the island and continue on D26. At 2nd roundabout turn right, marked Dolus and Le Château. Proceed 500 m. and take first right (Campings). Site is 1 km. GPS: 45.88207, -1.20648

Charges guide

Per unit incl. 2 persons and electricity	€ 22.00 - € 33.50
extra person	€ 6.00 - € 8.90

Les Mathes

Camping l'Orée du Bois

225 route de la Bouverie, la Fouasse, F-17570 Les Mathes (Charente-Maritime) T: 05 46 22 42 43.
E: info@camping-oree-du-bois.fr **alanrogers.com/FR17050**

L'Orée du Bois has 429 pitches of about 100 sq.m. in a very spacious, pinewood setting. There are 130 for touring units, mainly scattered amongst the permanent chalets and tents. They include 40 large pitches with individual sanitary facilities (in blocks of four with shower, toilet, washbasin and dishwashing sink). Pitches are on flat, fairly sandy ground, separated by trees, shrubs and hedges and all have electrical connections (6A, some Europlugs). The forest pines offer some shade. This is a family site with an excellent aqua park amongst the amenities as well as a splendid children's playground.

Facilities

Four main toilet blocks include some washbasins in cabins. Three have a laundry and facilities for disabled visitors. Shop. Excellent bar, restaurant, crêperie and takeaway service, heated swimming pools, water slide and paddling pool (trunks, not shorts). Large play areas. Boules, football and basketball. Games room and TV lounge. Gym equipment. Bicycle hire. Discos. Communal barbecues provided in special areas only. WiFi throughout (charged). Entertainment for adults and club for children (high season). Tree-top adventure park (adjacent, owned by site). Off site: Riding 300 m. Fishing 4 km. Golf 5 km.

Open: 24 May - 14 September.

Directions

From north follow D14 La Tremblade. At roundabout before Arvert turn on D268 (Les Mathes). Site is on right in Fouasse. From south, at Royan take D25 (La Palmyre). In town turn north to Les Mathes. At first roundabout in Les Mathes follow sign (Fouasse, La Tremblade). Site is on left after 2 km.
GPS: 45.7326, -1.1785

Charges guide

Per unit incl. 2 persons and electricity € 20.00 - € 46.00

Min. stay 7 days in high season, when no arrival/departure on Saturdays.

Camping Cheques accepted.

Les Mathes

Camping Atlantique Parc

26 avenue des Mathes, F-17570 Les Mathes (Charente-Maritime) T: 05 46 02 17 17.
E: info@camping-atlantique-parc.com **alanrogers.com/FR17975**

Camping Atlantique Parc is a large, well equipped holiday complex that has something to offer for campers of all ages, but particularly for families with children. It is ideally situated on the edge of Forêt de Saint Augustin-les-Mathes, only a short drive from the beautiful beaches of La Palmyre. The site has almost 400 large pitches, the majority used for chalets and mobile homes for rent. There are 50 touring pitches with electricity, water and drainage, many with good shade from attractive mature trees.

Facilities

Three well maintained toilet blocks include facilities for disabled visitors and babies. Motorcaravan services. Shop, bar and restaurant (all 1/6-10/9). Swimming pools with four slides. Good play areas. Pet corner. Bicycle hire. Boules. Archery. Video games room and TV. Football, volleyball and basketball. Entertainment and children's club (high season). WiFi in some areas (charged).
Off site: Riding 2 km. Beach 3 km. Golf 5 km.

Open: 1 May - 13 September.

Directions

From Royan take D25 towards La Palmyre. Pass the zoo on the right and at large roundabout take D141 towards Les Mathes. Site is on right after 500 m.
GPS: 45.701348, -1.167686

Charges guide

Per unit incl. 2 persons and electricity € 35.00 - € 57.00

Administration charge € 22 per stay.

Les Mathes-La Palmyre

Palmyre Loisirs

28 avenue des Mathes, F-17570 Les Mathes-La Palmyre (Charente-Maritime) T: 05 46 23 67 66.
E: info@palmyreloisirs.com **alanrogers.com/FR17995**

Camping Palmyre Loisirs is a very large and lively campsite lying on a peninsula 16 km. north west of Royan and only a 10 minute drive from several long sandy beaches. The site is surrounded by a pine forest and has over 600 pitches laid out in sandy, grassy, woodland areas. There are just 22 fairly small pitches for touring, all with 6A electricity (2-pin French style). These are a long walk from activities and pools. The campsite is very popular with families who enjoy plenty of entertainment (July and August) including the very popular circus school. The site is not suitable for large units.

Facilities

Modern toilet block with all necessary facilities. Washing machine/dryer. Shop. Bar and takeaway with adjacent open air amphitheatre and stage. Outdoor and indoor pools, water slide and flume. Play area. Children's and teenager's clubs. Discos. Tennis. Minigolf. Volleyball. Boules. Multisports area. Bicycle hire. Barbecues must be hired from site. WiFi on part of site (charged).

Open: 1 April - 11 September.

Directions

Leave A10 autoroute at exit 35 (Saintes). Take N137 south about 3 km. then N150 west about 32 km. (signed Royan). On outskirts Royan take D25 northwest 18 km. towards La Palmyre. Take D141 northeast to site for 3 km. GPS: 45.70229, -1.15716

Charges guide

Per unit incl. 2 persons and electricity € 30.00 - € 45.00

Les Mathes-La Palmyre

Camping Caravaning Monplaisir

26 avenue de la Palmyre, F-17570 Les Mathes-La Palmyre (Charente-Maritime) T: 05 46 22 50 31.
E: camping-monplaisir@orange.fr **alanrogers.com/FR17110**

Monplaisir provides a small, quiet haven in an area with some very hectic campsites. It is ideal for couples or families with young children. Quite close to the town and set back from the road, the entrance leads through an avenue of trees, past the owner's home to a well kept, garden-like site with many trees and shrubs. There are 114 level, marked pitches and all have 10A electrical connections. On 14 there are caravans for hire and a modern building provides flats and studios for rent. There is no shop, bar or restaurant but it is a happy, friendly site. Visitors return year after year.

Facilities

The toilet block has some washbasins in cabins and facilities for disabled visitors. Bread delivered daily. TV, games room and library. Heated swimming and paddling pools (early May-30/9). Small play area. WiFi throughout (charged). Off site: Bicycle hire opposite. Supermarket short walk. Minigolf adjacent (owned by the site). Fishing 200 m. Riding 500 m. Beach 4 km. Golf 5 km.

Open: 1 April - 30 September.

Directions

From north on D14 (La Tremblade) turn onto D268 (Les Mathes and La Palmyre) at roundabout just before Arvert. Keep straight on to Les Mathes, road becomes D141. Turn left (north) at roundabout. Site is 600 m. on left. GPS: 45.71530, -1.15533

Charges guide

Per unit incl. 2 persons and electricity	€ 25.00
extra person	€ 7.00

Les Mathes-La Palmyre

Camping Beausoleil

20 avenue de La Coubre, la Palmyre, F-17570 Les Mathes (Charente-Maritime) T: 05 46 22 30 03.
E: camping.beausoleil@wanadoo.fr **alanrogers.com/FR17430**

Beausoleil is ideally placed just 200 m. from the beach and a short walk away from the centre of La Palmyre. This area has many long sandy beaches. A friendly, family run site for over 60 years offering a warm welcome to its visitors. Of the 236 pitches, 119 are for touring units. Pitches are grassy, level and offer some shade; 10A electricity is available (Europlug). Whilst most are easily accessible, some are irregularly shaped, so visitors with large units should telephone in advance to ensure availability. The remaining pitches are for mobile homes/chalets, 23 of which are available for rent.

Facilities

One unheated sanitary block with preset pushbutton showers and facilities for babies and disabled visitors. Some Turkish style WCs. Two washing machines and dryer. Basic motorcaravan services. Fresh bread available. Snack bar and pizzeria (15/6-31/8). TV. Heated swimming pool and paddling pool (1/6-31/8). Play area. Pétanque. Gas barbecues only on pitches. Communal areas for charcoal. Bicycle hire. WiFi throughout (charged).

Open: 1 April - 31 August.

Directions

At main roundabout in La Palmyre, take D25 towards La Tremblade and site is 200 m. on the right. GPS: 45.69261, -1.18301

Charges guide

Per unit incl. 2 persons and electricity	€ 23.30 - € 34.80
extra person (over 10 yrs)	€ 5.10

Les Mathes-La Palmyre

Camping l'Estanquet

La Fouasse, F-17570 Les Mathes-La Palmyre (Charente-Maritime) T: 05 46 22 47 32.
E: contact@campinglestanquet.com **alanrogers.com/FR17690**

L'Estanquet is a large, lively campsite located in the vast Forêt de la Coubre, close to the pretty resort of La Palmyre and its beaches. Of the 387 pitches, just 92 are for tourers, they are of a good size and well shaded by the towering pines. All have electrical connections (10A). Some are in a group close to the leisure amenities and are separated by neat hedges; others are scattered among the mobile homes and chalets, many of which are for rent. The forest separates the site from the beaches and can be crossed using the miles of good cycle tracks, some leading to La Tremblade, the region's oyster capital.

Facilities

Four toilet blocks provide controllable showers and washbasins in cubicles, plus facilities for babies and for disabled visitors, only open in high season. One small prefabricated unit close to pool and main touring pitches is open all season. Excellent food shop and bakery. Bar, snack bar/restaurant with takeaway. Swimming pool with new flume and water slides. Children's pool. New floodlit area with adventure playground, boulodrome and multisports pitch. Activities and entertainment in high season. Bicycle hire. Free WiFi over site. Mobile homes and chalets for rent.

Open: 1 April - 30 September.

Directions

Les Mathes is 20 km. northwest of Royan. From A10 at Saintes, follow signs for Royan on N159, then head northwest on D14 towards Marennes. After Arvent, turn south on D268 towards Les Mathes and site is on right at La Fouasse. GPS: 45.73211, -1.17646

Charges guide

Per unit incl. 2 persons and electricity	€ 21.00 - € 40.00
extra person	€ 6.50
child (up to 4 yrs)	€ 3.20

Les Mathes-La Palmyre

Camping la Clé des Champs

1188 route de la Fouasse, F-17570 Les Mathes-La Palmyre (Charente-Maritime) T: 05 46 22 40 53.
E: contact@la-cledeschamps.com **alanrogers.com/FR17540**

On the edge of the large Forêt de la Coubre and around 1.5 km. from the village of Les Mathes, la Clé des Champs is a large site (7.6 hectares) with 119 grass touring pitches (90 sq.m). Set amongst avenues of small trees, 80 have electricity (6/10A). They are perhaps unsuitable for heavy units after wet weather, but large motorcaravans can sometimes be accommodated on a hardstanding area. The 185 mobile homes and fixed tents (60 for rent) occupy the central part of the site, beyond which is a field for tents. Various cycle routes lead through the forest to the beaches of the Côte Sauvage. These stretch for 70 km. and sandy beaches alternate with rocky coves. The nearby zoo at La Palmyre, with over 1,600 animals, is France's second largest. La Palmyre is a stylish resort with many cafés and restaurants, as well as a fine sandy beach. Also close by is La Tremblade, a starting point for some excellent boat trips and for a fascinating excursion on a little steam train past oyster beds to Mornac-sur-Seudre or on to Saujon. Close to the site are an amusement park, an aerial adventure park (accrobranche), paintball and quad biking centres, and riding stables.

Facilities

New toilet block, heated in cool weather. Washing machine. Shop. Bar. Snack bar and takeaway (April-Sept). Swimming pool. Paddling pool. Games room. Play area. Bicycle hire. Activity and entertainment programme (July/Aug). WiFi (charged). New wellness (jacuzzi, sauna) and fitness rooms. Mobile homes for rent. Off site: Riding centre nearby. Minigolf 800 m. Les Mathes village 1.5 km. (good range of shops and restaurants). Beach 4 km.

Open: 1 April - 15 November.

Directions

From Saujon take the D14 northwest towards La Tremblade. At Arvert head south on the D141 to Les Mathes. Beyond the village, head right on the Route de la Fouasse and the site is on the right after a further 500 m. GPS: 45.72098, -1.17149

Charges guide

Per unit incl. 2 persons and electricity	€ 19.68 - € 35.38
extra person	€ 4.30 - € 6.00
child (2-6 yrs)	€ 3.80 - € 4.80

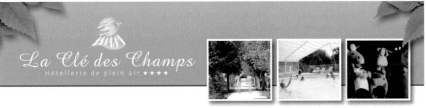

Les Mathes-La Palmyre

Camping la Pinède

2103 route de la Foasse, F-17570 Les Mathes-La Palmyre (Charente-Maritime) T: 05 46 22 45 13.
E: contact@campinglapinede.com **alanrogers.com/FR17740**

Camping la Pinède is a lively site located on a long stretch of land in a shady pine forest, slightly off the bustling coast. It is a few kilometres from the beach between Les Mathes and La Palmyre. The 8-hectare site provides a total of 372 pitches, of which 84 are available for touring units, all with 10A electricity and 60 also with water and drainage. They are level and a mixture of sand and grass, many hedged by bushes. Tall pines provide shade in places. On-site amenities include an impressive pool complex.

Facilities

Three toilet blocks provide showers and washbasins in cabins. Facilities for babies and visitors with disabilities. Laundry. Shop, restaurant, bar and takeaway. Indoor pool complex (all season). Outdoor pools (July/Aug). Play area. Mini-farm for children. Bicycle hire. Minigolf. TV room. Games room. Boules. Tennis. Multisport courts. Entertainment and activities. Communal barbecue area provided. Max. one dog. WiFi throughout (charged).

Open: 4 April - 26 September.

Directions

From Rochefort and Marennes follow directions to La Tremblade and join D14. At roundabout before Arvert turn on D268 (Les Mathes). Site is on right in Fouasse. From Saintes take N150. At Saujon take D14 (Marennes). After 13 km. turn south on D268. Site on right (3 km). GPS: 45.727603, -1.175601

Charges guide

Per unit incl. 2 persons and electricity	€ 19.00 - € 49.00

Loix

Flower Camping les Ilates

Route du Grouin, F-17111 Loix (Charente-Maritime) T: 05 46 29 05 43.

E: camping.les.ilates@flowercampings.com **alanrogers.com/FR17770**

Camping Ilates is a no frills campsite centrally located on the Ile de Ré and well situated to explore the 100 km. of cycle paths in the area. The site offers mobile homes and bungalows as well as 68 attractive touring pitches. These are all neatly hedged, of a good size and with 10A electricity, water and a drain. Units over 7 m. are not encouraged due to some road restrictions. At peak times, children's clubs and animation are organised and the site becomes very busy.

Facilities

Three modern and well maintained sanitary blocks. Hot showers. Facilities for disabled visitors and children. Washing machine. Laundry. Shop, bar and restaurant (15/6-15/9). Swimming pool (unheated). Jacuzzi (July/Aug). Tennis. Clubs for children (July/Aug). Bicycle hire. Free WiFi throughout. Off site: Fishing 300 m. Beach 800 m. Shops, restaurants and Internet café 1.5 km. Riding 2 km. Canoeing 4 km. Golf 18 km.

Open: 4 April - 27 September.

Directions

Cross toll bridge to Ile de Ré and take D201 towards Ars-en-Ré. Join D735 and at roundabout turn right on D102 towards Loix (do not enter village). Before Centre Ville, fork right for la Plage du Grouin. Cross 3 small roundabouts, then follow signs to site on left. Very tight turn at entrance. Park outside and sign in first. GPS: 46.226611, -1.429424

Charges guide

Per unit incl. 2 persons and electricity	€ 20.00 - € 45.00

Magné

Camping le Martin Pêcheur

155 av. du Marais Poitevin, F-79460 Magné (Deux-Sèvres) T: 05 49 35 71 81.

E: info@camping-le-martin-pecheur.com **alanrogers.com/FR79130**

On the edge of the Marais Poitevin and just six kilometres west of Niort, this is a simple family campsite on the bank of the Sèvre Niortaise river. There are 57 shaded pitches with electrical connections (10A, Europlug) available. The site is conveniently located close to the town centre where there are shops, bars and restaurants as well as a post office and bank. The area is ideal for walking and cycling and Magné is just a short drive (or ride) from several embarcadères, starting point for delightful excursions by boat or canoe along the waterways of la Venise Verte.

Facilities

The single toilet block has free hot water to showers, washbasins and sinks for dishwashing and laundry. Facilities for children and disabled visitors. Motorcaravan services. Play area. Boules. Volleyball. Free WiFi on part of site. Off site: Municipal swimming pool, free if staying at site (July/Aug), boules, tennis courts and canoeing base adjacent. Magné 600 m. Fishing 100 m. Coulon 4 km. Niort 6 km. Riding 6 km. Bicycle hire 8 km.

Open: 1 May - 28 September.

Directions

From north on A10 (Paris/Bordeaux) leave at exit 32 (Limoges/Marais Poitevin) and take D948 (Niort). Turn southeast on southern bypass (D611) for 7 km. and at roundabout turn north on D811 (Niort). In 1 km. turn west for Venise Verte, Coulon and Magné. Site is before village. From south on A10, leave at exit 33 (Marais Poitevin), turn north (Niort), then west on bypass as above. GPS: 46.31294, -0.53637

Charges guide

Per unit incl. 2 persons and electricity	€ 19.00 - € 27.50
extra person	€ 4.50 - € 6.00

Mazières

Camping Le Paradis

Mareuil, F-16270 Mazières (Charente) T: 05 45 84 92 06. E: info@le-paradis-camping.com

alanrogers.com/FR16130

Camping le Paradis is a small, immaculate, family run site, open all year. You are assured of a very warm welcome here. There are 28 large, well spaced pitches with 24 for touring, separated by hedging and a variety of maturing trees give some shade. Nine are on grass and 15 have hardstanding. All have 10/16A electricity and many have a water tap. Five very large pitches are fully serviced with satellite TV point and drainage; ideal for very large units. This delightful site is situated in the beautiful but lesser known region of the Charente. It is an ideal spot for couples and quiet families to get away from it all.

Facilities

Superb toilet facilities with rooms having toilet, washbasin and shower, part heated in winter. Room for disabled visitors. Washing machine and dryer. Motorcaravan services. Small shop for basics, bread to order (July/Aug). Internet point near reception. Small library. Communal barbecue. Caravan storage. Four mobile homes to rent. Off site: Bakers and fishing 3 km. Beach 5 km.

Open: All year.

Directions

Midway between Angoulême and Limoges leave N141 at La Péruse. Take D16 south, continue through Mazières. About 1 km. after Mazières turn right to site (signed). GPS: 45.832836, 0.558114

Charges guide

Per unit incl. 2 persons and electricity	€ 23.00 - € 26.00

No credit cards.

Médis

Sites et Paysages le Clos Fleuri

8 impasse du Clos Fleuri, F-17600 Médis (Charente-Maritime) T: 05 46 05 62 17. E: clos-fleuri@wanadoo.fr

alanrogers.com/FR17160

Camping le Clos Fleuri really does live up to its name. The profusion of different trees and the lawns and flower beds give this small site a very rural atmosphere. There is always a warm welcome from the Devais family who created this pretty site in 1974. The 103 touring pitches are mostly of generous size (a little uneven in places). They vary from being in full sun to well shaded and the majority have 5/10A electricity connections. The bar/restaurant is a converted barn providing a very convivial venue for evening gatherings and entertainment. Services here are only fully open in the height of the summer.

Facilities

Toilet facilities are kept clean. One block is segregated male and female, the other is unisex with each unit in its own cubicle. Facility for disabled visitors. Baby baths. Laundry facilities. Basic motorcaravan services. Small unheated pool and paddling pool. Sauna. Shop (from 10/7). Restaurant, bar and takeaway (10/7-30/8). In high season there are twice-weekly soirées and boules and archery competitions. Trampoline. Minigolf. WiFi on part of site (free). Large units should call in high season to check there is space. Off site: Riding 1 km. Médis 2 km.

Open: 1 June - 15 September.

Directions

Médis is on the N150 from Saintes, halfway between Saujon and Royan. Drive into village. Site signed to south at various points in Médis and is 2 km. outside village. GPS: 45.63011, -0.9458

Charges guide

Per unit incl. 2 persons and electricity	€ 23.00 - € 38.00
extra person	€ 6.50 - € 9.50
child	€ 5.00 - € 7.50
dog	€ 2.50 - € 3.50

Montbron

Castel Camping les Gorges du Chambon

Eymouthiers, F-16220 Montbron (Charente) T: 05 45 70 71 70. E: info@camping-gorgesduchambon.com

alanrogers.com/FR16020

This is a wonderful Castel site with 28 hectares of protected natural environment to be enjoyed in the rolling Perigord Vert countryside. Of 132 pitches, the 92 for touring are extremely generous in size (150 sq.m), some level, others on a gentle slope, and they enjoy a mixture of sunshine and shade. There are 85 with water and 10A electricity, the remaining seven are fully serviced. This spacious site offers fine walks through the woodlands and around the grounds. Flora and fauna are as nature intended. There has been much work done with the ecology association. Dogs are not accepted.

Facilities

Traditional style sanitary blocks include facilities for disabled visitors. Washing machine, dryer. Shop. Bar, restaurant and takeaway. New swimming pool (heated 1/5-13/9), children's pool (high season). Play area. Games room, TV and library with English books. Tennis. Archery. Minigolf. Volleyball. Multisports pitch. Bicycle hire. Beach and canoe hire. Organised activities July/Aug, children's club, youth disco, teenagers' corner. WiFi (charged).

Open: 25 April - 13 September.

Directions

Leave N141 Angoulême-Limoges road at Rochefoucauld take D6 to Montbron (14 km). Continue on D6 for 4 km, turn north on D163, site is signed. After 2 km. turn right and follow lane up to site. GPS: 45.6598, 0.557667

Charges guide

Per unit incl. 2 persons and electricity	€ 20.20 - € 34.10
extra person	€ 4.50 - € 9.10

Rivedoux-Plage

Campéole le Platin

125 avenue Gustave Perreau, F-17940 Rivedoux-Plage (Charente-Maritime) T: 05 46 09 84 10.
E: platin@campeole.com **alanrogers.com/FR17560**

Located at the gateway to the Ile de Ré, le Platin is just a short walk from the pleasant village of Rivedoux Plage where there are several good restaurants and shops. In high season a small market is held every morning in the village square. A long, narrow site, the beach is on one side and the main road on the other. It is divided into small avenues with around 20 pitches in each. All have 10A electricity and most are shaded (with 45 hardstanding), although the pitches nearest the beach have little shade. Of the 182 pitches, 50 are used for canvas bungalows for hire, the rest are seasonal and for touring.

Facilities

The toilet facilities here are a little below standard, although one block has good showers and an en-suite bathroom for disabled visitors. Children's room. Motorcaravan services. Small bar. Swimming pool (July/Aug). Play area. Trampoline. Entertainment in high season. Communal barbecues provided. Fishing. Bicycle hire. WiFi (charged). Off site: Baker opposite. Shops and restaurants in Rivedoux Plage 200 m. Beach 500 m.

Open: 5 April - 27 September.

Directions

After crossing the toll bridge from La Rochelle, continue on the D735 into Rivedoux Plage. Site is well signed on the right. GPS: 46.1588, -1.2708

Charges guide

Per unit incl. 2 persons and electricity	€ 19.10 - € 24.40
extra person	€ 7.80 - € 13.00
child (over 6 yrs)	€ 4.10 - € 6.20

Rivedoux-Plage

Campéole la Redoute

504 avenue Gustave Perreau, F-17940 Rivedoux-Plage (Charente-Maritime) T: 05 46 09 84 10.

E: redoute@campeole.com **alanrogers.com/FR17565**

La Redoute is a member of the Campéole group and is located on the Ile de Ré, just 100 m. from one of the island's fine sandy beaches. This site has a range of mobile homes for rent but no touring pitches (although these are available on the adjacent Camping du Platin). Rental accommodation includes the new, top quality three bedroom Fisherman's Huts. All accommodation is provided with a fully equipped kitchen, including fridge freezer, and a terrace. On-site amenities include a play area with bouncy castle, entertainment room and a communal barbecue area. The site is attractively located close to the 100 km. of cycle tracks for which the island is renowned.

Facilities

Laundry. Bar on sister site. Play area. Heated outdoor swimming pool (1/7-20/9). Terraced sunbathing area. Entertainment room. Bouncy castle. WiFi (charged).
Off site: Shops and restaurants in Rivedoux Plage 200 m. Chaveau Lighthouse. Bicycle hire 200 m. Beach 300 m.

Open: 5 April - 27 September.

Directions

From La Rochelle take N237 and continue over the bridge to the Ile de Ré. Continue towards Rivedoux and at the island immediately left (rue de Garenne). Site on right in 100 m. GPS: 46.158956, -1.267545

Charges guide

Contact the site for details.

Ronce-les-Bains

Camping la Clairière

Rue des Roseaux, F-17390 Ronce-les-Bains (Charente-Maritime) T: 05 46 36 36 63.

E: info@camping-la-clairiere.com **alanrogers.com/FR17480**

This site is attractively laid out with flowers, shrubs and trees. It is set away from the other campsites in the area and only 2.5 km. from the sea. Tranquil and peaceful, there is a feeling of spaciousness due to its setting within 12 hectares. The 150 touring pitches are level, shady and have easy access for large units. Eleven of these have their own sanitary facilities, fridge and barbecue. There are 38 mobile homes and chalets for rent. On-site facilities are impressive and include a covered and heated pool, as well as an outdoor water slide and flume. The gym here is well equipped and massages are also on offer.

Facilities

Two modern sanitary blocks. Baby room. No facilities for disabled visitors. Washing machines. Shop, bar, restaurant and takeaway (from June). Indoor heated swimming pool, children's pool, slide and flume. Games room. Gym. Massage. Children's club. Entertainment in July/Aug. Tennis. Pétanque. Minigolf. Basketball, volleyball and football pitch. Play area. Bicycle hire. No charcoal barbecues. WiFi in some areas (charged). Dog shower.

Open: 29 June - 7 September.

Directions

From Rochfort on D733 join D123 to Marennes and La Tremblade. In La Tremblade join D14 and take first right 1 km. after 'paper boat' roundabout. From Saujon on N150 join D14 (La Tremblade). 3 km. after Arvert, turn left at site sign. GPS: 45.772933, -1.166734

Charges guide

Per unit incl. 2 persons and electricity	€ 28.50 - € 36.50

Royan

Camping les Chèvrefeuilles

11 allée des Chèvrefeuilles, F-17200 Royan (Charente-Maritime) T: 05 46 02 61 94.

E: contact@leschevrefeuilles.com **alanrogers.com/FR17075**

Purpose-built in a wooded area on the outskirts of Royan and opened in 2012, les Chèvrefeuilles has 85 level, grassy pitches, separated by freshly planted bushes and hedging. Forty-five are for tourers, all with 16A electricity. A few extra large pitches (200 sq.m) are available and there are 40 mobile homes for hire. The aim of the friendly, English-speaking manager is to ensure that the site remains peaceful and tranquil. The beaches and all the attractions of Royan and Saint Palais-sur-Mer are within easy reach. The open sea and the Gironde Estuary provide endless opportunities for swimming, sailing and watersports, and the port is a starting point for a variety of boat trips.

Facilities

Modern heated sanitary block is kept spotless and has preset showers and washbasins in bright cubicles, baby room and en-suite unit for disabled visitors. Laundry facilities. Motorcaravan services. Small shop selling basics. Breakfasts delivered to pitch. Pizza van calls twice weekly. Heated swimming and paddling pools (1/5-30/9). Playground (2-12 yrs). Playroom (2-5 yrs). Games room. TV room. Multisports court. Boules pitch. Bicycle hire. Cots, high chairs and electric barbecues available. Free WiFi over site. Off site: Shops 3 km. Beach 2.5 km.

Open: 2 April - 12 November.

Directions

Royan is 110 km. northwest of Bordeaux. Site is on D733 Rochefort road north of town, signed to east at roundabout after Jaffe. From other directions take D25 road to bypass Royan and turn north on D733 to site on right at roundabout in about 2 km. GPS: 45.654242, -1.019827

Charges guide

Per unit incl. 3 persons and electricity	€ 31.00 - € 47.00
extra person (over 12 yrs)	€ 6.00

Royan

Campéole Clairefontaine

6 rue du Colonel Lachaud, F-17200 Royan (Charente-Maritime) T: 05 46 39 08 11.
E: clairefontaine@campeole.com **alanrogers.com/FR17100**

Campéole Clairefontaine is situated on the outskirts of Royan, 300 m. from a golden sandy beach and a casino. This is a busy site which has benefited from much recent investment and many of the facilities, especially the sanitary facilities, are of a high standard. There are 246 pitches, of which 123 are available for touring units. Electricity (10A) is available to all pitches but some may require long leads. The site is mostly shaded and level with easy access to pitches. American motorhomes are accepted but care is needed on the entrance road to the site as it is not wide enough for two vehicles to pass.

Facilities

Two very modern sanitary blocks. Good facilities for disabled visitors and children. Washing machines. Motorcaravan services. Bar and restaurant with takeaway (June-mid Sept). Large swimming and paddling pools (from June). Four play areas. Games room with TV. Tennis. Basketball. Entertainment in high season. WiFi in some areas (charged). Accommodation to rent. Off site: Beach and sailing 300 m. Bicycle hire 350 m.

Open: 3 April - 27 September.

Directions

Exit Royan on Avenue de Pontaillac towards La Palmyre. Turn right at the casino on the front, up Avenue Louise. Site is on left after 200 m. and is signed. GPS: 45.631388, -1.050122

Charges guide

Per unit incl. 2 persons and electricity	€ 20.70 - € 28.40

Saint Angeau

Camping Devezeau

F-16230 Saint Angeau (Charente) T: 05 45 94 63 09. E: ask@campingdevezeau.com
alanrogers.com/FR16040

Camping Devezeau has recently been acquired by its current English owners. They have lovingly restored the buildings and pitches to create an attractive and well equipped site, with water and 6A electricity available to all 29 pitches. There are eight mobile home pitches and the remainder are for touring units. Mature hedges divide the pitches and each is lit with its own solar lamp. The sanitary block is a restored barn with new facilities. Next to the swimming pool there is a restaurant serving food in a friendly and welcoming ambience. The owners clearly enjoy the company of their campers and do all they can to make their stay enjoyable.

Facilities

One sanitary block provides hot showers and a spacious, well equipped room for disabled visitors. Laundry facilities. Gas supplies. Bar and café/restaurant (1/3-1/11). Fish and chip van calls Sat. Solar-heated swimming pool (12x12 m; June-Sept). WiFi throughout (free). Off site: Shop and bar in village 1.5 km. Fishing and canoeing 2 km. Rivers Charente and Tardoire.

Open: Mid February - late November.

Directions

From north on N10 exit for Mansle. Turn left (east) at lights onto D6 for St Angeau (9 km). At St Angeau turn right on D15 (Tourriers). Take first left, after 300 m. site signed. GPS: 45.83927, 0.27196

Charges guide

Per unit incl. 2 persons and electricity	€ 17.00 - € 20.00

No credit cards.

Saint Augustin-sur-Mer

Le Logis du Breuil

36 rue du centre, F-17570 Saint Augustin-sur-Mer (Charente-Maritime) T: 05 46 23 23 45.
E: info@logis-du-breuil.com **alanrogers.com/FR17190**

The first impression on arrival at this impressive campsite is one of space. The site covers a 30-hectare expanse of farm pasture where (on different areas) cattle graze and children play. The nine-hectare camping areas are set among rows of mature and shady trees giving a dappled effect to the 229 grassy touring pitches. All have 3-10A electricity and are very large with direct access to wide, unpaved alleys which lead on to the few tarmac roads around the site. Some serviced pitches are available. The amenities are centred around the reception area and pool complex (a new facility is planned for 2016). The surrounding area is agricultural land and the beaches of the Atlantic coast are nearby.

Facilities

Four well maintained toilet blocks (one rebuilt in 2014). Laundry facilities. Motorcaravan services. Excellent shop, bar, restaurant and takeaway (20/5-15/9). Swimming pools (20/5-15/9). No evening entertainment. Play area. Indoor games area. TV room. Multisports pitch. Boules. Bicycle hire. Tennis. Archery (July/Aug). Excursions organised. WiFi on part of site (charged). Gîtes, mobile homes and chalets to rent.

Open: 9 May - 30 September.

Directions

From A10 exit 35, take the N150 to Saujon and continue on the N150 to Royan. Take the D25 towards La Palmyre (Zoo), then turn right onto the D145 towards St Augustin. Site is signed and is 2 km. on the left. GPS: 45.67448, -1.096232

Charges guide

Per unit incl. 2 persons and electricity (6A)	€ 23.00 - € 31.75
extra person	€ 4.60 - € 8.20

Saint Clément-des-Baleines

Camping les Baleines

Le Gillieux, F-17590 Saint Clément-des-Baleines (Charente-Maritime) T: 05 46 29 40 76.

E: contact@camping-lesbaleines.com **alanrogers.com/FR17400**

This campsite is situated at the western end of the Ile de Ré near the Balaines lighthouse and La Conche beach, considered to be one of the most beautiful beaches on the island. This is an attractive, well maintained, spacious site on different levels, occupying a good position close to the long golden sandy beach. It has 199 pitches of which 164 are for touring (120 with 10A electricity) and the remainder are occupied by mobile homes. They are level, mostly open and easily accessible, with some of a generous size. This end of the island is quieter and less crowded than the eastern part and the whole island has a network of paths for walkers and cyclists. This is a good base to explore the island's many places of interest, such as the ornithological park, the salt marshes and the charming little ports, each with its own character. The lighthouse, just a short walk away, is an historical monument surrounded by gardens, with a museum and the original lighthouse tower dating from 1682. It is worth climbing to the top on a good day just for the views. The island's capital, Saint Martin, is of historical interest having fortifications created by Vauban; it also offers a good range of shops, restaurants and bars.

Facilities

Three modern sanitary blocks (two recently renovated) have washbasins in cubicles, controllable showers and excellent facilities for babies and disabled visitors. New laundry room. Snack bar (7/7-25/8). Small shop (15/6-15/9). Takeaway food (July/Aug). Boules. Play area. Organised activities for children in July/Aug. Minigolf. TV room. WiFi over part of site (free). Bicycle hire. No charcoal barbecues outside communal area. Off site: Beach and fishing 200 m. Riding 500 m. Golf 5 km. Cycling and walking trails.

Open: 19 April - 24 September.

Directions

Cross to island from La Rochelle and take D201/D735 to Ars-en-Ré and Phare des Baleines. When you turn towards the lighthouse, look out for Camping de la Plage on your right and turn left into road opposite (rue du Chaume/rue de la Madeleine). Continue ahead for 500 m. to third crossroads; site is along track to right. GPS: 46.23975, -1.5599

Charges guide

Per unit incl. 6 persons and electricity	€ 21.00 - € 38.00
extra person (over 2 yrs)	€ 4.70 - € 5.60

Saint Clément-des-Baleines

Village Center la Côte Sauvage

336 rue de la Forêt, F-17590 Saint Clément-des-Baleines (Charente-Maritime) T: 08 25 00 20 30.

E: contact@village-center.com **alanrogers.com/FR17965**

Camping la Côte Sauvage is a member of the Village Center Group, located on the Ile de Ré, close to the pretty village of Saint Clement-des-Baleines. There are 274 pitches here (80-100 sq.m), as well as a number of fully equipped tents which are available for rent. The site also offers ten traditional yurts which have been attractively prepared in traditional style. Activities here are designed to take advantage of the site's natural setting and include ornithology and twilight nature trails. Shops, bars and restaurants can be found within walking distance.

Facilities

Three (unheated) toilet blocks include mainly open washbasins and preset showers in cubicles. Facilities for children and disabled visitors. Laundry. Motorcaravan services. Mobile snack bar. Play area. Activities for children. Small library. Volleyball. Boules. Bicycle hire. WiFi over part of site (charged). Off site: Shops and restaurants at St Clement-des-Baleines.

Open: 2 April - 1 October.

Directions

Approaching from the toll bridge, follow D735 past La Couarde-sur-Mer and Ars-en-Ré as far as St Clement des Baleines. The site is well signed from here. GPS: 46.225423, -1.54462

Charges guide

Per unit incl. 2 persons and electricity	€ 17.00 - € 25.00

Saint Georges-d'Oléron

Camping les Gros Joncs

850 route de Ponthezieres, les Sables Vignier B.P. 17, F-17190 Saint Georges-d'Oléron (Charente-Maritime)

T: 05 46 76 52 29. E: info@camping-les-gros-joncs.com **alanrogers.com/FR17070**

Situated on the west coast of the island of Ile d'Oléron, les Gros Joncs is owned and run by the Cavel family who work hard to keep the site up to date and of high quality. There are 50 or so touring pitches of a good size (some extra large) with tall pine trees providing a choice between full sun and varying degrees of shade. All have water and 10A electricity to hand. The main building not only houses a light and airy reception, but also a modern, beautifully presented bar and restaurant, a fully stocked and competitively priced shop, an attractive indoor swimming pool and a magnificent spa. The indoor pool, with water jets and jacuzzi, has glass sides which in good weather are opened out onto an outdoor pool area where there are also water slides, a paddling area and plenty of sunbathing terraces. Both pools are heated. The spa offers hydrotherapy and beauty treatments, sauna and a comprehensive fitness room. Much attention has been given to the needs of disabled visitors here, including chalets where space and equipment are specially adapted. All the amenities are of a standard unusual on a campsite.

Facilities

Traditional style toilet facilities are kept to a high standard and include provision for disabled visitors. Laundry facilities. Motorcaravan services. Well stocked shop with bakery. Restaurant and bar (15/4-15/9). Indoor pool with first class spa and wellness centre (all year, with professional staff). Outdoor pool (heated, 15/4-15/9). Play area. Bicycle hire. Children's clubs and entertainment (July/Aug). Internet access and free WiFi throughout. ATM. No charcoal barbecues. Off site: Beach 200 m. and 400 m. via a sandy path. Bus service from Chéray. Fishing 2 km. Riding 2 km. Golf 12 km.

Open: April - mid November.

Directions

Cross the viaduct onto the Ile d'Oléron. Take D734 (St Georges-d'Oléron). At traffic lights in Chéray turn left. Follow signs for camping and Les Sable Vignier. After prominent speed bumps turn right and follow site signs to les Gros Joncs.
GPS: 45.95356, -1.37979

Charges guide

Per unit incl. 2 persons and electricity	€ 20.30 - € 50.50
extra person	€ 6.80 - € 13.30
child (under 7 yrs)	€ 3.10 - € 8.10
dog	free - € 3.00

Saint Georges-d'Oléron

Camping l'Anse des Pins

Chemin du Râteau-Domino, F-17190 Saint Georges-d'Oléron (Charente-Maritime) T: 02 51 56 08 78.
E: contacts@camping-apv.com **alanrogers.com/FR17270**

Rock pools, sand dunes and spectacular sunsets, with sea views from some of the pitches, help to make this site attractive to those seeking an 'away from it all' holiday in a quiet part of the Ile d'Oléron. The campsite, which has direct access to a beautiful, sandy beach, is arranged in three areas, some with good shade, others in full sun. Of the 352 pitches, 137 are for touring units, most with electricity (3-10A), water and drainage. The nearest village (Domino) is about 500 m. away and has a daily market.

Facilities

Two fairly basic toilet blocks (plus two small blocks, open as needed) with mainly British style toilets, preset showers and washbasins in cabins. Laundry facilities. Bar, shop with limited takeaway and snack bar (June-Aug). Heated indoor pool (all season) and outdoor swimming and paddling pools with slides (April-Sept). Play area. Activities in high season. Tennis. Boules. Bicycle hire. WiFi over part of site (charged). Off site: Beach and fishing 50 m. Village 500 m. St Georges 5 km. Sailing 9 km. Shops, bars, restaurants and hypermarket in St Pierre 10 km.

Open: 11 April - 26 September.

Directions

Cross bridge onto Ile d'Oléron and follow D26/D734 (St Pierre then St Georges). In 18 km. at Chéray, turn left at traffic lights (signed Camping). Continue to and through Domino (narrow streets). Follow green signs to l'Anse des Pins (avoid side roads). GPS: 45.97059, -1.3864

Charges guide

Per unit incl. 2 persons and electricity	€ 23.15 - € 34.78
extra person	€ 8.26 - € 8.77

Saint Georges-d'Oléron

Camping la Campière

Chemin de l'Achnau, Chaucre, F-17190 Saint Georges-d'Oléron (Charente-Maritime) T: 05 46 76 72 25.
E: contact@la-campiere.com **alanrogers.com/FR17275**

Close to the Côte Sauvage and the Plage de Chaucre, this friendly, family run site is probably best suited to couples looking for a quiet, relaxing break. It is in a protected area of the state forest, 400 m. from one of the most beautiful beaches on the island. There are 66 good sized, grassy pitches, some open, others among tall pine trees. Most have electricity (10A), water and drainage. The surrounding area is well worth exploring and has numerous cycling and walking routes. The focal point of the site is a small wine bar. Owners of large outfits should phone ahead to reserve the larger pitches.

Facilities

One unheated toilet block has washbasins (some in cubicles) and controllable showers. Family room. Facilities for disabled visitors and children. Laundry facilities. Motorcaravan services. Small wine bar and takeaway (7/4-30/9). Bread can be ordered. Small outdoor heated swimming pool. Library. TV room. Play area. Boules. Basketball. Bicycle hire. Communal barbecue. Free WiFi throughout. Accommodation to rent. Off site: Beach 400 m. Fishing 400 m. Riding 6 km.

Open: 11 April - 26 September.

Directions

Take exit 35 from A10 (at Saintes), then west on D728 to Marennes. Cross viaduct to Ile d'Oléron and follow D26 and D734 to St Pierre d'Oléron. Continue on D734 to Cheray. At end of village take second left turn to Chaucre then follow campsite signs. GPS: 45.992475, -1.38001

Charges guide

Per unit incl. 2 persons and electricity	€ 22.84 - € 37.84
extra person	€ 4.80 - € 8.60

Saint Georges-d'Oléron

Chadotel le Domaine d'Oléron

La Jousselinière, F-17190 Saint Georges-d'Oléron (Charente-Maritime) T: 05 46 76 54 97.
E: info@chadotel.com **alanrogers.com/FR17470**

This is a neat, well presented and well managed site where you will receive a warm and friendly welcome from Anneke and Freddy who speak excellent English. The site is set in a peaceful rural location between Saint Pierre and Saint Georges and is part of the Chadotel group. At present there are 172 pitches of which 60 are for touring units. The pitches are generously sized (100-150 sq.m) and are mostly sunny, level and easily accessible, all with 10A electricity. The site is just 3 km. from the beach and the Forest of Saumonards. The local port, shops and restaurants are also nearby.

Facilities

Two modern sanitary blocks include facilities for disabled visitors and babies. Laundry facilities. Motorcaravan services. Snack bar and takeaway, bar with TV (all 15/5-10/9). Bread delivered daily. Swimming pool with slides (1/5-14/9). Adventure style play area. Six pétanque lanes. Bicycle hire. Entertainment (July/Aug). WiFi over site (charged). Max. 1 dog per pitch. Off site: Fishing and riding 2 km. Golf 8 km. Royan Zoo.

Open: 6 April - 21 September.

Directions

Take D734 to St Pierre. Turn right in St Pierre after Leclerc supermarket. At next roundabout turn left (Le Bois Fleury). After airfield, turn right and left and site is on the left. GPS: 45.9674685, -1.3192605

Charges guide

Per unit incl. 2 persons and electricity	€ 17.00 - € 32.00
extra person	€ 6.00

Saint Georges-les-Baillargeaux

Camping le Futuriste

RD 20, F-86130 Saint Georges-les-Baillargeaux (Vienne) T: 05 49 52 47 52.
E: camping-le-futuriste@wanadoo.fr **alanrogers.com/FR86040**

Le Futuriste is a neat, modern site, open all year and very close to Futuroscope. Its location is also very convenient for the A10 and N10 motorway network. There are 123 individual, level, grassy pitches of a generous size, divided by flowering hedges, 76 with 6A electricity and 64 also with water and waste water connections. The pitches are mostly open, although some do have the benefit of shade from trees. All are accessed via tarmac roads. There are lovely panoramic views from this site and the popular attraction of Futuroscope can be clearly seen across the valley. Large units are accepted by prior arrangement. A pleasant restaurant on site offers good food at reasonable prices. Entertainment takes place in the daytime rather than in the evenings. This site is ideal for a short stay to visit Futuroscope, but it is equally good for longer stays to explore the region.

Facilities

Excellent, clean sanitary facilities in two heated blocks. Good facilities for disabled visitors and babies. Laundry facilities. Shop (1/5-30/9, bread to order). Bar/restaurant snack bar and takeaway (July/Aug). Heated outdoor pool with slide and paddling pool (July/Aug). Covered pool. Games room. Boules. Multisports area. Lake fishing. Daily activities in season. Youth groups not accepted. Only gas and electric barbecues allowed. WiFi throughout (charged). Off site: Hypermarket 600 m. Futuroscope 2 km. Golf 5 km. Riding 10 km.

Open: All year.

Directions

From either A10 autoroute or N10, take Futuroscope exit. Site is east of both roads, off D20 (St Georges-les-Baillargeaux). Follow signs to St Georges. Site on hill; turn by water tower and site is on left.
GPS: 46.66447, 0.394564

Charges guide

Per unit incl. 2 persons and electricity	€ 23.30 - € 31.70
extra person (over 5 yrs)	€ 2.90 - € 3.80
dog	€ 2.80

Camping Cheques accepted.

Saint Georges-de-Didonne

Camping Bois Soleil

2 avenue de Suzac, F-17110 Saint Georges-de-Didonne (Charente-Maritime)
T: 05 46 05 05 94. E: camping.bois.soleil@wanadoo.fr **alanrogers.com/FR17010**

Close to the sea, Bois Soleil is a large site in three parts, with 165 serviced pitches for touring units and a few for tents. All the touring pitches are hedged and have electricity (all 10A), with water and drainage between two. The main part, Les Pins, is attractive with trees and shrubs providing shade. Opposite is La Mer with direct access to the beach, some areas with less shade and an area for tents. The third part, La Forêt, is for caravan holiday homes. It is best to book your preferred area as it can be full mid June to late August. Excellent private sanitary facilities are available to rent, either on your pitch or at a block (subject to availability). There are a few pitches with lockable gates. The areas are all well tended and are cleared and raked between visitors. This lively site offers something for everyone, whether it be a beach-side spot or a traditional pitch, plenty of activities or the quiet life. Recent additions include a new toilet block and some accommodation to rent with sea views. The wide sandy beach is popular with children and provides a pleasant walk to the pretty town of Saint Georges-de-Didonne.

Facilities

Each area has one large and one small sanitary block. Heated block near reception. Cleaned twice daily, they include facilities for disabled visitors and babies. Launderette. Supermarket, bakery, beach shop (all 15/4-15/9). Restaurant, bar and takeaway (all 15/4-15/9). Swimming pool (heated 15/6-15/9). Steam room. Tennis. Play area. TV room and library. WiFi throughout (charged). Charcoal and electric barbecues are not permitted. Dogs are not accepted 29/6-25/8. Off site: Bicycle hire adjacent. Fishing 200 m. Riding 500 m. Golf 20 km.

Open: 1 April - 8 October.

Directions

From Royan centre take coast road (D25) along the seafront of St Georges-de-Didonne towards Meschers. Site is signed at roundabout at end of the main beach. GPS: 45.583583, -0.986533

Charges guide

Per unit incl. 3 persons and electricity	€ 16.00 - € 47.00
extra person	€ 6.00 - € 12.00
child (under 7 yrs)	free - € 8.00
dog	€ 3.00 - € 5.00

Less 20% outside July/Aug.

Camping Cheques accepted.

Saint Hilaire-la-Palud

Flower Camping le Lidon

F-79210 Saint Hilaire-la-Palud (Deux-Sèvres) T: 05 49 35 33 64. E: info@le-lidon.com
alanrogers.com/FR79060

Le Lidon is located within the Marais Poitevin, an enchanting region of over 400 km. of rivers, canals and fens lying to the west of Niort. This site has 140 grassy pitches scattered across three hectares, 119 for touring, all with 10A electricity. The site's selection of rented accommodation includes fully equipped, Canadian-style tents and chalets. The Marais Poitevin is undeniably best explored by canoe or punt and it is possible to rent these on site. During high season, an activity and entertainment programme is organised including a children's club and various family activities. The site bar/restaurant is open all season and specialises in local cuisine. The Marais Mouillé makes up around a third of the Marais Poitevin, but it is the best known part, otherwise known as La Venise Verte (Green Venice), with miles of conches (channels) and drainage ditches overshadowed by ash and poplars.

Facilities

Two toilet blocks (one heated and one is closed in low season). Facilities for disabled visitors. Motorcaravan services. Shop. Bar. Snack bar. Restaurant (from where bread is available to order). Laundry. Heated swimming pool (July/Aug). Games room. Play area. Direct access to river. Fishing. Bicycle and canoe hire. Entertainment and activities (July/Aug). Tents, Trigano bungalows and chalets for rent. WiFi on part of site (charged). Off site: St Hilaire-la-Palud with a good selection of shops and cafés, as well as an open-air cinema. Fishing (river). La Maison des Oiseaux (ornithological centre). Tennis 3 km. Riding 15 km. Golf 25 km. Vendée beaches 50 km. Cycle and walking tracks.

Open: 11 April - 19 September.

Directions

St Hilaire-la-Palud is midway between Niort and La Rochelle. From the north (Niort) leave A10 at exit 33 and head west on N248 as far as Epannes. Head north here on D1 to Sansais, then west on D3 to St Hilaire-la-Palud. Site is signed to right just after village. Long access road. GPS: 46.2838, -0.74345

Charges guide

Per unit incl. 2 persons and electricity	€ 19.50 - € 28.00
extra person	€ 5.50 - € 6.50
child (3-6 yrs)	€ 2.00 - € 3.50
dog	€ 2.00 - € 3.50

Camping Cheques accepted.

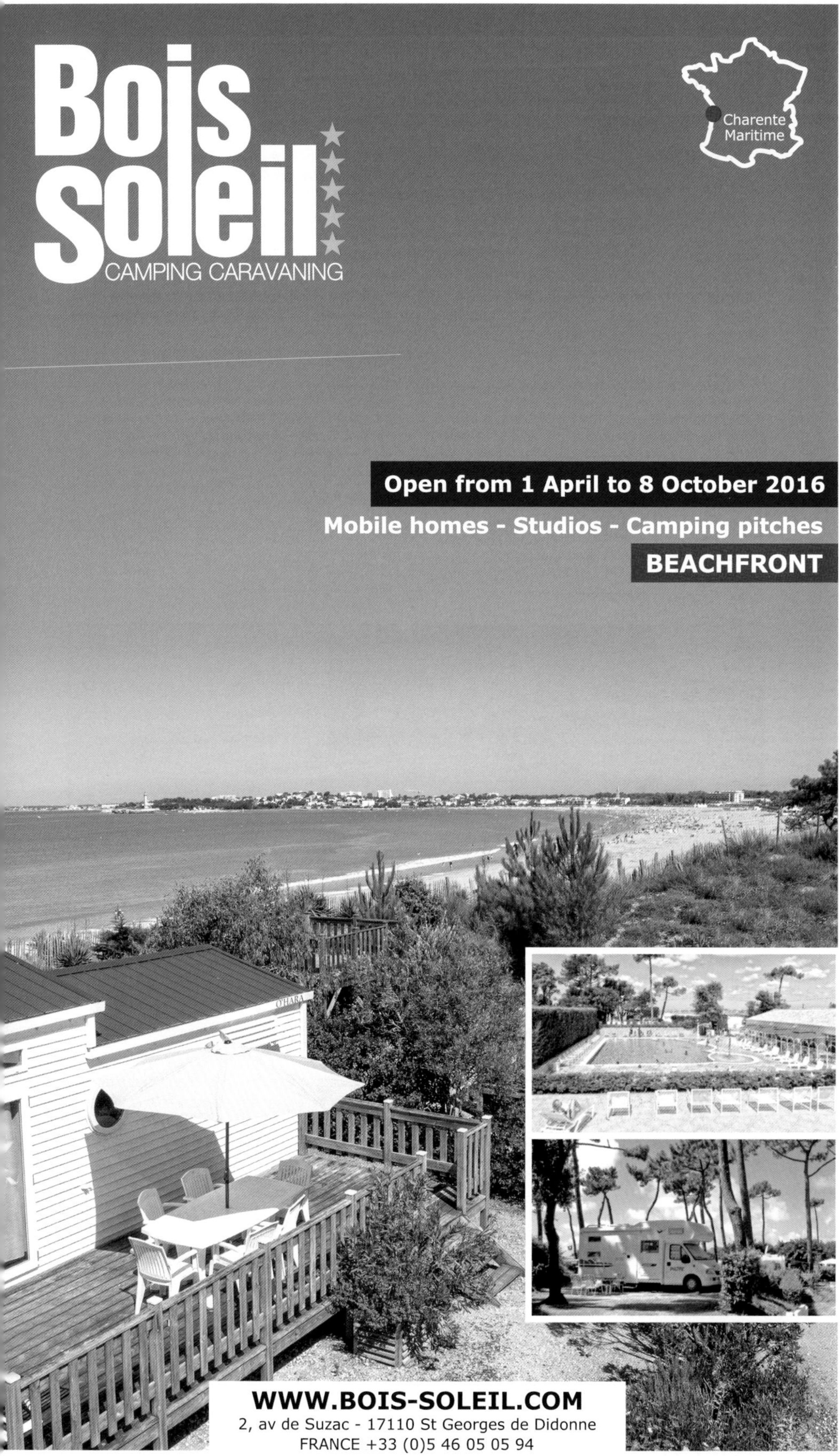
Bois Soleil
CAMPING CARAVANING
Charente Maritime
Open from 1 April to 8 October 2016
Mobile homes - Studios - Camping pitches
BEACHFRONT
WWW.BOIS-SOLEIL.COM
2, av de Suzac - 17110 St Georges de Didonne
FRANCE +33 (0)5 46 05 05 94

Saint Just-Luzac

Castel Camping Séquoia Parc

La Josephtrie, F-17320 Saint Just-Luzac (Charente-Maritime) T: 05 46 85 55 55. E: info@sequoiaparc.com

alanrogers.com/FR17140

This is definitely a site not to be missed. Approached by an avenue of flowers, shrubs and trees, Séquoia Parc is a Castel site set in the grounds of La Josephtrie, a striking château with beautifully restored outbuildings and courtyard area with a bar and restaurant. Most of the 640 pitches are about 140 sq.m. with 6/10A electricity connections and separated by mature shrubs providing plenty of privacy. The site has 350 mobile homes and chalets, with a further 65 used by tour operators. This is a popular site and reservation is necessary in high season. Children's clubs are run all season, with entertainment provided in high season. The site is designed to a high specification with reception in a large, light and airy room leading to the courtyard area. The pool complex with water slides is impressive and a new terraced area, adjacent to the snack bar, allows you to enjoy your food in a very pleasant garden setting with sunshades. A member of Leading Campings group.

Facilities

Three spotlessly clean luxurious toilet blocks (one heated) include units with washbasin and shower and facilities for disabled visitors and children. Large laundry. Motorcaravan services. Gas supplies. Large supermarket. Boutique. Restaurant/bar and takeaway. Swimming pool complex with water slides and large paddling pool. Massage (July/Aug). Multisports pitch. Tennis. Games and TV rooms. Bicycle hire. Updated play areas. Excursions and entertainment (high season). Clubs for children. Pony trekking. Children's farm. WiFi zones (charged). Off site: Supermarket and bank 5 km. Beach fishing 5 km. Golf 15 km. Flying trips. Ile d'Oléron. La Rochelle.

Open: 13 May - 4 September.

Directions

Site is 5 km. southeast of Marennes. From Rochefort take D733 south for 12 km. Turn west on D123 to Ile d'Oléron. Continue for 12 km. Turn southeast on D728 (Saintes). Site signed, in 1 km. on left. From A10 at Saintes take D728 and turn right shortly after St Just. Site signed. GPS: 45.81095, -1.06109

Charges guide

Per unit incl. 2 persons and electricity	€ 21.00 - € 56.00
extra person	€ 8.00 - € 11.00
child (3-11 yrs)	free - € 8.00
dog	€ 7.00

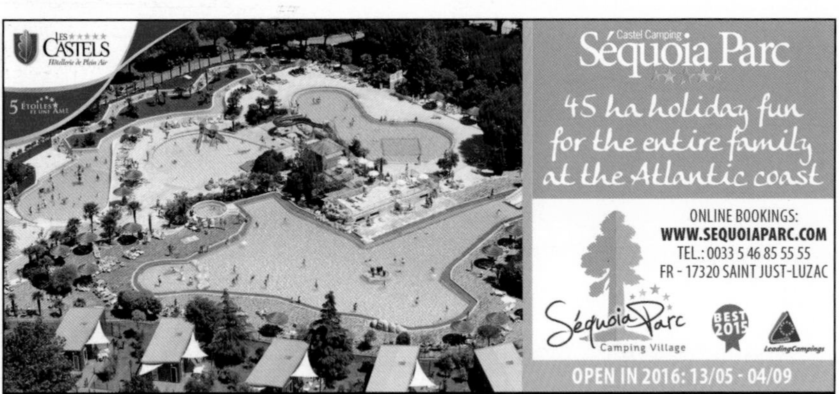

Saint Laurent-de-Céris

Camp Laurent

Le Fournet, F-16450 Saint Laurent-de-Céris (Charente) T: 06 02 22 37 15. E: lecamplaurent@gmail.com

alanrogers.com/FR16080

Camp Laurent is a small and peaceful CL style, dog friendly, caravan, motorcaravan and camping site for adults only. There are ten pitches (six for touring), with electricity (6A Europlug), set within eight acres of beautiful countryside just on the outskirts of the village of Saint Laurent-de-Ceris. The site borders the River Charente with great views over the valley, open fields and oak forest. The river can be accessed at the bottom of a lovely wooded bank from where you can fish and canoe.

Facilities

New toilet and shower facilities and washing up area. Facilities for disabled visitors. Washing machine. Swimming pool. Fishing. Canoeing. Picnic areas. Free WiFi. Off site: St Laurent-de-Céris (shops and a bar/restaurant). Cycle and walking trails. Riding.

Open: All year.

Directions

Leave the A20 motorway, exit 23. Head west on the N145 to Bellac and then to Confolens on the D951. Continue on the D951 (St Claud), but before arriving there turn right on the D15 to St Laurent-de-Céris. Just before village, turn right on D345 and site is on right after a builder's yard. GPS: 45.95995, 0.5296

Charges guide

Per unit incl. 2 persons and electricity	€ 25.00
No credit cards.	

Saint Nazaire sur Charente

Camping l'Abri-Côtier

26 la Bernardière, F-17780 Saint Nazaire sur Charente (Charente-Maritime) T: 05 46 84 81 65.
E: abri-cotier@wanadoo.fr **alanrogers.com/FR17815**

Ideally situated for discovering some of the best tourist attractions of Charente-Maritime, Abri Côtier is a family friendly site some 1,800 metres from the sea, and three kilometres from the Anses beach with its seawater pool and views of the Ile d'Oléron and Fort Boyard. The 54 touring pitches (90 sq.m) are delineated by mature hedges and have 6A electricity (French 2-pin plug, long leads useful). The indoor pool has a splash pool for young children and a sun terrace.

Facilities

One traditional sanitary block is fully equipped with free hot showers, washbasins in cubicles and facilities for children and disabled visitors. Laundry facilities. Motorcaravan services. Tourist market (July/Aug). Small shop, bar, snack bar and takeaway (4/7-29/8). Heated indoor pool and paddling pool. Play area. Bouncy castle. Trampoline. Volleyball. Boules. Games/TV rooms. Entertainment (high season). Communal barbecue area. Bicycle hire. Mobile homes and chalets to rent. WiFi throughout (charged). Off site: Greengrocer 800 m.

Open: 1 April - 30 September.

Directions

Travelling south on D733, pass Rochefort crossing River Charente, take exit for Soubise and St Agnant. At roundabout take first exit onto D238 (Soubise). In Soubise, follow road round to right (St Nazaire) and continue to Fontrouet. At roundabout take 2nd exit (Port des Barques). Turn left at sign for St Froult and Camping, then right for St. Bernardette. Site on right as you leave the hamlet. GPS: 45.93381, -1.06013

Charges guide

Per unit incl. 2 persons and electricity € 16.50 - € 28.50

Saint Palais-sur-Mer

Camping le Logis

22 rue des Palombes, F-17420 Saint Palais-sur-Mer (Charente-Maritime) T: 05 46 23 20 23.
E: reservations@yukadivillages.com **alanrogers.com/FR17530**

Le Logis is a member of the Yukadi Villages group and is a popular site close to the attractive resort of Saint Palais-sur-Mer, on the edge of the forest of Saint Augustin. The site was established back in 1936 and there are now 647 pitches here. The majority of these are occupied by mobile homes and chalets (many for rent) but there are 208 touring pitches also available. These are grassy and of a reasonable size, and all have 5A electrical connections. This is a lively site in high season with a varied programme of entertainment and activities, including concerts and discovery excursions into the forest.

Facilities

Four heated sanitary blocks are well situated around the site. Facilities for disabled visitors. Laundry. Shop, bar and snack bar. Excellent water park with heated pools, children's pool and water slides. Games room. Tennis. Play area. TV room. New multisports area. Bicycle hire. Activities and entertainment. Mobile homes and chalets for rent. WiFi in some areas (free). Off site: Fishing and golf 600 m. Beach 600 m. Riding 800 m. Royan 8 km.

Open: 27 April - 9 September.

Directions

From Royan, head west on D25 towards La Palmyre. Pass the golf course (on the right), and then turn left immediately towards St Palais-sur-Mer. Turn left at the next crossroads and site is 200 m. further on the right. GPS: 45.65208, -1.1159

Charges guide

Per unit incl. 2 persons and electricity € 22.20 - € 42.70
extra person € 4.40 - € 8.80

Saint Sornin

Flower Camping les Etangs Mina

17 route de Rochefort, lieu-dit Cadeuil, F-17600 Saint Sornin (Charente-Maritime) T: 05 46 22 82 61.
E: contact@campingmina.com **alanrogers.com/FR17325**

Les Etangs Mina is set in the heart of the Charente-Maritime, the varied landscapes of the Brouage Marshes including grasslands, salt meadows and reed beds, all rich in flora and fauna. The site is generally quiet and peaceful, offering a programme of activities during the summer season. The 7-hectare site has 109 flat grassy pitches of which 43 are used for touring units. Most of the pitches have 10A electricity (some Europlug), although long leads will be required on some pitches. For those interested in fishing, there are three lakes to choose from. Mobile homes are available to rent.

Facilities

Two sanitary blocks (unheated) provide toilets, showers and washbasins in cubicles. Facilities for children and disabled visitors. Laundry. No motorcaravan service point. Small shop. Bread to order. Bar, snack bar and takeaway (July/Aug and w/ends). Swimming pool (15/6-15/9). Playground. Bouncy castle. Bicycle hire. TV and games room. Boules. Fishing. Activities and entertainment in high season. Communal barbecue area. WiFi throughout (free). Off site: Riding 5 km. Watersports 10 km. Beach 20 km.

Open: 4 April - 29 September.

Directions

From A10 motorway exit 35 follow signs for Ile de Oléron. Join D137 and then D728. Pass through La Clisse, Balanzac and Nancras. At junction with the D733 turn north. The site is then on the left after 500 m. GPS: 45.76171, -0.94192

Charges guide

Per unit incl. 2 persons and electricity € 18.50 - € 26.50
extra person € 3.60 - € 5.50

Saint Trojan-les-Bains

Camping Indigo Oléron les Pins

11 avenue des Bris, F-17370 Saint Trojan-les-Bains (Charente-Maritime) T: 05 46 76 02 39.

E: oleron@camping-indigo.com **alanrogers.com/FR17580**

This attractive five hectare site is a member of the Indigo group. It can be found close to the popular seaside resort of Saint Trojan-les-Bains on the south side of the island. There are 163 pitches (56 for touring), which vary in size, most of which have electrical connections (10A French type). Indigo Oléron is situated in a lightly wooded setting on undulating, sandy terrain, just 1 km. from the nearest sandy beach. A number of specially designed wood and canvas safari-style tents are available for hire; the latest range are equipped with a shower, WC and sink. Large units should telephone ahead to ensure suitable pitch availability. Although quiet in low season, this site becomes much livelier during the peak months with daily entertainment and activities.

Facilities

Two very modern toilet blocks provide washbasins in cabins, showers and British style toilets. Ramped facilities for disabled visitors. Laundry. Motorcaravan services. Heated outdoor swimming pool (all season). Small bar, snack bar and takeaway (July/Aug). Bicycle hire. Sandy play area with equipment for young children. Activity and entertainment programme. Gas or electric barbecues only. Free WiFi. Max. 1 dog. Off site: Nearest beach and fishing 1.5 km. Tourist train at St Trojan. Walking and cycling tracks. Supermarket 3 km. Riding 5 km. Golf 7 km.

Open: 4 May - 12 September.

Directions

From Marennes, cross bridge to Ile d'Oléron (D26) then follow signs to St Trojan on D126. In town, drive along coast road to second roundabout. Turn right and continue ahead. Follow the railway track and where the road bends left, follow the road and the site is on your left. GPS: 45.831247, -1.213591

Charges guide

Per unit incl. 2 persons and electricity	€ 20.20 - € 30.30
extra person	€ 3.70 - € 5.90
child (2-7 yrs)	free - € 3.80
dog	€ 2.20 - € 4.40

Saint Trojan-les-Bains

Flower Camping Saint Tro'Park

6 avenue des Bris, F-17370 Saint Trojan-les-Bains (Charente-Maritime) T: 05 46 76 00 47.

E: la-combinette@wanadoo.fr **alanrogers.com/FR17865**

Saint Tro'Park can be found at the heart of a pine forest and just 1 km. from the sandy Gatseau beach on the beautiful Ile d'Oléron. This four-hectare site has 208 marked, sandy pitches (80-120 sq.m); the 93 for touring units are shaded and have 10A electricity hook-ups. The remainder are occupied by cottages and mobile homes for rent. There is a heated swimming pool with fenced paddling area and plenty to keep youngsters busy, including a miniclub in July and August. Families with older children can hire bikes on site and explore the island. A route from the site leads to the bustling seaside town of Saint Trojan. There is also a tourist train nearby that runs through the forest to a deserted beach.

Facilities

Two modern sanitary blocks have hot showers and washbasins in cubicles. Facilities for babies and disabled visitors. Landry. Motorcaravan services. Shop. Fresh bread and pastries (June-Sept). Bar. Snack bar and takeaway. Heated swimming pool with paddling area. (1/6-15/9). Fitness. Hammam, sauna and spa. Play area. Boules. Volleyball. Multisports pitch. Bicycle hire. No charcoal barbecues. WiFi throughout (charged). Off site: Riding 1 km. Theme park 1 km. Fishing and sailing 1.5 km.

Open: 1 April - 15 October.

Directions

From Marennes, cross bridge to Ile d'Oléron (D26) then follow signs to St Trojan on D126. In town, drive along coast road. At second island, turn right into Ave des Bris. Continue, following railway track and where road bends to left, follow road to site a little further along on the right. GPS: 45.82927, -1.21612

Charges guide

Per unit incl. 2 persons and electricity	€ 22.00 - € 33.90
extra person	€ 6.40 - € 9.70
child (1-5 yrs)	€ 2.70 - € 4.90
dog	€ 2.60 - € 3.60

Sainte Marie-de-Ré

Camping les Chardons bleus

Route de La Flotte, F-17740 Sainte Marie-de-Ré (Charente-Maritime) T: 05 46 30 23 75.
E: chardonsbleus@camping-indigo.com **alanrogers.com/FR17856**

Camping les Chardons Bleus is a simple 4.8-hectare site situated in a pine forest on the Ile de Ré, only 1,500 m. from the sea. It is often a very busy site in the high season due to its low prices. The site is divided into two areas on either side of the entrance road. Some of the 229 level but uneven touring pitches are separated by hedges and mature trees give plenty of shade from the hot sun; all have electricity (6A Europlug). In high season there is a full programme of family entertainment and a snack bar provides takeaway food.

Facilities

Three rather dated sanitary blocks provide preset showers and washbasins in cubicles. Facilities for disabled visitors. Washing machines and dryer. Motorcaravan services. Snack bar/takeaway (July/Aug). Swimming pool planned for 2016. Playground. TV/games room. Bingo, karaoke, family entertainment (July/Aug). Basketball. Table tennis. Tennis. Volleyball. Boules. Picnic areas. Bicycle hire. WiFi over part of site (free). Communal barbecues only. Off site: Village 1.2 km. Beach and fishing 1.5 km.

Open: 3 April - 18 October.

Directions

Cross bridge to Ile de Ré, take D735 then D201 to Ste. Marie de Ré. At roundabout turn north D103 to site shortly on left. GPS: 46.16568, -1.3347

Charges guide

Per unit incl. 2 persons and electricity	€ 16.80 - € 26.30
extra person	€ 5.00 - € 6.50
child (2-7 yrs)	free - € 4.00
dog	€ 3.00

Sainte Marie-de-Ré

Camping Nature Sainte Marie-de-Ré

Plage de la Basse Benaie, F-17740 Sainte Marie-de-Ré (Charente-Maritime) T: 05 46 30 21 74.
E: info@camping-saintemariedere.com **alanrogers.com/FR17857**

Just 20 m. from the beach and 1.5 km. from the centre of Sainte Marie-de-Ré, this peaceful site is in a wonderful location for a family beach holiday. There is direct access to the Basse Banaie beach, but there are several others to enjoy, whether you want to swim, surf or collect shellfish. There are 152 level, grass and sand pitches, a few with views over the Atlantic. The Ile de Ré is a picturesque island of salt pans, marshes and vineyards and, being level, it is a pleasure to explore by bike. For the freshest produce visit one of the colourful food markets held at La Flotte and Le Bois-Plage-en-Ré.

Facilities

Two sanitary blocks with hot showers and some washbasins in cubicles. Facilities for disabled visitors in one block. Laundry facilities. Motorcaravan services. Bar, snacks and bread to order (6/7-31/8). Playground. Fishing. Miniclub and entertainment (July/Aug). Fridge and barbecue hire. Bicycle hire. Direct beach access. WiFi on part of site (free). Off site: Shops and services in Sainte-Marie-de-Ré 1.5 km.

Open: 21 April - 26 September.

Directions

From La Rochelle follow directions for Ile de Ré. At roundabout before Rivedoux take road to the south. At Sainte Marie follow signs for centre at second roundabout, then camping signs.
GPS: 46.1451, -1.31513

Charges guide

Per unit incl. 2 persons and electricity	€ 13.00 - € 19.00
extra person	€ 5.50 - € 7.70

Saintes

Camping Municipal Au Fil de l'Eau

6 rue de Courbiac, F-17100 Saintes (Charente-Maritime) T: 05 46 93 08 00. E: campingaufildeleau@sfr.fr
alanrogers.com/FR17200

Saintes is a 2,000-year-old Gallo-Roman city, well worth a couple of days to visit the cathedral, the abbey, the Arch of Germanicus, the amphitheatre and several museums, all within walking distance of the site (reception can provide a city map). Do take a stroll through the well tended, very pretty public gardens by the riverside. This large, pleasant site is run as a franchise from the local municipality and has 214 mostly shady and generally grassy level pitches, with 132 electric hook-ups, and six mobile homes for rent.

Facilities

The main toilet block is a large building with two smaller older units opened at peak times. Washbasins in cubicles. Facilities for disabled visitors. Laundry building. Motorcaravan services. Shop. Bar. Restaurant and takeaway (July/Aug). TV room. Boules. Badminton. Minigolf. Playground. Fishing. WiFi in some areas (charged). Barrier system and guardian lives on site. Twin-axle caravans not accepted. Off site: Adjacent open-air Olympic size pool complex, free for campers.

Open: 1 May - 30 September.

Directions

From east and northeast follow signs for town and site, turning right after river. Avoiding centre and from all other directions, use bypass following signs for N137 La Rochelle to large roundabout at northern end. Turn right for town centre and Camping Municipal. Left at next roundabout, ahead at two more, right at next. Left at mini roundabout. Site is 200 m. on right. GPS: 45.755283, -0.628133

Charges guide

Per unit incl. 2 persons and electricity	€ 17.80

Vaux-sur-Mer

Camping le Val Vert

108 avenue Frederic Garnier, F-17640 Vaux-sur-Mer (Charente-Maritime) T: 05 46 38 25 51.
E: camping-val-vert@wanadoo.fr **alanrogers.com/FR17310**

Situated in seven acres of lush countryside, this is a charming campsite, just 200 metres from the village of Vaux-sur-Mer, and 900 metres from the sandy beach at Nauzan. There are 95 touring pitches, all with 6/10A electricity (Europlug) and extra long cables may be required. Pitches are of average size (100 sq.m) with good access, even for larger units, and some are terraced. Although entertainment and a children's club are organised in high season, facilities on the site are minimal. Accommodation for rent. Val Vert is a haven of peace and tranquillity, ideal for a relaxing holiday. The site is situated in a long, green valley – hence its name. The valley includes an attractive park. Nauzan Plage, a popular cove with an excellent beach, often sheltered from the winds by the cliffs on either side. Roller skates are not allowed on site.

Facilities

There are ample toilet and shower facilities. Separate facilities for children and disabled visitors. Laundry facilities. Motorcaravan services. Shop, bar, restaurant and takeaway (all 10/6-10/9). Bread to order. Heated swimming and paddling pools (29/4-10/9; supervised in high season). Play area. Games room. Pétanque. WiFi over site (charged). Off site: Village facilities including bar, supermarket and bank with ATM 200 m. Bicycle hire. Beach 900 m. Fishing 1 km. Boat launching 5 km. Golf and riding 10 km.

Open: 11 April - 26 September.

Directions

Follow camping signs from the village of Vaux-sur-Mer. GPS: 45.64400, -1.0632

Charges guide

Per unit incl. 1-3 persons and electricity	€ 23.20 - € 38.70
extra person	€ 4.20 - € 8.00
child (1-7 yrs)	€ 3.15 - € 6.00
dog	€ 2.00

Camping Cheques accepted.

Vaux-sur-Mer

Camping le Nauzan Plage

39 avenue de Nauzan Plage, F-17640 Vaux-sur-Mer (Charente-Maritime) T: 05 46 38 29 13.
E: contact@campinglenauzanplage.com **alanrogers.com/FR17825**

Le Nauzan Plage is a well equipped family site close to the popular resort of Royan. This is a lively site in peak season with a wide range of amenities and activities. These include swimming pools for adults and children, a children's playground and bouncy castle, as well as a snack bar with takeaway food and a well stocked shop. The nearest beach (Nauzan Plage) is just 450 m. away. The 170 touring pitches (90 to 150 sq.m.) are grassy and generally well shaded; most have electricity (10A). The site is divided into two parts by a small stream. A number of fully equipped mobile homes are available for rent. Vaux-sur-Mer is a stylish resort with a market, shops and easy access to Royan, the Côte Sauvage and its vast forest.

Facilities

Four (unheated) toilet blocks have washbasins and showers in cubicles. Separate facilities for children and disabled visitors. Laundry facilities. Motorcaravan services. Shop, bar, snack bar and takeaway (all 15/6-30/9). Outdoor heated swimming pool (all season). Games and TV room. Sports field. Play area. Children's farm. Activity and entertainment programme. Bicycle hire. WiFi throughout (charged). Mobile homes for rent. Off site: Nearest beach 450 m. Golf and riding 4 km. Cycle and walking tracks. Royan.

Open: 1 May - 30 September.

Directions

From Royan head west towards La Palmyre and St Palais. Upon reaching Vaux, head inland on Avenue de Nauzan Plage and the site is well signed. GPS: 45.642683, -1.071905

Charges guide

Per unit incl. 2 persons and electricity	€ 23.00 - € 40.30
extra person	€ 4.00 - € 8.90
child (2-10 yrs)	€ 3.17 - € 6.70
dog	€ 3.55 - € 5.20

DÉPARTEMENTS: 21 CÔTE D'OR, 58 NIÈVRE, 71 SAÔNE-ET-LOIRE, 89 YONNE

MAJOR CITY: DIJON

Burgundy is a wonderfully evocative region offering breathtaking châteaux and cathedrals, rolling hills and heady mountain views, vineyards and superlative cuisine, not to mention of course, a wide variety of world-renowned wines.

In the rich heartland of France, Burgundy was once a powerful independent state and important religious centre. Its golden age is reflected in the area's magnificent art and architecture: the grand palaces and art collections of Dijon, the great pilgrimage church of Vézelay, the Cistercian Abbaye de Fontenay and the evocative abbey remains at Cluny, once the most powerful monastery in Europe.

However, Burgundy is best known for its wine, including some of the world's finest, notably from the great vineyards of the Côte d'Or and Chablis, and also for its sublime cuisine. You'll also notice how driving through the country villages is like reading a wine merchant's list with plenty of opportunities for tasting and choosing your wine.

The area is criss-crossed by navigable waterways and includes the Parc Régional du Morvan; good walking country amidst lush, rolling wooded landscape.

Places of interest

Autun: 12th-century St Lazare cathedral.

Beaune: medieval town; Museum of Burgundy Wine.

Cluny: Europe's largest Benedictine abbey.

Dijon: Palace of the Dukes; Fine Arts Museum; Burgundian Folklore Museum.

Fontenay: Fontenay Abbey and Cloister.

Joigny: medieval town.

Mâcon: Maison des Vins (wine centre).

Paray-le-Monial: Romanesque basilica; pilgrimage centre.

Sens: historic buildings; museum with fine Gallo-Roman collections.

Vézelay: fortified medieval hillside.

Cuisine of the region

Many dishes are wine based and use fine ingredients such as Charolais beef, Bresse poultry, snails, truffles and mushrooms.

Boeuf Bourguignon: braised beef simmered in a red wine-based sauce.

Garbure: heavy soup, a mixture of pork, cabbage, beans and sausages.

Gougère: cheese pastry based on Gruyère.

Jambon persillé: parsley-flavoured ham, served cold in jelly.

Matelote: freshwater fish soup, usually based on a red wine sauce.

Meurette: red wine-based sauce with small onions, used with fish or poached egg dishes.

www.burgundy-tourism.com
documentation@crt-bourgogne.fr
(0)3 80 28 02 80

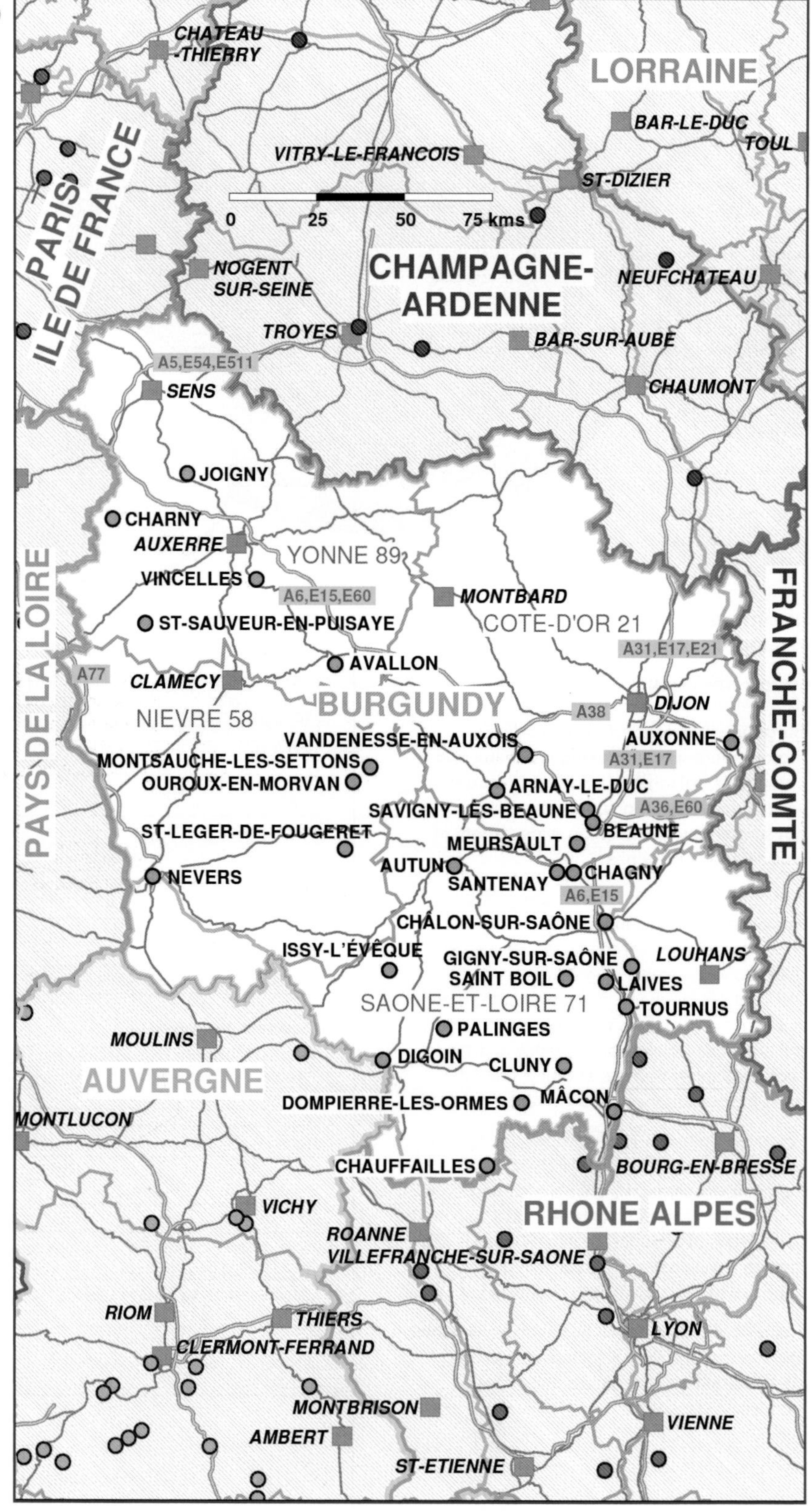
CHATEAU-THIERRY
LORRAINE
BAR-LE-DUC
TOUL
VITRY-LE-FRANCOIS
ST-DIZIER
PARIS
ILE DE FRANCE
0 25 50 75 kms
NOGENT SUR-SEINE
CHAMPAGNE-ARDENNE
NEUFCHATEAU
TROYES
BAR-SUR-AUBE
A5,E54,E511
SENS
CHAUMONT
JOIGNY
CHARNY
AUXERRE
YONNE 89
VINCELLES
A6,E15,E60
MONTBARD
ST-SAUVEUR-EN-PUISAYE
COTE-D'OR 21
FRANCHE-COMTE
PAYS DE LA LOIRE
A31,E17,E21
AVALLON
A77
CLAMECY
BURGUNDY
DIJON
A38
NIEVRE 58
AUXONNE
VANDENESSE-EN-AUXOIS
A31,E17
MONTSAUCHE-LES-SETTONS
OUROUX-EN-MORVAN
ARNAY-LE-DUC
SAVIGNY-LES-BEAUNE
A36,E60
BEAUNE
ST-LEGER-DE-FOUGERET
MEURSAULT
AUTUN
CHAGNY
NEVERS
SANTENAY
A6,E15
CHÂLON-SUR-SAÔNE
ISSY-L'ÉVÊQUE
GIGNY-SUR-SAÔNE
LOUHANS
SAINT BOIL
LAIVES
SAONE-ET-LOIRE 71
TOURNUS
PALINGES
MOULINS
DIGOIN
CLUNY
AUVERGNE
DOMPIERRE-LES-ORMES
MÂCON
MONTLUCON
CHAUFFAILLES
BOURG-EN-BRESSE
VICHY
RHONE ALPES
ROANNE
VILLEFRANCHE-SUR-SAONE
RIOM
THIERS
LYON
CLERMONT-FERRAND
MONTBRISON
VIENNE
AMBERT
ST-ETIENNE

Arnay-le-Duc

Camping de l'Etang de Fouché

Rue du 8 mai 1945, F-21230 Arnay-le-Duc (Côte d'Or) T: 03 80 90 02 23. E: info@campingfouche.com
alanrogers.com/FR21040

This quite large but peaceful, lakeside site with its new bar/restaurant and swimming pool complex, is useful as a stopover, or indeed for longer stays to explore the region. It can be very busy during the school holidays, but is quiet and relaxing outside the main season. There are over 200 good sized pitches, on fairly level grass and all with 10A electricity (some with water). Many are hedged and offer a choice of shade or more open aspect. There is direct access to the adjacent lake and beach facilities. A 2 km. stroll around the lake can be pleasant. This part of Burgundy is popular and Arnay-le-Duc itself is an attractive little town with an interesting history and renowned for its gastronomy.

Facilities

Two new toilet blocks and third (totally refurbished) provide all the necessary modern facilities (male and female are separate). Facilities for disabled visitors. Baby room. Washing machines. Shop, bar, restaurant, takeaway (all 15/5-15/9). New small heated outdoor swimming pool (15/5-10/9). Boules. TV/games room. Playground. Fishing. Activities and entertainment (July/Aug). Bicycle hire. WiFi. Off site: Lakeside beach adjacent with playground. Town centre 800 m.

Open: 15 April - 15 October.

Directions

From A6 (exit 24) take D981, 16 km. to the town. Turn left on D906 for 400 m. and site is signed to left. GPS: 47.13411, 4.49840

Charges guide

Per unit incl. 2 persons and electricity	€ 17.00 - € 27.00
extra person	€ 5.00 - € 7.00
child (2-12 yrs)	€ 2.00 - € 4.00
dog	€ 3.00

Autun

Camping de la Porte d'Arroux

Rue du Traité d'Anvers, les Chaumottes, F-71400 Autun (Saône-et-Loire) T: 03 85 52 10 82.
E: camping.autun@orange.fr **alanrogers.com/FR71260**

Camping de la Porte d'Arroux is a quiet, country site in the heart of the Burgundy region, on the banks of a river just outside the town of Arroux. The 79 level, grassy touring pitches have electricity (10A, Europlug) and water nearby. High hedges and trees separate the pitches to one side of the central thatched building housing the reception and bar, with those to the other side in a more open area. In addition, nine mobile homes to rent. There is direct access to the river and cycle routes are nearby. A big attraction here are the historic structures surviving from the Gallo-Roman period.

Facilities

Two sanitary blocks provide hot showers and washbasins (some in cubicles). Laundry facilities. Motorcaravan services. Small shop. Bar and restaurant (May-Sept). Play area. TV/games room. Communal barbecue. Accommodation for hire, incl. three new mobile homes. Bicycle hire (incl. electric). Fishing. Beach and canoeing on river. WiFi throughout (charged). Off site: Cycle path and river swimming 500 m. Autun 1.5 km. Shopping 2 km.

Open: 7 March - 6 November.

Directions

Camping de la Porte d'Arroux is 50 km. west of Beaune. From A6 exit 24, take D981 towards Autun, then follow D681 into Autun. Site is well signed on reaching town. GPS: 46.96468, 4.29297

Charges guide

Per unit incl. 2 persons and electricity	€ 16.90 - € 19.80
extra person	€ 3.70

Camping Cheques accepted.

Auxonne

Camping de l'Arquebuse

Route d'Athée, F-21130 Auxonne (Côte d'Or) T: 03 80 31 06 89. E: camping.arquebuse@wanadoo.fr
alanrogers.com/FR21090

This is a peaceful, verdant site located in the Northern Jura with a riverside setting on the Saône. L'Arquebuse has 100 level, unmarked pitches on grass, of which 17 are occupied by mobile homes and chalets. Most have 10A electricity and a variety of trees give shade to some pitches. Auxonne is close to both the A36 and A39 motorways and this site may prove a useful overnight stop. The site has a bar/restaurant, Le Pinocchio (open to the public), and the adjacent Base Nautique offers a good range of leisure activities, including canoeing, windsurfing, mountain biking as well as a large swimming pool.

Facilities

Basic toilet block, heated in winter, provides British and Turkish style toilets and open washbasins (cleaning can be variable). Washing machine and dryer. Small shop (1/5-31/10). Restaurant/bar. Pizzeria. Takeaway. Play area. TV room. WiFi. Chalets for rent. Off site: Swimming pool adjacent. Windsurfing, canoeing, boat trips and fishing. Town of Auxonne with shops, bars, restaurants and Friday market 1 km. Dijon 34 km.

Open: 29 March - 15 December.

Directions

From the A39 autoroute take exit 5 and the D905 for 6 km. to Auxonne. Site is signed to the left just before crossing the bridge over the Saône. Site is a few hundred metres. GPS: 47.19941, 5.38365

Charges guide

Per unit incl. 2 persons and electricity	€ 19.00 - € 22.00
extra person	€ 3.30 - € 4.00

Avallon

Camping Municipal Sous Roche

Rue Sous Roche, F-89200 Avallon (Yonne) T: 03 86 34 10 39. E: campingsousroche@ville-avallon.fr
alanrogers.com/FR89180

This attractive and tranquil site is one of those municipal gems one finds from time to time. Tucked away next to the pretty River Cousin, at the bottom of the hill on which Avallon stands, there are 94 medium to large pitches, of which 80 have access to electricity (16A). Long leads may be necessary on some smaller pitches. All are on grass except for three hardstandings, and are divided by shrubs and small trees. A separate eating room, with a tea and coffee machine and a microwave oven, is a welcome consideration for those under canvas. This is an excellent place to relax and break your journey when travelling south on the A6 motorway.

Facilities

Modern, clean and well maintained heated toilet block with washbasins in cabins and controllable showers. Baby room and excellent facilities for disabled visitors. Laundry facilities. Small well stocked shop. Separate eating and coffee room. Bread to order. Bicycle hire. Play area. Free WiFi over site. Off site: Shops, restaurants and museums in Avallon. Markets on Thursday and Saturday mornings.

Open: 1 April - 15 October.

Directions

From A6 take J22 and follow D606 signed Avallon. At central crossroads (with traffic lights) turn left onto D944, signed Municipal Camping. Follow road for 2 km. and turn left immediately before the bridge over the River Cousin. Site is approximately 100 m. on left. GPS: 47.48007, 3.91364

Charges guide

Per unit incl. 2 persons and electricity	€ 17.80
extra person	€ 3.70

Beaune

Camping Municipal les Cent Vignes

10 rue Auguste Dubois, F-21200 Beaune (Côte d'Or) T: 03 80 22 03 91.
E: campinglescentvignes@mairie-beaune.fr **alanrogers.com/FR21020**

Les Cent Vignes is a municipal site maintained to a high standard. Offering 116 individual pitches of good size, separated by neat beech hedges. Over half of the pitches are on grass, with the remainder on hardstandings. Most have electricity (10A) and 50 are fully serviced. A popular site with a good restaurant and within walking distance of the town, it becomes full mid June to early September with many short-stay campers. With daily departures, arrivals start around midday, however reservations can be made. This is an excellent site for a stopover en route, and equally good for exploring the town.

Facilities

Two large, very modern and fully equipped sanitary blocks, one of which can be heated, have washbasins mainly in cabins. Laundry facilities. Basic shop, bar, above average restaurant with takeaway (all 1/4-15/10). Playground. Sports area with tennis, basketball, volleyball and boules. TV room. Barbecue area. WiFi over site (free). Off site: Beaune 1 km. Bicycle hire 1 km. Riding 2 km.

Open: 15 March - 31 October.

Directions

From autoroute A6 take exit 24 to Beaune. Follow signs for Beaune centre and signs to site in 1 km. Signed from other routes. GPS: 47.03304, 4.83911

Charges guide

Per unit incl. 2 persons and electricity	€ 19.00 - € 22.40
extra person	€ 4.30 - € 4.90
child (under 7 yrs)	€ 2.20 - € 2.50

Chagny

Camping Paquier Fané

20 rue de Paquier Fané, Camping du Paquier Fané, F-71150 Chagny (Saône-et-Loire) T: 03 85 87 21 42.
E: camping-chagny@orange.fr **alanrogers.com/FR71250**

This small, welcoming, family run site is located at the edge of the cultural town of Chagny, and next to the Voie Vert which runs along the Canal de Centre. Of the 101 pitches, ten are used for high quality chalets and 91 for touring units. All are on grass (some with all-weather bases), separated by hedges and tall trees. Electricity (16A) is available to all, although some pitches may need longer leads. This is a relaxing base from which to explore the interesting town and the surrounding area either on foot or bicycle. The bar/restaurant is the perfect place to unwind after a busy day.

Facilities

One main, heated, modern sanitary block with a purpose built annexe for disabled visitors. Baby room. Laundry facilities. A second smaller block is behind reception. Bread to order. Bar/restaurant and takeaway (May-Aug, closed Tues). Small play area. WiFi over site (free). Ten chalets for rent, including one adapted for disabled visitors. WiFi throughout (free). Off site: Sports complex and pool adjacent, with fishing pond and family friendly picnic area. Tennis. Cycle tracks and wine route.

Open: 1 April - 31 October.

Directions

From A6 autoroute take exit 24.1 (D974 Beaune Centre) towards Chalon-sur-Sâone. Then take D62 towards Chagny. Follow signs for 'Complex Sportif/Camping'. GPS: 46.91187, 4.74567

Charges guide

Per unit incl. 2 persons and electricity	€ 18.80 - € 21.80
extra person	€ 3.20 - € 4.20
child (3-17 yrs)	€ 2.50 - € 3.00
dog	€ 1.50 - € 1.70

Châlon-sur-Saône

Camping du Pont de Bourgogne

Rue Julien Leneveu, Saint Marcel, F-71380 Châlon-sur-Saône (Saône-et-Loire) T: 03 85 48 26 86.
E: campingchalon71@wanadoo.fr **alanrogers.com/FR71140**

This is a well presented and cared for site, useful for an overnight stop or for a longer stay to explore the local area. It is close to the A6 autoroute, and the interesting market town of Châlon-sur-Saône is within 2 km. There are 100 mainly level pitches (90 sq.m) all with 10A Europlug, most on grass, but 30 have a gravel surface. They are separated by beech hedging, and a variety of mature trees provide shade. Many pitches overlook the river, a good spot to watch the passing boats, and a cycle route runs alongside. Access is easy for large outfits. The sanitary blocks are of a high standard and kept very clean. The bar, restaurant and terrace is close to the entrance and overlook the river. Takeaway meals are available from the bar all season but the restaurant is open only in July and August. The site gets crowded in the third week of July during the Châlon street theatre festival. Across the river is a large municipal swimming pool, and a golf club and sailing club are within 1 km.

Facilities

Three sanitary blocks, two of which are superb modern buildings, are kept very clean and have high quality fittings including a children's bathroom, disabled bathroom and family shower. Motorcaravan services. Laundry facilities. No shop but essentials kept in the bar (bread to order). Modern bar/restaurant (July/Aug). Simple play area. Bicycle hire arranged. WiFi (free in bar). Chalets for rent, one adapted for disabled visitors. Off site: Fishing and boat ramp 200 m. Municipal swimming pool 300 m. Golf 2 km. Riding 10 km. Châlon-sur-Saône with many shops, bars, banks etc.

Open: 1 April - 30 September.

Directions

From A6 exit 26 (Châlon-Sud), take N80 (signed Dôle) to second roundabout. Take fourth exit (signed Roseraie) and fork right (les Chavannes). At traffic lights turn right (signed Roseraie) under bridge to site entrance 500 m. GPS: 46.78448, 4.87295

Charges guide

Per unit incl. 2 persons and electricity	€ 22.50 - € 29.50
extra person	€ 5.60 - € 7.40
child (under 7 yrs)	€ 3.90 - € 5.50
dog	€ 2.20 - € 2.60

Camping Cheques accepted.

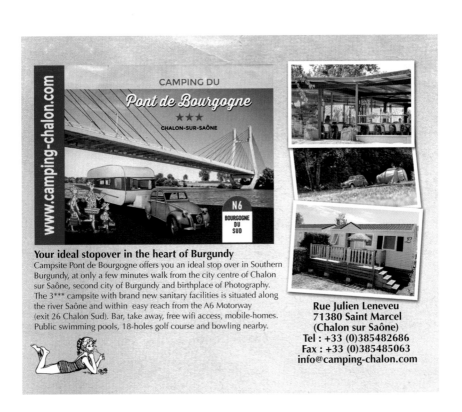

Charny

Camping des Platanes

41 route de la Mothe, F-89120 Charny (Yonne) T: 03 86 91 83 60. E: campingdesplatanes@wanadoo.fr
alanrogers.com/FR89070

Situated in the charming market town of Charny, this is a tranquil, welcoming site within easy reach of the A6 autoroute. There are currently 91 level, grass pitches, all with 16A electricity. The majority are used for touring units (some with water and waste water), and ten are occupied by chalets and safari-style tents, plus a few seasonal units. The important archaeological site of Guédelon castle is nearby, the Chablis wines of the Yonne are ready for discovery and there are delightful walks around two local lakes. Charny has a very old covered market and opposite is a 17th-century hotel/restaurant and some bars. The Loire Valley is easily accessed, as is Paris (only 1.5 hours).

Facilities

Modern, purpose-built, heated toilet block provides separate areas for men and women. Washbasins in cabins. Facilities for disabled visitors. Laundry. Motorcaravan services. Small bar with TV. Takeaway (June-Sept). Heated swimming pool (1/5-30/9). Bicycle and barbecue hire. Play area for under fives. WiFi. Off site: Town centre 5 mins. walk. Fishing 500 m. Historic town of Joigny. Riding 7 km.

Open: 1 April - 31 October.

Directions

Leave A6 at exit 18 and follow D943 towards Montargis for 14 km. Turn left on D950 and site is on right at start of village. GPS: 47.891, 3.092

Charges guide

Per unit incl. 2 persons and electricity	€ 18.50 - € 24.50
extra person	€ 5.00 - € 7.00
child (4-7 yrs)	€ 3.00 - € 5.00
dog	€ 2.00 - € 3.00

Chauffailles

Camping Municipal les Feuilles

18 rue du Chatillon, F-71170 Chauffailles (Saône-et-Loire) T: 03 85 26 48 12. E: infos@campinglesfeuilles.fr
alanrogers.com/FR71230

Les Feuilles is a small, attractive, well cared for municipal site in the Burgundy village of Chauffailles. There are 63 pitches here and a number of chalets for rent. The pitches are a mixture of all-weather surface and grass and are of a good size (80-100 sq.m), and most have 5/10A electricity connections. This is a good base to explore lesser known southern Burgundy. Chauffailles is a pretty village with a weaving museum and a regular market. The nearby town of Chateauneuf is renowned for its large number of antique shops and charming museum depicting the former life of the village.

Facilities

Two traditional clean toilet blocks with preset showers. Facilities for disabled visitors (key). Laundry facilities with hot water. Play area. Traditional wooden chalets to rent. English spoken. Off site: Direct access from site to municipal pool, tennis courts, town centre and château. Bicycle hire 1 km. Cycle and walking tracks in the surrounding hills. Châteauneuf.

Open: 1 May - 30 September.

Directions

From Charolles, head south on D985, passing through La Clayette until you reach Chauffailles, from where the site is clearly signed. GPS: 46.199671, 4.337363

Charges guide

Per unit incl. 2 persons and electricity	€ 14.60 - € 17.90
extra person	€ 2.75 - € 3.30

Cluny

Camping Municipal Saint Vital

Rue des Griottons, F-71250 Cluny (Saône-et-Loire) T: 03 85 59 08 34. E: cluny-camping@wanadoo.fr
alanrogers.com/FR71030

Saint Vital is conveniently situated close to the attractive and historic town of Cluny (300 m. walk) with its magnificent abbey, next to the municipal swimming pool, and alongside a Voie Verte route. This site has 174 pitches, two of which are occupied by chalets. On gently sloping grass, with some small hedges and shade in parts, 6A electricity is available (long leads may be needed). Some rail noise is noticeable during the day but we are assured that trains do not run between 23.30-07.00. On Monday and Thursday evenings during high season, there is a presentation of local produce in the 'salle de réunion'.

Facilities

Two sanitary buildings provide British and Turkish style WCs, some washbasins in cubicles and controllable showers. Facilities for disabled visitors. Motorcaravan services. Laundry facilities. Shop (July/Aug). Outdoor swimming pool (June-Sept). Play area. WiFi by reception (charged). Two chalets for rent, one adapted for disabled visitors. Off site: Fishing and bicycle hire 100 m. Bars, restaurants, shops and bank in Cluny 300 m.

Open: 26 April - 30 September.

Directions

Site is east of town, by the D15 road towards Azé and Blanot. From A6 exit 29 take N79 north and then D980 signed Cluny. Site is signed from town. GPS: 46.43196, 4.66755

Charges guide

Per unit incl. 2 persons and electricity	€ 15.30
extra person	€ 4.00
child (under 7 yrs)	€ 2.50

Digoin

Camping la Chevrette

41 rue de la Chevrette, F-71160 Digoin (Saône-et-Loire) T: 03 85 53 11 49. E: info@lachevrette.com

alanrogers.com/FR71180

This pretty town site has been leased from the municipality for some years by an enthusiastic, friendly couple. There are 81 neat and tidy pitches which are separated by hedges and flowers decorate the site. The level pitches include 71 with electricity (10A) for touring units and 50 for tents. There are four chalets for rent. At the far end of the site there is a slipway onto the River Loire and it is this aspect that attracts campers with canoes. The site also has its own canoes for hire and include free transfers. Situated on the route of the Voie Verte cycle path, this is a popular destination for walkers and cyclists.

Facilities

Four small toilet blocks, one with cold water only, each provide separate facilities for men and women and some washbasins in cabins. Facilities for disabled visitors. Laundry facilities. Small restaurant/snack bar and takeaway (all July/Aug). Bread to order. Heated outdoor pool (1/5-7/9). Club room/library with TV for bad weather. Canoe hire and transfers. Fishing and boat launching. Free WiFi over part of site. Off site: Municipal pool (free to campers 15/6-7/9). Supermarket 500 m. Restaurants and bars in the town. Cycle paths along the canals.

Open: 1 April - 8 October.

Directions

Digoin is off the N79 and site is well signed from all directions. Look for signs showing Piscine Camping. The site is located beside the bridge over the River Loire and the D979 and behind the municipal pool. GPS: 46.47973, 3.96755

Charges guide

Per unit incl. 2 persons and electricity	€ 16.90 - € 18.50
extra person	€ 3.70 - € 4.50

Twin-axle units are charged much more.

Dompierre-les-Ormes

Sites et Paysages Village des Meuniers

344 rue du Stade, F-71520 Dompierre-les-Ormes (Saône-et-Loire) T: 03 85 50 36 60.
E: contact@villagedesmeuniers.com **alanrogers.com/FR71020**

In a tranquil setting with panoramic views, the large and welcoming reception building sets the tone for the rest of this superb site. It is set on the gentle slopes of a hill top that has been tastefully landscaped. There is a feeling of spaciousness throughout with modern and well kept facilities. The 76 terraced, grassy touring pitches range from 100 to 250 sq.m. They are fairly level and all have electricity (10A) and ample water points, and 25 also have waste water outlets. All pitches enjoy stunning views.

Facilities

Heated sanitary facilities with modern fittings. Excellent facilities for disabled visitors. Smaller unit (also heated) in the lower area of the site, plus further toilets in the main reception building. Motorcaravan services. Shop, bar, restaurant and takeaway (all 1/5-30/10). Swimming pool complex (1/5-15/9). Play area. Activities for children (high season). Minigolf. WiFi in bar and reception (free). Chalets and lodge tents with own shower and WC for rent.
Off site: Dompierre 500 m. Bicycle hire 1 km.

Open: 2 April - 30 October.

Directions

Town is 35 km. west of Mâcon. Leave the A6 at exit 29 and follow N79/E62 (Charolles, Paray, Digoin) road and turn south onto D41 to Dompierre-les-Ormes (3 km). Site is clearly signed through village. GPS: 46.36369, 4.47460

Charges guide

Per unit incl. 2 persons and electricity	€ 20.00 - € 29.00
extra person	€ 5.00 - € 7.00

Issy-l'Évêque

Camping les Portes du Morvan

L'Etang Neuf, F-71760 Issy-l'Evêque (Saône-et-Loire) T: 03 85 24 96 05.

alanrogers.com/FR71080

Formerly known as Camping l'Etang Neuf, this is a well tended, tranquil campsite overlooking a lake, with views of a forest and the 19th-century Château de Montrifaut. It is a real countryside haven for relaxation and the birdsong includes nightingales and golden orioles. The 70 marked, grass pitches have 6A electricity, a small hardstanding area for a car and are separated by a variety of maturing trees giving some shade. A separate area nearer the lake is used for tents. There is a heated swimming pool and a fenced area of the lake with a beach. The new owners have recently built new amenities.

Facilities

Two clean sanitary blocks include washbasins in cabins. Laundry facilities. Baby room. Separate shower and toilet rooms for disabled visitors are in the lower block. Motorcaravan services. Shop with bread to order. Restaurant and bar. Swimming and paddling pools (1/5-15/9). Lake beach and swimming. Bicycle hire incl. electric bikes. Boules. TV/games room. WiFi throughout (free). Off site: Minigolf just outside the site entrance.

Open: 1 April - 25 October.

Directions

From Autun travel southwest on N81/D681/D981 to Luzy. Continue through the town on D973 towards Bourbon-Lancy. Just before leaving Luzy turn left. The site is clearly signed from here (possibly still Camping de l'Etang Neuf). GPS: 46.70773, 3.96018

Charges guide

Per unit incl. 2 persons and electricity	€ 18.00 - € 20.90
extra person	€ 4.20 - € 4.90

Joigny

Camping d'Epizy

68 Quai d'Epizy, F-89300 Joigny (Yonne) T: 03 86 62 07 55. E: camping.joigny@orange.fr

alanrogers.com/FR89190

This small, inexpensive campsite is on the banks of the River Yonne, beside a forest and surrounded by 40 hectares of vineyards. There are 41 large individual pitches surrounded by hedges, all with electricity (10A, some with old style French two-pin socket) and water supply. The toilet/shower block is modern and spotless and also houses the washing-up and laundry facilities. There is a large area for sports with table tennis, volleyball and crazy golf etc. The historic medieval town centre of Joigny is just a short walk away, with numerous restaurants and local shops.

Facilities

Toilet block with showers and washbasins in cubicles. Facilities for disabled visitors. Baby changing area. Laundry. Motorcaravan services. Small shop for essentials (from 1/5). Bread van visits. Volleyball court. Boules. Playground. Minigolf. Picnic tables. Free WiFi on part of site. Off site: Municipal swimming pool, karting, hiking, mountain biking, fishing, Wednesday and Saturday morning market. Sens 20 km. Montargis 35 km.

Open: 1 May - 30 September.

Directions

A6/E60 from northwest (Paris) exit 18, D943 to Joigny. A6/E60 from south east (Beaune) exit 19, D606 to Joigny. Cross river and turn left, follow signs for campsite which is next left on Quai d'Epizy. GPS: 47.98155, 3.37446

Charges guide

Per unit incl. 2 persons and electricity	€ 11.50
extra person	€ 3.50

Laives

Camping la Héronnière

Lac de Laives, F-71240 Laives (Saône-et-Loire) T: 03 85 44 98 85. E: contact@camping-laheronniere.com

alanrogers.com/FR71120

Camping la Héronnière is a quiet relaxing site on the edge of a leisure lake in pleasant rolling woodland countryside. Two further lakes are reserved for fishing. The 80 touring pitches are good sized, grassy and level. About half have shade, with 10A electricity connections and there are plenty of water points. The site is within 4 km of the village of Laive and within reach of Chalon-sur-Saône, Tournus and the Chalonnais vineyards and wine route. A pleasant walk can be accessed directly from the site and runs along the edge of the lake, plus there are numerous footpaths through the woods. The Voie Verte, a 117 km. long linear cycling route, is 15 km. to the west.

Facilities

Well equipped modern sanitary block includes facilities for disabled campers. Washing machine. Snack bar (June-Aug). Covered area outside reception with bread, drinks, ice-cream, basic provisions and French breakfast. Heated outdoor pool. Boules. Bicycle hire. Fishing. Marquee with TV, board games. Playground. WiFi (charged). Off site: Lake swimming, grass area, beach, bar and restaurant 300 m. Exercise circuit, canoeing, windsurfing, pedaloes. Historic buildings and old wash house in Laives 4 km. Riding 10 km. Golf 15 km. Cluny, Chalon, Le Creusot and Montceau-les-Mines. La Voie Verte, a 117 km. track for cycling or walking near the site.

Open: 6 April - 30 September.

Directions

Leave D906 (Chalon-sur-Saône-Mâcon) at Sennecey-le-Grand (about 18 km. south of the centre of Chalon), taking D18 west to Laives (4 km). In centre of village, take right fork and continue along D18, 4 km. to the northwest. GPS: 46.67198, 4.8333

Charges guide

Per unit incl. 2 persons and electricity	€ 26.80
extra person	€ 5.80
child (under 7 yrs)	€ 3.90
dog	€ 1.70

Gigny-sur-Saône

Castel Camping Château de l'Epervière

517

6 rue du Château, F-71240 Gigny-sur-Saône (Saône-et-Loire) T: 03 85 94 16 90.
E: info@domaine-eperviere.com **alanrogers.com/FR71070**

This popular and high quality site is peacefully situated in the wooded grounds of a 16th-century château, close to the A6 and near the village of Gigny-sur-Saône. It is within walking distance of the river where you can watch the cruise boats on their way to and from Châlon-sur-Saône. There are 160 pitches arranged over two areas separated by a small fishing lake, 120 are used for touring. All have 10A electricity, some are on hardstanding and 30 are fully serviced. Close to the château and fishing lake, the pitches are hedged and have shade from mature trees; whilst the area behind the lake has a more open aspect. Red squirrels, ducks, the occasional heron and even a coypu can be found on the campsite and the pitches around the periphery are good for birdwatchers. The château's main restaurant serves regional dishes and takeaway meals. Gert-Jan and the team enthusiastically organise many activities, mainly for younger children, but including wine tasting in the cellars of the château from mid May to mid September. Here you are in the Maconnais and Châlonnaise wine regions, so don't miss the opportunity to arrange some visits to the local caves to sample their wines.

Facilities

Two very clean toilet blocks with all necessary facilities including those for babies and disabled visitors. Washing machine/dryer. Motorcaravan services. Basic shop and takeaway (both 30/4-18/9). Restaurant with good menu. Cellar with wine tasting. Converted barn with bar, large TV. Heated outdoor swimming pool and new heated paddling pool with slides (30/4-18/9) partly enclosed by old stone walls. Smaller indoor heated pool. Play areas and open field. Fishing. Bicycle hire. Free WiFi in bar area. Off site: Boat launching 500 m. Riding 15 km. Golf 20 km. Historic towns of Châlon and Tournus, both 20 km. The Monday market of Louhans, to see the famous Bresse chickens 26 km.

Open: 1 April - 30 September.

Directions

From A6 heading south, take exit 26 Châlon-Sud, or from A6 heading north take exit 27 Tournus. Then D906 to Sennecey-le-Grand, turn east D18, signed Gigny. Follow site signs to site (6.5 km). GPS: 46.65485, 4.94463

Charges guide

Per unit incl. 2 persons and electricity	€ 25.20 - € 39.90
extra person	€ 6.20 - € 8.90
child (2-9 yrs)	€ 4.00 - € 6.50
dog	€ 2.40 - € 3.00

Mâcon

Camping Municipal Mâcon

1 rue des Grandes Varennes, F-71000 Sancé (Saône-et-Loire) T: 03 85 38 16 22. E: camping@ville-macon.fr
alanrogers.com/FR71010

A well cared for site worth considering as a stopover or for longer stays, as it is close to the main route south. The 256 good sized, level, grassy pitches, 190 with 6A electricity and 60 with fresh and waste water points, are easily accessed by tarmac roads. This is a pleasant site, remarkably quiet considering its location, and with a generally bright and cheerful ambience. Extra charge for outfits over 3,5 tonnes and with twin axles. Only gas and electric barbecues. Reservations are not accepted so, in July and August, arrive by late afternoon to avoid disappointment. Some road and rail noise.

Facilities

Four modern, well maintained toilet blocks. All necessary facilities including those for campers with disabilities. Washing machine and dryer. Motorcaravan services. Shop/tabac, bar, takeaway and restaurant open midday and evenings. Heated swimming and paddling pools (campers only, 15/5-15/9). TV lounge. Playground. WiFi throughout (free). Off site: Sports centre on banks of river close by. Supermarket 400 m. Fishing 500 m. Golf 10 km.

Open: 15 March - 31 October.

Directions

Site is on northern outskirts of Mâcon on main N6/D906, 3 km. from the town centre, well signed (just south of A40 autoroute exit). GPS: 46.33027, 4.84366

Charges guide

Per unit incl. 2 persons and electricity	€ 21.80 - € 24.00
extra person	€ 4.80 - € 5.40
child (under 7 yrs)	€ 2.70 - € 2.80

Meursault

Camping la Grappe d'Or

2 route de Volnay, F-21190 Meursault (Côte d'Or) T: 03 80 21 22 48. E: info@camping-meursault.com
alanrogers.com/FR21050

Meursault, the capital of the great white wines of Burgundy, is southwest of Beaune and Camping la Grappe d'Or offers terraced pitches overlooking the vineyards. Most of the 131 touring pitches are flat, of varying sizes and some have shade from mature trees; 125 have electrical connections (12A). A second part of the site is located 100 m. towards the village, in the grounds of the owners' house. Sited here are caravan holiday homes for rent, with use of the site facilities. This is a comfortable site to enjoy the cycling/walking tours around the local vineyards, or as a stopover en route. English is spoken.

Facilities

Sanitary facilities are in three blocks with some washbasins in cabins. Child/baby room. Facilities for visitors with disabilities. Laundry facilities. Shop and bar (16/5-15/9). Restaurant and takeaway (15/4-30/9). Swimming pool (15/6-15/9). Play area. Tennis. Bicycle hire. WiFi over part of site (charged). Off site: Fishing 2 km. Golf and riding 7 km. Beaune 9 km.

Open: 6 April - 15 October.

Directions

Site is north of Meursault. Take D974 from Beaune, then D973 and follow the sign for Meursault. Site is signed, but not very clearly (tents with three stars). GPS: 46.98574, 4.76858

Charges guide

Per unit incl. 2 persons and electricity	€ 20.00 - € 24.50
extra person	€ 3.30 - € 4.20

Montsauche-les-Settons

Camping les Mésanges

Rive Gauche amont, l'Huis Gaumont, F-58230 Montsauche-les-Settons (Nièvre) T: 03 86 84 55 77.
E: campinglesmesanges@orange.fr **alanrogers.com/FR58170**

A warm welcome awaits you at this rural haven, located in the heart of the beautiful Morvan national park. Just 100 metres from the Lac des Settons, there are many water based activities available as well as walking and cycling. This attractive and carefully landscaped site has its own well stocked fish pond with a few of the pitches along its bank. There are 100 spacious pitches (100-200 sq.m), all for touring, set among trees and neatly trimmed hedges. One side of the site has an open area, ideal for small groups of campers. All have 10-16A electricity and access to water. Built by the owner in 1986, this is a good example of traditional camping at its best with no mobile homes or chalets.

Facilities

Three toilet blocks have individual washbasins and facilities for disabled visitors. Baby bath. Laundry facilities. Shop with essentials and fresh bread daily. Takeaway (July/Aug). Play area. Swings. Large multisports court. Volleyball. Basketball. Pétanque. Games room. Free WiFi over part of site. Off site: Swimming, boating and fishing on Lac des Settons 150 m. Several bars and restaurants around the lake. Bicycle hire 3 km. Montsauche 7 km. Supermarket in Château-Chinon 20 km.

Open: 14 May - 15 September.

Directions

Site is 40 km. from exit 22 of A6 Avallon and Bierre-les-Semur. Take the D606 towards Saulieu. At Cussey les Forges take D60 (Quarre des Tombes). At Quarre follow signs to Lac des Settons and on to D193, continuing on to D520. Site signed. Access to site is via C4. GPS: 47.181683, 4.052733

Charges guide

Per unit incl. 2 persons and electricity	€ 19.50 - € 21.00
extra person	€ 5.30

Nevers

Camping de Nevers

Rue de la Jonction, F-58000 Nevers (Nièvre) T: 06 84 98 69 79. E: info@campingnevers.com

alanrogers.com/FR58100

On the banks of the Loire in Nevers, facing the cathedral and the Palais des Ducs across the river, this site has just 73 pitches. The area nearest the river is for tents and the terraces above for touring pitches, mainly grass but five hardstandings; there are 25 pitches with electricity (6/10A). The pitches are quite tight but larger units can be accommodated on the lower terrace. This site is ideal for those who enjoy being able to wander into town or as a base to explore the region with its famous Burgundy wines of Sancerre and Pouilly Fumé. Note: the site is closed 12.00-15.00 and there is no waiting place outside.

Facilities

One modern unisex toilet block with washbasins in cabins and controllable showers. Bright and clean, they may be under pressure in high season. Baby area. En-suite unit for disabled visitors. Laundry facilities. Motorcaravan services. Simple bar with basic snacks (June-Sept). Bicycle hire. Play area. Pétanque. Internet (charged). Eight mobile homes for hire. Free WiFi at reception. Off site: All the amenities of Nevers, including shops, restaurants, bars and supermarkets within easy reach.

Open: 3 April - 9 October.

Directions

Nevers is 150 km. north of Clermont-Ferrand. Do not approach through the town. From A77/N7 (Paris-Lyon) take exit 37 onto D976 (Bourges). Turn north at first roundabout towards 'Centre Ville'. Site is signed to right immediately before bridge across the Loire. GPS: 46.98209, 3.16098

Charges guide

Per unit incl. 2 persons and electricity	€ 18.80 - € 22.40
extra person	€ 2.30 - € 3.30

Ouroux-en-Morvan

Camping les Genêts du Morvan

Route de Lormes, F-58230 Ouroux-en-Morvan (Nièvre) T: 03 86 78 22 88. E: camping.ouroux@orange.fr

alanrogers.com/FR58020

Les Genêts du Morvan is a small, comfortable site with just 50 pitches, under the same ownership as FR58040. It can be found between the region's two largest lakes: Lac de Pannecière and Lac des Settons. The pitches are large and have 10A electricity. There are also some fully equipped mobile homes for rent. On-site amenities include a small swimming pool with a sunbathing terrace, a convivial snack bar and a small, but well stocked shop. There are many excellent footpaths in the vicinity and the site's friendly owners will be pleased to recommend routes.

Facilities

Two sanitary blocks have facilities for babies and disabled visitors. Washing machine and dryer. Motorcaravan services. Shop (1/5-15/9; bread to order). Bar. Snack bar (July/Aug, closed Tues). Small outdoor swimming pool (July/Aug). Play area. Mobile homes for rent. Free WiFi over part of site. Off site: Fishing 500 m. Shops and restaurants in Ouroux-en-Morvan. Château Chinon 25 km.

Open: 14 May - 15 September.

Directions

From the north (Avallon), take D606 (Cussey les Forges). Then take D60 and follow signs to Quarre de Tombes and then to Montsauche les Settons. Take 977b (Ouroux), then D12 (Ouroux-en-Morvan). Site is well signed. GPS: 47.188611, 3.939166

Charges guide

Per unit incl. 2 persons and electricity	€ 16.00 - € 18.00

No credit cards.

Palinges

Camping du Lac

Le Fourneau, F-71430 Palinges (Saône-et-Loire) T: 03 85 88 14 49. E: camping.palinges@gmail.com

alanrogers.com/FR71110

Camping du Lac is a very special campsite and it is all due to M. Labille and his wife, the owners, who think of the campsite as their home and every visitor as their guest. The campsite has 40 touring pitches in total, of which 32 have 10A electricity and 16 are fully serviced. There are also seven chalets to rent. The site is adjacent to a lake with a beach and safe bathing. Set in the countryside yet within easy reach of many tourist attractions, especially Cluny, the local Château de Digoine and Mont Saint Vincent with distant views of Mont Blanc on a clear day.

Facilities

The central sanitary block provides all necessary facilities. Site is particularly well adapted for disabled visitors. Motorcaravan services. Washing machine and fridge. Bread and croissants to order. Boules. Play area. TV room. Sports field. Lake beach, swimming and fishing adjacent. Simple locally sourced food from the 'resto-bus' (1/5-30/9). WiFi in part of site (free). Off site: Snack bar outside entrance (July/Aug). Palinges (walking distance).

Open: 1 April - 30 October.

Directions

Palinges is midway between Montceau-les-Mines and Paray-le-Monial. From Montceau take N70, then turn left onto D92 to Palinges. Follow campsite signs. Site is also well signed from D985 Toulon-sur-Arroux to Charolles road. GPS: 46.56095, 4.22492

Charges guide

Per unit incl. 2 persons and electricity	€ 23.00
extra person	€ 4.10

No credit cards.

Saint Boil

Camping le Moulin de Collonge

Moulin de Collonge, F-71390 Saint Boil (Saône-et-Loire) T: 03 85 44 00 32. E: millofcollonge@wanadoo.fr
alanrogers.com/FR71050

This small campsite is situated on the wine route between Baume and Cluny and close to the long cycle route through the Burgundy vineyards. This well run, family site offers an 'away from it all' location and it will appeal to those seeking a quiet, relaxing environment in a garden-like setting. There are 63 small to average sized, level, grassy pitches, with 50 for touring (6A electricity; long leads may be required). Most pitches are well shaded by a wide variety of mature trees making access for tall outfits quite difficult. No twin-axle caravans or large outfits accepted.

Facilities

Well kept toilet facilities housed in a converted barn. Washing machine and dryer. Bread each morning. Basic shop (1/5-30/9). Restaurant/pizzeria, snack bar. Games room. Swimming pool, covered but some walls can be opened in good weather (all season). Playgrounds. Bouncy castle. Bicycle hire. Fishing. Pony trekking. Free WiFi over part of site. Off site: La Voie Verte, a 117 km. track for cycling or walking near the site. Riding 4 km.

Open: 1 April - 30 September.

Directions

From Chalon-sur-Saône, take N80 west 9 km. Turn south on D981 through Buxy (6 km). Continue south to St Boil 7 km. and site is signed at south end of the village. GPS: 46.64621, 4.69479

Charges guide

Per unit incl. 2 persons and electricity	€ 19.95 - € 23.65
extra person	€ 4.90 - € 5.95

Saint Léger-de-Fougeret

Sites et Paysages l'Etang de la Fougeraie

Hameau de Champs, F-58120 Saint Léger-de-Fougeret (Nièvre) T: 03 86 85 11 85.
E: info@campingfougeraie.fr **alanrogers.com/FR58040**

This is a tranquil and spacious campsite laid out on a hillside deep in the Parc Naturel Régional du Morvan, with views over their own lake, across the valley and surrounding hills. The spring water lake is ideal for fishing and swimming. There is a small bar and restaurant serving good quality regional meals and a well stocked shop with local produce. There are 73 terraced pitches, with 67 for touring, 58 with electricity (10/16A). Recent renovations have included redesigned, level pitches overlooking the lake, fewer steep paths, a new heated, outdoor pool and heated sanitary block.

Facilities

Heated sanitary block with family/disabled room close to entrance, but a fair distance uphill from the lower pitches. Washing machine and dryer. Shop, bar, restaurant and takeaway, heated outdoor pool (all season). Lake swimming. Fishing. Playgrounds. Paintball. Bicycle hire. Caravan storage. American RVs and twin-axle units not accepted. Chalets for rent with TV and DVD player. WiFi (free). Off site: Riding 3 km. Shops, bank with ATM and services 11 km.

Open: 28 March - 3 October.

Directions

St Léger-de-Fougeret is 10 km. south of Château-Chinon. From Château-Chinon, on D978, take D27 south for 3 km, then fork right on D157 for 5.5 km. to St Léger. Continue through village, follow signs to site 1 km. GPS: 47.00587, 3.90548

Charges guide

Per unit incl. 2 persons and electricity	€ 20.50 - € 26.50
extra person	€ 7.00
child (0-16 yrs)	€ 4.00 - € 5.50

Saint Sauveur-en-Puisaye

Camping Parc des Joumiers

F-89520 Saint Sauveur-en-Puisaye (Yonne) T: 03 86 45 66 28. E: biotic@wanadoo.fr
alanrogers.com/FR89040

This is an attractive, spacious, family run site in the north of Burgundy and east of the Loire. It is set beside a lake and a forest which offers many opportunities for walks and bike rides. There are 200 large, slightly sloping, grass pitches separated by hedges with a variety of trees giving varying amounts of shade. All 174 for touring have 16A electricity, water, drainage and TV point. There are no organised on-site activities but within 10 km. there are many interesting old towns, a medieval-style castle being built using traditional methods, and Château de Saint Fargeau with its pageants and 'son-et-lumière'.

Facilities

Two well appointed toilet blocks with all necessary facilities, including those for children. Good provision for disabled visitors. Washing machine. Motorcaravan services. Small infinity pool and paddling pool (June-mid-Sept). Play area with bouncy castle. Bar, restaurant and takeaway (all season) overlooking lake (fishing only). WiFi near bar. Fishing. Off site: Large village of St Sauveur with small shops, bar, restaurant 1 km. Riding 5 km. Bicycle hire 8 km. Children's pedal cars.

Open: 28 March - 5 November.

Directions

Leave A77 at exit 21 and take D965 east for 17 km. to St Fargeau. Turn right on D85 southeast to St Sauveur-en-Puisaye in 11 km. In village turn hard left on D7. In 800 m. turn right (site well signed) to site in 800 m. GPS: 47.63083, 3.19405

Charges guide

Per unit incl. 2 persons and electricity	€ 18.50 - € 20.50
extra person	€ 4.00 - € 4.80

Santenay

Camping des Sources

Avenue des Sources, F-21590 Santenay (Côte d'Or) T: 03 80 20 66 55. E: camping-de-santenay@orange.fr
alanrogers.com/FR21080

Santenay lies in the heart of the Côte de Beaune, a region renowned for its wine and châteaux, and within easy reach of Beaune. This is a peaceful place to unwind after a day's sightseeing or wine tasting. It is near a long distance cycle and walking track and next to the village sports and leisure area with free access to the swimming pool and paddling pool (1/6-31/8; token from reception). There are 144 comfortable level grassy touring pitches (from 90 to 150 sq. m.) delineated by a variety of trees offering some shade and all with 6A electricity. Twin-axle caravans are not accepted.

Facilities

The modern, well equipped and very clean toilet block includes facilities for disabled visitors. Motorcaravan services. Laundry facilities. Gas supplies. Shop (15/5-31/8). Games room. Playground. Playing field. Minigolf. Boules. Volleyball. Six new mobile homes for hire. Internet point and WiFi. Off site: Municipal swimming pool adjacent (1/6-31/8 and charged). Tennis courts, skateboarding. Casino 300 m. Spa 400 m. Santenay 1.5 km. Bicycle hire 1.5 km. Riding 2 km. Fishing 4 km.

Open: 25 March - 23 October.

Directions

From Beaune take D974 southwest towards Mersault and Chagny. After 12 km. pass under N6 and in 3 km. turn right (D113) into Santenay. Site is signed from village. GPS: 46.90718, 4.6856

Charges guide

Per unit incl. 2 persons
and electricity € 18.20 - € 21.50
extra person € 3.40 - € 4.10

Camping Cheques accepted.

Savigny-lès-Beaune

Camping les Premier Prés

Route de Bouilland, F-21420 Savigny-lès-Beaune (Côte d'Or) T: 03 80 26 15 06.
E: contact.camping@x-treme-bar.fr **alanrogers.com/FR21030**

This popular and attractive site is ideally located for visiting the Burgundy vineyards, for use as a transit site or for spending time in the town of Beaune. During the high season it is full every evening, so it is best to arrive by 4 pm. The 90 level pitches are marked and numbered with 6A electric hook-ups and room for an awning. A former municipal site, now privately owned, it is quiet and peaceful, situated alongside a small river. A one-kilometre walk along the riverbank brings you to the village, which has a château and a weekly market. Whilst the famed wine region alone attracts many visitors, Beaune, its capital, is unrivalled in its richness of art from times gone by.

Facilities

Well kept sanitary facilities are housed in a building behind reception. Additional WCs and water points are conveniently placed towards the middle of the site. Motorcaravan services. Ice available to purchase. Torch useful. Fishing. Bicycle hire. WiFi. Off site: Village with Sunday market 1 km. Château housing Abarth racing collections and motorbikes and aircraft. Beaune 7 km.

Open: 15 March - 15 October.

Directions

From A6 autoroute take exit 24 signed Beaune and Savigny-les-Beaune onto D2. Turn right towards Savigny-les-Beaune (3 km) and follow signs to site. GPS: 47.069, 4.803

Charges guide

Per unit incl. 2 persons
and electricity € 14.00 - € 16.00
extra person € 2.70 - € 3.10

No credit cards.

Tournus

Camping de Tournus

14 rue des Canes, F-71700 Tournus (Saône-et-Loire) T: 03 85 51 16 58. E: camping-tournus@orange.fr
alanrogers.com/FR71190

This very well maintained, pleasant site is just 1.5 km. from exit 27 of the A6 'Autoroute du Soleil'. It is therefore an ideal stop en route to and from the south of France, and reservation may be necessary in high season. The site is 200 metres from the River Saône and 1 km. from the centre of the interesting old market town of Tournus. All the 90 pitches are for touring and are equipped with 10A electricity; 27 have hardstanding. A few trees give some pitches varying amounts of shade. Access is very easy for large units. A municipal outdoor swimming pool is adjacent to the site and open for the high season.

Facilities

Two clean toilet blocks near the entrance provide all necessary facilities, including those for disabled visitors. Motorcaravan services. Small bar and shop in the reception area where bread can be ordered daily and light snacks purchased. Small play area. Bicycle hire. WiFi near the bar (free). Off site: Municipal pool next door. Fishing 100 m. Riding 10 km. Golf 15 km.

Open: 1 April - 30 September.

Directions

From the A6 take exit 27 for Tournus and the N6 south for just over 1 km. In Tournus (opposite railway station), turn left signed camping and follow signs to site, 1 km. GPS: 46.57372, 4.909349

Charges guide

Per unit incl. 2 persons
and electricity € 21.50 - € 26.80

Camping Cheques accepted.

Vandenesse-en-Auxois

Sunêlia Lac de Panthier

1 chemin du lac, F-21320 Vandenesse-en-Auxois (Côte d'Or) T: 03 80 49 21 94. E: info@lac-de-panthier.com

alanrogers.com/FR21000

Camping Lac de Panthier is an attractively situated lakeside site in the Burgundy countryside. It is divided into two areas, one housing the reception, shop, restaurant, indoor pool and sauna. The other, larger area is 200 m. along the lakeside road and is where the other site activities take place and the outdoor pools can be found. Many of the pitches here have views across the countryside. The 210 pitches (149 for touring) all have 6A electricity and are mostly on gently sloping grass, although in parts there are shallow terraces. The restaurant and some pitches have views over the lake which offers many watersports and is popular with anglers. Used by tour operators.

Facilities

Each area has two adequate unisex toilet blocks including provision for babies and disabled visitors. Shop, bar, restaurant and takeaway. Games and TV rooms. Swimming pool, children's pool and slide (1/6-31/8). Indoor pool, sauna and gym. Fishing. Bicycle hire (including electric bikes with trailers for children). Canoe hire. Watersports. Entertainment and activities in high season and clubs for children and teenagers. WiFi throughout (charged). Trampoline. No electric barbecues. Max. 1 dog. Off site: Golf 10 km. Riding 18 km.

Open: 17 April - 11 October.

Directions

From the A6 join the A38 and exit immediately at exit 24. Take N81 south towards Arnay Le Duc, over A6, shortly turn left on D977 for 5 km. Fork left for Vandenesse-en-Auxois. Through village on D977 for 2.5 km, turn left and site is on left. A car park is on the right where one can stop before entering the site. GPS: 47.23661, 4.62810

Charges guide

Per unit incl. 2 persons and electricity	€ 19.00 - € 28.00
extra person	€ 5.00 - € 7.00

Vincelles

Camping les Ceriselles

Route de Vincelottes, F-89290 Vincelles (Yonne) T: 03 86 42 50 47. E: camping@cc-payscoulangeois.fr

alanrogers.com/FR89060

A modern and well managed site, les Ceriselles was created in 1998 on land adjacent to the Canal du Nivernais and is owned by a group of communities. A very level site, it has 92 pitches on grass (74 for touring), all with electricity and 38 with full services. There are also 18 mobile homes. Staff live on site and the gates are locked 22.00-07.00 hrs. A popular site with Dutch and English visitors making it busy in high season. A covered terrace houses a restaurant with a good range of meals, takeaway and drinks. Twin-axle caravans are not accepted. This good value site is just off the D606 and ideal for exploring the Yonne valley and Auxerre region.

Facilities

Four small, heated toilet blocks each provide one WC, 2 washbasins in cubicles and two showers per sex, with a unit for disabled visitors in block one (nearest reception). A further block has a baby room, WCs and laundry. Restaurant (all season, hours vary acc. to demand). Clubroom with TV. Playground. Bicycle hire. Fishing. Boules. Volleyball. Basketball. Archery, canoeing and kayaking on certain days in high season. WiFi over site (charged). Off site: Supermarket and restaurant within walking distance. Cycle path along canal for 8 km.

Open: 1 April - 30 September.

Directions

Vincelles is 10 km. south of Auxerre. From A6 take Auxerre Sud exit and follow N65 towards Auxerre. After 4 km. turn south on D606 towards Avallon and after 10 km. turn left on D38. Site entrance is on left just before canal. GPS: 47.706644, 3.635678

Charges guide

Per unit incl. 2 persons and electricity	€ 16.00 - € 20.20
extra person	€ 3.40 - € 4.50
child (3-10 yrs)	€ 1.30 - € 3.20

Camping Cheques accepted.

DÉPARTEMENTS: 25 DOUBS, 39 JURA, 70 HAUTE-SAÔNE, 90 TRE. DE BELFORT

MAJOR CITY: BESANÇON

Located to the south of Alsace, the historic province of Franche-Comté boasts a varied landscape ranging from flat plains to dense woodlands, rugged dramatic mountains and limestone valleys.

Franche-Comté is a beautiful rural area bordered by Burgundy, Alsace, Champagne and Switzerland. It is an immensely varied landscape – the rolling farmland and small towns of the Haute-Saône contrasting with the dense forests, soaring cliffs and thundering waterfalls of the Jura. A paradise for nature lovers, there are endless opportunities for hiking, cycling and caving, with some skiing in winter. The streams and lakes provide world-class fishing, while more therapeutic waters can be found in spa towns such as Luxeuil-les-Bains, Salins-les-Bains and Lons-le-Saunier.

The historic capital, Besançon, with its walled citadel, lies on a loop of the River Doubs and is listed as a UNESCO World Heritage Site. The city remains unspoilt by development and has some charming old buildings. Visitors should not miss the impressive Musée des Beaux Arts which houses works by Titian, Rembrandt, Rubens and other old masters.

Places of interest

Arbois: Pasteur Family Home and Museum; Museum of Wine and Wine Growing.

Belfort: sandstone lion sculpted by Bartholdi; Memorial and Museum of the French Resistance.

Besançon: citadel with good views over the city.

Champlitte: Museum of Folk Art.

Dole: lovely old town, Louis Pasteur's birthplace.

Gray: Baron Martin Museum.

Luxeuil-les-Bains: Tour des Echevins Museum.

Ornans: Gustave Courbet birthplace, museum.

Ronchamp: Chapel of Notre-Dame du Haut de Ronchamp designed by Le Corbusier.

Salins-les-Bains: Salt mines and tunnels.

Sochaux: Peugeot Museum.

Cuisine of the region

Freshwater fish such as trout, grayling, pike and perch are local specialities. The region has a rare wine known as *vin de paille* as well as *vin jaune* (deep yellow and very dry) and *vin du jura*, Jura wine.

Brési: water-thin slices of dried beef; many local hams.

Gougère: hot cheese pastry based on the local *Comté* cheese.

Jésus de Morteau: fat pork sausage smoked over pine and juniper.

Papet jurassien: orange blossom tart.

www.franche-comte.org
info@franche-comte.org
00800 2006 2010 (free from the UK)

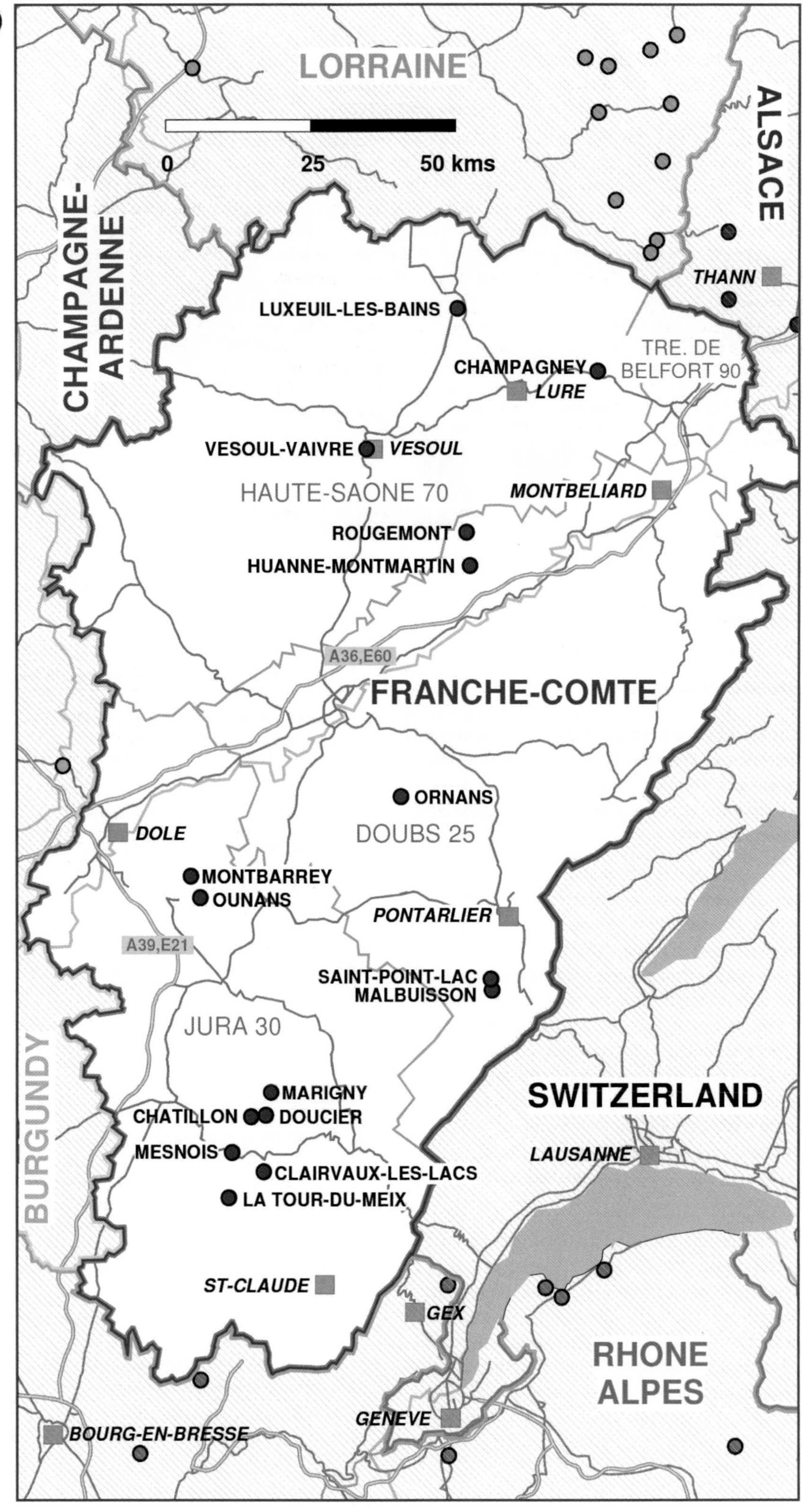
LORRAINE
0
25
50 kms
ALSACE
CHAMPAGNE-ARDENNE
THANN
LUXEUIL-LES-BAINS
TRE. DE BELFORT 90
CHAMPAGNEY
LURE
VESOUL-VAIVRE
VESOUL
HAUTE-SAONE 70
MONTBELIARD
ROUGEMONT
HUANNE-MONTMARTIN
A36,E60
FRANCHE-COMTE
ORNANS
DOLE
DOUBS 25
MONTBARREY
OUNANS
PONTARLIER
A39,E21
SAINT-POINT-LAC
MALBUISSON
JURA 30
MARIGNY
CHATILLON
DOUCIER
SWITZERLAND
BURGUNDY
MESNOIS
LAUSANNE
CLAIRVAUX-LES-LACS
LA TOUR-DU-MEIX
ST-CLAUDE
GEX
RHONE ALPES
GENEVE
BOURG-EN-BRESSE

Champagney

Camping des Ballastières

20 rue du Paguis, F-70290 Champagney (Haute-Saône) T: 03 84 23 11 22.
E: campingdesballastieres@orange.fr **alanrogers.com/FR70030**

Within easy reach of the historic town of Belfort, les Ballastières opened in 2008 in private ownership, but it is now run as a municipal site. The landscaping is becoming established and the 90 touring pitches are very large, level and easily accessible, all with 6/16A electricity. At the time of our visit, wooden lodges to rent were being installed on ten pitches. The reception building also houses a bar and snack bar, while outside a patio with tables and chairs overlooks the pool and adjacent lake. The site has been designed with disabled campers in mind; there is a sloping path down to the pool, a hoist has been installed, and one of the ten mobile homes is ramped for easy access.

Facilities

Three toilet blocks each with good facilities including those for disabled visitors. Washbasins in cabins. Laundry. Motorcaravan services. Shop (July/Aug). Bar with TV and snack bar. Swimming and paddling pools (July/Aug). Climbing facilities for children (3-11 yrs) with supervision. Kayaks and canoes. Play area for under 5s. WiFi on part of site (free). Off site: Riding 500 m.

Open: 1 April - 31 October.

Directions

Site is 20 km. northwest of Belfort. From roundabout on east side of Ronchamp on D19, take D4 eastwards for 2 km. Site is signed on left.
GPS: 47.706842, 6.67351

Charges guide

Per unit incl. 2 persons and electricity	€ 13.50 - € 22.00
extra person	€ 3.70

Chatillon

Camping Domaine de l'Epinette

15 rue de l'Epinette, F-39130 Chatillon (Jura) T: 03 84 25 71 44. E: info@domaine-epinette.com
alanrogers.com/FR39080

This site is set in charming wooded countryside on land sloping down to the River Ain, which is shallow and slow moving. There are 150 grassy pitches, some slightly sloping, and 110 are available for touring units. These are arranged on terraces and separated by hedges, bushes and trees, about half being shaded. Nearly all have electricity hook-ups, although some long leads are needed. Ten pitches have hardstanding. There is an attractive swimming pool with a paddling pool. An activity club for children takes place in high season. Guided canoe trips on the river start and finish at the campsite.

Facilities

Two modern toilet blocks. Unit for disabled visitors. Baby bath. Washing machine and dryer. Small shop for basics. Snack bar and takeaway (evenings). New reception, bar, TV room and shop. Takeaway (1/7-7/9). Swimming pool with toboggan. Playground. Boules. Direct access to river for fishing, swimming and canoeing. WiFi (free). Gas and charcoal barbecues permitted. Off site: Riding 6 km. Shops, etc. in Doucier 6 km. Golf 25 km.

Open: 15 June - 7 September.

Directions

From Lons-le-Saunier take D471 eastwards towards Pontarlier-Genève. After 8 km. fork right onto D39 towards Vevy. After 11 km. at Chatillon turn right onto D151 south towards Blye. Site is less than 2 km. on the left. GPS: 46.65252, 5.72106

Charges guide

Per unit incl. 2 persons and electricity	€ 17.00 - € 27.00

Camping Cheques accepted.

Clairvaux-les-Lacs

Yelloh! Village Fayolan

B.P. 52, F-39130 Clairvaux-les-Lacs (Jura) T: 03 84 25 88 52. E: lefayolan@odesia.eu
alanrogers.com/FR39050

This large, spacious site is modern and well equipped. Backed by wooded hills, it is situated on the shores of Le Petit Lac amid the lakes and forests of the Jura, about a mile from the town of Clairvaux-les-Lacs. It is in two parts with 516 pitches either on terraces overlooking the lake or on the flatter area near the shore. With 456 for touring units, all have electricity (10A) and 200 are fully serviced. The pitches are separated by hedges and mature trees giving most some shade. Many activities are organised on site, some in low season. Used by tour operators (130 pitches).

Facilities

Four modern well equipped toilet units. Baby room. Washing and drying machines. Shop. Restaurant. Bar. Snack bar/pizzeria and takeaway. Swimming pool complex with indoor pool (all season), outdoor pool (7/5-9/9; heated 5/6-31/8). Fitness centre with sauna, steam bath, massage (16/5-2/9). Entertainment area. Playground. Organised activities, children's club. Internet access. Fishing. Beach sports area and lake swimming. Boules. Off site: Bicycle hire 800 m. Riding 15 km.

Open: 28 April - 9 September.

Directions

Clairvaux-les-Lacs is on the D678 23 km. southeast of Lons-le-Saunier. In Clairvaux follow signs for 'Lacs Campings' and Fayolan (1.5 km. southeast of town). GPS: 46.56438, 5.75621

Charges guide

Per unit incl. 2 persons and electricity	€ 18.00 - € 44.00
extra person	€ 6.00 - € 8.00
child (3-7 yrs)	free - € 6.00

Doucier

Camping les Mérilles

215 route des Trois Lacs, F-39130 Doucier (Jura) T: 03 84 25 73 06. E: camping.lesmerilles@wanadoo.fr
alanrogers.com/FR39170

Camping les Mérilles is a small, good quality, family run campsite 500 m. from the small town of Doucier and only 2 km. from the beautiful Lac de Chalain. Despite speaking very little English, the owner, Christine Gras, is particularly friendly and she is justifiably proud of her site. It has 96 good sized, grass pitches separated by hedging. A variety of trees give shade. There are 76 pitches for touring units with 16 having a private bathroom. All have 10A electricity connections. This site is a quieter alternative to the much busier sites near the lake. Owners of large outfits should phone to reserve the larger pitches.

Facilities

One well appointed, heated toilet block with family shower room and facilities for disabled guests, one older small block plus 16 private cabins to rent with certain pitches. Motorcaravan services. Simple shop and bar with TV (1/6-30/9). Takeaway (1/7-30/9). Outdoor heated pool and paddling pool (1/5-30/9). Playground. Outdoor fitness equipment. Multisports pitch. Bicycle hire. Riding. Family activities (July/Aug). WiFi in some areas (free).

Open: 1 April - 30 September.

Directions

Doucier is 25 km. east of Lons-le-Saunier. The site is 500 m. east of Doucier on the D39 with the entrance on the right. GPS: 46.65178, 5.77491

Charges guide

Per unit incl. 2 persons and electricity	€ 17.10 - € 21.70
incl. private bathroom	€ 21.40 - € 30.85
extra person	€ 4.00 - € 4.30

Huanne-Montmartin

Camping du Bois de Reveuge

F-25680 Huanne-Montmartin (Doubs) T: 03 81 84 38 60. E: info@campingduboisdereveuge.com
alanrogers.com/FR25030

Bois de Reveuge is an attractive, spacious site with a total of 320 pitches, including 154 mobile homes located in woodland to one side of the site. The more open pitches on the lower terraces have good views across the surrounding countryside and overlook two lakes which may be used for fishing and canoeing. The 176 pitches available for touring have water and 6A electricity. Those on the upper terraces have more shade. There is a heated swimming pool which is covered in cool weather and another pool with four water slides and children's aquapark, supervised in high season.

Facilities

Four sanitary blocks (two open in low season). Facilities for disabled visitors, children and babies. Laundry facilities. Bar, restaurant/pizzeria (5/7-28/8). Kiosk for basics (from 1 May). Swimming pools. Play areas. Miniclub (high season). Boules. Shooting range. Archery. Tree walk. BMX track. Bicycle hire. Aquagym. Fishing. Pedalos and canoes. Reception closed 11.00-15.00 in low season. WiFi throughout (charged).

Open: 25 April - 5 September.

Directions

From A36 autoroute south of the site, take exit 5 for Baume-les-Dames and head north on D50 towards Villersexel for 7 km. Take D26 then follow D113. Site is on the right after Huanne. GPS: 47.4405, 6.34335

Charges guide

Per unit incl. 2 persons and electricity	€ 20.00 - € 35.00
extra person	€ 4.50 - € 8.50

Luxeuil-les-Bains

Domaine du Chatigny

14 rue Gramont, F-70300 Luxeuil-les-Bains (Haute-Saône) T: 03 84 93 97 97.
E: camping.ot-luxeuil@wanadoo.fr **alanrogers.com/FR70010**

An excellent example of a well cared for municipal site, Domaine du Chatigny is located on a hillside backing onto woods, yet is only a five minute walk from the centre of the interesting old spa town of Luxeuil-les-Bains. There are 98 good sized, level or slightly sloping, grass pitches separated by young shrubs and trees with not much shade. All the 78 touring pitches have 16A electricity and 11 are on hardstanding. Swimming and paddling pools are opened daily in high season and at weekends during June and September. Some activities are organised on site.

Facilities

Two modern, heated toilet blocks, plus toilet facilities at the pool provide all necessary facilities. Motorcaravan services. Bread to order. Snack bar, swimming and paddling pool (open weekends June, Sept and daily July/Aug). Games/TV room. Tennis. Internet access. WiFi throughout (free). Off site: Spa town of Luxeuil-les-Bains with good range of shops, bars, restaurants, Casino, Saturday market and many organised events, 5 minutes' walk. Bicycle hire 1 km. Fishing and riding 2 km.

Open: 15 March - 31 October.

Directions

No vehicle access from centre of Luxeuil-les-Bain – follow campsite signs rather than sat nav. Bypass Luxeuil-les-Bains on the N57. From south take exit to Luxeuil (after Auchan sign) head west (Luxeuil), first right (north, La Route des Retables). At next roundabout, left then left again (Auchan) following signs. From north exit 38 at roundabout take first exit then follow as above. GPS: 47.8236, 6.381667

Charges guide

Per unit incl. 2 persons and electricity	€ 16.50 - € 20.50

La Tour-du-Meix

Camping de Surchauffant

Le Pont de la Pyle, F-39270 La Tour-du-Meix (Jura) T: 03 84 25 41 08. E: info@camping-surchauffant.fr

alanrogers.com/FR39020

With only 200 pitches, this site may appeal to those who prefer a more informal atmosphere, however it can be lively in high season. It is pleasantly situated above the beaches bordering the Lac de Vouglans, which can be reached quickly on foot directly from the site. The 157 touring pitches are of a reasonable size and are informally arranged, some are fully serviced and most have electricity (10A). They are divided by hedges and there is some shade. The lake offers a variety of watersports activities, boat trips, etc. and is used for fishing and swimming (guarded in high season as it shelves steeply). Two signposted walks start from within 100 m. of the site entrance. English is spoken.

Facilities

The sanitary facilities are older in style and adequate rather than luxurious, but reasonably well maintained and clean when we visited. They include some washbasins in private cabins. Laundry. Heated swimming pool (200 sq.m), paddling pool and surround (15/6-14/9). Three playgrounds. Entertainment (July/Aug). Bicycle hire. Safety deposit boxes. Off site: Riding 5 km. Restaurant, takeaway and shops adjacent.

Open: 24 April - 14 September.

Directions

From A39 take exit 7 and N1082 to Lons-le-Saunier. Continue south on D52 for 20 km. to Orgelet. Site is by the D470, at La Tour-du-Meix, 4 km. east of Orgelet. GPS: 46.5231, 5.67401

Charges guide

Per unit incl. 2 persons and electricity	€ 15.00 - € 26.00
extra person	€ 3.00 - € 6.00
dog	free - € 2.00

Malbuisson

Camping les Fuvettes

24 route de la Plage et des Perrières, F-25160 Malbuisson (Doubs) T: 03 81 69 31 50.

E: les-fuvettes@wanadoo.fr **alanrogers.com/FR25080**

High in the Jura and close to the Swiss border, les Fuvettes is a well established family site beside Lac Saint Point. The 306 reasonably sized grass pitches are separated by hedges and small trees with varying degrees of shade and many are slightly sloping. There are 200 for touring with 150 having 6/10A electricity. Only a few have views over the lake. A very good outdoor, heated pool complex includes water slides and a separate children's pool. The site's bar/snack bar is housed in an attractive, steep roofed building and offers panoramic views across the lake. The lake is large – over 1,000 hectares and a wide range of watersports is possible from the site including sailing, windsurfing and pedaloes.

Facilities

Three toilet blocks include facilities for babies and disabled visitors. Shop (1/6-5/9). Bar (1/6-31/8). Snack bar (1/7-31/8). Swimming pool with water slides, jacuzzi and paddling pool (1/6-31/8). Play area. Trampolines. Minigolf. Archery. Bicycle hire. Sports pitch. Fishing (permit needed). Boat and pedalo hire. Games room. TV room. Children's club in peak season. Entertainment and excursion programme (July/Aug). Mobile homes and chalets for rent. No electric barbecues. WiFi (charged). Off site: Lakeside beach. Sailing school. Tennis. Riding 1 km. Bicycle hire 3 km. Many cycling and walking trails. Many restaurants, cafés and shops in nearby Malbuisson.

Open: 1 April - 30 September.

Directions

From Besançon, head south on the N57 to just beyond Pontarlier. Take the D437 signed Lac St Point and Mouthe. The road skirts the lake and through Malbuisson. Site is on right at the end of the village. GPS: 46.79197, 6.29334

Charges guide

Per unit incl. 2 persons and electricity	€ 20.60 - € 27.90
extra person	€ 3.80 - € 5.00
child (2-7 yrs)	€ 2.00 - € 3.40
dog	€ 1.00 - € 1.80

Marigny

Camping la Pergola

1 rue des Vernois, F-39130 Marigny (Jura) T: 03 84 25 70 03. E: contact@lapergola.com

alanrogers.com/FR39040

Close to the Swiss border and overlooking the sparkling waters of Lac de Chalain, la Pergola is a good quality terraced site set amongst the rolling hills of the Jura. Neat and tidy, and very well maintained, it has 350 large pitches, 100 for touring, mainly on grass and gravel and separated by small hedges. Ten are 'super' pitches. All have electricity (10/12A), water and drainage and some have shade from a variety of mature trees. The remainder are occupied by chalets. The bar/restaurant and terrace are next to the pool complex and enjoy views over the lake. This is a good holiday base for families with young children.

Facilities

Three good quality toilet blocks provide all the necessary facilities including facilities for disabled visitors and excellent provision for children. Laundry facilities. Motorcaravan services. Shop (14/6-6/9). Self-service restaurant (14/6-6/9). Bar, takeaway. Pool complex. Play areas and children's clubs. Boules. Lake swimming. Fishing. Bicycles, pedaloes, canoes and small boats for hire. Activities in high season. Evening entertainment with disco twice weekly. WiFi (charged). Chalets for rent. Off site: Hang-gliding 2 km. Riding 5 km. Golf 25 km.

Open: 8 May - 6 September.

Directions

Doucier is 25 km. east of Lons-le-Saunier on D471. From D471 turn south towards Doucier onto D27, site signed. Site in 3 km. beside Lac de Chalain. GPS: 46.6771, 5.78094

Charges guide

Per unit incl. 2 persons and electricity	€ 20.00 - € 47.00
extra person	€ 5.50 - € 8.00
child (5-12 yrs)	€ 3.00 - € 7.00

Camping Cheques accepted.

Mesnois

Sites et Paysages Beauregard

2 Grande rue, F-39130 Mesnois (Jura) T: 03 84 48 32 51. E: reception@juracampingbeauregard.com

alanrogers.com/FR39120

A hillside site on the edge of a small village with views of the rolling countryside, Beauregard has 192 level, grass pitches. There are 143 for touring units, all with 6A electricity (long leads may be necessary). The newer pitches on the lower level are drier so could be more suitable for motorcaravans, but they have no shade. The remaining pitches are used for mobile homes and tents for rent. The heated indoor pool area includes a paddling pool with a small water slide, a spa area with hydromassage jets, jacuzzi and a sauna. The heated outdoor pool has a 40 metre water slide.

Facilities

Three very clean toilet blocks (the newest one is only opened in peak season). Baby room and facilities for disabled visitors. Motorcaravan services. Shop (1/7-30/9). Bar, restaurant and takeaway (1/5-30/9). Indoor (all season) and outdoor pools (15/6-10/9) with toilet and shower facilities. Play areas. Outdoor fitness equipment. Minigolf. Tennis. Football. Volleyball. WiFi throughout (charged). Off site: Fishing 500 m. Pont de Poitte 2 km.

Open: 28 March - 30 September.

Directions

From Lons-le-Saunier (easily accessed from A39) take N78/D678 southeast towards Clairvaux-les-Lacs. After 17 km. in Thuron (before Pont-de-Poitte) turn left on D151 to Mesnois. Site is 1 km. on left by road junction. GPS: 46.59976, 5.68824

Charges guide

Per unit incl. 2 persons and electricity	€ 25.14 - € 31.30
extra person	€ 4.56 - € 5.70

Montbarrey

Flower Camping les Trois Ours

28 rue du Pont, F-39380 Montbarrey (Jura) T: 03 84 81 50 45. E: contact@camping-les3ours-jura.com

alanrogers.com/FR39150

This pretty and well cared for site is in a pleasant location at the edge of the Forêt de Chaux. The adjacent River Loué will be an attraction for fishermen and river bathing is also possible. There are 20 mobile homes and chalets to rent, and 70 shady level grassy touring pitches all with 6-10A electricity, 17 of which are premium riverside pitches. During peak season, various activities are organised including canoeing trips and themed evenings. The restaurant has a riverside terrace and offers a varied menu. The friendly owners can recommend numerous footpaths and cycle routes though the forest.

Facilities

One modern sanitary block provides all the usual facilities. Facilities for disabled visitors and children. Washing machine. Good restaurant and bar with TV. Outdoor pool (1/6-15/9). Trampoline. Small adventure style playground. Boules. Volleyball court. Table tennis. Small lake for fishing (free), river fishing (permit required). WiFi in bar area. Off site: Bicycle hire 3 km. Adventure centre and canoes 3 km. Shops in Ounans 3 km. Golf and riding 15 km.

Open: 10 April - 27 September.

Directions

From D472 Salins-les-Bains-Dole road, turn north on D11, 3.5 km. west of Ounans. Site is 3 km. on left just after river bridge. GPS: 47.011917, 5.6305

Charges guide

Per unit incl. 2 persons and electricity	€ 15.50 - € 29.00
extra person	€ 3.90 - € 5.50
child (2-7 yrs)	€ 2.90 - € 4.50

Ornans

Domaine le Chanet

9 chemin du Chanet, F-25290 Ornans (Doubs) T: 03 81 62 23 44. E: contact@lechanet.com

alanrogers.com/FR25070

Located in the heart of the Jura, in the Loue valley on the edge of historic Ornans, this traditional site is on a fairly steep slope with terraced pitches. The area has plenty of outdoor activities including canoeing and kayaking, mountain biking, caving, and fishing nearby. With 95 pitches (65 for touring), there are around 50 with electricity hook-ups (3-16A), including nine with multi-services. There are also 25 mobile homes, caravans or tents to rent on the site and three gîtes. Larger units will find access difficult. In the main season, entertainment and a children's club are arranged.

Facilities

Two toilet blocks. Baby room, facilities for children and disabled visitors. Small laundry area. Shop. Café, bar and takeaway (1/5-15/9). Heated outdoor eco-pool and paddling pool (1/5-30/9). Sauna and gym (charged). Washing facility for caving suits and equipment. Games room. Play area. Boules. Bicycle hire. Safety deposit boxes. Entertainment and a children's club in high season. WiFi on part of site (free). Off site: Fishing 500 m. Riding 10 km. Golf 20 km.

Open: 4 April - 15 October.

Directions

From Besançon take D67 to Ornans. At first and second roundabouts continue straight on towards town centre. Take first right on D241 (Chassagne St Denis), cross river, follow signs and turn right by school. Continue for 500 m. and then fork right, site is on left. GPS: 47.10055, 6.12795

Charges guide

Per unit incl. 2 persons and electricity	€ 17.00 - € 32.00
extra person	€ 4.10 - € 6.20

Ornans

Sites et Paysages la Roche d'Ully

Allée de la Tour de Peiltz, F-25290 Ornans (Doubs) T: 03 81 57 17 79. E: contact@larochedully.com

alanrogers.com/FR25150

Situated in the heart of the Jura mountains and close to historic Ornans, Roche d'Ully is a spacious, attractive and modern site, surrounded by views of wooded hills and rocky outcrops. There are 106 large grassy pitches, 65 of which are for tourers, most have electricity (10A) and all have access to water. Divided by a variety of bushes and young trees, there is not a great deal of shade. A feature here is the aquatic centre adjacent with two pools and many other facilities, with free entry to campers. The restaurant and bar are open all season and, being open to the public, both are busy at weekends.

Facilities

One modern and clean sanitary block with massage showers. Baby room. Facilities for disabled visitors. Laundry facilities. Motorcaravan services. Small shop. Bar/restaurant with terrace and takeaway (from 1/5). Games room and TV in bar. Play area. Bicycle hire. Pétanque. WiFi on part of site (free for 1 hour). Off site: Adjacent aqua centre (free entry to campers). Fishing 100 m. Dino Zoo 8 km. Golf (18 hole) 15 km.

Open: 2 April - 13 October.

Directions

From Besançon, take D67 to Ornans. Go through town and pass under arch of bridge, turning left immediately after in order to cross same bridge, following signs to Espace Nautiloue. Site is adjacent through car park. GPS: 47.10273, 6.1596

Charges guide

Per unit incl. 2 persons and electricity	€ 24.00 - € 33.00
extra person	€ 6.50

Ounans

Camping Indigo la Plage Blanche

3 rue de la Plage, F-39380 Ounans (Jura) T: 03 84 37 69 63. E: plageblanche@camping-indigo.com

alanrogers.com/FR39010

La Plage Blanche is a recent addition to the Indigo Group and is located in the Jura, by the rippling waters of the River Loue. This spacious eight-hectare site has 218 pitches (171 for touring, 40 of these on the riverbank). All are large, grassy and level with 10A electricity (Europlugs). This is a great site for family holidays with its children's activities and themed evenings in the bar/restaurant (DJ or live music) in high season. Other activities include kayaking, canoeing, fishing, fly fishing and woodland walks in the site's own wood. A number of distinctive safari style tents are available to rent.

Facilities

Three sanitary blocks include showers, washbasins in cabins and facilities for babies and disabled campers. Launderette. Motorcaravan service area. Shop with basics. Bar/snack bar/pizzeria with terrace. Takeaway. Heated swimming and paddling pools. Play area. Adults only spa with small pool, jacuzzi and sauna. Entertainment and activities. TV room. Library. Volleyball. Boules. Fishing. Canoeing. WiFi (free). Off site: Activities centre at site entrance. Bicycle hire 200 m. Shop 1.5 km.

Open: 4 May - 26 September.

Directions

Ounans is 20 km. southeast of Dole. From autoroute A39 exit 6 (Dole Choisey) follow signs for Pontarlier. In Ounans turn left just before the pizzeria (campsite signed). GPS: 47.00284, 5.663

Charges guide

Per unit incl. 2 persons and electricity	€ 19.00 - € 29.90
extra person	€ 5.50
child (1-6 yrs)	free - € 4.00

Rougemont

Castel Camping le Val de Bonnal

1 chemin du Moulin, F-25680 Bonnal (Doubs) T: 03 81 86 90 87. E: val-de-bonnal@wanadoo.fr

alanrogers.com/FR25000

This is an impressive, generally peaceful, well managed site in a large country estate, well away from main roads and other intrusions. The site itself is very busy, with a wide range of activities and amenities. The 280 very good sized, landscaped pitches (200 for touring units) with 6/10A electricity are separated by a mixture of trees and shrubs. Six of these pitches are fully serviced with water, drainage, fridge and garden furniture. As well as the 30 mobile homes the site has to rent, there many belonging to major tour operators. A main attraction here is the variety of watersports on the three large lakes and nearby river.

Facilities

Four toilet blocks include a new one with excellent facilities. Washbasins in cabins, suites for disabled visitors and facilities for children and babies. Laundry facilities. Riverside restaurant, snack bar/takeaway, bar and terrace, shop. Swimming pool complex and a splash park for children. Play areas. Sport and fitness facilities. Boules. Bicycle hire. Watersports. Fishing on the river and lake. Fitness suite. WiFi in some areas (charged).

Open: 7 May - 7 September.

Directions

From Vesoul take D9 (Villersexel). After 20 km. turn right in Esprels (Val-de-Bonnal). Continue for 3.5 km. to site on left. From autoroute A36, exit Baume-les-Dames; go north on D50, then D486 to Rougemont and follow site signs. GPS: 47.50768, 6.35596

Charges guide

Per unit incl. 2 persons and electricity	€ 28.15 - € 47.70

Min. stay 3 nights in high season.

Saint Point-Lac

Camping Municipal de Saint Point-Lac

8 rue du Port, F-25160 Saint Point-Lac (Doubs) T: 03 81 69 61 64. E: camping-saintpointlac@wanadoo.fr

alanrogers.com/FR25050

This pleasant, well run municipal site occupies a fine position on the shore of the third largest natural lake in France, with views across to the distant hills. The 84 level, numbered pitches are on grass and 61 have electricity (16A). It could be used for an overnight stop if passing Pontarlier, but above all it is an ideal base for those who enjoy fishing, walking, cycling and watersports. You can fish or swim in the lake and, just outside the entrance, you can have a drink at the open-air bar, hire canoes and rowing-boats or play boules and volleyball. The village is just a 200 m. walk from the site entrance.

Facilities

Well maintained, traditional style sanitary block is now fully enclosed and heated. Modern preset showers, warm water to washbasins (open-style except two for ladies). Basic en-suite unit for disabled visitors. Washing machine and dryer. Play area. Shop with terrace. Fishing and swimming in lake. Bicycle hire. WiFi over most of site (charged). Off site: Motorcaravan services opposite. Beach and swimming area (supervised in high season).

Open: 15 April - 15 October.

Directions

From Pontarlier take N57 south (Lausanne). After station, take exit for D437 (Malbuison) and in 5 km. turn right along west side of lake (D129) to St Point Lac; from south exit N57 at Les Hôpitaux-Neufs and turn west via D9 to lake then north on D129. GPS: 46.8118, 6.3031

Charges guide

Per unit incl. 2 persons and electricity	€ 18.00 - € 20.00
extra person	€ 3.50 - € 4.00

Vesoul-Vaivre

Camping International du Lac

Avenue des Rives du Lac, F-70000 Vesoul-Vaivre (Haute-Saône) T: 03 84 76 22 86.
E: camping_dulac@yahoo.fr **alanrogers.com/FR70020**

Part of a leisure park around a large lake, this campsite has 160 good sized, level pitches, mostly on grass, but with 29 hardstandings; they are separated by shrubs and bushes and 133 have electricty (6A). There is a large area in the centre of the site with a play area, a volleyball court and boules. Just outside the gate is a bar/restaurant and a pleasant beach for swimming and fishing. A five kilometre path has been created around the lake for jogging, walking and cycling and there are zones for boating and windsurfing. Watersports are professionally organised and there is also night-time carp fishing.

Facilities

Three traditional but well maintained toilet blocks, one heated, provide a mix of British (seatless) and Turkish style WCs, some washbasins in cabins and preset showers. Baby room. Three superb suites for disabled visitors. Laundry facilities. Motorcaravan services outside site. Baker calls daily (July/Aug); bread ordered from reception at other times. Entertainment and activities (July/Aug). Bicycle hire. TV and games rooms. Volleyball. Boules. WiFi (charged). Off site: Restaurant adjacent.

Open: 4 January - 19 December.

Directions

Vesoul is 50 km. north of Besançon. Site is 2 km. west of town. From D457 Epinal/Besançon turn west at roundabout following signs for Vaivre-et-Montoille and campsite. GPS: 47.63054, 6.12946

Charges guide

Per unit incl. 2 persons and electricity	€ 14.90
extra person	€ 4.00
child (under 7 yrs)	€ 19.00
dog	€ 2.15

DÉPARTEMENTS: 19 CORRÈZE, 23 CREUSE, 87 HAUTE-VIENNE

MAJOR CITIES: LIMOGES, BRIVE-LA-GAILLARDE

This quiet and deeply rural province is right in the centre of France to the south of the tourist region of the Loire Valley. Unspoilt and thinly populated, it is unknown to many but by others is considered close to paradise.

On the western side of the Massif Central, this stunningly beautiful region of still lakes, fast flowing streams, gentle rolling valleys and forested mountains has been one of the best kept secrets in France. Lush green meadows are grazed by the Limousin breed of cattle, numerous ancient villages and churches dot the landscape, as well as more imposing abbey churches and fortresses. The region's moorland has made it popular with horse breeders and the Anglo-Arab horse originated from the famous studs of Pompadour.

The city of Limoges, synonymous with porcelain production, produced the finest painted enamelware of Europe in the 16th and 17th centuries and today remains the porcelain capital of France. Aubusson is renowned for its beautiful and intricate tapestries.

But Limousin's appeal is more than anything the freedom of the countryside and it has not yet been discovered except by the discerning traveller. It is said that in Limousin a discovery awaits you at the end of every path and we consider this to be a fairly accurate description.

Places of interest

Aubusson: long tradition of tapestry making, Hotel de Ville tapestry collections.

Grimel-les-Cascades: a pretty hamlet set in a deep gorge.

Gueret: built around a monastery founded in the 8th century, the municipal museum houses a fine collection of porcelain.

Limoges: porcelain, enamel and faience work; château; church of St Michel-de-Lions; cathedral of St Etienne.

Oradour sur Glane: war-damaged village preserved from 1944.

Segur-le-Château: picturesque village dominated by its fortified château; Henry IV's house.

Treignac: Rocher des Folles with a view of the Vézères gorges.

Tulle: 12th-century cathedral and cloister; City museum; Maison de Loyac.

Cuisine of the region

Traditional dishes include a variety of stews such as pote, cassoulet, beans and pork and sauced dishes accompanied by chestnuts or rye pancakes. Limousin beef is tender and full of flavour.

Bréjaude: a soup eaten with rye bread and so thick with cabbage and other vegetables that a spoon will stand up in it.

Clafoutis: a pancake batter poured, for example, over fruit.

Galette Corrzienne: almond cake.

Pâté aux pommes de terre: potatoes and crème fraîche in a puff pastry crust.

www.tourismelimousin.com or
www.massifcentral-tourisme.com
documentation@crt-limousin.fr
(0)5 55 11 05 90

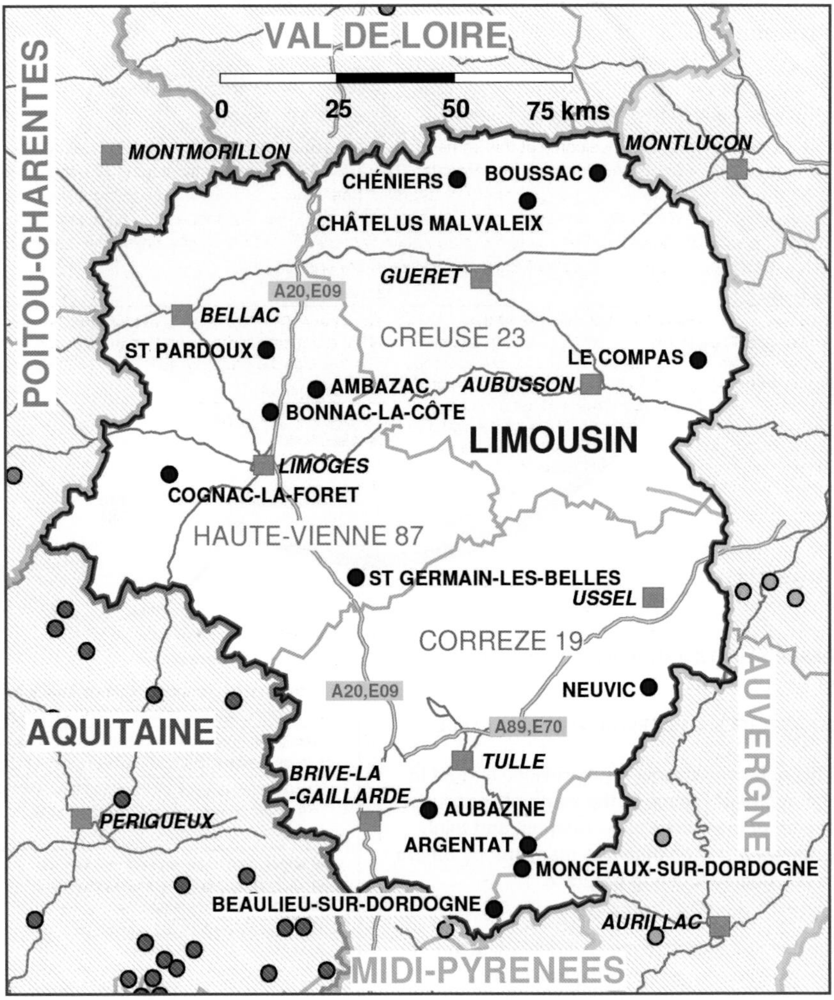

Ambazac

Camping l'Ecrin Nature

Etang de Jonas, F-87240 Ambazac (Haute-Vienne) T: 06 52 92 71 65. E: contact@campinglecrinature.com

alanrogers.com/FR87180

L'Ecrin Nature is a friendly site, attractively located close to Ambazac, with good access to the key sights of the Limousin. Some of the site's 54 touring pitches are well shaded and of a good size, many with fine views across the plan d'eau de Jonas towards the Monts d'Ambazac. Most have 6A electricity connections. A number of mobile homes and fully equipped tents are available for rent. On-site leisure facilites include a heated swimming pool, volleyball and badminton. There are many footpaths close to the site, and the managers will be pleased to recommend routes. A day trip to Limoges is recommended, a beautiful city with a wealth of tourist attractions and a thriving porcelain industry.

Facilities

Sanitary facilities include hot showers, washbasins in cabins and provision for families and disabled visitors in the main block. Laundry facilities. Motorcaravan services. Essentials available including local produce and wine. Bread to order (July/Aug). Heated swimming pool (June-Sept). Games room. Play area. Volleyball. Badminton. Tourist information. Entertainment and activities. Finnish Kota grill hire. Bicycle hire. Accommodation for rent. WiFi over site (charged). Off site: Ambazac 2 km. Riding, tennis and squash 2.5 km. Limoges 25 km.

Open: 11 April - 16 October.

Directions

The site is located to the north of Limoges. Approaching from the north, leave A20 autoroute at exit 26 (from the south exit 27) and follow signs to Ambazac, then Plan d'Eau de Jonas and site. The site is well signed. Use intercom to gain entry. GPS: 45.97155, 1.41346

Charges guide

Per unit incl. 2 persons and electricity	€ 16.00 - € 18.00
extra person	€ 3.00 - € 4.00

Min. € 12 spend for credit cards.

Argentat

Camping le Vaurette

Monceaux-sur-Dordogne, F-19400 Argentat (Corrèze) T: 05 55 28 09 67. E: info@vaurette.com

alanrogers.com/FR19090

You are assured of a warm welcome at this immaculate site, beautifully situated beside the shallow River Dordogne and just a few kilometres from Argentat. There are 120 large, gently sloping grass pitches, 118 for touring. Separated by a large variety of beautiful trees and shrubs offering varying amounts of shade, all have 6A electricity and many have good views over the River Dordogne as the pitches nearest the river are slightly terraced. The owners run an active campsite for all the family whilst maintaining an air of tranquillity (no radios). Excellent English and Dutch are spoken.

Facilities

Two very clean traditional toilet blocks offer all the expected facilities, including those for disabled visitors. Further facilities are near the bar and heated outdoor pool. Motorcaravan services. Shop. Two bars with terrace and takeaway. Football. Gym. Badminton. Boules. Tennis. Fishing. River bathing. Accompanied canoe trips, walks and mountain bike rides. Organised activities for all the family (July/Aug) but no late night discos etc. WiFi (charged). Off site: Argentat 9 km. Riding and golf 30 km.

Open: 1 May - 21 September.

Directions

From the A20 or A89 take the exit for Tulle then the N120 to Argentat, onto the D12 towards Beaulieu. The site is on the left. GPS: 45.0464, 1.8821

Charges guide

Per unit incl. 2 persons and electricity	€ 21.30 - € 32.70
extra person (over 2 yrs)	€ 4.30 - € 6.80
dog	€ 3.00 - € 4.50

Argentat

Camping Au Soleil d'Oc

Monceaux-sur-Dordogne, F-19400 Argentat (Corrèze) T: 05 55 28 84 84. E: info@dordogne-soleil.com

alanrogers.com/FR19100

You will be assured of a very warm welcome, throughout the long season, at this attractive family run site set amongst a variety of tall trees on the banks of the River Dordogne. The 120 large, level, grass pitches, 80 for touring units, all with electricity (6A, Europlug), are mostly separated by neatly trimmed shrubs and hedges. They are set out on two levels; the lower level nearer the river, with fewer static pitches, being some distance from the toilet facilities and sports area. This site should appeal to lovers of watersports and other activities, particularly in July and August when there is plenty to do for all.

Facilities

Two unisex toilet blocks offer all the facilities one would expect. Baby facilities. Motorcaravan services. Shop (July/Aug). Bar (1/7-30/9). Restaurant and takeaway (1/6-30/9). Outdoor pool (15/6-15/10). Indoor pool (19/4-31/10). Swimming in the Dordogne. Canoe hire and organised trips. Volleyball. Football. Electronic games. Archery. Minigolf. Fishing. Bicycle hire. Guided walks and bike rides. Entertainment (July/Aug). WiFi. Torches useful. Off site: River Dordogne. Argentat 4 km. Riding 15 km.

Open: 19 April - 15 November.

Directions

Leave Argentat on D12 heading southwest (Beaulieu). In 3.5 km. (village of Laygue) turn left across a single track bridge spanning the River Dordogne. Immediately turn left and site is a few hundred metres on left. GPS: 45.0753, 1.91699

Charges guide

Per unit incl. 2 persons and electricity (6A)	€ 18.90 - € 32.80
extra person	€ 4.50 - € 6.50

Camping Cheques accepted.

Aubazine

Campéole le Coiroux

Centre Touristique du Coiroux, F-19190 Aubazine (Corrèze) T: 05 55 27 21 96.

E: coiroux@campeole.com **alanrogers.com/FR19140**

Le Coiroux, part of the Campéole group, is set in a picturesque location in the heart of a forest on the edge of a large leisure park and lake. There are 174 large pitches, 62 for touring all with 10A electricity. They are flat and grassy with small dividing hedges and trees giving shade. The large number of mobile homes and chalets on site are separate from the camping area and not intrusive. There is everything one needs for a family holiday at this site which caters for adults and children of all ages.

Facilities

One large, modern, very well equipped sanitary block with all necessary facilities including those for campers with disabilities and baby room. Second smaller sanitary block. Laundry facilities. Motorcaravan services. Large heated swimming pool (1/5-30/9). Poolside bar, snack bar and large shop (July/Aug). Boules. Tennis. Organised daytime activities (July/Aug). Accommodation for hire. WiFi (free in low season). Off site: Leisure park (reduced fees charged). Lake fishing 300 m. Golf complex 800 m.

Open: 1 April - 30 September.

Directions

Leave A20 exit 49 Tulle, take D1089 (Tulle). At the village of Gare d'Aubazine turn right to Aubazine. Continue for 6 km. through village, take road to Chastang and follow signs to Parc Touristique du Coiroux 4 km. GPS: 45.18633, 1.70775

Charges guide

Per unit incl. 2 persons and electricity	€ 16.10 - € 28.20

Camping Cheques accepted.

Beaulieu-sur-Dordogne

Camping Indigo Beaulieu

Boulevard Rodolphe de Turenne, F-19120 Beaulieu-sur-Dordogne (Corrèze) T: 05 55 91 02 65.
E: beaulieu@camping-indigo.com **alanrogers.com/FR19130**

This is a very pleasant and well equipped site in a beautiful location on a small island in the River Dordogne. Camping Indigo Beaulieu is a very attractive site only two minutes' walk away from the centre of the medieval town of Beaulieu-sur-Dordogne with its ancient streets, old churches, many shops and restaurants. This seven-hectare site has 185 shady, grass pitches, 80 of which are available for touring, all with 10A electricity. The added bonus of its close proximity to the centre of the village makes this an ideal site for tourers. As part of the Indigo group, there are plans to make further improvements.

Facilities

Three modern, clean toilet blocks. Baby room. Laundry room. Motorcaravan services. Small shop for basics with local produce and bread to order. Heated pool (May-Sept), poolside bar, snacks. Boules. Canoe hire can be arranged. Fishing. Children's entertainment (3-12 yrs) 4 days per week. Evening soirées (2 evenings per week in July/Aug). WiFi. Off site: Pizzeria and takeaway 200 m. Tennis 600 m. Bicycle hire 8 km. Golf and riding 18 km. Gouffre de Padirac, Rocamadour, Collonges-la-Rouge (less than 1 hour). Caves, museums, several beautiful ancient villages.

Open: 4 May - 26 September.

Directions

The site is in the centre of Beaulieu-sur-Dordogne on the D940. From Tulle turn right or from Montal turn left. Approach site with care through the narrow streets. Enter site through narrow archway (3 m. high). GPS: 44.979705, 1.840146

Charges guide

Per unit incl. 2 persons and electricity	€ 15.50 - € 30.50
extra person	€ 3.90 - € 7.70
child (2-7 yrs)	free - € 5.10
dog	€ 1.00 - € 2.00

Low season reductions.

Bonnac-la-Côte

Castel Camping le Château de Leychoisier

Domaine de Leychoisier, 1 route de Leychoisier, F-87270 Bonnac-la-Côte (Haute-Vienne) T: 05 55 39 93 43.
E: contact@leychoisier.com **alanrogers.com/FR87020**

You will receive a warm welcome at this beautiful, family run site with its 9th-century château. It offers peace and quiet in superb surroundings. It is ideally situated for short or long stays being only 2 km. from the A20 and 10 km. north of Limoges. The large, slightly sloping and grassy pitches are in a parkland setting with many magnificent mature trees offering varying amounts of shade. The 78 touring pitches have 10A electricity and many have a tap. The small heated swimming pool with sunbathing area is accessed through the reception and bar, and the restaurant serves high quality, freshly prepared meals. The château grounds are free for visitors to explore and a walk through the woodland leads to the four-hectare lake (children must be supervised).

Facilities

The sanitary block is very clean with separate provisions for disabled visitors. Some washbasins in cabins. Family bathroom. Washing machine and dryer. Basic grocery provisions (bread can be ordered daily). Restaurant, bar, TV room, small heated swimming pool with sunbathing area (all open all season). Lake. Fishing. Play area. Tennis and boules courts. Torch useful. WiFi (charged). Off site: Shop 2 km. Riding 2 km. Limoges 12 km. Bicycle hire 15 km. Golf 18 km. Oradour-sur-Glane 28 km.

Open: 15 April - 20 September.

Directions

From A20, north of Limoges, take exit 27 (west) signed Bonnac-La-Côte. In village turn left and follow signs to site. GPS: 45.93299, 1.29006

Charges guide

Per unit incl. 2 persons and electricity	€ 28.00 - € 34.00
extra person	€ 6.50 - € 9.50
child (under 7 yrs)	€ 5.00 - € 6.00
dog	€ 2.00 - € 3.00

Credit cards in July/Aug. only.

Boussac

Castel Camping le Château de Poinsouze

Route de la Châtre, B.P. 12, F-23600 Boussac-Bourg (Creuse) T: 05 55 65 02 21.
E: info.camping-de.poinsouze@orange.fr **alanrogers.com/FR23010**

Le Château de Poinsouze is a well established site arranged on an open, gently sloping, grassy park with views over a small lake and château. It is an attractive, well maintained, high quality site situated in the unspoilt Limousin region. The 116 very large, grassy touring pitches, some with lake frontage, all have electricity (6-20A Europlug), water and drainage, and 68 have sewerage connections. The site has a friendly-family atmosphere with many organised activities in main season including a children's club. There are marked walks around the park and woods. All facilities are open all season.

Facilities

High quality sanitary unit includes suites for disabled visitors. Washing machines and dryers. Motorcaravan services. Shop for basics. Takeaway. Bar and restaurant. Swimming pool, slide, children's pool and new water play area with fountains. Fenced playground. Pétanque. Bicycle hire. Free fishing in the lake, boats and lifejackets can be hired. Sports facilities. Accommodation to rent. WiFi over site (charged). No dogs (14/7-18/8). Off site: Boussac (2.5 km) with Thursday morning market.

Open: 15 May - 16 September.

Directions

Boussac is 35 km. west of Montluçon, between the A20 and A71 autoroutes. Site is 2.5 km. north of Boussac on D917 (towards La Châtre) and is well signed. GPS: 46.37243, 2.20268

Charges guide

Per unit incl. 2 persons and full services	€ 19.00 - € 36.00
extra person	€ 3.00 - € 6.00
child (2-7 yrs)	€ 2.00 - € 5.00

Châtelus Malvaleix

Camping la Roussille

Plan d'Eau de la Roussille, F-23270 Châtelus Malvaleix (Creuse) T: 05 55 80 70 31.
E: contact@revea-vacances.com **alanrogers.com/FR23080**

Camping La Roussille is a small site which is part of the municipal park and lake. It is located in the heart of the Creuse, 25 km. from Gueret and 400 m. from the village. At the borders of the Berry and la Marche, the site has 26 touring pitches, all with electricity (long leads may be needed). Nearby is a five-hectare lake with sandy beach and supervised swimming in July/August. There is also a very conveniently placed bar with a terrace overlooking the beach. There are numerous on-site activities for children. The owners organise hiking and mountain biking trips. Rental accommodation is in eight chalets (2-6 persons) with one specially adapted for disabled visitors.

Facilities

One small toilet block provides hot showers and washbasins with hot water. Laundry room. Bar with terrace by the beach (July/Aug). TV room. Games room. Games for children. Fishing. Tennis. Bicycle hire. Barbecue area. Barbecues to loan. WiFi on part of site (charged). Off site: Shops, restaurant, pharmacy, doctor and Friday street market in Chatelus 400 m.

Open: 1 May - 30 September.

Directions

From N145 E62 at Gueret take D940 north bound. In village after the Mairie, turn left onto D40. Site is on left. GPS: 46.30445, 2.0188

Charges guide

Per unit incl. 2 persons and electricity	€ 13.00
extra person	€ 3.00
child	€ 2.00

Chéniers

Camping le Moulin de Piot

Rue du Moulin de Piot, F-23220 Chéniers (Creuse) T: 05 55 62 80 90. E: moulin-de-piot@orange.fr
alanrogers.com/FR23020

Camping le Moulin de Piot can be found on the banks of the Petite Creuse river. It is a popular site with anglers and kayaking enthusiasts. The 75 grass touring pitches are large and most are equipped with 10A electricity (long lead may be required). A number of mobile homes and gîtes are available to rent. The site is close to the village of Chéniers, and a good range of services are on offer there, including a small supermarket, baker and restaurant. On site, there is a small restaurant/snack bar, which also supplies takeaway meals, ice creams and regional specialities.

Facilities

Sanitary facilities with hot showers, some private cabins, family room and facilities for children and disabled visitors. Washing machine. Shop. Snack bar/restaurant and takeaway (1/5-30/9). Fishing. Craft workshop. Play area. Canoe and mountain bike hire. Free WiFi over part of site. Chalets and mobile homes for rent. Off site: Walking and mountain biking in the Creuse. Wildlife park.

Open: 1 April - 31 October.

Directions

The site can be found to the north of Guéret. From there, head north on D940 and D6 as far as Bonnat. From there, take the westbound D15 to Le Temple, and then head north to Cheniers, from where the site is well signed. GPS: 46.346512, 1.838912

Charges guide

Per unit incl. 2 persons and electricity	€ 13.15 - € 15.50
extra person	€ 2.65 - € 3.65

Cognac-la-Forêt

Camping des Alouettes

1, les Alouettes, F-87310 Cognac-la-Forêt (Haute-Vienne) T: 05 55 03 26 93.
E: info@camping-des-alouettes.com **alanrogers.com/FR87100**

Camping des Alouettes, located in the Perigord Limousin Nature Park, 25 kilometres west of Limoges, is run by a young Dutch couple who will do all they can to ensure your stay is enjoyable. The site has 68 large, level, grass pitches, mostly open, all with 10A electricity. Almost all pitches enjoy panoramic views of the area. There is a mixture of mature and young trees providing some shade and pitches are separated by new shrubs or hedging. Six mobile homes and three safari tents are for rent. On arrival you are given a guided tour and an explanation of what is available both on and off site.

Facilities

Well kept, very modern sanitary block includes facilities for disabled visitors, children and a family shower room. Washing machine. Bread can be ordered daily and delivered to your pitch. Bar. Restaurant (Mon. and Fri). Takeaway spit roast chicken (Wed). Heated swimming pool (15/5-30/9). Football, volleyball, badminton, pétanque and table tennis. Small play area. Small library. No charcoal barbecues. Internet access at bar. WiFi on most pitches (charged). Off site: Village 1 km. with shops, bar and restaurant. Walking and cycle routes.

Open: 1 April - 30 September.

Directions

From the north take exit 28 from the A20 onto the D2000/N520. Continue towards Perigueux until Cognac-la-Forêt is signed to the right at the roundabout. Continue through village on the D10. Site on the left after 250 m. GPS: 45.8247, 0.99657

Charges guide

Per unit incl. 2 persons and electricity	€ 17.25 - € 22.25
extra person	€ 3.75 - € 5.00
child (under 10 yrs)	€ 2.25 - € 3.25

Le Compas

Le Moulin des Jarasses

F-23700 Le Compas (Creuse) T: 06 48 44 52 75. E: info@moulindesjarasses.com
alanrogers.com/FR23040

Camping Le Moulin des Jarasses is owned by a young Dutch couple who have created their ideal campsite; small and natural, set in the heart of the Creuse countryside. Chickens and small animals have free range over the campsite in low season. There are just 25 pitches for touring and ten mobile homes to rent. Most pitches have electricity (10A) and are on level grass. Afternoon tea and communal evening meals are available in peak season. A small swimming pool with paddling pool along with the free loan of bicycles and go-karts make this a good site for young families. There are no organised events.

Facilities

One shower block includes showers, open style washbasins and a new family room. Facilities for babies. Laundry facilities. Motorcaravan services. Small shop with bread to order. Evening meals and afternoon tea in high season. Outdoor heated swimming pool and paddling pool. Basic play room. Bicycle and go-cart hire. Free WiFi on part of site. Off site: Supermarket 4 km. Riding 4 km. Fishing 15 km. Cycling.

Open: 1 May - 30 September.

Directions

Le Moulin des Jarasses is 20 km. to the northeast of Aubusson. From Auzances take D988 towards Aubusson. At Jarasse (2.5 km), turn left and follow signs to site on right. GPS: 46.01204, 2.46517

Charges guide

Per unit incl. 2 persons and electricity	€ 22.50 - € 35.00

No credit cards.

Monceaux-sur-Dordogne

Camping le Saulou

Lieu-dit Vergnolles, F-19400 Monceaux-sur-Dordogne (Corrèze) T: 05 55 28 12 33. E: le.saulou@orange.fr
alanrogers.com/FR19220

Camping le Saulou lies between Tulle and Aurillac, just south west of Argentat and alongside the River Dordogne which it fronts for about 400 metres. The site has 158 pitches with 128 for touring, all with 10A electricity (mostly Europlugs). They are on level grass separated by some hedging and a variety of trees give varying amounts of shade. There are some excellent pitches along the river's edge, well worth the small, additional charge in high season. This section of the river attracts many fishermen and some travel up to 300 km. for its excellent fly fishing.

Facilities

Adequate toilet blocks, facilities for disabled campers and babies. Washing machine/dryer. Shop (with fresh bread to order), bar, snack/bar and takeaway (1/7-31/8). Swimming/paddling pools (15/6-15/9). TV room. Library. Two playgrounds (2-5 yrs, 6-12 yrs). Multisports area. Family entertainment, children's clubs, disco (July/Aug). River fishing. Canoeing, kayaking and rafting. WiFi (€ 5 for duration of stay). Off site: Bicycle hire 5 km.

Open: 28 March - 31 October.

Directions

Leave Argentat on D1120 (southeast) and 500 m. after crossing River Dordogne turn right and follow D116 towards Vergnolles to site on right in 5 km. GPS: 45.05728, 1.91443

Charges guide

Per unit incl. 2 persons and electricity	€ 19.40 - € 26.90
extra person	€ 5.00 - € 6.50

Neuvic

Camping Domaine de Mialaret

Route d'Egletons, F-19160 Neuvic (Corrèze) T: 05 55 46 02 50. E: info@lemialaret.com

alanrogers.com/FR19060

Mialaret is 4 km. from the village of Neuvic and only 6 km. from the Gorges of the Dordogne. It is set in a 44-hectare estate with a 19th-century château, now a hotel and restaurant offering gastronomic dishes. More simple meals are served at the brasserie/pizzeria. Most of the 113 touring pitches are set in a gently sloping parkland situation with trees and shrubs. Some are level and separated by small bushes, most have some shade and 10A electricity. Each pitch has been provided with a wooden picnic table. A feature of the site is the 340 sq.m. pool designed by the Art Deco architect, Hector Guimard.

Facilities

Refurbished sanitary blocks, one heated, are adequate, with facilities for disabled visitors, and washing machines. Motorcaravan services. Bar. Brasserie/pizzeria. Takeaway. Shop with bread. Dinner at hotel. Large swimming pool with shallow area (15/6-15/9). Pool. Play areas. Tennis. Football. Volleyball. Pétanque. 2 fishing ponds. WiFi (free). Safari lodge tents, chalets and teepees for rent. Off site: Village with shops 4 km. Golf 4 km.

Open: 27 April - 31 October.

Directions

From Clermont-Ferrand or Brives on the A89, take exit 23 and follow signs for Neuvic (20 km). In Neuvic follow signs for le Mialaret (take first right after Intermarche). Site is 4 km. GPS: 45.38242, 2.22910

Charges guide

Per unit incl. 2 persons and electricity	€ 24.00 - € 34.00
extra person	€ 6.00 - € 9.00

Saint Germain-les-Belles

Camping de Montréal

Rue du Petit Moulin, F-87380 Saint Germain-les-Belles (Haute-Vienne) T: 05 55 71 86 20.
E: contact@campingdemontreal.com **alanrogers.com/FR87150**

You can be sure of a warm welcome from Hans and Leonie, the new Dutch owners of Camping de Montréal, in the heart of the Limousin countryside. The site provides 58 terraced pitches; 13 are occupied by chalets, mobile homes or bungalows, while 45 pitches are reserved for touring units. The pitches are mainly level and most have good views over the eight-hectare leisure lake. All have electricity (10A), some have shade and many are separated by tall cypress hedges. The single toilet block has recently been refurbished to a high standard. The small restaurant is popular with campers and users of the lake. The site is open at Christmas.

Facilities

One refurbished toilet block on the lower level has preset showers, baby changing and good facilities for disabled visitors. Laundry. Bar/restaurant with takeaway. Swimming pool. Play area. Small library. Lake for fishing and swimming. WiFi (charged). Off site: Riding and bicycle hire 2 km.

Open: All year.

Directions

From A20 take exit 42 and head northeast towards St Germain-les-Belles. In village follow signs for office de tourisme and on to campsite. GPS: 45.61159, 1.501348

Charges guide

Per unit incl. 2 persons and electricity	€ 17.10 - € 20.10
extra person	€ 3.00 - € 4.00

Saint Pardoux

Camping de Fréaudour

Lac de Saint-Pardoux, F-87250 Saint-Pardoux (Haute-Vienne) T: 05 55 76 57 22.
E: camping.freaudour@orange.fr **alanrogers.com/FR87070**

A member of the Aquadis Loisirs group who specialise in countryside holidays, Camping de Fréaudour is located in the Haute-Vienne region of Limousin. This peaceful site is situated in a wood on sloping ground and is next to Saint-Pardoux lake and village. The 107 grassy touring pitches (min. 80 sq.m) are separated by trees and shrubs which give some shade and have electricity (10/16A, Europlug). There are ten chalets and 20 mobile homes to rent. Visitors have direct access to the lake where they can relax on the lake beach and enjoy a wide variety of water-based activities and sports.

Facilities

Sanitary facilities include provision for children and disabled visitors. Motorcaravan services. Laundry. Baby equipment on request. Shop (essentials only outside July/Aug). Bar, snack bar and takeaway (June-Aug). Bread to order (May-Sept). Swimming pool (1/6-15/9). Playground. Pool table. TV/Games room. Children's club (once or twice a week, July/Aug). Entertainment for all (July and Aug). Yoga (weekly July/Aug). Lake fishing (charged). WiFi (free in reception). Off site: Watersports and activities on lake adjacent. Restaurant 1.7 km.

Open: 7 March - 6 November.

Directions

Site is 35 km. north of Limoges. From north or south take A20/E9 exit 25 onto D219 briefly then D44 and follow signs to Lac St Pardoux. Continue through village of St Pardoux onto D103a and follow signs to Site de Fréaudour and site. GPS: 46.04959, 1.27881

Charges guide

Per unit incl. 2 persons and electricity	€ 16.90 - € 18.90
extra person	€ 5.20 - € 5.30

Camping Cheques accepted.

DÉPARTEMENTS: 03 ALLIER, 15 CANTAL, 43 HAUTE-LOIRE, 63 PUY-DE-DÔME

MAJOR CITY: CLERMONT-FERRAND

Set in the heart of the Massif-Central, the Auvergne was formed by a series of volcanic eruptions and is a dramatic region of awe-inspiring, non-active volcanoes, lakes, sparkling rivers, green valleys and forests.

The ancient province of Auvergne is a largely mountainous and sparsely populated region reputed for its natural environment and the thermal spa resorts of Vichy, Chatel Guyon and Le Mont Dore.

The 'Parc Naturel Régional des Volcans d'Auvergne' – the Auvergne Volcano Park – is the largest national park in France and is a protected environment for exceptional flora and fauna. The mountains provide three classified downhill ski resorts and excellent cross-country skiing. The area around Clermont-Ferrand is characterised by mineral-rich volcanic rock and is the source of prominent mineral waters including Vichy and Volvic.

Popular destinations for visitors include the Vulcania theme park, where adults and children can learn about the fascinating science of volcanoes, and the vibrant city of Clermont-Ferrand with its black rock buildings and views of the Dôme mountains.

Places of interest

Aurillac: old town; wax museum; archaeology museum.

Clermont-Ferrand: old city centre; 11th-12th-century Notre Dame du Port Basilica; 13th-century cathedral; known as 'ville noire' for its houses built in local black volcanic rock.

Le Mont-Dore: spa; winter sports; panoramic view.

Le Puy en Velay: old city with cathedral and chapel in a dramatic volcanic landscape.

Puy-de-Dôme: Gallo-Roman site; television tower and observatory.

Vichy: spa buildings; opera house; riverside gardens.

Vulcania: 15 km. from Clermont-Ferrand. A scientific exploration park, designed for children and adults who want to discover and understand the fascinating world of volcanoes and the earth sciences.

Cuisine of the region

Local specialities include ham and andouille sausages, stuffed cabbage and bacon with lentil and cèpes (mushrooms). Le Puy is famed for its lentils and Vereine du Velay – yellow and green liqueurs made from over 30 mountain plants.

Aligot: purée of potatoes with Tomme de Cantal cheese, cream, garlic and butter.

Perdrix à l'Auvergnate: partridge stewed in white wine.

Potée Auvergnate: a stew of vegetables, cabbage, pork and sausage.

www.auvergne-tourisme.info.uk or
www.massifcentral-tourisme.com
documentation@crt-auvergne.fr
(0)4 73 29 49 99

BOURGES
0
25
50
75kms
VAL DE LOIRE
BRAIZE
MOULINS
DOMPIERRE-SUR-BESBRE
BURGUNDY
A71,E11
ALLIER 03
MONTLUCON
LIMOUSIN
BELLERIVE-SUR-ALLIER
VICHY
EBREUIL
ABREST
ROANNE
RHONE ALPES
AUVERGNE
RIOM
CLERMONT-FERRAND
THIERS
A72,E70
ROYAT
COURNON-D'AUVERGNE
NÉBOUZAT
ORCET
OLLIERGUES
ST BONNET-PRÈS-ORCIVAL
A89,E70
PUY-DE-DOME 63
ST NECTAIRE
MONTBRISON
TAUVES
MUROL
ISSOIRE
AMBERT
USSEL
ST-ETIENNE
SINGLES
CHAMBON-SUR-LAC
NONETTE
LEMPDES-SUR -ALLAGNON
ST DIDIER-EN-VELAY
LA TOUR-D'AUVERGNE
VIELLE BRIOUDE
CHAMALIÈRES-SUR-LOIRE
STE-SIGOLENE
CANTAL 15
ST-PAULIEN
A75,E11
LE PUY-EN-VELAY
ST-MARTIN-CANTALES
ST-FLOUR
RUYNES-EN-MARGERIDE
AURILLAC
NEUVÉGLISE
HAUTE-LOIRE 43
LACAPELLE-VIESCAMP
RHONE ALPES
LANGUEDOC ROUSSILLON
CASSANIOUZE
MIDI PYRENEES
MENDE
RODEZ
VILLEFRANCHE-DE-ROUERGUE
ALES
NIMES

Abrest

Camping de la Croix Saint Martin

Allée du Camping, 99 avenue des Graviers, F-03200 Abrest/Vichy (Allier) T: 04 70 32 67 74.
E: camping-vichy@orange.fr **alanrogers.com/FR03110**

La Croix Saint Martin is in Abrest on the edge of the attractive spa town of Vichy and close to the Bourbonnais mountains. The site is on the right bank of the Allier and extends over three hectares of wooded parkland. There are 89 level, grassy pitches with 71 for touring and 67 with 10A electricity. They are separated by some hedging and a variety of mature trees give varying amounts of shade. Vichy's elegant parks are less than 30 minutes on foot and the town centre is only another ten minutes. Twin-axle caravans are not accepted. A convenient site for sightseeing in Vichy and for short stopovers.

Facilities

One central toilet block has all necessary facilities. Separate toilet and shower for disabled visitors doubles as baby room. Motorcaravan services. Takeaway (1/5-15/9). Small swimming pool (1/5-30/9). Fishing. Play area. Tennis. Boules. Miniclub (July/Aug). Canoeing. Bicycle hire. Free WiFi. Off site: Vichy centre 40 minutes' walk. Bus to Vichy. Windsurfing 3 km. Golf 5 km.

Open: 2 April - 2 October.

Directions

Abrest is just south of Vichy. From town centre, head south D906 (Avenue de Thiers) to Abrest. Follow signs onto D426 and across a level crossing. Site signed on left. GPS: 46.1073, 0.057222

Charges guide

Per unit incl. 2 persons and electricity	€ 15.60 - € 19.90
extra person	€ 3.90 - € 5.10

Bellerive-sur-Allier

Camping Beau Rivage

F-03700 Bellerive-sur-Allier (Allier) T: 04 70 32 26 85. E: camping-beaurivage@wanadoo.fr
alanrogers.com/FR03030

This well maintained, compact, urban site is beside the River Allier and just over the water from the famous spa town of Vichy. It has recently been completely refurbished by the enthusiastic new owners. There are 74 medium sized, reasonably level, grass pitches with 37 for touring. Some have views across the river to the Parc Napoléon beyond. They are separated by shrubs and some tall hedging. All pitches have 10A electricity and 12 are fully serviced. On-site access is not easy for large outfits, though a new all-year motorcaravan service point adjacent to the site can accommodate these. No twin-axle caravans.

Facilities

Very clean, modern airy sanitary facilities in individual cubicles. Baby room and facilities for disabled visitors. Laundry facilities. Motorcaravan services. Small bar with snacks. Indoor and heated outdoor swimming pools (May-Sept). River fishing. Play area. Bicycles and pedaloes. Minigolf. Archery. WiFi (first two hours free). No electric barbecues. Off site: Riding, canoeing and tennis nearby. Several bars and restaurants are close to site. Hypermarket complex within 1 km. Vichy 2 km.

Open: 1 April - 9 October.

Directions

From A71 exit 12 (Vichy), head east, A719 then D2209 to Bellerive-sur-Allier. Right at roundabout with fountains, follow signs to Berges des Allier, Campings and then Beau Rivage. Site is in 3 km. Do not follow GPS co-ordinates due to a road closure. GPS: 46.11567, 3.43012

Charges guide

Per unit incl. 2 persons and electricity (6A)	€ 16.40 - € 24.80

Camping Cheques accepted.

Bellerive-sur-Allier

Camping les Acacias

Rue Claude Decloître, F-03700 Bellerive-sur-Allier (Allier) T: 04 70 32 36 22.
E: camping-acacias03@orange.fr **alanrogers.com/FR03080**

Les Acacias is a 2.5-hectare urban site on the west bank of the Allier river. It is opposite the historic spa town of Vichy, which has many attractions including parks, spas, theatres, a racecourse, ample sporting opportunities and numerous shops bars and restaurants. There are 105 level, average sized, grass and gravel pitches and 30 mobile homes for hire. The 75 pitches for touring have 10A electricity and 57 are fully serviced. Access is possible for large units although some busy roads must be negotiated. It is a good short stay site for visiting Vichy.

Facilities

Adequate sanitary blocks with some private cubicles and facilities for disabled visitors. Washing machine. Motorcaravan services. Basic supplies, bread (1/5-15/9). Soft drinks and simple takeaway (1/6-15/9). Heated swimming and paddling pools with slides (15/5-15/9). Boules. Play area. Games/TV rooms. Organised family activities (July/Aug). Multisports stadium. Canoes and boats loaned. Fishing. WiFi (free). Off site: Restaurant adjacent. Shops and hypermarket 500 m.

Open: 1 April - 10 October.

Directions

From A71 take exit 12 (Vichy), head east on A719 then D2209 to Bellerive-sur-Allier. Turn right at roundabout with fountains, follow signs to Berges des Allier, Campings and then Acacias. Site in 3 km. with entrances in rue Claude Decloître and rue Eugénie Desgouttes. GPS: 46.11645, 3.42559

Charges guide

Per unit incl. 2 persons and electricity	€ 18.10 - € 22.80
extra person	€ 4.00 - € 6.00

Braize

Camping Champ de la Chapelle

F-03360 Braize (Allier) T: 04 70 06 15 45. E: info@champdelachapelle.wanadoo.fr

alanrogers.com/FR03040

Champ de la Chapelle is a five-hectare site in the Forest of Troncais. It is mainly well maintained and there is mature parkland with a large area for those who prefer a taste of wild camping. It is ideal for families who want to get away from it all. The 72 touring pitches are slightly sloping, up to 250 sq.m. and there is plenty of shade and open space. Electricity (10A) and water is available to 64 of the pitches. It is the policy of the owner to keep the site quiet and unsophisticated (no discos here) and the reward is the wealth of wildlife. The area is a paradise for nature lovers, cyclists and walkers.

Facilities

Sanitary block includes washbasins in cabins. Low toilets for children. Laundry facilities. Small snack kiosk. Small shops with basics and bread to order (high season). Very small unheated pool (from 15/5). Play area. Courts for volleyball, flip-ball, netball, football and pétanque. English and Dutch books can be borrowed. Free WiFi. Off site: Supermarket and restaurant at St Bonnet 5 km. Lake with fishing, bathing, pedaloes, canoes, sail-boarding, minigolf, volleyball, tennis 5 km.

Open: 10 April - 30 October.

Directions

From N144 Bourges-Montlucon road, 14 km. south of St Amand Montrond, take D978A east, signed Clermont-Ferrand. At roundabout take D28 north (Braize). After 3 km. turn right for church and campsite (easy to miss). Follow site signs for 3 km. (narrow). From south, final km. of unpaved road could be challenging. GPS: 46.64291, 2.6557

Charges guide

Per unit incl. 2 persons and electricity	€ 16.00 - € 23.00

Cassaniouze

Camping de Coursavy

D141, F-15340 Cassaniouze (Cantal) T: 04 71 49 97 70. E: camping.coursavy@wanadoo.fr

alanrogers.com/FR15110

This is a tranquil, rural site located on the banks of the Lot river. There are just 50 pitches, of which four are used for chalets. Most have electricity, although some require long leads. Many have shade and some are separated by hedges. Very large units may have difficulties reaching a few pitches. Fishing from the river bank on the site is possible, as is swimming. The site also has a small, unheated swimming pool. Many interesting walks are possible in the surrounding hills. A well equipped, basic site for a taste of the real countryside, popular with Dutch visitors.

Facilities

One central, very clean toilet block includes facilities for disabled visitors and family and baby rooms. Washing machine, mangle and washing line. Fresh bread daily, fresh vegetables twice weekly. Small swimming pool. Sports field. Fishing. Chalets for rent. Free WiFi over site. Torches required. Off site: Walking and mountain biking. Riding. Golf. River sports. Bicycle hire 7 km. Historic village of Conques 7 km. Canoe hire 8 km.

Open: 20 April - 20 September.

Directions

Site is best approached from the west. North of Decazeville turn onto D42 at Port d'Agres (for Conques). Follow Lot Valley for 13 km. and turn right on D141 (Entraygues). Site is signed on the right. GPS: 44.642551, 2.366282

Charges guide

Per unit incl. 2 persons and electricity	€ 16.25 - € 22.40
extra person	€ 4.50

Chamalières-sur-Loire

CosyCamp

Les Ribes, F-43800 Chamalières-sur-Loire (Haute-Loire) T: 06 28 06 83 04. E: contact@cosycamp.fr

alanrogers.com/FR43070

CosyCamp is a superbly designed and equipped, car-free site in a tranquil, four-acre wild park close to Le Puy en Velay. It enjoys views towards the high hills and ruins of the Château d'Artias. The 86 pitches (65 for touring) are very large (100-300 sq.m) and have 16A electricity connections. There are nine motorcaravan pitches (100 sq.m) in a special meadow. Everyone will enjoy the outdoor pool and the indoor pool with water jets and counter-current feature. A range of rental accommodation is on offer including Safari lodges, tree houses, wood and canvas tents and a Romany-style caravan.

Facilities

New toilet blocks (one heated in low season) have modern facilities, including those for babies and disabled visitors. Launderette. Motorcaravan services. Shop and bar (1/6-30/9), snack bar and restaurant (14/6-14/9). Heated outdoor swimming pool and paddling pool (1/6-30/9). Indoor pool with water jets. Play area. Bicycle and canoe hire. Fishing. Free WiFi over site. Accommodation for rent. Max. 1 dog.

Open: 1 May - 3 October.

Directions

Approaching from the north (N88), head towards Le Puy as far as Monistrol-sur-Loire. Join the southbound D46, D9 and then D102 as far as Chamalières-sur-Loire, from where the site is well signed. GPS: 45.207915, 3.995343

Charges guide

Per unit incl. 2 persons	€ 18.00 - € 28.00
extra person	€ 3.00 - € 4.00

Camping Cheques accepted.

Chambon-sur-Lac

Camping les Bombes

Chemin de Pétary, F-63790 Chambon-sur-Lac (Puy-de-Dôme) T: 04 73 88 64 03. E: lesbombes@orange.fr
alanrogers.com/FR63250

Les Bombes is a beautifully situated and well maintained site within easy walking distance of Lac Chambon and the nearby amenities. On-site there is a heated swimming pool and sunbathing area, a snack bar and a number of chalets for rent (single night bookings accepted in low season). The site extends over five hectares and has 130 touring pitches. These are large (minimum 100 sq.m), flat, grassy and with 16A electricity (Europlug). The site is well located for walking and mountain biking, with a number of tracks leading directly from the site. The site owners will recommend possible routes.

Facilities

Three well maintained toilet blocks have washbasins in cabins and preset showers. Baby room. Facilities for disabled visitors. Motorcaravan services. Laundry facilities. Bread to order (July/Aug). Bar/snack bar (15/6-30/8). Swimming pool (1/6-15/9, no Bermuda shorts). Paddling pool. Games room. Play area. Giant chess. Fitness equipment. TV and games room. Bicycle hire. Weekly entertainment (high season). Free WiFi over part of site. Chalets for rent. Off site: Lac Chambon.

Open: 1 May - 15 September.

Directions

Site is west of Lac Chambon. From Murol, head west on D996 skirting the lake to Chambon-sur-Lac and follow signs to site. GPS: 45.56979, 2.90185

Charges guide

Per unit incl. 2 persons and electricity	€ 18.50 - € 24.90
extra person	€ 4.30 - € 5.30
child (1-7 yrs)	€ 3.00 - € 4.30
dog	€ 2.00 - € 2.50

Cournon-d'Auvergne

Camping le Pré des Laveuses

Rue des Laveuses, F-63800 Cournon-d'Auvergne (Puy-de-Dôme) T: 04 73 84 81 30.
E: camping@cournon-auvergne.fr **alanrogers.com/FR63230**

A well equipped municipal site, le Pré des Laveuses is adjacent to a boating and fishing lake and its beach, alongside the River Allier, close to Cournon-d'Auvergne and the A75 autoroute. This site will be busy in the high season due to its public bar/restaurant, heated swimming pool with flume, nearby activities and its proximity to Clermont-Ferrand. There are 100 large, grassy, mostly level touring pitches (all with 10A electricity, long leads advised). They are in small groups separated from other groups by neat low hedges. Mature trees give shade to some pitches and many have pleasant views.

Facilities

Two modern toilet blocks with all necessary facilities, including those for disabled visitors and babies. Laundry facilities. Public bar/restaurant with TV. Swimming and paddling pools. Children's room (TV). Play area. Boules. Overnight parking and services for motorcaravans outside gate. WiFi. Many high season sporting and family activities, children's club. Off site: Bathing, boating and free fishing in adjacent lake. Supermarket 800 m.

Open: 1 April - 9 October.

Directions

Site is 12 km. southeast of Clermont-Ferrand. Leave autoroute A75 at exit 1, taking D212 to Cournon-d'Auvergne. Site is well signed to east of town, beside River Allier. Follow Zone de Loisirs. GPS: 45.74019, 3.22266

Charges guide

Per unit incl. 2 persons and electricity	€ 20.40 - € 24.70
extra person	€ 5.10 - € 5.70

Dompierre-sur-Besbre

Camping les Bords de Besbre

F-03290 Dompierre-sur-Besbre (Allier) T: 04 70 34 55 57. E: camping@dsb.fr
alanrogers.com/FR03170

This immaculate and attractive municipal site has 67 level, partly shaded, individually hedged, grassy pitches, all with easy access. They are level and larger than average with electricity (10A) and most have their own water point and drainage. Situated by the municipal sports complex and the adjacent parkland, this site has much to offer. A footbridge from the site takes you across the river to the well tended park and to the town centre and supermarket (700 m). The friendly managers are justly proud of their well run site and its award-winning floral displays. Twin-axle caravans are not accepted.

Facilities

Two heated blocks have been renovated and are very clean with facilities for disabled visitors. Some washbasins in curtained cubicles. Washing machine (token). Motorcaravan services. No shop but bread van calls daily. Modern, heated indoor swimming pool and children's pool. No charcoal barbecues. WiFi (free). Off site: Walking and cycling routes. The small town has shops, restaurants and a Saturday market.

Open: 15 May - 15 September.

Directions

Dompierre is 35 km. east of Moulins. From N7 exit 49 onto N79 signed Dompierre-sur-Besbe. Leave N79 at eastern end of Dompierre bypass, turn southwest on D779 towards town. Entrance to sports complex and campsite is on left beyond D55 before river bridge and town centre. GPS: 46.51564, 3.68434

Charges guide

Per unit incl. 2 persons and electricity	€ 12.10
extra person	€ 2.65

Ebreuil

Camping de la Filature

Route de Chouvigny, F-03450 Ebreuil (Allier) T: 04 70 90 72 01. E: camping.filature@gmail.com

alanrogers.com/FR03010

Beside a fine fly fishing river and not far from the spa town of Vichy, this spacious family campsite makes a good base for exploring the Auvergne, the nearby river gorges, châteaux, mountains and lakes. There are 80 spacious, grassy pitches, 74 for touring, in a parkland setting. Most have 6A electricity and some shade from mature trees. Many are directly by the river, which is clean, shallow and pleasant to play in. There is a deeper area for swimming 500 m. away. You will receive a warm welcome from the English owners, who also provide good value and very popular takeaway food. In May and June, the fields abound with wild flowers, some quite rare. Bird songs are many and varied. Listen for the songs of the nightingale and golden oriole, often heard but seldom seen. The quiet country roads are ideal for walking and cycling, especially mountain biking and for touring by car. The interesting village of Ebreuil with its Thursday market, is just a 15 minute level stroll. Just west of the site are the gorges of the River Sioule, and the extinct volcanoes of the Puy-de-Dôme with the Vulcania Exhibition are well worth a visit.

Facilities

Clean, fully equipped sanitary facilities in original site buildings, bathroom and facilities for disabled visitors. Laundry facilities. Motorcaravan services. Small shop for essentials (1/5-30/9). Baker calls. Bar (15/5-15/9). Excellent takeaway (1/6-15/9). Barbecues and pizza nights organised in high season. River bathing and fishing. Large play areas. Minigolf. Pétanque. Free WiFi over part of site. Off site: Riding, canoeing, tennis and bicycle hire 500 m. Ébreuil with shops, bar, restaurants 1 km. Spa town of Vichy with shops, bars and restaurants 30 km.

Open: 15 April - 1 October.

Directions

Site is well signed from exit 12 of A71 autoroute to Clermont-Ferrand towards Ebreuil. It is 6 km. from the A71 and 1 km. west of Ebreuil beside the river on the D915 towards the Chouvigny gorges. From the south avoid exit 12.1. GPS: 46.10877, 3.07338

Charges guide

Per unit incl. 2 persons and electricity	€ 24.50
extra person	€ 6.00
child (under 16 yrs)	€ 3.50
dog	free

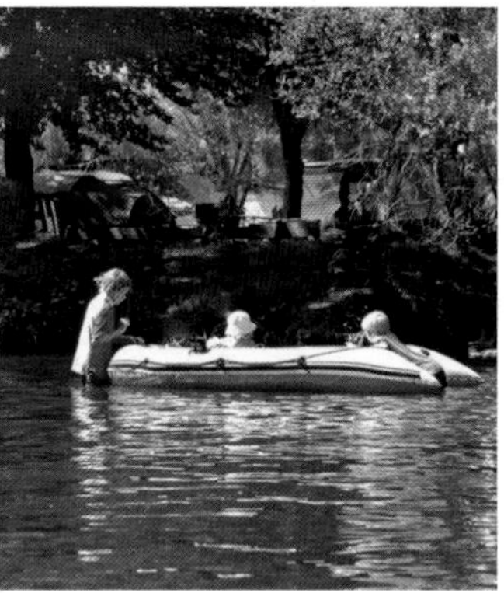

Issoire

Château Camping la Grange Fort

Les Pradeaux, F-63500 Issoire (Puy-de-Dôme) T: 04 73 71 02 43. E: chateau@lagrangefort.com

alanrogers.com/FR63040

This tranquil campsite of seven hectares is within the 25 hectare estate of the picturesque 15th-century Château of Grange Fort. There are 127 pitches (90 for touring units) some with panoramic views over the River Allier, others with views of the historic château. There is a mix of well drained grass and hardstanding pitches with varying degrees of shade. A short, steep path leads down to the river. Guided tours of the château are available and high quality evening meals are provided in its vaulted restaurant. The campsite is just ten minutes from the A75.

Facilities

Three good sanitary blocks have facilities for disabled visitors and a hydra-shower. Laundry room. Bread to order. Restaurant and takeaway (1/5-15/9). Bar (15/6-15/9). Indoor pool, sauna and massage table (15/4-15/10). Large outdoor swimming pool with jacuzzi (15/6-1/10). Play area. Games room. WiFi (charged). Tennis. Football. Boules. Activities in season. Torches useful. Off site: Fishing 250 m. Shops in Issoire 4 km.

Open: 10 April - 15 October.

Directions

From A75 autoroute take exit 13 onto D996 east towards Parentignat. At first roundabout take first exit on D999 new road (St Remy, La Vernet). At next roundabout take first exit (D34) and follow campsite signs. GPS: 45.50875, 3.28488

Charges guide

Per unit incl. 2 persons and electricity	€ 22.50 - € 30.45
extra person	€ 4.40 - € 6.25

La Tour-d'Auvergne

Camping la Chauderie

Route de Besse, F-63680 La Tour-d'Auvergne (Puy-de-Dôme) T: 06 33 78 53 45. E: info@la-chauderie.com

alanrogers.com/FR63350

La Chauderie is owned and run by an enthusiastic young Dutch couple. It boasts its own beautiful and totally natural waterfall on the small La Burande river. There are 75 terraced pitches arranged in small groups radiating from the winding central site road. All have 6A electricity and some are separated by hedging. A bar with terrace serving light meals adds to the relaxed, family atmosphere at this happy, well run site. Views from the site include the Puy de Sancy and the village of La Tour-d'Auvergne. Cycling and sightseeing are available in the surrounding Parc des Volcans national park.

Facilities

Two very clean sanitary blocks (one small and unisex, the other larger with separate facilities for ladies and men and includes provision for disabled visitors). Baby room. Laundry facilities in lower block. Bar and snack bar. Takeaway (June-Aug). TV room. Games room. Playground. Football. Volleyball. Boules. WiFi (free for 30 mins/day, then charged). Off site: Shops, bars and restaurants in village. Lake swimming and fishing 900 m.

Open: 9 May - 30 September.

Directions

Leave A89 at exit 25 (St Julien Puy Laveze) and head south on D98. Join D922 Westbound for 8 km. then take D203 south to site 9 km. on left.
GPS: 45.527824, 2.700008

Charges guide

Per unit incl. 2 persons and electricity	€ 17.50 - € 22.00
extra person	€ 4.00

Lacapelle-Viescamp

Camping la Presqu'ile du Puech des Ouilhes

F-15150 Lacapelle-Viescamp (Cantal) T: 04 71 46 42 38. E: contact@cantal-camping.fr

alanrogers.com/FR15080

La Presqu'île du Puech des Ouilhes is a small, family site located on a peninsula within the large Saint Etienne Cantales lake. There are 76 pitches set amongst mature trees, of which 68 have electrical connections. There are 21 chalets/simple camping huts (without bathrooms) available for rent. On-site amenities include a heated swimming pool (with sun terrace) and adjacent paddling pool. A number of activities are focused on the lake, including canoeing, windsurfing and fishing. This is excellent walking country with a number of long distance footpaths passing close to the site.

Facilities

Separate toilet and shower facilities for men and women. Laundry facilities. Shop (July/Aug). Takeaway. Outdoor heated swimming pool. Paddling pool. Play area. Fishing (boat available and tuition during high season). Watersports. Tennis. Chalets and mobile homes for rent. Torches useful. WiFi around bar area. Off site: Walking and mountain biking in the Cantal mountains. Adventure sports. Golf 7 km.

Open: 15 June - 31 August.

Directions

The site can be found to the west of Aurillac. From there, head west on D120 and follow signs to Puech des Ouilhes. Continue through Lacapelle-Viescamp and follow signs to Base de Loisirs.
GPS: 44.913058, 2.248887

Charges guide

Per unit incl. 2 persons and electricity	€ 18.00 - € 26.00
extra person	€ 5.50
child (1-8 yrs)	€ 4.50

Le Puy-en-Velay

Camping de Bouthezard

Chemin de Bouthezard-Aiguilhe, F-43000 Le Puy-en-Velay (Haute-Loire) T: 04 71 09 55 09.
E: camping.puyenvelay@orange.fr **alanrogers.com/FR43020**

This city site is located at the foot of a towering needle of volcanic rock with a church on top which is spectacularly lit at night. This is one of three major attractions in Le Puy-en-Velay, a World Heritage site. The excellent location, in a wooded area within walking distance of the medieval city, is protected by a good security barrier and the manager, who speaks good English, lives on site. Tarmac roads lead to 80 marked, grassy pitches with 6A electricity and a designated area for tents. Access is good and as the site may be popular in high season, early arrival is advised.

Facilities

Main unisex toilet block with facilities for disabled visitors. Second unisex unit at rear of site. The facilities may be stretched in high season. Motorcaravan services. Bread to order. Volleyball and badminton. TV room. WiFi (free near reception). Off site: Tennis and fishing adjacent. Baker and small supermarket 5 minutes' walk. Several other shops, bars and restaurants close by. Swimming pool 2 km. Golf 4 km. Riding 5 km.

Open: 25 March - 30 October.

Directions

Site is northwest of town, close to where N102 crosses River Borne and Rocher St Michel d'Aiguilhe (a church on a rocky pinnacle). Site is well signed from around town. GPS: 45.05042, 3.88094

Charges guide

Per unit incl. 2 persons and electricity	€ 15.20
extra person	€ 3.50
child (2-10 yrs)	€ 1.60

Lempdes-sur-Allagnon

Camping le Pont d'Allagnon

Rue René Filiol, F-43410 Lempdes-sur-Allagnon (Haute-Loire) T: 04 71 76 53 69.
E: centre.auvergne.camping@orange.fr **alanrogers.com/FR43240**

Camping le Pont d'Allagnon is a popular and friendly municipal site which is very well run and managed. There are 60 pitches (52 with 10A electricity for tourers) set mainly in rows with shade from mature trees and separated by hedges. The outdoor swimming pool is heated and is open only to campers, while other leisure facilities such as beach volleyball/football, minigolf and boules are shared with the village. This is a tranquil site with a convivial bar/snack terrace. No entertainment is provided though the pleasant village is only 50 metres away with easy access by a footbridge over the river.

Facilities

Clean sanitary block with separate room for families and disabled visitors. Heated baby room. Small laundry. Motorcaravan services. Bar/snack bar with terrace. Heated swimming pool with disabled access (13/6-15/9). Beach volleyball/football pitch. Basketball. Boules. Fishing in river. Playground. Free WiFi on part of site. Communal barbecue. Chalets for rent. Max. 1 dog. Off site: Shops, restaurant and bank in village 50 m. Riding 3 km.

Open: 28 March - 19 October.

Directions

From A75 take exit 20, then follow D909 north to Lempdes-sur-Allagnon. The site is then signed. GPS: 45.386994, 3.266083

Charges guide

Per unit incl. 2 persons and electricity	€ 17.20 - € 20.60
extra person	€ 3.00 - € 4.50

No credit cards.

Murol

Sunêlia la Ribeyre

Jassat, F-63790 Murol (Puy-de-Dôme) T: 04 73 88 64 29. E: info@laribeyre.com
alanrogers.com/FR63050

The friendly Pommier family have put much care into this spacious and well tended site. There are 460 level, grassy pitches, of which 290 are for tourers and 250 of these have electricity (6/10A). Electricity, water and drainage is available for 71 pitches. A superb large indoor/outdoor water park includes slides, toboggan and lazy river. A small man-made lake at one end of the campsite provides facilities for water sports. It is a great base for touring being only 1 km. from Murol, dominated by its ancient château, 6 km. from Saint Nectaire and about 20 km. from Le Mont Dore and Puy-de-Sancy.

Facilities

Six excellent, very clean modern toilet blocks with facilities for disabled campers. Washing machines, dryers. Snack bar in peak season (15/6-31/8). Large indoor/outdoor water park (heated July/Aug). TV. Games room. Tennis. Fishing. Lake swimming and canoeing. Many organised activities in high season. WiFi (charged). Off site: Riding 300 m. Bicycle hire 1 km. Shops, restaurants and large Wed. market (high season) in Murol 1.5 km. Fishing and watersports at Lac Chambon 3 km.

Open: 1 May - 15 September.

Directions

Site is 40 km. southwest of Clermont-Ferrand. From A75 autoroute, exit 6 signed St Nectaire. Take D978 signed St Nectaire and Murol, then D996 to Murol. Turn left up hill, D5, turn right immediately after tourist office car park onto D618, site signed. Site is second campsite on left. GPS: 45.56251, 2.93852

Charges guide

Per unit incl. 2 persons and electricity	€ 26.20 - € 36.05
extra person	€ 6.00 - € 7.90

Murol

Yelloh! Village le Pré Bas

Lac Chambon, F-63790 Chambon-sur-Lac (Puy-de-Dôme) T: 04 73 88 63 04.
E: prebas@campingauvergne.com **alanrogers.com/FR63070**

Le Pré Bas is an excellent site for families and those seeking the watersports on offer at the lake. Some 72 level, grassy touring pitches have mature hedging and trees, all with electricity (6A). A gate leads to the lakeside where, in high season, there is windsurfing, pedaloes, canoes and fishing, and 50 m. away is a beach with supervised bathing. The restaurant has an upper terrace with lake views. A pool complex has two heated swimming pools, slides and a paddling pool with splashpad. An exceptional spa/sauna centre offers complete relaxation for adults. There are 108 mobile homes for rent.

Facilities

Refurbished heated toilet building with facilities for disabled visitors, plus four smaller units. Laundry facilities. Baby room. Motorcaravan services. Bar, restaurant and takeaway (from 24/5). Three pools of different depths (24/5-14/9, lifeguard in July/Aug). Wellness centre. Watersports, fishing in lake. Games room, TV, library. Adventure-style playground. Football. Basketball. Bicycle hire. Children's club (supervised). Organised activities. WiFi. Max. 1 dog. Off site: Murol 3 km. St Nectaire.

Open: 23 April - 18 September.

Directions

Leave A75 autoroute at exit 6 and take D978 signed St Nectaire and Murol, then D996. Site is located on left, 3 km, west of Murol at the far end of Lac de Chambon. GPS: 45.57516, 2.91428

Charges guide

Per unit incl. 2 persons and electricity	€ 18.00 - € 36.00
extra person	€ 6.00 - € 7.00

No credit cards.

Murol

Camping le Repos du Baladin

Groire, F-63790 Murol (Puy-de-Dôme) T: 04 73 88 61 93. E: reposbaladin@free.fr

alanrogers.com/FR63130

A lovely, small and friendly campsite that offers an excellent alternative to the larger sites in this area. The owners are aiming for a quiet, relaxing site, attracting nature lovers who want to spend time walking, cycling or touring in this beautiful region. Attractively and well laid out, there are 91 good sized pitches, some with superb views of the château, 67 for touring (all with 5/10A electricity, 19 also with water and drainage), and many with good privacy. They are separated by conifer hedges with mature trees offering varying amounts of shade. Murol and its ancient 12th-century château are half an hour's walk away.

Facilities

One excellent, very clean and central, heated toilet block provides all the necessary facilities including those for babies and disabled visitors. Bar with TV. Restaurant, snacks and takeaway (all 15/6-30/8). Heated swimming pool and sunbathing area (15/6-10/9). Large play area. Boules. Free WiFi near reception. Off site: Supermarket 1 km. Murol 1.5 km. Fishing, bicycle hire and boat launching at Lac Chambon 2 km.

Open: 30 April - 10 September.

Directions

Site is 40 km. southwest of Clermont-Ferrand. Leave A75 at exit 6. Follow signs to St Nectaire then Murol (34 km). At far end of Murol at small roundabout turn left up hill on D5. At crossroads, straight across onto D146, signed Groire and site. Entrance on right in 900 m. GPS: 45.57373, 2.95708

Charges guide

Per unit incl. 2 persons and electricity	€ 17.30 - € 24.85

Murol

Domaine du Lac Chambon

Plage Est, F-63790 Murol (Puy-de-Dôme) T: 04 44 05 21 58. E: lac.chambon@wanadoo.fr

alanrogers.com/FR63510

In the heart of the Parc Naturel Régional des Volcans d'Auvergne, the Domaine occupies an attractive position on the lakeside, surrounded by wooded hills and with direct access to the beach and facilities. There are 119 touring pitches, 80 with electricity connection (16A), either in the open or part-shaded and some have views directly across the lake towards the Volcan de Tartaret. A separate area has 15 motorcaravan parking spaces equipped with electricity, water and a service point, available at a reduced rate. Accommodation is also available for rent.

Facilities

Two sanitary blocks. Washing machine and dryer. Motorcaravan services. Shop and takeaway (July/Aug). Bar/brasserie with terrace (12/4-31/8). Bread to order. Heated outdoor swimming pool (from 15/6). TV and activity room. Activities for children (5-11 yrs) and family sporting activities, entertainment and themed meals (July/Aug). Play areas. Boules. Minigolf and pedalo hire. Sandy beach (with lifeguard July/Aug). Fishing. WiFi (free). Off site: Footpath around lake for 3.5 km.

Open: 12 April - 13 September.

Directions

From north on A75 free motorway (Clermont-Ferrand/Béziers) leave at exit 6 and head south on D978 to Champeix, then turn west on D996 for 19km. to Murol. From south leave at exit 14 to Issoire then west on D996 to Champeix and Murol. At roundabout west of Murol, turn south on D996B to lake and campsite. GPS: 45.5715, 2.93053

Charges guide

Per unit incl. 2 persons and electricity	€ 18.00 - € 26.50
extra person	€ 4.50 - € 6.00

Nébouzat

Camping les Dômes

Les Quatre routes de Nébouzat, F-63210 Nébouzat (Puy-de-Dôme) T: 04 73 87 14 06.

E: camping.les-domes@orange.fr **alanrogers.com/FR63090**

A popular site, it is ideally situated for exploring the beautiful region around the Puy-de-Dôme. The site has 62 small to medium sized pitches, most for touring, all with 10A electricity, separated by trees and hedges. Hardstandings have been provided for a number of motorcaravans and caravan awnings. The attractive reception area comprising the office, a small shop for essentials and a meeting room has lots of local information and interesting artefacts. The small swimming pool is heated and has a cover which can be opened in good weather. There is entertainment on most days in high season for all ages.

Facilities

Well appointed, clean toilet block with limited facilities for disabled visitors. Basic shop including bread and pastries. Breakfast, snacks. Small bar. Boules, pool table, table football, table tennis, giant chess, draughts. Small play area. TV and games room. Free WiFi on part of site. Off site: Fishing 100 m. Restaurant 200 m. Nébouzat 1.3 km. (shops etc). Riding 8 km. Hang-gliding and paragliding in Puy-de-Dôme. Golf 10 km.

Open: 26 April - 4 October.

Directions

Site is 18 km. southwest of Clermont-Ferrand and is well signed from the roundabout at the junction of the D2089 and the D941A. It is a few hundred metres from the roundabout along the D216 towards Orcival. GPS: 45.72562, 2.89005

Charges guide

Per unit incl. 2 persons and electricity (10A)	€ 20.30 - € 25.70

Neuvéglise

Flower Camping le Belvédère

Lanau, F-15260 Neuvéglise (Cantal) T: 04 71 23 50 50. E: contact@campinglebelvedere.com

alanrogers.com/FR15010

This is a very steeply terraced, family run site situated in the heart of the Gorges de la Truyère. Of the 116 pitches, 63 are for touring (18 fully serviced). The highest pitches have no electricity and are only suitable for tents. The lower pitches have 15A electricity and some have a sink, draining and a barbecue. All have stunning views. The pitches are of average size and separated by tall conifers offering good shade. The site roads are very steep and have sharp bends, so access may be difficult for large units. Many pitches are some distance from the toilet blocks and access may involve climbing a large number of steep steps. The nearby lake is good for fishing and watersports but swimming is not allowed.

Facilities

Two basic toilet blocks include some washbasins in cabins. Baby room. Facilities for disabled visitors. Laundry facilites. Motorcaravan services. Small shop, spacious bar/restaurant and TV room provides meals and takeaways. Covered, heated swimming pool (18/4-15/9). Sauna. Exercise room. Organised activities for all the family (July/Aug). WiFi over part of site (free). Off site: Boat launching 500 m. Fishing 1 km. Bicycle hire 5 km.

Open: 18 April - 29 September.

Directions

Site is 5 km. north of Chaudes-Aigues. Leave A75 exit 29 signed St Flour D926. Then take D921 signed Neuvéglise. Site is 5 km. south. Turn west at site sign, entrance is just beyond the Belvédère Centre de Vacances. GPS: 44.89518, 3.00130

Charges guide

Per unit incl. 2 persons and electricity	€ 17.00 - € 29.00
extra person	€ 4.00 - € 6.00

Nonette

Camping les Loges

F-63340 Nonette (Puy-de-Dôme) T: 04 73 71 65 82. E: les.loges.nonette@wanadoo.fr

alanrogers.com/FR63140

A pleasant, spacious, rural site bordering the River Allier and close to the A75 autoroute, making it convenient as a stopover when travelling north or south. There are 126 good sized, mostly level, grassy pitches with mature trees offering plenty of shade, 96 of which are for touring and all with 6A electricity. This site would suit those seeking a quieter holiday without too many organised activities, although it was busy when we visited on a bank holiday. A good sized swimming pool with water slide is a popular attraction in high season. A path leads directly from the site to a stony river beach.

Facilities

Two basic toilet blocks contain all the usual facilities. Small shop (July/Aug). Bar, restaurant, takeaway (mid June-mid Sept). TV room. Heated swimming pool with water slide, paddling pool (June-Sept). Sauna (June-Sept, charged). Volleyball. Play areas, play room. River fishing, bathing and canoeing (canoe hire). Evening dances in high season. Off site: Walking and cycling routes. Small village of Nonette 3 km. Supermarket 4 km. Riding 5 km.

Open: 1 April - 13 September.

Directions

From A75 exit 17 (south of Issoire), turn left (D214, Le Breuil). Bypass Le Breuil, turn left (D123, Nonette). Cross river, turn left then immediately very sharp left after 100 m. – take care. Site is 600 m (narrow road). Follow signs not sat nav. GPS: 45.47310, 3.27223

Charges guide

Per unit incl. 2 persons and electricity	€ 17.60 - € 21.50
extra person	€ 4.10 - € 4.90

Olliergues

Camping les Chelles

Lieu-dit les Chelles, F-63880 Olliergues (Puy-de-Dôme) T: 04 73 95 54 34. E: info@camping-les-chelles.com

alanrogers.com/FR63220

A very rural, rustic site, les Chelles is run by enthusiastic Dutch owners. It is situated in the Parc Naturel Livradois, 25 km. south of Thiers, and is ideal for nature lovers and those seeking a quiet retreat. There are 65 pitches with 55 slightly sloping, grassy pitches for touring, most with views over the surrounding wooded hills (minimum 10A electricity, long leads advised). The distant mountains, visible from the site, can be snow-covered for up to six months of the year. Pitches are naturally laid out on woodland terraces but not ideal for those with walking difficulties or for large or underpowered units due to the hilly terrain. Ensure you have stocked up on provisions prior to arrival as this is a very remote site.

Facilities

Centrally placed basic toilet block. Facilities for disabled visitors and babies. Laundry facilities. Motorcaravan services. Bar/restaurant with TV. Bread to order. Heated swimming and paddling pools (1/6-15/9). Small play area. Tennis. Boules. Small fishing lake. Some activities for younger children, bike rides (high season). Free WiFi near bar. Off site: Olliergues 5 km. Thiers 25 km.

Open: 1 April - 30 October.

Directions

Olliergues is on D906 25 km. south of Thiers. On entering Olliergues bear left up hill, D37. Shortly turn sharp left on D87. In 4.5 km. at church turn right and shortly left to site. GPS: 45.68987, 3.63336

Charges guide

Per unit incl. 2 persons and electricity	€ 17.20 - € 19.20
extra person	€ 3.00

Orcet

Camping le Clos Auroy

15 rue de la Narse, F-63670 Orcet (Puy-de-Dôme) T: 04 73 84 26 97. E: orcet@wanadoo.fr

alanrogers.com/FR63060

Le Clos Auroy is a well established and attractive family run campsite with English-speaking Dutch owners. It is just 300 metres away from Orcet, a typical Auvergne village just south of Clermont-Ferrand. Being close (3 km) to the A75, and open all year, it makes an excellent stopping off point. It has a calm atmosphere, which may tempt you to stay longer. The 85 good sized pitches are on level grass, separated by high, neatly trimmed conifer hedges, offering lots of privacy and some shade. All have 10A electricity and eight are fully serviced. Situated on a gentle hillside, the higher pitches have better views but less shade than those lower down. The bar, restaurant and pool areas are close to the reception and entrance thus ensuring the remainder of the site is more tranquil. In winter, only 20 pitches are available. The local village of Orcet is a short but steep walk away.

Facilities

Three very clean, high quality toilet blocks. Two washing machines, dryer. Motorcaravan services. Small shop, bar and takeaway (July/Aug). Heated pool, jacuzzi, pool for children with slides (15/6-15/9), terrace near bar (1/6-31/8). Playground. Coffee evenings. Children's activities. Chalets for rent. Off site: Large playground and tennis court nearby and riverside walk just outside gate. Village with shops and three wine cellars 300 m. Fishing and canoeing 500 m. Golf 900 m. Parc des Volcans with fantastic scenery, walking and cycling.

Open: All year.

Directions

From A75 take exit 4 or 5 towards Orcet and follow campsite signs. It is just before the village. GPS: 45.70018, 3.16902

Charges guide

Per unit incl. 2 persons and electricity	€ 31.80
extra person	€ 6.30
child (4-14 yrs)	€ 2.30 - € 4.40
dog	€ 2.40

Less for longer stays in low season.

Royat

Camping Indigo Royat

Route de Gravenoire, Quartier l'Oclède, F-63130 Royat (Puy-de-Dôme) T: 04 73 35 97 05.
E: royat@camping-indigo.com **alanrogers.com/FR63120**

This is a spacious site sitting high on a hillside and set in natural woodland. Royat is on the outskirts of Clermont-Ferrand, but close to the beautiful Auvergne countryside. There are 196 terraced pitches on part hardstanding with 132 available for touring units; 107 with 10A electricity (long leads may be needed). A further five pitches offer water and drainage. The pitches are informally arranged in groups with each group separated by natural trees and shrubs. The central lodge and reception area have been completely renovated. The bar and terrace overlooks the irregularly shaped swimming pool area and play areas. Although very peaceful off season, the site could be busy in July and August. This site would be ideal for those who would like a taste of both the town and the countryside.

Facilities

Five toilet blocks, some heated, have all the usual amenities but it could be a long walk from some pitches. Small shop (all season). Bar, restaurant and takeaway (July/Aug). Attractive heated swimming and paddling pools (30/4-18/9), sunbathing area. Tennis. Boules. Two grassy play areas. Organised entertainment in high season. Central lodge for coffee/board games/relaxation. Free WiFi in bar area. Only electric barbecues permitted. Torches advised. Max. 1 dog. Off site: Royat 20 minutes' walk. Bus service every 30 minutes in the mornings. Golf 7 km. Clermont-Ferrand, Puy-de-Dôme, Parc des Volcans and Vulcania Exhibition.

Open: 24 March - 2 November.

Directions

From A75 exit 2 (Clermont-Ferrand) follow signs for Bordeaux on D2089. At second roundabout take exit signed Bordeaux and Ceyrat. Shortly after take exit right then turn right, signed Ceyrat. At traffic lights go straight across onto D944 (formerly D941C) signed Royat and Puy-de-Dôme. At top of hill turn left (D5), site signed. GPS: 45.758594, 3.054516

Charges guide

Per unit incl. 2 persons and electricity	€ 21.80 - € 32.10
extra person	€ 5.60 - € 6.60
child (2-7 yrs)	free - € 4.40
dog	€ 2.20 - € 4.40

Ruynes-en-Margeride

Camping le Petit Bois

F-15320 Ruynes-en-Margeride (Cantal) T: 04 71 23 42 26. E: contact@revea-vacances.com

alanrogers.com/FR15190

With views across the Auvergne countryside, this pleasant site on the edge of a small traditional French village is a comfortable and convenient break in your journey when using the A75 motorway. The interesting village has a bar and a small restaurant serving inexpensive meals. There are 90 touring pitches, all with electricity (6A); 16 also have water and drainage. Some are level with views over the village, some on the hilltop among trees and others on sloping, grassy land with panoramic views of the Monts du Cantal and the distant volcanic mountains.

Facilities

The main central heated toilet block has preset showers, washbasins in cabins, toilets for children and excellent en-suite units for disabled visitors (although building is on a hill, so access may not be easy). Baby bath can be borrowed and used in disabled unit. Washing machines. Motorcaravan services. Play areas. Children's club and family entertainment evenings (July/Aug). TV room. Pétanque. Mobile homes and wooden huts for rent. WiFi (free). Off site: Municipal swimming pool adjacent.

Open: 23 April - 18 September.

Directions

Leave A75 exit 30 taking D4 signed Ruynes-en-Margeride. After 6 km. follow signs for village and campsite. Site is 500 m. southwest of village and is clearly signed. GPS: 44.99904, 3.21908

Charges guide

Per unit incl. 2 persons and electricity	€ 12.00 - € 18.00
extra person	€ 3.00 - € 4.00
child (2-7 yrs)	€ 2.50 - € 3.50

Saint Bonnet-près-Orcival

Camping de la Haute Sioule

Route du Camping, F-63210 Saint Bonnet-près-Orcival (Puy-de-Dôme) T: 04 73 65 83 32.

E: info@chalets-auvergne.info **alanrogers.com/FR63210**

This simple, small site is family run in a quiet, rural location in the heart of the beautiful Parc des Volcans. With good views over the surrounding hills, it is close to the Puy-de-Dôme and several winter and summer resorts. Developed from a farm with sheep and geese roaming freely until mid June, the site has winding access roads with 70 sloping, slightly uneven, grassy pitches with about 45 for touring (4-13A electricity (Europlug), long leads needed). Access is not easy for large outfits. This open-all-year site, with great views from many pitches, offers a peaceful family atmosphere in a very rural setting.

Facilities

New heated sanitary block with baby changing and facilities for disabled visitors. Second basic toilet block (open in high season). Motorcaravan services. Washing machine and dryer. Shop. Bar with TV. Restaurant (July/Aug). Play area for younger children. Minigolf. Boules. Fishing (permits from reception). Free WiFi throughout. Off site: St Bonnet 200 m. with some small shops, a restaurant and a bar. Orcival 4 km.

Open: All year.

Directions

A75 just south of Clermont-Ferrand at exit 2, signed Bordeaux and La Bourboule. Continue on D2089 until Les Quatre Routes. Turn left at roundabout, D216. Bear left to site entrance in just over 500 m. Well signed. GPS: 45.7084, 2.86087

Charges guide

Per unit incl. 2 persons and electricity (4-13A)	€ 21.00 - € 24.40
extra person	€ 4.80

Saint Didier-en-Velay

Camping la Fressange

F-43140 Saint Didier-en-Velay (Haute-Loire) T: 01 71 66 25 28. E: camping.lafressange@orange.fr

alanrogers.com/FR43010

Situated in rolling Haute-Loire countryside, this pleasant municipal site is ideal for exploring the area and the historic old town of St Didier. The sheltered site is attractively laid out on three grassy terraces – with the lower terraces mostly for tourers. There are 74 pitches (18 occupied by private mobile homes and 11 chalets for rent). All have electricity (15A) and 15 have water and drainage. There is plenty of shade from the surrounding trees. There is an excellent municipal pool and sports ground opposite, free to campers. The town has markets on Wednesdays and Sundays.

Facilities

Two older style sanitary blocks include washbasins in cabins (warm water). Facilities for disabled visitors double as family room. Washing machine. Playground. Barrier card deposit. WiFi (free). Off site: Municipal pool complex adjacent (July/Aug). Town 5-10 minutes' walk. Fishing, tennis 200 m. Riding 1 km. Tennis courts 2 km.

Open: 1 May - 30 September.

Directions

Site is southwest of St Etienne and signed on N88 just south of Pont Salomon. Take D471 (St Didier) and at La Séauve turn left on D12 and follow signs to St Didier. On entering town take second right (Lichemialle), descend hill and turn left immediately at tennis courts. GPS: 45.301319, 4.28302

Charges guide

Per unit incl. 2 persons and electricity	€ 12.55 - € 17.95

Saint Martin Cantalès

Camping Pont du Rouffet

Pont du Rouffet, F-15140 Saint Martin Cantalès (Cantal) T: 04 71 69 42 76. E: pontdurouffet@live.nl
alanrogers.com/FR15060

A tranquil and very rural site located on the banks of the lac d'Enchanet. There are just 30 pitches, four of which have mobile homes for hire. All pitches have electricity (4/6/10A) and some require long leads. Many have shade and some are separated by young hedges. Fishing from the banks by the site is possible, as is swimming. Large units are advised to telephone in advance for suitable pitches. This is a well equipped but basic site aimed at those wishing to get away from the fast pace of city life. The main facilities are at the top of a steep site road and may prove difficult for those with limited mobility.

Facilities

Refurbished shower block. Washing machine and dryer. No shop but bread to order (mid July-end Aug). Fishing. Indoor games. Mobile homes for rent. Torches required. Free WiFi. Boat hire. Dogs may be accepted but only by prior arrangement (max. 1 in high season). Off site: Nearest supermarket 9 km. Walking on marked routes and along disused railway viaducts and through tunnels. Mountain trails for bikes. Bicycle hire 13 km. Riding 17 km. Golf 38 km. Lake sports.

Open: 16 May - 13 September.

Directions

The site is 80 km. southeast of Clermont-Ferrand. From Mauriac take D922 onto Aurillac. Half way, after St Martin Valmeroux, turn right onto D42 to Besse. Follow D42 until the end. Site is on right. Last few kilometres of single track road are very narrow with few passing places. GPS: 45.072187, 2.258865

Charges guide

Per unit incl. 2 persons and electricity	€ 13.00 - € 18.20
extra person	€ 2.50 - € 3.50

Saint Nectaire

Flower Camping la Vallée Verte

Route des Granges, F-63710 Saint Nectaire (Puy-de-Dôme) T: 04 73 88 52 68. E: contact@valleeverte.com
alanrogers.com/FR63180

La Vallée Verte is a very well tended, peaceful site at the edge of the village of St Nectaire, famous for its cheese of the same name. The 91 pitches are thoughtfully laid out with 74 for touring and 17 mobile homes and chalets. All pitches are separated by neatly trimmed hedges and mature trees offering shade if preferred. The pitches are generally flat and level, with some on more sloping ground reserved for tent campers. Most pitches have 8A electricity (Europlugs) and water is not far from any of them. There is an excellent heated, covered swimming pool with access for wheelchair users and a hoist.

Facilities

Excellent toilet block with all necessary facilities including a superb room for families and disabled visitors. Motorcaravan services. Laundry facilities. Shop, bar and snack bar with takeaway (July/Aug, other periods on reservation). Heated, covered swimming pool with ramp and hoist for disabled visitors. Play areas. Boules. Volleyball. Free WiFi near bar. Off site: Fishing 100 m. St Nectaire with shops, bars, restaurants. Casino. Caves.

Open: 16 April - 18 September.

Directions

Leave autoroute A75 at exit 6 south of Clermont-Ferrand. Take D978 then D996 to St Nectaire. On entering St Nectaire turn left, D642 (site signed). Entrance is a few hundred metres on the left. GPS: 45.57523, 2.99981

Charges guide

Per unit incl. 2 persons and electricity	€ 18.50 - € 25.50
extra person	€ 4.50 - € 7.00

Saint Nectaire

Camping la Clé des Champs

Route des Granges, F-63710 Saint Nectaire (Puy-de-Dôme) T: 04 73 88 52 33.
E: campingcledeschamps63@orange.fr **alanrogers.com/FR63270**

This extremely pretty and immaculate site is run by the friendly Blanc family in traditional French style. It is bisected by a small river, and is a short walk to the picturesque spa town of Saint Nectaire in the heart of the Auvergne. Pitches are of a good size and most have some shade, and many have 2-6A electrical connections. A number of fully equipped mobile homes and chalets are available for rent. On-site amenities here include a swimming pool, a children's playground and a snack bar. The nearby Lac de Chambon is a popular centre for a variety of watersports.

Facilities

Two toilet blocks, one central with all facilities including a washing machine. Swimming pool. Shop, bar/snack bar and takeaway (July/Aug). Games room. Play area. Entertainment and activity programme. Mobile homes and chalets for rent. Free WiFi. Torches useful. Off site: St Nectaire with tours of the thermal springs and cheese making at Farm Bellonte. Watersports at Lac de Chambon. Walking and mountain biking. Riding.

Open: 11 April - 26 September.

Directions

Leave A75 at exit 6 signed St Nectaire and Murol. Take D978 then D996 to St Nectaire. The site is well signed at the entrance to the town. Site has two entrances, the second offers better access for large units. GPS: 45.575498, 3.001741

Charges guide

Per unit incl. 2 persons and 6A electricity	€ 16.30 - € 24.00
extra person	€ 3.50 - € 6.20

Saint Paulien

Flower Camping de la Rochelambert

Route de Lanthenas, F-43350 Saint Paulien (Haute-Loire) T: 04 71 00 54 02.
E: infos@camping-rochelambert.com **alanrogers.com/FR43060**

This attractive and welcoming site can be found in the heart of Auvergne. Extending over four hectares, it is located at the foot of the Château de la Rochelambert and is bordered by a river and a wooded nature trail. There are 80 large pitches here (120 sq.m), mostly well shaded and equipped with 16A electricity. Twelve riverside pitches (no electricity) are perfect for anglers, and the site has a special hut for storing tackle and bait. A number of good quality timber chalets are for rent. The emphasis here is on peace and tranquillity in an idyllic natural setting, and for this reason the site is run along very environmentally friendly lines. Activities in high season include children's workshops, treasure hunts, themed meals and outdoor cinema. The nearby village of Saint Paulien has a good range of shops and other amenities. There are many mountain bike and walking trails in the area and the site's friendly owners will be pleased to make recommendations. This campsite is well run and maintained and prides itself on offering a place in the countryside with easy access to nature. The château can be seen above the trees at the entrance to the campsite and is open for visiting.

Facilities

Two well positioned toilet blocks (one heated) are well maintained and kept clean. Baby room. Excellent room for disabled visitors. Motorcaravan services. Small shop for basic needs. Snack bar serving pizza and regional specialities. Pleasant bar and terrace. Swimming and paddling pools. New sauna (charged). Fishing with chalet for preparation and freezing. Tennis. Archery. Boules. Play area. Entertainment and activities. Wooden chalets and two roulottes to rent. WiFi (free). Off site: St Paulien 2.5 km. Riding 10 km. Golf 15 km. Le Puy-en-Velay.

Open: 1 April - 30 September.

Directions

Site is north of Le Puy-en-Velay. From there, head north on N102 and turn onto D906 signed St Paulien from where the château and the site are well signed. GPS: 45.120173, 3.793674

Charges guide

Per unit incl. 2 persons and electricity	€ 16.30 - € 21.90
extra person	€ 3.80 - € 5.00
child (2-7 yrs)	€ 3.00 - € 4.00
dog	€ 1.50 - € 1.70

Sainte Sigolène

Sites et Paysages de Vaubarlet

Vaubarlet, F-43600 Sainte Sigolène (Haute-Loire) T: 04 71 66 64 95. E: camping@vaubarlet.com
alanrogers.com/FR43030

Expect a warm welcome at this peaceful and spacious, family run site. Located in a beautiful riverside setting, it has 131 marked, level, grassy, pitches, with those around the perimeter having shade (young trees and shrubs provide separation between the large pitches). The family has made great efforts to ensure all guests benefit equally from its facilities. There are 101 pitches, all with 16A electricity for touring units. The remaining places are occupied by site-owned tents and mobile homes including two fully equipped for disabled guests. Excellent facilities for guests with disabilities.

Facilities

Very good, clean toilet blocks include a baby room. Two family bathrooms (also suitable for disabled visitors). Laundry facilities. Small shop, bread. Bar, restaurant and takeaway (mid May-mid Sept). Swimming pool. Children's pool. Solarium. Boules. Games area. Playground. Activities in season include camp fire, music evenings, children's canoe lessons. Trout fishing. WiFi (free).

Open: 1 May - 30 September.

Directions

Site is 10 km north of Yssingeaux. From N88 exit on D44 east, signed Ste Sigolène, turn south on D43 signed Grazac. Keep left by river bridge, site signed. Site is shortly on right. GPS: 45.2163, 4.2124

Charges guide

Per unit incl. 2 persons and electricity	€ 20.00 - € 31.00

Camping Cheques accepted.

Singles

Camping le Moulin de Serre

Vallée de la Burande (D73), F-63690 Singles (Puy-de-Dôme) T: 04 73 21 16 06. E: moulindeserre@orange.fr

alanrogers.com/FR63080

A pleasant scenic drive brings you to this spacious and well maintained site. It is set in a wooded valley beside a pretty river where, we are told, the locals still pan for gold. You will find a warm welcome and a relaxing atmosphere here in this lesser known area of the Auvergne. The 99 large pitches (63 for touring) are separated by a variety of trees and hedges giving good shade. Some pitches have hardstanding and all have electricity (5-10A), long leads may be necessary. Fresh bread and croissants are baked daily on site, as are snacks and pizzas to order.

Facilities

Two clean and well equipped central toilet blocks, one heated, have good facilities for babies and disabled visitors. Washing machine, dryer. Motorcaravan services. Takeaway, bar/snack bar. Restaurant. Bread to order. Heated swimming pool (27/5-9/9). Play area. Tennis. Trampolines. Canoe hire in high season. Organised activities (July/Aug). Bicycle hire. Communal barbecues. WiFi throughout. Mobile homes for rent, one adapted for disabled visitors. Off site: Fishing lake 2 km.

Open: 9 April - 18 September.

Directions

Site is 25 km. southwest of La Bourboule. Leave A89 at exit 23, follow D979 signed Bort-les-Orgues, then take D922 north for 10 km. Turn west off D922 just south of Tauves at site sign. Follow site signs along D29 and then the D73 for 10 km. Site is well signed. GPS: 45.54317, 2.54275

Charges guide

Per unit incl. 2 persons and electricity	€ 14.50 - € 24.75
extra person	€ 2.50 - € 5.00

Tauves

Camping les Aurandeix

F-63690 Tauves (Puy-de-Dôme) T: 04 73 21 14 06. E: contact@camping-les-aurandeix.fr

alanrogers.com/FR63200

This site, at an altitude of 850 m, is under a long term management contract by a friendly family. It is only a few minutes' walk from the centre of the village of Tauves in the beautiful Parc des Volcans with its many extinct volcanoes and is ideal for touring on foot, bike or in the car. There are 75 grass pitches on terraces, many with views of the Massif du Sancy. Of these, 45 are for touring, separated by hedges and trees offering good shade and some privacy (10A electricity). This is a tranquil site keen on nature conservation. Part of the site is left wild to encourage wildlife.

Facilities

Two well appointed toilet blocks with facilities for disabled visitors. Motorcaravan services. Small shop (July/Aug). Bread to order. Heated swimming and paddling pools (mid June-mid Sept). Play area. Volleyball, basketball, football. Walks with guides in summer. Communal barbecue. WiFi throughout (charged). Self-catering facilities for campers on foot or bicycle.

Open: Early April - end September.

Directions

Site is well signed in Tauves, 9 km. southwest of La Bourboule, just off the D922. GPS: 45.56089, 2.62446

Charges guide

Per unit incl. 2 persons and electricity	€ 17.75 - € 19.75
extra person	€ 4.30 - € 5.20

Camping Cheques accepted.

Vieille Brioude

Camping la Bageasse

Avenue de la Bageasse, F-43100 Brioude (Haute-Loire) T: 04 71 50 07 70. E: labageasse@orange.fr

alanrogers.com/FR43040

La Bageasse is a member of the Aquadis Loisirs group. Popular with anglers, it is located on the banks of the River Allier, barraged to form a large lake with canoeing and bathing possible. It is near the stunning Gorges de l'Allier and the town of Brioude, home to the largest Romanesque church of the Auvergne, the Saint Julien basilica. The 49 touring pitches here are large and grassy, most are equipped with electrical connections (12A Europlug). There are 15 fully equipped chalets for rent. During peak season, several activities are organised, including a children's club (6-12 yrs).

Facilities

Two sanitary blocks are in traditional style and have been recently renovated. En-suite unit for disabled visitors. Laundry facilities. Small grocery shop at snack bar with bread and pastries to order and local produce. Bar and snack bar with games (15/5-30/9). Swimming and paddling pools (1/6-15/9). Fishing. Play area. Activity and entertainment programme (July/Aug). Chalets for rent. WiFi near reception (free). Off site: Shops and restaurants in Brioude, 5 km. The medieval village of Lamothe.

Open: 7 March - 6 November.

Directions

Brioude is midway between Clermont-Ferrand and Le Puy-en-Velay. Head south from Clermont-Ferrand on A75 as far as exit 20, then follow the southbound N102 to Brioude. Site well signed from town. Follow Vieille Brioude and site signs. Do not use sat nav due to new road layout. GPS: 45.28127, 3.40548

Charges guide

Per unit incl. 2 persons and electricity	€ 15.90 - € 17.20

Camping Cheques accepted.

DÉPARTEMENTS: 01 AIN, 07 ARDÈCHE, 26 DRÔME, 38 ISÈRE, 42 LOIRE, 69 RHÔNE, 73 SAVOIE, 74 HAUTE-SAVOIE

MAJOR CITIES; LYON, GRENOBLE

With a rich and varied landscape, the Rhône Alpes offers a spectacular region that includes the craggy gorges and scented hills of the Rhône Valley, the deep valleys and mountain slopes of the Savoy Alps and the forbidding Dauphiné Alps, all offering spectacular scenery.

The Rhône valley holds areas of great interest and natural beauty. From the sun-baked Drôme, with its ever changing landscapes and the isolated mountains of the Vercors, to the deep gorges and high plateaux of the Ardèche, studded with prehistoric caves and lush valleys filled with orchards; and encompassing the vineyards of the Beaujolais and the Rhône Valley. For the energetic there are cycling, horse riding and even white-water rafting opportunities, while for the more leisurely inclined, the remote areas are a haven for birdwatching and walking.

Lying between the Rhône Valley and the Alpine borders with Switzerland and Italy are the old provinces of Savoie and Dauphiné. This is an area of enormous granite outcrops, deeply riven by spectacular glacier hewn valleys. One of the world's leading winter playgrounds, there is also a range of outdoor activities in the summer. Despite development, great care has been taken to blend the old with the new and many villages still retain their charm and historical interest. It is an opportunity to enjoy some clean air, unusual wildlife, stunning views and hidden lakes.

Places of interest

Aix-les-Bains: spa resort on the Lac du Bourget; boat excursions to the Royal Abbey of Hautecombe.

Annecy: canal-filled lakeside town; 12th-century château; old quarter.

Bourg en Bresse: late Gothic Eglise de Brou; wetlands centre rich in birdlife.

Bourg-Saint-Maurice: centre of Savoie café society.

Chambéry: old quarter; Dukes of Savoie château; Savoie museum.

Chamonix: site of first Winter Olympics in 1924; world capital of mountain climbing.

Grenoble: Fort de la Bastille by cable car; museum with 19th- and 20th-century art.

Lyon: Gallo-Roman artifacts; Renaissance quarter; historical Fabric Museum; silk museum.

Vallon-Pont d'Arc: base from which to visit Gorges de l'Ardèche.

Cuisine of the region

Bresse (Poulet, Poularde, Volaille de): the best French poultry, fed on corn and when killed bathed in milk.

Farcement (Farçon Savoyard): potatoes baked with cream, eggs, bacon, dried pears and prunes.

Gratin Dauphinois: potato dish with cream, cheese and garlic.

Gratin Savoyard: another potato dish with cheese and butter.

Tartiflette: potato, bacon, onions and Reblochon cheese.

www.rhonealpes-tourism.co.uk
info@rhonealpes-tourisme.com
(0)4 72 59 21 59

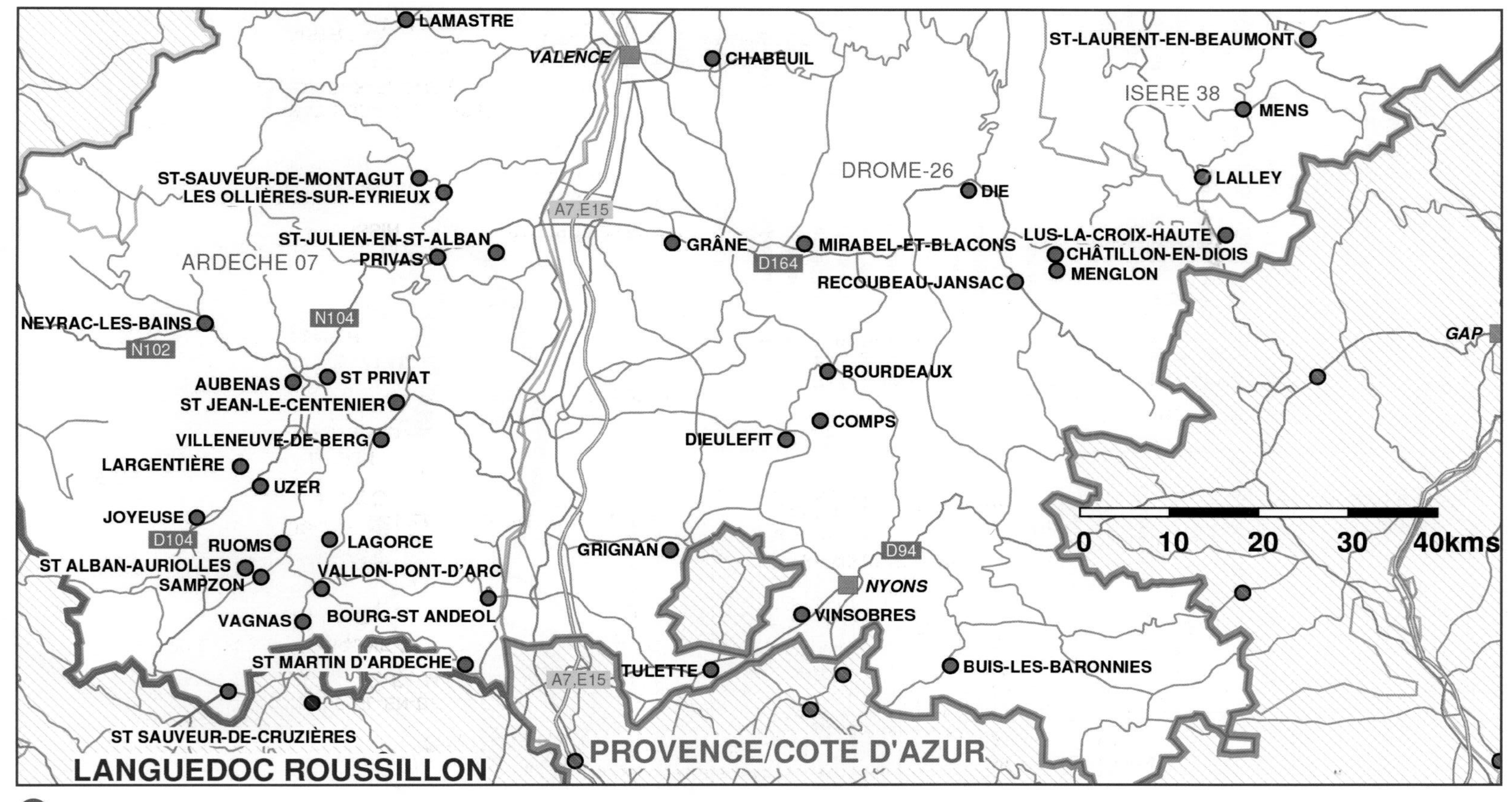
LAMASTRE
VALENCE
CHABEUIL
ST-LAURENT-EN-BEAUMONT
ISERE 38
MENS
ST-SAUVEUR-DE-MONTAGUT
LES OLLIÈRES-SUR-EYRIEUX
DROME-26
DIE
LALLEY
A7,E15
ST-JULIEN-EN-ST-ALBAN
PRIVAS
ARDECHE 07
GRÂNE
MIRABEL-ET-BLACONS
D164
LUS-LA-CROIX-HAUTE
CHÂTILLON-EN-DIOIS
MENGLON
RECOUBEAU-JANSAC
NEYRAC-LES-BAINS
N104
N102
GAP
BOURDEAUX
AUBENAS
ST PRIVAT
ST JEAN-LE-CENTENIER
COMPS
VILLENEUVE-DE-BERG
DIEULEFIT
LARGENTIÈRE
UZER
JOYEUSE
D104
RUOMS
LAGORCE
GRIGNAN
D94
0
10
20
30
40kms
ST ALBAN-AURIOLLES
SAMPZON
VALLON-PONT-D'ARC
NYONS
VAGNAS
BOURG-ST ANDEOL
VINSOBRES
ST MARTIN D'ARDECHE
A7,E15
TULETTE
BUIS-LES-BARONNIES
ST SAUVEUR-DE-CRUZIÈRES
PROVENCE/COTE D'AZUR
LANGUEDOC ROUSSILLON

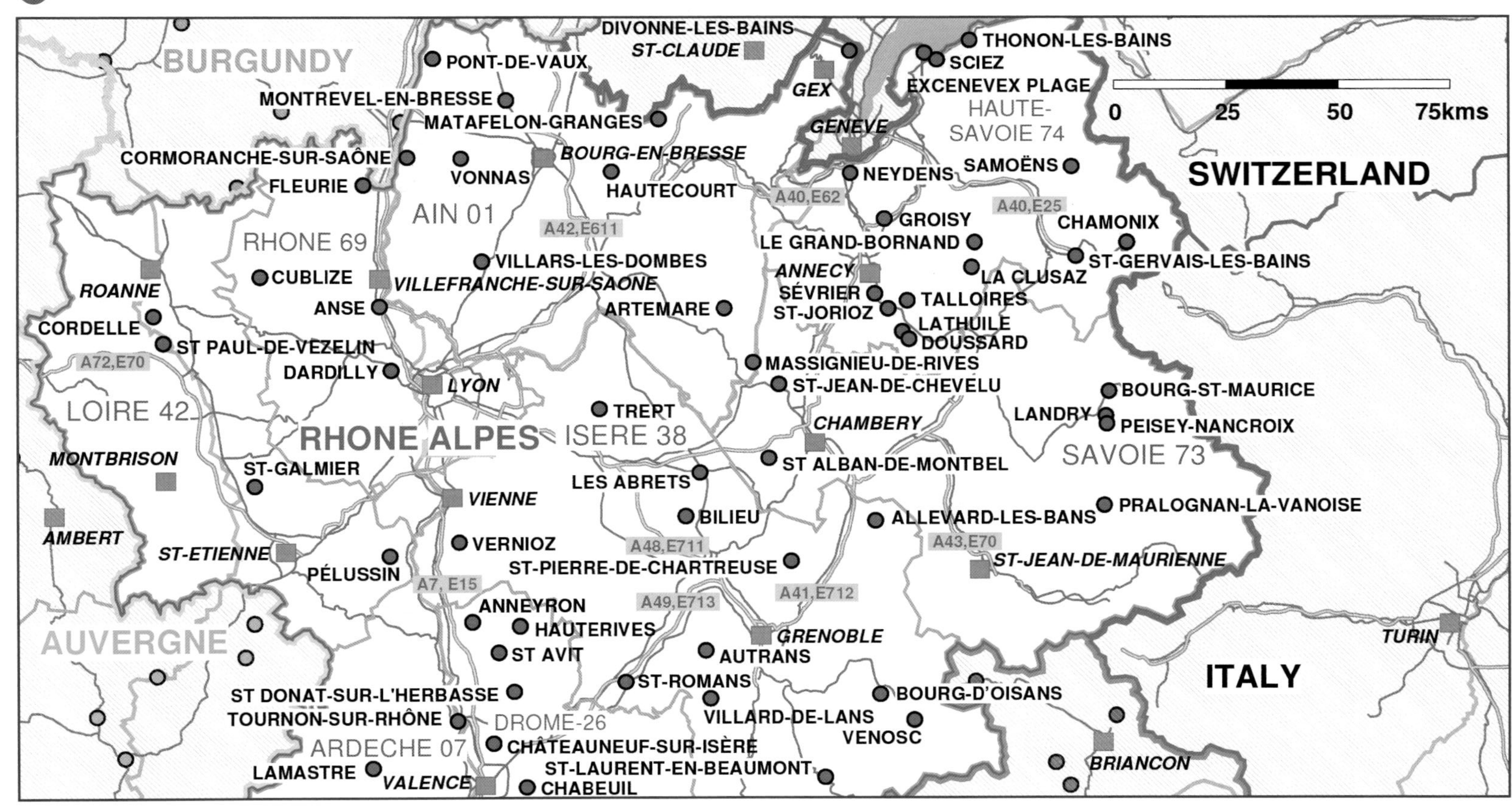
BURGUNDY
AUVERGNE
LOIRE 42
RHONE 69
AIN 01
RHONE ALPES
ISERE 38
ARDECHE 07
DROME 26
SAVOIE 73
HAUTE-SAVOIE 74
SWITZERLAND
ITALY
A72,E70
A7, E15
A42,E611
A48,E711
A49,E713
A41,E712
A43,E70
A40,E62
A40,E25
0
25
50
75kms
ROANNE
CORDELLE
AMBERT
MONTBRISON
ST PAUL-DE-VEZELIN
ST-ETIENNE
ST-GALMIER
DARDILLY
CUBLIZE
ANSE
CORMORANCHE-SUR-SAÔNE
FLEURIE
MONTREVEL-EN-BRESSE
MATAFELON-GRANGES
VONNAS
PONT-DE-VAUX
VILLEFRANCHE-SUR-SAÔNE
VILLARS-LES-DOMBES
LYON
PÉLUSSIN
VIENNE
VERNIOZ
ST-PIERRE-DE-CHARTREUSE
ANNEYRON
HAUTERIVES
ST AVIT
ST DONAT-SUR-L'HERBASSE
TOURNON-SUR-RHÔNE
LAMASTRE
VALENCE
CHÂTEAUNEUF-SUR-ISÈRE
ST-LAURENT-EN-BEAUMONT
CHABEUIL
ST-ROMANS
VILLARD-DE-LANS
AUTRANS
GRENOBLE
VENOSC
BOURG-D'OISANS
BRIANCON
LES ABRETS
TREPT
BILIEU
ST ALBAN-DE-MONTBEL
CHAMBERY
ALLEVARD-LES-BANS
ST-JEAN-DE-MAURIENNE
PRALOGNAN-LA-VANOISE
ARTEMARE
BOURG-EN-BRESSE
HAUTECOURT
MASSIGNIEU-DE-RIVES
ST-JEAN-DE-CHEVELU
ANNECY
SÉVRIER
ST-JORIOZ
LATHUILE
DOUSSARD
TALLOIRES
LE GRAND-BORNAND
GROISY
LA CLUSAZ
ST-GERVAIS-LES-BAINS
CHAMONIX
LANDRY
PEISEY-NANCROIX
BOURG-ST-MAURICE
NEYDENS
SAMOËNS
GENEVE
GEX
ST-CLAUDE
DIVONNE-LES-BAINS
EXCENEVEX PLAGE
SCIEZ
THONON-LES-BAINS
TURIN

Allevard-les-Bans

Camping Clair Matin

20 rue des Pommiers, F-38580 Allevard-les-Bans (Isère) T: 04 76 97 55 19.
E: contact@camping-clair-matin.com **alanrogers.com/FR38370**

Clair Matin can be found at the heart of the Belledonne Massif, 35 km. northeast of Grenoble. The nearby spa town of Allevard-les-Bains is a popular winter sports resort but has much appeal for summer holidays too. The three hectare site has 118 pitches, of which the 87 for touring have 2-10A electricity (seven also with water and waste water), are grassy and offer reasonable shade. Thirrty-one are occupied by mobile homes and chalets (available for rent). An area has been allocated to motorcaravans and a special overnight rate is available.

Facilities

Bar, snack bar and takeaway (all season). Bakery service (July/Aug). Outdoor swimming pool and children's pool (15/6-15/9). Activity and entertainment programme. Play area. Fully equipped chalets and mobile homes for rent. WiFi (charged). Off site: Fishing 300 m. Allevard-les-Bains centre 600 m. (shops, restaurants and cafes). Cycle and walking tracks. Riding 1.5 km. Grenoble 35 km.

Open: 25 April - 11 October.

Directions

Head north from Grenoble on A41 motorway and leave at the exit to Goncelin and Le Touvet. Head east on D29 to Goncelin and then north on D525 to Allevard. The site is signed to the left before reaching the town centre. GPS: 45.388413, 6.06492

Charges guide

Per unit incl. 2 persons and electricity	€ 19.05 - € 24.80

Anneyron

Flower Camping la Châtaigneraie

50 route de Font Flacher, F-26140 Anneyron (Drôme) T: 04 75 31 43 33. E: contact@chataigneraie.com
alanrogers.com/FR26140

La Châtaigneraie is a small, attractive, terraced site run by a very friendly family (English spoken). It is tucked away in the countryside high above the village of Anneyron with magnificent far reaching views over the valley of the Rhone. There are 71 medium sized, slightly sloping, grassy pitches, 30 for touring, away from the permanent units. Separated by hedges and young trees providing varying degrees of shade, all have 6-10A electricity. This site is popular with English and Dutch visitors, it has a comfortable and friendly atmosphere. Twin-axle caravans and large outfits are not accepted.

Facilities

Well appointed and very clean toilet block has all the necessary facilities including those for disabled campers. Motorcaravan services. Bar and small shop (all season). Good restaurant/takeaway with full menu at weekends and high season, otherwise a 'menu du jour'. Swimming and paddling pools (15/5-15/9). Jacuzzi. Massage and beauty therapies. Short tennis. Two small play areas, TV and games room. Bicycle hire. Farmers' market twice a week. Entertainment for children and adults (June-Aug). WiFi (free by reception). Gas barbecues only.

Open: 4 April - 27 September.

Directions

Leave A7 autoroute, exit 12, then N7 south for 7 km. Turn east, D1, to Anneyron (7 km). In the village turn right D161, signed Mantaille. In 3 km. turn right on to D301, signed Albon, to site immediately on right (well signed). GPS: 45.2547, 4.9039

Charges guide

Per unit incl. 2 persons and electricity	€ 17.00 - € 32.50
extra person	€ 4.00 - € 6.00
child (3-12 yrs)	free - € 4.50

Anse

Camping les Portes du Beaujolais

Avenue Jean Vacher, F-69480 Anse (Rhône) T: 04 74 67 12 87. E: contact@camping-beaujolais.com
alanrogers.com/FR69030

Situated just off the A6 at Anse, a warm welcome awaits you from Valerie and her enthusiastic team. This well run site has much to offer, both on site and locally. The reception area is comfortable and welcoming, and has a selection of local wines for tasting offered by the knowledgeable staff. There are 133 touring pitches, some open and some with shade, with neatly trimmed grass and hedges. All have 16A electrical connections and many have water. There are 65 chalets for rent which include two eco lodges (with plants growing on the roof).

Facilities

Modern toilet blocks include facilities for disabled visitors. Baby rooms. Motorcaravan services. Washing machines. Shop (all season). Gas supplies. Bar, restaurant, takeaway (30/6-31/8). Swimming and paddling pools (1/5-30/9). Playground. Playing field. Bicycle hire. Tennis. Minigolf. Boules. Games room. Internet access and WiFi over site (charged). Chalets, mobile homes and teepees (sleeping up to 4 persons) to rent. Off site: Narrow gauge railway outside entrance. Fishing 200 m. (permits sold on site).

Open: 1 March - 31 October.

Directions

Leave A6 at exit 32 and join D306 (N6) to Anse. Site is signed from northern and southern ends of village. There are height limits on all approaches (3 m. from south and 2.8 m. from north). GPS: 45.9405, 4.7268

Charges guide

Per unit incl. 2 persons and electricity	€ 23.70 - € 30.30
extra person	€ 4.50 - € 5.20
child (2-7 yrs)	€ 3.40 - € 3.80

Artemare

Sites et Paysages le Vaugrais

Chemin du Vaugrais, F-01510 Artemare (Ain) T: 04 79 87 37 34. E: contact@camping-le-vaugrais.fr

alanrogers.com/FR01100

This quiet, well cared for, family run site is near the small village of Artemare, nestling peacefully between low mountains and the Séran river. In addition to seven mobile homes to rent, there are 48 level grass pitches of varying sizes, divided by hedges. There are 45 with 6A electricity. Some of the pitches are shaded by mature trees, others are open. This area would suit couples or families with young children looking for a quiet site and the opportunity for activities such as walking and cycling. The site is a good starting point for walks. The welcoming owners are happy to tell you all about this pleasant area.

Facilities

Two traditional style sanitary blocks have the usual facilities including provision for disabled visitors. Washing machine. Shop in reception for essentials and snack bar (1/6-30/9). Swimming pool with lifeguard (1/6-30/9). Play area. Fishing. Bicycle hire. Activities and entertainment in season (archery, aquagym, themed evenings) all over by 23.00. WiFi in some areas (free). Off site: Supermarket 50 m. Village 500 m. Riding 1 km.

Open: 1 March - 10 December.

Directions

From Lyon, take A42 towards Bourg en Bresse and Genève. Take exit 8 to Ambérieu-en-Bugey, then St Rambert en Bugey. Turn left on D904 before Pugieu and go towards Artemare. GPS: 45.87463, 5.6839

Charges guide

Per unit incl. 2 persons and electricity	€ 19.00 - € 24.50
extra person	€ 4.00 - € 7.00

Aubenas

Camping Domaine de Gil

91 Route de Vals, Ucel, F-07200 Aubenas (Ardèche) T: 04 75 94 63 63. E: resa@domaine-de-gil.com

alanrogers.com/FR07150

This very attractive and well organised site is set in a less busy part of the Ardèche and should appeal to couples and families with younger children. The 80 good sized, level pitches, 28 for touring, are surrounded by a variety of trees offering plenty of shade. All have 10A electricity. The focal point of the site is formed by the very attractive heated swimming pool and paddling pool and their large sunbathing area. The bar, restaurant and well appointed play areas for children are all adjacent. A spacious sports area and shady picnic and play area are alongside the River Ardèche.

Facilities

Modern well appointed sanitary block with hot showers, some washbasins in cubicles, facilities for children and disabled visitors. Washing machine and iron. Motorcaravan services. Basic shop. Bar. Restaurant and takeaway (July/Aug). Heated swimming and paddling pools. Two play areas. Boules. Minigolf. Football. Tennis. Boating and fishing. Organised activities in high season. No charcoal barbecues. WiFi over site (charged). Max. 1 dog, low season only. Off site: Shops at Vals-les-Bain 1.5 km. and Aubenas 3 km.

Open: 29 April - 18 September.

Directions

Site north of Aubenas. From south east (N102), after tunnel, turn right, roundabout (signed Ucel), cross river into Pont d'Ucel (3.5 tonne limit). Bear right and at roundabout, last exit (signed Ucel). Shortly turn left (signed Ucel D218), then right (Ucel D578B). Site is 2 km. beyond Ucel. GPS: 44.64263, 4.37958

Charges guide

Per unit incl. 2 persons and electricity	€ 22.00 - € 40.00
extra person	€ 5.00 - € 7.00
child (under 7 yrs)	€ 3.00 - € 5.50

Autrans

Yelloh! Village Au Joyeux Reveil

Le Château, F-38880 Autrans (Isère) T: 04 76 95 33 44. E: camping-au-joyeux-reveil@wanadoo.fr

alanrogers.com/FR38080

This superb site is run by a very friendly family (English is spoken). It is on the outskirts of Autrans, high on a plateau (1,050 m) in the Vercors region close to a ski jump and short lift. There are 101 pitches with 70 for touring, all with electricity (6A). They are mainly on gently sloping grass, in a sunny location with fantastic views over the surrounding wooded mountains with small trees giving just a little shade. There is a new swimming pool with two pools, one covered, a river and slide plus a separate paddling pool.

Facilities

The spotless toilet block is very well appointed with underfloor heating and all the expected facilities. Another chalet-style building houses a bar with terrace, snack bar/takeaway. Two pools, one covered, toboggan for children, sunbathing area and a separate paddling pool. New wellness facilities with sauna and jacuzzi (1/5-30/8). Small play area. TV room. Internet point and WiFi (free). Family entertainment (July/Aug). Off site: Fishing 200 m. Autrans with a few shops 500 m. Bicycle hire 500 m.

Open: 1 May - 30 September.

Directions

Leave A48, northwest of Grenoble, exit 13 (going south) or 3A (north). Follow N532 to Sassenage, turn west at roundabout, D531 to Lans-en-Vercors. At roundabout turn right, D106 Autrans. At roundabout in Autrans turn right and very shortly right again. Site is on left. GPS: 45.17517, 5.54762

Charges guide

Per unit incl. 2 persons and electricity	€ 18.00 - € 43.00
extra person	€ 6.00 - € 8.00

Bilieu

Camping le Bord du Lac

687 route du Bord du Lac, Hameau du Petit Bilieu, F-38850 Bilieu (Isère) T: 04 76 06 67 00.
E: camping.bilieu@live.fr **alanrogers.com/FR38470**

Le Bord du Lac is located on the banks of the large Lac du Paladru, close to the village of Bilieu. It is a pleasant, terraced site with 76 grassy pitches, all with 6/10A electricity and some shade from mature birch trees. There is direct access to the lake where swimming is possible as well as various watersports, including sailing and windsurfing, and launching of your own boat can be arranged. There are many excellent walking and cycling opportunities in the area and the campsite managers will be pleased to recommend routes. The steep access roads may be difficult for large units.

Facilities

Two traditional toilet blocks include preset showers. Facilities for disabled visitors (key access). Laundry facilities. Motorcaravan services. Small shop, bar and takeaway (all 1/4-30/9). Direct lake access for swimming and watersports. Small play area. Covered recreation space. Free WiFi over site. Off site: Shops, cafés and restaurants in Bilieu. Bicycle hire 2 km. Riding.

Open: 15 March - 30 September.

Directions

From north on N75 3 km. after Abrets, take D50 to right, signed Paladru. After a further 3 km. turn left onto D90 and follow the lake for 5 km. The site is signed to your right. GPS: 45.446127, 5.53132

Charges guide

Per unit incl. 2 persons and electricity (10A)	€ 29.10 - € 30.60
extra person	€ 4.70 - € 4.90

Bourdeaux

Yelloh! Village les Bois du Chatelas

Route de Dieulefit, F-26460 Bourdeaux (Drôme) T: 04 75 00 60 80. E: reservation@chatelas.com
alanrogers.com/FR26210

Located in the heart of the Drôme Provençale, les Bois du Chatelas is a very high quality, family run site just 1.5 km. from the delightful village of Bourdeaux which offers some shops, cafés, etc. There are 169 level, good sized, terraced pitches, 70 for touring (rock pegs advised). They are separated by hedges and maturing trees give some shade; all have electricity, water and drainage, not to mention stunning views. There is a superb swimming pool complex with fitness room, jacuzzi and sauna. Overlooking the pool area is a restaurant with a full menu and superb views over the valley and mountains beyond. Air-conditioned chalets can be rented. Les Bois du Chatelas is a good choice for those seeking an active holiday and the fact that all facilities are open between April and September is a big attraction.

Facilities

Two excellent toilet blocks (one heated), on upper and lower levels, with facilities for babies and visitors with disabilities (though site is not ideal for those with mobility problems). Shop. Bar. Restaurant/takeaway/pizzeria. Indoor and outdoor pools with water slide, waterfall, sauna, aquagym and jacuzzi. Sports field. Archery. Play area. Bicycle hire. Entertainment and excursion programme. Accommodation for rent. WiFi over site (charged). Off site: Fishing 1 km. River bathing 1.5 km. Bourdeaux with some shops 1.5 km. Riding 5 km.

Open: 8 April - 11 September.

Directions

Leave A7 autoroute, exit 16 (Loriol). Take D104 east to Crest. Leave Crest bypass at traffic lights, take D538 south to Bourdeaux and continue towards Dieulefit for 1.5 km. Site is on the left (well signed). GPS: 44.57825, 5.12761

Charges guide

Per unit incl. 2 persons and electricity	€ 20.00 - € 48.00
extra person	€ 6.00 - € 8.00
child (3-6 yrs)	free - € 7.00

Bourg-d'Oisans

Camping la Cascade

Route de l'Alpe d'Huez, F-38520 Bourg-d'Oisans (Isère) T: 04 76 80 02 42. E: lacascade@wanadoo.fr
alanrogers.com/FR38030

La Cascade has a long season as it is at the heart of a popular skiing and cycling area. It is within sight and sound of the waterfall from which it takes its name. It is only 2 km. from Bourg-d'Oisans, which lies in the Romanche valley 725 m. above sea level, surrounded by high mountains. The area is a sun trap and gets very hot in summer. The site has 118 individual grassy pitches, 100 for touring units, all with 16A electricity, on mainly flat ground and of varying sizes. Although most are quite adequate, larger units are best sited near the entrance as the pitches and roads do become narrow.

Facilities

Two heated sanitary blocks are of good quality with mainly British style toilets, washbasins in cabins and showers. Laundry. Bar and snack bar (25/6-30/8). Fresh bread daily and takeaway pizzas (July/Aug). Good sized, heated swimming and paddling pools (1/6-30/9). TV in bar. Chalets for rent. WiFi throughout (free).

Open: 20 December - 30 September.

Directions

From Grenoble take D1091 (previously N91) to Bourg d'Oisans, cross river bridge, after 730 m. turn left on to D211, signed Alpe d'Huez. Site is on right in 600 m. GPS: 45.06408, 6.03903

Charges guide

Per unit incl. 2 persons and electricity	€ 27.40 - € 36.50

Bourg-d'Oisans

Sites et Paysages à la Rencontre du Soleil

Route de l'Alpe d'Huez, B.P. 33, F-38520 Bourg-d'Oisans (Isère) T: 04 76 79 12 22.
E: contact@rencontresoleil.fr **alanrogers.com/FR38040**

The Isère is an attractive and popular region with exceptional scenery. Bourg-d'Oisans lies in the Romanche valley 725 m. above sea level surrounded by high mountains. This compact site, pleasant, friendly and family run, nestles between two impressive mountain ranges, at the base of France's largest national park, Le Parc des Ecrins. It is a real sun trap and gets very hot in summer. It is only 2 km. from the busy town of Bourg-d'Oisans. It has 77 level, hedged pitches of small to average size with mature trees offering good shade (50 for touring with 10A electricity). Rock pegs are advised.

Facilities

Heated toilet block provides all the usual amenities with facilities for disabled visitors. Washing machine and dryer. Motorcaravan services. Bread to order. Restaurant and takeaway (all season). Room with TV, children's play room. Small, sheltered swimming pool (all season). Play area. Club for children. Fishing. Activities in high season include walking, mountain biking. WiFi throughout. Off site: Supermarket 1 km. Bicycle hire and riding 2 km. Golf and skiing 13 km. Cable car at Alpe d'Huez.

Open: 1 May - 30 September.

Directions

From Grenoble bypass Bourg-d'Oisans on N1091 towards Briançon. At end of bypass turn left at roundabout on D211 (Alpe-d'Huez). Site is on left beyond Camping la Piscine and just before a sharp left-hand bend – take care. GPS: 45.06547, 6.0394

Charges guide

Per unit incl. 2 persons and electricity	€ 22.05 - € 34.00
extra person	€ 6.10 - € 8.20

Bourg-d'Oisans

RCN Camping Belledonne

Rochetaillée, F-38520 Bourg-d'Oisans (Isère) T: 04 76 80 07 18. E: info@rcn-belledonne.fr
alanrogers.com/FR38100

This spacious site is owned by the RCN group and many improvements are planned. It has 180 well drained, level, generous, grassy pitches, most for touring, all with electricity (6-10A). Beech hedges and abundant mature trees provide ample privacy and shade. A bar/restaurant with terrace is open all season next to the attractive pool complex, comprising two heated swimming pools, a paddling pool and large sunbathing space surrounded by gardens and grassy areas. In July and August the site becomes quite lively with many organised activities. No twin-axle caravans are accepted and large outfits should phone ahead.

Facilities

Two well appointed sanitary blocks (one new) include baby rooms and facilities for disabled visitors. Shop. Bar/restaurant and takeaway (all open all season). Two swimming pools and a paddling pool. Sauna. Tennis. Good play area. Large meadow with fitness course. Football field. Bicycle hire (June-Sept). WiFi throughout (charged). Max. 1 dog. Off site: Riding 500 m. Allemont with shops 2 km. Fishing 4 km. Bourg-d'Oisans, shops, bars, restaurants and Saturday market 8 km.

Open: 25 April - 19 September.

Directions

Site is 8 km. west of Bourg-d'Oisans. From Grenoble take N85 to Vizille and then N91/D1091 towards Bourg-d'Oisans. In Rochetaillée branch left (site signed) onto D526, signed Allemont. Site is 250 m. on right. GPS: 45.11423, 6.00765

Charges guide

Per unit incl. 2 persons and electricity	€ 24.70 - € 46.50
extra person (over 2 yrs)	€ 3.25 - € 6.50

Camping Cheques accepted.

Bourg-d'Oisans

Camping le Colporteur

Le Mas du Plan, F-38520 Bourg-d'Oisans (Isère) T: 04 76 79 11 44. E: info@camping-colporteur.com
alanrogers.com/FR38140

Le Colporteur is within a few minutes level walk of an attractive market town and ski resort, making this an ideal spot for motorcaravanners. There are 150 level, grassy pitches, 120 for touring. All pitches have 16A electricity and rock pegs are advised. They are mostly separated by hedging and a variety of mature trees that offer some shade. There is no pool on site but campers have free entry to the adjacent municipal pool. In July and August the attractive bar/restaurant is the focal point for evening activities.

Facilities

Two large, clean toilet blocks are well equipped, modern and airy with all the necessary facilities including washbasins in cabins, baby room and en-suite room for disabled campers. Shop with fresh bread to order (July/Aug). Restaurant, bar and takeaway (1/6-31/8). Games room. Boules. Small play area. Organised family activities (July/Aug). Fishing. WiFi over site (charged). Off site: Open-air swimming pool adjacent.

Open: 1 April - 30 September.

Directions

Site is in Bourg-d'Oisans. From Grenoble follow the N91. Take the town bypass to the first roundabout. Site is signed from the first exit. Follow signs to site, a few hundred metres. GPS: 45.0526, 6.0355

Charges guide

Per unit incl. 2 persons and electricity	€ 28.60 - € 35.60
extra person	€ 7.00 - € 9.00

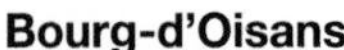

Bourg-d'Oisans

Castel le Château de Rochetaillée

Chemin de Bouthean, Rochetaillée, F-38520 Bourg-d'Oisans (Isère) T: 04 76 11 04 40.

E: jcp@camping-le-chateau.com **alanrogers.com/FR38180**

Set in the grounds of a small château with spectacular views, this site's ratings have recently been upgraded and it provides high quality amenities. The grounds are shared with chalets and tents to rent, with these in a separate area. There are 88 touring pitches, all with 6/10A electricity hook-ups on level areas (some large) separated by hedges and trees. The site has an excellent heated swimming pool, a fitness room, sauna, bar/restaurant and takeaway food together with a small shop selling bread and basic groceries. The site is in the centre of an area ideal for walkers, cyclists and climbers.

Facilities

The three very good sanitary blocks (two large) are colourful and very clean. Family room with facilities for babies. Excellent, spacious facilities for disabled visitors. Small launderette with ironing. Freezer space. Shop. Bar, snacks, takeaway and separate restaurant (all from 21/5). Heated swimming pool (all season). Sauna, fitness room and jacuzzi). Climbing wall. Daily activities for children (July/Aug). Minigolf. Guided mountain walks and other activities. Fishing. Barbecue area. WiFi over site (charged).

Open: 14 May - 11 September.

Directions

South of Grenoble take exit 8 from A480 (Stations de l'Oisans) and follow the D1091 to Briançon. Site is signed just north of Rochetaillée at junction with D526. Turn here and site is immediately on the left. GPS: 45.11530, 6.00548

Charges guide

Per unit incl. 2 persons and electricity	€ 26.20 - € 43.40
extra person	€ 6.20 - € 9.60
child (under 13 yrs)	€ 3.90 - € 6.10

Bourg-Saint-Andéol

Camping du Lion

Quartier Ile Chenevier, F-07700 Bourg-Saint-Andéol (Ardèche) T: 04 75 54 53 20.

E: contact@campingdulion.com **alanrogers.com/FR07550**

Du Lion is a spacious site bordering the River Rhône, just on the outskirts of the interesting old market town of Bourg-Saint-Andéol. Close to the A7 autoroute, this site makes a good overnight stop and is also a good base for exploring the famous Ardèche Gorges. There are 140 good sized, level pitches, 119 for touring; all have 6A electricity and long leads may be needed. They are informally laid out, most with good shade from mature trees, others more sunny. In high season, there is a full activity programme with themed dinner and dance evenings, barbecues and sports tournaments, nevertheless the camping area remains peaceful.

Facilities

Two dated but clean toilet blocks. Laundry room. Bar, snack bar and takeaway, swimming and paddling pools (all 1/5-15/9). Bread ordering service. Boules. Play area. Trampoline. TV/games room. Fishing. Entertainment and activity programme for adults and children (July/Aug). Free WiFi on part of site. Torches required. Off site: Supermarket 500 m. Town 800 m.

Open: 1 April - 30 September.

Directions

From N7, exit west on D59 for Bourg-Saint-Andéol. Cross river, at roundabout before Bourg-Saint-Andéol take first exit. At T-junction, turn right on D86, then first right onto Ch. du Chenevier. Continue under bridge (max. 4 m) and site entrance is on right. GPS: 44.38140, 4.64839

Charges guide

Per unit incl. 2 persons and electricity	€ 17.00 - € 28.00
extra person	€ 5.00 - € 8.00

Bourg-Saint-Maurice

Camping Indigo Bourg-Saint-Maurice

Route des Arcs, F-73700 Bourg-Saint-Maurice (Savoie) T: 04 79 07 03 45. E: leversoyen@wanadoo.fr

alanrogers.com/FR73020

Bourg-Saint-Maurice is on a small, level plain at an altitude of 830 m. on the River Isère, surrounded by mountains and the campsite attracts visitors all year round (except for a short time when they close). The site's 153 unseparated, flat pitches (135 for touring) are marked by numbers on the tarmac roads and all have electrical connections (10A). Most are on grass but some are on tarmac hardstanding making them ideal for use by motorcaravans or in winter. Trees give shade in most parts, although some pitches have almost none. Duckboards are provided for snow and wet weather.

Facilities

Two well maintained toilet blocks can be heated and have British and Turkish style WCs. No facilities for disabled visitors. Laundry. Motorcaravan services. No shop but bread to order. Small bar with takeaway in summer. Play area. Free shuttle to funicular railway (July/Aug). Free WiFi in central lodge. Off site: Municipal swimming pool adjacent (discounted entry). Bicycle hire 200 m.

Open: All year excl. 28/4-27/5 and 1/10-10/12.

Directions

Site is 1.5 km. east of Bourg-Saint-Maurice on CD119 Les Arcs road. GPS: 45.62248, 6.78475

Charges guide

Per unit incl. 2 persons and electricity	€ 19.70 - € 22.70
extra person	€ 4.70 - € 5.70
child (4-13 yrs)	free - € 4.00

Buis-les-Baronnies

Camping Domaine de l'Ecluse

Bénivay, F-26170 Buis-les-Baronnies (Drôme) T: 04 75 28 07 32. E: camp.ecluse@wanadoo.fr

alanrogers.com/FR26200

Tucked away in the beautiful Drôme Provençale region, this quiet, rural site is situated high in the hills, northeast of the Roman city of Vaison-la-Romaine and surrounded by vineyards. There are 75 level, stony pitches of average size, with 53 for touring (6A electricity, long leads necessary). They are separated by hedges and mature poplar trees giving varying amounts of shade. Some 15 of these are on an upper level, larger and more open, and separate from the rest of the site, with views of the surrounding hills. Rock pegs are advised. The attractive, L-shaped swimming pool has a toboggan and sunbathing area.

Facilities

Two toilet blocks with all the necessary modern facilities include rooms for babies and campers with disabilities. Small shop. Bar/restaurant and takeaway (all July/Aug). Swimming pool (April-Sept). Games field. Simple programme of events and some excursions (July/Aug). Gas barbecues only. Internet (cable). Max. 1 dog.
Off site: Restaurant nearby. Bicycle hire, fishing, lake bathing and riding 8 km. Buis-les-Baronnies 8 km. Mollans 8 km. Vaison la Romaine 14 km.

Open: 5 April - 15 November.

Directions

Site is northeast of Vaison la Romaine. Best access is via Buis-le-Baronnies. Just south of village turn northwest on D147 for 7 km. over pass to Propiac. Turn right on D347 and climb to site in 2 km. At entry use turning area provided to take sharp left-hand bend down to site. GPS: 44.28995, 5.1917

Charges guide

Per unit incl. 2 persons and electricity	€ 24.00 - € 30.00
extra person	€ 6.00 - € 7.00

Chabeuil

Camping le Grand Lierne

Les Garalands, F-26120 Chabeuil (Drôme) T: 04 75 59 83 14. E: grand-lierne@franceloc.fr

alanrogers.com/FR26030

Le Grand Lierne is part of the FranceLoc group, and is convenient for the A7 autoroute. It has 274 marked, stony pitches, 38 for touring units and tents (10A electricity, Europlug), separated by hedges and oak trees offering varying amounts of shade. Some pitches offer a fridge, barbecue, table and chairs, all stored in their own cabin. The site is clearly aimed at families with young children and has an excellent pool complex including a children's fun pool, a spacebowl flume (1.4 m. minimum height) and a covered heated pool. There is a small circus adjacent, aimed at children aged 2-6 years.

Facilities

Two sanitary blocks with modern facilities including those for disabled visitors. Fridge rental. Washing machines, dryers. Motorcaravan services. Restaurant (July/Aug). Shop, bar/takeaway, four pools (all season), one covered and heated. Paddling pool, water slide and spacebowl flume, toboggans and lazy river. Adventure playgrounds and climbing structure with slide. Minigolf. Archery and entertainment programme (July/Aug). No charcoal barbecues. Dogs are not accepted in July/Aug. WiFi (free).

Open: 24 April - 13 September.

Directions

Site signed from Chabeuil 17 km. east of Valence. Best approached from south side of Valence via Valence ring road. D68 to Chabeuil/Châteaudouble. Take D125 signed Charpey then follow site signs onto D143. Site just ahead on right.
GPS: 44.915833, 5.064722

Charges guide

Per unit incl. 2 persons and electricity	€ 19.00 - € 39.00
extra person	€ 4.70 - € 7.00

Chamonix

Camping les Deux Glaciers

80 route des Tissières, les Bossons, F-74400 Chamonix (Haute-Savoie) T: 04 50 53 15 84.
E: info@les2glaciers.com **alanrogers.com/FR74010**

A pleasant and well kept, naturally laid out, small mountain site for summer and winter use. Les Deux Glaciers lies at the foot of two glaciers and is close to the well known ski resort of Chamonix. The site has 130 terraced pitches, 100 for touring, with 2-10A electricity. Rock pegs are advised. It is pleasantly laid out with trees and floral displays. There are magnificent views of the Mont Blanc Range and the Aiguille-de-Midi. There is significant road noise. Reservations are not taken in summer. Not ideal for large outfits and those with walking difficulties.

Facilities

Two small, heated, sanitary blocks, one refurbished to include facilities for babies and disabled visitors. Washing machine and drying room. Baker calls (July/Aug) or order bread from reception. Restaurant and takeaway (all year). Small play area. WiFi in some areas (free). Off site: Shop 500 m. Fishing 600 m. Bicycle hire and riding 3 km.

Open: All year (except 15 November - 15 December).

Directions

From Geneva (N205) take 2nd exit for Les Bossons; site shortly on right. From Chamonix turn right at sign for Les Bossons, left at T-junction and pass under the main road. GPS: 45.90206, 6.83685

Charges guide

Per unit incl. 2 persons and electricity	€ 19.80 - € 25.20

Chamonix

Camping de la Mer de Glace

200 chemin de la Bagna, Les Praz, F-74400 Chamonix (Haute-Savoie) T: 04 50 53 44 03.
E: info@chamonix-camping.com **alanrogers.com/FR74150**

This attractive site is convenient for Chamonix, yet in a tranquil setting away from its hustle and bustle. The buildings are of typical regional timber construction, decorated with traditional painted flower designs. Returning in 2015, the English-speaking owners are making every effort to keep it as natural as possible, therefore it is without a pool, restaurant, bar or disco and is well suited to those looking for quiet and relaxation. There are 150 pitches of varying sizes, most with shade and 75 have electricity connections (3-6A). Visitors are provided with a free bus or train pass in order to visit Chamonix town, as well as the surrounding area, during their stay. The site is in a large level clearing, within a wooded area with a stunning view of the Mont Blanc range. The area is rich in trails for walking and mountain biking and many pass nearby. Alpinists are made especially welcome in low season.

Facilities

Three sanitary blocks with facilities for disabled visitors. Washing machine, dryer. Motorcaravan services. Small shop for essentials. Bread. Buvette for drinks and snacks. Pizza and crêpe vans twice weekly in July/Aug. Meeting room, snack preparation. Playground for young children. Free WiFi over part of site. Free charging point for mobile phones etc. Off site: Fishing and golf 500 m. Shops etc. in Les Praz 700 m. Bicycle hire 1 km. Shops and indoor and outdoor swimming pools in Chamonix 1.5 km. Riding 5 km. Free bus/train pass in locality.

Open: 24 April - 11 October.

Directions

From Chamonix take D1506 (previously N506) northeast towards Les Praz. After 1 km. site signed to right. NOTE: the first two signs direct you under a 2.4 m. high bridge. Continue to small roundabout at entrance to Les Praz, turn right and follow signs. GPS: 45.93805, 6.89267

Charges guide

Per unit incl. 2 persons and electricity	€ 24.10 - € 30.70
extra person (over 3 yrs)	€ 7.30 - € 9.50
dog	free

Neydens

Sites et Paysages la Colombière

Saint Julien-en-Genevois, F-74160 Neydens (Haute-Savoie) T: 04 50 35 13 14. E: la.colombiere@wanadoo.fr
alanrogers.com/FR74060

La Colombière, a family owned site, is on the edge of the small village of Neydens, a few minutes from the A40 autoroute and only a short drive from Geneva. It is an attractive site with 117 pitches (10/16A electricity), all reasonably level and separated by fruit trees, flowering shrubs and hedges. Forty-one new pitches and a toilet block have recently been added in an attractive, landscaped field. Neydens makes a good base for visiting Geneva and the region around the lake. It is a very pleasant, friendly site where you may drop in for a night stop – and stay for several days! The site is open all year for motorcaravans and suitable caravans. There are views to the east and west of the mountain ridges. M. Bussat owns a small vineyard close to the site, has the wine made in Switzerland and sells it in his restaurant. One of France's long distance footpaths (GR65) passes close to the site. English is spoken.

Facilities

Three sanitary blocks (one heated) include facilities for disabled visitors. Motorcaravan services. Fridge hire. Gas supplies. Good bar/restaurant (all season) and terrace overlooking the pool (1/5-15/9). New heated, indoor pool, spa pool and jacuzzi. Games room. Organised visits and activities (all season). Bicycle hire. Hire car. Archery. Boules. Playground. WiFi throughout (charged). Max. 1 dog. Off site: Fishing and riding 1 km. Switzerland 3 km. St Julien-en-Genevois 5 km. Golf 7 km. Lake beach and windsurfing 12 km. Bus to Geneva with its magnificent old town. Lake Geneva and beautiful surrounding area with many walks and cycle rides.

Open: 1 April - 31 October.

Directions

From A40 south of Geneva take exit 13 and then N201 towards Annecy. After 2 km. turn left into village of Neydens and follow campsite signs to site in just over 1 km. GPS: 46.1201, 6.10552

Charges guide

Per unit incl. 2 persons and electricity (16A)	€ 24.00 - € 41.00
extra person	€ 5.00 - € 6.00
child (3-16 yrs)	€ 3.00 - € 5.00
dog	€ 3.00

Châteauneuf-sur-Isère

Camping le Soleil Fruité

Les Peches, 480 chemin des Communaux, F-26300 Châteauneuf-sur-Isère (Drôme) T: 04 75 84 19 70.
E: contact@lesoleilfruite.com **alanrogers.com/FR26220**

This immaculate site opened in 2006 and is run by friendly, English-speaking owners. Conveniently located a little to the north of Valence, it is only 6 km. from the autoroute. The site lies amidst a large fruit farm growing peaches, apricots and olives with views over the Ardèche mountains. It is possible to pick fruit and there is a twice weekly market featuring the farm's produce. There are 138 large, level, grassy pitches with 104 for touring (electricity 10A). They are separated by attractive shrubs and trees giving some shade. All the facilities here are of a high standard. Twin-axle caravans are not accepted.

Facilities

Excellent, clean toilet block with facilities for babies and disabled visitors. Bar, TV/snack bar, small shop (all season). Swimming pool complex with outdoor pool, covered pool, water slide and 2 paddling pools. Play area. Bicycle hire. WiFi (free). Motorcaravan services. Trampolines. Twice weekly market in high season. Entertainment for under 10s and excursion programme (July/Aug). Off site: Canoeing on the River Drôme. Minigolf. Health club with steam bath and massage.

Open: 28 April - 15 September.

Directions

Leave A7 autoroute exit 14 (Valence Nord) take N7 north for 2 km. Turn right, D877, site signed. After 2 km. turn left, then left at roundabout then left again to site. GPS: 45.002716, 4.895514

Charges guide

Per unit incl. 2 persons and electricity	€ 24.00 - € 34.40
extra person	€ 5.90 - € 7.50
child (under 13 yrs)	€ 4.50 - € 5.50

Châtillon-en-Diois

Camping Lac Bleu

Quarter la Touche, F-26410 Châtillon-en-Diois (Drôme) T: 04 75 21 85 30. E: info@lacbleu-diois.com
alanrogers.com/FR26150

This spacious and peaceful site is run by a very friendly family who have made many improvements, making it comfortable and welcoming. It lies in a beautiful valley surrounded by mountains, south of the Vercors National Park. The 130 pitches (70 for touring) are level with rough grass, slightly uneven and separated by a variety of trees offering some shade (rock pegs advised). All have electricity (10A). At the centre of the site is an attractive lake of 2.5 hectares with warm, clean water fed by springs, making it ideal for swimming and fishing. A good bar, restaurant and terrace overlook the lake and there is plenty of space for children to play.

Facilities

Two clean toilet blocks, one new, the other refurbished, with all the necessary facilities. Baby room. Facilities for disabled campers. Bar/restaurant, takeaway. TV/games room (all season). Covered heated swimming pool and paddling pool (all season). Motorcaravan services. Play area bordering the lake which has footpaths around it, bathing and fishing. Pedalos. Large sports/play area. Bicycle hire. Visitors with dogs should contact site first. WiFi in bar/terrace area (charged).

Open: 1 April - 30 September.

Directions

Take D93 southeast from Die, signed Gap. In 5 km, at Pont de Quart, turn left on D539 (Châtillon-en-Diois). After 4 km. bear right onto D140, site signed. Site shortly on left. GPS: 44.6824, 5.44795

Charges guide

Per unit incl. 2 persons and electricity	€ 19.00 - € 29.90
extra person	€ 4.50 - € 7.00

No credit cards.

Comps

Sites et Paysages la Source du Jabron

D538, Comps, F-26220 Dieulefit (Drôme) T: 04 75 90 61 30. E: contact@campinglasource.com
alanrogers.com/FR26390

A warm and friendly welcome awaits you at this spacious, family run site, set in the beautiful Drôme countryside, yet within 3 km. of Dieulefit. There are 100 pitches, over gentle terraces, with 55 for touring (6-10A electricity). Attractively laid out in irregular shapes, in natural woodland, sizes vary from 80 to 180 sq.m. A modern and welcoming bar/restaurant with terrace is beside the pool complex which is arranged over three levels. Dieulefit is renowned for its pottery and has a number of studios and workshops open to the public. This is a comfortable base to explore, exercise or relax as you choose.

Facilities

Two sanitary blocks with facilities for disabled visitors and good facilities for children. Laundry facilities. Motorcaravan services. Small, well stocked shop. Bar/restaurant and takeaway (daily in July/Aug, then w/ends). Excellent pool complex (unheated). TV/games room. Adventure play area. Chalets for rent, 3 adapted for disabled visitors. Bicycle hire. No charcoal barbecues. WiFi over site (free).

Open: 30 April - 27 September.

Directions

Site is 3 km. north of Dieulefit. From A7 take exit 118 onto N7 signed Montelimar. Take D540 to Dieulefit, and then D538 north for 3 km. Site is well signed from Dieulefit. GPS: 44.55193, 5.08775

Charges guide

Per unit incl. 2 persons and electricity	€ 16.50 - € 33.80
extra person	€ 5.00 - € 7.00

Cordelle

Camping de Mars

RD56, route du Château de la Roche, F-42123 Cordelle (Loire) T: 04 77 64 94 42.
E: campingdemars@gmail.fr **alanrogers.com/FR42060**

Situated on the Mars peninsula in the Gorge de Loire, this picturesque site has stunning views across the gorge to the hillsides beyond. Of the 63 flat, grassy pitches, 48 are for tourers with the remainder for chalets and mobile homes. The site is gently terraced, with good access to all pitches. All have 10A electricity and water points. The charming husband and wife team will offer a warm welcome and information on local facilities and water based activities. There is a bar with an attractive terrace where visitors enjoying their evening meal will be rewarded with a stunning sunset in summer. Located between Clermont Ferrand and Lyon, there are many scenic drives through the countryside to historic sites and villages. Its rural location makes this site ideal for walkers, hikers and cyclists. Fishing is also available on the riverbank a short distance below the site. The owner will gladly offer advice on wine tasting; he has a wide knowledge of local wines as well as those further afield. Dutch and English are spoken in summer.

Facilities

Two modern sanitary blocks (one heated) have some washbasins in cabins. Preset timed showers. Facilities for disabled visitors. Baby room. Laundry room with washing machine and dryer (token). Small shop for basics. Bread ordered daily. Bar. Restaurant. Takeaway and pizzeria. Heated swimming pool and children's pool (May-Sept). WiFi (free). Off site: Fishing 500 m. Sailing and boat launching 3 km. Mini-market 4 km. Riding 5 km. Golf 10 km.

Open: 1 April - 15 October.

Directions

Situated 20 km. south of Roanne. Leaving A89 at exit 32 take D8 north (St Jean St Maurice). At St Polgues follow D45 east for 10 km. Turn right on to D56 and site is signed after 3 km. GPS: 45.915278, 4.060833

Charges guide

Per unit incl. 2 persons and electricity	€ 19.00 - € 29.50
extra person	€ 7.00 - € 7.80
child (2-13 yrs)	€ 4.50

Camping Cheques accepted.

Cublize

Campéole du Lac des Sapins

Pays d'Amplepuis-Thizy, F-69550 Cublize (Rhône) T: 04 74 89 52 83.
E: camping@lac-des-sapins.fr **alanrogers.com/FR69060**

Lac des Sapins is deep within the Beaujolais countryside, close to the large lake that gives the site its name, and the pretty village of Cublize. There are 181 pitches with 84 large, reasonably level, grassy touring pitches, all with electricity (6A). They are separated by high hedges and mature trees give some shade. On-site amenities include a multisports pitch, a tennis court and entertainment in high season. A bathing area and various watersports, including pedalos for hire, are available on the nearby lake. Supplementary charges are made for twin-axle caravans.

Facilities

Two older style toilet blocks have been renovated and have some washbasins in cubicles, generous controllable showers and a separate shower and WC for disabled visitors. Snack bar by lake (July/Aug). Swimming lake. Play area with bouncy castle. Miniclub (July/Aug). Evening events 3 times a week. Multisports terrain. Tennis. Boules. WiFi on part of site (charged). Accommodation for rent. Off site: Shops and restaurants in Cublize. Golf.

Open: 1 May - 30 September.

Directions

Approaching from the east (Meaux la Montagne), head west on D504 to Cublize and the site is well signed in the village. GPS: 46.013093, 4.381496

Charges guide

Per unit incl. 2 persons and electricity	€ 18.00 - € 22.00
extra person	€ 5.00 - € 6.00

Camping Cheques accepted.

Cormoranche-sur-Saône

Base de Loisirs - Camping du Lac

Base de Loisirs, 365 chemin du lac, F-01290 Cormoranche-sur-Saône (Ain) T: 03 85 23 97 10.
E: contact@lac-cormoranche.com **alanrogers.com/FR01090**

This attractive, family orientated site forms part of a landscaped recreation park that surrounds a tree lined lake. The 117 generous pitches, with a modern sanitary block in the centre, are level, grassed and enclosed by hedges. All have electricity (10A) and drainage. An area has been set aside for three teepees, and a further area for chalets. The whole site has been well thought out. A small dam divides the lake into two areas, one for swimming, with a beach, the other larger section for fishing, kayaks and pedaloes. Children will love the adventure playground in front of the beach area. There is some train noise from the nearby TVR, but only during daytime, and only a moderate rumble. Situated in a region famous for its wines, gastronomy and picturesque villages, there is much to explore locally. The town of Mâcon is only 5 km. distant. There are some 220 km. of cycle paths, on and off road, which are all marked and newly signed. Maps are available at reception. During the summer there are monthly events organised around and on the lake, which are supported by 12 local communes. There is something here for everyone. If one chose this site purely as an overnight stop because of its proximity to the A6, it is fairly certain that they would stay longer.

Facilities

A recently built sanitary building provides clean, well maintained facilities with showers and washbasins in cabins. Facilities for babies and disabled visitors. Laundry room with washing machine. Motorcaravan services. Small shop (order bread for following morning). A mobile shop selling fresh produce calls each morning. Bar and restaurant with takeaway, overlooking lake. Lake swimming with a separate area for small children. Adventure playground. Lifeguards and first aid during high season. Bicycle hire. WiFi (free). Off site: Riding 8 km. Golf 10 km. Macon, Bourg-en-Bresse and the village of Perouges.

Open: 1 May - 30 September.

Directions

Site is 5 km. south-southwest of Mâcon on the eastern side of the Saône. It is signed Base de Loisirs Cormoranche. From A6 J28 or A40 J1 follow N6 to Mâcon centre. At roundabout by Pont Urban Sud take third exit signed Bourge-en-Bresse over bridge. Then follow D51 signed Cormoranche. On entering village go right on D51B and follow signs for site. GPS: 46.25167, 4.8261

Charges guide

Per unit incl. 2 persons and electricity	€ 17.20 - € 22.50
extra person	€ 4.80 - € 5.80
child (under 12 yrs)	€ 2.00 - € 3.00
dog	€ 2.40

Dardilly

Camping Indigo Lyon

Porte de Lyon, allée du Camping International, F-69570 Dardilly (Rhône) T: 04 78 35 64 55.
E: lyon@camping-indigo.com **alanrogers.com/FR69010**

This is a short stay, city site just off the A6 autoroute and within easy reach of Lyon centre. Kept busy with overnight trade, the reception and the café (in July and August) are open until quite late. There are 159 separate numbered plots all with 6/10A electricity and 140 of these also provide water and waste water drainage. Those for caravans and motorcaravans are mostly on hardstandings on a slight slope, while those for tents are on a flatter area of grass. All have shade. A large commercial centre is just outside the site, with restaurants and shops. There is some road noise from the adjacent motorway.

Facilities

One large, modern (heated) sanitary block is in the central lodge with two further blocks (solar heated) for July/Aug. Facilities for babies. Washing machines. Motorcaravan services. Bar (all year, limited hours in low season). Snack bar, pizzas and takeaway (July/Aug). Heated swimming and paddling pools (30/4-18/9). TV, games and reading rooms. Playground. Boules. Picnic and barbecue area. No charcoal barbecues allowed. WiFi in bar (free).

Open: All year.

Directions

Travelling south, do not take A46 motorway around Lyon, continue on A6, take exit Limonest, Dardilly, Porte de Lyon. 8 km. north of Lyon tunnel; turn left for Porte de Lyon. GPS: 45.819739, 4.761196

Charges guide

Per unit incl. 2 persons and electricity	€ 24.55 - € 27.60
extra person	€ 4.70 - € 5.20

Die

Camping de la Pinède

135 impasse du Pont Neuf, F-26150 Die (Drôme) T: 04 75 22 17 77. E: info@camping-pinede.com
alanrogers.com/FR26180

Situated on the edge of the river in the narrow Drôme valley, this site is within walking distance of the historic market town of Die, famous for its Clairette de Die sparkling wines. There are 163 pitches with 93 good sized, level, stony pitches for touring. Laid out under pine trees offering some shade, all have 5/10A electricity, although long leads may be necessary. The site is not suitable for large outfits. There is a full programme of events for all the family in July/Aug. The multilingual Belgian owners will offer you a warm welcome.

Facilities

Two clean, modern sanitary blocks have all the necessary facilities including some showers with washbasins in cubicles and rooms for babies. Facilities for disabled visitors. Washing machines. Shop. Bar, restaurant with terrace, and takeaway. Two heated swimming pools with slide and loungers, one with good disability access. TV/games room. Large play area. Tennis. Wellness centre with sauna, jacuzzi, Hammam and massage (charged). Canoe, kayak and bicycle hire. Fishing. River bathing. Communal barbecue. WiFi throughout (charged July/Aug).

Open: 24 April - 30 September.

Directions

Site is 63 km. east of the A7 exit 16. Head east to Die and before the town, just after first campsite on right, turn right and follow signs down narrow lane, under low bridge (2.95 m) and across narrow river bridge (2.75 m) to site. To avoid low bridge go past first right turn, take next right signed Gap, then right again. GPS: 44.757233, 5.3535

Charges guide

Per unit incl. 2 persons and electricity	€ 23.00 - € 44.00
extra person	€ 7.00 - € 9.00

Dieulefit

Huttopia Dieulefit

Quartier d'Espeluche, F-26220 Dieulefit (Drôme) T: 04 75 54 63 94. E: dieulefit@huttopia.com
alanrogers.com/FR26580

This site is located just north of the town of Dieulefit and is set in a managed forest, by a small lake, with stunning views over the town and across the valley. There are 74 pitches with rental accommodation in the form of Cahuttes, Cabanes or Canadiennes, and a variety of clever wood and canvas structures. The remaining 91 pitches (66 with electricity) are for camping amongst the trees, although there are some closer to the central lodge which are more open. 'Bivouac' outdoor cooking and eating areas are dotted around the site. There are two pools and a good range of on-site amenities including a restaurant.

Facilities

Modern well equipped heated sanitary facilities in the central lodge, plus strategically placed outlying 'rondavels' containing family rooms and toilets and water points. Heated outdoor pool. Bar/restaurant, pizzeria (July/Aug and weekends). Small shop (all season). Large central lodge with wood burning fire and communal area. Conference Centre. Bicycle hire. Fishing. Only electric barbecues. Max. 1 dog per pitch.

Open: 14 April - 3 October.

Directions

From A7 take exit 18 onto N7 to Montélimar. Go right on ring road and follow D540 towards La Batise Rolland. Continue on D540 to Dieulefit. In town go left at roundabout onto D538 (north). Continue, passing fire station on right and following campsite signs. GPS: 44.538556, 5.056944

Charges guide

Per unit incl. 2 persons and electricity	€ 21.50 - € 47.80

Divonne-les-Bains

Camping Indigo Divonne

Quartier Villard - 2465 Vie de l'Etraz, F-01220 Divonne-les-Bains (Ain) T: 04 50 20 01 95.
E: divonne@camping-indigo.com **alanrogers.com/FR01170**

Camping Indigo Divonne is situated in the Haut Jura National Park, close to the Swiss border. It is in a large natural area surrounded by mountains and open countryside, only 3 km. from the lakeside spa town of Divonne-les-Bains. There are many swimming and watersports areas on the lake as well as on the much larger Lake Geneva, which is only 9 km. away. The wooded, nine hectare, terraced site has 274 pitches of which 181 are for touring units. These vary in size greatly so offer something for backpackers as well as those with large units. Drivers of motorcaravans may find levelling an issue on some of the sloping pitches. Most pitches have 10A electricity, many have shade and some have views over the lake and magnificent Mont Blanc.

Facilities

Five sanitary blocks. Washing machine and dryer. Bar, restaurant and takeaway (July-Sept). Heated swimming and paddling pools with sunbathing area and loungers (April-Sept). Volleyball. Boules. Tennis. Play area. Games/TV room. Children's club, sports tournaments, evening entertainment (July/Aug). Family area, library, board games, table football. No charcoal barbecues. WiFi.

Open: 23 March - 16 November.

Directions

From A1 motorway (in Switzerland) exit 10 (Coppet) onto D15 northwest into France. Continue to Divonne-les-Bains (2.7 km) and follow signs for 1.4 km. to site. GPS: 46.37506, 6.12134

Charges guide

Per unit incl. 2 persons and electricity	€ 19.20 - € 29.90
extra person	€ 3.70 - € 6.10

Doussard

Camping la Ravoire

Bout-du-Lac, route de la Ravoire, F-74210 Doussard (Haute-Savoie) T: 04 50 44 37 80.
E: info@campinglaravoire.com **alanrogers.com/FR74040**

La Ravoire is a high quality site, 800 m. from Lake Annecy. The site is noted for its neat and tidy appearance and the quietness of its location in this popular tourist region. The 124 level pitches are on well mown grass with some shade and separated by small shrubs and some hedging. All 90 pitches for touring units have 5-15A electricity, seven have water and drainage also. Those looking for a campsite in this attractive region without the 'animation' programmes that many French sites consider necessary, will find this a peaceful base. A tour operator has 26 mobile homes and tents to rent.

Facilities

Very good toilet block with facilities for disabled visitors. Bathroom for children. Laundry room with washing machines, dryers and irons. Shop (15/5-7/9). Outdoor pool, water slide and paddling pool (15/5-7/9). Good play area. Sports areas. WiFi throughout (charged). Off site: Lake with restaurants 800 m. Fishing, boat launching, bicycle hire 1 km. Riding 6 km. Golf 8 km. Shops in Doussard and Annecy (18 km). Canyoning and hang-gliding. Boat trips.

Open: 7 May - 15 September.

Directions

Site is signed from D1508 (previously N508) Annecy-Albertville road. 13 km. south of Annecy, at lights in Brédannaz, turn right and then immediately left. Site on left in 1 km. Large units use alternative access at the next right turn after the traffic lights.
GPS: 45.80256, 6.20977

Charges guide

Per unit incl. 2 persons and electricity	€ 25.20 - € 31.50
extra person	€ 6.50 - € 8.00

Camping Cheques accepted.

Doussard

Campéole la Nublière

30 allée de la Nublière, F-74210 Doussard (Haute-Savoie) T: 04 50 44 33 44. E: nubliere@wanadoo.fr
alanrogers.com/FR74190

If you are looking for large pitches, shady trees, mountain views and direct access to a lakeside beach, this site is for you. There are 271 touring pitches, of which 243 have 6A electrical hook-ups. The pitches are arranged in neat rows and access is good. This area is very popular and the site is very likely to be busy in high season. There may be some noise from the road and the public beach. La Nublière is 16 km. from old Annecy and you are spoilt for choice in how to get there. Take a ferry trip, hire a sailing boat or pedalo, or walk or cycle along the traffic free track towards the town. The local beach and sailing club are close and there is a good restaurant on the site perimeter.

Facilities

Large modern sanitary blocks are very well equipped. Good facilities for disabled visitors. Facilities for children and babies. Laundry. Shop (1/5-15/9). Restaurant on site perimeter (closed Mon). Miniclub (3/7-26/8, 4-8 yrs). Play area. Multisports area. Boules. WiFi (charged).

Open: 15 April - 23 September.

Directions

Site is 16 km. south of Annecy on Route d'Albertville, well signed. GPS: 45.79030, 6.21767

Charges guide

Per unit incl. 2 persons and electricity	€ 21.30 - € 31.20
extra person	€ 6.00 - € 7.90

Doussard

Camping International le Lac Bleu

Route de la Plage, F-74210 Doussard (Haute-Savoie) T: 04 50 44 30 18. E: contact@camping-lac-bleu.com

alanrogers.com/FR74180

This lakeside site has its own beach and jetty and a short walk brings you to the lake ferry. The site has breathtaking views and around 240 pitches divided by privet and beech hedges. This site is perfect for walking, cycling or sailing and in low season provides a tranquil base for those just wishing to relax. In high season it will be busy and popular. The proximity of the public lakeside area, which is often used as a festival venue, could become either a source of noise or an exciting place to be, depending on your point of view. A nearby cycle track on a disused railway line to Annecy gives a level 16 km. ride with mountains on the left and the lake to the right. In high season there is a children's club for the under eights. The restaurant is open early in the morning for breakfast and remains open until late in the evening, offering a large menu. Takeaway meals are also available, including pizza.

Facilities

Three toilet blocks are of a high standard with free hot showers. Good provision for babies and disabled visitors. Laundry facilities. Excellent motorcaravan services. Restaurant, bar and integral small shop. Takeaway. Pizzeria. Swimming pool and 'fun pool' (19/4-10/9). Play area. Bicycle hire. Boat launching (sailing lessons and boat hire nearby). Multisports pitch. Private beach. Free WiFi on most of site. Off site: Small supermarket 100 m. Village nearby with bars and restaurants. Fishing 100 m. Hypermarket 4 km. Riding and golf 7 km.

Open: 3 April - 21 September.

Directions

Site is 16 km. south of Annecy on Route d'Albertville, well signed. GPS: 45.790946, 6.216468

Charges guide

Per unit incl. 2 persons and electricity	€ 23.50 - € 48.70
extra person (over 3 yrs)	€ 4.00 - € 7.20
dog	€ 3.80 - € 4.80

Excenevex-Plage

Campéole la Pinède

10 avenue de la plage, F-74140 Excenevex-Plage (Haute-Savoie) T: 04 50 72 85 05.
E: pinede@campeole.com **alanrogers.com/FR74280**

La Pinède is a member of the Campéole group and has direct access to Excenevex beach, the only naturally sandy beach on Lake Geneva. The site has a pleasant woodland setting and the 364 touring pitches are of a good size, all with 16A electricity. Accommodation for rent includes specially adapted units for wheelchair users. There is a supervised bathing area on the beach which shelves gradually, and a small harbour suitable only for boats with a shallow draught. Other amenities include a shop and takeaway food service, as well as an entertainment marquee and a play area. The water complex has two pools, a jacuzzi, a sauna and a massage room.

Facilities

Heated toilet blocks include some private cabins, family shower room and facilities for children and disabled visitors. Washing machine. Motorcaravan services. Shop with fresh bread (June-Aug). Small swimming pool (15/6-10/9). Wellness area with sauna, massage and treatments. Play area. Bouncy castle. Activities and entertainment programme. Bicycle hire. Lake beach. Mobile homes, chalets and equipped tents for rent. WiFi over part of site (charged). Off site: Supermarket.

Open: 18 April - 15 September.

Directions

From Geneva head along south side of lake on the D1005 as far as Massongy and shortly beyond here take the northbound D324 to Escenevex. The site is well signed from here. GPS: 46.34492, 6.35808

Charges guide

Per unit incl. 2 persons and electricity	€ 19.30 - € 30.40
extra person	€ 4.70 - € 7.90

Camping Cheques accepted.

Fleurie

VivaCamp la Grappe Fleurie

La Lie, F-69820 Fleurie (Rhône) T: 04 74 69 80 07. E: info@beaujolais-camping.com

alanrogers.com/FR69020

With easy access from both the A6 autoroute and the N6, this attractive and welcoming site is situated in the heart of Beaujolais. It is perfect for overnight stops and equally inviting for longer stays to explore the vineyards and historic attractions of the region. Virtually surrounded by vineyards, but within walking distance (within 1 km) of the pretty village of Fleurie, this popular site has 60 generous, grassy and fairly level touring pitches with individual access to water, drainage and electricity connections (10A). Wine tasting on site is arranged twice weekly in high season. Shopping facilities are available in the village.

Facilities

Two modern sanitary blocks provide more than ample facilities (showers closed 22.00-07.00). Facilities for disabled visitors. Washing machine and dryer. Fridge. Bread to order. Snack bar with pizza and roast chicken (May-Sept). Outdoor swimming pool (15x7 m). Playground. Tennis court. Large TV/games room. Pétanque. Bicycle hire. Wine tasting (Tues. & Fri). No charcoal barbecues. Accommodation to rent. WiFi (code). Off site: Shops and restaurants 600 m.

Open: 11 April - 10 October.

Directions

From D906 at Le Maison Blanche/Romanech-Thorins, take D32 to village of Fleurie from where site is well signed. GPS: 46.1879, 4.69916

Charges guide

Per unit incl. 2 persons and electricity	€ 19.00 - € 26.00
extra person	€ 4.50 - € 6.00
child (2-12 yrs)	€ 2.00 - € 3.00
dog	€ 3.00

Grâne

Camping les Quatre Saisons

Route de Roche-sur-Grâne, F-26400 Grâne (Drôme) T: 04 75 62 64 17. E: contact@camping-4-saisons.com

alanrogers.com/FR26110

This small, terraced site nestles in the hillsides of the lower Drôme valley, close to the Vercors Mountains. There are a total of 80 pitches, 60 of which are for touring. Pitches are level and stony and of larger than average size, cut out of the hillside and reached by a one-way system on tarmac roads. All pitches have electricity (6A), some with water and drainage. The modern main building houses reception on the upper level as you enter the site, with the pool, bar and other facilities to the side and below.

Facilities

Good sanitary facilities include baby room, en-suite facilities for disabled visitors (but site is very sloping and not suitable for wheelchairs). Washing machine. Bar. TV/games room. Three swimming pools (1/5-30/9). Play area. Bouncy castle. Children's club (high season). Only electric and gas barbecues are allowed on the pitch. Chalets available to rent. No charcoal barbecues. WiFi throughout (charged). Off site: Village nearby with shops catering for most needs.

Open: 1 April - 30 September.

Directions

From A7 exit 17, or the N7 at Loriol, take the D104 towards Crest. After 8 km. in Grâne take D113 south. Site is on left 600 m. beyond the village. GPS: 44.7277, 4.9265

Charges guide

Per unit incl. 2 persons and electricity	€ 18.00 - € 31.50
extra person (over 3 yrs)	€ 4.00 - € 6.00
child (3-6 yrs)	€ 3.00 - € 4.50

Camping Cheques accepted.

Grignan

Camping les Truffières

1100 chemin Belle Vue d'air, route de Chamaret, F-26230 Grignan (Drôme) T: 04 75 46 93 62.
E: info@lestruffieres.com **alanrogers.com/FR26090**

This small, pleasant site in a rural setting next to a lavender field and within walking distance of the picturesque ancient village of Grignan, provides a haven of peace and tranquillity. The 85 good sized pitches are level and fairly stony with 78 for touring units, all with 10A electricity. They are shaded by oak trees and separated by rosemary or laurel hedging. The Croze family is most welcoming and achieves high standards while maintaining a friendly and relaxed atmosphere. The Drôme is one of the most beautiful regions of France; vineyards, olive orchards, lavender, sunflowers and meadows abound.

Facilities

Good toilet block provides all necessary facilities. Motorcaravan services. Bar (all season), snack bar, takeaway (1/6-30/8). Heated swimming pool, smaller pool for children (all season). Boules. Little in the way of on site entertainment but many off site activities can be booked. No dogs. Gas and electric barbecues only. Free WiFi in bar area. Off site: Riding 200 m. Fishing 2 km. Bicycle hire 5 km. Golf 6 km. Grignan with its château and Tues. market. Nyons with excellent market (Thurs) 26 km.

Open: 20 April - 20 September.

Directions

From N7 (or A7 autoroute exit 18) south of Montélimar, take D133 (changes to D541) signed Grignan. After 9 km, just before entering Grignan, take D71 towards Charamet and site is shortly on the left. GPS: 44.41131, 4.8911

Charges guide

Per unit incl. 2 persons and electricity	€ 20.00 - € 24.00

No credit cards.

Groisy

Camping Moulin Dollay

206 rue du Moulin Dollay, F-74570 Groisy (Haute-Savoie) T: 04 50 68 00 31. E: moulin.dollay@orange.fr

alanrogers.com/FR74170

Nestling between Annecy (15 km) and Geneva (35 km), this spacious site is a gem with only 45 pitches, 30 for touring. The friendly and enthusiastic owner has worked hard to develop this site to a high quality. The large to very large, level, grass pitches are partially separated by hedging and a variety of trees provide some shade. All pitches have 6A electricity and rock pegs are recommended. As there are only a few activities organised for youngsters on site, it is perhaps better suited to those who would appreciate a peaceful site in a parkland setting alongside a rushing stream.

Facilities

Spacious, well appointed, heated toilet block, including facilities for disabled visitors and a baby room. Washing machine, dryer. Motorcaravan services. Bar, TV corner. Large open play and sports area. Fishing and bathing in shallow river. Off site: Some shops, restaurants, bank and supermarkets at Groisy 1 km. Riding 4 km. Interesting little town of Thorens-Glières with its 11th-century château 5 km. Golf 6 km. Lake Annecy and watersports 15 km.

Open: 1 May - 30 September.

Directions

Site is north of Annecy. Heading north on N1203 Annecy-Bonneville road, turn right on D2 signed Thorens-Glières and site, then immediately right again. Site is 300 m. GPS: 46.00238, 6.19079

Charges guide

Per unit incl. 2 persons and electricity	€ 18.00 - € 22.00

No credit cards.

Hautecourt

Camping de l'Ile Chambod

3232 route du Port, F-01250 Hautecourt (Ain) T: 04 74 37 25 41. E: contact@campingilechambod.com

alanrogers.com/FR01020

This small, attractive rural site is situated in a valley close to the Gorges de l'Ain and within walking distance of the lake facilities. The 110 medium sized, slightly sloping, grassy pitches (many with views of the surrounding wooded hills) are separated by low hedges and most have some shade. All have access to water points and electricity (5/10A) although some may need extremely long leads. A lakeside beach is just 300 m. away on the delightful Ile de Chambod (charged for in high season) and is an idyllic spot for picnics, beach bathing, paddling, boat launching, simple watersports and minigolf.

Facilities

Two modern toilet blocks include some washbasins in cabins, dishwashing, laundry and vegetable preparation sinks. Washing machines and dryer. Both blocks have facilities for disabled visitors and one has a baby room. Bread available to order. Small shop (June-Aug). Bar/restaurant and takeaway (May-Aug). Swimming pool (May-Aug). Small play area. Activities organised in high season for all the family. Canoe and bicycle hire.

Open: 17 April - 20 September.

Directions

Site is 23 km. southeast of Bourg-en-Bresse via the D979. It is well signed from the crossroads in Hautecourt and is a further 4 km. south east down a long lane. GPS: 46.12777, 5.42818

Charges guide

Per unit incl. 2 persons and electricity	€ 13.70 - € 18.00
extra person	€ 4.10 - € 5.10

Hauterives

Flower Camping le Château

5 route de Romans, F-26390 Hauterives (Drôme) T: 04 75 68 80 19. E: camping-hauterives@orange.fr

alanrogers.com/FR26360

Le Château is a former municipal campsite which is now run by the friendly and very helpful Stéphanie and Marc. It is a family oriented site set an hour south from Lyon, near the motorway. In high season, activities are organised for the whole family. This site comprises 126 neat, good sized touring pitches and 29 for rental accommodation, well spread over an area of four hectares. There is also a dedicated area for tent campers near the entrance of the site. The old château buildings and courtyard are used for entertainment, bar and snacks, with the pools adjacent. The village of Hauterives is just a short walk from the site. A city trip to Lyon or Vienne is also recommended.

Facilities

Sanitary buildings include controllable showers. Facilities for disabled visitors. Bar/snack bar (May-Sept). Heated, supervised outdoor pools and children's pool. TV room. Playground. Library. Boules. Bicycle hire. Accommodation to rent. WiFi throughout (free at reception, elsewhere charged). Off site: Supermarket by entrance. Shops, restaurants and weekly market in village. Fishing 1 km. Riding 5 km. Golf 15 km.

Open: 1 April - 26 September.

Directions

Leave A7 at exit 12 (Chanas) and take third exit from roundabout (D519 for Grenoble-Beaurepaire). At Beaurepaire take D538, through Lens Lestang, then Hauterives. At roundabout by church, left to Romans. Site is 200 m. on left. GPS: 45.252796, 5.026717

Charges guide

Per unit incl. 2 persons and electricity	€ 12.00 - € 28.00
extra person (over 2 yrs)	€ 4.00 - € 5.50

Joyeuse

Camping Caravaning les Cruses

Ribes, F-07260 Joyeuse (Ardèche) T: 04 75 39 54 69. E: les-cruses@wanadoo.fr

alanrogers.com/FR07260

High in the quiet hills of the southern Ardèche, among the sweet chestnut trees, a warm welcome awaits you at this small, terraced site. M. and Mme. Rouvier are very keen to promote a quiet, family atmosphere; personal contact with their guests is important and weekly entertainment is tailored to guests' needs. For instance, M. Rouvier will lead walks, arrange boules competitions against other campsites and canyoning and canoe trips on the river. There are 45 pitches (23 with 6/10A electricity), and 22 mobile homes and chalets for hire. Pitches are of varying sizes, some on grass and some gravel, and some are only accessible for tents.

Facilities

The toilet block is up to date and clean with preset showers and a few en-suite shower, toilet and basin cabins. Baby room. Facilities for disabled visitors. Laundry room. Bar, restaurant and pizzeria providing good food (weekends only in low season). Swimming pool (1/5-20/9). Play area. Covered area for pétanque. Games room. Activities arranged. Good air-conditioned chalets, mobile homes and Romany-style caravans for rent. Gas barbecues only. WiFi and Internet access PC (charged).

Open: 11 April - 20 September.

Directions

From Joyeuse take D203 towards Ribes. Turn left at D450 (Ribes), continue for 1 km. Site is signed on left 1 km. before village. GPS: 44.492417, 4.207267

Charges guide

Per unit incl. 2 persons and electricity	€ 17.00 - € 29.00
extra person	€ 4.30 - € 6.80
child (under 2 yrs)	free
dog	free - € 2.80

La Clusaz

Camping le Plan du Fernuy

1800 route des Confins, F-74220 La Clusaz (Haute-Savoie) T: 04 50 02 44 75. E: info@plandufernuy.com

alanrogers.com/FR74090

This neat and open site has separate summer and winter seasons. It has 80 average sized, stony, grassy pitches, 42 for touring units (4-13A electricity) and 15 fully serviced. There are good mountain views but little shade and rock pegs are essential. The site's crowning glory is an excellent indoor heated pool with large windows looking out on to the mountains. This is a good site for skiing in winter (with access to a ski-tow from the campsite and a free bus to other centres). In summer, it is a good base for walking and cycling with other sporting opportunities nearby. The manager of this site speaks good English.

Facilities

Very good heated sanitary provision with controllable hot showers and some washbasins in cabins. Baby room. Limited facilities for disabled visitors. Washing machine and dryer. Drying room for ski clothing and boots. Motorcaravan services. Very limited shop. snacks, takeaway. Games, TV room. Heated indoor pool and paddling pool. Skiing from site and ski excursions organised. Only gas barbecues permitted on pitches (available to rent). WiFi throughout (30 mins. free).

Open: 6 June - 6 September, 13 December - 19 April.

Directions

From Annecy take D909 to La Clusaz and at roundabout turn towards Les Confins. Site is on right after 2 km. (well signed). It is best to avoid using D909 from Flumat particularly with caravans or motorcaravans. GPS: 45.90922, 6.45203

Charges guide

Per unit incl. 2 persons and electricity	€ 24.00 - € 36.00
extra person	€ 4.70 - € 7.00

Lagorce

Castel Domaine de Sévenier

Sévenier, F-07150 Lagorce (Ardèche) T: 04 75 88 29 44. E: domainedesevenier@orange.fr

alanrogers.com/FR07660

There are no touring pitches at this site. Le Domaine de Sévenier is a modern, high quality chalet complex enjoying a hilltop location with fine panoramic views over the surrounding garrigue, a unique mix of oak trees, juniper, rosemary and thyme. Located 4 km. from Vallon-Pont-d'Arc and 800 m. from the pretty village of Lagorce, the domaine is an old winery which has been sensitively converted and offers accommodation in well appointed wooden chalets serving the needs of families, both large and small. Rest and relaxation is the theme here and the restaurant has a good reputation. The site has links to Nature Parc Camping de l'Ardèche and guests are welcome to enjoy the site's evening entertainment.

Facilities

The sanitary block includes hot showers and provision has been made for disabled visitors. Washing machine. Shop. Bar. Restaurant. Outdoor heated swimming pool. Paddling pool. Activity programme. Play area. Minigolf. Bicycle hire. Fully equipped chalets for rent.

Open: 30 March - 4 November.

Directions

Head north from Vallon-Pont-d'Arc (at western end of the Ardèche gorges) on D1, and 800 m. before Lagorce site is on the right.
GPS: 44.434151, 4.410989

Charges guide

Contact the site for details.

Lalley

Sites et Paysages Caravaning Belle Roche

F-38930 Lalley (Isère) T: 04 76 34 75 33. E: camping.belleroche@gmail.com

alanrogers.com/FR38090

Belle Roche is very spacious, level and well maintained by the Durand family. The site has great views over the surrounding wooded mountains, in the relatively unknown Trièves area of the Isère. There are 57 large (minimum 150 sq.m), slightly uneven pitches, many part grass with gravel hardstanding. They are partially delineated by shrubs and young trees offering little shade. All have 10A electricity and rock pegs are necessary. This is a good site for an overnight stop being close to the N75, and also a quiet base from which to explore the Vercors National Park. It is a super location, surrounded by mountains.

Facilities

Two modern, clean and well equipped sanitary blocks. Facilities for disabled visitors. Laundry. Motorcaravan services. Bar/TV room, terrace where simple meals are served, also delivered to your pitch (all season). Bread. Swimming pool (mid May-Sept.) with large sunbathing area and sun beds. Very large play area. WiFi throughout (charged). Off site: Village shop 400 m. Fishing 500 m. Bicycle hire 1 km. Riding 10 km.

Open: 1 April - 30 September.

Directions

Follow N75 south from Grenoble (about 65 km). Turn east onto D66B, signed Lalley, Mens and campsite, and then follow camping signs through the village. Site is on right just beyond village. From south, leave N75 on D66. GPS: 44.75492, 5.67893

Charges guide

Per unit incl. 2 persons and electricity € 17.90 - € 27.90
extra person € 3.50 - € 8.00

Lamastre

Camping de Retourtour

1 rue de Retourtour, F-07270 Lamastre (Ardèche) T: 04 75 06 40 71. E: campingderetourtour@wanadoo.fr

alanrogers.com/FR07460

This family run site is situated in the lesser known, but beautiful, northern Ardèche and you can be sure of a warm and friendly welcome here. Set in a wooded valley close to a tiny village below the ruins of a chateau, there are 130 good sized, level, grass pitches with 80 for touring (all with 4-13A electricity). Separated by hedges and mature trees, most have good shade. The town of Lamastre is often used as a stage for cycling events and has markets on Tuesdays and Saturdays. The site is close to the Doux river with a beautiful natural river swimming area within 150 m.

Facilities

Three very clean, refurbished toilet blocks with hot showers, washbasins in cubicles, family shower room and facilities for disabled visitors. Washing machine. Motorcaravan services. Small shop. Bar (all season). Restaurant/takeaway (15/5-15/9). Good play area. Multisports area. Fitness room with covered patio for use in wet weather. Boules. Minigolf. Climbing. Fishing. Family entertainment (July/Aug). Bicycle hire. WiFi on part of site (charged). Only gas and electric barbecues are allowed. Mobile homes to rent. Off site: Restaurant 50 m.

Open: 17 April - 30 September.

Directions

Site is 25 km. west of Valence. Leave A7 autoroute at exit 13 or 15 (Valence). Go west to Lamastre following D533 signs to Le Puy. Continue through Lamastre. After 1.5 km. turn right (site signed) down lane to site. GPS: 44.99165, 4.56477

Charges guide

Per unit incl. 2 persons and 13A electricity € 15.86 - € 23.96
extra person € 3.98 - € 4.98

No credit cards.

Landry

Camping Qualité l'Eden de la vanoise

Avenue de la Gare, F-73210 Landry (Savoie) T: 04 79 07 61 81. E: campingleden@gmail.com

alanrogers.com/FR73060

L'Eden is open to touring units in summer and winter. It is beside the Isere river, set in beautiful woodland glades, and is perfect for winter skiing and walking and cycling in summer. The site is set in a valley with the Alpine peaks as a backdrop. The 117 good, spacious pitches all have 16A electricity hook-ups and individual water supplies and there are 20 mobile homes, bungalows etc. for hire. The clean, modern sanitary blocks are heated in colder weather and include a large drying room. There is a pool, a bar and a welcoming communal area with bar and TV.

Facilities

Two heated toilet blocks with drying rooms, good facilities for disabled visitors and for babies. Small launderette. Motorcaravan service point. Communal area with bar and TV. Snack bar and takeaway. Covered, heated swimming pool. Bicycle hire. Games room. Play area. Fishing. Ski passes for sale on-site. WiFi throughout (free). Shop and restaurants in village.

Open: 15 December - 25 September.

Directions

From the RN90 take D87 towards Landry. Site is on left after 250 m. and is well signed from the RN90. GPS: 45.57652, 6.73457

Charges guide

Per unit incl. 2 persons and electricity € 23.10 - € 37.60
extra person € 5.25 - € 7.15
child (3-6 yrs) € 2.95 - € 5.75

Largentière

Domaine les Ranchisses

Route de Rocher, F-07110 Largentière (Ardèche) T: 04 75 88 31 97. E: reception@lesranchisses.fr

alanrogers.com/FR07070

This is a very well equipped, modern campsite in a lesser known area of the Ardèche. There are 97 good sized, level pitches, all for touring with electricity (10A) including 76 which are fully serviced, both shaded and part shaded. Good quality mobile homes and chalets are available to rent. A small river pool provides opportunities for bathing, fishing or canoeing (free life jackets), with one part of the area quite safe for youngsters. A new spa has a sauna, jacuzzi, Hammam, ice fountain and a boutique. Well run and with the emphasis on personal attention, this is a highly recommended site.

Facilities

Comprehensive toilet buildings include facilities for babies and disabled visitors. Laundry facilities. Motorcaravan services. Shop. Bar. Restaurant (regional specialities), takeaway/pizzeria and terrace. Two large pools, paddling pool (heated). Separate water slides. Wellness centre with sauna, gym, jacuzzi and Hammam and semi-covered pool. Adventure-style playground. Organised amusements for adults and children (from 1/7). Very good miniclub including a mini theatre. Skate park. Tennis. Minigolf. Boules. Canoeing. Internet access. Chalets for rent. WiFi throughout (charged). Max. 2 dogs per pitch.

Open: 11 April - 20 September.

Directions

Largentière is southwest of Aubenas and best approached using D104. Just beyond Uzer, 16 km. from Aubenas, turn northwest on D5. After 5 km. at far end of Largentière, fork left downhill signed Rocher and Valgorge. Site on left in 1.8 km. just beyond rocky gorge. The approach from Valgorge is not recommended. GPS: 44.56071, 4.28463

Charges guide

Per unit incl. 2 persons and electricity	€ 19.00 - € 55.00
extra person	€ 5.00 - € 11.00

Lathuile

Camping l'Idéal

715 route de Chaparon, F-74210 Lathuile (Haute-Savoie) T: 04 50 44 32 97. E: camping-ideal@wanadoo.fr

alanrogers.com/FR74200

For panoramic views of mountains and the lake, this family run site is excellent. Trim and neat, the site is well cared for and the welcome is warm. The 300 pitches are generally large and well drained, some with small hedges but mostly open and with 10A electricity. These pitches share the site with chalets which are located at the top of the site, well away from the tourers. L'Idéal is far enough from the lake to avoid the noise and crowds but close enough to take advantage of the facilities there. From the site you can cycle downhill to join the Annecy cycle route.

Facilities

Three very well designed toilet blocks, one newly renovated, were fairly clean and include excellent facilities for babies and disabled visitors. A further new block is planned. Laundry facilities. Shop (May-Sept). Bar. Restaurant, snack bar and takeaway (May-September). Two swimming pools. Tennis. Paragliding lessons. Bicycle hire. Play area. Children's club. Activities and excursions in high season. WiFi (charged). Off site: Lake 900 m.

Open: 1 May - 19 September.

Directions

Lathuile is 18 km. southeast of Annecy and site is well signed in the village. GPS: 45.79514, 6.20564

Charges guide

Per unit incl. 2 persons and electricity	€ 26.00 - € 36.00
extra person	€ 4.70 - € 8.00
child (0-2 yrs)	free
dog	€ 4.50

Lathuile

Camping les Fontaines

1295 route de Chaparon, F-74210 Lathuile (Haute-Savoie) T: 04 50 44 31 22.
E: info@campinglesfontaines.com **alanrogers.com/FR74320**

Les Fontaines can be found close to the Forclaz pass, backed by the Taillefer mountains and around 1 km. from the crystal waters of Lake Annecy. There are 170 pitches here, 50 for touring, all on level ground, with 6A electricity, and reasonably well shaded. A number of mobile homes, chalets and teepees are available for rent. The site's aqua park comprises a large covered, heated swimming pool surrounded by a terrace with sun loungers and an attractive children's pool with water features. There is also a multi-track water slide. The campsite shop is well stocked with all necessary provisions and, in high season, there is a minimarket of local produce.

Facilities

Heated sanitary block with washbasins in cubicles. Facilities for children and disabled visitors. Washing machine. Shop (10/6-5/9). Bar/restaurant (all season). Covered, heated pool and water slides. Playground. Multisport terrain. Trampoline. Archery. Activity and entertainment programme. WiFi on part of site (charged).

Open: 15 May - 15 September.

Directions

Site is at southern end of Lake Annecy. From Annecy head south on N508 towards Albertville. Pass through Duingt. Then follow signs to Lathuile (to right) then site. GPS: 45.80042, 6.20468

Charges guide

Per unit incl. 2 persons and electricity	€ 25.50 - € 35.40

Le Grand-Bornand

Camping Caravaning l'Escale

33 chemin du Plein Air, F-74450 Le Grand-Bornand (Haute-Savoie) T: 04 50 02 20 69.

E: contact@campinglescale.com **alanrogers.com/FR74070**

You will receive a good welcome in English from the Baur family at this beautifully maintained and picturesque site, situated at the foot of the Aravis mountain range. There are 149 pitches with 123 for touring. Of average size, part grass, part gravel they are separated by trees and shrubs that give a little shade. All have 2-10A electricity and 86 are fully serviced. Rock pegs are essential. A 200-year-old building houses a bar/restaurant decorated in traditional style, overlooking the indoor pool; it offers regional dishes in a delightful, warm ambience. The village is 200 m. away and has all the facilities of a resort with activities for summer and winter holidays. In summer, a variety of well signed footpaths and cycle tracks provide forest and mountain excursions. In winter the area provides superb facilities for downhill and cross-country skiing. This very popular campsite, set beside the picture postcard ski resort of Le Grand-Bornand, has wonderful views and is surrounded by fields of flowers in summer.

Facilities

Good toilet blocks (heated in winter) have all the necessary facilities for disabled campers. Drying room for skis, clothing and boots. Superb pool complex with interconnected indoor (all season) and outdoor pools and paddling pools (July/Aug), jacuzzi and water jets. Cosy bar/restaurant and takeaway (all season). Play area. Tennis. Activities for adults and children. Video games. Discounts on organised walks and visits to Chamonix-Mont Blanc. Traditional chalets and mobile homes to rent. WiFi in some areas (free). Off site: Village (5 mins. walk).

Open: 27 May - 27 September, 19 December - 12 April.

Directions

From Annecy follow D16 and D909 towards La Clusaz. At St Jean-de-Sixt, turn left at roundabout D4 (Grand-Bornand). Just before village fork right (Vallée de Bouchet). Site entrance is on right at roundabout in 1.2 km. GPS: 45.94036, 6.42842

Charges guide

Per unit incl. 2 persons and electricity	€ 19.00 - € 33.20
extra person (over 2 yrs)	€ 3.20 - € 4.50
dog	€ 2.80 - € 3.60

Les Ollières-sur-Eyrieux

Flower Camping le Chambourlas

D2 le Chambon de Bavas, F-07360 Les Ollières-sur-Eyrieux (Ardèche) T: 04 75 66 24 31.

E: info@chambourlas.com **alanrogers.com/FR07190**

Tucked away in a beautiful setting, in the hills above Privas, this is a small, neat and tidy, family owned site. The 78 large, grassy, some slightly sloping pitches (62 for touring, electricity 10A) are set on low terraces, separated by an interesting variety of trees with excellent views over the wooded hills. The attractive reception, restaurant and shop are in one building close to all the facilities. There is a private lake with a beach making it a tranquil place for fishing or canoeing. The site is not ideal for very large units due to the steep and narrow local roads.

Facilities

One modern, very clean toilet block with all the necessary facilities including those for disabled visitors and children. Bar and takeaway (from 1/5). Restaurant (1/6-15/9). Small shop (from 1/6). Swimming pool, paddling pool and sunbathing area (all season, heated 8/5-1/9). Play area. Boules. Good range of activities, some in low season, no discos. River fishing. No charcoal barbecues. WiFi (free). Wooden chalets and tents for rent. Off site: Many walks and bike rides. Bicycle hire 6 km. Excursions.

Open: 20 April - 20 September.

Directions

At traffic lights in Privas take D2 north, signed Les Ollieres/Le Cheylard. Follow road over two river bridges climbing gradually through the hills before descending to site entrance on right after 14 km. Site access road appears more steep and narrow than it actually is. GPS: 44.78155, 4.61806

Charges guide

Per unit incl. 2 persons and electricity	€ 17.00 - € 29.00
extra person	€ 4.50 - € 6.00

Les Abrets

Camping le Coin Tranquille

6 chemin des Vignes, F-38490 Les Abrets (Isère) T: 04 76 32 13 48.

E: contact@coin-tranquille.com **alanrogers.com/FR38010**

Le Coin Tranquille is well placed for visits to the Savoie regions and the Alps. It is an a maintained site of 192 grass pitches (178 for touring units), all with 10A electricity. They a by neat hedges of hydrangea, flowering shrubs and a range of trees to make a lovely ...ment doubly enhanced by the rural aspect and marvellous views across to the mountains. This is a popular, family run site with friendly staff, making it a wonderful base for exploring the area. Set in the Dauphiny countryside north of Grenoble, le Coin Tranquille is truly a quiet corner, especially outside school holiday times, although it is still popular with families in high season. The Chartreuse caves near Voiron are well worth a visit, as is the Monastery, and a mountain railway goes to the summit of the Chartreuse Massif.

Facilities

The central well appointed sanitary block is well kept, heated in low season. Facilities for disabled visitors. Two smaller blocks provide facilities in high season. Busy shop. Excellent restaurant. Heated swimming pool and paddling pool (1/5-30/9; no Bermuda style shorts) with sunbathing areas. Play area. TV and games in bar. Quiet reading room. Weekly entertainment for children and adults (July/Aug) including live music (not discos). Bicycle hire (limited). WiFi near reception (free).
Off site: Les Abrets with shops and supermarket 2 km. Riding 6 km. Fishing 8 km. Golf 30 km.

Open: 1 April - 31 October.

Directions

Les Abrets is 70 km. southeast of Lyon at junction of D1006 (previously N6) and D1075 (previously N75). From roundabout in town take N6 towards Chambéry, turning left in just under 2 km. (signed restaurant and camping). Follow signs along country lane for just over 1 km. and entrance is on right. GPS: 45.54115, 5.60778

Charges guide

Per unit incl. 2 persons and electricity	€ 19.00 - € 37.00
extra person	€ 4.00 - € 8.00

Camping Cheques accepted.

Les Ollières-sur-Eyrieux

Camping Mas de Champel

Quartier Champel, F-07360 Les Ollières-sur-Eyrieux (Ardèche) T: 04 75 66 23 23.

E: masdechampel@wanadoo.fr **alanrogers.com/FR07440**

At Mas de Champel you will be encouraged by the friendly owners to relax in a region of natural beauty. Once a farm with orchards located at the heart of the valley of the Eyrieux, rounded river worn boulders are featured in the buildings that house the site's very good terraced restaurant with its stunning views. With 56 generously sized touring pitches with 6A electricity and varying degrees of shade and 44 chalets and mobile homes to rent, the campsite is able to provide a programme of entertainment for all family members. Two good sized pools and a paddling pool, plus a riverside beach, offer fishing, bathing and canoeing. On weekdays in July and August there are programmes of activities for children of all ages.

Facilities

Two clean toilet blocks with all the necessary facilities with a third opened in high season. Motorcaravan services. Bar, good restaurant with terrace (beautiful views) and takeaway (from 2/5). Swimming pool, heated paddling pool, fun pool, jacuzzi and sunbathing area. Wellness centre with visiting masseuse. Games/TV room. Play area. Pétanque. Bicycle hire. Fishing. Canoe hire. Many organised family activities (July/Aug). Only gas barbecues permitted. WiFi (free).

Open: End April - 23 September.

Directions

From A7 exit 15 take N7 south for 7 km. turn west onto D11 to join N86 heading south. Leave N86 just south of Beauchastel. Turn west, D120, to Ollières-sur-Eyrieux (about 20 km). Site on right at entrance to village and is signed. GPS: 44.80721, 4.61489

Charges guide

Per unit incl. 2 persons and electricity	€ 19.00 - € 29.90
extra person	€ 4.50 - € 7.00

…-la-Croix-Haute

…amping Champ la Chèvre

F-26220 Lus-la-Croix-Haute (Drôme) T: 04 92 58 50 14. E: info@campingchamplachevre.com

alanrogers.com/FR26270

This is a pleasant, unpretentious site with some really magnificent views across towards the western Alps. Formerly a farm (hence its name) and now under new management, Champ la Chèvre is undergoing a steady process of refurbishment and is attractively located just 200 m. from the village and 500 m. from the D1075. There are 100 pitches, for the most part sunny and quite spacious, and many with fine mountain views. Some pitches are sloping and most pitches have 6A electrical connections.

Facilities

Centrally located toilet block with facilities for disabled visitors. A second block by the entrance. Motorcaravan services. Bar, restaurant and takeaway. Heated swimming pool (15/6-31/8). Play area. Children's club (July/Aug). Minigolf. Mobile homes and chalets for rent. WiFi.
Off site: Riding 100 m. Lus-la-Croix-Haute 200 m. Railway station 300 m. Bicycle hire 500 m. Fishing 3 km. Tennis. Walking and cycle trails.

Open: 23 April - 17 September.

Directions

From the north, head south from Grenoble initially on the A480 and then the A51 towards Sisteron. Then join the southbound N75 for 35 km. to Lus-La-Croix-Haute. Drive through the village and site is well signed. GPS: 44.66440, 5.70742

Charges guide

Per unit incl. 2 persons and electricity	€ 19.00 - € 27.30

Camping Cheques accepted.

Massignieu-de-Rives

Camping du Lac du Lit du Roi

La Tuillière, F-01300 Massignieu-de-Rives (Ain) T: 04 79 42 12 03. E: info@camping-savoie.com

alanrogers.com/FR01040

This attractive and well cared for, family run site is ideal for those seeking an active holiday in a peaceful lakeside setting. This picturesque area offers wonderful opportunities for exploration by foot, bicycle, car and boat. Sample the wines and other local produce on offer. Of 120 pitches (electricity 10A), 90 are available for touring. All are close to the lake and many have wonderful views over the lake and beyond. The slightly sloping, grassy pitches are set on low terraces and are partly separated by hedging and trees giving some shade. Two raised teepees, with verandas and set on the lakeside, are a recent addition to the rental accommodation available.

Facilities

Two modern toilet blocks offer all necessary facilities, with provision for disabled visitors. Washing machines. Small shop, bar, restaurant and terrace (May-Sept). Bread. Swimming pool, play area with water features. Tennis. Play area beside lake. Grassy beach, pedaloes, canoes, surf bikes for hire. Bicycle hire. Lake fishing. Winter caravan storage. Free WiFi over part of site. Fridge and barbecue hire. Off site: Shops at Belley 8 km. Lac du Bourget (watersports, boat hire). Nature reserve.

Open: 11 April - 4 October.

Directions

Travelling south on N504 towards Aix-les-Bains bypass Belley and at roundabout (Champion supermarket) turn east D992 (Culoz and Seyssel). After 4 km. turn right over bridge, D37 signed Massignieu. Follow signs to site in 2 km. GPS: 45.76883, 5.76942

Charges guide

Per unit incl. 2 persons and electricity	€ 18.00 - € 28.00
extra person	€ 4.50 - € 6.70

Matafelon-Granges

Camping des Gorges de l'Oignin

Rue du Lac, F-01580 Matafelon-Granges (Ain) T: 04 74 76 80 97. E: camping.lesgorgesdeloignin@orange.fr

alanrogers.com/FR01050

This attractively landscaped, terraced site (English spoken) offers stunning views across the lake to the hills beyond. There are 123 good sized pitches, 120 for touring, which are thoughtfully laid out and separated by young trees and flowering shrubs. Most have grass and hardstanding. Forty-five have their own water point and most have 10A electricity. The reception, bar/restaurant and the pool complex are at the top of the site with a gently sloping road down to the lower terraces and lake. At the lowest part of the site is a large grassy area by the lake for relaxing. Twin-axle caravans are not accepted.

Facilities

Two modern, well equipped and clean toilet blocks with all the usual facilities. There are no facilities for disabled visitors. Washing machine and dryer (tokens). Bar and restaurant, takeaway and TV room (all season). Outdoor, heated swimming pool, paddling pool and new lazy river (1/6-30/9). Play and sports areas. Pétanque. Swimming, fishing and boating on the lake (no motorboats). Free WiFi over part of site. Off site: Matafelon 800 m. Golf 2 km. Oyonnax with range of shops, market, restaurants 10 km.

Open: 15 April - 30 September.

Directions

Matafelon is 40 km. east of Bourg-en-Bresse. Leave autoroute A404 at Nantua, exit 9 and turn right towards D18 road and continue to Matafelon (10 km). On entering village and opposite the Mairie turn left, signed camping, and descend to site (800 m). GPS: 46.25535, 5.55717

Charges guide

Per unit incl. 2 persons and electricity	€ 19.00 - € 29.00
extra person	€ 4.10 - € 7.10

Menglon

Camping l'Hirondelle

Bois Saint Ferreol, F-26410 Menglon (Drôme) T: 04 75 21 82 08. E: contact@campinghirondelle.com

alanrogers.com/FR26130

This is a natural, deceptively spacious and popular, family run site; you are assured of a good welcome. It lies in a beautiful valley, south of the Vercors mountains and the Vercors National Park, beside the River Bez. The 170 large to very large pitches, 118 for touring, are stony and slightly uneven (rock pegs advised). They lie in natural openings in woodland and some have views over the fields and hills beyond. In 2012, 53 new, large pitches were added, some with good views and 16 with a private bathroom. All have electricity (3/6A) and long leads are advised.

Facilities

Six large toilet blocks offer all the necessary facilities (16 private bathrooms). Good bar/restaurant/takeaway. Small shop, including bread. Excellent pool complex with toboggans, paddling pool, water games and river beach areas (1/5-15/9). Ample play room. River bathing. Club/TV room. Fishing. Football, boules, volleyball, archery. Multisports court. Bicycle hire. Organised events (high season). WiFi throughout (charged). No charcoal barbecues, communal available.

Open: 28 April - 15 September.

Directions

From Die follow D93 southwards and after 5 km. at Pont de Quart, turn left on D539 signed Châtillon. After 4 km. turn right on D140, signed Menglon. Site entrance is shortly on right just after crossing a small river. GPS: 44.68142, 5.44743

Charges guide

Per unit incl. 2 persons and electricity	€ 22.50 - € 41.80
extra person	€ 5.60 - € 10.25

Mens

Camping le Pré Rolland

Rue de la Piscine, F-38710 Mens (Isère) T: 04 76 34 65 80. E: contact@prerolland.fr

alanrogers.com/FR38230

Camping le Pré Rolland is a small, well maintained family run site on the outskirts of the little town of Mens. It is surrounded by beautiful mountain scenery making it an ideal base for nature lovers touring this little known region of the Trièves. There are 90 mainly level, good sized grass pitches, 80 for touring and all having electricity (10A). Some are delineated by flowering shrubs and mature trees and are quite shady, others are more open and sunny. The snack bar and bar, with terrace overlooking the pool, is a peaceful place to unwind after a day exploring the region. There is no on-site entertainment.

Facilities

Two well maintained and clean toilet blocks with all the necessary facilities, including those for babies and campers with disabilities. Covered area with tables, small kitchen and bunk room. Bar/snack bar. Adjacent municipal swimming pool, free (1/6-31/8). TV/day room. Playground. Bicycle hire. WiFi (free). Electric barbecues only on pitches, communal barbecue areas provided. Off site: Small town of Mens with range of small shops, bar and restaurant 500 m. Fishing 1.5 km.

Open: 1 May - 30 September.

Directions

From the A51 going south from Grenoble take the N75 towards Sisteron. After 50 km, at Clelles, turn east on D521 to Mens. On entering town turn right, signed site and 'piscine'. GPS: 44.814807, 5.7485

Charges guide

Per unit incl. 2 persons and electricity	€ 19.28 - € 24.98
extra person	€ 5.00 - € 8.50
child (3-12 yrs)	€ 3.50 - € 6.50

Mirabel-et-Blacons

Gervanne Camping

1175 avenue des 3 Becs, F-26400 Mirabel-et-Blacons (Drôme) T: 04 75 40 00 20.
E: info@gervanne-camping.com **alanrogers.com/FR26120**

This very attractive and spacious, riverside site has been run by a friendly family since 1965. There are 174 pitches, with 150 for touring (6A electricity), arranged over two sections either side of a road. The two parts are connected by a short underpass under the river bridge. One section is adjacent to the bar, restaurant and good pool with mountain views. The pitches are of larger than average size with some shade and are separated by shrubs and trees. The lower section, closer to the river, is less formally laid out with mature trees offering plenty of shade and with access to the beach area.

Facilities

Four well appointed, very clean toilet blocks including good facilities for babies and disabled visitors. Laundry. Good motorcaravan services. Bar/restaurant (1/5-20/9) with simple menu and takeaway service. Heated swimming pool (1/5-30/9). Small play area. Football pitch. Boules. Bicycle hire. Electric and gas barbecues only. WiFi over site (charged). Off site: Supermarket next door. Canoeing and bathing in adjacent Drôme river.

Open: 1 April - 30 September.

Directions

Leave A7 autoroute at exit 16 for Loriol. Take D104 then D164 bypassing Crest. After 6 km, at roundabout, turn left on D164A. Cross river into Mirabel-et-Blacons, left at roundabout, site in 200 m. GPS: 44.71110, 5.09015

Charges guide

Per unit incl. 2 persons and electricity	€ 19.20 - € 31.00

No credit cards.

Montrevel-en-Bresse

Camping la Plaine Tonique

Base de Plein Air, F-01340 Montrevel-en-Bresse (Ain) T: 04 74 30 80 52. E: plaine.tonique@wanadoo.fr

alanrogers.com/FR01010

This excellent site, ideal for active families, belongs to a syndicate of several local villages. It is a very well maintained, large site with 560 marked, numbered pitches, 400 with 10A electricity, 96 taken by accommodation and 70 seasonal pitches. The majority are of a good size, hedged and on flat grass, with shade in most parts. The site is spacious and broken up into sections by trees and hedges. One area has been allocated for eight teepees to rent, with cooking facilities. It is on the edge of an attractive, 235-acre lake with its own beach and adjacent public beach.

Facilities

Very clean sanitary facilities are in ten blocks and include some washbasins in cabins, baby rooms and washing machines. Motorcaravan services. Restaurant, bar (all season), takeaway and shop (July/Aug) next to site. Aquatic centre with five pools (no Bermuda shorts). Indoor pool (all season) and outdoor pool (25/6-31/8). Fishing and watersports. Minigolf. Tennis. Play area. TV room. Archery and bicycle hire. Fitness trail. WiFi (charged).

Open: 21 April - 16 September.

Directions

Montrevel is 20 km. north of Bourg-en-Bresse and 25 km. east of Mâcon. Site is on D28 500 m. east of town towards Etrez. GPS: 46.33972, 5.13592

Charges guide

Per unit incl. 2 persons and electricity	€ 25.20 - € 30.70
extra person	€ 6.10 - € 7.30
child (3-7 yrs)	€ 4.20 - € 4.70

Neydens

Sites et Paysages la Colombière

Saint Julien-en-Genevois, F-74160 Neydens (Haute-Savoie) T: 04 50 35 13 14. E: la.colombiere@wanadoo.fr

alanrogers.com/FR74060

La Colombière, a family owned site, is on the edge of the small village of Neydens, a few minutes from the A40 autoroute and only a short drive from Geneva. It is an attractive site with 117 pitches (10/16A electricity), all reasonably level and separated by fruit trees, flowering shrubs and hedges. Forty-one new pitches and a toilet block have recently been added in an attractive, landscaped field. Neydens makes a good base for visiting Geneva and the region around the lake. It is a very pleasant, friendly site where you may drop in for a night stop – and stay for several days! The site is open all year for motorcaravans and suitable caravans. There are views to the east and west of the mountain ridges. M. Bussat owns a small vineyard close to the site, has the wine made in Switzerland and sells it in his restaurant. One of France's long distance footpaths (GR65) passes close to the site. The village of Neydens is the first stage for pilgrims from Northern Europe on the pilgrim route to Santiago de Compostella on their way to cross the Pyrénées at Saint Pied-de-Port. The site has a dormitory with eight beds for pilgrims or for anyone else who may need a bed. English is spoken.

Facilities

Three sanitary blocks (one heated) include facilities for disabled visitors. Motorcaravan services. Fridge hire. Gas supplies. Good bar/restaurant (all season) and terrace overlooking the pool (1/5-15/9). New heated, indoor pool, spa pool and jacuzzi. Games room. Organised visits and activities (all season). Bicycle hire. Hire car. Archery. Boules. Playground. WiFi throughout (charged). Max. 1 dog. Off site: Fishing and riding 1 km.

Open: 1 April - 31 October.

Directions

From A40 south of Geneva take exit 13 and then N201 towards Annecy. After 2 km. turn left into village of Neydens and follow campsite signs to site in just over 1 km. GPS: 46.1201, 6.10552

Charges guide

Per unit incl. 2 persons and electricity (6A)	€ 24.00 - € 41.00
extra person	€ 5.00 - € 6.00
child (3-16 yrs)	€ 3.00 - € 5.00

Neyrac-les-Bains

Sites et Paysages la Plage

Neyrac-les-Bains, F-07380 Aubenas (Ardèche) T: 04 75 36 40 59. E: contact@lecampingdelaplage.com
alanrogers.com/FR07570

A great deal of care and attention to detail has gone into developing this compact site and its superb facilities. Of its 45 pitches, only 12 are available for camping and advance booking is essential. The site is beautifully landscaped with flora and fauna and the facilities are sympathetically incorporated into a former textile factory. It has a very attractive solar heated pool and sunbathing terrace, with bar and snack service, on-site shop, games room and library. The river is directly accessed from the site with a delightful bridge walkway crossing a waterfall and leading to a sports and picnic area.

Facilities

Modern sanitary facilities include superb facilities for disabled visitors although access around the site is quite steep. Comprehensive laundry room. Fridge hire. Microwave and oven facilities. Gas. Bar. Snack service. Shop. Solar heated swimming pool and poolside bar. Large games room, library and TV room. Pétanque. Play area. Multisports area. Entertainment and children's animation programmes. Fishing. Canoeing excursions with site pickup. WiFi (free). Off site: Thermal baths 700 m.

Open: 29 March - 23 October.

Directions

From A7 exit 17 take N7 (Montélimar) for 20 km. Turn west on N102 to Aubenas. Continue on N102 for 30 km. towards Neyrac-les-Bains. Cross river at Pont-de-Labeaume and site is 2 km, on left just before entering village. GPS: 44.6733, 4.2594

Charges guide

Per unit incl. 2 persons and electricity	€ 21.00 - € 40.00
extra person	€ 4.00 - € 8.00

Peisey-Nancroix

Camping les Lanchettes

Route de Boverêche (D87), F-73210 Peisey-Nancroix (Savoie) T: 04 79 07 93 07. E: lanchettes@free.fr
alanrogers.com/FR73030

This site is close to the beautiful Vanoise National Park and at 1,470 m. is one of the highest campsites we feature. There is a climb to the site but the spectacular scenery is well worth the effort. It is a natural, terraced site with 78 good sized, reasonably level and well drained, grassy pitches, with 69 used for touring units, all having electricity (5-10A). Outside taps are only available in summer because of the altitude and cold winters. For those who love walking and mountain biking, wonderful scenery, flora and fauna, this is the site for you. A fast-flowing river runs alongside the site.

Facilities

Well appointed heated sanitary block with roomy hot showers and washbasins in cabins. Facilities for disabled visitors (but site itself not recommended). Motorcaravan services. Restaurant, takeaway (July/Aug. and winter). Playground. Club/TV room. Large tent/marquee used in bad weather. In winter a small bus (free) runs to the ski lifts every 30 mins. Free WiFi in reception. Off site: Riding next to site. Shops and restaurants in Peisey-Nancroix 3 km. Golf 6 km. Indoor pool 8 km.

Open: 15 December - 1 May, 6 June - 12 September.

Directions

From Albertville take N90 towards Bourg-St Maurice, through Aime. In 9 km. turn right on D87 (Peisey-Nancroix). Follow a winding hilly road (hairpin bends) for 10 km. Go through Peisey-Nancroix; site on right 1 km. beyond Nancroix. GPS: 45.53137, 6.77560

Charges guide

Per unit incl. 2 persons and electricity	€ 18.50 - € 23.60
extra person	€ 4.40 - € 4.75

Pélussin

Sites et Paysages Bel'Epoque du Pilat

Route de Malleval, F-42410 Pélussin (Loire) T: 04 74 87 66 60. E: contact@camping-belepoque.fr
alanrogers.com/FR42030

This is a peaceful, family run site located within the relatively little known Pilat Regional Park, overlooking the attractive town of Pélussin. There are 70 good sized, slightly uneven and sloping, grassy pitches, of which 50 are for touring (electricity 6A). They are separated by trees and some hedging with most having some shade and some having good views over the valley below. The site is well maintained with an attractive new pool and new, large bar with terrace having panoramic views over the Rhône Valley and the mountains beyond. Large outfits accepted but care needed on narrow winding roads.

Facilities

Well appointed toilet block with facilities for children and disabled visitors. Laundry facilities. Motorcaravan services. Fridge available to hire. Bar (1/5-30/9), snack bar, takeaway meals (July/Aug). Outdoor, heated swimming and paddling pools (May-Sept). Tennis. Play area. Bicycle hire. Entertainment for young children everyday in peak season. WiFi throughout the site (charged). Off site: Fishing and riding 500 m.

Open: 1 April - 30 September.

Directions

Leave A7 autoroute, exit 10 Condrieu, 34 km. south of Lyon. Take N86 south to Chavanay, turn west on D7, climb to Pélussin. On entering the village bear left, site signed. Site on right in 1.5 km. Only recommended route. GPS: 45.4139, 4.69139

Charges guide

Per unit incl. 2 persons and electricity (6A)	€ 18.00 - € 27.00
extra person	€ 5.50

Pont-de-Vaux

Camping les Ripettes

Chavannes-sur-Reyssouze, F-01190 Pont-de-Vaux (Ain) T: 03 85 30 66 58.
E: info@camping-les-ripettes.com **alanrogers.com/FR01030**

A friendly welcome is assured from the owners of this spacious site situated in quiet, flat countryside near the pleasant small town of Pont-de-Vaux. The 2.5 hectare site has 54 large (100-400 sq.m), level, grassy pitches, all of which are available to tourers. Almost all are separated by hedges and most are shaded by trees. All but three have electrical connections (10A) and water. Because of its friendly and tranquil atmosphere, the site is popular with English and Dutch visitors alike, who choose to break their journey here for several days to or from the South of France.

Facilities

Two well appointed, small sanitary blocks contain a suite for disabled visitors. Washing machine and dryer. Limited range of food stocked and wine and ice-cream at reception. Two swimming pools. Play area. Areas for ball games. Board games, books. Free WiFi over part of site. Off site: Supermarket within 1 km. Restaurant 1 km. Riding 2 km. Amenities in Pont-de-Vaux 4 km. Fishing 4 km. Golf 15 km.

Open: 1 April - 30 September.

Directions

Leave N6 at Fleurville (14 km. south of Tournus). Go east on D933A to Pont-de-Vaux (5 km). In town turn left briefly onto D933 then take D2 east towards St Trivier-de-Courtes. After 3 km. turn left after water tower, then almost immediately left again (100 m). Site is 300 m. GPS: 46.44455, 4.98067

Charges guide

Per unit incl. 2 persons and electricity	€ 15.70 - € 19.00
extra person	€ 3.60 - € 4.00

Pont-de-Vaux

Camping Champ d'Eté

F-01190 Pont-de-Vaux (Ain) T: 03 85 23 9610. E: camping.champdete@wanadoo.fr
alanrogers.com/FR01480

This is a spacious, modern site adjacent to an excellent pool complex and wellness centre. There is also a small fishing lake just a short walk from the entrance. Just off the A6 autoroute, it is an ideal overnight halt, yet being close to the town and leisure centre, it is worth a longer stay. There are 134 pitches (106 for tourers), all with easy access and some hardstanding. All have 10A electricity (Europlug) and 30 are fully serviced. The mainly level, grass pitches are of varying sizes and partially separated by a variety of flowering shrubs and trees. Children's clubs are organised daily in peak season.

Facilities

Two sanitary blocks are modern with adequate provision. Facility for disabled visitors. Washing machine and dryer. Small shop (July/Aug). Bread to order. Playground. Volleyball. Pétanque. Play area. Boules. Fishing permits. Organised daytime and evening entertainment (July/Aug). No twin-axle caravans or charcoal/gas barbecues. WiFi over most of site (free). Off site: Modern pool complex with wellness centre (free to campers). Shops and Wed. a.m. market in Pont de Vaux, 5 mins. walk. Tennis 800 m.

Open: 1 May - 15 October.

Directions

Between Tournus and Mâcon leave D906 at roundabout in Fleurville (or J28 on A6). Take D933A east for 5 km. to Pont de Vaux. In town turn right, signed Base de Loisirs, follow signs to the site. GPS: 46.42878, 4.93365

Charges guide

Per unit incl. 2 persons and electricity	€ 17.00 - € 23.00
extra person	€ 3.00 - € 5.00
child (under 8 yrs)	free - € 3.00

Pralognan-la-Vanoise

Alpes Lodges le Parc Isertan

Quartier Isertan, F-73710 Pralognan-la-Vanoise (Savoie) T: 04 79 08 75 24.
E: camping@camping-isertan.com **alanrogers.com/FR73200**

Alpes Lodges Le Parc Isertan is open for both summer and winter seasons and can be found at the heart of the Vanoise National Park. It is located on the scenic GR55 long distance footpath. The 152 good sized pitches here are mainly flat and grassy and have 2/10A electricity connections. Many have fine views of the surrounding mountains, including La Grande Casse (3855 m). There is a small hotel located within the site and a restaurant, La Table des Lodges, which specialises in local Savoyard cuisine. The attached bar is a good place to relax after a day exploring the mountains.

Facilities

Three sanitary blocks are heated, airy and modern with washbasins in cubicles. Family bathroom. Facilities for disabled vistors. Bar/restaurant and takeaway (7/6-15/9 and 15/12-31/3). Heated indoor pool. Games room. TV room. Ski shuttle in winter (free). Play area. Fishing. Chalets for rent. WiFi in some areas (free). Off site: Shops 500 m. Riding 200 m. Bicycle hire 1 km.

Open: 29 May - 30 September.

Directions

From the west, leave N90 at Moutiers and head south on D915 towards Courchevel. Continue along route Pralognan (not Courchevel). The site is well signed in the village. GPS: 45.37642, 6.7226

Charges guide

Per unit incl. 2 persons and electricity	€ 18.20 - € 32.80
extra person	€ 5.00 - € 6.00

Privas

Ardèche Camping

Boulevard de Paste, F-07000 Privas (Ardèche) T: 04 75 64 05 80. E: jcray@wanadoo.fr

alanrogers.com/FR07180

This spacious, family run site is on the southern outskirts of Privas and aims to provide a warm and friendly atmosphere. The site has 166 large, grass, mostly level pitches, of which 112 are for touring units with 10A electricity and trees offering varying degrees of shade. It is a comfortable base for exploring the lesser known parts of the Ardèche with bus and coach trips available. On site there is something for all ages with a bar, restaurant, heated swimming pool complex and a multisports area with outdoor gym equipment. A welcome drink is offered each Sunday evening when details of the attractions in the area are given.

Facilities

Three toilet blocks, only two open in low season. Excellent children's area in the main block. Facilities for disabled visitors. Motorcaravan services. Bar (all season) and restaurant/pizzeria (1/5-15/9). Outdoor swimming pool (1/5-26/9) and covered heated pool. Boules. Play area. Trampoline. Multisports court. Miniclub (mainly 6-12 yrs; 1/5-11/9). Entertainment (high season). WiFi at the bar (free). Only gas barbecues are permitted.

Open: 11 April - 26 September.

Directions

From A7 (Loriol) take exit 16 towards Privas. At Le Pouzin use heavy goods route, D86, D22 then D2. In Privas at roundabout (Intermarché) look for signs Espace Ouvéze exit left and take 2nd left, signed site and Espace Ouvéze. GPS: 44.72611, 4.59845

Charges guide

Per unit incl. 2 persons and electricity	€ 21.00 - € 32.00

Camping Cheques accepted.

Recoubeau-Jansac

Camping le Couriou

F-26310 Recoubeau-Jansac (Drôme) T: 04 75 21 33 23. E: contact@lecouriou.fr

alanrogers.com/FR26340

Le Couriou is a family run site in the beautiful Drôme countryside, just south of Die. There are 131 stony and grassy, level pitches of varying sizes with 101 for touring (10A electricity). They are laid out on high terraces with superb views over the surrounding wooded hills, so not ideal for those with walking difficulties. The pitches are separated by some shrubs and a variety of trees giving some shade. Though the site roads can be quite steep, access is not difficult for large outfits. It has a large pool complex, terraced bar and restaurant (all open to the public) with views across to the Vercors mountains.

Facilities

Three adequate toilet blocks with facilities for babies and campers with disabilities. Washing machines/dryer. Shop, bar, restaurant/takeaway (1/7-30/8, or sooner depending on demand). Four heated swimming pools, toboggans, paddling pool. Multisport area. Boules. No charcoal barbecues. Communal barbecues. WiFi on part of site (charged). Off site: Fishing 1 km. Recoubeau 1 km.

Open: 1 May - 15 September.

Directions

From Die take D93 south for 14 km. Just before Recoubeau turn right. GPS: 44.658534, 5.407172

Charges guide

Per unit incl. 2 persons and electricity	€ 20.20 - € 33.00
extra person	€ 5.20 - € 7.30

Camping Cheques accepted.

Ruoms

Yelloh! Village la Plaine

F-07120 Ruoms (Ardèche) T: 04 75 39 65 83. E: info@yellohvillage-la-plaine.com

alanrogers.com/FR07250

This is a high quality campsite with full provision for families of all ages with a beautiful riverside location. La Plaine is quiet in low season, but in high season with all day and evening activities for both teenagers and adults, and a miniclub each day, there should be something for everyone! There are 217 pitches in total, of which 130 are for touring with 6A electricity. They are protected from the sun by trees with a high canopy making access easy. This is a young family site with lots of activities in high season, but if you prefer to spend time more quietly, many pitches are near the river and well away from the action centred around the pool and bar area. There are 77 pitches used for air-conditioned mobile homes.

Facilities

Three sanitary blocks, clean and modern provide all facilities under cover. Young children's toilet facilities. Good facilities for disabled visitors. Excellent laundry room. Fridge hire. Shop, restaurant, bar and takeaway. Heated swimming pool complex with good slides (all season). Gym. Games area and TV. Boules. Play area. Fitness room. Massage and beauty treatments. Activity and entertainment (high season). Miniclub (5-12 yrs). Fishing. River beach. Bicycle hire. WiFi over site (charged).

Open: 18 April - 14 September.

Directions

Site is 20 km. south of Aubenas. From Aubenas take D579 to Ruoms. 2 km. south of Ruoms take D111 signed St Ambroix. Site is on the left and signed. GPS: 44.427067, 4.335617

Charges guide

Per unit incl. 2 persons and electricity	€ 18.00 - € 47.00
extra person	€ 6.00 - € 8.00

No credit cards.

Ruoms

Sites et Paysages le Petit Bois

87 rue du Petit Bois, F-07120 Ruoms (Ardèche) T: 04 75 39 60 72. E: vacances@campinglepetitbois.fr

alanrogers.com/FR07360

Situated only 800 metres from the historic town centre of Ruoms, and yet within an area of trees and rocky outcrops, this site provides an ideal base for those wishing to explore this part of the Ardèche valley. The 110 pitches are of irregular shape and size and a mix of stone and grass, with 70 spaces for touring units, all reasonably flat and with shade. Situated high up on the side of the gorge, there are superb views from the luxury tents and chalets available for rent. A cliff path leads down to the river.

Facilities

Refurbished toilet block, older second block open in high season. Facilities for disabled visitors. Motorcaravan services. Bar (all season). Restaurant/pizzeria and takeaway (July/Aug). Heated swimming pool, covered in early season (1/4-30/6) and solarium. Slides and splash pool. Sauna and massage services. Pétanque. Play area. Games and TV rooms in season. Entertainment organised in high season. Mobile homes and tents for rent. WiFi in the bar (free). By local decree the use of barbecues is restricted to April, May and June. Off site: Fishing 600 m.

Open: 1 April - 30 September.

Directions

Site is 20 km. south of Aubenas. Frome Aubenas take the D579 to Ruoms. At first roundabout take exit signed Largentier and centre ville. At 'give way' junction, turn right and follow site signs (500 m). GPS: 44.46063, 4.3373

Charges guide

Per unit incl. 2 persons and electricity	€ 24.90 - € 37.00
extra person	€ 7.00 - € 7.50
child (2-7 yrs)	€ 5.50 - € 6.20

No credit cards.

Ruoms

Camping la Chapoulière

F-07120 Ruoms (Ardèche) T: 04 75 39 64 98. E: camping@chapouliere.com

alanrogers.com/FR07410

Camping la Chapoulière is a medium sized site, alongside the Ardèche river, some two kilometres south of Ruoms. Grassy banks allow easy access to the river with a deeper area for bathing. The site is in two areas: the upper level, above the pool, has chalets and touring pitches; the older, more established area is for touring pitches nearer the river, with some chalets close to the restaurant. Trees provide dappled shade. There are 164 fairly level touring pitches (no hedges) on sand and grass, all with 6/8A electricity. This site is a good choice for those who prefer to make their own entertainment, and many visitors return year after year, creating a lively community and a sociable atmosphere. The gym and wellness centre are popular, and some activities are organised in high season. It is a good base for exploring the medieval villages in this area.

Facilities

Modern and adequate sanitary blocks. Facilities for babies and disabled visitors in main block. Preset hot showers and some washbasins in cabins. Washing machine. Shop (July/Aug), bread to order all season. Bar (April-Sept). Restaurant (July/Aug and w/ends). Pizza takeaway. Heated swimming pool. Spa and fitness centre with Hammam and massage. Play area. Games room with large TV screen. Organised activities (July/Aug). Riding trips. River bathing. Fishing. Canoe trips. WiFi on most of site (free). Off site: Bicycle hire and riding 2 km. Rafting, canyoning and caving. Cycle and walking tracks.

Open: 28 March - 31 October.

Directions

South from Ruoms on D579, after 2.5 km. at a roundabout turn right on D111 signed St Ambroix. Site is shortly on right just beyond La Chapoulèire Restaurant. GPS: 44.431189, 4.32959

Charges guide

Per unit incl. 2 persons and electricity	€ 23.60 - € 38.60
extra person	€ 6.70 - € 9.30
child (1-13 yrs)	free - € 7.40
dog	€ 1.00 - € 3.10

Saint Alban-Auriolles

Sunêlia le Ranc Davaine

Saint Alban-Auriolles, F-07120 Ruoms (Ardèche) T: 04 75 39 60 55. E: camping.ranc.davaine@wanadoo.fr

alanrogers.com/FR07050

Le Ranc Davaine is a large, busy, family oriented site with direct access to the River Chassezac. There are 435 pitches with 87 for touring, all with electricity (10/16A) for which very long leads are required (some may cross roads). Most pitches are scattered between static caravan and tour operator pitches on fairly flat, stony ground under a variety of trees, some of which are quite low giving much needed shade. The site can get very busy for much of the season. A lively entertainment programme is aimed at young children and teenagers with an enclosed disco four nights a week until 03.00.

Facilities

Three fully equipped, very clean and modern toilet blocks include facilities for disabled visitors. Washing machines, dryers. Large shop. Internet. Bar/restaurant, pizzeria, takeaway. Swimming pool, covered pool (heated), two small square pools, slide and water park (no shorts allowed). Large play area. Tennis. Minigolf. Fishing. Activities and entertainment (July/Aug). Discos. Fitness hall (charged). WiFi on part of site. Off site: Canoe hire nearby for excursions down the River Ardèche.

Open: 4 April - 13 September.

Directions

Take D579 to Ruoms and 2.5 km. south of Ruoms, at roundabout, take D111. Just before Grospierres turn right onto D246, cross the river bridge (2.5 m. width restriction) and then left on D208 towards Chandolas and site. GPS: 44.4141, 4.2729

Charges guide

Per unit incl. 2 persons and electricity	€ 27.00 - € 51.00
extra person	€ 6.70 - € 12.10

No credit cards.

Saint Alban-de-Montbel

Camping le Sougey

Lac Rive Ouest, F-73610 Saint Alban-de-Montbel (Savoie) T: 04 79 36 01 44. E: info@camping-sougey.com

alanrogers.com/FR73120

In scenic surroundings, this site is only 200 m. from Lake Aiguebelette, the third largest natural lake in France. The 165 pitches (140 for touring units) all have 6/10A electricity and are set amongst many mature trees and well manicured hedges, giving plenty of shade and privacy. Most pitches are level, but some are on a steep hillside and therefore sloping. There are adequate water points around the site and there are 30 serviced pitches available. This is a very peaceful, quality site with good views of the surrounding countryside and mountains. The owner, Philippe Kremer, is very friendly and speaks excellent English. The restaurant and shop, open during the high season, are in a converted barn just outside the main entrance. The patio has terrific views across the lake. A traditional wood oven is used for pancakes and pizzas or there is a good choice of speciality Savoyard dishes. The lake offers many types of watersports but to maintain the purity of the water, motorboats are not allowed. The beach is free for campsite users and lifeguards are present in July and August (dogs are not permitted).

Facilities

Two identical sanitary blocks provide excellent facilities, washbasins in cabins, controllable showers, baby bath, 2 shower units with en-suite washbasin. Good facilities for disabled visitors. Separate laundry. Freezer. Shop (1/7-21/8). Bar and restaurant (open to public, just outside main gate). Small play area. Miniclub. TV room. Chalets to rent. WiFi throughout (charged). Off site: Fishing, boating, swimming, rafting at lake 200 m. Bicycle hire 3 km.

Open: 1 May - 16 September.

Directions

From A43 Chambéry-Lyon motorway, take exit 12 and D921 south towards Lac d'Aiguebelette. Follow signs to Plage du Sougey. Site is on the left just before the beach. GPS: 45.55582, 5.79081

Charges guide

Per unit incl. 2 persons and electricity	€ 15.50 - € 28.80

Saint Avit

Domaine la Garenne

156 chemin de Chablezin, F-26330 Saint Avit (Drôme) T: 04 75 68 62 26.
E: contact@domaine-la-garenne.com **alanrogers.com/FR26160**

This very spacious and cleverly terraced rural site lies in pleasant countryside hidden from the roads by its own wood, to the east of the Rhône valley. The very large pitches appear to form natural clearings under pine trees, creating a pleasant feeling of seclusion. A grassy lower area is more open and young trees give little shade. Although the pitches have electricity (6A) some long leads may be necessary. Fifty of the 112 pitches are for touring; all are level and grassy and many have their own water. The lower level pitches are easily accessed, while those on the upper levels have stunning views. The pool complex has an upper level solarium for serious sunbathing with a pleasant shaded area below. Good English is spoken by the friendly owners.

Facilities

Five small, but adequate sanitary blocks have washbasins in cabins and some facilities for children and disabled visitors (steep paths and terracing make only lower levels accessible). Washing machine. Motorcaravan services. Baker calls July/Aug. Small bar plus takeaway (July/Aug). Swimming pool, shallow pool and fun pool (heated June-Sept). Large sports area. Play area. Communal barbecues only. Some family activities (July/Aug). WiFi by reception and bar (free). Torches and rock pegs advisable.

Open: 10 April - 5 October.

Directions

Leave the N7 16 km. north of Tournon. Turn east on D51, signed Châteauneuf. After 15 km. at Mureils, turn right on D363, signed St Avit. After 2 km. turn left on D53 (site signed) and site entrance is shortly on the right. GPS: 45.20205, 4.95719

Charges guide

Per unit incl. 2 persons and electricity € 18.30 - € 33.80
extra person € 6.80

Saint Donat-sur-Herbasse

Camping des Ulèzes

Route de Romans, F-26260 Saint Donat-sur-Herbasse (Drôme) T: 04 75 47 83 20.
E: contact@domaine-des-ulezes.com **alanrogers.com/FR26330**

A neat and tidy family run site with a long season only five minutes' walk from Saint Donat and only 16 km. from the A7 and A49 autoroutes. There are 85 level, grassy pitches with 77 for touring; all have 10A electricity and are close to one of the nine toilet blocks. Occupying both sides of the access road, those in the older section are separated by hedging and a variety of mature trees giving good shade to most pitches. The hedges and trees in the newer section offer less shade. All are a convenient distance from the bar and pool. A site for the quieter family to unwind and to explore this lesser known region.

Facilities

Nine small toilet blocks with all the necessary facilities, some new, others to be refurbished soon. Facilities for children and disabled campers. Washing machines. Basic shop with bread to order. Bar, restaurant with simple menus and takeaways (15/4-15/9). Small swimming pool (8/5-15/9). Play area. Minigolf. Boules. Games/TV room. Free WiFi throughout. Gas and electric barbecues only.

Open: 1 April - 31 October.

Directions

Leave A7 autoroute (exit 13), take D532 east for 5 km. to Curson. Take D67 north 10 km. through St Donat. At a roundabout turn south, D53 and follow signs to site (1 km). GPS: 45.1192, 4.9927

Charges guide

Per unit incl. 2 persons and electricity € 20.10 - € 24.80
extra person € 4.80

Saint Galmier

Campéole Val de Coise

Route de la Thiéry, F-42330 Saint Galmier (Loire) T: 04 77 54 14 82. E: val-de-coise@campeole.com
alanrogers.com/FR42040

Val de Coise is a member of the Campéole group and is situated in the undulating landscape of the Massif Central, north of Saint Etienne. It is an attractive site located between the River Coise and a dense forest. Of the 92 grassy pitches, 30 are for tourers (28 with 16A electricity); a further 20 house mobile homes, chalets and fully equipped tents for rent. There is plenty of activity here in high season with a children's club and regular discos and karaoke evenings. This is rugged, dramatic country – ideal for walking and mountain biking. The nearby spa town of Saint Galmier is home to the Badoit water plant, a casino, restaurants and a number of art galleries.

Facilities

The single toilet block is central. It is kept clean and is neatly tiled and painted. Small baby room. Facilities for disabled visitors. Good motorcaravan services. Fridge hire. Small shop in reception. No bar or snacks. Heated outdoor swimming pool (15/6-15/9). Multisports terrain. TV room. Play area. Minigolf. Boules. Bouncy castle. Fishing. Activities and entertainment. WiFi (charged).

Open: 3 April - 27 September.

Directions

From St Etienne, head north on A72 and leave at exit 9a (Andrezieux Bouthéon St Galmier). Take the D100, then the D12 to St Galmier. Site is well signed from here. GPS: 45.59272, 4.33542

Charges guide

Per unit incl. 2 persons and electricity € 12.00 - € 22.00
extra person € 4.30 - € 6.30

Saint Gervais-les-Bains

Camping les Dômes de Miage

197 route des Contamines, F-74170 Saint Gervais-les-Bains (Haute-Savoie) T: 04 50 93 45 96.
E: info@camping-mont-blanc.com **alanrogers.com/FR74140**

Saint Gervais is a pretty spa town in the picturesque Val-Monjoie valley and this site is 2 km. from its centre, with wonderful views of Mont Blanc. It is 22 km. west of Chamonix and centrally located for discovering this marvellous mountain region. Nestled among the mountains, this sheltered, well equipped site provides 151 flat, grass pitches of a good size. About half have shade and there are 100 with 10A electricity (long leads may be needed). The remainder are on terraced ground and are used for tents. Third generation hosts, Stéphane and Sophie, will welcome you to the site and their passion for this area is infectious. An original Savoyard granary, converted into a superb two-storey chalet and finished internally to a very high standard, is for rent. This is a good site for large motorcaravans.

Facilities

Two sanitary blocks, one heated, with a suite for disabled visitors and baby room. Washing machines, dryer and ironing board. Motorcaravan services. Small simple shop (1/6-31/8). Bar/restaurant. TV room. Library. Excellent playground. Playing field. Herb garden for campers. Communal barbecue. WiFi (free). Off site: Fishing 100 m. Bicycle hire 1 km. Skiing 2.5 km. Riding 7 km. Golf 15 km.

Open: 18 May - 20 September.

Directions

From St Gervais take D902 towards Les Contamines. Site is on left after 2 km. GPS: 45.87372, 6.72008

Charges guide

Per unit incl. 2 persons and electricity	€ 23.40 - € 29.80
extra person	€ 3.00 - € 5.80
child (2-9 yrs)	€ 2.50 - € 4.60
dog	free - € 2.00

Saint Jean-de-Chevelu

Camping Lacs de Chevelu

F-73170 Saint Jean-de-Chevelu (Savoie) T: 06 59 49 83 94. E: campingdeslacs73@gmail.com
alanrogers.com/FR73080

This beautifully kept, small, family orientated campsite was recently acquired by a young, enthusiastic couple. It is surrounded by delightful scenery, not far from Lac du Bourget. Beside the site is a small lake which is fed by springs and has a small sandy beach ideal for swimming and playing around in small boats. The site has 120 average to large sized, grass pitches with 90 for touring. There are 80 with 16A electricity (long leads advised). They are numbered and marked by very small trees with a few having some shade. This site is ideal for families who are happy to make their own entertainment. This is a lovely setting and the site has some very good facilities.

Facilities

Excellent newly refurbished sanitary block with all necessary facilities including those for babies and disabled campers. Motorcaravan services. Very basic shop. Bar (1/7-30/8). Takeaway snacks (1/7-30/8). Fishing. Lake bathing. Organised walks and bike rides. Covered games area. Boules. TV room. Play area. Family entertainment in high season. WiFi (free). Off site: Bicycle hire 5 km. Sailing, golf and riding 10 km. Chambéry 13 km.

Open: 15 April - 15 September.

Directions

Leave A43 at exit 13 (Chambéry) and take D1504 (previously N504) north towards Belley. After Tunnel du Chat, continue into St Jean-de-Chevelu, turn right at roundabout (site signed). Site is just over 1 km. GPS: 45.69378, 5.82491

Charges guide

Per unit incl. 2 persons and electricity	€ 18.00 - € 30.50
extra person	€ 4.00 - € 6.00
child (2-7 yrs)	€ 3.00 - € 5.00
dog	€ 3.80 - € 4.30

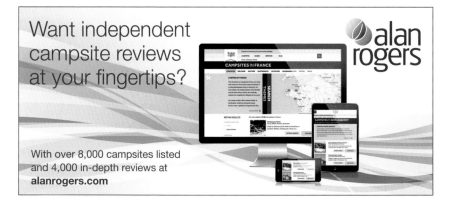

Saint Jean-le-Centenier

Camping les Arches

Route de Mirabel, F-07580 Saint Jean-le-Centenier (Ardèche) T: 04 75 36 75 19.
E: info@camping-les-arches.com **alanrogers.com/FR07280**

Situated behind the arches of a 19th-century viaduct, not presently in use, this ten-hectare site is a real delight, being divided by a small river, which is dammed for swimming, and a short causeway crossing. The owners have developed a site which shuns the razzmatazz of many holiday sites yet is welcoming and relaxing, making the most of its natural setting. There are 137 touring pitches ranging from small to very large, all with 10A electricity. Although one side of the site is on a gentle hill, all pitches are flat and almost all are shaded. A few have wooden terraces overlooking the river.

Facilities

Two refurbished toilet blocks and a newly built block are kept very clean and tidy. Baby room. Facilities for disabled visitors. Laundry facilities. Bread is available in high season from reception. Outdoor heated pool (15/5-31/8). Bar (15/6-31/8). Small restaurant (July/Aug). Play areas. Boules. Fishing. River swimming. Bicycle hire. Chalets for rent (plus 2 gîtes at the farm).

Open: 27 April - 14 September.

Directions

From Montélimar (20 km) take exit for Mirabel and right onto D458. Site is signed. Do not enter village while towing. GPS: 44.58756, 4.525766

Charges guide

Per unit incl. 2 persons and electricity	€ 14.00 - € 25.50
extra person	€ 4.00 - € 6.00
child (1-6 yrs)	€ 3.00 - € 3.50

Saint Jorioz

Village Camping Europa

1444 route Albertville, F-74410 Saint Jorioz (Haute-Savoie) T: 04 50 68 51 01. E: info@camping-europa.com
alanrogers.com/FR74100

You will receive a friendly welcome at this quality, family run site. The flowers, shrubs and trees are lovely and everything is kept neat and tidy. There are 194 medium to large sized pitches (110 for touring) on level, stony grass. Rock pegs are advised. All pitches have 6A electricity and 18 have 10A electricity, water and drainage. The static units are to one side of the site giving the impression that you are on a small site. There may be some noise from the adjacent main road. This is a good base from which to tour the Lake Annecy area and there is direct access to a 42 km. cycle path along the lake.

Facilities

Two very good toilet blocks, modernised to a high standard, have all the necessary facilities including some large cubicles with both showers and washbasins. Good bar and restaurant (26/5-31/8). Boulangerie with fresh bread daily (1/6-15/9). Traditional swimming pool (14/5-13/9) and aquatic complex (14/5-13/9). Bicycle hire. Miniclub. Some musical evenings. WiFi (charged). Off site: Fishing 300 m. Boat launching 500 m. Lakeside beach 2 km. Riding 3 km. Golf 8 km.

Open: 25 April - 19 September.

Directions

From Annecy take D1508 (previously N508) signed Albertville. Site is well signed on the right on leaving St Jorioz. GPS: 45.8246, 6.1758

Charges guide

Per unit incl. 2 persons and electricity	€ 21.00 - € 40.00
serviced pitch	€ 25.00 - € 44.00
extra person	€ 5.00 - € 8.50
dog	€ 4.00

Saint Jorioz

Camping International du lac d'Annecy

1184 route d'Albertville, F-74410 Saint Jorioz (Haute-Savoie) T: 04 50 68 67 93.
E: contact@camping-lac-annecy.com **alanrogers.com/FR74270**

International du Lac d'Annecy is a good quality, family run campsite within 500 m. of the crystal clear water of Lac d'Annecy which, in high season, offers a very wide range of watersports and other leisure activities. Passing close to the site is an excellent 42 km. cycle route running alongside the full length of the lake. The site has 163 level, grass pitches of a good size. There are 130 for touring units, all with electricity (6/10A). The pitches are arranged in pairs separated by a few flowering shrubs with mature trees giving some shade. Access is easy for large outfits.

Facilities

Very good toilet block with all necessary facilities including those for disabled campers. Bar/restaurant and takeaway (all season). Heated swimming pool. Play areas. Multisports pitch. Boules. Bicycle hire. Children's club and family entertainment (July/Aug). WiFi (free). Off site: Fishing and bathing in lake 500 m. Beach, boat ramp, windsurfing 1 km. St Jorioz with bar/restaurants and shops 1 km. Annecy with shops, bar/restaurants, museums, market and interesting old town 10 km.

Open: 25 April - 18 September.

Directions

From Annecy take D1580 south, signed Albertville, for 10 km. to Jorioz. Site is on the right 1 km. after traffic lights. GPS: 45.83084, 6.17842

Charges guide

Per unit incl. 2 persons and electricity	€ 20.00 - € 41.00
extra person (over 2 yrs)	€ 5.00 - € 8.00
dog	€ 4.00

Saint Julien-en-Saint Alban

Camping l'Albanou

Quartier Pampelonne, F-07000 Saint Julien-en-Saint Alban (Ardèche) T: 04 75 66 00 97.
E: campingalbanou@orange.fr **alanrogers.com/FR07210**

Guests are warmly welcomed at this small, very clean and attractive site. It is situated in the beautiful northern Ardèche region with its many old villages, markets and museums – well worth exploring. The site's 87 large, level and easily accessible pitches (84 for touring) are in groups separated by tall hedges, all with electricity (10A). An attractive modern building houses the reception and a small bar with a terrace. Snacks and bread are available to order. In high season a few games are organised for younger children but the emphasis here is on a quiet and peaceful site.

Facilities

Refurbished toilet block has all the necessary facilities including those for disabled visitors. Motorcaravan services. Small shop. Bar and takeaway. Good heated swimming pool, paddling pool and small slide (1/5-30/9). Jacuzzi. Spacious play area. Area for ball games. Information and maps. No charcoal barbecues. WiFi (free). Off site: Fishing 1 km. Shops and restaurants in St Julien 2 km. Supermarket 5 km. Bicycle hire 10 km.

Open: 17 April - 30 September.

Directions

From A7 autoroute take exit 16 for Loriol, head west across the Rhône to Le Pouzin. At roundabout take N104, signed Aubenas, follow road up hill. Turn left in 4 km. just before St Julien. Site is signed.
GPS: 44.757194, 4.712611

Charges guide

Per unit incl. 2 persons and electricity	€ 22.50 - € 26.50
extra person	€ 4.50 - € 5.50
child (0-13 yrs)	€ 3.50 - € 4.00
dog	€ 2.00 - € 3.00

Saint Laurent-en-Beaumont

Camping Belvédère de l'Obiou

Les Egats, F-38350 Saint Laurent-en-Beaumont (Isère) T: 04 76 30 40 80. E: info@camping-obiou.com
alanrogers.com/FR38130

This extremely good and well maintained small Alpine site, with just 45 pitches, is close to the Ecrins National Park, with great mountain views. It is therefore ideal for walkers and cyclists looking to take advantage of the well marked trails. It has most things a good site should have, with its restaurant, heated pool and sitting room with TV and library. The welcoming owners will even supply you with breakfast. The views from the 45 terraced pitches are spectacular and there is a wealth of activities in the area ranging from bungee jumping and high walkways across the lake to a more sedate trip by boat to take in the stunning views. Mobile homes are available to rent as well as two comfortable rooms.

Facilities

Two modern toilet blocks, one part of the main building, the other a prefabricated unit, are immaculate and can be heated. High standard facilities for disabled visitors. Excellent laundry. Motorcaravan services (€ 5). Small shop for ice-cream and soft drinks. Restaurant (May-Sept) with local speciality menu, high quality takeaway and breakfast. Heated swimming pool (May-Sept). Good play area. Small dog exercise area. WiFi on pitches (free). Off site: Fishing 5 km. Walking, cycling and mountain activities.

Open: 15 April - 15 October.

Directions

The site is just off the N85 (Route Napoleon) between Grenoble and Gap, 7 km. south of La Mure and is clearly signed on the left.
GPS: 44.876067, 5.837833

Charges guide

Per unit incl. 2 persons and electricity	€ 17.50 - € 28.20
extra person	€ 3.80 - € 6.00
child (2-10 yrs)	€ 2.40 - € 4.00
dog	free - € 2.00

Camping Cheques accepted.

Saint Martin-d'Ardèche

Camping Indigo le Moulin

F-07700 Saint Martin-d'Ardèche (Ardèche) T: 04 75 04 66 20. E: moulin@camping-indigo.com

alanrogers.com/FR07650

Le Moulin is a member of the Indigo group and is situated just 300 m. from the centre of Saint Martin-d'Ardèche. The site has its own river beach and is well placed for canoe trips on the Ardèche. There are 121 touring pitches here, extending over the site's seven hectares. The pitches have varying degrees of shade and most have 10A electricity. Rental accommodation includes eight modern wood chalets, 39 safari tents (many with a bathroom) and 16 Romany-style caravans. Amenities include a pleasant snack bar and a café. A children's club operates in peak season, focusing on craft activities and games.

Facilities

Three modern, well appointed sanitary units placed over the site. Snack bar/café. Pizza. Bread to order and local produce at reception. Heated outdoor swimming pool and paddling pool (April-Sept). New play area. Activity programme for children. Direct river access. Canoeing. Football. Bicycle hire. WiFi (free). Safari tents, chalets and caravans for rent. Max. 1 dog per pitch. Off site: St Martin 300 m. (shops, cafés, restaurants and weekly market). Aiguèze (picturesque medieval village) 3 km.

Open: 28 April - 26 September.

Directions

From A7 motorway, leave at exit 19 on D994 (west), then follow N86 signed Pont St Esprit. At Pont St Esprit take D6086 north and join D290 to St Martin-d'Ardèche. The site is clearly signed. GPS: 44.300272, 4.571171

Charges guide

Per unit incl. 2 persons and electricity	€ 21.60 - € 34.20
extra person	€ 4.40 - € 7.10

Saint Paul-de-Vezelin

Camping d'Arpheuilles

Lieu-dit Arpheuilles, F-42590 Saint Paul-de-Vezelin (Loire) T: 04 77 63 43 43.

E: arpheuilles.camp@gmail.com **alanrogers.com/FR42050**

Enjoying a good position on the banks of the River Loire, with gentle slopes down to a sandy beach, Camping d'Arpheuilles is a good choice for an active family holiday and the new owners are busy making many improvements. The river is wide and shallow here, resembling a very long lake, fed from the foothills of the Massif Central. There are 87 pitches, 76 are generous, slightly sloping, grass pitches for tourers, the majority having 6A electricity. Twenty are reserved for tents. Some pitches have good views over the river and canoes are available for hire.

Facilities

One central sanitary block is rather dated but very clean, with small preset showers, some washbasins in cubicles and some Turkish toilets. Separate facility for disabled campers. Washing machine and dryer. Small shop. Bread to order. Bar. Snack bar and takeaway. Swimming pool (1/5-15/10). Minigolf. Badminton. Games room (with billiards, table football). Playground. Barbecue and fire pit. Canoe and bicycle hire. Fishing. River bathing and beach. Canoe hire. Free WiFi in bar. Off site: Sailing. Windsurfing.

Open: 12 April - 30 September.

Directions

Leave A89 at exit 5 St Germain. Take D8 north (1.5 km) then D26 east 4 km. to St Paul-de-Vézelin. In village turn north onto narrow lane downhill to site in 3 km. GPS: 45.911615, 4.06595

Charges guide

Per unit incl. 2 persons and electricity	€ 19.10 - € 27.10
extra person	€ 6.00
child (3-7 yrs)	€ 3.00 - € 3.50

Saint Pierre-de-Chartreuse

Sites et Paysages de Martinière

Route du Col de Porte, F-38380 Saint Pierre-de-Chartreuse (Isère) T: 04 76 88 60 36.

E: camping-de-martiniere@orange.fr **alanrogers.com/FR38160**

Chamechaude, the 2,082 m. Eiger-like peak, presides benevolently over the 90 touring pitches at this beautiful, high alpine site open from May to mid September for the summer season. The large touring pitches, all with electricity (6A), have some shade and are slightly sloping. The site has a heated pool in the open air so that not a moment of the views is lost. This well run, family owned enterprise, set around a traditional Savoyard farmhouse, is a peaceful centre for walking, climbing, cycling or just soaking up the air and ambience. It is in the centre of the Chartreuse National Forest.

Facilities

Two heated toilet blocks, one at each end of the site provide excellent, clean facilities. Facilities for babies and disabled visitors. Laundry facilities. Shop (1/6-13/9). Bar (10/6-13/9) with snacks (July/Aug). Swimming and paddling pools (1/6-5/9; heated July/Aug). Play area. Indoor sitting area for poor weather. Paperback library (NL, IT, FR, UK). Off site: Restaurant at site entrance.

Open: 1 May - 13 September.

Directions

From St Laurent-du-Pont (north from Voiron or south from Chambery), take D512 signed St Pierre-de-Chartreuse. Site is well signed in the village (the road south from St Pierre-d'Entremont is not recommended for towing). GPS: 45.3258, 5.7972

Charges guide

Per unit incl. 2 persons and electricity	€ 19.90 - € 27.90
extra person	€ 5.30 - € 6.40

Saint Privat

Camping le Plan d'Eau

Route de Lussas, F-07200 Saint Privat (Ardèche) T: 04 75 35 44 98. E: info@campingleplandeau.fr
alanrogers.com/FR07430

This well cared for site is owned by a very friendly French family who speak excellent English. It is in the heart of the region, on the quieter upper reaches of the River Ardèche, just two kilometres from St Privat and surrounded by magnificent countryside. A nature trail leads to the river bank where it is possible to swim. There are 100 level, grassy pitches (75 for touring) with hedges and large trees providing good shade. Pitches are 100 and 150 sq.m, all with 8A electricity (long leads required on some).

Facilities

The toilet block is of very good quality. Some washbasins in cabins, good size, preset showers. Facilities for children and babies. Roomy facilities for disabled visitors. Washing machines. Small shop. Bar and restaurant. Takeaway with simple menu. Heated outdoor swimming and paddling pools (all season). Excellent multisports court. Fishing, boating, bathing in river. Play area. Organised family events in July/Aug and programme of off site events. No barbecues are allowed (communal area available). WiFi throughout (charged). Off site: St Privat 2 km.

Open: 30 April - 24 September.

Directions

Leave N304 northeast of Aubenas at St Privat. Near river bridge turn east on D259, signed Lussas. Site is on right in just over 1 km. GPS: 44.61916, 4.4321

Charges guide

Per unit incl. 2 persons and electricity	€ 19.50 - € 46.50
extra person	€ 4.00 - € 7.20
child (2-13 yrs)	€ 2.70 - € 7.00
dog	€ 2.10 - € 3.20

Saint Romans

Flower Camping Lac du Marandan

657 route des Marandans, F-38160 Saint Romans (Isère) T: 04 76 64 41 77.
E: contact@camping-lac-marandan.com **alanrogers.com/FR38250**

Lac du Marandan is ideally situated at the foot of the regional park of the Vercors. It has direct access to an inviting lake which has a temperature of 28 degrees at its shallowest point and is surrounded by a fine sandy beach. The resident manager will make sure you enjoy your stay. The site has 100 pitches (74 for touring, all with 10A electricity) from 100-200 sq.m. in size and located in a wooded area where old oaks will provide shade. Many activities are possible around the lake and the area itself also offers a rich variety of sporting activities and sightseeing.

Facilities

One modern sanitary block has free hot showers and excellent facilities for babies and disabled visitors. Washing machine. Shop. Bar/restaurant (all season). Tennis courts. Boules pitch. Playground. Canoe hire. Fishing. Accommodation to rent. WiFi (charged). Off site: Lakeside restaurant and takeaway 200 m. St Roman 2 km. Mountain bike hire and riding 5 km.

Open: 30 April - 13 September.

Directions

South of Grenoble, leave the A49 at exit 9 and follow the D518 towards St Romans. Then take the D1532, to Base de Loisirs du Marandan (signed). GPS: 45.103198, 5.292631

Charges guide

Per unit incl. 2 persons and electricity	€ 18.00 - € 30.00
extra person	€ 4.00 - € 5.50

Saint Sauveur-de-Cruzières

Camping de la Claysse

La Digue, F-07460 Saint Sauveur-de-Cruzières (Ardèche) T: 04 75 35 40 65. E: camping.claysse@wanadoo.fr
alanrogers.com/FR07940

Camping de la Claysse is an attractive small site run by a very friendly family. It is located in a natural setting in the heart of the Southern Ardèche countryside just on the outskirts of the small village of Saint Sauveur de Cruzières. It is an ideal base from which to explore the Ardèche Gorges on foot, by bike or in the car. The site has 58 pitches with 45 medium size (80-90 sq.m), level, grass pitches for touring, all with 10A electricity. They are separated by small hedges and mature trees offer varying amounts of shade. A restaurant and takeaway service is available at lunch and dinner.

Facilities

Two toilet blocks (one new in 2012 and heated) with facilities for babies and disabled visitors. Laundry. Bread to order. Bar. Restaurant. Swimming pool. Aquagym (July/Aug). Playground for children. Climbing wall. Mountain biking. Volleyball. Football. Boules. River swimming. WiFi over site (charged). No charcoal barbecues on pitches. Off site: Walking and cycling routes pass site. Village shop 500 m. Canoeing trips arranged. Riding 2 km. Barjac with Fri. market 8 km.

Open: 1 April - 15 September.

Directions

From A7 autoroute take exit 19 (Bollène). Go west towards Pont-St Esprit then D6086, D901 through Barjac to St Saviour-de-Cruzières. Through village on D901, site on left just beyond village. Do not take outfit off D901 in village. GPS: 44.300453, 4.250279

Charges guide

Per unit incl. 2 persons and electricity	€ 20.00 - € 30.00
extra person	€ 4.50
child (2-7 yrs)	€ 2.00

Saint Sauveur-de-Montagut

Camping Caravaning l'Ardéchois

Le Chambon, Gluiras, F-07190 Saint Sauveur-de-Montagut (Ardèche) T: 04 75 66 61 87.

E: ardechois.camping@wanadoo.fr **alanrogers.com/FR07020**

This attractive site is quite a way off the beaten track but it is worth the effort to find it as it is in such a spectacular and peaceful setting. This site has 106 spacious pitches (83 for touring with 10A electricity) laid out on steep terraces and many separated by trees and plants. Some are alongside the Glueyre river that tumbles between pools, while the rest are on higher, terraced ground nearer the restaurant, bar and pool. The main site access roads are quite steep but are made of good tarmac. A convivial family atmosphere is encouraged by the owners and entertainment is tailored to the guests' needs. There is weekly live music and an entertainment package for children in a room near a fenced play area.

Facilities

Two very good sanitary blocks include facilities for families and disabled visitors. Laundry facilities. Motorcaravan services. Shop. Cosy restaurant. Swimming and paddling pools (heated), adjacent bar, snack bar, terrace. TV. Bicycle hire, archery, fishing. Large sports field. Two adventure play areas. Comprehensive entertainment programme. No charcoal barbecues. WiFi (charged). Off site: Aquarock Adventure Park. Canyoning, climbing, river walking and canoeing trips organised.

Open: 11 May - 20 September.

Directions

From Valence take N86 south for 12 km. At La Voulte-sur-Rhône turn right onto D120 to St Sauveur-de-Montagut (site well signed), in centre turn left onto D102 towards Mézilhac for 8 km. to site. The road narrows in places with compensating wider stretches. GPS: 44.82842, 4.52332

Charges guide

Per unit incl. 2 persons and electricity	€ 21.00 - € 34.40

Camping Cheques accepted.

Samoëns

Camping Caravaneige le Giffre

1064 route du Lacs aux Dames, la Glière, F-74340 Samoëns (Haute-Savoie) T: 04 50 34 41 92.

E: camping.samoens@wanadoo.fr **alanrogers.com/FR74230**

Surrounded by magnificent mountains in this lesser known Alpine area, yet accessible to major ski resorts, le Giffre could be the perfect spot for those seeking an active, yet relaxing holiday. There are 212 firm, level pitches on stony grass (rock pegs advised) with 154 for touring units. Most have electricity (6/10A) but long leads may be needed. They are spaced out amongst mature trees which give varying amounts of shade and some overlook the attractive lake and leisure park. The small winter/summer resort of Samoëns is only a 15 minute, level stroll away. There is little in the way of on-site entertainment but there are many activities available in Samoëns and the surrounding area.

Facilities

Three adequate toilet blocks, heated in winter with facilities for campers with disabilities. Games room. Play area. Boules. Fishing. Lake swimming. Accommodation for hire. WiFi throughout (free). Off site: Leisure park next to site with pool (entry free summer), ice skating (entry free winter), tennis (summer), archery, adventure park. Paragliding. Rafting, many walks and bike rides (summer) and ski runs (winter). Snack bar and baker (high season) 100 m. Samoëns with a good range of shops, bars, restaurants 1 km. Grand Massif Express cable car 150 m. Bicycle hire 200 m. Riding 2 km.

Open: All year.

Directions

Leave A40 autoroute at Cluses (exit 18 or 19). Go north on D902 towards Taninges. In Taninges turn east on D907 to Samoëns (avoiding weight and width restriction on D4). The site is signed from the village. Park outside the entrance. GPS: 46.07731, 6.71851

Charges guide

Per unit incl. 2 persons and electricity	€ 17.55 - € 29.25
extra person	€ 4.30
child (4-12 yrs)	€ 2.95
dog	€ 2.35

Sampzon

Yelloh! Village Soleil Vivarais

F-07120 Sampzon (Ardèche) T: 04 75 39 67 56. E: info@yellohvillage-soleil-vivarais.com

alanrogers.com/FR07030

A large, lively, high quality site bordering the River Ardèche, complete with beach, Soleil Vivarais has much to offer visitors, particularly families with children. Of the 350 pitches, 110 generously sized, shaded, level pitches are for touring units, all with 10A electricity and many are situated beside the river bank. During the day the proximity of the swimming pools to the bar and restaurant terraces make it a pleasantly social area. In the evening the purpose built stage, with professional lighting and sound system, provides regular family entertainment programmes, six evenings a week. An additional attractive pool complex can be used by guests located in a separate mobile home section beyond the beach.

Facilities

Modern, clean, well equipped toilet blocks. Attractive facilities for babies and children. Facilities for campers with disabilities. Washing machines, dryers. Motorcaravan services. Small supermarket. Bar/restaurant (all season). Takeaways and pizzas in high season (cooked in a wood-burning oven). Heated pool complexes and paddling pool. Water polo. Aquarobics. Fishing. Boules. Archery. Bicycle and canoe hire. River bathing. Entertainment programme (June-Aug). WiFi near bars (free).

Open: 3 April - 13 September.

Directions

From Aubenas take the D579 (Ruoms). 4 km. south of Ruoms take the D161 (Sampzon). Cross river bridge at traffic lights and site is on the right. GPS: 44.42917, 4.35531

Charges guide

Per unit incl. 2 persons and electricity	€ 18.00 - € 51.00
extra person	€ 6.00 - € 8.00

No credit cards.

Sampzon

RCN la Bastide en Ardèche

Route d'Alès (D111), Sampzon, F-07120 Ruoms (Ardèche) T: 04 75 39 64 72. E: bastide@rcn.fr

alanrogers.com/FR07080

You are assured of a warm welcome at this site and much recent attention has been paid to the layout of the park with floral areas around the buildings and the separation of rented accommodation and touring pitches. There are 300 good sized, level, grassy pitches marked out by trees giving plenty of shade. There are 260 for touring units, all with 6A electricity and 86 with full services. Canoe trips can be arranged and annually a large section of the river bank next to the site is cleared of boulders and sand put down. Security patrols ensure quiet nights. There is an emphasis on families and there is good entertainment and activities to suit all.

Facilities

A large and impressive, central sanitary block includes a designated children's area. Two further well equipped toilet blocks, one new and one refurbished, with baby room and facilities for disabled visitors. Shop, attractive restaurant and bar. Heated swimming pool. Play area. Tennis. Fishing. Organised activities. Recreation room. Area for teenagers. Bicycle hire. River beach (July/Aug). WiFi over site (charged). No charcoal barbecues.

Open: 28 March - 26 September.

Directions

Site is 20 km. south of Aubenas. From Aubenas take D579 to Ruoms. 2.5 km. south of Ruoms, at roundabout, take D111. After 1 km. cross river bridge and site is 200 m. on the left. GPS: 44.42292, 4.32162

Charges guide

Per unit incl. 2 persons and electricity	€ 19.00 - € 52.50

No credit cards.

Sampzon

Flower Camping le Riviera

3319 route du Rocher, F-07120 Sampzon (Ardèche) T: 04 75 39 67 57. E: leriviera@wanadoo.fr

alanrogers.com/FR07400

This well organised, family run and orientated site is situated beside the River Ardèche not far from Vallon-Pont-d'Arc. There are 176 pitches in total with 114 of varying size for touring units, although access to certain pitches may prove difficult for larger units. Separated by hedges and trees, pitches have varying degrees of shade and 10A electricity connections. The site's facilities are of a high standard and it has a pleasant and welcoming atmosphere. In high season, day and evening activities are laid on for all the family. The site has a sandy beach by the river with opportunities for fishing and canoeing.

Facilities

Two modern toilet blocks have cubicles with washbasins, showers, baby room and excellent facilities for disabled visitors. Washing machines and dryer. Bar, restaurant with covered terrace, takeaway (1/5-10/9). Shop (July/Aug). Heated swimming and paddling pools. Play area. Multisports pitch. Bicycle and canoe hire (July/Aug). Fishing. Riding. River beach (July/Aug). WiFi throughout.

Open: 13 April - 22 September.

Directions

From Aubenas take D579 (Ruoms). 4 km. south of Ruoms, take D161 (Sampzon). Cross river bridge at traffic lights. Site on left. GPS: 44.42838, 4.35527

Charges guide

Per unit incl. 2 persons and electricity (10A)	€ 15.00 - € 44.50
extra person	€ 5.50 - € 8.50
child (under 7 yrs)	€ 4.50 - € 7.50

Sciez

Camping le Chatelet

658 chemin des Hutins Vieux, F-74140 Sciez (Haute-Savoie) T: 04 50 72 52 60.

E: info@camping-chatelet.com **alanrogers.com/FR74480**

Le Chatelet is a 3.5-acre site nestling in the Alps and close to the shore of Lake Geneva. This is an ideal location for visitors who enjoy water-based activities and sports, in addition to discovering the wealth of local culture. Close to the small town of Sciez, the site is just a five-minute walk away from the beach and the marina. There are 147 flat, grassy pitches (95 sq.m. on average), 45 for touring units, the remainder occupied by 12 chalets for rent and 86 residential mobile homes. All have 10A electricity. The site owner works hard to maintain high ecological standards, for example with solar heating and waste recycling initiatives.

Facilities

The two toilet blocks are modern and well maintained with facilities for children and disabled visitors. Washing machine and dryer. Motorcaravan services. Adventure playground (3-12 yrs). Bouncy castle. Boules. Mountain bike hire. Evenings organised in high season. Chalets for rent. WiFi in some parts (charged). Off site: Restaurants. Fishing and local diving school at lake 300 m. Riding 2 km. Thonon-Les-Bains 5 km. Golf 15 km.

Open: 1 April - 25 October.

Directions

From Thonon-les-Bains, follow signs for Geneva and join D1005. In four-lane section (ave de Bonnatrait) take slip road on right signed Renouillère, le Lac then turn left onto Chemin des Viex Hutins. Site is on right in 300 m. GPS: 46.340773, 6.396822

Charges guide

Per unit incl. 2 persons and electricity	€ 17.50 - € 23.50
extra person	€ 4.50 - € 5.80

Sévrier

Camping Rives du Lac

331 chemin des Communaux, F-74320 Sévrier (Haute-Savoie) T: 04 50 52 40 14.

E: lesrivesdulac-annecy@ffcc.fr **alanrogers.com/FR74250**

This attractive and well maintained site borders Lake Annecy with its own small private beach and mooring for small boats. The lake water is very clean and there are opportunities nearby for a wide range of activities both on and off the water. The site has 100 average sized, level grass pitches for touring units with 10A electricity. Trees give some pitches good shade. Occasional activities are organised, but this a good base for those who are seeking a more relaxed site and are happy to organise their own programme. A water taxi direct from the site makes twice weekly trips for Annecy market.

Facilities

A new, modern toilet block provides excellent facilities for all, including for campers with disabilities. Laundry facilities. Lake fishing, bathing and boating. Bicycle hire. Boules. Communal barbecue. Charcoal barbecues are not permitted. WiFi throughout (free). Off site: Cycle track of 20 km, almost the length of the lake, passes next to site. Riding, fishing and windsurfing 500 m.

Open: 28 March - 27 September.

Directions

Leave N508 6 km. south of Annecy at Sévrier. Turn left just beyond Lidl supermarket on the C3, signed Grand Prés. Follow site signs to site in 800 m. GPS: 45.84802, 6.15138

Charges guide

Per unit incl. 2 persons and electricity	€ 22.80 - € 28.50

Camping Cheques accepted.

Talloires

Camping la Chapelle Saint Claude

125 rue du Ponton, Angon, F-74290 Talloires (Haute-Savoie) T: 04 50 60 36 97.

E: contact@lachapellesaintclaude.com **alanrogers.com/FR74310**

La Chapelle Saint Claude is an attractively located site with direct access to Lake Annecy. The site can be found on the eastern shore of the lake, close to the pretty town of Talloires. There are 110 pitches here, many of which have fine views across the lake. All have electrical connections (10A). A number of chalets are available for rent. A private beach is available (with beach volleyball) and a larger, gently shelving public beach is around 200 m. distant. Boats can be moored on site but these must be booked beforehand (additional charges are applicable).

Facilities

Toilet facilities, in a modern block, are adequate and well maintained. Excellent facilities for children and disabled visitors. Bar and takeaway (July/Aug). Morning bread delivery. Direct lake access. Fishing. Beach volleyball. Playground. Activity and entertainment programme (July/Aug). Children's club. Chalets for rent. Limited WiFi (charged). Fishing. Off site: Public beach and several restaurants 200 m. Supermarket 1 km. Bicycle hire 1 km. Golf and riding 5 km. Annecy 15 km.

Open: 11 April - 27 September.

Directions

Approaching from the north (Annecy), take the D909 along the eastern shores of the lake and continue to Talloires. Drive through Talloires towards Faverges and continue as far as Angon. Site is well signed from here. GPS: 45.825869, 6.220526

Charges guide

Per unit incl. 2 persons and electricity	€ 20.00 - € 30.00
extra person	€ 4.00 - € 7.00

No credit cards.

Thonon-les-Bains

Camping Saint Disdille

117 avenue de Saint Disdille, F-74200 Thonon-les-Bains (Haute-Savoie) T: 04 50 71 14 11.
E: camping@disdille.com **alanrogers.com/FR74220**

Saint-Disdille is situated 300 m. from the beautiful Lake Geneva and the famous spa towns of Thonon-les-Bains, which can be reached on a bus that passes the site, and Evian-les-Bains. There are 297 large, level touring pitches on stone and rough grass (rock pegs are essential). Large trees give some shade. Those reserved for touring have 10A electricity and are scattered amongst mobile homes and permanent weekender caravans and can be some distance from the facilities situated by the entrance. The site is ideally placed for the large range of watersports in the area, and Switzerland is easily accessible by car, bus, train or boat.

Facilities

Five adequate toilet blocks. Shop. Bar with TV, restaurant and takeaway (all 1/4-30/9). Diving and rafting clubs. Play area with bouncy castle. Multisports court. Boules. Games room with pool table. Tennis court. Beach volleyball. Bicycle hire. Internet and WiFi (free in reception). Off site: Small lakeside public beach, nature reserve and disco 300 m. Fishing 500 m. Open-air pool 1 km. Boat ramp, windsurfing, bicycle hire 2 km.

Open: 1 April - 30 September.

Directions

From Annemasse take N5 to Thonon-les-Bains. In Thonon follow signs for Evian to Intermarché supermarket. At next roundabout follow signs to campsite and Parc de la Chataigneraie. GPS: 46.39765, 6.50335

Charges guide

Per unit incl. 2 persons and electricity	€ 18.00 - € 31.00

Tournon-sur-Rhône

Camping et Hôtel le Manoir

222 route de Lamastre, F-07300 Tournon-sur-Rhône (Ardèche) T: 04 75 08 02 50.
E: info@lemanoir-ardeche.com **alanrogers.com/FR07520**

Le Manoir is a small, family owned site by the banks of the Doux river, in a wooded valley. The 71 pitches (30 for tourers) are grassed and level and many have a gravel surface. Established trees shade the pitches and the site is attractively landscaped. There is a good sized swimming pool and adventure play area. During July and August, some on and off-site entertainment programmes are organised. There is direct access to the river from the site enabling fishing, canoeing and swimming. Some pitches may require long leads. The site is not recommended for large outfits. Good English is spoken.

Facilities

One sanitary block with reasonable facilities, which may be stretched in high season. Limited water points. Facilities for disabled visitors doubles as baby room. Laundry room. Motorcaravan services. Fridges and secure mobile phone charging. Small shop. Bar, snack bar and takeaway service. Outdoor swimming pool. TV room. Play area. Outdoor fitness area with machines. Pétanque. Activity and entertainment programmes (high season). Fishing, river swimming. Gas. Charcoal barbecues are not permitted. Chalet and hotel rooms available. WiFi.

Open: 7 April - 23 September.

Directions

From A7 exit 13 (Tain l'Hermitage) follow RN86 towards Tournon crossing river. Pass through Tournon, turn left at Sport 2000 roundabout (Lamastre) and take D532 under bridge. Le Manoir is 1.5 km. on the right. GPS: 45.06489, 4.79264

Charges guide

Per unit incl. 2 persons and electricity	€ 17.20 - € 24.70
extra person	€ 3.00 - € 4.70
child (under 7 yrs)	€ 2.00 - € 3.20

Trept

Camping les Trois Lacs du Soleil

La Plaine, F-38460 Trept (Isère) T: 04 74 92 92 06. E: les3lacsdusoleil@hotmail.fr
alanrogers.com/FR38060

Les Trois Lacs is a 30-hectare site situated on the edge of three lakes in flat, open country in the north of Dauphiné. The camping area is on one side of the largest lake with tall trees on one edge and views of distant mountains. The 212 good sized pitches, with 150 for touring units, are well spaced and separated by trees and hedges. All have 6A electricity. There is plenty of activity on offer for the whole family including fishing in one lake, swimming in the other two and, for the more energetic, roller blading. There is plenty of space around the lake for children to play.

Facilities

Two modern fully equipped toilet blocks with WCs for children. Excellent baby room. Laundry facilities. Small shop (May-Aug). Bar/snack bar and restaurant (June-Aug). Outdoor pool and paddling pool (May-Aug). Lakeside beach and water slide. Discos and entertainment in high season. TV and sports hall. Fitness. Minigolf. Archery. Bicycle hire. Riding (high season). Fishing. Electric barbecues not permitted. WiFi throughout (free).

Open: 2 May - 17 September.

Directions

From A43 exit 7 take D522 north. Turn left after 7 km. on D65. After 5 km. turn right on the D517. Site is 2 km. east of Trept with signs in village. GPS: 45.68699, 5.35191

Charges guide

Per unit incl. 2 persons and electricity	€ 20.50 - € 35.50
extra person	€ 4.00 - € 7.00

Tulette

Camping les Rives de l'Aygues

142 chemin des Rives de l'Eygues, route de Cairanne, F-26790 Tulette (Drôme) T: 04 75 98 37 50.
E: camping.aygues@wanadoo.fr **alanrogers.com/FR26240**

As the name implies, this spacious, family run site is situated by the bank of the river. Set in beautiful countryside and surrounded by vineyards for the famous Côtes du Rhône wines, this is a delightful site to unwind in and explore this picturesque region. There are 100 very large, stony pitches with some grass laid out in the natural landscape and separated by attractive shrubs and trees giving good shade and privacy. There are 92 for touring units (electricity 6A, long leads advised). A number of pitches back onto the bank separating the site from the river, which is accessible for sunbathing and paddling. The area around the site is fairly flat and ideal for cycling. For the more serious, Mont Ventoux is not far away.

Facilities

A single, large building provides adequate facilities including some washbasins in cabins. Family shower room. It is quite a walk from some pitches. Bread to order. Bar, restaurant and takeaway (July/Aug). Games room. Swimming and paddling pools (May-Sept). Play areas. Boules. Playing field. Only gas barbecues are permitted. WiFi throughout (charged July/Aug).

Open: 1 May - 25 September.

Directions

Leave A7 at exit 19 (Bollène) and take D94 towards Nyons. On entering Tulette (about 16 km) turn hard right onto D193 (site signed) and follow signs to site (2 km). GPS: 44.26518, 4.93149

Charges guide

Per unit incl. 2 persons and electricity	€ 23.50 - € 28.60
extra person	€ 6.10

Uzer

Camping la Turelure

Quartier Fontane, F-07110 Uzer (Ardèche) T: 04 75 89 29 21. E: camping-la-turelure@orange.fr
alanrogers.com/FR07920

Set on the banks of the rivers La Lande and La Ligne, la Turelure is in the heart of the Southern Ardèche with easy access to the many nearby tourist sights and activities. This friendly, family site has a secluded atmosphere being set in natural surroundings and away from the road. Of the 65 pitches, 45 are for tourers and are large, grassy and well drained. Some are open, though many have shade, and all have 10A electricity. In high season you can swim in a private stretch of the river. Canoes and fishing are also allowed. The approach track is a little narrow, so care is needed. Good English is spoken.

Facilities

Two modern sanitary blocks (one very new, which is covered rather than inside) with nursery area and a family cabin, and good facilities for disabled visitors. Washing machine (tokens). Fridge rental. Bar. Snack bar and takeaway (July/Aug). Swimming and paddling pools (15/5-30/9). Play area. Pétanque. River swimming (unsupervised; July/Aug). Fishing. WiFi (first 30 mins. free). Off site: Boat launching 10 km. Bicycle hire 3 km.

Open: 1 April - 31 October.

Directions

From north on A7, take exit 16 (D104 Privas). Continue through Aubenas on D104 (signed Uzer and Ales). Just after Uzer, 3rd exit on roundabout, still on D104, and after 100 m. turn left onto track through farm and vineyards. Follow signs to site and river (500 m). GPS: 44.50665, 4.32264

Charges guide

Per unit incl. 2 persons and electricity	€ 14.50 - € 27.40

Vagnas

Huttopia Sud Ardèche

RD217, F-07150 Vagnas (Ardèche) T: 04 75 38 77 27. E: sud-ardeche@huttopia.com
alanrogers.com/FR07475

This site only accepts tents. The gorges of the Ardèche are acknowledged to be among the most stunning tourist destinations in France, with the symbolic natural stone bridge, the Chauvet cave, and the charming town of Vallon-Pont-d'Arc. Just five kilometres to the south is Huttopia Sud Ardèche, richly planted with oaks, junipers and Montpellier maple trees. Its 171 spacious, grassy tent pitches have 10A electricity hook-ups and are divided into different areas to provide a more intimate atmosphere. There is a wide choice of rental accommodation on offer, including wood cabins, cahuttes and canvas and wood tents. Canoeing down the gorge, with or without a guide, is one of the most popular activities here.

Facilities

Five sanitary blocks with hot showers, private cubicles and family room. Washing machine. Shop selling regional produce. Bar, restaurant/pizzeria and takeaway (6/7-31/8). Breakfast service (July/Aug). Bread and pastries to order. Two outdoor swimming pools (one heated). TV/games room. Playgrounds. Activity and entertainment programme (July/Aug). Miniclub (5-12 yrs, 5/7-29/8). No charcoal barbecues. Fridge hire (€ 6/day). Bicycle hire. Off site: Vallon-Pont-d'Arc 5 km.

Open: 14 April - 17 October.

Directions

From A7, take exit 18 onto N7 (Pierrelatte). Follow signs for Bourg-Saint-Andéol, Vallon-Pont-d'Arc. In town, follow Toutes Directions, then Salavas on D290. Continue on route de Barjac for 3.5 km, then after metal bridge over stream turn left (Orgnac l'Aven) to site on left. GPS: 44.366839, 4.369712

Charges guide

Per unit incl. 2 persons and electricity	€ 21.50 - € 47.80

Vallon-Pont-d'Arc

Castel Camping Nature Parc l'Ardéchois

Route touristique des Gorges, F-07150 Vallon-Pont-d'Arc (Ardèche) T: 04 75 88 06 63.
E: ardechoiscamping@wanadoo.fr **alanrogers.com/FR07120**

This very high quality, family run site is within walking distance of Vallon-Pont-d'Arc. It borders the River Ardèche and canoe trips are run, professionally, direct from the site. This campsite is ideal for families with younger children seeking an active holiday. The facilities are comprehensive and the central toilet unit is of an extremely high standard. Of the 250 pitches, there are 225 for touring units, separated by trees and individual shrubs. All have electrical connections (6/10A) and with an additional charge, 125 larger pitches have full services (22 include a fridge, patio furniture, hammock and free WiFi). Forming a focal point are the bar and restaurant (excellent menus) with an attractive terrace and a takeaway service. A member of Leading Campings group.

Facilities

Two very well equipped toilet blocks, one superb with everything working automatically. Facilities are of the highest standard, very clean and include good facilities for babies, children and disabled visitors. Laundry. Four private bathrooms to hire. Well stocked shop. Excellent restaurant, bar and takeaway. Heated swimming pool and paddling pool (no Bermuda shorts). Massage. Gym. Tennis. Very good play area. Organised activities, canoe trips. Bicycle hire. Only gas barbecues are permitted. Communal barbecue area. WiFi throughout (charged). Off site: Canoeing, rafting, walking, riding, mountain biking, golf, rock climbing, bowling, wine tasting and dining. Vallon-Pont-d'Arc 800 m. Explore the real Ardèche on the minor roads and visit Labaume, Balazuc and Largentière (market Tuesday).

Open: 1 April - 30 September.

Directions

From Aubenas take D579 towards Ruoms. Continue south on D579 at Ruoms towards Vallon-Pont-d'Arc (western end of the Ardèche Gorge) at a roundabout go east on the D290. Site entrance is shortly on the right. GPS: 44.39804, 4.39878

Charges guide

Per unit incl. 2 persons and electricity	€ 33.00 - € 55.00
extra person	€ 6.50 - € 10.90
child (2-13 yrs)	€ 5.00 - € 8.60
dog	€ 5.00 - € 8.40

No credit cards.

Vallon-Pont-d'Arc

Camping la Roubine

Route de Ruoms, F-07150 Vallon-Pont-d'Arc (Ardèche) T: 04 75 88 04 56. E: roubine.ardeche@wanadoo.fr
alanrogers.com/FR07310

This site on the bank of the Ardèche has been in the same family ownership for some 30 years. During this time there has been constant upgrading and it must now be considered one of the best sites in the area. There are 97 touring pitches, all with electricity (10A) and quite spacious. Well tended grass, trimmed hedging and mature trees and smart tarmac roads create a calm and well kept atmosphere. The proprietors, M. Moulin and Mme. Van Eck like to welcome their guests and are available to help during the day – they are rightly proud of their well run campsite.

Facilities

Several small sanitary blocks include washbasins in cubicles. The main toilet block has showers, washbasins in vanity units, a baby bathroom and facilities for disabled visitors. Laundry. Swimming pools, paddling pool and separate children's pool. Wellness centre. Tennis. Boules, Fishing. Barbecues only permitted on communal sites. River beach. WiFi throughout (charged). Off site: Footpath to town 700 m. Supermarket in town. Bicycle hire and riding 1 km.

Open: 26 April - 18 September.

Directions

From Vallon take the D579 towards Ruoms. Site is well signed on left 400 m. from town. From west (Ruoms) site signed on right near Vallon town sign. If missed proceed to roundabout at entrance to Vallon, go around and return some 400 m. (as above). GPS: 44.40547, 4.37916

Charges guide

Per unit incl. 2 persons and electricity	€ 25.20 - € 51.00
extra person	€ 4.60 - € 10.10
child (0-13 yrs)	€ 2.70 - € 8.80
dog	free

Vallon-Pont-d'Arc

Mondial Camping

Route des Gorges de l'Ardèche, F-07150 Vallon-Pont-d'Arc (Ardèche) T: 04 75 88 00 44.
E: reserv-info@mondial-camping.com **alanrogers.com/FR07370**

Located at the head of the spectacular Ardèche Gorge, Mondial Camping is a friendly, family run site. Situated on the bank of the river, it offers the experience of canoe trips downstream with minibuses provided for the return. There are 211 pitches with 6/10A electricity and 33 of these also provide water and drainage. The grass pitches are an acceptable size with good shade and separated by some topiary styled hedges. There are 24 mobile homes and five tents available for rent. The site has a good sports provision and a pool complex with one pool for swimming, one for children and another with water slides. Mondial is close to Vallon-Pont-d'Arc with its many shops, bars, restaurants and weekly market. A full length canoe trip takes nine hours and can include an overnight stop. Alternatively, shorter trips are available and both can be organised from the site. The Gorges d'Ardèche has a route for those who prefer tarmac. A good wide road, the D290, takes you along the sides of the valley with numerous stunning viewpoints conveniently sited on your side of the road.

Facilities

Three modern sanitary units are tiled, very clean and heated in low season. Good facilities for disabled visitors. A fourth smaller block services the multisport court and outdoor heated pools and has facilities for babies. Full motorcaravan service point. Restaurant and takeaway, bar. Good mini-supermarket. Games room. Play area, organised entertainment for children and sports in high season. Archery. Canoe hire and launching. Fishing (licence required). Internet access. WiFi throughout (charged). Off site: Bicycle hire 500 m. Riding 100 m.

Open: 19 March - 25 September.

Directions

From Aubenas take D579 towards Ruoms. Continue south on D579 at Vallon Pont d'Arc take the Route Gorges d'Ardèche (D290). Site is 1 km. on right and well signed. GPS: 44.397313, 4.40107

Charges guide

Per unit incl. 2 persons and electricity	€ 26.00 - € 45.50
extra person	€ 6.00 - € 9.50
child (under 13 yrs)	free - € 6.50
dog	€ 3.00 - € 5.00

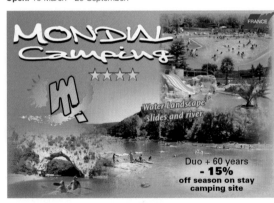

Venosc

Camping le Champ du Moulin

Bourg d'Arud, F-38520 Vénosc (Isère) T: 04 76 80 07 38. E: info@champ-du-moulin.com
alanrogers.com/FR38110

Le Champ du Moulin is in the narrow Vénéon valley at an altitude of 960 m, so the days may be hot but the nights are cool. It is open summer and winter and has 83 level stone and grass pitches, 65 for touring. They are delineated by a variety of trees that offer some shade and all have electricity (6/10A, long leads useful). Rock pegs are essential. When the mountain snow melts in spring, the river beside the site changes from a trickle to an impressive torrent, so parents and dog owners need to be especially vigilant. Large units are accepted but please book ahead.

Facilities

One heated, well equipped sanitary block with washbasins in cabins. Facilities for disabled visitors (key). Laundry and drying room. Motorcaravan services. Small shop in reception stocks basics. Chalet restaurant/bar with home cooking. Small play area. Sauna. TV room. Boules. Fishing. WiFi (free 5 h/day). Off site: Municipal swimming pools and flume adjacent. Bicycle hire 1 km.

Open: 30 May - 15 September,
15 December - 3 January, 6 February - 24 April.

Directions

From Grenoble bypass Bourg-d'Oisans on the RD1091, signed Briançon. After 3 km. turn right on D530 signed Venosc. In 8 km. pass the telecabin on left. Site on right in 400 m. GPS: 44.98596, 6.11986

Charges guide

Per unit incl. 2 persons and electricity	€ 22.10 - € 24.20
extra person	€ 5.20 - € 6.30

Vernioz

Camping le Bontemps

5 impasse du Bontemps, F-38150 Vernioz (Isère) T: 04 74 57 83 52. E: info@campinglebontemps.com

alanrogers.com/FR38120

This spacious, attractive and extremely well cared for site, between Lyon and Valence in the Rhone Alpes, is enhanced by a variety of trees planted by the original owner over 30 years ago. The 192 large, level and grassy pitches (75 for touring) are arranged in groups, partly separated by neat hedges, all with water and 10A electricity. Many of the pitches are used for mobile homes and chalets, with a group at the back used by weekenders. This is an excellent site for both short and long stays and the resident French director and his wife, who speak excellent English, have spared no efforts in ensuring that this continues to be a most attractive and comfortable site.

Facilities

Two toilet blocks, one recently refurbished to a high standard. Motorcaravan services. Shop (4/5-15/9). Bar, restaurant and takeaway (all 6/4-15/9). Heated swimming pool, children's fun pool and slide pool (all season). Several play areas. Minigolf. Tennis. Badminton. Electronic games. Fitness equipment. Bicycle hire. Family activities (high season). Small fishing lake. WiFi (charged).

Open: 4 April - 27 September.

Directions

Exit 9 on A7 south of Lyons. Continue for 7 km. on N7. Just north of Auberives turn left on D37. Follow campsite signs for 7 km. Entrance is on right 4 km. beyond Vernioz. GPS: 45.2531, 4.5542

Charges guide

Per unit incl. 2 persons and electricity	€ 18.00 - € 29.00
extra person	€ 6.00 - € 7.00

Camping Cheques accepted.

Villard-de-Lans

Camping Caravaneige l'Oursière

F-38250 Villard-de-Lans (Isère) T: 04 76 95 14 77. E: oursiere@franceloc.fr

alanrogers.com/FR38070

This friendly, family run site is within easy walking distance of the attractive resort of Villard-de-Lans. The town provides a wide range of summer and winter activities and therefore little is organised on site. It is ideal for those who prefer a peaceful site in a more natural setting. The 189 good sized grass and stone pitches are slightly uneven but with magnificent views over the surrounding mountains. There are 113 for touring, most have electricity (10A). A variety of trees offer some shade. Rock pegs are essential. A fast flowing, unfenced stream runs through the site, so children should be supervised. This is an excellent value for money site and a good base for those seeking a relaxing or active holiday.

Facilities

Clean, heated toilet blocks with all necessary facilities including those for disabled visitors. Ski store and drying room. Motorcaravan services. Cosy lounge with open fireplace, TV room, games rooms. Heated indoor and outdoor swimming pools. Play area. Boules. Trout fishing. WiFi (free). Off site: Bus to Autrans and Grenoble. Free bus to ski resorts (winter). Supermarket and bicycle hire 1 km. Skiing 2 km. Riding 4 km. Golf 8 km.

Open: All year excl. 23 September - 15 December.

Directions

Northwest of Grenoble, leave autoroute A48 exit 13/ 3A. Follow N532 to Sassenage, at roundabout take D531. In 25 km. at Villard-de-Lans, fork left (Villard Centre), site is shortly on left. Do not use other routes. GPS: 45.077583, 5.55616

Charges guide

Per unit incl. 2 persons and electricity	€ 22.00 - € 27.00
extra person	€ 4.70 - € 7.00

Villars-les-Dombes

Camping le Nid du Parc

164 avenue des Nations, F-01330 Villars-les-Dombes (Ain) T: 04 74 98 00 21.

E: camping@parcdesoiseaux.com **alanrogers.com/FR01110**

The Parc des Oiseaux is one of Europe's largest and most popular ornithological parks and can be found at Villars-les-Dombes, northeast of Lyon. The 190 pitches here are large and grassy, and are mostly supplied with electricity (6A). A range of wooden chalets and specially made tents are available for rent. On-site amenities include a swimming pool and a small bar/restaurant. The River Chalaronne runs alongside the site and fishing is popular. A children's activity programme is run in high season, focusing on nature and the countryside.

Facilities

Hot showers, private cabins and family shower room. Facilities for children and disabled visitors. Washing machine. Motorcaravan services. Fridge hire. Shop. Bar/restaurant (Apr-Aug). Takeaway (July/Aug). Swimming pool. Fishing. Play area. Activity programme for children. Bicycle hire. Free WiFi over part of site. Max. 1 dog. Romany-style caravans, wood and canvas tents for rent.

Open: 4 April - 1 November.

Directions

From A46, northeast of Lyons take exit 3 (Bourg-en-Bresse). Take N83 northeast to Villars-les-Dombes, 20 km. On entering town turn right to site (D904) which is well signed. GPS: 45.99723, 5.03047

Charges guide

Per unit incl. electricity	€ 20.90 - € 26.90
per person	€ 4.50 - € 5.50

Camping Cheques accepted.

Villeneuve-de-Berg

Domaine le Pommier

RN 102, F-07170 Villeneuve-de-Berg (Ardèche) T: 04 75 94 82 81. E: info@campinglepommier.com

alanrogers.com/FR07110

Domaine le Pommier is an extremely spacious, Dutch owned, first class site of ten hectares in 32 hectares of wooded grounds centred around a spectacular pirate themed water park. The site is steeply terraced and has wonderful views over the Ardèche mountains and beyond. Of the 611 pitches, 275 are for touring units, the rest used for a variety of mobile homes and chalets for rent. They are on flat, sandy grass, of a good size and well spaced. Separated by trees and hedges, some have less shade. All have shade and access to electricity and water and all facilities are of a very high standard. The site is not recommended for very large units.

Facilities

Four excellent toilet blocks, one with underfloor heating, provide all the necessary facilities. Comprehensive shop. Bar/restaurant. Swimming pool complex with exciting slides, paddling pools, etc. Boules. Minigolf. Large multisports area. Activities including games in the woods, archery, water polo and tug-of-war. Watercolour classes. Tennis. Soundproofed disco. Extensive programme of events on and off site. Entertainment programme only in Dutch. WiFi (charged). Off site: Villeneuve-de-Berg 1.5 km.

Open: 26 April - 6 September.

Directions

From N86 west of Montélimar, take D107 west (Aubenas), then N102 (Villeneuve-de-Berg). The entrance is adjacent to roundabout at eastern end of Villeneuve bypass. GPS: 44.57250, 4.51115

Charges guide

Per unit incl. 2 persons and electricity	€ 26.50 - € 46.50
extra person	€ 5.50 - € 10.50

Vinsobres

Camping le Sagittaire

Pont de Mirabel, F-26110 Vinsobres (Drôme) T: 04 75 27 00 00. E: sagittaire@franceloc.fr

alanrogers.com/FR26100

Le Sagittaire is a FranceLoc site, situated in this picturesque region with its Côtes du Rhône vineyards, lavender fields and medieval hilltop villages. It is only 2.5 km. from Vinsobres and 6 km. from Nyons, well known for its olives and its Provençal market. There are 297 level, grassy pitches with 100 for touring, all with 10A electricity. Most are separated by hedges and there are mature trees offering some shade. The hub of the site is a water park with indoor and outdoor pools, slides and toboggans, a restaurant, bar and small supermarket.

Facilities

Three excellent modern toilet blocks. Facilities for families and disabled campers. Motorcaravan services. Shop. Bar with TVs. Restaurant. Takeaway. Outdoor swimming pool, toboggan, slides, lazy river, cascades (1/5-30/8). Heated covered pool, paddling pool, jacuzzi (1/4-30/9). Games room (1/4-30/9). Cinema room. Small lake with sandy beach. Excellent range of sporting facilities. Play areas. Fitness room. Extensive activity programme (July/Aug). Fishing. Bicycle hire. Minigolf. WiFi. Cycling is forbidden.

Open: 28 March - 15 November.

Directions

Leave A7 at exit 19 (Bollène) and follow signs for Nyons (D94). Site is well signed on right just beyond Vinsobres (about 30 km) just before junction with D4. GPS: 44.32773, 5.07905

Charges guide

Per unit incl. 2 persons and electricity	€ 23.00 - € 40.00
extra person	€ 4.70 - € 8.00
child (under 7 yrs)	€ 3.50 - € 5.00

Vonnas

Camping le Renom

240 avenue des Sports, F-01540 Vonnas (Ain) T: 04 74 50 02 75. E: campingvonnas@wanadoo.fr

alanrogers.com/FR01490

Le Renom is an attractive, well maintained municipal site close to the picturesque village of Vonnas and bordered by an unfenced river. It is listed as a Station Verte de Vacances and was chosen as the first gastronomy town of France, thanks to the local chef, Georges Blanc. There are 80 pitches (69 for touring), 64 with 10A electricity. The pitches are level and spacious and are separated by neat beech hedges with a variety of mature trees giving some shade. Most are on grass but nine have hardstanding for motorcaravans. This quiet campsite is ideal for those prepared to make their own entertainment.

Facilities

Three toilet blocks have showers and washbasins in cubicles, facilities for children and disabled visitors. Washing machine and dryer. Motorcaravan services. Bar (1/6-31/8). Playground. Boules. Tennis. Football. Basketball. River fishing. No twin-axle caravans. Free WiFi. Off site: Outdoor swimming pool adjacent with flume and a small children's pool (1/6-3/9). Riding 10 km.

Open: 30 March - 29 September.

Directions

From A40 Mâcon-Bourg-en-Bresse autoroute, take exit 4 and D1079 westbound. Turn south onto D80. In Vonnas, take D96 westbound. Site is on right in 500 m. GPS: 46.22168, 4.98771

Charges guide

Per unit incl. 2 persons and electricity	€ 18.85 - € 23.60

Camping Cheques accepted.

DÉPARTEMENTS: 24 DORDOGNE, 33 GIRONDE, 40 LANDES, 47 LOT-ET-GARONNE, 64 PYRÉNÉES-ATLANTIQUES

MAJOR CITY: BORDEAUX

From the endless shimmering beaches and dunes, and the fragrant pine forests of the Atlantic coast to the historical and beautiful Dordogne with its gastronomic delights, it's easy to see the attraction of this popular holiday region.

The history of Aquitaine goes back many thousands of years to when man lived in the caves of the Périgord and left cave paintings at sites such as Les Eyzies and Lascaux. The ancient dukedom of Aquitaine was ruled by the English for 300 years following the marriage of Eleanor of Aquitaine to Henry Plantagenet, the future king, in 1154. The fortified villages and castles of the area bear evidence of the resulting conflict between the French and the English for control of Aquitaine, and today add character to the countryside.

This is a diverse region of mountains and vineyards, vast beaches, fertile river valleys, rolling grasslands and dense forests. The beaches of the Atlantic are renowned for their surfing, which was first introduced to Biarritz during the 1950s, and France's most complete long distance cycle route runs from La Baule to Biarritz.

Some of the world's most famous vineyards are around Bordeaux, the capital of the region. These are especially famous for their Médoc, Sauternes and St Emilion wines and most châteaux allow visits to their cellars and wine tastings.

Places of interest

Biarritz: a cosmopolitan seaside resort with surfing beaches and sea museum.

Bordeaux: riverside, streets and markets; art gallery; Grand Theatre.

Les Eyzies: pre-history museum and troglodyte houses.

Sarlat: attractive small town with preserved historic centre and medieval houses.

St Emilion: visit the castle ramparts or drink 'premier cru' St Emilion at pavement cafés.

St Jean-de-Luz: seaside resort and fishing village.

St Jean-Pied-de-Port: ancient city with citadel, bright Basque houses in steep streets.

Cuisine of the region

Local specialities include fish dishes: carp stuffed with foie gras, mullet in red wine and besugo (sea bream), plus cagouilles (snails from Charentes).

Canelé: a small fluted cake flavoured with rum and vanilla.

Cassoulet: a hearty stew of duck, sausages and beans.

Cèpes: fine, delicate mushrooms; sometimes dried.

Chou farci: stuffed cabbage, sometimes aux marrons (with chestnuts).

Confit of duck: duck legs preserved with spices and herbs.

Magret de canard: duck breast fillets.

Lamproie: eel-like fish with leeks, onions and red Bordeaux wine.

www.tourisme-aquitaine.fr/en
tourisme@tourisme-aquitaine.fr
(0)5 56 01 70 00

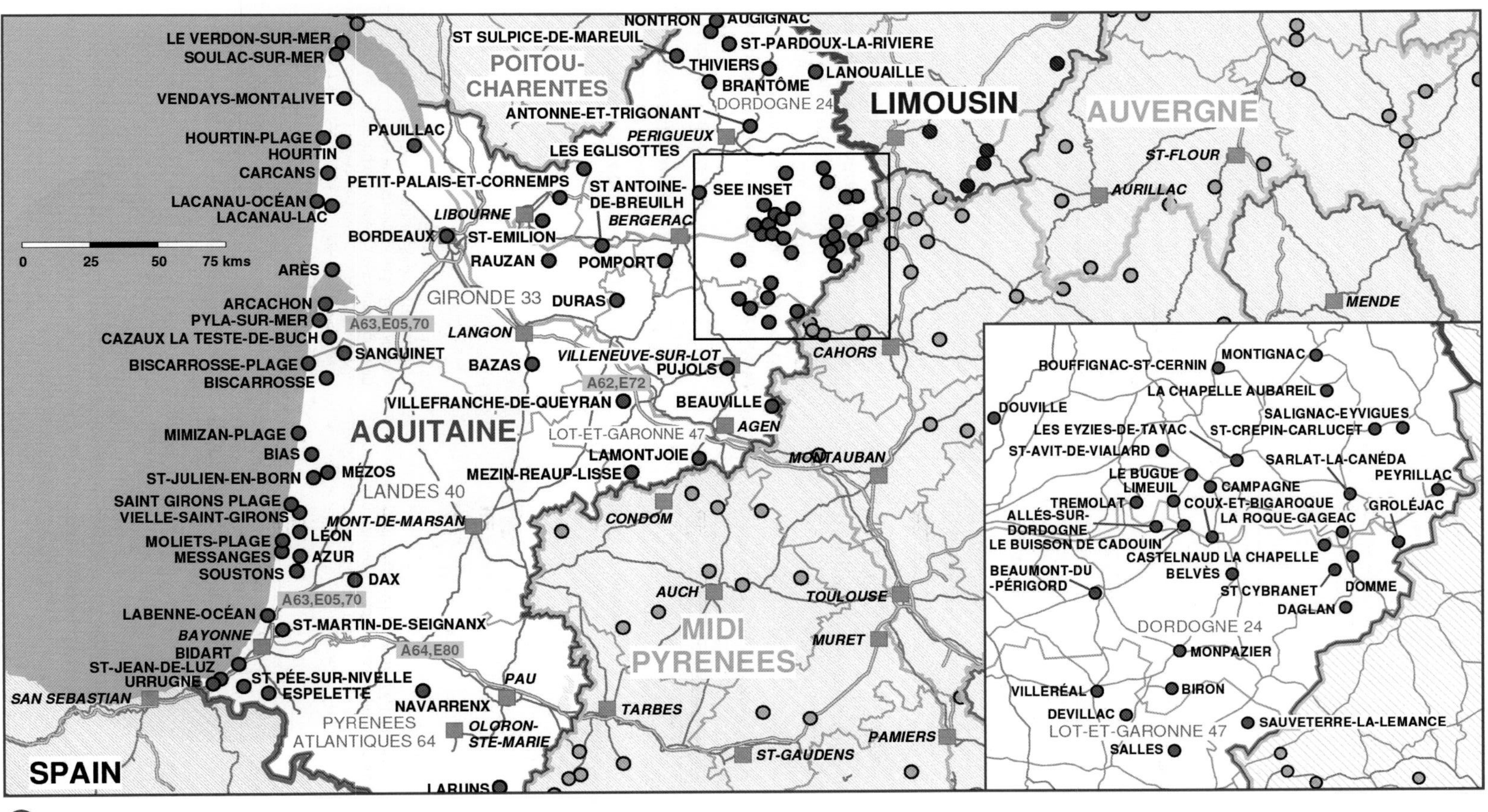
LE VERDON-SUR-MER
SOULAC-SUR-MER
VENDAYS-MONTALIVET
HOURTIN-PLAGE
HOURTIN
CARCANS
LACANAU-OCÉAN
LACANAU-LAC
0 25 50 75 kms
ARÈS
ARCACHON
PYLA-SUR-MER
CAZAUX LA TESTE-DE-BUCH
BISCARROSSE-PLAGE
BISCARROSSE
MIMIZAN-PLAGE
BIAS
ST-JULIEN-EN-BORN
SAINT GIRONS PLAGE
VIELLE-SAINT-GIRONS
MOLIETS-PLAGE
MESSANGES
SOUSTONS
LABENNE-OCÉAN
BAYONNE
BIDART
ST-JEAN-DE-LUZ
URRUGNE
SAN SEBASTIAN
SPAIN
PAUILLAC
PETIT-PALAIS-ET-CORNEMPS
LIBOURNE
BORDEAUX
ST-EMILION
RAUZAN
GIRONDE 33
A63,E05,70
SANGUINET
LANGON
BAZAS
VILLEFRANCHE-DE-QUEYRAN
AQUITAINE
MÉZOS
LANDES 40
LÉON
AZUR
DAX
MONT-DE-MARSAN
A63,E05,70
ST-MARTIN-DE-SEIGNANX
A64,E80
ST PÉE-SUR-NIVELLE
ESPELETTE
NAVARRENX
PAU
PYRENEES ATLANTIQUES 64
OLORON-STE-MARIE
LARUNS
ST SULPICE-DE-MAREUIL
POITOU-CHARENTES
ANTONNE-ET-TRIGONANT
LES EGLISOTTES
ST ANTOINE-DE-BREUILH
BERGERAC
POMPORT
DURAS
VILLENEUVE-SUR-LOT
PUJOLS
A62,E72
BEAUVILLE
LOT-ET-GARONNE 47
AGEN
LAMONTJOIE
MEZIN-REAUP-LISSE
CONDOM
AUCH
MIDI PYRENEES
TARBES
ST-GAUDENS
MURET
TOULOUSE
PAMIERS
MONTAUBAN
CAHORS
NONTRON
AUGIGNAC
ST-PARDOUX-LA-RIVIERE
THIVIERS
LANOUAILLE
BRANTÔME
DORDOGNE 24
PERIGUEUX
SEE INSET
LIMOUSIN
AUVERGNE
ST-FLOUR
AURILLAC
MENDE
BOUFFIGNAC-ST-CERNIN
MONTIGNAC
LA CHAPELLE AUBAREIL
DOUVILLE
SALIGNAC-EYVIGUES
LES EYZIES-DE-TAYAC
ST-CREPIN-CARLUCET
ST-AVIT-DE-VIALARD
SARLAT-LA-CANÉDA
LE BUGUE
LIMEUIL
CAMPAGNE
PEYRILLAC
TREMOLAT
COUX-ET-BIGAROQUE
GROLÉJAC
ALLÉS-SUR-DORDOGNE
LA ROQUE-GAGEAC
LE BUISSON DE CADOUIN
CASTELNAUD LA CHAPELLE
BEAUMONT-DU-PÉRIGORD
BELVÈS
ST CYBRANET
DOMME
DAGLAN
DORDOGNE 24
MONPAZIER
VILLERÉAL
BIRON
DEVILLAC
SAUVETERRE-LA-LEMANCE
LOT-ET-GARONNE 47
SALLES

Allés-sur-Dordogne

Camping le Port de Limeuil

F-24480 Allés-sur-Dordogne (Dordogne) T: 05 53 63 29 76. E: didierbonvallet@aol.com

alanrogers.com/FR24170

At the confluence of the Dordogne and Vézère rivers, opposite the picturesque village of Limeuil, this delightful and popular family site exudes a peaceful and relaxed ambience. There are 75 marked touring pitches on grass or hardstanding, some spacious and all with electricity (6/10A). The buildings are in traditional Périgourdine style and surrounded by flowers and shrubs. A sports area on a large, open, grassy space between the river bank and the main camping area adds to the feeling of space and provides an additional recreation and picnic area (there are additional unmarked pitches for tents and camper vans along the river bank).

Facilities

Two clean, modern toilet blocks provide excellent facilities. Bar. Restaurant with snacks and takeaway (15/5-15/9). Small shop. Swimming pool (heated in low season) with jacuzzi, paddling pool and children's slide. Badminton. Tennis. Beach volleyball. Football. Boules. Trampoline. Play areas. Mountain bike hire. Canoe hire. launched from the site's own pebble beach. Fishing. Free WiFi in bar area (charged on pitches).

Open: 1 May - 24 September.

Directions

From D51/D31E Le Buisson-Le Bugue road turn west towards Limeuil. Just before bridge into Limeuil, turn left (site signed), across another bridge. Site shortly on the right. GPS: 44.87977, 0.88587

Charges guide

Per unit incl. 2 persons and electricity	€ 15.00 - € 29.90
extra person	€ 4.00 - € 7.50

Antonne-et-Trigonant

Camping Caravaning le Bois du Coderc

Route des Gaunies, F-24420 Antonne-et-Trigonant (Dordogne) T: 05 53 05 99 83.

E: coderc-camping@wanadoo.fr **alanrogers.com/FR24410**

Located in the scenic Périgord region, 10 km. from Périgueux, le Bois du Coderc is a picturesque, part wooded, riverside site. It is ideally situated for visiting many interesting places in the area. The 45 touring pitches cover field and woodland, have 10A electricity and water points, and are separated by young hedging. This family run campsite has a calm, relaxing atmosphere. The River Isle runs through the site and is suitable for paddling but not swimming. The site is well placed near the historic town of Périgueux, with cobbled streets and delightful squares with restaurants, bars and shops.

Facilities

The single sanitary block is clean and well maintained. Preset showers. Baby changing area and the family shower are located in the room for disabled visitors. Laundry facilities. Small shop (fresh bread in July/Aug). Bar. Restaurant and takeaway. Games room. Heated outdoor swimming pool (1/5-30/9). Small play area. Bouncy castle. Volleyball. River beach. Fishing. WiFi (free). Off site: Riding 3 km. Golf 15 km.

Open: All year.

Directions

Heading north on N21 Périgueux-Limoges road, 2.5 km. north of Antonne-et-Trigonant turn right at Routier Restaurant (near km. marker 49). Continue along this country road following signs. South from Limoges, turn is on left 3 km. south of Sarliac-sur-l'Isle. GPS: 45.2194, 0.8636

Charges guide

Per unit incl. 2 persons and electricity	€ 16.40 - € 20.20
extra person	€ 3.80 - € 5.00

Antonne-et-Trigonant

Huttopia Forêt Domaniale de Lanmary

Camp forestier ONF, RD69, F-24420 Antonne-et-Trigonant (Dordogne) T: 05 53 45 88 63.

E: lanmary@huttopia.com **alanrogers.com/FR24415**

Lanmary, the first Huttopia forest camp, opened in 2013 has been carefully integrated into the landscape of the Lanmary National Forest. Some of the access routes in the campsite are quite rough and steep. Cars are only allowed on arrival and departure days. There are several designs of pre-erected tents and chalets, some on substantial stilts. Two chalets are adapted for disabled use (car access permitted). The touring tents can be pitched in defined areas and have plenty of space around each pitch, while other units must use the level pitches by the entrance.

Facilities

One sanitary block has facilities for families and disabled visitors. Three smaller blocks in the tent area. Laundry facilities. Fridge hire. Fresh bread daily and grocery corner. Bar/restaurant and pizzeria (July/Aug, weekends and public holidays). Heated swimming and paddling pools (14/4-18/9). Play area. Children's club. Pétanque. Evening entertainment. Mountain bike hire. Forest skills and nature activities. Internet in reception.

Open: 14 April - 28 September.

Directions

This site is approximately 12 km. northeast of Perigueux. From Perigueux take N21 and 2 km. after Antonne-et-Trigonant turn left onto D69 for 3.2 km. to site. GPS: 45.24247, 0.83072

Charges guide

Per unit incl. 2 persons and electricity	€ 21.30 - € 44.80
extra person	€ 4.70 - € 7.50

Arcachon

Camping Club Arcachon

5 allée Galaxie, B.P. 46, F-33312 Arcachon Cedex (Gironde) T: 05 56 83 24 15.
E: info@camping-arcachon.com **alanrogers.com/FR33030**

This campsite enjoys a position well back from the hustle and bustle, where nights are quiet and facilities are of a high standard. The 300 touring pitches are divided into areas for caravans, motorcaravans and tents and are on neatly formed terraces beneath tall pine trees. One third have electricity (6/10A), water and drainage. The site is quite hilly and the narrow roads that wind around it could possibly make it difficult for larger motorcaravans to manoeuvre and find suitable pitches. At night, wardens ensure that security and noise levels are controlled. A 1 km. walk takes you to the town of Arcachon.

Facilities

Three sanitary blocks include facilities for children and disabled visitors. Motorcaravan services. Laundry facilities. Fridge hire. Shop, bar, restaurant, snack bar and takeaway (all April-Oct). Swimming pool (1/5-30/9). Bicycle hire. Play area. Games room. Children's club and entertainment for all age groups (July/Aug). Electric barbecues only, communal area provided. Internet access. Free WiFi throughout. Off site: Beach 1 km.

Open: All year (excl. 12 November - 12 December).

Directions

Approaching Arcachon from Bordeaux on the N250 take exit for Pyla-sur-Mer (D217E1). Cross over bypass following signs for Abatilles. Pass golf club. At next roundabout follow signs for Camping. Take care as the route travels through suburban housing. Follow campsite signs. GPS: 44.651389, -1.174167

Charges guide

Per unit incl. 2 persons and electricity	€ 25.00 - € 56.50

Camping Cheques accepted.

Arès

Camping la Cigale

53 rue du Général de Gaulle, F-33740 Arès (Gironde) T: 05 56 60 22 59. E: contact.lacigale@gmail.com
alanrogers.com/FR33120

La Cigale is an attractive little site with charm and ambience where the owners extend a very warm welcome. Small and beautifully maintained, it is set amid a variety of trees that give some dappled shade. M. Pallet's floral displays add colour to the 44 neatly hedged, grassy touring pitches (100 sq.m. all with 6A electricity, 26 also with water and a drain). There is a small, unheated swimming pool and a paddling pool. The bar has a terrace where drinks, meals and snacks are served under the shade of large plane trees. Nine delightful chalets for rent are spacious, modern and very well presented.

Facilities

Well equipped toilet block includes a family room with two showers and facilities for disabled visitors. Laundry facilities. Motorcaravan services. Simple shop, bar, terrace, meals, snacks, pizza takeaway (all 24/6-10/9). Swimming and paddling pools (25/5-12/9). Small play area. Entertainers in July/Aug. Free donkey cart rides every Sunday in season. No charcoal barbecues. WiFi (free). Off site: Village centre 800 m. Fishing 1 km.

Open: 27 April - 26 September.

Directions

Leave Bordeaux ring road at exit 10 (D213) or exit 11 (D106) and continue direct to Arès. Turn into Arès following road to church square. Turn right following signs for Lège-Cap Ferret. Site is 800 m. on left. GPS: 44.77287, -1.14147

Charges guide

Per unit incl. 2 persons and electricity	€ 24.00 - € 41.50
extra person	€ 7.00 - € 8.00

Arès

Flower Camping la Canadienne

Route de Lège, 82 rue General de Gaulle, F-33740 Arès (Gironde) T: 05 56 60 24 91.
E: info@lacanadienne.com **alanrogers.com/FR33420**

La Canadienne is situated between Arcachon and Lège-Cap-Ferret, just 7 km. from the beach and 1 km. from the centre of Arès. There is direct access to 150 km. of cycle tracks. The campsite has 41 mobile homes for rent and 24 touring pitches, all with 15A electricity. Good shade is provided by tall oak trees. Swimming and paddling pools are centrally located, along with a shop, bar, restaurant and snack bar. In July and August, dancing, musical and paella evenings are organised, together with children's clubs and sports tournaments. Large units may have difficulty manoeuvring onto some pitches.

Facilities

Modern, well designed sanitary building. Shop, bar, restaurant, snack bar and takeaway (July/Aug). Heated outdoor swimming pool (1/6-15/9). Play area. Bicycle hire. TV room. Activity and entertainment programme. Mobile homes and equipped tents for rent. Solarium. Only gas or electric barbecues permitted on pitches. Communal barbecue area. WiFi near bar (free). Off site: Village centre 1 km. Riding 5 km. Fishing 7 km. Golf 15 km.

Open: 1 March - 15 November.

Directions

Leave the Bordeaux ring road at exit 10 (D213) and drive to Arès. Continue to the village centre and then follow signs for Lège and Cap Ferret. Site is on this road after a further 1 km. GPS: 44.77792, -1.1428

Charges guide

Per unit incl. 2 persons and electricity	€ 20.00 - € 40.00
extra person	€ 4.00 - € 8.00

Augignac

Manzac Ferme

Manzac, F-24300 Augignac (Dordogne) T: 05 53 56 31 34. E: info@manzac-ferme.com

alanrogers.com/FR24645

A gem of a small but spacious, family run, adults only campsite nestling in the beautiful Périgord Regional Park; you are sure of a very warm welcome here. At the entrance to the site is the old farmhouse which houses the reception and the toilet facilities. There are only six pitches, all for touring, all with electricity (6A) and all hardstanding, with varying amounts of shade. Lower down, close to a small fishing river, are four very spacious, grassy tent pitches of irregular shape, laid out in a woodland glade.

Facilities

One excellent, small toilet block with modern facilities is kept spotlessly clean. Washing machine and dryer. Emergency supplies only. Fishing. WiFi throughout (free). Off site: Riding, restaurant, bar and boulangerie in Abjat-sur-Bandiat 5 km. Lake swimming, canoeing, restaurant at St Estephe 9 km. Wider range of shops and bars in Nontron 7 km. St Jean de Cole, the village reputed to have the best rooftops in France 18 km. Many walking and cycling routes.

Open: 15 May - 15 September.

Directions

Leave A20 autoroute north of Limoges, exit 28. Take N520 west then D2000 bypassing Limoges. Take N21 southwest for 11 km. Turn west, D699, to St Mathieu (27 km). Turn south, D675 to Augignac (16 km). At crossroads turn left (Abjat) then immediately right to Manzac, follow signs to site, 4 km. GPS: 45.562088, 0.71956

Charges guide

Per unit incl. 2 persons and electricity	€ 22.00 - € 24.00
extra person	€ 5.00 - € 6.00

Azur

Camping Village la Paillotte

66 route des Campings, F-40140 Azur (Landes) T: 05 58 48 12 12. E: paillotte@franceloc.fr

alanrogers.com/FR40040

La Paillotte, in the Landes area of southwest France, is a site with a character of its own. It lies beside the Soustons Lake only 1.5 km. from Azur village, with its own sandy beach. This is suitable for young children because the lake is shallow and slopes gradually. All 310 pitches are mostly shady with shrubs and trees. The 75 pitches for touring vary in price according to size, position and whether they are serviced. La Paillotte is an unusual site with its own atmosphere which appeals to many regular clients. The campsite buildings (reception, shop, restaurant, even sanitary blocks) are all Tahitian in style.

Facilities

Well equipped toilet blocks include facilities for disabled visitors. Washing machines, dryers. Shop (15/6-6/9). Good restaurant with terrace overlooking lake, bar, takeaway, swimming pool complex. Sports, games and organised activities. Miniclub. TV room, library. Fishing. Bicycle hire. Sailing, rowing boats and pedaloes for hire. Torches useful. Free WiFi on part of site. Dogs are not accepted. Off site: Riding 8 km. Atlantic beaches 10 km.

Open: 12 April - 21 September.

Directions

Coming from the north along N10, turn west on D150 at Magescq. From south go via Soustons. In Azur turn left before church (site signed). GPS: 43.78696, -1.3093

Charges guide

Per unit incl. 2 persons and electricity	€ 16.00 - € 44.00
extra person (over 4 yrs)	€ 3.00 - € 8.00

No credit cards.

Bazas

Camping Le Paradis de Bazas

Route de Casteljaloux, F-33430 Bazas (Gironde) T: 05 56 65 13 17. E: paradis@franceloc.fr

alanrogers.com/FR33140

In a rural position, where the owners stated philosophy of tranquillity is realised. At present, there are only five grass pitches for touring units, up to 200 sq.m. Separated by flowering shrubs and bushes, all have electricity (6A), water and drainage. A further 39 pitches are available for tents. Reception facilities and a bar are in a very tastefully converted old barn, where you may have breakfast or collect bread. There is a traffic free footpath from the site to the town, which we can recommend. A new cycle path runs from Bazas to the Atlantic coast (on 80 km. of old railway track).

Facilities

Small, high quality toilet block. Facilities for disabled visitors. Baby room. Washing machine and dryer. Motorcaravan services. Restaurant/takeaway (July/Aug). Bar (all season). New swimming pool with large slide and paddling pool. Sunbathing area. Small playground. Boules. Minigolf. Bicycle hire. Free WiFi on part of site. Off site: Shops, bars, restaurants, gas supplies available in Bazas 1.5 km.

Open: 24 April - 6 September.

Directions

From Bazas centre take the D655 east towards Casteljaloux, and the site entrance is 1 km. on your right at the top of the hill (well signed). Take care not to use the road leading to the château. GPS: 44.42611, -0.198333

Charges guide

Pitch incl. 2 persons and electricity	€ 20.00 - € 40.00
extra person	€ 4.70 - € 7.00

Beaumont-du-Périgord

Camping Village le Moulin de Surier

Le Surier, F-24440 Beaumont-du-Périgord (Dordogne) T: 05 53 24 91 98. E: contact@lemoulindesurier.com

alanrogers.com/FR24950

Le Moulin de Surier is a very spacious and peaceful site located on the site of a former water mill, midway between Bergerac and Sarlat, and is close to Beaumont-du-Périgord, a delightful, 13th-century, fortified village. Please note that this is a camping village with accommodation to rent (47 attractive wooden chalets and mobile homes). There are no touring pitches here. The chalets and mobile homes are all fully equipped and occupy large shady pitches. Some are on high terraces and others are on a level area adjacent to a lake with its own sandy beach. The lake is used for swimming and fishing, and canoes and pedaloes are available. Leisure amenities include a swimming pool, a play area and a small animal park. Various activities and entertainment are organised in high season including karaoke, discos and a children's club. The bar, takeaway and shop all function throughout the high season. The attractive village of Beaumont-du-Périgord has a small selection of shops. To the west, Monbazillac has a fine château and is renowned for its sweet white wines.

Facilities

Shop and bar (all season). Snack bar and takeaway (1/6-27/9). Outdoor swimming pool. Swimming lake. Fishing lake. Play area. Bicycle hire. Activity and entertainment programme. WiFi. Off site: Walking and cycle trails. Canoeing. Riding 10 km. Golf 15 km.

Open: 19 April - 27 September.

Directions

From Bergerac head east, D660 to Couze, then head south (still on D660) towards Beaumont-du-Périgord for 6 km. Turn right, C3 and follow signs to the site. GPS: 44.78596, 0.7554

Charges guide

Contact the site for details.

An exceptional natural site surrounded by vineyards, medieval towns and castles
Moulin de Surier
village vacances
Dordogne Périgord
A really quiet family place
Special prices in low season : May-June-September-October
• Lake with a sandy beach • Swimming pool • Free fishing & Canoeing on site • Comfortable Chalets & Mobile homes • Paradise for Children • Glamping
www.lemoulindesurier.com • contact@lemoulindesurier.com • Tel : +33 5 53 24 91 98 • facebook.com/lemoulindesurier

Beauville

Camping les 2 Lacs

D122, F-47470 Beauville (Lot-et-Garonne) T: 05 53 95 45 41. E: camping-les-2-lacs@wanadoo.fr

alanrogers.com/FR47170

Les 2 Lacs is a spacious family campsite, attractively situated at the heart of a 19-hectare estate, with two lakes suitable for swimming and fishing. The 70 pitches are large (minimum 100 sq.m) and surrounded by hedges. It is a good site for anglers and the 3-hectare fishing lake is stocked with bream, carp, perch and pike, amongst others. It is possible to hire rowing boats, pedaloes and canoes. The site's bar and restaurant are located between the two lakes. There is plenty of activity in peak season with campfires, evening walks and musical evenings but these activities do not disturb the site's tranquillity. A walk around the site may offer the opportunity to see badgers, deer or even wild boar, with large birds of prey overhead. The village of Beauville is 10 minutes' walk from the campsite.

Facilities

One traditional toilet block has good clean facilities including controllable hot showers, washbasins in cabins, a baby bath and facilities for disabled visitors. Washing machine and dryer. Restaurant (April-Oct) and snack bar (July/Aug). Swimming and fishing lakes (no lifeguard). Boat, pedalo and canoe hire. Country walks. Volleyball. Tennis. Play area. Entertainment and activities in peak season. Mobile homes and equipped tents for rent. WiFi. Off site: Shops, cafés and restaurants in Beauville 800 m. Agen and Villeneuve-sur-Lot.

Open: 1 April - 31 October.

Directions

From Cahors head west on the D656 to Tournon d'Agenais and then to St Amans du Pech. Here, head south on the D80 and then the D215 to Beauville. The site is well signed from this point. GPS: 44.27217, 0.88821

Charges guide

Per unit incl. 2 persons and electricity	€ 16.55 - € 23.90
extra person	€ 3.70 - € 5.50
child (2-10 yrs)	€ 2.10 - € 2.85

Belvès

Camping les Hauts de Ratebout

Lieu-dit Ratebout, F-24170 Sainte Foy- de-Belves (Dordogne) T: 05 53 29 02 10. E: ratebout@franceloc.fr

alanrogers.com/FR24050

A member of the FranceLoc chain of sites, les Hauts de Ratebout is situated in the hills of the Perigord Noir. There are stunning views of the surrounding countryside from many of the 220 terraced pitches (41 for touring) which are mostly shady and level. They vary in size (90-100 sq.m), all with 10A electricity and some with water and drainage. There are 157 mobile homes, tents and chalets to rent, together with five gîtes. A tour operator has 25 pitches for tents. There is a good restaurant with an extensive menu and reasonable prices. Large motorhomes and twin-axled caravans are accepted by prior arrangement.

Facilities

Three high standard toilet blocks offer the usual amenities including private washbasins and facilities for children and disabled visitors. Washing machines and dryers. Small shopand takeaway service. Restaurant/bar with terrace. Swimming pool complex. Adventure playground. TV/games room. Tennis. Boules. Multisports pitch. Organised activities in season. Nightly videos and sporting events. Gas barbecues only. Free WiFi over part of site. No dogs. Off site: Fishing 6 km. Riding 10 km. Golf 8 km.

Open: 18 April - 6 September.

Directions

From Belvès, take D710 southwards for 2 km. then turn east on D54. After 2 km. turn left, and after a further 500 m. left again (following campsite signs all the way). Site is 1.5 km. along on a narrow, one-way road. GPS: 44.74175, 1.04513

Charges guide

Per unit incl. 2 persons and electricity	€ 16.00 - € 32.00
extra person	€ 4.70 - € 7.00

No credit cards.

Belvès

RCN le Moulin de la Pique

Le Moulin de la Pique, F-24170 Belvès (Dordogne) T: 05 53 29 01 15. E: moulin@rcn.fr

alanrogers.com/FR24350

This high quality campsite, set in the heart of the Dordogne, has fine views looking up to the fortified town of Belvès. It is a splendid rural estate where there is plenty of space and a good mixture of trees and shrubs. Set in the grounds of a former mill, the superb traditional buildings date back to the 18th century. There are 219 level pitches with 159 for touring units, all with 10A electricity, a water point and drainage. The remainder are used for mobile homes to rent. The site is ideally suited for families with young and teenage children as there is so much to do, both on site and in the surrounding area.

Facilities

Four modern sanitary blocks include facilities for disabled visitors. Launderette. Shop (bread to order), bar, restaurant, snack bar and takeaway. Swimming pools (two heated). Recreational lake. Playgrounds. Outdoor fitness area. Library. Fossil field. Sports field. Tennis. Minigolf. Boules. Satellite TV. WiFi (charged). Off site: Bars, restaurants and shops in the village of Belvès 2 km. Canoeing 10 km. Riding 5 km. Golf 7 km.

Open: 23 April - 24 September.

Directions

Site is 25 km. southwest of Sarlat on the D710, 7 km. south of Siorac-en-Périgord. GPS: 44.76228, 1.01412

Charges guide

Per unit incl. 2 persons, electricity and water	€ 19.00 - € 54.25
extra person (over 3 yrs)	€ 3.25 - € 6.75

Camping Cheques accepted.

Belvès

Flower Camping les Nauves

Le Bos Rouge, F-24170 Belvès (Dordogne) T: 05 53 29 12 64. E: campinglesnauves@hotmail.com

alanrogers.com/FR24470

Les Nauves is a pretty and well maintained site, 4 km. from the beautiful medieval village of Belvès in the Périgord Noir region of the Dordogne. The site consists of 100 pitches, 60 for touring (slight slope, 12A electricity, long leads necessary) and 45 dedicated to mobile homes, chalets and bungalow tents. There are some pitches that are separated and shaded by mature trees, while others are open with good views of the surrounding countryside. The ground on most of the pitches is soft, sandy soil and may cause some difficulty for large vehicles in wet weather. The French owners are warm, friendly and welcoming and very dedicated to providing a quality site.

Facilities

The single sanitary block is clean and well maintained. Facilities for disabled visitors. Baby room (with adult shower). Washing machine. Good shop (July/Aug). Bar. Restaurant with patio, and takeaway on request (July/Aug). Swimming pool and paddling pool. Play area. Boules. Library (FR, NL). Games room. WiFi (free). Off site: Fishing 200 m. Riding 500 m.

Open: 4 April - 24 September.

Directions

From Belvès take D53 southwest towards Monpazier. Site is 4 km. from Belvès on the left hand side. Follow signs and site is 800 m. off the main road. GPS: 44.75275, 0.98445

Charges guide

Per unit incl. 2 persons and electricity	€ 15.50 - € 26.90
extra person	€ 3.00 - € 5.50

Bias

Camping de Tatiou

Route de Lespecier, F-40170 Bias (Landes) T: 05 58 09 04 76. E: camping-le-tatiou@bias40.fr

alanrogers.com/FR40610

Camping de Tatiou is a friendly, welcoming and spacious municipal site near Bias in the Landes region, famous for its superb long sandy beaches, sand dunes and pine forests. The site is only 4 km. from the sea. It is naturally laid out in a sandy forest with tall pines giving plenty of shade. There are around 500 pitches, half are for touring and some have 10A electricity. The site has a good swimming pool and a paddling pool for children. This region has a huge choice of hiking trails and if you enjoy cycling, 'La Vélodyssée' is a cycle route along the Atlantic coast between Brittany and the Spanish border.

Facilities

Five modern toilet blocks with all necessary facilities including those for babies and disabled visitors. Laundry facilities. Shop, bar and restaurant (15/6-15/9). Takeaway (July/Aug). Swimming and paddling pools (lifeguard, 15/6-15/9). Playgrounds. Activity room. Volleyball. Handball. Football. Boules. Tennis. Minigolf. Karaoke and entertainment, organised sport (7/7 to 30/8). Bicycle hire. No charcoal barbecues on pitches (communal available). WiFi (free). Off site: Fishing 1 km. Village of Bias 2 km.

Open: 3 April - 30 September.

Directions

Leave E5 autoroute at exit 14 and take D38 west for 21 km. to roundabout near Bias. Take Route de Lespecier southwest for 2 km. to site. GPS: 44.1446, -1.24042

Charges guide

Per unit incl. 2 persons and electricity	€ 19.00 - € 23.30
extra person	€ 3.50 - € 6.10
child (3-12 yrs)	€ 2.00 - € 3.05

Bidart

Castel Camping le Ruisseau des Pyrénées

Rue Burruntz, F-64210 Bidart (Pyrénées-Atlantiques) T: 05 59 41 94 50. E: contact@camping-le-ruisseau.fr

alanrogers.com/FR64070

This busy site, with a large play area filled with equipment, is ideal for young families. It is about 2 km. from Bidart and 2.5 km. from a sandy beach. There are two swimming pools with slides on the main site and across the road there is an indoor heated pool and new spa complex (charged in July/August) with outdoor fitness equipment. There are 480 pitches with many units for hire and 14 for touring units. They are individual, marked and of a good size, either on flat terraces or around the lake. The terrain is wooded so the great majority of them have some shade. Electrical connections are available throughout.

Facilities

Two main blocks and some extra smaller units. Washing machines. Motorcaravan services. Shop, large self-service restaurant with takeaway and bar with terraces, and TV, outdoor swimming pools, indoor heated pool and spa complex. Sauna. Large play area. Two tennis courts (free outside July/Aug). Fitness track. TV and games rooms. Minigolf. Fishing. Small animal sanctuary. Gas barbecues only (communal available). WiFi throughout (charged). Off site: Riding and golf 3 km.

Open: 17 April - 20 September.

Directions

Site is east of Bidart on a minor road towards Arbonne. From A63 autoroute take Biarritz exit (4), turn towards St Jean-de-Luz and Bidart on N10. After Intermarché turn left at roundabout and follow signs to site. GPS: 43.4367, -1.5677

Charges guide

Per unit incl. 2 persons and electricity	€ 22.00 - € 49.00
extra person	€ 5.00 - € 8.00

Bidart

Sunêlia Berrua

Rue Berrua, F-64210 Bidart (Pyrénées-Atlantiques) T: 05 59 54 96 66. E: contact@berrua.com

alanrogers.com/FR64140

Berrua is in a useful situation on the Basque coast, 10 km. from the Pyrenees, 20 km. from Spain and a five minute drive from Biarritz. Just 1 km. from the sea, it is an ideal location for visiting the beaches in southwest France. A neat and tidy site, it has 270 level pitches (71 for touring units) set amongst trees. Most have electricity (6A) and some are fully serviced. The focal point of the site is an excellent swimming pool complex, surrounded by sunbeds. A member of the Sunêlia group.

Facilities

Toilet facilities are good (unisex) consisting of two blocks with washbasins in cabins. Baby rooms. Facilities for disabled visitors. Washing machines. Motorcaravan services. Shop, bar/restaurant and takeaway. Large pool complex with loungers and slide for children. Games room. Play area (3-10 yrs). Archery. Boules. No gas or electric barbecues. Evening entertainment for adults (June-Aug). WiFi throughout (charged). Off site: Fishing and beach 1 km. Golf and riding 3 km.

Open: 1 April - 28 September.

Directions

From A63 exit 4, take N10 south towards Bidart. At roundabout after the Intermarché supermarket, turn left. Bear right then take next right (site signed). GPS: 43.43822, -1.58237

Charges guide

Per unit incl. 2 persons and electricity	€ 19.90 - € 45.20
extra person	€ 3.30 - € 7.90
child (2-9 yrs)	€ 2.40 - € 4.90

Bidart

Camping le Pavillon Royal

Avenue du Prince de Galles, F-64210 Bidart (Pyrénées-Atlantiques) T: 05 59 23 00 54.
E: info@pavillon-royal.com **alanrogers.com/FR64060**

Le Pavillon Royal has an excellent situation on raised ground overlooking the sea (100 m. from the beach), with good views along the coast to the south and to the north coast of Spain beyond. There is a large heated swimming pool and sunbathing area in the centre of the site. The camping area is divided up into 325 marked, level pitches, many of a good size. Seventy-five are reserved for tents and are only accessible on foot. The remainder are connected by asphalt roads. All have electricity. Much of the campsite is in full sun, although the area for tents is shaded. Beneath the site – and only a very short walk down – stretches a wide sandy beach where the Atlantic rollers provide ideal conditions for surfing. A central, marked out section of the beach is supervised by lifeguards (from mid June). There is also a section with rocks and pools. Reservation in high season is advisable.

Facilities

Good quality toilet blocks with baby baths and two units for disabled visitors. Washing facilities (only two open at night). Washing machines, dryers. Motorcaravan services. Shop (including gas), restaurant and takeaway, bar, heated swimming and paddling pools, wellness facilities, fitness room. Playground. General room, TV room, games room, films. Fishing. Surf school. Dogs are not accepted. WiFi throughout (charged). Off site: Golf 500 m. Bicycle hire 2 km. Riding 3 km. Sailing 5 km. New oceanographic centre at Biarritz.

Open: 15 May - 30 September.

Directions

From A63 exit 4, take the N10 south towards Bidart. At roundabout after the Intermarché supermarket turn right (signed for Biarritz). After 600 m. turn left at site sign. GPS: 43.45458, -1.57649

Charges guide

Per unit incl. 2 persons, electricity and water	€ 33.00 - € 58.00
tent pitch	€ 27.00 - € 48.00
extra person (over 4 yrs)	€ 8.00 - € 14.00

Bidart

Yelloh! Village Ilbarritz

Avenue de Biarritz, F-64210 Bidart (Pyrénées-Atlantiques) T: 04 66 73 97 39.
E: info@yellohvillage-ilbarritz.com **alanrogers.com/FR64150**

This is a very pleasant Yelloh! Village group site (formerly Résidence des Pins), which will appeal greatly to couples, young families and surfers. Set on a fairly gentle hillside, the upper level has reception, shops and a bar. Slightly lower are the impressive paddling and swimming pools in a sunny location with sunbeds. Next comes the tennis courts and the 288 pitches. Some slightly sloping pitches are under trees and separated by hydrangea hedges, while others are more open and level. Fifty-five of the 115 touring pitches have electricity (10A, long leads required) and water. There is a varied entertainment programme in July and August. The site is unsuitable for American-style motorhomes, and large outfits should telephone to check availability. There is a little daytime road noise but not intrusive.

Facilities

The single toilet block has some washbasins and showers together. Washing machines, dryers, ironing boards and facilities for disabled campers. Shop and bar (open all season). Restaurant (1/6-10/9) and takeaway (July/Aug). Two swimming pools (one open all season). Games room. Tennis (charged in July/Aug). Play area (3-8 yrs). Bicycle hire. WiFi (30 hours free). Off site: Beach with lifeguard, fishing (no licence required) and surfing 800 m.

Open: 5 April - 4 November.

Directions

Heading south on the A63 towards Spain, take exit J4 onto the N10 towards Bidart. At the roundabout straight after Intermarché turn right towards Biarritz. The site is on the right after 1 km.
GPS: 43.4531, -1.5737

Charges guide

Per unit incl. 2 persons and electricity	€ 18.00 - € 50.00
extra person	€ 6.00 - € 9.00

Bidart

Camping Ur-Onea

Rue de la Chapelle, F-64210 Bidart (Pyrénées-Atlantiques) T: 05 59 26 53 61. E: contact@uronea.com
alanrogers.com/FR64280

Situated on the outskirts of Bidart and 600 m. away from a fine sandy beach, this large, attractively terraced site has 255 grass pitches with little shade, 150 are for touring, 118 have electricity (10A) and 18 have water and drainage also. There are some hardstandings for motorcaravans. Mobile home accommodation is also available. During the summer months, aquarobics, dancing and discos are arranged together with organised sports events and children's clubs. With local transport available all year (600 m) this campsite is ideal for exploring the surrounding areas.

Facilities

Three well maintained and clean sanitary blocks are of good size with large showers (all also have washbasins) and hairdryers. Facilities for babies and disabled visitors. Laundry. Shop, bar, restaurant and takeaway. New swimming pool complex with heated indoor (all season) and outdoor pools (2/5-18/9). Play areas. Organised activities in high season. WiFi throughout (charged). Off site: Beach, bars, restaurants and shops 600 m.

Open: 9 April - 18 September.

Directions

Take N10 north from St Jean-de-Luz. Continue through Guethary and site sign is on the right. Turn right and site is on the left in 800 m. GPS: 43.43397, -1.59074

Charges guide

Per unit incl. 2 persons and electricity	€ 22.00 - € 44.00
extra person	€ 5.00 - € 8.00

Biron

Camping le Moulinal

F-24540 Biron (Dordogne) T: 05 53 40 84 60. E: lemoulinal@franceloc.fr
alanrogers.com/FR24100

A rural, lakeside site in woodland, now owned and run by the FranceLoc company, le Moulinal offers activities for campers of all ages. Of the 313 grassy pitches, 55 are available for touring units and these are spread amongst the site's own mobile homes, chalets and a small number of Dutch tour operator tents. Most pitches are flat, grassy and have 6/10A electricity, but vary considerably in size (75-100 sq.m). The five-acre lake has a sandy beach and is suitable for boating, swimming and fishing. Well organised animation is run throughout the season including craft activities and a children's club.

Facilities

Sanitary facilities include those for disabled visitors and babies. Washing machines, dryers. Motorcaravan services. Excellent restaurant. Bar. Snack bar/takeaway. Large, heated swimming pool with flumes, slides, jacuzzi and paddling pool. Play area. Children's club. Multisports court. Boules. Tennis. Archery. Roller skating. Mountain bike hire. Canoeing. Fishing and swimming in lake. Free WiFi over part of site. Evening entertainment (July/Aug). Max. 1 dog. Off site: Riding and climbing 5 km. Potholing 10 km. Shops and supermarket in Villeréal 12 km.

Open: 13 April - 14 September.

Directions

Site is 53 km. southeast of Bergerac. From D104 Villeréal-Monpazier road take the D53/D150 south. Just before Lacapelle Biron turn right onto D255 towards Dévillac (site signed). Site is 1.5 km. on the left. GPS: 44.5998, 0.8708

Charges guide

Per unit incl. 2 persons and electricity	€ 19.00 - € 37.00
extra person	€ 4.70 - € 7.00
dog (max. 30 kg)	€ 5.00

Biscarrosse

Camping Bimbo

176 chemin du Bimbo, Navarrosse, F-40600 Biscarrosse (Landes) T: 05 58 09 82 33.
E: info@campingbimbo.fr **alanrogers.com/FR40460**

Camping Bimbo is a well maintained site in the popular resort of Biscarrosse. The aquapark features a spa pool and an excellent children's pool with many water games. The complex is surrounded by a large 700 sq.m. sun terrace. The 50 touring pitches are 80 sq.m. and are well shaded. Most have 6/8A electrical connections. A good range of 50 mobile homes and chalets are available for rent. Bimbo is a lively site in peak season with a varied activity and entertainment programme. The site is located on the south side of the massive Etang de Cazaux, where a wide range of water sports are possible.

Facilities

Toilet blocks have hot showers, washbasins in cabins and facilities for disabled visitors. Shop (July/Aug). Restaurant, bar/snack bar and takeaway (15/6-15/9, weekends in low season). Swimming pool complex (15/4-30/9). Sports area. Play area. Games room. Fitness room. Sauna and spa. Entertainment and activities (high season). Bicycle hire. Mobile homes and chalets for rent. WiFi on part of site (charged). Off site: Fishing and sailing 600 m.

Open: 1 April - 30 September.

Directions

Approaching Biscarrosse on D652 from Sanguinet, follow signs to Navarrosse. Pass through the hamlet of En Belliard, and the site is soon signed, and can be found on the right. GPS: 44.426828, -1.161091

Charges guide

Per unit incl. 2 persons and electricity	€ 19.80 - € 50.00
extra person	€ 5.00 - € 8.00

Biscarrosse

Camping Mayotte Vacances

368 chemin des Roseaux, F-40600 Biscarrosse (Landes) T: 05 58 78 00 00.
E: camping@mayottevacances.com **alanrogers.com/FR40240**

This appealing site is set amongst pine trees on the edge of Lac de Biscarrosse. Drive down a tree- and flower-lined avenue and proceed toward the lake to shady, good sized pitches which blend well with the many tidy mobile homes that share the area. Divided by hedges, all 137 touring pitches have electricity (16A) and water taps. There may be some aircraft noise at times from a nearby army base. The pool complex is impressive with various pools, slides, chutes, jacuzzi and sauna, all surrounded by paved sunbathing areas. The excellent lakeside beach provides safe bathing for all ages with plenty of watersports available. A comfortable restaurant and bar overlook the pool and there is a new, fully equipped gym. Children are catered for with organised clubs, play and sports areas and a games room. This well managed, clean and friendly site should appeal to all and the facilities are open all season.

Facilities

Four good quality, clean toilet blocks (one open early season). Good facilities for visitors with disabilities. Motorcaravan services. Laundry. Supermarket, bar, restaurant and takeaway. Comprehensive rental shop (July/Aug). Boutique. Heated swimming pools, supervised July/Aug. and weekends. Spa and sauna. Play area. Further children's area (extra cost) with trampolines, inflatables and a small train. Bicycle hire. Fishing. Watersports. Activities and entertainment (July/Aug). Clubs for toddlers and teenagers (July/Aug). TV room. Hairdressers (seasonal). ATM. WiFi throughout (charged). Off site: Riding and golf 4 km. Town 2 km. Beach 10 km.

Open: 4 April - 26 September.

Directions

From the north on D652 turn right on D333 (Chemin de Goubern). Pass through Goubern and Mayotte village. Take next right (signed to site) into Chemin des Roseaux. GPS: 44.43495, -1.15505

Charges guide

Per unit incl. 2 persons	€ 19.00 - € 53.00
extra person	€ 6.00 - € 9.50
child (3-7 yrs)	free - € 5.00
dog	€ 6.50

Biscarrosse-Plage

Campéole Plage Sud

230 rue des Bécasses, F-40600 Biscarrosse-Plage (Landes) T: 05 58 78 21 24. E: plage-sud@campeole.com
alanrogers.com/FR40420

Biscarrosse-Plage is a lively holiday resort with a fabulous beach. La Plage Sud is a member of the Campéole group and is located around 800 m. from the beach. This is a massive site with 601 touring pitches (most with 6A electricity) and a further 593 pitches occupied by mobile homes, chalets and fully equipped tents (many available for rent). The site is lively in peak season with a varied programme of activities and entertainment. On-site amenities include a swimming pool and paddling pool.

Facilities

Four modern and clean toilet blocks with some washbasins in cabins, warm water and preset showers. Facilities for children and disabled visitors. Motorcaravan services. Bar/snack bar/takeaway (July/Aug). Heated outdoor swimming pool (1/6-27/9). Paddling pool. Multisport terrain. Play area. Bicycle hire. Activities and entertainment. Mobile homes, chalets and tents for rent. WiFi throughout (charged). No charcoal barbecues. Off site: Beach 800 m. Surfing. Riding 8 km. Golf 10 km.

Open: 11 April - 27 September.

Directions

From A63 motorway, take A66 (Biscarrosse). Take Biscarrosse exit, then D216 (Sanguinet/Biscarrosse). In Biscarrosse, take right turning off 2nd roundabout, towards la Plage. Site is before Biscarrosse-Plage. Narrow entrance – large units ask at reception for access via side gate. GPS: 44.4419, -1.2455

Charges guide

Per unit incl. 2 persons and electricity	€ 19.20 - € 36.00

No credit cards.

518

Biscarrosse

Resort & Spa La Rive

Route de Bordeaux, F-40600 Biscarrosse (Landes) T: 05 58 78 12 33. E: info@larive.fr

alanrogers.com/FR40100

Surrounded by pine woods, la Rive has a superb beach-side location on Lac de Sanguinet. With a total of 764 pitches, it provides 220 mostly level, numbered and clearly defined touring pitches of 80-100 sq.m. all with electricity connections (10A), 100 also with water and waste water. The swimming pool complex is wonderful with pools linked by water channels and bridges. There is also a jacuzzi, paddling pool and two large swimming pools all surrounded by sunbathing areas and decorated with palm trees. An indoor pool is heated and open all season. This is a friendly site with a good mix of nationalities. The latest additions are a super children's aquapark with various games, and a top quality bar/restaurant complex where regular entertainment is organised. There are plans to extend the outdoor pools with the addition of new slides more than 200 m. long. The beach is excellent, shelving gently to provide safe bathing. There are windsurfers and small craft can be launched from the site's slipway.

Facilities

Three good clean toilet blocks have washbasins in cabins and mainly British style toilets. Facilities for disabled visitors. Baby baths. Motorcaravan services. Shop with gas. New bar/restaurant complex with entertainment. Swimming pool complex (supervised July/Aug) with aquapark for children. Games room. Play area. Tennis. Bicycle hire. Boules. Fishing. Water skiing. Watersports equipment hire. Tournaments (June-Aug). Skateboard park. Trampolines. Miniclub. No charcoal barbecues on pitches. Communal barbecue areas. WiFi throughout (charged). Off site: Riding 2 km. Golf 8 km. Beach 18 km.

Open: 2 April - 21 August.

Directions

Take D652 from Sanguinet to Biscarrosse and site is signed on the right in 6 km. Turn right and follow tarmac road for 2 km. GPS: 44.46052, -1.13065

Charges guide

Per unit incl. 2 persons and electricity	€ 27.50 - € 54.00
extra person	€ 5.30 - € 10.60
child (3-7 yrs)	€ 3.80 - € 8.70
dog	€ 6.20 - € 11.30

No credit cards.

Camping Cheques accepted.

Biscarrosse-Plage

Campéole le Vivier

681 rue du Tit, F-40600 Biscarrosse-Plage (Landes) T: 05 58 78 25 76. E: vivier@campeole.com

alanrogers.com/FR40430

Le Vivier is a member of the Campéole group and can be found 2 km. from the seaside resort of Biscarrosse-Plage. The nearest beach is 800 m. away and the crashing Atlantic breakers can be heard on site. The touring pitches (462) are located amongst the towering pine trees and around half have electrical connections. Mobile homes, chalets and equipped tents (372) are available for rent (including specially adapted units for wheelchair users). Although close to the beach, there is a large swimming pool on site and other sports amenities include volleyball, basketball and tennis. This large, lively site in high season has plenty going on, including discos and karaoke evenings, as well as sports tournaments. The Arcachon Basin is easily accessible to the north, as well as the Dune de Pyla, Europe's highest sand dune and the Aqualand water theme park.

Facilities

Sanitary facilities include provision for disabled visitors. Laundry facilities. Bar (25/6-4/9). Snack bar and takeaway (25/6-31/8). Outdoor heated swimming pool (15/6-15/9). Tennis. Bicycle hire. Bouncy castle. Play area. Activities and entertainment. Mobile homes, chalets and equipped tents for rent. Only communal barbecues are permitted. WiFi on part of site (charged). Off site: Nearest beach 800 m. Treetop adventure park 2 km. Lake beach 5 km. Hiking and cycle tracks. Golf 2 km. Riding 10 km.

Open: 27 April - 15 September.

Directions

Head south from Arcachon on D218 passing the Dune de Pyla and continue to Biscarrosse-Plage. The site is well signed from here. GPS: 44.45804, -1.23968

Charges guide

Per unit incl. 2 persons and electricity	€ 19.20 - € 36.00
extra person	€ 4.80 - € 10.30
child (2-6 yrs)	free - € 6.10
dog	€ 2.50 - € 3.80

No credit cards.

Bordeaux

Camping Village du Bordeaux Lac

Boulevard Jacques Chaban Delmas, F-33520 Bruges (Gironde) T: 05 57 87 70 60.
E: contact@village-du-lac.com **alanrogers.com/FR33410**

Bordeaux is undeniably one of France's 'must see' cities and now it has a superior campsite. Adjacent to the exhibition centre and beside Bordeaux Lac, the site opened in 2009 and is open all year. The facilities and accommodation are of top quality. There are 119 touring pitches, some on well kept grass, others, primarily for motorcaravans, have hardstanding. Some have electricity, water and drainage. Within the 14-hectare campsite there are also 175 well equipped chalets and mobile homes for rent. The site is arranged around five attractive, man-made lakes and set amongst tall trees.

Facilities

Modern, heated sanitary block with facilities for disabled visitors. Laundry. Supermarket (bread to order). Restaurant/bar. Swimming pool (1/6-30/9). Play area. Table tennis, handball and basketball court. Mobile homes and chalets for rent. No charcoal barbecues. Free WiFi (charged). Off site: Golf and fishing (Bordeaux Lac complex). Large shopping centre. Bordeaux centre 5 km.

Open: All year.

Directions

At Bordeaux, take the A630 ring road and exit 4A. Follow signs for Parc des Expositions and signs for campsite. At roundabout take second exit (right) and site is 700 m. on the right. GPS: 44.89805, -0.58194

Charges guide

Per unit incl. 2 persons and electricity	€ 21.00 - € 33.00
extra person	€ 5.50 - € 9.00

Brantôme

Camping Brantôme Peyrelevade

46 avenue André Maurois, F-24310 Brantôme (Dordogne) T: 05 53 05 75 24. E: info@camping-dordogne.net
alanrogers.com/FR24540

Le Peyrelevade is a quiet and peaceful site in the Périgord Vert region. Of a very good standard, it comprises 137 spacious and well kept touring pitches and 23 mobile homes for rent. All pitches have 10A electricity and 12 are fully serviced. The site is set in an area that is part open, part wooded and most pitches have partial shade from well sited trees and hedges. The beautiful island town of Brantôme is a short walk away. Its abbey is built into the cliff face and the town is served by five medieval bridges taking you to small bars, restaurants and other amenities. There is a 3.5 tonne weight restriction on the main road through the town. The River Dronne runs through the rear of the site and adds to its charm.

Facilities

Two heated sanitary blocks are well maintained, clean and adequate for the number of pitches. One is new, heated and includes good facilities for disabled visitors. Baby area with bath. Laundry with washing machine. Shop (1/6-15/9). Bar. Restaurant and takeaway (July/Aug). Games room with TV. Open-air heated swimming pool. Play area. River beach suitable for paddling. Fishing. WiFi (low speed free). Max. 2 dogs accepted. Off site: Boat trips. Riding 3 km. Golf 20 km.

Open: 1 May - 30 September.

Directions

Take D939 south from Angoulême, or north from Périgueux. Brantôme is 20 km. north of Périgueux. Drive through town and look for sign for site which is 1.5 km. north outside Brantôme. There is a 3.5 tonne weight restriction on the main road through the village. GPS: 45.361, 0.661

Charges guide

Per unit incl. 2 persons and electricity	€ 16.60 - € 26.00
extra person	€ 3.50 - € 5.00

Campagne

Camping le Val de la Marquise

Le Moulin, F-24260 Campagne (Dordogne) T: 05 53 54 74 10. E: contact@levaldelamarquise.com
alanrogers.com/FR24340

This well kept little campsite, between Le Bugue and Les Eyzies, is an ideal base to explore the châteaux and prehistoric sites of the Périgord region. The 104 pitches (72 for touring, all with 15A electricity) are flat, grassy and all of a good size. The pitches are divided by shrubs and some have shade from mature trees, whilst others are more open. Reception stocks a range of basic groceries including bread and croissants made freshly on site every morning. The site retains a relaxed peaceful air and is an ideal retreat after a busy day of sightseeing in the area. Car hire can be arranged on site.

Facilities

Clean toilet block provides first rate facilities. Baby bath. Smaller block near reception houses good facilities for disabled visitors. Washing and drying machines. Shop, good bar, takeaway (July/Aug). Swimming pool (heated 1/5-30/9), sun terrace, paddling pool. WiFi (charged 4/7-27/8). Small fishing lake. Bicycle and go-kart hire. Communal barbecue. Off site: Bars and restaurants in the village of Campagne 500 m. Riding 2 km.

Open: 1 April - 30 September.

Directions

Site is 5 km. southeast of Le Bugue. Take D703/D706 Le Bugue-Les Eyzies road. At Campagne take D35 southeast towards St Cyprien (there is a peculiar 'Y' junction with 3 roads). Site is 500 m. on right. GPS: 44.906509, 0.974334

Charges guide

Per unit incl. 2 persons and electricity	€ 15.60 - € 27.50
extra person	€ 3.30 - € 5.80

Carcans

Camping Indigo Lac de Carcans

Domaine de Bombannes, F-33121 Carcans (Gironde) T: 05 56 03 95 02.

E: bombannes@camping-indigo.com **alanrogers.com/FR33860**

On the shore of an extensive lake, surrounded by 250 hectares of pine forest and close to the long, sandy beaches of the Atlantic ocean, Indigo Lac de Carcans has plenty to offer lovers of the great outdoors, whilst being within easy reach of the châteaux and vineyards of Médoc and the bustling city of Bordeaux. The site has 280 pitches on sandy soil among the pine trees, with accommodation available in well equipped canvas tents on wooden platforms. The Lac d'Hourtin-Carcans is France's largest freshwater lake and provides numerous opportunities for water-based activities.

Facilities

Sanitary blocks provide hot showers, dishwashing and laundry sinks, washing machine and chemical disposal. Motorcaravan service point. Small shop with bread to order and basic supplies. Snack bar with takeaway facilities. Swimming and paddling pools. Playground. Volleyball, pétanque, basketball, handball and tennis courts. Organised activities in high season. Direct access to lake shore. Off site: Beach adjacent.

Open: 10 June - 12 September.

Directions

From north on A10 continue onto Rocade A630 towards airport (Mérignac). From south on A62 or A63 head west on Rocade towards airport. Leave at exit 8 and head north on D1215 (Lacanau). After Ste. Hélène turn north on D104/D207 to Carcans and continue to Maubuisson. North at roundabout to Domaine de Bombannes. GPS: 45.09604, -1.14756

Charges guide

Per unit incl. 2 persons and electricity	€ 17.50 - € 28.50

Castelnaud-la-Chapelle

Camping Maisonneuve

Vallée du Céou, F-24250 Castelnaud-la-Chapelle (Dordogne) T: 05 53 29 51 29.

E: contact@campingmaisonneuve.com **alanrogers.com/FR24450**

This family run site is beautifully situated in the Céou Valley, in the Périgord. There are 140 spacious touring pitches, all with 6/10A electricity. Some are well separated, whilst others are on two open, grassy areas. Most pitches have some shade. Swimming, fishing and canoeing are all possible in the Céou river which borders the site and can be accessed directly. There are also swimming and paddling pools on site and in high season, entertainment is organised several evenings each week. This is an excellent location from which to explore the beautiful region of the Périgord.

Facilities

Three heated sanitary blocks, one has been totally refurbished, are kept clean and tidy. Facilities for babies and disabled visitors. Family shower room. Laundry. Bar. Shop with bread, snack bar, takeaway (all July/Aug). Swimming and paddling pools (1/5-15/10). Minigolf. Play areas. TV room. Games room. Dance evenings. Karaoke. Sports tournaments. Canoe trips. Climbing. WiFi in reception and courtyard (free). Off site: Small shops and restaurants 800 m. Fishing and bicycle hire 1 km.

Open: 1 April - 31 October.

Directions

From A20 exit 55 take D703 (Sarlat and Beynac). Follow signs for D57 (Castelnaud la Chappelle). Site signed on edge of village. Outfits over 5 m. continue on D57 for 2 km. then turn left. Narrow road – passing difficult. Site is signed here at junction with D50. GPS: 44.80367, 1.15533

Charges guide

Per unit incl. 2 persons and electricity (6A)	€ 19.70 - € 29.40
extra person	€ 5.10 - € 7.40

Castelnaud-la-Chapelle

Camping Lou Castel

F-24250 Castelnaud-la-Chapelle (Dordogne) T: 05 53 29 89 24. E: contact@loucastel.com

alanrogers.com/FR24465

Lou Castel is attractively located close to Castelnaud-la-Chapelle, at the heart of the Périgord Noir, and close to many of the region's major attractions. There are 115 stony pitches here with just a little grass, 40 are available for touring under oak trees which provide good shade. All have electricity (10A). A range of mobile homes, chalets and bungalow style tents are available for hire. The pool complex is impressive, with three water slides, two swimming pools and a separate children's paddling pool. There is a bar/restaurant with a large terrace which is used for entertainment in peak season.

Facilities

The modern toilet block includes facilities for babies and disabled visitors. Family shower room. Basic shop. Restaurant/snack bar, takeaway and terrace. Heated swimming pool complex. Games room. Play area. Activity and entertainment programme (July/Aug). WiFi in bar. Off site: River beach and fishing 3.5 km. Bicycle hire 3.5 km. Riding 5 km. Golf 8 km. Castelnaud. Canoe trips.

Open: 18 April - 13 September.

Directions

From west (Bergerac) take D660, D29, D25, D703 and pass through Bezenac and Beynac. Shortly after Beynac, take D57 south to Castelnaud-la-Chapelle, then follow signs to site. GPS: 44.79768, 1.13121

Charges guide

Per unit incl. 2 persons and electricity	€ 18.00 - € 36.00
extra person	€ 3.00 - € 7.50

Castelnaud-la-Chapelle

Sites et Paysages les Pastourels

Le Brouillet, F-24250 Castelnaud la Chapelle (Dordogne) T: 05 53 29 42 17. E: camping@lespastourels.com
alanrogers.com/FR24970

Les Pastourels is a very spacious site enjoying an excellent location at the heart of the Périgord Noir, with views stretching across towards the Château de Milandes. The region's capital, Sarlat, can be reached in around 15 minutes. There are just 48 very large touring pitches (and 12 mobile homes) here, all with 6A electricity and six are fully serviced. Some pitches are laid out informally in woodland and others are on grass, separated by hedges. Much of the estate is covered by forest and pasture. A number of footpaths converge at the site, including the long-distance GR64.

Facilities

The modern toilet block includes facilities for babies and disabled visitors. Small shop for basics. Snack bar/pizzeria and takeaway (mid June-mid Sept). Outdoor swimming pool and paddling pool (heated 13/5-15/9). Playground. Large sports/play area. Bicycle hire. Organised family activities in July/Aug. WiFi.
Off site: Riding 3 km. Shops and restaurants at Castelnaud (3 km) and Beynac (4 km). Golf 15 km.

Open: 13 May - 15 September.

Directions

From Sarlat head southwest towards Bergerac (D57). At Castelnaud-la-Chapelle turn right (D53) and follow signs to Château de Milandes and the site. GPS: 44.815504, 1.10014

Charges guide

Per unit incl. 2 persons and electricity	€ 18.50 - € 27.50
extra person	€ 4.00 - € 5.50

Cazaux la Teste-de-Buch

Camping la Pinèda

Route de Cazaux, F-33260 Cazaux la Teste-de-Buch (Gironde) T: 05 56 22 23 24.
E: info@campinglapinede.net **alanrogers.com/FR33040**

La Pinèda is a popular, family site with an attractive forest setting, close to the Dune de Pyla and the lively resort of Arcachon. The site boasts a very impressive swimming pool complex which includes a large children's pirate ship, a covered pool and water slides. There are 200 pitches here, 178 of which are occupied by mobile homes for hire. These are positioned amongst tall trees with good shade. There are 30 touring pitches available with 6A electricity. The site is just 3 km. from Lac de Cazaux where there are many watersports. It also has direct access to a canal with mooring opportunities.

Facilities

One modern sanitary block is generally clean and well maintained providing facilities mostly in private cabins. Facilities for disabled visitors (access is fairly steep). Laundry rooms. Shop. Restaurant, bar and takeaway. Swimming pool complex and covered pool. Games room. Playground. Fishing. Bicycle hire. Canoe hire. Mobile homes and chalets for rent. Off site: Hiking and cycling trails through the Landes forest. Riding 1 km. Golf 5 km.

Open: 13 April - 21 September.

Directions

From Arcachon head south towards Cazaux on the D112. Site is located north of the village and is well signed to the left. GPS: 44.55500, -1.15067

Charges guide

Contact site for details.

Coux-et-Bigaroque

Camping les Valades

Les Valades, F-24220 Coux-et-Bigaroque (Dordogne) T: 05 53 29 14 27. E: info@lesvalades.com
alanrogers.com/FR24420

Sometimes we come across small but beautifully kept campsites which seem to have been a well kept secret, and les Valades certainly fits the bill. Set on a hillside overlooking lovely countryside between the Dordogne and Vézère rivers, each pitch is surrounded by a variety of shrubs and trees. The 70 pitches are flat and grassy, mostly on terraces, all with 10A electricity and most with individual water and drainage as well. Ten very large pitches (over 300 sq.m) are available for weekly hire, each having a private sanitary unit, dishwashing, fridge and barbecue. At the bottom of the hill, away from the main area, is a swimming pool and a good sized lake for carp fishing, swimming and canoeing (free canoes).

Facilities

Two clean modern toilet blocks, both with family shower rooms. Facilities for disabled visitors. Washing machine. Shop (1/6-30/9), bar and restaurant (1/6-30/9), takeaway (1/6-30/9) and a terrace overlooking the valley. Outdoor heated swimming pool with sun terrace and paddling pool (15/5-30/9). Play area near the lake and pool. Fishing. Canoeing. Free WiFi on part of site. No gas barbecues. Off site: Small shop, bar, restaurant in Coux-et-Bigaroque 3 km. Riding and bicycle hire 3 km. Golf 6 km.

Open: 1 May - 30 September.

Directions

Site is signed down a turning on west side of D703 Le Bugue-Siorac-en-Perigord road, 3.5 km. north of village of Coux-et-Bigaroque. Turn off D703 and site is 1.5 km. along on right. GPS: 44.86056, 0.96385

Charges guide

Per unit incl. 2 persons and electricity	€ 17.00 - € 30.00
extra person	€ 7.00
child (under 7 yrs)	€ 5.00

Daglan

Camping le Moulin de Paulhiac

F-24250 Daglan (Dordogne) T: 05 53 28 20 88. E: Francis.Armagnac@wanadoo.fr

alanrogers.com/FR24230

You will be guaranteed a friendly welcome from the Armagnac family who are justifiably proud of their well kept and attractive site, built in the grounds surrounding an old mill. The facilities have been continually updated and improved over the years. The 160 shady pitches (98 for touring) are separated by hedges and shrubs, all fully serviced and have 10A electricity. Many pitches are next to a small river that runs through the site and joins the River Ceou along the far edge. A tent field slopes gently down to the river which is quite shallow and used for swimming. This site with its superb new pool complex will appeal in particular to families with younger children.

Facilities

Two clean toilet blocks provide modern facilities, including those for disabled visitors. Shop. Restaurant. Takeaway. Heated swimming pool (with cover), children's pool, wave machine, toboggan and slides. Boules. Bicycle hire. Small river with beach. Fishing. Canoe trips organised on the Dordogne. Evening activities. Children's club in high season. WiFi (charged). Off site: Riding 5 km. Golf 10 km.

Open: 15 May - 15 September.

Directions

Site is 17 km. south of Sarlat and is on the east side of the D57, 5 km. north of the village of Daglan. GPS: 44.76762, 1.17635

Charges guide

Per unit incl. 2 persons and electricity	€ 31.10 - € 33.05
extra person	€ 8.00 - € 8.40
child (0-10 yrs)	€ 5.50 - € 6.00

Dax

Camping les Chênes

Bois de Boulogne, F-40100 Dax (Landes) T: 05 58 90 05 53. E: camping-chenes@wanadoo.fr

alanrogers.com/FR40020

Les Chênes is a well established site, popular with the French themselves and situated on the edge of town amongst parkland (also near the river) and close to the spa for thermal treatments. The 176 touring pitches are of two types, some large and traditional with hedges, 109 with electricity (5A), water and drainage, and others more informal, set amongst tall pines with electricity if required. This is a reliable, well run site, with a little of something for everyone, but probably most popular for adults taking the spa treatments or wanting a quiet holiday close to many small shops.

Facilities

Two main toilet blocks, one with heating, washbasins in cubicles, facilities for disabled visitors, babies and young children. The older block has been refurbished. Laundry facilities. Shop also providing takeaway (27/3-10/11). Swimming pool with paddling area (5/5-15/9). Play area. Field for ball games. Boules. Bicycle hire. Miniclub (July/Aug). Occasional special evenings for adults. No charcoal barbecues. Free WiFi over site. Mobile homes and bungalows for rent. Off site: Restaurant opposite.

Open: 16 March - 10 November.

Directions

Site is west of town on south side of river, signed after main river bridge and at many junctions in town – Bois de Boulogne (1.5 km). In very wet weather the access road to the site may be flooded (but not the site). GPS: 43.71182, -1.07329

Charges guide

Per unit incl. 2 persons and electricity	€ 17.80 - € 23.60
extra person	€ 6.00

Devillac

Sites et Paysages Fontaine du Roc

Les Moulaties, F-47210 Villeréal/Devillac (Lot-et-Garonne) T: 05 53 36 08 16.
E: reception@fontaineduroc.com **alanrogers.com/FR47070**

Situated on the border between the lovely region of Périgord (Dordogne) and the Lot-et-Garonne, in the heart of the Pays des Bastides, is Camping Fontaine du Roc. It is a natural environment on a wooded hillside and quite isolated. The three hectare site has panoramic views of the nearby Château Biron. Each of the 70 pitches has access to electricity (5/10/15A, 35 Europlugs); some are in the sun and others in the shade to suit your needs. The approach road is single track and narrow, and may cause difficulties for large units. A long established site now run by Dutch owners.

Facilities

One centrally located sanitary block is kept spotlessly clean and includes good facilities for babies, children and disabled visitors. Washing machine and dryer. Small shop. Bar and snack bar serving pizzas. Large swimming pool, children's pool, whirlpool (15/5-1/10). New wooden chalet with sauna, massage, whirlpool and bunkhouse. Two play areas. Library with TV. Boules. Two purpose built stone barbecues (wood provided). Activities for children (high season). WiFi (free). Off site: Fishing 200 m. Riding 2 km.

Open: 1 April - 1 October.

Directions

From Monflanquin, take D272 heading north towards Monpazier. Fontaine du Roc is 10 km. along the road on the left hand side. GPS: 44.61405, 0.81885

Charges guide

Per unit incl. 2 persons and electricity	€ 18.50 - € 24.50
extra adult	€ 4.50 - € 6.00
child (under 6 yrs)	€ 3.00 - € 3.50
dog	€ 3.50

Domme

Camping le Perpetuum

La Rivière, F-24250 Domme (Dordogne) T: 05 53 28 35 18. E: luc.parsy@wanadoo.fr

alanrogers.com/FR24520

Located alongside the Dordogne river, this is a small and friendly, family run site. Attractive and mature, the site is in an ideal location where you can make the most of the river and the Périgord region. The French owners are dedicated to providing a comfortable site and are warm and welcoming, particularly to families with young children. There are 120 pitches including 89 for touring units with 10A electricity. There are 31 mobile homes to rent. The pitches are level and most offer some shade. Access round the site is easy thus facilitating large motorcaravans and twin-axle caravans.

Facilities

Three well maintained sanitary blocks. En-suite toilet for disabled visitors. Newly renovated toilet block. Toilet, shower, washbasins for children. Baby room. Laundry room. Motorcaravan services. Shop (June-Sept). Bar and snack bar with TV (high season). Swimming pool and paddling pool. Two play areas. Covered games area. Bicycle hire. Canoeing on the river. River fishing (permit). WiFi (charged). Activities and entertainment most days (high season). Off site: Sarlat less than 3 km. Golf 2 km.

Open: 1 May - 10 October.

Directions

Take D703 to Vitrac Port. At Vitrac, head south for several hundred metres and take bridge over river. Follow for 1.5 km. until crossroads at the end D50. Turn right following signs to site. Do not use sat nav, and avoid Domme. GPS: 44.81579, 1.22052

Charges guide

Per unit incl. 2 persons and electricity	€ 18.00 - € 25.80
extra person	€ 5.00 - € 7.10

No credit cards.

Domme

Camping le Bosquet

La Riviere, F-24250 Domme (Dordogne) T: 05 53 28 37 39. E: info@lebosquet.com

alanrogers.com/FR24760

Located between Sarlat and Bergerac, this great little campsite is set in lovely countryside close to the River Dordogne. It is beautifully landscaped with flowers, shrubs and trees, maintained to a good standard and kept very clean. There are 57 level grass pitches of average size, 36 of which are for touring units. All have 10A electricity and are separated by shrubs and mature trees providing shade. The remainder are used for mobile homes to rent. The river is only 300 metres away and a canoeing centre can be found near the site entrance.

Facilities

The modern, high quality toilet block includes facilities for babies and disabled visitors. Washing machine and iron. Small shop (all season). Takeaway (1/5-20/9). Heated outdoor swimming pool (all season). Library. Entertainment (July/Aug). Play area. Boules. TV. WiFi (two hours free per day). Twin axle caravans are not accepted Off site: River beach, canoeing and fishing 300 m. Bicycle hire 1 km. Golf and tennis 2 km. Riding 3 km.

Open: 9 April - 25 September.

Directions

Take the D46 from Sarlat to Vitrac. Cross the river bridge in Vitrac and the site is on the right hand side 1 km. further on (signed). GPS: 44.82241, 1.225319

Charges guide

Per unit incl. 2 persons and electricity	€ 15.80 - € 21.30
extra person	€ 3.90 - € 5.20
child (2-7 yrs)	€ 2.10 - € 3.30
dog	€ 1.00 - € 2.00

Douville

Camping d'Orpheo Negro

Les Trois Frères (RN 21), F-24140 Douville (Dordogne) T: 05 53 82 96 58. E: camping@orpheonegro.com

alanrogers.com/FR24880

Camping d'Orpheo Negro can be found midway between Périgueux and Bergerac. There are 60 grassy pitches in a park which extends over 16 hectares. Pitches are large and generally well shaded. Most have electrical connections (6A). A few chalets and mobile homes are available for rent. The site has been developed on the banks of a three hectare lake which is well stocked with carp, so this is a popular site with anglers. Rowing boats and pedaloes are provided free of charge. Other leisure amenities include a swimming pool (with water slide), tennis, an open-air bowling alley and minigolf.

Facilities

The single toilet block has been refurbished to a high standard. Shop. Bar/pizzeria. Swimming pool. Water slide. Fishing. Rowing boats and pedalos. Tennis. Minigolf. Open-air bowling alley. Games room. Playground. Activity programme. WiFi throughout (charged). Off site: Campers can use the facilities of the adjacent hotel. Cycle and walking tracks. Riding 1 km. Vergt 8 km. Périgueux and Bergerac 25 km.

Open: 1 April - 31 October.

Directions

Site is at Douville, north of Bergerac. From Bergerac, take northbound N21 towards Périgueux and follow signs to Douville (D36). Then, follow signs to site. GPS: 45.024654, 0.615967

Charges guide

Per unit incl. 2 persons and electricity	€ 19.90 - € 24.90
extra person	€ 4.70 - € 5.50
child (3-9 yrs)	€ 3.30 - € 4.30

Duras

Le Cabri Holiday Village

Route de Savignac, F-47120 Duras (Lot-et-Garonne) T: 05 53 83 81 03. E: holidays@lecabri.eu.com

alanrogers.com/FR47110

This countryside site of 5.5 hectares is divided into three areas: camping, chalets and open fields. It is on the border of the Dordogne and the Lot-et-Garonne departments. Le Cabri Holiday Village is an English owned and run, small holiday complex. The owners, Peter and Eileen Marston, who are keen caravanners themselves, have developed 24 new spacious pitches (generally 150 sq.m), all with electricity (4/16A) and water. The open, level pitches are all on hardstandings surrounded by grass and separated by young trees, so with limited shade. Access for large motorcaravans using the rear entrance is possible as this was considered when the site was planned. Open all year round, the site has a swimming pool, a small fishing pond and other leisure facilities. Le Cabri also benefits from its own high quality restaurant which specialises in local cuisine.

Facilities

The sanitary block is centrally located, heated in low season and includes three new private cabins. Separate cabin for disabled visitors. Washing machines, dryers and ironing board. Small charity shop. Restaurant with occasional entertainment year round and Internet access. Swimming pool (June-Sept). Large play area. Boules. Well stocked fishing pond. WiFi (charged). Off site: Shops and Mon. am market in Duras 500 m. Riding and tennis 1 km. Watersports 7 km. Canoeing 8 km. Golf (international course) 10 km. Aquatic park 45 minutes drive.

Open: All year.

Directions

In Duras, look for the D203 and follow signs for site. It is less than 1 km. away. GPS: 44.68296, 0.18615

Charges guide

Per unit incl. 2 persons and 10A electricity	€ 17.00 - € 24.00
extra person	€ 4.00 - € 6.00
child (under 12 yrs)	€ 2.00 - € 3.00
dog	€ 2.00

Espelette

Camping Biper Gorri

Chemin de Lapitxague, F-64250 Espelette (Pyrénées-Atlantiques) T: 05 59 93 96 88.

E: info@camping-biper-gorri.com **alanrogers.com/FR64390**

Camping Biper Gorri can be found at the heart of Basque country, south of Cambo-les-Bains. This is a small site of 70 touring pitches, all of which are grassy and mostly shaded. There are a number of mobile homes and fully equipped bungalow-style tents available for rent. The site boasts an attractive pool complex with a large main pool and separate children's pool. The site is livelier in peak season with a children's club, regular entertainment and activities for all the family. Excursions include accompanied rafting and canoe trips. Trout fishing is popular in the fast flowing mountain streams close at hand, and mountain biking is also a very popular pursuit. The fashionable seaside resort and fishing port of Saint Jean-de-Luz is also within easy access.

Facilities

One toilet block is partly heated and includes some washbasins in cabins and preset showers. Facilities for disabled visitors. Motorcaravan services. Basic but good shop (15/6-15/9). Bar, restaurant, snack bar and takeaway (all season). Heated swimming pool. Spa. Play area. Entertainment and activity programme. Woodland walks. Mobile homes and tents for rent. WiFi throughout (charged). Torches useful. Off site: Shops, bars and restaurants in Espelette. Mountain sports. Walking and mountain bike trails. Cambo-les-Bains (Edmond Rostand museum). Fishing.

Open: 1 April - 6 November.

Directions

Take the exit for Bayonne Sud from A64 motorway (Maignon) and take D932 to Ustaritz. Continue to Cambo-les-Bains and then take D10 to Espelette. The site is well signed in the village.
GPS: 43.353374, -1.449635

Charges guide

Per unit incl. 2 persons and electricity	€ 19.45 - € 35.35
extra person	€ 3.20 - € 7.30
child (3-10 yrs)	€ 2.20 - € 5.90
dog	€ 0.65 - € 2.15

Hourtin-Plage

Airotel Camping de la Côte d'Argent

518

F-33990 Hourtin-Plage (Gironde) T: 05 56 09 10 25. E: info@cca33.com

alanrogers.com/FR33110

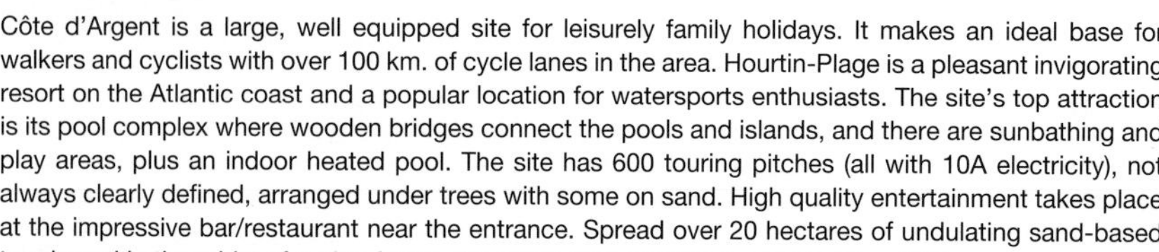

Côte d'Argent is a large, well equipped site for leisurely family holidays. It makes an ideal base for walkers and cyclists with over 100 km. of cycle lanes in the area. Hourtin-Plage is a pleasant invigorating resort on the Atlantic coast and a popular location for watersports enthusiasts. The site's top attraction is its pool complex where wooden bridges connect the pools and islands, and there are sunbathing and play areas, plus an indoor heated pool. The site has 600 touring pitches (all with 10A electricity), not always clearly defined, arranged under trees with some on sand. High quality entertainment takes place at the impressive bar/restaurant near the entrance. Spread over 20 hectares of undulating sand-based terrain and in the midst of a pine forest, the site is well organised and ideal for children.

Facilities

Very clean sanitary blocks include provision for disabled visitors. Washing machines. Motorcaravan services. Large supermarket, restaurant, takeaway, pizzeria and bar. Four outdoor pools with slides and flumes (1/6-18/9). Indoor pool (all season). Fitness room. Massage (Institut de Beauté). Tennis. Play areas. Miniclub, organised entertainment in season. Bicycle hire. WiFi throughout site (charged). ATM. Charcoal barbecues are not permitted. Hotel (12 rooms). Off site: Path to the beach 300 m. Fishing and riding. Golf 30 km.

Open: 13 May - 18 September.

Directions

Turn off D101 Hourtin-Soulac road 3 km. north of Hourtin. Then join D101E signed Hourtin-Plage. Site is 300 m. from the beach. GPS: 45.22297, -1.16465

Charges guide

Per unit incl. 2 persons and electricity	€ 30.00 - € 58.00
extra person	€ 5.00 - € 10.00
child (3-9 yrs)	€ 4.00 - € 9.00
dog	€ 3.00 - € 7.00

Camping Cheques accepted.

Groléjac

Camping du Lac de Groléjac

Le Roc Percé, F-24250 Groléjac (Dordogne) T: 05 53 59 48 70. E: contact@camping-dulac-dordogne.com

alanrogers.com/FR24850

There are 95 pitches, 67 for touring with electricity (10A) and 15 mobile homes for rent. The pitches are delightfully positioned in a circular formation, the toilet and shower block being at the hub. Shaded or sunny they are of a good size and divided by trees, shrubs and bamboo. By the side of a large lake, which is directly accessible from the site, swimming from the sandy beach area is supervised in high season by a lifeguard. In July and August the facilities at the lake are free of charge to campers. A new swimming pool, playground, bar and snack bar with decking have been added. The aim of the new owners is to provide a haven of peace where you can enjoy the luxuriant nature surrounding the lake and from where you can discover this wonderful region.

Facilities

One central, modern and well equipped toilet and shower block with washbasins in cabins and preset. Facilities for babies and campers with disabilities. Covered laundry and washing up area. Bar and takeaway. Heated outdoor pool (1/5-22/9). Fridge hire. Bicycle hire. Fishing. WiFi (free). Communal meals. Weekly welcoming drink. Off site: Restaurant at far side of lake. Golf 7 km. Gourdon for shopping and the Grottes de Cougnac 11 km. Sarlat for Saturday market.

Open: 30 April - 22 September.

Directions

From Sarlat on D704 go through Groléjac and at end of village turn right on to D50 signed Domme. After 100 m. turn left, site is 500 m. on left GPS: 44.802103, 1.294493

Charges guide

Per unit incl. 2 persons and electricity	€ 15.40 - € 19.60
extra person	€ 3.55 - € 5.00
child	€ 2.20 - € 2.90
dog	€ 1.00 - € 1.50

Camping Caravaning
La Côte d'Argent
★★★★★

Club Airotel

A forest of majestic pine trees, beauty, calmness and nature at its purest: that's what makes this station at the Atlantic Coast an ideal holiday site, also for lovers of surfing and sailing...

33990 HOURTIN-PLAGE
Tél : +33 (0)5 56 09 10 25
Fax : +33 (0)5 56 09 24 96
info@cca33.com

www.cca33.com

Groléjac

Camping Caravaning les Granges

Lieu-dit les Granges, F-24250 Groléjac (Dordogne) T: 05 53 28 11 15. E: contact@lesgranges-fr.com

alanrogers.com/FR24020

Situated only 500 metres from the village of Groléjac, les Granges is a lively and well maintained campsite set on sloping ground in woodland. There are 188 pitches, of which 100 are available for touring units. The pitches are marked and numbered on level terraces, some shaded by mature trees and shrubs whilst others are sunny. Outside high season you can choose your pitch when checking in at reception. All pitches have electricity (6A) and water either on the pitch or close by. The site has a swimming pool and a fun pool with water slides. Around 88 pitches are used by tour operators.

Facilities

The toilet blocks are of a very high standard with good facilities for children and disabled visitors. Bar. Restaurant, snack and takeaway. No shop, but bread can be ordered (July/Aug). Heated swimming pool. Play area. Minigolf. Canoe and bicycle hire. Outdoor gym equipment. Quad bikes. Paintball. Canoe trips. Sporting tournaments, entertainment and children's club in high season. WiFi over site (charged). Off site: Shops in the village of Groléjac 550 m. Riding 6 km. Golf 20 km.

Open: 23 April - 10 September.

Directions

In centre of village of Groléjac on main D704 road. Site signed through a gravel parking area on west side of road. Drive through this area and follow road around to T-junction. Turn right, under railway bridge, and immediately left (site signed). Site is just along this road on left. GPS: 44.81593, 1.29086

Charges guide

Per unit incl. 2 persons and electricity	€ 15.30 - € 30.80
extra person (over 2 yrs)	€ 5.70 - € 8.00

Hourtin

Camping les Ourmes

90 avenue du Lac, F-33990 Hourtin (Gironde) T: 05 56 09 12 76. E: info@lesourmes.com

alanrogers.com/FR33050

Located just 500 metres from the largest freshwater lake in France, this level, well maintained campsite is only ten minutes' drive from the beach and, with its own pool, is an attractive holiday site for those who enjoy watersports. Of the 300 pitches, 232 are for touring units. These are marked but not actually separated and arranged amongst trees that give good shade. All have electricity (10A). The site's amenities are arranged around a pleasant entrance courtyard with an evening entertainment programme in season. In low season, this is a quiet site with the added bonus of the bar and restaurant being open.

Facilities

Four refurbished toilet blocks. Facilities for disabled visitors. Laundry facilities. Small shop (July/Aug). Bar/restaurant with outdoor tables, takeaway snacks and reasonably priced meals (1/6-15/9). Medium sized swimming pool, paddling pool. Leisure area, play area, volleyball. TV, games rooms. Boules. WiFi throughout (charged). 37 mobile homes to rent. Off site: Watersports and fishing possible on the lake.

Open: 23 April - 30 September.

Directions

It is essential to follow Hourtin Port (Ave du Lac) from the town centre and site is signed on left. GPS: 45.182067, -1.0756

Charges guide

Per unit incl. 2 persons and electricity	€ 22.00 - € 35.90
extra person	€ 4.00 - € 7.00
child (3-13 yrs)	€ 2.00 - € 4.00

La Chapelle Aubareil

Camping la Fage

La Chapelle Aubareil, F-24290 Montignac (Dordogne) T: 05 53 50 76 50. E: contact@camping-lafage.com

alanrogers.com/FR24485

A warm welcome awaits you at Camping la Fage, a rural, hillside site on the edge of the village of La Chapelle Aubareil. It is situated between the valleys created by the Dordogne and Vezere rivers. The Crété family have created a peaceful place to stay in beautiful countryside and offer 60 spacious touring pitches, all with 10A electricity. These are well laid out, numbered and separated by shrubs and hedges. There are also 32 pitches occupied by a range of accommodation types available to rent. For outdoor enthusiasts there are hiking routes to explore, canoeing, climbing, caving and fishing opportunities.

Facilities

One unisex toilet block provides showers and washbasins in cubicles and facilities for disabled visitors. Washing machines and dryers. Basic shop, restaurant, bar and snack bar (all July/Aug). Bread to order. Covered outdoor swimming pool (heated from 1/5) and small children's pool. Play area. Trampolines. Pedal car hire. Tennis. Volleyball. Games room. Library. Activities for children and family entertainment (high season). Free WiFi over site. Off site: Riding 5 km. Fishing 7 km. Lascaux caves.

Open: 13 April - 13 October.

Directions

From north, leave A89/E70 at exit 17 and take D6089 and D704 (Montignac and Sarlat). 6 km. after leaving Montignac look for sign to Chapelle Aubareil. Site signed. NB: In July/August check traffic report for delays. GPS: 45.01765, 1.18811

Charges guide

Per unit incl. 2 persons and electricity	€ 18.30 - € 32.00
extra person	€ 4.80 - € 6.50

La Roque Gageac

Camping Beau Rivage

Gaillardou, F-24250 La Roque Gageac (Dordogne) T: 05 53 28 32 05. E: contact@beaurivagedordogne.com

alanrogers.com/FR24800

Beau Rivage has a fine location, just 7 km. from Sarlat, close to La Roque Gageac, with its ancient, honey-coloured houses, sheer rock face and Dordogne river frontage. There are 199 level or slightly sloping grass pitches of which 151 are for touring units with 6A electricity available to all. The pitches are of a good size, separated by shrubs and tall trees provide shade. Large units should phone ahead to check availability. The site has a good range of amenities including a swimming pool, a restaurant, a well stocked shop and a bar. Canoeing is very popular on the River Dordogne and there is direct access to the river and a small beach. Beau Rivage is popular with families and couples as it has something for everyone.

Facilities

Two toilet blocks include facilities for babies and disabled visitors. Washing machines. Shop, bar, restaurant and takeaway (all July/Aug). Heated swimming and paddling pools. Play area. Pétanque. Tennis. Canoeing. Fishing. WiFi in bar area. Electric barbecues are not permitted. Max. 2 dogs. Off site: Bicycle hire 2 km. Riding 5 km. Historic towns and villages with châteaux and museums.

Open: 25 April - 12 September.

Directions

From Sarlat, take the D46 to Vitrac and then D703 towards La Roque Gageac. Site is on the left, well signed. GPS: 44.81621, 1.21488

Charges guide

Per unit incl. 2 persons	€ 13.50 - € 24.00
extra person	€ 3.30 - € 5.60
electricity	€ 3.80

Labenne-Océan

Yelloh! Village le Sylvamar

Avenue de l'Océan, F-40530 Labenne-Océan (Landes) T: 05 59 45 75 16. E: camping@sylvamar.fr

alanrogers.com/FR40200

Less than a kilometre from a long sandy beach, this campsite has a good mix of tidy, well maintained chalets, mobile homes, a tree house and touring pitches. The 289 touring pitches (592 in total) are level, numbered and mostly separated by low hedges. A number of new, less shaded pitches have recently been added. Following development, all now have electricity (10A), water and drainage. Some have additional facilities and are charged accordingly. Pitches are set around a superb pool complex with pools of various sizes (one heated, one not) with a large one for paddling, a wild water river, toboggans and slides. In a sunny setting, all are surrounded by ample sunbathing terraces and overlooked by the excellent bar/restaurant. A member of Leading Campings group.

Facilities

Four modern toilet blocks have washbasins in cabins. Excellent facilities for babies and disabled visitors. Laundry. Fridge hire. Shop, bar/restaurant and takeaway. Swimming pool complex. Play area. Games room. Cinema, TV and video room. Fitness centre. Wellness amenities. Tennis. Football pitch. Bicycle hire. Library. Extensive entertainment programme. WiFi over site (charged). No charcoal barbecues. Off site: Beach 900 m. Fishing and riding 1 km. Golf and boat launching 7 km.

Open: 27 March - 4 October.

Directions

Labenne is on the N10. In Labenne, head west on D126 signed Labenne-Océan and site is on right in 4 km. GPS: 43.59570, -1.45638

Charges guide

Per unit incl. 2 persons and electricity	€ 18.00 - € 52.00
extra person	€ 6.00 - € 9.00
child (3-6 yrs)	free - € 6.00
dog	€ 5.00

Labenne-Océan

Camping le Boudigau

45 avenue de l'Ocean, F-40530 Labenne-Océan (Landes) T: (0)2 51 20 41 94.
E: contact@camp-atlantique.com **alanrogers.com/FR40540**

This site no longer accepts touring units. Taking its name from a little river that runs alongside, and situated just a kilometre from the extensive beach at Labenne-Océan, le Boudigau is a site that becomes very lively in high season. There are 301 pitches in total, mainly occupied by mobile homes and chalets for rent, with a few privately owned. In July and August, the site is very much geared to children and young people, with kids' clubs for ages 3-11 years and a full programme of sporting activities and entertainment for the whole family.

Facilities

Laundry facilities. Small supermarket. Bar/restaurant and takeaway with themed meals in high season. Heated outdoor pool (1/5-25/9) and new indoor pool. Play area. Clubs for children. Entertainment room with programme of activities (July/Aug). Multisports court. Beach volleyball and beach soccer. Outdoor fitness equipment. Bicycle hire. WiFi throughout (charged). Communal barbecue. Off site: Beach 700 m. Surf school, rafting, canoeing and kayaking, quad biking, riding, children's farm and minigolf.

Open: 2 April - 25 September.

Directions

Labenne-Océan is 4 km. west of Labenne. From north on A85 leave at exit 8 and take D28 east, then turn south on D810 to Labenne. In Labenne turn west on D126 Avenue de l'Océan. Site is on right in 3 km. immediately after crossing river. GPS: 43.59634, -1.46136

Charges guide

Contact site for details.

Lacanau-Océan

Yelloh! Village les Grands Pins

Plage Nord, F-33680 Lacanau-Océan (Gironde) T: 05 56 03 20 77. E: reception@lesgrandspins.com
alanrogers.com/FR33130

This Atlantic coast holiday site with direct access to a fine sandy beach, is on undulating terrain amongst tall pine trees. A large site with 576 pitches, there are 341 hardstanding pitches of varying sizes for touring units, all with 10A electricity. One half of the site is a traffic free zone (except for arrival or departure day, caravans are placed on the pitch, with separate areas outside for parking). There are 71 tent pitches, those in the centre of the site having some of the best views. This popular site has an excellent range of facilities available for the whole season. Mobile homes are available for hire.

Facilities

Four well equipped toilet blocks (one heated). Baby room and facilities for disabled campers. Laundry facilities. Motorcaravan services. Dog showers. Supermarket. Bar with TV. Restaurant and takeaway. Part-covered, heated swimming pool complex (lifeguard July/Aug) and jacuzzi. Fitness activities (charged) and wellness suite. Games room. Multisports pitch. Boules. Tennis. Playgrounds. Adventure playground. BMX course. Bicycle hire. WiFi throughout (charged). Communal barbecue areas. Off site: Golf 3 km. Fishing 5 km. Riding 12 km.

Open: 25 April - 29 September.

Directions

From Bordeaux take N125/D6 west to Lacanau-Océan. At second roundabout, take second exit: Plage Nord, follow signs to 'campings'. Les Grand Pins signed to right at the far end of road. GPS: 45.01107, -1.19337

Charges guide

Per unit incl. 2 persons and electricity	€ 18.00 - € 57.00
extra person	€ 6.00 - € 9.00
child (3-6 yrs)	free - € 7.00

Lacanau-Océan

Camping Talaris Vacances

Route de l'Océan, F-33680 Lacanau-Océan (Gironde) T: 05 56 03 04 15. E: talaris@franceloc.fr
alanrogers.com/FR33320

Camping Talaris Vacances is now a member of the FranceLoc group. It is located near a large lake and just 6 km. from the Atlantic coast at Lacanau-Océan, so there are opportunities for swimming in either lake or sea, for surfing, water-skiing or sailing. On site, there is plenty going on for youngsters – the many activities take place in front of the bar, restaurant and swimming pool area, so it is probably not the place for parents to relax! However, the part of the campsite allocated to the 150 touring pitches is amongst mature trees at the far end of the site, so is surprisingly peaceful and relaxed.

Facilities

One large, centrally located toilet block is well equipped. Laundry facilties. Baby room and facilities for disabled visitors. Shop. Bar/restaurant and takeaway with covered terrace. Swimming pools and toboggan runs (1/5-13/9). Bicycle hire. Electric barbecues only. Communal barbecue area. Off site: Lake 1 km. Riding 1 km. Fishing 2 km.

Open: 11 April - 21 September.

Directions

From Bordeaux, take N125/D6 west to Lacanau and continue on D6 towards Lacanau-Océan. Site is on right in 4 km. GPS: 45.0048, -1.10738

Charges guide

Per unit incl. 2 persons and electricity	€ 24.00 - € 44.00
extra person	€ 4.70 - € 7.00

Lacanau-Lac

Camping le Tedey

Par le Moutchic, route de Longarisse, F-33680 Lacanau-Lac (Gironde) T: 05 56 03 00 15.
E: camping@le-tedey.com **alanrogers.com/FR33290**

With direct access to a large lake and beach, this site enjoys a beautiful tranquil position set in an area of 14 hectares amidst mature pine trees. There are 680 pitches, of which 620 are for touring units, with just 38 mobile homes and chalets available for rent. The pitches are shady with dappled sunlight breaking through the trees, generally level and grassy although parts of the site are on a slope. Electricity (10A, Europlug) is available to 213 pitches. The bar/crêperie is close to the lake and has a large indoor and outdoor seating area. In July and August there is entertainment and a children's club is also organised. The takeaway sells a variety of food and the shop next door is well stocked. This is an attractive, well maintained site where you get a feeling of space and calm. There are many places of interest nearby and it is a short drive from Bordeaux. The owners and staff are friendly and helpful and English is spoken.

Facilities

Four modern sanitary blocks (recently refurbished) with facilities for disabled visitors, children and babies. Laundry facilities. Motorcaravan services. Shop (8/5-15/9). Bar with terrace (1/6-15/9). Crêperie (16/6-11/9). Takeaway (25/6-3/9). Bicycle hire. Boating on the lake. Fishing. Pétanque. Playground. Minigolf. Volleyball. Gas barbecues only on pitches. Dogs are not accepted in July/Aug. WiFi on part of site (charged). Off site: Riding and golf 3 km. Beach 5 km. Surfing. Cycling.

Open: 23 April - 23 September.

Directions

From Lacanau take the D6 to Lacanau-Océan. Take Route de Longarisse and the site is well signed.
GPS: 44.98620, -1.13410

Charges guide

Per unit incl. 2 persons and electricity	€ 23.00 - € 33.70

Le Tedey
CAMPING CARAVANING ★★★
ROUTE DE LONGARISSE
33680 LACANAU
TEL: 0033(0) 5 56 03 00 15
FAX: 0033(0) 5 56 03 01 90
LACANAU - COTE ATLANTIQUE
E-MAIL: CAMPING@LE-TEDEY.COM - INTERNET: WWW.LE-TEDEY.COM

Lamontjoie

Sites et Paysages Saint Louis

Lac de Lamontjoie, F-47310 Lamontjoie (Lot-et-Garonne) T: 05 53 99 59 38.
E: accueil@camping-lamontjoie.fr **alanrogers.com/FR47230**

Camping Saint Louis lies on the border of the department of Gers, in some 20 hectares of unspoilt countryside. It now has a good sized swimming pool and offers some unusual accommodation, including a floating raft for two. The 70 touring pitches are fairly level, some with good shade, others more open. Some are on terraces, others are on level ground where separating hedges are due to be planted. All have 10A electricity (long leads required). The 13-hectare lake can be used for fishing and canoeing. The old swimming pool on the campsite is now home to large numbers of freshwater crayfish, which can be easily seen in the shallows.

Facilities

The single sanitary block is well equipped and has modern facilities for disabled campers, but may be busy at peak times. Bar/restaurant with takeaway (all season). Swimming pool (June-Sept). Play areas. Trampoline. Football, volleyball and basketball areas. Large fishing lake. Canoe and bicycle hire. Communal barbecue. WiFi in bar (free). Off site: Walibi amusement park. Riding 17 km.

Open: 16 April - 16 October.

Directions

From Condom take D931 northeast for 19 km. At Lamontjoie watch for signs on left to site.
GPS: 44.07742, 0.51821

Charges guide

Per unit incl. 2 persons and electricity	€ 17.90 - € 28.20
extra person	€ 4.00 - € 6.00
child (5-12 yrs)	€ 3.00 - € 4.00

Lanouaille

Moulin de la Jarousse

F-24270 Lanouaille (Dordogne) T: 05 53 52 37 91. E: contact@location-en-dordogne.com

alanrogers.com/FR24960

Moulin de la Jarousse is in the Périgord Vert Regional Park covering 15 hectares of hilly forest, ponds and meadows. Please note that there are no touring pitches here. The accommodation includes the Gîtes de Clément, a restored farmhouse with its own private swimming pool and meadow, log cabins in the forest overlooking the lake and yurts in an open meadow. Scattered around the site are some tree houses accessed via scramble nets or rope bridges. Most of these have few facilities and are a long way from the toilet blocks. The site is unsuitable for those with walking difficulties and torches are essential.

Facilities

Two small, heated toilet blocks, one near the yurts, the other by the tree houses. Facilities for disabled visitors. Table d'hôte. Covered swimming pool. Waterslide. Canoe hire. Large children's playground. 2 fishing lakes. Football. Volleyball. Badminton. Organised children's activities. Wellness centre. Scandinavian treatments and a beauty salon. Free WiFi in reception area. Off site: Rouffiac recreational centre at Payzac. Tree climbing. Golf 15 km.

Open: All year.

Directions

Leave A20 autoroute south of Limoges, exit 36. Take D704 south through St Yrieix-la-Perche. After a further 12 km. at l'Hépital, turn east at site sign. Follow narrow lanes to site in 4 km. GPS: 45.437, 1.18421

Charges guide

Contact site for details.

Lanouaille

Camping de Rouffiac

F-24270 Lanouaille (Dordogne) T: 05 53 52 68 79. E: hebergements@semitour.com

alanrogers.com/FR24965

In the heart of an extensive wooded park on the bank of one of the largest lakes in Périgord, the Rouffiac leisure resort offers a wide range of activities. The campsite has 76 pitches in the shade of mature oak trees and separated by hedges. Fifty-one are for touring units, most with electrical connections, the remainder being occupied by chalets and mobile homes for rent. This corner of Périgord Vert in northeast Dordogne has a number of attractive villages, the nearest being Lanouaille where there are a few shops, bars and restaurants. Périgueux and Limoges are both well worth a visit.

Facilities

Sanitary block includes baby room and laundry facilities. Facilities for disabled visitors. Bar and restaurant. TV room. Play area. Boulodrome. Organised activities and supervised swimming in July/Aug. Fishing. Accrobranche (tree-top climbing), rock climbing, paintball and archery. Numerous watersports. Water ski school (April-Sept). Mountain biking. WiFi in bar area. Off site: Large watersports lake adjacent. Lanouaille 8 km.

Open: 1 May - 30 September (accommodation February - November).

Directions

From north on A20 at Limoges, leave at exit 36, head south on D704 to St Yrieux. Stay on D704 for 12 km. and turn east on D80 (Payzac). Follow signs to Base de Loisirs de Rouffiac. From south on A89 at exit 17 for St Yrieux head north on D704 for 35 km. then east on D80 as above. GPS: 45.41431, 1.16539

Charges guide

Per unit incl. 2 persons and electricity	€ 6.60 - € 8.40
extra person	€ 4.40 - € 5.50

Laruns

Camping des Gaves

Quartier Pon, F-64440 Laruns (Pyrénées-Atlantiques) T: 05 59 05 32 37. E: campingdesgaves@wanadoo.fr

alanrogers.com/FR64040

Set in a secluded valley, Camping des Gaves is a clean, small and well managed site, open all year, with very friendly owners and staff. It is set high in Pyrenean walking country on one of the routes to Spain and is only 30 km. from the Spanish border. There are 99 pitches including 43 level grassed touring pitches of which 38 are fully serviced (3/10A electricity, 2-pin plugs), numbered and separated; the remainder are used for seasonal units. Mature trees provide plenty of shade. The river runs alongside the site (well fenced) and fishing is possible. The busy little tourist town of Laruns is only a short walk.

Facilities

The very clean toilet block can be heated in cool weather and has modern fittings. Washbasins for ladies in curtained cubicles and one shower. Basic facilities for disabled visitors. Laundry room. Motorcaravan services. No shop but baker calls daily (July/Aug). Two bars, one with large screen TV, pool and video games (July/Aug). Small play area. Boules. Volleyball. Fishing. Free WiFi. 16 mobile homes/chalets to rent. Off site: Bicycle hire 500 m. Shops, restaurant and bars 1 km.

Open: All year.

Directions

Take N134 from Pau towards Olorons and branch left on D934 at Gan. Follow to Laruns and just after town, turn left following signs to site. Note: the D918 to the east of Laruns is not recommended for large units. GPS: 42.98241, -0.41591

Charges guide

Per unit incl. 2 persons and electricity	€ 15.20 - € 26.90
extra person	€ 4.10 - € 7.80

Le Bugue

Camping le Rocher de la Granelle

Route de Buisson, la Borie, F-24260 Le Bugue (Dordogne) T: 05 53 07 24 32. E: info@lagranelle.com

alanrogers.com/FR24225

Le Rocher de la Granelle is a friendly site, attractively located on the banks of the River Vézère, and close to the lively market town of Le Bugue. There are 150 good sized, level grass pitches, 120 of which are for touring, all with 10A electricity. Most are well shaded and some have pleasant views across the Vézère. On-site amenities include a swimming pool, water slide and a bar/snack bar which is the base for activities and entertainment during the peak season. Many of the facilities here are being upgraded. The river is good for fishing and canoeing but bathing is not recommended.

Facilities

Two toilet blocks are being refurbished and provide all the necessary facilities. Shop. Snack bar/bar (May-mid Sept). Swimming pool, children's pool, water slide (May-mid Sept). Sports field. Play area. Activity and entertainment programme. Direct river access. Fishing. Tennis. Pétanque. Bicycle hire. Motorcaravan service point. WiFi (10 minutes free per day). Off site: Shops and restaurants in Le Bugue 1 km. Beach and riding 5 km. Golf 15 km.

Open: 1 April - 1 October.

Directions

From Bergerac, head east on D660, D703 then D29 to le Buisson-de-Cadouin. Take D51 then D31E north towards Le Bugue. Follow signs to site on left, just south of Le Bugue. GPS: 44.911738, 0.916666

Charges guide

Per unit incl. 2 persons and electricity	€ 15.00 - € 29.00
extra person	€ 5.30
child (under 12 yrs)	€ 1.50 - € 4.00

Le Bugue

Camping Caravaning la Linotte

F-24260 Le Bugue (Dordogne) T: 05 53 07 17 61. E: lalinotte@vagues-oceanes.com

alanrogers.com/FR24260

This is a pleasant, good quality site with plenty of space and fantastic views from the bar, restaurant and pool complex. It is located in the heart of the Périgord Noir and is conveniently placed to visit many of the attractions in the area. The amenities are very good and include a heated swimming pool, a children's pool, a jacuzzi and two toboggans. Of the 120 level pitches, 90 are for mobile homes and chalets, leaving just 30 pitches for touring units. These are of a good size, all with electricity (5A), separated by hedges for privacy and tall trees provide good shade.

Facilities

A modern toilet block includes facilities for babies and disabled visitors. Bar/restaurant also providing takeaway (1/7-30/8). Small shop with bread to order. Pool complex (1/6-mid Sept). Swimming pool and water slides. Splash pool and paddling pool (both heated). Jacuzzi. Small playground with trampolines. Bicycle hire. Boules. WiFi near reception (charged). Off site: Riding 8 km. Canoes. Ancient market towns and villages, châteaux and caves.

Open: 4 April - 27 September.

Directions

From Le Bugue follow signs for Périgueux north, D710. On outskirts of Le Bugue turn right onto D32E (site signed). After 1.5 km. turn right along narrow lane to site (900 m). GPS: 44.934117, 0.9371

Charges guide

Per unit incl. 2 persons and electricity	€ 21.00 - € 33.00
extra person	€ 4.50 - € 6.70
child (under 5 yrs)	free - € 4.10

Le Bugue

Camping les Trois Caupain

725 allée Paul Jean Souriau, F-24260 Le Bugue (Dordogne) T: 05 53 07 24 60. E: info@camping-bugue.com

alanrogers.com/FR24510

A superb, mature, ex-municipal site, les Trois Caupain is less than 1 km. from Le Bugue, which has a range of supermarkets and tourist attractions. The site carefully blends mobile homes and camping pitches, and fruiting plum trees abound on the site. The 119 well marked touring pitches are neat, level and mostly shaded, with water and 6-16A electricity hook ups close by (16 are full service). The current owners, the three Caupain family members, will do all they can to make your stay a pleasant one. The campsite is less than 50 metres away from the river in an area that is popular with tourists.

Facilities

Two clean and well maintained sanitary blocks include toilet and shower for disabled visitors. Excellent laundry room. Baby room with bath. Motorcaravan services. Small shop selling local produce. Bar with pool table and TV. Restaurant with terrace (May-Aug). Takeaway. Heated swimming pool and paddling pool (1/5-30/10). Play area. Boules. Fishing. Entertainment in high season. WiFi in bar area. Off site: Aquarium and amusement park next door. Boat launch 800 m. Supermarkets in Le Bugue.

Open: 1 April - 30 October.

Directions

From Le Bugue, take D703 heading southeast and site is less than 1 km. from the town centre, well signed. Turn right off the main road and site is less than 800 m. along this road on the left. GPS: 44.90932, 0.93144

Charges guide

Per unit incl. 2 persons and electricity (6A)	€ 16.40 - € 23.00
extra person	€ 3.50 - € 5.50

Le Bugue

Camping Brin d'Amour

Saint Cirq Fonvidal, F-24260 Le Bugue (Dordogne) T: 05 53 07 23 73. E: campingbrindamour@orange.fr

alanrogers.com/FR24660

This attractive Dordogne site is situated in the Périgord Noir with wonderful views across the undulating hills and the Vézère valley. Here there is a feeling of tranquillity, spaciousness and calm. The owners offer a welcome and outstanding customer service. Of the 90 pitches, 56 are for touring units and the remaining 30 are for chalets and mobile homes which are all for rent. The pitches are level, easily accessible and mostly shaded. There is a pond at the far end of the site. The main building houses a pleasant restaurant and bar. This is a small site where you can relax in a friendly, family atmosphere.

Facilities

The single sanitary block is old, but clean, with family room, facilities for disabled visitors and two large rooms for children. Washing machine. Shop (1/6-15/10). Bar (1/4-15/9). Restaurant and takeaway (1/7-15/9). Heated swimming and paddling pools (1/4-30/9). Tennis. Fishing. Pétanque. Play area. Children's club (July/Aug). Bicycle hire. WiFi (free). Max. 1 dog. Off site: Canoeing 5 km. Sailing, riding and golf 10 km. Prehistoric Park. Caves.

Open: 1 May - 15 October.

Directions

Take D710 from Périgueux to Le Bugue and 500 m. after Le Bugue entry sign turn sharp left on D32E to St Cirq. Site signed. GPS: 44.944837, 0.960145

Charges guide

Per unit incl. 2 persons and electricity	€ 13.50 - € 23.00
extra person	€ 3.00 - € 6.00
child (1-10 yrs)	€ 2.50 - € 4.00

Le Buisson-de-Cadouin

Camping Domaine de Fromengal

F-24480 Le Buisson-de-Cadouin (Dordogne) T: 05 53 63 11 55. E: fromengal@domaine-fromengal.com

alanrogers.com/FR24810

Fromengal is a good quality site in the Périgord Noir. Set in over 22 acres, it was formerly an ancient farm and now offers a relaxed family atmosphere amid a calm, tranquil and natural setting. The pitches are of a good size, separated by shrubs and hedging with a mixture of sunshine and shade. There are 93 pitches, 37 for touring units, all with 6A Europlug (ten also with water and drainage). The remaining pitches are used for chalets and mobile homes to rent. There is a good range of new amenities, notably a fine heated swimming pool and a restaurant built in the local style and serving food from the area.

Facilities

The single heated sanitary block includes washbasins in cabins, baby room and facilities for disabled visitors. Laundry facilities. Bar, takeaway and shop (July-Aug), restaurant (June-Sept). Swimming pools (one heated) and slides (1/5-30/9). Pétanque. BMX circuit. Play area. Entertainment. Children's club. Library. Bicycle hire. Tennis, archery and quad bikes for children (charged). WiFi throughout (charged). No electric barbecues. Off site: Fishing 3 km. River beach and riding 5 km.

Open: 11 April - 30 September.

Directions

Take the D703 Bergerac-Sarlat road turning off at Lalinde towards Le Buisson-de-Cadouin. Site is probably the best signed in the Dordogne. GPS: 44.82298, 0.8604

Charges guide

Per unit incl. 2 persons and electricity	€ 17.00 - € 36.00
extra person	€ 5.00 - € 9.00
child (1-10 yrs)	€ 3.00 - € 8.00

Le Verdon-sur-Mer

Sunêlia la Pointe du Medoc

Route de la Pointe de Grave, F-33123 Le Verdon-sur-Mer (Gironde) T: 05 56 73 39 99.
E: info@camping-lapointedumedoc.com **alanrogers.com/FR33210**

Situated roughly equidistant between a sandy Atlantic beach (accessed by a walk through the forest opposite the site) and the Gironde estuary, this site has 260 pitches. There are 112 for touring units with 10A electricity, 70 with water and drainage. Heavier units will need to use those pitches with plastic runners to ensure easy access on and off the sandy ground. The pitches are generally large and most are in full sun but some smaller ones towards the rear of the site offer shade. Out of season this is a quiet campsite, but in July and August it becomes busy with families enjoying the excellent facilities.

Facilities

Good clean sanitary facilities. Shop (July/Aug). Bar, restaurant and takeaway. Outdoor swimming pool (heated) with water jets, jacuzzi and paddling pool. Indoor pool. Massage. Minigolf. Multisports terrain. Bicycle hire. Communal barbecues. Organised entertainment and children's club (4-11 yrs) all season. Small farm and children's garden. Activities for teenagers in July/Aug. Internet access and WiFi. Max. 1 dog. Off site: Sea fishing 1 km. Riding 5 km.

Open: 12 April - 14 September.

Directions

Site is on the N215 (D1215) just south of Le Verdon. Approaching Le Verdon it is important to follow the signs for Royan and Point de Medoc. Site is on the right. It is possible to take the ferry from Royan, but this can be expensive with long queues in high season. GPS: 45.54540, -1.07950

Charges guide

Per unit incl. 2 persons and electricity	€ 18.00 - € 28.00
extra person (over 4 yrs)	€ 3.00 - € 6.00

Léon

Camping Lou Puntaou

Avenue du Lac, F-40550 Léon (Landes) T: 05 58 49 24 40. E: loupuntaou@franceloc.fr

alanrogers.com/FR40290

Eight hundred metres from the charming village of Léon, this site offers 177 above average size, level, grass touring pitches (some sandy). Ninety have electricity (10A), water and drainage and they are separated by hedges. Shade on most pitches is provided by the tall oak trees. Amenities include a heated indoor and outdoor swimming pools, a sauna, a spa and gym room. Village Punta Largo has a good bar and restaurant and provides comprehensive entertainment for children in July and August. The lake is a short stroll away and offers many watersports, fishing, larger restaurants and small bars.

Facilities

The single toilet block is clean and well maintained. Facilities for children and disabled visitors. Laundry facilities. Large shop, restaurant and takeaway (June-Sept). Bar. Heated indoor (April-Sept) and outdoor pools. Sauna and jacuzzi. TV room. Bicycle hire. Play area. Fridge hire. Pétanque. Beach volleyball. Miniclub. Entertainment and activities (July/Aug). Communal barbecues only. WiFi over site (charged). Off site: Lake 300 m. for watersports and fishing. Léon 800 m.

Open: 1 April - 27 September.

Directions

From N10 take exit 12 towards Castets. Take D142 to Léon and at island take first exit to 'Centre Ville'. At T-junction turn left on D652 and after 300 m. turn left at sign for site and lake. After 800 m. site is on the left. GPS: 43.88469, -1.31497

Charges guide

Per unit incl. 2 persons and electricity	€ 17.00 - € 44.00
extra person	€ 5.00 - € 7.00

Les Eglisottes

Camping l'Eau Vive

6bis Fond de Bournac, F-33230 Les Eglisottes (Gironde) T: 05 57 69 56 09. E: camping-leau-vive@sfr.fr

alanrogers.com/FR33830

This spacious, well maintained campsite with 75 larger than average, level pitches is slightly out of the normal tourist areas, but ideal for a quiet break. The pitches are separated by small hedges and with various specimen trees including acers, catalpas and 'mushroom' trees. All pitches have water and electricity (6/10/16A). This is a family run site and the friendly new owners speak some English. It borders onto the Dronne river for fishing and is next to a swimming pool. There is a small, very reasonable restaurant and shop on site and the town of Les Eglisottes is a ten-minute walk.

Facilities

One clean and well equipped toilet block with facilities for babies. Laundry facilities. Motorcaravan services. Shop. Bar. Restaurant and takeaway meals. Three play areas. Football. Basketball. Volleyball. Boules. Gym equipment and spa with jacuzzi. Communal barbecue. Mobile homes to rent. Free WiFi. Off site: River fishing and swimming. Riverside walks. Large swimming pool with diving area (lifeguard July/Aug) 50 m. Tennis 100 m.

Open: April - October.

Directions

Located 50 km. northeast of Bordeaux. From La Roche-Chalais take D674 south for 7.5 km. to Les Eglisottes-et-Chalaures where the site is well signed. GPS: 45.097196, -0.04976

Charges guide

Per unit incl. 2 persons and electricity	€ 16.40 - € 21.40
extra person	€ 4.00 - € 5.00
child (3-10 yrs)	€ 2.00 - € 2.50

Les Eyzies-de-Tayac

Camping la Rivière

3 route du Sorcier, F-24620 Les Eyzies-de-Tayac (Dordogne) T: 05 53 06 97 14. E: la-riviere@wanadoo.fr

alanrogers.com/FR24680

This is a site with some Périgordine character situated beside the Vézère river. The 400-year-old buildings, in the traditional style of the area, create an impressive entrance to the site. It is owned and run by a French family who are friendly and helpful and visitors to the site speak highly of them. They are proud of the site's ecological credentials. There are 120 pitches of which 13 are used for chalets and mobile homes. All have 6/10A electricity connections, 75 also have water and drainage. The pitches are level, easily accessible and offer full shade. Access to the river provides opportunities for canoeing.

Facilities

Three sanitary blocks, two of them new. Facilities for disabled visitors and babies in the new, heated blocks. Washing machine and dryer. Motorcaravan services. Small shop. Bar/restaurant (open July/Aug for lunch and dinner, evenings only in low season) and outside eating area. Takeaway. Swimming pools (one heated) and toddlers' pool. Play area. Half-tennis court. Canoeing. Fishing. Boules. Music evenings and children's shows. WiFi (free). Off site: Fishing 200 m. Bicycle hire 1 km.

Open: 12 April - 12 October.

Directions

From Périgueux take D47 to Les Eyzies. After Manaurie and approaching Les Eyzies, turn right just before the bridge over the river. Then take the next left. Site is signed from D47. GPS: 44.93769, 1.00603

Charges guide

Per unit incl. 2 persons and electricity	€ 19.13 - € 30.19
extra person	€ 4.24 - € 7.20

Limeuil

Camping la Ferme de Perdigat

F-24510 Limeuil (Dordogne) T: 05 53 63 31 54. E: accueil@perdigat.com

alanrogers.com/FR24750

The delightful French owners, Michel and Noelle Paille, make this a happy place to stay and everyone we spoke to praised it highly. The site nestles beautifully in a very natural environment at the base of tree-lined hills which provide a wonderful scenic background. Flowers, bushes and trees give a superb sense of well being and much care and attention is given to the environment. There are only 52 touring pitches (all with electricity 10A) and 15 mobile homes to rent. A superb lake is 100 m. from the site where visitors staying at the farm may fish without charge. The river is also the same distance away in a different direction. This site will appeal to couples of all ages and families with young children.

Facilities

The completely refurbished shower block is bright and airy. Laundry facilities. Motorcaravan services. Shop (1/5-30/9). Bar (1/5-30/9) and restaurant with terrace (newly refurbished, 1/5-20/9). Swimming and paddling pools. Games room. WiFi in the bar area. Play area. Private fishing lake and the Vézère river. Canoes and kayaks. Max. 2 dogs. Off site: Bicycle hire 2 km. Riding 2 km. Supermarkets in Le Bugue 3 km. Golf 14 km.

Open: 21 March - 12 October.

Directions

From Le Bugue, take the D703 to La Borie and turn left to Limeuil. Campsite is well signed. GPS: 44.894765, 0.912509

Charges guide

Per unit incl. 2 persons and electricity	€ 14.80 - € 23.40
extra person	€ 3.90 - € 6.20
child (under 8 yrs)	free - € 3.80

Messanges

Camping Village Resort & Spa le Vieux Port

Plage Sud, F-40660 Messanges (Landes) T: 05 58 48 22 00. E: contact@resasol.com

alanrogers.com/FR40180

A well established destination appealing particularly to families with teenage children, this site has 1,546 pitches (398 for touring) of mixed sizes, most with electricity (6A). The camping area is well shaded by pines and pitches are generally of a good size, attractively grouped around the toilet blocks. There are many tour operators here and well over a third of the site is taken up with mobile homes and chalets. An enormous 7,000 sq.m. aquatic park is exceptional, boasting five outdoor pools (all 25°C), three large water slides plus waves and a heated spa. This is a lively site with a great deal to offer an active family.

Facilities

Nine well appointed, recently renovated toilet blocks with facilities for disabled visitors. Motorcaravan services. Good supermarket. Smaller shops in high season. Restaurants, takeaway and three bars. Large pool complex (no Bermuda shorts) including new covered pool and bar. Tennis. Multisports pitch. Minigolf. Outdoor fitness area. Fishing. Bicycle hire. Riding centre. Discos and karaoke evenings (1/4-12/9). Spa, massages and beauty area. WiFi over site (charged). Off site: Beach 400 m.

Open: 19 March - 25 September.

Directions

Leave RN10 at Magescq exit heading for Soustons. Pass through Soustons following signs for Vieux-Boucau. Bypass this town and site is signed to the left at 2nd roundabout. GPS: 43.79778, -1.40111

Charges guide

Per unit incl. 2 persons and electricity	€ 21.55 - € 61.80
extra person	€ 4.85 - € 9.10

Camping Cheques accepted.

Messanges

Camping les Acacias

101 chemin du Houdin, route du Quartier Caliot, F-40660 Messanges (Landes) T: 05 58 48 01 78.
E: lesacacias@lesacacias.com **alanrogers.com/FR40220**

Close to the Atlantic beaches of Les Landes, this small, well designed campsite is quiet and peaceful. Family run and well cared for, it is a site for couples looking for relaxation or families who want a safe environment for young children to play. There are 76 flat touring pitches, all with 6/10A electricity, ten also with water and separated by trees and shrubs. Forty-nine mobile homes (13 for hire) are arranged unobtrusively on two sides. Units longer than 7 m. may have some difficulty with access to the pitches. M. and Mme. Dourthe are constantly seeking to improve this charming campsite.

Facilities

One new sanitary block is modern and very clean with facilities for disabled visitors and babies. Laundry facilities. Motorcaravan services. Fridge hire. Shop (15/6-15/9). Takeaway (July/Aug). Games room. Play area. Outdoor fitness area. Children's entertainment (July/Aug). Small library. Boules. Football field. Bicycle hire. Communal, gas and electric barbecues only. WiFi throughout (free). Off site: Riding 1.5 km. Beach and supermarket 2 km.

Open: 25 March - 25 October.

Directions

Approaching Messanges from the north, continue through centre of village on the D652 (site signed). At roundabout turn left Route du Quartier Caliot and site is 1.5 km. on left. GPS: 43.79836, -1.37550

Charges guide

Per unit incl. 2 persons and electricity	€ 18.00 - € 27.50
extra person	€ 3.50 - € 4.90

Messanges

Camping de Moisan

1077 avenue de l'Océan, F-40660 Messanges (Landes) T: 05 58 48 92 06. E: camping.moisan@orange.fr

alanrogers.com/FR40470

This family site is located in the pine forests of the southern Landes and close to the region's magnificent broad, sandy beach. There are 360 pitches here, dispersed beneath the pines. These are mostly equipped with 5/6A electricity (Europlug, long leads may be required). A wide range of mobile homes and chalets are available for rent. On-site amenities include a well stocked shop, a snack bar and cycle hire. There are miles of marked cycle tracks through the surrounding forest, including a track to the beach. The site is part of the village of Messanges, a pleasant small resort.

Facilities

Two clean toilet blocks have equal number of Turkish and British style toilets, some washbasins in cabins, and preset showers. Facilities for disabled visitors. Laundry facilities. Shop (14/6-14/9). Bar/restaurant, snack bar and takeaway (21/6-20/9). Play area. Beach volleyball. Surf school (charged). Multisports court. Bicycle hire. Activities and entertainment. Mobile homes and chalets for rent. Electric barbecues only. WiFi throughout (charged). Max. 1 dog. Off site: Fishing 200 m. Shops and restaurants in Messanges 800 m. Riding 3 km. Golf 4 km.

Open: 1 May - 30 September.

Directions

Head south from Léon on 652 as far as Messanges. Turn right on Avenue de la Plage and the site is well signed. GPS: 43.816121, -1.390319

Charges guide

Per unit incl. 2 persons and electricity	€ 12.50 - € 25.20
extra person	€ 2.50 - € 5.80
child (2-13 yrs)	free - € 3.50
dog	€ 1.50 - € 2.00

Mézin-Réaup-Lisse

Camping du Lac de Lislebonne

Le Bétous, F-47170 Mézin-Réaup-Lisse (Lot-et-Garonne) T: 05 53 65 65 28. E: domainedelislebonne@free.fr

alanrogers.com/FR47090

Lac de Lislebonne can be found on the eastern edge of the vast Landes forest, in the Lot et Garonne département. This small site has just 40 touring pitches and 40 attractive wooden chalets (available for rent). The touring pitches are of a good size and most have electricity (10A Europlug). They are well spaced out over the 18-hectare site. The lake is a pleasant spot to cool off and has a sandy beach. Various activities are organised in and around the lake, including water polo, canoeing and beach volleyball. Bicycle hire is available on site and there are over 250 km. of marked cycle tracks in the area.

Facilities

The modern heated toilet block is clean and has a baby room and facilities for disabled visitors. Laundry. Basic shop. Bar, snack bar and takeaway (July/Aug). Swimming pool (15/5-15/9). Lake swimming. Play area. Fishing. TV room. Children's club. Entertainment programme. Bicycle and canoe hire. Chalets for rent. Free WiFi in bar/reception. Off site: Tennis 2 km. Village 3 km.

Open: 1 May - 15 September.

Directions

Leave the A62 autoroute at exit for Agen and head southwest on the D656 to Nérac and then Mézin. Join the 149 towards Réaup-Lisse and follow signs to Base de Loisirs. GPS: 44.07262, 0.201517

Charges guide

Per unit incl. 2 persons and electricity	€ 17.50 - € 28.50
extra person	€ 4.00 - € 6.00

Mézos

Le Village Tropical Sen-Yan

Le Village Tropical, F-40170 Mézos (Landes) T: 05 58 42 60 05. E: reception@sen-yan.com

alanrogers.com/FR40110

This exotic family site is about 12 km. from the Atlantic coast in the Landes forest area, just outside the village. There are 100 touring pitches set around a similar number of mobile homes. Pitches are marked with hedges and have electricity (6A). The reception, bar and pool area is almost tropical with the luxuriant greenery of its banana trees, palm trees, tropical flowers and its straw sunshades. The covered, heated pool, new water slide, gym with sauna and jacuzzi all add to the attractiveness. A new covered animation area provides entertainment and discos during high season.

Facilities

Three well maintained and clean toilet blocks with showers and washbasins in cabins. The newest block is especially suitable for low season visitors with a special section for babies, plus excellent facilities for disabled campers. Shop (from 15/6). Bar, restaurant and snacks (July/Aug). Outdoor swimming pools. Heated indoor pool. Archery. Golf practice. Bicycle hire. No charcoal barbecues. WiFi (charged). Off site: Fishing 500 m. Riding 6 km. Beach 12 km.

Open: 1 June - 31 August.

Directions

From N10 take exit 14 (Onesse-Laharie), then D38 Bias/Mimizan road. After 13 km. turn south to Mézos from where site is signed. GPS: 44.07208, -1.15671

Charges guide

Per unit incl. 2 persons and electricity	€ 20.00 - € 45.50
extra person	€ 6.00 - € 9.00
dog	free - € 5.50
child (under 7 yrs)	free - € 6.50

Mimizan-Plage

Airotel Club Marina-Landes

Rue Marina, F-40200 Mimizan (Landes) T: 05 58 09 12 66. E: contact@clubmarina.com

alanrogers.com/FR40080

Well maintained and clean, with helpful staff, Club Marina-Landes would be a very good choice for a family holiday. Activities include discos, play groups for children, specially trained staff to entertain teenagers and concerts for more mature campers. There are numerous sports opportunities and a superb sandy beach nearby. The site has 355 touring pitches (312 with 10A electricity) and 147 mobile homes and chalets for rent. The pitches are on firm grass, most with hedges and they are large (mostly 100 sq.m. or larger). A nightly curfew ensures that all have a good night's sleep. If ever a campsite could be said to have two separate identities, then Club Marina-Landes is surely the one. In early and late season it is quiet, with the pace of life in low gear – come July and until 1 September, all the facilities are open and there is fun for all the family with the chance that family members will only meet together at meal times. A new leisure pool is planned.

Facilities

Five toilet blocks (opened as required) are well maintained with showers and many washbasins in cabins. Facilities for babies, children and disabled visitors. Laundry facilities. Motorcaravan services. Fridge hire. Shop (freshly baked bread) and bar. Restaurant, snack bar, pizzas and takeaway. Covered pool and outdoor pools. Minigolf. Tennis. Bicycle hire. Play area. Entertainment and activities (high season). Gas or electric barbecues only. WiFi throughout (charged). Off site: Beach and fishing 500 m. Bus service and riding 1 km. Golf 8 km. Mimizan 8 km.

Open: 25 April - 19 September.

Directions

Heading west from Mimizan centre, take D626 passing Abbey Museum. Straight on at lights (crossing D87/D67), at next lights turn left. After 2 km. at T-junction turn left. Follow signs to site. GPS: 44.20447, -1.29099

Charges guide

Per unit incl. 3 persons and electricity	€ 21.00 - € 57.00
extra person	€ 5.00 - € 10.00
child (3-12 yrs)	€ 4.00 - € 8.00
dog	€ 3.00 - € 6.00

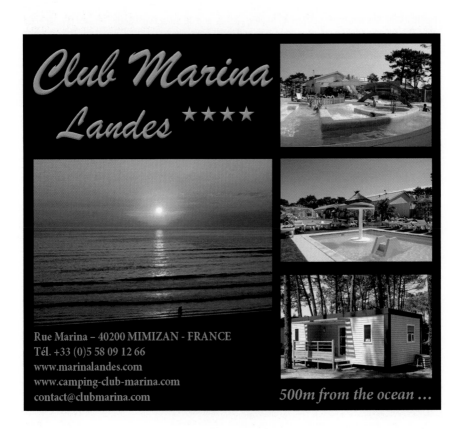

Moliets-Plage

Camping le Saint-Martin

Avenue de l'Océan, F-40660 Moliets-Plage (Landes) T: 05 58 48 52 30. E: contact@camping-saint-martin.fr

alanrogers.com/FR40190

A family site aimed mainly at couples and young families, le Saint-Martin offers 383 touring pitches and 173 mobile homes and chalets available for rent. First impressions are of a neat, tidy, well cared for site and the direct access to a wonderful fine sandy beach is an added bonus. The pitches are mainly typically French in style with low hedges separating them and with some shade. Electricity hook ups are 10/15A and a number of pitches also have water and drainage. Entertainment in high season is low key – daytime competitions and occasional evening entertainment, with the emphasis on quiet nights.

Facilities

Seven toilet blocks of a high standard and very well maintained, have washbasins in cabins, large showers, baby rooms and facilities for disabled visitors. Laundry facilities. Motorcaravan services. Supermarket. Bars, restaurants and takeaways. Indoor pool, jacuzzi and sauna (charged July/Aug). Outdoor pool area (15/6-15/9). Multisports pitch. Play area. Bicycle hire. Beach access. WiFi throughout (charged). Off site: Fishing 300 m.

Open: Easter - 1 November.

Directions

From the N10 take D142 to Lèon, then D652 to Moliets-et-Mar. Follow signs to Moliets-Plage, site is well signed. GPS: 43.85242, -1.38732

Charges guide

Per unit incl. 2 persons and electricity	€ 22.70 - € 50.00
extra person	€ 6.00 - € 8.90

Prices are for reserved pitches.

Monpazier

Camping le Moulin de David

D2, Gaugeac, F-24540 Monpazier (Dordogne) T: 05 53 22 65 25. E: contact@moulindedavid.com

alanrogers.com/FR24080

Set in a 14-hectare wooded valley, le Moulin de David has 160 pitches split into two sections, 102 are available for touring units – 33 below the central reception complex in a shaded situation and 69 above on partly terraced ground with varying degrees of shade. All pitches have electricity (10-16A). Spacing is good and there is no crowding. The variety of shrubs and trees, combined with the small stream that runs through the centre of the site, create a beautiful and tranquil setting. This site is one for those who enjoy peace, away from the main Dordogne attractions, yet sufficiently close for them to be accessible.

Facilities

Three good toilet blocks, including facilities for disabled visitors and babies. Laundry room. Shop. Bar/restaurant with shaded patio, takeaway. Outdoor swimming pool and paddling pool, freshwater pool with waterslide. Play area. Boules. Half-court tennis. Volleyball. Basketball. Football. Trampoline. Library. Events, games and canoe trips. Barbecues for hire. Mobile homes for rent. Bicycle hire. WiFi throughout (charged). Off site: Small supermarket in Monpazier 2.5 km. Riding 3 km. Fishing 8 km.

Open: 12 April - 28 September.

Directions

From Monpazier take the D2 Villeréal road. Take third turning left (after 2 km), signed to Moulin de David and Gaugeac Mairie. Site is 500 m. along this road on the left. GPS: 44.65949, 0.87898

Charges guide

Per unit incl. 2 persons and electricity	€ 20.00 - € 31.00
extra person	€ 4.00 - € 6.00
dog	€ 3.00

Montignac

Camping le Paradis

La Rebeyrolle, F-24290 Montignac (Dordogne) T: 05 53 50 72 64. E: le-paradis@perigord.com

alanrogers.com/FR24060

Le Paradis is an excellent, very well maintained riverside site, halfway between Les Eyzies and Montignac. The site is landscaped with a variety of mature shrubs and trees. The gardens are beautiful which gives a wonderful sense of tranquillity. This is a family run site and you are guaranteed a warm and friendly welcome. There are 200 good sized pitches with 62 with mobile homes to rent. The 134 touring pitches are level and with easy access, all with 10A Europlug, water and drainage. The new covered pool complements the good open-air pools.

Facilities

High quality, well equipped, heated toilet blocks are kept very clean. Well stocked shop. Restaurant and takeaway. Good pool complex heated in low season, paddling pool. Play area. Tennis. BMX track. Multisports court. Canoe hire. Fishing. Bicycle hire. Quad bike and horse riding excursions. WiFi (charged). Large units accepted by arrangement. Mobile homes to rent including one for visitors with disabilities (no smoking or dogs). Off site: Riding 8 km.

Open: 1 April - 20 October.

Directions

Site is 12 km. north of Les Eyzies and 3 km. south of St Léon-sur-Vézère, on the east side of the D706. GPS: 45.00207, 1.0711

Charges guide

Per unit incl. 2 persons and electricity	€ 24.00 - € 35.70
extra person	€ 6.20 - € 8.70
child (3-12 yrs)	€ 5.20 - € 7.50
dog	€ 3.00

Montignac

Camping le Moulin du Bleufond

Avenue Aristide Briand, F-24290 Montignac (Dordogne) T: 05 53 51 83 95.
E: campinglemoulindubleufond@gmail.com **alanrogers.com/FR24290**

Built on flat ground around a 17th-century mill, this friendly, family run site is proving to be very popular, especially for visiting the prehistoric cave paintings in Lascaux and the picturesque town of Montignac. It is separated from the banks of the Vézère river by a quiet road. Located in the Pérgord Noir, it is a five minute walk into the town. There are 83 level pitches (66 for touring) which are marked and divided by mature hedges, all with electricity and most with some shade from mature trees. Pitches tend to be on the smaller size (80 sq.m) and not suitable for large outfits. There is a sizeable river bank for fishing.

Facilities

Two modern, clean and heated sanitary blocks include facilities for disabled visitors. Laundry facilities. Bread and a few essentials available at reception. Bar, snack bar, terrace restaurant (fully open June-Aug, provides takeaways in low season). Heated swimming pool and paddling pool. Sauna. Jacuzzi. Play area. Games room with library and giant TV. Bicycle hire. Canoe trips. Weekly musical evenings (high season). Free WiFi (in bar area). Off site: Montignac 5 minutes' walk. Riverside walks.

Open: 1 April - 15 October.

Directions

Site is just south of Montignac, on D65 to Sergeac. Just after crossing old stone bridge on one way system in centre of town turn sharp right (allow for a wide sweep!) The site is 750 m. on left.
GPS: 45.05740, 1.16480

Charges guide

Per unit incl. 2 persons and electricity	€ 20.25 - € 29.10
extra person	€ 4.80 - € 7.20
child (2-8 yrs)	€ 2.50 - € 4.80

Navarrenx

Camping Beau Rivage

Allée des Marronniers, F-64190 Navarrenx (Pyrénées-Atlantiques) T: 05 59 66 10 00. E: beaucamping@free.fr
alanrogers.com/FR64120

This well cared for site lies just outside the walls of the bastide town of Navarrenx. It is owned and run by a British couple, Richard and Wendy Curtis, who take great pride in their site. Many bushes and trees have been planted and a total of 54 touring pitches are available either on hardstanding with full services or on grass, the latter having more shade. A traffic-free track leads to the town where all essential shops can be found. Richard trained as a pizzaiolo and offers fresh pizzas in the evenings. Located within driving distance of the Atlantic coast and the Pyrenees mountains, this is a good site for touring.

Facilities

Two very clean sanitary blocks with separate facilities for ladies and men include modern facilities for babies and disabled visitors. Laundry facilities. Locally produced good quality wines available in reception. Homemade pizzas. Small swimming pool (1/5-30/9). Playground for small children. Max. 2 dogs. Chalets for rent. Caravan storage. WiFi throughout (free). Off site: Municipal pool adjacent. Shop at end of road. Five minutes' walk into town.

Open: 28 March - 11 October.

Directions

From the north take D936 to Navarrenx. Turn left at first roundabout on D115 into Navarrenx. Turn left at T-junction, go over bridge and follow walls of town all the way around. At next island right on D947 and site is signed from here. GPS: 43.32001, -0.76216

Charges guide

Per unit incl. 2 persons and electricity	€ 20.10 - € 26.75
extra person	€ 4.95 - € 5.85

Nontron

Camping de Nontron

Saint Martial de Valette, F-24300 Nontron (Dordogne) T: 05 53 56 02 04. E: camping-de-nontron@orange.fr
alanrogers.com/FR24640

Open for almost all the year, this well presented, family run site is ideally situated in the Périgord Vert either as a first stop en route South, or for a much longer stay. There are 64 level, grassy pitches, 60 for touring (10A electricity), two for mobile homes and eight are studios available for rent. All are level with easy access and separated by hedges and trees providing some good shade. In Nontron you can see the famous French pocket knives being made, together with crayons that look like twigs. A sports complex adjacent to the site includes a swimming pool, toboggan, jacuzzi, sauna, solarium and tennis.

Facilities

Refurbished and well equipped toilet block with facilities for disabled visitors and babies. Laundry with washing machines and ironing boards. Motorcaravan services. Shop and takeaway (1/4-1/11). TV and games room. Boules. Play area. Charcoal barbecues only. Free WiFi over part of site. Off site: New sports complex next to site. Riding, karting and golf 10 km. Bicycle hire 20 km.

Open: 7 January - 14 December.

Directions

From Angoulême take D939 to Périgueux. Branch left on D4, then D75 to Nontron. After Nontron take D675 towards Brantôme, campsite is 200 m. on left after entering St Martial de Valette.
GPS: 45.519967, 0.65875

Charges guide

Per unit incl. 2 persons and electricity	€ 15.50 - € 16.80
extra person	€ 4.00

Pauillac

Camping Municipal les Gabarreys

Route de la Rivière, le Pastain, F-33250 Pauillac (Gironde) T: 05 56 59 10 03.
E: camping.les.gabarreys@wanadoo.fr **alanrogers.com/FR33150**

An attractive, small site with well tended flower beds, les Gabarreys is surrounded by vineyards of the Médoc region. An excellent site, it has 58 pitches, with 35 hardstandings for caravans or motorcaravans (so pegging out awnings could be a problem), some grass pitches for tents and six mobile homes, most with electric hook-ups (5/10A, some may require long leads). The Maison du Tourisme et du Vin should be your first port of call. The surrounding area is well supplied with wine caves and being fairly level you could perhaps cycle to some of them. The site is popular with the grape pickers in September.

Facilities

Two immaculate toilet blocks provide open and cubicle washbasins and excellent facilities for disabled visitors. Motorcaravan services. General room with satellite TV, fridge freezer and a small library. New play area. Minigolf (free) and volleyball. Spa and sauna (June-Sept). Communal barbecue. WiFi on part of site (free).
Off site: Fishing and bicycle hire 1 km. Riding 8 km. Golf 20 km. Beach 35 km.

Open: 26 March - 9 October.

Directions

Pauillac is northwest of Bordeaux. From Bordeaux take D1 to St Laurent, then D206 to Pauillac. At roundabout turn right to Pauillac Guais, then straight ahead at next roundabout and turn right before the Maison du Tourisme. GPS: 45.1852, -0.742397

Charges guide

Per unit incl. 2 persons and electricity	€ 18.70 - € 22.00
extra person	€ 3.80 - € 5.00

Petit-Palais-et-Cornemps

Airotel Camping le Pressoir

29 Queyrai, F-33570 Petit-Palais-et-Cornemps (Gironde) T: 05 57 69 73 25.
E: contact@campinglepressoir.com **alanrogers.com/FR33090**

Nestling in the famous wine producing countryside of the Lussac, Pomerol and Saint Emilion areas north of Bordeaux, le Pressoir is surrounded by fields of vines. The 100 large pitches are arranged on either side of a gravel road leading up a slight hill. Most are shaded by attractive trees, but almost all are sloping. They are over 100 sq.m. and equipped with electricity (10A, Europlug). The old barn has been converted into a stylish bar and a really charming, separate restaurant. A quiet, family site, le Pressoir provides a comfortable base for a holiday in this area famous for good food and wine.

Facilities

Fully equipped toilet block with excellent facilities for disabled visitors. Washing machine. Bar and pleasant restaurant with indoor and outdoor seating. Heated swimming pool (15/4-15/10, no Bermuda shorts). Sauna. Wellness (15/5-15/9). Playground with timber equipment. Bouncy castle. Trampoline. Kids' club. Pétanque. Mountain bike hire. Free WiFi throughout. Mobile homes and bungalow tents to rent. Bicycle hire. Off site: Tennis nearby. Fishing 1 km. Riding 5 km. St Emilion 11 km.

Open: All year.

Directions

From A89 Bordeaux-Périgueux take exit 11 to St Médard-de-Guizières then south towards Lussac on the D21 (signed from St Médard). From Castillon-la-Bataille on D936 Libourne-Bergerac road, south of site, take D17 north (St Médard) then D21 through Petit-Palais. Site signed. GPS: 44.9971, -0.06326

Charges guide

Per unit incl. 2 persons and electricity	€ 18.00 - € 34.00
extra person	€ 4.00 - € 7.00

Peyrillac

Camping Au P'tit Bonheur

Millac, F-24370 Peyrillac (Dordogne) T: 05 53 29 77 93. E: auptitbonheur24@gmail.com
alanrogers.com/FR24365

Camping Au P'tit Bonheur is in the heart of the Dordogne region, between Sarlat and Rocamadour, set in open countryside 250 m. above the River Dordogne and not far from the small village of Peyrillac-et-Millac. It is a quiet, spacious, family run site and in July and August there is a varied entertainment programme for all the family. There are 100 average sized pitches with 59 for touring. Many are on terraces, all have 10A electricity and some have a water supply. A variety of shrubs and trees give shade to many of the pitches and some have good views over the countryside below the campsite.

Facilities

Two modern toilet blocks including provision for babies and disabled campers. Laundry. Swimming/paddling pool, sauna and jacuzzi with terrace overlooked by the bar/restaurant. Play area. Volleyball. Football. Boules. Entertainment in high season. Miniclub (6-12 yrs). No electric barbecues. WiFi over part of site (charged).
Off site: Hiking, riding, cycling, canoeing and fishing. Souillac 8 km. Sarlat 22 km. Rocamadour 25 km.

Open: 1 April - 30 September.

Directions

A20 exit 55 near Souillac. Take D904 southwest around Souillac, road number changes to D703. In Peyrillac, follow signs to site. GPS: 44.8986, 1.4032

Charges guide

Per unit incl. 2 persons and electricity	€ 18.50 - € 22.70
extra person	€ 4.40 - € 5.65
child (0-7 yrs acc. to age)	free - € 2.55
dog	€ 2.00

Pomport

Camping Pomport Beach

Route de la Gardonnett, F-24240 Pomport (Dordogne) T: 05 24 10 61 13. E: info@pomport-beach.com
alanrogers.com/FR24865

In the heart of the Bergerac region, Pomport Beach is a recently much improved site now boasting 130 pitches, of which 85 are for touring, all with electricity (10A) and a shared water supply. The pitches have been levelled and new grass sown; young hedges and trees do not as yet offer much shade. Visitors can enjoy the heated pool or bathe in the lake, which has a sandy beach and is overlooked by the restaurant. This site is quiet and peaceful but becomes more lively in peak season, when children's entertainment takes place, and the tennis courts, minigolf and multisports court come into their own.

Facilities

Two recently refurbished sanitary blocks. Separate unit for disabled visitors. Laundry facilities. Motorcaravan services. Bar. Restaurant. Swimming pool. Play area. Multisports area. Playing field. Tennis courts. Minigolf. Fishing. Bicycle hire. Watersports. WiFi throughout (free). Off site: Supermarket and restaurant in Sigoulès 1 km.

Open: 22 May - 12 September.

Directions

From Bergerac take D933 (Sigoulès/Marmande) for 15 km. to Pomport. Site is on right. GPS: 44.77125, 0.41182

Charges guide

Per unit incl. 2 persons and electricity	€ 18.00 - € 30.00
extra person	€ 6.00 - € 7.00
child (1-17 yrs)	free - € 6.00

Pujols

Camping Lot & Bastides

Allée de Malbentre, F-47300 Pujols (Lot-et-Garonne) T: 05 53 36 86 79.
E: contact@camping-lot-et-bastides.fr **alanrogers.com/FR47060**

Close to the medieval village of Pujols and the Bastide of Villeneuve sur Lot, this purpose built campsite was opened in 2012 and offers 83 level touring pitches. A central area has 62 grassy pitches separated by young hedges and equipped with electricity (16A, mostly Europlug, long leads may be required), water tap and drainage; a further 21 pitches, currently with little shade, are dedicated to motorcaravans. There are 26 mobile homes and chalets plus four Canada tents for hire. The region is rich in historical sites and the valley of the River Lot provides opportunities for exploration, adventure and exercise.

Facilities

One fairly busy, modern sanitary block includes facilities for disabled visitors and laundry room. Motorcaravan service point. Small shop. Bar (18.00-21.00). Snack bar with bar and takeaway (daily in high season with breakfasts and bread to order in low season). Swimming pool and jacuzzi (April-Sept). Communal barbecue. Giant chess and draughts. Pétanque. Volleyball. Play area. Bicycle hire. Free WiFi. Off site: Shops, pharmacy, bars and restaurants in Villeneuve sur Lot 2 km. Pujols 2.5 km.

Open: 26 March - 29 September.

Directions

From A62 Bordeaux/Toulouse motorway leave at exit 7, follow signs for Agen (D931) then head north on N21 to Villeneuve sur Lot. Before river, turn south (D118, Pujols) and look for signs to right to Piscine de Malbentre and site (new road scheme may not appear on sat navs). GPS: 44.39498, 0.6874

Charges guide

Per unit incl. 2 persons, electricity, water and waste water	€ 15.00 - € 21.00
extra person	€ 3.00 - € 5.00

Pyla-sur-Mer

Yelloh! Village Panorama du Pyla

Grande Dune du Pyla, route de Biscarrosse, F-33260 Pyla-sur-Mer (Gironde) T: 04 66 73 97 39.
E: mail@camping-panorama.com **alanrogers.com/FR33310**

Panorama is set amongst pine trees and the entrance is inviting with well tended flower beds and a pleasant, airy reception. There is a steep climb up to the first of the touring pitches, passing the swimming pool and play area. Some pitches are suitable for caravans and motorcaravans and others suitable for tents. The 350 touring pitches are on terraces amongst the tall pines and almost all have electricity (3-10A). The sea views from some pitches are stunning. A track leads down to the beach with a staircase and right next door is Europe's largest dune, the Dune du Pyla. Access to the toilet blocks may involve a steep climb (the site is probably not suitable for those with disabilities).

Facilities

Seven toilet blocks (only two open in low season) are clean and well maintained with baby rooms and facilities for disabled campers. Laundry facilities. Motorcaravan services. Restaurant with panoramic view of the ocean. Three heated swimming pools and jacuzzi. 45 m. water slide. Adjacent play area. Tennis. Minigolf. Paragliding. Sub-aqua diving. Gym equipment. Bicycle hire. Entertainment in high season. Library. WiFi over site (charged). ATM. Off site: Riding and golf 10 km.

Open: 11 April - 29 September.

Directions

From N250, just before La Teste, take D259 signed Biscarrosse and Dune du Pyla. At roundabout at end of road turn left (south) on D218 coast road signed Biscarrosse and Dune du Pyla. Site is 4 km. on right. GPS: 44.57265, -1.22053

Charges guide

Per unit incl. 2 persons and electricity	€ 18.00 - € 47.00
extra person	€ 6.00 - € 8.00

Rauzan

Camping du Vieux Château

D123, F-33420 Rauzan (Gironde) T: 05 57 84 15 38. E: contact@vieuxchateau.fr

alanrogers.com/FR33440

Camping du Vieux Château is located in the heart of the Bordeaux vineyards and adjacent to the fortress town of Rauzan. It is an ideal starting point for walking and cycling along small tracks through the vineyards, and for day trips. The flat, grassy 2.6 hectare site has 78 well shaded pitches, many with views of the château. There are 47 pitches for touring (25 with 6/A electricity); some are rather uneven and require long leads. Mobile homes, cottages and bungalows are available to rent. There are swimming and paddling pools, plus jacuzzi. The village is within walking distance.

Facilities

Traditional sanitary block is kept clean and offers some washbasins and preset showers in cubicles. Facilities for babies and disabled visitors. Laundry facilities. Small shop (June-Sept, bread to order). Bar, snack bar and takeaway. Heated outdoor swimming pool and children's pool (May-Sept). Play area and mini farm. Television. Small library. Outdoor sports area. Boules. Communal barbecue. Mobile homes and chalets to hire. Free WiFi on part of site. Max. 1 dog. Off site: Rauzan 200 m.

Open: 1 April - 17 October.

Directions

From Libourne, join D670 towards St Emilion and Castillon-la-Bataille. At St Laurent-des-Combes turn right towards Sauveterre-de-Guyenne. At sign for Rauzan turn right onto D231. Campsite is signed from the village. GPS: 44.782472, -0.127139

Charges guide

Per unit incl. 2 persons and electricity	€ 14.50 - € 20.60
extra person	€ 3.50 - € 5.50
child (1-11 yrs)	€ 3.10 - € 4.12

Rouffignac-Saint Cernin

Camping Bleu Soleil

Domaine Touvent, F-24580 Rouffignac-Saint Cernin (Dordogne) T: 05 53 05 48 30.

E: infos@camping-bleusoleil.com **alanrogers.com/FR24380**

Camping Bleu Soleil is quietly located in the countryside and has magnificent views from all areas of the site across onto the wooded flanks of the hills opposite. It comprises 70 acres and, at present, has 120 pitches, 96 for touring units and 24 used for wooden chalets and two bungalow tents. Electricity (10A) is available on every pitch (long cables may be necessary). The area is famous for its walnut trees, which provide partial shade. There is some terracing. The site is divided by a very quiet minor road and the circular area in front of reception may prove narrow for larger units manoeuvring.

Facilities

Three modern unisex sanitary blocks are clean, well maintained and adequate for the number of pitches. En-suite toilet for disabled visitors. Baby room with bath. Enclosed laundry area. Small bar with TV (1/6-15/9). Restaurant (1/6-15/9). Large swimming pool and paddling pool (15/5-15/9). Multisports area. Boules. Small play area and a pen with donkeys and goats. Bicycle hire. WiFi (free). Off site: Supermarket 2 km. Riding 4 km. Fishing 10 km. Golf 14 km. Sunday market at Rouffignac.

Open: 11 April - 27 September.

Directions

From Périgueux take N89 east for 17 km. to Thenon, then D31 south signed Balou. Continue from Balou for 3 km. to the outskirts of Rouffignac-St Cernin-de-Reilhac and look for site sign on the left. Turn off main road to site (less than 1 km). GPS: 45.05497, 0.98691

Charges guide

Per unit incl. 2 persons and electricity (10A)	€ 14.90 - € 22.90
extra person	€ 3.00 - € 5.70

Saint Antoine-de-Breuilh

Camping la Rivière Fleurie

180 rue Théophile Cart, F-24230 Saint Antoine-de-Breuilh (Dordogne) T: 05 53 24 82 80.

E: info@la-riviere-fleurie.com **alanrogers.com/FR24300**

This quiet and pleasant campsite, beside the Dordogne, is close to the vineyards of Pomerol and Saint Emilion and not far from the towns of Saint Foy-la-Grande and Bergerac. There are 66 level, grass pitches of average size, 47 of which are for touring. All have electricity (10A) and 20 are fully serviced. They are separated by shrubs and mature trees provide varying amounts of shade. The site has a tranquil and peaceful ambience, suitable for anyone looking for a quiet and relaxing holiday. You will receive a warm and friendly welcome from the new owners and there is a convivial, family atmosphere.

Facilities

Two modern toilet blocks provide all the necessary facilities. Bar, terrace and restaurant/takeaway. Heated outdoor swimming pool and paddling pool. TV room. Weekly soirées. Canoe trips. WiFi near reception and bar/restaurant (free). Kid's club. Charcoal barbecues are not permitted. Off site: Walks beside the Dordogne 30 m. Tennis adjacent. Fishing 500 m. Riding 3 km.

Open: 10 April - 20 September.

Directions

Leave D936, Bergerac-Bordeaux road at roundabout just west of St Foy-la-Grande (site signed). Follow signs to site, about 3 km. GPS: 44.82905, 0.12238

Charges guide

Per unit incl. 2 persons and electricity	€ 31.10 - € 38.20
extra person	€ 4.60 - € 6.00

Camping Cheques accepted.

Saint Avit-de-Vialard

Castel Camping Caravaning Saint-Avit Loisirs

Le Bugue, F-24260 Saint Avit-de-Vialard (Dordogne) T: 05 53 02 64 00. E: contact@saint-avit-loisirs.com

alanrogers.com/FR24180

Although Saint-Avit Loisirs is set amidst rolling countryside, far from the hustle and bustle of the main tourist areas of the Dordogne, the facilities are first class, providing virtually everything you could possibly want without the need to leave the site. This makes it ideal for families with children. One part of the site is dedicated to chalets and mobile homes which are available to rent, whilst the main section contains 199 flat and mainly grassy, good sized pitches, 99 for touring, with electricity (6/10A).

Facilities

Three modern unisex toilet blocks provide high quality facilities, but could become overstretched in high season. Motorcaravan services. Shop, bar, good restaurant, cafeteria. Outdoor swimming pool, children's pool, water slide, crazy river, heated indoor pool with jacuzzi. Fitness room. Soundproofed disco. Minigolf. Boules. Tennis. Quad bikes. Play area. Bicycle hire. Canoe trips on the Dordogne. WiFi over site (charged). Off site: Riding 2 km.

Open: 28 March - 27 September.

Directions

Site is 6 km. north of Le Bugue. From D710 Le Bugue-Périgueux road, turn west on narrow and bumpy C201 towards St Avit-de-Vialard. Follow road through St Avit, bearing right and site is 1.5 km. GPS: 44.95161, 0.85042

Charges guide

Per unit incl. 2 persons and electricity	€ 20.50 - € 48.00
extra person	€ 4.00 - € 12.00

Saint Crépin-Carlucet

Camping les Péneyrals

Le Poujol, F-24590 Saint Crépin-Carlucet (Dordogne) T: 05 53 28 85 71. E: infos@peneyrals.com

alanrogers.com/FR24320

Within easy reach of all the attractions of the Périgord region, M. and Mme. Havel have created an attractive and friendly family campsite at les Péneyrals. There are 250 pitches, 114 of which are for touring. The pitches at the bottom of the hill tend to be quieter as they are further from the main facilities, but are all level and grassy (some on terraces), with electricity (5/10A), and most have some shade. An attractive bar and restaurant with terrace overlook the excellent pool complex and at the bottom of the site is a small fishing lake. The site is set on a wooded hillside with flowers in abundance (thanks to the dedication of Mme. Havel's mother). Activities are organised over a long season including archery, various sports tournaments, aquagym, discos and a children's club. On-site entertainment is provided in and around the bar and terrace area every night except Saturdays. The site is used fairly unobtrusively by a UK tour operator. Flights from London arrive at a new airport some 30 km. away; this may prove to be popular with visitors using the rental accommodation. Sarlat la Canéda is just 11 km. away.

Facilities

Three modern, unisex toilet blocks provide good quality facilities, including provision for babies and disabled visitors. Motorcaravan services. Good shop. Excellent restaurant and takeaway. Pool complex, paddling pool with games and four slides with splash pool. Indoor heated pool. Bicycle hire. Minigolf. Tennis (charged). Badminton. Play area. Games room, WiFi over site (charged), TV room and small library. Fishing.
Off site: Sarlat 11 km. Châteaux of the Dordogne. Prehistoric caves of the Vézère. Golf 15 km.

Open: 4 May - 11 September.

Directions

Site is 11 km. north of Sarlat. From D704 Sarlat-Montignac road turn east on D60 towards Salignac-Eyvigues. After 4 km. turn south on D56 towards St Crépin-Carlucet. Site is 500 m. along this road on the right. GPS: 44.95776, 1.2729

Charges guide

Per unit incl. 2 persons and electricity	€ 20.40 - € 39.60
extra person	€ 5.10 - € 10.20
child (under 7 yrs)	free - € 8.20
dog	€ 1.70 - € 3.10

Saint Cybranet

Camping Bel Ombrage

L'Albarède, F-24250 Saint Cybranet (Dordogne) T: 05 53 28 34 14. E: belombrage@wanadoo.fr

alanrogers.com/FR24140

Bel Ombrage is a quiet, well maintained site in a pretty location by the little River Céou with a pebble beach that is safe and clean for bathing. The site has a good pool complex but otherwise there are few on-site facilities because the owner has a deliberate policy of providing peace and quiet during the evening. The 180 well shaded, good sized and flat grass pitches are marked by trees and bushes and all have electricity. The quiet and tranquil setting makes the site particularly popular with couples. Bel Ombrage is very close to Domme and Castelnaud and would make an ideal and inexpensive base for visiting the southern Dordogne area. Adjacent to the site is a snack bar and pizzeria which is popular with campers. It is a short walk to the village of Saint Cybranet with bar, restaurant and a small, well stocked supermarket, and a short drive takes you to the beautifully restored village of Daglan. A park and ride service operates from the school in Sarlat during July and August; you can park your car or motorcaravan and take the bus into town for a small charge.

Facilities

Two modern toilet blocks with individual cubicles are kept spotlessly clean with facilities for disabled visitors and babies. Laundry facilities. Bread van. Large swimming pool with sun terrace, paddling pool. Play area. Fishing. Excursions can be booked at reception. WiFi (free).
Off site: Pizzeria next door. Tennis and canoeing nearby. Riding and bicycle hire 3 km. Golf 6 km. Shops at Cénac.

Open: 1 June - 5 September.

Directions

Site is 14 km. south of Sarlat, on the east side of the D57 Castelnaud-la-Chapelle-St Cybranet road, 1 km. north of the junction with the D50.
GPS: 44.79128, 1.16214

Charges guide

Per unit incl. 2 persons and electricity	€ 23.40
extra person	€ 5.90
child (under 7 yrs)	€ 3.90
dog	free

Saint Emilion

Yelloh! Village Saint Emilion

Domaine de la Barbanne, 2 Lieu-dit Les Combes, F-33330 Saint Emilion (Gironde) T: 05 57 24 75 80.
E: info@camping-saint-emilion.com **alanrogers.com/FR33080**

Yelloh! Village Saint Emilion (formerly La Barbanne) is a pleasant site in the heart of the Bordeaux wine region, only 2.5 km. from the famous town of Saint Emilion. With 173 pitches, 125 for touring, the owners have created a carefully maintained, well equipped site. The large, level and grassy pitches have dividing hedges and electricity (long leads necessary). The original parts of the site bordering the lake have mature trees, good shade and pleasant surroundings, whilst in the newer area the trees have yet to provide full shade and it can be hot in summer.

Facilities

Two modern, fully equipped toilet blocks include facilities for children and disabled visitors. Motorcaravan services. Well stocked shop. Bar, terrace, takeaway, restaurant. Breakfast service. Two swimming pools, one heated with water slide. Enclosed play area. Children's club. Tennis. Boules. Volleyball. Fishing. Minigolf. Bicycle hire. Evening entertainment. WiFi over site (charged). Max. 1 dog. Off site: St Emilion 2.5 km. Riding 8 km.

Open: 29 April - 26 September.

Directions

Site is 2.5 km. north of St Emilion. Caravans and motorcaravans are forbidden in the village of St Emilion and they must approach the site from Libourne on D243 or from Castillon leave D936 and take D130/D243. GPS: 44.91679, -0.14148

Charges guide

Per unit incl. 2 persons and electricity	€ 18.00 - € 40.00
extra person	€ 6.00 - € 7.00

Saint Girons-Plage

Camping Club International Eurosol

Route de la Plage, F-40560 Saint Girons-Plage (Landes) T: 05 58 47 90 14.
E: contact@camping-eurosol.com **alanrogers.com/FR40060**

Privately owned, Eurosol is an attractive, friendly and well maintained site extending over 15 hectares of undulating ground, amongst mature pine trees giving good shade. Of the 356 touring pitches, 231 have electricity (10A) with 120 fully serviced. A wide range of mobile homes and chalets, which are being updated, are available for rent. This is very much a family site with multi-lingual entertainers. Many games and tournaments are organised and a beach volleyball competition is held regularly in front of the bar. The adjacent boules terrain is floodlit. An excellent sandy beach 700 metres from the site has supervised bathing in high season and is ideal for surfing. The landscaped swimming pool complex is impressive with three large pools, one of which is covered and heated, and a large children's paddling pool. There is a convivial restaurant and takeaway food service. A number of cycle trails lead from the site through the vast forests of Les Landes, and a riding centre is located just 500 m. from Eurosol. To the south, the Basque country and Biarritz are within easy access.

Facilities

Four main toilet blocks and two smaller blocks are comfortable and clean with facilities for babies and disabled visitors. Motorcaravan services. Well stocked shop and bar. Restaurant, takeaway (1/6-7/9). Stage for live shows arranged in July/Aug. Outdoor swimming pool, paddling pool (all season) and heated, covered pool (May-July). Tennis. Multisports court. Bicycle hire. WiFi (charged). No charcoal barbecues. Off site: Riding (July/Aug) 500 m. Surf school 500 m. Beach 700 m.

Open: 10 May - 18 September.

Directions

Turn off D652 at St Girons on D42 towards St Girons-Plage. Site is on left before coming to beach (4.5 km). GPS: 43.95166, -1.35212

Charges guide

Per unit incl. 2 persons and electricity	€ 23.00 - € 41.00
extra person (over 5 yrs)	€ 7.00
dog	€ 4.00

Saint Jean-de-Luz

Camping Tamaris Plage

Quartier Acotz, 720 route des Plages, F-64500 Saint Jean-de-Luz (Pyrénées-Atlantiques) T: 05 59 26 55 90.
E: tamaris1@wanadoo.fr **alanrogers.com/FR64080**

This small, pleasant and popular site is well kept and open all year. It is situated outside the town and just across the road from a sandy beach. The 30 touring pitches, all with 7/10A electricity, are of a good size and separated by hedges, on slightly sloping ground with some shade. The site becomes full for July and August with families on long stays, so reservation for that period is essential. Mobile homes for rent occupy a further 40 pitches. A leisure centre and club provide a heated pool and various other free facilities. A gym, Turkish bath, massage and other relaxing amenities are available at an extra charge.

Facilities

The single heated toilet block of good quality should be an ample provision. Facilities for disabled guests. Laundry facilities. Wellness health club with free facilities: swimming pool, TV/playroom and club for children, and some on payment: gym, Turkish bath and other spa facilities, sunbathing area, jacuzzi, adult TV lounge. WiFi. Off site: Beach, fishing, surfing (with instruction) 30 m. Ghéthary with supermarket 2 km. St Jean-de-Luz 4 km. Bicycle hire, boat launching and golf 5 km. Riding 7 km.

Open: 3 April - 1 November.

Directions

Proceed south on N10 and 1.5 km. after Ghéthary take first road on right (before access to the motorway and Carrefour centre commercial) and follow site signs. GPS: 43.41795, -1.623817

Charges guide

Per unit incl. 2 persons and electricity	€ 20.00 - € 34.00
extra person	€ 8.00 - € 11.00
child (2-13 yrs)	€ 7.00 - € 10.00

Saint Jean-de-Luz

Camping International Erromardie

235 avenue de la Source, F-64500 Saint Jean-de-Luz (Pyrénées-Atlantiques) T: 05 59 26 07 74.
E: info@chadotel.com **alanrogers.com/FR64170**

There are not many sites right by the sea in this region. Erromardie, a new member of the Chadotel group, is a good one, with only a small access road to cross to reach a beach of coarse sand and fine shingle. The site is mainly flat and grassy, with several different parts separated by hedges, but not much shade. There are 215 pitches, mainly adjoining access roads and backing onto hedges, including 70 for tourers with 6A electricity, of which 20 also have water and waste water drainage. Some pitches have ocean views and others have views of the Pyrenees.

Facilities

The large sanitary buildings are of good quality, with individual cabins and free hot water. Baby area. Facilities for disabled visitors. Laundry room. Motorcaravan services. Shop, bar, restaurant and takeaway (May-Sept). Basic outdoor heated swimming pool (15/5-10/9). Water play area. Playground. Boules. Fishing. Mobile homes for hire. Barbecue rental. WiFi throughout (charged). Off site: Beach 50 m. Golf 1 km. Boat ramp 2 km. Biarritz and Spain 15 km.

Open: 3 April - 19 September.

Directions

Take exit 3 from the A63 (E05, E70) St Jean-de-Luz Nord towards St Jean-de-Luz/Guéthary/Ascain onto ave de Lahanchipia, then left onto ave André Ithurralde (D810), first right ave Claude Farrère and follow site signs. GPS: 43.406247, -1.637286

Charges guide

Per unit incl. 2 persons and electricity	€ 21.00 - € 37.00
extra person	€ 6.00
child (2-13 yrs)	€ 4.00

Saint Jean-de-Luz

Camping Atlantica

Quartier Acotz, 15 chemin mikelenia, F-64500 Saint Jean-de-Luz (Pyrénées-Atlantiques) T: 05 59 47 72 44.
E: info@campingatlantica.com **alanrogers.com/FR64250**

This is a friendly, family run site with 200 shady and well kept grass pitches set amongst many shrubs, flowers and hedges. There are 70 pitches for touring, 48 have 6A electricity. The excellent swimming pool area is attractively landscaped with plenty of sunbeds. With a bar, restaurant and takeaway open April to September, the beach 500 m. and the cosmopolitan town of Saint Jean-de-Luz only 3 km. away, this site is suitable for families and couples of all ages. If excessively wet, motorcaravans are advised to call ahead to check availability.

Facilities

Three immaculate toilet blocks include facilities for babies and campers with disabilities. Excellent laundry. Motorcaravan services. Shop, bar, restaurant and takeaway, heated outdoor swimming pool and fitness room. Games room. Multisports court. Bicycle hire. Modern, fenced play area. Family entertainment (July/Aug). WiFi throughout (charged). Off site: Bus to major town 400 m. Large supermarket 1 km. Golf 4 km.

Open: 1 April - 30 September.

Directions

Leave A63, exit 3, taking N10 toward Bayonne. Take the second left turn signed Acotz-Campings-Plages. At T-junction turn right and follow signs. Campsite is on the right. GPS: 43.41569, -1.61646

Charges guide

Per unit incl. 2 persons and electricity	€ 19.00 - € 39.70
extra person	€ 3.50 - € 8.20
child (2-6 yrs)	€ 2.50 - € 4.50

Saint Jean-de-Luz

Camping Duna Munguy

Quartier Acotz, 881 chemin Duhartia, F-64500 Saint Jean-de-Luz (Pyrénées-Atlantiques) T: 05 59 47 70 70.
E: contact@camping-dunamunguy.com **alanrogers.com/FR64520**

Situated close to two fine beaches and only six kilometres from the centre of Saint-Jean-de-Luz, this small and somewhat basic campsite is worth considering when visiting this region. The attractive site has 28 fully equipped bungalows available for rent but at the site entrance there are also eight good sized pitches available for touring units, each with electricity (10A, Europlug). The resident owners provide an incredible level of service and are available at all times with information and assistance on plenty of things to see and do in the area. Dogs are accepted according to weight.

Facilities

The clean sanitary facilities include hot showers, washbasins, dishwashing and laundry sinks. No shop but bread is available. Heated swimming pool. Play area. Small games room. Communal barbecue area. Free WiFi throughout. Off site: Beach, fishing, surfing (with instruction available) nearby. Supermarket 2 km. Bicycle hire, boat launching and golf 5 km. Riding 7 km. Spanish border 15 km.

Open: Easter - October.

Directions

Leave A63 at exit 3 and take N10 toward Bayonne. Take second left turn signed Acotz-Campings-Plage. At T-junction turn right and follow signs. Campsite is on left down a hill and 200 m. past railway bridge. GPS: 43.41832, -1.62106

Charges guide

Per unit incl. 2 persons and electricity	€ 21.50 - € 36.50
extra person	€ 6.00 - € 8.00

Saint Julien-en-Born

Yelloh! Village Lous Seurrots

606 avenue de l'Ocean, Contis Plage, F-40170 Saint Julien-en-Born (Landes) T: 05 58 42 85 82.
E: info@seurrots.com **alanrogers.com/FR40070**

Lous Seurrots is only a short 500 m. walk from the beach with parts of the site having views across the estuary. There are 550 pitches, mainly in pine woods on sandy undulating ground. They are numbered but many are only roughly marked out, some with good shade. All 215 touring pitches have 10A electricity (adaptors required). The site has a brand new Aquatic Centre with excellent access for wheelchairs and disabled campers. The complex has a superb setting among palm trees and flower beds, the decked sunbathing areas having wonderful views out to the estuary and the sea. For all its size, Lous Seurrots is a family site with the emphasis on peace and tranquillity with some well organised entertainment in peak season.

Facilities

Three well kept, modern toilet blocks have baby rooms and facilities for disabled visitors. Washing machines. Motorcaravan services. Large shop and bar, restaurant and takeaway, heated indoor and outdoor pools (all open all season). Jacuzzi with keep fit classes (July/Aug). Tennis. Archery. Minigolf. Canoeing. Bicycle hire. Fishing. Miniclub. Evening entertainment twice weekly in high season in open-air auditorium. Gas and electric barbecues are permitted. WiFi (charged).
Off site: Beach 500 m. Riding 3 km.

Open: 27 March - 27 September.

Directions

Turn off D652 on D41 (15 km. south of Mimizan) to Contis-Plage and site is on left as you reach it.
GPS: 44.08881, -1.31634

Charges guide

Per unit incl. 2 persons and electricity	€ 18.00 - € 51.00
extra person	€ 8.00
child (3-7 yrs)	free - € 6.00
dog	€ 5.00

No credit cards.

Saint Martin-de-Seignanx

Sites et Paysages Caravaning Lou P'tit Poun

110 avenue du Quartier Neuf, F-40390 Saint Martin-de-Seignanx (Landes) T: 05 59 56 55 79.
E: contact@louptitpoun.com **alanrogers.com/FR40140**

The manicured grounds surrounding Lou P'tit Poun give it a well kept appearance, a theme running throughout this very pleasing site which celebrated its 20th anniversary in 2009. It is only after arriving at the car park that you feel confident it is not a private estate. Beyond this point an abundance of shrubs and trees is revealed. Behind a central sloping flower bed lies the open plan reception area. The avenues around the site are wide and the 168 pitches (142 for touring) are spacious. All have 10A electricity, many also have water and drainage and some are separated by low hedges. The jovial owners not only make their guests welcome, but extend their enthusiasm to organising weekly entertainment (at the café/restaurant) for young and old during high season.

Facilities

Two unisex sanitary blocks, maintained to a high standard and kept clean, include washbasins in cabins, a baby bath and provision for disabled visitors. Laundry facilities with washing machine and dryer. Motorcaravan services. Shop, bar and café/restaurant (all 7/7-31/8). Outdoor swimming pool. Play area. Games room, TV. Half-court tennis. No charcoal barbecues. WiFi on part of site (charged). Off site: Bayonne 6 km. Fishing and riding 7 km. Golf 10 km. Sandy beaches of Basque coast ten minute drive. Trips to the Pyrenees.

Open: 14 June - 13 September.

Directions

Leave A63 at exit 6 and join D817 towards Pau. Site is signed at Leclerc supermarket. Continue for 3.5 km. and site is clearly signed on right.
GPS: 43.52406, -1.41196

Charges guide

Per unit incl. 2 persons and electricity	€ 24.45 - € 36.50
extra person	€ 7.90 - € 8.40
child (under 7 yrs)	€ 5.85 - € 6.45
dog	€ 4.65 - € 5.65

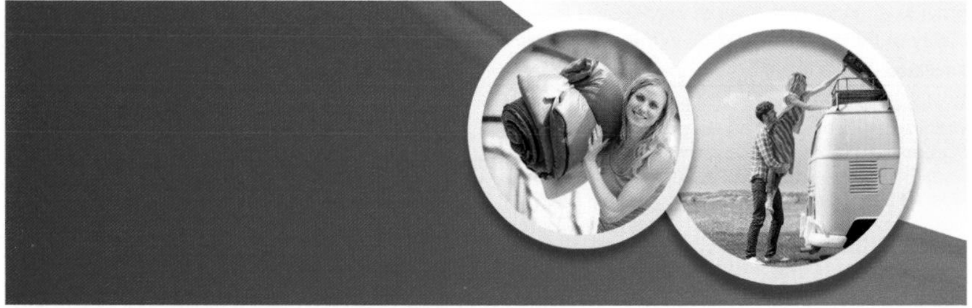

Saint Pardoux-la-Rivière

Camping Château le Verdoyer

Champs Romain, F-24470 Saint Pardoux-la-Rivière (Dordogne) T: 05 53 56 94 64. E: chateau@verdoyer.fr

alanrogers.com/FR24010

Château le Verdoyer has been developed in the park of a restored château and is owned by a Dutch family. This 22-hectare estate has three lakes, two for fishing and one with a sandy beach and safe swimming area. There are 135 good sized touring pitches, level, terraced and hedged. With a choice of wooded area or open field, all have electricity (5/10A) and most share a water supply between four pitches. There is a swimming pool complex and high season activities are organised for children but there is no disco. This site caters well for disabled visitors with wheelchair access to all facilities.

Facilities

Well appointed sanitary blocks include baby baths and facilities for disabled visitors. Serviced launderette. Motorcaravan services. Fridge rental. Shop and takeaway (15/5-15/9). Bar (15/5-30/9). Restaurant (25/4-30/9). Bistro (July/Aug). Two swimming pools, slide and paddling pool. Play areas. Tennis. Minigolf. Bicycle hire. Fishing. Small library. Kids' club (July/Aug). WiFi (free in courtyard). Computer in reception for Internet access. Off site: Golf 3 km. Riding 12 km. 'Circuit des Orchidées'.

Open: 23 April - 30 September.

Directions

Site is 2 km. from the Limoges (N21)-Chalus (D6bis-D85)-Nontron road, 20 km. south of Chalus and is well signed from main road. Site on D96 4 km. north of village of Champs Romain. GPS: 45.55035, 0.7947

Charges guide

Per unit incl. 2 persons and electricity	€ 22.00 - € 37.00
extra person	€ 5.00 - € 7.00

Camping Cheques accepted.

Saint Pée-sur-Nivelle

Camping Goyetchea

F-64310 Saint Pée-sur-Nivelle (Pyrénées-Atlantiques) T: 05 59 54 19 59. E: info@camping-goyetchea.com

alanrogers.com/FR64300

Camping Goyetchea is located at the heart of Basque country, close to the area's celebrated Atlantic beaches and the classic seaside town of Biarritz. There are 104 pitches with electrical connections (6A). Pitches vary in size (80-100 sq.m) and most have shade from tall trees. There are 27 mobile homes and two Romany-style caravans and three tents available for rent. Facilities include a good sized swimming pool with children's pool. This is a green and pleasant site away from the busy coastal areas of Saint Jean-de-Luz and Biarritz, both only a short drive away, and a good base for hiking and cycling.

Facilities

Two main toilet blocks are very clean and have preset showers, washbasins in cabins, baby bath and changing mat. Facilities for disabled visitors. Laundry facilities. Snack bar, pizzeria (July/Aug). Heated swimming pool (May-Sept). Children's pool. Play area. TV room. Library. Board games. Volleyball. Pétanque. Sports tournaments. Hiking trips. Accommodation for rent. WiFi throughout. ff site: Supermarket 800 m.

Open: 14 May - 16 September.

Directions

Take N10 from Bordeaux and continue on A63 towards Biarritz leaving at exit 4 (St Pée-sur-Nivelle). Continue following signs to St Pée-sur-Nivelle via D810 and D655. Then take D855 for 6 km. and follow signs to site. GPS: 43.36344, -1.56752

Charges guide

Per unit incl. 2 persons and electricity	€ 16.50 - € 28.50
extra person	€ 4.00 - € 6.00

Saint Sulpice-de-Mareuil

Camping Domaine de Corneuil

Lieu-dit Corneuil, F-24340 Saint Sulpice de Mareuil (Dordogne) T: 05 53 60 79 48. E: camping@corneuil.com

alanrogers.com/FR24085

Camping Domaine de Corneuil is situated in 25 hectares of park and woodland in the Périgord Vert region of the Dordogne. There are 50 mainly level, touring pitches (100-200 sq.m. with 10A Europlug) for tents and caravans as well as mobile homes and furnished tents to rent, mostly set on the woodland fringes of the park. Some are particularly suitable for those seeking peace and tranquillity, while others are specifically for families. Fresh bread is available daily and there are several villages and towns within a 25 km. radius for other provisions. Several improvements are planned for the 2016 season.

Facilities

Modern heated sanitary block with provisions for disabled visitors. Laundry. Restaurant, takeaway, bar with terraces. Bakery. Use of fridge and freezer. Swimming pool. Lounge with table games, board games and a DVD corner for children. Woodland play area. Activities for children (high season). A special house menu (Sat, Sun, Wed, high season). Riding. Bicycle hire. WiFi (free in courtyard). Off site: Riding 20 m. Fishing 10 km.

Open: 20 June - 13 September.

Directions

From Périgueux follow D939 north, then at Mareuil take D708 to Nontron. Follow signs to Corneuil and after very small village of St Sulpice-de-Mareuil, Camping Corneuil is 3 km. on right. GPS: 45.4745, 0.536267

Charges guide

Per unit incl. 2 persons and electricity	€ 24.50 - € 26.50
extra person	€ 5.00 - € 6.00

Sanguinet

Camping les Grands Pins

1039 avenue de Losa, F-40460 Sanguinet (Landes) T: 05 58 78 61 74.
E: info@campinglesgrandspins.com **alanrogers.com/FR40250**

Approached by a road alongside the lake, this Airotel group site is surrounded by tall trees. Of the 345 pitches, the 80 sand/gravel pitches are of average size, mostly level with varying degrees of shade. All have 6A electricity connections. Low hedges and young trees divide those available for tourers and most are set away from the mobile homes and chalets. An impressive central pool complex is open all season and includes a covered heated indoor pool, an outdoor pool, water slide and flume, children's pool and jacuzzi. There are plenty of walks, cycle rides and the lake to enjoy. The poolside bar and restaurant are open all season and the shop is open in July and August when the site becomes busier. The site offers watersports, minigolf, a children's club, boat trips and organised activities. Volleyball, tennis, boules and fishing are also available. The charming small village of Sanguinet is 2 km. away with supermarket and shops, bank, bars, restaurants and an archaeological museum.

Facilities

Four toilet blocks include washbasins in cabins, showers and British style toilets (not all open in low seasons). Provisions for disabled visitors. Laundry facilities. Motorcaravan services. Shop, bar, restaurant and takeaway. Indoor and outdoor pool complex with jacuzzi. Play area. Games room and TV in bar. Tennis, volleyball, boules. Sports equipment available to hire. Bicycle hire. Club for children. Dogs are not accepted in July/Aug. Gas barbecues only. Off site: Fishing 200 m. Boat launching 1 km. Horse riding 1.5 km. Golf 17 km. Beach and windsurfing 20 km.

Open: 2 April - 25 September.

Directions

Enter Sanguinet from the north on the D46. At one way system turn right. Do not continue on one way system but go straight ahead toward lake (signed) on Rue de Lac. Site is 2 km. on left.
GPS: 44.48396, -1.089716

Charges guide

Per unit incl. 2 persons and electricity	€ 20.00 - € 46.50
extra person	€ 6.90 - € 10.00
child (3-7 yrs)	€ 5.20 - € 7.20
dog	€ 4.00

Salignac-Eyvigues

Flower Camping le Temps de Vivre

Malmont, F-24590 Salignac-Eyvigues (Dordogne) T: 05 53 28 93 21. E: contact@temps-de-vivre.com
alanrogers.com/FR24460

Le Temps de Vivre is situated in the centre of the Périgord Noir, in the countryside and lies about 250 m. above sea level. The area of the campsite covers about 6.5 hectares in total, with 1.5 acres in use at present. It is a small, friendly, family run site with 50 pitches, 28 of which are for touring and 22 for mobile homes available for rent. The pitches are wide and terraces separate some of them. All have 10A Europlug and you will find a variety of trees and bushes often as a natural separation. This is a delightful and peaceful rural site. Due to its size and the small number of touring pitches, large units are advised to contact the site in advance to check availability.

Facilities

One modern unisex sanitary block is very clean, well maintained and serviced. En-suite toilet for disabled visitors. Baby room with bath. Covered laundry area. Small shop in the reception area. Small bar (15/5-15/9), restaurant and takeaway (July/Aug). Two swimming pools (one for children). Boules. Play area. Pottery and painting workshops for young children (weekly in high season). Themed meals (one evening a week in high season). Wellness (July/Aug). WiFi in reception area (free). No electric barbecues. Off site: Shops and restaurants within walking distance in nearby Salignac-Eyvigues. Riding and golf 5 km. Canoe hire. Walking (maps from reception).

Open: 21 April - 23 September.

Directions

From Brive-La-Gaillarde heading south on the A20 continue for 30 km. to exit 55 signed Souillac. Take D62/D15 northwest for 12 km. until Salignac-Eyvigues. As you drive through the town centre look for blue sign for site. Follow the sign off the main road for 2 km. GPS: 44.96374, 1.32813

Charges guide

Per unit incl. 2 persons and electricity	€ 15.50 - € 27.90
extra person	€ 3.00 - € 5.50
child (3-7 yrs)	€ 2.00 - € 3.50
dog	€ 2.00 - € 3.00

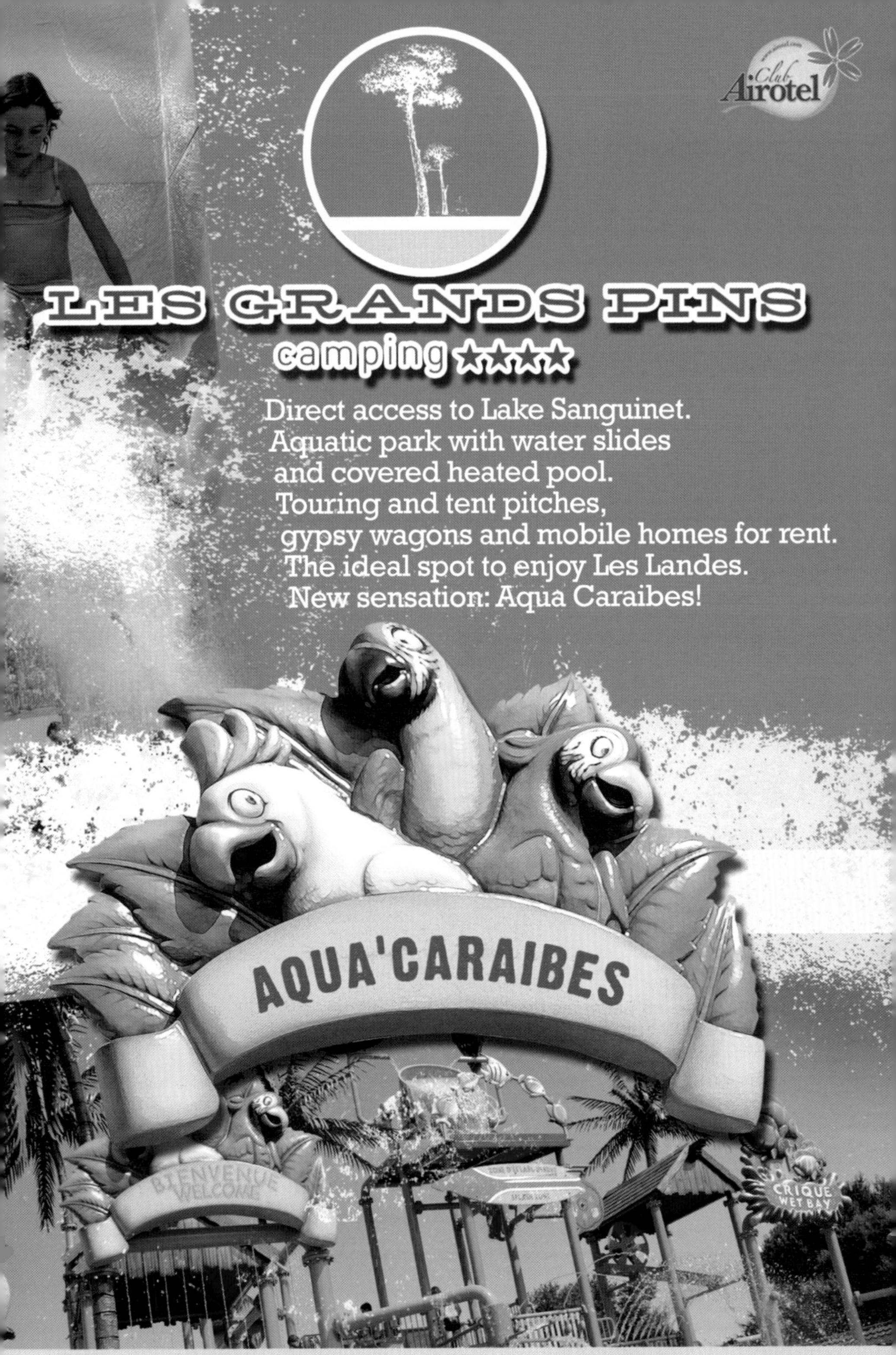
Club Airotel
LES GRANDS PINS
camping ★★★★
Direct access to Lake Sanguinet.
Aquatic park with water slides
and covered heated pool.
Touring and tent pitches,
gypsy wagons and mobile homes for rent.
The ideal spot to enjoy Les Landes.
New sensation: Aqua Caraibes!
AQUA'CARAIBES
BIENVENUE
WELCOME
CRIQUE
WET BAY

Salles

Camping des Bastides

Terre Rouge, F-47150 Salles (Lot-et-Garonne) T: 05 53 40 83 09. E: info@campingdesbastides.com
alanrogers.com/FR47130

Attractive and well maintained, this six and a half-hectare site is hilly and terraced with good views from the top of the site. The new French owners, Gaelle and Christian, are warm and welcoming. Although the terrain is hilly, most of the 80 medium sized touring pitches are fairly level and moderately shaded (all with 6A electricity). Tight turns with narrow gravel paths and overhanging trees may cause some difficulties for larger units. A range of different types of accommodation, including Mongolian tents, are available to rent. Reception keeps information on a variety of local walking and cycling routes.

Facilities

Two modern, clean and well maintained sanitary blocks can be heated. Facilities for disabled visitors. Excellent children's facilities and baby bath. Private en-suite facilities for hire. Shop for essentials. Bar/reception and snack restaurant (including takeaway). Swimming pool complex and spa. Boules. Play area. Small indoor play area with TV and small library. Entertainment (high season) and activities. Free WiFi on part of site. Off site: Fishing 1 km.

Open: 7 April - 30 October.

Directions

From Fumel, take D710 north towards Cuzorn. Before reaching Cuzorn, turn northwest on D162 and site is 6 km. on the right hand side (well signed). GPS: 44.5525, 0.8815

Charges guide

Per unit incl. 2 persons and electricity	€ 16.60 - € 33.90
extra person	€ 4.70 - € 5.70

No credit cards.

Sarlat-la-Canéda

Camping le Capeyrou

Le Capeyrou, F-24220 Beynac et Cazenac (Dordogne) T: 05 53 29 54 95.
E: contact@campinglecapeyrou.com **alanrogers.com/FR24005**

Le Capeyrou is an excellent and very well maintained site. It is situated by the River Dordogne, within easy walking distance of the picturesque château village of Beynac. The friendly Dutch and French owners pride themselves on maintaining the traditions of a true camping site, but with the benefits of modern facilities. Most of the 120 level pitches have good views of the hilltop château, and all have access to electricity (6/10A, mainly Europlug). Four fully equipped tents are available to hire. The village of Beynac et Cazenac can be reached on foot along the riverside footpath.

Facilities

Two high quality and very clean toilet blocks include preset and controllable showers, some washbasins in cabins, baby room and facilities for disabled visitors. Laundry room. Motorcaravan services. Fridge hire. Bar. Heated swimming pool and paddling pool. TV room for major events only. Play areas. Direct river access. Fishing. WiFi (free). Off site: Small supermarket 75 m. Canoe hire.

Open: 26 April - 30 September.

Directions

Site is 500 m. southeast of Beynac et Cazenac on the southern side of the D703.
GPS: 44.83809, 1.1486

Charges guide

Per unit incl. 2 persons and electricity	€ 18.00 - € 28.85
extra person	€ 4.40 - € 6.75

Sarlat-la-Canéda

Camping Indigo Sarlat les Perières

Rue Jean Gabin, F-24200 Sarlat-la-Canéda (Dordogne) T: 05 53 59 05 84. E: sarlat@camping-indigo.com
alanrogers.com/FR24030

Les Perières is a pleasant small site set on an attractive, wooded, terraced hillside within walking distance of the beautiful medieval town of Sarlat. The 107 pitches (all with 10A electricity) are arranged around the semi-circle of a fairly steep slope, overlooking a central leisure area that includes indoor and outdoor swimming pools and a tennis court. They range from 80-100 sq.m; most have water and drainage points. Mixed pine and deciduous trees provide dappled shade. Fully equipped wood and canvas tents, Romany-style caravans, mobile homes and traditional stone cottages available to rent.

Facilities

The sanitary blocks were renovated in 2014. Facilities for disabled visitors, baby bathroom, washing machines and dryers. Motorcaravan services. Small shop, pleasant bar (all season). Small snack bar/takeaway (July/Aug). Outdoor swimming pool (24/4-26/9), paddling pool, indoor spa pool and sauna (all season). Tennis, football, fitness track. Stone cottages to rent. Bicycle hire. Free WiFi in reception/bar area. No charcoal barbecues.
Off site: Sarlat 10 minutes' walk. Bicycle hire 1 km. Riding 4 km. Fishing 14 km.

Open: 24 March - 2 November.

Directions

Site is on the east side of Sarlat, on the D47 to Ste Nathalène (try to avoid Sarlat town centre during peak hours). From north leave A89/E70 at exit 17 and take D6089 and D704 (Montignac and Sarlat). Just before entering Sarlat, pass McDonalds on left and at 2nd island go round to face north and shortly turn right. Site signed. NB: In July and August check traffic reports for delays. GPS: 44.8937, 1.22747

Charges guide

Per unit incl. 2 persons and electricity	€ 24.30 - € 36.90

Sarlat-la-Canéda

Castel Camping le Moulin du Roch

Route des Eyzies, Allas - D47, F-24200 Sarlat-la-Canéda (Dordogne) T: 05 53 59 20 27.
E: contact@moulin-du-roch.com **alanrogers.com/FR24040**

The site has 209 large pitches, of which 136 are for touring units. They are mostly flat (some slope slightly) and grassy and all have electricity (10A). Mature trees provide shade to all pitches at different times of the day. Entertainment and activities are organised from mid-June to the end of August, with something for everyone, from quizzes and sports tournaments to canoeing and riding for the more adventurous. An excellent multi-lingual children's club runs in July and August. Walking and mountain biking routes lead from the site through surrounding woodland. Le Moulin du Roch is set on natural sloping woodland in the grounds of a former water mill and the Dutreux family have worked hard to ensure that it is an attractive and well run family campsite.

Facilities

Well maintained, very clean toilet blocks. Washing machines, dryers. Good shop. Bar and terrace. Takeaway. Superb restaurant. Attractive swimming pool, paddling pool and sun terrace. Fishing lake. Multisports area. Boules. Playground. Evening entertainment in high season. Pets are not accepted. WiFi throughout (charged). Off site: Supermarkets, banks, etc. at Sarlat 10 km. Bicycle hire and riding 10 km. Golf 15 km.

Open: 14 May - 17 September.

Directions

Site is 10 km. west of Sarlat-la-Canéda, on south side of D47 Sarlat-Les Eyzies road.
GPS: 44.90867, 1.1148

Charges guide

Per unit incl. 2 persons and electricity	€ 19.00 - € 40.00
extra person	€ 5.00 - € 10.50
child (3-7 yrs)	free - € 6.00

Camping Cheques accepted.

Sarlat-la-Canéda

Domaine de Soleil Plage

Caudon par Montfort, Vitrac, F-24200 Sarlat-la-Canéda (Dordogne) T: 05 53 28 33 33. E: info@soleilplage.fr
alanrogers.com/FR24090

This site is in one of the most attractive sections of the Dordogne valley, with a riverside location. There are 238 pitches, in three sections, with 118 for touring units. Additionally, there are a number of mobile homes and fully renovated chalets for rent. The site offers river swimming from a sizeable sandy bank or there is a very impressive heated pool complex. All pitches are bound by hedges and are of adequate size, with electricity (16A, Europlug), 44 also have water and a drain. Most pitches have some shade. If you like a holiday with lots going on, you will enjoy this site. It is busy and reservation is advisable. You pay more for a riverside pitch, but these have fine river views.

Facilities

Three modern unisex toilet blocks (designated male and female facilities in one). One has been completely renovated to a high standard with heating and family shower rooms. Washing machines and dryer. Motorcaravan services. Shop, bar with TV and attractive restaurant with local menus and a terrace with views towards the cliffs (all 3/5-18/9). Picnics available to order. Very impressive heated main pool, new covered pool, paddling pool, spa pool and two slides. Tennis. Minigolf. Three play areas. Fishing. Canoe and kayak hire. Bicycle hire. Currency exchange. Small library. WiFi throughout (charged). Activities and social events (high season). Max. 2 dogs. Off site: Riding 5 km. Sarlat 6 km.

Open: 9 April - 30 September.

Directions

Site is 6 km. south of Sarlat. From A20 take exit 55 (Souillac) towards Sarlat. Follow the D703 to Carsac and on to Montfort. After Montfort castle site is signed on left. Continue for 2 km. down to the river and site. GPS: 44.825, 1.25388

Charges guide

Per unit incl. 2 persons and electricity	€ 23.00 - € 40.50
extra person	€ 5.20 - € 8.20
child (2-8 yrs)	€ 3.10 - € 4.90
dog (max. 2)	€ 2.60 - € 3.60

Camping Cheques accepted.

Sarlat-la-Canéda

Camping les Grottes de Roffy

Sainte Nathalène, F-24200 Sarlat-la-Canéda (Dordogne) T: 05 53 59 15 61. E: contact@roffy.fr

alanrogers.com/FR24130

About 6 km. east of Sarlat, les Grottes de Roffy is a pleasantly laid out, family site. There are 162 clearly marked pitches, some very large, set on very well kept grass terraces. They have easy access and good views across an attractive valley. Some have plentiful shade, although others are more open, and all have 6A electricity. Those with very large units are advised to check availability in advance. The reception, bar, restaurant and shop are located within converted farm buildings surrounding a semi-courtyard. The site shop is well stocked with a variety of goods and a tempting épicerie. A good heated outdoor pool complex is open all season. In season there is something for all the family, with evening entertainment (including jazz and Latin evenings) and daily activities including clown shows for children. A variety of activities and excursions includes quad biking, hiking, pottery and massage. Conveniently located for Sarlat (a bus calls at the site on a Saturday to take visitors to and from the market) and all other Dordogne attractions, this is a good site for families. Accommodation is available to rent.

Facilities

Two toilet blocks with modern facilities are more than adequate. Shop. Bar and gastronomic restaurant with imaginative and sensibly priced menu. Takeaway. Good swimming pool complex comprising one heated and deep pool, a fountain, paddling pool and heated jacuzzi. Tennis. Games room. Room for teenagers. Play area. Bicycle hire. Entertainment and activities. WiFi in courtyard area. Off site: Fishing 2 km. Riding 10 km. Golf 15 km.

Open: 18 April - 13 September.

Directions

Take D47 east from Sarlat to Ste Nathalène. Just before Ste Nathalène the site is signed on the right hand side of the road. Turn here and the site is 800 m. along the lane. GPS: 44.90404, 1.2821

Charges guide

Per unit incl. 2 persons and electricity	€ 16.50 - € 32.40
extra person	€ 5.70 - € 8.50
child (2-7 yrs)	€ 4.30 - € 6.50

Sarlat-la-Canéda

Camping les Tailladis

Marcillac-Saint Quentin, F-24200 Sarlat-la-Canéda (Dordogne) T: 05 53 59 10 95. E: tailladis@wanadoo.fr

alanrogers.com/FR24480

Les Tailladis is a well situated, mature 4.5-hectare campsite set in 17 hectares of woodland, and owned by the same Dutch and French family since 1964. It is about 12 km. from Sarlat, Eyzies and Montignac-Lascauax, and 35 km. from Souillac. There are 78 medium to large pitches which are grassy, terraced and partially shaded with electricity (10A, some Europlugs) and water points close by. There is also a small stream and pond. The access road and campsite roads/tracks are narrow and winding, which may cause difficulties for some larger units. The hosts are welcoming and provide a very friendly service.

Facilities

One heated sanitary block is well sited for all pitches. En-suite toilet for disabled visitors. Baby bath and changing area. Laundry room. Motorcaravan services. Large shop (fresh bread and milk to order). Restaurant, bar. Swimming pool and paddling pool. Play area. Library with 2 computers. Activities during high season. WiFi in bar area (charged). Fishing. Accommodation for rent. Off site: Riding 3 km. Bicycle hire 13 km. Golf 25 km. Boat launching 25 km. Sarlat 12 km.

Open: 15 May - 30 November.

Directions

From Sarlat-la-Canéda, take D704 heading north. After 10 km. look for signs on left for Marcella-St Quentin. Take this road heading northwest, and site is less than 3 km. after Marcella-St Quentin on left. Access and site roads are narrow for large units. GPS: 44.97450, 1.18832

Charges guide

Per unit incl. 2 persons and electricity	€ 20.60 - € 25.45
extra person	€ 5.15 - € 6.75

Sarlat-la-Canéda

Camping la Palombière

Sainte Nathalène, F-24200 Sarlat-la-Canéda (Dordogne) T: 05 53 59 42 34. E: contact@lapalombiere.fr

alanrogers.com/FR24570

This site is set in a gorgeous, rural part of France amongst the beauty of the Périgord countryside with its rolling green hills and ancient buildings. The restored and preserved buildings at la Palombière add to the pleasure of this delightful site. It is evident that much investment has gone into making this holiday destination a place to remember. There are 200 pitches of which 68 are for touring caravans and tents. All have 10A electricity and some are fully serviced. Most are level and shaded from the sun, with some terracing because of the different levels. The remaining pitches are used for chalets and mobile homes, of which 61 are for rent. The site has a relaxed ambience and a tranquil atmosphere.

Facilities

Three modern sanitary blocks include facilities for babies and disabled visitors. Laundry facilities. Shop. Bar. Restaurant, snack bar and takeaway. Heated swimming pool complex with slide and toboggan. Gymnasium. Playgrounds. Library. Sports field. Tennis. Minigolf. Boules. Trampoline. Satellite TV. Games room. Bicycle hire. WiFi (free). Off site: Riding and canoeing 3 km.

Open: 26 April - 14 September.

Directions

Take the D47 east from Sarlat to Ste Nathalène. Site is signed from village and is reached by taking a left turn just beyond it. GPS: 44.90819, 1.29252

Charges guide

Per unit incl. 2 persons and electricity	€ 16.00 - € 33.80
extra person	€ 4.90 - € 8.90

Sarlat-la-Canéda

Camping la Bouysse de Caudon

Caudon, F-24200 Vitrac (Dordogne) T: 05 53 28 33 05. E: info@labouysse.com

alanrogers.com/FR24590

La Bouysse is a very attractive site situated on one of the most picturesque stretches of the Dordogne river. The views of the river and cliffs from some of the pitches and the pool area are magnificent. There are 160 large pitches; 147 of them for touring units. All are flat with trees providing shade, dividing hedges and 10A electricity. The pitches nearer the river are a little more open but very pleasant. The site has its own beach, slipway and canoe hire is provided. There are 13 very good chalets to rent. Housed in a traditional style building, the bar has a large, covered terrace.

Facilities

Two modern toilet blocks are very clean and house showers and washbasins in cubicles. Excellent facilities for disabled visitors. Laundry facilities. Motorcaravan services. Well stocked shop (15/6-31/8). Bar/restaurant with large covered terrace and takeaway with extensive menu (15/6-31/8). Swimming pool (1/5-15/9). Play area. Tennis. Boules. Fishing in the river. Canoe hire. WiFi (free in low season). Off site: Bicycle hire 4 km. Riding 5 km.

Open: 15 April - 20 September.

Directions

From A20 take exit 55 (Soulliac) towards Sarlat. Follow D703 to Carsac and on to Monfort. At Monfort castle turn left and follow for 2 km. down to the river. GPS: 44.82358, 1.25072

Charges guide

Per unit incl. 2 persons and electricity	€ 19.30 - € 26.50
extra person	€ 4.90 - € 6.60
child (2-7 yrs)	€ 2.30 - € 3.40

Sarlat-la-Canéda

Camping le Montant

Saint André-d'Allas, F-24200 Sarlat-la-Canéda (Dordogne) T: 05 53 59 18 50.

E: contact@camping-sarlat.com **alanrogers.com/FR24610**

Camping le Montant is a family run site, located on a hillside overlooking beautiful countryside, only 2 km. from Sarlat. There are 131 pitches, of which 92 are large pitches for touring units, the remainder being used for a variety of high quality furnished accommodation for rent. The touring pitches, all with 6/10A electricity, are divided into two areas, each with its own sanitary block. One part of the site is shaded with hedges, the other area is more open with flat terraced pitches looking out over the wooded hills. Access to these however, via narrow site roads, may be difficult for large units.

Facilities

Both toilet blocks are very well equipped especially a newer one with a family bathroom. Large laundry. Bar, restaurant and takeaway (limited opening hours in low season). Swimming pool complex with outdoor pool (from 9/5), slides, heated indoor pool and large indoor jacuzzi. New playground. Tennis. Multisports area. Minigolf. Boules. Bicycle hire. Activities organised for children, teenagers and adults day and evening (July/Aug). Free WiFi in bar and reception area. Off site: Historic Sarlat 2 km. Riding 3 km. Fishing and golf 5 km.

Open: 11 April - 30 September.

Directions

Site is 2 km. south of Sarlat off the D57 Sarlat-Baynac road. If approaching from Sarlat, site is signed to the right. Follow this road for 1 km. GPS: 44.865344, 1.187704

Charges guide

Per unit incl. 2 persons and electricity	€ 15.90 - € 40.50
extra person	€ 4.00 - € 8.90
child (3-8 yrs)	€ 2.00 - € 5.90
dog	free - € 2.50

Sarlat-la-Canéda

Camping les Terrasses du Périgord

Pech-d'Orance, F-24200 Sarlat-la-Canéda (Dordogne) T: 05 53 59 02 25.
E: terrasses-du-perigord@wanadoo.fr **alanrogers.com/FR24670**

Set on a hilltop on the edge of Sarlat, this site has panoramic views across the Périgord. There are 90 pitches, of which 70 are for touring units, with the remaining 20 for chalets and mobile homes for rent. The site is terraced and the pitches are generally level. All are shady, marked and separated by trees, and have 10/16A electricity. For those with larger units, it is essential to phone in advance for pitch availability, as not all are suitable. A warm and friendly welcome is given by the French owners, whose keen gardening skills are in evidence throughout. This well appointed site offers good value for money.

Facilities

One modern sanitary block divided into two provides all facilities including those for disabled visitors and babies. Washing machine and dryer. Motorcaravan services. Shop and bar (15/6-15/9). Snack bar and takeaway (July/Aug). Wine tastings. Swimming pool and toddler's pool (19/4-15/9). Indoor spa pool with jacuzzi. Play area with cable slide. Minigolf. Bicycle hire. Gas and electric barbecues only. Evening entertainment. Off site: Medieval town of Sarlat. Caves. Châteaux. Fishing 2 km.

Open: 18 April - 20 September.

Directions

From Sarlat, take D47 to Proissans. Continue on D56 to Proissans and site is 500 m. on the left. In Sarlat, follow the signs for hospital as it is nearby. GPS: 44.9058, 1.23598

Charges guide

Per unit incl. 2 persons and electricity	€ 18.80 - € 24.70
extra person	€ 4.70 - € 5.90
child (under 7 yrs)	€ 2.00 - € 3.50

Credit cards (June-Sept only).

Sarlat-la-Canéda

Camping Domaine des Mathevies

Les Mathevies, Sainte Nathalène, F-24200 Sarlat-la-Canéda (Dordogne) T: 05 53 59 20 86.
E: info@mathevies.com **alanrogers.com/FR24740**

This gem of a small, family run site is situated in the rural heart of the Périgord and the delightful owners will give you a warm and friendly welcome. There are only 50 slightly sloping, grass pitches, 40 for touring, and all have 10A electricity. They are separated by hedging and flowering shrubs and trees give varying amounts of shade. A shaded terrace is next to the beautiful, original Perigordine building and the barn has been lovingly converted into a bar/restaurant, a superb playroom and the toilet facilities. The play area makes this a paradise for toddlers.

Facilities

Excellent, very clean toilet block includes a good room for young children and disabled campers. Laundry facilities. Bar. Snacks. Swimming and paddling pools. Tennis court. Library. Selection of games. Satellite TV. Playground. Indoor playroom. Pétanque. Crèche (under 5 yrs). Basketball. Bicycle hire. WiFi over part of site (free). Special interest groups catered for. Off site: Shops, restaurant, bars and Saturday market (bus) in Sarlat.

Open: End April - end September.

Directions

Leave A20 exit 55, head west through Souillac to Roufillac. Take D61 north then D47B to Ste Nathalène. Site well signed from there. GPS: 44.918056, 1.277778

Charges guide

Per unit incl. 2 persons and electricity	€ 21.00 - € 32.00
extra person	€ 5.00 - € 8.50

Sarlat-la-Canéda

Camping la Sagne

Lieu-dit Lassagne, Vitrac, F-24200 Sarlat (Dordogne) T: 05 53 28 18 36. E: info@camping-la-sagne.com
alanrogers.com/FR24940

Camping la Sagne is a family run site and was significantly rebuilt for the 2012 season. The rebuilding programme included a new reception, bar and snack bar complex and a covered swimming pool and paddling pool with jacuzzi. There are 100 large, level pitches with 65 for touring, all with 16A electricity but long leads are required. Trees and hedges separating the pitches in the new area give little shade as yet, while pitches in the older section are separated by hedges and mature trees providing good shade. Access to the Dordogne river is available via a track down through the trees.

Facilities

The old toilet block has been refurbished and a new one built with family bathroom, child size toilet, baby bath and facilities for disabled visitors. Washer/dryers. Small shop. Bread service daily. Bar with TV, snack bar and takeaway (July/Aug). Library. Games room. Covered, heated swimming pool, paddling pool and jacuzzi. Playground. River fishing and bathing. Bicycle hire. WiFi over site (charged). Accommodation to rent. Off site: Golf 800 m. Sarlat with range of shops, bars and restaurants 8 km.

Open: 12 April - 28 September.

Directions

Site is 6 km. south of Sarlat. Leave autoroute A20, exit 55 (Souillac) towards Sarlat. Take D703 to Montfort, turn left following site signs. Site entrance on right in 1 km. GPS: 44.825452, 1.242346

Charges guide

Per unit incl. 2 persons and electricity	€ 15.70 - € 31.00
extra person	€ 4.70 - € 6.70
child (2-13 yrs)	€ 3.10 - € 4.10

Sauveterre-la-Lemance

Flower Camping Moulin du Périé

F-47500 Sauveterre-la-Lemance (Lot-et-Garonne) T: 05 53 40 67 26. E: moulinduperie@wanadoo.fr

alanrogers.com/FR47010

Set in a quiet area and surrounded by woodlands, this peaceful little site is well away from much of the tourist bustle. It has 95 reasonably sized, grassy touring pitches, all with 6A electricity, divided by mixed trees and bushes with most having good shade. All are extremely well kept, as indeed is the entire site. The attractive front courtyard is complemented by an equally pleasant terrace at the rear. Two small, clean swimming pools overlook a shallow, spring water lake, ideal for inflatable boats and paddling, and bordering the lake, a large grass field is popular for games.

Facilities

Two clean, modern and well maintained toilet blocks include facilities for disabled visitors. Motorcaravan services. Basic shop. Bar/reception, restaurant and takeaway. Spring-water swimming lake with sandy beach and two small swimming pools (15/6-24/9). Boules. Volley-Badminton. Playground. Small indoor play area. Children's activities in high season. Barbecues. Gourmet meals. WiFi in bar/restaurant. Off site: Fishing 3 km.

Open: 14 May - 24 September.

Directions

From D710, Fumel-Périgueux, turn southeast into Sauveterre-la-Lemance. Turn left (northeast) at road signed Loubejec for 3.5 km. along this valley road to site on right. GPS: 44.59016, 1.04761

Charges guide

Per unit incl. 2 persons and electricity	€ 16.00 - € 28.80
extra person	€ 4.00 - € 7.30

Camping Cheques accepted.

Soulac-sur-Mer

Camping le Palace

65 boulevard Marsan de Montbrun, F-33780 Soulac-sur-Mer (Gironde) T: 05 56 09 80 22.
E: info@camping-palace.com **alanrogers.com/FR33060**

Le Palace is close to the beach in Soulac-sur-Mer, south of Royan across the estuary. It is an impressive, traditional site, large and level, with 580 good sized individual pitches, regularly laid out amongst a variety of trees that provide good shade. On the very sandy ground, pitches for caravans have hardened areas. Electricity (10A) is available. Most pitches have water taps and some also have sewerage connections. The pool complex could be described as a small water park with several pools, slides, a jacuzzi and a children's pool with galleon in the centre. A wide, sandy beach is 400 m. away.

Facilities

Six separate toilet blocks include washbasins in private cabins. Baby bathrooms. Facilities for disabled visitors. Laundry facilities. Supermarket (Apr-Sept). Restaurant and bar (May-Sept). Indoor and outdoor swimming pools (from mid May) and paddling pool. Sauna and Hammam. Gym. Playground. Games room. Snooker. Bicycle hire. Sports, entertainment and excursions in July/Aug. Miniclub. Minigolf. Winter caravan storage. Free WiFi (around bar/restaurant area). Off site: Tennis courts adjacent. Riding 400 m. Supermarkets in Soulac 1.5 km.

Open: 4 April - 27 September.

Directions

From Bordeaux head north on D1215 to Soulac-sur-Mer. Site is 1 km. south of Soulac and well signed. The shortest and simplest way is via the ferry which runs from Royan across the Gironde estuary to the Pointe de Grave, but this is quite expensive with a caravan. GPS: 45.501384, -1.131785

Charges guide

Per unit incl. 2 persons, electricity and water	€ 19.00 - € 44.00
extra person	€ 4.00 - € 8.00

Soulac-sur-Mer

Yelloh! Village Soulac-sur-Mer

8 allée Michel Montaigne, F-33780 Soulac-sur-Mer (Gironde) T: 05 56 09 77 63. E: contact@lelilhan.com

alanrogers.com/FR33330

This is a well established woodland site, popular with families. Now part of the Yelloh! Village group, it has benefited from an extensive programme of investment and development. There are 82 large touring pitches (all with 10A electricity), the remainder used for mobile homes and chalets to rent. Most pitches are heavily shaded and on natural woodland floor terrain. A special area is kept for younger campers away from the quieter family areas. There is a well laid out pool complex, a bar and a restaurant.

Facilities

Three unisex toilet blocks fitted to a high standard. These provide a family bathroom, facilities for babies, washbasins in cubicles and a suite for disabled campers. Laundry facilities. Swimming pool complex, new Balnéo, sauna and jacuzzi. Shop, bar, restaurant and pizzeria, takeaway. Entertainment and children's club (high season). Playground. Minigolf. Tennis. Archery. Riding. Bicycle hire. WiFi throughout (charged). No gas or charcoal barbecues. Off site: Town and beach 3 km.

Open: 24 April - 6 September.

Directions

Soulac-sur-Mer is on the Atlantic coast just south of the tip of the Gironde peninsula. Site signed off D101 – turn east on a minor road 3 km. south of Soulac town and site is on left. GPS: 45.48576, -1.1179

Charges guide

Per unit incl. 2 persons and electricity	€ 20.00 - € 46.00
extra person	€ 6.00 - € 7.00

Credit cards accepted but debit cards preferred.

Soulac-sur-Mer

Flower Camping des Pins

Passe de Formose, F-33780 Soulac sur Mer (Gironde) T: 05 56 09 82 52. E: contact@campingdespins.fr

alanrogers.com/FR33405

Tucked away in a pine forest, close to an interesting little seaside town at the northern end of the Médoc peninsula, this family run site offers a range of possibilities for holidaymakers. It has just 150 pitches of which 75 are available for touring units; electrical connections (6A) are available for 60 and 10 pitches also have individual taps and waste water drains. There are various styles of mobile home for rent as well as a number of pre-erected, well equipped tents. The beach is within easy reach, just 800 m. from the site, through woodland. This environmentally friendly site has a small permaculture garden and animal area aimed at educating children to understand the natural world.

Facilities

Two toilet blocks. Laundry. Greengrocer/bakery, bar, snack bar/takeaway (July/Aug). Heated outdoor swimming pool, paddling pool and jacuzzi (1/5-30/9). Playground. Mini soccer/volleyball field. Archery (July/Aug). Clubs for children and teenagers. Communal barbecues (no charcoal barbecues on pitches). Bicycle hire. WiFi (free). One pet only per pitch. Off site: Beach 800 m. Shops 1 km. Riding 1 km. Fishing 2 km. Golf 8 km. Le Verdon-sur-Mer/ferry to Royan 10/12 km.

Open: 29 April - 30 September.

Directions

From the A630 Bordeaux Rocade leave at exit 8 (Le Verdon, Lacanau) and head north on D1215 to Soulac. Site is to south of town via D101 and D101/E2 (signed L'Amélie and site). Alternatively turn west before Soulac along minor road (not signed). GPS: 45.482787, -1.127401

Charges guide

Per unit incl. 2 persons and electricity	€ 21.00 - € 34.00
extra person	€ 5.00 - € 6.00

Soustons

Camping le Framissima Nature

63 avenue du Port d'Albret, F-40140 Soustons (Landes) T: 05 58 77 70 00. E: resa.soustons@fram.fr

alanrogers.com/FR40760

Framissima Nature is a new site located in the heart of the vast Landes pine forest. It is close to Soustons and its huge lake and around six kilometres from the Atlantic beaches. There are 249 pitches, all occupied by chalet-style mobile homes and other rentable accommodation. There are no touring pitches. There is little natural shade but this is provided in the bar areas. There is an impressive pool complex and clubs for children are well organised, with different ages catered for. In order to preserve a pleasant, tranquil aspect, cars must be left in a separate parking area at all times.

Facilities

Bar. Restaurant. Takeaway. Swimming pool complex (including covered pool). Play area. Football. Volleyball. Basketball. Tennis. Multisports terrain. Gym. Activities and entertainment for all. Cinema. Mobile homes and chalets for hire. Free WiFi over part of site. Off site: Supermarket 500 m. Shops and restaurants in Soustons. Cycle tracks through the forest. Golf 5 km. Beach 6 km. Watersports.

Open: 14 April - 1 October.

Directions

The site is located on the eastern side of the Etang de Soustons. Heading south on N10, leave at the Magesq exit and head for Soustons on D116. From there follow signs for the site. GPS: 43.75579, -1.35384

Charges guide

Contact site for details.

Trémolat

Camping de la Base Nautique Trémolat

D30, F-24510 Trémolat (Dordogne) T: 05 53 05 65 60. E: contact@semitour.com

alanrogers.com/FR24315

This site is set on the banks of the beautiful Dordogne river just a few hundred metres outside the typical Périgord Noir village of Trémolat, about halfway between Bergerac and Sarlat. Although the site's emphasis is on peace and tranquillity, there is no shortage of activities available. Touring units have a choice of 65 shaded or open pitches alongside the river (63 have 10A electricity, long leads required). There are 18 fully equipped mobile homes for rent. Amenities on the site include a swimming pool and a bar/restaurant, the Pyramid. The pleasant pitches and riverside location may be all that you require, but the Périgord countryside is dotted with châteaux and deep, cool caves with dramatic stalactites.

Facilities

Sanitary facilities include shower and toilet for disabled visitors. Washing machine. Shop. Bar. Restaurant/snack bar (both 15/3-30/9). Swimming pool (15/6-30/9). Adventure playground. TV room. Fishing. Water ski club. Volleyball. Tennis. Canoe, kayak and pedalos for hire. Entertainment (July/Aug). Free WiFi. Off site: Shops 600 m. Riding 6 km. Bicycle hire 12 km.

Open: 15 March - 31 October.

Directions

Trémolat is roughly halfway between Bergerac (30 km) and Sarlat (40 km) on the north bank of the Dordogne. The site is signed from the D30e to the north of the village. GPS: 44.8792, 0.82504

Charges guide

Per unit incl. 2 persons and electricity	€ 18.10 - € 23.50
extra person	€ 4.40 - € 5.70

Thiviers

Camping le Repaire

Le Repaire, F-24800 Thiviers (Dordogne) T: 05 53 52 69 75. E: contact@camping-le-repaire.fr

alanrogers.com/FR24210

Set in quiet countryside in the heart of the Périgord Vert, next to a small fishing lake, le Repaire is a beautiful, spacious and peaceful municipal site, well situated for visiting towns such as Périgueux and Brantôme. There are 110 good sized, slightly sloping, grassy pitches (90 for touring), all with electricity (6A). They are in small groups, separated by shrubs and a variety of trees providing shade to some pitches. A few shadier pitches are available at the edge of the adjoining woodland. The interesting town of Thiviers can be reached in 20 minutes along a footpath and is just 2 km. by road. On-site facilities include a small fishing lake near the entrance (no swimming) and small swimming and paddling pools open mid-June to mid-September. It also has a new bar and restaurant (July/August). There are many walking and cycle routes in the surrounding area. Bungalows are available to rent.

Facilities

Two clean and functional toilet blocks provide washbasins in cabins and cubicles for disabled visitors. One unit is shut in low season. Laundry facilities. No chemical disposal point. Reception area (no shop but bread to order). Terrace bar and snack/takeaway service (July/Aug). Swimming pool (heated) and paddling pool (15/6-15/9). Small fishing lake. Play area. Tennis. Boules. Pétanque. Exercise track. Barbecue area. Free WiFi in reception area. Off site: Tennis 300 m. Bicycle hire 1 km. Shops, bars and restaurants in Thiviers 1 km.

Open: 1 April - 1 November.

Directions

Leave N21 at Thiviers, about 60 km. southwest of Limoges. At roundabout turn east, D707, signed Lanouaille. Site is on right in 2 km.
GPS: 45.413116, 0.932022

Charges guide

Per unit incl. 2 persons and electricity	€ 14.00 - € 19.00
extra person	€ 3.00 - € 4.50
child (2-12 yrs)	free - € 3.00

No credit cards.

Urrugne

Camping Larrouleta

210 route de Socoa, F-64122 Urrugne (Pyrénées-Atlantiques) T: 05 59 47 37 84. E: info@larrouleta.com

alanrogers.com/FR64180

Camping Larrouleta is an all year site located at the heart of the Basque country. The site has been developed around a 7.5 hectare lake which has a sandy beach and is ideal for fishing. On-site amenities include a swimming pool which is covered in low season. There is also a bar/restaurant which specialises in local cuisine and where occasional Basque folk evenings are held in high season. The 327 touring pitches are of a good size (90 sq.m) and are generally shaded by poplars. Most have electrical connections (5A). A number of 'grand confort' pitches are available (large pitches with electricity, water and drainage – supplement charged).

Facilities

Toilet block (can be heated) with hot showers, washbasins in cabins and facilities for disabled visitors. Washing machine. Shop (July/Aug). Bar (1/3-20/9). Restaurant and takeaway (15/6-15/9). Swimming pool (covered in low season). Lake. Fishing. Tennis. Play area. Entertainment and activity programme. WiFi throughout (charged). Off site: Nearest beach, sailing, golf and bicycle hire, all 3 km. Col d'Ibardin (Pyrenees) 7 km. Hendaye 8 km. Spanish border 10 km.

Open: All year.

Directions

Take exit 2 from A63 motorway (St Jean-de-Luz Sud) and follow signs to Port Fort, crossing N10. From here follow signs to the site.
GPS: 43.37024, -1.686161

Charges guide

Per unit incl. 2 persons and electricity	€ 20.00 - € 36.00
extra person	€ 6.00 - € 8.50
child (under 7 yrs)	€ 2.50 - € 3.50

Urrugne

Sunêlia Col d'Ibardin

220 route d'Olhette, F-64122 Urrugne (Pyrénées-Atlantiques) T: 05 59 54 31 21. E: info@col-ibardin.com

alanrogers.com/FR64110

This family owned site at the foot of the Basque Pyrenees is highly recommended and deserves praise. It is well run with emphasis on personal attention, the friendly family and their staff ensuring that all are made welcome, and is attractively set in the middle of an oak wood with a mountain stream cascading through it. Behind the forecourt, with its brightly coloured shrubs and modern reception area, various roadways lead to the 203 pitches. These are individual, spacious and enjoy the benefit of the shade (if preferred, a more open aspect can be found). There are electricity hook-ups (6/10A) and adequate water points. A very attractive chalet 'village' has been added. From this site you can enjoy the mountain scenery, be on the beach in 7-10 km. or cross the border into Spain in about 14 km.

Facilities

Two toilet blocks, one rebuilt to a high specification, are kept very clean. WC for disabled visitors. Laundry facilities. Motorcaravan services. Shop for basics and bread orders (15/6-15/9). Restaurant, takeaway service and bar (1/6-15/9). Heated swimming pool and paddling pool. Playground and club (adult supervision). Tennis. Boules. Video games. Multisports area. Free WiFi on part of site. Not suitable for American-style motorhomes. Off site: Supermarket and shopping centre 5 km. Fishing, boat launching, sailing, bicycle hire and golf 7 km.

Open: 1 April - 30 September.

Directions

Leave A63 at St Jean-de-Luz sud, exit no. 2 and join RN10 towards Urrugne. Turn left at roundabout (Col d'Ibardin) on D4. Site on right after 5 km. Do not turn off to the Col itself, carry on towards Ascain. GPS: 43.33376, -1.68458

Charges guide

Per unit incl. 2 persons and electricity	€ 17.50 - € 41.00
extra person	€ 3.50 - € 6.50
child (2-7 yrs)	€ 2.50 - € 4.00
dog	€ 2.80

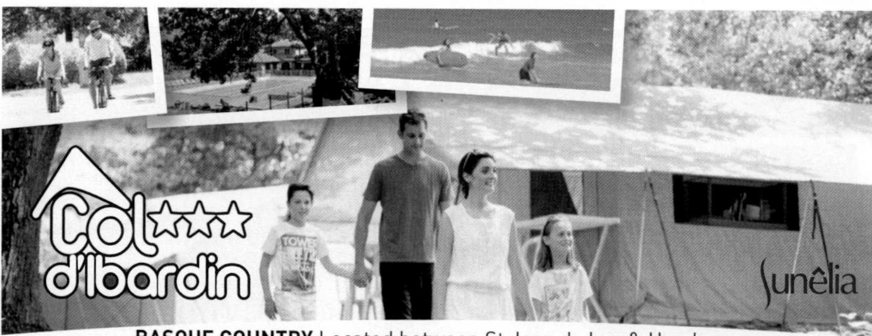

Vendays-Montalivet

Campéole Médoc Plage

Avenue de l'Europe, F-33930 Vendays-Montalivet (Gironde) T: 05 56 09 33 45. E: montalivet@campeole.com

alanrogers.com/FR33840

This is a large site (905 pitches) with 393 touring pitches (150 with 10A electricity) and a further 212 pitches occupied by mobile homes, chalets and Trigano tents, all of which are available for rent. The site has a woodland setting and is 1,200 m. from the vast, sandy beach, which can be accessed via a footpath from the site. On-site amenities here include a swimming pool, a snack bar and a shop. All amenities are open in July and August, but may be closed in the low season. Cycling is very popular and a number of trails lead from the site through the surrounding forest.

Facilities

Four toilet blocks have British style WCs, washbasins and showers in cubicles. Facilities for children and disabled visitors. Laundry. Motorcaravan services. Shop, bar, snack bar/takeaway (all July/Aug). Heated swimming pool with slides (1/5-14/9). Beach volleyball. Boules. All-weather sports pitch. Play area. Children's club and entertainment programme (July/Aug). Bicycle hire. WiFi (charged). Mobile homes and chalets for rent. Off site: Shops, restaurants and tourist information in Vendays-Montalivet. Supermarket 200 m. Cycling and walking trails through the forest. Médoc vineyards.

Open: 19 April - 14 September.

Directions

From the north, use toll ferry across the Gironde then head south on D1215, then D102 to Vendays-Montalivet. 8 km. beyond village, turn left at traffic lights, site is on left after 800 m. GPS: 45.369989, -1.144606

Charges guide

Per unit incl. 2 persons and electricity	€ 17.80 - € 28.50

Camping Cheques accepted.

Vielle-Saint-Girons

Sunêlia le Col-Vert

Lac de Léon, 1548 route de l'Etang, F-40560 Vielle-Saint-Girons (Landes) T: 08 90 71 00 01.

E: contact@colvert.com **alanrogers.com/FR40050**

This large, well maintained campsite is well laid out on the shores of Lac de Léon and offers 380 touring pitches and 185 mobile homes for rent. The pitches range from simple ones to those with water and a drain and there are eight with private, well designed, modern sanitary facilities. In low season it is a quiet site and those pitches beside the lake offer a wonderful backdrop to relaxing pastimes. During the main season it is a lively place for children of all ages. A pool complex offers a standard pool for swimming, a pool for children with a water canon and fountains, plenty of sunbeds and a heated indoor pool. Swimming is also permitted in the lake. A fitness and beauty spa offers a wide range of treatments. This extensive but natural site edges a nature reserve and stretches along the Lac de Léon, a conservation area, for 1 km. on a narrow frontage. This makes it particularly suitable for those who want to practise watersports such as sailing and windsurfing, there is also a water playground with inflatable games. An overall charge is made for some of the leisure activities.

Facilities

Four toilet blocks, one heated. Fun facilities for children in one block. Facilities for disabled guests. Laundry facilities. Motorcaravan services. Shops, bar/restaurant, takeaway (1/4-6/9; limited hours until June). Swimming pool complex with three pools. Spa, fitness centre and sauna. Play area. Games room. Sports areas. Boules. Tennis. Bicycle hire. Minigolf. Fishing. Riding. Sailing school (15/6-15/9). Communal barbecues only. WiFi (charged). Free bus to beach (July/Aug). Off site: Walking and cycle ways in the forest. Shops in Léon 4 km. Beaches 5 km.

Open: 1 April - 20 September.

Directions

Site is off D652 Mimizan-Léon road, 4 km. south of crossroads with D42 at St Girons. The road to the lake and the site is signed at Vielle.
GPS: 43.90285, -1.3125

Charges guide

Per unit incl. 2 persons and electricity (10A)	€ 17.20 - € 51.10
extra person	€ 2.30 - € 7.20
child (3-12 yrs)	€ 1.70 - € 6.20

Camping Cheques accepted.

Vielle-Saint-Girons

Campéole les Tourterelles

Route de Saint Girons-Plage, F-40560 Saint-Girons Plage (Landes) T: 05 58 47 93 12.

E: tourterelles@campeole.com **alanrogers.com/FR40450**

Les Tourterelles is a large site extending over 20 hectares of forest and is a member of the Campéole group. The site has direct access to the beach, using two footpaths, one of which is decked. The beach is vast and very popular with surfers. A lifeguard is in attendance during the high season. There are 882 pitches at les Tourterelles, of which around 271 are occupied by mobile homes, chalets and fully equipped bungalow tents, all available for rent, and including some units specially adapted for disabled visitors. Pitches are well shaded by pines and most have electrical connections (6A).

Facilities

Toilet blocks have hot showers, washbasins in cabins and facilities for disabled visitors. Motorcaravan service. Laundry facilities. Bar (1/6-15/9). Takeaway (29/6-30/8). Direct beach access. Volleyball. Beach volleyball. Bicycle hire. Bouncy castle. Play areas. Games room. Activity and entertainment programme. Mobile homes, chalets and equipped tents for rent. Communal barbecues only. WiFi (charged). Off site: St Girons Plage 200 m. Fishing.

Open: 25 April - 30 September.

Directions

From Bordeaux, take A63 (Bayonne). Leave at Castets-Vielle-St Girons exit and continue to Vielle-St Girons. At traffic lights follow signs to St Girons Plage. At St Girons-Plage turn right at roundabout and site is a further 50 m. GPS: 43.95435, -1.35683

Charges guide

Per unit incl. 2 persons and electricity	€ 21.20 - € 36.00

Camping Cheques accepted.

Villefranche-de-Queyran

Camping Moulin de Campech

F-47160 Villefranche-de-Queyran (Lot-et-Garonne) T: 05 53 88 72 43. E: camping@moulindecampech.co.uk

alanrogers.com/FR47050

This well shaded, pretty site is run by Sue and George Thomas along with Sue's parents, Dot and Bob Dunn. At the entrance to the site, a trout lake with graceful weeping willows feeds under the restored mill house, which is home to the owners as well as housing the bar and restaurant. Children will need supervision around the lake and at the pool which is on an elevated area above the mill house. The 46 large sized pitches are mostly divided by hedges, with electricity (6A, long leads may be necessary in places, but can be borrowed free of charge). A cheery welcome awaits you along with a determination to ensure that you enjoy your stay. All campers are provided with a folder on arrival that contains useful information about the site and the surrounding area.

Facilities

The single, rather dated toilet block has modern fittings. Washing machine and tumble dryer. Shop (1/5-20/9). Restaurant (1/5-20/9). Fish and chips (Sat pm). Heated swimming pool (access via steep steps, 7/5-20/9). Open grassy games area. Board games and English library. Boules. Barbecue and quiz night (Wed) in high season. Fishing (discounted rate for campers, no permit required). Torch useful. WiFi in reception (charged). Off site: Watersports, bicycle hire, golf and riding 10 km. Markets daily in villages and towns around the region. Numerous wine caves and Armagnac products.

Open: 1 April - 7 October.

Directions

Take A10 south to Bordeaux. Join A62 for Toulouse and take exit 6 for Damazan. Follow D8 to Mont de Marsan, at Cap du Bosc turn right onto D11 for Casteljaloux. Site is signed, 5 km. on right. GPS: 44.27179, 0.19093

Charges guide

Per unit incl. 2 persons and electricity	€ 18.50 - € 30.00
extra person	€ 3.65 - € 6.75
child (under 7 yrs)	€ 3.00 - € 4.50
dog	€ 2.40

Villeréal

Yelloh! Village le Chateau de Fonrives

Rives, F-47210 Villeréal (Lot-et-Garonne) T: 05 53 36 63 38. E: chateau.de.fonrives@wanadoo.fr

alanrogers.com/FR47030

Le Château de Fonrives is situated in Lot-et-Garonne. The site is set in pretty part-farmed, part-wooded countryside. It is a mixture of hazelnut woodland with a lake and château (mostly 17th century). An attractive tree-lined avenue leads to the barns adjacent to the château, which have been converted to house the site's amenities. There are 301 pitches, 131 of which are for touring units, with electricity. They are of a generous size and are well defined by neatly trimmed hedges and small shrubs. Pitches near the woodland receive moderate shade, but elsewhere there is light shade from hedges and young trees. There are also a large number of mobile homes here but they do not detract from the general feeling of spaciousness and due to the position of the touring pitches they appear well separated.

Facilities

Three well positioned, modern sanitary blocks with facilities for disabled visitors. Laundry facilities. Shop. Restaurant, snacks and takeaway. Bar with disco area and terrace. Covered swimming pool, outdoor pool, water slides, paddling pool. Jacuzzi. Gym. Sauna. Trim trail. Bouncy castle. Small play area. Small field for volleyball and football. Library. Minigolf, tennis, bicycle hire (all charged). Activities organised for children and adults in season, including excursions and walks. Caravan storage. Hairdresser (July/Aug). WiFi in bar area (charged). Off site: Riding 8 km. Golf, walking and cycling.

Open: 13 April - 29 September.

Directions

Site is 2 km. northwest of Villeréal, on west side of the D14/D207 Bergerac-Villaréal road. Pass through Rives and site is signed on the left. GPS: 44.65723, 0.72847

Charges guide

Per unit incl. 2 persons and electricity	€ 18.00 - € 40.00
extra person	€ 7.00 - € 8.00
child (3-6 yrs)	free - € 7.00
dog	€ 5.00

DÉPARTEMENTS: 09 ARIÈGE, 12 AVEYRON, 31 HAUTE-GARONNE, 32 GERS, 46 LOT, 65 HAUTES-PYRÉNÉES, 81 TARN, 82 TARN-ET GARONNE.

MAJOR CITY: TOULOUSE

Rolling fields of sunflowers, the Armagnac vineyards and crumbling, ancient stone buildings amidst the sleepy villages make this region popular with those who enjoy good food and wine and a taste of the good life.

Extending from the Dordogne in the north to the Spanish border in the south, Midi-Pyrénées is the largest region in France at over 45,000 sq.km. It incorporates parts of historic provinces, including Languedoc and Gascony, whose heritage and traditions lend much to its identity.

It is blessed by radiant sunshine and a fascinating range of scenery. South of the cultivated fields and cliffside villages beside the Lot river, lie the stony lands of the Quercy Causse and the rocky gorges of the Aveyron and Tarn rivers. Centered around Millau, there are tortuous gorges and valleys, spectacular rivers, underground caves and grottoes, and forested mountains. Further south, high chalk plateaux, majestic peaks, tiny hidden valleys and small fortified sleepy villages seem to have changed little since the Middle Ages.

The vibrant university city of Toulouse is the regional capital; it has a wealth of attractions from a Roman amphitheatre to an aerospace museum. Do not miss historic Albi with its magnificent fortified cathedral and dramatic Rocamadour clinging to the side of the Alzou canyon.

Places of interest

Albi: birthplace and Museum of Toulouse-Lautrec; imposing Ste Cécile cathedral with 15th-century fresco of The Last Judgement.

Auch: capital of ancient Gascony, boasts a fine statue of d'Artagnan.

Collonges-la-Rouge: picturesque village of medieval- and Renaissance-style mansions and manors.

Foix: 11th-/12th-century towers on a rocky peak above town; 14th-century cathedral.

Lourdes: famous pilgrimage site where Ste Bernadette is said to have spoken to the Virgin Mary in a grotto and known for the miracles said to have been performed there.

Martel: home of the Haute Quercy heritage railway with steam trains in July and August.

Cuisine of the region

Food is rich and strongly seasoned, making generous use of garlic and goose fat, and there are some excellent regional wines. Seafood such as oysters, saltwater fish and piballes from the Adour river are popular.

Cassoulet: stew of duck, sausages and beans.

Confit de Canard (d'oie): preserved duck meat.

Croustade aux pommes: caramelised apple tart sometimes containing Agen prunes.

Magret de canard: duck breast fillets

Ouillat (Ouliat): Pyrénées soup with onions, tomatoes, goose fat and garlic.

Piperade Basque: an omelette of tomatoes, peppers and local pimentos.

www.tourisme-midi-pyrenees.com
information@crtmp.com
(0)5 61 13 55 48

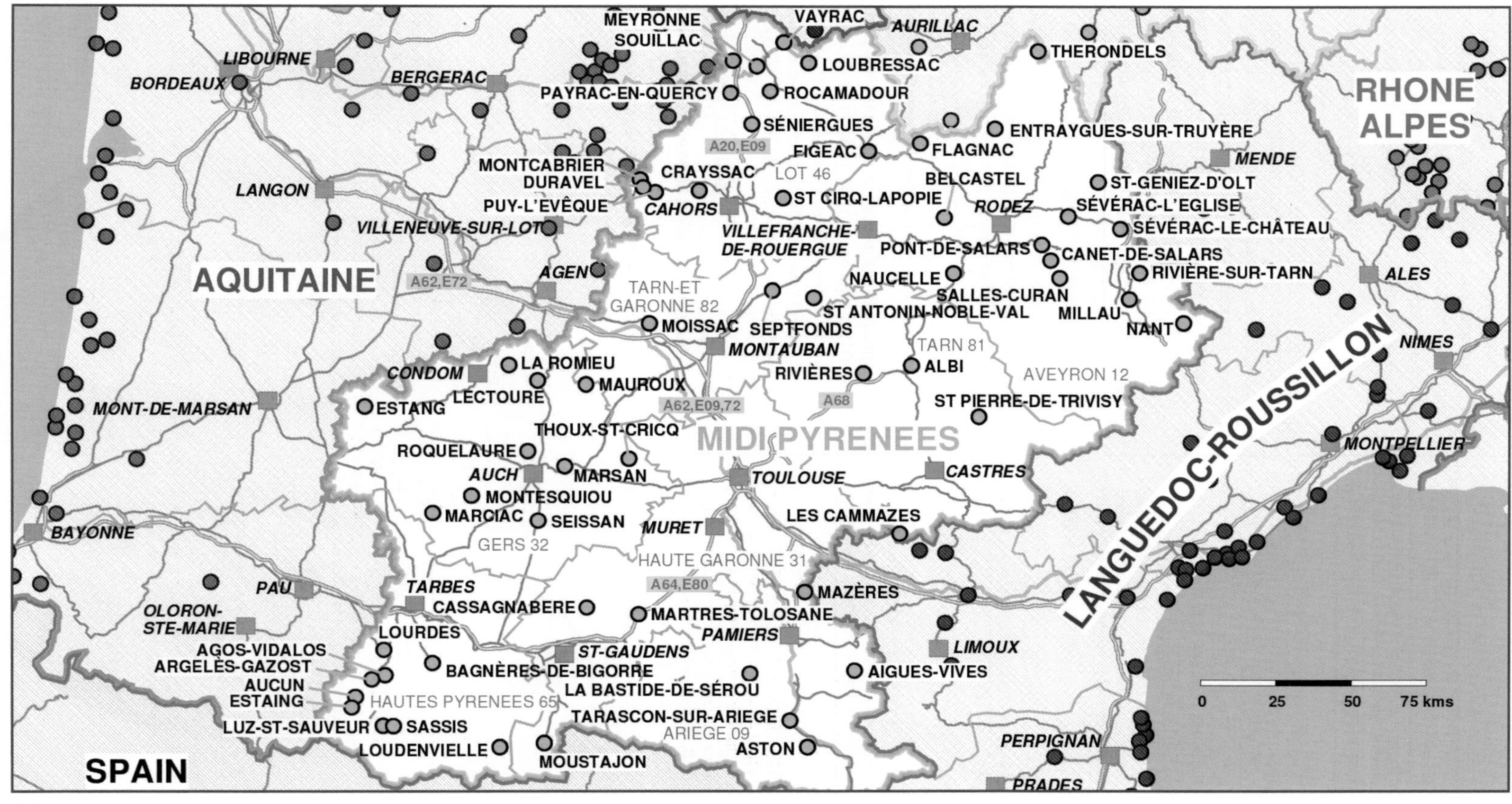
MEYRONNE
SOUILLAC
VAYRAC
AURILLAC
LIBOURNE
BORDEAUX
BERGERAC
PAYRAC-EN-QUERCY
LOUBRESSAC
ROCAMADOUR
THERONDELS
RHONE ALPES
SÉNIERGUES
ENTRAYGUES-SUR-TRUYÈRE
A20,E09
FIGEAC
FLAGNAC
MENDE
MONTCABRIER
DURAVEL
CRAYSSAC
LOT 46
BELCASTEL
ST-GENIEZ-D'OLT
LANGON
PUY-L'EVÊQUE
CAHORS
ST CIRQ-LAPOPIE
RODEZ
SÉVÉRAC-L'EGLISE
VILLENEUVE-SUR-LOT
VILLEFRANCHE-DE-ROUERGUE
SÉVÉRAC-LE-CHÂTEAU
PONT-DE-SALARS
CANET-DE-SALARS
AQUITAINE
A62,E72
AGEN
NAUCELLE
RIVIÈRE-SUR-TARN
ALES
TARN-ET GARONNE 82
SALLES-CURAN
ST ANTONIN-NOBLE-VAL
MILLAU
MOISSAC
SEPTFONDS
NANT
MONTAUBAN
TARN 81
NIMES
CONDOM
LA ROMIEU
RIVIÈRES
ALBI
AVEYRON 12
MAUROUX
MONT-DE-MARSAN
ESTANG
LECTOURE
A62,E09,72
A68
ST PIERRE-DE-TRIVISY
THOUX-ST-CRICQ
MIDI-PYRENEES
MONTPELLIER
ROQUELAURE
AUCH
MARSAN
TOULOUSE
CASTRES
MONTESQUIOU
MARCIAC
SEISSAN
LES CAMMAZES
BAYONNE
MURET
GERS 32
HAUTE GARONNE 31
LANGUEDOC-ROUSSILLON
PAU
TARBES
A64,E80
MAZÈRES
OLORON-STE-MARIE
CASSAGNABERE
MARTRES-TOLOSANE
LOURDES
PAMIERS
AGOS-VIDALOS
ST-GAUDENS
LIMOUX
ARGELÈS-GAZOST
BAGNÈRES-DE-BIGORRE
AIGUES-VIVES
AUCUN
LA BASTIDE-DE-SÉROU
ESTAING
HAUTES PYRENEES 65
0
25
50
75 kms
TARASCON-SUR-ARIEGE
LUZ-ST-SAUVEUR
SASSIS
ARIEGE 09
PERPIGNAN
LOUDENVIELLE
ASTON
MOUSTAJON
SPAIN
PRADES

Agos-Vidalos

Flower Camping Soleil du Pibeste

16 avenue du Lavedan, F-65400 Agos-Vidalos (Hautes-Pyrénées) T: 06 72 32 17 04.
E: info@campingpibeste.com **alanrogers.com/FR65090**

The Dusserm family, the owners, are very proud of their regional culture and heritage and will ensure you are made welcome. The reception is friendly and has an area for local foods, maps and good tourist information. This site is special because of the range and type of activities that it offers. These include tai chi, qi gong, massage, archery, walking, climbing and canoeing. Choral and creative activities are offered. There are 40 touring pitches all with 6-10A electricity. Mobile homes and chalets are available to rent. The mountain view from the terrace is magnificent.

Facilities

Two heated toilet blocks. Baby room. Facilities for disabled visitors (key). Cleaning can be variable. Washing machine, dryer. Motorcaravan services. Bar, snack bar, restaurant and pizzeria (June-Sept). Shop for essentials (bread to order). Swimming pool (opening dates vary with weather). New play areas. Multisports pitch. Volleyball. Tennis. Badminton. Bowling. Basketball. 4 free activities weekly (July/Aug). Entertainment, children's activities and craft workshops (July/Aug). Massage (charged). Library. Free WiFi over site. Off site: Fishing 800 m. Rafting 2 km.

Open: 1 May - 30 October.

Directions

Agos-Vidalos is on the N21, which becomes the D821, 5 km. south of Lourdes. Leave expressway at second exit, signed Agos-Vidalos and continue on D921B to site, a short distance on the right.
GPS: 43.03557, -0.07093

Charges guide

Per unit incl. 2 persons and electricity	€ 26.00 - € 37.00
extra person	€ 8.00
dog	€ 5.00

Aigues-Vives

Sites et Paysages la Serre

Chemin de la Serre 5, F-09600 Aigues-Vives (Ariège) T: 05 61 03 06 16. E: contact@camping-la-serre.com
alanrogers.com/FR09170

A beautiful site set in ten hectares of gentle hillside and run by Corinne and Patrick, a hardworking and very friendly French couple. There are 66 spacious pitches, 46 for touring, all with electricity (5/10A). Most are on well drained grass with shade and privacy, some are on hardstanding and there is additional hardstanding for motorcaravans in wet weather. There is a small, friendly bar and the site takes pride in not having a disco or karaoke, but preferring to enjoy and respect nature – there are superb views towards the Pyrenees. A range of well specified chalets are available for hire.

Facilities

Two main modern sanitary blocks and one small block. Good facilities for disabled campers. Child size toilets, Baby room. Family shower rooms. Laundry facilities. Motorcaravan services. Bar, takeaway and outdoor swimming pool (July/Aug). Tennis. Volleyball. Pétanque. Mountain bike track. Play area. Observation telescope. Small film theatre. Farming museum. Bicycle hire. Free WiFi over part of site. Telephone kiosk. Nature trails. Orchid and butterfly fields. Off site: Shops 3 km.

Open: 1 April - 31 October.

Directions

From Foix take D117 (15 km) south at Lavelanet turn left onto D625 (7.5 km) to Aigues-Vives, site clearly signed on left just after town.
GPS: 42.997617, 1.87201

Charges guide

Per unit incl. 2 persons and electricity	€ 20.00 - € 29.00
extra person	€ 5.00

No credit cards.

Albi

Albirondack Park Camping Lodge & Spa

31 allée de la Piscine, F-81000 Albi (Tarn) T: 05 63 60 37 06. E: albirondack@orange.fr
alanrogers.com/FR81230

Albirondack Park is ideal for campers seeking something out of the ordinary. This site has a selection of rental accommodation, including Airstream caravans and chalets raised to tree top height. The 54 touring pitches are well shaded and all have 10A electricity. Some of the pitches, which are separated by low wooden barriers giving no privacy, vary in size (60-100 sq.m) so can be a little awkward for large units. The outdoor heated swimming pool, sauna and steam rooms are open all year, as is the modern restaurant which is open to non-residents.

Facilities

One well equipped, modern toilet block has en-suite showers and washbasins in cabins. Facilities for disabled campers. Laundry facilities. Motorcaravan services. Restaurant. Bar. Takeaway. Daily bread. Heated swimming pool. Paddling pool. Sauna and steam room. Jacuzzi. Large screen TV room. Play area (July/Aug). WiFi (charged). Off site: Shopping centre 600 m.

Open: 1 April - 15 November, 15-31 December.

Directions

Approaching Albi from the east on the Route de Millau (D999) follow signs for Camping.
GPS: 43.9337, 2.1663

Charges guide

Per unit incl. 2 persons, electricity, water and waste water	€ 21.70 - € 35.70
extra person	€ 5.00 - € 7.50
child (2-7 yrs)	€ 3.00 - € 5.00

Argelès-Gazost

Sunêlia les Trois Vallées

Avenue des Pyrénées, F-65400 Argelès-Gazost (Hautes-Pyrénées) T: 05 62 90 35 47.
E: 3-vallees@wanadoo.fr **alanrogers.com/FR65020**

Attractive outdoor pools, jacuzzi, water chutes and heated indoor pool with opening roof are features of this large and lively site. It has 200 level grassy touring pitches, with some mountain views, and 283 mobile homes. All have electricity (3,6A). Reception staff are helpful and friendly. Visitors can gather in the new, imaginatively designed centre to eat, drink, chat, use the WiFi, watch events on the overhead TVs and, in season, enjoy the daily programme of professional entertainers. All visitors can enjoy an impressive programme of activities. The pilgrimage town of Lourdes is nearby.

Facilities

One slightly dated toilet block, the other one superb with washbasins and twin power showers. Facilities for disabled visitors. Bar/disco (15/6-30/9). Café, takeaway, restaurant (15/6-15/9). Bread. Swimming pool complex (15/5-15/9), heated indoor pool (all year), paddling pool, spa bath, large jacuzzi and two water slides. TV room. Good playground. Volleyball, football, boules, archery. Entertainment and activities in high season. Large TV screens for major events. WiFi throughout (charged in high season). Off site: Supermarket across the road.

Open: 11 April - 16 October.

Directions

Argelès-Gazost is 13 km. south of Lourdes. Take D821 towards Argelès-Gazost, then onto 'La Voie Rapide' and turn right at the first roundabout, after 300 m. right at the new roundabout and you are at the site. GPS: 43.01216, -0.09711

Charges guide

Per unit incl. 2 persons and electricity	€ 18.50 - € 39.00
extra person	€ 6.00 - € 12.50
child (2-13 yrs)	€ 4.00 - € 10.50

Argelès-Gazost

Camping du Lavedan

Lau-Balagnas, 44 route des Vallees, F-65400 Argelès-Gazost (Hautes-Pyrénées) T: 05 62 97 18 84.
E: contact@lavedan.com **alanrogers.com/FR65080**

Camping du Lavedan is a well established, family owned site set in the Argelès-Gazost valley south of Lourdes, where a warm welcome and an impressive mountain view await you. There are 60 level touring pitches, all with electricity (3-10A) and most have shade from trees. They are set away from the 48 mobile homes, of which 12 are for rent. Planting of bushes and trees has been carefully considered. The large restaurant and bar area is the scene of some lively evening entertainment in the summer.

Facilities

Recent well maintained toilet block. Baby room. Facilities for disabled visitors. Laundry facilities. Shop, bread delivery (1/5-15/9). Restaurant with terrace, pizzeria and snacks (1/5-15/9). Bar, TV (all year). Swimming pool (15/5-15/9; can be covered). Paddling pool. Play area. Boules. WiFi over site (charged). Off site: Trout fishing and bicycle hire 1 km. Supermarket 2 km. Riding 5 km.

Open: All year.

Directions

From Lourdes take the N21 (Voie rapide) south. This becomes the N821/N821A. Take exit 3 (Argelès-Gazost). Take D921 then D921B to Lau-Balagnas. Site is on right at southern edge of town.
GPS: 42.98822, -0.089

Charges guide

Per unit incl. 2 persons and electricity	€ 19.30 - € 37.70
extra person	€ 6.30 - € 10.35

Camping Cheques accepted.

Aston

Camping le Pas de l'Ours

F-09310 Aston (Ariège) T: 05 61 64 90 33. E: contact@lepasdelours.fr
alanrogers.com/FR09110

In the small town of Aston, which is located in the heart of the scenic Vallées d'Ax in the Haute-Ariège region, you will find the secluded campsite of le Pas de l'Ours. With panoramic views of the mountains, this charming site has a total of 57 pitches, although only 30 of these are for tourers, as the rest are taken up by chalets to rent. Six of the smaller touring pitches are reserved for tents and have no electricity, but the other 24 grassy and mainly level pitches are well kept and attractively laid out, separated by shrubs and bushes, and have 6A electricity (French sockets).

Facilities

Two modern sanitary blocks are well equipped and include preset showers. Large en-suite room for disabled visitors. Motorcaravan services. Baker's van calls every morning in July/Aug. Communal covered purpose built barbecue area with picnic tables. Small play area. Tennis court. Off site: Heated outdoor swimming pool in village adjacent to site (charged). Shops and restaurant 2 km.

Open: 1 June - 14 September.

Directions

From N20 between Ax-les-Thermes and Tarascon take exit to Les Cabannes on D522a signed Verdun and Aston. After 1.8 km. turn left on D520 to Château Verdun and Aston. Site is well signed.
GPS: 42.772283, 1.67155

Charges guide

Per unit incl. 2 persons and electricity	€ 20.00 - € 27.00

Aucun

Camping Azun Nature

1 route des Poueyes, F-65400 Aucun (Hautes-Pyrénées) T: 05 62 97 45 05. E: azun.nature@wanadoo.fr
alanrogers.com/FR65190

This site is attractively located on the edge of the National Park of the High Pyrenees with superb walking, mountain biking and paragliding opportunities. The 25 open and grassy touring pitches, most with electricity (3-6A, long leads may be required), have fine views of the surrounding mountains. There are 12 rental chalets. A small shop is provided and drinks can be served on the terrace in summer. The site prides itself on its relative simplicity and its environmental ethos. The friendly and enthusiastic owners are delighted to recommend walking or cycling itineraries and to help organise excursions.

Facilities

Good quality sanitary block with facilities for babies and disabled visitors. Washing machine and dryer. Motorcaravan services. No restaurant/snack bar but drinks and coffee served on the terrace in high season. Shop selling organic and local produce, ice creams, bread and pastries (1/6-30/9). Play area. Activities room. Maps and tourist information. Free WiFi throughout. Large field for sports and games. Off site: Paragliding schools opposite site. Fishing 800 m. Riding 1 km.

Open: 1 May - 30 September.

Directions

From Argelès-Gazost take 921B then D918 following signs for Aucun. At sign for Aucun village turn left for Las Poueyes and drive for 100 m. Azun Nature's entrance is on the right between the barns.
GPS: 42.97344, -0.18501

Charges guide

Per unit incl. 2 persons and electricity	€ 17.00 - € 21.50
extra person	€ 4.50

Bagnères-de-Bigorre

Camping le Monlôo

Route de la Plaine, F-65200 Bagnères-de-Bigorre (Hautes-Pyrénées) T: 05 62 95 19 65.
E: campingmonloo@yahoo.com **alanrogers.com/FR65160**

Le Monlôo is set in a wide valley in the Pyrenees. The immediate surroundings of farmland, with crops growing and cows at pasture, give way to some magnificent views of the mountains towering away from the front of the site, whilst the back is right at the foot of some smaller foothills. It is a relatively small site of 120 touring pitches and 70 mobile homes and chalets, some for rent. There is shade on many pitches with some tall dividing hedges. Electricity (10A) is available. The friendly family take their job seriously and will even show you a selection of available pitches from the comfort of their electric car.

Facilities

Ample toilet facilities are provided in four blocks (one heated). Facilities for disabled visitors. Washing machines and dryer. Motorcaravan services. Bread to order. Snacks, bar and takeaway (July/Aug). Indoor heated pool with slide. Outdoor lagoon pool with sandy beach (15/7-15/9). Tennis court. Bouncy castle. Simple play area. Gas or electric barbecues are permitted. WiFi over site (charged). Off site: Fishing, golf and bicycle hire 1 km.

Open: 1 January - 15 December.

Directions

From the A64 take exit 14 signed Bagnères-de-Bigorre. Enter town and take D8 road to the right for Ordizan. Site is just a few hundred metres along this road, well signed. GPS: 43.08180, 0.15139

Charges guide

Per unit incl. 3 persons and electricity	€ 17.50 - € 26.50
extra person	€ 2.50 - € 5.00
child (2- 8 yrs)	€ 2.00 - € 3.90

Belcastel

Camping le Bourg

F-12390 Belcastel (Aveyron) T: 05 65 63 95 61. E: camping@mairie-belcastel.fr
alanrogers.com/FR12670

A 2 km. drive through woodland, along a single track road (do not despair, it will get you there!), opens up to a stunning landscape. This little gem of a campsite shaded by trees on the banks of the Aveyron, is linked by an ancient bridge to the medieval hillside village of Belcastel, classed as one of the most beautiful in France. It is a small municipal site with 30 grassy pitches, all for touring and most with 10A electricity. It has all the necessary facilities, but they are basic. With no activities or entertainment, this site will appeal to the purist and those seeking a peaceful retreat in beautiful surroundings.

Facilities

One basic toilet block with hot showers and hot water for washing up. Washing machine and drying area. Motorcaravan service point. Shop, bar and snack bar. Communal room with fridge and games. Library. Play area. Direct access to river. Fishing. WiFi (free on bar terrace). Off site: Belcastel with two restaurants. Supermarket, shops, municipal swimming pool, riding and ATM in Rignac 6 km. Golf 25 km.

Open: 1 April - 31 October.

Directions

From Rodez, take D994 west toward Rignac. At junction for Rignac, turn south towards Belcastel. At river, turn right over bridge. Site well signposted on left, 2 km along single track road (50% hardcore). GPS: 44.387597, 2.336158

Charges guide

Per unit incl. 2 persons and electricity	€ 14.00 - € 16.00
extra person	€ 5.00

Canet-de-Salars

Camping Soleil Levant

Lac de Pareloup, Pont des Vernhes D993, F-12290 Canet-de-Salars (Aveyron) T: 05 65 46 03 65.
E: contact@camping-soleil-levant.com **alanrogers.com/FR12140**

Soleil Levant has a superb lakeside beach as part of the campsite with shady grassy banks for picnics. Very reasonably priced, this is a site for lovers of nature, peace and quiet. There are competitions and games for all ages in July and August, but at other times there is just the sound of the birds. The 205 level pitches (151 for touring) all have electricity (6/10A) and water nearby. Most have shade from the maturing trees. Many activities are possible on the lake and there is a ramp for launching boats. This is a good area for walking and biking with several marked routes. The nearby gorges of the River Tarn provide many spectacular views and scenic picnic locations. They also offer white-water rafting and canyoning experiences for the more adventurous. The towns of Rodez, Albi and Millau can be visited by car, each having their own special character. The medieval village of Pegayrolles with a château and 11th-century church is also worth a visit.

Facilities

Three toilet blocks provide British and Turkish style WCs, preset showers and most washbasins in the main blocks are in cubicles. Superb facilities for disabled visitors. Baby rooms with bath, shower and child's WC. Washing machines. Fridge hire. No shop, but bread and gas are available at the bar. Snack bar/pizzeria (27/6-10/9). Bar with TV and video games. Pedalo, zodiac and canoe hire. Free WiFi in bar. Off site: Riding 4 km. Golf 30 km.

Open: 1 May - 30 September.

Directions

From the A75, take exit 44.1, then D911 towards Pont de Salars for 28 km. Before Pont de Salars follow signs for Salles Curan. After 7 km. site is on the left just before the large bridge over the Lac de Pareloup. GPS: 44.21512, 2.77788

Charges guide

Per unit incl. 2 persons and electricity	€ 14.00 - € 28.90
extra person	€ 4.70 - € 7.20
child (2-6 yrs)	free - € 5.20

Canet-de-Salars

Castel Camping le Caussanel

Lac de Pareloup, F-12290 Canet-de-Salars (Aveyron) T: 05 65 46 85 19. E: info@lecaussanel.com
alanrogers.com/FR12170

This is an attractive site which is well cared for and with amenities for all the family. It has 228 large, fairly level, grassy pitches, 108 for touring. Most have some shade, 6A electricity (very long leads may be necessary) and 45 are fully serviced. The pitches are defined by lines and offer little privacy but some have wonderful views over the lake. The site has swimming pools and a paddling pool, both with slides. The adjacent 1,200-hectare lake offers a large area for swimming and all the usual watersports. This large, extremely spacious site on the banks of Lac de Pareloup is greatly improved.

Facilities

Modern toilet blocks have all the necessary facilities including those for disabled visitors. Washing machine. Small shop and bar (27/6-26/8). Grill with takeaway (reduced opening in low season). Swimming pool complex. Large play area. Boules. Tennis. Football. Organised activities (July/Aug). Fishing. Bicycle hire (July/Aug). Watersports (July/Aug). Swimming in lake. Max. 2 dogs (1 in rentals). WiFi over site (charged). Off site: Paths by lake. Shops, banks, restaurants 8 km.

Open: 2 May - 3 September.

Directions

From D911 Rodez-Millau road, just east of Pont de Salars, turn south on D993 signed Salles-Curan. In 6 km. at crossroads turn right on D538 signed le Caussanel. Very shortly turn left and continue to site. GPS: 44.21462, 2.76658

Charges guide

Per unit incl. 2 persons and electricity	€ 18.80 - € 36.60
extra person	€ 4.10 - € 7.90

Camping Cheques accepted.

Cassagnabère

Camping Pré Fixe

Route de Saint-Gaudens, F-31420 Cassagnabère (Haute-Garonne) T: 05 61 98 71 00.
E: campingprefixe@orange.fr **alanrogers.com/FR31090**

Camping Pré Fixe is a friendly family site, located on a sunny south-facing slope. The site is a member of La Via Natura, a small group of campsites in attractive rural settings, with a strong environmental awareness. There are 43 good sized, level, grassy pitches (80-100 sq.m), most with electricity (6/10A), and some with views across to the distant Pyrenees. Some site roads are steep (but the owner can assist with his tractor if necessary) and a maximum unit length of seven metres is suggested. The site is well equipped with a bistro and wine bar, as well as a swimming pool and small shop.

Facilities

One central unisex sanitary block with hot showers and facilities for children and disabled visitors. Motorcaravan services. Shop for essentials and local produce. Bread to order. Bistro and wine bar. Heated swimming pool. Play area. Badminton. Boules. Children's club. Some evening entertainment. Chalets and safari-style tents for rent. Communal barbecue. WiFi in bar (free).
Off site: Tennis 200 m. Aurignac and supermarket 7 km.

Open: 1 May - 30 September.

Directions

Site is close to Cassagnabere-Tournas, south of Toulouse. From Toulouse on A64 motorway, leave at Boussens exit (no. 21) and follow the northbound D635 as far as Cassagnabere-Tournas. The site is well signed from here. GPS: 43.22628, 0.78886

Charges guide

Per unit incl. 2 persons and electricity	€ 17.50 - € 24.80
extra person	€ 4.20 - € 6.20

Crayssac

Campéole les Reflets du Quercy

Mas de Bastide, F-46150 Crayssac (Lot) T: 05 65 30 00 27. E: reflets-du-quercy@campeole.com
alanrogers.com/FR46170

Set in the west of the Lot department, this site is located on a wooded hill about 16 km. from the large town of Cahors. It is owned by the Campéole group and is classed as a holiday village. It is very lively here during July and August but otherwise very quiet. There are 136 uneven, stony pitches with shade, just 39 of which are for touring, most with 6A electricity (rock pegs are essential). At the rear of the site is a large area of independently owned mobile homes and residents here also have access to the campsite facilities. There are many ancient market towns and villages to explore.

Facilities

One adequate toilet block with facilities for disabled visitors. Baby room with bath. Laundry facilities. Motorcaravan services (charged). Shop, bar and snack bar (April-Sept). Swimming and paddling pools (May-Sept). TV and games room, bouncy castle (June-Sept). Boules. Tennis. Multisports court. Play area. Entertainment (July/Aug). WiFi (charged). Off site: Shop, bar and restaurant at Mercuès 4 km. Canoeing and fishing on the River Lot. Riding 7 km. Bicycle hire 15 km.

Open: 12 April - 28 September.

Directions

At Cahors leave the D820 and take D811 northwest signed Fumel, through Mercuès. After a further 4.5 km. turn left D23, signed Crayssac. Just before Crayssac turn right, site signed, entrance in 1.5 km. GPS: 44.50993, 1.32269

Charges guide

Per unit incl. 2 persons and electricity	€ 15.70 - € 27.50
extra person	€ 4.20 - € 6.90

Camping Cheques accepted.

Duravel

Domaine Duravel

Port de Vire (D58), F-46700 Duravel (Lot) T: 05 65 24 65 06. E: duravel@franceloc.fr
alanrogers.com/FR46140

This quality site is beautifully situated on the banks of the River Lot, only 35 km. from the historic town of Cahors. The site has 293 clearly defined, large pitches (135 for touring) all with electricity. Some of these are fully serviced with water and drainage and private sanitary facilities. The reception, bar, restaurant, snack bar and the shop are all located beside the river and from the terrace you can enjoy lovely views over the water. The pool complex offers two large heated pools with water slides and a children's pool. Duravel would particularly suit families with children of all ages.

Facilities

Two clean toilet blocks include facilities for disabled visitors. Baby rooms. Laundry facilities. Serviced pitch facility provides a toilet, shower and sink. Well stocked shop. Restaurant, bar, pizzeria and takeaway (30/5-14/9). Heated outdoor swimming pool complex. Two tennis courts. New adventure play area. Miniclub (high season). Bicycle hire. Canoe hire. Free WiFi at bar. Off site: Fishing and boat trip on an underground river 500 m.

Open: 25 April - 20 September.

Directions

From Paris A10 towards Orléans and A71 towards Vierzon. Follow A20 and take exit 57 to Villeneuve-sur-Lot. Take the D811 to Cahors, Puy l'Evêque and the D58 to Duravel. Site is well signed as Club Vacances Duravel. GPS: 44.49636, 1.08176

Charges guide

Per unit incl. 2 persons and electricity	€ 15.00 - € 29.00
extra person	€ 3.50 - € 7.00

Entraygues-sur-Truyère

Camping du Val de Saures

Village de Gîtes le Bastie, F-12140 Entraygues-sur-Truyère (Aveyron) T: 05 65 44 56 92.
E: info@camping-valdesaures.com **alanrogers.com/FR12260**

Camping du Val de Saures is a well presented, value-for-money site only five minutes across a river bridge from the interesting old town of Entraygues. Situated at the confluence of the Lot and Truyère rivers, it is a good base for relaxing and exploring this beautiful area of Aveyron. There are 110 good sized, level, grassy pitches (10A electricity) separated by small hedges and trees with varying amounts of shade. Many overlook the River Lot. Although the site has no shop, bar or restaurant, these are all available in the town. There are marked paths to explore on foot, on horseback or by bike.

Facilities

Two very clean and well appointed toilet blocks with all the necessary facilities including baby room and facilities for disabled campers in one block. Laundry. Motorcaravan services. TV/games room. Play area. Activities and entertainment (July/Aug). WiFi (free). River fishing but no bathing. Communal barbecues. Off site: Entraygues 400 m. (by footbridge) with shops, banks, bars and restaurants. Bicycle hire 500 m.

Open: 1 May - 30 September.

Directions

Entraygues-sur-Truyère is 42 km. southeast of Aurillac on the D920. At southern end of Entraygues on the D920 turn right (site signed), over river bridge onto the D904 and immediately right again. Just past the tennis courts fork right and follow lane down to site. GPS: 44.64243, 2.56414

Charges guide

Per unit incl. 2 persons and electricity	€ 14.80 - € 23.30

Estaing

Camping Pyrénées Natura

Route du Lac, F-65400 Estaing (Hautes-Pyrénées) T: 05 62 97 45 44. E: info@camping-pyrenees-natura.com
alanrogers.com/FR65060

Pyrénées Natura, at an altitude of 1,000 m. on the edge of the national park, is the perfect site for lovers of nature. The 66 pitches (47 for tourers), all with electricity (3-10A), are in a landscaped area with 75 varieties of trees and shrubs – but they do not spoil the fantastic views. There is a small, well stocked shop in the former watermill. Prices are very reasonable and homemade bread can be purchased. On the river there is a small beach belonging to the site for supervised water play. The owners, the Papin family, will do all they can to make your stay a pleasant one. Their aim is that you return home feeling at peace with the world and having learnt something about the area and its flora and fauna, especially the birds which soar above the site. There are several unusual hens on site and you are encouraged to use the free birdspotting telescope! Pyrénées Natura belongs to the prestigious Via Natura group of 17 campsites in France, committed to eco-tourism principles.

Facilities

First class toilet blocks. Facilities for disabled visitors and babies. Laundry facilities (no lines allowed). Motorcaravan services. Bar and small shop. Takeaway 1/5-1/10). Lounge, library, TV, upstairs games/reading room. Birdwatching (equipment is available). Infrared sauna and jacuzzi. Play area. Small beach beside river. Boules. Giant chess. Weekly evening meal in May, June and Sept. Wine tasting and barbecues (July-Aug). WiFi throughout (free in bar). Off site: Village with two restaurants. Riding 4 km. Bicycle hire 11 km. Lac d'Estaing 4 km. Lourdes 26 km.

Open: 18 April - 10 October.

Directions

At Argelès-Gazost, take D918 towards Aucun. After 8 km. turn left on D13 to Bun, cross the river, then right on D103 to site (5.5 km). Narrow road, few passing places. GPS: 42.94152, -0.17726

Charges guide

Per unit incl. 2 persons and electricity	€ 19.60 - € 37.00
extra person	€ 6.00
child (under 8 yrs)	€ 3.90
dog	€ 3.00

Estang

Camping les Lacs de Courtès

Route de Panjas, F-32240 Estang (Gers) T: 05 62 09 61 98. E: contact@lacsdecourtes.com

alanrogers.com/FR32100

This pleasant site is situated on a gentle hillside overlooking a lake at the edge of the village of Estang, famous for its unique wooden arènes where the traditional 'courses landaises' (an ancient form of bullfighting) take place several times a year. There are 104 pitches neatly arranged on terraces. The 50 level touring pitches, a small number of hardstandings, each has an adjacent 6/10A electricity supply (French sockets); the remaining pitches are used for mobile homes and chalets of which 29 are for rent. The touring pitches are mainly grassed and are well separated by hedges and mature trees which provide shade. Some are situated alongside a private lake that is used for fishing and canoeing.

Facilities

Main sanitary block with showers, WCs, washbasins and baby facilities. Facilities for disabled visitors. Laundry room. Motorcaravan services. Bar and snack bar (daily July/Aug, then w/ends) with covered entertainment area. Two outdoor pools and paddling pool. Jacuzzi. Play area. Private lake for fishing and canoeing. WiFi throughout (charged). Off site: Shops, restaurant and bars in Estang 400 m. Supermarket in Cazaubon 10 km. Riding 10 km.

Open: 1 April - 31 October.

Directions

From Condom take D931 to Eauze then N524 west to Cazaubon. After 4 km. take D30 to Estang. Site is on left as you enter the village of Estang. GPS: 43.86767, -0.10167

Charges guide

Per unit incl. 2 persons and electricity	€ 19.00 - € 27.50
extra person	€ 3.00 - € 5.25

Camping Cheques accepted.

Figeac

Camping le Domaine du Surgié

Domaine du Surgié, F-46100 Figeac (Lot) T: 05 61 64 88 54. E: contact@marc-montmija.com

alanrogers.com/FR46320

Very conveniently placed, this site is only 2 km. from the centre of the interesting old town of Figeac. There are 193 pitches, of which 137 are for touring, the remaining 56 are split between 20 mobile homes, 30 gîtes and six fully equipped large tents, all of which are for rent. The grass pitches are level with a mixture of shade and sun, and all have 10A electricity. Access is easy for large outfits. The pool complex, restaurant and reception area are at one end of the site. There are many organised activities, details of which are given out on Sunday mornings. This is an ideal choice for an active family.

Facilities

Three sanitary blocks include facilities for babies and disabled visitors. Laundry. Shop, bar, restaurant and takeaway. Swimming pool complex adjacent (July/Aug, open to the public). Sports competitions and party nights with themed dining. Children's clubs. Canoeing. Fishing. Minigolf. Boules. Bicycle hire. WiFi near reception (free). Off site: Riding 2 km. Shops and restaurants in medieval town of Figeac 2 km.

Open: 1 April - 30 September.

Directions

From the west, enter Figeac on the D802 and then turn right across river, signed Base de Loisirs. Shortly turn left at small roundabout and then, at traffic lights, branch left uphill to site. Well signed from the centre of Figeac. GPS: 44.60989, 2.05015

Charges guide

Per unit incl. 2 persons and electricity	€ 19.00 - € 26.00
extra person	€ 5.00 - € 7.50

Flagnac

Flower Camping le Port de Lacombe

F-12300 Flagnac (Aveyron) T: 05 65 64 10 08. E: accueil@campingleportdelacombe.fr

alanrogers.com/FR12290

Le Port de Lacombe is well kept, situated on the banks of the Lot river, a location ideal for walking, cycling, fishing and canoeing. The 97 grass touring pitches (with 10A electricity) are level and range in size from 100-130 sq.m. A large natural swimming pool is fed by the river and provides a separate paddling area and a large slide. Using the D42, one can wind through the valley and climb to over 2,000 feet to the Plateau de la Viadene. Running past the site, the Lot river provides a very relaxing environment to laze away your holiday, should you wish to do so.

Facilities

Two separate sanitary blocks, each with the usual facilities including provision for disabled visitors. Washing machine. Shop and bar (all season) with restaurant and takeaway (both 15/6-15/9). TV in function room. Play area. Swimming pool fed from the river. Paddling pool (15/6-15/9). Bicycle hire. Fishing in river. Entertainment (July/Aug). WiFi throughout (charged).

Open: 1 April - 30 September.

Directions

Driving south from Brive-la-Gaillarde, take N140 to Decazeville, turning north on D963 to Flagnac. Site is well signed on the left. From Rodez take N140 to Decazeville, then as above. GPS: 44.60915, 2.23597

Charges guide

Per unit incl. 2 persons and electricity	€ 16.50 - € 26.40
extra person	€ 2.50 - € 5.50

La Bastide-de-Sérou

Flower Camping l'Arize

Lieu-dit Bourtol, F-09240 La Bastide-de-Sérou (Ariège) T: 05 61 65 81 51. E: mail@camping-arize.com
alanrogers.com/FR09020

The site sits in a delightful, tranquil valley among the foothills of the Pyrenees and is just east of the interesting village of La Bastide-de-Sérou, beside the River Arize (good trout fishing). The river is fenced for the safety of children on the site, but may be accessed just outside the gate. The 71 large touring pitches are neatly laid out on level grass within the spacious site. All have 6/10A electricity and are mostly separated into bays by hedges and young trees. Full services are available to some pitches with access to a small toilet block. You will receive a warm welcome from Dominique and Brigitte.

Facilities

Toilet block includes facilities for babies and disabled visitors. Laundry room. Motorcaravan services. Shop. Bar (1/7-31/8). Takeaway (5/7-30/8) Small swimming pool (1/6-30/9) and sunbathing area. Entertainment in high season. Weekly barbecues and welcome drinks on Sundays. Fishing. Bicycle hire. WiFi (charged).
Off site: The nearest restaurant is located at the national stud for the famous Merens horses just 400 m. away.

Open: 4 April - 30 October.

Directions

Site is southeast of the village La Bastide-de-Sérou. Take the D15 towards Nescus and site is on right after 1 km. GPS: 43.00182, 1.44538

Charges guide

Per unit incl. 2 persons and electricity	€ 15.60 - € 28.60
extra person	€ 4.30 - € 6.40
child (2-13 yrs)	€ 2.30 - € 5.00

Lectoure

Yelloh! Village le Lac des Trois Vallées

F-32700 Lectoure (Gers) T: 05 62 68 83 33. E: contact@lacdes3vallees.fr
alanrogers.com/FR32060

This is a very large (140 hectares), hilly site with many facilities. It is a large holiday complex and good for families with young children or teenagers. The large lake provides the opportunity for canoeing and swimming. There is a large safe paddling area and a separate fishing lake. The impressive heated pool complex, complete with gymnasium and jacuzzi, has paved areas for sunbathing and a large paddling pool. Of the 600 pitches, over 200 are well situated for tourers on shaded terraces or open ground, all with electricity (10A) and many with water also. There is a range of rental accommodation.

Facilities

Eight modern sanitary blocks, each with baby bathing facilities. Provision for disabled visitors. Laundry facilities. Motorcaravan services. Supermarket. Restaurants and bars. Lakeside snack bar and drinks kiosk. Heated swimming pool complex (supervised). Lake complex with water slides. Multisports pitch. BMX/skateboard area. Fishing. Tennis. Minigolf. Video games room. Disco. Children's club. Evening entertainment. WiFi (free in bar). Off site: Golf 10 km. Riding 20 km. Hot air balloon rides.

Open: 1 June - 6 September.

Directions

Take N21 south from Lectoure and turn left at Yelloh! Village flags just before river bridge. Site is well signed and is a further 2 km. along this road. GPS: 43.91250, 0.64852

Charges guide

Per unit incl. 2 persons and electricity	€ 18.00 - € 50.00
extra person	€ 6.00 - € 9.00
child (3-7 yrs)	free - € 8.00

Les Cammazes

Camping de la Rigole

Route de Barrage, F-81540 Les Cammazes (Tarn) T: 05 63 73 28 99. E: campings.occitanie@orange.fr
alanrogers.com/FR81100

La Rigole is located high in the hills above Lac des Cammazes. Although the site slopes, of the 65 pitches, the 34 for touring are on small terraces and many have quite deep shade. All have electricity (8-13A). There are nine privately owned mobile homes and 13 mobile homes and chalets for rent. These are well separated from the touring area. There is a small bar and snack bar. One evening each week in main season, a regional meal is organised. Small children are well catered for and there is a delightful children's farm. The site is totally unsuitable for American RVs and large units.

Facilities

Fairly modern toilet block. Baby room. Facilities for disabled visitors (although the slopes might be difficult). Washing machines, dryer. Small shop. Bar. Takeaway. Swimming pool and children's pool. All open in high season. Bicycle hire. Badminton. Volleyball. Boules. WiFi on part of site (free). Off site: Lac des Cammazes with its dam 400 m. Fishing 400 m. Riding 1.5 km. Lac de St Ferréol with large sandy beach 5 km.

Open: 27 April - 30 September.

Directions

Les Cammazes is 25 km. northeast of Castelnaudary, 10 km. southeast of Revel. From Revel take D629 to Cammazes, continue through village, after 1 km. turn left towards Barrage (site signed), site entrance 200 m. on right. GPS: 43.407867, 2.0866

Charges guide

Per unit incl. 2 persons and electricity	€ 18.70 - € 25.00
extra person	€ 4.10 - € 5.50

La Romieu

Castel Camping Le Camp de Florence

Route Astaffort, F-32480 La Romieu (Gers) T: 05 62 28 15 58. E: info@lecampdeflorence.com

alanrogers.com/FR32010

Camp de Florence is an attractive and very well equipped site on the edge of an historic village in pleasantly undulating Gers countryside. The 197 large, part terraced pitches (100 for touring units) all have 10A electricity, 20 with hardstanding and 16 fully serviced. They are arranged around a large field with rural views, giving a feeling of spaciousness. The 13th-century village of La Romieu is on the Santiago de Compostela pilgrims' route. The Pyrenees are a two hour drive, the Atlantic coast a similar distance. The site has been developed by the friendly Mijnsbergen family. They have sympathetically converted the old farmhouse buildings to provide facilities for the site. The Collegiate church, a UNESCO World Heritage monument, is visible from the site and well worth visiting (the views from the top of the tower are magnificent). The local arboretum has the biggest collection of trees in the Midi-Pyrénées.

Facilities

Three toilet blocks provide all the necessary facilities. Washing machines and dryers. Motorcaravan services. Restaurant (1/5-27/9, also open to the public). Takeaway. Bread. Swimming pool area with water slide (1/5-30/9). Bubble bath. Protected children's pool (open to public in afternoons). New playgrounds, games and animal park. Bouncy castle. Trampoline. Outdoor fitness machines. Games room. Tennis. Pétanque. Bicycle hire. Discos, picnics, musical evenings. WiFi over site (charged, free in bar). Max. 2 dogs. Off site: Shop 500 m. in village. Fishing 5 km. Riding 10 km. Walking tours. Walibi theme park nearby.

Open: 1 April - 10 October.

Directions

Site signed from D931 Agen-Condom road. Small units turn left at Ligardes (signed), follow D36 for 1 km, turn right at La Romieu (signed). Otherwise continue to outskirts of Condom and take D41 left to La Romieu, through village to site.
GPS: 43.98299, 0.50183

Charges guide

Per unit incl. 2 persons and electricity	€ 17.00 - € 36.00
extra person	€ 3.90 - € 8.00
child (4-17 yrs)	free - € 7.60
dog (max. 2)	€ 2.00 - € 3.00

Special prices for groups, rallies, etc.

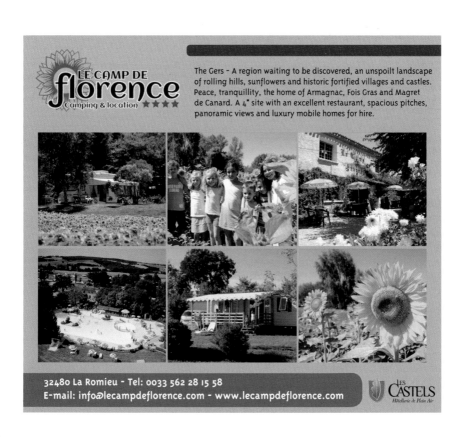

Loubressac

Camping la Garrigue

F-46130 Loubressac (Lot) T: 05 65 38 34 88. E: infos@camping-lagarrigue.com

alanrogers.com/FR46420

Camping la Garrigue is a quiet, friendly, family-run site on the outskirts of Loubressac, one of the most beautiful villages in France. The village is perched on a promontory that offers wonderful views over the Dordogne valley with the River Dordogne close by. The site has 50 pitches with 29 reasonably level, on grass for touring, all with 6/10A electricity. Some are separated by hedges with mature trees giving varying amounts of shade. This well run site is ideal for couples and families with small children seeking to holiday in wonderful surroundings.

Facilities

Modern toilet block, facilities for campers with disabilities. Washing machine and dryer. Motorcaravan services. Shop. Bar and snack bar with takeaway (1/6-15/9). Meals and picnic baskets to order. Swimming pool (15/5-30/9). Library. Playground. Games room. Barbecue area. Family activities. Mobile homes for rent. WiFi on part of site (charged). Off site: Loubressac 300 m. Hiking, climbing, biking, canoeing. Fishing 4 km. Golf and riding 10 km.

Open: 1 April - 30 September.

Directions

From Tulle take the D940 south 45 km. to Bretenoux. Cross river, turn right D14 to le Pont de Maday. Turn left on D30, then right on D118. Site is signed in the village. GPS: 44.869876, 1.800814

Charges guide

Per unit incl. 2 persons and electricity	€ 17.20 - € 20.40
extra person	€ 4.50 - € 5.50
child (under 7 yrs)	€ 2.40 - € 3.30

Loudenvielle

Camping la Vacance Pène Blanche

9 chemin de la Mainette, F-65510 Loudenvielle (Hautes-Pyrénées) T: 05 62 99 68 85.

E: info@peneblanche.com **alanrogers.com/FR65140**

La Pène Blanche is spacious and well kept, in an idyllic location close to Lake Loudenvielle and surrounded by high mountains. The approach is on good roads through spectacular scenery. There are 120 small pitches which are not separated; 80 are for touring (40 have 5/10A electricity, long leads required). The area is ideal for walking, hiking and biking in the mountains. An outdoor swimming pool is just 200 m. away and nearby is the Balnéa Centre with its spa waters. The resorts of Val Louron and Peyragudes are within easy reach for skiing.

Facilities

Two toilet blocks, one traditional, one modern and heated include facilities for disabled visitors. Laundry facilities. Play area. WiFi (part site, free). Off site: Restaurant, snack bar, bar and local shops all within 100 m. Cinema, fishing and golf 200 m. Motorcaravan services 300 m. Within walking distance is the Balnéa Centre with its spa water baths and adjacent swimming pool with waterslide. Bicycle hire 1 km. Tennis. Minigolf. Hiking. Mountain biking. Paragliding. Hang-gliding. Skiing.

Open: 11 April - 2 November.

Directions

From A64 (Tarbes-Toulouse) exit 16 take D929 and follow signs to Arreau, then D618 to D25 signed Loudenvielle. GPS: 42.796107, 0.406679

Charges guide

Per unit incl. 2 persons and electricity	€ 16.50 - € 26.90
extra person	€ 4.00 - € 6.00
child (3-7 yrs)	€ 3.00 - € 4.50

No credit cards.

Lourdes

Camping le Moulin du Monge

28 avenue Jean Moulin, F-65100 Lourdes (Hautes-Pyrénées) T: 05 62 94 28 15.

E: camping.moulin.monge@wanadoo.fr **alanrogers.com/FR65100**

A well organised, family run site with a friendly welcome, Moulin du Monge is an ideal base for visiting Lourdes, only 3 km. away, and a bus service stops just outside the site. There will be some traffic noise from the nearby N21 and railway line. This attractive garden-like site has 55 pitches, all with electricity (2-6A) in three grassy areas, mostly shaded by trees and easy to access. The swimming pool is slightly apart from most of the pitches. There is a separate adjacent pool for children. There are ten mobile homes available to rent. The region is good for sightseeing, with the cities of Pau and Tarbes fairly near.

Facilities

The heated toilet blocks have all necessary facilities, including washing machine and dryer. Facilities for disabled campers and children. Baby room. Motorcaravan services. Shop (15/6-20/9). Heated swimming pool, sliding cover (20/5-20/9), paddling pool. Sauna. Games/TV room. Barbecue, terrace. Boules. Volleyball. Playground. Trampolines. Free WiFi throughout the site. Off site: Good transport links to the city centre. Bicycle hire 500 m. Riding 2 km. Fishing 3 km. Golf 4 km.

Open: 1 April - 10 October.

Directions

Site is just off the N21 on northern outskirts of Lourdes. From north, on N21 (2 km. south of Adé) be prepared to take slip lane in centre of road. Turn left into Avenue Jean Moulin. Site is shortly on left. GPS: 43.115516, -0.031583

Charges guide

Per unit incl. 2 persons and electricity	€ 18.95 - € 21.45
extra person	€ 5.65

Lourdes

Sites et Paysages la Forêt

Route de la Forêt, F-65100 Lourdes (Hautes-Pyrénées) T: 05 62 94 04 38. E: info@campingdelaforet.fr

alanrogers.com/FR65450

As its name suggests, Camping de la Forêt can be found in a peaceful wooded valley just 1 km. from Lourdes. This 4.5-hectare site has a relaxed atmosphere and a popular restaurant serving traditional specialities. The 130 grass pitches are level and shaded; 74 are for touring and have 3-10A electricity (French plugs) and easy access. The remainder are occupied by tastefully arranged chalets and mobile homes for rent. The new attractive heated swimming pool with jacuzzi and paddling pool area has splendid views of 'The Grande Convent' at the Sanctuary of Lourdes. This campsite is perfect for visiting Lourdes (a bus runs from the site every day). The 7.5 km. petite train ride will take you via the old quarter, the upper town and the major monuments.

Facilities

Sanitary block has hot showers and washbasins in cubicles. Facilities for babies, children and disabled campers. Washing machine and dryer. Motorcaravan services. Small shop. Bread to order. Bar with TV. Restaurant (evenings only in low season). Snack bar. Heated swimming pool, paddling pool and jacuzzi (1/6-30/9). Play area. Trampoline. Volleyball. Boules. Basketball. Junior football. WiFi throughout (charged). No charcoal barbecues. Bread to order. Daily bus service to Lourdes. Off site: All major amenities in Lourdes 1 km.

Open: 28 March - 31 October.

Directions

From Pau take D937 towards Lourdes, turn south on D13 before Lourdes and follow signs to site. GPS: 43.09566, -0.07468

Charges guide

Per unit incl. 2 persons and electricity	€ 15.95 - € 24.95
extra person	€ 5.50
child (4-7 yrs)	€ 2.70
dog	€ 1.50

Lourdes

Camping le Vieux Berger

2 route de Julos, F-65100 Lourdes (Hautes-Pyrénées) T: 05 62 94 60 57. E: levieuxberger@gmail.com

alanrogers.com/FR65510

Le Vieux Berger, under new ownership, is a small campsite on the edge of the town and within easy reach of the Sanctuaire Notre Dame de Lourdes, just under two kilometres away. There are views of the Pyrenees from many of the 63 touring pitches, with electricity connections (6/10A) available; trees provide shade and the owners' aim is to ensure a peaceful, green environment. There is a new separate area for motorcaravans with hardstandings and grass verges; open all year, it would be an ideal stopover for visiting Lourdes. A shuttle bus service runs to the entrance of the sanctuary area several times a day in season. The shops, bars and restaurants of the town are within easy reach. There is a little road noise.

Facilities

Sanitary blocks have a mixture of Turkish and British style WCs, controllable hot showers and facilities for disabled visitors. Laundry room with washing machine and dryer. Tourist information. Bread to order (July/Aug). Takeaway (April-Sept). Playground with trampoline. Pétanque. WiFi throughout (free). Off site: Town centre 1.2 km. Fishing 2 km. Sanctuary 3.7 km. Golf and Pic du Jer 4 km. Riding 8 km. Argelès-Gazost 16 km.

Open: 1 April - 15 November.

Directions

Lourdes is 30 km. south of Tarbes. From A64 (La Pyrénéenne) motorway take exit 12 (Lourdes/Tarbes Ouest) and head south on N21 towards Lourdes. In 16 km. at roundabout take third exit D821 (Bagnères) and in 600 m. bear left onto Route de Julos to site on right in 150 m. GPS: 43.10443, -0.03314

Charges guide

Per unit incl. 2 persons and electricity	€ 15.50 - € 17.50
extra person	€ 4.00 - € 4.50
child (under 10 yrs)	€ 3.00 - € 3.50
dog	€ 2.50

Luz-Saint Sauveur

Sites et Paysages Pyrenevasion

Route de Luz-Ardiden, Sazos, F-65120 Luz-Saint Sauveur (Hautes-Pyrénées) T: 05 62 92 91 54.
E: info@campingpyrenevasion.com **alanrogers.com/FR65130**

In the heart of the Pyrenees, Camping Pyrenevasion has panoramic views of the mountains and the town of Luz-Saint Sauveur in the valley below. This welcoming, family run site has 60 well laid out touring pitches, all with electricity (3-10A), on level, grassy hillside terraces partially shaded by young trees. There are 12 modern chalets for rent (all year), ideal for the nearby skiing, and in summer guided walks are arranged, with one free weekly walk. There is an outdoor swimming pool and a new indoor pool with a sauna. In July and August, activities are organised for 4-12 year olds and weekly entertainment for adults. The site is on a fairly steep hillside and the sanitary block is at the top of the site near the new bar, restaurant and reception areas, both accessed by stairs. There is good provision for games with a five-a-side football and basketball court and outdoor table tennis. The playground is designed for smaller children. The area is excellent for touring and walking with sights such as the Cirque de Gavarnie fairly close. Luz-Saint Sauveur is an interesting town with thermal spa facilities.

Facilities

Refurbished heated sanitary block with showers, WCs, washbasins (cubicles and open area). Facilities for disabled visitors, steep access. Baby bath. Laundry facilities. Motorcaravan services. Bread to order. Bar. Takeaway (1/6-20/9). Heated outdoor swimming and paddling pools (1/6-15/9). Indoor pool (15/5-30/9). Small play area. Sports area. WiFi (charged). Off site: Fishing 200 m. Shops, restaurant and bar 2 km. Bicycle hire 3 km. Riding and skiing 10 km. Golf 30 km. Jazz festival in Luz-St Sauveur in early July.

Open: All year excl. 21 October - 19 November.

Directions

From the north take the D921 to Luz-St Sauveur. Follow signs from Luz-St Sauveur to Luz-Ardiden (D12). Site is on right as you enter the village of Sazos. GPS: 42.88283, -0.02241

Charges guide

Per unit incl. 2 persons and electricity	€ 19.50 - € 34.00
extra person	€ 6.20
child (2-7 yrs)	free - € 3.70
dog	€ 2.60

Marciac

Camping du Lac

F-32230 Marciac (Gers) T: 05 62 08 21 19. E: info@camping-marciac.com
alanrogers.com/FR32020

Summer wine and cheese tastings from local producers are a feature of this site, set in the beautiful Gers region and close to the ancient fortified town of Marciac. Rob and Louise Robinson, the English owners since 2002, offer a quiet, relaxing stay. The well shaded site has 95 pitches, including 16 used for mobile homes and chalets for rent. There are 73 spacious touring pitches, 60 with electrical connections (6/10A, Europlug) and water. There are five with hardstanding for motorcaravans and an attractive natural terrace has 20 pitches without electricity for tents.

Facilities

The centrally situated sanitary block uses solar energy to help heat the water. Washbasins in cubicles. Facilities for disabled visitors. Washing machine. Motorcaravan services. Small shop, bar, takeaway. Bread delivered daily (order at reception). Swimming pool (15/4-30/9). Small library and communal room. Play area. WiFi throughout (charged). Off site: Fishing, watersports, sailing and riding 300 m. Shops, restaurant and bars 1 km.

Open: 21 March - 10 October.

Directions

From Auch take N21 south and 9 km. after Mirande turn west on D3 to Marciac. In Marciac turn west on D943 towards Bassoues. Site is signed on the left after 500 m. GPS: 43.5323, 0.1667

Charges guide

Per unit incl. 2 persons and electricity (6A)	€ 14.50 - € 26.00
extra person	€ 2.50 - € 5.00

Marsan

Camping Aramis

Quartier Gaubette, F-32270 Marsan (Gers) T: 05 62 65 60 11. E: contact@camping-aramis.com
alanrogers.com/FR32170

Aramis is a pretty, family campsite located 10 km. east of Auch, just off the N124. There are 65 large pitches with those for touring units positioned at the lower end of the site near the lake. They are mostly well shaded and have 6/10A electricity connections. A number of mobile homes, chalets and tents are available for rent. A swimming pool complex includes a heated, covered pool (open all season) and a larger pool with a shallow area for young children and a long water slide. Activities take place around the site's convivial bar, particularly during peak season.

Facilities

Toilet blocks with hot showers and facilities for disabled visitors and babies. Launderette. Motorcaravan services. Small shop, bar, restaurant and takeaway (all July/Aug). Fresh bread and pastries can be ordered (July/Aug). Swimming pools. Tennis. Boules. Minigolf. Play area. Entertainment and activities (July/Aug). Mobile homes for rent. WiFi throughout (charged). Off site: Auch 10 km. Walking and cycle tracks. Riding 2 km. Golf 12 km.

Open: 1 April - 30 September.

Directions

From the N124 exit 17 follow signs to Marsan and then follow campsite signs.
GPS: 43.658577, 0.733429

Charges guide

Per unit incl. 2 persons and electricity	€ 15.50 - € 26.50
extra person	€ 2.50 - € 5.50
child (3-6 yrs)	€ 1.50 - € 4.50

Martres-Tolosane

Sites et Paysages le Moulin

Lieu-dit le Moulin, F-31220 Martres-Tolosane (Haute-Garonne) T: 05 61 98 86 40.
E: info@campinglemoulin.com **alanrogers.com/FR31000**

With attractive, shaded pitches and many activities, this family run campsite incorporates 12 hectares of woods and fields beside the River Garonne. It is close to Martres-Tolosane, an interesting medieval village. Some of the 60 level and grassy pitches are super-size and all have 6/10A electricity. There are 24 chalets to rent. Summer brings opportunities for guided canoeing, archery and walking. Tennis, volleyball, basketball, boules and birdwatching are all available on site. The site is very child-friendly and provides many amenities to occupy and entertain young visitors. There is slight road noise.

Facilities

Large sanitary block with separate toilets for men and women. Communal area with showers and washbasins in cubicles. Area for disabled visitors. Baby bath. Laundry facilities. Motorcaravan services. Outdoor bar. Restaurant (1/7-20/8). Snack bar and takeaway (1/6-15/9). Bread to order. Heated swimming and paddling pools (1/6-15/9). Fishing. Tennis. Canoeing. Archery. Fitness area. Two playgrounds. Games room. Bouncy castle. Entertainment. Children's club (high season). Massage by arrangement (charged). Car rental service. WiFi throughout (charged).

Open: 1 April - 30 September.

Directions

From the A64 motorway (Toulouse-Tarbes) take exit 21 (Boussens) or exit 22 (Martres-Tolosane) and follow signs to Martres-Tolosane. Site is well signed from village. GPS: 43.19048, 1.01788

Charges guide

Per unit incl. 2 persons and electricity	€ 18.90 - € 31.90
extra person	€ 5.00 - € 7.00
child (under 7 yrs)	€ 3.00 - € 5.00
dog	€ 3.00

Maroux

Camping le Néri

Le Nery, F-32380 Maroux (Gers) T: 05 81 67 50 10. E: contact@campingleneri.com
alanrogers.com/FR32190

This is a calm, pleasant and very friendly, family run site, sitting on ten hectares in beautiful wooded countryside, where visitors can totally relax. There is a real family atmosphere and everyone is made to feel welcome. The 40 large, partly shaded pitches have 6/10A electricity. The cool, traditional reception building houses a bar, games room and seasonal brasserie. The swimming pool is away from the pitches in a very sunny spot on the lower part of the site. Activities are easy going: woodland walks, boules, lake fishing, minigolf and volleyball, with extra entertainment in high season.

Facilities

All necessary toilet facilities (unisex), including those for disabled visitors. Laundry facilities. No motorcaravan services. Brasserie, bread and pastries to order (July/Aug). Bar and takeaway. Swimming pool. Sauna. Lake for fishing. Indoor games. Communal barbecue. Playground. Boules. Some lighting switched off after midnight. Bicycle hire. Baby equipment hire. Torches needed. WiFi over part of site (free).

Open: 1 April - 31 October.

Directions

From Lectoure take D7 to St Clar. At St Clar turn left onto D13 then after 1 km, right onto D167 to Gaudonville. Site is along a fairly narrow, bumpy roadway. GPS: 43.898035, 0.811234

Charges guide

Per unit incl. 2 persons and electricity	€ 14.00 - € 23.00
extra person	€ 3.50 - € 6.00

Mazères

Camping la Bastide

Route de Belpech, F-09270 Mazères (Ariège) T: 05 61 69 38 82.

alanrogers.com/FR09180

La Bastide is a spacious and attractive site bordering the River Hers (children need to be supervised as access to the river is unfenced) and only a short walk away from Mazères. A variety of trees provide ample shade for the 127 pitches, 91 for touring and the remainder occupied by mobile homes and chalets for rent. The pitches are level, grassy and separated by hedges and trees; most have electricity and water. In peak season, activities are organised every day except Saturday for all the family to enjoy.

Facilities

Six small adequate toilet blocks, one reserved for disabled visitors. Laundry. Motorcaravan service point. Bar, snack bar/takeaway (July/Aug). Swimming and paddling pools (July/Aug). Play area. Boules. Basketball. Tennis. Volleyball. Activities (July/Aug). Games area. Canoeing and fishing on the river. WiFi. Off site: Shops, cafés and a small supermarket 400 m. Riding 5km. Hypermarkets in Pamiers 20 km.

Open: 1 May - 15 September.

Directions

From the A66 take exit 2 then the D14 and then D624 to Mazères. In centre of town, turn southeast on D11 towards Belpech. In 400 m site is signed on left. Access is difficult from the opposite direction. GPS: 43.2498, 1.68252

Charges guide

Per unit incl. 2 persons and 10A electricity	€ 15.70 - € 30.40
extra person	€ 4.20 - € 6.90

Meyronne

Camping la Plage

Rive gauche de la Dordogne, F-46200 Meyronne (Lot) T: 05 65 32 23 26. E: contact@camping-laplage.com

alanrogers.com/FR46580

Camping la Plage is set in an attractive walnut grove on the banks of the Dordogne, on the edge of the village of Meyronne. The 57 grass touring pitches are level and of a good size. Although not delineated by hedging, they are clearly marked and all have 6A electricity. This family run site is well cared for and the enthusiastic owners organise entertainment for children in high season. Canoe hire is available immediately adjacent to the site. A well placed site for visiting nearby Rocamadour, Souillac and Martel. The more central area of the Dordogne also has plenty of beautiful villages waiting to be explored.

Facilities

Two sanitary blocks (one new in 2013). Family bathrooms and facilities for disabled visitors. Shop for basics. Bar, snack bar and takeaway. Attractive outdoor swimming pool. Play area. Bicycle hire. Boules. River fishing. Kayak hire. Weekly disco (high season). Free WiFi throughout. Off site: Shops, bars and restaurants in St Sozy less than 2 km. Riding 8 km.

Open: 1 June - 15 September.

Directions

From the north, exit A20 motorway at exit 55 for Souillac. At roundabout follow D803 towards Martel. After about 5 km. turn right onto D15 through St Sozy and cross the River Dordogne into Meyronne. Site is immediately on the right. GPS: 44.87602, 1.577072

Charges guide

Per unit incl. 2 persons and electricity	€ 17.70
extra person	€ 4.50

Millau

Camping Caravaning les Rivages

860 avenue de l'Aigoual, F-12100 Millau (Aveyron) T: 05 65 61 01 07. E: info@campinglesrivages.com

alanrogers.com/FR12020

Les Rivages is a large, well established site on the outskirts of the town. It is well situated being close to the high limestone Causses and the dramatic gorges of the Tarn and Dourbie. Smaller pitches, used for small units, abut a pleasant riverside space suitable for sunbathing, fishing and picnics. Most of the 314 pitches are large and well shaded. A choice of site packages is offered with 'Privilège' being the largest at 130-150 sq.m. All pitches have electricity (10A) and 42 have water and drainage. The site offers a very wide range of sporting activities, close to 30 in all.

Facilities

Four well kept, modern toilet blocks. Special block for children. Small shop (30/6-15/9). Terrace, restaurant and bar overlooking heated swimming pool complex with paddling pool and spa (from 1/5). Play area. Impressive sports centre with tennis), squash and badminton. Boules. River activities, walking, birdwatching, fishing. Entertainment, largely for children, child-minding, miniclub. WiFi (free in bar area). Off site: Rafting and canoeing arranged. Bicycle hire 1 km. Riding 10 km.

Open: 15 April - 30 September.

Directions

From Millau, cross the Tarn bridge and take D991 road east towards Nant. Site is 400 m. from the roundabout on the right, on the banks of the Dourbie river. GPS: 44.10123, 3.095604

Charges guide

Per unit incl. 2 persons and electricity	€ 19.50 - € 45.00
extra person	€ 3.50 - € 8.00
child (3-10 yrs)	€ 2.00 - € 5.00

Millau

Camping Indigo Millau

455 avenue de l'Aigoual, F-12100 Millau (Aveyron) T: 05 65 61 18 83. E: millau@camping-indigo.com

alanrogers.com/FR12350

Camping Indigo Millau is just 500 m. from the lively market town of Millau which lies in the valley below the imposing Millau suspension bridge. There are 160 good sized, slightly sloping grassy pitches with varying degrees of shade, good views over the wooded hills and some enjoy a riverside location. There are 119 pitches for touring with 6/10A electricity for which long leads are needed. The site has a heated swimming pool and snack bar/bar, pleasant for unwinding after a busy day touring making it ideal for long or short stays.

Facilities

Modern, well equipped and clean toilet block with all necessary facilities including those for disabled visitors. Laundry facilities. Breakfast service. Snack bar/bar (June/July). Swimming pool (May-Sept). Small TV room. Family recreation room. Play area. Kids' club. Activities and entertainment, mainly off site. River fishing and bathing. Free WiFi on part of site. Glamping tents for hire. Off site: Bicycle hire 300 m. Millau town centre 500 m.

Open: 4 May - 26 September.

Directions

Leave A75 autoroute at exit 45 before crossing viaduct and follow signs to Millau. On entering Millau turn left at roundabout (Zone Commerciale). Follow signs for Campings. Left at roundabout, cross river and shortly right to site. GPS: 44.10240, 3.09100

Charges guide

Per unit incl. 2 persons and electricity	€ 19.40 - € 29.80
extra person	€ 3.90 - € 6.50

Millau

Campéole le Millau Plage

Avenue de Millau-Plage, F-12100 Millau (Aveyron) T: 05 65 61 43 69. E: millauplage@campeole.com

alanrogers.com/FR12390

Millau Plage is a recent addition to the Campéole group and is located on the banks of the Tarn river, 3 km. from the interesting town of Millau, and with good access to the Tarn gorges. Trees provide ample shade for the 251 pitches, 211 for touring; over half have electricity (5A). Forty pitches are occupied by mobile homes for rent. There is a pleasant pool next to the restaurant and bar area. Millau is an historic town with shops, bars and restaurants, and is a very popular place for hang-gliding and watersports.

Facilities

Five toilet blocks (one completely renovated) along the middle of the site. Motorcaravan services. Small shop, bar with TV (July/Aug) and snack type restaurant with takeaway (15/6-31/8). New heated outdoor swimming pool (1/6-20/9). Children's club in high season. Fishing and river swimming. Activity and entertainment programme. WiFi over part of site (charged). Off site: Millau 1.5 km. Riding 2 km. Bicycle hire 3 km. Lake beach 25 km.

Open: 25 April - 20 September.

Directions

From north leave A75 (Clermont-Ferrand/Béziers) at exit 44.1 and follow Aguessac (D29) then Paulhe and join D187 towards Millau. Site on right in 4 km. From south leave D909 (Millau) at exit 47. Follow signs for Campings at each roundabout, turn right across river and take third exit at next roundabout. Site is on left in 1.5 km. GPS: 44.11552, 3.08692

Charges guide

Per unit incl. 2 persons and electricity	€ 15.70 - € 28.70
extra person	€ 4.20 - € 6.60

Moissac

Camping du l'ile de Bidounet

Saint Benoit, F-82200 Moissac (Tarn-et-Garonne) T: 05 63 32 52 52. E: camping-bidounet@moissac.fr

alanrogers.com/FR82030

Located on an island in the Tarn river, this rustic site has a rather unique location. Reception is in the entrance to an old watermill and you reach the pitches by passing through a three metre high passageway through the building itself, then over a short, curved bridge onto the island. There are 97 touring pitches, arranged in groups of three and most give views of the river. Others have views of the old buildings of Moissac on the river bank. A small pool complex is situated in the grass area before the pitches and you can watch people sailing and fishing on the river.

Facilities

Two traditional toilet blocks should be adequate. Some washbasins in cubicles, modern showers. Facilities for babies and young children. Excellent unit for disabled visitors. Laundry facilities. Motorcaravan services. Basic provisions from reception, bread delivery. Games room with small bar (july/Aug). Swimming pool (1/5-30/9). Boules. Play area. Activities for children (1/7-31/8). Communal barbecue area. Fishing. WiFi room (free).

Open: 1 April - 30 September.

Directions

From the A62 leave at exit 9 (Castelsarrasin) and head due north for 8 km. on N113 for Moissac. On arriving at the town take the first exit from roundabout and follow for 300 m. to site on the left. GPS: 44.09644, 1.08862

Charges guide

Per unit incl. 2 persons	€ 16.00 - € 23.10
extra person	€ 3.70 - € 5.00

Montcabrier

Camping Moulin de Laborde

Laborde, F-46700 Montcabrier (Lot) T: 05 65 24 62 06. E: moulindelaborde@wanadoo.fr

alanrogers.com/FR46040

Based around a converted 17th-century watermill, Moulin de Laborde has been created by the van Bommel family to provide a tranquil and uncommercial campsite for the whole family to enjoy. Bordered by woods, hills and a small river, there are 90 flat and grassy pitches, all of at least 100 sq.m. with 6/10A (Europlug) electricity. A variety of pretty shrubs and trees divide the pitches and provide a moderate amount of shade. A gate at the back of the site leads walkers onto a Grande Randonée footpath which passes through the village of Montcabrier, 1 km. away.

Facilities

Well designed, clean toilet block, unit for disabled visitors. Washing machine, dryer. Basic shop, small bar, restaurant, takeaway, swimming pool with small slide, sunbathing area, paddling pool. Play area. Small lake, free rafts and rowing boats. Fishing. Volleyball. Covered recreation area. Football and boules area. Rock climbing. Archery. Dogs are not accepted. WiFi (free). Off site: Tennis nearby and canoeing on the Lot.

Open: 7 May - 9 September.

Directions

Site is on the north side of the D673 Fumel-Gourdon road 1 km. northeast of the turn to village of Montcabrier. GPS: 44.5475, 1.083883

Charges guide

Per unit incl. 2 persons and electricity	€ 24.15 - € 29.30
extra person	€ 6.00 - € 7.50

No credit cards.

Montesquiou

Camping Château le Haget

Route de Mielan, F-32320 Montesquiou (Gers) T: 05 62 70 95 80. E: lehaget@orange.fr

alanrogers.com/FR32210

Château le Haget can be found very close to the delightful village of Montesquiou. Set within a magnificent park, many exotic trees were brought back by the first owner from his travels around the world. Pitches here are large and well shaded, surrounded by colourful shrubs and bushes. Electrical connections (3A) are available. A number of chalets, mobile homes and bungalow-style tents are available for rent. The restaurant is in the former coach house and specialises in typically Gascon cuisine. Short, guided tours of the château are available.

Facilities

The sanitary facilities are in the 19th-century former orangery and include hot showers. Facilities for disabled visitors. Shop (July/Aug). Bar, restaurant and takeaway (5/7-15/8). Swimming pool. Children's pool. Play area. Accommodation for rent. Hotel. Free WiFi on part of site. Off site: Walking and cycle trails. Fishing 2 km. Riding 3 km. Bicycle hire 4 km. Golf 10 km.

Open: 1 May - 30 September.

Directions

From Auch follow the road towards Tarbes/Mirande (N21). After Miramont d'Astarac turn right, toward Isle de Noé/Montesquiou (D2). In Isle de Noé turn left to join D943 for 8 km. as far as Montesquiou, and then follow signs to Château le Haget. GPS: 43.564891, 0.319762

Charges guide

Per unit incl. 2 persons and electricity	€ 17.00 - € 27.50

No credit cards.

Montesquiou

Camping l'Anjou

F-32320 Montesquiou (Gers) T: 05 62 70 95 24. E: clemens.van-voorst@wanadoo.fr

alanrogers.com/FR32220

Camping l'Anjou is a very small, quiet, rural, family run site set in a lesser known area of the Midi Pyrénées, to the west of Auch and halfway between the small villages of Montesquiou and Bassoues. You will receive a warm welcome from the friendly Dutch owners. The site has rural views over the surrounding countryside and is open from May to September. There are 38 small to medium size, level grass pitches with 32 for touring and electricity (6A) is available. The shrubs and trees around the pitches offer some privacy and varying amounts of shade.

Facilities

Excellent toilet blocks with all necessary facilities including room for babies and campers with disabilities. Washing machine/dryer. Bar with terrace, snack bar and bread to order (July/Aug). Small outdoor swimming pool with sunbathing terrace (July/Aug). Shaded garden with play area. Communal barbecue. Small farm. Boules. WiFi in one area (free). Off site: Montesquiou, shop. 3.5 km. Old town of Mirande with shops 15 km. Paint ball.

Open: 1 May - 30 September.

Directions

From Auch take N21 southwest for about 18 km. Just after Miramont d'Astarac take D2 northwest to l'Isle de Noé, then D943 west to Montesquiou for 9 km. Continue on D943 and site is signed on the left after 3 km. GPS: 43.5772, 0.2911

Charges guide

Per unit incl. 2 persons and electricity	€ 14.50 - € 19.00
extra person	€ 3.00 - € 4.00

Moustajon

Camping Pradelongue

CD125, Moustajon, F-31110 Luchon (Haute-Garonne) T: 05 61 79 86 44.
E: camping.pradelongue@wanadoo.fr **alanrogers.com/FR31060**

Located within a half hour walk of Bagneres-de-Luchon, this green and pleasant site provides an ideal base for touring. Of the 135 pitches, 121 are for touring with the remainder being occupied by mobile homes for rent. The grassy pitches are level and separated by a mixture of hedges and small trees. Shade is provided by large mature trees. All have electricity (2-10A) and 18 also have water and waste water drainage. Just inside the gate is a tarmacked area for motorcaravans. This very well maintained site, situated in the Luchon valley, is surrounded by the Pyrenean mountains.

Facilities

Three toilet and shower blocks, one heated, some en-suite cabins. Facilities for children and disabled visitors. Laundry facilities. Fridge hire. Motorcaravan services. Heated swimming pool (1/6-30/9). Paddling pool. Football pitch. Boules. Volleyball. Basketball. New multisports area. Play areas. Trampoline. Adult exercise equipment. Games room. Two TV rooms. Small library. WiFi over site (30 mins. free daily). Off site: Supermarket 50 m.

Open: 1 April - 30 September.

Directions

Driving south of D125, take D125c for Antignac and Moustajon for 2.4 km. Site is well signed on left, next to supermarket. GPS: 42.808143, 0.597253

Charges guide

Per unit incl. 2 persons and electricity	€ 17.40 - € 25.60
extra person	€ 4.90 - € 6.95
child (under 7 yrs)	€ 2.00 - € 3.50

Nant

Sites et Paysages les 2 Vallées

Route de l'estrade basse, F-12230 Nant (Aveyron) T: 05 65 62 26 89. E: contact@lesdeuxvallees.com
alanrogers.com/FR12420

Les 2 Vallées is an attractive site with very welcoming and informative young owners. It is located in a valley at the confluence of the Dourbie and the Durzon, deep in the countryside south of Millau. There are 80 pitches in total, extending over two hectares. The 64 touring pitches are of a good size and all are equipped with electrical connections (6A, Europlug). Sixteen fully equipped mobile homes and chalets are available for rent. The site is situated around 800 m. from the pretty village of Nant with shops and restaurants. One side of the site runs along the Durzon and fishing is popular here. A varied activity and entertainment programme is organised in peak season, including special activities for children, such as treasure hunts and nature discovery sessions. This is, of course, excellent country for mountain biking and walking (the long distance GR71D runs close by). The site owners will be happy to recommend routes. Other activity sports include canoeing, canyoning, rock climbing and potholing.

Facilities

Heated sanitary block is very clean and well maintained and includes some washbasins in cubicles, hot showers and facilities for disabled visitors. Small laundry. Motorcaravan services. Basic shop. Snack bar and takeaway (15/6-15/9). Heated swimming pool (30/5-26/9). Fishing. Bicycle hire. Play area. Games room. Activities and entertainment. Fitness equipment. New communal barbecue area. Mobile homes for rent. WiFi over site. Off site: Restaurant and tennis 600 m. River fishing. Shops and restaurants in Nant. River beach 1 km.

Open: 15 April - 17 October.

Directions

Nant is southeast of Millau. Leave the A75 motorway at exit 47 (La Cavalerie) and head east on D999 to Nant. From here, follow signs to the site. GPS: 44.01702, 3.30162

Charges guide

Per unit incl. 2 persons and electricity	€ 15.00 - € 21.00
extra person	€ 4.00
child (under 7 yrs)	€ 2.00

Nant

RCN Val de Cantobre

Domain de Vellas, F-12230 Nant (Aveyron) T: 05 65 58 43 00. E: cantobre@rcn.fr
alanrogers.com/FR12010

Imaginatively and tastefully developed by the Dupond family over the past 30 years, this very pleasant terraced site is now owned by the RCN group. Most of the 215 pitches (109 for touring, all with 6A electricity, and most with water) are peaceful, generous in size and blessed with views of the valley. The terrace design provides some peace and privacy, especially on the upper levels. Rock pegs are advised. An activity programme is supervised by qualified instructors in July and August and a new pleasure pool has been added.

Facilities

The fully equipped toilet blocks are well appointed and include facilities for disabled visitors. Fridge hire. Shop, bar, restaurant, pizzeria and takeaway. There is some fairly steep up-and-down walking from furthest pitches to some facilities. Swimming pools. Minigolf. Play area. Activity programme. Bicycle hire. All-weather multisports pitch. Torch useful. WiFi over site (charged).
Off site: Fishing and riding 4 km.

Open: 3 April - 10 October.

Directions

Site is 4 km. north of Nant, on D991 road to Millau. From Millau take D991 signed Gorge de la Dourbie. Site is on left, just past turn to Cantobre. GPS: 44.04467, 3.30228

Charges guide

Per unit incl. 2 persons, electricity and water	€ 18.00 - € 51.50
extra person (4 yrs and over)	€ 3.75 - € 6.50

Camping Cheques accepted.

Naucelle

Flower Camping du Lac de Bonnefon

L'Etang de Bonnefon, F-12800 Naucelle (Aveyron) T: 05 65 69 33 20.
E: camping-du-lac-de-bonnefon@wanadoo.fr **alanrogers.com/FR12250**

This small, family run site, popular with French campers, lies in a picturesque region waiting to be discovered, with rolling hills, deep river valleys, lakes and many old fortified villages. This site is more suitable for those seeking a quieter holiday with less in the way of entertainment, although there is a range of activities available during the summer should you wish to participate. There are 112 good sized, grassy, slightly sloping pitches with 69 for touring (all with access to 10A electricity). Some are separated by hedging with others more open and maturing trees provide some shade. The enthusiastic and friendly owners have recently extended the site and refurbished the facilities to a high standard.

Facilities

Two main toilet blocks include some washbasins in cabins and good facilities for disabled visitors. No shop but bread to order. Bar with TV. Snack bar and restaurant (July/Aug) with occasional themed 'Breton' evenings. Swimming and paddling pools (1/5-30/9). Jacuzzi. Playground. Lake fishing. Activities for all the family in July/Aug. Bicycle hire. WiFi on part of site. Off site: Riding 800 m. Naucelle 1 km.

Open: 1 April - 15 October (accommodation all year).

Directions

Site is just off the N88 halfway between Rodez and Albi. From Naucelle Gare take D997 (Naucelle). In just over 1 km. turn left on D58 and follow signs to site in just under 1 km. GPS: 44.18805, 2.34827

Charges guide

Per unit incl. 2 persons and electricity	€ 16.50 - € 27.90
extra person	€ 3.50 - € 6.00

Pont-de-Salars

Flower Camping les Terrasses du Lac

Route du Vibal, F-12290 Pont-de-Salars (Aveyron) T: 05 65 46 88 18. E: campinglesterrasses@orange.fr
alanrogers.com/FR12050

A terraced site, it provides 180 good sized, level pitches, 104 for touring, with or without shade, all with 6A electricity. Some pitches have good views over the lake to which there is direct access from the site in two places – one for pedestrians and swimmers, the other for cars and trailers for launching small boats. This site is well placed for excursions into the Gorges du Tarn, Caves du Roquefort and nearby historic towns and villages. Although there are good facilities for disabled visitors, the terracing on the site may prove difficult.

Facilities

Four toilet blocks with all necessary facilities including those for disabled visitors. Washing machine. Motorcaravan services. Fridge hire. Shop. Bar/restaurant serving full meals, snacks and takeaway (July/Aug). New heated swimming pool complex with paddling pool, slides and jacuzzi (1/6-15/9). Solarium. Play area. Pétanque. Billiards. Games/TV rooms. Activities in high season. Fishing. WiFi (free by reception). Accommodation for rent. Off site: Supervised beach 1 km.

Open: 1 April - 30 September.

Directions

Using D911 Millau-Rodez road, turn north at Pont-de-Salars towards lake on D523. Follow site signs. Ignore first site and continue, following lake until les Terrasses du Lac on right (about 5 km).
GPS: 44.30498, 2.73556

Charges guide

Per unit incl. 2 persons and electricity	€ 17.50 - € 30.90
extra person	€ 3.50 - € 6.00

Payrac-en-Quercy

Camping Yelloh! Village Payrac les Pins

F-46350 Payrac-en-Quercy (Lot) T: 05 65 37 96 32. E: info@les-pins-camping.com

alanrogers.com/FR46030

Set amongst 3.5 hectares of beautiful pine forest, Camping Yelloh! Village Payrac les Pins is well situated for exploring the historical and natural splendours of the Dordogne region, as well as being a convenient overnight stop when heading north or south. There are 137 clearly marked, level pitches (100 sq.m), of which 49 are for touring units, separated by small shrubs or hedges. Many have shade from the abundant pine trees and all have 10A electricity connections. There is a bar and a good value restaurant with a terrace overlooking the pool area. The friendly and welcoming owners are keen to encourage visitors to explore the region and have negotiated reductions for their guests when visiting certain local attractions. Closer to the site there are trails for walkers leading out from the grounds and through the woods. The site has become very popular and is extremely busy in the high season.

Facilities

Three toilet blocks (heated April/May) are well maintained and include washbasins in cabins and good baby facilities. Laundry facilities. Motorcaravan services. Shop with basics. Bar with TV. Restaurant and takeaway. Indoor heated swimming pool. Heated outdoor pool with slides and paddling pool. Wellness centre with jacuzzi and sauna. Tennis. Small library. Free WiFi over site. Some entertainment in season, including weekly family discos. Walking routes starting from site. Off site: Riding 5 km. Fishing 7 km. Rocamadour 19 km. Sarlat 25 km.

Open: 9 April - 11 September.

Directions

Site entrance is 16 km. from Souillac on western side of the D823 just south of the village of Payrac-en-Quercy. GPS: 44.78946, 1.47204

Charges guide

Per unit incl. 2 persons and electricity	€ 19.00 - € 37.00
extra person	€ 6.00 - € 7.00
child (3-6 yrs)	free - € 6.00
dog	€ 2.00 - € 3.00

Puy-l'Evêque

Camping le Ch'Timi

La Roque, Touzac, F-46700 Puy-l'Evêque (Lot) T: 05 65 36 52 36. E: info@campinglechtimi.com

alanrogers.com/FR46120

This is a small and friendly site which has all the requirements for a peaceful holiday. There is a really nice rural feel to the site which adds to the ambience, and the Dutch owners are keen to ensure you enjoy your stay with them. Set high up above the Lot with a steep staircase down to the river bank, the views are breathtaking and you can fish or hire the campsite's own canoes (a short drive down to the river may be easier). The 77 pitches are grassy and slightly sloping, all with 6A electricity. There is an open feel to the site with a mixture of sunshine and shade.

Facilities

The modern toilet block includes washbasins in cabins. Washing machines, spin dryer and ironing board. Small shop in reception and bar (1/5-30/9). Restaurant (1/5-30/9). Motorcaravan services. L-shaped swimming pool and well fenced paddling pool with sunbathing surround. Play areas. Boules. Canoe and bicycle hire. Internet access. WiFi in bar area (free). English and Dutch spoken. Off site: Riding 5 km. Shops and restaurants at Puy-l'Eveque 8 km. Many châteaux. Golf 10 km.

Open: 1 April - 30 September.

Directions

From D911 Villeneuve-sur-Lot-Cahors road turn south at village of Duravel (11 km. east of Fumel) onto D58. At Port Vire cross the river, then take first exit at roundabout onto the D8 heading west towards Touzac. Site is 1.8 km. on right. GPS: 44.49756, 1.06588

Charges guide

Per unit incl. 2 persons and electricity	€ 21.30 - € 27.25
extra person	€ 6.55

Rivières

Camping les Pommiers d'Aiguelèze

Aiguelèze, F-81600 Rivières (Tarn) T: 05 63 33 02 49. E: info@camping-lespommiers.com
alanrogers.com/FR81180

This pleasant site is located between Albi and Gaillac at the heart of the Tarn. Of the 74 pitches, 54 are reserved for touring with the remainder for mobile homes. The pitches are of a good size and located in a natural setting around the site. All are separated by hedges and have 13A electricity and water points nearby. There is a heated swimming pool with spa facilities planned. The River Tarn is very close, as well as a marina where you can fish, canoe or take boat trips to the nearby city of Albi.

Facilities

Sanitary facilities include provision for disabled visitors. Small shop for basics. Bar. Fresh bread and croissants all season. Heated swimming pool with spa. Paddling pool. Trampolines. Ball games area. Pétanque. Play area. Bicycle hire. No charcoal barbecues. WiFi over site (charged). Off site: Golf club adjacent (reduced rate for campers). La Javanaise bar and restaurant opposite the site. Marina with canoe and pedalo hire adjacent.

Open: 1 April - 30 September.

Directions

From Toulouse take A68 motorway to Albi. Take exit 10 to Lagrave and follow signs for 'Espace Loisirs d'Aigueleze. GPS: 43.908889, 1.982778

Charges guide

Per unit incl. 2 persons and electricity	€ 20.30 - € 26.80
dog	€ 1.50 - € 2.00

Rivière-sur-Tarn

Flower Camping Caravaning de Peyrelade

Route des Gorges du Tarn, F-12640 Rivière-sur-Tarn (Aveyron) T: 05 65 62 62 54.
E: contact@campingpeyrelade.com **alanrogers.com/FR12000**

Although shady, this well managed site has an open feel with a long stony beach frontage to the River Tarn, one of the best in the area. All the 137 touring pitches (100-150 sq.m) are level and have 10A electricity. There are also 53 mobile homes for rent. Extensive refurbishment of the site's facilities has taken place over the last two years, with a new attractive reception, restaurant and bar area together with a large swimming pool complex. The site is ideally placed for visiting the Tarn, Jonte and Dourbie gorges, and having its own canoes, round trips of 5 and 17 km. are organised daily.

Facilities

Two very well equipped toilet blocks with excellent facilities for young children and disabled visitors. Laundry facilities. Motorcaravan services. Bar, restaurant, pizzeria, takeaway (all from 15/5). New aquapark with several pools (no Bermuda shorts). Playground. Games room. Miniclub. Activities for adults and teenagers, evening entertainment (July/Aug). Fishing. Large screen for major sporting events. WiFi over site (charged), free in bar area. Off site: Bicycle hire 2 km. Riding 6 km.

Open: 15 May - 15 September.

Directions

Take autoroute A75 to exit 44-1 Aguessac then onto D907 (follow Gorges du Tarn signs). Site is 2 km. past Rivière-sur-Tarn, on the right. The access road is quite steep. GPS: 44.19047, 3.15638

Charges guide

Per unit incl. 2 persons and electricity	€ 20.00 - € 38.00
extra person	€ 3.50 - € 8.00

Rivière-sur-Tarn

Camping les Peupliers

Route des Gorges du Tarn, F-12640 Rivière-sur-Tarn (Aveyron) T: 05 65 59 85 17.
E: lespeupliers12640@orange.fr **alanrogers.com/FR12160**

Les Peupliers is a friendly, family site on the banks of the Tarn river. Most of the 103 good sized touring pitches have shade, all have electricity (6/10A), water and a waste water point and are divided by hedges giving some privacy. It is possible to swim in the river and there is a landing place for canoes. The site has its own canoes and organises round trips of 10, 15 and 20 km. In a lovely, sunny situation on the site is a swimming pool with a paddling pool, sunbeds and a slide, all protected by a clipped hedge and with a super view of the surrounding hills and the Château du Peyrelade perched above the village.

Facilities

Three very well equipped and clean toilet blocks with facilities for children and disabled visitors. Washing machines. Motorcaravan service point. Shop (1/5-30/9). Bar, TV. Internet. Snack bar, takeaway (1/5-30/9). Swimming pool with water slide (heated 1/5-30/9). Paddling pool. Play area. Games, competitions, weekly dances and family entertainment July/Aug. Fishing. Canoe hire. Bicycle hire. WiFi over site (free). Off site: Village with shops and restaurant 300 m. Bicycle hire 2 km.

Open: 1 April - 30 September.

Directions

Heading south from Clermont-Ferrand to Millau on the A75 autoroute take exit 44-1 signed Aguessac/Gorges du Tarn. In Aguessac turn left and follow signs to Riviere-sur-Tarn (5 km). Site is clearly signed down a short road to the right. GPS: 44.18577, 3.13068

Charges guide

Per unit incl. 2 persons and electricity	€ 20.00 - € 37.00
extra person	€ 4.00 - € 8.00

Camping Cheques accepted.

Rocamadour

Camping Padimadour

La Châtaigneraie, F-46500 Rocamadour (Lot) T: 05 65 33 72 11. E: camping@padimadour.fr

alanrogers.com/FR46410

Camping Padimadour is a small friendly, family run campsite in beautiful Quercy countryside, not far from the ancient town of Rocamadour in the Vallée de la Dordogne. There are 52 very large, grassy and slightly sloping pitches with 25 for touring. There is some shade from maturing trees. Extensive refurbishment has taken place to provide a superb new toilet block, small bar/snack bar and a games room. A new swimming pool is overlooked by the bar. The site is aimed at couples and families with pre-teen children and family entertainment is provided in July and August. This region is popular for all manner of adventure sports – including rock climbing, potholing, canyoning and mountain biking. The nearby town of Gramat is a noted riding centre. For a more relaxed holiday, a visit to Rocamadour is a must. This unique town is an important pilgrimage destination, thanks to the wooden Black Madonna, said to have been carved by Saint Amator (Saint Amadour) and housed in the church of Notre Dame.

Facilities

Superb new toilet block with all necessary facilities including those for disabled visitors. Laundry facilities. Small shop for essentials (from 1/5). Bar, snack bar and takeaway (1/6-31/8). Swimming pool (1/6-30/9). Play area. Trampolines. Boules. Games room with library. Activities and family entertainment (July/Aug). Free WiFi over site. Chalets for rent. Off site: Fishing. Rock climbing. Alvignac with shop and restaurant 2 km. Riding 4 km. Rocamadour 5 km. Padirac, Gouffre de Padirac 8 km.

Open: 30 April - 12 October.

Directions

From D840 (Figeac to Brive-la-Gaillarde road) turn east 7 km. northwest of Gramat, site signed. Follow small lane to site in just under 2 km.
GPS: 44.817742, 1.686267

Charges guide

Per unit incl. 2 persons and electricity	€ 22.50 - € 32.50
extra person	€ 6.00 - € 9.00
child (3-12 yrs)	€ 3.00 - € 6.00

Roquelaure

Yelloh! Village le Talouch

F-32810 Roquelaure (Gers) T: 05 62 65 52 43. E: info@camping-talouch.com

alanrogers.com/FR32080

Although enjoying a quiet and rural location, this neat and tidy site is only a short drive from the town of Auch with its famous legendary son, d'Artagnan. The entrance is fronted by a parking area with reception to the right and the bar and restaurant facing. Beyond this point lies the top half of the touring area with generous pitches of at least 120 sq.m. located between mature trees and divided by hedges, some with chalets. There are 100 pitches for touring, with electricity (6/10A). The rear half of the site has unshaded pitches in a more open aspect.

Facilities

Two toilet blocks with open style washbasins and controllable showers. Baby unit. One toilet for disabled visitors. Coin operated washing machine and laundry sinks. Small shop. Bar, restaurant and takeaway. Two excellent swimming pools, one heated and covered. Sauna and spa. Bicycle hire. GPS hire with pre-programmed walking routes. Activities for children. Play areas. Tennis and sports area. Entertainment in high season. Small library. Internet and WiFi (charged) in reception. Off site: Walking routes from the campsite.

Open: 8 April - 18 September.

Directions

Situated some 11 km. north of Auch on the D149, and 64 km. east of Toulouse the site is well signed. From the north approach via the A62 motorway, leaving at Layrac and heading towards Auch on the N21. GPS: 43.71283, 0.5645

Charges guide

Per unit incl. 2 persons and electricity	€ 15.00 - € 40.00
extra person	€ 6.00 - € 8.00
child (3-7 yrs)	free

Saint Antonin-Noble-Val

Flower Camping les Gorges de l'Aveyron

Marsac bas, F-82140 Saint Antonin-Noble-Val (Tarn-et-Garonne) T: 05 63 30 69 76.
E: info@camping-gorges-aveyron.com **alanrogers.com/FR82040**

This is a friendly, family site which is undergoing a process of renovation by its new owners, Stéphane and Johanna Batlo. A superb new toilet block was added in 2014 along with a fun paddling pool. The site has an attractive wooded location, sloping down to the River Aveyron and facing the Roc d'Anglars. There are 80 pitches, 49 are for touring units, all with electricity connections (3-10A). The pitches are grassy and well shaded and may become very soft in wet weather. Some pitches are available close to the river but we would suggest that these are unsuitable for younger children as the river is unfenced.

Facilities

Two toilet blocks with excellent facilities for children and disabled visitors. Laundry facilities. Motorcaravan service point. Small shop, bar, snack bar and takeaway (June-Sept). Swimming and paddling pools (May-Sept). Direct access to river. Fishing. Canoeing. Play area. Games room. Entertainment and activities in high season. WiFi in bar area (free). No gas barbecues. Mobile homes for rent. Off site: St Antonin-Noble-Val 1.5 km.

Open: 18 April - 28 September.

Directions

From the north, take exit 59 from the A20 autoroute joining the D926 and follow signs to St Antonin. Site can be found on the D115, 1.5 km. east of the town. GPS: 44.1519, 1.7715

Charges guide

Per unit incl. 2 persons and electricity	€ 15.00 - € 30.50
extra person	€ 3.00 - € 6.00

Saint Cirq-Lapopie

Camping de la Plage

Porte Roques, F-46330 Saint Cirq-Lapopie (Lot) T: 05 65 30 29 51. E: camping-laplage@wanadoo.fr
alanrogers.com/FR46070

You will continue to receive a warm welcome at Camping de la Plage from the new owners, the Defosse family. The site is situated beside the River Lot and is within walking distance of the beautiful historic village of Saint Cirq-Lapopie. It provides a good base for those who want an active holiday with many organised activities available either on site or in the immediate area. There are 120 good sized, level stony/grass pitches, 93 of which are for touring. Forty are fully serviced (6/10A electricity) and have hardstandings. They are separated by hedges and shrubs and mature trees give good shade.

Facilities

Three sanitary blocks are clean and well maintained. Facilities for disabled visitors. Laundry facilities. Shop. Bar. Restaurant and takeaway (1/5-30/9). Play area. Children's activities. Canoeing, kayaking and swimming from beach at the rear of the site (lifeguard July/Aug). Fishing. Bicycle hire. Occasional evening entertainment. Communal barbecue. Free WiFi over part of site. Off site: Walking, rock climbing, caving, canyoning and shops all nearby.

Open: 11 April - 30 September.

Directions

From Cahors take D653 east to Vers, then D662 for 17 km. to Tour de Faure. Cross river and site entrance is on right by bar/restaurant. Do not approach via St Cirq-Lapopie (very steep, winding and narrow roads). GPS: 44.46926, 1.68135

Charges guide

Per unit incl. 2 persons and electricity	€ 21.00 - € 28.00
extra person	€ 6.00 - € 7.00

Saint Geniez-d'Olt

Camping la Boissière

Route de la Cascade, F-12130 Saint Geniez-d'Olt (Aveyron) T: 05 65 70 40 43. E: boissiere@campeole.com
alanrogers.com/FR12090

With trout in the river and carp in the lakes, la Boissière is a fisherman's paradise. The site is situated on the banks of the River Lot, surrounded by wooded hills. Walking, swimming, canoeing or cycling are alternative pursuits here. Mature trees provide plenty of shade on 154 generous, partly hedged, grassy pitches, 80 of which are for touring with 6A electricity. Ten pitches are specially reserved for tents. Reception is housed in an old, converted farmhouse. The nearby old town of Saint Geniez-d'Olt should satisfy all shopping needs and day, or longer, fishing licences can be obtained there.

Facilities

Two modern, clean toilet blocks with washbasins in cubicles and preset showers. Baby changing facilities. Basic facilities for visitors with disabilities (no rails in shower). Small laundry. Shop with basic provisions, bar/snack bar with terrace (July/Aug). New heated swimming pool and paddling pool (July/Aug). New multisports terrain. Tennis. Playground. Entertainment is organised in July/Aug. Mobile homes, chalets and tents for rent. Free WiFi on part of site. Max. 2 dogs. Off site: St Geniez-d'Olt 700 m. Bicycle hire nearby.

Open: 29 March - 30 September.

Directions

From St Geniez-d'Olt follow the D988 eastwards towards Banassac. After 500 m. follow signs on right to la Boissière campsite. GPS: 44.4686, 2.9825

Charges guide

Per unit incl. 2 persons and electricity	€ 15.70 - € 25.90
extra person	€ 4.20 - € 6.50
child (2-6 yrs)	free - € 4.20

Camping Cheques accepted.

Saint Geniez-d'Olt

Village Marmotel

F-12130 Saint Geniez-d'Olt (Aveyron) T: 05 65 70 46 51. E: info@marmotel.com

alanrogers.com/FR12150

The road into Marmotel passes various industrial buildings and is a little off-putting – persevere, as they are soon left behind. The campsite itself is a mixture of old and new with a total of 90 touring pitches available and a similar number of mobile homes for rent. The old part provides many pitches with lots of shade and separated by hedges. The new area is sunny until the trees grow. These 40 pitches each have a private sanitary unit with shower, WC, washbasin and dishwashing. New and very well designed, they are reasonably priced for such luxury. All the pitches have electricity (10A). A lovely restaurant has a wide terrace with views of the hills and overlooks the heated swimming and paddling pools.

Facilities

Good sanitary facilities include baby baths and facilities for disabled visitors. Washing machines. Bar/restaurant, takeaway. Swimming pools. Small play area. Multisports area. Entertainment (July/Aug) including disco below bar, cinema, karaoke, dances, miniclub for 4-12 yrs. Bicycle hire. Fishing. Canoeing. WiFi on part of site. Off site: Large supermarket 500 m. Riding 10 km.

Open: 25 April - 22 September.

Directions

Heading south on autoroute 75 (free) take exit 41 and follow signs (St Geniez-d'Olt). Site is at western end of village (signed onto D19 to Prades d'Aubrac, then 500 m. on left). GPS: 44.46165, 2.96318

Charges guide

Per unit incl. 1 or 2 persons and electricity	€ 22.90 - € 45.90

No credit cards.

Saint Pierre-de-Trivisy

Camping la Forêt

F-81330 Saint Pierre-de-Trivisy (Tarn) T: 05 63 50 48 69. E: tourisme@saint-pierre-de-trivisy.net

alanrogers.com/FR81250

This beautifully landscaped and very unusual municipal site is set on the edge of a 40-hectare woodland leisure park offering a wide range of sporting activities for all the family. Just 150 m. from the heart of the village, the site provides 64 pitches (40 for touring), plus 24 chalets and Bengali tents for rent. The slightly sloping, grassy pitches are of a good size, mostly shaded and all have 6A electricity. You are always made welcome at the bar/restaurant which is open seven days a week throughout the season and serves local specialities as well as children's favourites.

Facilities

The two toilet blocks are well maintained and include provision for babies, children and disabled visitors. Laundry. Motorcaravan service point. Fridge hire. Bar/restaurant/snack bar and takeaway (1/5-30/9). Aqua park (16/6-31/8). Play area. Games/TV room. Tennis. Minigolf (charged). Fitness trail. Multisports court. Volleyball. Football/rugby pitch. Boules. Bicycle hire. Two communal barbecues and picnic area. Adventure park (charged). WiFi (first hour free daily).

Open: 1 May - 30 September.

Directions

From A68/N88 motorway at Albi take D81 south, then D53 and finally D57. From Albi, take D612 south to Réalmont, then turn southeast on D86 to Montredon-Labessonnié and northeast on D59 to St Pierre-de-Trivisy. Site is in centre of village on left, follow 'Base de Loisirs'. GPS: 43.76140, 2.43664

Charges guide

Per unit incl. 2 persons and electricity	€ 14.00
extra person	€ 3.50

Salles-Curan

Camping les Genêts

Lac de Pareloup, F-12410 Salles-Curan (Aveyron) T: 05 65 46 35 34. E: contact@camping-les-genets.fr

alanrogers.com/FR12080

This family run site is on the shores of Lac de Pareloup and offers both family holiday and watersports facilities. The 163 pitches include 80 grassy, mostly individual pitches for touring units. These are in two areas, one on each side of the entrance lane, and are divided by hedges, shrubs and trees. All have 6A electricity and many also have water and waste water drainage. The site slopes gently down to the beach and lake with facilities for all watersports including water-skiing. A full entertainment and activities programme is organised in high season and there is much to see and do in this corner of Aveyron.

Facilities

Two sanitary units, one refurbished (in a quirky gothic style), with suite for disabled guests. Baby room. Laundry. Well stocked shop and heated outdoor pool (1/6-14/9). Bar (1/6-7/9). Restaurant and takeaway (23/6-7/9). Play area. Minigolf. Boules. Bicycle hire. Pedalos, windsurfers, kayaks. WiFi throughout (free). Off site: Riding 6 km. Medieval village of Castelnau Pegayrolles. Canyoning and many walking routes. Millau for shopping.

Open: 11 May - 12 September.

Directions

From Salles-Curan take D577 for 4 km. and turn right into a narrow lane immediately after a sharp right hand bend. Site is signed at junction. GPS: 44.18933, 2.76693

Charges guide

Per unit incl. 2 persons and electricity	€ 21.60 - € 38.60
extra person	€ 4.20 - € 8.30

Camping Cheques accepted.

Sassis

Camping le Hounta

Le Village, F-65120 Sassis (Hautes-Pyrénées) T: 05 62 92 95 90. E: le-hounta@wanadoo.fr

alanrogers.com/FR65440

This friendly, family run site is set in spectacular mountain scenery close to the head of la Vallée de Lumière in the Pyrenees, making it an ideal base from which to explore the Parc National des Pyrénées and to visit the Col du Tourmalet and the Cirque de Gavarnie. Winter sports enthusiasts have a choice of three ski stations, with cross-country skiing, snow-boarding and snow-biking among the options. There are 125 level, grassy pitches, of which 89 are available for touring units and electrical connections (2-10A, Europlug) are charged accordingly. Nearby Luz-Saint-Sauveur has shops, bars and restaurants.

Facilities

Two sanitary blocks with mainly British style toilets, hot showers and washbasins in cabins. Facilities for disabled visitors. Baby bath. Laundry facilities. Motorcaravan services. Small shop selling basics. Bread delivery (July/Aug). Fast food to order (19.00-20.00, July/Aug). TV room. Pétanque. Playground. Charcoal barbecues only. WiFi on part of site (charged). Off site: Thermal baths 800 m. Swimming pool 1 km. Bicycle hire 1 km.

Open: 1 February - 20 October.

Directions

From A64 at exit 12 (Tarbes) head south on N21 to Lourdes, then D821 (Bagnères/Argelès) and follow signs for Argelès-Gazost, then Luz-St Sauveur (D100). Finally turn right on D12 1.5 km. past Sassis to site on left. GPS: 42.87242, -0.01512

Charges guide

Per unit incl. 2 persons and electricity	€ 13.60 - € 20.60
extra person	€ 3.70 - € 4.10

Seissan

Domaine Lacs de Gascogne

Rue du Lac, F-32260 Seissan (Gers) T: 05 62 66 27 94. E: info@domainelacsdegascogne.eu

alanrogers.com/FR32180

This spacious, Dutch-owned site is located at Seissan in the Pyrenean foothills. Its impressive drive sweeps around the largest of three lakes into the spacious and relaxing Domaine. The 50 large, grassy touring pitches mostly have shade and fine lake views. Electricity is 16A (some long leads required). Comfortable chalets and 23 mobile homes can be rented. On-site amenities include swimming pools, a sauna and a gym. The bar and restaurant are open all season and the food is very good. The lakes are perfect for fishing and kayaking and there is a private beach for a cooling dip (no lake swimming).

Facilities

Excellent sanitary facilities are well maintained. Facilities for disabled visitors. Laundry facilities. Restaurant. Breakfast service. Lounge. TV room. Swimming pool. Health pool. Sauna. Gym. Fishing (carp). Kayaks. Rope raft across lake. Play area. Play room. Tennis. Football. Basketball. Bicycle hire. Entertainment and activities. Accommodation to rent. WiFi (first 150 mb per week free). Off site: Seissan with supermarket and amenities 1 km.

Open: 1 April - 1 November.

Directions

Head south from Auch on N21 and at Beaulieu join the southbound D929. Continue on this road as far as Seissan and then follow signs to the site. GPS: 43.49535, 0.57826

Charges guide

Per unit incl. 2 persons and electricity	€ 18.00 - € 30.00
extra person	€ 4.00 - € 7.00

Séniergues

Domaine de la Faurie

Lieu-dit la Faurie, F-46240 Séniergues (Lot) T: 05 65 21 14 36. E: contact@camping-lafaurie.com

alanrogers.com/FR46190

A stunning array of tended shrubs and thoughtful flower planting is spread throughout this very pretty seven-hectare site which is located on a hilltop with wide open views of the surrounding hills and valleys. Although hidden away, it is an excellent base for exploring the Lot and Dordogne regions. The site is separated into two distinct areas, an open, lightly shaded front section and a much more densely shaded area with tall pine trees all around the pitches. The 56 touring pitches, with 6A electricity, are large and most are at least 100 sq.m. A small number also have water and drainage. The friendly French owners will tell you that they consider the site their personal garden.

Facilities

The two sanitary blocks are clean and well maintained. Facilities for children and disabled visitors. Washing machine. Motorcaravan services. Gift shop selling regional and local produce (bread available). Bar, restaurant and takeaway. Swimming pool and paddling pool. TV and games rooms. Boules. Bicycle hire. Play area. Small library. Weekly soirées in high season. No charcoal barbecues. Free WiFi over part of site. Max. 2 small dogs.

Open: 2 April - 28 September.

Directions

From the A20 take exit 56 and follow D2 towards St Germain-du-Bel-Air. Continue for 5 km. and the site is on the right. GPS: 44.69197, 1.53461

Charges guide

Per unit incl. 2 persons and electricity	€ 19.50 - € 30.00
extra person	€ 4.50 - € 7.00

Camping Cheques accepted.

Septfonds

Camping de Bois Redon

10 chemin de Bonnet, F-82240 Septfonds (Tarn-et-Garonne) T: 05 63 64 92 49.
E: info@campingdeboisredon.com **alanrogers.com/FR82020**

Charlotte and Hans de Bruin welcome their guests at Bois Redon, which is situated away from the hustle and bustle of everyday life. The 40 pitches are level and grassy, each with electricity (10A), and most are shaded. On-site activities include boules, basketball, volleyball and badminton, and close by you can go fishing, canoeing, climbing or caving. Small meals and fresh drinks are available on site - or in any of the charming local villages. In spring, orchids are mostly in bloom. Just 6 km. away is the artisan town of Saint Antonin-Noble-Val which dates back to the eighth century.

Facilities

Centrally located heated sanitary block with showers and basic facilities for disabled visitors. Snack bar/takeaway (June-end Aug). Bread to order. Outdoor swimming pool (mid June-15/9). Play area. Sports pitch. Basketball. Volleyball. Badminton. Communal barbecue. Free WiFi. Tents and bungalows for hire. Guided walks and boules evenings. Off site: Fishing 1 km. Tennis 3 km. Riding 5 km. Caving and climbing 4 km. Gorges de l'Aveyron 12 km. Golf 20 km.

Open: All year.

Directions

Septfonds is halfway between Cahors and Montauban. From E9/A20 exit 59 take D926 towards Caussade and Caylus. In Septfonds follow signs for Cayriech, via the Boulevard des Morgues and Route de Cayriech. Chemin de Bonnet and the site are shortly on your left. Follow signs in village. Do not use sat nav. GPS: 44.18271, 1.6051

Charges guide

Per unit incl. 2 persons and electricity	€ 18.50 - € 23.50
extra person	€ 4.00 - € 5.50

No credit cards.

Sévérac-le-Château

Camping les Calquières

17 avenue Jean Moulin, F-12150 Sévérac-le-Château (Aveyron) T: 05 65 47 64 82.
E: contact@camping-calquieres.com **alanrogers.com/FR12190**

This site is ideally situated, 3 km. from the free A75 autoroute, making an excellent short stay for those en route to the south and a good base for those wishing to visit the Cévennes National Park with its beautiful and rugged scenery. This quiet, neat, family run site nestles below the old village, close to the lower part of the town, all within easy walking distance. There are spectacular views from the château, floodlit at night. There are 97 good sized, level, grassy pitches, all with electricity (6A) and mostly separated by hedges with maturing trees providing some shade. A snack bar, restaurant and bar are near the covered and heated swimming pool. These are all more recent additions to the site's facilities.

Facilities

Two good toilet blocks include facilities for disabled visitors. Washing machine. Shop (15/6-30/9). Bar/restaurant, snack bar and takeaway (all 15/4-30/9). Covered and heated swimming pool with sliding roof. TV room. Games room. Trampoline. Play area. Bicycle hire. Entertainment for children. WiFi throughout. Off site: Tennis. Fishing 800 m. Riding 1 km. Sévérac-le-Château 1 km. small range of shops, restaurants and bank. Old, upper part of the town, with the château is a similar walking distance but involves a good climb.

Open: 1 April - 15 October.

Directions

From A75 exit 42 take N9 signed Sévérac le Château. Shortly hard right (N88), at crossroads straight on, signed Centre Ville. At station roundabout turn left, follow road beside railway through town. Turn left at site sign, immediately left again and site is on right. GPS: 44.31841, 3.06412

Charges guide

Per unit incl. 2 persons and electricity	€ 19.40 - € 27.50
extra person	€ 3.00 - € 5.50
child (0-7 yrs)	€ 2.00 - € 4.50

Sévérac-l'Eglise

Camping la Grange de Monteillac

F-12310 Sévérac-l'Eglise (Aveyron) T: 05 65 70 21 00. E: info@la-grange-de-monteillac.com

alanrogers.com/FR12070

La Grange de Monteillac is a modern, well equipped site in the beautiful, well preserved small village of Sévérac-l'Eglise. A spacious 4.5-hectare site, it provides 104 individual pitches, 61 for touring (eight extra large), on gently sloping grass, separated by flowering shrubs and trees offering some shade. All pitches have electricity (6/10A, long leads may be required). There are 43 chalets, mobile homes and tents for rent in separate areas. The friendly owners will advise about the many interesting activities in the region. An evening stroll around this delightful village is highly recommended.

Facilities

Modern toilet block with good facilities for babies and disabled visitors. Washing machine, dryer. Shop (10/5-15/9). Two swimming pools (1/5-15/9). Poolside restaurant/snack bar. Takeaway (July/Aug). Music or groups feature in the bar (July/Aug). Playground. Bicycle hire. Archery. Floodlit boules court. Organised activities. Children's and teens' clubs. Jacuzzi. WiFi (free).
Off site: Fishing 1 km. Shops in village 3 km. Riding 9 km.

Open: 27 April - 15 September.

Directions

Site is on the edge of Sévérac-l'Eglise village, just off N88 Rodez-Sévérac-le-Château road. From A75 use exit 42. At Sévérac-l'Église turn south onto D28, site is signed. Site entrance is very shortly on left. GPS: 44.3652, 2.85142

Charges guide

Per unit incl. 2 persons and electricity	€ 21.50 - € 50.50
extra person	€ 3.30 - € 6.80

Souillac

Castel Camping le Domaine de la Paille Basse

F-46200 Souillac-sur-Dordogne (Lot) T: 05 65 37 85 48. E: info@lapaillebasse.com

alanrogers.com/FR46010

Originally three abandoned farmsteads which the owners have sympathetically restored, Domaine de la Paille Basse is set in a rural location some 9 km. from Souillac. It is easily accessible from the A20 and well placed to take advantage of excursions into the Dordogne. The 262 pitches are in two main areas – one is level in cleared woodland with good shade, and the other is on grass with limited shade. Of these, 169 are available for touring. Numbered and marked, the pitches are a minimum 100 sq.m. and often considerably more. All have electricity (10A) and 80 are fully serviced.

Facilities

Three main toilet blocks are kept very clean. Laundry. Small shop with a large selection of wine (from 1/7). Restaurant, bar (open until 02.00 in high season), terrace, pizza takeaway. Crêperie. Main swimming pool, a smaller one, paddling pool (unheated), water slides. Sun terrace. Soundproofed disco (three times weekly in season). TV. Cinema. Tennis. Play area. Library. WiFi in office/bar area (charged). Mini farm. Entertainment for all (July/Aug). No electric barbecues. Off site: Golf 4 km. Souillac 9 km.

Open: 15 May - 15 September.

Directions

From Souillac take D15 and then D62 roads leading northwest (Salignac-Eyvignes) and after 6 km. turn right at site sign and follow steep and narrow approach road for 2 km. GPS: 44.94728, 1.43924

Charges guide

Per person incl. 2 persons and electricity	€ 19.00 - € 36.50
extra person	€ 5.00 - € 9.50

Camping Cheques accepted.

Souillac

Flower Camping les Ondines

Rue des Ondines, F-46200 Souillac (Lot) T: 05 65 37 86 44. E: info@camping-lesondines.com

alanrogers.com/FR46390

Souillac is a picturesque town lying between the Dordogne and Lot. It is just a five minute walk from les Ondines to the town's attractive pedestrianised centre where there are many cafés, restaurants and shops, as well as an abbey and, unusually, a robotic toy museum! There are 229 grassy and well sized touring pitches, all with 6A electricity. The site has recently been completely refurbished and now includes a new, heated swimming pool. In peak season, various activities are organised, including a children's club. The site lies on the banks of the Dordogne and canoe rental is available nearby.

Facilities

Three modern toilet blocks. Provision for babies and disabled visitors. Laundry facilities. Motorcaravan services. Snack bar (1/5-31/8). Heated outdoor swimming pool (1/5-15/9). Fishing. Pétanque. Play area. Communal barbecue. Activities and entertainment (July/Aug).
WiFi throughout (free). Mobile homes and tents for rent.
Off site: Bicycle hire 200 m. Riding 500 m. Golf 2 km. Cafés, shops, restaurants and takeaway in Souillac.

Open: 1 May - 29 September.

Directions

From the north, leave the A20 motorway at exit 55 and head for Souillac. Drive through the town and, 500 m. beyond the traffic lights, turn right following signs to les Ondines and Quercyland. Continue to follow signs to the site. GPS: 44.888871, 1.474196

Charges guide

Per unit incl. 2 persons and electricity	€ 15.00 - € 27.90
extra person	€ 3.00 - € 6.00

Tarascon-sur-Ariege

Yelloh! Village le Pré Lombard

B.P. 90148, F-09400 Tarascon-sur-Ariege (Ariège) T: 05 61 05 61 94. E: leprelombard@wanadoo.fr

alanrogers.com/FR09060

This busy, good value site is located beside the attractive River Ariège and near the town. There are 94 level, grassy, touring pitches with shade provided by a variety of trees (electricity 10A). At the rear of the site are 115 site owned chalets and mobile homes for hire. A gate in the fence provides access to the riverbank for fishing. Open for a long season, it is an excellent choice for early or late breaks, or as a stopover en-route to the winter sun destinations in Spain. This region of Ariège is in the foothills of the Pyrenees and 85 km. from Andorra. At Tarascon itself you can visit the Parc de la Préhistoire to view prehistoric rock paintings, take full-day guided walks and the really adventurous can take to the air for paragliding, hang-gliding or microlighting.

Facilities

Five toilet blocks of varying ages. Facilities for disabled visitors. Laundry. Motorcaravan services. Shop, bar and takeaway, restaurant, heated swimming pool (all 30/4-4/10). Entertainment and dancing. Play areas. Video game machines. Boules. Multisport court. Fishing. Satellite TV. Entertainment (high season), nightclub, children's club, sports tournaments. Activity programmes. Free WiFi. Off site: Supermarket 300 m. Town 600 m. Archery, kayaking and fishing nearby. Riding 5 km.

Open: 2 March - 4 October.

Directions

Site is 600 m. south of town, adjacent to the river. From north, turn off main N20 into the town, site well signed. From south (Andorra) site signed at roundabout on town approach.
GPS: 42.83985, 1.612

Charges guide

Per unit incl. 2 persons and electricity	€ 18.00 - € 36.00
extra person	€ 6.00 - € 8.00
child (3-6 yrs)	free - € 7.00
dog	€ 5.00

Thérondels

Flower Camping la Source

Presqu'île de Laussac, F-12600 Thérondels (Aveyron) T: 05 65 66 27 10. E: info@camping-la-source.com

alanrogers.com/FR12210

This extremely spacious, steeply terraced site borders the long and narrow Lac de Sarrans with its steep wooded sides. The site is run by a very friendly family and is better suited to the younger family wanting to 'get away from it all'. All the facilities are first class although the layout of the site means that pitches may be some distance and a steep climb away. The owners prefer to provide tractor assistance for caravans. There are 101 medium to large, slightly sloping, grassy pitches with 62 for touring, all with 6/10A electricity, water and drainage. They are separated by mostly silver birch trees offering some shade and have views through the trees over the lake. Rock pegs are essential. The site is not suitable for very large units or for those with walking difficulties.

Facilities

Two large, well appointed and clean toilet blocks with all the necessary facilities including those for babies and campers with disabilities. Bar with TV (all season). Shop, restaurant and takeaway (30/6-31/8). Heated swimming pool with toboggan and paddling pool (all season). Play area. TV room. Activities in high season for all the family. Lake fishing. Barbecues permitted. WiFi (charged). Off site: Boat ramp 500 m. Golf 6 km. Riding and bicycle hire 15 km.

Open: 5 June - 6 September.

Directions

Leave the A75 at exit 28 or 29 (St Flour). Go through town and take D921 towards Rodez. After 12 km. turn right on D990 to Pierrefort and 3 km. after village turn left on D34, signed Laussac. Follow narrow twisting lanes down to site (about 9 km).
GPS: 44.853716, 2.77105

Charges guide

Per unit incl. 2 persons and electricity	€ 17.00 - € 29.50
extra person	€ 3.00 - € 5.80
child (0-7 yrs)	free - € 4.80
dog	free - € 2.00

Camping Cheques accepted.

Thoux-Saint-Cricq

Camping Lac de Thoux Saint-Cricq

Lieu-dit en Castellan, F-32430 Thoux (Gers) T: 05 62 65 71 29. E: contact@camping-lacdethoux.com

alanrogers.com/FR32130

Camping Lac de Thoux Saint-Cricq in the Gers Gascogne region is a mature, family run site set alongside a 70-hectare lake with lots of watersports on offer. The site is well shaded by mature trees in most parts and provides 130 pitches with 80 available for touring units, the remainder taken up with mobile homes and chalets for rent. All the touring pitches are grass and slope slightly towards the lake. All have 10A electricity. There is an attractive, new water park complex adjacent to the site which includes a large bar area, a lakeside sandy beach and a play area. A sailing club operates within the site and offers tuition as well as boat, canoe and windsurfer hire. The lake is accessible from the campsite to fish for carp, pike and perch. Toulouse is only 50 km. away, so the site is a good base for visiting Space City and the very popular Airbus sites.

Facilities

One sanitary block provides all necessary facilities including a baby room and an en-suite unit for disabled visitors. Laundry facilities. Motorcaravan services. Shop (1/5-20/9). Bar (15/6-20/9). Snack bar and takeaway (15/6-20/9). Water park (15/6-20/9). Play area. Trampoline and multisport court. Boules. Lakeside beach (supervised July/Aug). WiFi throughout (charged). Off site: Gourmet restaurant 50 m. Golf, riding, bicycle hire 10 km.

Open: 1 May - 20 September.

Directions

From Auch head east on N124 to Toulouse. At L'Isle-Jourdain take the D654 north towards Cologne. Site is on right after 11 km. and is signed. GPS: 43.685533, 1.002417

Charges guide

Per unit incl. 2 persons and electricity	€ 20.00 - € 33.00
extra person	€ 6.00 - € 8.00
child (3-6 yrs)	€ 4.00 - € 6.00
dog	€ 3.00 - € 4.00

Vayrac

Camping les Granges

Lieu-dit les Granges, F-46110 Vayrac (Lot) T: 05 65 32 46 58. E: info@les-granges.com

alanrogers.com/FR46310

Situated just over 3 km. outside Vayrac in a very rural position, this site nestles quietly beside the river in a tranquil and peaceful area. Pitches along the river frontage are popular but children will need to be supervised as the river is unfenced. There is access to the river at one end of the site, ideal for those wishing to discover the pleasures of the River Dordogne. There are 150 level grassy pitches, shaded by a variety of mature trees, with 116 for touring. Most have 10A electricity. In July/August there is some family entertainment, but only in French. The owners are friendly and helpful and are keen to ensure you enjoy your holiday whilst on their family orientated site. This part of France offers many places of interest to visit with many fine châteaux and historic sites.

Facilities

Two toilet blocks include facilities for babies and disabled visitors. Washing machine and ironing board. Small shop, bar, snack bar and takeaway (July/Aug). Swimming pool and paddling pool (May-Sept). Play area. Family entertainment (12/7-16/8). Fishing and river beach. Max. 1 dog. Electric barbecues are not permitted. WiFi in reception (free). Off site: Bicycle hire 3 km. Shops, bars and restaurant in Vayrac 3 km. Golf and riding 10 km.

Open: 1 May - 13 September.

Directions

Leave A20 at exit 52 and go east on D158 then south on D8 and D720 to Vayrac. Turn right just before the church at sign for 'Espace loisir les Granges'. Site is signed from here in 3 km. GPS: 44.93462, 1.67981

Charges guide

Per unit incl. 2 persons and electricity	€ 17.60 - € 20.70
extra person	€ 4.30 - € 5.30
child (2-10 yrs)	€ 2.50 - € 3.10
dog (max. 1)	€ 1.50 - € 1.80

DÉPARTEMENTS: 11 AUDE, 30 GARD, 34 HÉRAULT, 48 LOZÈRE, 66 PYRÉNÉES-ORIENTALES

MAJOR CITIES: MONTPELLIER, PERPIGNAN, CARCASSONNE

Languedoc and Roussillon form part of the Massif Central. With its huge sandy beaches, the mountainous Languedoc region is renowned for its long sunshine records, and the pretty coastal villages of Roussillon are at their most beautiful at sunset, erupting in a riot of colour.

Stretching from the Rhône Valley in the east to the Spanish border in the south west, Languedoc-Roussillon is a mixture of rugged mountains, fertile coastal plains and a long sandy coastline dotted with modern resorts. Yet, away from the brash developments there is plenty of opportunity to discover reminders of the region's dramatic history – the Roman remains at Nîmes, the walled city of Carcassonne and the many Cathar castles perched on rocky hilltops.

Today, the plains are given over to agriculture and wine; fruit and vegetables in the Roussillon in particular, while Languedoc is responsible for around one third of France's total wine production, with appellations such as Corbières, Minervois and the sparkling Blanquette de Limoux.

Above all, the uncrowded expanses of sand and long hours of sunshine draw holidaymakers, both to the old coastal villages of Collioure and Banyus, and to the vibrant resorts of La Grande Motte and Cap d'Agde, which are a popular alternative to the Côte d'Azur.

Places of interest

Aigues-Mortes: medieval city.

Béziers: wine capital of the region; St Nazaire cathedral; Canal du Midi.

Carcassonne: largest medieval walled city in Europe.

Collioure: picturesque coastal village popular with artists.

Limoux: medieval town; Notre Dame de Marseille Basilica; St Martin church.

Montpellier: universities; Roman sites; Gothic cathedral.

Nîmes: Roman remains; Pont du Gard.

Perpignan: Kings' Palace; Catalan characteristics; old fortress.

Sigean: 700-acre African safari park.

Cuisine of the region

Cooking draws heavily on local produce: garlic, olive oil, tomato sauces and herbs from the 'garrigue'; apricots, peaches and cherries in jams and puddings.

Aïgo Bouido: garlic soup.

Boles de picoulat: small balls of diced beef and pork, garlic and eggs.

Bourride: a fish stew with garlic mayonnaise.

Boutifare: a sausage-shaped pudding of bacon and herbs.

Cargolade: snails, stewed in wine.

Cassoulet: hearty stew of haricot beans, sausage or pork and preserved goose.

Touron: a pastry of almonds, pistachio nuts and fruit.

www.sunfrance.com
contact.crtlr@sunfrance.com
(0) 4 67 20 02 20

ST-FLOUR
AUVERGNE
RHONE ALPES
VALENCE
AURILLAC
A75,E11
MENDE
LOZERE 48
ST PRIVAT-DE-CHAMPCLOS
ISPAGNAC
STE ENIMIE
RODEZ
BOISSON
GOUDARGUES
GARD 30
VILLENEUVE-LEZ-AVIGNON
MEYRUEIS
ST-JEAN-DU-GARD
ALES
MIDI PYRENEES
ANDUZE
UZÈS
LE VIGAN
REMOULINS
CRESPIAN
NIMES
SOMMIÈRES
BOISSERON
VAUVERT
A75,E11
LA GRANDE MOTTE
ARLES
CLAPIERS
ISTRES
HERAULT 34
MONTPELLIER
AIGUES-MORTES
PORT CAMARGUE
CASTRES
ST CHINIAN
FONTÈS
BESSAN
AGDE
LE GRAU-DU-ROI
ST PONS-DE-THOMIÈRES
BROUSSES-ET-VILLARET
VIAS
FRONTIGNAN-PLAGE
BALARUC-LES-BAINS
VILLENEUVE-LES-BÉZIERS
SÈTE
SAISSAC
VENDRES
MARSEILLAN-PLAGE
NARBONNE
CAP D'AGDE
CARCASSONNE
VIAS PLAGE
MONTCLAR
PORTIRAGNES-PLAGE
LEZIGNAN-CORBIERES
SÉRIGNAN-PLAGE
LIMOUX
VENDRES-PLAGE
VALRAS-PLAGE
LA PALME
NARBONNE-PLAGE
ALET-LES-BAINS
A9,E15
PORT BARCARES
LE BARCARÈS
TORREILLES-PLAGE
LANGUEDOC ROUSSILLON
AUDE 11
PERPIGNAN
STE MARIE-LA-MER
NEFIACH
CANET-EN-ROUSSILLON
ST-CYPRIEN-PLAGE
PRADES
PALAU-DEL-VIDRE
VERNET-LES-BAINS
CERET
ARGELÈS-SUR-MER
FONT-ROMEU
LAROQUE DES ALBERES
PYRENEES-ORIENTALES 66
SPAIN
0 25 50 75 kms

Agde

Camping le Neptune

46 boulevard du Saint Christ, F-34300 Agde (Hérault) T: 04 67 94 23 94. E: info@campingleneptune.com
alanrogers.com/FR34130

Camping le Neptune is a rare find in this area. This small, family run site with only 165 pitches makes a delightful change. The pitches are mostly separated by flowering bushes, with some shade, most with 6/10A electricity. There are 20 mobile homes to rent. The site's swimming pool is in a sunny position and is overlooked by the bar. The Fray family are welcoming and even though this is a busy area, this site is an oasis of calm, suited to couples and young families. Situated alongside the splendid Hérault river, one can cycle or walk into the village of Le Grau d'Agde or on into the historic centre of Agde itself.

Facilities

Two toilet blocks provide preset showers, washbasins in cabins, three cold showers for hot weather. Facilities for disabled visitors and babies. Laundry. Small shop, bar (15/5-15/9). Snacks and takeaway (26/6-21/8). Heated swimming pool (bracelets required July/Aug). Field for sports. Free WiFi. Boat mooring facility on the River Hérault across the road. Gas barbecues only permitted. Max. 1 dog. Off site: Canal du Midi and round lock 2 km.

Open: 6 April - 5 October.

Directions

From A9 exit 34 follow signs for Agde, Bessan, Vias, then Cap d'Agde. Exit for Grau d'Agde. At roundabout (with statue) turn left (Grau d'Agde), and left again at 2nd roundabout. Straight on to 5th roundabout turning left and under bridge. Site is 600 m. on left. GPS: 43.29803, 3.45628

Charges guide

Per unit incl. 2 persons and electricity € 19.90 - € 35.20

Agde

Camping les Champs Blancs

76 route de Rochelongue, F-34300 Agde (Hérault) T: 04 67 94 23 42.
E: contact@campingleschampsblancs.com **alanrogers.com/FR34190**

Les Champs Blancs celebrated its 50th birthday in 2015 and is still run by the same family that started it all those years ago. The trees and flowering shrubs have matured to provide a shady, green, calm environment two kilometres from the sea at Rochelongue. There are over 300 pitches with 155 level, sandy pitches for touring units. All have 10A electricity and water and, unusually, 110 also have private sanitary cabins, which are popular. Mobile homes and chalets can be rented. The area nearest the main road, where you will find the leisure facilities, is well screened by trees to deaden possible road noise.

Facilities

Two modern, fully equipped toilet blocks but 110 pitches have their own private cabins. Two units for disabled visitors. Laundry facilities. Motorcaravan services. Small shop (21/4-23/9, bread only in low season). Bar (from 10/6). Restaurant (17/5-14/9). Takeaway (24/6-3/9). Swimming complex (from 8/4 depending on weather). Good play area. Miniclub (July/Aug). Minigolf. Tennis. Multisports court. Bicycle hire (from mid June). WiFi throughout (charged). Off site: Supermarket 1 km.

Open: 1 April - 15 October.

Directions

From A9 exit 34, follow N312 for Agde, joins N112 Béziers-Sète road. Cross bridge over river, take first turn (Rochelongue), turn right at roundabout, next left, then next left (Agde). Site on left before another bridge back over N112. GPS: 43.29702, 3.47547

Charges guide

Per unit incl. 2 persons and electricity € 16.00 - € 50.50
Camping Cheques accepted.

Agde

Camping les Romarins

Route du Grau, F-34300 Agde (Hérault) T: 04 67 94 18 59. E: contact@romarins.com
alanrogers.com/FR34420

A welcoming and popular, family owned campsite beside the River Hérault, les Romarins is only 1 km. from a wide sandy beach and 800 metres from the village. With 120 level grassy pitches separated by flowering shrubs, 80 are available for touring units, the rest are taken by mobile homes and chalets (40 to let). Electricity (6A) is available on all pitches, some of which have more shade than others. A pleasant walk beside the river takes you to the shops, restaurants and beach of Grau d'Agde.

Facilities

Two modern toilet blocks are fully equipped. Good facilities for babies and disabled visitors. Motorcaravan services (charged). Bar with snacks. Bread can be ordered. Heated pool. Large playing field. Play area. Bicycle hire. Multisports court. Outdoor gym equipment. Sports activities and evening entertainment in season. WiFi (charged on pitch). Off site: Boat launching 50 m. Shops and restaurants 700 m. Beach 900 m. Riding, swimming pool and golf 2 km. Cap d'Agde 3 km.

Open: 28 March - 3 October.

Directions

From A9 exit 34 (Agde) picking up N112. Cross river, then exit for Grau d'Agde/Rochelonge. Left at roundabout, left again by Hyper U, and over two roundabouts towards river. Left at roundabout beside river following 'Campings les Berges de l'Hérault' along riverside (one way). Site is third on left. GPS: 43.29446, 3.45005

Charges guide

Per unit incl. 2 persons and electricity € 18.00 - € 34.00
Camping Cheques accepted.

Agde

Camping la Pepinière

3 route du Grau, F-34300 Agde (Hérault) T: 04 67 94 10 94. E: reception@campinglapepiniere.com

alanrogers.com/FR34850

La Pepiniere is a quiet family campsite located on the banks of the Hérault. A cycle path leads direct from the site to Le Grau, the beach (1.2 km) and shops (or a pleasant 20 minute walk). In the opposite direction is the town of Agde alongside the river. There are 100 flat, grassy pitches with limited shade, of which 37 are reserved for touring units, each with electricity (10A). Additionally, there are a number of mobile homes and canvas bungalows to rent. Leisure amenities include a swimming pool with a daily water aerobics session in peak season. Entertainment and activities are organised in high season.

Facilities

Sanitary facilities with showers, washbasins in cubicles and provision for disabled visitors. Laundry. Motorcaravan services. Snack bar/restaurant. Bread to order. Heated outdoor swimming pool and whirlpool, bar (all 11/4-30/9). Entertainment in high season. Library. Water aerobics (free). Outdoor fitness area. Trampoline. Play area. Sports field. Miniclub (July/Aug). No charcoal barbecues (communal available). Bicycle hire. WiFi throughout (free).

Open: 14 March - 17 October.

Directions

From A9 exit 34 (Cap d'Agde) take D612 south (Vias and Agde). After 7 km. cross the River Hérault and almost immediately turn south on D32 signed Le Grau d'Agde. Site is then signed from here. Entrance is beside boatyard. GPS: 43.29621, 3.45238

Charges guide

Per unit incl. 2 persons and electricity	€ 14.00 - € 29.50
extra person	€ 3.00 - € 6.50

Agde

Camping les Sablettes

55 chemin de Baluffe, F-34300 Agde (Hérault) T: 04 67 94 36 65. E: lessablettes@hotmail.fr

alanrogers.com/FR34970

Les Sablettes is quietly situated approximately one kilometre back from the beach in the residential area of Grau d'Agde. It is quite pleasant with a mixture of pine and other trees providing some shade, interspersed with some flowering shubs. The site is accessed via gravel roads and regularly laid out in squares, with the pool and bar area centrally situated. There is a mixture of 90 touring pitches and 74 mobile homes and chalets to rent. The level pitches are of average size, on sandy/grassy soil with 6A electricity. The walled entrance is a little tight so care is needed if towing.

Facilities

Two fully equipped toilet blocks open on demand, baby bath and unit for disabled campers. Washing machines. Shop (bread to order). Bar, restaurant and takeaway (15/5-15/9). Swimming pool with slides and paddling pool (15/5-29/9). Play area with bouncy castle. Children's club and evening entertainment (July/Aug). Bicycle hire. WiFi (charged on pitch). Gas and electric barbecues only. Off site: Bus stop. Beach and fishing 800 m.

Open: 1 April - 29 September.

Directions

From A9 exit 34 follow N312 for Agde. Join N112 Béziers/Sète road, cross bridge over river and take first turn (Rochelongue). Right at two roundabouts, over speed humps to just past restaurant Baluffee. Site on right in 0.25 km. GPS: 43.28812, 3.46273

Charges guide

Per unit incl. 2 persons and electricity	€ 14.00 - € 36.00
extra person	€ 3.50 - € 7.50

Aigues-Mortes

Yelloh! Village la Petite Camargue

B.P. 21, D62, F-30220 Aigues-Mortes (Gard) T: 04 66 53 98 98. E: info@yellohvillage-petite-camargue.com

alanrogers.com/FR30020

La Petite Camargue sets a very high standard and is a well organised site with much to offer. With the fascinating Camargue on its doorstep, the medieval walled city of Aigues Mortes and the Mediterranean beaches close by, it makes an ideal holiday centre. A large site (532 pitches) on 40 hectares, it has a swimming pool complex and other sporting amenities, including a riding school. There are 144 good sized touring pitches (6/10A electricity) on level, sandy grass, laid out in shady avenues with flowering shrubs. They are interspersed among more than 300 mobile homes and 145 tour operator pitches.

Facilities

Three toilet blocks provide modern facilities including many combined showers and washbasins. Provision for disabled visitors. Laundry facilities. Motorcaravan services. Shops, bar/restaurant with pizzeria and takeaway. Beauty centre. Swimming pool with jacuzzi. Aquagym. Scuba diving. Play area. Children's club. Mini animal park. Tennis. New multisports court. Bicycle hire. Diving school. Free shuttle bus to beach (July/Aug). Disco/nightclub (over 16 yrs). WiFi throughout (free).

Open: 23 April - 19 September.

Directions

From A9, exit 26 (Gallargues), towards Le Grau-du-Roi, site 18 km. Continue past Aigues-Mortes on D62, site is 2 km. on the right, just before large roundabout for La Grand-Motte and Le Grau-du-Roi junction. GPS: 43.56307, 4.15888

Charges guide

Per unit incl. 2 persons and electricity	€ 18.00 - € 52.00
extra person	€ 5.00 - € 9.00
child (3-7 yrs)	free - € 8.00

Alet-les-Bains

Camping Val d'Aleth

F-11580 Alet-les-Bains (Aude) T: 04 68 69 90 40. E: camping@valdaleth.com

alanrogers.com/FR11110

In the Cathar country of the upper Aude valley, and open all year round, this popular, small site is run by Christopher and Christine Cranmer who offer a warm welcome. The mellow, medieval walls of Alet-les-Bains form one boundary of the site while on the other, and popular with anglers, is the River Aude (fenced). Beyond this is the D118 and a railway which produces noise at times. The 37 mainly small, numbered pitches, around half of which are on hardstandings, all have electricity (4-10A) and are separated by hedges and mature trees which give shade. Try the local sparkling wine, Blanquette de Limoux, said to be the first Champagne.

Facilities

Modern, heated sanitary blocks are fully equipped with controllable hot showers and vanity style washbasins. Facilities for disabled visitors. Laundry facilities. Motorcaravan services. Reception stocks essentials, drinks, wine, beer, use of freezer. Small play area. Small library area. Barbecue. Mountain bike hire. WiFi over part of site (charged). Off site: Swimming pool in village.

Open: All year.

Directions

From Carcassonne take D118 south for 32 km. Ignore first sign to Alet (avoiding narrow bridge) and after crossing the river, turn into town. Site is 800 m. on the left (tight turn). GPS: 42.99482, 2.25605

Charges guide

Per unit incl. 2 persons and electricity	€ 18.75 - € 22.00
extra person	€ 3.95 - € 4.95

Anduze

Domaine de Gaujac

Boisset-et-Gaujac, F-30140 Anduze (Gard) T: 04 66 61 67 57. E: contact@domaine-de-gaujac.com

alanrogers.com/FR30000

The 293 level, well shaded pitches include 175 for touring with electricity (4-10A) and 22 are fully serviced. Access to some areas can be difficult for larger units due to narrow winding access roads, trees and hedges. Larger units should ask for lower numbered pitches (1-148) where access is a little easier. In high season this region is dry and hot, thus grass quickly wears off many pitches leaving just a sandy base. There are 12 special hardstanding pitches for motorcaravans near the entrance. The site has a covered entertainment area and courtyard terrace.

Facilities

Toilet blocks (one heated) include facilities for disabled visitors. Washing machines and dryer. Motorcaravan services. Good shop (2/6-27/8). Newsagent. Bar, restaurant and takeaway/crêperie (5/5-15/9). New heated swimming, paddling pool (lifeguard 5/7-15/8) and jacuzzi. Playground, sports field. Tennis. Minigolf. Communal barbecue, on pitches only gas or electric. Dog agility course. WiFi in bar/terrace area (free). Off site: Fishing 100 m. Riding, golf 8 km. Bicycle hire 10 km.

Open: 1 April - 20 September.

Directions

From Alès take N110 towards Montpellier. At St Christol-les-Alès fork right on D910 (Anduze) and in Bagard, at roundabout, turn left on D246 to Boisset et Gaujac. Follow signs to site in 5 km. GPS: 44.03580, 4.02425

Charges guide

Per unit incl. 2 persons and electricity	€ 22.80 - € 30.70

Credit cards accepted in high season only.

Camping Cheques accepted.

Anduze

Camping Cevennes-Provence

Corbés-Thoiras, F-30140 Anduze (Gard) T: 04 66 61 73 10. E: info@campingcp.com

alanrogers.com/FR30200

You are sure of a very warm welcome at this spacious, family owned site. New arrivals are taken on a tour in order to select a good pitch. There are 226 touring pitches on the various levels, 220 with electricity (10A). Some are on the level land close to the river and others are scattered on high terraces, having privacy and fine views across the Cévennes countryside. The river is very popular for swimming, otherwise there are few on-site activities. Advice is given to visitors who wish to explore off site.

Facilities

Ten excellent, modern, clean toilet blocks (one new for 2014). Good facilities for disabled visitors. Family shower room. Well stocked shop (1/4-1/10). Restaurant, takeaway, bar (19/4-15/9). Excellent play area. Tennis. Minigolf. Volleyball. River bathing and fishing. Many off-site activities arranged at reception. Internet point. Free WiFi near reception. Communal barbecue areas. Bicycle hire. Off site: Riding 4 km. Golf 10 km.

Open: 20 March - 1 October.

Directions

Only viable access. From D907 Anduze, take D284 alongside the river. Site signed on right 3 km. from town. Take care on the approach – narrow lane for 100 m, then a narrow bridge, visibility good. GPS: 44.07763, 3.96484

Charges guide

Per unit incl. 2 persons and electricity	€ 20.90 - € 32.00
extra person	€ 4.40 - € 8.60

Anduze

Camping Castel Rose

610 chemin de Recoulin, F-30140 Anduze (Gard) T: 04 66 61 80 15. E: castelrose@wanadoo.fr
alanrogers.com/FR30360

Spacious and wooded, Castel Rose stretches for more than a kilometre along the banks of one of France's most beautiful rivers, the Gardon d'Anduze. The site's long, private river beach is protected from the currents of the river by an artificial breakwater. The 218 touring pitches, all with 10A electricity, are level and marked out with mature trees. The site is set away from the busy main road and at night all you will hear is the sound of the water. The pretty town of Anduze is a 15 minute walk from the site.

Facilities

Five toilet blocks with open style washbasins, private cabins and spacious shower cubicles. Baby bath and toilets for children. Laundry facilities. Bar and restaurant with terrace. Spa, sauna and steam room. Games room. Children's club (July/Aug). Fishing, swimming and canoeing in the river. Play area. Boules. Multisports area. Free WiFi over part of site. Off site: Anduze with small shops, cafés, crafts. Nearby supermarkets. Steam train. Riding 2 km.

Open: 1 April - 30 September.

Directions

From Alès take N110 (D6110) towards Sommières, then D910a to Anduze. From village centre follow signs for St Jean-du-Gard and then campsite. There is a railway viaduct over road and shortly after a sign on right: 'Chemin de Recoulin'. Sharp right here, descending towards river. GPS: 44.0643, 3.97694

Charges guide

Per unit incl. 2 persons and electricity	€ 18.00 - € 32.00

No credit cards.

Anduze

Camping le Pradal

200 chemin d'Anduze-Generargues, F-30140 Anduze (Gard) T: 04 66 61 79 81.
E: camping-le-pradal@orange.fr **alanrogers.com/FR30550**

A friendly welcome awaits at this family run site which is situated beside the Gardon river, just a ten minute walk from the historic town of Anduze, the gateway to the Cevennes and beautiful unspoilt countryside. The site has direct access to an attractive, private, pebble beach. There are 133 grass and sand pitches set amongst mature trees, most with good shade. Of these, 100 are for touring units, all with 10A electricity connections, 20 also with water and drainage. Most pitches are level with some terracing to allow views of the river and surrounding mountainside. Some English is spoken.

Facilities

Two toilet blocks in traditional buildings. Most washbasins in cabins. Good showers for children. Facilities for babies and for disabled visitors. Laundry facilities. Motorcaravan service point. Fridge rental. Small shop. Bar. Snack bar and takeaway (high season). Swimming pool complex. TV in bar. Games room. Playground. Trampoline. Tennis. Volleyball. Private pebble beach. Fishing. WiFi on bar terrace (free). Off site: Shops and town 1 km.

Open: 29 March - 30 September.

Directions

From the N106 Nîmes-Ales road, turn west on D982 to Anduze. In Anduze cross the river and turn north on D129 to Generargues. Site is 900 m. along this road to the west. GPS: 44.06231, 3.98286

Charges guide

Per unit incl. 2 persons and electricity	€ 17.00 - € 30.00
extra person	€ 5.00 - € 6.00

Argelès-sur-Mer

Camping le Soleil

Route du Littoral, F-66702 Argelès-sur-Mer (Pyrénées-Orientales) T: 04 68 81 14 48.
E: camping.lesoleil@wanadoo.fr **alanrogers.com/FR66040**

Le Soleil is an attractive site with direct access to the sandy beach but also with an impressive heated pool complex. It is a busy, popular, family owned site which over the years has developed into a small village. It has over 800 pitches of ample size, of which 132 are used by tour operators and a further 430 for touring units, on sandy/grassy ground and with a mixture of tall trees and shrubs providing light shade. All have electricity (6A) and 24 are fully serviced. Caravans sometimes need to take care on the narrow access roads. The site offers a wide range of amenities, activities and entertainment for all.

Facilities

Six toilet blocks (one heated in low season) of the type with external access to individual units. Some family cabins with washbasins, showers. Washing machines. Supermarket. General shop, restaurant, takeaway and bar. Disco (July/Aug), beach bar. Heated swimming pool complex and entertainment area. Adventure playground. TV room. WiFi throughout (free). Tennis. Diving and riding in high season (charge). Gas and electric barbecues only. No dogs. Off site: Fishing on the adjacent river.

Open: 7 May - 24 September.

Directions

Site is at north end of the beach, 1 km. from Argelès-Plage village. GPS: 42.57552, 3.04232

Charges guide

Per unit incl. 2 persons and electricity	€ 20.00 - € 46.80
extra person (over 5 yrs)	€ 5.00 - € 12.10
dog	€ 3.00 - € 4.00

Less 25% in May, June and August - no booking fee.

Argelès-sur-Mer

MS Vacances Camping Club Le Littoral

Route du Littoral, F-66700 Argelès-sur-Mer (Pyrénées-Orientales) T: 02 53 81 70 00.

E: reservation@ms-vacances.com **alanrogers.com/FR66060**

Le Littoral is only 800 metres from a fine, sandy beach via a footpath. The site offers plenty of accommodation in mobile homes as well as 25 good sized, level touring pitches with shade and 6A electricity. The site is well looked after and the pool area is particularly impressive. Argelès is a very popular holiday resort with good sandy beaches. A free shuttle bus runs to the beach and town centre in July and August. The border with Spain is only 30 km. away.

Facilities

Large modern toilet block, fully equipped and with some washbasins in cabins. Baby bath. Some facilities for disabled visitors. Washing machines. Shop, bar, restaurants and takeaway. Outdoor and covered heated swimming pools with slides. Solarium. Entertainment for all in high season. Gas barbecues only. Play area. Fitness room. Bicycle hire. WiFi throughout (charged). Path to beach. Max. 1 dog per pitch. Free shuttle to beach and city centre (July-Aug).

Open: 11 April - 20 September.

Directions

From A9 take exit 43 (Le Boulou) and follow N114 for Argelès. At exit 10 follow directions for Taxo d'Avall then Plage Nord. Site is clearly signed off coast road in the St Cyprien direction. GPS: 42.58066, 3.03324

Charges guide

Per unit incl. 2 persons and electricity	€ 25.00 - € 47.00
extra person	€ 6.20 - € 12.40

Argelès-sur-Mer

Castel Camping les Criques de Porteils

Corniche de Collioure (RD 114), F-66701 Argelès-sur-Mer (Pyrénées-Orientales) T: 04 68 81 12 73.

E: contactcdp@lescriques.com **alanrogers.com/FR66150**

This is an amazing site situated on the cliff top with views across the sea to Argelès, set against a backdrop of mountains and close to Collioure, the artists' paradise. A lot of work has been carried out to improve the facilities here, including a new bar and restaurant and pitches have been redesigned for easier access. There are around 204 of varying sizes and shapes due to the nature of the terrain, level in places, up and down in others. All have 10A electricity available and either a sea view or views towards the mountains. There are eight small coves accessed by steep steps (gated).

Facilities

Two renovated toilet blocks (one can be heated) are fully equipped with super children's room. Laundry room with Internet point. Motorcaravan services. Shop. New bar and terraced restaurant with takeaway. Swimming pool. TV/games room. Play area. Golf practice. Tennis. Volleyball. Boules. Fishing. Yoga classes. Guided hikes. Duck pond and small animal area. No charcoal barbecues. WiFi over site (charged). Off site: Collioure and beach (both 30 mins. walk). Bicycle hire 6 km.

Open: 26 March - 29 October.

Directions

Exit A9 at Perpignan Sud or Le Boulou. Head for Argelès to pick up signs for 'Collioure par la Corniche'. Watch for site signs coming into a bend as you come down a hill by hotel. Sharp left in front of hotel and follow road to site which is in front of you as you exit bridge. GPS: 42.53372, 3.06792

Charges guide

Per unit incl. 2 persons and electricity	€ 29.50 - € 53.50
extra person	€ 7.00 - € 12.50

Argelès-sur-Mer

Camping la Chapelle

Avenue du Tech, F-66700 Argelès-sur-Mer (Pyrénées-Orientales) T: 04 68 81 28 14.

E: contactlc@camping-la-chapelle.com **alanrogers.com/FR66830**

A shaded, neat and tidy haven just off the main square within easy walking distance of the beach. There is a super pool complex at the far end of the site including a heated pool with sliding cover, a large outdoor pool and various other small pools with slides and a jacuzzi. Most of the sandy, grass pitches are 100 sq. m. with hedging, shade from tall trees, regularly laid out with 6A electricity. The site is under the same ownership as Les Criques de Porteils near Collioure and is popular with tour operators. Shops are within very easy reach, just outside the site. This does mean that there could be some night time noise at busy times and choosing a pitch at the back of the site might be a good idea.

Facilities

Five toilet blocks with modern facilities. Facilities for children/babies and disabled visitors (key). Laundry. Bread shop. Snacks. Bar (evenings). Swimming pool complex with bar. Play areas. Tennis. Multisports court. Minigolf. Gym. Children's club run by tour operator. No charcoal barbecues. Mobile homes to rent. WiFi (charged).
Off site: Restaurants, bars and shops are a short walk from the site. Sandy beach 200 m. Collioure 7 km.

Open: 18 April - 27 September.

Directions

Follow signs for the Office de Tourism and site clearly signed opposite. GPS: 42.553038, 3.043492

Charges guide

Per unit incl. 2 persons and electricity	€ 25.70 - € 46.30
extra person	€ 7.80 - € 12.50
child (3-5 yrs)	€ 4.70 - € 8.30
dog	free - € 4.00

Balaruc-les-Bains

Sites et Paysages le Mas du Padre

4 chemin du Mas du Padre, F-34540 Balaruc-les-Bains (Hérault) T: 04 67 48 53 41.
E: contact@mas-du-padre.com **alanrogers.com/FR34100**

Mas du Padre is a very pleasant little site run by the Durand family and it makes a good base from which to explore the Sète area or 'take the waters' at Balaruc-les-Bains. Madame Durand speaks excellent English. On a hillside, just 2.5 km. from Balaruc-les-Bains and near the Etang de Thau (famous for oysters), this small site is unusually situated in a residential area that has obviously developed around it over the years. The 113 secluded pitches are of varying sizes and are marked by hedges, mature trees and shrubs. Some are on a very gentle slope and hard ground. There are 88 touring pitches with 6/10A electricity and 25 mobile homes to let including one adapted for disabled visitors.

Facilities

Well equipped toilet blocks include baby changing area. Facilities for disabled visitors. Washing machines. Reception sells bread, drinks and ice cream. Heated swimming pool (18/4-27/9), plus one for children. Half-court tennis. Boules. Mini adventure playground. Sports programme, tournaments, aquarobics, entertainment for children, weekly dance (all in high season). WiFi on part of site (free for half an hour).
Off site: Seaside beach 10 km. Golf 12 km.

Open: 1 April - 31 October.

Directions

From A9, exit Sète, follow N800 to Balaruc-le-Vieux, first roundabout (D2), second roundabout both following Balaruc-les-Bains/Sète. After 50 m. right for Balaruc-les-Bains, immediately left across road, double back down it (50 m). Immediately right, follow Chemin du Mas du Padre. GPS: 43.45219, 3.69241

Charges guide

Per unit incl. 2 persons and electricity	€ 17.90 - € 42.50
extra person (over 13 yrs)	€ 3.90 - € 5.50

Bessan

Domaine de Sainte Veziane

F-34550 Bessan (Hérault) T: 04 67 77 58 58. E: info@domainesainteveziane.com
alanrogers.com/FR34980

Just 15 minutes from the Mediterranean coast at Agde, Domaine de Sainte Veziane is a residential park that is ideal for families with younger children. There are no touring pitches here, but 120 chalets and mobile homes, of which 75 are for hire. The original part of the site requires some up-and-down walking, but is very pretty, with flowering shrubs, mature trees and hedged pitches. The newer part is more open and may be subject to road noise. The pool area is the focal point of the site and has plenty to keep the whole family busy – slides and games for the children and a jacuzzi and sun terrace for adults.

Facilities

Laundry. Bar/restaurant and takeaway. Bread service. Water park with swimming pool, wading pool, 3 slides, a river and whirlpool (1/5-30/9). Volleyball court. Pétanque pitch. Play area. Children's club (July/Aug). Evening entertainment (July/Aug). No charcoal barbecues. WiFi throughout (charged). Off site: Fishing 2 km. Golf 10 km.

Open: All year.

Directions

From A9 take exit 34 (Pézenas/Agde/Vias) for Bessan. In Bessan at first set of traffic lights turn right. At first roundabout go straight on, at second follow signs for Montblanc, go under blue bridge. In 300 m. turn right to site. GPS: 43.37039, 3.41364

Charges guide

Contact site for details.

Boisseron

Flower Camping Domaine de Gajan

Rue de Pie Bouquet, F-34160 Boisseron (Hérault) T: 04 66 80 94 30. E: info@campingdomainedegajan.com
alanrogers.com/FR34910

Domaine de Gajan lies midway between the Cevennes hills and the Mediterranean, with good access to the Camargue. Pitches here are of a good size, flat and well shaded by trees. Most have electrical connections (16A). A range of fully equipped mobile homes and chalets are available for rent and four wooden safari tents on stilts fit well into the rural environment overlooking the countryside. On-site amenities include a bar/snack bar overlooking the large swimming pool. A wellness centre with spa pool and sauna is a great addition. The site becomes livelier in July and August.

Facilities

Large, central, fully equipped toilet block has facilities for babies and for disabled visitors. Washing machines and dryer. Bar/snack bar (July/Aug). Takeaway. Outdoor swimming pool (all season). Aquagym. Spa and wellness centre. Sports field. Play area. Free WiFi in bar/terrace area. Mobile homes and chalets for rent. Off site: Small shop in Boisseron 800 m. Fishing 1 km. Supermarket 2 km. Bicycle hire 3 km. Riding 5 km. Golf 20 km. Cycling and walking routes. Shops and restaurants in Sommières.

Open: 1 April - 30 September.

Directions

Leave A9 autoroute at exit 27 (Lunel) and take D34 (Boisseron/Sommières). After passing Saturargues and St Sériès, turn right (roundabout, Boisseron and Sommières). On to Boisseron and, on approach to village centre, turn right following sign to Camping Domaine de Gajan. GPS: 43.76667, 4.07472

Charges guide

Per unit incl. 2 persons and electricity	€ 18.00 - € 30.50
extra person	€ 3.50 - € 5.00

Boisson

Castel Camping le Château de Boisson

Boisson, F-30500 Allègre-les-Fumades (Gard) T: 04 66 24 85 61. E: reception@chateaudeboisson.com

alanrogers.com/FR30070

Château de Boisson is a quiet, welcoming, high quality family site within easy reach of the Cévennes, Ardèche and Provence. The site is hilly and the 178 pitches, with 87 for touring, are on two levels. They are separated by neat hedges and a variety of trees providing some shade. All have 6/10A electricity. Twenty-eight are fully serviced and seven have private bathrooms. Rock pegs are essential. The large swimming pools, one indoor with paddling pool and toboggan, are in a sunny location at the top of the site, close to the château. Gas and electric barbecues only. Dogs are not accepted in July and August.

Facilities

Two excellent, very clean toilet blocks with all necessary facilities including those for disabled visitors. Dishwashers (free). Small shop (13/4-15/9). Good restaurant, bar, snacks (all season). Play area. Pools – indoor (all season), outdoor (1/5-28/9). Bridge tournaments in low season. Painting classes. Tennis. Boules. Bicycle hire (July/Aug). No charcoal barbecues. WiFi throughout (charged).
Off site: Fishing 2 km. Riding 4 km. Golf 30 km. Many market towns and villages to explore. Alès 16 km.

Open: 11 April - 26 September.

Directions

From Alès take D16 northeast through Salindres and Auzon. After Auzon turn right across river, immediately left, signed Barjac and site. Shortly turn right to site entrance. Only route for trailers and motorcaravans. Do not drive through the village of Boissons. GPS: 44.20967, 4.25625

Charges guide

Per unit incl. 2 persons and electricity	€ 19.90 - € 43.90
extra person	€ 3.50 - € 10.50

Brousses-et-Villaret

Camping le Martinet Rouge

F-11390 Brousses-et-Villaret (Aude) T: 04 68 26 51 98. E: camping.lemartinetrouge@orange.fr

alanrogers.com/FR11040

Le Martinet Rouge provides a peaceful retreat in the Aude countryside to the north of Carcassonne, in Cathar country. Isobelle and John are very proud of the improvements they have made to their site and provide a warm welcome. An unusual feature of the site are the massive granite boulders (outcrops of smooth rock from the last ice age). The site offers 53 pitches for touring units, all with electricity (6/10A), in two contrasting areas. The original one is well secluded with irregularly shaped, fairly level, large pitches amongst trees and shrubs, while the other is on a landscaped gentle hill with some mature trees.

Facilities

One modern sanitary block with facilities for babies and disabled visitors can be heated in low season. Two refurbished blocks used in high season. Laundry facilities. Shop for basics (no others locally). Bar, terrace, TV (1/7-15/9). Snack bar (July/Aug). Swimming pool and water slide (15/6-15/9). Croquet. Half-court tennis. Multisports court. Play area. WiFi over site (charged).

Open: 27 March - 6 September.

Directions

Site is 20 km. northwest of Carcassonne and best approached via D118, Carcassonne-Mazamet road. Turn onto D103 15 km. north of Carcassonne to Brousses-et-Villaret. Western outskirts of village turn south to site in 50 m. GPS: 43.33932, 2.25201

Charges guide

Per unit incl. 2 persons and electricity	€ 16.00 - € 34.00
extra person	€ 7.50

Canet-en-Roussillon

Camping Ma Prairie

1 avenue des Coteaux, F-66140 Canet-en-Roussillon (Pyrénées-Orientales) T: 04 68 73 26 17.
E: contact@maprairie.com **alanrogers.com/FR66020**

Ma Prairie is an excellent site and its place in this guide goes back over 30 years to when it was simply a field surrounded by vineyards. Trees and colourful shrubs provide a comfortable, park-like setting with 208 touring pitches, 197 with 10A electricity and 15 with water and drainage. There are also 50 mobile homes available to rent and ten privately owned. It is a peaceful haven some 3 km. back from the sea but within walking distance of Canet village itself. The Gil family still provide a warm welcome.

Facilities

Fully equipped toilet blocks including baby bath. Laundry facilities. No shop but baker calls every morning June-Sept. Covered snack bar and takeaway. Air-conditioned bar and restaurant. Heated swimming pool, water chute and children's pool (15/5-15/9). Multisports court. Gym. TV. Amusement machines. Daily activities and entertainment in season for children (6-12 yrs). WiFi over site (charged). No charcoal barbecues. Several small communal barbecue areas. Tourist train stops at site (April-June and Sept). Off site: Supermarket 150 m.

Open: 12 April - 20 September.

Directions

Leave autoroute A9 at Perpignan North (Barcarès). Exit the D11 Perpignan road (exit 5). Turn left at junction (direction St Nazaire). Go under bridge, take first turning right at roundabout then left off small roundabout. Site on left. GPS: 42.70135, 2.99968

Charges guide

Per unit incl. 2 persons and electricity	€ 19.00 - € 50.00
extra person	€ 5.00 - € 9.00

Camping Cheques accepted.

Canet-en-Roussillon

Camping Mar Estang

Route de Saint Cyprien, Voie des Flamants Roses, F-66140 Canet-en-Roussillon (Pyrénées-Orientales)
T: 04 68 80 35 53. E: contactme@marestang.com **alanrogers.com/FR66090**

Le Mar Estang is a large, impressive, 'all singing, all dancing' site with something for everyone. Situated on the edge of Canet, between the Etang (part of the Réserve Naturelle de Canet/Saint Nazaire) and the sea, there is access to the sandy beach from the site by two tunnels under the road. If you don't fancy the beach, the site has not one but two attractive pool complexes linked by a bridge. They are amazing, providing slides, toboggans, hot tub, paddling pool and a heated pool, all with lifeguards. You can swim seriously, learn to swim or scuba dive or just enjoy the fun pools. Who needs the beach! There are 600 pitches in total, some 150 for touring units, with 6A electricity, and some degree of shade, on sandy ground. The rest are used by tour operators or have site-owned mobile homes to rent. A very wide range of activities and entertainment is organised all season with children's clubs in high season and a beach club for watersports. Children and teenagers would have a great time here and parents would enjoy Canet-Plage with its esplanade, shops and restaurants.

Facilities

Nine well equipped sanitary blocks. Facilities for babies. Laundry. Motorcaravan services. Shops, bars, restaurant and takeaway, swimming pools with lifeguards, jacuzzi and solarium. Fitness club. Children's clubs. Artistic workshops. Daily sports and entertainment. Day trips. Evening entertainment with cabaret. Disco. Communal barbecue only. Sailing club. Beach club. Tennis. Bicycle hire. Play areas. WiFi throughout (charged). Direct access to beach. Off site: Fishing 100 m. Riding and golf 4 km. Rafting, canoeing and quad bike treks by arrangement. Canet 500 m. with tourist train in high season.

Open: 16 April - 18 September.

Directions

Take exit 41 from A9 autoroute and follow signs for Canet. On outskirts of town follow signs for St Cyprien/Plage Sud. Site is very clearly signed on southern edge of Canet Plage.
GPS: 42.6757, 3.03135

Charges guide

Per unit incl. 2 persons and electricity	€ 24.20 - € 50.20
extra person	€ 8.00 - € 15.00
child (0-5 yrs)	free - € 7.50

No credit cards.

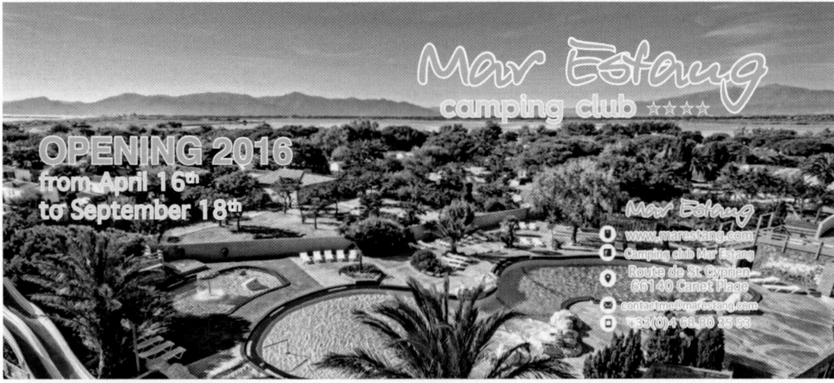

Canet-en-Roussillon

Camping les Peupliers

Avenue des Anneaux du Roussillon, F-66141 Canet-en-Roussillon (Pyrénées-Orientales) T: 04 68 80 35 87.
E: contact@camping-les-peupliers.fr **alanrogers.com/FR66720**

Camping les Peupliers is situated in the harbour area 500 m. from a fine sandy beach. It is a neat, tidy and well organised site with shade from tall trees and shrubs. There is an attractive pool complex here, a spa bath and a shallower area for children. It is a lively site in peak season with music evenings and various games and competitions. There are 245 pitches in total with 124 level, grass pitches for touring units. Most are supplied with 10A electricity. Mobile homes are available for rent.

Facilities

Two very clean sanitary blocks with facilities for disabled visitors. Baby room. Individual wash cubicles. Dog shower. Shop. Bar and snack bar. Excellent water park with water slides. Games room. Play area. Small fitness area. Activity and entertainment programme. Communal barbecue. WiFi. Mobile homes for rent. Off site: Beach 500 m. Fishing and boat launching 200 m. Golf 600 m. Riding 1 km. Spanish border 45 km.

Open: 1 May - 20 September.

Directions

From A9 take exit 41 for Le Barcarès and Caneton D83 for 10 km. Then follow D81 towards Canet-en-Roussillon. At first Canet roundabout (Ch. de Gaulle) turn fully back on yourself to Barcarès-Ste Marie. Turn right (ZA Las Bigues). At end of road, turn right, then first left to site. GPS: 42.706793, 3.030447

Charges guide

Per unit incl. 2 persons and electricity	€ 22.00 - € 54.00

Canet-en-Roussillon

Yelloh! Village le Brasilia

2 avenue Anneaux du Roussillon, F-66141 Canet-en-Roussillon (Pyrénées-Orientales)

T: 04 68 80 23 82. E: info@lebrasilia.fr **alanrogers.com/FR66070**

Situated across the yacht harbour from the resort of Canet-Plage, le Brasilia is an impressive, well managed family site directly beside the beach. The state-of-the-art reception incorporates an information centre. Although large, it is pretty, neat and well kept with an amazingly wide range of facilities – indeed, it is camping at its best. There are 418 neatly hedged touring pitches, all with electricity (6-10A) and 304 with water and drainage. They vary in size from 80 to 120 sq.m. and some of the longer pitches are suitable for two families together. There is a variety of shade from pines and flowering shrubs, with less on pitches near the beach. There are 288 pitches with mobile homes and chalets to rent (the new ones have their own gardens). The sandy beach here is busy with a beach club and a naturist section to the west of the site. An exciting pool complex with pools catering for all ages and hydrotherapy facilities for adults is overlooked by its own snack bar and restaurant. The village area of the site offers a good range of shops, a busy restaurant and bar, entertainment (including a nightclub) and clubs for children of all ages. In fact you do not need to stir from the site which is almost a resort in itself. A free tourist train runs to Canet-Plage in summer. A member of Yelloh! Village and Leading Campings group.

Facilities

Nine modern sanitary blocks are very well equipped and maintained, with British style WCs and washbasins in cabins. Good facilities for children and for disabled campers. Laundry room. Motorcaravan services. Range of shops. Gas supplies. Bars and restaurant. Renovated pool complex (heated). New wellness centre including jacuzzi, massage and beauty rooms. Play areas. Sports field. Tennis. Sporting activities. Library, games and video room. Hairdresser. Internet café and WiFi. Daily entertainment programme. Bicycle hire. Fishing. ATM. Exchange facilities. Post office. Weather forecasts.
No charcoal barbecues. Free WiFi in bar. Off site: Boat launching and sailing 500 m. Riding 5 km. Golf 12 km.

Open: 23 April - 8 October.

Directions

From A9 exit 41 (Perpignan Centre, Rivesaltes) follow signs for Le Barcarès and Canet on D83 for 10 km. then for Canet (D81). At first Canet roundabout, turn fully back on yourself (Ste Marie) and watch for Brasilia sign almost immediately on right. GPS: 42.70467, 3.03483

Charges guide

Per unit incl. 2 persons and electricity (6A)	€ 24.00 - € 60.50
extra person	€ 6.00 - € 9.00
child (3-7 yrs)	free - € 8.50
dog (max. 2)	€ 5.00

No American Express cards.

Cap d'Agde

Yelloh! Village Mer et Soleil

Chemin de Notre Dame à Saint Martin, Rochelongue, F-34300 Cap d'Agde (Hérault) T: 04 67 94 21 14.
E: contact@camping-mer-soleil.com **alanrogers.com/FR34290**

Close to Cap d'Agde, this is a popular, well equipped site which continues to impress with its innovative development and many facilities. The pool area, at the heart of the site, is particularly attractive with toboggans, whirlpool and slides as well as a gym and wellness centre. An upstairs restaurant, bar and stage overlooks this area. There are 467 pitches in traditional rows, around half taken by mobile homes and chalets (some to let, some privately owned). The touring pitches are hedged and have good shade from tall trees, all with 6A electricity. A 1 km. long path leads to the sandy beach at Rochelongue.

Facilities

Three well equipped and modern toilet blocks. Units for children. Units for disabled visitors. Washing machine. Shop. Bar, snacks and restaurant. Heated swimming pools with fun pool for children. Gym. State-of-the-art Balnéo with hydro pools, massage rooms, sauna and Turkish bath. Play area. Tennis. Archery. Bicycle hire. Sporting activities and evening entertainment. Miniclub for kids and teens. Library. Hairdresser. Doctor. Video games. TV room. Bakery. WiFi over site (charged).

Open: 11 April - 3 October.

Directions

From A9 exit 34, follow N312 for Agde. It joins the N112 Béziers-Sète road. Cross bridge over Hérault river and turn right for Rochelongue. Take the second exit at next roundabout and site is a little further on the right. GPS: 43.286183, 3.478

Charges guide

Per unit incl. 2 persons and electricity	€ 18.00 - € 47.00
extra person	€ 4.00 - € 8.00

Carcassonne

Camping la Cité

Route de Saint Hilaire, F-11000 Carcassonne (Aude) T: 04 68 10 01 00. E: camping@carcassonne.fr
alanrogers.com/FR11100

A visit to the medieval city of Carcassonne is a must and Camping la Cité is within walking distance along a shaded footpath beside a stream. The majority of pitches are very large, separated by hedges and with good shade. There are also some undefined places under trees for small tents. In total there are 200, with 143 for touring, 95 having 10A electricity and the rest used for mobile homes and chalets to hire. Because of its situation it is very popular and you need to arrive early in the high season. A swimming pool, snack bar/restaurant make this a very comfortable and useful site.

Facilities

Three traditional, fully equipped toilet blocks. Laundry. Motorcaravan services. Fridge hire. Bar and snack bar/restaurant with takeaway meals (limited opening outside July/Aug). TV and games room. Multisports pitch. Swimming and paddling pools (15/6-15/9). Play area. Entertainment (July/Aug). Communal barbecue. Chalets and mobile homes to rent. WiFi (charged). Off site: Bicycle hire 2 km. Riding 3 km. Lake with beaches 6 km.

Open: 23 March - 5 October.

Directions

From A61 autoroute take exit 24 onto N113 following signs for la Cité. Site signed (look carefully) from all roads into the city. Avoid arrival 12.00 and 14.00 outside July/Aug – reception is closed and queues block entrance. GPS: 43.200315, 2.353767

Charges guide

Per unit incl. 2 persons and electricity	€ 32.50 - € 50.60
extra person	€ 6.00 - € 9.10

Clapiers

Camping le Plein Air des Chênes

Route de Castelnau, F-34830 Clapiers (Hérault) T: 04 67 02 02 53. E: pleinairdeschenes@sandaya.fr
alanrogers.com/FR34230

Le Plein Air des Chênes is situated just outside the village of Clapiers, about 5 km. from the interesting city of Montpellier, yet merely 20 km. from a choice of Mediterranean beaches. However, the site itself has much to offer, with an amazing pool complex with toboggans, cascades, pools and a wonderful children's pool area. In the main season there is plenty of entertainment. There are 73 touring pitches with 10A electricity (some large with individual toilet cabin), all in a shaded, terraced setting. There are some 175 chalets and mobile homes to rent, mixed in with the touring pitches.

Facilities

Two well equipped modern toilet blocks provide washbasins in cabins and facilities for babies and disabled visitors. Washing machines. Fridge hire. Excellent restaurant open to the public. Bar, pool side bar, café/takeaway (1/6-15/9). Swimming pools (1/6-15/9; mornings reserved for campers). Aqua bicycles. Tennis courts. Multisports court. Play area. Miniclub. Evening entertainment in main season. WiFi over site (charged). Off site: Shops in Clapiers 800 m. Montpellier 5 km.

Open: April - October.

Directions

Site is north of Montpellier, 8 km. from A9. Exit 28 on N113 towards Montpellier passing Vendargues. Follow signs for Millau on D65, then Clapiers and follow site signs. GPS: 43.65135, 3.89607

Charges guide

Per unit incl. 2 persons and electricity	€ 25.00 - € 48.00
incl. water and drainage	€ 20.00 - € 59.00
extra person	€ 4.00 - € 9.00

Crespian

Camping le Mas de Reilhe

Chemin du Mas de Reilhe, F-30260 Crespian (Gard) T: 04 66 77 82 12. E: info@camping-mas-de-reilhe.fr

alanrogers.com/FR30080

This is a pleasant family site in the heart of the Gard region with a favourable climate. There are 92 pitches, 64 for tourers, 60 have electricity (10A), 31 also have water and waste water and some of the upper ones may require long leads. The large lower pitches are separated by tall poplar trees and hedges, close to the main facilities but may experience some road noise. The large terraced pitches on the hillside are scattered under mature pine trees, some with good views, more suited to tents and trailer tents but with their own modern sanitary facilities. The heated swimming pool and spa is in a sunny position and overlooked by an attractive bar/restaurant. There are no shops in the village, the nearest being in the medieval city of Sommières 10 km. away (and well worth a visit). From here you can explore the Cévennes gorges, enjoy the Mediterranean beaches, visit the Petite Camargue or Nîmes with its Roman remains, and other old Roman cities. In July and August, there are clubs for children (from 4 years), sports competitions and evening entertainment for adults.

Facilities

Excellent, very clean toilet blocks with facilities for disabled visitors. Laundry. Motorcaravan services. Limited shop (bread to order). Bar, restaurant and takeaway (1/6-4/9). Heated swimming and paddling pools and spa (1/5-18/9). TV room. Trampolines. Fitness area. Multisports court. Pétanque. Bicycle hire. Fridge hire. Only gas or electric barbecues on pitches. Communal barbecue area. Internet access. WiFi over site (charged). Off site: Marked walking and cycling routes 500 m. Fishing 3 km. Riding 10 km. Golf 25 km. The sea and the gorges are about 30 km. and Nîmes 25 km.

Open: 23 April - 18 September.

Directions

From the A9 take exit 25, Nîmes-ouest signed Alès, then D999 towards Le Vigan (about 23 km). Turn north on the D6110, site shortly on right at southern edge of Crespian. Entrance is on a bend - care needed. GPS: 43.87931, 4.09637

Charges guide

Per unit incl. 2 persons and electricity	€ 20.90 - € 31.90
extra person	€ 5.50 - € 7.40
child (2-6 yrs)	free - € 6.50

Camping Cheques accepted.

Camping Le Mas de Reilhe****
SPECIAL OFFERS IN LOW SEASON
Camping Qualité
www.camping-mas-de-reilhe.fr
info@camping-mas-de-reilhe.fr
Le Mas de Reilhe
Camping Le Mas de Reilhe
30260 CRESPIAN
Tel : 33 (0)4 66 77 82 12

Fontès

Camping les Clairettes

Route de Péret D128, F-34320 Fontès (Hérault) T: 04 67 25 01 31. E: info@campinglesclairettes.net

alanrogers.com/FR34715

Les Clairettes is a quiet, all year, family site situated among vines and olive trees in the Hérault countryside, west of Montpellier. It is within easy reach of Cap d'Agde and neighbouring beaches and resorts. There are just 75 pitches of which 19 are for tourers with 10A electricity and a number of mobile homes and caravans, both private and for hire. A small bar and a pleasant swimming pool with a paddling pool provide opportunities for relaxation on site, and the nearby town of Paulhan has a range of shops, bars and restaurants. The Lac du Salagou is a short drive (or cycle ride) away.

Facilities

Heated toilet block with hot showers, baby room, launderette and ironing facilities. Basic shop with bread to order. Bar/snack bar with TV and takeaway. Outdoor swimming and paddling pools (1/6-30/9). TV room. Playground. Games field. Boules. Volleyball. Activities for all in high season. WiFi (charged). Off site: Riding 100 m. Village 1.7 km. Fishing 4 km. Paulhan 4.5 km.

Open: All year.

Directions

Adissan is 45 km. due west of Montpellier. From A75 autoroute leave at exit 58 for Paulhan and Adissan. Head northwest on D128 through Adissan. Site is almost 1 km. on right after village. GPS: 43.54491, 3.41742

Charges guide

Per unit incl. 2 persons and electricity	€ 15.00 - € 22.00

Font-Romeu

Huttopia Font-Romeu

Route de Mont-Louis, F-66120 Font-Romeu (Pyrénées-Orientales) T: 04 68 30 09 32.
E: font-romeu@huttopia.com **alanrogers.com/FR66250**

This is a large, open site of some seven hectares, with 123 touring pitches (72 with 10A electricity), nestling on the side of the mountain at the entrance to Font-Romeu. This part of the Pyrenees offers some staggering views and the famous Mont Louis is close by. An ideal base for climbing, hiking and cycling, it would also provide a good stopover for a night or so whilst travelling between Spain and France, or to and from Andorra. The terraced pitches for caravans and motorcaravans are at the top of the site, whilst tents go on the lower slopes. Trees provide shade to many of the pitches.

Facilities

Three bright and clean toilet blocks. Toilet for children and excellent facilities for disabled visitors. Laundry facilities. Shop (for basics). Bar, restaurant and takeaway service (weekends only outside July/Aug). Outdoor heated swimming pool. Large games hall. No charcoal barbecues (communal area available). Max. 1 dog. Off site: Bicycle hire 300 m. Golf and riding 2 km. The small town of Font-Romeu is very near. Beach 8 km.

Open: 16 June - 12 September.

Directions

Font-Romeu is on the D118, some 12 km. after it branches off the N116 heading west, just after Mont Louis. An interesting road with magnificent views. Site is just before the town, on the left and accessed before the public car park. GPS: 42.50593, 2.04564

Charges guide

Per unit incl. 2 persons and electricity	€ 21.80 - € 40.30
extra person	€ 5.80 - € 7.70

Frontignan-Plage

Camping les Tamaris

140 avenue d'Ingril, F-34110 Frontignan-Plage (Hérault) T: 04 67 43 44 77. E: les-tamaris@wanadoo.fr
alanrogers.com/FR34440

This is a super site, unusually situated on a strip of land that separates the sea from the étang, or inland lake, and therefore Frontignan-Ville from Frontignan-Plage. We were lucky enough to see flamingos when we visited. The design of the site is unusual which adds to its attractiveness. The pitches are laid out in hexagons divided by tall hedging and colourful shrubs. In total, there are 250 pitches with 100 taken by mobile homes which are let by the site. All are 'grand confort' with 10A electricity, water and waste water and on level sandy grass. Direct access to the sandy beach is possible via three gates.

Facilities

Three modern and colourful toilet blocks with some en-suite showers and washbasins. Excellent facilities for children. Unit for disabled visitors. Motorcaravan services. Shop, bar, restaurant, takeaway, swimming pool. Hairdresser. Gym. Play area. Miniclub. Archery. Bicycle hire. Fishing. Internet access in reception and WiFi throughout (free). Entertainment for all ages. Charcoal barbecues only. Off site: Riding 150 m. Sailing 1 km. Boat launching 2.5 km. Golf 15 km.

Open: 3 April - 28 September.

Directions

From north on A9 take exit 32 and follow N112 towards Sète and Frontignan. After 16 km. ignore sign for Frontignan town and continue to Frontignan-Plage following site signs along road between the sea and étang for 2 km. GPS: 43.44970, 3.80603

Charges guide

Per unit incl. 2 persons and all services	€ 28.00 - € 51.00
extra person	€ 6.00 - € 9.50

No credit cards.

Goudargues

Camping les Amarines

La Vérune Cornillon, F-30630 Goudargues (Gard) T: 04 66 82 24 92. E: les.amarines@wanadoo.fr
alanrogers.com/FR30340

In the heart of the picturesque Southern French valley of the River Cèze, Amarines offers a friendly family atmosphere and you will be made most welcome. This rural site is a good place to enjoy a restful and relaxing stay. It is well equipped and under good professional family management. The site has 120 spacious, grass pitches separated by tall hedges, all with 6A electricity. There is plenty of shade, yet many spots bask in the southern sunshine. The swimming pool is heated all season and the small bar offers a pleasant atmosphere.

Facilities

One very well equipped toilet block. Provision for wheelchair users is good. Toilet for children. Baby bath and changing mat. Good quality laundry facilities. Limited restaurant service and takeaways. Heated swimming pool (1/4-30/9). Summer entertainment programme. WiFi throughout. Off site: Small village Goudargues 1 km. Hiking trails, horse and pony rides, tennis courts. Caves, museums and tourist train.

Open: 28 March - 3 October.

Directions

From the A7 exit 19 (Bollène) take D994 to Pont-St Esprit and the N86 south towards Bagnols-sur-Cèze. Shortly before Bagnols turn right onto D980 to Cornillon. Site is signed. GPS: 44.219946, 4.479858

Charges guide

Per unit incl. 2 persons and electricity	€ 20.50 - € 27.60
extra person	€ 3.40 - € 5.90
child (2-7 yrs)	€ 2.00 - € 2.80

Goudargues

Camping la Grenouille

Avenue du Lavoir, F-30630 Goudargues (Gard) T: 04 66 82 21 36. E: campingard@orange.fr

alanrogers.com/FR30740

Situated in the centre of Goudargues (the Venice of the Gard), close to the Cèze river, la Grenouille is a gem of a campsite. A friendly welcome is guaranteed from Renaud who takes great pride in keeping the 50 grassy, hedged, mostly shaded touring pitches and first class facilities neat and tidy. All have 6A or 10A electricity connections (long leads may be required for some). Most are easily accessible and there are views of the historic village and church. Care should be taken with small children as a shallow stream runs through the site. In Goudargues (a short walk) you will find shops, bars and restaurants.

Facilities

Two sanitary blocks include washbasins in cabins and hot showers. Good facilities for disabled visitors. Baby bath. Laundry facilities. Motorcaravan service point. Fridge hire. Enclosed swimming pool (1/4-15/9, no Bermudas). Paddling pool. Playground. Fishing in river. Free WiFi on part of site. Tourist information. Off site: Shops, restaurants and bars in village. Kayak and canoe hire (5 minutes' walk). Riding 1 km.

Open: 1 April - 25 September.

Directions

From the A7 take exit 19 to Bollène. Take D994 to Pont St-Esprit and the N86 south to Bagnols-sur-Cèze. Shortly before Bagnols turn west, D980 to Goudargues. In Goudargues turn south and site is well signed. GPS: 44.21428, 4.468877

Charges guide

Per unit incl. 2 persons and electricity	€ 18.40 - € 25.50
extra person	€ 2.00 - € 5.50

Ispagnac

Camping du Pré Morjal

Pré Morjal, F-48320 Ispagnac (Lozère) T: 04 66 45 43 57. E: lepremorjal@gmail.com

alanrogers.com/FR48090

Le Pré Morjal lies at the head of the Tarn Gorges with easy access, so would be ideal for large units with secondary transport to explore the spectacular gorges and the Cévennes National Park. The site is very welcoming and peaceful with a good range of amenities but no organised activities, only live music once a week in high season. It offers a real sense of getting back to nature. There are 123 good sized, level, grassy pitches with 107 for touring. Most have shade and all have electrical connections (10A), long leads may be required for some.

Facilities

Three adequate, heated toilet blocks include provision for children and disabled campers. Motorcaravan services. Bar (soft drinks only; all season). Heated outdoor swimming and paddling pools (15/6-1/9). Play area. Communal room with TV, library, pool table. Volleyball. Entertainment and activities (July/Aug). Gas and electric barbecues only. Communal barbecue. WiFi (free in bar area). Off site: Fishing 100 m. Riding 400 m.

Open: 3 April - 2 November.

Directions

Leave A75 autoroute, exit 39 (Le Monastier). Take N88 east to Balsièges (25 km). Then turn southeast on N106. After 26 km. turn east on D907 (Ispagnac). Site signed in village. GPS: 44.372168, 3.530474

Charges guide

Per unit incl. 2 persons and electricity	€ 16.10 - € 22.30
extra person	€ 3.10 - € 4.30
child (under 13 yrs)	€ 2.00 - € 3.20

La Palme

Flower Camping Domaine de la Palme

79 chemin du Stade, F-11480 La Palme (Aude) T: 04 68 48 50 40. E: info@camping-la-palme.com

alanrogers.com/FR11360

Domaine de la Palme was a run down municipal site until three years ago when Delphine and Michel Munck bought it. They have worked hard to upgrade it and provide good clean facilities and some unusual tents to rent. The site is situated on the edge of the village, next to the sports stadium and close to the salt étang, with the beach and sea beyond. Of the 69 level grass pitches, 42 are for touring units. They are of a good size and divided by low fencing and the odd shrub; all have 6/10A electricity. Rental accommodation includes mobile homes, chalets and wooden pods in addition to two bivouac tents.

Facilities

One central toilet block is fully equipped with some washbasins in cabins and preset showers. Facilities for disabled visitors. Washing machine. Bread and pastries to order. Tennis. Small play area. Children's club (weekly in July/Aug). Bicycle hire. Only gas or electric barbecues. Communal barbecue. Outside TV. Free WiFi on part of site. Off site: Shop within walking distance. Windsurfing. Birdwatching. Fishing 1 km. Beach 5 km. Riding 10 km.

Open: 1 April - 30 September.

Directions

Take A9 autoroute exit 39 signed Sigean/Port Nouvelle but pick up D6009/La Palme. Do not take first turn for La Palme but second (D709) and continue 1-2 km. until left turning for village. Watch for immediate left turn for site. GPS: 42.97254, 2.99783

Charges guide

Per unit incl. 2 persons and electricity	€ 14.50 - € 23.00
extra person	€ 3.50 - € 5.00

La Grande Motte

Camping le Garden

44 place des Tamaris, F-34280 La Grande Motte (Hérault) T: 04 67 56 50 09. E: campinglegarden@orange.fr
alanrogers.com/FR34020

Le Garden is a well cared for and pretty site, situated amongst tall pines and flowering shrubs, some 400 m. back from a fine sandy beach at La Grande Motte. The pitches are of a good size (100 sq.m) on sandy grass. There are 121 mobile homes to rent and 86 touring pitches, most with 10A electricity, water and drainage. An attractive pool is overlooked by the restaurant. The site also has a small 'centre commercial' with a range of shops and a bar next door, which is open to the public. Le Garden is a very comfortable and well ordered site (possible road noise during the day) within pleasant walking distance of the town centre and port. La Grande Motte is a product of the sixties tourist boom when much building went on, and at the time the apartment blocks seemed very futuristic. It has now matured into a smart, upmarket seaside resort with plenty of green space. There is much to see in the area, being on the edge of the Petite Camargue and only a few kilometres from the old walled town of Aigues-Mortes. A regular bus service (half hourly) runs from outside the site to Montpellier and other places.

Facilities

Three well situated toilet blocks, smartly refurbished, include washbasins in cabins and baby bath. Laundry facilities. Unit for disabled visitors. Shops with groceries, cigarettes, newspapers and boutique (1/3-30/9). Bar, restaurant and takeaway on site (15/5-30/9). Swimming pool and paddling pool (15/5-30/9). Play area. TV room. Internet access and WiFi. Gas and electric barbecues only. Off site: Beach 400 m. Tennis, riding, bicycle hire and boat launching 500 m. Golf and fishing 2 km.

Open: 1 April - 15 October.

Directions

Entering La Grande Motte from D62 dual carriageway, keep right following 'campings' signs and petite Motte. Right at traffic lights by the casino, and right again by the Bar Le Garden. Site is almost immediately on right. GPS: 43.56322, 4.07278

Charges guide

Per unit incl. 1-3 persons, electricity, water and drainage	€ 44.00
extra person	€ 9.80
dog	€ 2.00

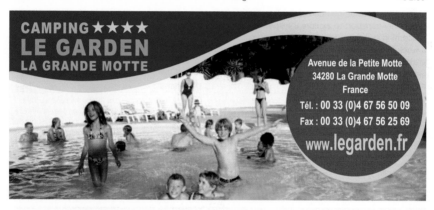

Laroque des Albères

Camping des Albères

Route Moulin Cassagnes, F-66740 Laroque des Albères (Pyrénées-Orientales) T: 04 68 89 23 64.
E: lesalberes@cybelevacances.com **alanrogers.com/FR66900**

In the Languedoc Roussillon region of the Pyrénées Orientales, Camping des Albères lies between the Pyrenees mountains and the Mediterranean sea at the foot of the Massif des Albères. There are 124 touring pitches, 105 with electricity (16A) and three also with water, located in a grove of oak trees and mimosa, together with 87 mobile homes, chalets and tents to rent. The swimming and paddling pool area has expansive views of the Pyrenees and the site is very well situated for exploring both coastal and inland areas. The well known resorts of Collioure and Argelès are nearby.

Facilities

Sanitary facilities with provision for disabled visitors. Separate baby room. Laundry. Restaurant and bar, snack bar, grocery, bread and pastries (all July/Aug). Swimming pool and paddling pool (a new indoor pool should be ready for 2016). Playground. Basketball. Volleyball. Entertainment and activities (July/Aug). Fridges for hire. Bicycle hire. No charcoal barbecues. WiFi at bar (charged). Off site: Nearby off-road biking and walks.

Open: 4 April - 26 September.

Directions

Camping des Albères is south of Perpignan. From Perpignan take A9/E15 south to Le Boulou, exit 43, then D115 and D618 (Argelès/Port Vendres). Exit at Laroque des Albères slip road. Take D50 for 3 km. to village, follow signs. GPS: 42.52396, 2.94403

Charges guide

Per unit inc. 2 persons and electricity	€ 19.00 - € 31.00
extra person	€ 5.00 - € 6.00

Le Barcarès

Camping Club le Floride et l'Embouchure

Route de Saint Laurent, F-66420 Port-Barcarès (Pyrénées-Orientales) T: 04 68 86 11 75.
E: campingfloride@orange.fr **alanrogers.com/FR66290**

A well established and multilingual, family run enterprise, le Floride et l'Embouchure is really two sites in one – l'Embouchure the smaller one with direct access to the beach and le Floride on the opposite side of the road. Fifty pitches have their own individual sanitary facility and in total the site offers 632 reasonably sized pitches, 140 for touring, all with 10A electricity. A good range of chalets and mobile homes are available for rent, including a recent Polynesian-style village. It is relatively inexpensive, especially outside the July/August peak period and the majority of the facilities are open from 1st May. The busy town of Le Barcarès is within easy walking distance and has an increasing range of shops and supermarkets. The Voie Verte runs for 15 km. from Le Barcarès to Rivesaltes alongside the River Agly, which borders l'Embouchure and is popular with cyclists, walkers, runners and roller skaters.

Facilities

Four fully equipped toilet blocks on le Floride and two on l'Embouchure where 50 pitches near the beach have individual facilities. Facilities for babies and disabled visitors. Family shower room. Motorcaravan services. Shop, bar, and restaurant (from 10/4), takeaway (15/6-5/9). Excellent pool complex with indoor heated pool. Play area. Multisports court. Gym. Tennis. Bicycle hire. Multilingual entertainment and sports programmes (1/5-30/9). No charcoal barbecues. Max. 1 dog. WiFi over site (free). Off site: Beach 100 m. Fishing 1 km. Riding 1.5 km.

Open: 1 April - 2 October.

Directions

From A9 take exit 41 (Perpignan Nord) and follow signs for Canet and Le Barcarès via D83. At exit 9 follow D81 (Canet) then next left into Le Barcarès Village. Site is 1 km. on the left and right sides of the road. GPS: 42.77855, 3.0301

Charges guide

Per unit incl. 2 persons and electricity	€ 16.90 - € 49.70
incl. individual sanitary facility	€ 19.00 - € 58.60
extra person	€ 2.90 - € 6.70
child (1-3 yrs)	free - € 3.90
dog	€ 5.00 - € 8.00

Le Barcarès

Yelloh! Village le Pré Catalan

Route de Saint Laurent, F-66420 Le Barcarès (Pyrénées-Orientales) T: 04 68 86 12 60.
E: info@yellohvillage-pre-catalan.com **alanrogers.com/FR66300**

The green foliage from the mixed trees and the flowering shrubs makes this 4.5-hectare site very attractive. There has been a campsite here since 1960, but the present owners, the Galidie family, took over in 1982 and the site is now run to a very high standard by their son, François, and his English wife, Jenny. With 250 pitches in total, 140 are taken by mobile homes and chalets, either to let or privately owned. These are mixed amongst the 80 touring pitches which are on level, sandy ground, clearly divided by hedging and all with 10A electricity. An upstairs bar overlooks the attractive pool complex.

Facilities

Good modern facilities include small showers for children. Laundry. Small shop. Bar, restaurant and takeaway. Heated swimming pool complex including fun pools, whirlpool and paddling pool. Excellent play area. Tennis. Archery. Internet access. Library. Activities for children with miniclub and evening entertainment (most of the season). Bicycle hire. No charcoal barbecues. WiFi over site (charged). Off site: Beach 900 m. River fishing 1 km.

Open: 25 April - 20 September.

Directions

From A9 exit 41 (Perpignan Nord), follow signs for Le Barcarès and Canet (D83). At exit 9 take D81 (Canet), then first left to Le Barcarès (D90). Site is on left after 500 m. next to Le California. Follow narrow lane to site entrance. GPS: 42.78106, 3.02282

Charges guide

Per unit incl. 2 persons and electricity	€ 18.00 - € 44.00
extra person	€ 5.00 - € 8.00

Le Barcarès

Camping California

F-66423 Le Barcarès (Pyrénées-Orientales) T: 04 68 86 16 08. E: camping-california@wanadoo.fr
alanrogers.com/FR66770

Situated just outside Le Bacarés and close to five miles of sandy beaches, Camping California is located beside a busy main road – however, traffic noise is light on most pitches. The 81 separated touring pitches are 80-100 sq.m. in size and have 10A electricity (long cables may be needed). There are a further 179 pitches occupied by mobile homes and chalets, 28 of which are privately owned and the rest are available to rent. This is an extremely busy site in high season when daytime and evening entertainment is organised and this can be noisy.

Facilities

Two toilet blocks include individual cabins, hot showers, toilets and facilities for babies and visitors with disabilities. Laundry. Shop (15/6-15/8). Bar, restaurant and takeaway. Swimming pool, paddling pool and slide. Outdoor fitness centre. Large field for games. Entertainment and club for children in high season. Excursions. WiFi on part of site (charged). Off site: Watersports, riding, fishing and golf. Carcassonne, Perpignan, Barcelona, Pyrénées.

Open: 1 May - 28 September.

Directions

From the A9 take exit 41 (Perpignan-Nord) and follow signs for Le Barcarés. After 9 km. take exit 9 (Canet/Toreilles), then first right to Le Barcarés village. Pass under the motorway (passing Lidl) and site is third on the left. GPS: 42.77588, 3.02279

Charges guide

Per unit incl. 2 persons and electricity	€ 14.50 - € 44.50
extra person	€ 4.00 - € 8.00

Le Barcarès

Camping l'Ile des Pêcheurs

Route des Sanills, F-66420 Le Barcarès (Pyrénées-Orientales) T: 04 68 73 66 00.
E: iledespecheurs@franceloc.fr **alanrogers.com/FR66920**

This is a FranceLoc holiday complex and there are no touring pitches here. There are two types of accommodation: the Mas are large oval huts with reed roofs which recall the traditional dwellings of the Catalan fisher-folk; the Marinas are houses with tiled roofs and colourful facades. On the Mediterranean coast close to the Catalan Pyrenees, l'Ile des Pêcheurs has been designed to 'recreate an atmosphere of an authentic village, where generous green spaces complement the private gardens and central village square, where various services and activities are brought together'.

Facilities

Small supermarket. Restaurant, bar, snack bar and takeaway. Aquatic area with two pools (one heated in low season), paddling pool with slides. Jacuzzi. Sauna. Hammam. 'Activ' club. Aerobics. Volleyball. Pétanque. Canoe tour. Football. Badminton. Water polo. Miniclub with crafts, sporting activities and games. Teenagers' club with canyoning, diving, rafting and hydro-speed. Evening entertainment and music. WiFi. Off site: Minigolf 500 m.

Open: 28 March - 31 October.

Directions

L'Ile des Pêcheurs is 24 km. northeast of Perpignan. From north on A9 motorway (La Catalane), leave at exit 40 (Leucate) and follow D627 towards Port Barcarès for about 20 km. Take exit 13 La Grande Plage/Coudalère and at roundabout turn right then right again after 500 m. GPS: 42.82075, 3.02535

Charges guide

Contact the site for details.

Le Grau-du-Roi

Camping Caravaning le Boucanet

B.P. 206, route de Carnon, F-30240 Le Grau-du-Roi (Gard) T: 04 66 51 41 48. E: boucanet@franceloc.fr
alanrogers.com/FR30160

Le Boucanet has a superb situation beside the beach between La Grande Motte and Le Grau-du-Roi, and we received a friendly welcome. Many trees have been planted and give some shade. The 462 pitches are sandy and are on the small side, but they are level and all have 6A electricity (long leads and adaptors useful). The 122 touring pitches are mixed amongst those used for mobile homes and chalets and are separated by small bushes. There are five pitches with hardstanding. Plenty of flowers decorate the site and the pleasant restaurant (open lunchtimes and evenings) overlooks the pool area.

Facilities

The fully equipped toilet blocks include facilities for disabled visitors. Baby rooms. Laundry facilities. Fridge hire. Motorcaravan services. Range of shops, restaurant, bar, snacks and takeaway. Large swimming pool, smaller covered pool, toboggans and paddling pool. Large castle adventure play area (4-13 yrs). Miniclub (July/Aug). Bicycle hire. Hire of windsurfing boards, pedalos, kayaks (July/Aug and w/ends). WiFi in some areas (free). Gas barbecues only. No dogs. Off site: Riding 500 m.

Open: 3 April - 27 September.

Directions

Site is between La Grande Motte and Le Grau-du-Roi on the D255 coastal road, on the seaward side of the road. GPS: 43.5543, 4.11749

Charges guide

Per unit incl. 2 persons and electricity	€ 24.00 - € 41.00
extra person	€ 6.00 - € 9.00
child (2-7 yrs)	€ 4.50 - € 7.90

Le Grau-du-Roi

Yelloh! Village Secrets de Camargue

Route de l'Espiguette, F-30240 Le Grau-du-Roi (Gard) T: 04 66 80 08 00.
E: info@yellohvillage-secrets-de-camargue.com **alanrogers.com/FR30380**

Les Secrets de Camargue is part of the same group as la Petite Camargue and les Petits Camarguais, and is of the same high standard. Les Secrets, however, is rather special for two reasons: firstly, it is reserved for over 18s and for families with children under 3 years old; secondly, it is environmentally aware and the identity of the Camargue area is maintained by careful planting and the use of thatch and timber. This can be clearly seen in the pool area, which appears to blend seamlessly into the sand dunes beyond. In total there are 177 pitches with 26 for touring units (with 10A electricity) on level sandy grass. The remainder of the pitches are for mobile homes and chalets all with thatched roofs.

Facilities

Fully equipped sanitary block includes excellent provision for babies and facilities for disabled visitors. Small shop (2/4-19/9). Bar/restaurant (all season). Heated swimming pool. Aquagym. Bicycle hire. Small play area (under 3s). Activities and entertainment. Mobile homes and chalets for rent. Off site: Large shop at les Petites Camargues 400 m. Riding 800 m. Beach 1.5 km. Fishing 5 km.

Open: 12 April - 11 October.

Directions

Leave the A9 at exit for Gallargues and head for Aigues-Mortes on the D979. Continue to Le Grau-du-Roi and then follow signs to Port Camargue on the D62, continuing to join the D255. Site is well signed from this point. GPS: 43.48736, 4.14202

Charges guide

Per unit incl. 2 persons	€ 18.00 - € 52.00
extra person	€ 5.00 - € 9.00

Le Vigan

Camping le Val de l'Arre

Route du Pont de la Croix, F-30120 Le Vigan (Gard) T: 04 67 81 02 77. E: valdelarre@wanadoo.fr
alanrogers.com/FR30230

Camping Val de l'Arre is situated along the Arre river, a tributary of the Hérault river and in the centre of the Cévennes National Park. The site is well managed by the very friendly Triaire family. There are 170 grassy, level pitches, 135 for touring, many have some shade and most have electricity (10A). There is a pleasant swimming pool with an outdoor bar. A pebble beach at the river bank provides opportunities for play and fishing enthusiasts will also certainly appreciate the river. There are numerous possibilities for outdoor activities such as white-water rafting, canoeing and mountain biking.

Facilities

Three clean and well appointed toilet blocks include controllable showers. Facilities for babies and disabled visitors. Washing machines. Motorcaravan services. Shop and open-air snack bar, restaurant and takeaway (1/6-31/8). Swimming and paddling pools (1/6-15/9). Boules. Play area. Guided walks organised. WiFi over site (charged). Off site: Bicycle hire 2.5 km. Riding 5 km. Many opportunities for walkers, cyclists and mountain bikers.

Open: 1 April - 30 September.

Directions

Leave A75 at exit 48 and follow D7 and then D999 east to Le Vigan (43 km). Drive through town, signed Nîmes, at roundabout turn right D110D, site signed. Cross river, turn left, site in 800 m.
GPS: 43.992067, 3.6374

Charges guide

Per unit incl. 2 persons and electricity	€ 19.00 - € 28.00
extra person	€ 4.50 - € 7.50

Lézignan-Corbières

Camping la Pinède

Rue des Rousillons, F-11200 Lézignan-Corbières (Aude) T: 04 68 27 05 08. E: reception@campinglapinede.fr
alanrogers.com/FR11030

Within walking distance of the town and only 28 km. from Narbonne Plage, la Pinède is set on terraces on a hillside, with good internal access on made-up roads, but some up-and-down walking. The 66 individual, level pitches vary in size and are divided up mainly by various trees and shrubs with 6A electricity (20 mobile homes and two lodge tents). There is now a very pleasant terrace with a restaurant with good 'plat du jour'. Wine tasting and local walks are organised. Outside the gates are a municipal swimming pool (free June-Sept), a restaurant and tennis courts.

Facilities

Three fully equipped sanitary blocks, one with facilities for babies, are a little dated. Not all blocks are opened outside high season. Outdoor heated swimming pool (1/6-30/9). Washing machine. Motorcaravan services. Gas. Bar and restaurant (July/Aug). Fresh vegetables can be sampled from the garden (small charge). Shop, restaurant and takeaway (20/6-31/8). Communal barbecue only. Torches necessary. Caravan storage. WiFi throughout (free). Off site: Town centre 500 m.

Open: 1 April - 30 October.

Directions

Access is directly off the main N113 on west side of Lézignan-Corbières. From A61 (to avoid low bridge) exit at Carcassonne or Narbonne onto N113 and follow to site. GPS: 43.2046, 2.7526

Charges guide

Per unit incl. 2 persons and electricity	€ 14.70 - € 18.30
extra person	€ 4.00 - € 5.00
child (under 10 yrs)	€ 2.30 - € 3.70

Marseillan-Plage

Camping les Méditerranées Beach Garden

Avenue des campings, F-34340 Marseillan-Plage (Hérault) T: 04 67 21 92 83.
E: info@beach-garden-camping.com **alanrogers.com/FR34155**

Under the same ownership as Les Méditerranées Beach Club, but further along the road, with beach access and views across the Bagnas Nature Reserve. This is a pretty site with a mixture of trees and shrubs. In all it provides 653 pitches with 350 for touring units on mainly level, sandy grass with a variety of shade and 6A electricity. The remainder are occupied by mobile homes and by tour operators. The site is divided by the beach road, with all the facilities on the beach side. They are comprehensive and excellent with a rather stylish upstairs restaurant overlooking the pool area, sea and countryside.

Facilities

One large, newly renovated toilet block has cold water to washbasins, controllable hot showers, a baby bath and an en-suite unit for disabled visitors. Laundry. Shop. Bar, restaurant and takeaway. Good sized swimming pool area with children's pool and sunbathing space. Miniclub (5-12 yrs), sporting activities and evening entertainment. Motorcaravan services. Free WiFi in bar area. No charcoal barbecues. Shuttle to Sète, Agde and Cap d'Agde (high season). Off site: Riding 2 km. Fishing 5 km. Golf 7 km.

Open: 12 April - 27 September.

Directions

From A9 autoroute exit 34, follow N312 towards Agde, then follow N112 for Sète. About 5 km. after Agde turn right at first roundabout then right again at end of road. Go past the first Les Méditerranées camping to site. GPS: 43.30583, 3.53797

Charges guide

Per unit incl. 2 persons and electricity	€ 19.00 - € 51.00
extra person	€ 6.00 - € 10.00

Marseillan-Plage

Camping la Créole

74 avenue des Campings, F-34340 Marseillan-Plage (Hérault) T: 04 67 21 92 69.
E: campinglacreole@orange.fr **alanrogers.com/FR34220**

This is a surprisingly tranquil, well cared for small campsite in the middle of this bustling resort and will appeal to those seeking rather less of the frenetic ambience typical of many sites in this area. The Chaput family, who run the site, originally worked the land as a vineyard but developed it into a campsite in 1973. It offers 100 good sized, level, sandy pitches, all with 6A electricity and most with shade from mature trees and shrubs. There are also 18 mobile homes available to rent. It benefits from direct access to an extensive sandy beach (secure gated access).

Facilities

Good sanitary facilities include some washbasins in private cabins, a baby room and en-suite facilities for disabled visitors. Motorcaravan services. Newly developed fitness and sports area near the beach. Beach games, dances, sangria evenings for families (July/Aug) along with a small bar/snack bar (all season). Only gas barbecues on pitches. Communal barbecue area. WiFi over site (charged). Off site: Bicycle hire 100 m.

Open: 1 April - 11 October.

Directions

From A9 exit 34 take N312 towards Agde, then N112 towards Sète keeping a look-out for signs to Marseillan-Plage off this road. Site is well signed in Marseillan-Plage. GPS: 43.3206, 3.5501

Charges guide

Per unit incl. 2 persons and electricity	€ 18.00 - € 38.00
extra person (over 2 yrs)	€ 3.00 - € 7.00

Meyrueis

Camping Caravaning le Jardin des Cévennes

Route de la Brèze, F-48150 Meyrueis (Lozère) T: 04 66 45 60 51. E: infocamping@jardindescevennes.com
alanrogers.com/FR48000

You can be sure of a warm welcome at this traditional, family run site, set in the heart of the Cévennes and its magnificent gorges. Le Jardin des Cévennes is well kept and run with young families in mind. The 90 slightly sloping grass pitches, 66 for touring, are mostly shady and hedged. All have electricity (6/10A) but some may require long leads. The site is ideally situated only a few minutes' walk from the picturesque market town of Meyreuis with its narrow streets, colourful shops and Wednesday market. The area has some narrow, winding roads, which may be challenging for large and underpowered units.

Facilities

The toilet block is kept very clean and has all the necessary facilities. A new block is planned. Baby room. Facilities for disabled visitors. Laundry facilities. Shop and small bar (from 1/5) and takeaway (1/6-20/9). Heated swimming and paddling pools (from 20/5). Play area. Games room. Boules. Activities arranged (July/Aug). Communal barbecue. Charcoal barbecues not permitted. WiFi throughout (charged). Off site: The small town of Meyrueis (500 m) has many good shops and restaurants.

Open: 29 April - 20 September.

Directions

Leave A75 at exit 44-1, east on D29 through Aquessac, D907 to Le Rozier then D996 to Meyrueis. In Meyrueis (narrow roads) cross river and follow signs for Ayres. Site is 500 m. east of the town. GPS: 44.18077, 3.43507

Charges guide

Per unit incl. 2 persons and electricity	€ 14.50 - € 29.00
extra person	€ 3.80 - € 5.30
child (under 7 yrs)	€ 2.10 - € 3.60

Meyrueis

Camping le Capelan

Route de Millau, F-48150 Meyrueis (Lozère) T: 04 66 45 60 50. E: info@campingcapelan.com

alanrogers.com/FR48020

Le Capelan is a very attractive site with a warm and friendly welcome, only one kilometre from the picturesque market town of Meyrueis. It has 66 level, grassy touring pitches (10A electricity), most with some shade. It is on the banks of the (unfenced) River Jonte, so families with young children may prefer a pitch further from the river. For fishermen and rock climbers, this is a special site with three kilometres of trout fishing river and climbs of up to 25 metres, all on site. The swimming pool, across the road, is set high on the mountainside and is reached via steps or a longer path.

Facilities

Well maintained toilet blocks, facilities for disabled visitors (site is not ideal for those with walking difficulties). Three bathrooms for rent. Family shower room. Small shop. Bar and takeaway (1/6-17/9). Swimming, paddling pools, sunbathing terrace (1/6-17/9), access via 60 steps. Multisports terrain. Satellite TV. Play area. Rock climbing. Fishing. WiFi throughout (charged). Communal barbecue area. No charcoal barbecues. Off site: Town centre with shops, bars and restaurants 1 km. Bicycle hire 1 km.

Open: 4 May - 17 September.

Directions

Exit A75 at 44-1, take D29 to Aguessac, D907 to le Rozier, then D996 towards Meyrueis. The site is on the right 1 km. before town and is well signed. GPS: 44.18583, 3.41988

Charges guide

Per unit incl. 2 persons and electricity	€ 18.70 - € 29.50
extra person	€ 3.90 - € 5.90

Camping Cheques accepted.

Meyrueis

Camping la Cascade

Salvinsac, F-48150 Meyrueis (Lozère) T: 04 66 45 45 45. E: contact@camping-la-cascade.com

alanrogers.com/FR48040

A delightful small site run by a friendly family, la Cascade is located in the Lozère, where there is some truly spectacular, rugged scenery, wonderful flora and fauna and old towns and villages. This site has 54 good sized, grassy pitches, separated by trees giving varying amounts of shade. There are 41 for touring and 35 with 10A electricity. The small river just outside the campsite is lovely, with a low waterfall, shallow water running over stones, and deeper pools. The access road is narrow at the entrance but is passable with care by most units. An ideal site for exploring this wonderful region.

Facilities

Two small heated toilet blocks with good facilities including baby bath. Washing machine. Bread to order, cold drinks and local specialities. Takeaway (July/Aug). Family room. Play area. Trout fishing. Communal barbecue. Bicycle hire. Guided walks. Fitness equipment. Boules. Free WiFi. Off site: Trout fishing and natural pool in adjacent river (unsupervised). Meyrueis, shops, bars, restaurant, banks 3 km. Riding 3 km. Canoeing.

Open: 4 April - 11 October.

Directions

From Clermont Ferrand on the A75 take exit 44-1, Aguessac-le Rozier, towards Meyrueis. Pass through Meyrueis on to the D996 (signed Florac). In 3 km. turn right down ramp onto narrow road to site. GPS: 44.19498, 3.45559

Charges guide

Per unit incl. 2 persons and electricity	€ 15.00 - € 22.00
extra person	€ 3.00 - € 4.00

Montclar

Yelloh! Village Domaine d'Arnauteille

F-11250 Montclar (Aude) T: 04 68 26 84 53. E: info@yellohvillage-domaine-arnauteille.com

alanrogers.com/FR11060

Enjoying some beautiful and varied views, this site is ideal for exploring the little known Aude département and for visiting the walled city of Carcassonne. The site is set in 12 hectares of farmland on hilly ground with the original pitches on gently sloping, lightly wooded land. Newer ones are on open ground, of good size, with water, drainage and electricity (10A), semi-terraced and partly hedged. The most recent have views of Montclar village. Of the 198 level grass pitches, 138 are for touring. Access, although much improved, could be difficult for large, twin-axle caravans.

Facilities

Three toilet blocks are fully equipped with some en-suite provision. Facilities for disabled visitors, children and babies. Laundry, Motorcaravan services. Small shop (10/5-15/9). Bar, restaurant and takeaway (all 15/5-15/9). Swimming pool (1/5-15/9), two toboggans, paddling pool, river with water massage and sunbathing terrace. Multisports court. Boules. Play area. Riding (July/Aug). Day trips. Library, games room, TV. WiFi (charged). Gas barbecues only. Off site: Fishing 3 km. Bicycle hire 8 km.

Open: 17 April - 15 September.

Directions

D118 from Carcassonne, pass Rouffiac d'Aude. At new roundabout turn right to Montclar up narrow road (passing places) for 2.5 km. Site signed very sharp left up hill before village. GPS: 43.12714, 2.25953

Charges guide

Per unit incl. 2 persons and electricity	€ 18.00 - € 39.00
extra person	€ 6.00 - € 8.00

Narbonne

Yelloh! Village les Mimosas

Chaussée de Mandirac, F-11100 Narbonne (Aude) T: 04 68 49 03 72. E: info@lesmimosas.com

alanrogers.com/FR11070

Six kilometres inland from the beaches of Narbonne and Gruissan, this family owned site benefits from a less hectic situation than others by the sea. Set amongst the vineyards, it is welcoming, peaceful in low season, but lively in July and August with plenty to amuse and entertain the younger generation, including a separate paddling pool for toddlers, but still offering facilities for the whole family. A free club card is available in July/August for use at the children's club, gym, sauna, tennis, minigolf, billiards etc. There are 266 pitches, 153 for touring, hedged and on level grass, and of a very good size, most with 6/10A electricity. There are a few 'grand confort' pitches with reasonable shade, mostly from two-metre-high hedges. There are also 113 mobile homes and chalets to rent. This could be a very useful site meeting a variety of needs, on-site entertainment and easy access to popular beaches. Nearby Gruissan is a fascinating village with its wooden houses on stilts, beaches, ruined castle, port and salt beds. Narbonne has Roman remains and inland Cathar castles are to be found perched on rugged hill tops.

Facilities

Sanitary buildings refurbished to a high standard include a baby room. Washing machines. Shop and restaurant (incl. breakfast). Takeaway. Bar (low season only at w/ends). Small lounge, amusements (July/Aug). Heated pool with slides and islands (12/4-mid Oct), plus the original large pool and excellent new paddling pool and play room. Play area. Minigolf. Mountain bike hire. Tennis. Wellness area. Sauna. Gym. Children's activities, sports, entertainment (high season). Bicycle hire. Multisports court. WiFi throughout (charged). Off site: Riding adjacent. Fishing and windsurfing/sailing school 300 m. Kite surfing.

Open: 22 March - 1 November.

Directions

From A9 exit 38 (Narbonne Sud) take last exit on roundabout, back over the autoroute (site signed from here). Follow signs for La Nautique and then Mandirac and site (6 km. from autoroute). Also signed from Narbonne centre.
GPS: 43.13662, 3.02562

Charges guide

Per unit incl. 2 persons and electricity	€ 17.00 - € 47.00
extra person	€ 5.00 - € 8.00
child (3-6 yrs)	free - € 7.00

Narbonne-Plage

Campéole la Côte des Roses

Route de Gruissan, F-11100 Narbonne-Plage (Aude) T: 04 68 49 83 65. E: cote-des-roses@campeole.com

alanrogers.com/FR11130

This large site, between Gruisson and Narbonne Plage, on the edge of a vast sandy beach, is now owned by the Campéole group. There are over 700 pitches with 90 Bengali tents, and over 200 mobile homes and chalets which vary in style. The 400 touring pitches are well spaced out amongst the sort of trees and shrubs which grow near the beach, providing varying degrees of shade. Pitches are on sandy grass with 6A electricity. On-site amenities include a shop, bar, snack bar and a pool complex.

Facilities

The colourful renovated toilet blocks are fully equipped with some en-suite showers and washbasins. Attractive provision for children and babies and facilities for disabled visitors. Washing machines. Motorcaravan services. Shop, bar, restaurant (high season). Swimming pool complex (1/6-31/8). Multisports court. Play area. Communal barbecue. WiFi around reception (charged). Off site: Beach 500 m. Sailing, jet skis, go-karting 1 km.

Open: 27 April - 30 September.

Directions

From A9 exit 37 follow D168 to roundabout by Narbonne Plage then take D332 towards Gruissan and watch for site on left at roundabout.
GPS: 43.143677, 3.144708

Charges guide

Per unit incl. 2 persons and electricity	€ 18.70 - € 32.10

No credit cards.

Camping Cheques accepted.

Narbonne

Camping la Nautique

Chemin de la Nautique, F-11100 Narbonne (Aude) T: 04 68 90 48 19. E: info@campinglanautique.com

alanrogers.com/FR11080

This well established site is owned and run by a friendly Dutch family. It is an extremely spacious site situated on the Etang de Bages, where flat water combined with strong winds make it one of the best windsurfing areas in France. La Nautique has 390 huge, level pitches, 270 for touring, all with 10A electricity and fully equipped individual sanitary units. Six or seven overnight pitches with electricity are in a separate area. A range of mobile homes are available to rent. The flowering shrubs and trees give a pleasant feel while providing some shade. Hedges separate the pitches making some quite private and providing shade. The ground is quite hard and stony. Entertainment is organised from Easter to September (increasing in high season), plus windsurfing, sailing, rafting, walking, pedaloes and canoeing. The unspoilt surrounding countryside is excellent for walking and cycling and locally there is riding and fishing. This site caters for families with children of all ages and is fenced off from the water. Windsurfers can have a key for the gate (with deposit) that leads to launching points on the lake.

Facilities

Each pitch has its own fully equipped sanitary unit. Extra facilities for disabled visitors. Laundry. Motorcaravan services. Shop. Bar/restaurant with terrace, TV and takeaway (all 1/5-30/9). Snack bar (July/Aug). Outdoor heated swimming pool, water slide and paddling pool (1/5-30/9). Play areas. Tennis. Minigolf. Pétanque. Miniclub (high season). Games room. Bicycle hire. WiFi (charged). Electric barbecues only. Torch useful. Off site: Narbonne 4 km. Sandy beaches at Gruissan (12 km) and Narbonne Plage (20 km). Kite surfing. Canoeing, sailing and windsurfing on the Etang.

Open: 1 March - 31 October.

Directions

From A9 take exit 38 (Narbonne Sud). Go round roundabout to last exit and follow signs for la Nautique and site, then further site signs to site on right in 2.5 km. GPS: 43.14696, 3.00439

Charges guide

Per unit incl. 2 persons, electricity, water and sanitary unit	€ 21.20 - € 46.50
extra person	€ 5.00 - € 8.60
child (2-12 yrs)	free - € 7.60
dog	€ 3.00

Narbonne-Plage

Flower Camping Soleil d'Oc

Route de Gruissan, F-11100 Narbonne-Plage (Aude) T: 04 68 49 86 21. E: info@soleildoc.fr

alanrogers.com/FR11270

This family oriented campsite with just over 200 pitches and a friendly atmosphere, is just a short walk from a wide sandy beach on the Mediterranean sea. There is a wide choice of marked pitches (135 for touring) which vary in size, with or without electricity (6A), and a variety of rental accommodation. The facilities at the front of the site have been redeveloped and create quite an impact on arrival. The bar/restaurant with a wide terrace has carefully constructed access suitable for disabled visitors.

Facilities

The sanitary block includes preset showers and open style washbasins. Facilities for disabled visitors. Laundry. Shop (fresh bread, fruit and vegetables, June-Sept). Bar and restaurant with takeaway and entertainment in high season. TV room. Large play area and bouncy castle. Boules. Football. Basketball. No charcoal barbecues. Communal barbecue. WiFi (free for 1 hr per day). Off site: Bicycle hire 100 m. Riding 400 m. Beach 600 m.

Open: 1 April - 15 October.

Directions

From A9 motorway leave at exit 37 Narbonne Est and follow signs for Narbonne Plage D168, then turn west on D332 towards Grouissan and site is signed to right in 1.8 km. GPS: 43.144994, 3.142227

Charges guide

Per unit incl. 2 persons and electricity	€ 16.50 - € 30.50

No credit cards.

Camping Cheques accepted.

Néfiach

Flower Camping la Garenne

RD 916, F-66170 Néfiach (Pyrénées-Orientales) T: 04 68 57 15 76. E: contact@camping-lagarenne.fr
alanrogers.com/FR66490

Situated beside the N116 which runs through the foothills of the Pyrenees from Perpignan to Andorra, this site is well situated for hiking, climbing, cycling and canoeing. The grass pitches are all level with very easy access and have a degree of privacy to them. There are 73 pitches in total, with 10A electricity available for some of the 36 touring pitches, plus several privately-owned mobile homes and some site-owned chalets available to rent. Great views of the surrounding hills and mountains are enjoyable from most areas of the site whilst at the back there are vineyards and orchards in abundance.

Facilities

A single heated toilet block provides modern facilities. Baby area and facilities for disabled visitors. Washing machine. Motorcaravan services. Bar area and snack type restaurant (May-mid Oct) with covered area for singing and dancing. Weekly paella or moules evening in summer. Small pool (April-Nov) and paddling pool. Play area. Outdoor fitness machines. Gas or electric barbecues only. WiFi (charged). Max. 1 dog. Off site: Fishing 2 km.

Open: 1 March - 30 November.

Directions

From the N116 (Perpignan-Andorra), take exit for Néfiach and head up the old road to Ile-sur-Têt and the site is on the right. GPS: 42.69067, 2.65785

Charges guide

Per unit incl. 2 persons and electricity	€ 16.20 - € 29.00
extra person	€ 4.10 - € 5.50
child (3-6 yrs)	€ 3.10 - € 4.50

Palau-del-Vidre

Le Haras

1 ter avenue Joliot Curie, Domaine Sant Galdric, F-66690 Palau-del-Vidre (Pyrénées-Orientales)
T: 04 68 22 14 50. E: contact@camping-le-haras.com **alanrogers.com/FR66050**

Situated in the mature grounds of an old hunting lodge, later developed into an arboretum, le Haras is a rather special site. The 131 pitches are in bays of four arranged amidst an amazing variety of trees and shrubs that provide colour and shade for 100 touring units and some 34 mobile homes (16 to rent). All the touring pitches have 10A electricity, 29 are fully serviced. Some of the access roads are narrow. Under the same family management as Ma Prairie at Canet Village (FR66020), this is a comfortable site popular with British visitors. Rail noise is possible, although the line is screened by large trees.

Facilities

Fully equipped toilet blocks. Facilities for disabled visitors. Washing machines. Motorcaravan services. Fridge hire. Bar, restaurant and takeaway (all 2/4-27/9). Swimming and paddling pools (1/4-30/9). Play area. Archery (10/7-25/8). No charcoal barbecues. Max. 1 dog. WiFi throughout (free). Off site: Shops in the village. Fishing 500 m. Riding 2 km. Bicycle hire 6 km. Golf 7 km. Beaches 10 minutes' drive.

Open: 1 April - 30 September.

Directions

From A9, exit 43 (Le Boulou) follow D618 towards Argelès for 13 km. From the bypass at St André, turn left for Palau-del-Vidre (D11). Bear right through village, on D11 (Elne). Site on right at end of village, before railway bridge. GPS: 42.57581, 2.96481

Charges guide

Per unit incl. 2 persons and electricity (5A)	€ 20.00 - € 41.00

Camping Cheques accepted.

Port Barcarès

Camping la Presqu'île

Avenue de la Presqu'ile, F-66420 Port Barcarès (Pyrénées-Orientales) T: 04 68 86 12 80.
E: lapresquile@cybelevacances.com **alanrogers.com/FR66470**

La Presqu'île sits on a peninsula overlooking the Etang de Leucate, behind the resort of Port Barcarès. It is set in a pinewood, some 2 km. from the beaches and the port. The site is split in two with 163 pitches (28 for touring with 6A electricity) irregularly arranged under the pine trees. Some are very large and marked with flowering shrubs, others are smaller and used for tents, all mixed in amongst a range of mobile homes and chalets, many for hire. Amenities include a large pool and an impressive toboggan and are all situated across the road overlooking the Etang.

Facilities

Two fully equipped toilet blocks. Laundry room. Shop, bar, snack bar and takeaway (July/Aug. plus weekends in low season). Large, heated outdoor swimming pool with toboggan and paddling pool. Tennis. Multisport court. Gym. Amusements. TV. Inflatable castle. Bicycle hire. Fishing. Play area. Sporting activities, children's club and evening entertainment (July/Aug). Charcoal barbecues are not permitted. WiFi throughout (charged). Off site: Boat launching 500 m. Beach 2 km.

Open: 4 April - 27 September.

Directions

From the A9 take exit 40 signed Leucate. Follow D627 then D83 for Le Barcarès and Port area. Take exit 11 and follow site signs.
GPS: 42.80521, 3.02675

Charges guide

Per unit incl. 2 persons and electricity	€ 16.00 - € 41.00
extra person	€ 3.00 - € 6.50
child (3-12 yrs)	€ 2.00 - € 5.00

Port Camargue

Camping Abri de Camargue

320 route du Phare de l'Espiguette, Port Camargue, F-30240 Le Grau-du-Roi (Gard) T: 04 66 51 54 83.
E: contact@abridecamargue.fr **alanrogers.com/FR30030**

Abri de Camargue is a well established family site within easy reach of beaches and the town of Le Grau-du-Roi. The welcoming pool area is overlooked by the bar with a pleasant sheltered terrace, and the larger outdoor pool has surrounds for sunbathing. The smaller indoor pool is heated. With 277 level and hedged pitches, there are 47 for touring units (mainly of 100 sq.m), 101 mobile homes or chalets to rent and the remainder are privately owned. Electricity (6A) and water are available on most, and the pitches are well maintained and shaded, with trees and flowering shrubs, quite luxuriant in parts.

Facilities

Two renovated toilet blocks. Facilities for disabled visitors. Washing machines. Motorcaravan services. Shop. Bar with TV. Restaurant and takeaway. Heated indoor pool, outdoor pool and paddling pool. New multisports court. Outdoor fitness room. Cinema. Play area. Bicycle hire. Entertainment and children's club and music room (all high season). Pétanque. WiFi on part of site (charged) and free at the restaurant. Site access card (deposit € 15).

Open: 3 April - 30 September.

Directions

From A9 exit 26, Gallargues to Le Grau-du-Roi. From bypass follow signs Port Camargue and Campings. Then follow Rive gauche signs towards Phare l'Espiguette. Site is on right opposite Toboggan Park. GPS: 43.5225, 4.1491

Charges guide

Per unit incl. 2 persons and electricity	€ 27.00 - € 51.00

Portiragnes-Plage

Camping Caravaning les Mimosas

Port Cassafières, F-34420 Portiragnes-Plage (Hérault) T: 04 67 90 92 92.
E: les.mimosas.portiragnes@wanadoo.fr **alanrogers.com/FR34170**

Les Mimosas is quite a large site with 400 pitches – 200 for touring units, the remainder for mobile homes – in a rural situation. The level, grassy pitches are of average size, separated and numbered in regular avenues, all with 6A electricity (long leads may be required), some have good shade, others have less. The pool area, a real feature of the site, includes a most impressive wave pool, various toboggans, the 'Space Hole' water slide, a large swimming pool and a super paddling pool (nine pools in all) with lots of free sun beds. This is a friendly, family run site with families in mind, with something new for each year. Les Mimosas has a less hectic situation than sites closer to the beach. However, it is possible to walk to a lovely sandy beach (1.2 km). There is lots going on including day trips and excursions, from canoeing to visiting castles. Portiragnes-Plage is about 2 km. away and can be reached by cycle tracks. The Canal du Midi runs along the edge of the site (no access), providing another easy cycle route.

Facilities

Good, modern toilet blocks include baby rooms, children's toilets, facilities for disabled visitors (whole site wheelchair friendly). En-suite facilities on payment. Washing machines and dryers. Motorcaravan services. Fridge hire. Large shop. Bar, restaurant and takeaway. Swimming pool complex (lifeguards). Play area. Miniclub. Boules. New gym with sauna, games room, beauty salon and massage. Multisports court. Bicycle hire. Games/TV room. Variety of evening entertainment. WiFi throughout (charged). Communal barbecue (only gas and electric permitted on pitches). Off site: Fishing and riding 1 km.

Open: 28 May - 10 September.

Directions

From A9 exit 35 (Béziers Est) take N112 south towards Sérignan (1 km). Large roundabout follow signs for Cap d'Agde, watch carefully for D37, Portiragnes (1-2 km), follow signs for Portiragnes-Plage. Site well signed before Portiragnes-Plage (5 km). GPS: 43.29153, 3.37348

Charges guide

Per unit incl. 2 persons and electricity	€ 21.00 - € 46.00
extra person	€ 5.00 - € 10.50
child (under 4 yrs)	free - € 5.00

Portiragnes-Plage

Camping les Sablons

Avenue des Muriers, F-34420 Portiragnes-Plage (Hérault) T: 04 67 90 90 55. E: contact@les-sablons.com
alanrogers.com/FR34400

Les Sablons is an impressive and popular site with 680 pitches and lots going on, a village in itself. Most of the facilities are arranged around the entrance with shops, a restaurant, a bar and a large pool complex with no less than five slides and three heated pools. There is also direct access to a white sandy beach at the back of the site, close to a small lake. There is good shade on the majority of the site, although some of the newer touring pitches have less shade. On level sandy grass, all 220 touring pitches have 6A electricity. The remainder are taken by a range of mobile homes and chalets.

Facilities

Well equipped, modernised toilet blocks include large showers, some with washbasins. Baby baths and facilities for disabled visitors. Supermarket, bakery and newsagent. Restaurant, bar and takeaway. Swimming pool complex. Entertainment and activity programme with sports, music and cultural activities. Children's club. Beach club. Tennis. Archery. Play areas. Bicycle hire. Electronic games. ATM. Internet access. WiFi throughout (charged). Off site: Village and bicycle hire 100 m. Beach and riding 200 m.

Open: 1 April - 25 September.

Directions

From A9 exit 35 (Béziers Est) follow signs for Vias and Agde (N112). After large roundabout pass exit to Cers then take exit for Portiragnes (D37). Follow for 5 km. and pass over Canal du Midi towards Portiragnes-Plage. Site is on left after roundabout. GPS: 43.28003, 3.36396

Charges guide

Per unit incl. 2 persons and electricity	€ 22.00 - € 55.00
extra person	€ 7.00 - € 11.00

Remoulins

Camping la Soubeyranne

1110 route de Beaucaire, F-30210 Remoulins (Gard) T: 04 66 37 03 21. E: soubeyranne@franceloc.fr
alanrogers.com/FR30140

Owned by the group FranceLoc, this site is well positioned for visiting the Pont du Gard, Nîmes and Uzès, famed for their Roman connections. The 200 pitches offer extremely generous amounts of shade and keeping the 14 hectares watered involves over 5 km. of hose pipe. The touring pitches, of which there are 79, are large, level, numbered and separated and all have 6A electricity connections. An entertainment programme (July and August) is aimed mainly at young children. The site has a very good swimming pool complex, complete with both indoor and outdoor pools and water slides. An ideal site as a base from which to explore the Camargue, Cévennes, Ardèche and Luberon.

Facilities

Two refurbished toilet blocks. Motorcaravan services. Small shop selling basics. Restaurant, bar and takeaway. Heated swimming pool complex including smaller toddlers' pool (unsupervised). New heated indoor pool. Multisports court. Play area including inflatable castle. Minigolf. Boules. Tennis. Bicycle hire. No charcoal barbecues permitted. Free WiFi in bar area. Off site: Fishing 1 km.

Open: 11 April - 13 September.

Directions

Leave A9, exit 23 (Remoulins). Go over river bridge, left at roundabout, then left again (signed D986 Beaucaire). Site is 1.5 km. further on left. GPS: 43.9259, 4.56422

Charges guide

Per unit incl. 2 persons and electricity	€ 19.70 - € 31.20
extra person	€ 4.70 - € 7.00
child (under 7 yrs)	€ 3.50 - € 4.50

Saint Chinian

Camping les Terrasses

555 route de Saint Pons, F-34360 Saint Chinian (Hérault) T: 06 12 90 14 55.
E: contact@campinglesterrasses.net **alanrogers.com/FR34950**

Les Terrasses is a small, friendly site located next to the wine growing area of Saint Chinian in the Hérault hinterland, set back from the busy Mediterranean coastline. There are 50 terraced, grass pitches here, all with 10A electricity and views across the vineyards to the hills of the garrigue. On-site facilities include a good little swimming pool with decking for sunbathing, or for a more rustic setting, the river (800 m) has natural pools for a cooling dip. The site was orignally a municipal, but is now run by the enthusiastic Cathy Dubost, who makes you very welcome and does a great deal for motorcaravanners.

Facilities

The traditional, fully equipped sanitary block has facilities for babies and disabled visitors. Washing machine and freezer. Motorcaravan services. Bar. Fresh bread to order. Swimming pool (15/6-15/9). Small play area. Tennis. Communal barbecues only. WiFi. Off site: Supermarket 800 m. Bars and restaurants 1.5 km. Bicycle hire 1 km.

Open: 1 April - 30 September.

Directions

From Béziers take D612 towards St Chinian, continue through town following signs for St Pons to pick up municipal camping signs just outside town. GPS: 43.421243, 2.934374

Charges guide

Per unit incl. 2 persons and electricity	€ 16.80 - € 26.80

Saint Cyprien-Plage

Camping Cala Gogo

Avenue Armand Lanoux, les Capellans, F-66750 Saint Cyprien-Plage (Pyrénées-Orientales)

T: 04 68 21 07 12. E: camping.calagogo@wanadoo.fr **alanrogers.com/FR66030**

This is an excellent, well organised site and it is agreeably situated by a superb sandy beach with a beach bar and boat launching. There are 649 pitches in total with 378 average sized, level, pitches for touring, regularly laid out, with electrical connections (6/10A) and some shade. Twenty fully serviced pitches have been added. The site has a most impressive pool complex, part heated and attractively laid out with palm trees and sunbathing areas. The large bar complex overlooking the pool area becomes very busy in season and dancing or entertainment is arranged on some evenings. A feature of the site is the provision of special beach buggies for visitors with disabilities.

Facilities

Fully equipped toilet blocks with some Turkish style WCs are of a high standard. Motorcaravan services. Good supermarket and small shopping mall. Two restaurants. Takeaway. Bar. Small beach bar (high season). Three swimming pools (heated) plus one for children, water-jets, jacuzzi, waterfall. Play area. Tennis. Fishing. Diving club. Disco. TV. Free WiFi over part of site. Bicycle hire. Events, sports and entertainment in season. Torches useful.

Open: 4 May - 21 September.

Directions

Using D81 (southward) avoid St Cyprien-Plage and continue towards Argelès. Turn right at roundabout signed St Cyprien Sud and Aquapark and pick up site signs. Site is just past the Aquapark. GPS: 42.59939, 3.03761

Charges guide

Per unit incl. 2 persons and electricity	€ 20.00 - € 46.10
extra person	free - € 11.70

Saint Jean-du-Gard

Camping les Sources

Route de Mialet, F-30270 Saint Jean-du-Gard (Gard) T: 04 66 85 38 03. E: camping-des-sources@orange.fr **alanrogers.com/FR30150**

This is a small, family run site situated in the foothills of the beautiful Cévennes and close to Saint Jean-du-Gard and the River Gardon. There are 92 average to good sized, slightly sloping pitches on small terraces with 69 for touring units, all with electricity (6/10A). A number of attractive mobile homes and chalets are also available for rent. They are separated by a variety of flowering shrubs and trees offering good shade. Near the entrance is the attractive reception, bar, restaurant and terrace overlooking the swimming pools and children's play area. There is a range of daily activities on offer for all ages and also evening entertainment once a week. Nearby, one can walk in the footsteps of Robert Louis Stevenson (Travels with a Donkey), ride on a picturesque steam train, explore deep underground caverns, visit a giant bamboo forest and explore the region by foot, on bike or by car.

Facilities

Three well appointed, modern toilet blocks (heated) with washbasins in cabins. Facilities for babies and disabled visitors. Washing machine. Motorcaravan services. Bar/restaurant with takeaway. Small shop. Heated swimming and paddling pools. Games/TV room. Play area. Gas barbecues only. Daily activities. Family evening meals (July/Aug). WiFi throughout. Off site: St Jean-du-Gard 1.5 km. Bus service to Nîmes and Alès a few times daily. Fishing and bathing 1.5 km. Riding 10 km. Bicycle hire 10 km. Golf 20 km.

Open: 1 April - 30 September.

Directions

From Alès take D910A to Anduze, then D907 to St Jean-du-Gard. Take ring road (autre directions) towards Florac. Turn right at traffic lights on D983. Right onto D50 (site signed). Very shortly, on sharp right-hand bend, fork right to site. Access impossible from the north. GPS: 44.11322, 3.89052

Charges guide

Per unit incl. 2 persons and electricity	€ 16.50 - € 28.00
extra person	€ 3.50 - € 5.50

Camping Cheques accepted.

Saint Jean-du-Gard

Camping Mas de la Cam

Route de Saint André de Valborgne, F-30270 Saint Jean-du-Gard (Gard) T: 04 66 85 12 02.
E: camping@masdelacam.fr **alanrogers.com/FR30180**

Camping Mas de la Cam is a superb, high quality, family run touring site on the edge of the Cévennes National Park and you are assured of a warm welcome here. It is a very pleasant and spacious site with well trimmed grass and hedges and a profusion of flowers and shrubs. Lying alongside the small Gardon river, the banks have been left free of pitches, just neat grass and some trees for shade. The 200 medium to large pitches, all for touring, are on low level terraces, with varying amounts of shade and have electricity (6/10A). Entrance is via a narrow unfenced bridge, so not ideal for large outfits.

Facilities

Three high quality, very clean toilet blocks (one recently rebuilt) include baby bath and facilities for disabled visitors. Washing machines. Plans for a motorcaravan service point. Restaurant/takeaway (1/6-10/9). Small shop (20/5-15/9). Bar (26/5-10/9). Large swimming pool (heated) and paddling pools (15/5-15/9). Play area with new equipment. Sports areas and multisports court. Tennis. Boules. Fishing. WiFi. Gas and electric barbecues only. Off site: St Jean-du-Gard with shops. Riding 5 km.

Open: 27 April - 20 September.

Directions

Site is 3 km. northwest of St Jean-du-Gard towards St André-de-Valborgne on D907, site signed, fork left, descend across a narrow unfenced bridge to site. Site entrance not accessible from north. GPS: 44.11235, 3.8541

Charges guide

Per unit incl. 2 persons and electricity	€ 19.00 - € 38.50
extra person	€ 3.90 - € 8.50

Saint Pons-de-Thomières

Camping les Cerisiers du Jaur

Route de Bédarieux, F-34220 Saint Pons-de-Thomières (Hérault) T: 04 67 95 30 33.
E: info@cerisierdujaur.com **alanrogers.com/FR34640**

Saint Pons-de-Thomières lies in a valley in the Parc Régional du Haut Languedoc, just east of the village. It was purchased six years ago by Domian and Virginie, who have worked hard to develop it, adding an attractive pool area and extra pitches. The original part of the site has pitches in the shade of old cherry trees, while the newer section is more open, but with new planting. Of the 98 touring pitches, 88 have water, 10-16A electricity and drainage. The Jaur river running alongside the campsite has a number of little cascades, is a great fishing spot and a new sandy beach has been made.

Facilities

Fully equipped toilet blocks with facilities for children and disabled visitors. 10 pitches have their own private sanitary facility. Washing machine. Motorcaravan services. Swimming and paddling pools, spa area. Playground. Morning bread delivery. Pizza delivery. Communal barbecue. Ice creams and fresh drinks. Chalets, mobile homes and a Romany-style caravan for hire. WiFi (1st hour free). Off site: Shops and restaurants in village 2 km.

Open: 4 April - 25 October.

Directions

From A9 exit 36 (Béziers Ouest), head north on D64 then D612 Mazamet and St Pons. Before village, turn north on D908 Olargues. Site is on right in 500 m. past block of flats. GPS: 43.4905, 2.7852

Charges guide

Per unit incl. 2 persons and electricity	€ 20.00 - € 29.00

Saint Privat-de-Champclos

Domaine le Clos des Capitelles

Les Lacs, F-30430 Saint Privat-de-Champclos (Gard) T: 04 66 60 24 57.
E: contact@camping-closdescapitelles.fr **alanrogers.com/FR30730**

Le Clos des Capitelles was opened in 2006 by the present owner and is ideally situated for exploring this beautiful area between Provence, Cévennes and Ardèche. It is a peaceful site, with 88 pitches set in four hectares of young oak trees offering shade to the 17 terraced touring pitches (16A electricity). All are individually landscaped to give space and privacy, but trees could be a problem for large units on some pitches. On-site facilities have been designed to promote wellbeing and relaxation and include a sauna, gym, attractive swimming pool area and beauty and therapy treatments.

Facilities

One modern, well maintained, open toilet block has controllable showers and washbasins in cubicles. Facilities for babies and disabled visitors (gravel access roads). Laundry. Small shop in reception. Bar, restaurant/takeaway (July-Aug). Good sized heated swimming pool (from 1/6). Wellness facility (April-Sept; by appt). Play area. Sports field. WiFi throughout. Chalets for rent. Electric barbecues only. Off site: Tennis 1 km. Fishing and river beach 3 km. Bicycle hire 6 km.

Open: 1 April - 30 September.

Directions

From Alès take D16 then D979 northeast towards Barjac. 5 km. beyond St Jean-de-Maruejols turn right on D266 signed St Privat. After 3 km. turn right at junction and follow signs to site (1 km). GPS: 44.274, 4.34879

Charges guide

Per unit incl. 2 persons and electricity	€ 29.00 - € 35.00
extra person	€ 5.00 - € 6.00

Sainte Enimie

Camping Couderc

Route de Millau, F-48210 Sainte Enimie (Lozère) T: 04 66 48 50 53. E: contact@campingcouderc.fr

alanrogers.com/FR48080

A spacious rural site, Couderc stretches for 1 km. along the clear shallow River Tarn, with access possible at each end of the site. The beautiful Gorges du Tarn and the high plateaux are well worth exploring. In May and June there are wonderful flowers and butterflies and vultures soaring overhead. There are 130 good sized, level, grassy/stony pitches here, separated by vines and mature trees. With 123 for touring units, most have welcome shade and 10A electricity (long leads may be needed). Rock pegs are advised. Although the local roads are winding and narrow, access on the site is good.

Facilities

Four toilet blocks with adequate facilities including those for children. Facilities for disabled visitors. Bar/TV room. Breakfast. Basic shop, bread to order. Swimming and paddling pools. Play area. Canoe/kayak hire and trips run from site. Boules. River fishing. Electric barbecues only. Communal barbecues. WiFi. Off site: Ste Enimie with shops and restaurants, bars and a bank 1.5 km. Grottos, canyoning, rock climbing, caving. Gorges of the Tarn.

Open: 1 April - 26 September.

Directions

Leave A75 at exit 40 for La Canourgue. Take the D998 to Ste Enimie (28 km) following signs for Millau, Gorges du Tarn. Take the D907 to site on left in 1.5 km. Approach from south not recommended for large outfits. GPS: 44.353606, 3.401347

Charges guide

Per unit incl. 2 persons and electricity	€ 17.00 - € 28.00
extra person	€ 3.00 - € 5.00

Sainte Marie-la-Mer

Camping la Pergola

21 avenue Frederic Mistral, F-66470 Sainte Marie-la-Mer (Pyrénées-Orientales) T: 02 51 20 41 94.
E: contact@camp-atlantique.com **alanrogers.com/FR66100**

La Pergola is an attractive, tranquil campsite with 183 pitches which include 56 for tourers, all with 10A electricity. It is located in a mainly residential area of this up-and-coming and, at times, quite lively, seaside resort. Orientated towards family holidays, it offers a choice of mainly large pitches, some with lots of shade and some with less. It has a very pleasant ambience and a nice quiet pool area. It is about five minutes' walk from the beach. Many improvements have been made to the campsite during the last few years and the management team recognise that there is still some work to be done.

Facilities

Three modern toilet blocks include facilities for babies and disabled visitors. Laundry facilities. Bar, restaurant and takeaway (all season). Heated outdoor swimming and paddling pools (all season). TV. Play area. Bicycle hire. Some evening entertainment. Max. one dog. No charcoal barbecues allowed. WiFi throughout (charged). Off site: Beach and boat launching 500 m. Riding 1 km.

Open: 2 April - 25 September.

Directions

From A9 take exit 41 and follow signs towards Canet via the D83 and D81 until a roundabout signed Ste Marie-la-Mer Plage. Turn left into Ste Marie-Plage and follow campsite signs. GPS: 42.72665, 3.03300

Charges guide

Per unit incl. 2 persons and electricity	€ 18.00 - € 38.00
extra person	€ 5.00 - € 9.00

Saissac

Camping la Porte d'Autan

Rue Boris Vian, F-11130 Saissac (Aude) T: 04 68 76 36 08. E: laportedautan@yahoo.fr

alanrogers.com/FR11170

The small village of Saissac, on the edge of the Black Mountains, is a scenic base for exploring the rich heritage of the Languedoc-Roussillon. La Porte d'Autan is in a peaceful, verdant location (the site is reminiscent of an English park) within walking distance of the village, which has a good range of amenities, including a bakery, butcher, pharmacy, vet and petrol station. The 2.5 acre site's 69 level, grass pitches are separated by hedges and have access to 6A electricity. They are well shaded by mature trees. On Mondays in July and August, campers are invited to enjoy a welcome drink.

Facilities

One fully equipped sanitary block with hot showers and washbasins in cubicles. Facilities for disabled visitors. Washing machine. Shop. Outdoor swimming and paddling pools (1/7-1/9, no Bermuda shorts). Playground and trampoline. Activities for children (July/Aug). Pétanque pitch. Communal barbecue. Fridge hire. Bicycle hire. Mobile homes for rent. WiFi on part of site (free).
Off site: A wide choice of outdoor pursuits, including riding, climbing, archery, canoeing, rafting and fishing.

Open: 11 April - 19 October.

Directions

West on A61, exit 22 (Bram). At roundabout take 2nd exit onto D4 (Bram), continue as far as Saissac. At junction turn left onto D629 (signed Cammazes and Gendarmarie), proceed to top of hill and mini roundabout, take 2nd exit by service station and butchers. Continue to site. GPS: 43.36149, 2.16084

Charges guide

Per unit incl. 2 persons and electricity	€ 17.00 - € 28.00
extra person	€ 4.20 - € 5.20

No credit cards.

Sérignan-Plage

Yelloh! Village le Sérignan-Plage

519

Le Sérignan Plage, F-34410 Sérignan-Plage (Hérault) T: 04 67 32 35 33. E: info@leserignanplage.com

alanrogers.com/FR34070

A lively and vibrant site with direct access onto a superb 600 m. sandy beach (including a naturist section), plus two swimming pool complexes and an indoor pool, this is a must for a Mediterranean holiday. It is a busy, friendly, family orientated site with a very comprehensive range of amenities and activities for children. There are now over 1,200 pitches with 260 for touring units. They are fairly level, on sandy soil and all have 10A electricity. The collection of spa pools (balnéo) built in Romanesque style with colourful terracing and columns is overlooked by a very smart restaurant, Le Villa, available to use in the afternoons (used by the adjacent naturist site in the mornings). The owners, Jean-Guy and Catherine, continually surprise us with their flair and unique style in developing and organising the site. Their latest project is a shallow fun pool with colourful play equipment (watch out for the buckets of water!). There are over 300 mobile homes and chalets to let, plus some 400 privately owned units and a good number of tour operator pitches. The busy heart of the site is some distance from reception – a busy and informal area with shops, another good restaurant, the Au Pas d'Oc, an indoor pool and a super roof-top bar. There is a range of sporting activities, children's clubs and evening entertainment, indeed something for all the family – a good holiday choice.

Facilities

Seven modern blocks of individual design with good facilities including showers with washbasin and WC. Facilities for disabled visitors. Baby bathroom. Laundry facilities. Motorcaravan services. Supermarket, bakery and newsagent. Other shops (2/6-14/9). ATM. Restaurants, bars and takeaway. Hairdresser. Balnéo spa (afternoons). Gym. Heated indoor pool. Outdoor pools. Tennis courts. Multisports courts. Play areas. Trampolines. Children's clubs. Evening entertainment. Sporting activities. Bicycle hire. Bus to Sérignan village (July/Aug). Beach (lifeguards 15/6-15/9). WiFi over site (charged). Gas barbecues only. Off site: Fishing 1 km. Riding 1.5 km. Golf 15 km. Sailing and windsurfing school on beach. Local markets. Ferry to Valras Plage.

Open: 23 April - 28 September

Directions

From A9 exit A75 (Béziers Centre) and exit 64 towards Sérignan, D64 (9 km). Before Sérignan, turn left, Sérignan-Plage (4 km). At small sign (blue) turn right. At T-junction turn left over small road bridge and after left hand bend. Site is 100 m.
GPS: 43.26308, 3.31976

Charges guide

Per unit incl. 2 persons and electricity	€ 19.00 - € 65.00
extra person	€ 6.00 - € 10.00
child (3-7 yrs)	free - € 9.00
dog	€ 5.00

Low season offers.

Sérignan-Plage

Yelloh! Village Aloha

F-34410 Sérignan-Plage (Hérault) T: 04 67 39 71 30. E: info@alohacamping.com

alanrogers.com/FR34390

An impressive and well run site beside the beach at Sérignan-Plage. Split into two halves with a small beach running inbetween, Aloha offers a wide range of good quality facilities, all open when the site is open. There are 431 pitches with 192 mobile homes for hire, some in attractive garden settings. The 170 pitches for touring units are of a good size, regularly laid out on level, sandy grass with light shade. Easily accessed from tarmac roads, all have 10A electricity. The swimming pool complex is very impressive and there is an emphasis on activities for children with a popular play area and miniclub. The large main pool is unusually situated upstairs on the roof top with views of the sea and with landscaped fun pools below. There is direct access to the beach where you can windsurf or try sailing a catamaran.

Facilities

Good toilet blocks, one of which is new and very impressive. They offer all modern facilities and are well equipped for children. Laundry. Motorcaravan services. Supermarket including fresh produce market. Bakery. Newsagent. Bazaar. Hairdresser. Bar, restaurant, snack bar, pizzeria and takeaway. Large heated pool and fun pools. Paddling pool. Playground. Tennis. Multisports facility. Large gym. Bicycle hire. Miniclub. Activity programme and evening entertainment. WiFi on part of site (charged). ATM. Off site: Minigolf and trampolines 500 m. Riding 800 m. Boat launching 8 km. Golf 20 km.

Open: 20 April - 16 September.

Directions

From A9 exit 35 (Béziers Est) follow signs for Sérignan then Sérignan-Plage (D37, 10 km). Once at Sérignan-Plage continue straight. Follow the sign for Aloha to right after the pink building.
GPS: 43.273333, 3.348333

Charges guide

Per unit incl. 2 persons and electricity	€ 20.00 - € 58.00
extra person	€ 6.00 - € 9.00
child (3-6 yrs)	free - € 8.00
dog	€ 5.00

Long-stay early season discounts.

Imagine - hot sunshine, blue sea, vineyards, olive and eucalyptus trees, alongside a sandy beach - what a setting for a campsite - not just any campsite either ! With three pool areas, one with four toboggans surrounded by sun bathing areas, an indoor pool for baby swimmers plus a magnificent landscaped, Romanesque spa-complex with half Olympic size pool and a superb range of hydromassage baths to let you unwind and re-charge after the stresses of work. And that's not all - two attractive restaurants, including the atmospheric "Villa" in its romantic Roman setting beside the spa, three bars, a mini-club and entertainment for all ages, all add up to a fantastic opportunity to enjoy a genuinely unique holiday experience.

yelloh! VILLAGE

34410 Sérignan France - Tel : +33 4 67 32 35 33 Fax : +33 4 67 32 68 39
info@leserignanplage.com www.leserignanplage.com

Sète

Village Center le Castellas

RN 112, F-34200 Sète (Hérault) T: 04 99 57 21 21. E: contact@village-center.com
alanrogers.com/FR34240

Le Castellas is an amazingly large site stretching for 2 km. alongside a super 14 km. sandy beach with the Etang du Thau behind. Although there is a main road and railway line, once within the confines of this site there is everything one could want for a happy beach holiday. Over 800 mobile homes, chalets and ready erected tents to rent occupy various areas of the site. There are also 125 sandy and hedged pitches for touring units, most with 6A electricity and some 25 purpose-built for motorcaravans.

Facilities

Adequate toilet facilities. Laundry. Provision for disabled visitors and babies. Supermarket, shops and cafés. Restaurant, bars, snack bars. Swimming pool complex (heated April-June). Toboggans. Games room. Multisport court. Sports field. Archery. Bicycle hire. Play area. Outdoor fitness area. WiFi (charged). Entertainment. Children's clubs (July/Aug). Sea fishing. Watersports.

Open: 6 April - 29 September.

Directions

Site is beside the RN112 which links Marseillan-Plage and Sète (nearer Marseillian-Plage). Road can get very busy in main season but it is being re-routed behind the site. GPS: 43.34192, 3.58449

Charges guide

Per unit incl. 2 persons and electricity	€ 16.00 - € 44.00

Camping Cheques accepted.

Sommières

Camping Domaine de Massereau

Les Hauteurs de Sommières, route d'Aubais, F-30250 Sommières (Gard) T: 04 66 53 11 20.
E: camping@massereau.com **alanrogers.com/FR30290**

Two brothers, one a wine producer and one an hotelier, opened Domaine de Massereau in August 2006. It is set within a 50-hectare vineyard dating back to 1804, and the idea was to promote their wine, so tours are arranged and they now produce their own olive oil as well. There are 149 pitches, with 75 available for touring units, all with electricity (45 with 16A electricity, water and drainage). Pitch sizes range from 150-250 sq.m. but the positioning of trees on some of the pitches could limit the usable space. The area is lightly wooded and most pitches are now hedged with flowering shrubs. The other pitches are used for chalets and mobile homes to rent. Amenities include an attractive pool area, a trim trail, mountain bike path and large grass play area. The camping area is accessed over a narrow bridge (3 m. wide) passing over a section of the 25 km. of cycle routes which enable the area to be explored safely. The riverside town of Sommières is a 1.5 km. ride away and its historic centre is full of narrow streets lined with traditional shops. This is a high quality site which is extremely good value for money.

Facilities

The modern toilet block incorporates excellent facilities for children and disabled visitors. Laundry area. Motorcaravan services. Shop. Restaurant. Bar. Pizzeria and outdoor grill. Takeaway, (all 2/4-30/9). Heated swimming pool and paddling pool. Sauna, steam bath, jacuzzi and massage. Play area. Trampoline. Minigolf. Bicycle hire. Multisports area. Fitness trail. Pétanque. Short tennis. TV room. Barbecue and fridge hire. Tent hire (2 person). Gas. WiFi (charged). Off site: The site's own, new adventure park nearby with private riverside beach (charged). Fishing 500 m. Riding 3 km. Golf 30 km.

Open: 2 April - 29 October.

Directions

From south A9 take exit 27 and D12 (Sommières). Site is 5 km. on right. From north (width and weight restriction in Sommières). To avoid, remain on N110, then take N2110 into Sommières, crossing river over narrow bridge (traffic lights). Turn right onto the D12. Site is on left in 1 km. GPS: 43.765786, 4.097426

Charges guide

Per unit incl. 2 persons and electricity	€ 24.70 - € 48.50
extra person	€ 4.10 - € 11.60
child (under 7 yrs)	€ 3.40 - € 7.60

Torreilles-Plage

Village Camping Spa Marisol

Boulevard de la Plage, F-66440 Torreilles-Plage (Pyrénées-Orientales) T: 04 68 28 04 07.
E: marisol@camping-marisol.com **alanrogers.com/FR66170**

Good quality sites with direct access to the beach are hard to find and Marisol is a useful option. It is a fairly large site, having 377 pitches with a significant number of mobile homes, but with 170 available for touring. These are sandy grass pitches of a good size with some shade. All have electricity (10A). This is essentially a holiday site with all the popular facilities and an extensive entertainment programme, gym and fitness courses and a children's club throughout the main season. At the beauty centre you can also enjoy a sauna, Turkish or spa bath. The owners have fulfilled their plans to add a heated children's pool along with an 8.5 metre high multi-waterslide feature.

Facilities

Three fully equipped toilet blocks, baby bath. Washing machine. Small supermarket. Bar. TV. Restaurant. Takeaway. Heated swimming pool. New heated children's pool. New waterslides. Beauty centre (including special packages). Fitness room. Play area. Tennis. Archery. Children's club. Gates with access to path across dunes to sandy beach. Watersports. Evening entertainment. WiFi. Max. 1 dog. Off site: Sea fishing and watersports.

Open: 9 April - 24 September.

Directions

From A9 take exit 41 (Perpignan Nord) towards Le Barcarès for 9 km. Then south on D81 towards Canet for 3 km. before turning to Torreilles-Plage. Site is signed. GPS: 42.78432, 3.0329

Charges guide

Per unit incl. 2 persons and electricity	€ 24.00 - € 64.00
extra person	€ 6.40 - € 11.60

Torreilles-Plage

Camping Sunêlia les Tropiques

Boulevard de la Plage, F-66440 Torreilles-Plage (Pyrénées-Orientales) T: 04 68 28 05 09.
E: contact@campinglestropiques.com **alanrogers.com/FR66190**

Les Tropiques is a very attractive site with a large pool complex, only 400 metres from a sandy beach. It will provide families with children of all ages with an ideal seaside holiday. There are 450 pitches with 78 for touring units, all with 10A electricity. Pleasant pine and palm trees with other Mediterranean vegetation give shade and provide a pleasant environment. Activities are provided for all including a large range of sports, activities, cabarets and shows. The pool complex at les Tropiques is very impressive with four pools, two heated with good provision for children, including a range of toboggans.

Facilities

Modern, fully equipped sanitary facilities with provision for disabled visitors. Launderette. Shop. Bar and restaurant. Takeaway and pizzeria (July/Aug). Swimming pool (heated in low season) and water slides. Paddling pool. Wellness centre. Outdoor fitness equipment. Tennis. Multisports area. Pétanque. Archery (July/Aug). TV/billiards room. Play area. Disco. Miniclub and teenagers' club (July/Aug). Bicycle hire. WiFi throughout (charged).

Open: 4 April - 4 October.

Directions

From A9 exit Perpignan Nord, follow D83 towards Le Barcarès for 9 km. Take D81 south (Canet) for 3 km. and left at roundabout for Torreilles-Plage. Site is last but one on left. GPS: 42.7675, 3.02972

Charges guide

Per unit incl. 2 persons and electricity	€ 18.00 - € 51.00
extra person	€ 3.85 - € 9.60

Torreilles-Plage

Chadotel Camping le Trivoly

Route des Plages, F-66440 Torreilles-Plage (Pyrénées-Orientales) T: 04 68 28 20 28. E: info@chadotel.com
alanrogers.com/FR66240

The popularity of Torreilles derives mainly from its huge sandy beach and for some off-site nightlife, shopping, etc. but for smarter resorts one really needs to visit Le Barcarès or Canet a few kilometres distance in either direction. Le Trivoly (a member of the French Chadotel Group) is about 800 m. gentle stroll from the beach, in a fairly tranquil setting. In total there are 273 pitches, of which 33 are used for touring units. These are of a good size, well shaded and hedged with electricity (10/16A). The remainder are either used by tour operators or for site-owned mobile homes to rent.

Facilities

Four toilet blocks, although not new, provide modern, well cared for facilities, including washbasins in (rather small) cabins. Facilities for disabled visitors. Laundry facilities. Small shop, snack bar/restaurant and takeaway (all May-mid Sept). Heated pool (15/5-15/9) with water slide and paddling pool. Terraced restaurant. Play area. Tennis. Minigolf. Bicycle hire. Entertainment (high season). Gas barbecues only. WiFi throughout (charged).

Open: 5 April - 21 September.

Directions

From A9 exit 42 (Perpignan-Nord) towards Le Barcarès for 9 km, then turn south on D81 towards Canet. After 3 km. turn left at roundabout, signed Torreilles-Plage. Site is on left, in 500 m. GPS: 42.765808, 3.02681

Charges guide

Per unit incl. 2 persons and electricity	€ 21.50 - € 38.50
extra person	€ 6.00

Uzès

Camping du Mas de Rey

Arpaillargues, F-30700 Uzès (Gard) T: 04 66 22 18 27. E: info@campingmasderey.com

alanrogers.com/FR30110

A warm welcome from the English-speaking Maire family is guaranteed at this small, attractive, 70 pitch site. Most of the 60 large (up to 200 sq.m) touring pitches are separated by bushes, many are shaded and all have 10A electricity. There are plans to increase the number of touring pitches by using an adjacent field. A good site for couples and families with young children. Due to the wonderful climate, grass can at times be hard to find. The reception, bar, restaurant and shop are in the same large, airy building. The owners are always willing to give advice on the numerous things to see and do in the area.

Facilities

Two excellent, well maintained and very clean toilet blocks, both quite new, with solar heating, facilities for disabled visitors, baby room and en-suite family cubicles. Laundry facilities. Shop (July/Aug), bread to order (all season). Takeaway (1/5-30/9). Restaurant (July/Aug). New heated swimming pool and paddling pool (1/5-15/10, closed lunchtimes). New chalets. Free WiFi over site. No charcoal barbecues. Off site: Golf 4 km.

Open: 10 April - 15 October.

Directions

Leave A9 autoroute, exit 23 (Pont du Gard). Take N100 to Remoulins. Follow D981 to Uzès (18 km). Take D982 west, signed Arpaillargues, Moussac. Site signed on left, 3 km. GPS: 43.99843, 4.38424

Charges guide

Per unit incl. 2 persons (3 in high season) and electricity	€ 21.20 - € 40.00
extra person	€ 5.60 - € 8.00

Credit cards accepted in July/August only.

Valras Plage

Camping du Levant

Avenue Charles Cauquil, F-34350 Valras Plage (Hérault) T: 04 67 32 04 45. E: camping.dulevant@free.fr

alanrogers.com/FR34435

Camping du Levant is an attractive little site tucked away on the outskirts of Valras Plage, which can be somewhat hectic at times. Richard, his French wife, Nadini, and their children run the site and are really keen to welcome more English and Dutch visitors. It is ideal for couples and families with small children who do not seek organised entertainment but are happy just enjoying the pool. The site has some 47 static units and 32 medium sized grassy touring pitches. These are separated by trees and some hedging, giving shade to many. The beach is 800 m. away and the village is within walking distance.

Facilities

Toilet block (accessed by steps) with family room and facilities for disabled campers (ramp). Washing machine, dryer, ironing board. Bread to order. Heated swimming and paddling pools. Shop. Bar stocks essentials. Simple takeaway (July/Aug). Children's playroom and outdoor playground. Library. Boules, table tennis. WiFi throughout (charged). Parking outside barrier for late arrivals.
Off site: Valras Plage, bicycle hire and fishing 800 m.

Open: 18 April - 20 September.

Directions

Leave A9 autoroute at exit 36 south of Béziers. At roundabout head south, D64 for 8.2 km. to roundabout. Head east, D64 for 2.2 km. to roundabout. Take D19 south for 400 m. site on left before garage. GPS: 43.25407, 3.28865

Charges guide

Per unit incl. 2 persons and electricity	€ 19.00 - € 40.00
extra person	€ 5.00 - € 7.00

Valras-Plage

Camping Caravaning Domaine de la Yole

CS 10715, F-34350 Valras-Plage (Hérault) T: 04 67 37 33 87. E: info@campinglayole.com

alanrogers.com/FR34090

An impressive, busy, happy holiday village with over 1,200 pitches with a wide range of facilities. There are 590 pitches for touring with the remainder occupied by a range of mobile homes plus some special tents to rent. Pitches are of a good size, all are level, hedged and have electricity (5A), water and waste water points and, very importantly for this area, they all have shade. Some fully serviced pitches are now available. The extensive pool area is impressive, more like an aqua park with its six pools and water slides (heated in low season). The central shopping and entertainment area form the heart of the site.

Facilities

Well maintained toilet blocks include baby rooms. Facilities for families and/or disabled visitors. Laundry facilities. Motorcaravan services. Fridge hire. Shops. Good restaurant, terrace, amphitheatre for daily entertainment. Large pool complex. Tennis. Multisports court. Play areas. High wire adventure park. Bicycle hire. Minigolf. Miniclub. Youth club. Boules. WiFi over site (charged). Site-owned farm, vineyard and winery. No electric barbecues. Max. 2 dogs. Off site: Beach 500 m (no dogs). Fishing 2 km.

Open: 25 April - 19 September.

Directions

From A9 autoroute take Béziers Ouest exit for Valras-Plage (13-14 km) and follow Casino signs. Site is on left, just after sign for Vendres-Plage. GPS: 43.23708, 3.26234

Charges guide

Per unit incl. 2 persons and all services	€ 21.00 - € 55.00
extra person	€ 6.20 - € 9.75
child (3-16 yrs)	free - € 6.30

Valras-Plage

Camping Blue Bayou

Vendres-Plage Ouest, avenue du Port, F-34350 Valras-Plage (Hérault) T: 04 67 37 41 97.
E: infobluebayou@orange.fr **alanrogers.com/FR34370**

The Amiel family have worked hard to make Blue Bayou a comfortable and pleasant place to stay. It is situated at the far end of Vendres-Plage near Le Grau Vendres (the port of Vendres). It is therefore in a much quieter location than many other sites, away from the more hectic, built-up areas of Vendres and Valras-Plage. The beach is 300 m. away across sand dunes and there are open views from the site creating a feeling of spaciousness. There are 286 pitches, all with 10A electricity, with 37 privately owned mobile homes and 120 to let, including some chalets. The level grass touring pitches are of a good size, arranged in avenues with shade from tall trees, some with their own sanitary arrangements. The new, larger restaurant and bar area is an attractive focal point, overlooking two swimming pools, one with a toboggan, joined by a bridge where lifeguards station themselves. The owners and their family are very proud of their site and you are made to feel very welcome. The site would make a good choice for couples and families, with a good range of activities and entertainment on offer for all.

Facilities

Fully equipped and modern toilet block. Individual toilet units for 56 touring pitches. Baby bath. Facilities for disabled visitors. Laundry. Shop. Bar and restaurant. Takeaway (July/Aug). Swimming pool (heated all season). Tennis court. Play area. Miniclub and entertainment in high season. WiFi throughout (charged). Bouncy castle (free) Tuesdays and Thursdays. Only electric barbecues permitted. Off site: Beach 300 m. Fishing, boat launching and riding 1 km. Bicycle hire 3 km. Golf 25 km.

Open: 23 April - 17 September.

Directions

From A9 exit 36 (Béziers Ouest) follow directions for Valras-Plage and Vendres-Plage over four roundabouts. At fifth roundabout (Port Conchylicole) follow sign for Vendres-Plage Ouest. Site is 500 m. on the left past the Ranch and tourist office. The entrance is quite tight. GPS: 43.227408, 3.243536

Charges guide

Per unit incl. 2 persons and electricity	€ 22.00 - € 49.00
incl. private sanitary facility	€ 25.00 - € 56.00
extra person (over 4 yrs)	€ 5.00 - € 9.00

Camping Cheques accepted.

Valras-Plage

Camping Domaine les Vignes dOr

Route de Valras B.P. 34, F-34350 Valras-Plage (Hérault) T: 04 67 32 37 18. E: vignesdor@franceloc.fr
alanrogers.com/FR34360

Les Vignes d'Or, owned by the FranceLoc group, is a pretty site with a mix of site owned mobile homes and chalets to rent and privately owned units, some 250 in total. There are no pitches for touring units. It is set back from the busy beach area among the vineyards with shade from trees and flowering shrubs. There are two pools, one of which can be covered and heated. Toboggan slides and a space bowl are popular features. It is a good venue for families with activities and entertainment in season.

Facilities

Large, modern toilet block is fully equipped, with facilities for babies and disabled campers. Laundry. Restaurant, bar and takeaway. Swimming pool complex. Play area. Sports field. Miniclub and entertainment (July/Aug). Bicycle hire (arranged in July/Aug). WiFi (free by reception and bar). Off site: Shops 900 m. Golf and riding 2 km. Fishing 2.5 km.

Open: 11 April - 20 September.

Directions

From A9 exit 35 (Béziers Est) follow D64 towards Sérignan and Valras. At second roundabout turn right following site signs carefully (back on yourself on secondary road). The road is narrow in parts and involves a left turn just before a boat storage yard (500 m). GPS: 43.259134, 3.275532

Charges guide

Contact site for details.

Valras-Plage

Yelloh! Village l'Hermitage

F-34350 Valras-Plage (Hérault) T: 04 67 32 61 81. E: info@campinghermitage.fr

alanrogers.com/FR34630

Camping Club l'Hermitage is a pleasant park with 100 mobile homes and chalets to rent, although a few are still privately owned. Most are attractively situated with trees and flowering shrubs, except for the newer ones (where cars are parked separately). The central pool and entertainment area forms the heart of the site and has a covered heated pool for early and late season, along with three other pools equipped with slides and a jacuzzi. The bar with upstairs terrace and restaurant overlooks the area. It is situated in a quiet position close to the vineyards, just outside the village of Sérignan.

Facilities

One toilet block, mainly for swimming pool users, has facilities for babies and disabled campers. Laundry. Swimming pool complex with paddling pool, slides and indoor pool (heated May and Sept). Covered terrace with bar and restaurant. Play area. Children's club. Multisports court. Evening entertainment. No charcoal barbecues. WiFi (charged). Off site: Beach 1.5 km.

Open: All year.

Directions

From autoroute A9 exit Bézier-Est and follow signs towards Valras-Plage. At roundabout outside Valras follow signs to Yelloh Village l'Hermitage. GPS: 43.27, 3.28

Charges guide

Contact site for details.

Vauvert

Flower Camping Mas de Mourgues

Gallician, F-30600 Vauvert (Gard) T: 04 66 73 30 88. E: info@masdemourgues.com

alanrogers.com/FR30040

Sandra and Cyril are proud of their campsite on the edge of the Petite Camargue region, a unique area of France. It can be hot here, the Mistral can blow and you may have some road noise, but the situation between Nîmes and Arles is ideal for exploring the Camargue and visiting towns such as Aigues Mortes. There are 71 pitches with 46 for touring units on level grass (10A electricity), nine mobile homes/bungalow tents to rent and a further 16 privately owned. Originally a vineyard on stony ground (strong pegs needed), some of the vines are now used to mark the pitches.

Facilities

Two small toilet blocks provide for all needs. Facilities for disabled visitors. Washing machine. Motorcaravan services (charged). Chips and panini to takeaway (high season). Breakfast served. Reception keeps essentials and bottled water. Bread to order (evening before). Play area. Games for children once a week (July/Aug). WiFi (charged). Communal barbecue. Mobile homes and tents to rent. Off site: Fishing 2 km. (licence not required). Riding 8 km. Bicycle hire 1 km. Golf 20 km. Beach 26 km.

Open: 15 March - 31 October.

Directions

Leave A9 autoroute at exit 26 (Gallargues) and follow signs for Vauvert. At Vauvert take N572 towards Arles and St Gilles. Site is on left after 4 km. at crossroads for Gallician. GPS: 43.6575, 4.2943

Charges guide

Per unit incl. 2 persons and electricity	€ 17.50 - € 26.50
extra person	€ 3.00 - € 5.00
child (3-6 yrs)	€ 2.00 - € 3.00
dog	€ 2.00 - € 3.00

Vendres

Camping Club les Vagues

F-34350 Valras-Plage (Hérault) T: 04 67 37 33 12. E: vag@sandaya.fr

alanrogers.com/FR34120

Camping les Vagues is a member of the Sandaya group and is situated at the popular seaside resort of Valras-Plage, 500 m. from a fine sandy beach. Les Vagues has an excellent (28°C) swimming pool complex extending over 2,000 sq.m, complete with waves and a sandy beach. There is also a wide range of amenities, including a buffet-style restaurant (with carvery), a multisports pitch and a minigolf course. Pitches are well shaded, most with 6/10A electrical connections, and are mixed with mobile homes and chalets (for rent) over three sections of the site. Les Vagues is a lively site in peak season.

Facilities

Four modern toilet blocks provide large showers, washbasins mainly in cabins, baby baths and provision for disabled visitors. Laundry facilities. Shop, bar, restaurant and snack bar. Swimming pool complex. Play area. Minigolf. Games room. Multisports court. Entertainment and miniclub (July/Aug). Gas or electric barbecues. Tourist train (July/Aug). Bicycle hire. WiFi (charged). Mobile homes and chalets for rent. Off site: Sandy beach, shops, bars and restaurants in Valras-Plage 500 m. Riding 500 m. Boat launching 2 km. Sailing 3 km. Carcassonne.

Open: 3 April - 12 September.

Directions

Les Vagues is on the southern side of Valras-Plage. Approaching from A9 autoroute, leave at the Vendres exit and head south on the D64. Having passed Vendres and shortly before reaching Valras, watch for site signs at roundabout and turn right. GPS: 43.231023, 3.25356

Charges guide

Per unit incl. 2 persons and electricity	€ 21.00 - € 60.00
extra person	€ 2.00 - € 8.50

Vendres-Plage

Campéole les Mûriers

37E route départementale, F-34350 Vendres-Plage (Hérault) T: 04 67 37 25 79. E: muriers@campeole.com
alanrogers.com/FR34620

Les Mûriers is a member of the Campéole group and is located among a group of sites situated on the route to le Grau de Vendres, the port of Vendres at the mouth of the River Aude. A marina has been developed there recently and there is also access to a lovely sandy beach, an 800 m. walk across the flat dunes. Look carefully for the Campéole reception as there is a large reception for a separate mobile home site under the same name. There are 105 fully equipped bungalow tents available to rent. They are arranged in a circular layout on grass with hedging. There are no pitches for touring units here.

Facilities

Two fully equipped toilet blocks. Laundry. Bar/restaurant (28/6-30/8), takeaway, shop, heated swimming pool. Entertainment and miniclub (5-12 yrs, 28/6-28/8). Amusements. Play area. Volleyball/basketball court. Multisports court. WiFi (charged). No barbecues allowed. Off site: Beach, diving, jet ski and sailing 800 m. Fishing and boat launching 1 km. Riding and karting.

Open: 21 June - 5 September.

Directions

From A9 take exit 36 (Béziers Ouest), towards Valras-Plage and Vendres-Plage. Continue over four roundabouts. At fifth roundabout (Port Conchylicole) follow signs for Vendres-Plage Ouest. Continue for 800 m. and site is on the right signed Les Mûriers. GPS: 43.223433, 3.23945

Charges guide

Contact site for details.

Vernet-les-Bains

Hotel de Plein Air l'Eau Vive

Chemin de Saint-Saturnin, F-66820 Vernet-les-Bains (Pyrénées-Orientales) T: 04 68 05 54 14.
E: contact@leauvive-camping.com **alanrogers.com/FR66130**

Enjoying dramatic views of the Pic du Canigou (2,784 m), this rather special and peaceful natural site is only 1.5 km. from the centre of Vernet-les-Bains in the Pyrenees. The 62 touring pitches are on grass, with electricity (10A) and 45 fully serviced, are on a slight slope, part hedged and some terraced, with a separate tent field. Most pitches have some shade and there are 15 chalets and mobile homes to rent. Well situated for touring this area of the Pyrenees and with very comfortable amenities, including a small bar and restaurant. The French owners are very proud of the improvements they have made to the site.

Facilities

Fully equipped toilet facilities and provision for babies and disabled visitors. Washing machine. Bread, main season. Bar/restaurant/takeaway with terrace (15/6-15/9). Play area with trampoline, basketball and table tennis. Free WiFi throughout. Off site: Fishing 200 m. Swimming pool, thermal centre in village 1 km. Organised rafting, canoeing, hydrospeed trips. Bicycle hire 2 km.

Open: 4 April - 3 October.

Directions

Follow N116 (Andorra). At Ville Franche, turn south, D116 (Vernet-les-Bains). After 5 km. keep right (avoid town). Right over bridge (Sahorre), immediately right (ave de Saturnin) for 1 km. through residential area. Watch carefully for signs. GPS: 42.55506, 2.37779

Charges guide

Per unit incl. 2 persons and electricity	€ 20.50 - € 26.50
extra person (over 4 yrs)	€ 4.00 - € 5.00

Vias

Camping International le Napoléon

1171 avenue de la Méditerranée, F-34450 Vias-Plage (Hérault) T: 04 67 01 07 80.
E: reception@camping-napoleon.fr **alanrogers.com/FR34030**

Le Napoléon is a smaller, family run site situated in the main street of Vias-Plage bordering the Mediterranean. It is a well established site having been owned by the Graziani family for over 40 years. Vias-Plage is hectic to say the least in season, but once through the security barrier and entrance to le Napoléon, the contrast is marked – tranquillity, yet still only 150 m. from the beach and other attractions. With good shade from many tall trees, there are 239 hedged and level pitches, 92 for touring units, all with 10A electricity. These are mixed in with a range of mobile homes for rent.

Facilities

Fully equipped sanitary blocks are of a reasonable standard. Baby bath. Facilities for disabled visitors. Laundry. Motorcaravan services. Fridge hire. Supermarket and bakery. Bar. Restaurant/pizzeria. Swimming pool complex (heated in early and late season) includes a jacuzzi, Hammam and solarium. Gym/fitness room with new equipment. Bicycle hire. Tennis, archery, boules. TV. Rooms for young campers. Miniclub. Teenage club. Amphitheatre and free entertainment until midnight (high season). Disco (Easter-Sept). WiFi over site (charged).

Open: 8 April - 25 September.

Directions

From autoroute A9 take exit Agde-Pézenas, towards Béziers. Continue for 5 km. towards Sète and Vias. Follow sign for Vias-Plage. Site is on the right near the beach; watch carefully for turning between restaurant and shops. GPS: 43.29197, 3.41535

Charges guide

Per unit incl. 2 persons and electricity	€ 21.00 - € 50.00
extra person	€ 6.00 - € 8.00
child (4-13 yrs)	free - € 8.00

Vias

Yelloh! Village Club Farret

Chemin des Rosses, F-34450 Vias-Plage (Hérault) T: 04 67 21 64 45. E: farret@wanadoo.fr

alanrogers.com/FR34110

An excellent site for families, well maintained and attractively landscaped with flowering shrubs, giving a truly Mediterranean feel. The main area has beach frontage and touring pitches, the other half, across a lane, has high quality mobile homes. Staff are helpful and everywhere is neat and tidy. It is a large, busy site but well organised with a relaxed atmosphere. There are 756 good sized, level, grassy pitches, with 302 for touring (10A electricity) with some shade from many trees. Both areas have impressive pool complexes, the newest has a pool bar. The safe beach is alongside the site, so some pitches have sea views as does the restaurant high above the pool. Evening entertainment and cultural visits are arranged. After 50 years, the Giner family are still continually striving to improve the site and have added a spa and wellbeing facility, numerous activities and a beach club.

Facilities

Very clean toilet blocks (one heated) have children's facilities and showers shaped like clowns! Baby rooms, facilities for disabled visitors. Washing machines. Dog shower. Motorcaravan services. Supermarket. Hairdresser. Bars with pizzas, snacks, takeaway. Restaurant. Crêperie with minigolf. Heated swimming pool complex (1,000 sq.m) with lifeguard. Wellness centre with sauna, steam room, jacuzzi etc. Gym. Excellent play areas. Miniclub (5-12 yrs). Teenagers' club (13-17 yrs). Tennis. Archery. Programme of games. Multisports court. Bicycle hire. WiFi (charged). Off site: Shops, bars and Luna Park within walking distance. Riding 1 km. Boat launching 6 km. Golf 10 km. Canal du Midi.

Open: 9 April - 26 September.

Directions

Site is south of Vias at Vias-Plage. From N112 (Béziers-Agde) take D137 signed Vias-Plage. Site is signed on the left. GPS: 43.1727, 3.2507

Charges guide

Per unit incl. 2 persons and electricity	€ 18.00 - € 57.00
extra person	€ 7.00 - € 9.00
dog	€ 5.00

Vias

Camping le Méditerranée Plage

Côte Ouest, F-34450 Vias (Hérault) T: 04 67 90 99 07. E: contact@mediterranee-plage.com

alanrogers.com/FR34410

A somewhat unusual but comfortable beach site set in a quiet part of the coast with not only an impressive entertainment complex, but two good sized pools (one heated) and a children's farm with small animals. A supermarket and snack bar provide for daytime needs, with evening entertainment beside the main bar and restaurant. Méditerranée Plage is very well cared for, with 410 pitches (some 110 for touring units, all with 6A electricity) situated in tree-lined avenues on level grass. Nearer the beach, they become sandier and have smaller trees. The sand is built up high so the sea is not visible from the site. Very popular with Dutch and German visitors.

Facilities

Two large, heated toilet blocks are modern, one with a special smart nursery unit, plus two smaller ones. There is a mixture of British and Turkish style WCs Facilities for disabled visitors. Laundry. Motorcaravan services. Supermarket. Smart restaurant (facing stage for entertainment) and bar. Snack bar. Hairdressers. TV room. Play area. Games room. Multisports court. Tennis. Archery. Windsurfing possible from beach. Bicycle hire. Activity programme, children's entertainment, circus school (on specific dates). Evening entertainment. Minifarm. WiFi (charged). Off site: Riding and fishing 2 km. Golf 15 km. Canal du Midi nearby. Luna Park at Vias. Local markets in Vias, Agde and Beziers.

Open: 28 March - 27 September.

Directions

From A9 exit 35 (Béziers Est) follow directions for Agde and Sète on N112. After 4.2 km. turn for Portiragnes. Pass village and continue for 2.5 km. over Canal du Midi then turn left and follow site signs. GPS: 43.28202, 3.37105

Charges guide

Per unit incl. 2 persons and electricity	€ 17.00 - € 47.00
extra person	€ 3.30 - € 8.90
child (2-10 yrs)	€ 2.30 - € 6.80
dog	€ 2.20 - € 4.50

Vias

Sunêlia Domaine de la Dragonnière

RD 612, F-34450 Vias-sur-Mer (Hérault) T: 04 67 01 03 10. E: contact@dragonniere.com

alanrogers.com/FR34450

La Dragonnière offers an amazing selection of swimming pools and a wide range of sporting activities and entertainment which amply makes up for it being set back from the sea. It is a busy holiday village, located between the popular resorts of Vias and Portiragnes, and very well organised. In total, there are 879 pitches split into two areas, most occupied by a range of smart mobile homes and chalets, but there are still 38 grass touring pitches with shade from trees and shrubs. All have electrical connections (10A) as well as water and drainage and a number of individual en-suite sanitary units.

Facilities

Individual sanitary unit on every pitch. Baby room. Laundry. Supermarket. Stalls selling local produce. Bar and restaurant complex with takeaway service. Two heated swimming pool complexes with children's pools. Indoor pool. Play areas. Sauna and gym. Multisports pitch. Sports competitions, children's club and evening entertainment in high season. Activities in low season. Bicycle hire. WiFi (charged). Excursions. Mobile homes and chalets for rent. Communal or gas barbecues only.

Open: 3 April - 27 September.

Directions

Take the Béziers Est exit from the A9 autoroute. Follow directions to Villeneuve, Sérignan and Valras-Plage. After 800 m. at the large roundabout, follow signs to 'Vias aéroport' on the N112. After a further 7 km, site is on the right. GPS: 43.313, 3.36517

Charges guide

Per unit incl. 3 persons, water, waste water and electricity	€ 25.00 - € 65.00
extra person	€ 7.00 - € 11.00

Vias-Plage

Camping les Salisses

Route de la Mer, F-34450 Vias-Plage (Hérault) T: 04 67 21 64 07. E: info@salisses.com

alanrogers.com/FR34520

A traditional-style French campsite, les Salisses is well run and managed with an impressive range of swimming pools and other facilities. The 400 plus level, hedged pitches of average size are separated by flowering shrubs and trees that provide shade – all rather pretty. There are just over 100 places for touring units with 10A electricity, the rest being taken by a range of mobile homes, some to let. Vias-Plage is a busy, somewhat hectic resort and les Salisses has its own section of beach with a bar.

Facilities

Four fully equipped toilet blocks. Facilities for disabled visitors. Laundry. Motorcaravan services. Shop. Bar and restaurant. Takeaway pizzeria (July/Aug). One indoor pool (heated for low season; used by naturists in high season). Two other pool complexes, one for swimming and one with cascades and islands. Play area. Sports field (rugby posts). Multisports court. Tennis. Minigolf. Bicycle hire. Wide range of entertainment and activities. WiFi (free). Communal barbecue areas. Off site: Beach 800 m.

Open: 12 April - 13 September.

Directions

From the A9 take exit 34, then the N312 towards Vias and Agde. Join the N112 to avoid Vias town to pick up sign for Vias-Plage. Site is first on the right. GPS: 43.29657, 3.4164

Charges guide

Per unit incl. 2 persons and electricity	€ 27.00 - € 44.00
extra person	€ 7.50 - € 10.00

Camping Cheques accepted.

Villeneuve-les-Béziers

Camping les Berges du Canal

Promenade les Vernets, F-34420 Villeneuve-les-Béziers (Hérault) T: 04 67 39 36 09.
E: contact@lesbergesducanal.com **alanrogers.com/FR34210**

There are surprisingly few campsites that provide an opportunity to enjoy the rather special ambience for which the Canal du Midi is renowned, but this pleasant little site is right alongside the canal at Villeneuve-les-Béziers. It is in a peaceful and shady situation, separated from the canal by an unmade access road, with a total of 90 level pitches on sandy grass. Some are large with 6A electricity, and eight are fully serviced for motorcaravans. Of these, 20 are occupied by privately owned mobile homes and a further 25 are available to rent. Villeneuve-les-Béziers is just a few minutes' walk along the towpath.

Facilities

Fully equipped toilet block with some washbasins in cabins. Facilities for children and disabled visitors (key access). Laundry facilities. Motorcaravan services. Bar/snack bar with TV (serving breakfast too). Small restaurant attached to site. Two swimming pools. Beauty therapist visits weekly. Multisports court. Play area. Fishing. Evening entertainment during high season. Gas and electric barbecues only. Off site: Villeneuve-les-Béziers. Beach at Portiragnes-Plage. Bicycle hire 100 m.

Open: 15 March - 15 October.

Directions

From A9 exit 35, follow signs for Agde, at first roundabout take N112 (Béziers). First left onto D37 signed Villeneuve-les-Béziers and Valras-Plage. Pass traffic lights, left at roundabout and follow site signs (take care at junction beside bridge). GPS: 43.31673, 3.28433

Charges guide

Per unit incl. 2 persons and electricity	€ 20.00 - € 26.00

Camping Cheques accepted.

Villeneuve-lez-Avignon

Campéole Ile des Papes

1497 RD 780, F-30400 Villeneuve-lez-Avignon (Gard) T: 04 90 15 15 90. E: ile-des-papes@campeole.com
alanrogers.com/FR30120

Camping Ile des Papes is a large, open and very well equipped site. Avignon and its palace and museums are 8 km. away. The site has an extensive swimming pool area and a fishing lake with beautiful mature gardens. The railway is quite near but noise is not too intrusive. The 396 pitches, 195 for touring (all with 10A electricity), are of a good size on level grass, but with little shade. Games and competitions for all ages are organised in high season. This site is very popular with groups and is especially busy at weekends and in high season. A good base to explore the famous Routes des Vins and the old villages and ancient towns of the Provençale region. There are many walks and cycle routes close by.

Facilities

Good quality toilet blocks (may be stretched when busy) include baby rooms and facilities for disabled campers. Washing machines. Motorcaravan services. Shop (1/5-30/9). Bar, restaurant and takeaway (1/4-15/10, limited hours in low season). Large swimming pool complex and pool for children (1/5-30/9; all unheated). Play area. Lake for fishing. Archery, tennis, minigolf and basketball. Bicycle hire. Communal barbecue. WiFi over part of site (charged). Off site: Riding 3 km. Boat launching 5 km. Parachuting, paintball, jetski. Villeneuve-lez-Avignon with shops, bars and restaurants. Avignon 6 km. Golf 20 km.

Open: 28 March - 2 November.

Directions

Leave the A9 at exit 22 (Roquemaure) and take D976 to Roquemaure, turn south D980 towards Villeneuve. Near railway bridge turn hard left, D780 (site signed). Cross river, immediately turn right to site. GPS: 43.993842, 4.817988

Charges guide

Per unit incl. 2 persons and electricity	€ 19.90 - € 30.60
extra person	€ 4.70 - € 5.10
child (under 7 years)	free - € 4.00
dog	€ 2.00 - € 3.00

Camping Cheques accepted.

Villeneuve-lez-Avignon

Camping Municipal la Laune

Chemin Saint Honoré, F-30400 Villeneuve-lez-Avignon (Gard) T: 04 90 25 76 06.
E: campingdelalaune@wanadoo.fr **alanrogers.com/FR30420**

A well run municipal site just 1 km. from the interesting old town of Villeneuve-lez-Avignon and only 4 km. from the historic walled town of Avignon, on the opposite bank of the mighty River Rhône. Avignon is easily reached by bike using the nearby ferry or by bus. There are 126 spacious touring pitches, some with 6A electricity. They are separated by some hedging and a variety of tall trees give welcome shade. There are no problems here for large outfits. The adjacent municipal swimming pool, skate park and tennis courts are free to campers. The site is within easy walking distance of Villeneuve-lez-Avignon with its interesting old town and imposing Fort Saint-André high above the town.

Facilities

Two well appointed, clean toilet blocks with facilities for campers with disabilities. Motorcaravan services. Shop. Bar, restaurant, good value takeaway. TV room/library. Play area. Gas and electric barbecues only. Communal barbecue. Off site: Municipal swimming pool and tennis courts adjacent (free). Bicycle hire 100 m. Villeneuve-lez-Avignon and fort 1 km. Avignon with many shops, bars restaurants, museums 4 km. Fishing 1 km. Riding 4 km. Golf 9 km. Côte du Rhône vineyards. Many villages and towns of the Cévennes and Provence.

Open: 1 April - 20 October.

Directions

Leave autoroute A9 (exit 23) Remoulins. Take N100 east 17 km. to Villeneuve-lez-Avignon. Turn north, D980, just before the River Rhone. Just beyond castle walls turn right at traffic lights (signed piscine and camping). Site in 200 m. GPS: 43.97061, 4.798881

Charges guide

Per unit incl. 2 persons and electricity	€ 17.50 - € 20.50
extra person	€ 4.50 - € 5.60
child (3-7 yrs)	€ 2.50 - € 3.70
dog	€ 3.50

DÉPARTEMENTS: 04 ALPES-DE-HAUTE-PROVENCE, 05 HAUTES-ALPES, 06 ALPES-MARITIME, 13 BOUCHES-DU-RHÔNE, 83 VAR, 84 VAUCLUSE

MAJOR CITIES: NICE, CANNES, MONTE CARLO (MONACO), MARSEILLES

The sleepy villages, sunny vineyards and pretty lavender fields of Provence sit in stark contrast to the cosmopolitan towns and thronging beaches of the Côte d'Azur, one of France's most popular destinations.

Provence is characterised by bleached landscapes, olive groves and herb-scented garrigue. The colours and amazing intensity of light have encouraged artists and writers to settle in the quiet villages, their ancient dwellings topped by distinctive terracotta tiles, and their narrow streets fragrant with the perfume of wild herbs and lavender. Roman monuments can be seen at Orange and Vaison-la-Romaine, and the spectacular Palais des Papes at Avignon is a 'must see'. The extinct volcanic cone of Mont Ventoux provides dramatic views and is one of the most gruelling stages in the Tour de France.

In contrast, the glittering Côte d'Azur is a beautiful stretch of coast studded with sophisticated towns such as Monte Carlo, Nice and Cannes and, of course, the glamorous resort of St Tropez. With its vast expanses of golden sand and long hours of sunshine, this is a paradise for sun worshippers. The quaint harbours and fishing villages have become chic destinations full of luxury yachts, harbour-side cafés and crowded summertime beaches. Inland, St Paul-de-Vence with its shops and galleries and Grasse, perfume capital of the world, are popular destinations for visitors.

Places of interest

Aix-en-Provence: old town; cathedral of St. Sauveur; Cézanne museum.

Antibes: old city with 17th-century ramparts; 12th-century castle.

Camargue: wetland and nature reserve with white horses, flamingos and bulls.

Cannes: popular for conventions and festivals; la Croisette; old city.

Marseille: bustling port city with boat trips to the Château d'If prison on a nearby island.

Menton: warmest of coastal cities, year round resort.

Orange: Roman city, gateway to the Midi; Colline St Europe.

Cuisine of the region

Aigo Bouido: garlic and sage soup with bread (or eggs and cheese).

Aïoli (ailloli): a mayonnaise sauce with garlic and olive oil.

Bagna Cauda: raw vegetables in a fondue of hot olive oil, garlic and anchovies.

Bouillabaisse: fish soup served with rouille sauce, saffron and aioli.

Pissaladière: Provençal bread dough with onions, anchovies, olives.

Porquetta: stuffed suckling pig.

Salade niçoise: salad of anchovies, tuna, tomatoes, peppers, eggs and olives.

Socca: a crêpe made with chick pea flour and cooked in a wood-fired oven.

www.guideriviera.com
info@guideriviera.com
(0)4 93 37 78 78

www.discover-southoffrance.com
information@cft-paca.fr
(0)4 91 56 47 00

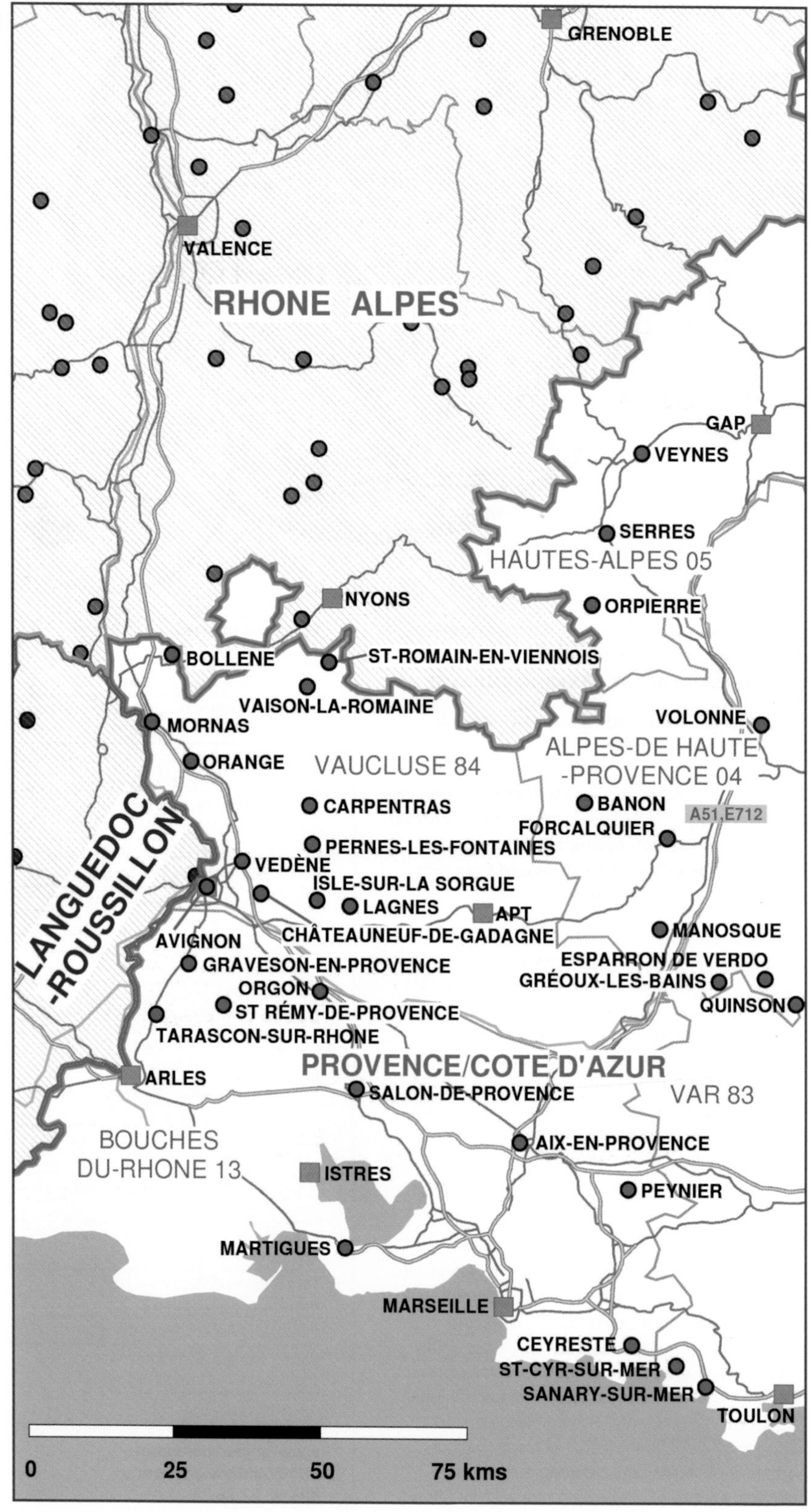
GRENOBLE
VALENCE
RHONE ALPES
GAP
VEYNES
SERRES
HAUTES-ALPES 05
NYONS
ORPIERRE
BOLLENE
ST-ROMAIN-EN-VIENNOIS
VAISON-LA-ROMAINE
MORNAS
VOLONNE
ALPES-DE HAUTE
-PROVENCE 04
ORANGE
VAUCLUSE 84
CARPENTRAS
BANON
A51,E712
FORCALQUIER
PERNES-LES-FONTAINES
VEDÈNE
LANGUEDOC
-ROUSSILLON
ISLE-SUR-LA SORGUE
LAGNES
APT
AVIGNON
CHÂTEAUNEUF-DE-GADAGNE
MANOSQUE
GRAVESON-EN-PROVENCE
ESPARRON DE VERDO
GRÉOUX-LES-BAINS
ORGON
QUINSON
ST RÉMY-DE-PROVENCE
TARASCON-SUR-RHONE
PROVENCE/COTE D'AZUR
ARLES
SALON-DE-PROVENCE
VAR 83
BOUCHES
DU-RHONE 13
AIX-EN-PROVENCE
ISTRES
PEYNIER
MARTIGUES
MARSEILLE
CEYRESTE
ST-CYR-SUR-MER
SANARY-SUR-MER
TOULON
0
25
50
75 kms

LA GRAVE
VAL-DES-PRÈS
BRIANCON
VALLOUISE
LES VIGNEAUX
HAUTES-ALPES 05
ITALY
GUILLESTRE
ST APOLLINAIRE
ST-VINCENT-LES-FORTS
MONTCLAR
MEOLANS-REVEL
SEYNE-LES-ALPES
ALPES-DE HAUTE
-PROVENCE 04
VILLARS-COLMARS
PROVENCE/COTE D'AZUR
DIGNE-LES-BAINS
ANNOT
SOSPEL
BRIANCONNECT
CONTES
CASTELLANE
MONTE-CARLO
MOUSTIERS-STE-MARIE
VENCE
NICE
LE BAR-SUR-LOUP
LA COLLE-SUR-LOUP
GRASSE
VILLENEUVE-LOUBET
VILLENEUVE-
LOUBET PLAGE
QUINSON
AURIBEAU-SUR-SIAGNE
RÉGUSSE
ST PAUL-EN-FORET
ANTIBES
PUGET-SUR-ARGENS
DRAGUIGNAN
A8,E80
LE MUY
AGAY
ROQUEBRUNE-SUR-ARGENS
ST RAPHAEL
FRÉJUS
ST AYGULF
BRIGNOLES
LES ISSAMBRES
VAR 83
A57
ST-TROPEZ
GRIMAUD
COGOLIN
GASSIN
RAMATUELLE
LA MOLE
CAVALAIRE-SUR-MER
BORMES-LES-MIMOSAS
TOULON
HYÈRES
LE LAVANDOU
HYERES-LES-PALMIERS
LE PRADET
HYÈRES-PLAGE

Parc Saint-James
Villages Club

Parc Saint-James is a small group of 4* campsites, all located in the South of France on the Côte d'Azur.

These three 'village-club' style campsites offer a warm welcome, a decent range of facilities with a real family atmosphere and a great location for beach-based holidays.

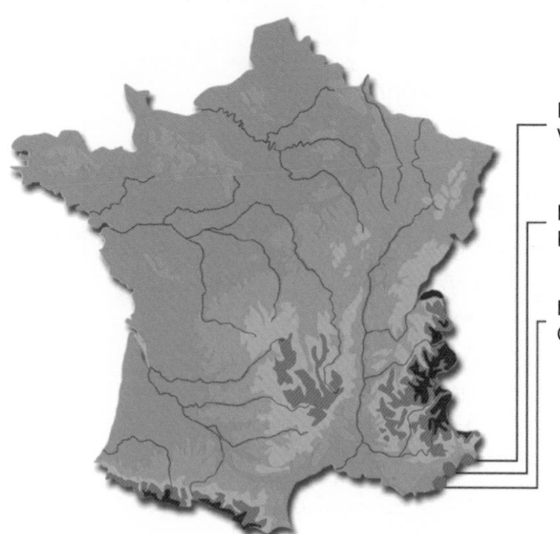

Parc Saint-James 'Le Sourire★★★★'
Villeneuve Loubet

Parc Saint-James 'Oasis Village★★★★★'
Puget sur Argens

Parc Saint-James 'Parc Montana★★★★'
Gassin

Parc Saint-James

In Their Own Words...

Come and discover the Côte d'Azur South of France

Enjoy the pleasure of spending your holidays outdoors in village-clubs where everything has been designed for your leisure and well being.

A superb environment, a warm welcome, a friendly setting where your family can get together in a privileged world and experience true moments of happiness.

Active holidays

According to campsite, Parc Saint-James offers the opportunity to enjoy many activities such as soccer, volleyball, tennis, badminton, cross-fit and fitness. Guests can also enjoy horse riding, windsurfing, rowing, diving and climbing.

...or relaxing holidays

Parc Saint-James campsites village club is for you! According to campsite, you'll find a Waterpark with swimming pools and jacuzzi, sun decks and shady trees. Each campsite works hard to ensure you don't need to lift a finger – just relax and we'll take care of you. Enjoy our bars, restaurants and TV lounges.

Your evening

Parc Saint-James ensures you are always close to some activity and entertainment. A short distance from Fréjus and Saint-Raphaël, or in the Gulf of St. Tropez or near Nice, our locations allow you to party through the night. And the Parc Saint-James campsites organise evenings exclusively for residents, with a different daily themed programme (musical groups and/or shows) and at Oasis, from 11pm, a disco party.

Children's kingdom

At Parc Saint-James campsites, children are heroes! Children from 4 to 10 years can enjoy our mini-club and a whole range of fun activities: treasure hunts, contests, make-up, crafts and sports. They will also enjoy our playground with slides and swings or go paddling safely under the eye of a lifeguard. Two of our campsites have new aquatic gardens. Older children can do battle with friends in our arcades or play ping-pong, soccer and volleyball.

www.camping-parcsaintjames.com

Agay

Camping Caravaning Esterel

Avenue des Golfs, Agay, F-83530 Saint Raphaël (Var) T: 04 94 82 03 28. E: contact@esterel-caravaning.fr
alanrogers.com/FR83020

Esterel is a quality, award-winning caravan site east of Saint Raphaël, set among the hills beyond Agay. The site is 3.5 km. from the sandy beach at Agay where parking is perhaps a little easier than at most places on this coast, but a shuttle from the site runs to and from the beach several times daily in July and August. It has 146 touring pitches (tents are not accepted) with 10A electricity and a water tap. A number of 'deluxe' pitches are available with heated bathroom, jacuzzi, dishwasher and washing machine. Pitches are on shallow terraces, attractively landscaped with good shade and a variety of flowers, giving a feeling of spaciousness.

Facilities

Heated toilet blocks (one newly refurbished with facilities for babies and children). New en-suite facilities for disabled visitors. Laundry room. Motorcaravan services. Small supermarket. Gift shop. Takeaway. Bar/restaurant. Swimming pool complex (two heated), separate 'jungle' pool for children (covered and heated). Fitness centre. Spa with sauna. Disco. Archery. Minigolf. Tennis. Pony rides. Pétanque. Squash. Nursery (4 mths.-3 yrs). Playground. Miniclubs. Family activities. TV room/library. Bicycle hire. Internet access. Organised events in season. No barbecues. WiFi throughout. Off site: Golf nearby. Trekking by foot, bicycle or pony in l'Esterel forest park. Fishing and beach 3 km.

Open: 19 March - 24 September.

Directions

From the D559 coast road at Agay, turn north on the D100 (route des Golf). Site is signed after 3 km. and is 400 m. up a small access road.
GPS: 43.453775, 6.832817

Charges guide

Per unit incl. 2 persons and electricity	€ 18.00 - € 38.00
extra person	€ 9.00 - € 10.00
child (acc. to age)	free - € 9.00
dog	free - € 4.00

Agay/Saint Raphaël

Campéole du Dramont

986 boulevard 36ème Division Texas, F-83530 Agay/Saint Raphaël (Var) T: 04 94 82 07 68.
E: dramont@campeole.com **alanrogers.com/FR83700**

Le Dramont stretches over a shady hillside, sloping gently down to a pebble beach (with direct access), close to the attractive resort of Agay. This site is popular with scuba divers and is an ideal base for exploring the turquoise waters. There is an international diving school on site and other amenities here include a beauty salon (July and August) and a sports field. Le Dramont has 400 pitches, of which 188 are occupied by mobile homes, chalets and fully equipped tents for rent. The 212 touring pitches are well shaded and generally of a good size, all with 6/10A electricity (although long leads may be necessary). Some are near the main road so there may be some road noise, others are overlooking the beach and shaded by pine trees. The site becomes lively in high season with a daily entertainment and activity programme, including activities for children.

Facilities

Three sanitary blocks include seatless toilets, modern preset showers and washbasins with hot and cold water. Very good facilities for babies in a seperate heated unit. Wet room for disabled visitors. Modern laundry facilities. Shop, bar, snack bar (all May-Aug). Swimming pool (from 1/6). Beauty salon. Takeaway. Games room. Playground. Diving school. Boat launching (charged). Multisport pitch. Activity and entertainment programme. Direct beach access. Charcoal barbecues not permitted. Mobile homes, chalets and tents for rent. WiFi in some areas (charged). Off site: Riding 200 m. Fishing. Golf. Rock climbing. Walking and mountain biking in the Esterel hills. St Raphaël and Fréjus.

Open: 23 March - 6 October.

Directions

From St Raphaël, take the RN98 towards Cannes. The site is 7 km. beyond St Raphaël (between Boulouris and Agay). It is in Dramont and is signed from the Dramont roundabout.
GPS: 43.417864, 6.848195

Charges guide

Per unit incl. 2 persons and electricity	€ 24.00 - € 47.20
extra person	€ 5.70 - € 10.30
child (2-6 yrs)	€ 3.00 - € 5.20
dog	€ 3.20 - € 4.30

Aix-en-Provence

Camping Chantecler

41 avenue du Val Saint André, F-13100 Aix-en-Provence (Bouches du Rhône) T: 04 42 .
E: info@campingchantecler.com **alanrogers.com/FR13120**

Aix is a busy, attractive town with a delightful pedestrian-friendly centre just waiting
There is much to visit in the area and Marseilles is within easy reach using the freque
Chantecler is a pleasant, eight-hectare campsite set in mixed woodland with an atmosp
and tranquillity. It is particularly well situated on the southeast edge of the town, close to t
and only minutes, by a good bus service, from the city centre and the main station. The s ovides 271 hedged and shaded pitches (over 200 for touring units) arranged in mature woodland with good facilities. Whilst this is a popular site which can get very busy in July and August, it is well run by a friendly, enthusiastic management.

Facilities

At the height of the season four sanitary blocks provide ample WCs, washbasins and hot showers around the site. Baby room and facilities for disabled visitors. Laundry facilities. Motorcaravan services. Bar and restaurant (1/5-15/9). Swimming pool (1/5-30/9). Boules. Internet. WiFi throughout (charged). No charcoal barbecues. Twin-axle units are not accepted. Mobile homes to rent.

Open: All year.

Directions

Leave the A8 at exit 31 (Aix-Sud) and at roundabout turn right. At second set of lights turn left and within 300 m. at roundabout turn right to the site in 200 m. GPS: 43.51636, 5.47495

Charges guide

Per unit incl. 2 persons and electricity	€ 24.00 - € 28.10
extra person	€ 6.30 - € 7.50

Annot

Camping la Ribière

Route du Fugeret, F-04240 Annot (Alpes-de-Haute-Provence) T: 04 92 83 21 44. E: info@la-ribiere.com
alanrogers.com/FR04520

This very welcoming family run site is set on the northern edge of Annot, a medieval village renowned for the Grès d'Annot, a chaos of massive sandstone boulders which attracts both geologists and climbers from all over the world. La Ribère is a small site with only 60 pitches, 52 of which are for touring. The majority are level and mainly grassy and all have 10A electricity; those by the river bank are stony, so rock pegs may be useful. The bar/snack bar is open all season, serving delicious home-made pizzas at very reasonable prices. In low season, there is a convivial meeting room heated by a wood burner.

Facilities

One new heated and very clean toilet block with facilities for babies and disabled visitors. Laundry with drying area. Motorcaravan services. Bread and pastries to order. Bar/snack bar with terrace (all season). Library. Meeting room (heated in low season). Small play area. Small football pitch. Boules. Communal barbecue area. No charcoal barbecues on pitches. Direct river access. WiFi throughout (free). Off site: Supermarket 200 m.

Open: 15 March - 31 October.

Directions

From Digne-les-Bains, head south on N85. At Barrême turn east on N202. After 37 km. turn north on D908 to Annot. Site is 700 m. past Annot, on left. GPS: 43.97176, 6.65805

Charges guide

Per unit incl. 2 persons and electricity	€ 18.40
extra person	€ 4.10
child (3-7 yrs)	€ 2.20
dog	€ 1.00

Antibes

Camping le Sequoia

Avenue du Pylone, F-06600 Antibes (Alpes-Maritimes) T: 04 93 74 44 75. E: sequoia-antibes@orange.fr
alanrogers.com/FR06170

Camping le Sequoia is a family run, family oriented site with carefully maintained facilities and a beautiful pool. The owner, who is justifiably proud of her oasis of calm greenery in this very busy tourist area, lives on site. It is only 800 metres from the new SNCF station at Biot with a very frequent train service that serves the entire coast from Monaco, Nice and Cannes to Antibes. A small, quiet site, there are just 20 touring pitches and 24 mobile homes for rent. Beaches are 800 m. distant and the spectacular theme parks of Marineland and Aquasplash are a short walk along the N7. The Riviera has something for everyone and this site would make an excellent base to explore the department of Alpes-Maritime.

Facilities

One unisex toilet block provides WCs, showers and washbasins. Facilities for disabled campers. Washing machine. Shop, bar and restaurant (15/6-30/8). Swimming pool. Play area. Boules. Mobile homes to rent. WiFi (charged). Off site: Beach 800 m. Antibes. Marineland, Aquasplash and much more.

Open: Mid April - 22 September.

Directions

East of Antibes on N7, drive past SNCF station Gare de Biot and at next roundabout turn to Biot. After 100 m. turn left into Ave Mozart, then right into Ave du Pylone. Follow signs. GPS: 43.61221, 7.11543

Charges guide

Per unit incl. 2 persons and electricity	€ 21.95 - € 31.70
extra person	€ 4.10 - € 5.95

au-sur-Siagne

mping le Parc des Monges

635 chemin du Gabre, F-06810 Auribeau-sur-Siagne (Alpes-Maritimes) T: 04 93 60 91 71.

E: contact@parcdesmonges.fr **alanrogers.com/FR06230**

This small and delightful, family run site is set amongst small trees and oleander hedges that give welcome shade. There are 40 level and grassy touring pitches each with electricity (4/6/10A). Some are on the banks of the Siagne river which provides excellent fishing. A small number of chalets and mobile homes are available for rent. In high season, activities are organised for children and adults, both on site and in the surrounding hills. The swimming pool and pleasant snack bar make a welcome relaxation point after a day exploring nearby Cannes. A regular bus service stops just outside the campsite.

Facilities

Modern sanitary block with hot showers, some washbasins in cabins and facilities for disabled visitors, children and babies. Laundry. Snack bar (13/6-15/9). Bread to order. Heated outdoor pool and jacuzzi. Aquagym. Play area. Evening entertainment and activities (July/Aug). Accommodation for rent. WiFi (charged). Charcoal barbecues not permitted. Communal barbecue.

Open: 25 April - 26 September.

Directions

Site is 13 km. northwest of Cannes. Take D9 northwest of Cannes for 11 km. then at roundabout take exit for Auribeau sur Saigne (D509). Continue for 1.5 km. to site on left. GPS: 43.60639, 6.90246

Charges guide

Per unit incl. 2 persons and electricity	€ 21.50 - € 38.50
extra person	€ 4.80 - € 6.10

Avignon

Camping du Pont d'Avignon

10 chemin de la Barthelasse, Ile de la Barthelasse, F-84000 Avignon (Vaucluse) T: 04 90 80 63 50.

E: camping.lepontdavignon@orange.fr **alanrogers.com/FR84090**

Pont d'Avignon is on the Ile de la Barthelasse in the centre of the river and within walking distance of the town centre via the bridge or on the free ferry. Separated by trees and flowering shrubs, there are 300 level pitches, some grassy and some with gravel; 276 have 10A electricity. All are shaded and neatly laid out with good access. A good play area, tennis courts and volleyball pitch are in the centre of the site separating the two halves. The restaurant, bar and terrace overlook the attractive pool. During the season there are musical and themed evenings in the restaurant. Good English is spoken at reception.

Facilities

Three adequate sanitary blocks (two open in low season) have good facilities for disabled visitors. Washing machines, dryer. Motorcaravan services. Well stocked shop. Bar/restaurant and takeaway. Swimming pool, paddling pool and jacuzzi (15/5-15/9). TV/games room. Boules. Play area with climbing frame. Tennis (free). Bicycle hire (and electric). Internet access. WiFi throughout (charged). Bungalow, tents and mobile homes for hire. Off site: Ferry to town centre. Riding 3 km.

Open: 29 February - 20 November.

Directions

From A7 exit 23 head for Avignon Centre. Follow D224 along river into Avignon. Follow signs for Barthelasse and over Pont Daladier. Take care on approach road before bridge – do not go under bridge. Just after crossing first section of river, fork right to site in 500 m. GPS: 43.95661, 4.80215

Charges guide

Per unit incl. 2 persons and electricity	€ 19.30 - € 31.00

Camping Cheques accepted.

Avignon

Camping Bagatelle

Ile de la Barthelasse, 25 allée Antoine Pinay, F-84000 Avignon (Vaucluse) T: 04 90 86 30 39.

E: camping.bagatelle@wanadoo.fr **alanrogers.com/FR84160**

Camping Bagatelle is a combination of a city campsite, backpackers' hostel and restaurant. It may be a bit noisy because of its location at the edge of the town – the city sights are just across the bridge. From the restaurant and terrace there are good views across the river of the historical Papal Palaces and the city walls of Avignon. There are 227 shaded gravel pitches, all for touring, 140 with 6/10A electricity (long leads required) and suitable for larger outfits. The site is a little hard to find and one must be very careful to follow the signs.

Facilities

Two toilet blocks, although quite old, are well equipped and kept very clean. One is heated in low season and is being slowly renovated. It is near the touring pitches. The second block is near the hostel. Private bathroom (key at reception). Heated baby room. Facilities for disabled visitors. Motorcaravan services. Good shop. Two restaurants and a bar with counter meals. Extensive tourist information and booking of city sightseeing at reception. Playground. Occasional organised activities. WiFi in reception and bar areas (free).

Open: All year.

Directions

From A9 exit 22 take N580 to Avignon. Follow signs for Barthelasse, then Camping Bagatelle. Use co-ordinates for sat navs, not address. GPS: 43.954, 4.798

Charges guide

Per unit incl. 2 persons and electricity	€ 20.42 - € 28.15
extra person	€ 3.36 - € 4.61
child (2-17 yrs)	€ 1.00 - € 4.55

Bormes-les-Mimosas

Camp du Domaine

B.P. 207 la Favière, 2581 route de Bénat, F-83230 Bormes-les-Mimosas (Var) T: 04 94 71 03 12.
E: mail@campdudomaine.com **alanrogers.com/FR83120**

Camp du Domaine, 3 km. south of Le Lavandou, is a large, attractive, beachside site with 1,173 touring pitches set in 45 hectares of pinewood, yet surprisingly it does not give the impression of being so big. The pitches are large and most are reasonably level; 957 have 10A electricity. The most popular pitches are beside the beach, but those furthest away are generally larger and have more shade. Amongst the trees, many pitches are more suitable for tents. There are also 147 mobile homes for rent, located on the hillside with super sea views. The beach is the attraction and everyone tries to get close. American motorhomes are accepted. Despite its size, the site does not feel too busy, except perhaps around the supermarket. This is mainly because many pitches are hidden in the trees, the access roads are quite wide and it all covers quite a wide area (some of the beach pitches are 600 m. from the entrance). Its popularity makes early reservation necessary over a long season (about mid June to mid September) since regular clients book from season to season. A good range of languages are spoken.

Facilities

Ten modern, well used but clean toilet blocks. Facilities for disabled visitors. Baby room with showers, WC and changing facilities. Washing machines. Fridge hire. Well stocked supermarket, bars, pizzeria (all open all season). No swimming pool, but direct beach access. Several excellent play areas for all ages. Entertainment and activities for children and teenagers (July/Aug). 6 tennis courts. Kayaks and paddle boards for hire. Wide range of watersports. Water games. New gym. Multisports courts (one indoor for wet or hot weather) for football, basketball. Only gas and electric barbecues are allowed. Direct beach access. Dogs are not accepted 12/7-16/8. Free WiFi at both bars. Off site: Sailing school, boat and jet ski hire 300 m. Bicycle hire 2.5 km. Riding and golf 15 km.

Open: 28 March - 31 October.

Directions

From Bormes-les-Mimosas, head east on D559 to Le Lavandou. At roundabout, take D298 south for 2.5 km. Campsite is well signed.
GPS: 43.11779, 6.35176

Charges guide

Per unit incl. 2 persons and electricity	€ 31.50 - € 51.00

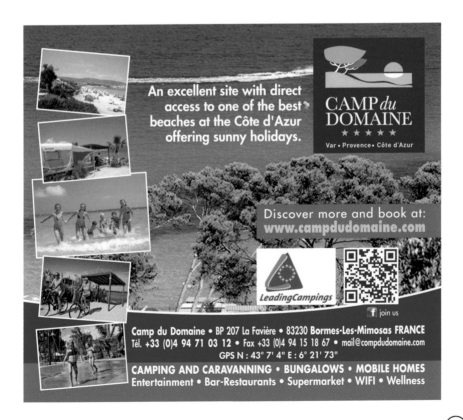

Banon

Flower Camping l'Epi Bleu

Lieu-dit les Gravières, F-04150 Banon (Alpes-de-Haute-Provence) T: 04 92 73 30 30.
E: campingepibleu@aol.com **alanrogers.com/FR04380**

L'Epi Bleu is a small and friendly family run site, set in the heart of Haute-Provence, close to the unspoilt hilltop village of Banon which gave its name to a renowned goat's cheese. Of the 90 level pitches, 40 are for touring (rock pegs advised), the remainder for mobile homes, chalets and lodges. Most pitches are shaded by trees and all have 10A electricity. Since joining the Flower Group in 2014, the site has undergone extensive refurbishment including new sanitary blocks. The convivial bar terrace overlooks the children's playground and the restaurant serves simple meals at lunchtime and in the evenings in the high season, when there is plenty of activity for all the family.

Facilities

Two heated sanitary blocks with hot showers and washbasins in cabins, one with facilities for babies and disabled visitors. Laundry facilities. Motorcaravan services. Bar, restaurant and takeaway. Heated swimming pool, paddling pool (15/5-15/9). TV. Small football pitch. Volleyball. Boules. Archery. Games room. Play area. Activities for children and entertainment programme in high season. Only electric barbecues on pitches. Large units are accepted. Riding. Bicycle hire. WiFi throughout.

Open: 15 April - 15 October.

Directions

From Sisteron take D4085 south towards Aix-en-Provence. After 4 km, head south on D951 through St-Etienne-les-Orgues; 7 km. further, take D950 to Banon. Campsite signed along D12, 1 km. south of Banon. GPS: 44.02647, 5.63113

Charges guide

Per unit incl. 2 persons and electricity	€ 19.00 - € 27.50
extra person	€ 3.30 - € 6.00

No credit cards.

Bollène

Camping la Simioune

Route de l'Embisque, F-84500 Bollène (Vaucluse) T: 04 90 63 17 91. E: camping@la-simioune.fr
alanrogers.com/FR84080

A warm welcome awaits you at this rural site. It is a peaceful and inexpensive base, especially for those who love horses and ponies, with the small stables adjacent. Off the beaten track, it is situated amongst tall pines on sandy, undulating ground, bordered by woods. The 80 touring pitches are of varying size and shape, most with electricity (10A). An area of woodland is set aside for those with tents. The family owners also keep some small animals with the horses; a few goats, rabbits and chickens are a delight for young visitors. The access road may be difficult for very large units.

Facilities

One clean, modern sanitary block (new in 2015) has facilities for children and a room for disabled visitors, although the site may be difficult for wheelchairs and those with mobility problems. Washing machine. Small bar, simple meals (mid June-Sept). Takeaway (all year). Small unheated swimming and paddling pools (May-Sept). Play area. Central barbecue area. Chalets for rent. WiFi throughout (free). Off site: Pony rides for children.

Open: 1 March - 30 November.

Directions

From A7 exit 19 (Bollène). At first roundabout, third exit signed Suze-la-Rousse (site signed). After traffic lights, before river, turn left, site signed (rue Alphonse Daudet), follow signs for 5 km. (along winding lane). GPS: 44.2968, 4.7874

Charges guide

Per unit incl. 2 persons and electricity	€ 17.50 - € 23.50
extra person	€ 4.00 - € 4.50

Carpentras

Flower Camping Lou Comtadou

881 avenue Pierre de Coubertin, F-84200 Carpentras (Vaucluse) T: 04 90 67 03 16.
E: info@campingloucomtadou.com **alanrogers.com/FR84180**

Lou Comtadou can be found 20 km. from Avignon at the foot of the Mont Ventoux. This is an area which is often considered to be the gateway to Provence. It is also a region of fine cuisine, lavender fields and wonderful sunlight, which has always attracted artists to this corner of the region. Lou Comtadou is open for a long season and has 97 pitches, some of which are occupied by mobile homes. The pitches are grassy and generally well shaded; all are equipped with 6A electricity. The site is close to the centre of Carpentras and is part of a sports complex; campers have access to the large municipal swimming pool.

Facilities

Two toilet blocks, one new. Large family room and facilities for disabled visitors. Baby room. Laundry sinks. Motorcaravan services. Small shop (15/6-15/9), snack bar and takeaway (all 1/6-30/9). Bar (1/5-15/9). Outdoor swimming pool (20/6-30/8). TV room. Playground. Bicycle hire. No charcoal barbecues. Mobile homes for rent. Free WiFi on part of site. Off site: Fishing 5 km. Golf 20 km.

Open: 1 March - 31 October.

Directions

From the north, leave A7 at exit 22 (Orange Sud) and follow signs to Carpentras on D907 and D950. In Carpentras follow signs to St Didier then Complexe Sportif. GPS: 44.04379, 5.05363

Charges guide

Per unit incl. 2 persons and electricity	€ 17.50 - € 28.50
extra person	€ 4.50 - € 6.50

Castellane

Castel Camping le Domaine du Verdon

Camp du Verdon, F-04120 Castellane (Alpes-de-Haute-Provence) T: 04 92 83 61 29.
E: contact@camp-du-verdon.com **alanrogers.com/FR04020**

Close to the Route des Alpes and the Gorges du Verdon, le Domaine du Verdon is a large, level site, part meadow, part wooded with an attractive range of planting. There are 500 partly shaded, rather stony pitches (390 for touring units), 360 with 16A electricity and 125 also with water and drainage. Numbered and separated by bushes, they vary in size and are mostly separate from 60 mobile homes and pitches used by tour operators. Some overlook the unfenced Verdon river so watch your children. This is a very popular holiday area, the gorge and the associated canoeing and rafting being the main attractions. Two heated pools and numerous on-site activities during high season help to keep non-canoeists here. This site is ideal for active families. One can walk to Castellane without using the main road where there are numerous shops, cafés and restaurants. Dances and discos in July and August suit all age groups. The latest finishing time is around 23.00, after which time patrols make sure that the site is quiet. The site is popular and very busy in July and August.

Facilities

Refurbished toilet blocks include facilities for disabled visitors. Washing machines and dryers. Fridge hire. Motorcaravan services. Supermarket. Restaurant, terrace, log fire for cooler evenings. Pizzeria/crêperie. Takeaway. Heated swimming pools, paddling pool with fountain. All amenities are open all season. Fitness equipment. Organised entertainment (July/Aug). Play areas. Minigolf. Archery. Organised walks. Bicycle hire. Riding. Small fishing lake. Room for games and TV. Internet access. Communal barbecue (charcoal not permitted on pitches). Babysitting service. WiFi in some parts (free). Off site: Bus stop outside main entrance (only one bus each day). Castellane and the Verdon Gorge 1 km. Riding 1.5 km. Boat launching 4.5 km. Watersports.

Open: 13 May - 15 September.

Directions

From Castellane take D952 westwards towards Gorges du Verdon and Moustiers. Site is 1 km. on left. GPS: 43.83921, 6.49396

Charges guide

Per unit incl. 2 persons (3 in high season) and electricity	€ 28.00 - € 48.00
extra person (over 4 yrs)	€ 9.00 - € 14.00
dog	€ 4.00 - € 5.00

Castellane

RCN les Collines de Castellane

Route de Grasse, F-04120 Castellane (Alpes-de-Haute-Provence) T: 04 92 83 68 96. E: collines@rcn.fr
alanrogers.com/FR04040

RCN, a Dutch company, runs a chain of nine good campsites in the Netherlands. They also operate eight sites in France, all with Dutch managers who speak good French and English. Les Collines de Castellane is pleasantly situated in the mountainous landscape of the Alpes-de-Haute-Provence. There are 160 touring pitches (with 10A electricity) spread over a series of flat terraces and most have shade provided by trees. Access roads are very steep and it is quite a long way down to the bottom of the site. At the top of the site, near the entrance, is a combined reception and attractive bar/restaurant area overlooking the pool complex with its water slides and a paddling pool for small children.

Facilities

Tiled, modern toilet facilities include individual cabins and facilities for disabled visitors and babies. Washing machines, dryers and ironing area. Well stocked shop. Library. Bar/restaurant (including takeaway) with terrace. Heated swimming pool with slides and paddling pool. Tennis court. Football pitch. Multisports court. Outdoor fitness area. Boules. 3 play areas. Tree-top adventure park. Organised activities (May-Sept). Bicycle hire. No charcoal barbecues. WiFi throughout (charged).

Open: 25 April - 19 September.

Directions

Take the D6085 (Route Napoléon) from Digné-les-Bains towards Castellane and Grasse. Site is 6 km. south of Castellane, on the right hand side of the road. GPS: 43.82412, 6.56962

Charges guide

Per unit incl. 2 persons, electricity and water	€ 17.50 - € 49.00
extra person	€ 3.75 - € 6.50
child (under 3 yrs)	free

Castellane

Camping International

Route Napoléon RD 4085, F-04120 Castellane (Alpes-de-Haute-Provence) T: 04 92 83 66 67.
E: info@campinginternational.com **alanrogers.com/FR04100**

Camping International has very friendly, English-speaking owners and is a reasonably priced, less commercialised site situated in some of the most dramatic scenery in France. The 274 pitches, 130 good sized ones for touring, are clearly marked, separated by trees and small hedges, some are on a slight slope and all have electricity and water. Access is good for larger units. The bar/restaurant overlooks the swimming pool with its sunbathing area set in a sunny location with fantastic views. In high season, English-speaking young people entertain children (3-8 years) and teenagers.

Facilities

Nine toilet blocks are distributed around the site, some of the smaller blocks are of an older design. One newer block has modern facilities, including those for disabled visitors. Washing machines and dryer. Motorcaravan services. Fridge hire. Shop. Bar, restaurant/takeaway (1/5-30/9). Swimming pool (1/5-30/9). Club/TV room. Children's entertainment, some evening entertainment (July/Aug). Play area. Boules. Bicycle hire. WiFi (charged).

Open: 31 March - 1 October.

Directions

Site is 1 km. north of Castellane on the N85 Route Napoléon. GPS: 43.85866, 6.49803

Charges guide

Per unit incl. 2 persons and electricity	€ 16.00 - € 32.00
extra person	€ 3.00 - € 5.00
dog	€ 2.00

Camping Cheques accepted.

Castellane

Camping Indigo Gorges du Verdon

D 952, F-04120 Castellane (Alpes-de-Haute-Provence) T: 04 92 83 63 64.
E: gorgesduverdon@camping-indigo.com **alanrogers.com/FR04250**

Located at an altitude of 660 metres, between pinewoods and the River Verdon, Indigo Gorges du Verdon is a family site with large, shaded or semi-shaded pitches and a range of chalets and mobile homes. The site has been entirely renovated. It has an inviting swimming pool and offers direct access to the Verdon (with its own river beach). The main sight here is, of course, the stunning canyon of the Gorges du Verdon, a grandiose area of vertiginous cliffs towering above the emerald river below. There are some superb walks and this is also an ideal location for white-water rafting or canoeing.

Facilities

Two modern sanitary blocks (one in each section of the site). Children's toilets. Facilities for disabled visitors and babies. Well stocked shop, bar/restaurant and takeaway. Swimming pool and new paddling pool. River beach. Play areas. Volleyball. Boules. Games room. Fishing. Kayaking. Children's club. Activities and entertainment (July/Aug). Mobile homes, wood and canvas tents and chalets for rent. WiFi around reception (free).

Open: 14 April - 26 September.

Directions

Site is west of Castellane. Leave the village on D952 headed towards the Gorges du Verdon and the site is 9 km. on the left. GPS: 43.82343, 6.43095

Charges guide

Per unit incl. 2 persons and electricity	€ 19.40 - € 30.80
extra person	€ 5.20 - € 7.90
child (2-7 yrs)	free - € 3.80
dog	€ 2.20 - € 4.40

Cavalaire-sur-Mer

Camping Cros de Mouton

F-83240 Cavalaire-sur-Mer (Var) T: 04 94 64 10 87. E: campingcrosdemouton@wanadoo.fr

alanrogers.com/FR83220

Cros de Mouton is an attractive and reasonably priced campsite in a popular area. High on a steep hillside, about 2 km. from Cavalaire and its popular beaches, the site is a calm oasis away from the coast. There are stunning views of the bay but, due to the nature of the terrain, some of the site roads are very steep – the higher pitches with the best views are especially so. There are 199 large terraced pitches (electricity 10A) under cork trees, with 125 for touring and 74 mobile homes for rent. Half of these are more suitable for tents, with parking nearby. English is spoken by the welcoming and helpful owners.

Facilities

Clean, well maintained toilet blocks have all the usual facilities including those for disabled visitors (but site is a little steep in places for wheelchairs). Washing machine. Motorcaravan services. Shop (1/4-15/10). Bar/restaurant with reasonably priced meals and takeaway (1/4-30/9). New swimming pool complex. Relaxation area with bar serving snacks and cold drinks. Play area. Multisports court. Games room. Entertainment (July/Aug). Bicycle hire. No charcoal barbecues. WiFi (free in reception).

Open: 22 March - 31 October.

Directions

Take the D559 to Cavalaire (not Cavalière 4 km. away). Site is 1.5 km. north of Cavalaire-sur-Mer, very well signed from the approach to the town. GPS: 43.18247, 6.5161

Charges guide

Per unit incl. 2 persons and electricity	€ 26.70 - € 34.80
extra person	€ 7.20 - € 9.80
child (under 7 yrs)	€ 4.50 - € 5.40

Ceyreste

Flower Camping de Ceyreste

Avenue Eugène Julien, F-13600 Ceyreste (Bouches du Rhône) T: 04 42 83 07 68.

E: campingceyreste@yahoo.fr **alanrogers.com/FR13220**

Camping de Ceyreste is located on the edge of an extensive pine forest in the heart of Provence, a five minute drive from the beach of La Ciotat and its beautiful bay, Le Golfe d'Amour. There are 160 shaded pitches, most terraced, of which about 70 are for touring units, all with electricity connections (6/10A), sink and water supply. The remainder are occupied by seasonal caravans and a range of mobile homes for rent. You can head off on foot or by mountain bike into the pine-covered slopes behind the site, or by car to explore the countryside of the Bouches-du-Rhône and the varied coastline of the Mediterranean between Marseille and Toulon.

Facilities

Two sanitary blocks, one older with some Turkish WCs, have hot showers, baby bath, family rooms and facilities for disabled visitors. Dog shower. Washing machine and dryer. Motorcaravan services. Grocery. Bar/snack bar (July/Aug). Water park (April-Sept) with heated pool, children's pool, water slide and solarium. Boules. Minigolf. Daytime activities and evening entertainment for children and families (July/Aug). Play area. WiFi (charged).

Open: 1 April - 30 September.

Directions

From A50 (Marseille-Toulon) leave at exit 9 and head south on D40B to La Ciotat. At roundabout in 8 km. turn east on D559 (Toulon/Ceyreste) then north on D40A /D3 to Ceyreste. Before village bear left (D40H) signed Simalègre and site on left in 1.5 km. GPS: 43.22034, 5.62878

Charges guide

Per unit incl. 2 persons and electricity	€ 26.00 - € 45.50

Châteauneuf-de-Gadagne

Camping Fontisson

1125 route d'Avignon, F-84470 Châteauneuf-de-Gadagne (Vaucluse) T: 04 90 22 59 77.

E: info@campingfontisson.com **alanrogers.com/FR84210**

Camping Fontisson is west of Avignon, near the pretty Provençal village of Châteauneuf-de-Gadagne. The site is well located for visiting the Luberon and close to the fascinating city of Avignon and its Palais des Papes. There are 55 pitches here, 24 of which are occupied by mobile homes, chalets and equipped tents (available for rent). Pitches are large and generally well shaded and all have 10A electricity hook-ups. On-site amenities include a swimming pool, as well as a tennis court and minigolf. During the high season there is a regular activity and entertainment programme.

Facilities

Recently refurbished toilet block. Bar and snack bar (July/Aug). Bread and milk service. Outdoor swimming pool (mid May-Sept). Tennis. Multisports field. Boules. Play area. Entertainment and activity programme. WiFi throughout (charged). Off site: Châteauneuf-de-Gadagne with shops, cafés and restaurants. Riding and fishing 2 km. Golf 5 km. Grottes de Thouzon at Le Thor 8 km.

Open: 2 April - 1 October.

Directions

Leave A7 motorway at exit 23 (Avignon North). Head south on D6 bypassing St Saturnin-lès-Avignon to Châteauneuf-de-Gadagne. The site is well signed from here. GPS: 43.92883, 4.93347

Charges guide

Per unit incl. 2 persons and electricity	€ 18.80 - € 30.60
extra person	€ 4.20 - € 7.20

Cogolin

Camping l'Argentière

37 route de Collobrières (CD 48), F-83310 Cogolin (Var) T: 04 94 54 63 63.

E: campinglargentiere@wanadoo.fr **alanrogers.com/FR83310**

This little jewel of a site is in a pleasant setting and the intervening wooded area seems to give it sufficient screening to make the campsite itself quite peaceful. It is only 5 km. from the beaches at Cogolin and Saint Tropez, so its position is handy for one of the showplaces of the Riviera, but away from the hustle and bustle of the beach resorts. There are 150 good sized touring pitches (out of 248 with the others used for mobile homes for rent). All have electricity (6-10A) although long leads may be necessary. The site is very well maintained.

Facilities

Four well appointed sanitary blocks (one new in 2015) with facilities for babies and disabled visitors. Washing machines. Water available at sanitary blocks. Fridge hire. Shop (July/Aug). Bar (1/6-30/9). Restaurant and takeaway (15/6-15/9). Large outdoor heated swimming pool complex with slides, jacuzzi, fun paddling pools (one from 11/4, others 15/6-15/9). Play area. Two tennis courts. Multisports court. Boules. Bicycle hire. Communal barbecue area. WiFi around bar area (free).

Open: 1 April - 30 September.

Directions

From A8 (Aix-en-Provence-Cannes) take exit 36 (Le Muy), then D25 to Ste Maxime and coast road D559 for St Tropez. After 6 km. take D14 west for Cogolin. Approaching village follow D48 west towards St Maur-en-Collobrière. Site is well signed after 1 km. GPS: 43.256083, 6.5124

Charges guide

Per unit incl. 2 persons and electricity € 20.00 - € 47.00

No credit cards.

Contes

La Ferme Riola

5309 route des Sclos, F-06390 Contes (Alpes-Maritimes) T: 04 93 79 03 02.

E: contact@campinglafermeriola.com **alanrogers.com/FR06220**

La Ferme Riola is a very small site with just 50 pitches for touring and six gîtes attractively dispersed around the four-hectare terrain. Areas for touring units are spread all around the site, mostly situated on the terraces amongst olive trees. Pitches are large and generally well shaded. All are equipped with electrical connections. Leisure facilities include a swimming pool, a volleyball court and a children's playground. This is a working farm and fresh produce, including olives, olive oil and fresh eggs, is available at the site's small shop.

Facilities

Two sanitary blocks have preset pushbutton showers and include a family shower room, baby room and facilities in one block for disabled visitors. Laundry. Small shop (bread to order in July/Aug). Swimming pool (April-Sept). Volleyball pitch. Games room. Play area. Large communal barbecue area. Sporting competitions and organised walks in high season. Free WiFi around reception area.

Open: 1 April - 30 September.

Directions

Head north from Nice on D2204 (Col de Nice). Continue towards Sospel and then join D215 and D115 to Sclos de Contes. The site is signed from here. GPS: 43.81612, 7.34324

Charges guide

Per unit incl. 2 persons and electricity € 25.50 - € 26.50

No credit cards.

Esparron de Verdo

Flower Camping la Beaume

Route d'Albiosc, F-04800 Esparron de Verdo (Alpes-de-Haute-Provence) T: 04 92 77 15 28.

alanrogers.com/FR04500

Hidden in the hillside 2 km. from Esparron-de-Verdon, this small family run site (61 pitches) offers some unusual, alternative rental accommodation; tree house, teepees and Romany-style caravans. Camping la Beaume is at one with its natural surroundings and the pitches mould themselves into the hillside. None of the 39 touring pitches (21 with 6/10A electricity) are visible from the hub of the site. The Blondé family are very friendly and accommodating and will do their best to make your stay an enjoyable one. Access to the site can be difficult for larger units and it is recommended that they stop in the lower car park before proceeding to reception.

Facilities

Two traditional unisex toilet blocks with showers and open style washbasins, with heated facilities for disabled visitors. Laundry facilities. Bar. Restaurant (15/6-15/9 and on demand). Snack bar (July/Aug). Bread to order. Heated, covered swimming pool with access and lowering device for disabled visitors. Play area. Children's club. Volleyball. Boules court. Fishing. Aquagym. Gas barbecues only. Free WiFi (in bar area).

Open: 1 April - 1 November.

Directions

From Gréoux-le-Bains head east on D952 toward Riez, after 6 km. in St-Martin-de-Brôme turn south on D82 to Esparron-de-Verdon. Follow D82 around outside of village and the site is signed after 2 km. up a short narrow road. GPS: 43.74224, 5.99502

Charges guide

Per unit incl. 2 persons and electricity	€ 21.00 - € 24.00
extra person	€ 8.50 - € 10.00

Forcalquier

Camping Indigo Forcalquier

Avenue Claude Delorme, F-04300 Forcalquier (Alpes-de-Haute-Provence) T: 04 92 75 27 94.

E: forcalquier@camping-indigo.com **alanrogers.com/FR04120**

Although Camping Indigo is an urban site, there are extensive views over the surrounding countryside where there are some excellent walks. The 72 touring pitches are on grass and of a good size, all with electricity, six fully serviced (long leads may be needed). The site is secure with an electronic barrier (card deposit required) and there is no entry between 22.30 and 07.00. This is an excellent base for visiting Forcalquier, a 15th-century fortified hill town, and the Monday market (the best in Haute-Provence). Local guides lead tours of the historic town and area. Since Camping Indigo acquired this site, an extensive modernisation programme has been put into effect.

Facilities

Three refurbished toilet blocks with washbasins in cubicles and excellent facilities for disabled visitors. Motorcaravan services. Bar (all season). Snack bar and takeaway (July/Aug). Heated swimming and paddling pools (May-Sept). Play area. Boules. Basketball. Range of activities in high season, often involving local people, including food tasting and storytelling. Max. 1 dog. WiFi in the central lodge (free). Off site: Town centre 200 m.

Open: 4 May - 26 September.

Directions

From town centre, follow D16 signed to Montlaux and Sigonce. Site is 500 m. on the right. Well signed from town. GPS: 43.96206, 5.78743

Charges guide

Per unit incl. 2 persons and electricity	€ 20.80 - € 33.80
extra person	€ 5.30 - € 6.60
child (2-7 yrs)	free - € 4.80

Fréjus

Camping Caravaning les Pins Parasols

3360 rue des Combattants d'Afrique du Nord, F-83600 Fréjus (Var) T: 04 94 40 88 43.

E: lespinsparasols@wanadoo.fr **alanrogers.com/FR83010**

Les Pins Parasols with its 200 pitches is a comfortably sized site, which is quite easy to walk around. It is family owned and run and very peaceful, to the extent that the owners make it quite clear in their brochure, 'no entertainment'. Although on slightly undulating ground, all of the pitches (with 6A electricity) are level, some terraced, and separated by hedges or bushes with pine and oak trees for shade. Of the 160 touring pitches, 48 have their own fully equipped sanitary unit. Naturally these cost more but may well be of interest to those seeking a little bit of extra comfort. The pool area is attractively laid out and for a small site, it is quite substantial. The site also has its own bar/restaurant and shop which are open most of the season. Some of the best beaches on the coast are only 6 km. away. Fréjus was a major port during the Roman Empire and a walk around the old town after dark, when it is floodlit, is a memorable experience. There is a useful bus service to Fréjus (5 km) from the site's entrance.

Facilities

Two toilet blocks (one heated) with facilities for babies and disabled visitors. Small shop with reasonable stock, bar/restaurant, takeaway (15/4-20/9). Swimming pool with attractive rock backdrop (heated in low season), separate long slide with landing pool and fun paddling pool. Half-court tennis. TV/games room. Volleyball. Basketball. Play area. Bicycle hire. WiFi in reception area (charged). Off site: Riding 2 km. Beach 6 km. Golf 10 km.

Open: 4 April - 26 September.

Directions

From west on A8 take exit 38 (Fréjus centre) and turn south at first roundabout onto D4a. After 1 km. turn north on D4 and site is 1 km. on right. GPS: 43.46290, 6.72570

Charges guide

Per unit incl. 2 persons and electricity	€ 19.50 - € 31.10
pitch with sanitary unit	€ 24.10 - € 38.50
extra person	€ 4.70 - € 6.80
child (under 7 yrs)	€ 3.10 - € 4.10

Fréjus

Camping Resort la Baume la Palmeraie

3775 rue des Combattants d'Afrique du Nord, F-83618 Fréjus (Var) T: 04 94 19 88 88.
E: reception@labaume-lapalmeraie.com **alanrogers.com/FR83060**

La Baume is a large, busy site about 5.5 km. from the long sandy beach of Fréjus-Plage, although with its fine and varied selection of swimming pools many people do not bother to make the trip. The pools, with their palm trees, are remarkable for their size and variety (water slides, etc) – the very large feature pool being a highlight. There is also an aquatic play area and two indoor pools with a slide and a spa area. The site has 240 adequately sized, fully serviced pitches, separated by hedges and most have shade. Although tents are accepted, the site concentrates mainly on caravanning. It becomes full in season. Adjoining la Baume is its sister site, la Palmeraie, providing self-catering accommodation, its own landscaped pool, sports facilities and some entertainment to supplement that at la Baume. There are 500 large pitches with mains sewerage for mobile homes. La Baume's convenient location has its downside as there is traffic noise on some pitches from the nearby autoroute – somewhat obtrusive at first but we soon failed to notice it. It is a popular site with tour operators.

Facilities

Five toilet blocks. Supermarket, several shops. Two bars, terrace overlooking pools, TV. Restaurant, takeaway, pizzeria. Six swimming pools (heated all season), one aquatic playground for children up to four years, two covered, plus steam room and jacuzzi, seven slides. Two renovated play areas. Large gym and fitness centre. Multisports court. Archery (July/Aug). Tennis. Skateboard park. Daytime and evening entertainment, organised events, some in English. Amphitheatre. Discos all season. Children's club (4-11 yrs) and teens' club (12-16 yrs. Easter and July/Aug). WiFi on part of site (charged). Off site: Bus to Fréjus passes gate. Riding 2 km. Beach 5 km. Golf 8 km.

Open: 26 March - 1 October.

Directions

From west on A8, exit 38 (Fréjus centre) and turn south at first roundabout onto D4a. After 1 km. turn north onto D4 and site is 1 km. on the left.
GPS: 43.45998, 6.72048

Charges guide

Per unit incl. 2 persons, electricity, water and drainage	€ 25.00 - € 55.00
extra person	€ 5.00 - € 15.00
child (under 7 yrs)	free
dog	€ 6.00

Min. stay for motorcaravans 2 nights.
Large units should book.

Gassin

Camping Parc Saint-James Parc Montana

Route du Bourrian, F-83580 Gassin (Var) T: 04 94 55 20 20. E: gassin@camping-parcsaintjames.com
alanrogers.com/FR83620

A member of the Parc Saint-James Group, this attractive campsite is very well positioned close to Saint Tropez. The majority of the pitches are occupied by privately owned mobile homes and chalets plus 127 bungalows for hire, but there are also 30 touring pitches on the lower part of the site. The 30-hectare estate clings to the hillside with fragrant woodland providing good shade to the mainly terraced pitches. There is a good range of activities here, many concentrated around the large, heated pool complex. There are plans to include another heated fun pool area with flumes and jacuzzi. The gradients on the site may make it a challenging choice for those with walking difficulties. In high season, the activity and entertainment programme is popular and includes soirées on the site's attractive bar terrace. The site lies close to many places of interest – Saint Tropez is close at hand, as well as Ramatuelle with its famous beach of Pampelone. The site is also well located for Port Grimaud, Sainte Maxime and Gassin itself with a range of restaurants offering superb views over the gulf.

Facilities

Five worn, dated toilet blocks provide barely adequate facilities with few hot showers. Basic facility for disabled visitors in one block. Laundry. Small supermarket, bar, restaurant and takeaway (9/4-15/9). Heated outdoor swimming pools and children's pool (9/4-30/9). Play area. Tennis. Multisports area. Games room. Children's club. Evening entertainment. Disco. Electric barbecues only. Mobile homes and chalets for rent. WiFi in some areas (charged). Off site: Riding 1 km. Golf 1.5 km. Beach, sailing and bicycle hire 3 km. Fishing 4 km. St Tropez, Port Grimaud and Cogolin. Walking trails.

Open: 11 January - 30 November.

Directions

From A8 take Le Muy exit and follow signs to St Tropez and La Croix-Valmer. Pass Ste Maxime and continue on the N98. At large roundabout take signs to Gassin and Croix Valmer. Cross first roundabout and turn left at next traffic lights. Site is also signed as Parc Montana in places. Do not drive through Gassin – the roads are very narrow.
GPS: 43.24035, 6.57345

Charges guide

Per unit incl. 2 persons and electricity	€ 19.00 - € 41.00
extra person	€ 2.50 - € 5.00
child (4-10 yrs)	€ 1.50 - € 4.00
dog	€ 5.00

Fréjus

Domaine du Colombier

1052 rue des Combattants en Afrique du Nord, F-83600 Fréjus (Var) T: 04 94 51 56 01.
E: info@domaine-du-colombier.com **alanrogers.com/FR83230**

Domaine du Colombier is located between Cannes and Saint Tropez, alongside a main road 2 km. from the centre of Fréjus and 4.5 km. from the fine sandy beaches of Fréjus and Saint Raphaël. There are 20 touring pitches, ranging in size from 80-100 sq.m. all with 16A electricity, plus 363 units of rental accommodation. Over recent years there has been much ongoing investment in high quality facilities. An attractive heated pool complex (3,600 sq.m) with a long river, paddling pool, waterslides, lagoon and whirlpool, all surrounded by sun loungers. Plenty of activities and excursions are arranged all season and the site caters principally for families. There are professionally organised themed evenings, visits to olive mills and wine caves, coach and boat excursions, horse riding, jet skiing, diving and three nearby golf courses (all with extra charges). A variety of accommodation to rent includes mobile homes and chalets (with nightly charges) and include new themed accommodation such as 'Africa' and 'Malibu'.

Facilities

Two high quality, fully equipped and heated sanitary blocks with baby rooms. Laundry. Well stocked shop. Bar/restaurant and takeaway. Large heated swimming pool complex. Spa. Balnéotherapy. Hairdresser. Fitness facilities. Three play areas and four sports areas. Soundproofed nightclub. Charcoal barbecues are not permitted. Picnic area with communal barbecue. Bicycle, fridge, safe and barbecue hire. Internet access and WiFi over site (charged). Off site: Bus stop 50 m. Riding 2 km. Beach, fishing and boat launching 4.5 km. Golf 8 km.

Open: 26 March - 10 October.

Directions

From A8 motorway take exit 38. From East (Nice) continue straight on at first 4 roundabouts after exit, then right at 5th and 6th roundabouts. Site 300 m. on right. GPS: 43.44583, 6.72727

Charges guide

Per unit incl. 2 persons and electricity	€ 18.00 - € 67.00
extra person	€ 7.00 - € 9.00
child (3-7 yrs)	€ 2.00 - € 8.00
dog	€ 5.00

Special low season offers.

Graveson-en-Provence

Camping les Micocouliers

445 route de Cassoulen, F-13690 Graveson-en-Provence (Bouches du Rhône) T: 04 90 95 81 49.
E: micocou@orange.fr **alanrogers.com/FR13060**

M. and Mme. Riehl started work on les Micocouliers in 1997 and they have developed a welcoming, comfortable site. On the outskirts of the town, the site is only some 10 km. from Saint Rémy and Avignon. Purpose built, modern terracotta houses in a raised position provide all the facilities at present. The 116 pitches radiate out from here with the pool and entrance to one side, and a central area for recreation. The pitches are on level grass, separated by small bushes, and shade is developing well. Electricity connections are possible (4-10A). There are also a few mobile homes. The popular swimming pool is a welcome addition. Bread can be ordered and a small shop is opened in July and August.

Facilities

Several unisex units provide toilets and very good facilities for disabled visitors (by key), showers and washbasins in cabins and laundry facilities. A new block has just been added. Small shop (July/Aug). Swimming pool (12x8 m; 15/5-15/9). Paddling pool (July/Aug). Play area. Gas and electric barbecues permitted. WiFi in some areas (charged). Off site: Supermarkets, shops, bars and restaurants 1 km. Riding and bicycle hire 1 km. Golf and fishing 5 km. Beach 60 km. at Ste Marie-de-la-Mer.

Open: 15 March - 15 October.

Directions

Site is southeast of Graveson. From the N570 at new roundabout take D5 towards St Rémy and Maillane and site is 500 m. on the left.
GPS: 43.84397, 4.78131

Charges guide

Per unit incl. 2 persons and electricity	€ 21.10 - € 33.20
extra person	€ 5.40 - € 8.50
child (1-10 yrs)	€ 4.00 - € 6.00
dog	€ 2.50

Domaine du Colombier

BALNÉO SPA RESORT

FRENCH RIVIERA

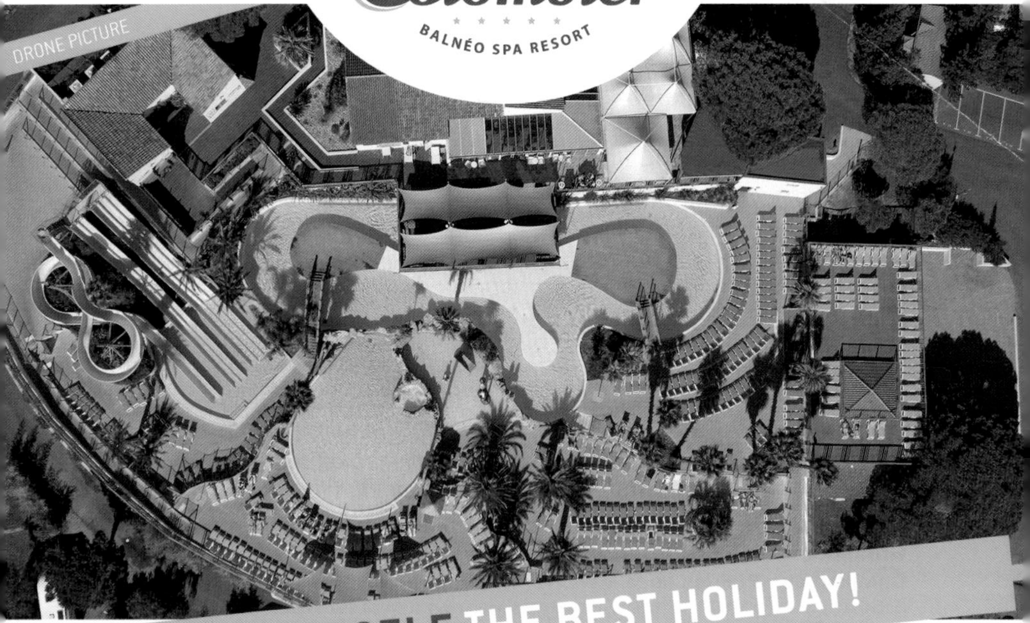

DRONE PICTURE

GIVE YOURSELF THE BEST HOLIDAY!

Everyone has their own favourites,

On the French Riviera, between Cannes and St Tropez, 4.5 km from the fine sandy beaches of the bay of Fréjus and Saint-Raphaël, Domaine du Colombier 5 star campsite boasts a vast, heated 'lagoon' of 3600m² with a lazy river, slides and games perfect for families, as well as a Vitality Pool and a beautiful Spa for those who seek rest and relaxation.

Luxury accommodation, restaurants, shows, kids clubs, fitness facilities... all of this can be found on the site spanning 10 hectares, full of palm trees, pines, and rose-bays...

1052 rue des combattants en Afrique du nord
83600 Fréjus

+33 (0)4.94.51.56.01

www.domaine-du-colombier.com

yelloh! VILLAGE

Gréoux-les-Bains

Yelloh! Village Verdon Parc

Domaine de la Paludette, F-04800 Gréoux-les-Bains (Alpes-de-Haute-Provence) T: 04 92 78 08 08.
E: info@campingverdonparc.fr **alanrogers.com/FR04110**

Friendly and family run, this very spacious site borders the River le Verdon and is close to the attractive spa town of Gréoux-les-Bains. The 210 medium to very large, stony or gravel touring pitches are in two sections. The main part of the campsite has large pitches laid out in rows separated by poplar trees. Along the river bank the larger, more natural pitches are scattered amongst the trees and are of irregular shape and size. These have very pleasant views across the river to the town beyond. Electrical connections (10A) and water taps are reasonably close to most pitches. Unfortunately, river swimming is forbidden but there is a large swimming pool on site.

Facilities

Several toilet blocks (one heated in low season) are clean and of a high standard, with all necessary facilities including for disabled visitors and families. Laundry room. Motorcaravan services. Small shop. Bar and courtyard terrace, restaurant and takeaway. Heated swimming pool. TV. Internet point. Large play area. Bicycle hire (July/Aug). Tennis. Volleyball. Miniclub for younger children (high season). Organised sports. Evening entertainment. Gas and electric barbecues only. WiFi over site (free at bar).

Open: 25 March - 2 November.

Directions

Leave A51 at Manosque, take D907 south east (Gréoux-les-Bains). Turn right on D4, then left on D82 to Gréoux-les-Bains. Follow main road downhill through town to roundabout with fountain. Take 2nd right (D8 St Pierre), descend for 1 km. Cross river, immediately left to site. GPS: 43.75198, 5.89403

Charges guide

Per unit incl. 2 persons and electricity	€ 18.00 - € 43.00

Grimaud

Camping des Prairies de la Mer

Quartier Saint-Pons (RN98), les Mûres, F-83310 Grimaud (Var) T: 04 94 79 09 09.
E: prairies@riviera-villages.com **alanrogers.com/FR83380**

This busy site is in the pleasant and popular holiday resort of Port Grimaud where there is an attractive harbour, restaurants, shops and a weekly market. A long, sandy beach runs right round the bay. The site is right on the beach and is very well equipped for a family holiday. In fact, it is a complete holiday resort, even including its own amusement park for children. There are 500 individual touring pitches on flat, sandy ground, all with electricity. A further 900 pitches are used for mobile homes and chalets. Trees have grown well to give plenty of shade but there is no swimming pool. English is spoken.

Facilities

Nine modern toilet blocks with three near the touring pitches include washbasins in cabins. Launderette. Large shopping complex. Bar. Attractive, Italian-style restaurant (all season). Good takeaway. Entertainment programme with live music evenings. Play area. Sports ground. TV room. Bicycle hire. Sailing and diving schools. Miniclub. ATM. Excursions. Beach. Off site: Riding 2 km. Golf 3 km.

Open: 31 March - 14 October.

Directions

From A8 (Aix-en-Provence-Cannes) exit 36 (Le Muy) take D25 to St Maxime, then coast road N98 towards St Tropez. Site is 6 km. on the left.
GPS: 43.277133, 6.581833

Charges guide

Per unit incl. 2 persons	€ 25.00 - € 58.00
extra person	€ 6.00
child (5-13 yrs)	free - € 4.00

Grimaud

Camping les Mûres

2721 route du littoral, F-83310 Grimaud (Var) T: 04 94 56 16 97. E: info@camping-des-mures.com
alanrogers.com/FR83390

Les Mûres is a friendly, family site situated northeast of the busy holiday centre of Port Grimaud and has been run by the Grau and Ferrari families for four generations. The site extends over 11 hectares of undulating ground with 600 of its 669 pitches reserved for touring. This high proportion of touring pitches is relatively unusual for this area. All have 6A electricity and the pitches are generally of a good size, well shaded by mature trees. Although there is no pool, the site lies right beside a lovely sandy beach with views across the bay to Saint Tropez.

Facilities

Six toilet blocks, all reasonably clean when visited. Three units for disabled visitors including a special block near the beach. Washing machines. Shop. Bar. Restaurant and takeaway. Snack bar on beach. Play area. Sports pitch. Bicycle hire all season. Sports facilities and miniclub in high season. Fishing. WiFi throughout (charged). Electric barbecues only. Mobile homes and chalets for rent. Off site: Golf 1 km. Riding 5 km.

Open: 28 March - 10 October.

Directions

From the A8 (Aix-en-Provence-Cannes) take exit 36 (Le Muy) and D25 to St Maxime, then the 2721 Route du Littoral towards St Tropez. Site is 4.5 km. on the right of this road. GPS: 43.284017, 6.5918

Charges guide

Per unit incl. 2 persons and electricity	€ 27.00 - € 41.00
extra person	€ 5.00 - € 9.00
child (2-12 yrs acc. to age)	free - € 6.00

Grimaud

Holiday Marina Resort

323 route du Littoral, F-83310 Grimaud (Var) T: 04 94 56 08 43. E: info@holiday-marina.com

alanrogers.com/FR83400

Owned and operated by an English family, this site is an established favourite with British families. It is in the busy holiday area of the Gulf of Saint Tropez. The site has a large and well kept pool area and its own adjacent moorings for small boats. Smaller than many sites in this area, there are 230 generous pitches of which 49 are for touring units. Each of these has its own spacious bathroom with a good shower, washbasin, WC and outdoor sink. The 'grand luxe plus' pitches have a small mobile home instead of the sanitary unit, with kitchen, bathroom, bedroom and terrace and are suitable for extra large motorcaravans. On level, rather sandy ground, with variable shade, all have 16A electricity. Some noise can be heard from the busy coast road and the D61.

Facilities

Private toilet blocks include washbasin, shower and WC, heated in low seasons. Facilities for disabled visitors include one fully adapted mobile home. Laundry. Shop. Two restaurants with varied and full menu. Snacks and takeaway. Separate building houses a bar and games room. TV room. Heated swimming and paddling pools and jacuzzi (1/4-31/9). New salon and spa. Miniclub and evening entertainment. Adventure playground. Multisports court. Mobile homes for hire. WiFi (charged).

Open: 1 March - 31 October.

Directions

From A8 (Aix-en-Provence-Cannes) take exit 36 (Le Muy) and D25 to St-Maxime. Follow D559 coast road towards St Tropez and site is 8 km. west at Port Grimaud. GPS: 43.26978, 6.57311

Charges guide

Per unit incl. 2 persons and electricity	€ 25.00 - € 65.00
extra person	€ 5.00 - € 15.00

Min. stays apply.

Grimaud

Domaine des Naïades

655 chemin des Mûres, F-83310 Grimaud (Var) T: 04 94 55 67 80. E: info@lesnaiades.com

alanrogers.com/FR83640

Les Naïades is a well equipped site with an enviable setting close to the modern resort of Port Grimaud and the Gulf of Saint Tropez. The 470 pitches (226 are used for mobile homes for rent) are of a good size and well shaded, most have 10A electricity. The site boasts an Olympic sized pool and two giant water slides, as well as a separate pool for children, and there is an attractive new bar/restaurant area. Les Naïades becomes lively in high season with a full activity and entertainment programme, as well as a miniclub. Car-free Port Grimaud is a stylish resort, built in the 1960s on the marshy delta of the Giscle.

Facilities

Five basic but adequate toilet blocks. Facilities for disabled visitors, but access can be difficult. Laundry facilities. Motorcaravan services. Supermarket. Bar. Restaurant. Swimming pool with water slides. Aquagym. Play area. Kid's club (July/Aug). Multisports court. Boules. Bicycle hire. Mobile homes for rent. WiFi (charged). Off site: Beach 900 m. Golf 2 km. Riding 5 km.

Open: 11 April - 3 October.

Directions

The site is 3 km. north of Port Grimaud. Take D559 towards St-Maxime. After 2 km. turn north at the island. Site is signed. GPS: 43.285278, 6.579722

Charges guide

Per unit incl. 2-3 persons and electricity	€ 26.00 - € 60.00
extra person (over 7 yrs)	€ 4.00 - € 8.00

Guillestre

Camping la Rochette

Route des Campings, F-05600 Guillestre (Hautes-Alpes) T: 04 92 45 02 15. E: guillestre@aol.com

alanrogers.com/FR05110

At a height of 800 metres, this attractive municipal site looks fresh and well kept. Located in a beautiful mountainous region, it is run under contract by a very welcoming young couple who are fully responsible for the day-to-day running of the site. There are 190 grassy pitches, separated by trees that give welcome shade, with 185 for touring; all have 4-10A electricity. The excellent, clean facilities are immaculately kept. Although there are few amenities on site, most can be found in the town, only ten minutes' walk away. The Monday market is well worth a visit. English is spoken.

Facilities

Three well appointed toilet blocks are clean and modern. Facilities for disabled visitors. Small shop, snack bar/takeaway and restaurant (July/Aug). Heated outdoor swimming pool (July/Aug). Play area. Boules. Bicycle hire. Only gas and electric barbecues are permitted. Internet access and WiFi throughout (free). Off site: Municipal heated swimming pool and tennis courts adjacent. Restaurant, shops and supermarket in Guillestre 800 m.

Open: 15 May - 30 September.

Directions

Between Briançon and Gap on the RN94, at roundabout signed Guillestre, turn towards the village. Site is signed with the entrance in 900 m. GPS: 44.65854, 6.63816

Charges guide

Per unit incl. 2 persons and electricity	€ 16.80 - € 20.10
extra person	€ 3.00 - € 4.00
child (under 10 yrs)	€ 2.00 - € 2.70

Hyères

Campéole Eurosurf

2947 route de Giens, F-83400 Hyères (Var) T: 04 94 58 00 20. E: eurosurf@campeole.com

alanrogers.com/FR83690

Facing the shimmering island of Porquerolles, Campéole Eurosurf has an enviable setting with direct access to a fine sandy beach. This is a large site with 402 pitches, all occupied by mobile homes, chalets and fully equipped tents for rent. There are no touring pitches here. Ferry tickets are sold on the site for trips to Porquerolles and its neighbouring islands. The campsite's bar/restaurant is on the beach and is a pleasant spot for an evening meal. Eurosurf becomes lively in peak season with frequent evening entertainment and activities for children.

Facilities

Laundry facilities. Shop. Bar (1/5-15/9). Restaurant. Takeaway (1/5-15/9). Games room. Playground. Diving school. Jet ski and boat hire. Boat launching (charged). All-weather sports area. Activity and entertainment. Internet point. WiFi (charged). Direct beach access. Mobile homes, chalets and tents for rent. Off site: Sentier des douaniers coastal walk. Fishing 200 m. Etang des Pesquiers (bird sanctuary). Windsurfing. Riding 1 km.

Open: 28 March - 2 November.

Directions

Take the A57 motorway as far as Hyères. Then follow signs to Giens/Les Iles. The site is on the left hand side of the road, 1 km. after the village of La Capte. GPS: 43.0332, 6.0852

Charges guide

Contact the site for details.

Hyères-les-Palmiers

Camping Domaine du Ceinturon 3

2 rue des Saraniers, F-83400 Hyères-les-Palmiers (Var) T: 04 94 66 32 65. E: contact@ceinturon3.fr

alanrogers.com/FR83810

Le Ceinturon 3 is located close to the popular resort of Hyères, just 80 m. from the beach. There are 160 shaded and partly shaded pitches, all with 6/10A electricity. A number of fully equipped chalets is available for rent. The site's modern amenities include a swimming pool and a convivial bar/restaurant. The pool has suitable access for those with limited mobility. A special bracelet system is in use to ensure that only campers have access. Free aqua gym sessions are held in peak season. The village of L'Ayguade is just 400 m. away; it has a supermarket and hosts a traditional market every Wednesday.

Facilities

Four modern, heated toilet blocks with most washbasins in cubicles, controllable showers and baby room (key). Facilities for disabled visitors (key). Excellent launderette. Motorcaravan services. Shop (24/6-31/8), bread to order in low season. Bar. Restaurant and takeaway. Outdoor heated swimming pool. Jacuzzi. New adventure play area. Tennis. Volleyball. Fitness park. Playing field. Multisports court. Fishing. Miniclub (July/Aug). Fully equipped chalets for rent. WiFi (charged). Off site: Bicycle hire 100 m.

Open: 12 April - 30 September.

Directions

Approaching from the north (A7, A52 and A570) follow signs to Hyères and at fifth traffic lights turn right towards L'Ayguade and Les Salins. At roundabout in L'Ayguade, take the coast road to the right. Site is 1.2 km. GPS: 43.10093, 6.16931

Charges guide

Per unit incl. 2 persons (3 in high season) and electricity	€ 23.65 - € 36.80
extra person	€ 6.25

Hyères-Plage

Camping la Presqu'île de Giens

153 route de la Madrague-Giens, F-83400 Hyères (Var) T: 04 94 58 22 86. E: info@camping-giens.com

alanrogers.com/FR83190

La Presqu'île de Giens is a well run, family campsite at the southern end of the Giens peninsula. The site is well maintained and extends over 17 acres of undulating terrain. Of the site's 427 pitches, 170 are for touring. These are generally of a good size and well shaded – there is a separate area of smaller pitches reserved for tents. Electrical connections (16A) are available on all pitches. In high season this becomes a lively site with a well run children's club (small charge) and an evening entertainment programme including discos, singers and dancers.

Facilities

Five toilet blocks, three very good new ones (heated in low season) and two refurbished. All was clean and well maintained. Facilities for disabled visitors. Washing machines and dryers. Motorcaravan services. Well stocked shop. Bar, restaurant and takeaway. Play area. Sports pitch. Diving classes. Club and workshops for children (high season). Evening entertainment. Sports tournaments. Excursion programme. No charcoal barbecues. WiFi throughout (charged).

Open: 31 March - 7 October.

Directions

From west, leave A57 at exit for Hyères on A570. At Hyères follow signs to Giens-les Iles (D97). At end of this road, after 11 km. turn right towards Madraque. Site is on the left. GPS: 43.04071, 6.1435

Charges guide

Per unit incl. 2 persons and electricity	€ 23.22 - € 35.62
extra person	€ 5.40 - € 8.60

Camping Cheques accepted.

Isle-sur-la Sorgue

Camping Airotel La Sorguette

871 route d'Apt, F-84800 Isle-sur-la Sorgue (Vaucluse) T: 04 90 38 05 71. E: sorguette@wanadoo.fr

alanrogers.com/FR84050

This popular, well organised municipal site is well placed, just 1.5 km. from the attractive small town of Isle-sur-la Sorgue, known for its antique galleries. There are 164 medium sized level pitches (109 for touring) arranged in groups of four; all have 10A electricity. Each group is separated by tall hedges and most have a little shade. In high season, a few competitions are organised (boules or volleyball), plus some children's entertainment, but this is quite low key. You will receive a warm welcome from the English-speaking staff.

Facilities

Well maintained toilet blocks. Washing machines. Units for disabled visitors. Baby room. Motorcaravan services. Fridge hire. Shop, bar and snacks (1/7-25/8). Play area. Volleyball. Half-court tennis. Basketball. Canoeing. Fishing. Entertainment (July/Aug). Bicycle hire. Internet point. WiFi over site (charged). Twin-axle caravans not accepted. Off site: Local markets (Sun. and Thurs) with free shuttle bus. Swimming pools (preferential rates) 2 km.

Open: 15 March - 15 October.

Directions

Site is 1.5 km. east of Isle-sur-la Sorgue on the D901 towards Apt. It is well signed from the town. GPS: 43.91462, 5.07215

Charges guide

Per unit incl. 2 persons and electricity	€ 21.90 - € 27.50
extra person	€ 6.15 - € 7.90
child (1-11 yrs)	€ 3.00 - € 3.90

La Colle-sur-Loup

Sites et Paysages les Pinèdes

Route du Pont de Pierre, F-06480 La Colle-sur-Loup (Alpes-Maritimes) T: 04 93 32 98 94.
E: info@lespinedes.com **alanrogers.com/FR06100**

Les Pinèdes is 7 km. inland from the busy coast, at the centre of all the attractions of the Côte d'Azur, yet far enough away to be a peaceful retreat at the end of a busy day. Run by the third generation of family owners, the site is terraced on a wooded hillside where olives and vines used to grow. All of the 108 touring pitches are level and have electricity (6-10A), most also have water and are separated by low bushes. There are also 41 mobile homes and chalets available to rent. In May the evenings are alive with fireflies.

Facilities

Three excellent toilet blocks. One has facilities for disabled visitors. Baby room. Laundry. Shop, bakery (1/6-5/9). Bar, restaurant, takeaway (all season). Heated outdoor swimming pool (from 15/4). Play area and paddling pool. TV/games room. Multisports court. Archery. Boules. Fitness area. Riding. Miniclub and activities (July/Aug). Weekly walks in the hills (June-Sept). WiFi throughout (charged). Car rental. Twin-axle caravans not accepted.

Open: 24 March - 30 September.

Directions

From A8 exit 47 take D6007 towards Nice. After 1.4 km. take D2085 towards Villeneuve Loubet for 2.5 km. At roundabout take D6 (Grasse) and site is signed on right after 6 km. GPS: 43.6819, 7.08335

Charges guide

Per unit incl. 2 persons and electricity	€ 25.90 - € 45.30
extra person	€ 4.70 - € 5.90
child (0-5 yrs)	free - € 4.10

La Grave

Camping de la Meije

Le Village, F-05320 La Grave (Hautes-Alpes) T: 04 76 79 93 34. E: nathalie-romagne@wanadoo.fr

alanrogers.com/FR05300

Camping de la Meije has a superb setting surrounded by majestic mountains. It is an ideal site for couples and families who are looking for either a relaxing holiday or an action packed one. Set at an altitude of 1,460 m. in the magnificent Parc des Ecrins in the Haut-Alpes, it can get chilly in the evenings. It is only 50 m. from the village of La Grave with its shops, bars and restaurants. There are 50 large, grass pitches, all with 6A electricity and on level ground. Separated by shrubs and trees that give some shade, most have magnificent views of the imposing, snow-capped la Meije. This is a wonderful area for those keen on skiing, hiking and mountain biking.

Facilities

Two sanitary blocks, one brand new, bright and airy with extra large showers. Facilities for disabled campers. Laundry facilities. Small heated pool with large deck area. Minigolf. Basketball. Tennis. Fishing. WiFi throughout (free). Off site: Play area. Rafting 100 m. Paragliding. Wellness centre. Many climbing, hiking and biking trails. Some summer skiing. Cable car to La Meije.

Open: 10 May - 30 September.

Directions

From A480 exit 8 just south of Grenoble take N85 (Route Napoléon) towards Gap, Briançon and Vizille. Continue on D1091 into La Grave. Site is well signed on right as you leave. GPS: 45.045192, 6.310302

Charges guide

Per unit incl. 2 persons and electricity	€ 19.00
extra person	€ 3.00
child (4-10 yrs)	€ 2.00
dog	€ 1.00

La Mole

Camping Pachacaïd

Route du Canadel, F-83310 La Mole (Var) T: 04 94 55 70 80. E: pachacaid@franceloc.fr
alanrogers.com/FR83720

Pachacaïd is a very popular holiday village on the edge of the Massif des Maures. Please note that there are no touring pitches here. The site is located 17 km. from Saint Tropez and 8 km. from Rayol Canadel with its famous creeks and beaches. At the heart of Pachacaïd is its amazing Niagara water park with seven massive water slides, a huge Californian-style swimming pool and numerous jacuzzis and other water features. Other on-site amenities are of a very high standard, such as the Pachacafé restaurant and well stocked shop. The site extends over a 50-hectare pine forest with a wide variety of mobile homes available for rent.

Facilities

Shop, bar, restaurant, café, Niagara water park (swimming pools and large water slides, all open all season). Water aerobics. Archery. Football. Volleyball. Play area. Entertainment and activity programme. Bicycle hire. Caravans for rent. Riding, bicycle and kayak activities organised. WiFi (charged). Dogs are not accepted. Off site: Riding 5 km. Beach 8 km. Golf 10 km.

Open: 11 April - 27 September.

Directions

From the A8, use the Le Luc exit and follow signs to St Tropez. On reaching Grimaud, take westbound N98 (Toulon) and continue beyond Cogolin and pass an aerodrome. Turn left following signs to the site (before reaching La Mole).
GPS: 43.190181, 6.470887

Charges guide

Contact the site for details.

Lagnes

Camping la Coutelière

2765 route de Fontaine de Vaucluse (D24), F-84800 Lagnes (Vaucluse) T: 04 90 20 33 97.
E: couteliere@wanadoo.fr **alanrogers.com/FR84370**

La Coutelière is a friendly, family run site nestling in the hills of the Lubéron National Park, at the heart of Provence. There are 103 pitches with 81 good sized grass touring pitches, all with 10A electricity and access to water points. They are separated by low hedges and mature trees provide good shade. Some very attractive pitches lie alongside the River Sorgue. Some family activities are arranged, but the owners aim to provide an attractive base for relaxing family holidays and peaceful retreats for couples. There are occasional family nights in the summer but no regular music or discos to disturb the peace.

Facilities

Two toilet blocks have been renovated and can be heated. Washbasins in cabins, controllable showers and facilities for disabled visitors. Fresh bread daily and local wine for sale. Bar (all season). Takeaway, groceries and ice creams (3/5-27/9). Heated outdoor swimming pool (25/4-30/9). Children's pool. Tennis. Basketball. Boules. Canoeing and fishing in the river. WiFi (charged).

Open: 18 March - 7 October.

Directions

From A7 autoroute take exit 24 (Avignon Sud) and D900 east for 9 km. Turn northeast on D24 towards Fontaine de Vaucluse. Site is on left in 2.5 km.
GPS: 43.91034, 5.107003

Charges guide

Per unit incl. 2 persons and electricity	€ 19.90 - € 33.90
extra person	€ 6.40 - € 8.70

Le Bar-sur-Loup

Camping Caravaning les Gorges du Loup

965 chemin des Vergers, F-06620 Le Bar-sur-Loup (Alpes-Maritimes) T: 04 93 42 45 06.
E: info@lesgorgesduloup.com **alanrogers.com/FR06090**

Les Gorges du Loup is situated on a steep hillside above Grasse. The one-kilometre lane which leads to the site is narrow with passing places. The 70 pitches are on level terraces (all with electricity 6/10A), shaded by oak and olive trees, some of which are several hundred years old. Some pitches are only suitable for tents and the site roads are quite steep but the very friendly and enthusiastic owners, who speak a little English, can provide 4x4 assistance. A quiet family site, there is no organised entertainment here. There are stunning views over the Gorges du Loup and Gourdon – a hilltop village, recognised as one of the most beautiful in France.

Facilities

Two clean and well equipped toilet blocks with facilities for young children and disabled visitors. Laundry facilities. Small shop (bread to order). Small bar/restaurant with terrace, takeaway (all 1/5-15/9). New heated swimming pool. Boules. Skittles. TV room, board games, library. Climbing frame and slide. No charcoal barbecues. Fridge hire. Chalets and mobile homes for hire. WiFi (charged). Off site: Bar-sur-Loup is only a 500 m. walk. Fishing 1 km.

Open: 11 April - 26 September.

Directions

From Grasse, D2085 Nice road. D3 briefly to Châteauneuf Pré du Lac. D2210 to Pont-de-Loup, Vence. Pass Bar-sur-Loup on left, after a sharp right turn site is well signed, follow narrow access road 750 m. Large units continue 2 km. to junction with D6 and turn around. GPS: 43.7017, 6.9948

Charges guide

Per unit incl. 2 persons and electricity	€ 20.60 - € 35.80

No credit cards.

Le Lavandou

Camping Saint Pons

Avenue Maréchal Juin, F-83980 Le Lavandou (Var) T: 04 94 71 03 93. E: info@campingsaintpons.com

alanrogers.com/FR83680

Camping Saint Pons enjoys an attractive setting within walking distance of the delightful family resort of Le Lavandou. This is a relatively small, quiet and uncomplicated site extending over two hectares, with many flowering shrubs and bushes. There are 155 pitches here, well shaded and of a fair size. All have electrical connections. A number of mobile homes are available for rent. There is no shop on site but there is a supermarket just 300 m. away. There is also a bar and restaurant next door. The Littoral cycle track runs close to the site and provides an appealing way of exploring the coast and a number of pretty Provençal villages. Good English is spoken.

Facilities

Two clean sanitary blocks with controllable pushbutton showers. Wet room for disabled visitors. Laundry facilities. Play area. Boules. New sports field. Mobile homes for rent. Dogs are not accepted 5/7-26/8. Off site: Le Lavandou 500 m. Nearest beach 800 m. Bicycle hire 800 m. Fishing 1.5 km. Sailing 2 km.

Open: 1 May - 4 October.

Directions

From Hyères (A570) head east on D98 to Bormes-les-Mimosas and then southeast on D559 to Le Lavandou. Then follow signs to the site. GPS: 43.136047, 6.354416

Charges guide

Per unit incl. 2 persons and electricity	€ 18.60 - € 30.50
extra person	€ 4.50 - € 6.60

Le Muy

RCN Domaine de la Noguière

1617 route de Fréjus, F-83490 Le Muy (Var) T: 04 94 45 13 78. E: noguiere@rcn.fr

alanrogers.com/FR83090

Domaine de la Noguière is located close to the town of Le Muy and is owned by RCN, a Dutch company with a chain of campsites in the Netherlands. Run by an enthusiastic team, this is a friendly and informal campsite. Set in 15 hectares, with delightful views of the beautiful Provençal scenery, it has 146 touring pitches, mainly level and with sizes up to 120 sq.m. to suit all units, all with electricity (6A). Reception has a small shop adjacent selling fresh bread daily, while the bar/restaurant serves local specialities. There is a good swimming pool complex with toboggan slides and a snack bar nearby. This site is ideally situated close to the Gorges du Verdon, yet only 16 km. from the Mediterranean beaches.

Facilities

Two modern sanitary buildings have been added with family showers and children's rooms. Toilets are fully tiled with individual cabins and access for disabled visitors. Laundry facilities. Shop, bar/restaurant with terrace plus takeaway service, swimming pool complex with slides and snack bar (all open all season). Small meeting room with library and large TV. Fishing. Tennis. Boules. Games field. Play area. WiFi (charged). No charcoal barbecues. Off site: Riding 5 km. Bicycle hire, golf and beach 15 km.

Open: 21 March - 31 October.

Directions

From A8 autoroute exit 36 Le Muy, take DN7 Le Muy. At roundabout in town, take signs for Route de Fréjus. Site is 2 km. on left from centre of village. GPS: 43.46832, 6.59202

Charges guide

Per unit incl. 2 persons, electricity and water	€ 19.50 - € 52.50
extra person (over 3 yrs)	€ 3.75 - € 7.00

Camping Cheques accepted.

Les Issambres

Camping Au Paradis des Campeurs

La Gaillarde-Plage, F-83380 Les Issambres (Var) T: 04 94 96 93 55.

alanrogers.com/FR83080

Family owned and run, this popular site has 180 pitches, all with 6A electricity and 132 with water and drainage. All pitches are of a good size, on grass and separated by a variety of Mediterranean trees and bushes; most offer a good level of shade. There is no entertainment which gives peaceful nights. The gates are surveyed by CCTV (especially the beach gate) and a night watchman is on duty. With direct access to a sandy beach (via an underpass) and being so well maintained, the site has become deservedly popular so it is essential to book for June, July and August. There is an Italian influence in the design and layout of the site and the central toilet block is built around an attractive courtyard reminiscent of a Roman villa. A coded exit gives access up steps to a small but well stocked supermarket, bar, restaurant and takeaway. The Camping Car Aire Chez Marcel which is adjoining the site is a separate business with no connections to the site.

Facilities

Excellent, refurbished and well maintained toilet blocks. Facilities for babies and children with shower at suitable height. En-suite for disabled visitors. Washing machines and dryer. Motorcaravan services. TV room. Excellent play areas with top quality safety bases, catering for the under and over 5s. Boules. Car wash area. Mobile homes for rent. WiFi (charged). Off site: Shop, restaurant and takeaway service. Bicycle hire 2.5 km. Riding 3 km. Golf 6 km.

Open: 29 March - 3 October.

Directions

From Frejus take the D559 south. Site is signed at La Gaillarde, 2 km. south of St Aygulf. GPS: 43.36593, 6.71230

Charges guide

Per unit incl. 2 persons and electricity	€ 21.00 - € 32.00
incl. water and drainage	€ 23.00 - € 35.00
extra person	€ 6.00
child (under 5 yrs)	€ 3.00

Les Vigneaux

Campéole le Courounba

Le Pont du Rif, D994, F-05120 Les Vigneaux (Hautes-Alpes) T: 04 92 23 02 09.

E: courounba@campeole.com **alanrogers.com/FR05140**

Le Courounba is a member of the Campéole group, located at the entrance to the magnificent Parc National des Ecrins. Pitches are shady and spacious, dispersed around 12 hectares of woodland. Many of the 160 touring pitches have superb views of the surrounding mountain scenery. Ninety mobile homes for rent (including specially adapted units for disabled campers). There is also a brand new ecological swimming pool with water slides and watergames and other on-site amenities include two tennis courts and a volleyball pitch. Most facilities are free of charge (including tennis). Adjacent to the site is a friendly bar/restaurant and a small, basic shop during high season only. There is dramatic mountain scenery all around. The Mont Brison is the highest limestone rock face in France and the Mont Pelvoux, and at 3,943 m. has an all-year snow cap. Le Courounba is on the banks of the River Gyronde, popular for fishing. A little further afield, Briançon is a superb town, fortified by Vauban and well worth a visit.

Facilities

Four modern sanitary blocks include washbasins and showers. Facilities for children and disabled visitors. Motorcaravan services. Washing machine. Heated swimming pool (14/6-20/9, closed Sat. in July/Aug). Sauna and jacuzzi. Volleyball. Tennis. Multisports court. Bouncy castle. Play area. BMX track. Activity and entertainment programme in high season. Mobile homes for rent. WiFi (charged). Electric barbecues and camp fires not permitted. Off site: Adjacent bar/restaurant and basic shop. Fishing 100 m. Hiking and cycle tracks. Golf, riding, bicycle hire 5 km. Briançon 17 km. White-water sports. Rock climbing and bouldering.

Open: 16 May - 20 September.

Directions

The site is close to the village of Les Vigneaux, south of Briançon. From Briançon, head south on N94 as far as Prelles and then join the D4 to Les Vigneaux. Drive through the village and take the direction to Puy St Vincent, when you cross the bridge, turn immediately right to join the road to the campsite. GPS: 44.82483, 6.52566

Charges guide

Per unit incl. 2 persons and electricity	€ 19.80 - € 30.20
extra person	€ 4.70 - € 7.90
child (2-6 yrs)	free - € 4.80
dog	€ 2.50 - € 3.90

Manosque

Flower Camping Provence Vallée

1138 avenue de la Repasse, F-04100 Manosque (Alpes-de-Haute-Provence) T: 04 92 72 28 08.
E: contact@provence-vallee.fr **alanrogers.com/FR04510**

On the edge of historic and picturesque Manosque, the largest town of the Alpes-de-Haute-Provence, this is an ideal base from which to explore the Luberon to the north, the Gorges du Verdon to the east and Mediterranean Provence to the south and west. There are 106 pitches separated by hedges and shaded by pine trees; 62 are for touring units, most with electrical connections (6A), whilst the remainder are occupied by mobile homes and canvas lodges. The medieval heart of Manosque has quaint, narrow streets and from the Mont d'Or you can enjoy views of the Durance Valley.

Facilities

Three well spaced sanitary blocks with facilities for disabled visitors. Washing machine and dryer. Motorcaravan services. Variety of takeaway meals provided by outside caterers. Shop for essentials. Swimming pool (1/6-15/9). Organised activities and entertainment (July/Aug). Bouncy castle and playground. Table tennis. Pétanque. Football field. Communal barbecue only. Sale of local produce. Entertainment (July/Aug). TV and fridge hire. WiFi throughout (charged).

Open: 1 April - 31 October.

Directions

Leave A51 motorway at exit 18 and head north east on D607 to Manosque. At third roundabout, take 3rd exit (Ste. Tulle, Apt). Continue across junction and at 2nd roundabout take 3rd exit following sign to site on right in 500 m. GPS: 43.82972, 5.76361

Charges guide

Per unit incl. 2 persons and electricity	€ 15.00 - € 26.00
extra person	€ 3.00 - € 5.00

Martigues

Flower Camping le Marius

Route de la Saulce, la Couronne, F-13500 Martigues (Bouches du Rhône) T: 04 42 80 70 29.
E: contact@camping-marius.com **alanrogers.com/FR13140**

Camping Marius is tucked away beside a calanque (or inlet) on the protected and wild coastline between Marseille and Martigues. The Cavalier family take great pride in making it a peaceful haven. A private gate leads to a challenging walk through the pine trees to the beach (200 m) across the rocky cliffs or you can walk along the road. The site is a colourful oasis, regularly laid out with shade from shrubs and mixed trees. It provides 103 pitches, of which 62 are occupied by mobile homes for rent (two specially adapted) and 21 are seasonal, leaving just 20 for touring units (all with 6A electricity, sink and water supply).

Facilities

A good modern toilet block is well equipped and is supplemented by a smaller one. Baby bath. Facilities for families. Good facilities for disabled visitors. Washing machine and dryer. Motorcaravan services. Small shop. Bar and restaurant (all season). Wellness. Play area. Bicycles and canoes loaned. Activity and entertainment (twice weekly, July/Aug). Chalets for rent. Max. 1 dog accepted. Only gas barbecues allowed. WiFi (free).

Open: 4 April - 11 October.

Directions

Approach Martigues from north on D5 and cross Canal de Caronte, continuing south on D5, then D49 to La Couronne. At roundabout on outskirts of town, turn left for Sausset-les-Pins and St Croix. Site is signed from there. GPS: 43.335, 5.0673

Charges guide

Per unit incl. 2 persons and electricity	€ 23.00 - € 36.00
extra person	€ 6.00 - € 9.00

Méolans-Revel

Camping du Rioclar

D900, F-04340 Revel (Alpes-de-Haute-Provence) T: 04 92 81 10 32. E: rioclar@orange.fr
alanrogers.com/FR04410

Camping le Rioclar is a friendly, family run site set in an eight-hectare forest 1,100 m. up in the heart of the Alpes de Haute Provence. Surrounded by high mountains and bordered by a section of the River Ubaye, famous for hosting kayaking championships. There are mobile homes, chalets and caravans for rent sleeping 4-6 people and an area for tourers set in a shaded wooded part of the site. The 170 touring pitches range from 60 to 120 sq.m. and have electricity (6-10A) and water points nearby. It is a perfect location for a multitude of outdoor activities including rafting, cycling, swimming and hiking.

Facilities

Three well equipped sanitary blocks with facilities for babies and disabled visitors. Laundry. Shop, bar, restaurant and takeaway (mid June-Aug). Heated outdoor swimming pool (mid June-Aug). Playground. Badminton court. Multisports court. Tennis. Fishing. Rafting. Kayaking. Hydro speed. Boules. Minigolf. Entertainment. Mountain bike hire (including electric). No charcoal barbecues. Free WiFi (in bar).

Open: 12 June - 6 September.

Directions

From Gap head south on D900B then D900 towards Barcelonnette, 1.8 km. west of Méolans-Revel. Site is on the right. GPS: 44.39953, 6.53181

Charges guide

Per unit incl. 2 persons and electricity	€ 29.00
extra person	€ 6.50
child (0-6 yrs)	€ 4.30
dog	€ 3.60

Montclar

Yelloh! Village l'Etoile des Neiges

F-04140 Montclar (Alpes-de-Haute-Provence) T: 04 66 73 97 39. E: info@yellohvillage-etoile-des-neiges.com
alanrogers.com/FR04080

This attractive, family run site near the mountain village and ski resort of Saint Jean Montclar is open most of the year, although touring units are only accepted in the summer months. Being at an altitude of 1,300 m. the nights can get quite cold in summer. The 150 shady, terraced pitches, with 55 for touring, are separated by small shrubs and alpine trees. All pitches are close to electricity and water points. An attractive bar and restaurant overlooks the two outdoor swimming pools with the shallow pool having a water slide ideal for children. A new indoor complex with a heated pool, gym, jacuzzi, sauna and steam room makes a splendid addition to the facilities.

Facilities

Central toilet block (heated in winter) and facilities for disabled visitors. Two washing machines. Motorcaravan services. Bar/restaurant. Two outdoor swimming pools with slides. Indoor complex for adults only with heated pool, gym, jacuzzi, sauna and steam room for adults only (all amenities 28/5-9/9). Tennis. Boules. Two play areas. Multisports pitch. WiFi in some areas (free).

Open: 28 May - 30 September (chalets all year).

Directions

Site is 35 km. south of Gap via D900B. Beyond Serre Ponçon, turn right, D900 signed Selonnet, St Jean Montclar. Entering St Jean Montclar turn left, pass chalets, shops, fork right down lane to campsite in 250 m. GPS: 44.40921, 6.34826

Charges guide

Per unit incl. 2 persons and electricity (6A)	€ 18.00 - € 37.00
extra person	€ 6.00 - € 8.00

Mornas

Camping Beauregard

Route d'Uchaux, F-84550 Mornas (Vaucluse) T: 04 90 37 02 08. E: beauregard@franceloc.fr
alanrogers.com/FR84140

Just a kilometre off the N7 and near an A7 exit, this FranceLoc site will appeal to families and couples looking for a busy site with every amenity you could think of. These include magnificent play areas, equipment and clubs, a heated, outdoor, four pool complex, flumes, a paddling pool and a heated indoor pool. Although there are many mobile homes, there are 60 pitches available for touring units. These pitches are under large pine trees and are rather sandy (firm pegging might be difficult). They are of various shapes and sizes, mainly about 100 sq.m. The site has been fully upgraded and this is now a great family site which can easily accommodate teenagers, toddlers, babies and pre-teens.

Facilities

Two toilet blocks, one heated when necessary, with washbasins in cabins, some with hairdryer and spacious showers, some with washbasins. Facilities for disabled visitors (key). Laundry facilities. Motorcaravan services. Shop, bakery, bar, restaurant and takeaway (April-Sept). Swimming pools, one covered. Tennis. Play area. Boules. Fitness trail. Entertainment (high season). Electric barbecues only. WiFi on part of site (free).

Open: 11 April - 21 September.

Directions

From the A7 take exit for Bollène, then N7 towards Orange. At north end of Mornas, turn left on D74 signed Uchaux. Site is on left after 1.7 km. Height restriction on bridge 3.4 m. GPS: 44.21540, 4.74530

Charges guide

Per unit incl. 2 persons and electricity	€ 30.00 - € 49.00
extra person	€ 4.70 - € 7.00

Moustiers-Sainte Marie

Camping Manaysse

Rue Fréderic Mistral, F-04360 Moustiers-Sainte Marie (Alpes-de-Haute-Provence) T: 04 92 74 66 71.
E: manaysse@orange.fr **alanrogers.com/FR04190**

Manaysse is a little gem of a family campsite on the outskirts of the famous hillside village of Moustiers-Sainte Marie (900 m) and is ideal for exploring the magnificent Gorges du Verdon region. There are 97 terraced pitches on grass and gravel, with 85 for touring (electricity 6/10A). Some of the pitches are on a slight slope, however those at the top of the site have a beautiful view of Moustiers-Sainte Marie. There are both shady and sunny pitches available and the abundance of flowers, trees and shrubs make the site look very attractive. An area of grassland is set aside to promote the growth of wild flowers and butterflies. Large units should approach with care as there is a short, steep incline up to reception.

Facilities

Simple but clean toilet blocks. Facilities for disabled visitors. Washing machines. Bread is delivered. Small play area. Boules. Minigolf. No charcoal barbecues. Torches may be useful. WiFi (charged but very reasonable).
Off site: Fishing 600 m. Moustiers 900 m. Bicycle hire 2 km. Lake, beach, watersports 4 km. Riding 12 km.

Open: 24 March - 26 October.

Directions

From Riez on D952 turn north at first roundabout in Moustiers, site signed, entrance in 200 m.
GPS: 43.84486, 6.21566

Charges guide

Per unit incl. 2 persons and electricity	€ 14.20 - € 15.50

No credit cards.

Orange

Camping Manon

1321 rue Alexis Carrel, F-84100 Orange (Vaucluse) T: 04 32 81 94 96. E: campingmanon@yahoo.fr

alanrogers.com/FR84320

This small, comfortable and well looked after site is something of a gem. Located on the outskirts of Orange, yet close to the town centre, it somehow retains a rural atmosphere. There are 80 pitches, some 50 for touring. All are flat and grassy with some larger pitches ideal for motorcaravans. Separated by high hedges and flowering bushes, with tall trees for shade, all have access to electricity (10A, some may need long leads) and water. Convenient for the N7 and the A7 motorway, this is definitely one to stop at en route, or spend a few days enjoying the interesting town of Orange.

Facilities

One clean, modern toilet block in the centre of the site. A second block by the pool and bar has facilities for disabled visitors. Baby room and children's toilets. Washing machine. Motorcaravan services. Shop with essentials. Bread to order. Breakfast service. Bar and snack bar/pizzeria (on demand). Small pool with attractive sunbathing area and paddling pool. Jacuzzi, gym and sauna. Multisports field. Tennis court. Pétanque. Playing field. Small playground. Communal barbecue only. Free WiFi throughout. Chalet accommodation to rent.

Open: 1 April - 30 October.

Directions

From A7, take J21 towards Orange centre. At first roundabout, turn left and follow signs. Or, from N7 south towards Orange centre, turn right just before the Arc de Triomphe, and right at second roundabout. Site signed. GPS: 44.14665, 4.79538

Charges guide

Per unit incl. 2 persons and electricity	€ 22.50 - € 28.50
extra person	€ 6.00
dog	€ 3.00

Orgon

Camping la Vallée Heureuse

Impasse Lavau, F-13660 Orgon (Bouches du Rhône) T: 04 90 44 17 13. E: contact@valleeheureuse.com

alanrogers.com/FR13310

A friendly welcome awaits you at Camping la Vallée Heureuse, which lies hidden in a valley of outstanding natural beauty, surrounded by cliffs and steep, wooded hills. This large site is very popular with hikers and climbers (a professional gives lessons on site). It is also close to the parks of the Cévennes, the Carmargue and the Luberon making it an ideal centre for touring this very interesting region, as well as the coast a little further south. The site is terraced with 180 stony, grassy pitches, some quite large, many hedged and with shade and 16A electricity. They are good for large outfits.

Facilities

Modern toilet block with all necessary facilities. Washing machine and dryer. Small shop. Bar (from March). Restaurant (Apr-Oct). Swimming and paddling pools (May-Sept). Play area. Boules. Fishing. Bicycle hire. TV room. Internet point. WiFi. Entertainment programme and children's club (July/Aug). Off site: Restaurant and snacks 1 km. Lake swimming and fishing close by. Rock climbing walls. Cavaillon 10 km. L'Isle-sur-la-Sorgue (antiques).

Open: 27 March - 31 October.

Directions

Leave A7 at exit 25 (St Rémy-de-Provence). Shortly, at roundabout, take D26 to Orgon and then the N7. Site is well signed on the right south of the village. GPS: 43.781891, 5.040225

Charges guide

Per unit incl. 2 persons and electricity	€ 19.80 - € 25.50

Camping Cheques accepted.

Orpierre

Camping des Princes d'Orange

F-05700 Orpierre (Hautes-Alpes) T: 04 92 66 22 53. E: campingorpierre@wanadoo.fr

alanrogers.com/FR05000

This attractive, terraced site, set on a hillside above the village has been thoughtfully developed. Muriel, the owner, speaks excellent English and the genuine, friendly welcome means many families return year upon year, bringing in turn new generations. Divided into five terraces, each with its own toilet block, some of its 100 generously sized pitches (68 for touring) enjoy good shade from trees and have electricity connections (10A). In high season, one terrace is reserved as a camping area for young people. Orpierre has an enchanting maze of medieval streets and houses, almost like going back in time.

Facilities

Six well equipped toilet blocks. Excellent bathrooms for children and babies. Laundry facilities. Fresh bread. Bar (15/6-15/9). Heated swimming pool and paddling pool (15/6-15/9). Play area with inflatable climbing tower. Boules. Games room. Fridge hire. No charcoal barbecues. WiFi throughout (charged). Off site: Orpierre with a few shops and bicycle hire 500 m. Fishing 7 km. Nearest shopping centre Laragne 12 km.

Open: 1 April - 31 October.

Directions

Turn off N75 road at Eyguians onto the D30. Site is signed on the left at crossroads in the centre of Orpierre village. Cross over bridge, narrow approach road. GPS: 44.31121, 5.69677

Charges guide

Per unit incl. 2 persons and electricity	€ 24.00 - € 39.00

No credit cards.

Pernes-les-Fontaines

Camping les Fontaines

125 chemin de la Chapelette, route de Sudre, F-84210 Pernes-les-Fontaines (Vaucluse) T: 04 90 46 82 55.
E: contact@campingfontaines.com **alanrogers.com/FR84190**

A warm welcome awaits visitors to Camping les Fontaines. It is a small, family run site set in two and a half hectares, with magnificent views of Mont Ventoux and the mountains of the Vaucluse. There are 90 level, grassy pitches, 60 for tourers, all with 6A electricity and some shade from mature trees. They are separated by hedging and flowering shrubs. On-site amenities include a 200 sq.m. lagoon-style pool, an excellent restaurant and a bar with a large terrace overlooking the pool complex.

Facilities

The modern, very clean, heated central toilet block has facilities for babies and disabled visitors. Laundry. Motorcaravan services. Small shop selling basics and fresh bread. Bar, restaurant, takeaway (all May-Sept). Lagoon-style pool with large 'beach' area (all season). Play area. Free WiFi. Twin-axle caravans are not accepted. Off site: Bicycle hire 2 km. Riding 4 km. Golf and fishing 10 km. Avignon, Gordes, Roussillon.

Open: 28 March - 20 October.

Directions

Leave autoroute A7 at exit 23 (Avignon Nord). Take D942 northeast towards Carpentras. Shortly turn southeast on D6 to St Saturnin. Take D28 northeast for 11 km. to Pernes-les-Fontaines. Follow signs to site 1 km. west of town. GPS: 44.006351, 5.038771

Charges guide

Per unit incl. 2 persons and electricity	€ 20.70 - € 36.80
extra person	€ 5.50 - € 8.80

Peynier

Camping le Devançon

451 chemin de Pourrachon, F-13790 Peynier (Bouches du Rhône) T: 04 42 53 10 06.
E: ledevancon@orange.fr **alanrogers.com/FR13360**

This small, attractive family run site is situated south east of Aix-en-Provence, just a short distance from Peynier. Set amongst pine trees, the 40 mainly level and mostly hedged touring pitches have plenty of shade with some enjoying views of the mountains beyond. All pitches have 6A or 10A electricity. There are also 20 mobile homes tastefully positioned and available for rent. This site has a warm, friendly and relaxed atmosphere and is a nature lover's paradise. It is surrounded by forest and there is a path through the fragrant pines and wild flowers into Peynier (600 m). From Peynier there is a regular bus service to Aix-en-Provence.

Facilities

One heated sanitary block includes showers, washbasins in cabins and British style toilets. Good provision for disabled visitors (key access). Baby bath and changing area. Motorcaravan service point. Laundry facilities. Takeaway (July-Aug). Fresh bread to order. Small gift shop, ice-cream, drinks. Swimming pool and paddling pool (June-Sept). Play area. Trampoline. Boules. Torches required after midnight. No charcoal barbecues. Covered WiFi area. Off site: Supermarket, bars and restaurants in Peynier 1 km. Hypermarket at Trets 4 km.

Open: 5 March - 1 November.

Directions

Follow the A7 and the A8 towards Nice and exit at 32. Continue in the direction of Trets D6. At the junction with the D568, turn right towards Peynier. Once in the village the site is signed.
GPS: 43.2652, 5.3776

Charges guide

Per unit incl. 2 persons and electricity	€ 23.00 - € 27.00
extra person	€ 5.00 - € 6.00
child (2-7 yrs)	€ 4.00 - € 5.00

Puget-sur-Argens

Camping Club la Bastiane

1056 chemin de Suvières, F-83480 Puget-sur-Argens (Var) T: 04 94 55 55 94. E: info@labastiane.com
alanrogers.com/FR83040

La Bastiane is an attractive, well established site which celebrated its 40th anniversary in 2012. It has good amenities and is well located for exploring the Côte d'Azur with easy access to nearby beaches. There are 180 pitches here of which 47 are reserved for touring. They are generally of a good size and are all supplied with electrical connections (10A). The terrain is somewhat undulating but most of the pitches are on level terraces. There is a good swimming pool and a range of amenities including a shop, bar and restaurant with a well priced menu.

Facilities

Three toilet blocks, clean and very well maintained. Facilities for disabled visitors. Washing machines, dryers. Shop, bar, restaurant and takeaway (all season). Heated swimming pool (all season). Tennis. Multisports terrain. Children's club. Play area. Games/TV room. Evening entertainment in peak season. Excursion programme. Only electric barbecues. Bicycle hire. WiFi throughout (charged). Max. 1 dog. Mobile homes and chalets for rent.

Open: 11 April - 20 October.

Directions

Leave A8 at exit 37 (Puget), take right turn at first roundabout (signed Roquebrune), join N7. Turn right, first traffic lights (200 m), then left at roundabout. Site signed from here, on the right 2.5 km. from the motorway. GPS: 43.46966, 6.67845

Charges guide

Per unit incl. 2 persons and electricity	€ 19.00 - € 47.00

Puget-sur-Argens

Parc Saint-James Oasis

Route de la Bouverie, F-83480 Puget-sur-Argens (Var) T: 04 98 11 85 60.
E: oasis@camping-parcsaintjames.com **alanrogers.com/FR83610**

Oasis Village, set in a 42-hectare forest, is a spacious site with 450 pitches exclusively for mo and chalets. As part of the Parc Saint-James Group, it has all the first class facilities you woul A superb swimming pool complex, with one pool equipped with a wave machine, takes centre s ge on the park. Close to the pool, a Provençal village area has been created, with shops, two bars, a restaurant and takeaway. Activities are organised daily in high season and in the evening the village square hosts shows, cabarets and karaoke; if you still have the energy, there is a disco from 11 pm in July and August.

Facilities

One modern sanitary block has controllable showers, some washbasins in cubicles and facilities for disabled visitors. Laundry. Supermarket and shopping area. Bar. Restaurant and takeaway. Large complex with heated swimming pool and children's pool. Water play area. Jacuzzis. Wellness centre (July/Aug). Fitness room and equipment. Play area. TV area and video games room. Tennis. Minigolf. Paintball. Boules. Archery (July/Aug). Miniclub (11/4-5/9). Only electric barbecues permitted. Evening entertainment. Disco. Bicycle hire. WiFi (charged).

Open: 9 April - 24 September.

Directions

Take the Puget-sur-Argens exit from the A8 autoroute and join the N7 towards Le Muy. After 2.5 km. turn right into the Route de la Bouverie. The site can be found after a further 1.5 km. on the right. GPS: 43.47158, 6.66150

Charges guide

Contact site for details.

Quinson

Village Center les Prés du Verdon

F-04500 Quinson (Alpes-de-Haute-Provence) T: 04 99 57 21 21. E: contact@village-center.com
alanrogers.com/FR04230

This family site is attractively located close to the River Verdon and it is a good base for exploring the famous gorges. The site boasts a fine pool complex with a large main pool and separate paddling pool. There are 47 touring pitches here (70-110 sq.m), some well shaded and others rather sunnier. Most are equipped with electrical connections. A further 163 pitches are used for mobile homes and bungalow tents, most of which are available for rent. This is a great region for an active holiday. Popular activities include rafting, canoeing on the Verdon and canyoning.

Facilities

Two toilet blocks have controllable pushbutton showers and washbasins with hot and cold water. Wet room for disabled visitors. Baby room. Swimming pool with paddling pool (from 1/5). Play area. TV room. Volleyball. Entertainment and activity programme with club for children. Off site: Tennis just beyond site entrance. Walking and cycling routes. River, lake, fishing and canoeing all 100 m. Supermarket 200 m. Climbing 500 m. Mon. morning market in Quinson (July/Aug).

Open: 10 April - 13 September.

Directions

Leave A51 at exit 18 and head east on D6 to Riez. From Riez take the D11 southeast to Quinson. 0.5 km. after village, site is signed to the east. GPS: 43.69713, 6.04162

Charges guide

Per unit incl. 2 persons and electricity	€ 17.00 - € 26.00
extra person	€ 4.00 - € 6.00
child (0-3 yrs)	free

Ramatuelle

Yelloh! Village les Tournels

Route de Camarat, F-83350 Ramatuelle (Var) T: 04 94 55 90 90. E: info@yellohvillage-les-tournels.com
alanrogers.com/FR83210

Les Tournels is a large site set on a hillside and pitches have panoramic views of the Gulf of Saint Tropez and Pampelonne beach. The hillside is covered in parasol pines and old olive trees. Of the 890 pitches, 535 are available for touring. They are reasonably level and shady, of variable size, all with electricity and many also with water and waste water drainage. The swimming pool, play area, shop and bar may be some distance away. The site has a superb new spa centre with gym, sauna and jacuzzi, with an excellent pool alongside, all reserved for over 18s, and a new restaurant with a large terrace. Competitions and shows are organised for adults and children in July and August.

Facilities

Well equipped toilet blocks, some heated, have baby baths, children's WCs and facilities for disabled visitors. Laundry. Bar and restaurant. Takeaway. Bar and disco well away from most pitches. Large heated swimming pool. Fitness centre and pool (from 1/4). Good quality play area. Boules. Archery. Miniclub (over 5 yrs). WiFi.

Open: 19 March - 30 October.

Directions

From A8 exit 36 take D25 to Ste Maxime, then D98 towards St Tropez. Take D93 to Ramatuelle. Site is clearly marked after 9 km. GPS: 43.20596, 6.65083

Charges guide

Per unit incl. 2 persons, electricity and water	€ 18.00 - € 67.00
extra person	€ 7.00 - € 8.00

..natuelle

Campéole la Croix du Sud

Route des Plages (CD93), F-83350 Ramatuelle (Var) T: 04 94 55 51 23. E: croix-du-sud@campeole.com

alanrogers.com/FR83710

La Croix du Sud is perched on a little hill and pleasantly shaded by parasol pines and eucalyptus trees. The nearby fine sandy beach of Pampelonne is maybe the most celebrated in France, famed for its association with Saint Tropez (although it is actually closer to Ramatuelle!). There are 120 pitches here, of which just 10 are available for touring units. Pitches are well shaded and mostly equipped with 10A electricity. The other pitches are occupied by mobile homes, chalets and tents for rent. The nearest beach (Pampelonne) is 1.6 km. away and can be accessed by cycle track with just one road to cross. There is a small swimming pool and a separate children's pool. Other amenities include a restaurant with terrace and a well stocked shop. The site becomes lively in peak season with plenty of activities and evening entertainment, as well as a children's club. Off-site, Saint Tropez is close at hand and there are many fine walks to enjoy in the surrounding hills.

Facilities

Sanitary facilities include a baby room but there is no provision for disabled visitors. Shop, restaurant, bar and snack bar (all 1/5-30/9). Takeaway pizza. Swimming pool (1/5-30/9). Children's pool. Games room. Playground. Sports field. Activity and entertainment programme. Bicycle hire. Mobile homes, chalets and tents for rent. Gas barbecues only. WiFi over part of site (charged). Off site: Ramatuelle 1.5 km. Nearest beach 2.5 km. Fishing 5 km. Golf. Walking and mountain biking. St Tropez 7 km. Gassin 10 km.

Open: 1 April - 14 October.

Directions

From the A8 (La Provençale) take exit to Le Luc. Take the D558 towards La Garde-Freinet and St Tropez, and then D93 towards Ramatuelle. In Ramatuelle, follow signs to Les Plages and Pampelonne. At second roundabout go straight on for 1.5 km. then turn left to site. GPS: 43.21422, 6.64096

Charges guide

Per unit incl. 2 persons and electricity	€ 24.00 - € 47.20
extra person	€ 5.70 - € 10.30
child (2-6 yrs)	€ 3.00 - € 5.20
dog	€ 3.20 - € 4.30

Régusse

Camping les Lacs du Verdon

Domaine de Roquelande, F-83630 Régusse (Var) T: 04 94 70 17 95. E: info@lacs-verdon.com

alanrogers.com/FR83140

In beautiful countryside and within easy reach of the Grand Canyon du Verdon and its nearby lakes, this site is only 90 minutes from Cannes. It is now part of the Homair Vacances chain and is currently run by Christophe Laurent and his team who are immensely proud of their site and the high standard they have achieved. The 30-acre wooded park is divided in two by a minor road. The 456 very stony but level pitches (rock pegs advised) are marked and separated by stones and trees. Of these, just 24 are available for touring units, many of an irregular shape, but all of average size with 16A electricity (long leads may be necessary). Booking for touring pitches in high season is strongly advised. The part across the road is used mainly for mobile homes but has three pitches for tourers, ideal for those wanting peace and quiet away from the main area. The site is very attractive, clean and well cared for and is most suitable for families with almost all facilities open from the beginning of the season.

Facilities

Five toilet blocks with all facilities including some for disabled visitors and young children. Laundry facilities. Well equipped supermarket. Bar and restaurant. Snack bar (July/Aug). Superb new heated swimming pool complex with water slides and paddling pool. Artificial grass tennis courts. Mulitsports court. Minigolf. Outdoor fitness area. Boules. Bicycle hire. Playground. TV and teenage games room. Entertainment programme (July/Aug). Discos, dances and theme nights. Electric barbecues only. WiFi (charged). Off site: Régusse 2.5 km. Aups 7 km. Riding 10 km. Fishing, beach, sailing and windsurfing at St Croix 15 km.

Open: 11 April - 27 September.

Directions

From A51 exit 17 take the D952 east to Vinon-sur-Verdon. Turn south on D554 to La Verdière. Turn east on D30 to Montmeyan, continue to Régusse. Site is well signed. GPS: 43.6602, 6.1511

Charges guide

Per unit incl. 1 or 2 persons and electricity	€ 15.50 - € 26.00
extra person	€ 3.00 - € 6.00
child (3-6 yrs)	free - € 4.50
dog	€ 1.50

Min. stay 2 nights in July/Aug.

Roquebrune-sur-Argens

Camping Caravaning Leï Suves

Quartier du Blavet, F-83520 Roquebrune-sur-Argens (Var) T: 04 94 45 43 95.
E: camping.lei.suves@wanadoo.fr **alanrogers.com/FR83030**

This quiet, pretty site is a few kilometres inland from the coast, 2 km. north of the DN7. Close to the unusual Roquebrune rock, it is within easy reach of Saint Tropez, Sainte Maxime, Saint Raphaël and Cannes. The site entrance is appealing – wide and spacious, with a large bank of well tended flowers. Mainly on a gently sloping hillside, the 309 pitches are terraced with shade provided by the many cork trees which give the site its name. All 162 touring pitches have 6A electricity and access to water. The large swimming pool and a new fun paddling pool together with the bar/restaurant and entertainment area create a very attractive and convivial setting. It is possible to walk in the surrounding woods. There are 149 mobile homes available to rent.

Facilities

Modern, well kept toilet blocks include excellent facilities for disabled visitors and children, washing machines and dryers. Shop (mornings only in low season). Good sized swimming pool, fun paddling pool. Bar, terrace, snack bar, takeaway. Outdoor stage near the bar for evening entertainment in high season. Excellent play area. Tennis. Multisports court. Aquagym. Water polo. WiFi (charged). Only gas barbecues are permitted. Off site: Bus stop at site entrance. Riding 1 km. Fishing 3 km. Bicycle hire 5 km. Golf 7 km. Beach at St Aygulf 15 km.

Open: 2 April - 14 October.

Directions

Leave A8 at exit 36 (Le Muy) and take the DN7 towards Frejus. After 9 km. turn left at roundabout onto D7 heading north signed La Bouverie (site also signed). Site on right in 2 km.
GPS: 43.47793, 6.63881

Charges guide

Per unit incl. 2 persons and electricity	€ 27.70 - € 51.20
extra person	€ 5.45 - € 11.00
child (under 7 yrs)	free - € 7.60
dog	€ 2.00 - € 3.50

Roquebrune-sur-Argens

Camping les Pêcheurs

F-83520 Roquebrune-sur-Argens (Var) T: 04 94 45 71 25. E: info@camping-les-pecheurs.com

alanrogers.com/FR83200

Les Pêcheurs will appeal to families who appreciate natural surroundings with many activities, cultural and sporting. Interspersed with mobile homes and cabins, the 110 good sized touring pitches (10A electricity) are separated by trees and flowering bushes. The Provençal-style buildings are delightful, especially the bar, restaurant and games room with its terrace down to the river and the site's own canoe station (locked gate). Across the road is a lake with a sandy beach and restaurant. Enlarged spa facilities include a swimming pool, a large jacuzzi, massage, a steam pool and a sauna (some charges apply). Developed over three generations by the Simoncini family, this peaceful, friendly site is set in more than four hectares of mature, well shaded countryside at the foot of the Roquebrune Rock. Activities include climbing the Rock with a guide, trips to Monte Carlo, Ventimiglia (Italy) and the Gorges du Verdon, etc. The medieval village of Roquebrune is within walking distance.

Facilities

Three toilet blocks, baby baths, facilities for disabled visitors and children. Washing machines. Shop. Bar and restaurant. Heated outdoor swimming pool, separate paddling pool, ice cream bar. Games room. Separate adults only pool and spa facilities. Multisports court. Playing field. Fishing. Canoes. Minigolf. Miniclub (July/Aug). Activities for children and adults (high season), visits to local wine caves. Only electric and gas barbecues allowed. WiFi throughout (charged). Security bracelets for all guests. French courses (3 levels). Off site: Bicycle hire 1 km. Golf 5 km. (reduced fees).

Open: 1 April - 30 September.

Directions

From A8 Aix/Cannes leave at exit 36 (Le Muy) and head east on the DN7 towards Fréjus. After 8 km. turn south on D7 towards Roquebrune-sur-Argens. Site is on left after 1 km. just before bridge over river. GPS: 43.450783, 6.6335

Charges guide

Per unit incl. 2 persons and electricity	€ 23.70 - € 50.50
extra person	€ 4.20 - € 9.60
child (acc. to age)	free - € 7.30
dog (max. 1)	€ 3.50

Roquebrune-sur-Argens

Camping Caravaning Moulin des Iscles

Chemin du Moulin des Iscles, F-83520 Roquebrune-sur-Argens (Var) T: 04 94 45 70 74.

E: moulin.iscles@wanadoo.fr **alanrogers.com/FR83240**

Moulin des Iscles is a small, pretty site beside the Argens river with access in places for fishing, canoeing and swimming, with some sought after pitches overlooking the river. The 80 grassy, level pitches have water and 6A electricity. A nice mixture of deciduous trees provides natural shade and colour and the old mill house is near the entrance, which has the security barrier closed at night. This is a quiet site with little on-site entertainment, but with a pleasant restaurant. Visitors with disabilities are made very welcome. Unusually for this area, this is a real campsite, not a camping village.

Facilities

Fully equipped toilet block, ramped access for disabled visitors. Some Turkish style toilets. Washbasins have hot water. Baby facilities. Washing machine. Restaurant, home cooked dish-of-the-day, well stocked shop, bar and takeaway (7/4-26/9). Library with some English books. TV, table tennis. Play area, minigolf, badminton, boules all outside the barrier. WiFi throughout (charged).

Open: 1 April - 30 September.

Directions

From A8, exit Le Muy, follow N7 towards Fréjus for 13 km. Cross over A8 and turn right at roundabout through Roquebrune-sur-Argens towards St Aygulf for 1 km. Site signed on left. Follow private unmade road for 500 m. GPS: 43.44513, 6.65783

Charges guide

Per unit incl. 2 persons and electricity	€ 20.70 - € 27.80

Roquebrune-sur-Argens

Castel Camping Domaine de la Bergerie

Vallée du Fournel, route du Col-du-Bougnon, F-83520 Roquebrune-sur-Argens (Var) T: 04 98 11 45 45.
E: info@domainelabergerie.com **alanrogers.com/FR83170**

This excellent site near the Côte d'Azur will take you away from all the bustle of the Mediterranean to total relaxation amongst the cork, oak, pine and mimosa in its woodland setting, whilst still only ten minutes away from the sea. The 60-hectare site is well spread out with semi-landscaped areas for mobile homes and 200 separated pitches for touring caravans and tents. All pitches average over 80 sq.m. and have electricity, with those in one area also having water and drainage. Eight premium pitches with cabins equipped with kitchenette and bathroom have been added. The restaurant/bar, in a converted farm building, is surrounded by shady patios, whilst inside it oozes character with high beams and archways leading to intimate corners. Activities are organised daily and, in the evening, shows, cabarets, discos, cinema, karaoke and dancing at the amphitheatre prove popular (possibly until midnight). A superb new pool complex supplements the original pool, with further outdoor pools with slides and a river feature, a jacuzzi, sauna, Turkish bath, massage, reflexology and gym.

Facilities

Four new toilet blocks are kept clean and include some washbasins in cubicles, facilities for babies and disabled visitors. Supermarket. Bar/restaurant with takeaway. Indoor heated pool with jacuzzi, sauna and steam bath. Outdoor pool complex, aquagym, slides and paddling pools. Fitness centre. Bicycle hire. Tennis. Archery. Roller skating. Minigolf. English-speaking children's and teenager's clubs. Mini-farm. Fishing. Paintball (July/Aug). WiFi throughout (charged). Only gas barbecues permitted. Off site: Riding and golf 2 km. Beach, St Aygulf and Ste Maxime 7 km. Water skiing, scuba diving, quad bikes and rock climbing nearby.

Open: 23 April - 30 September.

Directions

Leave A8 at Le Muy, exit on DN7 towards Frejus. After 9 km. turn south to Roquebrune on D7. Proceed for a further 5 km. then at roundabout turn southwest on D8 signed St Aygulf. Continue for 2 km. to site on the right. GPS: 43.3988, 6.675417

Charges guide

Per unit incl. 2 persons and electricity (6A)	€ 25.00 - € 43.50
extra person	€ 6.10 - € 12.10
child (under 7 yrs)	€ 4.50 - € 8.40
dog	€ 3.60 - € 5.80

Roquebrune-sur-Argens

Camping de Vaudois

Route Départementale 7, F-83520 Roquebrune-sur-Argens (Var) T: 04 94 81 37 70.
E: camping.vaudois@wanadoo.fr **alanrogers.com/FR83990**

In a quiet location, just a twenty minute cycle ride from the beach and close to the popular resort of Fréjus, Camping de Vaudois has been run by the Gonzalez family for over 30 years. It offers 110 level pitches, 41 of which are for touring with the remainder occupied by mobile homes both residential and for hire. Pitches are of a good size and separated by hedges and mature trees which provide plenty of shade; electricity (10A) is available to all. The beaches of Saint-Aygulf, Fréjus and Saint-Raphaël are all within easy reach by car or bike. This is a tranquil site with a very convivial atmosphere.

Facilities

Sanitary facilities include hot showers and washbasins in cabins. Facilities for disabled visitors and babies. Laundry facilities. Swimming pool (unsupervised; closed lunchtimes). Snack bar, bread to order. Play area. Boules. Table tennis. Electric and gas barbecues are permitted. Free WiFi in bar area. Off site: Fishing in nearby lake or River Argens 500 m. Riding 1.5 km. Golf 2 km. Beach and Saint-Aygulf 5 km. Fréjus and Roquebrune 6 km.

Open: 1 May - 30 September.

Directions

From A8 Aix/Cannes motorway leave at exit 36 (Le Muy) and head east on DN7 towards Fréjus. In 8 km. turn south on D7 to Roquebrune and site is signed on right in 8.5 km. GPS: 43.411, 6.692

Charges guide

Per unit incl. 2 persons and electricity	€ 15.50 - € 32.00
extra person	€ 2.50 - € 7.20

Saint Apollinaire

Campéole le Clos du Lac

Route des Lacs, F-05160 Saint Apollinaire (Hautes-Alpes) T: 04 92 44 27 43. E: clos-du-lac@campeole.com
alanrogers.com/FR05130

Le Clos du Lac can be found close to the little mountain village of Saint Apollinaire, on the southern fringe of the immense Ecrins National Park. The site is at an altitude of 1,450 m. and has 68 pitches, including 50 for touring units (most with 7A electricity) and 18 mobile homes. Many of the pitches have fine views of the scenery all around. There is a small lake nearby, for 'no kill' fly fishing and also for swimming. This is also a great place to watch the night sky with a special astronomy week in August. The nearby Boscodon forest has been officially acknowledged as the least polluted place in France. Access to the site is via a 2.2 km. steep, single track and therefore not suitable for large units.

Facilities

New, modern sanitary block provides preset showers and open style washbasins. Good facilities for babies and disabled visitors. Laundry facilities. Shop (July/Aug). New wellness centre includes jacuzzi, sauna and showers. Play area. Mobile homes for rent. No barbecues on pitches. Free WiFi over part of site. Off site: St Apollinaire (shops and restaurants). Canoe hire. Fishing. Minigolf. Watersports. Hiking and mountain biking. Bicycle hire.

Open: 13 May - 14 September.

Directions

St Apollinaire is on north side of Lac de Serre Ponçon. From Gap head west on N94 towards Embrun. At Chorges join D9 to St Apollinaire from where the site is well signed. GPS: 44.5647, 6.3652

Charges guide

Per unit incl. 2 persons and electricity	€ 15.70 - € 19.70
extra person	€ 3.80 - € 5.40

Camping Cheques accepted.

Saint Aygulf

Camping Riviera d'Azur

189 les Grands Chateaux de Villepey (RD 7), F-83370 Saint Aygulf (Var) T: 04 94 81 01 59.
E: residenceducampeur@sandaya.fr **alanrogers.com/FR83050**

This excellent site near the Côte d'Azur will take you away from all the bustle of the Mediterranean coast. Spread out over ten hectares, this is a well equipped holiday destination with pitches arranged along avenues. The 136 touring pitches average 100 sq.m. in size and all have electricity connections and, unusually, private sanitary facilities (although washbasins double as dishwashing sinks). There are 238 accommodation units for rent, the majority of which were installed after significant investment by the owners, Sandaya, in 2012.

Facilities

Private toilet blocks include a washbasin, shower and WC. Laundry area with washing machines. Very well stocked supermarket. Bar/restaurant with evening entertainment. Takeaway (all open all season). Large swimming pool complex with four water slides. Two tennis courts. Sports area. Minigolf. Boules. Fishing. Bicycle hire. Kindergarten and Kid's Club. Play area. Nightclub (July/Aug). WiFi over site (charged).

Open: 31 March - 14 October.

Directions

Leave A8 at Le Muy exit 36 on N555 towards Draguignan then onto the N7 towards Fréjus. Turn right on D7 signed St Aygulf and site is on the right 2.5 km. before the town. GPS: 43.40905, 6.70893

Charges guide

Per unit incl. 2 persons and electricity	€ 25.00 - € 60.00
extra person	€ 3.50 - € 7.00
child (3-7 yrs)	€ 1.00 - € 5.00

Saint Aygulf

Caravaning l'Etoile d'Argens

121 chemin des Etangs, F-83370 Saint Aygulf (Var) T: 04 94 81 01 41. E: info@etoiledargens.com

alanrogers.com/FR83070

First impressions of l'Etoile d'Argens are of space, cleanliness and calm. This is a site run with families in mind and many of the activities are free, making it an excellent choice for a good value holiday. There are 255 level, fully serviced grass touring pitches (all with 10/16A electricity). Separated by hedges, they range in size from 100-250 sq.m. and mainly have good shade. The pool and bar area is attractively landscaped with olive and palm trees. The very large pool complex has been designed very much with families in mind. Reception staff are very friendly and English is spoken.

Facilities

Twenty, well kept, spacious toilet blocks with facilities for disabled visitors, some with baby baths. Supermarket and gas supplies. Bar, restaurant, pizzeria and takeaway. Extensive pool complex (heated in low season). Floodlit tennis with coaching. Multisports court. Minigolf. Aerobics. Archery (July/Aug). Football and swimming lessons. Boules. Play area. Children's entertainment (July/Aug). Activity programme with games, dances and escorted walking trips to the surrounding hills within 3 km. Free water shuttle to beach (15/6-15/9). Fishing. Bicycle hire. WiFi over site (charged). Off site: Golf and riding 2 km.

Open: 1 April - 30 September.

Directions

From A8 exit 36 (Le Muy), head east on the DN7 towards Fréjus. After 8 km. turn south on D7 (Roquebrune, St Aygulf.) After 9.5 km. turn north (Fréjus) on D8. After 400 m. site is signed. GPS: 43.41581, 6.70545

Charges guide

Per unit incl. 3 persons and electricity	€ 20.00 - € 52.00
extra person	€ 5.00 - € 10.00
child (under 7 yrs)	€ 4.00 - € 8.00

No credit cards.

Saint Cyr-sur-Mer

Camping Clos Sainte-Thérèse

Route de Bandol, F-83270 Saint Cyr-sur-Mer (Var) T: 04 94 32 12 21. E: camping@clos-therese.com

alanrogers.com/FR83300

This is a very attractive, family run campsite set in hilly terrain four kilometres from the beaches of Saint Cyr. The terraced pitches are level, some with sea views, the helpful owners offering a tractor service if required. With good shade from pines, olives, almonds and evergreen oaks, there are 88 pitches for touring units, all with electricity and 35 for chalets or mobile homes. Five pitches are fully serviced. The landscaped pool complex is pretty and well kept, with a small slide, jacuzzi and a separate paddling pool. This is a friendly, small site, ideal for couples or families with younger children.

Facilities

Clean, well maintained toilet facilities. Fridge hire. Shop. Bar, restaurant and takeaway (15/6-15/9). Swimming pools (one heated) and paddling pool. Games room. TV room and library. Boules. Play area. Activities in high season. WiFi (charged). Off site: Golf course (9 and 18 holes, driving range) 500 m. Riding 2 km.

Open: 5 April - 30 September.

Directions

From A50 exit 10 take D559 to St Cyr. Continue towards Bandol and site is 3 km. on the left. GPS: 43.159783, 5.729004

Charges guide

Per unit incl. 2 persons and electricity	€ 21.90 - € 35.90
extra person	€ 4.00 - € 7.00

Saint Paul-en-Forêt

Camping le Parc

408 quartier Trestaure, F-83440 Saint Paul-en-Forêt (Var) T: 04 94 76 15 35. E: info@campingleparc.com

alanrogers.com/FR83835

Camping le Parc is a small and peaceful site just 35 minutes from the hustle and bustle of the Côte d'Azur, where you will receive a warm welcome by the Baccofin family. Set in the heart of Provence, there are 107 mostly level pitches, 30 of which are a good size for touring (all with 10A electricity), the remainder taken by mobile homes and chalets for rent or privately owned. Pitches are partly shaded by oak trees which let enough sunlight through to give an open feel to the site. It is a good base for visiting the nearby Provençal hilltop villages with colourful markets. These might include Fayence, Seillans (classed as one of the most beautiful villages in France), Caillan and Montauroux.

Facilities

One central toilet block, part heated in low season. Good facilities for babies and disabled visitors. Laundry. Bar, restaurant and takeaway (15/6-30/8). Small shop for basics (bread to order). Swimming and paddling pools (May-Sept) and jacuzzi (June-Aug). Play area. Trampoline. Minigolf (charged). Floodlit tennis court. Multisports court. Volleyball. Boules. Miniclub and low key entertainment for the family (July/Aug). Torches useful. WiFi (charged).

Open: 4 April - 30 September.

Directions

Leave A8 at exit 39 and head north on D37 towards Montauroux for 9 km, then east on D562. In 4 km. turn south (St Paul-en-Forêt) for 1.5 km. Site is signed on the left 400 m. up a small road. GPS: 43.58436, 6.68986

Charges guide

Per unit incl. 2 persons and electricity	€ 17.00 - € 42.80
extra person	€ 5.60 - € 7.20

Saint Raphaël

Castel Camping Douce Quiétude

3435 boulevard Jacques Baudino, F-83700 Saint Raphaël (Var) T: 04 94 44 30 00.
E: info@douce-quietude.com **alanrogers.com/FR83250**

Douce Quiétude is just ten minutes' drive from the sandy beaches at Saint Raphaël and Agay (with campsite shuttle transport) but is quietly situated at the foot of the Estérel Massif. There are 440 pitches, 78 for touring units and 257 for fully equipped mobile homes for rent, some with air conditioning, dishwasher and jacuzzi. The touring pitches are set in either pleasant pine woodland or in sunny and shaded green areas. They are of a comfortable size, separated by bushes and trees with 16A electricity (Europlug), water, drainage and telephone/TV points provided. Eight have private sanitary facilities. This mature site offers a wide range of services and facilities complete with a pool complex. It can be busy in the main season yet is relaxed and spacious.

Facilities

Fully equipped modern heated toilet blocks, facilities for babies and disabled visitors. Launderette. Shop, bar, restaurant and takeaway. Three swimming pools (two heated), water slide, jacuzzi. Play area. Children's club, activities for teenagers (all July/Aug). Sports area. Games room. Tennis. Minigolf. Archery. Fitness centre, sauna. Evening entertainment (July/Aug). Mountain bike hire. Shuttle bus service. WiFi throughout (charged).

Open: 11 April - 11 October.

Directions

From A8 exit 38 (Fréjus/St Raphaël) take D37, after 5 km. turn east on D100, (Valescure then Agay). Follow site signs. GPS: 43.44727, 6.80600

Charges guide

Per unit incl. 2 persons and electricity	€ 21.00 - € 62.00
extra person	€ 7.50 - € 11.50

Camping Cheques accepted.

Saint Rémy-de-Provence

Camping Monplaisir

Chemin de Monplaisir, F-13210 Saint Rémy-de-Provence (Bouches du Rhône) T: 04 90 92 22 70.
E: reception@camping-monplaisir.fr **alanrogers.com/FR13040**

Only a kilometre from the centre of Saint Rémy, in the foothills of the Alpilles mountains, this is one of the most pleasant and well run sites we have come across. Saint Rémy is a very popular town with tourists and the site is frequently fully booked. Everything about it is of a high standard and quality. The good impression created by the reception and shop continues through the rest of the site. In all there are 130 level grass touring pitches with nine taken by smart mobile homes, with 10A electricity throughout. Flowering shrubs and greenery abounds, roads are tarmac and all is neat and tidy.

Facilities

Six very modern, unisex toilet blocks were immaculate when we visited. All are heated in low season and have some washbasins in cabins. Family rooms and en-suite facilities for disabled visitors in two. Washing machines and dryers. Two motorcaravan service points. Recently refurbished shop with good range of essentials and regional produce. Bar with snacks (July/Aug). Swimming pool (from 1/5). Library. Play area. Boules. WiFi (free in library). Bicycle hire. Mobile homes and chalets for hire.

Open: 9 March - 24 October.

Directions

From St Rémy town centre follow signs for Arles and Nîmes. At roundabout on western side of town take D5 signed Maillane and immediately left by supermarket. Site is signed and is 500 m. on the left. GPS: 43.79695, 4.82372

Charges guide

Per unit incl. 2 persons and electricity	€ 20.60 - € 34.50
extra person	€ 5.10 - € 8.50
child (2-7 yrs)	€ 3.10 - € 6.30

Saint Rémy-de-Provence

Camping Mas de Nicolas

Avenue Plaisance du Touch, F-13210 Saint Rémy-de-Provence (Bouches du Rhône) T: 04 90 92 27 05.
E: contact@camping-masdenicolas.com **alanrogers.com/FR13050**

The site has a very spacious feel to it, due mainly to the central area of gently sloping grass, dotted with shrubs, that is kept clear of pitches and used for leisure and sunbathing. The 138 pitches are separated by hedges, trees and flowering shrubs, 34 for mobile homes, the remainder for touring units. The pitches all have 10A electricity, water and drainage and access roads are wide. Some pitches are an irregular shape and some are sloping, but many have views and they are mostly organised into groups of two and four. There is an attractive pool area with Balnéotherapie et Remise en form (spa and gym!).

Facilities

Good, modern sanitary blocks with baby bathroom and facilities for disabled visitors can be heated. Washing machines and dryer. Dog shower. Motorcaravan services. Small bar. Occasional paella evenings. Heated swimming pool and paddling pool. Sauna, steam room, spa bath, gym. Play area. Fridge hire. WiFi (free in bar and reception). Gas barbecues permitted.

Open: 14 March - 17 October.

Directions

St Rémy-de-Provence is where D571 from Avignon connects with D99 Tarascon-Cavaillon road. Site is signed from village centre on north side. Leave A7 at Cavaillon or Avignon-Sud. GPS: 43.79622, 4.83879

Charges guide

Per unit incl. 2 persons and electricity	€ 20.70 - € 31.20
extra person	€ 5.50 - € 8.50

Saint Romain-en-Viennois

Camping le Soleil de Provence

Route de Nyons, F-84110 Saint Romain-en-Viennois (Vaucluse) T: 04 90 46 46 00.

E: info@camping-soleil-de-provence.fr **alanrogers.com/FR84100**

This site has been developed to a high standard. The 194 average sized pitches, 172 for touring units, are separated by hedges and a variety of young trees offering only a little shade (10A electricity). The excellent pool, surrounded by a sunbathing terrace and overlooked by the bar, is an unusual shape with an island in the centre. A new paddling pool has been added and one end of the pool is very shallow. There is some organised entertainment in July and August but the emphasis is on a quiet and peaceful environment and is an ideal site for relaxing and unwinding. The views from this spacious, well organised, family run site must take some beating.

Facilities

Modern well appointed, heated toilet blocks. Facilities for disabled visitors. Baby room. Washing machine and dryer. Motorcaravan services. Small shop for bread, open on demand. Bar, snack bar (June-Sept). New aqua park with slides and paddling pool. Small gym. Play area. Volleyball. Boules. Free WiFi on part of site. Off site: Tennis 1 km. Rafting, hiking, cycling and mountain biking 4 km.

Open: 15 March - 31 October.

Directions

Site is 4 km. north of Vaison-la-Romaine on the D938 road to Nyons. Turn right to St Romain-en-Viennois. Site is signed from there. Take first left to site. GPS: 44.26902, 5.10597

Charges guide

Per unit incl. 2 persons, and electricity € 22.10 - € 40.80

No credit cards.

Saint Vincent-les-Forts

Campéole le Lac

Le Fein, F-04340 Saint Vincent-les-Forts (Alpes-de-Haute-Provence) T: 04 92 85 51 57.

E: lac@campeole.com **alanrogers.com/FR04210**

Le Lac is a member of the Campéole group and enjoys a fine location in the mountains of Haute-Provence. The site can be found at an altitude of 800 m. on the banks of the large Lac de Serre Ponçon and many of the site's 300 pitches (202 for touring units) have fine views of the lake and the surrounding mountains. All are of a good size with electricity hook-ups (long leads may be needed) and ample water points. The access road down to the site (3 km) is fairly steep and winding but it is certainly worth the effort. The waters of the lake have an alluring blue-green hue and shelve gradually from the site's beach. There is an ecological swimming pool, using natural water, consistent with this stunning natural setting.

Facilities

Several toilet blocks have all the usual facilities. Wet room for disabled visitors. Laundry areas. Bar (1/6-15/9), restaurant (15/6-10/9) and takeaway (10/6-31/8). Shop (15/6-10/9). Natural swimming pool (lifeguard July/Aug). Fishing. Volleyball. Tennis. Play area. Canoe and boat hire. Activity and entertainment programme. Mobile homes, chalets and equipped tents for rent. WiFi in reception area (free). Off site: Montagne aux Marmottes (animal park). Riding 10 km. Serre Ponçon dam.

Open: 22 May - 21 September.

Directions

Site is near St Vincent-les-Forts. From Gap, head south on N85, then join D900b following signs to Barcelonnette. Continue on this road along the Durance Valley passing the Barrage de Serre Ponçon and on to St Vincent-les-Forts. Site is well signed from here. GPS: 44.45682, 6.36529

Charges guide

Per unit incl. 2 persons and electricity € 19.80 - € 30.20

Camping Cheques accepted.

Salon-de-Provence

Camping le Nostradamus

Route d'Eyguières, F-13300 Salon-de-Provence (Bouches du Rhône) T: 04 90 56 08 36.

E: camping.nostradamus@gmail.com **alanrogers.com/FR13030**

Only some 5 km. from Salon-de-Provence, near the village of Eyguières, this is a very pleasant campsite with shaded grassy pitches thanks to the many trees which have been preserved here as a result of the imaginative irrigation scheme developed by the owners in the 18th century. The campsite, edging the canal, was first opened about 50 years ago as a farm site, but has been developed to offer 83 hedged pitches including 17 used for mobile homes. There are 20 with full services, the rest having 4-10A electricity connections. This is a good site for families but the canal at the entrance is unfenced.

Facilities

One large sanitary block with showers and toilets upstairs, and one small block (both recently renovated) provide all modern facilities. Very good facilities for disabled visitors (key). Washing machine. Motorcaravan services. Shop (fresh bread and basics). Bar. Restaurant with takeaway (from 15/5). Swimming and paddling pools (15/5-30/9). Pétanque. Fishing. WiFi in some areas (charged).

Open: 1 March - 31 October.

Directions

From A7 exit 26 (Senas) follow N538 south for 5 km. Take D175 west and pick up D17 south to Salon. Site is at junction of D17 and CD72 with entrance off the CD72. GPS: 43.67772, 5.06476

Charges guide

Per unit incl. 2 persons and electricity € 22.90 - € 28.15

extra person € 5.50 - € 6.50

Sanary-sur-Mer

Campasun Parc Mogador

167 chemin de Beaucours, F-83110 Sanary-sur-Mer (Var) T: 04 94 74 53 16. E: mogador@campasun.com
alanrogers.com/FR83320

This site in the Mediterranean countryside is very much geared for family holidays with children. Some 20 minutes on foot from the beach, the site has a very large and well kept pool area and a stage for entertainment. Somewhat smaller than other sites of this type, there are 122 good sized pitches (61 for touring units). The ground is mainly level, if rather stony and sandy. Variable shade is available and all pitches have 10A electricity. There are plans to enlarge some of the smaller, 80 sq.m. pitches. The attractive pool is surrounded by ample paved sunbathing areas.

Facilities

Two large, super deluxe toilet blocks, one including washbasins and showers in cabins. The high tech toilets are automatically cleaned and disinfected after every use. Laundry. Motorcaravan services. Restaurant with full menu (1/4-5/11), also snacks, pizzas and takeaway. Swimming and paddling pools (heated 1/4-20/9). Solarium. Boules. Bicycle hire. Miniclub and evening entertainment in season. WiFi (charged). Barbecues not permitted.

Open: 24 March - 10 November.

Directions

Take Bandol exit 12 from A50 and head for Six Fours on the N559. Arriving at Sanary-sur-Mer turn left towards Beaucours and site is on left after 100 m. GPS: 43.12377, 5.78767

Charges guide

Per unit incl. 2 persons and electricity	€ 23.70 - € 48.50
extra person	€ 6.50 - € 9.70

Serres

Flower Camping Domaine des 2 Soleils

Avenue des Pins la Flamenche, F-05700 Serres (Hautes-Alpes) T: 04 92 67 01 33.
E: dom.2.soleils@wanadoo.fr **alanrogers.com/FR05410**

At an altitude of 800 metres in the foothills of the Alps, Domaine des 2 Soleils could scarcely be in a more rural location. From the outskirts of the attractive town of Serres, it is reached along a winding country lane which climbs through pine woods. The lower part of the site has chalets and mobile homes for rent and looks out across fields and farmhouses. Sixty touring pitches, with 6A electrical connections, are attractively located on sloping ground among a variety of trees and bushes, with the pool and leisure complex beyond. Forested hills form an impressive backdrop.

Facilities

Three well equipped sanitary blocks include provision for disabled visitors and a baby room with bath. Washing machine. Restaurant/bar/takeaway with French family food and entertainment. Swimming and children's pools with water slide (15/6-15/9). Electronic games, table football and pool. Playground and multisports ground. Volleyball. Basketball. Pétanque. Pony riding (11/4-31/8). Entertainment (4-10 yrs and 11-18 yrs). Monday market with local produce in high season. Communal barbecue. Torches useful. Free WiFi in reception area.

Open: 11 April - 26 September.

Directions

Serres is 110 km. south of Grenoble via A51 and D1075, and 135 km. north of Aix-en-Provence via A51 and D4075. Site is signed to the east, 500 m. south of the town. Continue 1 km. up steep and winding access road. GPS: 44.42029, 5.72758

Charges guide

Per unit incl. 2 persons and electricity	€ 15.00 - € 27.00
extra person	€ 4.50
child (3-6 yrs)	€ 3.50

Seyne-les-Alpes

Camping les Prairies

Haute-Greyere, F-04140 Seyne-les-Alpes (Alpes-de-Haute-Provence) T: 04 92 35 10 21.
E: info@campinglesprairies.com **alanrogers.com/FR04140**

Les Prairies lies in a beautiful part of the French Alps, at the foot of the Grand Puy (1,800 m), at the entrance to the once fortified town of Seyne. With lovely views of the mountains and the river running beside the site, there are 84 attractively landscaped, grassy touring pitches (with 10A electricity) and 16 mobile homes. There is a new beach-effect swimming pool and a convivial bar area adjoining reception. A few picnic tables have been provided for visitors with tents. This is a family run site and attention to detail is evident throughout.

Facilities

The two toilet blocks near the pool are immaculate and regularly kept that way. Facilities for babies and disabled visitors. Laundry. Motorcaravan services. Bar (1/6-31/8). Snack bar/takeaway (15/6-25/8). Heated swimming pool (1/6-10/9). Pétanque. Table football. Large play area. Occasional entertainment in high season. Fishing. Gas and electric barbecues only, communal area provided. Max. 1 dog. WiFi (free).

Open: 6 May - 10 September.

Directions

Site is southeast of Gap. From Gap take D900B and turn right at T-junction where it joins D900. Cross Col de St Jean, go through Seyne to small airfield on left. Turn right, following signs (ignore earlier sign to very narrow road). GPS: 44.34232, 6.35896

Charges guide

Per unit incl. 2 persons and electricity	€ 18.50 - € 25.00
extra person	€ 5.90

Sospel

Camping Domaine Sainte Madeleine

Route de Moulinet, F-06380 Sospel (Alpes-Maritimes) T: 04 93 04 10 48.
E: camp@camping-sainte-madeleine.com **alanrogers.com/FR06010**

Domaine Sainte Madeleine is an attractive, peaceful site, with a swimming pool, in spectacular mountain scenery. It is about 20 km. inland from Menton and very near the Italian border. The approach to this site involves a 17 km. climb with hairpin bends and then a choice of going over the Col de Castillon or through an 800 m. long tunnel (3.5 m. high, 3 m. wide). Situated on a terraced hillside with mountain views towards Italy, manoeuvring within the site presents no problem as the pitches are on level, well drained grass. The lower ones have good shade but those higher up on the hill have less. Electricity (10A) is available to 80 of the 90 pitches. English is spoken.

Facilities

Good quality toilet block with hot showers (token required). Hot water (often only warm) for dishwashing and laundry sinks. Washing machines. Bread to order. Wine, beer and soft drinks from reception. Swimming pool (140 sq.m, heated in spring and autumn). WiFi throughout (charged). Charcoal barbecues not permitted. Chalets to rent. Off site: Fishing 200 m. Bicycle hire 4 km. The attractive town of Sospel is 4 km. with many restaurants, bars, cafés and shops and a Thursday market.

Open: 1 April - 30 September.

Directions

From A8 take Menton exit and head north towards Sospel on D2566. In Sospel continue on D2566 towards Moulinet. Site is 4 km. north of Sospel on the left. GPS: 43.89702, 7.41685

Charges guide

Per unit incl. 2 persons and electricity	€ 22.80 - € 27.50
extra person	€ 4.00 - € 5.00

No credit cards.

Tarascon-sur-Rhône

Camping Saint Gabriel

Quartier Saint Gabriel, route de Fontvielle, F-13150 Tarascon-sur-Rhône (Bouches du Rhône)
T: 04 90 91 19 83. E: contact@campingsaintgabriel.com **alanrogers.com/FR13300**

Camping Saint Gabriel has been developed from an attractive ancient Provençal farm. This friendly, environmentally committed, family run site is at the foot of the Alpilles and is situated almost opposite the famous Chapel of Saint Gabriel. It is close to the mighty River Rhône, between Avignon and Arles, and is only a short distance from the interesting towns of Tarascon and Beaucaire, making it an ideal base from which to explore this beautiful and historic area. The site has 68 average size pitches with 45 on grass for touring, separated with hedges and trees, most having some shade and all have 6A electricity, water and drainage.

Facilities

Sanitary facilities with hot showers and washbasins in cubicles. Facilities for children and very good facilities for disabled visitors. Washing machine. Small shop with fresh bread to order (15/4-30/10). Bar with TV (April-Sept). Snack bar, takeaway (20/4-20/9). Small heated pool and paddling pool with sunbathing terrace. Boules. Some entertainment (July/Aug). Small playground. Fishing (permits available). Fridge hire. Bicycle hire arranged. Communal barbecue. WiFi throughout (charged).

Open: 9 March - 20 November.

Directions

The site lies close to the D570N Avignon to Arles road about 27 km. south of Avignon. At roundabout take D32 east for 200 m. turn southwest, local road to site about 100 m. (Large sign off Route de Fontielle). GPS: 43.7675, 4.69341

Charges guide

Per unit incl. 2 persons and electricity	€ 20.20 - € 26.20

Camping Cheques accepted.

Vaison-la-Romaine

Camping de l'Ayguette

Faucon (D86), F-84110 Vaison-la-Romaine (Vaucluse) T: 04 90 46 40 35. E: info@ayguette.com
alanrogers.com/FR84060

This friendly, family run site is in the beautiful region of northern Provence, surrounded by vineyards and wooded hills. There are 99 slightly sloping, stony pitches, with 75 for touring, widely spaced out on terraces amongst pine and oak trees giving plenty of dappled shade, and all have 10A electricity (long leads and rock pegs necessary) and Europlugs. Some are a considerable distance from the amenities, so not ideal for those with walking difficulties. This spacious campsite is ideal for rest and relaxation and it makes an ideal base for touring this very interesting region.

Facilities

Two well equipped toilet blocks, one heated. Room for disabled campers and families. Washing machines. Motorcaravan services. Small shop with bread to order. Bar. Snack bar/takeaway (1/6-30/8). Heated outdoor swimming pool with terrace. Volleyball. Badminton. Multisports pitch. Playground. Occasional entertainment, some activities for children. Free WiFi in bar.

Open: 16 April - 25 September.

Directions

From D938, 1 km. north of Vaison-la-Romaine, turn right at roundabout onto D71, signed St Romaine, for 2.8 km. Turn right on D86, entrance to site is on right in 1 km. GPS: 44.26220, 5.129133

Charges guide

Per unit incl. 2 persons and electricity	€ 15.00 - € 33.00

Vaison-la-Romaine

Domaine le Carpe Diem

Route de Saint Marcellin, B.P. 68, F-84110 Vaison-la-Romaine (Vaucluse) T: 04 90 36 02 02.
E: carpe-diem@franceloc.fr **alanrogers.com/FR84070**

Carpe Diem is attractively themed with Greek statues and an amphitheatre surround to its older pool. The situation is quite impressive with magnificent views over one of the most beautiful parts of France, yet only 1 km. from the fascinating town of Vaison-la-Romaine. There are 349 pitches with 118 small to medium sized, grassy/stony touring pitches all with 10A electricity; most with little or no shade. A new area has mobile homes and a few touring pitches with no shade. This is a good site for active families seeking all day entertainment. The pool complex is impressive with outdoor and covered pools, paddling pools, toboggans and more.

Facilities

Two modern toilet blocks with facilities for children and campers with disabilities. Washing machine. Motorcaravan services. Small shop, bar, pizzeria and restaurant (all 11/4-15/9), takeaway (July/Aug). TV. Impressive pool complex with swimming pools, slides and flumes, one covered and heated (all season). Play area. Minigolf, archery, volleyball, football, basketball. Mountain bike hire. Miniclub. Entertainment (high season). Organised canoeing, riding, climbing, walking, mountain biking. No charcoal barbecues. Free WiFi on part of site.

Open: 11 April - 1 November.

Directions

Leave Vaison-la-Romaine on D938 heading south towards Carpentras. 1 km. beyond the 'Super U' roundabout turn left on D151, signed St Marcellin. Site entrance is on the left immediately after the junction. GPS: 44.23431, 5.08964

Charges guide

Per unit incl. 2 persons and electricity (10A)	€ 24.00 - € 40.00
extra person	€ 4.70 - € 7.00
child (2-7 yrs)	€ 3.50 - € 4.50

Vaison-la-Romaine

Camping du Théatre Romain

205 chemin du Brusquet, F-84110 Vaison-la-Romaine (Vaucluse) T: 04 90 28 78 66.
E: info@camping-theatre.com **alanrogers.com/FR84290**

This family friendly site is ideally situated within easy walking distance of the delightful town of Vaison and its excellent tourist office, shops, restaurants and museums. There are 66 level pitches and these all have electricity (5/10A), water and drainage and are of a good size (100 sq.m). Most pitches are part grass and part gravel and are generally separated by hedges and mature trees, giving partial shade. The site also has nine mobile homes for rent. This is a quiet site with no organised entertainment, perfect for a relaxing holiday and a good base for exploring the surrounding Provençal countryside.

Facilities

Two heated sanitary blocks include facilities for babies and disabled visitors. Launderette. Fresh bread daily. Pizza van twice a week. Hot and cold drinks machine. Heated outdoor swimming pool (1/4-31/10). Play area. Table football. Snooker. Pétanque. WiFi throughout (free). Off site: Bicycle hire 1 km. Riding 4 km. Shops, two supermarkets and restaurants in Vaison-la Romaine.

Open: 15 March - 5 November.

Directions

From the north, take A7 and exit at Bollène. Follow signs to Vaison-la-Romaine. Continue on D975 through the town and follow signs to site. GPS: 44.244959, 5.078508

Charges guide

Per unit incl. 2 persons and electricity	€ 21.50 - € 41.00
extra person	€ 3.50 - € 7.00

Val des Près

Camping la Clarée

8 route des Alberts le Rosier, F-05100 Val des Près (Hautes-Alpes) T: 04 92 21 06 01.
E: info@camping-la-claree.com **alanrogers.com/FR05470**

Camping la Clarée is a simple, quiet and remote campsite in a magnificent setting in the beautiful valley of la Clarée, high in the Hautes-Alpes. It only has a short season due to its altitude and even summer nights can be cold here. It is just 7 km. from the historic, fortified city of Briançon, only 10 km. from the Italian border. There are 200 large pitches with 180 on fairly level grass for touring with 10A electricity available. The pitches are laid out amongst pine trees offering some shade and mountain views. There are few rules and regulations and the site is ideal for those looking to get away from it all.

Facilities

Three rather old fashioned toilet blocks are clean and well maintained. Mixed British and Turkish style WCs. Facilities for children and disabled campers. Washing machine. Fridge hire. Small shop for basics at reception; bread to order. Bar and pizzas (July/Aug). Playground. Volleyball. Boules. Fishing (permits available). Max. 1 dog per unit. Wood and canvas tents to rent. Off site: Bus stop 100 m. Val des Prés with some shops, bars, restaurants 1.5 km.

Open: 10 June - 5 September.

Directions

Leave A480 south of Grenoble at exit 8 (Vizille) onto D1091 to Briançon for 110 km. At Briançon turn left on D940 towards Montgenèvre and Italy. Turn left on D201 (le Rosier) and on to site which is well marked. GPS: 44.93886, 6.68332

Charges guide

Per unit incl. 2 persons and electricity	€ 17.10 - € 18.70
extra person	€ 3.20 - € 3.80

Vallouise

Camping Indigo Vallouise

Chemin des Chambonnettes, F-05290 Vallouise (Hautes-Alpes) T: 04 92 23 30 26.

E: vallouise@camping-indigo.com **alanrogers.com/FR05440**

This former municipal site is a recent addition to the Indigo group of campsites and is located close to the pretty village of Vallouise, deep in the Hautes-Alpes. The site extends over 6.5 hectares and enjoys some magnificent views of the surrounding mountain scenery. There are 134 touring pitches here, bordered by two glacier streams. Most have 10A electricity. A number of fully equipped safari-style tents and chalets are available for rent. The site lies at the foot of the vast Ecrins National Park and is an ideal base for many adventure sports, including paragliding, rock climbing and mountain biking.

Facilities

Two excellent sanitary blocks (one heated) are well maintained and include facilities for babies and disabled visitors. Shop. Snack bar (July/Aug). Heated outdoor swimming pool. Play area. Boules. Tennis. Volleyball. TV room. Activity programme (July/Aug). Fully equipped tents and chalets for rent. WiFi over part of site (free). Off site: Fishing 100 m. Bicycle hire 200 m. Shops and restaurants in Vallouise. Mountain sports.

Open: 26 May - 3 October.

Directions

From Briançon, head south on N94 as far as Prelle, then join D4 to Les Vigneaux. Just past village turn right on D994 to Vallouise. The site is well signed. GPS: 44.844153, 6.490084

Charges guide

Per unit incl. 2 persons and electricity	€ 20.90 - € 28.80
extra person	€ 5.30 - € 6.35

No credit cards.

Vedène

Camping Flory

Route d'Entraigues, avenue Pasteur, F-84270 Vedène (Vaucluse) T: 04 90 31 00 51.

E: campingflory@wanadoo.fr **alanrogers.com/FR84150**

Camping Flory is a traditional, country site in the heart of Provence and only ten minutes drive from the historic Papal town of Avignon. The area dedicated to camping is somewhat sloping, with shade provided by mature pine trees. There are 135 touring pitches, 100 with 10A electricity. Mobile homes occupy a separate area. Vedène lies in a low area not far from the confluence of the Rhône and Durance rivers, but the site is on a hillside and the danger of flooding is minimal with excellent precautions in place. An award-winning warm welcome is offered by owners, Ernest and Jeannine Guindos.

Facilities

Three toilet blocks, two old but refurbished to a good standard, one new. Some washbasins in cabins and pre-set showers. Good facilities for disabled visitors. Motorcaravan services. Shop providing basic supplies. Small restaurant (1/7-30/8) with simple menu and takeaway. Bar (5/7-23/8). Swimming pool (no shorts) with paddling pool. Play area. Volleyball. Boules. Some organised activities in high season. Off site: Golf 2 km. Riding 3 km. Bicycle hire and fishing 10 km. Wine tasting.

Open: 30 March - 30 September.

Directions

From A7 autoroute du Soleil, take exit 23 (Avignon Nord) and follow D942 towards Carpentras for 3 km. then turn right at the second sign for Vedène. Site is also signed east from the centre of Vedène. GPS: 43.99057, 4.91398

Charges guide

Per unit incl. 2 persons and electricity	€ 19.20 - € 28.00
extra person	€ 5.00 - € 7.00

Camping Cheques accepted.

Vence

Camping Caravaning Domaine de la Bergerie

1330 chemin de la Sine, F-06140 Vence (Alpes-Maritimes) T: 04 93 58 09 36.

E: info@camping-domainedelabergerie.com **alanrogers.com/FR06030**

La Bergerie is a quiet, family owned site that celebrated its 60th anniversary in 2012. It is situated in the hills 3 km. from Vence and 10 km. from the sea at Cagnes-sur-Mer. An extensive, natural, lightly wooded site, it is in a secluded position at about 300 m. above sea level. Most of the pitches are shaded and all are of a good size. There are 450 pitches, 245 with electricity (2/5/10A), including 65 also with water and drainage. Because of the nature of this site, some areas are a little distance from the toilet blocks. With the aim of keeping this a quiet and tranquil place to stay, there are no organised activities.

Facilities

Refurbished toilet blocks are centrally positioned and include excellent provision for disabled visitors (pitches near the block are reserved for disabled visitors). Good shop. Small bar/restaurant, takeaway (all 1/5-30/9). Large swimming pool and smaller pool, spacious sunbathing area (1/5-30/9). Play area. Tennis. 12 shaded boules pitches (lit at night) with competitions in season. Charcoal barbecues are not permitted. Accommodation to rent.

Open: 25 March - 15 October.

Directions

From A8 exit 48 take Cagnes-sur-Mer road towards Vence (do not follow sat nav instructions to turn off this road before Vence). At first roundabout in Vence follow signs for Centre Ville and site is well signed from here. GPS: 43.71174, 7.0905

Charges guide

Per unit incl. 2 persons and electricity (2A)	€ 21.50 - € 32.00

Camping Cheques accepted.

Veynes

Camping les Rives du Lac

Plan d'eau les Iscles, F-05400 Veynes (Hautes-Alpes) T: 04 92 57 20 90. E: contact@camping-lac.com
alanrogers.com/FR05200

Les Rives du Lac lies within the Buech region of the Hautes-Alpes department, close to the small resort town of Veynes. This is a good base for outdoor activities, such as hiking, riding, paragliding, mountain biking, rock climbing or potholing. The site is located on the banks of the 5.5 ha. lake, Les Iscles, which offers good opportunities for various water based activities (swimming, pedaloes, fishing.) The lake is shallow and lifeguards are on duty during July and August. Campsite amenities include a convivial bar/restaurant, which is used for entertainment in peak season. There are 109 semi-shaded touring pitches, all with electricity connections (10A). Fifteen Alpine chalets and mobile homes are for rent.

Facilities

A central building provides modern sanitary facilities of a high standard. Facilities for disabled visitors (key). Baby room. Laundry. Fridge hire. Bar/snack bar and pizzeria. Takeaway. Covered swimming pool and paddling pool. Direct lake access. Fishing. Games room. Play area. Minigolf. Sports field. Activity and entertainment. Bicycle hire. Mobile homes and chalets for rent. No charcoal barbecues. Free WiFi over part of site. Max. 2 dogs.

Open: 28 April - 29 September.

Directions

Approaching from Gap or Grenoble, follow directions for Valence at large roundabout. About 1 km. after Veynes, follow signs to site. GPS: 44.51889, 5.7988

Charges guide

Per unit incl. 2 persons and electricity	€ 16.50 - € 34.00
extra person	€ 4.50 - € 9.00
child (2-9 yrs)	€ 2.50 - € 5.50

Villars-Colmars

Camping Caravaning le Haut-Verdon

RD 908, F-04370 Villars-Colmars (Alpes-de-Haute-Provence) T: 04 92 83 40 09.
E: campinglehautverdon@wanadoo.fr **alanrogers.com/FR04060**

For those seeking a quiet, family site set in most spectacular scenery, Camping le Haut-Verdon is ideal. It is on the banks of the Verdon, an excellent trout river, which flows through the spectacular gorge. The river can be fast flowing. Surrounded by the majestic peaks of the Alpes-de-Haute-Provence, it is on the doorstep of the Mercantour National Park. Set amongst the pines, the 109 pitches are mostly on the large size but are rather stony. With 66 for touring units, all have electricity (6/10A) but some require long leads. There is a small village nearby and the town of Saint André is 23 km. away.

Facilities

Two sanitary blocks (one heated) with hot showers and facilities for babies. Washing machines. Freezer for ice packs. Room for tent campers for inclement weather. Motorcaravan services. Small shop. Bar/restaurant, takeaway (19/6-31/8). Heated swimming, paddling pools (15/6-15/9). Play area. Boules. Skittle alley. Tennis. Volleyball. Basketball. Trim trail in the woods. TV room. Organised games and competitions (July/Aug). Fishing. Communal barbecues only. WiFi throughout (charged).

Open: 1 May - 30 September.

Directions

Follow D955 north from St André-les-Alpes towards Colmar. After 11 km. road changes to D908. Site on right at southern edge of Villars-Colmars. Caravans not advised to use the D908 from Annot or Col d'Allos from Barcelonnette. GPS: 44.1601, 6.60625

Charges guide

Per unit incl. 2 persons and electricity (6A)	€ 19.00 - € 32.00
extra person	€ 3.00 - € 5.00
child (2-7 yrs)	€ 2.00 - € 3.00

Villeneuve-Loubet

Parc Saint-James le Sourire

Route de Grasse, F-06270 Villeneuve-Loubet (Alpes-Maritimes) T: 04 93 20 96 11.
E: lesourire@camping-parcsaintjames.com **alanrogers.com/FR06190**

Le Sourire is a member of the Parc Saint-James group. There are 411 pitches here and many are occupied by mobile homes and chalets, many residential. However, there are about 80 touring pitches dispersed throughout the wooded terrain, some of which are on soft sandy soil. Electricity (6A) is available on 42. A stream runs through the camping area and it can flood. A large swimming pool has a regular programme of activities. Some pitches are close to the main road so there may be some noise.

Facilities

Sanitary facilities (with key access) include preset pushbutton showers and washbasins in cabins. Laundry. Motorcaravan services. Shop, bar, restaurant and takeaway (all July/Aug). Swimming pool and separate children's pool (1/6-15/9). Play area. Gym. Games room. Entertainment programme (July/Aug). Electric barbecues only. WiFi (charged). Off site: Bus stop outside entrance. Cannes and Nice. Golf 1 km. Nearest beaches 5 km. Riding 5 km. Fishing 6 km. Bicycle hire 7 km.

Open: 9 April - 24 September.

Directions

From the A8 take exit for Villeneuve-Loubet and follow signs to Grasse joining the D2085. The site is on the left, 2 km. from Villeneuve Loubet. GPS: 43.6603, 7.10429

Charges guide

Per unit incl. 2 persons and electricity	€ 18.00 - € 33.00
extra person	€ 2.50 - € 4.50

Villeneuve-Loubet-Plage

Camping la Vieille Ferme

296 boulevard des Groules, F-06270 Villeneuve-Loubet-Plage (Alpes-Maritimes) T: 04 93 33 41 44.
E: info@vieilleferme.com **alanrogers.com/FR06050**

In a popular resort area and open all year, la Vieille Ferme is an oasis of calm. A family owned site with good facilities, it has 119 level, gravel based touring pitches, all with 2/10A electricity and 95 fully serviced. The majority are separated by hedges. Some are only small, simple pitches for little tents. There are special winter rates for long stays with quite a few long stay units on site during the winter. The entrance to the site is welcoming and very colourful with well tended flower beds. English is spoken at reception and the whole place has a very friendly feel to it. There are 15 km. of cycle paths linking the village to the coast, with some routes passing through a nature park.

Facilities

Modern, heated, well kept sanitary blocks with toilets for children, baby room and facilities for disabled visitors. Motorcaravan services. Washing machines and dryer. Small shop (July/Aug). Bread to order. Vending machine in TV room. Snacks (May-Sept). Swimming and paddling pools, heated and covered in winter (closed mid Nov-mid Dec). Jacuzzi. Play area. Boules. Small outdoor gym. Games and competitions (July/Aug). WiFi (charged).

Open: All year.

Directions

From west, A8, exit 44 Antibes, D35, 3.5 km. Left towards Nice, N7. After 3.5 km. turn left for site between Marineland and Parc de Vaugrenier. Site is 150 m. on right. Avoid N98 Route du Bord de Mer (low bridge). GPS: 43.62002, 7.12586

Charges guide

Per unit incl. 2 persons and electricity	€ 22.50 - € 42.00

Volonne

Sunêlia L'Hippocampe

Quartier la Croix, route de Napoléon, F-04290 Volonne (Alpes-de-Haute-Provence) T: 04 92 33 50 00.
E: camping@l-hippocampe.com **alanrogers.com/FR04010**

Sunêlia L'Hippocampe is a friendly, family run, all action, riverside site (no swimming), with families in mind, situated in a beautiful area of France. The perfumes of thyme, lavender and wild herbs are everywhere and the higher hills of Haute-Provence are not too far away. There are 447 level, numbered pitches (177 for touring units), medium to very large (130 sq.m) in size. All have 10A electricity and 140 have water and drainage, most being separated by bushes and cherry trees. Some of the best pitches border the lake or are in the centre of the site. The restaurant, bar, takeaway and shop have all been completely renewed. Games, aerobics, competitions, entertainment and shows, plus a daily club for younger family members are organised in July and August and organised activities also at Easter and Whitsun. A soundproofed underground disco is set well away from the pitches and is very popular with teenagers. Staff tour the site at night ensuring a good night's sleep. English is spoken.

Facilities

Four refurbished toilet blocks, all with good clean facilities that include washbasins in cabins. Washing machines. Motorcaravan services. Bread available. Shop (July/Aug). Bar, restaurant and pizzeria (25/4-13/9). Large, heated pool complex with five waterslides. Tennis (free in low season). Fishing. Canoeing. Boules. Bicycle hire. Several sports facilities (some with free instruction). Charcoal barbecues are not permitted. WiFi throughout (charged). Off site: Village of Volonne 600 m. (Fri. market).

Open: 25 April - 30 September.

Directions

Approaching from north turn off N85 across river to Volonne, then right to site. From south right on D4 for 3 km. to site on left. GPS: 44.10462, 6.01688

Charges guide

Per unit incl. 2 persons and electricity	€ 16.00 - € 36.00
with full services	€ 16.00 - € 47.00
extra person (over 4 yrs)	€ 3.00 - € 8.00
dog	€ 2.00

Credit cards not accepted in low seasons.

DÉPARTEMENTS: 2A CORSE-DU-SUD; 2B HAUTE-CORSE

MAJOR CITIES: AJACCIO AND BASTIA

The island of Corsica is both dramatic and beautiful. The scenery is spectacular with bays of white sand lapped by the clear blue waters of the Mediterranean. At certain times of the year, the entire island is ablaze with exotic flowers aided by Corsica's excellent sunshine record.

The 'scented isle' of Corsica is a mountainous region of France with over 1,000 km. of largely unspoilt coastline with soaring cliffs, sandy beaches and hidden coves. The island has a complex and bloody history, having been disputed by the Greeks and Romans, invaded by the Byzantines and Moors, and ruled by the Genoese. This legacy has shaped the island with its hilltop villages featuring rustic, unadorned churches and a few Romanesque examples too.

The diverse landscape of glacial lakes, mountain streams, thick pine and chestnut forests and fragrant maquis makes it a paradise for walkers, who can choose from the many paths that criss-cross the island or tackle the famous GR20. The highest mountains lie to the west, while the gentler ranges, weathered to strange and often bizarre shapes, lie to the south and a continuous barrier forms the island's backbone.

Places of interest

Ajaccio: a dazzling white city full of Napoleonic memorabilia; Musée Fesch.

Bastia: historic citadel towering over the headland. The old town has preserved its streets in the form of steps connected by vaulted passages converging on the Vieux port (the old port). The new port is the real commercial port of the island.

Cuisine of the region

Brocchui: sheep's milk cheese is used much in cooking, in both its soft form (savoury or sweet) or more mature and ripened.

Capone: local eels, cut up and grilled on a spit over a charcoal fire.

Dziminu: fish soup, like bouillabaise but much hotter, made with peppers and pimentos.

Figatelli: a sausage made of dried and spiced pork with liver. A popular snack between meals.

Pibronata: a highly spiced local sauce.

Prizzutu: a peppered, smoked ham; resembles the Italian prosciutto, but with chestnut flavour added.

www.visit-corsica.com
info@visit-corsica.com
(0)4 95 51 00 00

SAINT FLORENT
BASTIA
N197
BELGODERE
CALVI
HAUTE-CORSE 2B
SAN NICOLAO
CORTE
PORTO
CORSICA
SAGONE
GHISONACCIA
N198
AJACCIO
CORSE-DU-SUD 2A
STE LUCIE-DE-PORTO-VECCHIO
SARTÈNE
PORTO-VECCHIO
BONIFACIO
0 25 50 75 kms

Belgodère

Camping le Belgodère

Hameau Lozari (RN 1197), F-20226 Belgodère (Haute-Corse) T: 04 95 60 20 20.
E: camping.lebelgodere@gmail.com **alanrogers.com/FR20190**

Belgodère is now a municipal site and offers neat and tidy camping pitches on grass and sand. They vary from 40-80 sq.m and most have 6A electricity. There is some shade for the tent pitches and limited shade for larger units. The site slopes upward from the reception area where there is a basic restaurant/bar with a menu of the day and also a small shop. The beach is a 400 m. walk after crossing the busy road at the front of the site. This is a simple, no-frills site which will suit many looking for peace and quiet and reasonable prices.

Facilities

One dated but clean toilet block with baby changing and facilities for disabled visitors. Shop stocks basics (limited opening hours). Bar, snack bar with fresh bread daily (July/Aug) and simple restaurant. TV/games room. Book exchange and games to borrow. Play area. Volleyball. WiFi in reception (charged). Dogs accepted. Information point by reception. Off site: Beach 400 m. Golf, riding, ATM and shops in Ile Rousse 7 km. Excursions to towns of Rousse, Calvi and Belgodère.

Open: 1 May - 28 September.

Directions

Site is in the north of the island. On the N197 Calvi/Bastia road, look for the D363 turn to Palasca near the N197 31 km. marker. The site is at this point on the N197 but not very well signed.
GPS: 42.637778, 9.019722

Charges guide

Per unit incl. 2 persons and electricity	€ 14.00 - € 24.00
extra person	€ 4.60 - € 7.00
child	€ 2.50 - € 5.00

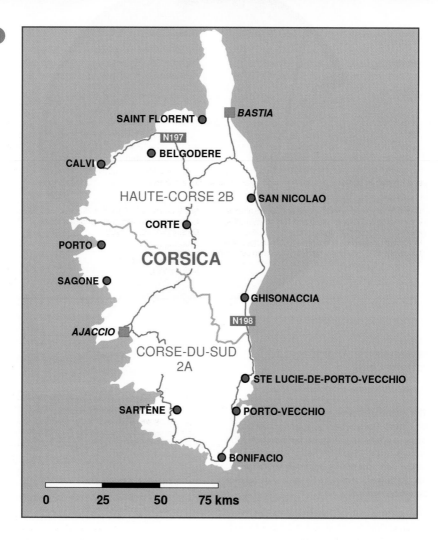

Bonifacio

Camping U-Farniente de Pertamina Village

RN 198, F-20169 Bonifacio (Corse-du-Sud) T: 04 95 73 05 47. E: pertamina@wanadoo.fr

alanrogers.com/FR20000

This is a smart, well run site with many activities for a family holiday. The 120 pitches, many in delightful settings with dry stone walls, have electricity (6A), are partially terraced and have trees and bushes providing shade. The touring area is near the entrance with the facilities at a lower level. The main features of the site are the large attractive swimming pool and amphitheatre surrounded by terraces. There is also a bar, restaurant and pizzeria/grill. There is a full entertainment programme for all in high season and some special activities for older children. Dogs accepted upon request. The site has a pleasant and peaceful feel with pitches kept separate from the activity areas. The staff are very friendly and English is spoken. It is busy in high season so a phone call to check availability is advised.

Facilities

Two toilet blocks (one refurbished) include washbasins in semi-private cubicles, British and Turkish style WCs, washing machines plus drying and ironing facilities. Motorcaravan services at entrance (public usage). Shop. Takeaway. Bar, restaurant, pizzeria/grill serving set meals and à la carte menu. Swimming pools. Tennis. Play area. TV room. Excellent gym. Extensive entertainment in high season. Off site: Excursions. Bonifacio 4 km.

Open: Easter - 15 October.

Directions

Site is on the RN198 road, 4 km. north of Bonifacio to the east. Well signed as Pertamina Village. GPS: 41.41790, 9.17990

Charges guide

Per unit incl. 2 persons and electricity	€ 25.00 - € 44.00
extra person	€ 6.50 - € 11.50
child (0-10 yrs)	free - € 7.00

Camping Cheques accepted.

Bonifacio

Camping Rondinara

Suartone, F-20169 Bonifacio (Corse-du-Sud) T: 04 95 70 43 15. E: reception@rondinara.fr

alanrogers.com/FR20240

The views from the facilities at this site are stunning, over the rolling hills and coast. 'The great outdoors' describes this campsite which is away from any tourist over-development and is at one with nature. The natural and informal pitches sit on the hillside above a superb bay with sheltered water, fine silver sand and safe swimming. Pitches have varied shade from foliage. Large boulders make natural divisions and some pitches need long leads for the 6A electricity. The beach is a 400 m. walk down a rough track through the maquis. Once down the track the walk is well worth while as the beach is wonderful. This site is unsuitable for disabled campers if they wish to use the beach.

Facilities

Three excellent, modern toilet blocks are very clean and offer hot water throughout, hot showers and single sex toilets. Facilities for disabled visitors. Motorcaravan services. Shop. Pizza restaurant. Bar. Beach bar. Infinity swimming pool. Play area. Games room. Electronic games. Entertainment and family activities. Torches are essential here. WiFi (charged). Off site: Beach, boat launching and fishing 400 m. Golf and riding 15 km.

Open: 15 May - 30 September.

Directions

Site is midway between Bonifacio and Porto-Vecchio off the RN198. Take the D158 to Baie de la Rondinara for 7 km. (site is well signed). The road is rough and narrow but large units will have no trouble negotiating it. GPS: 41.47323, 9.26316

Charges guide

Per unit incl. 2 persons and electricity	€ 24.20 - € 32.60
extra person	€ 6.60 - € 9.50
child (2-7 yrs)	€ 3.40 - € 4.90
dog	€ 2.50 - € 3.50

Calvi

Camping Paduella

Route de Bastia, F-20260 Calvi (Haute-Corse) T: 04 95 65 06 16. E: camping.paduella@wanadoo.fr

alanrogers.com/FR20170

Camping Paduella is a beautifully maintained, simple site which has been run by the friendly Peretti family for 40 years. As it is a popular site, it is best to book ahead for high season. There is a wide choice of pleasant pitches (137 in total), some shaded under pines, others grassed and hedged with less shade. They are all well maintained and on mostly level terraces with good access and 4/16A electricity. The surroundings are pleasant and the site is peaceful. The main reception area with its small shop, pizzeria and bar are at the front of the site. The lovely white sand beach is 300 m. away and the picturesque town of Calvi is a delightful 30-minute walk. Dogs are not permitted.

Facilities

Two centrally located modern and clean sanitary blocks (British style WCs). Well equipped showers with facilities for disabled visitors. Baby bathroom. Laundry with washing machines, ironing board. Small shop with basic supplies and fresh bread, snack bar and bar (all open June-Sept). Play area. Sports ground. TV. Charcoal barbecues not permitted. Fridge hire can be arranged. WiFi (charged high season). Off site: Supermarket 200 m. Adventure activities 200 m. Bicycle hire 700 m.

Open: 8 May - 8 October.

Directions

From the north, site is just before the town of Calvi. It is directly off the RN197 on the left and is well signed. GPS: 42.5521, 8.7641

Charges guide

Per unit incl. 2 persons and electricity	€ 20.00 - € 28.00
extra person	€ 6.70 - € 8.50
child (under 7 yrs)	€ 3.35 - € 4.25

No credit cards. Cash only.

Calvi

Camping la Pinède

Route de la Pinède, F-20260 Calvi (Haute-Corse) T: 04 95 65 17 80. E: info@camping-calvi.com

alanrogers.com/FR20180

Camping la Pinède offers 185 touring pitches, all with 4-16A electricity and is planted throughout with gum trees. The pitches are marked and level and there is access for large units in some areas. Water points are spread around the site and everything is kept tidy and clean. Under the mature trees it can be quite dark but there are plenty of places in the sunlight. The site is divided into sections – pitches for tour operators, mobile homes and tourers. Unusually, all amenities are in separate buildings. There is a very small pool, oddly sectioned and a restaurant that some may consider expensive.

Facilities

Three well maintained and well placed concrete sanitary buildings offer hot showers, facilities for disabled campers and unisex toilets and showers. Washing machines. Motorcaravan services. Shop (June-Sept). Bar. Restaurant (May-Sept). Swimming pool (no lifeguard). Play area. Tennis. Minigolf (charged). WiFi (charged). Overnight parking for late arrivals. Off site: Beach and fishing 200 m. Riding 500 m. Boat launching and bicycle hire 2 km.

Open: 1 April - 31 October.

Directions

Site is north of Calvi off the RN197, just south of the D251 road to the airport. Look for signs off the roundabout here and take care along a narrow road with leaning fir trees. GPS: 42.55320, 8.7686

Charges guide

Per unit incl. 2 persons and electricity	€ 21.00 - € 41.00

Camping Cheques accepted.

Corte

Camping Restonica

Faubourg Saint Antoine, F-20250 Corte (Haute-Corse) T: 04 95 46 11 59. E: camping.restonica@orange.fr

alanrogers.com/FR20110

Tucked away alongside the pretty Restonica river and near the Pont Neuf leading into the stunning old mountainside city of Corte, Camping Restonica is ideally placed for tourists wanting to visit Corte or travel on the popular inland mountain railway (the station is only a few hundred metres from the site). This is a small, simple site catering for those who want to enjoy the many delights of Corte. The entrance is steep but manageable and there are 110 flat, shady pitches for campers with many beautiful terraced pitches for tents dotted along the river bank under trees. The river is great for paddling or a shallow swim. The spectacular town is just above the site.

Facilities

Single, central toilet block is unisex and somewhat dated, although very clean. Toilet for disabled visitors but site not really suitable. Washing machine. Bread to order. Bar and snack bar. WiFi throughout (charged). No barbecues. Only certain breeds of dog accepted. Off site: Sightseeing. Famous train journeys across Corsica.

Open: 15 April - 30 September.

Directions

Site is south of Corte. Approaching the town, turn left at first roundabout onto Ave du 9 Septembre. Site is 300 m. on the right at the top of a steep, narrow access road. GPS: 42.3015, 9.152

Charges guide

Per unit incl. 2 persons and electricity	€ 21.00 - € 22.00

Ghisonaccia

Camping Arinella Bianca

Route de la Mer, F-20240 Ghisonaccia (Haute-Corse) T: 04 95 56 04 78. E: arinella@arinellabianca.com

alanrogers.com/FR20010

Arinella is a smart, lively, site with a strong family orientation, on Corsica's east coast. It has 137 good sized touring pitches with 10A electricity available (Europlug). Level and grassy, they are amply shaded by a variety of trees and shrubs. Some pitches overlook attractive lakes which have fountains and are lit at night. The site has direct access to a huge long beach of soft sand. The brilliantly designed resort-style pool complex with two pools and a paddling pool, is overlooked by a large restaurant, terraced bar and very professional entertainment area, forming the hub of Arinella Bianca. The very active and well organised children's club is impressive. Watch for some unmarked drops in level at one toilet block and near the restaurant. We feel that this site is not suitable for disabled campers.

Facilities

Four unisex, open plan sanitary blocks provide solar heated showers, washbasins in cabins, mainly British style WCs. Poor facilities for disabled visitors (unlocked). Baby room. Laundry. Motorcaravan services. Supermarket. Boutique. Bar and restaurant with terrace. Snack bar. Excellent swimming pools (heated). Wellness centre. Amphitheatre. Multisports centre. Windsurfing. Canoeing. Fishing. Tennis. Riding. Bicycle hire. Canyoning can be organised. Miniclub and teens' club (23/5-12/9). Unfenced play area. Superb entertainment programme (23/5-19/9). Disco. Communal barbecue area. WiFi (free). Only 1 dog per pitch (not July/Aug, under 10 kg).

Open: 16 April - 30 September.

Directions

Site is 4 km. east of Ghisonaccia. From N198 in Ghisonaccia look for sign 'La Plage, Li Mare'. Turn east on D144 at roundabout just south of town. Continue for 3.5 km. to further roundabout where site is signed to right. Site is 500 m.
GPS: 41.9984, 9.442

Charges guide

Per unit incl. 2 persons and electricity	€ 38.00 - € 54.00
extra person	€ 9.50 - € 16.00
child (2-15 yrs)	€ 7.00 - € 15.00
dog	€ 7.00

Porto

Camping les Oliviers

F-20150 Porto (Corse-du-Sud) T: 04 95 26 14 49. E: lesoliviersporto@wanadoo.fr

alanrogers.com/FR20220

This attractive and modern, resort style campsite is by the Bay of Porto, set alongside a charming river suitable for fishing and swimming. It is located on the difficult to access and remote west coast of Corsica and reservations are essential. The site is on very steep slopes and has 190 pitches (120 with 10A electricity). The mainly small and terraced pitches reflect the rugged terrain, are unsuitable for motorcaravans and extremely challenging for larger units. A new 'Bohemian' area offers Romany-style caravans for rent in a tranquil setting. The site is not suitable for disabled visitors.

Facilities

Toilet facilities are unisex and in four clean blocks dotted around the site. Some washbasins in cubicles, Four washing machines. Fridge hire. Bread supplies. Bar, restaurant and takeaway (1/6-15/9). Heated outdoor swimming pool (all season), gym and sauna. Play area. WiFi throughout (free). Fishing. Torches useful. Corsican trek agency. Gas barbecues only. Dogs are not accepted. Off site: Supermarket in village 50 m. Bicycle hire 200 m. Garage 750 m. Beach and fishing 1.5 km. Riding 30 km. Corsican Trek organises a variety of active sports. Visits to Scandola nature reserve. The surrounding area is listed as a World Heritage Site.

Open: 28 March - 2 November.

Directions

When approaching Porto from the north the road crosses a bridge over the river. Les Oliviers is on the left, well signed. The entrance is busy and soon congested in high season. Allow extra time for transits on this coast road, and take great care with larger units on the mountain roads.
GPS: 42.2619, 8.7103

Charges guide

Per unit incl. 2 persons and electricity	€ 18.90 - € 22.60
extra person	€ 7.60 - € 10.80
child (under 7 yrs)	€ 4.00 - € 5.50

Porto-Vecchio

Camping la Vetta

Route de Bastia, La Trinité, F-20137 Porto-Vecchio (Corse-du-Sud) T: 04 95 70 09 86.
E: info@campinglavetta.com **alanrogers.com/FR20060**

The French/English owners Marieline and Nick Long have created a peaceful country park setting for their great campsite, to the north of La Trinité village. The 8.5 hectares of well maintained campsite are part sloping, part terraced, with an informal pitch allocation system. It seems to stretch endlessly. The abundance of tree varieties, including many cork oaks, give shade to 111 pitches which all have 10A electricity. The site has a pleasant pool and lagoon-style paddling pool and also a bar serving pizza, snacks and ice cream. Visitors will experience 'real camping' here with high standards but none of the activity you would get on the resort-style sites.

Facilities

The sanitary facilities have been refurbished to a very high standard and include plenty of hot water. Laundry. Bread and milk. Lunchtime and evening pizzas/snacks and bar (July/Aug). Swimming pool, paddling pool, water play area and grassy relaxation area. Snooker table. Play area. TV. Occasional Corsican evenings with food typical of the area (high season). WiFi on part of site (charged).

Open: 1 June - 1 October.

Directions

Site is in La Trinité village, off the RN198 (east side), north of Porto-Vecchio. GPS: 41.6316, 9.2929

Charges guide

Per unit incl. 2 persons and electricity	€ 23.70 - € 33.70
extra person	€ 9.90 - € 14.90
child (3-17 yrs)	€ 2.90 - € 10.90

Sagone

Camping le Sagone

Route de Vico, F-20118 Sagone (Corse-du-Sud) T: 04 95 28 04 15. E: contact@camping-sagone.fr
alanrogers.com/FR20230

Part of the Campéole group, Camping le Sagone is situated outside the bustling seaside resort of Sagone, surrounded by protective hills. This campsite, which used to be a fruit farm, is in an ideal location for exploring Corsica's wild and rocky west coast or its mountainous interior. The large site borders a pleasant river and has 230 shaded pitches, with 6A electricity and water. The restaurant/bar and new snack bar overlook the modern pool and they are the focal point of this well managed site. The site provides an amazing array of sports and specialises in sports activities for groups in the low season.

Facilities

Clean, fully equipped toilet blocks with washbasins in cubicles (one block was closed when we visited, May 2015, and in need of attention). Facilities for disabled visitors. Baby baths. Washing machines, dryers. Motorcaravan services. Restaurant, pizzeria, bar. Swimming pools (June-Sept). Superb sports facilities. Fully equipped gymnasium. Tennis. Play area. Barbecues are not permitted. Satellite TV. WiFi (charged). Car wash. Putting and senior golf practice area.

Open: 1 February - 1 December.

Directions

From Ajaccio take the RD81 towards Cergése and Calvilby (by coast road). In Sagone take RD70 towards Vico, Sagone can be found on left after 1.5 km. next to supermarket. GPS: 42.1304, 8.7055

Charges guide

Per unit incl. 2 persons and electricity	€ 22.50 - € 39.05
extra person	€ 5.00 - € 9.25

Camping Cheques accepted.

Saint Florent

Camping d'Olzo

L. D. Strutta, F-20217 Saint Florent (Haute-Corse) T: 04 95 37 03 34. E: info@campingolzo.com
alanrogers.com/FR20150

The friendly Barenghi family, who own this site, are delightful. They are pleased to welcome you to their compact site and Dutch, Italian and English are spoken. The site is flat and very peaceful with a wide variety of trees, including gums and olives, which offer shade to most of the informal pitches and the area for motorcaravans. There is ample room to manoeuvre for large units. All 140 pitches have electricity (10A) and are not far from the central sanitary block or the facilities which are grouped near reception. The site is a 500 m. walk from the beach, 300 m. of which is along a road. This is a very quiet site in an unspoilt area which will suit those who enjoy being in a peaceful, friendly atmosphere.

Facilities

New central sanitary block has unisex toilets (Turkish and British style) and single sex hot showers. Water at the sinks is cold. Everything is kept very clean and smart. Washing machines. Motorcaravan services. Facilities for disabled visitors. Baby room. Small shop supplies most essentials (July/Aug), bread to order. Restaurant/pizzeria and bar. Swimming pool. Play area. Communal barbecue area. Mobile homes and cabins for hire. WiFi.

Open: 11 April - 20 September.

Directions

From Bastia take the D81 west to St Florent. After some 30 minutes the site is well signed as you enter the village on the right. GPS: 42.6936, 9.3265

Charges guide

Per unit incl. 2 persons and electricity	€ 16.00 - € 29.50
extra person	€ 4.50 - € 8.50
child (under 10 yrs)	€ 3.50 - € 6.00

Sainte Lucie-de-Porto-Vecchio

Camping Caravaning Santa Lucia

Lieu-dit Mulindinu, F-20144 Sainte Lucie-de-Porto-Vecchio (Corse-du-Sud) T: 04 95 71 45 28.
E: information@campingsantalucia.com **alanrogers.com/FR20070**

Camping Santa Lucia is a small, friendly, family run site in a delightful southern Corsican setting. Behind the little reception hut is a simple and attractive restaurant and bar which has terraces overlooking the pool. It is very pleasant in the evenings when ornamental lamps light up the area. There are 160 informal pitches, 60 with 6A electrical connections. Some of the pitches are in lovely enclosed bays created from huge boulders or trees and shrubs, making them very private. Most have shade from mature trees. This site is only minutes by car from Porto-Vecchio and with very reasonable prices, will suit many.

Facilities

Two excellent modernised (2015) toilet blocks include British style toilets and smart washbasins in cubicles. Charming bathroom area for children. Washing machines. Facilities for disabled visitors. Bread to order. Bar (15/6-15/9). Restaurant and takeaway (July/Aug). Swimming and paddling pools. Play area. Miniclub (July/Aug). Minigolf. Communal barbecues. Satellite TV. WiFi (charged). Off site: Supermarket near site entrance. Doctor, chemist, grocers and newsagent in village. Beach 5 km. Riding 8 km.

Open: 5 April - 4 October.

Directions

Site is at south end of Ste Lucie-de-Porto-Vecchio village, off N198 and well signed.
GPS: 41.69660, 9.3434

Charges guide

Per unit incl. 2 persons and electricity	€ 19.80 - € 33.75
extra person	€ 5.65 - € 9.90
child (2-12 yrs)	free - € 7.00

San Nicolao

Camping Merendella

Moriani-Plage, F-20230 San Nicolao (Haute-Corse) T: 04 95 38 53 47. E: contact@merendella.com
alanrogers.com/FR20030

This attractive site has direct access to a very pleasant, 300 m. sandy beach. It is situated on level grass and sand with many trees and shrubs providing shade and colour. There are 196 pitches, all large and well spaced with electricity (10A). There is a choice of pitch with some hedged for privacy under the cool shade of mature trees. Some have direct beach access with brilliant sea views and the sound of the waves. A pleasant bar, snack bar/pizzeria and restaurant are all available on the beach, providing great views and a wonderful atmosphere, particularly when dining in the evening.

Facilities

Two sanitary blocks with two smaller cabin units near the beach. Washbasins in private cubicles. Mostly British style WCs. Facilities for disabled visitors. Laundry facilities. Motorcaravan services. Shop. Bar/restaurant, pizzeria on the beach. Solar heated swimming pool with sliding cover (uncovered high season). TV room. Games room. Play area. Torches essential. WiFi (charged). Communal barbecue area. Night parking area for late arrivals. Dogs are not accepted. Off site: Supermarket outside gate.

Open: 1 April - 10 October.

Directions

Site is to seaward side of the RN198, 800 m. south of Moriani Plage. GPS: 42.3656, 9.5296

Charges guide

Per unit incl. 2 persons and electricity	€ 25.90 - € 33.90
extra person	€ 7.45 - € 9.60
child (4-12 yrs)	€ 4.80 - € 6.00

Sartène

Campéole l'Avena

Tizzano, F-20100 Sartène (Corse-du-Sud) T: 04 95 77 02 18. E: avena@campeole.com
alanrogers.com/FR20290

Part of the Campéole group, l'Avena is primarily a beach site which sits in an attractive valley. The beach is within ten minutes' walk away along a sandy track. There are 194 flat pitches with 69 for tourers, all with 16A electricity. Some are closely placed and there are differing levels of shade from young trees. The small snack bar, bar and shop provide an adequate service, but remember the closest village is 15 km. away for extra supplies. A small play area was to be supplemented with a bouncy castle when we visited. Visitors are left to their own devices here.

Facilities

Single, dated unisex sanitary block, which is under pressure during peak periods. Hot showers. Provision for disabled visitors. Washing machines. Shop/bar/snack bar (15/6-15/9). Motorcaravan services. WiFi (charged). Communal barbecue. Off site: Beach 10 mins. walk. Watersports and fishing. Riding 1 km. Archaeological sites. Walking. Diving.

Open: 30 May - 21 September.

Directions

Site is on the west coast of Corsica. From the RN196 take the D48 towards Tizzano, site is off to the left down a rough track and is well signed.
GPS: 41.5343, 8.8633

Charges guide

Per unit incl. 2 persons and electricity	€ 22.00 - € 32.70

Camping Cheques accepted.

Naturism is something of a way of life, and today many more people than one might think enjoy the freedom and sense of equality found in naturist campsites. Being in harmony with nature, whether by the sea or in a woodland setting, can be a unique and liberating experience.

Some are dedicated naturists who practise their way of life wherever they may be, and who, in the UK, may well belong to clubs of like-minded people. For others, especially those who have enjoyed sunbathing on one of the many designated naturist areas on European beaches and feel comfortable with it, the logical next step is to try a holiday in a naturist village or campsite.

This growing number of 'holiday naturists' clearly enjoy the relaxed atmosphere prevailing on naturist sites. If they are not members of British Naturism, they can pick up a naturist card on the first site they visit. The rules are simple: respect for the environment and for other visitors. You are encouraged to strip off but, in reality, it is up to you, except in and around the swimming pool where there is always a 'no clothes' rule. Clothes do tend to label people and without them there is a relaxed informality and sense of equality often missing in today's 'designer society'.

We feature some 34 naturist campsites in this guide and have been impressed by the friendly welcome and cultural aspects of their entertainment and range of activities – classical music beside the pool, walking trails to discover local wildlife or book-binding classes, for example.

Most campsites make an effort to provide good entertainment and to make your holiday memorable; on the naturist sites in particular, this is usually achieved quite elegantly without the frenzy that sometimes pervades more commercially-minded sites.

Saint Chéron

Centre Naturiste Héliomonde

La Petite Beauce, F-91530 Saint Chéron (Essonne) T: 01 64 56 61 37. E: heliomonde@heliomonde.fr

alanrogers.com/FR91040

Centre Naturiste is situated in a 47-hectare parkland setting surrounded by woodland and is ideal for visiting Paris. There are 500 pitches with 100 unmarked pitches for touring, all with 16A electricity and laid out naturally amongst the trees. The remaining pitches are used for mobile homes, tents and chalets, all but 28 of which are privately owned. This site is very popular with Parisian weekenders and is also open for day visitors to unwind in a calm and relaxing environment. Paris is only 50 minutes from the RER Saint Chéron Station, 2 km. from the site. Cars must be parked in the main car park away from pitches.

Facilities

Two sanitary blocks have washbasins in cubicles, preset showers (no dividers) and a mixture of Turkish and British style toilets (some without seats). The one nearest reception is heated. Toilets but no adapted showers for disabled visitors. Washing machines and dryers. Restaurant, bar and snack bar. Small shop. Games room. Heated swimming and paddling pools. Sauna. Hammam. Gym. Tennis. Volleyball. Badminton. Multisports pitch. Basketball. Archery. Organised activities in high season all week and low season at weekends. WiFi (free).
Off site: Golf 20 km. Paris 45 minutes.

Open: 6 March - 8 October.

Directions

Leave A10 autoroute southwest Paris, exit 10. Take D149 south to bypass Dourdan, road number changes to D116. Continue east on D116 east to Chéron. Site signed 3 km. from village.
GPS: 48.543448, 2.138077

Charges guide

Per unit incl. 2 persons and electricity	€ 18.80 - € 43.80
extra person	€ 4.00 - € 7.25
child (6-14 yrs)	€ 3.60 - € 4.60
dog	€ 4.20

Luzeret

Domaine Naturiste la Petite Brenne

La Grande Métairie, F-36800 Luzeret (Indre) T: 02 54 25 05 78. E: la.petite.brenne@wanadoo.fr
alanrogers.com/FR36220

La Petite Brenne is a spacious, family owned naturist site in the Parc Naturel Régional de Brenne. There is ample room for 150 families and you are free to choose one of the many places in and around the edges of the small fields. The pitches are grassy and flat and all have access to electricity (10A, long leads required on some) and water. Cars are not allowed on the pitches, except for the overnight area, whilst there is a designated, part-surfaced area for motorcaravans. Large floral hedges surround the site, which is decorated with mosaic sculptures. At its heart is the courtyard with terraces, bar, snack bar, pizzeria and restaurant.

Facilities

Six very clean, modern toilet blocks, facilities for babies and disabled campers. Small shop selling fresh bread. Bar, snack bar, restaurant. Outdoor and indoor heated swimming pools, paddling pool, sauna. Recreation room and library. Sports area. Outdoor fitness area. Play area. Extensive activity and entertainment programme for all the family. Dogs are not accepted. WiFi throughout (charged).

Open: 24 April - 30 September.

Directions

Leave A20 south of Châteauroux at exit 18 Argenton-sur-Creuse onto D55 west signed Prissac for 6 km. Turn south onto D55A for 3km. Turn right, campsite shortly on left. GPS: 46.541959, 1.40357

Charges guide

Per unit incl. 2 persons and electricity	€ 32.00
extra person	€ 9.00
child (0-15 yrs acc. to age)	€ 3.00 - € 6.00

Saint Martin-Lars-Ste Hermine

Camping Naturiste le Colombier

Le Colombier, F-85210 Saint Martin-Lars-Ste Hermine (Vendée) T: 02 51 27 83 84.
E: lecolombier.nat@wanadoo.fr **alanrogers.com/FR85140**

A countryside site for naturists near La Roche sur Yon, just right for those seeking a peaceful holiday. It provides 176 pitches (70 for touring) in seven very natural fields, on different levels linked by informal tracks. There are level, terraced areas for caravans and the marked pitches are around the edges, giving a feeling of spaciousness; all have electricity (6/10A) and some may need long leads. The bar/restaurant is in a converted barn. The site's 125 acres provide many walks throughout the attractive, wooded valley and around the lake. English is spoken by the Dutch owner and staff.

Facilities

Fully equipped toilet blocks are good, providing some showers in cubicles. Laundry. Facilities for children and disabled visitors. Small shop. Bar/restaurant with à la carte and full menu (order before 12.00). Takeaway. Heated swimming pool. Sauna. Jacuzzi. Turkish steam bath. Masseuse visits. Fishing. Volleyball, boules and table tennis. Playground. Pony rides. One day a week children can make their own bread. WiFi (€ 2). Off site: Charming towns such as Lucon, Bazoges and Fontenay-le-Comte. Small village of Vouvant (popular with artists in July/Aug).

Open: 1 April - 1 October.

Directions

From A83 at exit 7, join D137 towards St Hermine, continue ahead through town on D137, turn onto D52 eastward for 4 km. Turn left on D10 to St Martin-Lars. Site is then signed (very small signs). GPS: 46.59795, -0.96936

Charges guide

Per unit incl. 2 persons and electricity	€ 23.50 - € 28.50
extra person	€ 6.50 - € 7.80
child (3-16 yrs acc. to age)	€ 4.10 - € 5.65

Luzy

Centre de Vacances Naturiste Domaine de la Gagère

Lieu-dit La Gagère, F-58170 Luzy (Nièvre) T: 03 86 30 48 11. E: info@la-gagere.com
alanrogers.com/FR58060

At this secluded and attractive naturist campsite, you will receive a warm welcome from the enthusiastic owners, Thom and Betty. The site is spacious and well equipped with 105 good sized, level, grassy touring pitches, some shaded and some open. Many are arranged in groups around three sides of a rectangle, between hedges. Electricity (4-10A) is supplied to all pitches, four of which are fully serviced. There are plenty of water points. In high season, there are organised activities, barbecues and entertainment. A children's club meets twice a week.

Facilities

Three modern unisex toilet blocks, one heated, contain British style WCs, washbasins and preset communal showers. Facilities for disabled visitors. Baby room. Motorcaravan services. Laundry. Shop (15/5-15/9). Bar. Restaurant with snack bar and takeaway (1/5-15/9). Satellite TV. Two heated swimming pools (one 15/5-15/9). Sauna. Wellness. Playgrounds. Boules. Bicycle hire. No charcoal barbecues permitted. WiFi over site (free).

Open: 1 April - 30 September.

Directions

Leave Autun on D981, southwest towards Bourbon-Lancy. In 27 km. turn left (signed Gagère) down a 3 km. narrow lane with few passing places. Site is 3 km. GPS: 46.81692, 4.05636

Charges guide

Per unit incl. 2 persons and electricity	€ 24.85 - € 33.00
extra person	€ 5.65 - € 7.50
child (3-12 yrs)	€ 3.00 - € 4.00

Boussac

Creuse Nature Naturisme

Route de Bétête (D15), F-23600 Boussac (Creuse) T: 05 55 65 18 01. E: creuse.nature@wanadoo.fr

alanrogers.com/FR23030

You are sure of a warm welcome by the Dutch owners of this very spacious, naturally laid out and well maintained naturist site. It is set in the beautiful Limousin region in the centre of France. There are 100 large grassy/stony pitches, 80 of which are for touring with 10A electricity. Some are slightly sloping and there are varying degrees of shade. They are laid out in an open, wooded, parkland setting around the perimeter of the site or beside the small fishing lake. An attractive central feature is the swimming pool, sauna, bar and restaurant complex. There are many and varied activities organised for all the family. They range from bedtime stories for the very young, exciting games in the woods for the older children, convivial themed meals and Saturday evening campfires.

Facilities

Four modern, very clean toilet blocks with the usual facilities (open plan, so little privacy). Facilities for disabled visitors. Laundry facilities. Small shop (July/Aug) and baker calls. Indoor (all season, heated) and outdoor (June-Sept) pools. Paddling pool. Sauna. Bar and restaurant. Archery (high season). Boules. Bicycle hire. Lake fishing. WiFi throughout (charged). Charcoal barbecues not permitted. Accommodation for hire. Off site: Small, attractive town of Boussac with bank, post office, supermarket, bars and restaurants 3 km. Lake bathing 2 km. Riding 10 km. Golf 20 km. Interesting towns, villages and châteaux nearby.

Open: 1 April - 31 October.

Directions

Boussac is 35 km. west of Montluçon between the A20 and A71 autoroutes. In Boussac site is well signed. Take D15 west for 3 km. Site is on right. GPS: 46.34902, 2.18691

Charges guide

Per unit incl. 2 persons and electricity	€ 23.50 - € 34.50
extra person	€ 5.00 - € 8.50
child (3-11 yrs)	€ 2.50 - € 4.50
dog	€ 3.00 - € 5.50

Eyburie

Domaine Naturiste Aimée Porcher

Pingrieux, F-19140 Eyburie (Corrèze) T: 05 55 73 20 97. E: aimeeporcher@hotmail.com

alanrogers.com/FR19250

Aimée Porcher is a naturist site where you can relax and find your own space in an 11-hectare park, to the east of Uzerche. This very rural site, with a welcoming and uncommercial ambiance, has 55 spacious well shaded pitches (20 with 6A electricity) surrounded by a profusion of different trees and shrubs. Most have delightful views across the Limousin countryside. A small lake lies at the heart of the site and the River Vézère runs along the edge and is popular for trout fishing. Other amenities include a convivial bar/restaurant with shady terrace and play room. Campers can be collected from the train station on request. Meals can be booked once or twice a week, when you can meet fellow campers in a social and relaxed atmosphere. This is excellent walking and cycling country and maps are available.

Facilities

Two sanitary blocks include showers and open style washbasins. Facilities for disabled visitors (access may be difficult for wheelchairs). Bar/takeaway. Weekly meals to order. Lake with beach for swimming. Play area. Fishing. Volleyball. Boules. Activity and entertainment programme (July/Aug). No charcoal barbecues on pitches. Communal barbecue. WiFi (charged). Off site: Bicycle hire and riding 15 km. Canoeing and boating. Uzerche (shops and restaurants).

Open: 20 May - 7 September.

Directions

Approaching from Uzerche, head east on D3 as far as Eyburie. Here, follow signs to the site. GPS: 45.4518, 1.65074

Charges guide

Per unit incl. 2 persons and electricity	€ 20.30 - € 24.95
extra person	€ 3.65 - € 4.25
child (1-9 yrs)	€ 3.00 - € 3.50
dog	€ 2.85 - € 3.00

No credit cards.

Sussac

Camping Naturiste les Saules

Les Saulières, F-87130 Sussac (Haute-Vienne) T: 05 55 69 64 36. E: info@lessaules.com

alanrogers.com/FR87140

Les Saules is a quiet, naturist campsite in an attractive location in the valley of the River Combade, south east of Limoges. Its focal point is an old farmhouse, surrounded by tall trees, housing a bar and terrace. The site has 36 large, level, grassy pitches for touring units, of which 33 have electrical connections (6A). There are three rental units and three tent-only pitches. Bushes between the pitches provide privacy and to maintain the peaceful environment, cars are not allowed on pitches except for those intended for and used by persons with disabilities. A small, unfenced lake with a sandy beach is good for swimming.

Facilities

Very clean sanitary facilities include provision for children, babies and disabled visitors; hot water also to sinks. Washing machine and dryer. Chemical disposal only permitted if biological product used. Bar. Fresh bread daily. Communal meals twice weekly. Organised activities and informal evening entertainment. Swimming in lake, with roped-off shallow section for young children. Playroom and playground with trampoline. Boules. Badminton. Volleyball. WiFi (charged).

Open: 15 May - 15 September.

Directions

Sussac is 50 km. southeast of Limoges. Leave A20 at exit 39, east on D15/D12 to Châteauneuf-la-Forêt. Continue east then south on D39 to Sussac and follow signs to campsite, turning east towards Domps on D30A. then south (sharp right) to les Saules. Ignore sat nav. GPS: 45.65138, 1.6786

Charges guide

Per unit incl. 2 persons and electricity € 23.85 - € 27.85

No credit/debit cards.

Bouillac

Naturiste Camping Terme d'Astor

Terme d'Astor, F-24540 Saint Avit Rivière (Dordogne) T: 055 363 2452. E: termedastor@wanadoo.fr

alanrogers.com/FR24550

A welcoming Dutch-owned naturist site, Terme d'Astor is hidden amongst trees some two kilometres from Bouillac and is very private. On a plateau in wooded hills, there are 100 pitches, 90 used for touring and ten attractive wooden chalets. Most pitches have good shade, while some are open and unshaded. Electricity (6A, Europlug) is available for most pitches, although long leads are sometimes required. Access to the site is via a two kilometre, very narrow, hilly road and the gravel roads around the site are also very narrow with tight turns and overhanging trees. This may cause some difficulties for larger units, although big delivery lorries get through! The atmosphere is relaxed and friendly and English is spoken.

Facilities

Two very clean sanitary blocks include facilities for disabled visitors and a baby room. Washing machines and a spin dryer. Good shop. Bar/restaurant with shaded terrace. Pizza van (July/Aug). Swimming pool and paddling pool. Sauna (charged). Three play areas. Trampoline. Boules. Children's clubs, theme nights and wine tasting (July/Aug). WiFi (free).

Open: 1 May - 30 September.

Directions

From D53 take D26 west towards Bouillac. Look for signs to site. It is 5 km. along the road on the left. Take small single track road signed Terme d'Astor and follow for 1 km. GPS: 44.758026, 0.902245

Charges guide

Per unit incl. 2 persons and electricity € 20.50 - € 34.50

extra person € 4.00 - € 8.00

Frontenac

Domain Naturiste Château Guiton

Guiton, F-33760 Frontenac (Gironde) T: 05 56 23 52 79. E: accueil@chateau-guiton.com

alanrogers.com/FR33450

A small naturist site situated in the park of an 18th-century castle, just 8 km. south of the Dordogne. The owners offer a warm welcome and a family atmosphere. The site makes good use of the château's outbuildings and wisteria hangs over the tiny reception area. There are 29 large pitches (6A electricity) mainly on level grass, separated by mature hedges giving considerable privacy. A small number of chalets and gîtes are also available to rent. The site is an excellent starting point for walking and cycling along small tracks through the vineyards and for day trips.

Facilities

One small, unheated, unisex toilet block has washbasins (some in cubicles) and preset open showers. Baby bath and facilities for disabled visitors. Washing machine. Small shop, fresh bread daily. Bar and snack bar. Small swimming pool, but no children's pool. Entertainment programme (July/Aug). Play area. Boules. Badminton. Fitness room and sauna (charged). Communal barbecue area. Bicycle hire. WiFi (free). Ice packs frozen.

Open: 15 May - 20 September.

Directions

From Libourne, join D670 towards St Emilion and Castillon-la-Bataille. At St Laurent-des-Combes turn right towards Sauveterre-de-Guyenne. At sign for Rauzan turn right onto D231. Continue following signs to Frontenac. Site is signed from outskirts of village. GPS: 44.725512, -0.150767

Charges guide

Per unit incl. 2 persons and electricity € 25.50 - € 28.90

Grayan et l'Hôpital

Espace Naturiste Euronat

F-33590 Grayan-et-l'Hôpital (Gironde) T: 05 56 09 33 33. E: info@euronat.fr

alanrogers.com/FR33160

Euronat is a well established naturist resort with extensive facilities, direct access to 1.5 km. of sandy beach and a thalassotherapy centre. With a total of 3,000 pitches, those for touring (around 1,200) are in two areas separated from the chalets and mobile homes. A variety of good sized, fairly flat and sandy pitches include some suitable for large motorcaravans. All pitches have 5/10A electricity and some also have water and drainage. The recently enhanced centre is superb with supermarkets, cash point, butcher, fish shop, bakery, restaurants including fish, brasserie, pizzeria/crêperie and a takeaway with a selection of hot and cold dishes and desserts that you can eat in the square at picnic tables.

Facilities

Sanitary blocks are well maintained with some heated (some closed in low season). Facilities for disabled campers. Launderette. Motorcaravan services. Shops, restaurants. Swimming pool, flumes, children's pool. Swimming lessons. Activities and workshops, archery, pony club, riding, tennis, pétanque, fishing. Children's activities and day care. TV rooms, video/games centre. Library. Supervised beach. Skate park. Bicycle hire. No barbecues on pitches. Torches useful. WiFi (charged).

Open: 4 April - 1 November.

Directions

From Bordeaux ring road take exit 7, then D1215 to Lesparre and Vensac, then follow (large) signed route. GPS: 45.41627, -1.13178

Charges guide

Per unit incl. 2 persons and services	€ 19.90 - € 53.50
extra person	€ 4.00 - € 7.50
child (under 10 yrs)	free
dog	€ 5.00

Monflanquin

Camping Naturiste Domaine Laborde

Paulhiac, F-47150 Monflanquin (Lot-et-Garonne) T: 05 53 63 14 88. E: domainelaborde@wanadoo.fr

alanrogers.com/FR47140

Ideally situated on the border of Lot-et-Garonne and Dordogne, Domain Laborde is a naturist site of outstanding quality with sweeping views from many of the higher pitches. This hilly site, set in 20 hectares of countryside, has 150 well maintained pitches of at least 120 sq.m. all for touring, many shaded, some partially shaded and all surrounded by woodland. Electricity (6-15A) is available (long leads may be required). There are also 40 chalets and mobile homes for hire. The site has something for everyone and even in low season it is very popular. If you are new to naturist sites, then this is a must.

Facilities

The three sanitary blocks and a new wash block (one with underfloor heating) are well sited and clean. Washing machines and dryer. Shop with fresh bread and milk. Bar with TV. Snack bar serving pizzas. Restaurant (15/4-15/9). Two large swimming pools with slides, whirlpool, sauna, and paddling pool. Indoor heated pool. Massage. Hammam. Trampoline. Two play areas. Boules. Giant chess. Communal barbecue (no charcoal on pitches). Activities for children (high season). Free WiFi in cybercafé.

Open: 1 April - 30 September.

Directions

From Monflanquin take D272 towards Monpazier. 10 km. along the road look for the signs to site. It is very well signed at regular intervals and will read 'Domaine Laborde'. GPS: 44.613889, 0.835556

Charges guide

Per unit incl. 2 persons and electricity	€ 24.00 - € 32.50
extra person	€ 5.50 - € 7.00
child (under 6 yrs)	€ 4.00 - € 4.50

Naussannes

Camping Naturiste le Couderc

Le Couderc, F-24440 Naussannes (Dordogne) T: 05 53 22 40 40. E: info@lecouderc.com

alanrogers.com/FR24190

This is a very spacious naturist site set in 33 hectares of open countryside with large pitches naturally laid out around sloping meadows. There is a feeling of calm and tranquillity and the family owners ensure that visitors enjoy their stay. There are 193 pitches, of which 158 are for touring, all with 6A electricity and 35 accommodation units for hire. The site is on different levels with undulating slopes but the generous pitches are level and easily accessible. Generally open, but mature trees all around offer some shade. A varied programme of events for all the family are run throughout most of the season.

Facilities

Four very clean modern toilet blocks with facilities for children and disabled visitors. Outdoor showers. Washing machines and dryer. Well stocked shop. Bar. Restaurant and takeaway. Heated outdoor swimming pools. Jacuzzi. Sauna. Steam room. Two ponds, one for fishing. Miniclub. Sculpture and circus lessons. Play area. Bicycle hire. WiFi throughout (charged). Walking tracks. Torch essential.

Open: 1 April - 15 October.

Directions

From Bergerac take N21. Turn left D25 to Issigeac. Continue towards Naussannes for 8 km. Turn left at signpost indicating Naussannes 2 km. Le Couderc is 350 m. on the right. GPS: 44.75602, 0.70212

Charges guide

Per unit incl. 2 persons and electricity	€ 19.50 - € 39.20
extra person	€ 6.00 - € 8.70

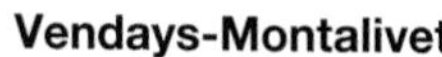

Vendays-Montalivet

Centre Naturiste Helio-Marin de Montalivet

46 avenue de l'Europe, F-33930 Vendays-Montalivet (Gironde) T: 05 56 73 73 73.
E: infos@chm-montalivet.com **alanrogers.com/FR33370**

This is a very large naturist village with everything that you could need during your holiday without leaving the site. It has direct access to the sea with its own beautiful, golden sandy beaches with coastguard surveillance in high season. Watersports are numerous with lessons if you require. The main emphasis here is to keep the family entertained. There are 3,082 pitches, of which 449 are for touring. Pitches are level, on grass or sand and mature trees provide shade in some areas. A circus school, dancing classes and skateboarding are just some of the activities organised here. Both the swimming pools are different, from tropical to traditional. Four slides and a toboggan are available to use in the aquatic park. The site also boasts a state-of-the-art spa and wellness centre.

Facilities

Numerous sanitary blocks. Facilities for disabled visitors. Launderette. Motorcaravan services. Shops, restaurants and bars. Two swimming pool complexes with slides and toboggan (30/4-28/9). Children's clubs. Evening entertainment. Playgrounds. Sports grounds. TV rooms and cinema. Large library. Wellness centre offering numerous treatments and massage as well as saunas and jacuzzi. Bicycle hire. Fishing. WiFi over site (charged). Max. 1 dog. Off site: Riding 1 km. Sailing 6 km.

Open: 2 April - 29 October.

Directions

From Royan, take the ferry to Verdon-sur-Mer and continue on N215 for 34 km. Turn right on D102 to Montalivet. Nearing the sea turn left for Hourtins and site is 1 km. on the right. GPS: 45.36348, -1.14575

Charges guide

Per unit incl. 2 persons and electricity	€ 19.00 - € 37.00
extra person	€ 4.50 - € 8.00
child (4-10 yrs)	free - € 3.00
dog (max. 1)	€ 5.00

Camping Cheques accepted.

Vielle-Saint-Girons

Domaine Naturiste Arnaoutchot

5006 route de Pichelebe, F-40560 Vielle-Saint-Girons (Landes) T: 05 58 49 11 11. E: contact@arna.com
alanrogers.com/FR40120

'Arna' is a large (500 pitches) naturist site with extensive facilities and direct access to the beach. Its layout in the form of a number of sections, each with its own character, makes it quite relaxing and very natural. These sections amongst the trees and bushes of the Landes provide a variety of reasonably sized pitches, most with electricity (3/6A), some with hardstanding, although the hilly terrain means that only a limited number are flat enough for motorcaravans. The centrally located amenities are extensive and of excellent quality. We suggest that new visitors telephone before arrival as the site can require them to be proposed by a family who have stayed at the campsite for at least three years. There are chalets, mobile homes and bungalow-style tents for rent. English is spoken at reception.

Facilities

Heated sanitary facilities include the usual naturist site type of blocks with communal hot showers and also a number of tiny blocks. Motorcaravan services. Supermarket, bar/restaurant, pizzeria and tapita (fish) bar (25/4-27/9). Heated indoor swimming pool with solarium, whirlpool and slide. Outdoor pool, sunbathing area. Paddling pool. Spa, sauna, steam room and massage. Gym. TV, games rooms. Cinema. Theatre. New tennis court. Library. Internet point. Bicycle hire. Fishing. Torches useful. No charcoal barbecues. American-style motorhomes not accepted. Off site: Riding and golf 5 km.

Open: 1 April - 27 September.

Directions

Site is signed off the D652 road at Vielle-St Girons. Follow D328 for 3-4 km. GPS: 43.9075, -1.361683

Charges guide

Per unit incl. 2 persons and electricity	€ 17.45 - € 48.65
extra person (over 3 yrs)	€ 2.80 - € 8.60
dog	€ 2.00 - € 4.00

Camping Cheques accepted.

Castelnau-Magnoac

Domaine Naturiste l'Eglantière

Aries-Espenan, F-65230 Castelnau-Magnoac (Hautes-Pyrénées) T: 05 62 39 88 00. E: info@leglantiere.com

alanrogers.com/FR65010

A delightful naturist site with an air of calm and repose, l'Eglantière is set within 50 hectares of organic farmland and woodland for walking and is a nature lovers' paradise. The fast-flowing River Gers runs through the site, bringing opportunities for watersports and fishing. Pitches are large and naturally shaped, most have electricity (16A, long leads). Many are separated by wild flowers, grasses and trees, ensuring shade and privacy. There is a separate wild area for tents. The clubhouse bar, restaurant and terrace have an extremely pleasing ambiance overlooking the attractive swimming pool area where nudity is compulsory. The owners are welcoming and keen to promote visitors' enjoyment of the area.

Facilities

Three sanitary blocks in typically naturist style, with covered, open facilities with individual cubicles. Motorcaravan services. Shop (June-Aug). Clubhouse with bar. Restaurant (1/6-30/9). Takeaway food. Heated swimming pool. Soundproofed activity/disco area. Playroom for younger children. Play area. Miniclub. Volleyball. Badminton. Pétanque. Archery. River activities. Canoe and mountain bike hire. Trekking. Cross-country cycling. Torches useful. WiFi in bar and reception areas.

Open: 11 April - 3 October.

Directions

From Auch take D929 south towards Lannemezan. After Castelnau-Magnoac continue past aerodrome and turn onto the D9 towards Monleon-Magnoac. Take the first left towards Ariès-Espénan and follow site signs. GPS: 43.26466, 0.52119

Charges guide

Per unit incl. 2 persons and electricity € 20.30 - € 38.30

Camping Cheques accepted.

Saint Clar

Centre Naturiste Devèze

Gaudonville, F-32380 Saint Clar (Gers) T: 05 62 66 43 86. E: deveze@deveze-nat.com

alanrogers.com/FR32040

This is a well established and very pleasant, French owned naturist site in 20 hectares of lovely Gers countryside. There are 153 pitches, most of which are for touring, all with electricity (6/10A, Europlug). They are set across several different areas and many are terraced. All are separated by mature hedges and trees with the amount of shade varying from area to area. The pitches higher up have fantastic views over the valley. As many of the site roads are quite steep and stony, the owner can use his tractor to position your caravan. The ambience at Devèze is warm and friendly with all social activities taking place at the centrepiece bar and terrace, leaving the pitch area quiet and peaceful.

Facilities

Sanitary facilities in three unisex blocks include hot showers (communal) and washbasins, all fitted out to a high standard and very well maintained. Shop for basic provisions (July/Aug). Bread to order. Takeaway, pub and snack bar (15/6-30/9). Small gym. Swimming and paddling pools (from 1/5). Adventure play area. Tennis, boules and archery. Fishing. TV rooms. Library. WiFi.

Open: 1 April - 30 September.

Directions

From Lectoure take D7 to St Clar. At St Clar turn left onto D13. In 1 km. right onto D167 to Gaudonville. After 4 km. turn left into narrow bumpy track to site in 0.8 km. GPS: 43.891011, 0.828545

Charges guide

Per unit incl. 2 persons and electricity € 17.50 - € 27.50

extra person € 3.70 - € 7.30

Varilhes

Naturiste Camping Millefleurs

Le Tuilier Gudas, F-09120 Varilhes (Ariège) T: 05 61 60 77 56. E: simone.groot@orange.fr

alanrogers.com/FR09090

Millefleurs is a beautifully quiet site in a secluded location for naturists. It is peaceful with some 70 acres of woods and meadows providing naturist walks in total privacy. The site has 40 large, flat, mostly terraced pitches (34 with 6/10A electricity), long leads required if pitching off the terraces. There are also very secluded pitches in wooded areas with shade, or you can pitch a tent in the meadows if you prefer. There are few of the normal commercial camping leisure facilities here and the site is definitely aimed at the more mature naturist camper but would provide a good introduction to the novice.

Facilities

Excellent toilet block with facilities for disabled campers. Bread to order (July/Aug). Guests dine together in the farmhouse two nights a week or just meet friends for a drink. Fridge with drinks. Pétanque. Guide book for walks and cycle rides. Torches useful. Pick ups from airports and stations arranged. There is no mobile phone reception, but a telephone is available.

Open: 1 April - 1 November.

Directions

From Varilhes, 8 km. south of Pamiers on D624 (parallel to N20). Take D13 for Dalou and Gudas cross railway and N20. The site is 2 km. past Gudas, on right. GPS: 42.9927, 1.6788

Charges guide

Per unit incl. 2 persons and electricity € 22.75 - € 25.75

No credit cards.

Barjac

Camping Naturiste de la Sablière

Domaine de la Sablière, Saint Privat-de-Champclos, F-30430 Barjac (Gard) T: 04 66 24 51 16.
E: contact@villagesabliere.com **alanrogers.com/FR30100**

Spectacularly situated in the Cèze Gorges, this well equipped, spacious naturist site, tucked away within its wild and dramatic terrain offers a wide variety of facilities, all within a really peaceful, wooded setting. There are 504 pitches, 240 for touring. Many are large and most have electricity (10A). Long leads and rock pegs may possibly be needed. Nudity is only obligatory around the pool complex. There are long and steep walks between many pitches and the facilities. Cars can be used in low season and there is a shuttle service in July and August. Large outfits not advised. No charcoal barbecues on site.

Facilities

Six good open-plan unisex sanitary blocks. Naturist style baths and facilities for disabled visitors. Laundry. Good supermarket. Bar, excellent open-air, covered restaurant and takeaway and small café/crêperie (all open until 25/9). Swimming pool complex. Fitness room. TV room. Disco. Tennis. New minigolf. Play areas. River bathing. Trim trail. Archery. Activities and entertainment. WiFi at reception. Off site: Fishing 2 km. Bicycle hire 8 km. Riding 10 km.

Open: 28 March - 4 October.

Directions

From Alès take D16 then D979 north east towards Barjac. 5 km. beyond St Jean-de-Maruéjols turn right D266 signed St Privat. After 3 km. turn right at junction and for site. Site is 5 km. along winding lane. GPS: 44.26713, 4.358195

Charges guide

Per unit incl. 2 persons and electricity	€ 21.50 - € 44.30

Camping Cheques accepted.

Cap d'Agde

Centre Naturiste Oltra

1 rue des Néréides, B.P. 884, F-34307 Cap d'Agde (Hérault) T: 04 67 01 06 36.
E: contact@centrenaturiste-oltra.fr **alanrogers.com/FR34270**

A large, naturist site situated within the Cap d'Agde Village Naturiste and alongside a wonderful sandy beach. Regularly laid out in sheltered avenues covering 35 hectares, it is well organised with 2,546 level sandy pitches and 1,038 privately owned mobile homes. The remainder is divided between touring pitches (5A electricity) and site owned mobile homes and chalets, some very smart and almost on the beach. Luxury cottages with garden, private spa, sun deck and communal pool are a new addition. A wide range of sports facilities, including archery, are available and children's clubs for 6-14 year olds. Bread, fresh fruit and vegetable stalls and several shops are at the Centre Naturiste. The site has its own smart beach bar, which is very popular. Visitors require a valid naturist card.

Facilities

Over 25 toilet blocks of varying sizes. Mainly open style showers typical of naturist sites. Laundry. Motorcaravan services. Two bars, snack bar selling pizzas. (1/5-30/9). Bread and fruit stalls (15/4-30/9). Miniclubs. Entertainment programme. Open-air cinema. Beauty centre. Outdoor fitness equipment. Multisports court. Football. Volleyball. Archery. Tennis. Play area. WiFi (charged).

Open: 15 March - 15 October.

Directions

Follow signs for Cap d'Agde Tourist office then pick up signs for 'Naturisme'. GPS: 43.29723, 3.52782

Charges guide

Per unit incl. 2 persons and electricity	€ 20.00 - € 42.30
extra person	€ 8.60 - € 16.50
child	free - € 6.50

Cesseras-en-Minervois

Camping Naturiste le Mas de Lignières

Montcélèbre, 2 chemin de la Source, F-34210 Cesseras-en-Minervois (Hérault) T: 04 68 91 24 86.
E: lemas1@wanadoo.fr **alanrogers.com/FR34050**

A quiet, rural naturist site hidden in the hills of the Minervois, only 3 km. from the medieval town of Minerve. There are marvellous views to the Pyrenees, the Corbières and the coast at Narbonne. The site now has just 20 very large pitches (electricity 6/10A) and six caravan holiday homes. Mainly on level grass, they are separated by mature hedges which give considerable privacy. There is natural shade and a variety of flora and fauna including four types of orchid and a warm welcome from Jeanne and her family. Her son is now qualified to accompany those interested on walking trips to the mountains.

Facilities

Clean toilet block has open washbasins and showers, facilities for disabled visitors. Washing machine. Bread (15/6-15/9). Swimming pool, sliding cover for use when cold. Paddling pool. Room for general use with TV, library, separate provision for young visitors. Playground. Tennis. Boules. Torch useful. WiFi (free). Only gas barbecues are permitted. Off site: Sailing, riding and canoeing at nearby Lac de Jouarres. Canal du Midi.

Open: 27 April - 30 September.

Directions

Take Lézignan-Corbières exit from A61, D611 to Homps, then D910 to Olonzac. Follow signs to Minerve (D10). In 4 km. left to Cesseras (D168). At Cesseras follow signs to Fauzan for 4 km. Site is on narrow, winding road. GPS: 43.34092, 2.70648

Charges guide

Per unit incl. 2 persons and 6A electricity	€ 24.50 - € 29.50
extra person	€ 6.00

La Palme

Camping Naturiste le Clapotis

2000 chemin de Prade, F-11480 La Palme (Aude) T: 05 56 73 73 73. E: infos@socnat.fr

alanrogers.com/FR11090

Le Clapotis is a six-hectare naturist site situated between Narbonne and Perpignan in a secluded pine wood above the Etang de La Palme (a large sea lagoon). There is a fairly steep walk down to the lagoon which is popular with those in pursuit of the ideal conditions provided for windsurfing. In total there are 230 pitches with 97 for touring, all with electricity (10A). They are of a good size on stony or sandy ground. Pitches in the older part have excellent shade from the pine trees and in the newer area shade is increasing. The site is now owned by the Socnat group.

Facilities

Two large and three small sanitary blocks, a little basic but fully equipped. Showers are both open and in cabins. Facilities for babies and disabled campers. Washing machines. Well stocked shop (15/5-15/9). Bar, restaurant and takeaway (all 15/6-31/8). Heated outdoor swimming pool. Massage (charged). Two half-tennis courts. Pétanque. Windsurfing. Kitesurfing. Fishing. Torches useful. Miniclubs (4-12, 13-17 yrs). Entertainment (July/Aug). Bicycle hire. WiFi over part of site (charged).

Open: 2 April - 1 October.

Directions

From N9 exit 40 (Port Leucate). At roundabout take N9 north for 3 km. to next roundabout. Turn right (Port-la-Nouvelle). Site signed in 500 m. on right. Follow narrow, poorly made road for 2 km. bearing left up hill to site. GPS: 42.958, 2.99586

Charges guide

Per unit incl. 2 persons and electricity	€ 24.70 - € 30.70
extra person	€ 3.60 - € 5.20

Camping Cheques accepted.

Lodève

Domaine Naturiste de Lambeyran

Hameau de Lambeyran, F-34700 Lodève (Hérault) T: 04 67 44 13 99. E: lambeyran@wanadoo.fr

alanrogers.com/FR34540

A wooded valley covering 348 hectares allows Domaine de Lambeyran a place in the Guinness Book of Records for having the largest area available for naturists in the world. It is a wonderful natural area with amazing views across to Lodève and the spectacular surrounding countryside. Naturists can enjoy the marked trails around the valley or the large, heated pool whilst choosing from 130 huge touring pitches, 100 with electricity (5/10A) and many quite private. Where necessary, the pitches have been levelled with local stone which has also been used to create short stairways in the terrain.

Facilities

Two large sanitary blocks and one smaller one are fully equipped including baby baths. No facilities for disabled visitors. Washing machine. Small shop, bar and snack bar (all 7/6-31/8). Large, solar-heated swimming pool (from 20/5) floodlit at night. Paddling pool and sunbathing terrace. Some play equipment for children and indoor area for older children. Dancing, films and organised trips such as canoeing down the Orb Gorges. Communal barbecue area. Dogs are only allowed in one area.

Open: 10 May - 20 September.

Directions

Lodève is 50 km. west of Montpellier. From A75 (Béziers, Clermont-Ferrand) take exit for Lodève and follow signs for town centre. Cross town following signs for Lunas (D35). Ignore right turn for les Plans and take next right (site signed) and continue up hill for 3 km. to site. GPS: 43.73648, 3.26483

Charges guide

Per unit incl. 2 persons and electricity	€ 21.60 - € 32.90
extra person	€ 5.40 - € 7.60

Méjannes-le-Clap

Camping Naturiste la Genèse

Route de la Genèse, F-30430 Méjannes-le-Clap (Gard) T: 05 56 73 73 73. E: infos@socnat.fr

alanrogers.com/FR30400

La Genèse is a well equipped naturist site close to the banks of the River Cèze, on the northern edge of the Cévennes national park. This is a large site with 483 well shaded pitches, 326 are for touring, most with 6A electricity. These are divided into 'sauvage', for those seeking peace and quiet, and 'prairie', closer to the main facilities. A wide variety of activities are on offer here, including art and craft workshops, bridge evenings and a cinema. Sports amenities include a large swimming pool with a daily aquagym session in high season, separate children's pool, tennis, archery and river bathing.

Facilities

Six clean and well maintained toilet blocks. Facilities for disabled campers. Motorcaravan services. Bar, restaurant and takeaway. Shop (1/5-30/9). New swimming pool and children's pool. Sauna. Archery. Games room. Art and craft workshops. Cinema. Canoe hire. Play area with new equipment. Activity and entertainment. Direct river access. Fishing. WiFi over part of site (charged).

Open: 2 April - 1 October.

Directions

From Alès take D16 via Salindres to Rochegude. Shortly beyond Rochegude, take D167 to Méjannes-le-Clap and follow signs to site (6 km). GPS: 44.26772, 4.37013

Charges guide

Per unit incl. 2 persons and electricity	€ 21.00 - € 30.00

Camping Cheques accepted.

Octon

Le Village du Bosc (Naturiste)

Ricazouls, F-34800 Octon (Hérault) T: 04 67 96 07 37. E: r.villagedubosc@free.fr
alanrogers.com/FR34930

Camping Village du Bosc is a family run naturist campsite in a secluded spot, with views over the Lac du Salagou. The 80 good sized touring pitches and 20 rental units are on 25 acres of gently sloping, terraced hillside with its distinctive red soil. Most have some shade and all have access to 6-10A electricity. The large swimming pool and friendly communal evening meals, with family entertainment, add to the warm atmosphere of this site. The extended estate of 200 acres surrounding the campsite provides many naturist walking routes with superb views down the valley towards the lake.

Facilities

Four shower blocks, two naturist. Baby bath. Washing machine. Motorcaravan services. Bar (July/Aug). Evening meals. Swimming pool. Trampoline. Family fitness exercises. Musical evenings. Pétanque competitions. Play area. Dogs accepted on one area of site. Naturist hiking trails. Off site: Lac du Salagou. Cycling. Watersports. Hiking. Riding. Rock climbing. Fishing. Supermarket 9 km.

Open: 1 April - 30 September.

Directions

From north on A75 take exit for D609 Lac du Salagou and Cartels, then follow D148 southwest towards Octon. Approaching Octon follow signs on right for Centre Naturiste. GPS: 43.6605, 3.32092

Charges guide

Per unit incl. 2 persons and electricity	€ 19.10 - € 23.10

Saint Michel-de-Dèze

Domaine Naturiste la Combe de Ferrière

La Combe de Ferrière, F-48160 Saint Michel-de-Dèze (Lozère) T: 04 66 45 52 43. E: info@la-combe.com
alanrogers.com/FR48190

La Combe de Ferrière is a naturist campsite with a wonderful welcome and a relaxing ambiance, hidden amid the dramatic hills of the southern Cevennes. This is a peaceful region where you can enjoy a Mediterranean lifestyle and climate. For the adventurous, a moonlit walk is on offer. There is a good swimming pool, sauna and dip pool and convivial evening meal once or twice a week. There are 35 pitches (6A electricity), all with something special, whether it be a spectacular view or a beautiful tree. Two gîtes and three studios are for hire all year. Site staff will arrange to collect you from the nearby railway station if you wish. No arrivals before 12 noon to avoid departing vehicles on the narrow road.

Facilities

Sanitary facilities include hot showers and open style washbasins. Room for families and disabled visitors (no wheelchair access). Small laundry. Daily delivery of bread and groceries (July/Aug). Evening meals once or twice weekly. Swimming pool (15/5-15/9) and sauna. Play area. Boules. Bicycle hire. Fishing possible in stream. Communal barbecue. Free WiFi. Dogs are accepted, but please inform reception before bringing dog in. Off site: Shops and restaurants in St Michel. Fishing 5 km. Riding 15 km. Skiing in winter 30 km.

Open: 15 May - 15 September.

Directions

From N106, between Alès and Florac, take D13 and follow twisting road for 10 km. until Col de Pendédis. Keep right and after 10 m. turn right, between two houses, then immediately into a small road. Continue for 2 km. NB: Units over 7 m. will need a lot of manoeuvring to negotiate final bend. GPS: 44.23016, 3.86326

Charges guide

Per unit incl. 2 persons and electricity	€ 25.25
extra person	€ 4.85

No credit cards.

Sérignan-Plage

Camping le Sérignan-Plage Nature

Route de l'Orpellière, F-34410 Sérignan-Plage (Hérault) T: 04 67 32 09 61. E: info@leserignannature.com
alanrogers.com/FR34080

Sérignan-Plage Nature benefits from the same 600 m. of white, sandy beach as its sister site next door but being a naturist site, it actually abuts the naturist section of the beach with direct access to it. It also has the use of the Sérignan-Plage balnéotherapy pool in the mornings, an excellent facility with spa and jacuzzi pools in a Romanesque-style setting for those over 16 years of age. The site has 286 good sized pitches on level sandy grass of which 99 are available for touring (6A electricity). There is plenty of shade except on the pitches beside the beach. Eighty-three mobile homes and chalets are available to rent.

Facilities

Two toilet blocks of differing designs offer modern facilities with some washbasins in cabins. All clean and well maintained. Washing machines. Supermarket, fresh fruit and vegetables, newsagent/souvenir shop and ice-cream kiosk. Small bar/café. Evening entertainment. Play area, miniclub and disco for children. Facilities and pools at Sérignan-Plage. Only gas barbecues are permitted. WiFi on part of site (charged). Off site: Bicycle hire 200 m.

Open: 25 April - 30 September.

Directions

From A9 exit 35 (Béziers Est) towards Sérignan, D64 (9 km). Before Sérignan, take road to Sérignan-Plage. At small sign (blue) turn right for 500 m. At T-junction turn left over bridge, site is 75 m. just after left-hand bend. GPS: 43.263409, 3.320148

Charges guide

Per unit incl. 2 persons and electricity	€ 17.00 - € 54.00

No credit cards.

Bédoin

Domaine Naturiste de Bélézy

132 chemin de Maraval, F-84410 Bedoin (Vaucluse) T: 04 90 65 60 18. E: info@belezy.com

alanrogers.com/FR84020

At the foot of Mont Ventoux, surrounded by beautiful scenery, Bélézy is an excellent naturist site with many amenities and activities and the ambience is relaxed and comfortable. The 326 pitches, 248 for touring (12A electricity, long leads required) are set amongst many varieties of trees and shrubs giving space and privacy. The attractive bar/restaurant and terrace overlook the swimming pool area and have superb views over the large recreational area and hills beyond. The site has an ecological theme with a small farm, a fish pond and a vegetable garden especially for the children.

Facilities

Four toilet blocks with very good facilities for campers with disabilities, some have hot showers in the open air. Superb children's section. Shop, bar, excellent restaurant with takeaway, swimming pools, hydrotherapy centre (all open 13/4-5/10). Sauna. Tennis. Adventure play area. Activities all season. Archery. Guided walks. Children's club. Only gas barbecues are allowed. WiFi throughout (charged). Pets are not accepted. Off site: Bédoin with shops and restaurants 1.5 km. Bicycle hire 2 km.

Open: 13 April - 10 October.

Directions

From A7 autoroute (exit 22) or RN7, south of Orange, take D950 southeast to Carpentras, then D974 northeast to Bédoin. In Bédoin turn right at roundabout, site is in 2 km. and signed. GPS: 44.13352, 5.18745

Charges guide

Per unit incl. 2 persons and electricity	€ 28.10 - € 46.60
extra person	€ 6.60 - € 10.00
child (3-8 yrs)	free - € 9.80

Brianconnet

Camping Naturiste le Haut Chandelalar

725/929 chemin de la Loubre, F-06850 Brianconnet (Alpes-Maritimes) T: 04 93 60 40 09.

E: lehaut.chandelalar@orange.fr **alanrogers.com/FR06060**

Camping le Haut Chandelalar is a spacious, family run naturist campsite high in the Alpes Maritimes, east of Castelallane and only 1 km. from Brianconnet. The site covers an area of ten hectares, laid out on terraces and the higher pitches have sweeping views of the surrounding mountains. The 70 pitches are car-free during high season, reasonably level, on grass and naturally laid out in woodland glades offering some shade. Forty have 10A electricity (Europlug). After an active day you can relax by the pool or around the bar and then enjoy a gourmet meal prepared by the very entertaining site owner.

Facilities

Five small modern toilet blocks, facilities for babies and campers with disabilities. Washing machine. Well stocked shop including homemade bread and pastries. Small bar at pool. Restaurant with gourmet menu. Takeaway. Heated pool. Boules. Multisports area. Games and TV room. WiFi (charged). Library. Large communal barbecue area. Dogs are not accepted. Off site: Tennis. Riding. Canyoning. Many marked walks, cycle routes. Roman village of Brianconnet 2 km. St Auban 7 km.

Open: 1 May - 15 September.

Directions

From Castellane east on D4085 for 10 km. to La Battie where left onto D452 for 7 km. Turn left, D2211 for 10 km. to St Auban. Continue with care for 6 km. through the Clue de St Abin towards Brianconnet. Site is well signed at sharp bend 1 km. to the left. GPS: 43.863859, 6.733289

Charges guide

Per unit incl. 2 persons and electricity	€ 25.50 - € 38.75
extra person	€ 6.00 - € 9.10
child (3-10 yrs)	free - € 5.40

Castellane

Camping Naturiste Castillon de Provence

La Grande Terre, La Baume, F-04120 Castellane (Alpes-de-Haute-Provence) T: 04 92 83 64 24.
E: info@castillondeprovence.com **alanrogers.com/FR04460**

Camping Castillon de Provence is a large (50 hectares) naturist site for families, 1,000 m. up in the heart of the Alpes de Haute Provence. There are 110 touring pitches of 100 sq.m. or greater, most with 6A electricity, plus 42 mobile homes, chalets and tents to rent, all with lake and mountain views. The bar, restaurant with terrace and swimming pool have spectacular views of the mountains. Sports, games and activities are organised for all ages while adventure activities including hang-gliding and white-water rafting are nearby. The road to the site is narrow with some sharp bends.

Facilities

Three new sanitary blocks have hot showers, facilities for disabled visitors and a family room. Washing machine. Well stocked shop. Bakery. Restaurant and bar with terrace. Heated swimming pool. Aquagym. Wellness centre. Sauna. Canoeing and kayaking (free hire). Outdoor fitness area. Clubs for children and adults (July/Aug). Play area and trampolines. Archery. Art and creative area. Fishing. Fridge rental. WiFi in bar (free).

Open: 26 April - 26 September.

Directions

From Castellane take D955 north (St. André-les-Alpes). In 3.5 km. turn left on D402 to La Baume. Leaving La Baume take road to the right. Campsite is in 1.3 km. NB: due to narrow access road, no arrivals before 14.00. GPS: 43.88354, 6.51455

Charges guide

Per unit incl. 2 persons and electricity	€ 25.35 - € 36.35
extra persoon	€ 4.90 - € 9.00

Forcalquier

Domaine Naturiste les Lauzons

Campagne de Briasse, F-04300 Forcalquier (Alpes-de-Haute-Provence) T: 04 92 73 00 60.
E: leslauzons@wanadoo.fr **alanrogers.com/FR04130**

This naturist site is set deep in the countryside, right in the heart of Haute Provence at an altitude of 450 metres. It is on a 60-hectare estate and offers peace and tranquillity. The owner, M. Cyril Kagenaar, does everything to make his guests feel welcome and the facilities are impeccably kept. There are 163 pitches in total, 111 for touring (all with electricity 6-10A) and large enough for bigger caravans (although the access is rather narrow). The remainder are occupied by chalets, mobile homes and lodges to rent. You can chose between open pitches on a grassy hill with views over the surrounding area or more sheltered places with enough shade. Even camping in the wild is possible on this large site.

Facilities

Four toilet blocks (one heated) are well spaced around the site. Some washbasins in cabins and mostly open showers. Baby room. Facilities for disabled visitors. Laundry. Shop and restaurant (May-Sept). Takeaway. Bar (June-Sept). Heated swimming pool (May-Sept) and large pool with water slides (July/Aug). Water polo. Aquagym. Sauna. Open-air gyms. Play area. Games room. Multisports court. Archery. Cinema. Entertainment and activities in high season. Walking trips. WiFi (charged).

Open: 15 April - 15 October.

Directions

Site is 2 km. south of Limans-en-Provence. From A51 (Sisteron-Aix-en-Provence) take exit 19. In La Brillane take D4100 towards Forcalquier, then Avignon. At Folcarquier take D950 towards St Etienne les Orgues. Site is signed 100 m. before Limans. GPS: 43.97273, 5.73386

Charges guide

Per unit incl. 2 persons and electricity	€ 24.00 - € 37.00
extra person	€ 6.00 - € 9.00

Puget-Theniers

Origan Village Naturiste

F-06260 Puget-Theniers (Alpes-Maritimes) T: 04 93 05 06 00. E: origan@orange.fr
alanrogers.com/FR06070

Origan, a member of Natustar, is a naturist site set in the mountains behind Nice at a height of 500 m. The access road is single track and winding with passing places. The site's terrain is fairly wild and some roads are stony, so it is unsuitable for caravans longer than six metres due to the steep slopes. The 100 touring pitches, in three areas, are irregular sizes and shapes with good views. Electricity connection (6A) is possible on most pitches (by long cable). The bar area, backing onto an impressive rock face (lit at night), overlooks a very attractive pool complex. Reservation is necessary in high season.

Facilities

Sanitary facilities are clean and typical of a naturist site – mostly open plan hot showers. Laundry facilities. Well stocked shop (15/5-15/9). Bar/restaurant. Takeaway. Heated swimming pools with toboggan and jacuzzi. Wellness centre (June-Sept). Sauna. Gym. Play area. Archery. Tennis. Fishing. Organised activities (July/Aug) season). Torches advised. Free WiFi around reception.

Open: 25 April - 30 September.

Directions

Heading west on the N202, just past the town of Puget-Theniers, turn right at campsite sign at level crossing; site is 2 km. GPS: 43.957633, 6.860883

Charges guide

Per unit incl. 2 persons and electricity	€ 22.00 - € 38.00
extra person	€ 4.00 - € 9.00
child (3-8 yrs)	free - € 7.00

Aléria

Riva Bella Nature Resort & Spa

Route de Riva Bella, F-20270 Aléria (Haute-Corse) T: 04 95 38 81 10. E: rivabella.corsica@gmail.com

alanrogers.com/FR20040

This is a relaxed, informal, spacious site alongside an extremely long and beautiful beach. Riva Bella is open all year and is exclusively naturist from 16 May to 29 September only. The site is divided into several areas with 199 pitches (with 6A electricity), some of which are alongside the sandy beach with little shade. Others are in a shady, wooded glade on the hillside. The huge fish-laden lakes are a fine feature of this site and a superb balnéotherapy centre offers the very latest beauty and relaxation treatments (men and women) based on marine techniques. An excellent, beachside restaurant offers a sophisticated menu and has superb sea views.

Facilities

High standard toilet facilities. Provision for disabled visitors, children and babies. Laundry. Large shop (15/5-15/10). Fridge hire. Lovely restaurant with sea views and menu for children. Ice creams. Excellent beach restaurant/bar. Watersports, sailing school, pedaloes, fishing. Balnéotherapy centre. Sauna. Aerobics. Giant chess. Petanque. Archery. Fishing. Mountain bike hire. Half-court tennis. Walking with llamas. Professional evening entertainment. Baby sitting. WiFi (charged).

Open: All year (naturist 16/5-29/9).

Directions

Site is 12 km. north of Aleria on N198 (Bastia) road. Watch for large signs and unmade road to site and follow for 4 km. GPS: 42.16151, 9.55269

Charges guide

Per unit incl. 2 persons and electricity	€ 23.90 - € 42.90
extra person	€ 5.00 - € 9.90
child (3-8 yrs)	€ 2.00 - € 7.00

Bravone

Camping Bagheera Naturisme

Route 198, F-20230 Bravone (Haute-Corse) T: 04 95 38 80 30. E: bagheera@bagheera.fr

alanrogers.com/FR20080

This naturist site is situated alongside a 3 km. beach of fine sand and has been owned by the same family for 40 years. There are 250 informal pitches on grass and sand which are well shaded under a variety of trees. All have 10A electricity. Some beach-side pitches have sea views, but all are within 200 m. of the sea. The pleasant main restaurant/bar and the beach restaurant/bar have superb panoramic views of the sea and offer extensive menus with good seafood served by enthusiastic staff.

Facilities

Modernised to a high standard, the five very comfortable sanitary blocks can be heated and offer hot water throughout. Baby rooms. Washing machines. Shop. Excellent restaurant. Lovely beach restaurant and bar. Pizzeria. Play area. Fitness circuit. Gym. Massage. Sauna. Pedalos. Windsurfing. Kayaking. Paddle boards. Beach umbrella rental. Pétanque. Tennis. Bicycle hire. Fishing. Entertainment (July/Aug). TV. WiFi (charged).

Open: All year.

Directions

Site is between Bastia and Aleria near Bravone, 7 km. north of Aleria on the RN198. It is well signed off the RN198. Follow site road 4 km. east to beach. GPS: 42.2206, 9.5380

Charges guide

Per unit incl. 2 persons and electricity	€ 17.50 - € 35.50
extra person	€ 10.80 - € 13.90

Camping Cheques accepted.

Porto-Vecchio

Village Naturiste la Chiappa

Route de Palombaggia, F-20137 Porto-Vecchio (Corse-du-Sud) T: 04 95 70 00 31. E: chiappa@wanadoo.fr

alanrogers.com/FR20050

This is a pleasant and large, non-textile naturist campsite on the Chiappa peninsula with 200 pitches, some with good sea views, for touring and tents, plus 230 bungalows. The pitches are informally marked and are a variety of shapes and sizes. Cars are parked separately. Very long electricity leads may be necessary. The superb beaches are between long rocky outcrops and it is safe to swim, alternatively you can enjoy the swimming pools beside the main beaches, along with the restaurants and bars. This is a well organised site with plenty of activities on offer.

Facilities

The sanitary facilities were clean when we visited. Washing machines. Well stocked shop. Two bars and restaurants with snacks. Bistro. Two swimming pools (one heated). Play area. Riding. Tennis. Minigolf. Fishing. Diving, windsurfing and sailing schools. Keep fit, yoga, sauna and massage (charged high season). Pottery. Riding. Satellite TV. Disco. WiFi over part of site (charged). Torches essential. Off site: Excursions.

Open: 14 May - 8 October.

Directions

From Bastia, south on N198, take Porto-Vecchio bypass (Bonofaccio). At southern end, take first left (Pont de la Chiappa) on to unclassified road. After 8 km. site signed. Turn left and follow rough track for 2 km. to site. GPS: 41.59387, 9.35713

Charges guide

Per unit incl. 2 persons and electricity	€ 28.80 - € 38.80
extra person	€ 8.40 - € 10.40

Accommodation

Over recent years many of the campsites featured in this guide have added large numbers of high quality mobile homes and chalets. Many site owners believe that some former caravanners and motorcaravanners have been enticed by the extra comfort they can now provide, and that maybe this is the ideal solution to combine the freedom of camping with all the comforts of home.

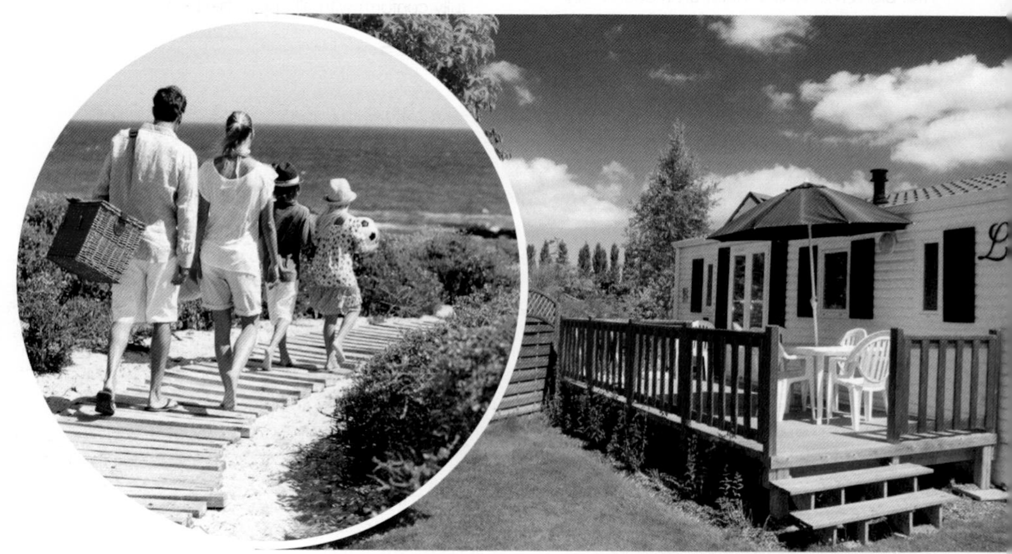

Quality is consistently high and, although the exact size and inventory may vary from site to site, if you choose any of the sites detailed here, you can be sure that you're staying in some of the best quality and best value mobile homes available.

Home comforts are provided and typically these include a fridge with freezer compartment, gas hob, proper shower – often a microwave and radio/cassette hi-fi too, but do check for details. All mobile homes and chalets come fully equipped with a good range of kitchen utensils, pots and pans, crockery, cutlery and outdoor furniture. Some even have an attractive wooden sundeck or paved terrace – a perfect spot for outdoors eating or relaxing with a book and watching the world go by.

Regardless of model, colourful soft furnishings are the norm and a generally breezy décor helps to provide a real holiday feel.

Although some sites may have a large number of different accommodation types, we have restricted our choice to one or two of the most popular accommodation units (either mobile homes or chalets) for each of the sites listed.

The mobile homes here will be of modern design, and recent innovations, for example, often include pitched roofs which substantially improve their appearance.

Design will invariably include clever use of space and fittings/furniture to provide for comfortable holidays – usually light and airy, with big windows and patio-style doors, fully equipped kitchen areas, a shower room with shower, washbasin and WC, cleverly designed bedrooms and a comfortable lounge/dining area (often incorporating a sofa bed).

In general, modern campsite chalets incorporate all the best features of mobile homes in a more traditional structure, sometimes with the advantage of an upper mezzanine floor for an additional bedroom.

Our selected campsites offer a massive range of different types of mobile home and chalet, and it would be impractical to inspect every single accommodation unit. Our selection criteria, therefore, primarily takes account of the quality standards of the campsite itself.

However, there are a couple of important ground rules:

- Featured mobile homes must be no more than five years old
- Chalets no more than ten years old
- All listed accommodation must, of course, fully conform with all applicable local, national and European safety legislation.

For each campsite we have given details of the type, or types, of accommodation available to rent, but these details are necessarily quite brief. Sometimes internal layouts can differ quite substantially, particularly with regard to sleeping arrangements, where these include the flexible provision for 'extra persons' on sofa beds located in the living area. These arrangements may vary from accommodation to accommodation, and if you're planning a holiday which includes more people than are catered for by the main bedrooms you should check exactly how the extra sleeping arrangements are to be provided!

Charges

An indication of the tariff for each type of accommodation featured is also included, indicating the variance between the low and high season tariffs. However, given that many campsites have a large and often complex range of pricing options, incorporating special deals and various discounts, the charges we mention should be taken to be just an indication. We strongly recommend therefore that you confirm the actual cost when making a booking.

We also strongly recommend that you check with the campsite, when booking, what (if anything) will be provided by way of bed linen, blankets, pillows etc. Again, in our experience, this can vary widely from site to site.

On every campsite a fully refundable deposit (usually between 150 and 300 euros) is payable on arrival. There may also be an optional cleaning service for which a further charge is made. Other options may include sheet hire (typically 30 euros per unit) or baby pack hire (cot and high chair).

FR29090 Camping le Raguénès-Plage

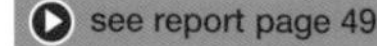
see report page 49

19 rue des Iles, F-29920 Névez (Brittany)

AR1 – VARIANTE – Mobile Home

Sleeping: 2 bedrooms, sleeps 5: 1 double, 3 singles, bunk bed, sofa bed, pillows and blankets provided

Living: heating, TV, shower, WC, separate WC

Eating: fitted kitchen with hobs, oven, microwave, coffee maker, fridge, freezer

Outside: table & chairs, parasol, 2 sun loungers, barbecue

Pets: accepted (with supplement)

AR2 – OHARA – Mobile Home

Sleeping: 2 bedrooms, sleeps 4: 1 double, 2 singles, sofa bed, pillows and blankets provided

Living: heating, TV, shower, WC, separate WC

Eating: fitted kitchen with hobs, microwave, coffee maker, fridge, freezer

Outside: table & chairs, parasol, 2 sun loungers, barbecue

Pets: accepted (with supplement)

Other (AR1 and AR2): bed linen, cot, highchair to hire

Open: 9 April - 30 September

Weekly Charge	AR1	AR2
Low Season **(from)**	€ 336	€ 364
High Season **(from)**	€ 749	€ 798

FR56240 Domaine d'Inly

see report page 50

Route de Couarne, F-56760 Pénestin-sur-Mer (Brittany)

AR1 – COTTAGE CONFORT 4/6 PERS 30m² – Mobile Home

Sleeping: 2 bedrooms, sleeps 6: 2 doubles, 2 singles, sofa bed, pillows and blankets provided

Living: heating, shower, WC, separate WC

Eating: fitted kitchen with hobs, microwave, coffee maker, fridge, freezer

Outside: table & chairs, parasol, 2 sun loungers

Pets: accepted (with supplement)

AR2 – COTTAGE VIP ZEN 4/6 PERS 40m² – Mobile Home

Sleeping: 2 bedrooms, sleeps 6: 2 doubles, 2 singles, bunk bed, sofa bed, pillows and blankets provided

Living: heating, TV, shower, WC, separate WC

Eating: fitted kitchen with hobs, microwave, dishwasher, coffee maker, fridge, freezer

Outside: table & chairs, parasol, 2 sun loungers, barbecue

Pets: accepted (with supplement)

Other (AR1 and AR2): bed linen, cot, highchair to hire

Open: 1 April - 25 September

Weekly Charge	AR1	AR2
Low Season **(from)**	€ 315	€ 595
High Season **(from)**	€ 910	€ 1420

FR27070 Camping l'Ile des Trois Rois

see report page 76

1 rue Gilles Nicolle, F-27700 Les Andelys (Normandy)

AR1 – MOBILE HOME 4 PERS – Mobile Home

Sleeping: 2 bedrooms, sleeps 4: 1 double, 2 singles, pillows and blankets provided

Living: heating, TV, shower, WC, separate WC

Eating: fitted kitchen with hobs, microwave, coffee maker, fridge

Outside: table & chairs, parasol, 1 sun lounger, barbecue

Pets: not accepted

AR2 – MOBILE HOME 6 PERS – Mobile Home

Sleeping: 2 bedrooms, sleeps 6: 2 doubles, 4 singles, pillows and blankets provided

Living: heating, TV, shower, WC, separate WC

Eating: fitted kitchen with hobs, microwave, coffee maker, fridge

Outside: table & chairs, parasol, 1 sun lounger, barbecue

Pets: not accepted

Open: 15 March - 14 November

Weekly Charge	AR1	AR2
Low Season **(from)**	€ 360	€ 405
High Season **(from)**	€ 560	€ 660

FR80150 Camping Airotel Le Walric

see report page 103

345 route d'Eu, F-80230 Saint Valery-sur-Somme (Picardy)

AR1 – 4 COUCHAGES – Mobile Home	AR2 – 6 COUCHAGES – Mobile Home
Sleeping: 2 bedrooms, sleeps 4: 1 double, 2 singles, pillows and blankets provided	Sleeping: 3 bedrooms, sleeps 6: 1 double, 4 singles, pillows and blankets provided
Living: heating, TV, shower, WC, separate WC	Living: heating, TV, shower, WC, separate WC
Eating: fitted kitchen with hobs, microwave, coffee maker, fridge, freezer	Eating: fitted kitchen with hobs, microwave, coffee maker, fridge, freezer
Outside: table & chairs, parasol, barbecue	Outside: table & chairs, parasol, barbecue
Pets: accepted (with supplement)	Pets: accepted (with supplement)

Other (AR1 and AR2): bed linen, cot, highchair to hire

Open: 1 April - 1 November

Weekly Charge	AR1	AR2
Low Season (from)	€ 294	€ 399
High Season (from)	€ 686	€ 791

FR02020 Camping les Etangs du Moulin

see report page 104

F-02320 Suzy (Picardy)

AR1 – ROULOTTE – Roulotte	AR2 – CABANES – Chalet
Sleeping: 3 bedrooms, sleeps 4: 1 double, 2 singles	Sleeping: 2 bedrooms, sleeps 5: 1 double, 3 singles, pillows and blankets provided
Living: heating, shower, WC	Living: heating, TV, shower, WC, separate WC
Eating: fitted kitchen with hobs, microwave, coffee maker, fridge	Eating: fitted kitchen with hobs, microwave, coffee maker, fridge
Outside: table & chairs, 2 sun loungers, barbecue	Outside: table & chairs, 2 sun loungers, barbecue
Pets: accepted (with supplement)	Pets: accepted (with supplement)

Other (AR1 and AR2): cot to hire

Open: All year

Weekly Charge	AR1	AR2
Low Season (from)	€ 287	€ 441
High Season (from)	€ 448	€ 686

FR41070 Camping la Grande Tortue

see report page 138

3 route de Pontlevoy, F-41120 Candé-sur-Beuvron (Val de Loire)

AR1 – IRM SUPER MERCURE – Mobile Home	AR2 – LOUISIANE ZEN – Mobile Home
Sleeping: 2 bedrooms, sleeps 4: 1 double, 2 singles, pillows and blankets provided	Sleeping: 3 bedrooms, sleeps 6: 1 double, 4 singles, bunk bed, pillows and blankets provided
Living: heating, shower, separate WC	Living: heating, shower, separate WC
Eating: fitted kitchen with hobs, microwave, coffee maker, fridge	Eating: fitted kitchen with hobs, microwave, coffee maker, fridge, freezer
Outside: table & chairs, parasol, 2 sun loungers	Outside: table & chairs, parasol, 2 sun loungers
Pets: accepted (with supplement)	Pets: accepted (with supplement)

Other (AR1 and AR2): bed linen, cot, highchair to hire

Open: 11 April - 21 September

Weekly Charge	AR1	AR2
Low Season (from)	€ 407	€ 639
High Season (from)	€ 837	€ 930

FR45030 Sites et Paysages Camping de Gien

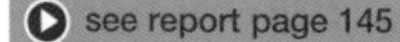
see report page 145

Rue des Iris, F-45500 Poilly-lez-Gien (Val de Loire)

AR1 – LOUSIANA OHARA – Mobile Home	AR2 – ROULOTTE DE CAMPAGNE – Roulotte
Sleeping: 3 bedrooms, sleeps 8: 1 double, 4 singles, sofa bed, pillows and blankets provided	Sleeping: 1 bedroom, sleeps 5: 1 double, 3 singles, sofa bed, pillows and blankets provided
Living: heating, shower, WC, separate WC	Living: heating, shower, WC
Eating: fitted kitchen with microwave, coffee maker, fridge, freezer	Eating: fitted kitchen with microwave, coffee maker, fridge, freezer
Outside: table & chairs, parasol, barbecue	Outside: table & chairs, parasol, 1 sun lounger, barbecue
Pets: not accepted	Pets: not accepted

Other (AR1 and AR2): bed linen, cot, highchair to hire

Open: 12 March - 31 October

Weekly Charge	AR1	AR2
Low Season (from)	€ 250	€ 400
High Season (from)	€ 600	€ 575

FR44220 Le Domaine de Léveno

see report page 155

Lieu-dit Léveno, F-44350 Guérande (Pays de la Loire)

AR1 – COTTAGE CONFORT – Mobile Home	AR2 – COTTAGE CONFORT – Mobile Home
Sleeping: 2 bedrooms, sleeps 6: 1 double, 2 singles, sofa bed, pillows and blankets provided	Sleeping: 3 bedrooms, sleeps 6: 1 double, 4 singles, pillows and blankets provided
Living: heating, shower, separate WC	Living: shower, separate WC
Eating: fitted kitchen with hobs, fridge	Eating: fitted kitchen with hobs, fridge
Outside: table & chairs, parasol	Outside: table & chairs, parasol
Pets: accepted (with supplement)	Pets: accepted (with supplement)

Other (AR1 and AR2): bed linen, cot, highchair to hire

Open: 7 April - 29 September

Weekly Charge	AR1	AR2
Low Season (from)	€ 315	€ 350
High Season (from)	€ 875	€ 903

FR44210 Camping de l'Océan

see report page 160

15 route de la Maison Rouge, F-44490 Le Croisic (Pays de la Loire)

AR1 – COTTAGE OCEAN ESPACE – Mobile Home	AR2 – COTTAGE OCEAN GRAND CONFORT ZEN 35m² – Mobile Home
Sleeping: 2 bedrooms, sleeps 4: 1 double, 2 singles, pillows and blankets provided	Sleeping: 2 bedrooms, sleeps 6: 2 doubles, 2 singles, sofa bed, pillows and blankets provided
Living: heating, shower, WC, separate WC	Living: heating, TV, shower, WC, separate WC
Eating: fitted kitchen with hobs, microwave, coffee maker, fridge	Eating: fitted kitchen with hobs, oven, microwave, grill, coffee maker, fridge
Outside: table & chairs, parasol	Outside: table & chairs, parasol, 2 sun loungers, barbecue
Pets: accepted (with supplement)	Pets: accepted (with supplement)

Other (AR1 and AR2): bed linen, cot, highchair to hire

Open: 1 April - 25 September

Weekly Charge	AR1	AR2
Low Season (from)	€ 329	€ 504
High Season (from)	€ 900	€ 1380

FR44180 Camping de la Boutinardière

see report page 165

Rue de la Plage de la Boutinardière 23, F-44210 Pornic (Pays de la Loire)

AR1 – COTTAGE 5 PERSONS – Mobile Home	**AR2 – COTTAGE 6 PERSONS – Mobile Home**
Sleeping: 2 bedrooms, sleeps 5: 1 double, 2 singles, sofa bed, pillows and blankets provided	Sleeping: 3 bedrooms, sleeps 6: 1 double, 4 singles, pillows and blankets provided
Living: heating, TV, shower, WC, separate WC	Living: heating, TV, shower, WC, separate WC
Eating: fitted kitchen with hobs, microwave, coffee maker, fridge, freezer	Eating: fitted kitchen with hobs, microwave, coffee maker, fridge, freezer
Outside: table & chairs, parasol, 2 sun loungers, barbecue	Outside: table & chairs, parasol, 2 sun loungers, barbecue
Pets: accepted (with supplement)	Pets: accepted (with supplement)

Other (AR1 and AR2): bed linen, cot, highchair to hire

Open: 2 April - 1 October

Weekly Charge	AR1	AR2
Low Season (from)	€ 260	€ 440
High Season (from)	€ 950	€ 1100

FR17010 Camping Bois Soleil

see report page 222

2 avenue de Suzac, F-17110 Saint Georges-de-Didonne (Poitou-Charentes)

AR1 – COTTAGE PRESTIGE – Mobile Home	**AR2 – COTTAGE MER – Mobile Home**
Sleeping: 3 bedrooms, sleeps 6: 1 double, 4 singles, pillows and blankets provided	Sleeping: 2 bedrooms, sleeps 4: 1 double, 2 singles, pillows and blankets provided
Living: heating, TV, air conditioning, shower, WC, separate WC	Living: heating, TV, air conditioning, shower, WC, separate WC
Eating: fitted kitchen with hobs, oven, microwave, grill, dishwasher, coffee maker, fridge, freezer	Eating: fitted kitchen with hobs, microwave, coffee maker, fridge, freezer
Outside: table & chairs, parasol, 2 sun loungers	Outside: table & chairs, parasol
Pets: not accepted	Pets: not accepted

Other (AR1 and AR2): bed linen, cot, highchair to hire

Open: 1 April - 8 October

Weekly Charge	AR1	AR2
Low Season (from)	€ 600	€ 350
High Season (from)	€ 1350	€ 980

FR71070 Castel Camping Château de l'Epervière

see report page 237

6 rue du Château, F-71240 Gigny-sur-Saône (Burgundy)

AR1 – LOUISIANE PACIFIQUE 3XL – Mobile home	**AR2 – CHATEAU GITE – Gîte**
Sleeping: 3 bedrooms, sleeps 6: 1 double, 4 singles, pillows and blankets provided	Sleeping: 2 bedrooms, sleeps 5: 1 double, 3 singles, bunk bed, pillows and blankets provided
Living: heating, TV, shower, separate WC	Living: heating, TV, shower, WC
Eating: fitted kitchen with hobs, microwave, dishwasher, coffee maker, fridge, freezer	Eating: fitted kitchen with hobs, oven, microwave, dishwasher, coffee maker, fridge, freezer
Outside: table & chairs, parasol, 2 sun loungers	Outside: table & chairs, parasol
Pets: not accepted	Pets: not accepted

Other (AR1 and AR2): bed linen, cot, highchair to hire

Open: 1 April - 30 September

Weekly Charge	AR1	AR2
Low Season (from)	€ 459	€ 479
High Season (from)	€ 899	€ 909

FR40100 Resort & Spa La Rive

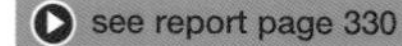
see report page 330

Route de Bordeaux, F-40600 Biscarrosse (Aquitaine)

AR1 – KEY WEST – Mobile Home	AR2 – DUO VIP – Mobile Home
Sleeping: 2 bedrooms, sleeps 4: 1 double, 1 single, pillows and blankets provided	Sleeping: 3 bedrooms, sleeps 8: 2 doubles, 3 singles, sofa bed, pillows and blankets provided
Living: heating, TV, shower, WC, separate WC	Living: heating, TV, shower, WC, separate WC
Eating: fitted kitchen with hobs, microwave, dishwasher, coffee maker, fridge, freezer	Eating: fitted kitchen with hobs, microwave, dishwasher, coffee maker, fridge, freezer
Outside: table & chairs, parasol, 2 sun loungers	Outside: table & chairs, parasol, 2 sun loungers
Pets: not accepted	Pets: not accepted

Other (AR1 and AR2): bed linen, cot, highchair to hire

Open: 2 April - 31 August

Weekly Charge	AR1	AR2
Low Season (from)	€ 1003	€ 1255
High Season (from)	€ 1997	€ 2305

FR33110 Airotel Camping de la Côte d'Argent

see report page 338

F-33990 Hourtin-Plage (Aquitaine)

AR1 – ALIZE – Mobile Home	AR2 – DUNE – Mobile Home
Sleeping: 2 bedrooms, sleeps 6: 2 doubles, 2 singles, sofa bed, pillows and blankets provided	Sleeping: 3 bedrooms, sleeps 8: 2 doubles, 4 singles, bunk bed, sofa bed, pillows and blankets provided
Living: shower, WC	Living: shower, WC
Eating: fitted kitchen with hobs, microwave, coffee maker, fridge, freezer	Eating: fitted kitchen with hobs, microwave, dishwasher, coffee maker, fridge, freezer
Outside: table & chairs, 2 sun loungers	Outside: table & chairs, 2 sun loungers
Pets: not accepted	Pets: not accepted

Other (AR1 and AR2): bed linen, cot, highchair to hire

Open: 13 May - 18 September

Weekly Charge	AR1	AR2
Low Season (from)	€ 260	€ 472
High Season (from)	€ 1190	€ 1883

FR40250 Camping les Grands Pins

see report page 362

1039 avenue de Losa, F-40460 Sanguinet (Aquitaine)

AR1 – COTTAGE TIVY 2 CH 4/6 PLACES – Mobile Home	AR2 – ROULOTTE 4 PLACES – Roulotte
Sleeping: 2 bedrooms, sleeps 6: 2 doubles, 2 singles, sofa bed, pillows and blankets provided	Sleeping: 2 bedrooms, sleeps 4: 1 double, 2 singles, bunk bed, pillows and blankets provided
Living: heating, TV, shower, WC, separate WC	Living: heating, shower, WC, separate WC
Eating: fitted kitchen with hobs, microwave, coffee maker, fridge, freezer	Eating: fitted kitchen with hobs, microwave, coffee maker, freezer
Outside: table & chairs, parasol, 1 sun lounger	Outside: table & chairs, parasol
Pets: not accepted	Pets: not accepted

Other (AR1 and AR2): bed linen, cot, highchair to hire

Open: 2 April - 25 September

Weekly Charge	AR1	AR2
Low Season (from)	€ 488	€ 412
High Season (from)	€ 1232	€ 1120

FR66070 Yelloh! Village le Brasilia

see report page 415

2 avenue Anneaux du Roussillon, F-66141 Canet-en-Roussillon (Languedoc-Roussillon)

AR1 – OKAVANGO – Mobile Home

Sleeping: 2 bedrooms, sleeps 5: 1 double, 3 singles, bunk bed, pillows and blankets provided

Living: heating, TV, shower, WC, separate WC

Eating: fitted kitchen with hobs, microwave, grill, coffee maker, fridge, freezer

Outside: table & chairs, parasol, 2 sun loungers

Pets: not accepted

AR2 – LES CRÉOLES – Mobile Home

Sleeping: 3 bedrooms, sleeps 6: 1 double, 4 singles, pillows and blankets provided

Living: heating, TV, air conditioning, shower, WC, separate WC

Eating: fitted kitchen with hobs, microwave, grill, dishwasher, coffee maker, fridge, freezer

Outside: table & chairs, parasol, 2 sun loungers

Pets: not accepted

Other (AR1 and AR2): bed linen, cot, highchair to hire

Open: 23 April - 8 October

Weekly Charge	AR1	AR2
Low Season (from)	€ 413	€ 595
High Season (from)	€ 1295	€ 1995

FR34070 Yelloh! Village le Sérignan-Plage

see report page 434

Le Sérignan Plage, F-34410 Sérignan-Plage Dept

AR1 – CHALET ORPELLIERES – Chalet

Sleeping: 2 bedrooms, sleeps 5: 1 double, 2 singles, bunk bed, pillows and blankets provided

Living: heating, TV, air conditioning, shower, WC, separate WC

Eating: fitted kitchen with hobs, microwave, dishwasher, coffee maker, fridge, freezer

Outside: table & chairs, 2 sun loungers

Pets: not accepted

AR2 – COTTAGE CABANE – Mobile home

Sleeping: 3 bedrooms, sleeps 6: 1 double, 2 singles, bunk bed, pillows and blankets provided

Living: heating, TV, air conditioning, shower, WC, separate WC

Eating: fitted kitchen with hobs, microwave, dishwasher, coffee maker, fridge, freezer

Outside: table & chairs, 2 sun loungers

Pets: not accepted

Other (AR1 and AR2): bed linen, cot, highchair to hire

Open: 23 April - 28 September

Weekly Charge	AR1	AR2
Low Season (from)	€ 413	€ 518
High Season (from)	€ 1687	€ 2198

FR04020 Castel Camping le Domaine du Verdon

see report page 455

Camp du Verdon, F-04120 Castellane (Provence)

AR1 – STANDARD – Mobile Home

Sleeping: 2 bedrooms, sleeps 4: 1 double, 2 singles, sofa bed, pillows and blankets provided

Living: heating, shower, WC, separate WC

Eating: fitted kitchen with hobs, microwave, coffee maker, fridge

Outside: table & chairs, 2 sun loungers

Pets: accepted (with supplement)

AR2 – CONFORT – Mobile Home

Sleeping: 2 bedrooms, sleeps 4: 1 double, 2 singles, sofa bed, pillows and blankets provided

Living: heating, shower, WC, separate WC

Eating: fitted kitchen with hobs, microwave, coffee maker, fridge

Outside: table & chairs, 2 sun loungers

Pets: accepted (with supplement)

Other (AR1 and AR2): bed linen, cot, highchair to hire

Open: 13 May - 15 September

Weekly Charge	AR1	AR2
Low Season (from)	€ 364	€ 406
High Season (from)	€ 847	€ 917

FR83060 Camping Resort la Baume la Palmeraie

see report page 460

3775 rue des Combattants d'Afrique du Nord, F-83618 Fréjus Dept

AR1 – BASTIDON 3 BEDROOMS – Bungalow

Sleeping: 3 bedrooms, sleeps 8: 1 double, 4 singles, bunk bed, sofa bed, pillows and blankets provided

Living: heating, TV, air conditioning, shower, WC, separate WC

Eating: fitted kitchen with hobs, microwave, grill, dishwasher, coffee maker, fridge, freezer

Outside: table & chairs, parasol, 4 sun loungers

Pets: not accepted

AR2 – ACAJOU 3 BEDROOMS – Mobile Home

Sleeping: 3 bedrooms, sleeps 6: 1 double, 4 singles, sofa bed, pillows and blankets provided

Living: heating, TV, air conditioning, shower, WC, separate WC

Eating: fitted kitchen with hobs, microwave, grill, dishwasher, coffee maker, fridge, freezer

Outside: table & chairs, parasol, 2 sun loungers, barbecue

Pets: not accepted

Other (AR1 and AR2): bed linen, cot, highchair to hire

Open: 26 March - 1 October

Weekly Charge	AR1	AR2
Low Season (from)	€ 497	€ 560
High Season (from)	€ 1680	€ 2030

Open All Year

The following sites are understood to accept caravanners and campers all year round. It is always wise to phone the site to check as the facilities available, for example, may be reduced.

Nord-Pas de Calais

FR62120	Eté Indien	93

Paris-Ile de France

FR75020	Indigo Paris	108
FR91010	Paris Beau Village	111

Champagne-Ardenne

FR08170	Motte	118

Lorraine

FR88050	Champé	121
FR88400	Gadémont Plage	123
FR88040	Lac de Bouzey	125
FR88090	Lac de la Moselotte	126

Alsace

FR68140	Bouleaux	132
FR67060	Indigo Strasbourg	133

Val de Loire

FR37210	Acacias	141

Pays de la Loire

FR44010	Nantes	163
FR44430	Pindière	155

Vendée

FR85045	Ambois	181
FR85540	Eden	173
FR85345	Grisse	179

Poitou-Charentes

FR86040	Futuriste	221
FR16080	Laurent	224
FR16130	Paradis	214

Burgundy

FR21090	Arquebuse	231

Limousin

FR87150	Montréal	257

Auvergne

FR63060	Clos Auroy	268
FR63210	Haute Sioule	269

Rhône Alpes

FR74230	Giffre	310
FR69010	Indigo Lyon	286

Aquitaine

FR33410	Bordeaux Lac	332
FR47110	Cabri	337
FR64040	Gaves	344
FR64180	Larrouleta	371
FR24960	Moulin de la Jarousse	344
FR33090	Pressoir	353

Midi-Pyrénées

FR82020	Bois Redon	401
FR65080	Lavedan	378

Languedoc-Roussillon

FR34715	Clairettes	417
FR34630	Hermitage	440
FR34980	Sainte Veziane	412
FR11110	Val d'Aleth	409

Provence/Côte d'Azur

FR84160	Bagatelle	452
FR13120	Chantecler	451
FR06050	Vieille Ferme	489

Corsica

FR20080	Bagheera (Naturist)	511
FR20040	Riva Bella (Naturist 16/5-29/9)	511

Dogs

Many British campers and caravanners prefer to take their pets with them on holiday. However, pet travel rules changed on 1 January 2012 when the UK brought its procedures into line with the European Union. From this date all pets can enter or re-enter the UK from any country in the world without quarantine provided they meet the rules of the scheme, which will be different depending on the country or territory the pet is coming from. Please refer to the following website for full details: www.gov.uk/take-pet-abroad

For the benefit of those who want to take their dogs to France, we list here the sites which have indicated to us that they do not accept dogs or have certain restrictions. If you are planning to take your dog we do advise you to phone the site first to check – there may be limits on numbers, breeds, or times of the year when they are excluded.

Never – sites that do not accept dogs at any time:

Brittany

FR29350	Atlantique	48

Normandy

FR14090	Brévedent	75

Alsace

FR68080	ClairVacances	133
FR67040	Ferme des Tuileries	132

Val de Loire

FR41020	Grenouillère	147
FR36220	Petite Brenne (Naturist)	500

Vendée

FR85020	Jard	178
FR85030	Loubine	183
FR85060	Pas Opton	179

Poitou-Charentes

FR17750	Côte Sauvage	208
FR16020	Gorges du Chambon	215

Rhône Alpes

FR26090	Truffières	289

Aquitaine

FR24050	Hauts de Ratebout	325
FR24040	Moulin du Roch	365
FR40040	Paillotte	323
FR24060	Paradis	351
FR64060	Pavillon Royal	327

Midi-Pyrénées

FR46040	Moulin de Laborde	392

Languedoc-Roussillon

FR30160	Boucanet	422
FR66040	Soleil	410

Provence/Côte d'Azur

FR84020	Bélézy (Naturist)	509
FR06060	Haut Chandelalar	509
FR83720	Pachacaïd	468

Corsica

FR20030	Merendella	497
FR20220	Oliviers	495

Sometimes – sites that accept dogs but with certain restrictions:

Brittany

FR29470	2 Fontaines	48
FR56260	Conguel	56
FR29430	Escale Saint-Gilles	28
FR29290	Grand Large (Fouesnant)	48
FR56120	Iles Pénestin	50
FR29940	Indigo Douarnenez	37
FR29000	Mouettes	31
FR29500	Plage Bénodet	29
FR22130	Port l'Epine	65
FR22000	Vallées	58

Normandy

FR50060	Grand Large (Les Pieux)	79
FR14070	Vallée (Houlgate)	74

Paris-Ile de France

FR78040	Huttopia Rambouillet	109
FR78060	Huttopia Versailles	111
FR75020	Indigo Paris	108

Champagne-Ardenne

FR10020	Lac d'Orient	117

Alsace

FR68110	Colmar	130
FR67060	Indigo Strasbourg	133

Val de Loire

FR45010	Bois du Bardelet	141
FR37140	Huttopia Rillé	145
FR28140	Huttopia Senonches	146
FR41120	Indigo Châteaux	137

Pays de la Loire

FR72040 Indigo Molières 168

Vendée

FR85500 Bahamas Beach 185
FR85870 Baie d'Aunis 177
FR85710 Bel Air 179
FR85385 Bellevue (Vendée) 184
FR85580 Blancs Chênes 178
FR85400 Bois Soleil 184
FR85430 Bolée d'Air 196
FR85440 Brunelles 181
FR85480 Chaponnet 173
FR85495 Cyprès 185
FR85013 Dive 195
FR85770 Ferme du Latois 175
FR85930 Forges 172
FR85030 Loubine 183
FR85110 Océan 173
FR85270 Océano d'Or 175
FR85280 Places Dorées 190
FR85310 Trévillière 174
FR85150 Yole 189

Poitou-Charentes

FR17010 Bois Soleil 222
FR17856 Camping les Chardons Bleus 227
FR17325 Etangs Mina 225
FR17985 Indigo Chênes Verts 204
FR17580 Indigo Oléron 226
FR17470 Oléron 220
FR17050 Orée du Bois 211
FR17290 Peupliers 207
FR17740 Pinède 213
FR17857 Sainte Marie de Ré 227
FR17600 Signol 202
FR17390 Varennes 209

Franche-Comté

FR39010 Indigo Plage Blanche 249
FR25000 Val de Bonnal 250

Limousin

FR87100 Alouettes 256
FR23010 Château Poinsouze 255
FR19130 Indigo Beaulieu 254

Auvergne

FR63120 Indigo Royat 268
FR15060 Pont du Rouffet 270
FR63070 Pré Bas 265
FR63050 Ribeyre 265

Rhône Alpes

FR07280 Arches 306
FR07080 Bastide 311
FR38100 Belledonne 279
FR38120 Bontemps 317
FR73020 Bourg-Saint-Maurice 280
FR74060 Colombière 298
FR26340 Couriou 301
FR07260 Cruses 291
FR01170 Divonne - Fleutron 287
FR26200 Ecluse 281
FR07150 Gil 277
FR26030 Grand Lierne 281
FR26580 Huttopia Dieulefit 286
FR07475 Huttopia Sud Ardèche 314
FR69010 Indigo Lyon 286
FR07650 Indigo Moulin 308
FR26150 Lac Bleu 283
FR01110 Nid du Parc 317
FR07070 Ranchisses 293
FR74250 Rives du Lac 312
FR26220 Soleil Fruité 283
FR07030 Soleil Vivarais 311

Aquitaine

FR40540 Boudigau 342
FR64170 Erromardie 359
FR40250 Grands Pins 362
FR24415 Huttopia Lanmary 321
FR24030 Indigo Sarlat Perières 364
FR33860 Lac de Carcans 333
FR40070 Lous Seurrots 360
FR40470 Moisan 349
FR24350 Moulin de la Pique 325
FR24290 Moulin du Bleufond 352
FR24100 Moulinal 328
FR24640 Nontron 352
FR33050 Ourmes 340
FR33040 Pinèda 334
FR33210 Pointe du Medoc 346
FR33320 Talaris 342
FR33290 Tedey 343
FR24315 Trémolat 370

Midi-Pyrénées

FR46190 Faurie 400
FR12070 Grange de Monteillac 402
FR46310 Granges 404
FR12350 Indigo Millau 391
FR32060 Trois Vallées 384

Languedoc-Roussillon

FR30070 Boisson 413
FR66290 Floride l'Embouchure 421
FR66490 Garenne 428
FR66050 Haras 428
FR66250 Huttopia Font-Romeu 418
FR66060 Littoral 411
FR66170 Mar I Sol 437
FR30080 Mas de Reilhe 417
FR34130 Neptune 407
FR66100 Pergola 433
FR66470 Presqu'île 428
FR34970 Sablettes 408
FR30140 Soubeyranne 430

Provence/Côte d'Azur

FR83040 Bastiane 474
FR84140 Beauregard 472
FR05470 Clarée 486
FR83120 Domaine 453
FR04250 Gorges du Verdon 456
FR04120 Indigo Forcalquier 459
FR05440 Indigo Vallouise 487
FR13140 Marius 471
FR83320 Mogador 484
FR04140 Prairies 484
FR83680 Saint Pons 469

Travelling in Europe

When taking your car (and caravan, tent or trailer tent) or motorcaravan to the continent you do need to plan in advance and to find out as much as possible about driving in the countries you plan to visit. Whilst European harmonisation has eliminated many of the differences between one country and another, it is well worth reading the short notes we provide in the introduction to each country in this guide in addition to this more general summary.

Of course, the main difference from driving in the UK is that in mainland Europe you will need to drive on the right. Without taking extra time and care, especially at busy junctions and conversely when roads are empty, it is easy to forget to drive on the right. Remember that traffic approaching from the right usually has priority unless otherwise indicated by road markings and signs. Harmonisation also means that most (but not all) common road signs are the same in all countries.

Your vehicle

Book your vehicle in for a good service well before your intended departure date. This will lessen the chance of an expensive breakdown. Make sure your brakes are working efficiently and that your tyres have plenty of tread (3 mm. is recommended, particularly if you are undertaking a long journey).

Also make sure that your caravan or trailer is roadworthy and that its tyres are in good order and correctly inflated. Plan your packing and be careful not to overload your vehicle, caravan or trailer – this is unsafe and may well invalidate your insurance cover (it must not be more fully loaded than the kerb weight of the insured vehicle).

There are a number of countries that have introduced low emission zones in towns and cities, including Germany, Czech Republic, Denmark, Italy and Sweden. For up-to-date-details on low emission zones and requirements please see: www.lowemissionzones.eu

CHECK ALL THE FOLLOWING:

- GB sticker. If you do not display a sticker, you may risk an on-the-spot fine as this identifier is compulsory in all countries. Euro-plates are an acceptable alternative within the EU (but not outside). Remember to attach another sticker (or Euro-plate) to caravans and trailers. Only GB stickers (not England, Scotland, Wales or N. Ireland) stickers are valid in the EU.
- Headlights. As you will be driving on the right you must adjust your headlights so that the dipped beam does not dazzle oncoming drivers. Converter kits are readily available for most vehicles, although if your car is fitted with high intensity headlights, you should check with your motor dealer. Check that any planned extra loading does not affect the beam height.
- Seatbelts. Rules for the fitting and wearing of seatbelts throughout Europe are similar to those in the UK, but it is worth checking before you go. Rules for carrying children in the front of vehicles vary from country to country. It is best to plan not to do this if possible.
- Door/wing mirrors. To help with driving on the right, if your vehicle is not fitted with a mirror on the left hand side, we recommend you have one fitted.
- Fuel. Leaded and Lead Replacement petrol is increasingly difficult to find in Northern Europe.

Compulsory additional equipment

The driving laws of the countries of Europe still vary in what you are required to carry in your vehicle, although the consequences of not carrying a required piece of equipment are almost always an on-the-spot fine.

To meet these requirements you should make sure that you carry the following:

- FIRE EXTINGUISHER
- BASIC TOOL KIT
- FIRST AID KIT
- SPARE BULBS
- TWO WARNING TRIANGLES – two are required in some countries at all times, and are compulsory in most countries when towing.
- HIGH VISIBILITY VEST – now compulsory in France, Spain, Italy and Austria (and likely to become compulsory throughout the EU) in case you need to walk on a motorway.
- BREATHALYSERS – now compulsory in France. Only breathalysers that are NF-approved will meet the legal requirement. French law states that one breathalyser must be produced, but it is recommended you carry two in case you use or break one.

Insurance and Motoring Documents

Vehicle insurance

Contact your insurer well before you depart to check that your car insurance policy covers driving outside the UK. Most do, but many policies only provide minimum cover (so if you have an accident your insurance may only cover the cost of damage to the other person's property, with no cover for fire and theft).

To maintain the same level of cover abroad as you enjoy at home you need to tell your vehicle insurer. Some will automatically cover you abroad with no extra cost and no extra paperwork. Some will say you need a Green Card (which is neither green nor on card) but won't charge for it. Some will charge extra for the Green Card. Ideally you should contact your vehicle insurer 3-4 weeks before you set off, and confirm your conversation with them in writing.

Breakdown insurance

Arrange breakdown cover for your trip in good time so that if your vehicle breaks down or is involved in an accident it (and your caravan or trailer) can be repaired or returned to this country. This cover can usually be arranged as part of your travel insurance policy (see below).

Documents you must take with you

You may be asked to show your documents at any time so make sure that they are in order, up-to-date and easily accessible while you travel.

These are what you need to take:

- Passports (you may also need a visa in some countries if you hold either a UK passport not issued in the UK or a passport that was issued outside the EU).
- Motor Insurance Certificate, including Green Card (or Continental Cover clause)
- DVLA Vehicle Registration Document plus, if not your own vehicle, the owner's written authority to drive.
- A full valid Driving Licence (not provisional). The new photo style licence is now mandatory in most European countries.

Personal Holiday insurance

Even though you are just travelling within Europe you must take out travel insurance. Few EU countries pay the full cost of medical treatment even under reciprocal health service arrangements. The first part of a holiday insurance policy covers people. It will include the cost of doctor, ambulance and hospital treatment if needed. If needed the better companies will even pay for English language speaking doctors and nurses and will bring a sick or injured holidaymaker home by air ambulance.

An important part of the insurance, often ignored, is cancellation (and curtailment) cover. Few things are as heartbreaking as having to cancel a holiday because a member of the family falls ill. Cancellation insurance can't take away the disappointment, but it makes sure you don't suffer financially as well. For this reason you should arrange your holiday insurance at least eight weeks before you set off.

Whichever insurance you choose we would advise reading very carefully the policies sold by the High Street travel trade. Whilst they may be good, they may not cover the specific needs of campers, caravanners and motorcaravanners.

Telephone 01580 214000 for a quote for our Camping Travel Insurance with cover arranged through leading leisure insurance providers.
Alternatively visit our website at: alanrogers.com/insurance

European Health Insurance Card (EHIC)

Make sure you apply for your EHIC before travelling in Europe. Eligible travellers from the UK are entitled to receive free or reduced-cost medical care in many European countries on production of an EHIC. This free card is available by completing a form in the booklet 'Health Advice for Travellers' from local Post Offices. One should be completed for each family member. Alternatively visit www.ehic.org.uk and apply on-line. Please allow time to send your application off and have the EHIC returned to you.

The EHIC is valid in all European Community countries plus Iceland, Liechtenstein, Switzerland and Norway. If you or any of your dependants are suddenly taken ill or have an accident during a visit to any of these countries, free or reduced-cost emergency treatment is available – in most cases on production of a valid EHIC.

Only state-provided emergency treatment is covered, and you will receive treatment on the same terms as nationals of the country you are visiting. Private treatment is generally not covered, and state-provided treatment may not cover all of the things that you would expect to receive free of charge from the NHS.

Remember an EHIC does not cover you for all the medical costs that you can incur or for repatriation - it is not an alternative to travel insurance. You will still need appropriate insurance to ensure you are fully covered for all eventualities.

Travelling with children

Most countries in Europe are enforcing strict guidelines when you are travelling with children who are not your own. A minor (under the age of 18) must be accompanied by a parent or legal guardian or must carry a letter of authorisation from a parent or guardian. The letter should name the adult responsible for the minor during his or her stay. Similarly, a minor travelling with just one of his/her parents, must have a letter of authority to leave their home country from the parent staying behind. Full information is available at www.fco.gov.uk

Getting the most from **off peak touring**

There are many reasons to avoid high season, if you can. Queues are shorter, there's less traffic, a calmer atmosphere and prices are cheaper. And it's usually still nice and sunny!

And when you use Camping Cheques you'll find great quality facilities that are actually open and a welcoming conviviality.

Did you know?

Camping Cheques can be used right into mid-July and from late August on many sites. Over 90 campsites in France alone accept Camping Cheques from 20th August.

Save up to 60% with Camping Cheques

Camping Cheque is a fixed price scheme allowing you to go as you please, staying on over 600 campsites across Europe, always paying the same rate and saving you up to 60% on regular pitch fees. One Cheque gives you one night for 2 people + unit on a standard pitch, with electricity. It's as simple as that.

Special offers mean you can stay extra nights free (eg 7 nights for 6 Cheques) or even a month free for a month paid! Especially popular in Spain during the winter, these longer-term offers can effectively halve the nightly rate. See Site Directory for details.

Check out our amazing Ferry Deals!

Why should I use Camping Cheques?

- It's a proven system, recognised by all 600+ participating campsites - so no nasty surprises.
- It's flexible, allowing you to travel between campsites, and also countries, on a whim - so no need to pre-book. (It's low season, so campsites are rarely full, though advance bookings can be made).
- Stay as long as you like, where you like - so you travel in complete freedom.
- Camping Cheques are valid at least 2 years - so no pressure to use them up. (If you have a couple left over after your trip, simply keep them for the following year, or use them up in the UK).

Tell me more... (but keep it brief!)

Camping Cheques was started in 1999 and has since grown in popularity each year (nearly 2 million were used last year). That should speak for itself. There are 'copycat' schemes, but none has the same range of quality campsites that save you up to 60%.

Ask for your **FREE** continental road map, which explains how Camping Cheque works

01342 336621

Order your 2016

Directory

campingcheque.co.uk

alan rogers

Been to any good campsites lately?

We have

You'll find them here...

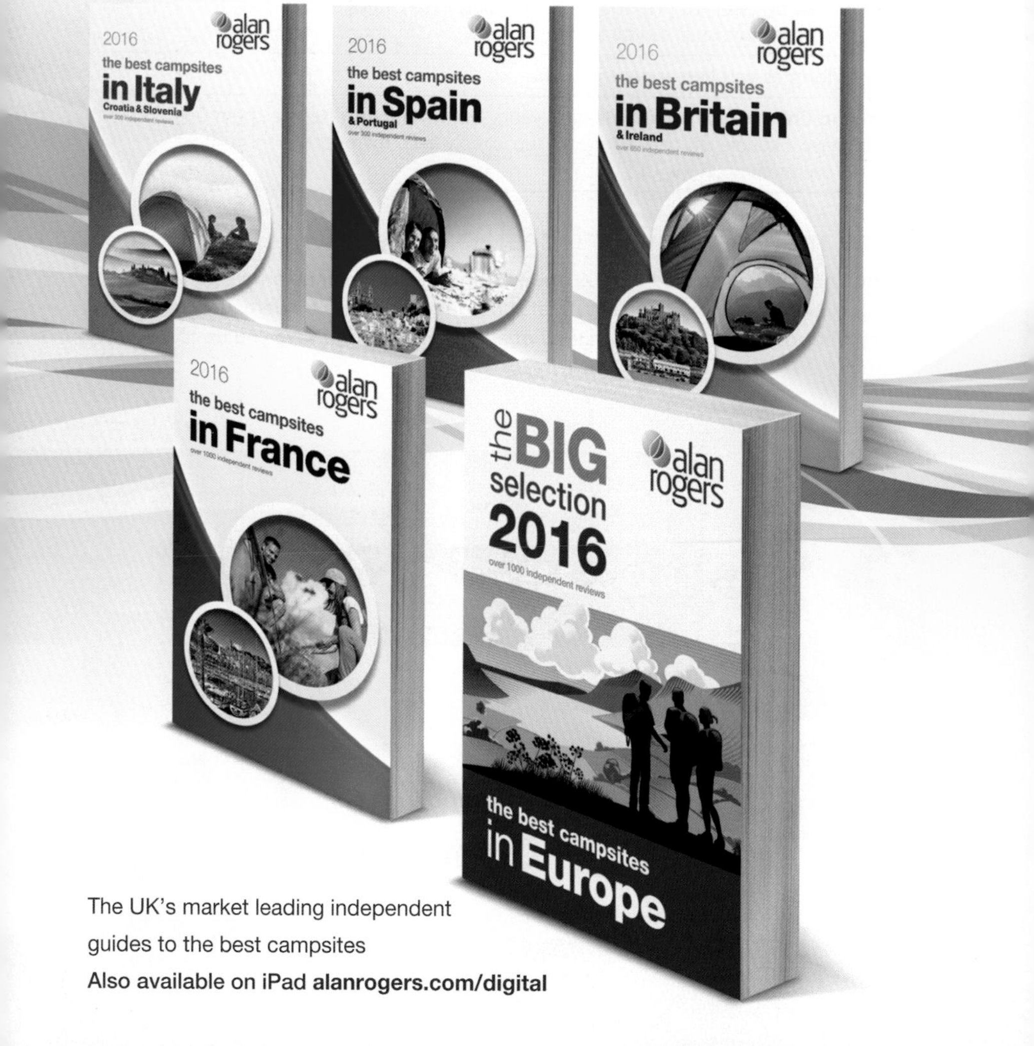

The UK's market leading independent
guides to the best campsites
Also available on iPad **alanrogers.com/digital**

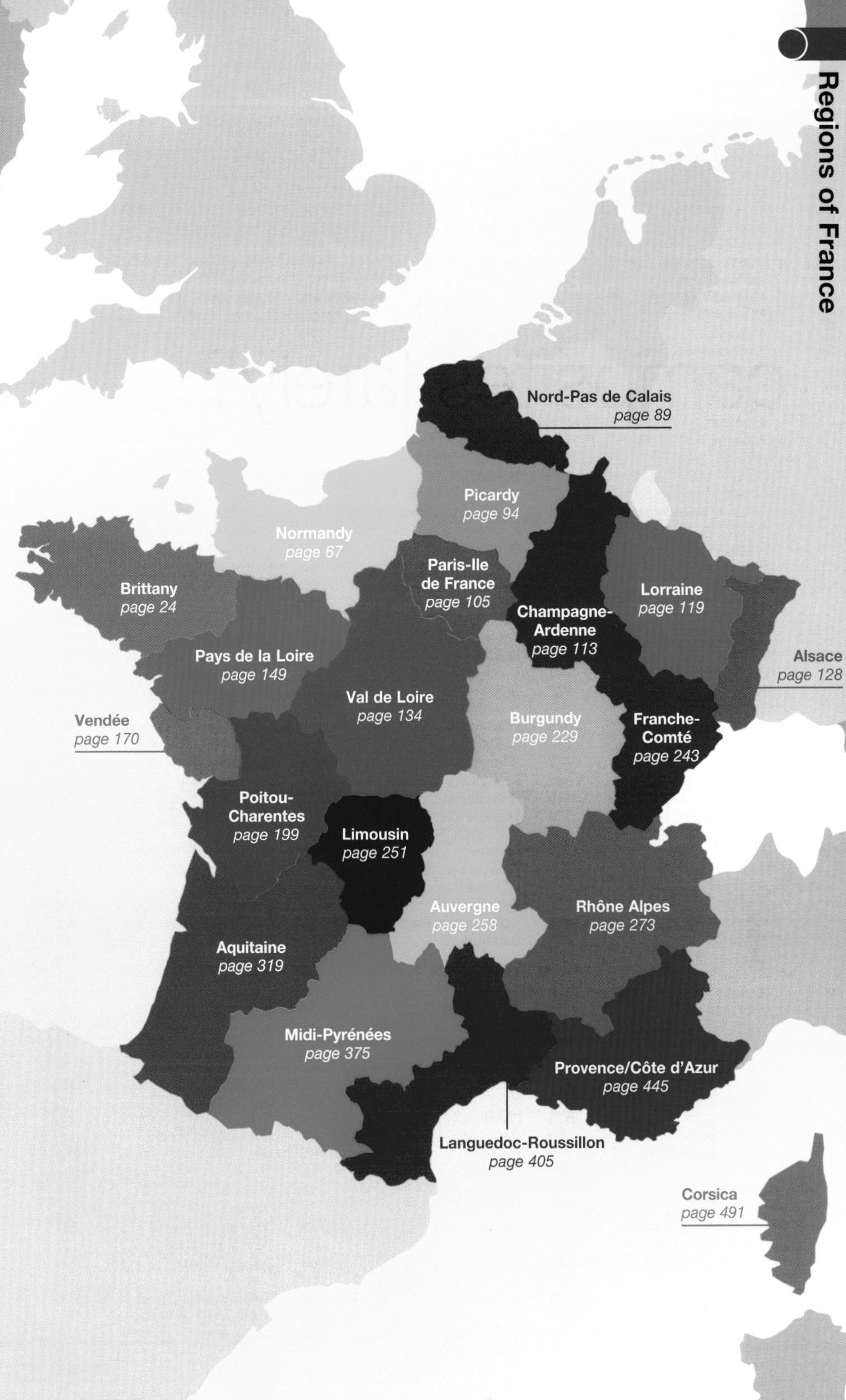
Nord-Pas de Calais
page 89
Picardy
page 94
Normandy
page 67
Brittany
page 24
Paris-Ile de France
page 105
Champagne-Ardenne
page 113
Lorraine
page 119
Alsace
page 128
Pays de la Loire
page 149
Val de Loire
page 134
Vendée
page 170
Burgundy
page 229
Franche-Comté
page 243
Poitou-Charentes
page 199
Limousin
page 251
Auvergne
page 258
Rhône Alpes
page 273
Aquitaine
page 319
Midi-Pyrénées
page 375
Provence/Côte d'Azur
page 445
Languedoc-Roussillon
page 405
Corsica
page 491

Town & Village Index

Index by Campsite Region & Name

Brittany

Normandy

Poitou-Charentes

Burgundy

Index by Campsite Region & Name

Aquitaine

Midi-Pyrénées

Languedoc-Roussillon

Provence/Côte d'Azur

Corsica